South University Library
Richmond Campus
2151 Old Brick Road
Glen Allen, Va 23060

MAR 2 0 2018

The Wiley Handbook of Disruptive and Impulse-Control Disorders

The Wiley Handbook of Disruptive and Impulse-Control Disorders

Edited by

John E. Lochman

and

Walter Matthys

WILEY Blackwell

This edition first published 2018
© 2018 John Wiley & Sons Ltd

All rights reserved. No part of this publication may be reproduced, stored in a retrieval system, or transmitted, in any form or by any means, electronic, mechanical, photocopying, recording or otherwise, except as permitted by law. Advice on how to obtain permission to reuse material from this title is available at http://www.wiley.com/go/permissions.

The right of John E Lochman and Walter Matthys to be identified as the authors of the editorial material in this work has been asserted in accordance with law.

Registered Office(s)
John Wiley & Sons, Inc., 111 River Street, Hoboken, NJ 07030, USA
John Wiley & Sons Ltd, The Atrium, Southern Gate, Chichester, West Sussex, PO19 8SQ, UK

Editorial Office
The Atrium, Southern Gate, Chichester, West Sussex, PO19 8SQ, UK

For details of our global editorial offices, customer services, and more information about Wiley products visit us at www.wiley.com.

Wiley also publishes its books in a variety of electronic formats and by print-on-demand. Some content that appears in standard print versions of this book may not be available in other formats.

Limit of Liability/Disclaimer of Warranty
While the publisher and authors have used their best efforts in preparing this work, they make no representations or warranties with respect to the accuracy or completeness of the contents of this work and specifically disclaim all warranties, including without limitation any implied warranties of merchantability or fitness for a particular purpose. No warranty may be created or extended by sales representatives, written sales materials or promotional statements for this work. The fact that an organization, website, or product is referred to in this work as a citation and/or potential source of further information does not mean that the publisher and authors endorse the information or services the organization, website, or product may provide or recommendations it may make. This work is sold with the understanding that the publisher is not engaged in rendering professional services. The advice and strategies contained herein may not be suitable for your situation. You should consult with a specialist where appropriate. Further, readers should be aware that websites listed in this work may have changed or disappeared between when this work was written and when it is read. Neither the publisher nor authors shall be liable for any loss of profit or any other commercial damages, including but not limited to special, incidental, consequential, or other damages.

Library of Congress Cataloging-in-Publication Data is Available

9781119092162 (hardback)
9781119092230 (epdf)
9781119092223 (epub)

Cover Design: Wiley
Cover Image: © Marko Kotilainen/EyeEm/Gettyimages

Set in 9.5/11.5 Galliard by SPi Global, Pondicherry, India
Printed and bound in Malaysia by Vivar Printing Sdn Bhd

10 9 8 7 6 5 4 3 2 1

*To Linda and Paula and to our children and grandchildren:
Lisa, Kara, Bryan, Garrett, Audrey, Jonathan, Lori, Ine, Joost,
Bram, Ellen, and Dorien*

Contents

Notes on Contributors		xi
Part 1 Introduction to the Handbook		**1**
1	A Framework for the Handbook's Exploration of Disruptive Behavior Disorders, Intermittent Explosive Disorder, and Impulse-Control Disorders *John E. Lochman and Walter Matthys*	3
Part 2 Diagnostic Issues for the Disruptive and Impulse-Control Disorders		**19**
2	Diagnostic Issues in Oppositional Defiant Disorder *Jeffrey D. Burke, Olivia J. Derella, and Oliver G. Johnston*	21
3	Conduct Disorder and Callous-Unemotional Traits *Paul J. Frick and Tina D. Wall Myers*	37
4	Diagnostic Issues for ODD/CD with ADHD Comorbidity *Kristen L. Hudec and Amori Yee Mikami*	55
5	Comorbidity with Substance Abuse *Naomi R. Marmorstein and Helene R. White*	73
6	Intermittent Explosive Disorder and the Impulse-Control Disorders *Emil F. Coccaro and Jon E. Grant*	89
7	Related Personality Disorders Located within an Elaborated Externalizing Psychopathology Spectrum *Martin Sellbom, Bo Bach, and Elizabeth Huxley*	103
Part 3 Etiological and Maintenance Factors		**125**
Child-Level Factors		
8	Genetic and Gene–Environment Influences on Disruptive Behavior Disorders *Edward D. Barker, Charlotte A. M. Cecil, Esther Walton, and Alan J. Meehan*	127
9	The Neurobiology of Oppositional Defiant Disorder and Conduct Disorder *Leah M. Efferson and Andrea L. Glenn*	143

10	Cognitive Functions Matthew A. Jarrett and Dane C. Hilton	159
11	Temperament Jinhong Guo and Sylvie Mrug	175
12	Prenatal and Perinatal Risk Factors D. Anne Winiarski, Cassandra L. Hendrix, Erica L. Smearman, and Patricia A. Brennan	189
13	Attachment and Disruptive Disorders Marleen G. Groeneveld and Judi Mesman	205
14	Emotion Regulation Megan K. Bookhout, Julie A. Hubbard, and Christina C. Moore	221
15	"It's Gonna End Up with a Fight Anyway:" Social Cognitive Processes in Children with Disruptive Behavior Disorders Bram Orobio de Castro and Anouk van Dijk	237

Family Factors — 255

16	Family Poverty and Structure Barbara Maughan, Richard Rowe, and Joseph Murray	257
17	Parent Psychopathology Tammy D. Barry, Rebecca A. Lindsey, Elizabeth C. Fair, and Kristy M. DiSabatino	275
18	Relationship Discord, Intimate Partner Physical Aggression, and Externalizing Problems of Children K. Daniel O'Leary and Ingrid Solano	291
19	Parenting Practices and the Development of Problem Behavior across the Lifespan Elizabeth A. Stormshak, Elisa DeVargas, and Lucía E. Cárdenas	307

Peer Factors — 323

20	Peer Rejection and Disruptive Behavioral Disorders Kristina L. McDonald and Carolyn E. Gibson	325
21	The Role of Deviant Peers in Oppositional Defiant Disorder and Conduct Disorder Damir S. Utržan, Timothy F. Piehler, and Thomas J. Dishion	339

Broader Social Context — 353

22	The Broader Context: School and Neighborhood Factors Contributing to ODD and CD Symptomatology Paula J. Fite, Sonia L. Rubens, Spencer C. Evans, and Jonathan Poquiz	355

Part 4 Assessment Processes — 371

23	Problem-Solving Structure of Assessment Walter Matthys and Nicole P. Powell	373

Part 5   Treatment and Prevention   391

24   Engaging Families in Treatment for Child Behavior Disorders:
A Synthesis of the Literature   393
Mary Acri, Anil Chacko, Geetha Gopalan, and Mary McKay

25   Pharmacotherapy of Disruptive and Impulse Control Disorders   411
Gloria M. Reeves, Heidi J. Wehring, and Mark A. Riddle

26   Psychosocial Treatment and Prevention of Conduct Problems
in Early Childhood   433
*Danielle Cornacchio, Laura J. Bry, Amanda L. Sanchez, Bridget Poznanski,
and Jonathan S. Comer*

27   Psychosocial Treatment and Prevention in Middle Childhood
and Early Adolescence   451
*Caroline L. Boxmeyer, Nicole P. Powell, Qshequilla Mitchell, Devon Romero,
Cameron E. Powe, and Casey Dillon*

28   Psychosocial Treatment and Prevention in the Adolescent Years
for ODD and CD   467
*Brian P. Daly, David DeMatteo, Aimee Hildenbrand, Courtney N. Baker, and
Jacqueline H. Fisher*

29   Factors Influencing Intervention Delivery and Outcomes   485
John E. Lochman, Francesca Kassing, Meghann Sallee, and Sara L. Stromeyer

Part 6   Concluding Comments   501

30   Future Directions   503
Walter Matthys and John E. Lochman

Index   519

Notes on Contributors

Mary Acri, PhD, currently holds the titles of Senior Research Scientist at the McSilver Institute for Policy, Poverty, and Research; Research Assistant Professor at New York University School of Medicine's Department of Child and Adolescent Psychiatry; and Adjunct Faculty at The Silver School of Social Work at New York University. She has published over 50 peer-reviewed journal articles on mental health, peer-delivered interventions, animal-assisted therapies, and developing and testing unique models of detection and outreach for families impacted by poverty.

Bo Bach, PhD, is a clinical psychologist and Senior Research Associate at the Psychiatric Research Unit, Slagelse Psychiatric Hospital, Denmark. He is co-founder of the Center of Excellence on Personality Disorder within the aforementioned hospital. As clinician, he is particularly experienced with assessment and treatment of personality disorders. His research interests are on the utility of diagnostic models of personality disorders, and on how pathological personality dimensions may inform treatment decisions as well as predict treatment benefit and outcome.

Courtney N. Baker, PhD, is an Assistant Professor in the Department of Psychology at Tulane University. Dr. Baker's research program aims to eliminate disparities in health and academic achievement by improving the delivery of high-quality evidence-based prevention and intervention programming. Her research focuses on low-income community settings serving children and their families. In line with best practices when working with underserved communities, Dr. Baker utilizes a community-based participatory research approach.

Edward D. Barker, PhD, is Associate Professor in the Department of Psychology at the Institute of Psychiatry, Psychology, and Neuroscience, King's College London, where he also directs the Developmental Psychology Lab. His research interests are in examining how stressful environments exacerbate underlying biological vulnerabilities to affect children's development. He is particularly interested in the impact of psychopathology in caregivers (and associated risks) on children's externalizing disorders, and the relative role of prenatal and postnatal risk exposures.

Tammy D. Barry, PhD, is an Associate Professor in the Department of Psychology at Washington State University and the Director of Clinical Training for the clinical psychology doctoral program. She has taught doctoral students at four other institutions. She currently serves on the Board of Directors of the Council of University Directors of Clinical Psychology. Her research focuses on biologically based and contextual correlates of child externalizing behaviors, including ADHD, aggression, and disruptive behaviors associated with autism.

Megan K. Bookhout, MA, is a fifth-year doctoral student in the Clinical Science Program in the Department of Psychological and Brain Sciences at the University of Delaware. Her research interests focus on the peer relations of children with obesity, particularly in the effects of weight-related victimization on children's psychosocial outcomes.

Caroline L. Boxmeyer, PhD, is an associate professor in the Department of Psychiatry and Behavioral Medicine at The University of Alabama. She is also a Research Scientist in UA's Center for Prevention of Youth Behavior Problems. Dr. Boxmeyer's federally funded program of research focuses on developing, testing, and disseminating preventive interventions that support children's social and emotional development and family well-being. She is a master trainer in the Coping Power program and has codeveloped several related interventions.

Patricia A. Brennan, PhD, is a Clinical Psychology Professor at Emory University. She obtained her doctorate from the University of Southern California, and for over two decades has studied the social and biological factors that contribute to aggression. As a Fellow at the Center for Advanced Studies in the Behavioral Sciences at Stanford, she coauthored a book on the prevention of aggression in youth. Her current work incorporates biological variables in treatment outcomes studies of delinquency.

Laura J. Bry, BA, is a doctoral student in the Clinical Science of Child and Adolescent Psychology program at Florida International University. She is a member of the Mental Health Interventions and Technology (MINT) program, where her research focuses broadly on improving access to care for children and families through novel intervention methods and models of care.

Jeffrey D. Burke, PhD, is an Associate Professor in the Department of Psychological Sciences at the University of Connecticut. His research focuses on describing the development of disruptive behavior problems and on improving the characterization of chronic irritability and its outcomes. His work also involves the evaluation of treatments and barriers to treatment engagement for irritability and antisocial behavior.

Lucía E. Cárdenas, BA, is a doctoral student in the Counseling Psychology program at the University of Oregon. Through a NIDA diversity supplement, she currently participates as a doctoral student investigator on a project evaluating the efficacy of a family-centered web program focused on the prevention of substance use in at-risk students (PI: Elizabeth Stormshak, PhD). Her research interests are on the implementation of school-based mental health services and the influence of parenting on emerging adulthood.

Charlotte A. M. Cecil, PhD, is an ESRC FRL Fellow in Developmental Psychopathology at the Institute of Psychology, Psychiatry, and Neuroscience, King's College London. Her work focuses on the impact of early adversity on children's emotions, behavior, and mental health. In particular, her aim is to identify how stressful experiences become biologically embedded, influencing children's development and long-term health, so as to improve current strategies for prevention and intervention.

Anil Chacko, PhD, is an Associate Professor in Applied Psychology in the Steinhardt School of Culture, Education, and Human Development at New York University. His clinical and research interests are in treatment engagement and the development, evaluation, and dissemination of psychosocial interventions for the prevention and treatment of child behavioral difficulties, primarily ADHD, oppositional and conduct problems in youth.

Emil F. Coccaro, MD, is the Ellen C. Manning Professor of Psychiatry and Behavioral Neuroscience at the Pritzker School of Medicine of the University of Chicago. His work involves neurobiologic and treatment studies of impulsive aggressive behavior in humans, work that led to the DSM-5 Criteria for Intermittent Explosive Disorder (IED).

Jonathan S. Comer, PhD, is Professor of Psychology at Florida International University, where he serves as Director of the Mental Health Interventions and Technology (MINT) Program. His research is focused on expanding the scope and accessibility of mental healthcare for youth with anxiety, traumatic stress, and/or disruptive behavior problems. Dr Comer is Associate Editor of *Behavior Therapy*, and has received several early career awards, including from the American Psychological Association and the Association for Behavioral and Cognitive Therapies.

Danielle Cornacchio, MS, is a fourth-year PhD student in the clinical science program in child and adolescent psychology at Florida International University. Her research interests are related to examining innovative treatment formats for difficult-to-treat child populations.

Brian P. Daly, PhD, is Associate Professor and Director of Clinical Training at Drexel University, where he also directs the Pediatric, Child, and Adolescent Psychology lab. He is a Consulting Editor for *Professional Psychology: Research and Practice* and the *Journal of Psychotherapy Integration*, and has been President of the Philadelphia Behavior Therapy Association. His areas of interest in research include prevention and resiliency in urban youth, school mental health promotion, and evidence-based psychosocial interventions for youth.

David DeMatteo, JD, PhD, ABPP (Forensic), is an Associate Professor of Psychology and Law at Drexel University, and Director of Drexel's JD/PhD Program in Law and Psychology. His interests include psychopathy, forensic assessment, and offender diversion. He is a Fellow of the American Psychological Association, a Fellow of the American Academy of Forensic Psychology, board-certified in forensic psychology by the American Board of Professional Psychology, and currently President of the American Psychology–Law Society (APA Div. 41).

Olivia J. Derella, BA, is a doctoral student in clinical psychology at the University of Connecticut, specializing in child clinical psychology under the mentorship of Dr Jeffrey D. Burke. Her research interests include transactional models of maladaptive parent–child relations and cognitive-behavioral treatment of childhood irritability and emotional dysregulation.

Elisa DeVargas is currently a fifth-year counseling psychology doctoral student at the University of Oregon. She will begin her predoctoral internship at the University of New Mexico Health Sciences Center in July 2017. Elisa's dissertation aims to investigate the treatment fidelity of the Family Check-Up by determining to what extent therapists adhere to motivational interviewing, and to understand which therapist behaviors are most related to improvements in emerging adult health risk behaviors one year after intervention.

Casey Dillon is a predoctoral intern at Boston Children's Hospital, Harvard Medical School, completing her final year as a doctoral candidate in clinical child psychology at the University of Alabama. Her research interests center on bullying, victimization, and bystander behavior, and her clinical work has emphasized child/adolescent and parent populations across outpatient, residential, forensic, and pediatric contexts. Looking forward, she aspires to build a career in the child advocacy and public policy domains.

Kristy M. DiSabatino, PhD, is a Psychology Resident at the University of Missouri-St. Louis with a postdoctoral fellowship in clinical psychology at the Community Psychological Service Center for Behavioral Health Clinic. Her clinical interests are in evidence-based treatment of children and families who have experienced trauma and in co-leading parenting groups. Her research interests are in at-risk families and the emotional factors that influence youth and family outcomes.

Thomas J. Dishion, PhD, is a child clinical psychologist who conducts research in developmental psychopathology and intervention science. He founded the Child and Family Center at the University of Oregon and was its director for 10 years, as well as a professor in psychology and school psychology. He is interested in studying how children's relationship dynamics with parents and peers influence the development of substance use, problem behavior, and emotional distress (anxiety and depression). His developmental work is translational with respect to directly informing the design of effective prevention and treatment strategies that are ecologically and culturally informed, including the development of the Family Check-Up model.

Leah M. Efferson, MA, is a PhD graduate student in the developmental concentration of the experimental program at the University of Alabama. She attended Hiram College in Ohio for her undergraduate degree and worked as a research coordinator at a prison before attending graduate school. Her research interests include how psychopathy influences punishment in criminal scenarios. She is also interested in gender differences in psychopathy and morality.

Spencer C. Evans, MA, is a doctoral candidate in the Clinical Child Psychology Program at the University of Kansas. He is currently completing his predoctoral psychology internship in the Department of Psychiatry and Behavioral Sciences at the Medical University of South Carolina. His research examines the relations between disruptive behavior and mood problems in youth, particularly focusing on irritability and related constructs (e.g., reactive aggression, emotion reactivity) and their implications for evidence-based assessment and treatment.

Elizabeth C. Fair, MA, is a graduate student at the University of Southern Mississippi. She is currently completing her predoctoral clinical internship year in the child specialty track of the UAB-BVAMC Clinical Psychology Internship Consortium in Birmingham, Alabama. As part of her internship, she is training at the Civitan-Sparks Interdisciplinary Clinics, which is a LEND/UCEDD training site. Her research interests include studying endophenotypes and behavioral characteristics of children with autism spectrum disorder.

Jacqueline H. Fisher is an Associate Research Scientist within the Adolescent and Family Research department at The National Center on Addiction and Substance Abuse (CASA). Her research focuses on understanding predictors and trajectories of adolescent delinquency, legal system involvement, and substance use. She uses this research to inform the development of evidence-based intervention techniques for youth involved in the behavioral healthcare system and to improve behavioral health service delivery to justice-involved youth.

Paula J. Fite, PhD, is an Associate Professor in the Clinical Child Psychology Program at the University of Kansas. She serves on several editorial boards, has received the American Psychological Foundation Division 37 Diane J. Willis Early Career Award, and has served as the early-career member-at-large for the Society for Children and Family Policy and Practice Board. Her research focuses on the etiology and developmental progression of child and adolescent problem behavior.

Paul J. Frick, PhD, is the Roy Crumpler Memorial Chair in the Department of Psychology at the Louisiana State University and Professor in the Learning Sciences Institute of Australia at Australian Catholic University. Dr Frick has received the Robert D. Hare Lifetime Achievement Award from the Society for the Scientific Study of Psychopathy. He has also been the editor of the *Journal of Clinical Child and Adolescent Psychology* and the *Journal of Abnormal Child Psychology*. Dr Frick's research focuses on the different pathways through which youth develop severe antisocial behavior.

Carolyn E. Gibson, MS, is pursuing her PhD in Developmental Science and Social Psychology at the University of Alabama. Her research interests broadly include peer relations in adolescence, specifically the effects of victimization and rejection and the accompanying social cognitions.

Andrea L. Glenn is an Assistant Professor in the Center for the Prevention of Youth Behavior Problems and the Department of Psychology at the University of Alabama. Her research focuses on understanding the biological factors that contribute to the development of antisocial behavior, as well as how such factors may influence responsiveness to interventions designed to reduce behavior problems in youth or be altered by them.

Geetha Gopalan is an Assistant Professor at the University of Maryland School of Social Work. Dr. Gopalan's research and practice interests focus on family-level interventions to improve youth mental health and reduce youth risk behavior, particularly for families with intensive service involvement and extreme psychosocial needs (such as those involved in the child welfare system).

Jon E. Grant is a Professor of Psychiatry and Behavioral Neuroscience at the University of Chicago where he directs a clinic and research lab on addictive, compulsive, and impulsive disorders. Dr. Grant is the author of over 300 peer-reviewed scientific articles, the Chair of the Scientific Advisory Board for the TLC Foundation for Body Focused Repetitive Behaviors, and the Director of a Center for Excellence in Gambling research supported by the National Center for Responsible Gaming.

Marleen G. Groeneveld, PhD, is an Assistant Professor at the Centre for Child and Family Studies at Leiden University, the Netherlands. Her research focuses on three important caregivers of children: mothers, fathers, and professional caregivers in home-based childcare and center-based childcare. She has experience in longitudinal observation studies, studying gender socialization and the relation with antisocial behavior of boys and girls, and randomized controlled trials focusing on improving caregivers' sensitivity in childcare.

Jinhong Guo, PhD, is Postdoctoral Research Fellow at the Center for Injury Research and Policy at the Research Institute at Nationwide Children's Hospital. Dr Guo received her PhD in Psychology from the University of Alabama at Birmingham in August 2015 on emotion socialization and emotional functioning in late adolescence and emerging adulthood. Her recent research focuses on applying developmental psychology to the prevention of sports-related injuries among college athletes.

Cassandra L. Hendrix, MA, is a current clinical psychology doctoral student at Emory University. She is a recipient of the Graduate Research Fellowship from the National Science Foundation. Her research explores prenatal as well as postnatal social and biological factors that shape early development and long-term risk for psychopathology.

Aimee Hildenbrand, MS, is a fifth-year doctoral student in clinical psychology at Drexel University. Her research interests include psychosocial and neurocognitive sequelae of pediatric injury and illness, with a particular emphasis on the intersection between pain and traumatic stress. She is also interested in developing and evaluating empirically based interventions for at-risk, underserved children and their families. Aimee completed her predoctoral internship at Cincinnati Children's Hospital Medical Center, graduating in June 2017.

Dane C. Hilton, MA, is a doctoral candidate studying clinical child psychology at the University of Alabama. His research interests are in the cognitive mechanisms underlying social deficits found in children with attention deficit hyperactivity disorder (ADHD) and related disorders. Additionally, he is interested in understanding how mindfulness-based interventions affect the core symptoms and functional impairments of ADHD in adults. His current research explores the relation between working memory and social encoding in children and adolescents with and without ADHD.

Julie A. Hubbard, PhD, is a Professor in the Clinical Science Program in the Department of Psychological and Brain Sciences at the University of Delaware. She is an Associate Editor of the *Merrill-Palmer Quarterly* and serves on the editorial boards of several other journals dedicated to child clinical and developmental psychology. Her research interests coalesce around children's peer relations, aggressive behavior, and emotion regulation, with a focus on both basic science and prevention/intervention.

Kristen L. Hudec, PhD, is a postdoctoral fellow under the supervision of Dr Amori Yee Mikami at the University of British Columbia. She completed her degree at Oklahoma State University, and her research interests include executive functioning and social-emotional impairment in individuals with attention deficit hyperactivity disorder.

Elizabeth Huxley is currently completing a PhD (clinical psychology) at the Australian National University on factors influencing the development of pathological narcissism. She is also a psychologist and a Research Fellow at the Project Air Strategy for Personality Disorders based at the University of Wollongong. Her research interests include narcissism, the impact of social factors on personality development, and models of care and interventions for personality disorders.

Matthew A. Jarrett, PhD, is Associate Professor in Clinical Psychology at The University of Alabama, where he also directs the Child and Adolescent Anxiety Clinic. His research and clinical interests are in the field of developmental psychopathology, particularly in relation to attention-deficit/hyperactivity disorder (ADHD) and commonly comorbid internalizing and externalizing disorders. His current research explores the interface of neuropsychological functioning and co-occurring symptomatology in children, adolescents, and emerging adults with ADHD.

Oliver G. Johnston, BS, is a second-year graduate student in the clinical psychology PhD program at the University of Connecticut. Under the mentorship of Dr Jeffrey D. Burke, Oliver's research focuses on the identification and developmental psychopathology of disruptive behavior disorders, as well as studying the factors that affect service engagement for families of children with disruptive behavior problems.

Francesca Kassing, MA, is currently a graduate student pursuing her PhD in child clinical psychology at The University of Alabama, under the direction of Dr John Lochman. Francesca's research interests include biological and social risk and protective factors for child aggression. She also has secondary research interests in the effects and treatment of early childhood trauma. Francesca completed her undergraduate degree in psychology with honors at Duke University, under the direction of Dr Terrie Moffitt.

Rebecca A. Lindsey, BA, is a graduate student in clinical psychology at Washington State University. Her research interests are on parenting stress and parenting behaviors for caregivers who have a child with a developmental disability.

John E. Lochman, PhD, ABPP, is Professor and Doddridge Saxon Chairholder in Clinical Psychology at The University of Alabama, where he also directs the Center for Prevention of Youth Behavior Problems. He is past-editor of the *Journal of Abnormal Child Psychology*, and has received the Distinguished Career Award from the Society of Clinical Child and Adolescent Psychology. His research interests are on risk factors, social cognition, and intervention and prevention with aggressive children.

Naomi R. Marmorstein, PhD, is a Professor of Psychology at Rutgers University (Camden campus). Her research focuses on comorbidities between mental health problems and substance abuse.

Walter Matthys, MD, PhD, is Professor Emeritus at Utrecht University, the Netherlands. His clinical work as a child and adolescent psychiatrist was based at the University Medical Centre, Utrecht. His research focuses on neurocognitive and social cognitive functions in children with oppositional defiant disorder and conduct disorder, and on interventions to prevent and treat these disorders.

Barbara Maughan is Professor of Developmental Epidemiology at the Institute of Psychiatry, Psychology, and Neuroscience, King's College London. She is a past editor of the *Journal of Child Psychology and Psychiatry*, and past section editor of *Longitudinal and Life Course Studies*. Her research focuses on psychosocial risks for disorder in childhood, and the implications of disorder and adversity in childhood for health, well-being and functioning across the life course.

Kristina L. McDonald, PhD, is an Assistant Professor and the Director of Undergraduate Studies in the Department of Psychology at The University of Alabama. She is also affiliated with the Center for Prevention of Youth Behavior Problems. Her research interests include aggression, social cognitions, peer relationships and friendships, and emotion regulation and reactivity.

Mary McKay, PhD, is Dean of the Brown School at Washington University in St Louis. Previously, she was Professor and the inaugural director of the McSilver Institute for Poverty Policy and Research at NYU Silver School of Social Work. Dr McKay has received substantial federal funding for research focused on meeting the mental health and health prevention needs of poverty impacted families. She has published more than 150 peer-reviewed journal articles on mental and behavioral health, HIV/AIDS prevention, and other urban health issues.

Alan J. Meehan, MSc, is a PhD candidate in Developmental Psychopathology at the Institute of Psychiatry, Psychology, & Neuroscience, King's College London. His doctoral research, funded by the National University of Ireland's Travelling Studentship Scheme and the Economic and Social Research Council, is focused on heterogeneity within callous-unemotional traits, primarily based around co-occurring levels of anxiety and low prosocial behaviour, and identifying distinct risk profiles and co-occurring psychological difficulties for these proposed subtypes.

Judi Mesman, PhD, is Professor of Diversity in Parenting and Education at Leiden, the Netherlands, where she also runs the Diversity in Parenting lab, which focuses on research into the role of culture and gender in parent-child interactions (www.diversityinparenting.nl). She has obtained over 6 million dollars worth of competitive research grants, is an expert coder of many observation instruments of parenting and child behavior, and specializes in the cross-cultural understanding of the sensitivity construct.

Amori Yee Mikami, PhD, is an Associate Professor of Psychology at the University of British Columbia, and a Michael Smith Foundation for Health Research Scholar. She is a previous recipient of the Young Scientist Research Award from Children and Adults with ADHD (CHADD). Her research focuses on peer relationships and interventions for peer problems among youth with attention deficit hyperactivity disorder, with current projects funded by the Canadian Institutes of Health Research and the Institute of Education Sciences.

Qshequilla Mitchell, PhD, MPH, is a Research Scientist at the Center for the Prevention of Youth Behavior Problems at the University of Alabama. She received her PhD in Health Education at the University of Alabama and a Master's of Public Health degree in Health Care, Organization and Policy at the University of Alabama at Birmingham. Her line of research focuses on the racial and ethnic disparities in adolescent health outcomes among youth from rural areas.

Christina C. Moore is a second-year graduate student in the clinical science program in the Department of Psychological and Brain Sciences at the University of Delaware. Her research focuses on topics including the psychophysiology of reactive and proactive aggression and the role of emotion regulation and temperament in externalizing behaviors among children and adolescents.

Sylvie Mrug, PhD, is a Professor of Psychology at the University of Alabama at Birmingham. She studies risk and protective factors for externalizing and internalizing problems in adolescence and the role of spiritual coping in adjustment to chronic illness. Dr. Mrug serves as an Associate Editor for the Journal of Early Adolescence.

Joseph Murray, PhD, is Professor in the Postgraduate Programme in Epidemiology, Federal University of Pelotas, Brazil, and Honorary Senior Visiting Fellow at the Department of Psychiatry, Cambridge University. His research interests are on life-course determinants of conduct problems and crime. He has received the Manuel Lopez-Rey prize and Nigel Walker prize in criminology from the University of Cambridge and the Distinguished New Scholar Award from the Division of Corrections and Sentencing, American Society of Criminology.

Tina D. Wall Myers, PhD, is the University of Dayton's Shea Hellervik Endowed Postdoctoral Fellow, a position which is dedicated to the explanation, prevention, and treatment of juvenile delinquency. Her research interests include studying psychopathy and callous-unemotional traits from a lifespan perspective. She is particularly interested in non-criminal or "successful" subtypes of psychopathy with a focus on investigating protective factors and treatment implications.

K. Daniel O'Leary, PhD, is Distinguished Professor of Psychology at Stony Brook University. His awards include: Distinguished Scientist Award, Clinical Division, APA; Family Psychologist of the Year in 2015, APA, and Elizabeth Beckman Award for mentoring graduate students in 2015. He published 266 manuscripts in edited journals, 34 chapters, and 13 books; the most recent was *The Couples Psychotherapy Treatment Planner* (2nd ed.), with R. E. Heyman and A. E. Jongsma (2015).

Bram Orobio de Castro, PhD, is Professor and Chair in Developmental Psychopathology at Utrecht University, the Netherlands. He received VENI, VICI, and Pearl awards for research excellence from the Netherlands Organization for Scientific Research and the Netherlands Organization for Health Research. He is chair of the Dutch review committee for evidence-based youth care and the Dutch national evaluation of interventions to reduce bullying in schools. He studies the roles of social-cognitive factors in the development of aggressive behavior problems and the effectiveness of cognitive and behavioral interventions.

Timothy F. Piehler, Ph.D., LP, is an Assistant Professor in the Department of Family Social Science at the University of Minnesota. He researches the etiology and prevention of behavior problems and substance use in children and adolescents. His work seeks to identify moderators and mechanisms of response to family and youth-focused preventive interventions with a goal of developing increasingly targeted and personalized intervention strategies.

Jonathan Poquiz is a graduate student in the Clinical Child Psychology Program at the University of Kansas. His interests are broadly within the area of contextual influences of child and adolescent behavior, with a particular interest in the role of school and community characteristics that contribute to the development of aggression, substance use, delinquency, and other problem behaviors.

Cameron E. Powe, MA, is a fifth-year doctoral clinical child psychology candidate working with Dr John Lochman at The University of Alabama. Her research interests include examining how negative parenting behaviors can serve as a risk factor for impaired decision making within disruptive children, how genetic markers might inform this relationship, and the dissemination of evidence-based treatments.

Nicole P. Powell, PhD, MPH, has been a Research Psychologist at the Center for the Prevention of Youth Behavior Problems at the University of Alabama since 2003. In this position, she has been involved in delivering the child and parent components of the Coping Power Program as well as training and supervising others in the implementation of the program. She is a licensed psychologist, specializing in children and families.

Bridget Poznanski, BS, is a doctoral student in the Clinical Science Program at Florida International University. Her research interests are focused on ways to prepare young children with, or at risk for the development of, disruptive behavior disorders and other mental health concerns for success in the transition to school. Additionally, her research focuses on ways to best prepare teachers for managing typical behavioral challenges in the classroom.

Gloria M. Reeves, MD, is a child and adolescent psychiatrist and Associate Professor at the University of Maryland School of Medicine. Her research focuses on medication safety issues and healthy lifestyle interventions for youth with special mental health needs. Dr Reeves also partners with parent consumers of child mental health services to develop "family-centered" peer support programs.

Mark A. Riddle, MD, is Professor of Psychiatry and Pediatrics at Johns Hopkins University School of Medicine and former Director of the Division of Child and Adolescent Psychiatry. Dr Riddle's 300 clinical and research publications include the book *Pediatric Psychopharmacology for Primary Care*, published by the American Academy of Pediatrics Press.

Devon Romero, MA, NCC, is a third-year PhD student in the CACREP-accredited Counselor Education and Supervision program at the University of Alabama, where she also works full-time as a research assistant in the Center for Prevention of Youth Behavior Problems. Her master's degree is in clinical mental health counseling with a specialization in marriage and family counseling. She is a National Certified Counselor and has a graduate certificate in quantitative educational research.

Richard Rowe, PhD, is Professor of Psychology at the University of Sheffield, UK. His research addresses the development of antisocial behaviour. He is an Associate Editor for *BioMedCentral Psychology* and sits on the Scientific Review Panel of the research charity Autistica.

Sonia L. Rubens, PhD, is an Assistant Professor of Psychology at the University of New Orleans. Her research focuses on the role of health behaviors (e.g., sleep) and contextual factors (e.g., peers, schools, neighborhood) in the link between trauma exposure and mental health outcomes among diverse youth.

Meghann Sallee is Psychology Fellow in Psychosocial Rehabilitation at the Durham, VA, Medical Center. She completed her predoctoral internship at Duke University Medical Center and received her PhD in clinical psychology from the University of Alabama. She received a master's in criminology from Queen's University Belfast in Northern Ireland. Her research interests include understanding and trying to reduce negative effects of the positive illusory bias in children and the dissemination of preventative interventions for aggression.

Amanda L. Sanchez, MS, is a third-year doctoral student in Clinical Science in Child and Adolescent Psychology at Florida International University. Her research interests are on understanding barriers to treatment engagement for underserved children and families.

Martin Sellbom, PhD, is an Associate Professor of Clinical Psychology at the University of Otago, Dunedin, New Zealand. His research program focuses on the conceptualization and operationalization of personality disorders (especially psychopathy) as well as personality assessment. He is the associate editor for four journals, including *Psychological Assessment* and the *Journal of Personality Disorders*. Dr Sellbom has won several awards, including the American Psychology-Law Society's Saleem Shah Award and the Society for Personality Assessment's Samuel and Anne Beck Award—both for early-career achievement.

Ingrid Solano is a doctoral candidate in clinical psychology at Stony Brook University. Her graduate adviser is Dr. K. Daniel O'Leary in the Relationship and Forensic Assessment Clinic. She earned her BA in Psychology with a concentration in Behavioral Neuroscience at Bryn Mawr College and her Masters in Marriage and Family Therapy at Hofstra University. Her research interest is in intimate relationships with a focus on aggression, intimate partner violence, personality, communication, and sexuality.

Erica L. Smearman, PhD, completed her doctorate in the Department of Behavioral Sciences and Health Education at Emory University and then pursued a one-year postdoctoral fellowship with Dr Brennan in the Psychology Department. She has now returned to complete her MD training as part of Emory's MD/PhD program. Her interests surround the bio-psycho-social approach to the study of human behavior, including how experiences influence and interact with biology in the development of behavioral outcomes.

Elizabeth A. Stormshak, PhD, is a Philip H. Knight Chair and Professor in Counseling Psychology and Human Services in the College of Education at the University of Oregon and the Director of the Prevention Science Institute. Her primary research focus is on the prevention of risk behavior from early childhood to adolescence, including substance use, conduct problems, and academic failure. Her research focuses on family-centered prevention programs that engage families in the intervention process and enhance long-term positive outcomes for youth.

Sara L. Stromeyer, PhD, is a Clinical Child and Adolescent Psychologist, currently working in private practice in Birmingham, AL. She is also an Adjunct Professor of Psychology at The University of Alabama. Sara trained at The University of Alabama, Children's National Health System in Washington, DC, and La Rabida Children's Hospital in Chicago, IL. Her research focuses on contextual influences on children's aggression.

Damir S. Utržan, MS, ABD, LMFT, is a licensed marriage and family therapist and doctoral candidate in family social science, couple and family therapy specialization, with a human rights concentration, in the Department of Family Social Science at the University of Minnesota. He researches the intersection of refugee resettlement, determinants of mental health problems, and immigration law.

Anouk van Dijk, MSc, is a PhD candidate in Developmental Psychology at Utrecht University, the Netherlands. She investigates the social cognitive processes that underlie aggressive behavior in young children. She studies parental modeling of hostile interpretational styles, the social cognitive underpinnings of bullying behavior, and intervention techniques to reduce aggression. She also teaches in psycho-diagnostic assessment for graduate and undergraduate students.

Esther Walton spent her PhD and postdoctoral fellowship focussing on the genetics and epigenetics of schizophrenia and their neuroimaging phenotypes. During her time as a postdoctoral researcher at King's College London, UK, she investigated mediating effects of epigenetic markers on the development of psychopathology in childhood. She has now taken a position at the University of Bristol applying causal inference methods such as Mendelian Randomization to psychopathological outcomes.

Heidi J. Wehring, PharmD, BCPP, is an Assistant Professor of Psychiatry with the Maryland Psychiatric Research Center, University of Maryland-Baltimore School of Medicine. Dr. Wehring is a board-certified psychiatric pharmacist who specializes in treatment and clinical research with a goal towards improving the lives of children and adults with serious mental illness.

Helene R. White, PhD, is Distinguished Professor at Rutgers, the State University of NJ, with a joint appointment in the Center of Alcohol Studies and Sociology Department. She has won career awards from the Alcohol, Drugs and Tobacco Section of the American Sociological Association, Society for Prevention Research, and American Society of Criminology. Her research focuses on the development of substance use and related problem behaviors over the life course.

D. Anne Winiarski, MA, is a doctoral candidate at Emory University, and a child and adolescent psychology intern at Rush University Medical Center in Chicago, IL. Her dissertation examined the mediating role of biological variables on the relationship between early life stress and aggression. Her research seeks to link early stress exposure to long-term externalizing behaviors in an effort to inform the next iteration of treatments for behavioral problems in children and adolescents.

Part 1
Introduction to the Handbook

1

A Framework for the Handbook's Exploration of Disruptive Behavior Disorders, Intermittent Explosive Disorder, and Impulse-Control Disorders

John E. Lochman and Walter Matthys

In this introductory chapter, we will provide a general description of the diagnostic conditions that are the focus of this book—Disruptive Behavior Disorders (DBDs; namely Oppositional Defiant Disorder and Conduct Disorder), Intermittent Explosive Disorder (IED), and Impulse-Control Disorders (Pyromania and Kleptomania), see Chapters 2, 3, and 6 for full descriptions of them. Although there are some obvious behavioral links across these disorders, they also, as will become apparent in subsequent chapters, have some important differences. DSM-5, the fifth edition of the *Diagnostic and Statistical Manual of Mental Disorders* (American Psychiatric Association [APA], 2013), included this set of disorders within one chapter, and we have decided to follow that convention for the *The Wiley Handbook of Disruptive and Impulse-Control Disorders*. This chapter will also include a brief background to the history of diagnostic classification and its purposes, explain our key assumptions, which are the basis for how the *Handbook* addresses these forms of psychopathology, and provide an overview of how the chapters are structured into the book's main sections.

The *Handbook* is designed to survey and integrate the most important and the most recent scholarship and research on these disruptive and impulse-control disorders in children and adolescents. Each chapter will contain a synthetic overview of the accumulated research in the area in question and identify important next directions for research. The chapters will thus serve as a stimulant for new advances in our understanding of the source, course, and treatment of these disorders. Key researchers have authored the chapters in this volume, and comment on the research methods being employed in each area, as well as the outcomes and implications of the findings. An overriding emphasis throughout the book is to comment on the applied "real-world" value of the accumulated research findings, and in that sense, the *Handbook* is expected to spur policy implications and recommendations.

The Wiley Handbook of Disruptive and Impulse-Control Disorders, First Edition.
Edited by John E. Lochman and Walter Matthys.
© 2018 John Wiley & Sons Ltd. Published 2018 by John Wiley & Sons Ltd.

DBDs, IED, and Impulse-Control Disorders

This set of disorders is primarily characterized by behaviors that adversely affect the well-being and safety of others. The three main types of behavioral problems evident in the criteria for the disorders are: (a) markedly defiant, disobedient, provocative behavior; (b) major violations of either the basic rights of others or of age-appropriate societal norms and rules, and (c) explosive episodes of aggression. Explosive aggressive behavior may involve violence toward people or animals, destruction of property, or overtly threatening behavior that is markedly out of proportion to any stressor, frustration, or provocation that might have preceded the episode. Many youth commit an isolated illegal act at some point, but this does not warrant the designation "conduct disorder."

Although the disorders (DBDs, IED, Impulse-Control Disorders) addressed in this *Handbook* involve problems in behavioral and emotional regulation, the disorders vary in the degree of these two areas of dysregulation. Conduct Disorder is defined by criteria that primarily address poorly controlled behaviors that violate societal norms, although some of the behavioral symptoms may be due to poor emotional control of anger. IED represents the other extreme, as the IED criteria primarily involve poorly controlled emotion, and Oppositional Defiant Disorder (ODD) lies in between, as the criteria are more evenly distributed between emotional and behavioral dysregulation. Pyromania and Kleptomania are relatively rare disorders that are diagnosed as poor impulse control that leads to the periodic behaviors (fire setting and stealing) that serve to relieve internal tension when expressed. This set of disorders tends to have first onset in childhood or adolescence. Many of the symptoms defining these disorders can occur in some degree in typically developing individuals, so a critically important step in diagnosis is to determine that the frequency, persistence, pervasiveness across situations, and impairment resulting from the behaviors is substantially different than what would be expected normatively for a child of the same age, gender, and culture.

The disorders described in this book have been linked to a common externalizing spectrum (e.g., Krueger & South, 2009; Witkiewitz et al., 2013) related to a disinhibited personality dimension (see Chapter 6 of this *Handbook* for a discussion of personality disorders), and to a lesser extent to negative emotionality. These personality dimensions may partially cause the high rates of comorbidity between these disorders and other conditions such as substance abuse (see Chapter 5 for a full discussion of this comorbidity). Disruptive behavior disorders may arise in individuals with some other serious underlying mental disorder; in those cases both should be diagnosed if the diagnostic criteria are met. However, a separate diagnosis of a DBD, IED or impulse-control disorder is not warranted if the disruptive behavior is limited to episodes of some other mental disorder (such as mania or depression) and where the other mental disorder can reasonably be viewed as primary.

Background on Diagnostic Classification and its Purposes

Before we embark on the description and treatment of the disruptive behavior disorders and their close relatives (IED and impulse-control disorders) throughout this *Handbook*, it is useful to think about the history and issues involved in psychiatric diagnoses in general (Fabrega, 1996, 2001; Pincus & McQueen, 2002). Early efforts to classify human problems started as human civilizations became more established, and people became attentive to the types of physical and emotional difficulties that were evident in themselves and their peers. The earliest known efforts by humans to classify mental disorders as they perceived them among their fellow humans included Egyptian and Sumerian references to senile dementia, melancholia, and hysteria evident in writings prior to 2000 B.C. In the fifth century before Christ, Hippocrates and his followers developed what could be regarded as the first classification system for mental illnesses. This system included classification of melancholia, paranoia, phobias, phrenitis, mania, epilepsy, and Scythian disease (transvestism). These disorders were presumed to be due to different imbalances of the four humors. Hippocrates' system placed these disorders within the medical domain, and was based on observation of patients, in contrast to the logical approach to categorization of mental disorders used by Plato, which distinguished between rational and irrational forms of madness that were created when the rational and irrational souls were separated.

On the other side of the world, the early history of the Mayan culture in the Americas also indicates that they identified several psychiatric syndromes in the period 500–100 B.C. Our understanding of the classification of mental disorders within the later Incan culture largely comes from Spanish chronicles, but suggests that differentiations were being made between anxiety, insanity (e.g., Utek cay), melancholy (e.g., Putirayay), and hysteria (Elferink, 1999). As with modern classification systems, these early descriptions of emotional and mental maladies led to intervention efforts, including efforts by Mayan priests to intervene with gods such as Ixchel, the patroness of medicine. A number of plants were used by Incans and pre-Incans to treat depression, including the seeds of the vilca tree, which has hallucinogenic properties, and the china root, which is still used in folk medicine today.

Mental disorders were thought in the ancient world to be the result of supernatural phenomena, and the mentally ill were scorned and feared. Children with mental or physical handicaps were viewed as sources of economic burden and embarrassment, and were often abandoned and sometimes put to death. In the Western world, advances in classification of mental illnesses were slow in the millennia after the Greek and Roman philosophers. Innovations in classification did not substantially develop until the seventeenth century. A function of these evolving classification systems was to move from assuming that causes of disorders were supernatural to determining the natural causes of diseases.

Thomas Sydenham (1624–1663), who has been characterized as the "English Hippocrates" and "father of modern medical thinking," emphasized careful clinical observation and diagnosis of patients, and pioneered the idea of syndromes in which associated symptoms would have a common course (Dewhurst, 1966). Sydenham described how different individuals with the same disease would have similar symptom presentations, and that there were different causes for different disorders. Sydenham's approach suggested that classification of mental disorders could be approached best through systematic observation and description of symptom patterns. This descriptive approach to classification became increasingly accepted by professional groups, as evident in Jean Columbier and Francois Doublet's publication of *Instruction sur la manière de gouverner les insensés . . .* in psychiatry in 1785, which involved information compiled from, and sanctioned by, a group of French physicians who were treating the mentally ill. The categories of mental illness described in this book included ones that were, in fact, similar to categories suggested by Hippocrates thousands of years earlier (mania, melancholy, frenzy, stupidity). Subsequent descriptive classification systems by Pinel and Jean-Etienne Esquirol identified finer distinctions within disorders, and were the first to use terms like "remission" to describe the course of mental illness.

However, this taxonomic system, which had evolved from the botanical sciences, was largely abandoned in the nineteenth century in favor of an anatomical-clinical approach which described the course of diseases and the accompanying brain lesions. The work of Bale, and especially of Greisinger, was particularly important in this effort to develop a classification system that incorporated then prevalent understandings of the cause of the disease. They believed that all mental disorders had an underlying physical cause that originated in the brain. Emil Kraepelin took the next step at the end of the nineteenth century and proposed that a classification system could be developed on the basis of etiology, symptomatology, and course of disorder. Contemporary classification systems have evolved from these predecessors, and the ICD and DSM are generally compatible systems of classification of mental disorders.

International Classification of Diseases (ICD)

After World War II, the US Army and the US Navy developed a more comprehensive diagnostic system which could also address less severe mental disorders evident in veterans. The system used by the armed forces and the ICD-6 (International Classification of Diseases – Revision 6) played a major role in serving as the foundation for the first edition of the *Diagnostic and Statistical Manual of Disorders* (DSM) published by the American Psychiatric Association in 1952. The ICD actually predates the DSM by nearly 100 years, and is the standard used throughout the world. The ICD developed out of efforts to statistically record and classify causes of death, such as the Bills of Mortality in London, and were not originally aimed to standardize medical diagnosis and treatment. A major change in the ICD classification occurred with ICD-6 in 1948, as it was expanded to classify morbidity as well as mortality information, and included for the first time a section on mental, psychoneurotic, and personality disorders. The ICD-6 and its successive revisions through ICD-10 proved to be adaptable enough to be extended for use in diagnosing illnesses and for classifying health statistics in hospitals (Goodheart, 2014). All 193 World Health Organization (WHO) member countries, including the United States, are required by international treaty to collect and report health statistics to the WHO using the ICD as a framework.

The next revision of the ICD, ICD-11, is undergoing field trials, and will appear in 2018. The WHO's priorities for the development of the classification of mental and behavioral disorders in ICD-11 include increasing its clinical utility in global mental health settings (Reed, 2010) and improving the identification and diagnosis of mental disorders among children and adolescents (Lochman et al., 2015; Rutter, 2012). The disruptive behaviors will appear in a section titled Disruptive Behavior and Dissocial Disorder. The inclusion of mental and behavioral disorders alongside all other diagnostic categories is an important advantage for ICD, as it can facilitate research on related mechanisms of etiology and comorbidity of disease processes across psychopathology and other medical conditions, and can increase the clinical use of the classification by all specialties and general health care workers all over the world (International Advisory Group, 2011).

Diagnostic and Statistical Manual (DSM)

The American Psychiatric Association published a predecessor to the DSM prior to the American Civil War, in 1844, as a way to develop a statistical classification of institutionalized mental patients. This pre-DSM was meant to improve communication about the types of patients in hospitals (APA, 2013), certainly a familiar aim today. Following efforts to address veterans' mental disorders after World War II, the American Psychiatric Association published the first edition of the DSM in 1952. This manual was heavily based on the diagnostic system used by the armed forces in World War II, and was published in collaboration with the roll-out of ICD-6. There were three major categories of dysfunction in DSM-I: organic brain syndromes, functional disorder, and mental deficiency, which then comprised 106 categories (the number of categories increased sharply in subsequent editions; there were 407 in DSM-IV). DSM-II followed in 1968, but these first two DSM versions experienced only limited success among mental health professionals, largely because of their reliance on theoretical descriptions and use of vague diagnostic criteria (Netherton, Holmes, & Walker, 1999). Because of professionals' frustration with the system, the APA task force, which was formed in 1974, aimed to modify the system substantially so that it would provide more objective, clinically useful, and reliable diagnostic information. It was hoped that this major revision would be more acceptable to clinicians and to scholars from various theoretical orientations.

In contrast to the first two DSM editions, which had only narrative descriptions of symptoms (requiring clinicians to form their own definitions to make diagnoses), the DSM-III had explicit criteria for the disorders. The dramatic changes in the DSM-III content were because of the "Feighner criteria" (Feighner et al., 1972) and the Research Diagnostic Criteria developed by Spitzer and colleagues (Spitzer, Endicott, & Robins, 1978). At the same time, inferences that were heavily embedded in psychoanalytic theory were dropped. DSM-III also introduced the idea of multiaxial diagnoses, and became a widely used diagnostic system. The increasing emphasis on the research basis for the diagnostic categories has become stronger with succeeding editions of the manual, which rely more on available data and field trials than was the case with early versions of DSM. The DSM-IV attempted to provide scientific support for its diagnostic criteria, in contrast to use of expert judgment in the development of prior versions of the DSM. In addition to literature reviews, the DSM-IV committees reanalyzed existing large datasets in an effort to refine diagnostic criteria and to test reliability and validity in field trials (Quay, 1999).

The most recent revision of the DSM, DSM-5, began in 1999 with a series of conferences evaluating the strengths and weaknesses of DSM by the American Psychiatric Association in conjunction with officials from the World Health Organization's Division of Mental Health, the World Psychiatric Association, and the National Institute of Mental Health (APA, 2013). The literature on diagnoses was reviewed from 2003 to 2008 in 13 international DSM-5 planning conferences sponsored by the APA in cooperation with WHO and three of the NIH institutes (NIMH; NIDA; NIAAA). The DSM-5 was published in 2013.

What Are the Purposes of, and Concerns about, Diagnostic Classification of Behavioral Problems?

Although concerns exist about diagnostic classification systems, as noted below, they are meant to serve a variety of clinical and scientific objectives—and can do so, if classification is done as reliably, accurately, and validly as possible. Experienced and perceptive clinicians have been aware for a long time that diagnostic categories are simply concepts that are meant to provide a useful framework for organizing clinical experiences so that effective clinical work can be done (Kendell & Jablensky, 2003). In order to do this, we need to distinguish between disorders and diagnoses, with "disorder" referring to the clinically relevant emotional and behavioral maladjustment of a client, and "diagnosis" to the label that represents the concept of, or information about, that condition (Helzer, Kraemer, & Krueger, 2006). These diagnostic labels or concepts are justified only if they provide part of the framework for organizing complex clinical case information in such a way that it helps with better understanding this type of client's array of symptoms and then assists researchers and the clinician in treatment decisions (Kendell & Jablensky, 2003). Chapter 23 of this *Handbook* presents a discussion of how categorical diagnoses should be augmented with a case formulation and targets for intervention in forming treatment decisions. Two of the most important purposes for diagnostic classification thus involve facilitation of research and clinical work.

To Facilitate Research on the Causes and Active Mechanisms That Contribute to the Development and Maintenance of Behavioral Disorders

Beyond identifying clues to the genesis of disorders through a focus on the clustering of cases, as in epidemiological research, diagnostic systems can be useful in providing the focus for research into the biological, social, cognitive, and emotional risk factors that promote the disorder and contribute to its course across time. Disorders that are defined lead researchers to focus their studies of etiology on those disorders as the outcomes to be predicted. Increasingly precise and specific definitions of disorders, and the development of instruments (typically structured clinical interviews) designed to assess for the symptoms, have become the norm in clinical research. Research often focuses on broad distal risk factors for a disorder (e.g., the role of poverty, neighborhood violence, and density of aggressive children in classrooms in predicting to adolescent conduct disorder) and the more proximal and mutable risk factors that in some cases are part of a mediational chain leading to the disorder (e.g., harsh and inconsistent parenting, peer rejection, deviant peer involvement, distorted social cognitions also predicting to adolescent conduct disorder). The more mutable risk factors typically become the targets of research-based intervention programs. But before the intervention can be developed and found to be effective, researchers should, in association with clinicians, explore the active risk mechanisms leading to the disorder that will be the focus of the intervention. And this chain of investigation cannot occur without the disorder being known. As will be discussed shortly, however, some would argue that a discrete categorical classification of disorder is not the only approach to etiological research, and that studies of risk and protective factors predicting continuous dimensions (rather than categories) of pathological behaviors has also proven to be a rich source of information leading to our understanding of disordered behaviors.

To Facilitate Treatment Planning

Whether one uses categorical or dimensional approaches to conduct research on a disorder, the clinical decision as to whether to treat or provide intervention is inherently a categorical one. Although we can decide to use different intensities of a treatment, we ultimately decide either to provide treatment of the client's disorder or not to treat a given client's signs and symptoms. Categorical diagnoses help the clinician to decide whether there is a condition that needs treatment and, perhaps more importantly, can assist in deciding which type of treatment would be most appropriate and effective for a client with a specific diagnosis. Thus, classification systems help professionals to organize services for clients in an effective, planned way, and permit one service provider to indicate to the next service provider (because of a client's move, or because of a step-down or step-up in services in a system-of-care) how they can best accommodate and serve the transferring client.

In many ways, the ability of a diagnostic system to guide clinical practice, evident in useful and effective treatment planning, is the penultimate indication of the diagnostic system's clinical utility. Clinical utility has been a widely used concept in descriptions of clinical decision making, tests, and treatments, but it has not been well defined. However, First and colleagues (2004) tackled this problem by defining clinical utility as the extent to which a diagnostic classification system assists clinical decision makers to fulfill clinical functions including communicating information among practitioners, patients, and health care system administrators, to choose effective treatments, and to predict future clinical management needs. It has also been argued that the clinical utility of a diagnostic system is perceived to be different than the validity of the system (First et al., 2004) and that, even in the absence of convincing overall evidence for the validity of diagnostic classification of mental disorders, it still can have functional utility by guiding treatment decisions (Kendell & Jablensky, 2003). However, there have been serious concerns about the clinical utility of prior diagnostic classification systems, in terms of their ability to coherently guide treatment planning (Reed, 2010).

Concerns about Diagnostic Systems

The degree of antipathy towards our diagnostic classification systems was highly visible and apparent as the rollout proceeded toward the release of the revised DSM classification, the DSM-5, in the spring of 2013. However, disagreement about the classification system is not new, has existed for decades, and was only to a certain degree specific to DSM-5 itself. Despite frequent agreement about the goals for a diagnostic system, consensus on the optimal diagnostic classification has not occurred. Research on diagnostic classifications and on other methods of identification of clusters or types of patients has led to growing agreement that the type of categorical diagnostic system used in the DSM and ICD systems has lagged behind our accrued knowledge about psychopathology and classification. Its focus on a purely categorical approach places limits on its reliability, validity and ability to account for cultural and contextual effects (Alarcon, 2009; Beutler & Malik, 2002; Freedman et al., 2013; Houts, 2002).

The strongest argument for categorical diagnostic systems is that clinicians need to make categorical decisions on a daily basis using typical clinical information (Helzer et al., 2006). Clinicians need to decide whether to treat a client and which type of treatment should be used, including whether to hospitalize a client (Kraemer, Noda, & O'Hara, 2004). One diagnostic label can potentially convey a considerable amount of useful clinical information in a vivid and succinct way (Widiger & Samuel, 2005). It has been noted that the clinicians' problem is not whether to use a categorical approach, but instead which one to use (e.g., DSM versus ICD—Helzer et al., 2006; Kraemer et al., 2004), since clinicians have to make "yes or no" decisions about treatment. The most obvious disadvantages of a categorical system are the limited validity of data that exist for some diagnostic categories, the dangers of reifying a presumptive diagnosis if little validity is evident, and, at a practical level, the fact that the degree to which someone is just above or below the decision line for the diagnosis can be lost. In the latter case, if a diagnosis is made, the diagnosis does not, by itself, indicate the intensity of the client's problem, while, if a diagnosis is not made, it is not clear whether the potential client had important subclinical levels of symptoms that could still warrant some clinical attention.

Dimensional approaches can have greater predictive validity than categorical methods, and have potential utility in clinical as well as research work (Widiger & Samuel, 2005). However, disadvantages exist for purely dimensional approaches to psychopathology as well. A dimensional approach introduces much more complexity into clinical communication, and may be very difficult to use in many clinical settings. Dimensional approaches provide information about degree of severity across a number of behavioral and emotional dimensions. At best, this wide range of information can be integrated into profiles, but the profiles (and definitely the single dimensions) are not likely to be as easily used by many clinicians to guide treatment in a clear and efficient manner. One potential resolution to this inherent conflict is to include both categories and dimensions in the diagnostic process (Drabick, 2009; Maser et al., 2009). Dimensional severity ratings could also be developed for existing categorical diagnoses (Brown & Barlow, 2005; Cantwell, 1996). Thus, a categorical diagnosis can be useful for epidemiology, treatment research, communication among professionals and permitting clients to obtain services, while dimensional information about the number and severity of symptoms can provide complementary information about risk and resilience and permit prevention or tiered levels of intervention (e.g., more intensive treatments for those clients with most symptoms) to be provided (Drabick & Kendall, 2010). Such an approach could permit clinicians and researchers to use quantitative scores that go along with specific diagnoses, and thus permit easier assessment of degree of improvement during therapy. Such a framework would also assist targeted prevention activities, where an individual displays some early levels of a disorder but is not diagnostic yet. The dimensional approach could be used to identify ranges of problem presentation that, though not yet diagnostic, could trigger the provision of targeted prevention services for that individual or their family. This *Handbook* will focus on both categorical diagnoses of disruptive behavior disorders AND dimensional ratings of children's behavior.

Handbook Structure: Key Assumptions about Exploration of Research and Treatment Planning

A first step in our planning for this *Handbook* was to think about the types of knowledge (and, therefore, chapters) that we felt would be very important in enhancing understanding of how this form of developmental psychopathology was guided by the empirical evidence that has been rapidly accumulating in recent decades, and how research has led to evidence-based intervention approaches. On the one hand, our thinking about the planned structure of the *Handbook* was guided by our own recent work on the second edition of our book on several of these disorders, *Oppositional Defiant Disorder and Conduct Disorder in Childhood* (Matthys & Lochman, 2017). Based on our reading of the literature, we had a sense of what key topics should be reviewed by important experts in the field. On the other hand, we also had certain principles in mind that we felt would be important for advancing the science and clinical work related to youths' disruptive behaviors. These principles underlie the chapters that will follow.

Integrative Science

Integrated science synthesizes the perspectives of individual disciplines, and integrates them during all phases of the approach to a question or problem (from understanding risk mechanisms to understanding intervention approaches that address those mechanisms), with the results having an influence on policy decisions. Integrated science is thus an interdisciplinary effort, involving researchers from diverse scientific and clinical backgrounds, and requiring syntheses and integration of varied clinical research paradigms.

Although this approach extends back in some form to the early years of psychological research, there has been a resurgence in thinking about how advances in our understanding of human behavior requires multidisciplinary research. Collaboration across disciplines focuses on how individual, interpersonal, and cultural factors contribute to behavioral actions across time, including the serious acts of aggression and conduct problems that are the behaviors of interest for this *Handbook*. In recent years, based on discoveries about the mind, brain, and behavior, an integrative science of the person has been advocated (McAdams & Pals, 2006; Mischel, 2004), examining the physiological correlates, often evident in the work of cognitive neuroscientists, of individuals' psychological and social functioning. Thus, even at the level of risks in the individual child, integration is required across a wide range of research on children's neurobiological and genetic risks, prenatal and perinatal risk factors, attachment patterns, and stable child characteristics involving their cognitive functioning, emotional regulation, and social cognitive processing. As a result, professional societies, such as the Association for

Psychological Science, have initiated symposia on integrative science, journals on this field of research have been founded (*Integrative Psychological and Behavioral Science*), and applications in a wide variety of areas have begun (including in non-psychological domains, such as advocacy for an integrative science framework to assist with understanding the functioning and management of animals and plants within the national park system; Myers et al., 2007).

Consistent with a developmental psychopathology approach, this book uses an integrative science framework to explore risk factors and mechanisms that predict and account for children's disruptive behaviors, reviewing research from different disciplines and across different levels of factors affecting children's behavioral functioning. Relevant processes are examined at a genetic level, at a neurobiological level, at the levels of children's cognitive functions, emotional regulation and social-cognitive processing, and, within the social context around the child, at the levels of family, peer, community and school influences on children's behavior. The reader's task will be to maintain an integrative science framework across rich chapters on these separate risk factors, to consider how they can be considered together.

Not Just Direct Effects: Complex and Dynamic Relations among Risk Factors, and between Risk Factors and Behaviors

Risk and protective factors that are associated with children's behavior do not typically operate in vacuums, but can have profound additive effects. In some cases in risk factor research no specific risk factor emerges, but the accumulation of risk factors can predict problem behavior outcomes (Sameroff, Gutman, & Peck, 2003). In an even more intriguing way, risk factors often dynamically affect each other. Poverty, neighborhood context, parental depression and stress, and poor parenting practices have all been identified as risk factors for children's disruptive behaviors. However, poverty can influence neighborhood context (poor families often have to live in disadvantaged, high-crime neighborhoods), and both poverty and poor neighborhood context can affect parents' levels of depression and stress, and parents' levels of depression and stress can have large effects on the kinds of parenting practices they employ. A central research challenge involves how to integrate findings that were generated in "single-risk" studies and how to design analyses and research designs to better address this complexity (Funderburk, Maisto, Sugarman, & Wade, 2008; Minney, Lochman, & Guadagno, 2015; Weiner, Schinka, & Velicer, 2003). One useful approach that takes advantage of longitudinal data has been to examine developmental cascades leading to serious psychopathological outcomes (e.g., Dodge, Greenberg, Malone, & Conduct Problems Prevention Research Group, 2008; Klimes-Dougan et al., 2010). This approach not only accounts for the direct and additive effects of risk factors, but also can model their primary impact at different time points in the child's development.

Children's behavior and the risk and protective factors in their social contexts also relate in complex ways, often making simple conclusions about causality difficult. In the middle of the last century, Leary (1957) described how certain behaviors can become self-sustaining because they elicit confirmatory behaviors from others. Experimental manipulation of higher levels of disapproving and lower levels of approving behaviors in couples' conflict discussions leads to strong reciprocal behaviors in the partner, serving to increase the occurrence of heightened levels of conflict behaviors (Lochman & Allen, 1979). In the parent–child literature, there has been notable attention to "child effects," indicating how child behavior problems can evoke harsher and less involved forms of parenting behaviors from their parents (Bell, 1968; Huh, Tristan, Wade, & Stice, 2006; Lansford et al., 2011). In a similar vein, changes in children's behavior can lead to radiating changes in their peer group (Lochman, 2007), as intervention-produced changes in students' behavior in classrooms can lead to improvements in the behavior of other problematic students (Allen, Chinsky,

Larcen, Lochman, & Selinger, 1976). Thus, understanding how children's problem behaviors can transform their environment should assist us in not being too quick to assume that the behavior that we are observing in a parent or child is causing the problem behavior.

Mechanisms

Related to the assumption that risk factors predicting children's disruptive behaviors have complex interrelationships is another, namely that some intermediate constructs have been found to be mechanisms, or putative causes, of behavioral difficulties. Thus, the *Handbook* includes an emphasis on active mechanisms that contribute to the development and maintenance of disordered behavior, rather than only addressing risk factors that empirically predict outcomes, but have not been found to have a causal role in the development or maintenance of the disorder. Thus, an active mechanism is a risk factor that is manipulable and, when manipulated (as with psychotherapeutic intervention targeted at the mechanism), can produce a change in the risk of the outcome (Kraemer et al., 1997). This approach addresses questions of "why" the behavioral disorders develop in the first place and what accounts for their occurrence in children's day-to-day interactions with others.

Mediation research has been a fruitful approach to exploring mechanisms and examining temporal relations between factors that can indicate which variables might be affected by earlier risk factors and then serve as proximal triggers for the problem behavior to occur (MacKinnon, 2008; O'Connell, Boat, & Warner, 2009). For example, parenting has been found to be a mediator of a variety of risk factors. Mothers who are more depressed, have been found to be more inconsistent when they discipline their children, and their inconsistent discipline is the mechanism that accounts for children's increased aggressive behavior (e.g. Barry, Dunlap, Lochman, & Wells, 2009). The active mechanisms can also be psychological or biological processes within the child, as, for example, shown by findings that diminished cortisol reactivity can mediate the relation between children's exposure to interparental conflict and increases in children's externalizing behavior across time (Davies, Sturge-Apple, Cicchetti, & Cummings, 2007), and that children's dominance- and revenge-oriented social goals tended to mediate the relation between African-American children's ethnic identity and their aggressive behavior (Holmes & Lochman, 2009). The identification of active mechanisms associated with a behavioral disorder has considerable importance for intervention development, as these mechanisms can inform the developmental model for the intervention and can become the key targets that the intervention is designed to change in order to prevent or treat the behavioral disorder (Conduct Problems Prevention Research Group, 1992; O'Connell, Boat, & Warner, 2009).

Interventions Exist on a Continuum from Prevention to Treatment

The scope of this *Handbook* covers not only disruptive behavior disorders in youth, but also the subdiagnostic aggressive and conduct problem behaviors, considered as continuous dimensions, that are associated with the disorders. From a developmental psychopathology perspective, children move along developmental trajectories from early forms of problem behaviors to the onset of frank disorder. Thus, prevention can serve the important function of helping to divert children off the developmental pathway to disorder before the disorder becomes entrenched, making intervention more efficient and less costly. This assumption about the importance of prevention is especially important with the externalizing behaviors that are part of the disruptive behavior disorders because of longitudinal research that demonstrates the escalating patterns of serious antisocial behaviors in children.

The Institute of Medicine (IOM) has provided a reconceptualization of treatment and prevention approaches, indicating how they exist as a continuum of services rather than as discrete and qualitatively separate endeavors (Mrazeck & Haggerty, 1994; O'Connell et al., 2009). The IOM conceptualized three classes of services: prevention (universal, selective, indicated); treatment (case identification, standard treatment); and maintenance (compliance with long-term care, after care)—and emphasized how certain forms of each blended into the next category. Thus, targeted preventive interventions (selective and indicated), which address children who are already showing behaviors associated with the disorder but who are not yet in the diagnosable range, differ from universal preventive interventions because of the population served (Weisz, Sandler, Durlak, & Anton, 2005), and are not conceptually far removed from efforts to identify existing diagnosable cases in the treatment category. Because the active mechanisms contributing to problem behavior may be similar for children who are on the developmental pathway to the disorder and those that are already diagnosed, some interventions may be used both in targeted prevention (with at-risk individuals) and in treatment (with diagnosed ODD or CD children).

Evidence-Based Interventions

An underlying assumption in the *Handbook* is that rigorous research designs should not only be evident in basic research clarifying the nature of the disruptive behavioral disorders in children, but are equally important in determining whether interventions (pharmacotherapy and psychosocial interventions) benefit the children and adolescents served. Considerable strides have been made in identifying evidence-based programs and practices in both treatment and prevention with children with externalizing behavior problems (e.g., Weisz & Kazdin, 2010). Active efforts have been made to evaluate research on the efficacy of interventions and to disseminate these conclusions on easily accessible websites (e.g., www.blueprintsprograms.com; www.crimesolutions.gov/Programs.aspx; www.ies.ed.gov/ncee/wwc).

Evidence in support of the effectiveness of a program or practice falls on a continuum ranging from very low to very high levels of confidence. The more rigorous the research design of the intervention trials and the greater the number of positive evaluations, the greater confidence users can have that the intervention will reach its goal of helping youth. Evidence with the lowest level of confidence is "opinion-informed," consists of data such as testimonials, and does not provide any real proof of effectiveness. At the higher end of the continuum are experimental studies that lead to conclusions about evidence-based programs. All experimental studies use designs that involve comparison or control groups to determine if the program had the intended effect. The levels of confidence and evidence of effectiveness attributed to experimental studies can vary depending on factors such as whether the study's design was quasi-experimental or a randomized control design. Research on the evidence base of programs is critically important from a policy perspective, to insure that effective programs can be disseminated and that ineffective and iatrogenic programs are not.

Implementation Science

Implementation science can assist in the often difficult process of translating evidence-based interventions into real-world settings. LaGreca, Silverman, and Lochman (2009) have noted that it is time for intervention research to extend beyond documenting the efficacy and effectiveness of specific psychological treatments or preventive interventions for children and adolescents. Only a small percentage of youths who suffer from emotional and behavioral problems receive psychological services, and many of these services are not evidence-based.

Thus, it is important to develop an implementation science that uses research designs and methods that are as rigorous as those used in efficacy research to examine how best to disseminate interventions in diverse community settings (exploring the transportability of treatment), and how to personalize and adapt evidence-based interventions to produce optimal outcomes for children and their families. Implementation research will require innovation and complex research designs and analytic methods.

Research can range from identifying, and providing solutions for, key barriers (such as difficulties in engaging parents) that interfere with successful implementation of treatments, to rigorous testing of planned adaptations of evidence-based programs for different cultures and contexts and for subgroups of children who do not fare as well in the typical administration of a program. Research can also determine optimal methods for training "real-world" staff in the use of evidence-based approaches, as well as the organizational characteristics of service settings and personal characteristics of staff that can promote, or undermine, useful implementation of programs. At a larger policy level, implementation science can assist with reforming the mental health care delivery system (Fisher, Shortell, & Savitz, 2016) and improving the availability of evidence-based services for children with disruptive behavior problems in a variety of primary health care settings (Asarnow et al., 2015).

Overview of the Handbook

With these assumptions in mind, we have planned and edited the *Handbook* to comprehensively address Disruptive Behavior Disorders, Intermittent Explosive Disorder, and the Impulsive-Control Disorders as they appear in children and adolescents. The book has four sections, and the chapters in these sections address topics related to the definitions, risk factors, and etiology of each disorder, and to intervention with families and with the children themselves.

The first section of the book (Chapters 2 through 7) addresses diagnostic issues, and begins with foundational chapters on Oppositional Defiant Disorder and Conduct Disorder, two of the most prominent disorders covered throughout the book. These chapters address recent changes in DSM-5, and upcoming changes in ICD-11, that relate to these disorders. The chapters describe the rationale for diagnostic changes. Two chapters discuss two of the common classes of comorbid disorders for disruptive behavior disorders, Attention Deficit Hyperactivity Disorder and the Substance Abuse Disorders. A separate chapter describes Intermittent Explosive Disorder and the Impulse-Control Disorders (Pyromania; Kleptomania). These disorders have received less attention in the past in the realm of developmental psychopathology, so the treatment approaches that have been used with them are included in the chapter. Finally, a chapter on personality disorders and psychopathy describes the later adult sequelae of the disruptive behavior disorders.

The second section of the book (Chapters 8 through 22) covers the broad literature on factors that indicate the development and maintenance of the externalizing behaviors in children. A subsection (Chapters 8 through 15) addresses child-level factors, ranging from biological characteristics to psychological characteristics, associated with the disruptive behavior disorders. Chapters explore recent evidence for and against genetic markers, and deal with the brain structures and neurochemical characteristics associated with these disorders. The functional cognitive expression of children's neurobiological characteristics is examined in a subsequent chapter that covers a range of topics from executive functions to intelligence to language, while a further chapter describes prenatal and perinatal risk factors and their behavioral outcomes. Finally, three chapters address stable characteristics that emerge in children and their relation to their environment, including the nature of the parent–child attachment, children's emotional regulation, and children's social-cognitive processes. Using a social contextual framework, the other three subsections address key aspects of children's environment and social context (family; peers; community). Four chapters (Chapters 16 through 19) describe how children's disruptive behaviors are linked, in complex ways, to broad family risk factors, including family poverty, family structure, parent psychopathology, and interparental aggression, and to parenting practices associated with children's aggression and conduct problems. Two chapters (Chapters 20 and 21) then describe how children's behavioral problems are related to their relationships with their peers, focusing on peer status and rejection, and on the considerable risks attached to involvement in deviant peer groups. Finally the last chapter in this section (Chapter 22) explores how broader risk factors in children's neighborhoods and schools are associated with their behavior.

A third section of the book includes one chapter (Chapter 23) on the clinical assessment process with disruptive behavior disorder children, which then contributes to the treatment plans for the children.

The fourth section of the book comprises six chapters that provide an overview of interventions and intervention issues for these children. Chapter 25 summarizes the current state of pharmacotherapy for children with CD and ODD. Three chapters offer a qualitative review of evidence-based family and child intervention approaches: for young children from birth through early elementary school (Chapter 26); for preadolescent children in late elementary school at the transition to middle school (Chapter 27); and for adolescents (Chapter 28). Consistent with the *Handbook*'s framework, prevention as well as treatment approaches are described. One of the most common and difficult barriers to effective treatment for these children is dealt with in Chapter 24, namely difficulties in engaging parents in the intervention process. Chapter 29 addresses a range of issues related to the implementation, dissemination, and adaptation of interventions. Finally, Chapter 30 will provide a summary overview and synthesis of key points and themes evident across the *Handbook*'s four sections.

References

Alarcon, R. D. (2009). Culture, cultural factors and psychiatric diagnosis: Review and projections. *World Psychiatry, 8,* 131–139.

Allen, G. J., Chinsky, J. M., Larcen, S. W., Lochman, J. E., & Selinger, H. V. (1976). *Community psychology in the schools: A behaviorally oriented multilevel preventive approach.* Hillsdale, NJ: Erlbaum.

American Psychiatric Association. (2013). *Diagnostic and statistical manual of mental disorders* (5th ed.). Arlington, VA: American Psychiatric Association.

Asarnow, J. R., Hoagwood, K. E., Stancin, T., Lochman, J. E., Hughes, J. L., Miranda, J. M., . . . Kazak, A. E., (2015). Psychological science and innovative strategies for informing health care redesign: A policy brief. *Journal of Clinical Child and Adolescent Psychology, 44,* 923–932.

Barry, T. D., Dunlap, S., Lochman, J. E., & Wells, K. C. (2009). Inconsistent discipline as a mediator between maternal distress and aggression in boys. *Child and Family Behavior Therapy, 31,* 1–19.

Bell, R. Q. (1968). A reinterpretation of the direction of effects in studies of socialization. *Psychological Review, 75,* 81–95

Beutler, L. E. & Malik, M. L. (2002). *Rethinking the DSM: A psychological perspective.* Washington, DC: American Psychological Perspective.

Brown, T. A., & Barlow, D. H. (2005). Categorical *vs* dimensional classification of mental disorders in DSM-V and beyond. *Journal of Abnormal Psychology, 114,* 551–556.

Cantwell, D. P. (1996). Classification of child and adolescent psychopathology. *Journal of Child Psychology and Psychiatry, 37,* 3–12.

Conduct Problems Prevention Research Group, (1992). A developmental and clinical model for the prevention of conduct disorders: The FAST Track Program. *Development and Psychopathology, 4,* 509–527.

Davies, P. T., Sturge-Apple, M. L., Cicchetti, D., & Cummings, E. M. (2007). The role of child adrenocortical functioning in pathways between interparental conflict and child maladjustment. *Developmental Psychology, 43*, 918–930.

Dewhurst, K. (1966). *Dr. Thomas Sydenham (1624–1689): His life and original writings.* Berkeley, CA: University of California Press.

Dodge, K. A., Greenberg, M. T., Malone, P. S., & Conduct Problems Prevention Research Group (2008). Testing an idealized dynamic cascade model of the development of serious violence in adolescence. *Child Development, 79*, 1907–1927.

Drabick, D. A. (2009). Can a developmental psychopathology perspective facilitate a paradigm shift toward a mixed categorical-dimensional classification system? *Clinical Psychology: Science and Practice, 16*, 42–49.

Drabick, D. A., & Kendall, P. C. (2010). Developmental psychopathology and the diagnosis of mental health problems among youth. *Clinical Psychology: Science and Practice, 17*, 272–280.

Elferink, J. G. (1999). Mental disorder among the Incas in ancient Peru. *History of Psychiatry, 10*, 303–318.

Fabrega, H. (1996). Cultural and historical foundation of psychiatric diagnosis. In J. Mezzich, A. Kleinman, H. Fabrega, & D. L. Parron (Eds.), *Culture and psychiatric diagnosis: A DSM-IV perspective* (pp. 3–14). Arlington, VA: American Psychiatric Association.

Fabrega, H. (2001). Cultural history in psychiatric diagnosis and practice. *Psychiatric Clinics of North America, 24*, 391–405.

Feighner, J. P., Robins, E., Guze, S. B., Woodruff, R. A., Winokur, G., & Munoz, R. (1972). Diagnostic criteria for use in psychiatric research. *Archives of General Psychiatry, 26*, 57–63.

First, M. B., Pincus, H. A., Levine, J. B., Williams, J. B., Ustun, B., & Peele, R. (2004). Clinical utility as a criterion for revising psychiatric diagnoses. *American Journal of Psychiatry, 161*, 946–954.

Fisher, E. S., Shortfell, S. M., & Savitz, L. A. (2016). Implementation science: A potential catalyst for delivery system reform. *Journal of the American Medical Association, 315*, 339–340.

Freedman, R., Lewis, D. A., Michels, R., Pine, D. S., Schultz, S. K., Tamminga, C. A., . . . Yager, J. (2013). The initial field trials of DSM-5: New blooms and old thorns. *American Journal of Psychiatry, 170*, 1–5. doi: 10.1176/appi.ajp.2012.12091189.

Funderburk, J. S., Maisto, S., Sugarman, D. E., & Wade, M. (2008). The covariation of multiple risk factors in primary care: A latent class analysis. *Journal of Behavioral Medicine, 31*, 525–535.

Goodheart, C. D. (2014). *A primer for ICD-10-CM Users: Psychological and behavioral conditions.* Washington, DC: American Psychological Association.

Helzer, J. E., Kraemer, H. C., & Krueger, R. F. (2006). The feasibility and need for dimensional psychiatric diagnosis. *Psychological Medicine, 36*, 1671–1680.

Holmes, K. J., & Lochman, J. E. (2009). Ethnic identity in African American and European American preadolescents: Relation to self-worth, social goals, and aggression. *Journal of Early Adolescence, 29*, 476–496.

Houts, A. C. (2002). Discovery, invention, and the expansion of the modern diagnostic and statistical manuals of mental disorders. In M. L. Malik & L. E. Beutler (Eds.), *Rethinking the DSM: A psychological perspective* (pp. 17–65). Washington, DC: American Psychological Association.

Huh, D., Tristan, J., Wade, E., & Stice, E. (2006). Does problem behavior elicit poor parenting? A prospective study of adolescent girls. *Journal of Adolescent Research, 21*, 185–204.

International Advisory Group for the Revision of the ICD-10 Mental and Behavioural Disorders. (2011). A conceptual framework for the revision of the ICD-10 classification of Mental and Behavioural Disorders. *World Psychiatry, 10*, 86–92.

Kendell, R., & Jablensky, A. (2003). Distinguishing between the validity and utility of psychiatric diagnoses. *American Journal of Psychiatry, 160*, 4–12.

Klimes-Dougan, B., Long, J. D., Lee, C. S., Ronsaville, D. S., Gold, P. W., & Martinez, P. E. (2010). Continuity and cascade in offspring of bipolar parents: A longitudinal study of externalizing, internalizing, and thought problems. *Development and Psychopathology, 22*, 849–866.

Kraemer, H. C., Kazdin, A. E., Offord, D. R., Kessler, R. C., Jensen, P. S., & Kupfer, D. J. (1997). Coming to terms with the terms of risk. *Archives of General Psychiatry, 54*, 337–343.

References

Kraemer, H. C., Noda, A., & O'Hara, R. (2004). Categorical versus dimensional approaches to diagnosis: Methodological challenges. *Journal of Psychiatric Research, 38,* 17–25.

Krueger, R. F., & South, S. C. (2009). Externalizing disorders: Cluster 5 of the proposed metastructure for DSM-V and ICD-11. *Psychological Medicine, 39,* 2061–2070.

Lansford, J. E., Criss, M. M., Laird, R. D., Shaw, D. S., Pettit, G. S., Bates, J. E., & Dodge, K. A. (2011). Reciprocal relations between parents' physical discipline and children's externalizing behavior during middle childhood and adolescence. *Development and Psychopathology, 23,* 225–238.

Leary, T. (1957). *Interpersonal diagnosis of personality: A functional theory and methodology for personality evaluation.* New York, NY: Ronald Press.

Lochman, J. E. (2007). Contextual factors in risk and prevention research. In G. W. Ladd (Ed.), *Appraising the human developmental sciences: Essays in honor of Merrill-Palmer Quarterly* (pp. 351–365). Detroit, MI: Wayne State University Press.

Lochman, J. E. & Allen, G. (1979). Elicited effects of approval and disapproval: An examination of parameters having implication for counseling couples in conflict. *Journal of Consulting and Clinical Psychology, 47,* 636–638.

Lochman, J. E., Evans, S. C., Burke, J. D., Roberts, M. C., Fite, P. J., Reed, G. M., . . . Garralda, M. E. (2015). An empirically based alternative to DSM-5's disruptive mood dysregulation disorder for ICD-11. *World Psychiatry, 14,* 30–33. doi: 10.1002/wps.20176.

MacKinnon, D. P. (2008). *Introduction to statistical mediation analysis.* Mahwah, NJ: Erlbaum.

Maser, J., Norman, S., Zisook, S., Everall, I., Stein, M., Schettler, P., & Judd, L. (2009). Psychiatric nosology is ready for a paradigm shift in DSM-V. *Clinical Psychology: Science and Practice, 16,* 24–40.

Matthys, W., & Lochman, J. E. (2017). *Oppositional defiant disorder and conduct disorder in childhood* (2nd ed.). Oxford, UK: Wiley-Blackwell.

McAdams, D. P., & Pals, J. L. (2006). A new Big Five: Fundamental principles for an integrative science of personality. *American Psychologist, 61,* 204–217.

Minney, J. A., Lochman, J. E., & Guadagno, R. (2015). SEARCHing for solutions: Applying a novel person-centered analysis to the problem of dropping out of preventive parent education. *Prevention Science, 16,* 621–632. doi: 10.1007/s11121-014-0526-7.

Mischel, W. (2004). Toward an integrative science of the person. *Annual Review of Psychology, 55,* 1–22.

Mrazek, P. J., & Haggerty, R. J. (1994). *Reducing risks for mental disorders: Frontiers for preventive intervention research.* Washington, DC: National Academies Press.

Myers, M. D., Ayers, J. S., Baron, P. R., Beauchemin, K. T., Gallagher, M. B., Goldhaber, D. R., . . . Wilde, W. (2007). U.S. Geological Survey updates science goals for the coming decade. *Science 318,* 200–201. doi: 10.1126/science.1147228.

Netherton, S. D., Holmes, D. L., & Walker, C. E. (1999). *Child and adolescent psychological disorders: A comprehensive textbook.* Washington, DC: American Psychological Association.

O'Connell, M. E., Boat, T., & Warner, K. E. (Eds.). (2009). *Preventing mental, emotional, and behavioral disorders among young people: Progress and possibilities.* Washington, DC: National Academies Press.

Pincus, H. A. & McQueen, L. (2002). The limits of evidence-based classification of mental disorders. In J. Z. Sadler (Ed.), *Description and prescription: Values, mental disorders, and the DSM* (pp. 9–24). Baltimore, MD: The Johns Hopkins University Press.

Quay, H. C. (1999). Classification of the disruptive behavior disorders. In H. C. Quay and A. E. Hogan (Eds.), *Handbook of disruptive behavior disorders* (pp. 3–21). New York, NY: Kluwer Academic/Plenum.

Reed, G. M. (2010). Toward ICD-11: improving the clinical utility of WHO's international classification of mental disorders. *Professional Psychology: Research and Practice, 41,* 457–64.

Rutter, M. (2012). Child psychiatric diagnosis and classification: concepts, findings, challenges and potential. *Journal of Child Psychology and Psychiatry, 52,* 647–660.

Sameroff, A. J., Gutman, L. M., & Peck, S. C. (2003). Adaptation among youth facing multiple risks: Prospective research findings. In S. S. Luthar (Ed.), *Resilience and vulnerability: Adaptation in the context of childhood adversities* (pp. 364–391). New York, NY: Cambridge University Press.

Spitzer, R. L., Endicott, J., & Robins, E. (1978). Research diagnostic criteria. *Archives of General Psychiatry, 35,* 773–782.

Weiner, I. B., Schinka, J. A., & Velicer, W. F. (2003). *Handbook of psychology (Vol. 2.), Research methods in psychology.* New York, NY: Wiley.

Weisz, J. R., & Kazdin, A. E. (2010). *Evidence-based psychotherapies for children and adolescents.* New York, NY: Guilford Press.

Weisz, J. R., Sandler, I. N., Durlak, J. A., & Anton, B. S. (2005). Promoting and protecting youth mental health through evidence-based prevention and treatment. *American Psychologist, 60,* 628–648.

Widiger, T. A., & Samuel, D. B. (2005). Diagnostic categories or dimensions? A question for the *Diagnostic and Statistical Manual of Mental Disorders*—Fifth Edition. *Journal of Abnormal Psychology, 114,* 494–504.

Witkiewitz, K., King, K., McMahon, R. J., Wu, J., Luk, J., Bierman, K. L., . . . Pinderhughes, E. E. (2013). Evidence for a multi-dimensional latent structural model of externalizing disorders. *Journal of Abnormal Child Psychology, 41,* 223–237.

Part 2

Diagnostic Issues for the Disruptive and Impulse-Control Disorders

2

Diagnostic Issues in Oppositional Defiant Disorder

Jeffrey D. Burke, Olivia J. Derella, and Oliver G. Johnston

Oppositional Defiant Disorder (ODD), which is characterized by a pattern of defiant and antagonistic behavior and angry or irritable mood, has at times been characterized as a childhood-restricted experience that is the product of bad parenting. This view is inconsistent with the breadth of empirical evidence, which establishes the indicia of ODD consistent with any other disorder. Evidence for the utility of the symptoms of the disorder, for meaningful dimensionality within those symptoms, for important gender differences and developmental considerations, and for understanding common comorbidities will be reviewed in this chapter. Of particular importance—emerging evidence for the irritability dimension of ODD has led to markedly varying diagnostic conceptualizations, raising potential challenges for clinicians and researchers. The evidence regarding these conceptualizations, their implications, and related key concerns is here reviewed.

The History of Oppositional Defiant Disorder

Since its introduction in the third edition of the *Diagnostic and Statistical Manual of Disorders* (DSM-III; American Psychiatric Association [APA], 1980), perhaps the most persistent diagnostic question regarding ODD has been whether or not it should even exist (Kelland, 2012; Moffitt et al., 2008; Rey et al., 1988). As described in the DSM-5 (APA, 2013: 313.81), the diagnosis of ODD is intended to represent "a pattern of angry/irritable mood, argumentative/defiant behavior, or vindictiveness." These features have been part of ODD since DSM-III-R (APA, 1987), but the DSM-5 characterization represents a marked shift in the prominence of an affective feature—chronic irritability—in what had historically been regarded as primarily, if not exclusively, a behavioral disorder. This new recognition is one of several important products of the research that has flowed from the empirical evaluation of diagnostic issues in ODD, which has clearly confirmed the validity and utility of ODD as a diagnostic construct by demonstrating that ODD plays a key role in the explanation of diverging psychopathological pathways and persisting functional difficulties across multiple domains from early childhood into adulthood. Important current issues involve understanding the substantial overlap with a controversial new diagnostic category, expanding developmental assessment, evaluating potential gender differences, and the further explication of comorbidities with other disorders.

The Wiley Handbook of Disruptive and Impulse-Control Disorders, First Edition.
Edited by John E. Lochman and Walter Matthys.
© 2018 John Wiley & Sons Ltd. Published 2018 by John Wiley & Sons Ltd.

The history of the definition and description of the disorder provides key insight into some vexing questions about ODD, including the controversy regarding Disruptive Mood Dysregulation Disorder (DMDD), as it helps to explain to some degree why researchers and clinicians may have failed to recognize irritability as an important dimension within the symptoms of ODD. ODD first appeared in the third edition of the DSM (APA, 1980) as "oppositional disorder," and was characterized as a "pattern of disobedient, negativistic and provocative opposition to authority figures." The text specified that the "oppositional attitude is toward family members, particularly the parents, and toward teachers" (p. 63). The five symptoms of "oppositional disorder" listed in the DSM-III included "temper tantrums." None of the other symptoms, however, related to affective experiences; in particular, there was no mention of chronic anger or irritability. Those symptoms first appeared in DSM-III-R (APA, 1987), but no distinctions regarding affective versus behavioral features were made.

It is arguable that, due to this characterization of ODD as a behavioral disorder particularly manifest in the form of poor parent–child interactions, researchers and clinicians may have overlooked the disorder, and the full understanding of the dimensional nature, prognostic utility, and developmental persistence of ODD may have been substantially delayed. However, over the past decade investigations into the constituent components of ODD have become of critical importance, driving recent changes to the DSM-5 and providing contrast to the new diagnostic category of DMDD.

Criteria

The text of the symptoms of ODD has undergone only modest changes from DSM-III-R through DSM-5. The symptoms have consistently included losing one's temper, arguing, defying others, annoying others, blaming others, being touchy, being angry, and being spiteful. Some changes have been made to the criteria in DSM-5 that might appear superficial, but actually reflect potentially dramatic differences in the understanding of the disorder. These include important developmental changes, which will be discussed later in this chapter, as well as evidence of dimensionality among the symptoms that is pertinent to questions about diagnostic subtyping or specification.

Symptom Dimensions within ODD

The criteria for oppositional defiant disorder in the DSM-5 include three subcategories. "Angry/Irritable Mood" includes often loses temper, often touchy or easily annoyed, and often angry and resentful. "Argumentative/Defiant Behavior" includes often argues with authority figures or adults, often defies, or refuses to comply with, authority figures or rules, often annoys others, and often blames others. Finally, "Vindictiveness" includes has been spiteful or vindictive. The inclusion of these subcategories was driven by evidence suggesting the existence of separate dimensions—distinguishing chronic irritability from oppositional behavior—among the symptoms (Burke, Hipwell, & Loeber, 2010; Burke et al., 2014; Ezpeleta, Granero, de la Osa, Penelo, & Domenech, 2012; Lavigne, Bryant, Hopkins, & Gouze, 2014; Rowe, Costello, Angold, Copeland, & Maughan, 2010; Stringaris & Goodman, 2009a).

A robust literature demonstrates the utility of distinguishing between these dimensions, as the irritability dimension predicts risk for depression and anxiety (Burke, 2012; Burke et al., 2010; Rowe et al., 2010; Stringaris, Cohen, Pine, & Leibenluft, 2009; Stringaris & Goodman, 2009b; Whelan, Stringaris, Maughan, & Barker, 2013). Importantly, these symptom dimensions show discriminant validity. While the irritability dimension, as noted, has been found to be a robust predictor of depression and anxiety, it has *not* predicted borderline personality disorder (Burke & Stepp, 2012; Stringaris et al., 2009), bipolar disorder, conduct disorder, attention deficit hyperactivity disorder (ADHD), and substance abuse (Vidal-Ribas, Brotman, Valdivieso, Leibenluft, & Stringaris, 2016). Conversely, the behavioral dimensions have not predicted depression and anxiety, whereas they are predictive of later conduct disorder (CD) and delinquency (Stringaris & Goodman, 2009b; Whelan et al., 2013).

The evidence is clear regarding the validity of distinguishing dimensions of irritability from oppositionality within the symptoms. There remains some disagreement about which symptoms best measure which dimensions. Much of the evidence tends to support the identification of at least the "Angry/Irritable Mood" dimension of the DSM-5 through the symptoms of losing temper, being touchy, and being angry (e.g., Burke et al., 2014). However, a number of comparisons of various dimensional models reach different conclusions (Herzoff & Tackett, 2016; Lavigne et al., 2015), finding support for the identification of irritability using the symptoms of being touchy, being angry, and being spiteful (Burke, Hipwell, & Loeber, 2010), and an alternate structure for the behavioral symptoms. As yet, there is no clear explanation for these differences, but further exploration of measurement approaches, including informant effects and the wording of items, as well as potential developmental differences, or possible gender differences, should be undertaken to ensure that the dimensions of ODD are identified and distinguished with the greatest clarity.

Irritability and Disruptive Mood Dysregulation Disorder

A pressing example of the importance of answering these remaining questions regarding symptom dimensions arises with the introduction of DMDD in the DSM-5 (APA, 2013). Although DMDD was presented as resting upon the evidence for a construct called severe mood dysregulation (SMD), it is important to clarify just how different SMD was from DMDD. SMD was operationalized using symptoms of ODD (irritability), depression (dysphoric mood), sleep problems, ADHD (hyperactivity, distractibility), mania (racing thoughts or flight of ideas and pressured speech; Brotman et al., 2006). Such an operationalization of SMD makes very good sense, given that it was intended to test important questions aimed at the misdiagnosis of pediatric bipolar disorder (Leibenluft, 2011; Margulies, Weintraub, Grover, & Carlson, 2011). However, it is clearly not equivalent to DMDD.

The core feature of DMDD is described in the DSM-5 as "chronic, severe persistent irritability," which has two manifestations, "frequent temper outbursts" and "chronic, persistently irritable or angry mood." Given this, the difficulty in distinguishing between DMDD and the irritability dimension of ODD is obvious. In an effort to help clinicians distinguish between the two, the DSM-5 suggests that "mood symptoms of disruptive mood dysregulation disorder are relatively rare in children with oppositional defiant disorder." However, this assertion seems at odds with other evidence regarding the relationship between ODD irritability and behavior symptoms (e.g., Burke et al., 2014; Boylan et al., 2016), and the evidence base regarding DMDD prior to its introduction in DSM-5 was very limited.

The DSM-5 asserts that most children who meet criteria for DMDD will also meet criteria for ODD, while the "reverse is not the case," and that only approximately 15% of those meeting criteria for ODD would meet criteria for DMDD. The first assertion has been empirically supported. In preschoolers, who are currently below the age cutoff established for DMDD in the DSM-5, 57.4 to 70.6% of those meeting criteria for DMDD also met criteria for ODD (Copeland, Angold, Costello, & Egger, 2013). In clinical samples, rates of overlap are higher. Among children with DMDD born of parents with bipolar disorder, 92% met criteria for ODD (Sparks et al., 2014). DMDD appears to be particularly associated with comorbid ODD and ADHD, with up to 89.7% of children meeting criteria for the three disorders (Mulraney et al., 2015).

However, the assertion that only 15% of those with ODD will meet criteria for DMDD appears to be a substantial underestimate. Across three data sets, Copeland et al. (2013) found that 23 to 38% of those with ODD would meet criteria for DMDD; Axelson et al. (2012) reported that 58% did so in their clinical sample. Further, Dougherty et al. (2014) found that children with ODD had worse functional impairment than those with DMDD alone or comorbid DMDD and ODD. The authors concluded that DMDD does not merely reflect more severe ODD symptomology (Dougherty et al., 2014). Others have also observed such high comorbidity involving DMDD as to question whether it occurs independently (Mayes et al., 2015). Similarly, chronic irritability as a dimension of ODD is consistently highly correlated with the behavioral dimension (e.g., Burke et al., 2014), calling into question any consideration for a separate category within a psychiatric nosology.

An ODD Specifier

The International Classification of Diseases, currently in its tenth edition (ICD-10; (World Health Organization, 1992) is currently undergoing revision. The task group making recommendations to the WHO for the next revision gave significant consideration to the nosological challenge presented by the new DMDD category, and ultimately proposed an alternative diagnostic solution (Lochman et al., 2015). Specific concerns against the inclusion of DMDD were the lack of empirical evidence supporting it as a valid and distinct diagnostic category, evidence that the ODD symptom dimensions are distinct but still highly correlated with one another, and evidence from latent class analysis suggesting classes of youth with ODD with and without the presence of symptoms of irritability (Burke, 2012). Rather than accepting DMDD as a diagnostic category, the task group proposed a specifier for ODD to reflect whether or not the presentation of ODD includes chronic irritability and anger (Lochman et al., 2015). This proposal, founded upon a firm empirical footing, would address the high overlap between ODD and DMDD, would highlight the proper diagnostic home for children with severe and chronic irritability, and would avoid the DSM-5's awkward, forced, and potentially clinically harmful exclusionary prohibition against assigning both ODD and DMDD when criteria are met for both.

Exclusionary Issues in the Diagnosis of ODD

The question as to the distinctiveness of ODD has been around since it was first introduced in DSM-III (APA, 1980). Overlap with CD was the primary concern, and it was believed that whenever criteria for CD were met, criteria for ODD would also have been met (APA, 1994). As a result, up through DSM-IV, clinicians were prohibited from assigning a diagnosis of ODD if criteria for CD were met. The empirical basis for these beliefs is somewhat unclear. Although in clinical samples many children who meet criteria for CD will also meet criteria for ODD, the same is not true for community samples, where two-thirds to three-quarters of children with CD do not meet criteria for ODD (see, e.g., Rowe, Maughan, Pickles, Costello, & Angold, 2002). Further, longitudinal analyses suggest that only approximately one-third of children with ODD go on to develop CD (Burke, Waldman, & Lahey, 2010). Other research has called into question the progression along a developmental pathway from ODD to CD, especially for girls (Rowe et al., 2010). Because of other evidence regarding the distinctiveness of ODD from CD, including in particular the role of ODD in the development of anxiety and depression (Burke, Loeber, Lahey, & Rathouz, 2005; Copeland, Shanahan, Costello, & Angold, 2009; Rowe, Maughan, & Eley, 2006), the prohibition against assigning a diagnosis of ODD if the criteria for CD are present was dropped in DSM-5.

However, DSM-5 introduced a new exclusion, prohibiting a diagnosis of ODD being given if criteria for DMDD are also met. There is good reason to agree that there will be overlap between the two disorders, since, as described above, DMDD was created to capture the same symptoms as the irritability dimension of ODD, with some qualifiers regarding the frequency or severity with which they are shown. Independent of the merits of DMDD, this exclusion is highly problematic. It has long been known that ODD predicts a greater risk for CD (Burke, Loeber, & Birmaher, 2002), which may be particularly due to the behavioral dimension of symptoms (Burke et al., 2010; Stringaris & Goodman, 2009b; Whelan et al., 2013), and thence a risk for other outcomes from CD, including antisocial personality disorder (APD) and substance use (Burke et al., 2002). If clinicians are prohibited from assigning an ODD diagnosis if DMDD criteria are met, it is not clear how they would be expected to represent the prognostic risks associated with the behavioral symptoms of ODD. DSM-5 has traded one exclusion, which previously obscured the risks for poor affective outcomes, for a new one that will obscure the risks for poor behavioral outcomes.

Prevalence

Estimates of the prevalence of ODD vary by gender, age, and study methodology, but center around an estimate of between 3 and 6% (Boylan, Vaillancourt, Boyle, & Szatmari, 2007). A recent meta-analysis (Demmer, Hooley, Sheen, McGillivray, & Lum, 2016) found similar results, with an average of 5.5% across 19 cross-sectional, non-referred samples of boys and girls in middle childhood to late adolescence. Of note, they reported that the gender disparity in prevalence was 1.59:1 for boys relative to girls, lower than the roughly 3:1 ratio for boys to girls seen in other behavioral disorders (namely ADHD and CD; Demmer et al., 2016).

Prevalence by Gender

The majority of community samples in both the United States and Europe have provided consistent evidence that ODD prevalence differs by gender, with girls presenting with the disorder at slightly lower rates. In a Spanish early childhood sample, 7.9% of boys and 3.2% of girls met criteria for ODD, though more girls than boys met subthreshold criteria in preschool (Ezpeleta, de la Osa, Granero, & Trepat, 2014). Between the ages of 7 and 9 in a Norwegian sample, 4% of boys and 1.3% of girls manifested four or more ODD symptoms (Munkvold, Lundervold, & Manger, 2011), while estimates in rural American settings demonstrate 11.6% of boys and 7.8% of girls met ODD criteria at least once between ages 9 and 16 (Rowe et al., 2010).

On the other hand, some studies find no gender differences: equal rates of ODD have been seen within a matched sample of clinic and non-referred American preschoolers (Keenan et al., 2007), as well as according to self-report in a representative population study of youths aged 9 to 17 (Keenan, Coyne, & Lahey, 2008). Gender differences in prevalence may depend in some part on respondent, as parent-reported higher rates of ODD in boys have contradicted youth-reported gender equivalence (Keenan et al., 2008). Similarly, lifetime prevalence rates from retrospective self-reported data find modest difference in rates by gender (11.2% for men and 9.2% for women; Nock, Kazdin, Hiripi, & Kessler, 2007).

Development and Gender Disparity

Some evidence suggests that the gender difference in prevalence rates between boys and girls may vary over development. While boys show a stability in the prevalence of ODD, girls show increasing rates into adolescence and young adulthood, where young women reach nearly equivalent rates with young men (Boylan et al., 2007; Leadbeater, Thompson, & Gruppuso, 2012). Further, the rates for women may be curvilinear, in that initial evidence suggests they show declining rates to age 24 (Leadbeater et al., 2012), again in contrast to greater stability for young men. Further clarification and explanation for different developmental trajectories for young men and women is hampered by a paucity of studies examining ODD beyond adolescence.

Gender Differences at the Level of the Construct?

Early investigations of gender and ODD sought to understand whether gender differences in prevalence were the result of underrecognition of the disorder in girls. Many have questioned whether symptom count thresholds, as well as symptom descriptions of ODD, are appropriate for both boys and girls. Research has juxtaposed the DSM–ODD threshold with "sex-specific" criteria to assess whether comparison of children to same-age same-sex peers would yield improved norms for evaluating clinical impairment in girls (Waschbusch & King, 2006). While essentially only girls met "sex-specific" but not DSM symptom count criteria, these children were no more impaired than average schoolchildren (Waschbusch & King, 2006), suggesting that DSM thresholds are appropriate across gender.

Ohan and Johnston (2005) addressed concerns that girls manifest ODD differently than boys and present with clinically significant symptoms not captured by current DSM indicators. Results of this work were inconclusive, such that community mothers perceived DSM–ODD symptoms as more problematic than the generated "female-sensitive portrayals" of ODD behavior, but severity ratings on "feminine" items were related to DSM symptomology, total CBCL (Child Behavior Checklist) problem behaviors, and impairment (Ohan & Johnston, 2005). Since girls with elevations on "feminine" ODD items also had elevated DSM symptoms, it appears unnecessary thus far to include gender-specific behavior symptoms. Additionally, gender differences in ODD rates do not appear to be due to referral bias, as research suggests teachers are equally likely to make treatment referrals for boys and girls who demonstrate the same impairing ODD symptomology (Kelter & Pope, 2011).

Researchers have also explored whether gender differences exist in the presentation of ODD dimensions, comorbid conditions, and symptom-related impairment. Across both school and clinical samples, research strongly suggests that the DSM symptoms of ODD demonstrate measurement invariance for gender (de Zeeuw, van Beijsterveldt, Lubke, Glasner, & Boomsma, 2015; Ezpeleta & Penelo, 2014; Lavigne, Hopkins, Bryant, & Gouze, 2015), and latent classes within a sample do not differ by gender either (Herzoff & Tackett, 2016). Studies of dimensional structure find no evidence for variation by gender, regardless of the structural model identified (Ezpeleta & Penelo, 2014; Herzoff & Tackett, 2016; Lavigne et al., 2015). However, other research suggests that girls with ODD score lower on temper and arguing symptoms, while boys with ODD are more likely to engage in defiance or noncompliance and annoying and blaming others (Carlson, Tamm, & Gaub, 1997; Trepat de Ancos & Ezpeleta, 2011).

Munkvold and colleagues (2011) found no gender differences in degree of comorbid symptomology, with most children with ODD demonstrating clinical dysfunction in multiple domains. On the other hand, others have found that boys with ODD have higher rates of aggression and externalizing symptoms (Carlson et al., 1997), and hyperactivity and diagnosed ADHD (Munkvold et al., 2011; Trepat de Ancos & Ezpeleta, 2011), while girls with ODD are more likely to have generalized anxiety disorder, depression, self-harming behaviors, somatic symptoms, and mood or emotional impairment (Trepat de Ancos & Ezpeleta, 2011). While ODD predicts risk for later depression across gender, girls with ODD may be at particularly high risk, with 41.6% of girls developing the disorder compared to 10.8% of boys in a large cross-sectional analysis (Rowe et al., 2002). It has not yet been identified to what extent these differences reflect general gendered rates of comorbid conditions, or whether the manner in which ODD exerts influence on functioning varies for boys and girls in such a way that it creates distinct risks of experiencing externalizing versus internalizing symptomology.

While among children with ODD in middle childhood and pre-adolescence, gender has been unrelated to functional impairment (Ezpeleta, Keeler, Erkanli, Costello, & Angold, 2001), boys with ODD in early childhood demonstrate greater impairment, which has been seen both with equal symptom counts across gender (Keenan et al., 2007) and with higher symptom counts than female peers (Ezpeleta et al., 2014). Problems with peers (Munkvold et al., 2011), school expulsions, police involvement, and impairment across school, community, and interpersonal domains are more common among boys with ODD (Trepat de Ancos & Ezpeleta, 2011). While ODD symptoms in girls are associated with lower rates of help seeking as compared to boys (Trepat de Ancos & Ezpeleta, 2011), girls with ODD have also been rated as more unhappy and disliked by peers than boys with ODD (Carlson et al., 1997). It is possible that ODD behaviors in girls are less noticeable or problematic for parents and teachers, but the behaviors may be engaged in at comparable rates according to youths themselves (Keenan et al., 2008) and result in negative experiences across gender (Carlson et al., 1997).

Developmental Issues: Is ODD a Childhood Disorder?

ODD, as noted above, has historically been considered a disorder of childhood, with many expressing concern that ODD might not be distinguishable from normal child defiance and non-compliance (see Rey et al., 1988 for a discussion), and that it may be "benign and transient" in childhood if not accompanied by ADHD or CD (Moffitt et al., 2008). This perception, along with the DSM prohibition (APA, 1994) against assigning a diagnosis of ODD when CD was present, has contributed to the dearth of evidence on the course of ODD beyond childhood.

However, when the criteria for the disorder are applied faithfully, ODD behaviors can be reliably distinguished from normative childhood behaviors in preschool (Keenan & Wakschlag, 2004), and are predictive of persisting problems with ODD and with subsequent comorbid conditions (Speltz, McClellan, DeKlyen, & Jones, 1999). The stability of ODD in childhood further challenges the suggestion that ODD reflects normative or transient child behaviors. For example, in a Dutch sample of children between the ages of 42 and 66 months who met criteria for ODD (Bunte, Schoemaker, Hessen, van der Heijden, & Matthys, 2014), 62% met criteria again 18 months later. Similarly, in a US sample of children with ODD between 3 and 5 years of age (Keenan et al., 2011) 73% met criteria at one year follow-up, and 52% did so at 3 years. Further, in the US sample, cumulative stability (meeting criteria again at any one of the three years of follow-up) was 82% (Keenan et al., 2011), while, conversely, in the Dutch sample, of those meeting criteria for ODD at baseline, only 2.1% showed a complete absence of symptoms of ODD at 18 months follow-up.

Evidence also suggests that the *dimensions* of ODD can be distinguished in preschool samples as well (Ezpeleta et al., 2012; Lavigne et al., 2014), with no evidence of variation by age or gender in early childhood (Lavigne et al., 2014). Initial evidence suggests that among children between ages 3 and 5, differing trajectories of irritability symptoms can be identified (Ezpeleta, Granero, de la Osa, Trepat, & Domènech, 2016). Trajectories reflecting irritability that is either high and persisting or is increasing over ages 3 to 5 was found to be associated with poorer affective and behavioral outcomes for both the general population of children and among children with ODD specifically (Ezpeleta et al., 2016). Thus, the criteria for ODD appear to function in early childhood in a manner consistent with evidence from late childhood through adolescence.

It is not yet clear how well the symptoms of ODD function to identify the disorder beyond adolescence. Only a relatively small number of studies have examined ODD in adulthood. In a clinical sample of adults, 28.7% met criteria for ODD as defined by the DSM-IV (Barry, Marcus, Barry, & Coccaro, 2013). Interestingly, this rate is consistent with the low end of the range of prevalence (28%) in clinical samples of children identified by Boylan et al. (2007).

ODD symptoms have been shown to persist from adolescence into adulthood (Leadbeater et al., 2012), with some differences between men and women. Thus, based on a very small set of findings, it seems that ODD symptoms can be identified in adulthood, showing some consistency with earlier developmental periods. On the other hand, one study suggests that, although the irritability symptoms of ODD may persist, there is desistence in behavioral symptoms (i.e. arguing and defying, deliberately annoying others, blaming others, spitefulness) into adulthood (Leadbeater & Homel, 2015). Additionally, the impairments associated with ODD also persist into adulthood. ODD symptoms through adolescence were shown to predict a number of functional problems in adulthood, including poorer romantic relationships, poorer functioning with peers, and having nobody to provide a job recommendation for them (Burke, Rowe, & Boylan, 2014) over and above the effects of CD, ADHD, depression, and anxiety. Similarly, among a population of adults with ADHD, those with a history of ODD experience greater psychosocial impairment than those with ADHD alone or those with neither disorder (Harpold et al., 2007).

The issue of ODD in adulthood has never been clearly addressed in the DSM. Despite the historical presentation of ODD as a disorder of childhood, driven largely by parent–child interactions, there has never been a diagnostic prohibition against assigning the diagnosis in adulthood if criteria were met. There was initially some belief that the progression of ODD into adulthood would lead to passive aggressive personality disorder (PAPD), reflected in a prohibition in the DSM III (APA, 1980) against assigning oppositional disorder for those over 18 if criteria for PAPD were met. PAPD reflected the use of procrastination, forgetfulness, or stubbornness to avoid adequate performance in occupational or social functioning, suggesting that ODD and PAPD might be linked by obstinacy and covert aggression. With DSM-IV (APA, 1994), PAPD was relegated to the "criteria sets and axes provided for further study," and the description of the course of ODD was limited to its being an antecedent to CD.

The criteria for ODD in the DSM-5 reflect a shift in regards to its developmental perspective. The language linking ODD to parents is softened, although the home is still named as the most frequent setting. Further, the symptoms of arguing and defying focus on "authority figures" rather than limiting the behavior to displays toward adults (APA, 2013). Additional changes imply that consideration should be given to these behaviors in adults as well. While these changes are concordant with the small literature on ODD in adulthood, questions arise regarding how well the current symptoms might measure the construct in adulthood. Further research is required to fully understand the presentation and clinical utility of an ODD diagnosis in adulthood.

Comorbidities

ODD and Conduct Disorder

ODD and CD often co-occur in youth (Angold, Costello, & Erkanli, 1999; Burke, Waldman, & Lahey, 2010; Rowe et al., 2002). Although some have interpreted this to suggest that they represent two parts of a single continuum or construct (Moffitt et al., 2008), sufficient evidence reveals that the two are distinct (e.g., Pardini, Frick, & Moffitt, 2010), and can be distinguished as early as preschool (Keenan & Wakschlag, 2004).

Given the relatively recent elucidation of the distinct dimensions of chronic irritability versus oppositional behavior within ODD, further research will need to be done to better explain the processes that lead to co-occuring or developmental associations between ODD and CD. Improved clarity may come from the consideration of callous-unemotional traits (CU) in early childhood. Although the DSM-5 places CU (within a Limited Prosocial Emotions specifier), as part of CD, evidence suggests that CU may co-occur with ODD independent of CD (Ezpeleta, Granero, de la Osa, & Domenech, 2015), improving the prediction of the development of aggressive behavior and conduct problems.

ODD and Internalizing Disorders

In the past, CD was seen as the point of comorbidity between behavioral and affective psychopathology, particularly depression (Puig-Antich, 1982), illustrated particularly in the ICD-10 diagnostic category of depressive conduct disorder (World Health Organization, 1992). More recent evidence implicated ODD and not CD (Burke et al., 2005; Copeland et al., 2009), and the surge in research on affective symptoms of ODD has pinpointed the irritability dimension of ODD symptoms as key to explaining comorbidity with depression as well as anxiety, as described above. This association holds across gender (Burke, 2012; Burke, Hipwell, & Loeber, 2010; Burke & Loeber, 2010; Stringaris & Goodman, 2009a, 2009b), though girls with ODDmay follow the trajectory to depression in greater numbers (Rowe et al., 2002, Burke & Loeber, 2010). In addition, girls with ODD more broadly appear to experience higher rates of concurrent depression and anxiety in childhood (Trepat de Ancos & Ezpeleta, 2011).

Research suggests a concurrent genetic link between irritability and depression, both sharing hallmark negative mood, may underlie the longitudinal relationship of the disorders (Stringaris, Zavos, Leibenluft, Maughan, & Eley, 2012). While irritability is included as a core mood symptom in the DSM-5's diagnosis of major depressive disorder or persistent depressive disorder in childhood, irritability is rarely present without depressed mood in children meeting MDD criteria (Stringaris, Maughan, Copeland, Costello, & Angold, 2013). Children with both irritable and depressed mood display higher rates of ODD than children with depressed mood alone, and boys with depression are more likely to present with irritability (Stringaris et al., 2013). High rates of irritability are also present among children with anxiety disorders (Stoddard et al., 2014).

ODD and ADHD

ODD is one of the most common comorbid psychological disorders for children with ADHD, though rates of comorbid ADHD are lower when considering all children with ODD (Carlson et al., 1997). Even among adults with ADHD, ODD is diagnosable in 43% and is present predominantly when ADHD co-occurs with high levels of emotional dysregulation, which is associated with greater impairment (Reimherr et al., 2010). Rates of comorbid ADHD and ODD differ depending on gender and sample, with 62 to 68.7% of boys, in comparison to the more wide-ranging 28.6 to 71% of girls (Biederman et al., 2008; Carlson et al., 1997; Munkvold et al., 2011; Trepat de Ancos & Ezpeleta, 2011). Consistent with general trends of ADHD diagnosis in boys, most studies suggest that girls are less likely than boys to present with both ADHD and ODD (Munkvold et al., 2011; Trepat de Ancos & Ezpeleta, 2011). In a Finnish population study, a lower proportion of girls with either ODD or CD have comorbid ADHD than do boys with disruptive behavior disorders (Nordström, Hurtig, Moilanen, Taanila, & Ebeling, 2013). However, some research finds equivalent rates of comorbidity across gender (Carlson et al., 1997), and girls with ADHD are more likely than population girls to have ODD (Biederman et al., 2008).

In comparison to either diagnosis alone, comorbidity of ADHD and ODD is associated with greater impairment and higher levels of psychological problems in multiple domains across both children (Biederman et al., 2008; Carlson et al., 1997; Kim et al., 2010) and adults (Gadow et al., 2007). Individuals with both ADHD and ODD present with lower self-directedness and persistence (Kim et al., 2010), greater likelihood of being ignored by peers (Carlson et al., 1997) and, among girls, being placed in a special classroom and having higher rates of suspensions (Biederman et al., 2008). Some evidence suggests that ODD symptoms underlie the risk of engaging in bullying and being victimized among children with ADHD (Fite, Evans, Cooley, & Rubens, 2014). Clinic adults with both ADHD and ODD have higher rates of unemployment, while community adults with comorbidity have lower rates of marriage (Gadow et al., 2007).

Among children with ADHD, ODD dimensions of irritability and oppositional behavior maintain their separate associations with internalizing and externalizing symptoms, respectively, and are uniquely related to impairment (de la Cruz et al., 2015). A higher level of irritability is correlated with more ADHD symptoms, and both medication and behavioral treatments for ADHD have demonstrated some effectiveness for irritability (de la Cruz et al., 2015). While emotion dysregulation in some form is common across most psychological disorders, its manifestation across ADHD and ODD, with prominent negative affect in the form of anger, irritability, and temper, appears to be similar (Barkley, 2010).

The high rate of comorbidity and increasing focus on these irritability symptoms has led some to suggest that the overlap reflects a core dimension of ADHD symptomology, such as emotional impulsivity, rather than emotion dysregulation rooted in ODD (Barkley, 2010). However, measures of emotional impulsivity include the DSM-5 irritability dimension of ODD (touchy, angry, and lose temper), as well as non-ODD items (impatient, easily frustrated, overreact emotionally, and easily excited; Barkley, 2010), making it difficult to attribute emotional impulsivity entirely to ADHD. Emotional impulsivity appears in the majority of adults with ADHD, is strongly correlated with both ADHD dimensions, is associated with greater impairment beyond ADHD severity, and individuals with ADHD are more emotionally impulsive than clinical comparison groups (Barkley, 2010). In addition, parent emotional impulsivity scores predict greater severity of ODD and CD symptoms in offspring (Barkley, 2010). However, since comparisons do not include individuals with ODD without ADHD, and emotional impulsivity contains ODD symptoms, this presentation cannot be ruled out as reflective of ADHD+ODD instead of tied uniquely to ADHD.

ODD and Autism Spectrum Disorder

Research into ODD in the context of autism spectrum disorder (ASD) has been sparse. However, ODD is as common, if not more so, in children with ASD as among neurotypical children (Gadow, DeVincent, & Drabick, 2008; Guttman-Steinmetz, Gadow, & DeVincent, 2009), and comorbid presentations of the disorders are of growing interest to the scientific and clinical community. A recent study examining verbally fluent mainstream schoolchildren with ASD indicated that over half met the symptom count threshold for ODD (Mandy, Roughan, & Skuse, 2014). Studies have sought to clarify whether ODD behaviors among children with ASD reflect the same disorder seen in children without ASD (Kaat & Lecavalier, 2013), rather than a "phenocopy" or "autistic epiphenomenon" resulting from core ASD symptoms (Mandy et al., 2014). Among children with ASD, comorbid ODD does appear to present distinctly from other ASD-related behavioral difficulties, and is associated with higher rates of psychiatric symptoms (Gadow et al., 2008). Research suggests that ASD symptomology is not uniquely associated with ODD behaviors, and that co-occurrence of the two disorders is likely a true comorbid presentation (Mandy et al., 2014).

ODD appears to present similarly across both ASD and neurotypical samples. ASD children, like their non-ASD counterparts, demonstrate high rates of ODD and ADHD co-occurrence (Kaat & Lecavalier, 2013; Simonoff et al., 2008). This comorbidity is associated with a more severe clinical presentation than that seen among ASD children with ODD alone (Gadow et al., 2008; Guttman-Steinmetz et al., 2009). DSM-5 ODD dimensions have also been identified, and share similar predictions as to outcomes as in typically developing children (Mandy et al., 2014). Among general clinically referred children (non-ASD-specific), the ODD irritability dimension has been linked to higher levels of ASD symptoms, though the generalizability of this finding to children with ASD may be limited (Gadow & Drabick, 2012).

Conclusion

The past 10 to 15 years have seen a marked increase in research on ODD that has helped to put to rest questions about the validity of the disorder and, relatedly, the issue of whether it is meaningfully distinct from CD. In particular, studies much less frequently lump ODD and CD together, a practice that plagued research in the past and made it impossible to discern differences between the disorders. With this more refined focus, it has become clear that dimensions within ODD of chronic irritability and oppositional behavior are distinct, but yet highly related to one another. These dimensions explain important differences in risk for internalizing versus externalizing disorders. Evidence demonstrates that not only can ODD be distinguished from normative behavior in preschool, but that it and its associated impairments persist into adulthood. However, on this latter point, research is sorely lacking, and basic questions regarding assessment, identification, and diagnosis have yet to be meaningfully addressed. Evidence suggests that gender differences do exist in prevalence rates, but not in the structure of dimensions or the adequacy of item content to measure the disorder. Differences in prevalence rates appear to vary across development, associated with a potentially curvilinear growth for girls that is not matched by boys. At this point, the perception of ODD as a transient, benign disorder caused by, or limited to, poor parent–child interactions is simply insufficient to account for the breadth of evidence on the etiology, course, persistence, and impact on functioning of ODD.

References

American Psychiatric Association. (1980). *Diagnostic and statistical manual of mental disorders* (3rd ed.). Washington, DC: Author.

American Psychiatric Association. (1994). *Diagnostic and statistical manual of mental disorders* (4th ed.). Washington, DC: Author.

American Psychiatric Association. (2013). *Diagnostic and statistical manual of mental disorders* (5th ed.). Arlington, VA: Author.

Angold, A., Costello, E. J., & Erkanli, A. (1999). Comorbidity. *Journal of Child Psychology and Psychiatry, and Allied Disciplines, 40*(1), 57–87.

Axelson, D., Findling, R. L., Fristad, M. A., Kowatch, R. A., Youngstrom, E. A., Horwitz, S. M., . . . Birmaher, B. (2012). Examining the proposed disruptive mood dysregulation disorder diagnosis in children in the longitudinal assessment of manic symptoms study. *Journal of Clinical Psychiatry, 73*(10), 1342–1350. doi:10.4088/Jcp.12m07674

Barkley, R. A. (2010). Deficient emotional self-regulation: A core component of attention-deficit/hyperactivity disorder. *Journal of ADHD and Related Disorders, 1*(2), 5–37.

Barry, T. D., Marcus, D. K., Barry, C. T., & Coccaro, E. F. (2013). The latent structure of oppositional defiant disorder in children and adults. *Journal of Psychiatric Research, 47*(12), 1932–1939.

Biederman, J., Petty, C. R., Monuteaux, M. C., Mick, E., Parcell, T., Westerberg, D., & Faraone, S. V. (2008). The longitudinal course of comorbid oppositional defiant disorder in girls with attention-deficit/hyperactivity disorder: Findings from a controlled 5-year prospective longitudinal follow-up study. *Journal of Developmental & Behavioral Pediatrics, 29*(6), 501–507.

Boylan, K., Rowe, R., Duku, E., Stepp, S., Hipwell, A. E., & Burke, J. D. (2016). Longitudinal profiles of girls' irritable, defiant and antagonistic oppositional symptoms: Evidence for group based differences in symptom severity. *Journal of Abnormal Child Psychology*. doi:10.1007/s10802-016-0231-z

Boylan, K., Vaillancourt, T., Boyle, M., & Szatmari, P. (2007). Comorbidity of internalizing disorders in children with oppositional defiant disorder. *European Child and Adolescent Psychiatry, 16*(8), 484–494. doi:10.1007/s00787-007-0624-1

Brotman, M. A., Schmajuk, M., Rich, B. A., Dickstein, D. P., Guyer, A. E., Costello, E. J., . . . Leibenluft, E. (2006). Prevalence, clinical correlates, and longitudinal course of severe mood dysregulation in children. *Biological Psychiatry, 60*(9), 991–997.

Bunte, T., Schoemaker, K., Hessen, D. J., van der Heijden, P. G., & Matthys, W. (2014). Stability and change of ODD, CD and ADHD diagnosis in referred preschool children. *Journal of Abnormal Child Psychology, 42*, 1213–1224.

Burke, J. D. (2012). An affective dimension within oppositional defiant disorder symptoms among boys: Personality and psychopathology outcomes into early adulthood. *Journal of Child Psychology and Psychiatry, 53*(11), 1176–1183. doi:10.1111/j.1469-7610.2012.02598.x

Burke, J. D., Boylan, K., Rowe, R., Duku, E., Stepp, S. D., Hipwell, A. E., & Waldman, I. D. (2014). Identifying the irritability dimension of ODD: Application of a modified bifactor model across five large community samples of children. *Journal of Abnormal Psychology, 123*(4), 841–851. doi:10.1037/a0037898

Burke, J. D., Hipwell, A. E., & Loeber, R. (2010). Dimensions of oppositional defiant disorder as predictors of depression and conduct disorder in preadolescent girls. *Journal of the American Academy of Child & Adolescent Psychiatry, 49*(5), 484–492.

Burke, J. D., & Loeber, R. (2010). Oppositional defiant disorder and the explanation of the comorbidity between behavioral disorders and depression. *Clinical Psychology: Science and Practice, 17*(4), 319–326.

Burke, J. D., Loeber, R., & Birmaher, B. (2002). Oppositional defiant disorder and conduct disorder: A review of the past 10 years, part II. *Journal of the American Academy of Child and Adolescent Psychiatry, 41*(11), 1275–1293.

Burke, J. D., Loeber, R., Lahey, B. B., & Rathouz, P. J. (2005). Developmental transitions among affective and behavioral disorders in adolescent boys. *Journal of Child Psychology and Psychiatry, 46*(11), 1200–1210. doi:10.1111/j.1469-7610.2005.00422.x

Burke, J. D., Rowe, R., & Boylan, K. (2014). Functional outcomes of child and adolescent oppositional defiant disorder symptoms in young adult men. *Journal of Child Psychology and Psychiatry and Allied Disciplines, 55*(3), 264–272.

Burke, J. D., & Stepp, S. D. (2012). Adolescent disruptive behavior and borderline personality disorder symptoms in young adult men. *Journal of Abnormal Child Psychology, 40*(1), 35–44. doi:10.1007/s10802-011-9558-7

Burke, J. D., Waldman, I., & Lahey, B. B. (2010). Predictive validity of childhood oppositional defiant disorder and conduct disorder: Implications for the DSM-V. *Journal of Abnormal Psychology*, *119*(4), 739–51. doi:10.1037/a0019708

Carlson, C. L., Tamm, L., & Gaub, M. (1997). Gender differences in children with ADHD, ODD, and co-occurring ADHD/ODD identified in a school population. *Psychiatry*, *36*(12), 1706–1714. doi:10.1097/00004583-199712000-00019

Copeland, W., Angold, A., Costello, E., & Egger, H. (2013). Prevalence, comorbidity and correlates of DSM-5 proposed disruptive mood dysregulation disorder. *American Journal of Psychiatry*, *170*(2), 173–179. doi:10.1176/appi.ajp.2012.12010132.

Copeland, W. E., Shanahan, L., Costello, E. J., & Angold, A. (2009). Childhood and adolescent psychiatric disorders as predictors of young adult disorders. *Archives of General Psychiatry*, *66*(7), 764–772.

de la Cruz, L. F., Simonoff, E., McGough, J. J., Halperin, J. M., Arnold, L. E., & Stringaris, A. (2015). Treatment of children with attention-deficit/hyperactivity disorder (ADHD) and irritability: Results from the multimodal treatment study of children with ADHD (MTA). *Journal of the American Academy of Child & Adolescent Psychiatry*, *54*(1), 62–70.

Demmer, D. H., Hooley, M., Sheen, J., McGillivray, J. A., & Lum, J. A. (2016). Sex differences in the prevalence of oppositional defiant disorder during middle childhood: A meta-analysis. *Journal of Abnormal Child Psychology*, *45*(2), 313–325. doi:10.1007/s10802-016-0170-8

de Zeeuw, E. L., van Beijsterveldt, C. E. M., Lubke, G. H., Glasner, T. J., & Boomsma, D. I. (2015). Childhood ODD and ADHD behavior: The effect of classroom sharing, gender, teacher gender and their interactions. *Behavior Genetics*, *45*(4), 394–408. doi:10.1007/s10519-015-9712-z

Dougherty, L. R., Smith, V. C., Bufferd, S. J., Carlson, G. A., Stringaris, A., Leibenluft, E., & Klein, D. N. (2014). DSM-5 disruptive mood dysregulation disorder: Correlates and predictors in young children. *Psychological Medicine*, *44*, 2339–2350. doi:10.1017/S0033291713003115

Ezpeleta, L., de la Osa, N., Granero, R., & Trepat, E. (2014). Functional impairment associated with symptoms of oppositional defiant disorder in preschool and early school boys and girls from the general population. *Anales de Psicologia*, *30*(2), 395–402. doi:10.6018/analesps.30.2.148141

Ezpeleta, L., Granero, R., de la Osa, N., Trepat, E., & Domènech, J. M. (2016). Trajectories of oppositional defiant disorder irritability symptoms in preschool children. *Journal of Abnormal Child Psychology*, *44*(1), 115–128.

Ezpeleta, L., Granero, R., de la Osa, N., & Domènech, J. M. (2015). Clinical characteristics of preschool children with oppositional defiant disorder and callous-unemotional traits. *PloS One*, *10*(9), e0139346. doi:10.1371/journal.pone.0139346

Ezpeleta, L., Granero, R., de la Osa, N., Penelo, E., & Domenech, J. M. (2012). Dimensions of oppositional defiant disorder in 3-year-old preschoolers. *Journal of Child Psychology and Psychiatry*, *53*(11), 1128–1138. doi:10.1111/j.1469-7610.2012.02545.x

Ezpeleta, L., Keeler, G., Erkanli, A., Costello, E. J. and Angold, A. (2001). Epidemiology of psychiatric disability in childhood and adolescence. *Journal of Child Psychology and Psychiatry*, *42*, 901–914. doi:10.1111/1469-7610.00786

Ezpeleta, L., & Penelo, E. (2015). Measurement invariance of oppositional defiant disorder dimensions in 3-year-old preschoolers. *European Journal of Psychological Assessment*, *31*(1), 45–53. doi:10.1027/1015-5759/a000205

Fite, P. J., Evans, S. C., Cooley, J. L., & Rubens, S. L. (2014). Further evaluation of associations between attention-deficit/hyperactivity and oppositional defiant disorder symptoms and bullying-victimization in adolescence. *Child Psychiatry and Human Development*, *45*(1), 32–41. doi:10.1007/s10578-013-0376-8

Gadow, K. D., DeVincent, C. J., & Drabick, D. A. G. (2008). Oppositional defiant disorder as a clinical phenotype in children with autism spectrum disorder. *Journal of Autism and Developmental Disorders*, *38*(7), 1302–1310. doi:10.1007/s10803-007-0516-8

Gadow, K. D., & Drabick, D. A. G. (2012). Symptoms of autism and schizophrenia spectrum disorders in clinically referred youth with oppositional defiant disorder. *Research in Developmental Disabilities*, *33*(4), 1157–1168. doi:10.1016/j.ridd.2012.01.004

Gadow, K. D., Sprafkin, J., Schneider, J., Nolan, E. E., Schwartz, J., & Weiss, M. D. (2007). ODD, ADHD, versus ODD+ADHD in clinic and community adults. *Journal of Attention Disorders, 11*(3), 374–383.

Guttmann-Steinmetz, S., Gadow, K. D., & Devincent, C. J. (2009). Oppositional defiant and conduct disorder behaviors in boys with autism spectrum disorder with and without attention-deficit hyperactivity disorder versus several comparison samples. *Journal of Autism and Developmental Disorders, 39*(7), 976–985. doi:10.1007/s10803-009-0706-7

Harpold, T., Biederman, J., Gignac, M., Hammerness, P., Surman, C., Potter, A., & Mick, E. (2007). Is oppositional defiant disorder a meaningful diagnosis in adults? Results from a large sample of adults with ADHD. *The Journal of Nervous and Mental Disease, 195*(7), 601–605.

Herzhoff, K., & Tackett, J. L. (2016). Subfactors of oppositional defiant disorder: Converging evidence from structural and latent class analyses. *Journal of Child Psychology and Psychiatry, 57*(1), 18–29. doi:10.1111/jcpp.12423

Kaat, A. J., & Lecavalier, L. (2013). Disruptive behavior disorders in children and adolescents with autism spectrum disorders: A review of the prevalence, presentation, and treatment. *Research in Autism Spectrum Disorders, 7*(12), 1579–1594. doi:10.1016/j.rasd.2013.08.012

Keenan, K., Boeldt, D., Chen, D., Coyne, C., Donald, R., Duax, J., . . . Humphries, M. (2011). Predictive validity of DSM-IV oppositional defiant and conduct disorders in clinically referred preschoolers. *Journal of Child Psychology and Psychiatry, 52*, 47–55.

Keenan, K., Coyne, C., & Lahey, B. B. (2008). Should relational aggression be included in DSM-V? *Journal of the American Academy of Child and Adolescent Psychiatry, 47*(1), 86–93. doi:10.1097/chi.0b013e31815a56b8

Keenan, K., & Wakschlag, L. S. (2004). Are oppositional defiant and conduct disorder symptoms normative behaviors in preschoolers? A comparison of referred and nonreferred children. *The American Journal of Psychiatry, 161*(2), 356–358.

Keenan, K., Wakschlag, L. S., Danis, B., Hill, C., Humphries, M., Duax, J., & Donald, R. (2007). Further evidence of the reliability and validity of DSM-IV ODD and CD in preschool children. *Journal of the American Academy of Child and Adolescent Psychiatry, 46*(4), 457–468. doi:10.1097/CHI.0b013e31803062d3

Kelland, K. (2012). New mental health manual is dangerous say experts. *Reuters*, February 9. Retrieved from http://www.reuters.com/article/us-mental-illness-diagnosis-idUSTRE8181WX20120209

Kelter, J. D., & Pope, A. W. (2011). The effect of child gender on teachers' responses to oppositional defiant disorder. *Child & Family Behavior Therapy, 33*(1), 49–57. doi:10.1080/07317107.2011.545013

Kim, H. W., Cho, S. C., Kim, B. N., Kim, J. W., Shin, M. S., & Yeo, J. Y. (2010). Does oppositional defiant disorder have temperament and psychopathological profiles independent of attention deficit/hyperactivity disorder? *Comprehensive Psychiatry, 51*(4), 412–418. doi:10.1016/j.comppsych.2009.09.002

Lavigne, J. V., Bryant, F. B., Hopkins, J., & Gouze, K. R. (2015). Dimensions of oppositional defiant disorder in young children: Model comparisons, gender and longitudinal invariance. *Journal of Abnormal Child Psychology, 43*(3), 423–439. doi:10.1007/s10802-014-9919-0

Lavigne, J. V., Gouze, K. R., Bryant, F. B., & Hopkins, J. (2014). Dimensions of oppositional defiant disorder in young children: Heterotypic continuity with anxiety and depression. *Journal of Abnormal Child Psychology, 42*(6), 937–951. doi:10.1007/s10802-014-9853-1

Leadbeater, B., & Homel, J. (2015). Irritable and defiant sub-dimensions of ODD: Their stability and prediction of internalizing symptoms and conduct problems from adolescence to young adulthood. *Journal of Abnormal Child Psychology, 43*(3), 407–421.

Leadbeater, B., Thompson, K., & Gruppuso, V. (2012). Co-occurring trajectories of symptoms of anxiety, depression, and oppositional defiance from adolescence to young adulthood. *Journal of Clinical Child and Adolescent Psychology, 41*(6), 719–730. doi:10.1080/15374416.2012.694608

Leibenluft, E. (2011). Severe mood dysregulation, irritability, and the diagnostic boundaries of bipolar disorder in youths. *American Journal of Psychiatry, 168*, 129–142.

Lochman, J. E., Evans, S. C., Burke, J. D., Roberts, M. C., Fite, P. J., Reed, G. M., . . . Elena Garralda, M. (2015). An empirically based alternative to DSM-5's disruptive mood dysregulation disorder for ICD-11. *World Psychiatry, 14*(1), 30–33. doi:10.1002/wps.20176

Mandy, W., Roughan, L., & Skuse, D. (2014). Three dimensions of oppositionality in autism spectrum disorder. *Journal of Abnormal Child Psychology, 42*(2), 291–300. doi:10.1007/s10802-013-9778-0

Margulies, D. M., Weintraub, S., Basile, J., Grover, P. J., & Carlson, G. A. (2012). Will disruptive mood dysregulation disorder reduce false diagnosis of bipolar disorder in children? *Bipolar Disorders, 14*(5), 488–496. doi:10.1111/j.1399-5618.2012.01029.x

Mayes, S. D., Mathiowetz, C., Kokotovich, C., Waxmonsky, J., Baweja, R., Calhoun, S. L., & Bixler, E. O. (2015). Stability of disruptive mood dysregulation disorder symptoms (irritable-angry mood and temper outbursts) throughout childhood and adolescence in a general population sample. *Journal of Abnormal Child Psychology, 43*(8), 1543–1549. doi:10.1007/s10802-015-0033-8

Moffitt, T. E., Arseneault, L., Jaffee, S. R., Kim-Cohen, J., Koenen, K. C., Odgers, C. L., . . . Viding, E. (2008). Research review: DSM-V conduct disorder: Research needs for an evidence base. *Journal of Child Psychology and Psychiatry, 49*(1), 3–33. doi:10.1111/j.1469-7610.2007.01823.x

Mulraney, M., Schilpzand, E. J., Hazell, P., Nicholson, J. M., Anderson, V., Efron, D., . . . Sciberras, E. (2016). Comorbidity and correlates of disruptive mood dysregulation disorder in 6–8-year-old children with ADHD. *European Child and Adolescent Psychiatry, 25*(3), 321–330. doi:10.1007/s00787-015-0738-9

Munkvold, L. H., Lundervold, A. J., & Manger, T. (2011). Oppositional defiant disorder—Gender differences in co-occurring symptoms of mental health problems in a general population of children. *Journal of Abnormal Child Psychology, 39*(4), 577–587. doi:10.1007/s10802-011-9486-6

Nordstrom, T., Hurtig, T., Moilanen, I., Taanila, A., & Ebeling, H. (2013). Disruptive behaviour disorder with and without attention deficit hyperactivity disorder is a risk of psychiatric hospitalization. *Acta Paediatrica, 102*(11), 1100–1103. doi:10.1111/apa.12383

Nock, M. K., Kazdin, A. E., Hiripi, E., & Kessler, R. C. (2007). Lifetime prevalence, correlates, and persistence of oppositional defiant disorder: Results from the national comorbidity survey replication. *Journal of Child Psychology and Psychiatry, and Allied Disciplines, 48*(7), 703–713. doi:JCPP1733 [pii]

Ohan, J. L., & Johnston, C. (2005). Gender appropriateness of symptom criteria for attention-deficit/hyperactivity disorder, oppositional-defiant disorder, and conduct disorder. *Child Psychiatry and Human Development, 35*(4), 359–381. doi:10.1007/s10578-005-2694-y

Pardini, D. A., Frick, P. J., & Moffitt, T. E. (2010). Building an evidence base for DSM-5 conceptualizations of oppositional defiant disorder and conduct disorder: Introduction to the special section. *Journal of Abnormal Psychology, 119*(4), 683–688. doi:10.1037/a0021441

Puig-Antich, J. (1982). Major depression and conduct disorder in prepuberty. *Journal of the American Academy of Child and Adolescent Psychiatry, 21*(2), 118–28.

Rey, J. M., Bashir, M. R., Schwarz, M., Richards, I. N., Plapp, J. M., & Stewart, G. W. (1988). Oppositional disorder—Fact or fiction. *Journal of the American Academy of Child and Adolescent Psychiatry, 27*(2), 157–162. doi:10.1097/00004583-198803000-00004

Reimherr, F. W., Marchant, B. K., Olsen, J. L., Halls, C., Kondo, D. G., Williams, E. D., & Robison, R. J. (2010). Emotional dysregulation as a core feature of adult ADHD: its relationship with clinical variables and treatment response in two methylphenidate trials. *Journal of ADHD & Related Disorders, 1*(4), 53–64.

Rowe, R., Costello, E. J., Angold, A., Copeland, W. E., & Maughan, B. (2010). Developmental pathways in oppositional defiant disorder and conduct disorder. *Journal of Abnormal Psychology, 119*(4), 726–738. doi:2010-23724-004 [pii] 10.1037/a0020798

Rowe, R., Maughan, B., & Eley, T. C. (2006). Links between antisocial behavior and depressed mood: The role of life events and attributional style. *Journal of Abnormal Child Psychology, 34*(3), 293–302.

Rowe, R., Maughan, B., Pickles, A., Costello, E. J., & Angold, A. (2002). The relationship between DSM-IV oppositional defiant disorder and conduct disorder: Findings from the great smoky mountains study. *Journal of Child Psychology and Psychiatry and Allied Disciplines, 43*(3), 365–373. doi:10.1111/1469-7610.00027

Simonoff, E., Pickles, A., Charman, T., Chandler, S., Loucas, T., & Baird, G. (2008). Psychiatric disorders in children with autism spectrum disorders: Prevalence, comorbidity, and associated factors in a population-derived sample. *Journal of the American Academy of Child and Adolescent Psychiatry, 47*(8), 921–929. doi:10.1097/CHI.0b013e318179964f

Sparks, G. M., Axelson, D. A., Yu, H., Ha, W., Ballester, J., Diler, R. S., . . . Birmaher, B. (2014). Disruptive mood dysregulation disorder and chronic irritability in youth at familial risk for bipolar disorder. *Journal of the American Academy of Child and Adolescent Psychiatry, 53*(4), 408–416. doi:10.1016/j.jaac.2013.12.026

Speltz, M. L., McClellan, J., DeKlyen, M., & Jones, K. (1999). Preschool boys with oppositional defiant disorder: Clinical presentation and diagnostic change. *Journal of the American Academy of Child & Adolescent Psychiatry, 38*(7), 838–845.

Stoddard, J., Stringaris, A., Brotman, M. A., Montville, D., Pine, D. S., & Leibenluft, E. (2014). Irritability in child and adolescent anxiety disorders. *Depression and Anxiety, 31*(7), 566–573. doi:10.1002/da.22151

Stringaris, A., Cohen, P., Pine, D. S., & Leibenluft, E. (2009). Adult outcomes of youth irritability: A 20-year prospective community-based study. *American Journal of Psychiatry, 166*(9), 1048–1054. doi:10.1176/appi.ajp.2009.08121849

Stringaris, A., & Goodman, R. (2009a). Longitudinal outcome of youth oppositionality: Irritable, headstrong, and hurtful behaviors have distinctive predictions. *Journal of the American Academy of Child and Adolescent Psychiatry, 48*(4), 404–412. doi:10.1097/CHI.0b013e3181984f30

Stringaris, A., & Goodman, R. (2009b). Three dimensions of oppositionality in youth. *Journal of Child Psychology and Psychiatry and Allied Disciplines, 50*(3), 216–223. doi:10.1111/j.1469-7610.2008.01989.x

Stringaris, A., Maughan, B., Copeland, W. S., Costello, E. J., & Angold, A. (2013). Irritable mood as a symptom of depression in youth: Prevalence, developmental, and clinical correlates in the Great Smoky Mountains study. *Journal of the American Academy of Child and Adolescent Psychiatry, 52*(8), 831–840. doi:10.1016/j.jaac.2013.05.017

Stringaris, A., Zavos, H., Leibenluft, E., Maughan, B., & Eley, T. C. (2012). Adolescent irritability: Phenotypic associations and genetic links with depressed mood. *American Journal of Psychiatry, 169*, 47–54.

Trepat de Ancos, E., & Ezpeleta, L. (2011). Sex differences in oppositional defiant disorder. *Psicothema, 23*(4), 666–671.

Vidal-Ribas, P., Brotman, M. A., Valdivieso, I., Leibenluft, E., & Stringaris, A. (2016). The status of irritability in psychiatry: A conceptual and quantitative review. *Journal of the American Academy of Child & Adolescent Psychiatry, 55*(7), 556–570.

Whelan, Y. M., Stringaris, A., Maughan, B., & Barker, E. D. (2013). Developmental continuity of oppositional defiant disorder subdimensions at ages 8, 10, and 13 years and their distinct psychiatric outcomes at age 16 years. *Journal of the American Academy of Child and Adolescent Psychiatry, 52*(9), 961–969. doi:10.1016/j.jaac.2013.06.013

Waschbusch, D. A., & King, S. (2006). Should sex-specific norms be used to assess attention-deficit/hyperactivity disorder or oppositional defiant disorder? *Journal of Consulting and Clinical Psychology, 74*(1), 179–185. http://doi:10.1037/0022-006X.74.1.179

World Health Organization. (1992). *ICD-10 classifications of mental and behavioural disorder: Clinical descriptions and diagnostic guidelines.* Geneva, Switzerland: Author.

3

Conduct Disorder and Callous-Unemotional Traits

Paul J. Frick and Tina D. Wall Myers

Conduct Disorder (CD) is defined as a repetitive and persistent pattern of behavior that violates the rights of others or that violates major age-appropriate societal norms or rules (American Psychiatric Association [APA], 2013). The symptoms of CD fall into four clusters: (a) aggression to people and animals, (b) destruction of property, (c) deceitfulness or theft, and (d) serious violations of rules (e.g., truancy, running away from home). To meet the criteria for the disorder, the person must show a repetitive and persistent pattern of behavior involving multiple symptoms from these groups (i.e., three or more). CD is an important mental health problem for a number of reasons. First, it is highly prevalent, with a meta-analysis of epidemiological studies estimating that the worldwide prevalence of CD among children and adolescents aged 6 to 18 is 3.2% (Canino, Polanczyk, Bauermeister, Rhode, & Frick, 2010). Second, CD often involves aggression and violence and it is highly related to criminal behavior (Frick, 2012). Thus, it has a significant impact on society through its effects on the victims of these acts. Third, CD is also related to significant and long-lasting impairments to the person with the disorder. That is, CD in childhood predicts later problems in adolescence and adulthood, including mental health problems (e.g., substance abuse), legal problems (e.g., risk for arrest), educational problems (e.g., school drop-out), social problems (e.g., poor marital adjustment), occupational problems (e.g., poor job performance) and physical health problems (e.g., poor respiratory function) (Odgers et al., 2008).

CD is listed in the fifth edition of the *Diagnostic and Statistical Manual of Mental Disorders* (DSM-5) as being part of the class of disorders labeled as "Disruptive, Impulse Control, and Conduct Disorders," which all involve problems in the self-control of emotions and behaviors (APA, 2013). However, the DSM-5 recognizes that the causes of the problems of self-control can vary, not only across the different disorders in this group, but can also differ among individuals with the same disorder. This heterogeneity in causes is not unique to these disorders or to CD (Sanislow et al., 2010). However, the best way to capture the multiple causal pathways to CD has been one of the most important and controversial issues related to defining the condition since it was first recognized in official classification systems.

A Brief History of Diagnostic Classification for Conduct Disorder

CD was first recognized as a mental health disorder in the second edition of the *Diagnostic and Statistical Manual of Mental Disorders* (DSM-II; APA, 1968). In its first definition, it was conceptualized as being a response to negative environmental factors that could result in

---

The Wiley Handbook of Disruptive and Impulse-Control Disorders, First Edition.
Edited by John E. Lochman and Walter Matthys.
© 2018 John Wiley & Sons Ltd. Published 2018 by John Wiley & Sons Ltd.

three distinct patterns of behavior: runaway reaction, undersocialized aggressive reaction, and group delinquent reaction. Thus, this first definition focused on the heterogeneity in how CD might be expressed behaviorally and not on different causes.

In the DSM-III (APA, 1980), a different method for subtyping persons with CD was introduced that focused more on potential differences in causes. Persons with CD were differentiated into those who were (a) aggressive or not and (b) those who were considered "socialized" (e.g., had lasting friendships, felt guilt/remorse) or not. Research on the undersocialized subtype of CD supported its validity, in that adolescents who were classified with this subtype tended to have poorer adjustment in juvenile institutions and were more likely to continue to show antisocial behavior into adulthood compared to other adolescents with CD (Quay, 1987). Further, the undersocialized group was also more likely to show several neurophysiological correlates to their antisocial behavior, such as low serotonin levels and autonomic irregularities, supporting the possibility that this subtype might be important for capturing the heterogeneity in causes of this disorder (Lahey, Hart, Pliszka, Applegate, & McBurnett, 1993; Quay, 1993).

Despite these promising findings, the name given to this group (i.e., "undersocialized aggressive") resulted in considerable confusion as to the core features of this subtype and the best way to operationalize these features (Lahey, Loeber, Quay, Frick, & Grimm, 1992). Some definitions focused on the child's ability to form and maintain social relationships, whereas others focused primarily on the context (alone or as a group) in which the antisocial acts were typically committed. Very few definitions focused directly on the interpersonal and affective characteristics that were central to the clinical descriptions of psychopathic individuals which purportedly formed the research basis for this method of subtyping (Quay, 1987). In response to this definitional confusion, the next revision of DSM revised its criteria to focus solely on whether the antisocial acts were committed alone and whether the pattern included aggressive symptoms, both of which were judged to be more easily assessed than the emotional and interpersonal features defining the undersocialized type (DSM-III-R; APA, 1987). It was renamed the solitary–aggressive subtype. The criteria for the second subtype focused solely on whether the antisocial acts were committed with other antisocial peers, and this subtype was assumed to be primarily nonaggressive in nature. It was renamed the group subtype.

The method of subtyping CD was changed yet again in the next edition of the manual. In the DSM-IV, subtypes of CD were largely based on when the severe conduct problems first occurred, with a childhood-onset group showing severe conduct problems well before adolescence (i.e., before age 10) and an adolescent-onset group showing the onset of severe conduct problems coinciding with puberty (APA, 1994). This distinction was chosen based on research showing that:

1. the two groups had very different outcomes (i.e., in the childhood-onset group, CD being more likely to persist into adulthood);
2. the two groups had very different correlates that would seem to implicate different etiologies;
3. the childhood-onset group was more likely to be aggressive, thus, it largely subsumed the aggressive subtypes from previous diagnostic definitions
4. there was minimal evidence supporting the validity of the solitary-group distinction (Moffitt et al., 2008).

Research supporting this distinction has continued to grow (Frick & Viding, 2009; Moffitt et al., 2008). This is especially true in terms of differential outcomes. For example, in a New Zealand birth cohort, boys who showed a childhood onset to their chronic conduct problems were over three times more likely to have been convicted of a violent offense, to have received psychiatric services, to have attempted suicide, and to be homeless as adults (i.e. by age 32) compared to boys who showed an adolescent onset (Odgers et al., 2008). Similarly, girls with the childhood-onset group were over three times more likely to be convicted for a violent offense and to be homeless as adults and they were twice as likely to exhibit substance use, major depression, anxiety, and to have hit a child as an adult compared to girls who showed an adolescent onset to their conduct problems. It is important to note that, although persons who show an adolescent onset to their serious conduct problems seem to be less impaired than their childhood-onset counterparts, they are still at risk for problems in adjustment as adults. These may result from the consequences of their adolescent antisocial behavior, such the consequences of having a criminal record, dropping out of school, abusing substances, or associating with deviant peers (Odgers et al., 2008).

Because of the substantial support for this method of subtyping youth with serious conduct problems, it was retained in the DSM-5. However, it is important to note a number of limitations in this approach. First, it is not firmly established what method (e.g., age or pubertal stage) should be used to differentiate childhood-onset from adolescent-onset groups (Frick & Nigg, 2010), and some have even argued that age of onset should be considered more dimensionally (Lahey, Waldman, & McBurnett, 1999). Second, it is sometimes difficult in both research and practice to accurately establish the age of onset for CD, given problems in persons' retrospective recall of past behaviors (Moffitt et al., 2008). Third, this approach to subtyping still appears to leave considerable heterogeneity in both outcomes (Odgers et al., 2007) and etiology (Frick, Ray, Thornton, & Kahn, 2014a) within the childhood-onset group.

Callous-Unemotional Traits and Developmental Pathways to Conduct Disorder

In order to further reduce the heterogeneity in CD, the DSM-5 included another specifier to designate those youth with serious conduct problems who also show elevated rates of callous-unemotional (CU) traits. The specifier of "with limited prosocial emotions" (LPE) is given if the individual (a) meets criteria for CD and (b) shows two more of the following CU traits persistently over 12 months in more than one relationship or setting:

- lack of remorse or guilt;
- callous lack of empathy;
- unconcern about performance at school, work, or in other important activities;
- shallow or deficient affect.

These four criteria are consistent with conceptualizations of the earlier DSM-III definition of the "undersocialized" subtype of CD that was proposed to be characterized by "a failure to establish a normal degree of affection, empathy, or bond with others" (APA, 1980, p. 45). However, the definition for the LPE specifier has critical features that are likely to enhance its ability to reliably and validly define an important subgroup of youth with serious conduct problems.

First, the indicators are more closely tied to the way psychopathy has been defined in adult samples by focusing on the affective features of this construct (Hare & Neumann, 2008). Second, these features are similar to affective components of conscience that have been the focus of substantial amount of research in normally developing children and, as a result, provide for an important integration of research on a normal developmental process that can go awry in some children leading to a mental health diagnosis (Frick & Viding, 2009). Third, and most importantly, the specifier was based on a rather substantial body of research showing that elevated CU traits designate a subgroup of children and adolescents with serious conduct problems who show a particularly severe, aggressive, and stable pattern of antisocial behavior and who show a number of distinct genetic, biological, cognitive, affective, and social characteristics that would seem to suggest that the causes of serious conduct problems for this group of youth are different from those leading to the behavior problems of children and adolescents without elevated CU traits (Frick et al., 2014a).

To form the symptoms of the LPE specifier, items that had been used to assess CU traits in research were selected based on their utility in capturing the overall construct across different types of samples from various countries (Kimonis et al., 2015). Further, the two-symptom cut-off was selected to designate elevated CU traits for the specifier because it captured about 25–30% of children with childhood-onset CD and this subgroup was more severely impaired than other children with childhood-onset CD in an ethnically diverse community sample (Kahn, Frick, Youngstrom, Findling, & Youngstrom, 2012; Rowe et al., 2010), a clinic-referred sample (Kahn et al., 2012), and a forensic sample (Kimonis et al., 2014). Further, this two-symptom cut-off predicted greater risk for future impairment for both boys (McMahon, Witkiewitz, Kotler, & The Conduct Problems Prevention Research Group, 2010) and girls (Pardini, Stepp, Hipwell, Stouthamer-Loeber, & Loeber, 2012).

The rest of this chapter provides a summary of the research that led to this change in the diagnosis of CD and its implications for research and practice. However, it is important to note that the name given to the specifier (i.e., with limited prosocial emotions) was not chosen to indicate that its criteria was capturing a construct that was intended to be different from CU traits and the way it had been measured in research. In fact, the DSM-5 explicitly states that, "the indicators of this specifier are those that have often been labelled as callous-unemotional traits in research" (APA, 2013, p. 471). Instead, the name was chosen in an attempt to minimize the potential stigma that is often associated with labels related to antisocial behavior, like "psychopathy," "delinquent," or "conduct disorder" (Rockett, Murrie, & Boccaccini, 2007). That is, "limited prosocial emotions" was judged to convey the construct which is defined by developmentally limited levels of the affective components of conscience that help to promote prosocial behaviors and to inhibit antisocial behaviors but in a way that is potentially less pejorative than terms like "psychopathy" or "callous."

Clinical Significance of Callous-Unemotional Traits

Perhaps the primary body of research that led to the inclusion of the LPE specifier in the DSM-5 was a large body of research indicating that elevated CU traits are typically present in only a minority of persons with serious conduct problems but it is a subgroup that is clinically important in a number of ways. Specifically, Frick et al. (2014a) reported that out of 118 published studies reviewed (70 cross-sectional and 48 longitudinal), 89% reported that CU traits (either alone or with other dimensions of psychopathy) were significantly associated with measures of antisocial and aggressive behavior, with an average correlation of .33. More importantly, CU traits designate children and adolescents with serious conduct problems who show a more stable pattern of problems (Frick, Stickle, Dandreaux, Farrell, & Kimonis, 2005; Ray, Thornton, Frick, Steinberg, & Cauffman, 2016a) and more severe aggression that results in greater harm to others (Kruh, Frick, & Clements, 2005; Lawing, Frick, & Cruise, 2010). Further, youth with severe conduct problems who also show elevated CU traits display more instrumental (i.e., for personal gain or dominance) and premeditated aggression compared to other children and adolescents with severe conduct problems (Fanti, Frick, & Georgiou, 2009; Frick, Cornell, Barry, Bodin, & Dane, 2003; Kruh et al., 2005; Lawing et al., 2010). Antisocial adolescents with CU traits are also more likely to report instigating and taking a leadership role in crimes committed with their peers (Thornton et al., 2015). Finally, Frick et al. (2014a) reviewed 20 studies that compared the treatment outcomes for youth with conduct problems with and without elevated levels of CU traits. Eighteen (90%) reported results suggesting that the group high on CU traits showed poorer treatment outcomes to traditional mental health interventions compared to other children and adolescents with serious conduct problems. In a later section of this chapter, we review several treatments that have proven to show some effectiveness for reducing the level and severity of antisocial behavior in youth with CU traits. However, it is important to note that even these studies indicate that youth with CU traits often start treatment with poorer levels of adjustment and still leave treatment with higher levels of antisocial behavior, despite any positive changes (Hawes, Price, & Dadds, 2014; White, Frick, Lawing, & Bauer, 2013; Wilkinson, Waller, & Viding, 2015).

Thus, there is a rather substantial amount of research suggesting that elevated CU traits designate a clinically important subset of children and adolescents with serious conduct problems. Importantly, very few of these studies actually used the criteria for the LPE specifier to define subgroups of youth with CD. However, there are some promising findings that the criteria adopted by the DSM-5 do adequately capture this clinically important group. Specifically, in a population-based sample ($n = 5,326$) of children and adolescents aged 5 to 16, Rowe et al. (2010) reported that children and adolescents with both CD and two or more symptoms of CU traits were five times more likely to continue to have a diagnosis of CD three years later, compared to youths with CD with less than two CU symptoms. Kahn et al., (2012) reported that children in both community ($n = 1,136$) and clinic-referred ($n = 566$) samples who met the criteria for the LPE specifier were more severe than those with CD only, especially in being more aggressive and cruel. Pardini et al. (2012) tested the LPE specifier in a community sample of 1,862 girls aged 6 to 8 and reported that girls who met criteria for CD and who also met criteria for the LPE specifier showed more bullying, more relational aggression, and more global impairment both at baseline and at a 6-year follow-up compared to girls with CD alone. Finally, McMahon et al. (2010) reported that CU traits assessed in the 7th grade significantly predicted adult antisocial outcomes (e.g., adult arrests, adult antisocial personality symptoms) independent of other indicators of poor outcome (e.g., number of conduct problems, level of inattention and impulsivity, age of onset of conduct problems) and that the combination of a CD diagnosis and the LPE specifier showed greater positive predictive power for adult antisocial outcomes than the diagnosis of CD alone.

Etiological Significance of Callous-Unemotional Traits

As noted previously, a critical issue in classifying youth with CD throughout the history of this disorder relates to determining the best methods for defining subgroups of individuals with the disorder who show distinct etiologies. There is substantial evidence to suggest that CU traits and the LPE specifier may have validity for this purpose as well. Specifically, Frick et al. (2014a) have provided a comprehensive review of research suggesting that CU traits define a group of youth with serious conduct problems who show very different genetic, cognitive, emotional, and social characteristics from other children and adolescents with serious conduct problems.

To briefly summarize these findings, behavioral genetic research suggests that the genetic influences on childhood-onset conduct problems are considerably greater in those with higher levels of CU traits compared to those who show normative levels (Viding, Blair, Moffitt, & Plomin, 2005; Viding, Jones, Frick, Moffitt, & Plomin, 2008). Further, children and adolescents with serious conduct problems and CU traits show an insensitivity to punishment cues, which includes responding more poorly to punishment cues after a reward-dominant response set is primed, responding more poorly to gradual punishment schedules, underestimating the likelihood that they will be punished for misbehavior, and being less sensitive to potential punishment when peers are present relative to other youth with serious conduct problems (Blair, Colledge, & Mitchell, 2001; Frick, Cornell, Bodin, et al., 2003; Muñoz-Centifanti & Modecki, 2013; Pardini, Lochman, & Frick, 2003). Children and adolescents with serious conduct problems and elevated CU traits endorse more deviant values and goals in social situations, such as viewing aggression as an acceptable means of attaining goals, blaming others for their misbehavior, and emphasizing the importance of dominance and revenge in social conflicts (Chabrol, Van Leeuwen, Rodgers, & Gibbs, 2011; Pardini, 2011; Pardini et al., 2003; Stickle, Kirkpatrick, & Brush, 2009).

Children and adolescents with elevated CU traits also show reduced emotional responsiveness in a number of situations including showing weaker responses to cues of distress in others, less reactivity to peer provocation, less fear of novel and dangerous situations, and less anxiety over the consequences of their behavior relative to other youth with serious conduct problems (Fanti, Panayiotou, Lazarou, Michael, & Georgiou, 2015; Kimonis et al., 2008; Munoz, Frick, Kimonis, & Aucoin, 2008; Viding et al., 2012). Finally, conduct problems tend to have a different association with parenting practices depending on whether or not the child or adolescent shows elevated levels of CU traits. Specifically, harsh, inconsistent, and coercive discipline is more strongly associated with conduct problems in youth with normative levels of CU traits in comparison to youth with elevated CU traits. In contrast, low warmth in parenting appears to be more strongly associated with conduct problems in youth with elevated CU traits (Pasalich, Dadds, Hawes, & Brennan, 2012; Wootton, Frick, Shelton, & Silverthorn, 1997). These associations with parenting are consistent with research suggesting that parental warmth may help a child develop emotional attachments to others and learn to recognize signs of distress in them (Dadds et al., 2013). These associations are also consistent with research suggesting that children with elevated CU traits may be more responsive to rewards than punishments (Frick et al., 2014a).

These findings on the different correlates to CD depending on the level of CU traits highlight the potential importance of CU traits for guiding etiological research. In other words, research studying the potential role of emotional responsiveness in the development of serious conduct problems can lead to erroneous conclusions if it does not consider the role of CU traits. To illustrate this, Viding et al. (2012) studied functional MRI responses to fearful and calm faces in a sample of boys (aged 10–16) and reported that amygdala responses to fearful faces (relative to calm faces) were stronger than controls in boys with conduct problems without elevated CU traits but were weaker compared to controls in boys with conduct problems who were elevated on CU traits. Similarly, in a sample of children (mean age of 11.21; SD = 1.06), Fanti et al. (2015) reported that on both physiological (i.e., startle reflex during fear imagery) and behavioral (i.e., ratings of fear and sensitivity to punishment) measures of fearfulness, children with chronic conduct problems with and without CU traits showed opposing responses, with those high on CU traits showing weaker startle reflex and lower ratings of fear and punishment sensitivity and those normative on CU traits showing enhanced physiological responses and higher behavioral ratings. Thus, while some studies find that emotional processes are associated with CD even without considering CU traits (Van Goozen, Matthys, Cohen-Kettenis, Buitelaar, & van Engeland, 2000; Van Goozen, Snoek, Matthys, Van Rossum, & van Engeland, 2004), it is also quite possible that the differences between the two groups high on conduct problems may obscure important associations and lead to erroneous conclusions on the potential importance of emotional responding for understanding the development of conduct problems.

The research on the different characteristics of children with serious conduct problems depending on their level of CU traits has led to a number of theories to account for these differences by hypothesizing distinct causal processes underlying the behavior problems in children with and without elevated CU traits. For example, Frick, Ray, Thornton, and Kahn,

(2014b) have proposed that children with serious conduct problems and elevated CU traits have a temperament (i.e., fearless, insensitive to punishment, low responsiveness to cues of distress in others) that can interfere wiith the normal development of conscience and place the child at risk for a particularly severe and aggressive pattern of antisocial behavior. In contrast, children and adolescents with childhood-onset antisocial behavior with normative levels of CU traits display higher levels of emotional reactivity to distress in others and to provocation from others. Further, the conduct problems in this group are strongly associated with hostile/ coercive parenting. Based on these findings, it appears that children in this group show a temperament characterized by strong emotional reactivity combined with inadequate socializing experiences that result in a failure to develop the skills needed to adequately regulate their emotional reactivity (Frick & Morris, 2004). The resulting problems in emotional regulation can result in the child committing impulsive and unplanned aggressive and antisocial acts, for which he or she may feel remorseful afterwards and show high rates of anxiety and distress, but which he or she may still have difficulty controlling in the future.

In summary, the presence of CU traits could be critical for guiding causal theories by helping to differentiate factors that may lead to distinct causal pathways to CD. However, this research has also suggested that there are some characteristics that are present in those with childhood-onset CD irrespective of these traits. For example higher rates of impulsivity and other symptoms of attention-deficit hyperactivity disorder appear to be present in both groups of children with CD (Caputo, Frick, & Brodsky, 1999; Christian, Frick, Hill, Tyler, & Frazer, 1997; Frick, Cornell, Bodin, et al. 2003). Similarly, certain impairments in contingency processing may be present for those high or low on CU traits as well (Matthys, Vanderschuren, & Schutter, 2013; White et al., 2016). Thus, causal theories need to consider both shared and unique etiological factors in the development of conduct problems. For example, the lack of concern over the consequences of behavior in those with CU traits and their difficulty in considering consequences in the context of intense emotional arousal may both lead to impulsive behavior problems and difficulties in learning from certain contingency schedules.

Linking Conduct Disorder to Personality Theory

As noted above, one potential advantage of using CU traits to subtype children with CD is the method's explicit attempt to provide a developmental extension of the construct of psychopathy. This extension is important because the construct of psychopathy has a long history of clinical research on incarcerated adults showing that psychopathic traits designate a clinically and etiologically important subgroup of antisocial individuals (see Skeem, Polaschek, Patrick, & Lilienfeld, 2011 for a comprehensive review of this research). Importantly, most definitions of psychopathy focus on a number of dimensions in addition to CU traits, including interpersonal (e.g., narcissism, manipulativeness) and behavioral (e.g., impulsivity and irresponsibility) facets (Hare & Neumann, 2008). However, CU traits focus only on the affective facet of psychopathy because these traits seem to be most important for designating distinct groups within antisocial individuals, especially groups that differ on etiologically important variables like emotional reactivity (Frick & Ray, 2015). Further, CU traits are the facet of psychopathy that is not captured by other constructs (e.g., impulsivity, oppositional behavior) that are frequently used to classify children with serious behavior problems (Frick & Ray, 2015). However, because CU traits were developed as a downward extension of the construct of psychopathy, it is important to determine how it relates to other measures of psychopathy. Frick and Ray (2015) reviewed eight studies investigating the correlations between self-report ratings of CU traits and clinician ratings of psychopathy in samples of youth and reported correlations ranging from .20 to .62, with an average correlation of .37. This modest correlation is not surprising given the differences in method of assessment (self-report ratings vs. clinician ratings) and the fact that CU traits only assess one dimension of the condition.

The use of CU traits can also be useful for integrating research on children and adolescents with serious behavior problems to research on normal personality dimensions. There is growing recognition of the importance of integrating research on pathological aspects of personality that contribute to problems in adjustment with research on normal personality dimensions found in the general population (Lynam & Widiger, 2001). One of the most commonly used systems for describing normal personality traits is the Five Factor Model (FFM; Costa & McCrae, 1989). Frick and Ray (2015) reviewed eight published studies linking measures of CU traits in children and adolescents to FFM dimensions and reported that the most consistent association was a negative association with Agreeableness, with an average association across studies being $r= -.36$. Further, these negative associations were consistent across the various lower-order facets of Agreeableness (i.e., trustfulness, straightforwardness, altruism, compliance, modesty, and tender-mindedness). CU traits were also negatively associated with Openness, with an average correlation across studies of $r = -.21$. Again, this negative association was generally consistent across the facets of Openness (i.e., fantasy, aesthetics, feelings, actions, ideas, and values). The associations between CU traits and other FFM dimensions (e.g., Neuroticism, Conscientiousness, and Extraversion) were not consistent across samples.

Considering CU traits as a dimension of personality opens the possibility that some level of these traits may be present in children and adolescents without serious conduct problems. However, in many community samples, the majority of children or adolescents with elevated CU traits show significant levels of them (Fontaine, McCrory, Boivin, Moffitt, & Viding, 2011; Frick, Bodin, & Barry, 2000). Kumsta, Sonuga-Barke, and Rutter (2012), on the other hand, reported that there were a significant number of children who were elevated on CU traits without significant conduct problems in a sample (n = 165) of Romanian adoptees exposed to severe early deprivation. Fanti (2013) also identified a group that was high on CU traits without significant conduct problems in a sample of young adolescents (aged 12) in Greek Cyprus using latent profile analysis. Importantly, they reported that those adolescents who were elevated on CU traits without conduct problems showed less impulsivity than those with elevated CU traits and conduct problems. Using a similar methodology in a younger sample (ages 7 to 11) of children in Greek Cyprus, Wall, Frick, Fanti, Kimonis, and Lordos (2016) also identified a group of children who were elevated on CU traits without significant conduct problems. They reported that this group scored better on measures of impulse control and executive functioning, came from families who used more warm and involved parenting, and were more connected to school. Thus it appears that, in some samples, elevated CU traits can occur without serious conduct problems. Further, certain factors within the child (e.g., better executive functioning) and his or her social context (more positive parenting, being connected to school) may help in inhibiting serious conduct problems despite the absence of the prosocial emotions that normally inhibit such antisocial behavior.

Assessment Implications

With the recent inclusion of CU traits in the LPE specifier for CD, it is likely that CU traits will be assessed in a wider range of contexts. It is important, therefore, to critically examine how it has been assessed in research to date. Because CU traits are one part of the overall construct of psychopathy, many assessments have relied on subscales from broader measures of psychopathy (Frick & Ray, 2015). These include rating scales assessing psychopathy, like the Antisocial Process Screening Devices (APSD; Frick & Hare, 2001), the Child Psychopathy

Scale (CPS; Lynam, 1997) and the Youth Psychopathic traits Inventory (YPI; Andershed, Kerr, Stattin, & Levander, 2002). It also includes the clinician rating system, the Psychopathy Checklist Youth Version (PCL-YV; Forth, Kosson, & Hare, 2003). However, because these systems were designed to assess psychopathy more generally, they are often quite limited in the number of items assessing CU traits, typically having as few as four (Forth et al., 2003) or six (Frick & Hare, 2001) items directly assessing these traits. Further, the response options for rating the severity or frequency of the CU items on these scales has been limited, often with only three response options (Forth et al., 2003; Frick et al., 2000). The small number of items, the limited range of response options, and the fact that ratings of CU traits are negatively skewed in most samples resulted in these measures having significant psychometric limitations for assessing CU traits, most notably showing poor internal consistency in many formats (Poythress, Dembo, Wareham, & Greenbaum, 2006).

In an effort to overcome these limitations in the assessment of CU traits, the Inventory of Callous-Unemotional Traits (ICU) was developed (Kimonis et al., 2008). The ICU was developed from the four items on the APSD that most consistently loaded on the callous-unemotional dimension across samples (Frick et al., 2000). These four core traits are also the ones that are directly linked to both the affective component of psychopathy (Hare & Neumann, 2008) and the DSM-5 specifier of LPE (Kimonis et al., 2015). To form the items on the ICU, six items (three positively and three negatively worded) were developed to assess a similar content to each of the four core traits. These 24 items were then placed on a 4-point Likert scale that could be rated from 0 (Not at all true) to 3 (Definitely true) and versions for parent, teacher, and self-report were developed to encourage multi-informant assessments. A separate version for use with preschool children was also developed (Ezpeleta, de la Osa, Granero, Penelo, & Domenech, 2013). Thus, the ICU content was designed to assess CU traits in a way similar to how they are operationalized for the DSM-5 specifier but to overcome limitations of past measures by a) including a more comprehensive assessment of CU traits (i.e., 24 items), b) using an expanded anchor system (i.e., four points), and c), including an equal number of items worded in the positive (e.g., "I do not care who I hurt to get what I want") and the negative (e.g., "I am concerned about the feelings of others") direction in an attempt to avoid response sets.

To date, the ICU has been translated into over 20 languages and has over 110 published studies testing its validity (http://sites01.lsu.edu/faculty/pfricklab/). Importantly, several studies have tested the construct validity of the ICU using factor analyses and reported that the best-fitting model tends to be one specifying a general CU factor and three subfactors: callousness (a lack of empathy and remorse), uncaring (an uncaring attitude toward performance on tasks and other's feelings), and unemotional (deficient emotional affect). This structure has been supported in samples of children and adolescents of various ages (Essau, Sasagawa, & Frick, 2006; Ezpeleta et al., 2013) and across multiple language translations (Ciucci, Baroncelli, Franchi, Golmaryami, & Frick, 2014; Essau et al., 2006; Ezpeleta et al., 2013; Fanti et al., 2009; Kimonis et al., 2008). Further, this factor structure has been invariant across boys and girls (Essau et al., 2006; Ciucci et al., 2013) and across rating formats (Roose, Bijttebier, Decoene, Claes, & Frick, 2010). Thus, it appears that this three dimensional structure of the ICU is robust across age, language, rater, and gender (although see Feilhauer, Cima, & Arntz, 2012; Houghton, Hunter, & Crow, 2013 for exceptions), and these analyses support the presence of an overarching dimension of CU traits. Further, the total score of the ICU shows acceptable internal consistency (Cronbach's alpha range between .77–89) and similar correlations with antisocial behavior and other emotional and cognitive characteristics that have been reported in studies using other measures of CU traits (Frick et al., 2014a). Thus, the total score from the ICU provides a continuous measure of the overall construct of CU traits that overcomes many of the limitations in past measures.

However, the available research also highlights several significant limitations of the ICU scale, especially in the use of the subscales. First, although the three subfactors, with an overarching general factor, consistently emerge as the best fitting factor structure across diverse samples, the fit indices tend to be modest and typically only reach acceptable fit after eliminating certain items with poor item–total correlations and after post-hoc modifications are made to the model (Hawes et al., 2014). Second, there was no a priori specification for this three-factor structure for CU traits based on a clear theoretical model, nor have the subfactors shown consistent associations with external criteria (Frick & Ray, 2015; Waller et al., 2014). Third, it is possible that the factors to some extent represent method variance, in that the callousness dimension tends to comprise largely positively scored items (e.g., "I do not care who I hurt to get what I want), whereas the uncaring dimension comprise largely negatively scored items (e.g., "I try not to hurt others' feelings"; Hawes et al., 2014). Ray, Frick, Thornton, Steinberg, and Cauffman (2016b) evaluated the item functioning of the ICU in an ethnically diverse sample of 1,190 adolescents and found that the positively worded items (i.e., items for which higher ratings were indicative of higher levels of CU traits) were more likely than negative worded items (i.e., items in which higher ratings were indicative or more prosocial emotions) to be rated in the lower response category. Youth, that is, were less likely to rate themselves as being highly callous than they were to rate themselves as being very low on prosocial emotions. Consequently, the positively worded items showed higher difficulty in item response theory analyses and the authors concluded that the factor structure may be an artifact of this differential item difficulty and recommended relying on the total score of the ICU to assess CU traits in future research.

Treatment Implications

As noted previously, children and adolescents who show elevated CU traits often don't respond as well as other youth with CD to typical mental health treatments. (Frick et al., 2014a). However, a number of treatment studies have shown some success in reducing the level of antisocial behavior in youth with CU traits (Hawes et al., 2014; Wilkinson et al, 2015). These treatments have generally been intensive treatments that are tailored to the unique cognitive and emotional risk factors that have been associated with CU traits. For example, Caldwell, Skeem, Salekin and Van Rybroek (2006) demonstrated that adolescent offenders with CU traits improved when treated using an intensive treatment program that utilized reward-oriented approaches, targeted the self-interests of the adolescent, and taught empathy skills. Specifically, they reported that adolescent offenders high on CU traits who received the intensive treatment were less likely to recidivate in a 2-year follow-up period than offenders with these traits who underwent a standard treatment program in the same correctional facility. White et al. (2014) tested whether or not CU traits moderated the treatment effectiveness of Functional Family Therapy (FFT) in a sample of adolescents who had been arrested and referred for mental health treatment at a community mental health center. FFT is a comprehensive and individualized approach to treatment that focuses on engaging the child and family in treatment and providing motivations for change that are individualized for each family and child (Alexander, Waldron, Robbins, & Neeb, 2013). Results indicated that CU traits were associated with poorer behavioral, emotional, and social adjustment prior to treatment but they were also associated with greater improvements in adjustment over the course of treatment, and this included improvements in their level of parent-rated conduct problems. Further, the association between CU traits and risk for violent charges decreased after treatment at 6-month and 12-month follow-ups.

Thus, while youth with CU traits present a treatment challenge, research suggests that certain intensive and individualized interventions can reduce the level and severity of conduct problems in children and adolescents with elevated CU traits. As noted before, despite this improvement, youth with CU traits typically start treatment with higher levels of conduct problems than other youth and end it still with higher levels. Thus, future research needs to continue to refine these interventions by focusing on enhancing treatment components that directly address the unique needs of youth with CU traits (Dadds, Allen, McGregor, Woolgar, Viding, and Scott, 2013; Kimonis & Armstrong, 2012; Miller et al., 2014). Furthermore, very little research has focused on whether CU traits themselves respond to treatment, although a few studies provide promising results (Hawes et al., 2014).

The strongest effects on CU traits appear to be achieved by intensive interventions implemented early in development that help parents learn methods for teaching children the skills needed for perspective taking. For example, Somech and Elizur (2012) demonstrated significant reductions in CU traits in a sample of young children (aged 3–5 years) who received an intensive parent-training program, which consisted of 14 two-hour treatment sessions and included components focused on both parent and child self-regulation and strategies to enhance the child's development of emotional recognition skills. Relative to a minimal intervention control group, there was a significant decline in level of CU traits from pre- to post-treatment ($d = 0.85$) and these gains were maintained at a 1-year follow-up. Although it appears that these treatment effects are stronger in younger samples, intensive interventions implemented later in development can also lead to significant reductions in CU traits as well (McDonald, Dodson, Rosenfield, & Jouriles, 2011; Kolko, Dorn, Bukstein, Pardini, Holden, & Hart, 2009). For example, Lochman et al. (2014) tested an intervention for children screened to have high levels of aggression in the 4th grade and then who received an intensive intervention for both the child (24 sessions) and parent (10 sessions) in the 5th grade. The intervention implemented at the child's school led to greater reductions in CU traits relative to children in the no-treatment control group.

In summary, children with CD and elevated CU traits present quite a treatment challenge, but research also clearly suggests that they are by no means untreatable nor are the CU traits themselves unchangeable. The most successful treatments are those that take into account research showing that youth with CU traits differ on a number of important characteristics from other children with CD, which seems to implicate different causal factors in the development of their conduct problems. Interventions that are tailored to the unique needs of these different groups with CD show the most effectiveness (Frick, 2012). As research accumulates and clarifies the different causal processes involved in the development of CD across these groups, it is highly likely that treatments will also continue to improve. These advances will be especially important for the group with elevated CU traits who seem to show a particularly severe, aggressive, and stable pattern of conduct problem behavior.

Conclusions

In conclusion, CD is a serious mental health condition that can lead to significant impairments in the child throughout the lifespan. While this diagnosis has been included in major systems for classifying psychopathology in children for several decades, there have been a number of changes in how this diagnosis captures the variability in the causes of CD and variability in the severity of behavior problems and outcome of children within this category. The most recent edition of the DSM manual focuses on two primary methods for parsing this heterogeneity using the timing of onset of the serious behavior problems (i.e., before or after age 10) and the presence or absence of non-normative levels of CU traits. While these distinctions have proven to have important clinical and etiological implications, there remain a number of important directions for future research.

As noted above, successful treatments have largely been ones that are tailored to the unique characteristics of children with CD across the developmental pathways. Therefore, improvements in treatments are likely to be guided by advances in research on the different causal factors that can lead to CD (Frick, 2012). To illustrate this, Hyde et al. (2016) reported on an adoption cohort of 561 families to the effect that CU traits at 27 months of age were predicted by biological mothers' antisocial behavior, despite limited or no contact with the biological mother, but that adoptive mothers' use of positive reinforcement reduced this risk in the child. Thus, it appears that positive parenting modified the biological risk for CU traits in this sample. Further, as noted above, studies of children with CU traits who do not show significant conduct problems suggest that these children are more likely to come from families that use more positive parenting techniques (Wall et al., 2016). These findings have led to the development of interventions for children to either prevent the development of CU traits or to reduce the level of conduct problems in children with elevated CU traits that focus on enhancing parental use of positive reinforcement and increasing parental warmth (Wilkinson et al., 2015).

Further, as research begins to study CU traits earlier in development, these interventions can be implemented in young children when these behaviors are more changeable. Specifically, studies have shown that CU traits can be assessed reliably in preschool samples (Hyde et al., 2013; Kimonis et al., 2016) and they are associated with aggression in children at this age (Kimonis et al., 2006). Further, Waller et al. (2016) reported that from age 3, CU traits predicted aggression and other types of conduct problems at age 9, even after taking into account the stability in behavior problems and controlling for method effects. Thus, as early as age 3 or 4, CU traits are associated with severe behavior problems and predict risk for later problems in adjustment. As a result, children with elevated CU traits are an important focus for early intervention programs to reduce this risk.

Recent research has also suggested that there may be even earlier signs of problems in the social connections of children who are at risk for CU traits. For example, Bedford, Pickles, Sharp, Wright, and Hill (2015) reported that lower preferential face tracking at 5 weeks of age predicted higher CU traits at age 2.5. Such face tracking is critical for healthy attachment between the infant and parent and for the development of other prosocial skills, such as empathy and perspective taking (Skuse, 2003). Moreover, it provides another difference between how CU traits develop and how autism develops, given that children with autism do not show impairments in selective attention to their mother's faces until 12 months of age (Jones & Klin, 2013). In short, studies that focus on the early processes related to the development of CU traits could not only be critical for guiding early intervention but they could also be critical for clarifying the early developmental processes that lead to these traits and for clarifying how they differ from the causal processes related to other disorders.

The potential for guiding both research and practice is why the DSM-5 added the specifier "with limited prosocial emotions" to its criteria for CD and why CU traits are also being considered for inclusion in the upcoming revision of the International Classification of Diseases (Salekin, 2016). However, with this inclusion in the major methods for diagnosing CD, it will become increasingly important to develop better methods for assessing these traits in clinical contexts. As noted above, the ICU is a multi-informant rating scale that was developed to overcome limitations in other measures of CU traits and it has been extensively used in research as a continuous measure of these traits, with evidence to support its validity for this purpose across gender, a large age range, and various language translations (Frick & Ray, 2015). However, research has only recently begun to test methods for defining cut-offs that can be used to designate individuals who show an impairing level of these traits (Docherty, Boxer, Huesmann, O'Brien, & Bushman, 2016; Kimonis, Fanti, & Singh, 2014) or methods for using this scale to approximate the criteria for the DSM-5 specifier (Kimonis et al., 2015). Further, research has not tested whether these structured methods approximate to how clinicians use the DSM-5 criteria for making this diagnosis nor have there been tests of whether certain tools (e.g., clinical interviews, clinician checklists) could enhance this clinical process.

Thus, the use of CU traits provides a promising method for defining important and distinct causal pathways to CD with great potential for advancing both treatment and causal theory. Specifically, these traits have proven to be useful for designating a subgroup of children and adolescents with serious conduct problems who differ on important emotional, cognitive, and contextual characteristics that would seem to implicate distinct causal processes leading to their antisocial behavior relative to antisocial youth who are normative on CU traits. Further, these traits designate a particularly severe, stable, and aggressive group of antisocial youth that respond differently to many of the existing treatments for CD. Nevertheless, despite the positive findings, there is also a great deal more research needed to increase the utility of this construct for both research and practice.

References

Alexander, J. F., Waldron, H. B., Robbins, M. S., & Neeb, A. A. (2013). *Functional family therapy for adolescent behavior problems.* Washington, DC: American Psychological Association. doi:10.1037/14139-000 DOI:10.1037/14139-000#_blank#https://doi.org/10.1037/14139-000

American Psychiatric Association. (1968). *Diagnostic and statistical manual of mental disorders* (2nd ed.). Washington, DC: Author.

American Psychiatric Association. (1980). *Diagnostic and statistical manual of mental disorders* (3rd ed.). Washington, DC: Author.

American Psychiatric Association. (1987). *Diagnostic and statistical manual of mental disorders* (3rd ed., rev.). Washington, DC: Author.

American Psychiatric Association. (1994). *Diagnostic and statistical manual of mental disorders* (4th ed.). Washington, DC: Author.

American Psychiatric Association. (2013). *Diagnostic and statistical manual of mental disorders* (5th ed.).Arlington, VA: Author.

Andershed, H., Kerr, M., Stattin, H., & Levander, S. (2002). Psychopathic traits in non-referred youths: A new assessment tool. In E. Blauuw & L. Sheridan (Eds.), *Psychopaths: Current international perspectives* (pp. 131–158). The Hague, Netherlands: Elsevier.

Bedford, R., Pickles, A., Sharp, H., Wright, N., & Hill, J. (2015). Reduced face preference in infancy: A developmental precursor to callous-unemotional traits? *Biological Psychiatry, 78,* 144–150. doi:10.1016/j.biopsych.2014.09.022

Blair, R. J. R., Colledge, E., & Mitchell, D. G. V. (2001). Somatic markers and response reversal: Is there orbitofrontal cortex dysfunction in boys with psychopathic tendencies. *Journal of Abnormal Child Psychology, 29,* 499–511. doi:10.1023/A:1012277125119

Caldwell, M., Skeem, J., Salekin, R., & Van Rybroek, G. (2006). Treatment response of adolescent offenders with psychopathy features: A 2-year follow-up. *Criminal Justice and Behavior, 33,* 571–596. doi:10.1177/0093854806288176

Canino, G., Polanczyk, G., Bauermeister, J. J., Rohde, L. A., & Frick, P. J. (2010). Does the prevalence of CD and ODD vary across cultures? *Social Psychiatry and Psychiatric Epidemiology, 45,* 695–704. doi:10.1007/s00127-010-0242-y DOI:10.1007/s00127-010-0242-y#_blank#https://doi.org/10.1007/s00127-010-0242-y

Caputo, A. A., Frick, P. J., & Brodsky, S. L. (1999). Family violence and juvenile sex offending: The potential mediating role of psychopathic traits and negative attitudes toward women. *Criminal Justice and Behavior, 26,* 338–356. doi:10.1177/0093854899026003004

Chabrol, H., Van Leeuwen, N., Rodgers, R. F., & Gibbs, J. C. (2011). Relations between self-serving cognitive distortions, psychopathic traits, and antisocial behavior in a non-clinical sample of adolescents. *Personality and Individual Differences, 51,* 887–892. doi:10.1016/j.paid.2011.07.008

Christian, R. E., Frick, P. J., Hill, N. L., Tyler, L., & Frazer, D. R. (1997). Psychopathy and conduct problems in children: Implications for subtyping children with conduct problems. *Journal of the American Academy of Child and Adolescent Psychiatry, 36,* 233–241. doi:10.1097/00004583-199702000-00014

Ciucci, E., Baroncelli, A., Franchi, M., Golmaryami, F. N., & Frick, P. J. (2014). The association between callous-unemotional traits and behavioral and academic adjustment in children: Further validation of the Inventory of Callous-Unemotional Traits. *Journal of Psychopathology and Behavioral Assessment, 36,* 189–200. doi:10.1007/s10862-013-9384-z

Costa, P. T., & McCrae, R. R. (1989). *The NEO-PI/NEO-FFI manual supplement.* Odessa, FL.: Psychological Assessment Resources.

Dadds, M. R., Allen, J. L., McGregor, K., Woolgar, M., Viding, E., & Scott, S. (2013). Callous-unemotional traits in children and mechanisms of impaired eye contact during expressions of love: a treatment target? *Journal of Child Psychology and Psychiatry, 55*(7), 771–780. doi:10.1111/jcpp.12155

Docherty, M., Boxer, P., Huesmann, L. R., O'Brien, M., & Bushman, B. (2016). Assessing callous-unemotional traits in adolescents: Determining cutoff scores for the Inventory of Callous and Unemotional Traits. *Journal of Clinical Psychology, 73*(3), 257–278. doi:10.1002/jclp.22313

Essau, C. A., Sasagawa, S., & Frick, P. J. (2006). Callous-unemotional traits in adolescents. *Assessment, 20,* 1–16. doi:10.1177/1073191106287354

Ezpeleta, L., de la Osa, N., Granero, R., Penelo, E., & Domenech, J. M. (2013). Inventory of callous-unemotional traits in a community sample of preschoolers. *Journal of Clinical Child & Adolescent Psychology, 42,* 91–105. doi:10.1080/15374416.2012.734221

Fanti, K. A. (2013). Individual, social, and behavioral factors associated with co-occurring conduct problems and callous-unemotional traits. *Journal of Abnormal Child Psychology, 41,* 811–824. doi:10.1007/s10802-013-9726-z

Fanti, K. A., Frick, P. J., & Georgiou, S. (2009). Linking callous-unemotional traits to instrumental and non-instrumental forms of aggression. *Journal of Psychopathology and Behavioral Assessment, 31,* 285–298. doi:10.1007/s10862-008-9111-3

Fanti, K. A., Panayiotou, G., Lazarou, C., Michael, R., & Georgiou, G. (2015). The better of two evils? Evidence that children exhibiting continuous problems high or low on callous-unemotional traits score on opposite directions on physiological and behavioral measures of fear. *Development and Psychopathology.* doi:10.1017/S0954579415000371

Feilhauer, J., Cima, M., & Arntz, A. (2012). Assessing callous-unemotional traits across different groups of youths: Further cross-cultural validation of the Inventory of Callous-Unemotional Traits. *International Journal of Law and Psychiatry, 35,* 251–262. doi:10.1016/j.ijlp.2012.04.002

Forth, A. E., Kosson, D. S., & Hare, R. D. (2003). *The psychopathy checklist: Youth version manual.* Toronto, Canada: Multi-Health Systems.

Fontaine, N., McCrory, E. J. P., Boivin, M., Moffitt, T. E., & Viding, E. (2011). Predictors and outcomes of joint trajectories of callous-unemotional traits and conduct problems in childhood. *Journal of Abnormal Psychology, 120,* 730–742. doi:10.1037/a0022620

Frick, P. J. (2012). Developmental pathways to Conduct Disorder: Implications for future directions in research, assessment, and treatment. *Journal of Clinical Child & Adolescent Psychology, 41,* 378–389. doi:10.1080/15374416.2012.664815

Frick, P. J., Bodin, S. D., & Barry, C. T. (2000). Psychopathic traits and conduct problems in community and clinic-referred samples of children: Further development of the psychopathy screening device. *Psychological Assessment, 12,* 382–393. doi:10.1037/1040-3590.12.4.382

Frick, P. J., Cornell, A. H., Barry, C. T., Bodin, S. D., & Dane, H. A. (2003). Callous-unemotional traits and conduct problems in the prediction of conduct problem severity, aggression, and self-report of delinquency. *Journal of Abnormal Child Psychology, 31,* 457–470. doi:10.1023/A:1023899703866

Frick, P. J., Cornell, A. H., Bodin, S. D., Dane, H. A., Barry, C. T., & Loney, B. R. (2003). Callous-Unemotional traits and developmental pathways to severe aggressive and antisocial behavior. *Developmental Psychology, 39,* 246–260. doi:10.1037/0012-1649.39.2.246

Frick, P. J. & Hare, R. D. (2001). *The antisocial process screening device.* Toronto, Canada: Multi-Health Systems.

References

Frick, P. J. & Morris, A. S. (2004). Temperament and developmental pathways to conduct problems. *Journal of Clinical Child and Adolescent Psychology, 33*, 54–68. doi:10.1207/S15374424JCCP3301_6

Frick, P. J., & Nigg, J. T. (2012). Current issues in the diagnosis of attention-deficit/hyperactivity disorder, oppositional defiant disorder, and conduct disorder. *Annual Review of Clinical Psychology, 8*, 77–107. doi:10.1146/annurev-clinpsy-032511-143150

Frick, P. J., & Ray, J. V. (2015). Evaluating callous-unemotional traits as a personality construct. *Journal of Personality, 83*, 710–722. doi:10.1111/jopy.12114

Frick, P. J., Ray, J. V., Thornton, L. C., & Kahn, R. E. (2014a). Can callous-unemotional traits enhance the understanding, diagnosis, and treatment of serious conduct problems in children and adolescents? A comprehensive review. *Psychological Bulletin, 140*, 1–57. doi:10.1037/a0033076

Frick, P. J., Ray, J. V., Thornton, L. C., & Kahn, R. E. (2014b). A developmental psychopathology approach to understanding callous-unemotional traits in children and adolescents with serious conduct problems. *Journal of Child Psychology and Psychiatry, 55*, 532–548. doi:10.1111/jcpp.12152

Frick, P. J., Stickle, T. R., Dandreaux, D. M., Farrell, J. M., & Kimonis, E. R. (2005). Callous-unemotional traits in predicting the severity and stability of conduct problems and delinquency. *Journal of Abnormal Child Psychology, 33*, 471–487. doi:10.1007/s10648-005-5728-9

Frick, P. J., & Viding, E. M. (2009). Antisocial behavior from a developmental psychopathology perspective. *Development and Psychopathology, 21*, 1111–1131. doi:10.1017/S0954579409990071

Hare, R. D. & Neumann, C. S. (2008). Psychopath as a clinical and empirical construct. *Annual Review of Clinical Psychology, 4*, 217–246. doi:10.1146/annurev.clinpsy.3.022806.091452

Hawes, D. J., Price, M. J., & Dadds, M. R. (2014). Callous-unemotional traits and the treatment of conduct problems in childhood and adolescence: A comprehensive review. *Clinical Child and Family Psychology Review, 17*, 248–267.

Hawes, S. W., Byrd, A. L., Henderson, C. E., Gazda, R. L., Burke, J. D., Loeber, R., & Pardini, D. A. (2014). Refining the parent-reported Inventory of Callous–Unemotional Traits in boys with conduct problems. *Psychological Assessment, 26*(1), 256–266. doi:10.1037/a0034718

Houghton, S., Hunter, S. C., & Crow, J. (2013). Assessing callous unemotional traits in children aged 7-to 12-years: A confirmatory factor analysis of the Inventory of Callous Unemotional Traits. *Journal of Psychopathology and Behavioral Assessment, 35*(2), 215–222. doi:10.1007/s10862-012-9324-3

Hyde, L. W., Shaw, D. S., Gardner, F., Cheong, J., Dishion, T. J., & Wilson, M. (2013). Dimensions of callousness in early childhood: Links to problem behavior and family intervention effectiveness. *Development and Psychopathology, 25*, 347–363. doi:10.1017/S0954579412001101

Hyde, L. W., Waller, R., Trentacosta, C. J., Shaw, D. S., Neidehiser, J. M., Ganiban, J. M., Reiss, D., & Leve, L. D. (2016). Heritable and nonheritable pathways to early callous-unemotional behaviors. *American Journal of Psychiatry, 173*(9), 903–910. Advance online publication: doi:10.1176/appi.ajp.2016.15111381

Jones, W. & Klins, A. (2013). Attention to eyes is present but in decline in 2-6-month-old infants later diagnosed with autism. *Nature, 504*, 427–431. doi:10.1038/nature12715

Kahn, R. E., Frick, P. J., Youngstrom, E., Findling, R. L., & Youngstrom, J. K. (2012). The effects of including a callous-unemotional specifier for the diagnosis of conduct disorder. *Journal of Child Psychology and Psychiatry, 53*, 271–282. doi:10.1111/j.1469-7610.2011.02463.x

Kimonis, E. R. & Armstrong, K. (2012). Adapting Parent-Child Interaction Therapy to treat severe conduct problems with callous-unemotional traits: A case study. *Clinical Case Studies, 11*, 234–252. do1:10.1177/1534650112448835

Kimonis, E. R., Fanti, K. A., Anastassiou-Hadjicharalambous, X., Mertan, B., Goulter, N., & Katsimicha, E. (2016). Can callous-unemotional traits be reliably measured in preschoolers? *Journal of Abnormal Child Psychology, 44*, 625–638. doi:10.1007/s10802-015-0075-y

Kimonis, E. R., Fanti, K. A., Frick, P. J., Moffitt, T. E., Essau, C., Bijjtebier, P., & Marsee, M. A. (2015). Using self-reported callous-unemotional traits to cross-nationally assess the DSM-5 "With Limited Prosocial Emotions" specifier. *Journal of Child Psychology and Psychiatry, 56*, 1249–1261. doi:10.1111/jcpp.12357

Kimonis, E. R., Fanti, K., Goldweber, A., Marsee, M. A., Frick, P. J., & Cauffman, E. (2014). Callous-unemotional traits in incarcerated adolescents. *Psychological Assessment, 26,* 227–237. doi:10.1037/a0034585

Kimonis, E. R., Fanti, K. A., & Singh, J. P. (2014). Establishing cut-off scores for the parent-reported Inventory of Callous-Unemotional traits. *Archives of Forensic Psychology, 1,* 27–48.

Kimonis, E. R., Frick, P. J., Boris, N. W., Smyke, A. T., Cornell, A. H., Farrell, J. M., & Zeanah, C. H. (2006a). Callous-unemotional features, behavioral inhibition, and parenting: independent predictors of aggression in a high-risk preschool sample. *Journal of Child and Family Studies, 15,* 745–756. doi:10.1007/s10826-006-9047-8

Kimonis, E. R., Frick, P. J., Skeem, J., Marsee, M. A., Cruise, K., Muñoz, L. C., . . . Morris, A. S. (2008). Assessing callous-unemotional traits in adolescent offenders: Validation of the Inventory of Callous-Unemotional Traits. *Journal of the International Association of Psychiatry and Law, 31,* 241–252. doi:10.1016/j.ijlp.2008.04.002

Kolko, D. J., Dorn, L. D., Bukstein, O. G., Pardini, D., Holden, E. A., & Hart, J. (2009). Community vs. clinic-based modular treatment for children with early-onset ODD or CD: A clinical trial with 3-year follow-up. *Journal of Abnormal Child Psychology, 37,* 591–609. do1:10.1007/s10802-009-9303-7

Kruh, I. P., Frick, P. J., & Clements, C. B. (2005). Historical and personality correlates to the violence patterns of juveniles tried as adults. *Criminal Justice and Behavior, 32,* 69–96. doi:10.1177/0093854804270629

Kumsta, R., Sonuga-Barke, E., & Rutter, M. (2012). Adolescent callous-unemotional traits and conduct disorder in adoptees exposed to severe early deprivation. *British Journal of Psychiatry, 200,* 197–201. doi:10.1192/bjp.bp.110.089441

Lahey, B. B., Hart, E. L., Pliszka, S., Applegate, B., & McBurnett, K. (1993). Neurophysiological correlates of conduct disorder: A rationale and a review of research. *Journal of Clinical Child Psychology, 22,* 141–153. doi:10.1207/s15374424jccp2202_2

Lahey, B. B., Loeber, R., Quay, H. C., Frick, P. J., & Grimm, J. (1992). Oppositional defiant disorder and conduct disorders: Issues to be resolved for DSM-IV. *Journal of the American Academy of Child and Adolescent Psychiatry, 31,* 539–546. doi:10.1097/00004583-199205000-00023

Lahey, B. B., Waldman, I. D., & McBurnett, K. (1999). The development of antisocial behavior: An integrative causal model. *Journal of Child Psychology and Psychiatry, 40,* 669–682. doi:10.1111/1469-7610.00484

Lawing, K., Frick, P. J., & Cruise, K. R. (2010). Differences in offending patterns between adolescent sex offenders high or low in callous-unemotional traits. *Psychological Assessment, 22,* 298–305. doi:10.1037/a0018707

Lochman, J. E., Baden, R. E., Boxmeyer, C. L., Powell, N. P., Qu, L., Salekin, K. L., & Windle, M. (2014). Does a booster intervention augment the preventive effects of an abbreviated version of the Coping Power Program for aggressive children? *Journal of Abnormal Child Psychology, 42,* 367–381. do1:10.1007/s10802-013-9727-y

Lynam, D. R. (1997). Pursuing the psychopath: Capturing the fledgling psychopath in a nomological net. *Journal of Abnormal Psychology, 106,* 425–438. doi:10.1037/0021-843X.106.3.425

Lynam, D. R. & Widiger, T. A. (2001). Using the five-factor model to represent the DSM-IV personality disorders: An expert consensus approach. *Journal of Abnormal Psychology, 110,* 401–412. doi:10.1037/0021-843X.110.3.401

Matthys, W., Vandershcuren, L. J. M. J., & Schutter, D. J. L. G. (2013). The neurobiology of oppositional defiant disorder and conduct disorder: Altered functioning in three mental domains. *Development and Psychopathology, 25,* 193–207. doi:10.1017/S0954579412000272

McDonald, R., Dodson, M. C., Rosenfield, D., & Jouriles, E. N. (2011). Effects of a parenting intervention on features of psychopathy in children. *Journal of Abnormal Child Psychology, 39,* 1013–1023. do1:10.1007/s10802-011-9512-8

McMahon, R. J., Witkiewitz, K., Kotler, J. S., & The Conduct Problems Prevention Research Group. (2010). Predictive validity of callous-unemotional traits measures in early adolescence with respect to multiple antisocial outcomes. *Journal of Abnormal Psychology, 119,* 752–763. doi:10.1037/a0020796

Miller, N. V., Haas, S. M., Waschbusch, D. A., Willoughby, M. T., Helseth, S. A., Crum, K. I., . . . Pelham, W. E. (2014). Behavior therapy and callous-unemotional traits: Effects of a pilot study examining modified behavioral contingencies on child behavior. *Behavior Therapy, 45,* 606–618. doi:10.1016/j.beth.2013.10.006

References

Moffitt, T. E., Arseneault, L., Jaffee, S. R., Kim-Cohen, J., Koenen, K. C., Odgers, C. L., . . . Viding, E. (2008). Research review: DSM-V conduct disorder: research needs for an evidence base. *Journal of Child Psychology and Psychiatry, 49*, 3–33. doi:10.1111/j.1469-7610.2007.01823.x.

Muñoz, L. C., Frick, P. J., Kimonis, E. R., & Aucoin, K. J. (2008). Types of aggression, responsiveness to provocation, and callous-unemotional traits in detained adolescents. *Journal of Abnormal Child Psychology, 36*, 15–28. doi:10.1007/s10802-007-9137-0

Muñoz Centifanti, L. C., & Modecki, K. (2013). Throwing caution to the wind: Callous-unemotional traits and risk taking in adolescents. *Journal of Clinical Child and Adolescent Psychology, 42*, 106–119. doi:10.1080/15374416.2012.719460

Odgers, D. L., Moffitt, T. E., Broadbent, J. M., Dickson, N., Hancox, R. J., Harrington, H., . . . Caspi, A. (2008). Female and male antisocial trajectories: From childhood origins to adult outcomes. *Developmental Psychopathology, 20*, 673–716. doi:10.1017/S0954579408000333

Pardini, D. A. (2011). Perceptions of social conflicts among incarcerated adolescents with callous-unemotional traits: 'You're going to pay. It's going to hurt, but I don't care.' *Journal of Child Psychology and Psychiatry, 52*, 248–255. doi:10.1111/j.1469-7610.2010.02336.x

Pardini, D. A., Lochman, J. E., & Frick, P. J. (2003). Callous-unemotional traits and social-cognitive processes in adjudicated youths. *Journal of the American Academy of Child and Adolescent Psychiatry, 42*, 364–371. doi:10.1097/00004583-200303000-00018

Pardini, D. A., Stepp, S., Hipwell, A., Stouthamer-Loeber, M., & Loeber, R. (2012). The clinical utility of the propose DSM-5 callous-unemotional subtype of conduct disorder in young girls. *Journal of the American Academy of Child and Adolescent Psychaitry, 51*, 62–73. doi:10.1016/j.jaac.2011.10.005

Pasalich, D. S., Dadds, M. R., Hawes, D. J., & Brennan, J. (2012). Do callous-unemotional traits moderate the relative importance of parental coercion versus warmth in child conduct problems? An observational study. *Journal of Child Psychology and Psychiatry, 52*, 1308–1315. doi:10.1111/j.1469-7610.2011.02435.x

Poythress, N. G., Dembo, R., Wareham, J., & Greenbaum, P. E. (2006). Construct validity of the youth psychopathic traits inventory (YPI) and the antisocial process screening devices (APSD) with justice-involved adolescents. *Criminal Justice and Behavior, 33*, 26–55. doi:10.1177/0093854805282518

Quay, H. C. (1987). Patterns of delinquent behavior. In H. C. Quay (Ed.), *Handbook of juvenile delinquency* (pp. 118–138). Oxford, UK: John Wiley & Sons.

Quay, H. C. (1993). The psychobiology of undersocialized aggressive conduct disorder. *Development and Psychopathology, 5*, 165–180. doi:10.1017/S0954579400004326

Ray, J. V., Frick, P. J., Thornton, L. C., Steinberg, L., & Cauffman, E. (2016a). Impulse control and callous-unemotional traits distinguish patterns of delinquency and substance use in justice involved adolescents: Examining the moderating role of neighborhood context. *Journal of Abnormal Child Psychology, 44*, 599–611. doi:10.1007/s10802-015-0057-0

Ray, J. V., Frick, P. J., Thornton, L. C., Steinberg, L., & Cauffman, E. (2016b). Positive and negative item wording and its influence on the assessment of callous-unemotional traits. *Psychological Assessment, 28*(4), 394–404. doi:10.1037/pas0000183

Rockett, J., Murrie, D. C., & Boccaccini, M. T. (2007). Diagnostic labeling in juvenile justice settings: Do psychopathy and conduct disorder findings influence clinicians? *Psychological Services, 4*, 107–122. doi:10.1037/1541-1559.4.2.107

Roose, A., Bijttebier, P., Decoene, S., Claes, L., & Frick, P. J. (2010). Assessing the affective features of psychopathy in adolescence: A further validation of the Inventory of Callous and Unemotional traits. *Assessment, 17*, 44–57. doi:10.1177/1073191109344153

Rowe, R., Maughan, B., Moran, P., Ford, T., Briskman, J., & Goodman, R. (2010). The role of callous and unemotional traits in the diagnosis of conduct disorder. *Journal of Child Psychology and Psychiatry, 51*(6), 688–695. doi:10.1111/j.1469-7610.2009.02199.x

Salekin, R. T. (2016). Psychopathy in childhood: Toward better informing the DSM-5 and ICD-11 conduct disorder specifiers. *Personality disorders: Theory, research, and treatment, 7*, 180–191. doi:10.1037/per0000150

Sanislow, C. A., Pine, D. S., Quinn, K. J., Kozak, M. J., Garvy, M. A., Heinssen, R. K., Wang, P. S., & Cuthbert, B. N. (2010). Developing constructs for psychopathology research: Research domain criteria. *Journal and Abnormal Psychology, 119*, 631–639.

Skeem, J. L., Polaschek, D. L. L., Patrick, C. J., & Lilienfeld, S. O. (2011). Psychopathic personality: Bridging the gap between scientific evidence and public policy. *Psychological Science in the Public Interest, 12*, 95–162. doi:10.1177/1529100611426706

Skuse, D. (2003). Fear recognition and the neural basis of social cognition. *Child and Adolescent Mental Health, 28*, 50–60. doi:10.1111/1475-3588.00047

Somech, L. Y. & Elizur, Y. (2012). Promoting self-regulation and cooperation in pre-kindergarten children with conduct problems: A randomized controlled trial. *Journal of the American Academy of Child and Adolescent Psychiatry, 4*, 412–422. doi:10.1016/j.jaac.2012.01.019

Stickle, T. R., Kirkpatrick, N. M., & Brush, L. N. (2009). Callous-unemotional traits and social information processing: multiple risk factor models for understanding aggressive behavior in antisocial youth. *Law and Human Behavior, 33*, 515–529. doi:10.1007/s10979-008-9171-7

Thornton, L. C., Frick, P. J., Shulman, E. P., Ray, J. V., Steinberg, L., & Cauffman, E. (2015). Callous-unemotional traits and adolescents' role in group crime. *Law and Human Behavior, 39*, 368–377. doi:10.1037/lhb0000124

Van Goozen, S. H. M., Snoek, H., Matthys, W., Van Rossum, I., & van Engeland, H. (2004). Evidence of fearlessness in behaviourally disordered children: A study on startle reflex modulation. *Journal of Child Psychology and Psychiatry, 45*, 884–892. doi:10.1111/j.1469-7610.2004.00280.x

Van Goozen, S., Matthys, W., Cohen-Kettenis, P. T., Buitelaar, J. K., & van Engeland, H. (2000). Hypothalamic-pituitary-adrenal axis and autonomic nervous system activity in disruptive children and matched controls. *Journal of the American Academy of Child and Adolescent Psychiatry, 39*, 1438–1445. doi:10.1111/j.1469-7610.2004.00280.x

Viding, E., Blair, R. J. R., Moffitt, T. E., & Plomin, R. (2005). Evidence for substantial genetic risk for psychopathy in 7-year-olds. *Journal of Child Psychology & Psychiatry, 46*, 592–597. doi:10.1111/j.1469-7610.2004.00393.x

Viding, E., Jones, A. P., Frick, P. J., Moffitt, T. E., & Plomin, R. (2008). Heritability of antisocial behaviour at nine-years: Do callous-unemotional traits matter? *Developmental Science, 11*, 17–22. doi:10.1111/j.1467-7687.2007.00648.x

Viding, E., Sebastian, C. L., Dadds, M. R., Lockwood, P. L., Cecil, C. A., De Brito, S. A., & McCrory, E. J. (2012). Amygdala response to preattentive masked fear in children with conduct problems: The role of callous-unemotional traits. *American Journal of Psychiatry, 169*, 1109–1116. doi:10.1176/appi.ajp.2012.12020191

Wall, T. D., Frick, P. J., Fanti, A., Kimonis, E., & Lordos, A. (2016). Factors differentiating callous-unemotional children with and without conduct problems. *Journal of Child Psychology and Psychiatry, 57*(8), 976–983. doi:10.1111/jcpp.12569

Waller, R., Dishion, T. J., Shaw, D. S., Gardner, F., Wilson, M. N., & Hyde, L. W. (2016). Does early childhood callous-unemotional behavior uniquely predict behavior problems or callous-unemotional behavior in late childhood? *Developmental Psychology, 52*, 1805–1819.

Waller, R., Wright, A. G., Shaw, D. S., Gardner, F., Dishion, T. J., Wilson, M. N., & Hyde, L. W. (2014). Factor structure and construct validity of the parent-reported Inventory of Callous-Unemotional Traits among high-risk 9-year-olds. *Assessment, 22*(5), 561–580. Advance online publication. doi:10.1177/1073191114556101

White, S. F., Frick, P. J., Lawing, S. K., & Bauer, D. (2013). Callous-unemotional traits and response to functional family therapy in adolescent offenders. *Behavioral Science and the Law, 31*, 271–285. doi:10.1002/bsl.2041

White, S. F., Tyler, P. M., Erway, A. K., Botkin, M. L., Kolli, V., Meffert, H., Pope, K., & Blair, J. R. (2016). Dsyfunctional representation of expected value is associated with reinforcement-based decision-making deficits in adolescents with conduct problems. *Journal of Child Psychology and Psychiatry, 57*, 938–946. doi:10.1111/jcpp.12557

Wilkinson, S., Waller, R., & Viding, E. (2015). Practitioner review: Involving young people with callous unemotional traits in treatment – does it work? A systematic review. *Journal of Child Psychology and Psychiatry, 57*(5), 552–565. doi:10.1111/jcpp.12494

Wootton, J. M., Frick, P. J., Shelton, K. K. & Silverthorn, P. (1997). Ineffective parenting and childhood conduct problems: The moderating role of callous-unemotional traits. *Journal of Consulting and Clinical Psychology, 65*, 301–308. doi:10.1037/0022-006X.65.2.292.b

4

Diagnostic Issues for ODD/CD with ADHD Comorbidity

Kristen L. Hudec and Amori Yee Mikami

Individuals with disruptive and impulse-control disorders, such as oppositional defiant disorder (ODD) and conduct disorder (CD), often experience comorbid attention-deficit/hyperactivity disorder (ADHD). Overlap between these disorders in symptomatic behavior and developmental considerations can create diagnostic challenges. However, accurate diagnosis of co-occurring ADHD is important, because its presence may exacerbate conduct problems and require additional intervention approaches. In this chapter, we provide an overview of ODD/CD with comorbid ADHD, discuss factors that contribute to variability in the presentation of the comorbid symptoms, review considerations for diagnosing ODD/CD with ADHD, and offer information on interventions suited to a comorbid presentation.

Overview of ODD/CD with Comorbid ADHD

Rates of Comorbidity with ADHD

Comorbid presentations of ODD/CD with ADHD are quite prevalent. Approximately 50% of individuals with ODD or CD are estimated to have co-occurring ADHD, and the comorbidity rates are similar (40–60%) for individuals with ADHD who also have ODD or CD (Angold, Costello, & Erkanli, 1999; Freitag et al., 2012). Though estimates vary, the co-occurrence of ADHD is generally observed to be higher among individuals with CD (47–64%; Maughan, Rowe, Messer, Goodman, & Meltzer, 2004; Pardini & Fite, 2010) compared to ODD (35–49%; Nock, Kazdin, Hiripi, & Kessler, 2007; Pardini & Fite, 2010).

Comorbidity rates may differ depending on the type (presentation) of ADHD. ADHD is characterized by difficulty in sustaining concentration (inattention) and/or excessive motor activity (hyperactivity) and acting without thinking (impulsivity; American Psychiatric Association [APA], 2013). Individuals with combined presentation of ADHD (ADHD-C) experience clinically significant inattentive and hyperactive-impulsive symptoms. However, individuals with the predominantly inattentive presentation (ADHD-I) display symptoms of inattention but not hyperactivity/impulsivity, whereas those with the predominantly hyperactive-impulsive presentation (ADHD-HI) display symptoms of hyperactivity/impulsivity but not inattention. Importantly, comorbidity with ODD/CD is most commonly found among individuals with ADHD-C, as opposed to individuals with ADHD-I or ADHD-HI (Freitag et al., 2012).

The Wiley Handbook of Disruptive and Impulse-Control Disorders, First Edition.
Edited by John E. Lochman and Walter Matthys.
© 2018 John Wiley & Sons Ltd. Published 2018 by John Wiley & Sons Ltd.

Impairment and Outcomes Associated with ADHD Comorbidity

For individuals with ODD/CD, the presence of co-occurring ADHD warrants concern. Individuals with ADHD in addition to ODD or CD are suggested to have more severe symptoms of both disorders (ODD/CD and ADHD) as well as greater impairment in functioning (Waschbusch, 2002). Children with comorbid ODD and ADHD demonstrate social impairment across more domains (e.g., parents, peers, siblings) and more school and sibling problems than do children with either ADHD or ODD alone (Tseng, Kawabata, & Gau, 2011). Children with conduct problems and ADHD tend to show more severe delinquent behaviors at a younger age compared to children with conduct problems alone (Sibley et al., 2011). The additional concerns that may come with comorbidity are not isolated to childhood. Adults with comorbid ODD and ADHD have been found to display more severe emotional-behavioral difficulties and impairment, including higher likelihood of being unemployed and unmarried, relative to adults with individual disorder presentations (Gadow et al., 2007). Collectively, these findings underscore the importance of accurately assessing ADHD among individuals with ODD/CD.

Common Factors Related to ODD/CD and ADHD

The high rates of comorbidity that exist between ODD/CD and ADHD may be attributable to naturally similar etiological factors across disorders, increasing the likelihood of both disorders emerging for youth experiencing certain high-risk life circumstances. First, the influence of shared genetic factors in ODD/CD and ADHD is quite large (35–57%) in accounting for the overlap among the disorders (Burt, Krueger, McGue, & Iacono, 2001; Tuvblad, Zheng, Raine, & Baker, 2009). Some findings suggest that genetic liability (and the effects of gene–environment interactions) explain the co-occurrence between disorders without environmental influences contributing significantly (Nadder, Rutter, Silberg, Maes, & Eaves, 2002; although see Burt et al., 2001).

However, ODD/CD and ADHD may also share similar environmental risk factors. Several factors in the family environment are known to contribute to childhood-onset CD and may influence the expression of ADHD symptoms as well (Freitag et al., 2012). Adverse parenting (e.g., lacking supervision, detached, negative) is associated with increased risk for CD + ADHD comorbidity (Freitag et al., 2012). A higher risk for co-occurring ODD/CD and ADHD is also related to environmental factors including maternal smoking during pregnancy (Freitag et al., 2012), use of spanking in childhood (Morgan et al., 2016), and experiencing childhood abuse (Bandou, Koike, & Matuura, 2010), though these factors may operate as intermediaries for risk associated with parental psychopathology.

Danforth, Connor, and Doerfler (2016) suggest the development of comorbid ADHD and conduct problems reflects the culmination of interactions among genetic and environmental factors. Specifically, genetic factors contribute to child behaviors that are challenging (e.g., impulsivity), and these behaviors are likely to elicit parenting approaches that negatively impact the parent–child relationship and limit the child's development of self-directive skills (e.g., verbal working memory, private speech), creating interactive circumstances that progress to increasing child oppositionality and conduct problems over time (Danforth et al., 2016).

Importantly, transmission of genetic and familial risk seems particularly strong for comorbid presentations. The risk of comorbid conduct problems and ADHD is five times greater if a sibling has the comorbid presentation rather than ADHD only (Christiansen et al., 2008). Even in young children, a family history of ODD + ADHD predicts an early emergence of co-occurrence of ADHD and ODD anger/irritability symptoms (Harvey, Breaux, & Lugo-Candelas, 2016). The increased family incidence of comorbidity is consistent with genetic findings that ODD + ADHD is associated with greater genetic risk severity (i.e., more of the risk alleles identified as contributing to clinical symptoms; Kotte, Faraone, & Biederman, 2013) relative to the genetic loading for either disorder in isolation.

An alternative perspective is that rates of ODD/CD with ADHD diagnoses may be artificially elevated because the comorbid symptom presentation represents a distinct disorder not currently included in the DSM. In support of this idea, some evidence suggests that the overlap and variability of ODD/CD and ADHD symptoms are accounted for by a single common factor rather than exclusively specific factors (Martel, Gremillion, Roberts, von Eye, & Nigg, 2010). Findings from performance studies also support the notion of a distinct ODD/CD+ADHD disorder, as individuals with this combined presentation exhibit a different pattern of responses and deficits across several domains (i.e., attentional orienting, response preparation, information processing; Banaschewski et al., 2003) than would be predicted by the additive effects of experiencing two co-occurring individual disorders. While there remains notable inter-individual variability in comorbid presentations and disagreement about how symptoms combine (i.e., synergistically, additively; Christiansen et al., 2008; Martel et al., 2010; Waschbusch, 2002), some have argued that comorbidity represents a distinct clinical presentation (King et al., 2005). Thus, comorbidity rates may reflect individuals who experience a distinct ODD/CD+ADHD disorder in addition to those who experience both individual disorders, artificially increasing the frequency of dual diagnoses using DSM criteria.

Sociodemographic Factors Affecting Comorbidity Rates and Symptom Trajectory

Overall comorbidity rates have been provided in the opening section of this chapter, but below we detail sociodemographic factors, such as gender and developmental stage, that may influence the prevalence rates and patterns of ODD/CD with comorbid ADHD.

Geographical Similarity in Rates

Comorbidity rates tend to be similar across geographic locations, though direct comparisons are challenging. Relatively similar comorbidity rates of ADHD for individuals with ODD have been estimated in Argentina (33.3%; Michanie, Kunst, Margulies, & Yakhkind, 2007), the United States (35%; Nock et al., 2007), England (29.5% for males; Maughan et al., 2004), and China (25.25%; Qu, Jiang, Zhang, Wang, & Guo, 2015). In Turkey, one study found comorbidity rates to be a bit lower for ODD+ADHD (9.4%; Ercan, Bilaç, Özaslan, & Rohde, 2015). That same study also reported lower rates in Turkey for CD with ADHD (15.1%; Ercan et al., 2015) compared to China (42.14%; Qu et al., 2015) and England (30.8% for males; Maughan et al., 2004), although they were not appreciably different from the comorbidity rate in a Danish sample (16.5%; Jensen & Steinhausen, 2015). Taken together, these findings suggest overall similarity in comorbidity rates across geographic locations, considering the variability in sample populations (e.g., nationwide inclusive group, children, adolescents) and study methods. Variability in comorbidity rates appears to reflect differences in diagnostic methodology and in cultural norms, which are revisited under diagnostic-related issues.

Gender Differences in ODD/CD+ADHD Comorbidity

The prevalence of ODD/CD with comorbid ADHD, as well as the expression of symptoms, may have important differences depending on the individual's gender. Crucially, ODD, CD, and ADHD are all less prevalent in females relative to males; however, the risk of comorbidity between these disorders may be higher for females (Loeber & Keenan, 1994). In epidemiological estimates, approximately 30% of males and 16% of females with ODD/CD are estimated to experience ADHD (Maughan et al., 2004). Other studies have found that females with ADHD-C are more likely to have conduct problems compared to their male counterparts (Loeber & Keenan, 1994), and estimates in the United States suggest the odds for ADHD and ODD comorbidity are 6.6 for males compared to 56.3 for females (Costello, Mustillo, Erkanli, Keeler, & Angold, 2003). Another study found that childhood ODD symptoms predicted the presence of CD in adolescence for youth of both genders, but childhood ADHD symptoms additionally contributed to adolescent CD in females only (Van Lier, Van der Ende, Koot, & Verhulst, 2007).

The high prevalence of comorbid symptoms in females may be connected to findings that conduct problems emerging in adolescent girls often follow a history of overlooked symptoms. Females with ADHD are frequently underdiagnosed and, as a result, undertreated (Biederman, 2005). Struggling with undetected ADHD may contribute to associated impairments that also happen to be risk factors for conduct problems, such as academic underachievement, peer rejection, and depressed mood. Moreover, females may tend to express their antisocial behavior via relational aggression as compared to males who are more physically aggressive (e.g., Abikoff et al., 2002). It is possible that because girls may show early conduct problems in more relational ways, symptoms are less likely to be noticed and treated, and, therefore, more likely to escalate (Abikoff et al., 2002). By adolescence, unidentified or poorly controlled early symptoms may have progressed to severe comorbid ODD/CD+ADHD, emphasizing the need to recognize ADHD or conduct symptoms earlier, especially for girls.

Developmental Onset of Comorbid ODD/CD+ADHD

The particular developmental stage in which ODD/CD+ADHD comorbidity emerges may be associated with a distinct pattern of symptom course, related impairment, and outcome prognosis. ADHD usually first presents in childhood and persists into adulthood, although hyperactive/impulsive symptoms may decline or be expressed in adult-relevant ways while inattention is more likely to continue (Biederman, 2005). Conduct problems may begin in one of several developmental stages and may or may not persist over time (Nock et al., 2007).

Early Childhood Among preschoolers, significant ODD behaviors (13.4%) and hyperactive-impulsive symptoms (6.9%) are common, though their comorbid occurrence happens less frequently (2.4%; Lavigne, LeBailly, Hopkins, Gouze, & Binns, 2009). However, although these behaviors signal risk for future problems, which disorder or comorbidity will develop or persist (e.g., ODD/CD, ADHD, ODD/CD+ADHD) may be more uncertain than in older children. Studies have found that early ADHD behaviors are not only associated with future diagnoses and clinically significant symptoms of ADHD (Bunte, Schoemaker, Hessen, Van der Heijden, & Matthys, 2014), but also predict later argumentative and defiant ODD symptoms (Harvey et al., 2016). Conversely, preschool children who display conduct problems are likely to exhibit both CD symptoms and ADHD-related hyperactive/impulsive symptoms during school-age years (Rolon-Arroyo, Arnold, & Harvey, 2014). Notably, Tandon, Si, and Luby (2011) found that the persistence of ADHD was nine times lower between the ages of 3 and 5 relative to persistence between the ages of 5 and 7. Children showing tantrums, excessive motor activity, emotion dysregulation, and aggression in preschool (sometimes referred to as "hard-to-manage" children; Campbell, 1994) may be best described as carrying a relatively undifferentiated risk for future ADHD/ODD/CD.

The predictive utility of early childhood conduct problems for subsequent ODD/CD and/or ADHD may also be tied to a few specific behaviors, such as fighting and breaking things, because these may indicate the presence of callous-unemotional (CU) traits. CU traits, captured with the DSM-5 diagnostic specifier for CD "with limited prosocial emotions," include lack of remorse, lack of empathy, shallow or absent affective response, and lack of concern about performance (APA, 2013). CU traits represent a unique dimension, distinguishable from conduct problems and ADHD, that is associated with proactive aggression and lower guilt and empathy (Waller, Hyde, Grabell, Alves, & Olson, 2015). CU traits may be challenging to discern in preschool but are associated with markedly more severe problem behaviors and impairment in later stages (Pardini & Fite, 2010).

Childhood Symptoms of ADHD are likely in children with ODD (48.9%) and CD (63.6%) at this developmental stage (Pardini & Fite, 2010). However, the presence of comorbid ODD/CD+ADHD imparts particularly high risk for poor future outcomes. School-age children with co-occurring ODD/CD and ADHD behaviors are more likely to experience continued difficulties with impulsivity and hyperactivity in adolescence and adulthood (Biederman, Petty, Clarke, Lomedico, & Faraone, 2011), and are at increased risk for psychiatric disorders in later years (Harpold et al., 2007), as compared to children with ADHD alone. The presence of ADHD among children with ODD may similarly hasten the age of onset of CD and predict problem persistence and worse outcomes, such as criminal involvement (Loeber, Burke, Lahey, Winters, & Zera, 2000, for review; Van Lier et al., 2007).

Functional impairment related to comorbid ODD/CD and ADHD is also noteworthy in this developmental period, because children with these disorders are more likely to evidence academic and social difficulties in elementary school than in preschool. This is related to parents, teachers, and peers having increased expectations for focusing, impulse control, and following directions during the elementary school years, and ADHD comorbid with ODD/CD is highly likely to lead to conflict with adults, academic disengagement, and peer rejection (Pardini & Fite, 2010). These impairments may escalate conduct problems or other psychopathology in the long term, above and beyond the contribution of the initial levels of ADHD or ODD/CD.

Adolescence The behavior profiles and projected outcomes of co-occurring conduct problems with ADHD in adolescence depend on whether the conduct problems persisted from childhood or began in adolescence. Three groups are often observed: (1) childhood-onset ADHD with adolescent-limited ODD/CD; (2) childhood-onset ADHD with adolescent-onset ODD/CD; and (3) childhood-onset ODD/CD+ADHD with comorbidity persisting into adolescence.

Regarding the first group: Children with ADHD may develop conduct problems that originate in adolescence and desist after this stage (Moffitt, 1993). For these youth, the ODD/CD with ADHD comorbidity is limited to adolescence, though ADHD (at least, the inattention) is likely to remain despite resolution of adolescent ODD/CD behaviors. The initiation of conduct problems in adolescence may reflect, to some extent, what is normative for typical teenagers in this developmental stage (e.g., arguing with adults, minor rule-breaking behavior, using alcohol). Adolescent-limited conduct problems are also likely to be less severe than conduct problems that originated in childhood, or that continue on past adolescence (Barker, Oliver, & Maughan, 2010; Moffitt, Caspi, Harrington, & Milne, 2002).

However, we speculate that adolescents with ADHD may be at greater risk than typically developing peers for impairment and negative consequences as a result of even minor, relatively age-appropriate conduct problems (Kuja-Halkola, Lichtenstein, D'Onofrio, & Larsson, 2015). Typical adolescent misbehavior may be more severe in the context of ADHD symptoms if ADHD leads to behaviors being exaggerated or compounded. For instance, if adolescents with ADHD ignore homework assignments or skip school like non-affected peers, this could potentially lead to a greater drop in grades. Although the severity and duration of comorbidity may be less intense, adolescent-limited conduct problems with ADHD can still have residual effects (e.g., scholastic failure, criminal record, internalizing disorders) even after the ODD/CD has resolved (Moffitt et al., 2002).

Regarding the second group: Many children with ADHD may develop conduct problems that emerge in adolescence and persist over time (Barker et al., 2010). Relative to youth with adolescent-limited conduct problems, youth with childhood ADHD and adolescent-onset, persistent conduct problems may have different characteristics and experiences in childhood (e.g., greater peer rejection; Rabiner, Coie, Miller-Johnson, Boykin, & Lochman, 2005) and adolescence (e.g., more CD behaviors, presence of CU-like traits; Byrd, Loeber, & Pardini, 2012) that increase the likelihood of symptoms continuing into adulthood.

Relative to those with no ADHD, adolescents who have histories of childhood ADHD, may be at higher risk for having their emerging conduct problems carry lasting effects into adulthood, a process often referred to as becoming trapped by "snares" (e.g., adolescent conduct problems result in substance addiction, teenage parenthood, or incarceration; McGee et al., 2015; Moffitt, 1993). Snares increase the likelihood of conduct problem persistence and poor prognosis later. This may be why the presence of comorbid ADHD, and problems such as social marginalization (Savolainen et al., 2010) and substance use (Hussong, Curran, Moffitt, Caspi, & Carrig, 2004) that are more common in comorbid ADHD + CD, predict a higher likelihood that adolescent-onset antisocial behaviors will persist into adulthood.

Regarding the third group: Other children with ADHD had conduct problems originating in childhood, and the comorbid ODD/CD + ADHD persists into adolescence. In adolescence this group likely displays the most severe conduct problems, relative to youth whose conduct problems originate then (Waschbusch, 2002). In addition, the long term prognosis for youth in this group is of greatest concern. For instance, recidivism rates are highest among juveniles in the justice system who have comorbid conduct problems and ADHD (Van der Put, Asscher, & Stams, 2016). This group is also at highest risk for development of antisocial personality disorder in adulthood (Storebø & Simonsen, 2016), as indicated by a longstanding and pervasive pattern of rule violations, aggressive and deceitful behavior, and lack of remorse.

Adulthood Considerably less is known about ODD/CD and/or ADHD in adulthood than in earlier developmental stages, perhaps because these disorders have historically been considered "disorders of childhood" that are naturally outgrown. However, ADHD is progressively being recognized as a lifelong condition (Biederman et al., 2011), where the symptoms and impairment associated with inattention typically persist, although hyperactivity/impulsivity may reduce (e.g., climbing on furniture becomes feelings of subjective restlessness) or be expressed in adult-relevant ways (e.g., blurting out answers becomes risky driving). Additionally, ODD/CD does persist into adulthood in some cases (Burke, Rowe, & Boylan, 2014).

It is worth noting that ODD/CD + ADHD is unlikely to manifest for the first time in adulthood. Nonetheless, among adults with ADHD, a large portion (42–45%) experience co-occurring ODD symptoms, and this presentation is associated with childhood ODD and ADHD (Reimherr, Marchant, Olsen, Wender, & Robison, 2013). Because symptoms of ODD/CD and ADHD in adulthood have typically been occurring for some time, problems may have progressed to serious aggressive or criminal behavior (Young et al., 2015). Independently, ODD/CD and ADHD impact interpersonal and occupational functioning in adulthood, but the combination of disorders has been found to predict the highest risk activities with consequences such as driver's license suspension, arrests, and gunshot/stabbing (Burke et al., 2014).

Considerations and Issues for Diagnosing Comorbid ODD/CD with ADHD

The diagnostic issues for ADHD, ODD, and CD are complex, and comorbid presentation introduces additional challenges in differential diagnosis that require special consideration. We begin this section by discussing the common factors that may influence informants' judgments of conduct problems or ADHD symptoms. Then, we review specific concerns related to differentiating the comorbid presentation of ODD/CD + ADHD from diagnosing the individual disorders.

General Diagnostic Challenges Related to ODD/CD or ADHD

Assessment of ODD/CD or ADHD commonly relies upon information provided by reporters on rating scales, sometimes supplemented with clinical interviews and behavioral observations. Crucially, characteristics of the reporter and the setting in which behavior is assessed may influence informant reports of the target's behavior in all of these formats.

Because rating scales are widely used, the issues reviewed in this section are often considered in the context of information provided by reporters via ratings. We note that clinical interviews may be less prone to bias as clinicians may elicit clarification or elaboration from the reporter in order to get a more accurate representation of behavior. However, many of the reporter issues discussed here may also apply to clinicians when gathering and filtering information from reporters, and the validity of clinical interviews may vary depending on the clinician's expertise. Finally, behavioral observations theoretically allow for more direct assessment of the target's behavior and functioning without the influence of reporter biases, but this process is not entirely bias free. Although observations confirm a diagnosis (or lack of one) in many cases (Bunte et al., 2013), a particular challenge is the potential difficulty in reconciling discrepancies between reported and observed behaviors. Regardless, parents may feel more confident and comfortable with clinical assessment that includes behavioral observation to determine a diagnosis (Bunte et al., 2013). In the sections below, we present issues that deserve attention when assessing ADHD and ODD/CD (see also Chapter 23), with consideration of whether rating scales, clinical interviews, or behavioral observations are being used.

Reporter Expectations Reporters' experience and knowledge regarding typical development may influence their impressions of symptom severity. The preschool, school-age, and adolescent periods are particularly difficult developmental periods in which to assess symptoms of ODD/CD and ADHD, because some of the diagnostic behavior is age-appropriate (to a certain extent). As a result, variations in reporters' understanding of behavioral norms may contribute to differences in severity judgments. For instance, some reporters may expect preschoolers to be more active than is actually warranted, whereas other reporters may deem age-appropriate hyperactive-impulsive behaviors as excessive.

Similarly, reporters may define the frequency of behaviors differently. A behavior occurring twice a day may be considered "often" by some but "almost always" by others. Reporters' perceptions of frequency are not only affected by their personal definitions of what the words "sometimes," "often," and "almost always" mean, but also influenced by their opinions about how frequently these behaviors ought to occur (e.g., talking out of turn may seem to occur "very often" for a 5-year-old if the reporter's expectations for the 5-year-old are on a par with the usual behavior of a 12-year-old). The DSM-5 (APA, 2013) includes guidance on distinguishing normal behavior from behavior symptomatic of ODD, according to the child's age. However, this type of guidance is not provided for ADHD.

Perceptions of symptoms may also vary among reporters as a result of differences in expectations about normative behavior due to culture. Given the same child behavior, a reporter who generally encourages children to ask questions of adults and permits unrestricted talking may not endorse any concerns, whereas a reporter who expects children to remain silent and believes speaking out of turn is rude may endorse clinical symptoms (e.g., arguing with adults, interrupting, oppositionality). Because these expectations are culturally influenced, authors have urged consideration of culture for several specific populations (e.g., for Chinese; Tseng et al., 2011; for Hispanics; Siegel, Laska, Wanderling, Hernandez, & Levenson, 2016).

Reporter expectations may particularly impact impressions of boys' versus girls' behavior. Reporters may expect fewer ADHD and ODD/CD behaviors in females. This may be why, even with equivalent descriptions, symptoms of hyperactivity/impulsivity are rated higher in females compared to males (Coles, Slavec, Bernstein, & Baroni, 2012).

To reduce the potential influence of reporter expectations, using rating scales with appropriately normed reference groups is recommended. In addition, semi-structured clinical interviews may be used to ask follow-up and clarification questions in order to help pinpoint the actual frequency and severity of behavior that is occurring. Observational methods are often useful in determining the objective behaviors as well, although it may be difficult to reliably assess infrequent (but highly severe) behaviors, or to capture nuances in severity.

Reporter's History with the Target A history of conflictual interactions between the reporter and the target individual may lead to an overly negative perspective that, consciously or unconsciously, surfaces in reports. This issue may be particularly relevant for assessment of ODD/CD and ADHD, since the nature of ODD/CD and ADHD symptoms – disruptive, confrontational, dysregulated, inconsistent – are likely to evoke frustration in the reporter (Ohan, Visser, Strain, & Allen, 2011). Informants may have cognitive biases that predispose them to interpret things that disliked targets do in a negative light. Specifically, they may be more likely to remember the negative behaviors of targets whom they dislike, while forgetting the positive behaviors; likewise, ambiguous behaviors of disliked targets may be more likely interpreted as negative rather than positive (Mikami, Chi, & Hinshaw, 2004). Crucially, one study of an ADHD sample found that teachers' personal dislike of children contributed to their being more likely to rate ODD/CD behaviors as present on rating scales, compared with more objective observations (Mikami et al., 2004). This source of bias may not be well addressed by clinical interviews, because if an informant exaggerates the negative behaviors of a target (owing to memory and interpretation biases), it may be difficult for a clinician to ascertain that this is the case. Objective observations may be more useful to address this source of bias.

Beliefs about the Utility of Reports Reporters may alter what they say based on beliefs about how the information will impact the target. For instance, a reporter may believe that diagnosis is the only means to help the individual receive the intervention and support services he or she requires. This may encourage the reporter to inflate reports of behavior problems. Conversely, another reporter may be hesitant to endorse symptoms for fear of the individual being labeled with a clinical disorder, and may underreport as a result. This factor is likely to affect both ratings and clinical interviews. Gathering information from several reporters within a setting may lessen the potential impact of reporters' personal motivations and feelings regarding the target. In addition, behavioral observations may help control for this source of bias.

Reporter Psychopathology Reporters' own psychopathology may further confound the information they provide. This concern may be especially pertinent in the diagnosis of ADHD or ODD/CD, given the high heritability of these conditions, such that parents of children with ADHD are more likely to experience similar issues themselves (Karakas et al., 2015), and the fact that spouses of individuals with externalizing and personality disorders are more likely to have these psychopathologies as well (Galbaud du Fort, Boothroyd, Bland, Newman, & Kakuma, 2002). As a result, the process of completing ratings may be affected (e.g., instructions may be misread, items accidentally skipped, events poorly recollected). Reporters' judgments may also be influenced by their perspective on behaviors that they have struggled with personally. This applies especially to fathers' perceptions of their children's ADHD symptoms (Karakas et al., 2015)—an issue that affects both rating scales and clinical interviews. When possible, incorporating measures of the reporter's psychopathology may inform the diagnostic process.

Self-Report Ratings Reliance on self-reports for diagnosis of ODD/CD or ADHD carries its own unique concerns. Self-reports are solicited from children less frequently due to concerns about reliability and validity, but adolescents and adults are considered more knowledgeable reporters and typically complete self-report ratings and/or clinical interviews about presenting symptoms. Self-report information may help to identify conditions often associated with ODD/CD and ADHD, such as anxiety or depression, that might otherwise remain undetected but do affect functioning. However, individuals with ADHD, as well as individuals with conduct problems, have difficulty recalling or acknowledging their behavioral difficulties (Sibley et al., 2010). The ratings of ADHD symptoms provided by individuals (including adults) with ADHD, as well as ratings of associated impairments, are often inconsistent with collateral reporters (Kooij et al., 2008). Further, like issues that affect the validity of other-informant reports, factors may motivate an individual to deliberately self-report in such a way as to present themselves in a positive light (Sibley et al., 2010), or conversely, to overstate symptoms for personal gain. In sum, self-report ratings and clinical interviews with targets may contribute to the diagnostic process, but information may need to be interpreted with caution and rating scales should contain validity and/or consistency scales as an added precaution.

Diagnostic Issues in Differentiating Comorbid ODD/CD with ADHD

This section focuses on specific issues associated with the diagnosis of comorbidity between ODD/CD and ADHD. Diagnosis of comorbid presentations is especially difficult, given the shared symptomology between disorders and the fact that distinguishing between ODD/CD and ADHD may depend upon reporter perceptions, which are prone to biases. Further complicating matters, referrals often focus on disruptive behavior problems in general (e.g., arguing with adults, difficulty following rules, interrupting conversations, acting impulsively) which may reflect ODD/CD, ADHD, or both conditions. The challenge, therefore, is in determining whether one disorder accounts for the exhibited clinical behaviors versus whether two disorders occur uniquely (above and beyond the other disorder) to a significant degree.

Issue: Shared Symptoms between Disorders Disentangling which symptoms are actually present (ODD/CD versus ADHD) is complicated by the fact that many of the diagnostic behaviors for ODD/CD also occur in ADHD. For example, an individual who does not seem to listen when spoken to directly or does not follow through on instructions (ADHD) may also be perceived as defying or refusing to comply with requests from authority figures (ODD). Other symptoms of ADHD (i.e., avoiding or being reluctant to engage in tasks that require mental effort, leaving a seat when expected to remain seated, running or climbing in inappropriate situations) are also consistent with that ODD criterion of defying rules or requests. On the other hand, ODD behaviors may contain components of ADHD. For example, deliberately annoying others (ODD) may include blurting out an answer before a question is completed, interrupting or intruding on others, and/or talking excessively (ADHD).

Other symptoms, such as not listening when spoken to directly (ADHD) and blaming others for mistakes or misbehaviors (ODD), may occur simultaneously or in the same situation, creating difficulty in knowing which symptom to endorse (e.g., an individual genuinely does not hear instructions for a task, then blames the incomplete task on not receiving proper instructions from a supervisor). Reflecting the overlap between core symptoms of each disorder, some researchers have argued that mild to moderate ODD behaviors may be an element of ADHD (not requiring a separate diagnosis), while moderate to severe behaviors may reflect ODD/CD uniquely (Reiff & Stein, 2003).

Thorough, multi-reporter assessment using ratings, clinical interviews, and observation is recommended to obtain the most comprehensive representation of the presenting problems. Providing clearer instructions for reporters (Johnston, Weiss, Murray, & Miller, 2011), using setting-specific phrasing, and using symptom anchors may help to address the subjectivity in ratings. Over-diagnosis and negative halo effects are perhaps related to overlap and/or difficult differentiation of symptoms, meaning the diagnostic criteria lack sufficient specificity to allow for clear diagnostic separation. However, the majority of presentations involve comorbid symptoms, so the major shortcoming of current diagnostic criteria may be the lack of a combined symptom disorder, a position that has garnered support in the literature (e.g., Christiansen et al., 2008).

Further complicating the problem of shared symptoms, the developmental immaturity inherent in ADHD may partially contribute to behaviors that fit ODD/CD criteria due to the contrast between the individual's abilities and age-based expectations, but may actually be better characterized as manifestations of ADHD. The 2- to 3-year neurodevelopmental lag in ADHD may manifest as behavioral and emotional immaturity relative to unaffected, same-age peers. Consequently, some ODD/CD behaviors may, in fact, reflect a child with ADHD's appropriate response to repeated demands to behave beyond his or her capabilities. To illustrate, consider a typically developing 6-year-old child who is asked to complete academic work, engage in social activities, and maintain household responsibilities at the proficiency level of a 9-year-old. This 6-year-old child is likely to experience frustration and failure as these requests are beyond his or her developmental abilities, but this child's actions do not warrant a diagnosis of ODD/CD. As far as ADHD is concerned, children with this condition may be frequently asked to do things legitimately beyond their capabilities (owing to their developmental immaturity), and the resulting failure and frustration may be mistakenly attributed to oppositionality and conduct problems. To ensure accurate diagnosis, ODD/CD symptoms should be considered in the context of impairments associated with ADHD.

Issue: Accurately Identifying Which Symptoms Are Present   The diagnostic criteria for ODD/CD and ADHD, as mentioned above, possess many overlapping objective behaviors. Frequently, the key distinction between whether the same behavior reflects ODD/CD or ADHD rests on whether the rater perceives the behavior to be intentional or unintentional (or what percent of the time the same behavior is perceived to be done intentionally versus unintentionally). Naturally, this attribution is a subjective judgment and makes differential diagnosis between ODD/CD and ADHD vulnerable to rater biases.

A child failing to follow directions may be perceived as acting unintentionally if the reporter believes the child wants to follow directions but is unable due to distractibility and mental disorganization (ADHD). On the other hand, the reporter may interpret the behavior as intentional if the child is believed to be capable of following through but does not like the direction given (ODD). Similarly, interrupting or intruding on conversations may be rated differently based on whether the reporter attributes the behavior to uncontrollable, impulsive excitement (ADHD) or to purposeful annoyance and disrespectful, argumentative intent (ODD). In summary, a reporter's attribution of intentionality will affect whether a behavior is interpreted as a symptom of ODD, ADHD, or both. Additional information gathered from multiple informants, or through observation, may help accurately discern the reason for the behavior.

CU traits in the context of conduct problems may lead to additional difficulties in distinguishing between ADHD and ODD/CD symptoms, because ADHD-like behaviors (e.g., impulsive physicality, poor emotion regulation, lacking theory of mind or consideration of others' emotions) may indicate conduct problems with CU traits rather than ADHD. For example, individuals with ADHD may lack emotional understanding and have impairments in demonstrating empathy (Deschamps, Schutter, Kenemans, & Matthys, 2015); individuals with high CU traits seem to understand emotions yet lack emotional empathy (Waller et al., 2015). However, lacking empathy (CU) may look similar to difficulty demonstrating empathy (ADHD) to reporters (Deschamps et al., 2015). Other behaviors (e.g., knocking over a classmate on the playground) may also be attributed to ADHD-related symptoms (e.g., impulsivity, poor body control) while CU traits are overlooked (e.g., proactive aggression, low guilt). The potential difficulty in discerning ODD/CD with CU traits from ODD/CD alone or ODD/CD with ADHD calls for routine assessment of CU behaviors and emotional responsivity.

Issue: Possible Artificial Comorbid Presentation While the legitimate co-occurrence of ODD/CD and ADHD is common, it is also possible that assessment may give the convincing, yet artificial, impression of a comorbid presentation owing to halo effects, or alternatively, to a third underlying disorder being mistaken for ODD/CD + ADHD. ODD/CD and ADHD symptoms are particularly susceptible to halo effects, whereby the presence of one disorder (ODD or ADHD) may lead raters to artificially increase ratings of the other disorder. Studies involving printed clinical vignettes and staged video interactions present the specific symptoms of interest while controlling for references to other symptoms, yet teachers (Jackson & King, 2004) and unbiased raters (Hartung et al., 2010) are susceptible to endorsing symptoms of the other disorder. That is, depiction of ODD behaviors results in inflated ratings of ADHD symptoms despite those not being present, and vice versa (Hartung et al., 2010). Although existing studies documenting halo effects have done so when behavior is measured via rating scales, halo effects may similarly affect informants' reports in clinical interviews.

Halo effects resulting in artificial co-occurrence ratings have been ascribed to reporters' expectations of observing comorbidity (since ODD/CD and ADHD are very often observed by the reporter, the other symptoms are assumed to be present). Alternatively, halo effects may result from stigma, considering that the ADHD diagnostic label itself results in less favorable ratings of not only behavior but also factors unrelated to diagnostic criteria, such as IQ and personality (Batzle, Weyandt, Janusis, & DeVietti, 2010). However, unclear differentiation of symptomology in assessment measures may be the greatest contributor to halo effects, especially given similar findings of halo bias between ODD and separation anxiety due to ambiguous wording of items (Hommersen & Johnston, 2010). In recognition of potential halo effects, behavioral observations may be necessary to tease apart the behaviors that are truly present versus the behaviors that are only thought to occur.

In addition, the inaccurate diagnosis of comorbid ODD/CD + ADHD may occur because of the presence of a different disorder entirely. Symptoms of ADHD are not pathognomonic, meaning that struggling with concentration or fidgetiness is commonly observed in other disorders (e.g., depression, anxiety, learning disorders) as well. Similarly, symptoms of ODD/CD (irritability, low frustration tolerance, angry outbursts) are also common in other disorders. This issue would affect ratings and behavioral observations equally. However, clinical interviews may be useful to tease apart the true source of the symptom.

Particularly in the adolescent and adult developmental periods, the occurrence of conduct problems with hyperactivity/impulsivity may be indicative of Borderline Personality Disorder (Burke & Stepp, 2012) rather than the assumed comorbid ODD/CD+ADHD. Although limited studies have been conducted, provocative work suggests that for some individuals, childhood symptoms of ADHD may not necessarily reflect ADHD as much as they represent an early stage of Borderline Personality Disorder (Storebø & Simonsen, 2014). This trajectory may be most relevant for females (Stepp, Burke, Hipwell, & Loeber, 2012). As a result, the co-occurrence of ODD/CD and ADHD symptoms for some individuals may signify the presence of Borderline Personality Disorder features rather than a true comorbidity between ODD/CD and ADHD. Deliberate monitoring and assessment of Borderline Personality Disorder is recommended.

Intervention Implications of Comorbid ODD/CD with ADHD

Unique challenges may arise in the treatment of comorbid ODD/CD with ADHD, though a combined (behavioral and pharmacological) intervention targeting both disorders is generally recommended. Early identification and appropriate intervention are crucial to reduce associated impairments that could escalate symptoms of both disorders.

Interestingly, behavioral family/parent treatment is often effective for addressing ODD/CD or ADHD alone, but some evidence suggests that behavioral parent training may not provide much utility for children with comorbid ODD/CD+ADHD symptoms (Ercan, Ardic, Kutlu, & Durak, 2014). In addition, behavioral family interventions for adolescents with ODD+ADHD may result in improvement for only a small portion of families (25%; Barkley, Edwards, Laneri, Fletcher, & Metevia, 2001). In fact, behavioral interventions alone do not appear to be beneficial for comorbid presentations (Jensen et al., 2001), and could, conceivably, be detrimental. It is thought that caregivers may have more difficulty engaging in psychosocial/behavioral interventions if their children have comorbid ODD/CD+ADHD, because the immediate emphasis on parenting strategies may provoke more problematic child behavior and lead to attrition (Barkley et al., 2001).

Psychostimulant medication appears to be a necessary, but not always sufficient, treatment in addressing comorbid ODD/CD+ADHD (Jensen et al., 2001), though reducing ODD symptoms may depend on the medication's ability to effectively reduce symptoms of ADHD (Biederman et al., 2007). For a discussion of pharmacotherapy, please refer to Chapter 25.

Multimodal or integrated treatment, including behavioral and pharmacological elements, is typically recommended to address the spectrum of concerns pertaining to ODD/CD with ADHD. In fact, treatment success for ODD with ADHD improves 20% when combined (psychosocial and pharmacological) intervention is used, relative to either psychosocial or pharmacological treatment alone (Swanson et al., 2001). Children's receipt of cognitive behavioral therapy plus behavioral parent training for ODD/CD combined with psychostimulant medication for ADHD has also been helpful in preventing adolescent problems with delinquency and substance use, even reducing behaviors to levels comparable with typically developing peers (Zonnevylle-Bender, Matthys, Van de Wiel, & Lochman, 2007). Children with ODD/CD+ADHD and CU traits may not respond to behavior therapy alone as well as children with ODD/CD+ADHD; the addition of stimulant medication, however, reduces these differences substantially, affirming that combined treatment may be especially necessary when CU traits are present (Waschbusch, Carrey, Willoughby, King, & Andrade, 2007).

Conclusion

ODD/CD and ADHD possess many similarities in terms of symptoms, etiology, and associated impairments. It is, therefore, not surprising that comorbidity between the two conditions is high, although comorbidity rates, expression of associated symptoms, and prognosis may vary depending on sociodemographic factors such as the individual's developmental stage and gender. Accurate assessment is important because the co-occurring presence of ADHD among individuals with ODD/CD may confer greater risk for poor outcomes and may have important implications for treatment planning.

There are many resulting issues to consider when making a differential diagnosis between ODD/CD and ADHD or establishing the presence of a true comorbidity. Specifically, reporter biases and overlap in diagnostic symptoms between ODD/CD and ADHD as well as other disorders may require particular attention during the assessment process. An approach that includes multiple reporters (e.g., parent, co-parent, teacher, spouse, self) and methods (e.g., in vivo observation, clinical interview, ratings scales) is important to conducting a thorough assessment. In summary, each disorder needs to be considered in the discussion of the other, so that comprehensive treatment recommendations can be offered.

References

Abikoff, H. B., Jensen, P. S., Arnold, L. L. E., Hoza, B., Hechtman, L., Pollack, S., . . . Wigal, T. (2002). Observed classroom behavior of children with ADHD: Relationship to gender and comorbidity. *Journal of Abnormal Child Psychology*, *30*(4), 349–359.

American Psychiatric Association. (2013). *Diagnostic and statistical manual of mental disorders* (5th ed.). Arlington, VA: Author.

Angold, A., Costello, E. J., & Erkanli, A. (1999). Comorbidity. *Journal of Child Psychology and Psychiatry*, *40*(1), 57–87.

Banaschewski, T., Brandeis, D., Heinrich, H., Albrecht, B., Brunner, E., & Rothenberger, A. (2003). Association of ADHD and conduct disorder—Brain electrical evidence for the existence of a distinct subtype. *Journal of Child Psychology and Psychiatry*, *44*(3), 356–376.

Bandou, N., Koike, K., & Matuura, H. (2010). Predictive familial risk factors and pharmacological responses in ADHD with comorbid disruptive behavior disorders. *Pediatrics International*, *52*, 415–419.

Barker, E. D., Oliver, B. R., & Maughan, B. (2010). Co-occurring problems of early onset persistent, childhood limited, and adolescent onset conduct problem youth. *Journal of Child Psychology and Psychiatry*, *51*(11), 1217–1226.

Barkley, R. A., Edwards, G., Laneri, M., Fletcher, K., & Metevia, L. (2001). The efficacy of problem-solving communication training alone, behavior management training alone, and their combination for parent-adolescent conflict in teenagers with ADHD and ODD. *Journal of Consulting and Clinical Psychology*, *69*(6), 926–941.

Batzle, C. S., Weyandt, L. L., Janusis, G. M., & DeVietti, T. L. (2010). Potential impact of ADHD with stimulant medication label on teacher expectations. *Journal of Attention Disorders*, *14*(2), 157–166.

Biederman, J. (2005). Attention-deficit/hyperactivity disorder: A selective overview. *Biological Psychiatry*, *57*, 1215–1220.

Biederman, J., Petty, C. R., Clarke, A., Lomedico, A., & Faraone, S. V. (2011). Predictors of persistent ADHD: An 11-year follow-up study. *Journal of Psychiatric Research*, *45*, 150–155.

Biederman, J., Spencer, T. J., Newcorn, J. H., Gao, H., Milton, D. R., Feldman, P. D., & Witte, M. M. (2007). Effect of comorbid symptoms of oppositional defiant disorder on responses to atomoxetime in children with ADHD: A meta-analysis of controlled clinical trials. *Psychopharmacology*, *190*, 31–41.

Bunte, T. L., Laschen, S., Schoemaker, K., Hessen, D. J., Van der Heijden, P. G. M., & Matthys, W. (2013). Clinical usefulness of observational assessment in the diagnosis of DBD and ADHD in preschoolers. *Journal of Clinical Child and Adolescent Psychology, 42,* 749–761.

Bunte, T. L., Schoemaker, K., Hessen, D. J., Van der Heijden, P. G. M., & Matthys, W. (2014). Stability and change of ODD, CD an ADHD diagnosis in referred preschool children. *Journal of Abnormal Child Psychology, 42,* 1213–1224.

Burke, J. D., Rowe, R., & Boylan, K. (2014). Functional outcomes of child and adolescent oppositional defiant disorder symptoms in young adult men. *Journal of Child Psychology and Psychiatry, 55*(3), 264–272.

Burke, J. D., & Stepp, S. D. (2012). Adolescent disruptive behavior and borderline personality disorder symptoms in young adult men. *Journal of Abnormal Child Psychology, 40*(1), 35–44.

Burt, S. A., Krueger, R. F., McGue, M., & Iacono, W. G. (2001). Sources of covariation among attention-deficit/hyperactivity disorder, oppositional defiant disorder, and conduct disorder: The importance of shared environment. *Journal of Abnormal Psychology, 110*(4), 516–525.

Byrd, A. L., Loeber, R., & Pardini, D. A. (2012). Understanding desisting and persisting forms of delinquency: The unique contributions of disruptive behavior disorders and interpersonal callousness. *Journal of Child Psychology and Psychiatry, 53*(4), 371–380.

Campbell, S. B. (1994). Hard-to-manage preschool boys: Externalizing behavior, social competence, and family context at two-year followup. *Journal of Abnormal Child Psychology, 22*(2), 147–166.

Christiansen, H., Chen, W., Oades, R. D., Asherson, P., Taylor, E. A., Lasky-Su, J., . . . Faraone, S. V. (2008). *Journal of Neural Transmission, 115,* 163–175.

Coles, E. K., Slavec, J., Bernstein, M., & Baroni, E. (2012). Exploring the gender gap in referrals for children with ADHD and other disruptive behavior disorders. *Journal of Attention Disorders, 16*(2), 101–108.

Costello, E. J., Mustillo, S., Erkanli, A., Keeler, G., & Angold, A. (2003). Prevalence and development of psychiatric disorders in childhood and adolescence. *Archives of General Psychiatry, 60,* 837–844.

Danforth, J. S., Connor, D. F., & Doerfler, L. A. (2016). The development of comorbid conduct problems in children with ADHD: An example of an integrative developmental psychopathology perspective. *Journal of Attention Disorders, 20*(3), 214–229.

Deschamps, P. K. H., Schutter, D. J. L. G., Kenemans, J. L., & Matthys, W. (2015). Empathy and prosocial behavior in response to sadness and distress in 6- to 7-year-olds diagnosed with disruptive behavior disorder and attention-deficit hyperactivity disorder. *European Child & Adolescent Psychiatry, 24,* 105–113.

Ercan, E. S., Ardic, U. A., Kutlu, A., & Durak, S. (2014). No beneficial effects of adding parent training to methylphenidate treatment for ADHD+ODD/CD children: A 1-year prospective follow-up study. *Journal of Attention Disorders, 18*(2), 145–157.

Ercan, E. S., Bilaç, Ö., Özaslan, T. U., & Rohde, L. A. (2015). Is the prevalence of ADHD in Turkish elementary school children really high? *Social Psychiatry and Psychiatric Epidemiology, 50,* 1145–1152.

Freitag, C. M., Hänig, S., Schneider, A., Seitz, C., Palmason, H., Retz, W., & Meyer, J. (2012). Biological and psychosocial environmental risk factors influence symptom severity and psychiatric comorbidity in children with ADHD. *Journal of Neural Transmission, 119,* 81–94.

Gadow, K. D., Sprafkin, J., Schneider, J., Nolan, E. E., Schwartz, J., & Weiss, M. D. (2007). ODD, ADHD, versus ODD+ADHD in clinic and community adults. *Journal of Attention Disorders, 11*(3), 374–383.

Galbaud du Fort, G., Boothroyd, L. J., Bland, R. C., Newman, S. C., & Kakuma, R. (2002). Spouse similarity for antisocial behaviour in the general population. *Psychological Medicine, 32,* 1407–1416.

Harpold, T., Biederman, J., Gignac, M., Hammerness, P., Surman, C., Potter, A., & Mick, E. (2007). Is oppositional defiant disorder a meaningful diagnosis in adults? Results from a large sample of adults with ADHD. *Journal of Nervous and Mental Disease, 195,* 601–605.

Hartung, C. M., Lefler, E. K., Tempel, A. B., Armendariz, M. L., Sigel, B. A., & Little, C. S. (2010). Halo effects in ratings of ADHD and ODD: Identification of susceptible symptoms. *Journal of Psychopathology and Behavioral Assessment, 32,* 128–137.

Harvey, E. A., Breaux, R. P., & Lugo-Candelas, C. I. (2016). Early development of comorbidity between symptoms of attention-deficit/hyperactivity disorder (ADHD) and oppositional defiant disorder (ODD). *Journal of Abnormal Psychology, 125*(2), 154–167.

Hommersen, P., & Johnston, C. (2010). Separation anxiety and oppositional defiant behavior: Perceived comorbidity resulting from ambiguous behavioral items. *Journal of Psychopathology and Behavioral Assessment, 32,* 96–107.

Hussong, A. M., Curran, P. J., Moffitt, T. E., Caspi, A., & Carrig, M. M. (2004). Substance abuse hinders desistance in young adults' antisocial behavior. *Development and Psychopathology, 16,* 1029–1046.

Jackson, D. A., & King, A. R. (2004). Gender differences in the effects of oppositional behavior on teacher ratings of ADHD symptoms. *Journal of Abnormal Child Psychology, 32*(2), 215–224.

Jensen, P. S., Hinshaw, S. P., Kraemer, H. C., Lenora, N., Newcorn, J. H., Abikoff, H. B., . . . Vitiello, B. (2001). ADHD comorbidity findings from the MTA study: Comparing comorbid subgroups. *Journal of the American Academy of Child and Adolescent Psychiatry, 40*(2), 147–158.

Jensen, C. M., & Steinhausen, H.-C. (2015). Comorbid mental disorders in children and adolescents with attention-deficit/hyperactivity disorder in a large nationwide study. *ADHD Attention Deficit and Hyperactivity Disorders, 7,* 27–38.

Johnston, C., Weiss, M., Murray, C., & Miller, N. (2011). The effects of instructions on mothers' ratings of child attention-deficit/hyperactivity disorder symptoms. *Journal of Abnormal Child Psychology, 39,* 1099–1110.

Karakas, S., Bakar, E. E., Dinçer, E. D., Ülsever, H., Ceylan, A. Ö., & Taner, Y. I. (2015). Relationship between diagnosis of ADHD in offspring and current and retrospective self-reports of parental ADHD. *Journal of Child and Family Studies, 24,* 3595–3609.

King, S., Waschbusch, D. A., Frankland, B. W., Andrade, B. F., Thurston, C. M., McNutt, L., . . . Northern Partners in Action for Child and Youth Services (2005). Taxonomic examination of ADHD and conduct problem comorbidity in elementary school children using cluster analyses. *Journal of Psychopathology and Behavioral Assessment, 27*(2), 77–88.

Kooij, J. J. S., Boonstra, A. M., Swinkels, S. H. N., Bekker, E. M., De Noord, I., & Buitelaar, J. K. (2008). Reliability, validity, and utility of instruments for self-report and informant report concerning symptoms of ADHD in adult patients. *Journal of Attention Disorders, 11*(4), 445–458.

Kotte, A., Faraone, S. V., & Biederman, J. (2013). Association of genetic risk severity with ADHD clinical characteristics. *American Journal of Medical Genetics, 162*(7), 718–733.

Kuja-Halkola, R., Lichtenstein, P., D'Onofrio, B. M., & Larsson, H. (2015). Codevelopment of ADHD and externalizing behavior from childhood to adulthood. *Journal of Child Psychology and Psychiatry, 56*(6), 640–647.

Lavigne, J. V., LeBailly, S. A., Hopkins, J., Gouze, K. R., & Binns, H. J. (2009). The prevalence of ADHD, ODD, depression, and anxiety in a community sample of 4-year-olds. *Journal of Clinical Child & Adolescent Psychology, 38*(3), 315–328.

Loeber, R., Burke, J. D., Lahey, B. B., Winters, A., & Zera, M. (2000). Oppositional defiant and conduct disorder: A review of the past 10 years, Part I. *Journal of the American Academy of Child and Adolescent Psychiatry, 39*(12), 1468–1484.

Loeber, R., & Keenan, K. (1994). Interaction between conduct disorder and its comorbid conditions: Effects of age and gender. *Clinical Psychology Review, 14*(6), 497–523.

Martel, M. M., Gremillion, M., Roberts, B., von Eye, A., & Nigg, J. T. (2010). The structure of childhood disruptive behaviors. *Psychological Assessment, 22*(4), 816–826.

Maughan, B., Rowe, R., Messer, J., Goodman, R., & Meltzer, H. (2004). Conduct disorder and oppositional defiant disorder in a national sample: Developmental epidemiology. *Journal of Child Psychology and Psychiatry, 45*(3), 609–621.

McGee, T. R., Hayatbakhsh, M. R., Bor, W., Aird, R. L., Dean, A. J., & Najman, J. M. (2015). The impact of snares on the continuity of adolescent-onset antisocial behaviour: A test of Moffitt's developmental taxonomy. *Australian & New Zealand Journal of Criminology, 48*(3), 345–366.

Michanie, C., Kunst, G., Margulies, D. S., & Yakhkind, A. (2007). Symptom prevalence of ADHD and ODD in a pediatric population in Argentina. *Journal of Attention Disorders, 11*(3), 363–367.

Mikami, A. Y., Chi, T. C., & Hinshaw, S. P. (2004). Behavior ratings and observations of externalizing symptoms in girls: The role of child popularity with adults. *Journal of Psychopathology and Behavioral Assessment, 26*(3), 151–163.

Moffitt, T. E. (1993). Adolescence-limited and life-course-persistent antisocial behavior: A developmental taxonomy. *Psychological Review, 100*(4), 674–701.

Moffitt, T. E., Caspi, A., Harrington, H., & Milne, B. J. (2002). Males on the life-course-persistent and adolescence-limited pathways: Follow-up at age 26 years. *Development and Psychopathology, 14,* 179–207.

Morgan, P. L., Li, H., Cook, M., Farkas, G., Hillemeier, M. M., & Lin, Y. (2016). Which kindergarten children are at greatest risk for attention-deficit/hyperactivity and conduct disorder symptomatology as adolescents? *School Psychology Quarterly, 31*(1), 58–75.

Nadder, T. S., Rutter, M., Silberg, J. L., Maes, H. H., & Eaves, L. J. (2002). Genetic effects on the variation and covariation of attention deficit-hyperactivity disorder (ADHD) and oppositional-defiant disorder/conduct disorder (ODD/CD) symptomatologies across informant and occasion of measurement. *Psychological Medicine, 32,* 39–53.

Nock, M. K., Kazdin, A. E., Hiripi, E., & Kessler, R. C. (2007). Lifetime prevalence, correlates, and persistence of oppositional defiant disorder: Results from the National Comorbidity Survey Replication. *Journal of Child Psychology and Psychiatry, 48*(7), 703–713.

Ohan, J. L., Visser, T. A. W., Strain, M. C., & Allen, L. (2011). Teachers' and education students' perceptions of and reactions to children with and without the diagnostic label "ADHD." *Journal of School Psychology, 49,* 81–105.

Pardini, D. A., & Fite, P. J. (2010). Symptoms of conduct disorder, oppositional defiant disorder, attention-deficit/hyperactivity disorder, and callous-unemotional traits as unique predictors of psychosocial maladjustment in boys: Advancing an evidence base for DSM-V. *Journal of the American Academy of Child and Adolescent Psychiatry, 49*(11), 1134–1144.

Qu, Y., Jiang, H., Zhang, N., Wang, D., & Guo, L. (2015). Prevalence of mental disorders in 6-16-year-old students in Sichuan Province, China. *International Journal of Environmental Research and Public Health, 12,* 5090–5107.

Rabiner, D. L., Coie, J. D., Miller-Johnson, S., Boykin, A.-S. M., & Lochman, J. E. (2005). Predicting the persistence of aggressive offending of African American males from adolescence into young adulthood: The importance of peer relations, aggressive behavior, and ADHD symptoms. *Journal of Emotional and Behavioral Disorders, 13*(3), 131–140.

Reiff, M. I., & Stein, M. T. (2003). Attention-deficit/hyperactivity disorder evaluation and diagnosis: A practical approach in office practice. *Pediatric Clinics of North America, 50,* 1019–1048.

Reimherr, F. W., Marchant, B. K., Olsen, J. L., Wender, P. H., & Robison, R. J. (2013). Oppositional defiant disorder in adults with ADHD. *Journal of Attention Disorders, 17*(2), 102–113.

Rolon-Arroyo, B., Arnold, D. H., & Harvey, E. A. (2014). The predictive utility of conduct disorder symptoms in preschool children: A 3-year follow-up study. *Child Psychiatry & Human Development, 45*(3), 329–337.

Savolainen, J., Hurtig, T. M., Ebeling, H. E., Moilanen, I. K., Hughes, L. A., & Taanila, A. M. (2010). Attention deficit hyperactivity disorder (ADHD) and criminal behaviour: The role of adolescent marginalization. *European Journal of Criminology, 7*(6), 442–459.

Sibley, M. H., Pelham, W. E., Molina, B. S. G., Gnagy, E. M., Waschbusch, D. A., Biswas, A., . . . Karch, K. M. (2011). The delinquency outcomes of boys with ADHD with and without comorbidity. *Journal of Abnormal Child Psychology, 39,* 21–32.

Sibley, M. H., Pelham, W. E., Molina, B. S. G., Waschbusch, D. A., Gnagy, E. M., Babinski, D. E., & Biswas, A. (2010). Inconsistent self-report of delinquency by adolescents and young adults with ADHD. *Journal of Abnormal Child Psychology, 38,* 645–656.

Siegel, C. E., Laska, E. M., Wanderling, J. A., Hernandez, J. C., & Levenson, R. B. (2016). Prevalence and diagnosis rates of childhood ADHD among racial-ethnic groups in a public mental health system. *Psychiatric Services, 67,* 199–205.

Stepp, S. D., Burke, J. D., Hipwell, A. E., & Loeber, R. (2012). Trajectories of attention deficit hyperactivity disorder and oppositional defiant disorder symptoms as precursors of borderline personality disorder symptoms in adolescent girls. *Journal of Abnormal Child Psychology, 40,* 7–20.

Storebø, O. J., & Simonsen, E. (2014). Is ADHD an early stage in the development of borderline personality disorder? *Nordic Journal of Psychiatry, 68,* 289–295.

Storebø, O. J., & Simonsen, E. (2016). The association between ADHD and antisocial personality disorder (ASPD): A review. *Journal of Attention Disorders, 20*(10), 815–824.

Swanson, J. M., Kraemer, H. C., Hinshaw, S. P., Arnold, L. E., Conners, C. K., Abikoff, H. B., Wu, M. (2001). Clinical relevance of the primary findings of the MTA: Success rates based on severity of

ADHD and ODD symptoms at the end of treatment. *Journal of the American Academy of Child and Adolescent Psychiatry, 40,* 168–179.

Tandon, M., Si, X., & Luby, J. (2011). Preschool onset attention-deficit/hyperactivity disorder: Course and predictors of stability over 24 months. *Journal of Child and Adolescent Psychopharmacology, 21*(4), 321–330.

Tseng, W.-L., Kawabata, Y., & Gau, S. S.-F. (2011). Social adjustment among Taiwanese children with symptoms of ADHD, ODD, and ADHD comorbid with ODD. *Child Psychiatry and Human Development, 42,* 134–151.

Tuvblad, C., Zheng, M., Raine, A., & Baker, L. A. (2009). A common genetic factor explains the covariation among ADHD ODD and CD symptoms in 9-10 year old boys and girls. *Journal of Abnormal Child Psychology, 37,* 153–167.

Van der Put, C. E., Asscher, J. J., & Stams, G. J. J. M. (2016). Differences between juvenile offenders with and without AD(H)D in recidivism rates and risk and protective factors for recidivism. *Journal of Attention Disorders, 20*(5), 445–457.

Van Lier, P. A. C., Van der Ende, J., Koot, H. M., & Verhulst, F. C. (2007). Which better predicts conduct problems? The relationship of trajectories of conduct problems with ODD and ADHD symptoms from childhood into adolescence. *Journal of Child Psychology and Psychiatry, 48*(6), 601–608.

Waller, R., Hyde, L. W., Grabell, A. S., Alves, M. L., & Olson, S. L. (2015). Differential associations of early callous-unemotional, oppositional, and ADHD behaviors: Multiple domains within early-starting conduct problems? *Journal of Child Psychology and Psychiatry, 56*(6), 657–666.

Waschbusch, D. A. (2002). A meta-analytic examination of comorbid hyperactive-impulsive-attention problems and conduct problems. *Psychological Bulletin, 128*(1), 118–150.

Waschbusch, D. A., Carrey, N. J., Willoughby, M. T., King, S., & Andrade, B. F. (2007). Effects of methylphenidate and behavior modification on the social and academic behavior of children with disruptive behavior disorders: The moderating role of callous/unemotional traits. *Journal of Clinical Child & Adolescent Psychology, 36*(4), 629–644.

Young, S., Sedgwick, O., Fridman, M., Gudjonsson, G., Hodgkins, P., Lantigua, M., & González, R. A. (2015). Co-morbid psychiatric disorders among incarcerated ADHD populations: A meta-analysis. *Psychological Medicine, 45,* 2499–2510.

Zonnevylle-Bender, M. J. S., Matthys, W., van de Wiel, N. M. H., & Lochman, J. E. (2007). Preventive effects of treatment of DBD in middle childhood on substance abuse and delinquent behavior. *Journal of the American Academy of Child and Adolescent Psychiatry, 46,* 33–39.

5
Comorbidity with Substance Abuse
Naomi R. Marmorstein and Helene R. White

Disruptive Behavior Disorders (DBDs) are highly comorbid with substance abuse. Links between DBDs and substance abuse have been the subject of multiple previous excellent reviews (e.g., Conner & Lochman, 2010; Stein, Hesselbrock, & Bukstein, 2008). We aim to build off this knowledge base, including an up-to-date discussion of possible explanatory mechanisms for this association as well as possible moderators. We first briefly review the nature of the specific associations of substance use with Conduct Disorder (CD) and Oppositional Defiant Disorder (ODD). Then we discuss underlying causes for this pattern of comorbidity and potential moderators of these associations. We conclude by briefly summarizing available evidence and recommending next steps for research in this area.

In order to limit the scope of our review, we concentrate on certain foci within the broad categories of DBDs and substance abuse. We focus specifically on CD and ODD as DBDs of interest and limit our discussion of other behavior problems (e.g., attention-deficit hyperactivity disorder, ADHD). Our emphasis is on the disorders CD and ODD, as defined by the Diagnostic and Statistical Manual of Mental Disorders (DSM; American Psychiatric Association, 2013) (see Chapters 2 and 3 of this book for definition and characteristics of both of these disorders), though when relevant we also include research on related constructs (e.g., delinquency). We focus on alcohol and illicit drug use and limit our discussion of nicotine, due to the somewhat separate literatures on these different substances.

When we use the term "substance abuse," we are referring to an umbrella category of substance use-related problems; within this category we are considering heavy use (e.g., frequent binge drinking), abuse (e.g., repeated driving under the influence), and/or dependence (including indications of physiological dependence such as tolerance and withdrawal) of or on alcohol and/or drugs. This approach to substance use-related problems is broadly consistent with the new DSM-5 categorization. In contrast to the DSM-IV (American Psychiatric Association, 1994), which contained separate diagnoses for substance abuse (the misuse of substances; for example, drinking while driving) and substance dependence (dependence on substances; for example, tolerance or withdrawal), the DSM-5 includes one primary diagnosis, "substance use disorder," capturing the construct of problematic substance use (American Psychiatric Association, 2013). This diagnosis includes most of the symptoms of both substance abuse and substance dependence from DSM-IV. The DSM-IV substance abuse symptom of problems with law enforcement related to use was eliminated (due to the potential confounding of cultural factors), and a symptom for craving was added in DSM-5. There are also now specifiers for mild, moderate, and severe substance use disorder, with the "mild" category requiring two to three symptoms (in contrast to the single symptom required for a diagnosis of substance abuse in DSM-IV).

The Wiley Handbook of Disruptive and Impulse-Control Disorders, First Edition.
Edited by John E. Lochman and Walter Matthys.
© 2018 John Wiley & Sons Ltd. Published 2018 by John Wiley & Sons Ltd.

Some of the substance use research we discuss comes from the psychopathology literature, which tends to focus on DSM diagnostic categories, while other studies utilize continuous approaches to characterizing substance use and related problems. In addition, some of the research we review focuses on substance use early in development. Because early use is a strong predictor of later use-related problems, abuse, and dependence (e.g., Grant & Dawson, 1997; Grant, Stinson, & Harford, 2001), we considered it appropriate to include along with already developed diagnoses. When relevant, we explicitly distinguish among these different substance-related outcomes.

Associations between DBDs and Substance Abuse

Conduct Disorder

CD symptoms are strongly associated, both cross-sectionally and longitudinally, with risk for numerous measures of early substance use, heavy and/or problem use, and abuse and dependence (e.g., Armstrong & Costello, 2002; Boyle & Offord, 1991; Chassin, Ritter, Trim, & King, 2003; Conner & Lochman, 2010; Disney, Elkins, McGue, & Iacono, 1999; Loeber, Burke, Lahey, Winters, & Zera, 2000; Stein et al., 2008; Weinberg, Rahdert, Colliver, & Myer, 1998; Whitmore et al., 1997; Windle, 1990). CD and substance-related behaviors are so intertwined that early substance use is sometimes considered to be an indicator of conduct problems, as opposed to the possible beginnings of a separate disorder (Angold & Costello, 2001).

CD is associated with increased risk for early first use of a variety of substances, including nicotine (e.g., Bagot et al., 2007; Brinkman, Epstein, Auinger, Tamm, & Froehlich, 2015), alcohol (e.g., Brinkman et al., 2015), and drugs (e.g., Elkins, McGue, & Iacono, 2007). CD is also linked to heavy use such as binge drinking (e.g., Chassin, Pitts, & Prost, 2002), as well as problem use, abuse, and dependence (Heron et al., 2013; Loeber, Stouthamer-Loeber, & White, 1999; McCarty et al., 2013; Pardini et al., 2007; Sung, Erkanli, & Costello, 2014; White, Xie, Thompson, Loeber, & Stouthame-Loeber, 2001). Across samples, CD tends to precede substance use disorders and is a strong predictor of future substance use-related problems (Huizinga, Menard, & Elliott, 1989). It also predicts progression from first use of substances to substance use disorders (e.g., Sung et al., 2014).

Potential pathways from substance use and abuse to CD (or the broader category of externalizing or antisocial behavior) have been the subject of less research attention (see White, 2015, 2016 for reviews). That said, available evidence supports the notion that substance abuse may place youth at risk for increasing antisocial behavior (Wymbs et al., 2014), and other research has supported bidirectional effects between delinquency and substance use across high school among boys (Mason & Windle, 2002), indicating that there may be reciprocal associations between these problem behaviors. Additional research indicates that being drunk or having a drug-use-related symptom (i.e., a symptom of abuse of or dependence on any illicit drug) by age 18 is associated with risk for antisocial behavior in adulthood, regardless of the presence or absence of conduct problems in childhood or adolescence (Ridenour et al., 2002), and higher levels of substance use predict higher rates of antisocial personality disorder in early adulthood (Brook, Cohen, & Brook, 1998). In addition, substance abuse may act as a "snare" in development, keeping youth who might otherwise mature out of delinquent behavior involved in a longer-lasting pattern of antisocial behavior (Hussong, Curran, Moffitt, Caspi, & Carrig, 2004; Moffitt, 1993a; see below for more discussion of this); in these cases, substance abuse acts to exacerbate pre-existing conduct problems.

Putting these strains of research together, it seems likely that there are reciprocal associations between CD-related behaviors and substance use and abuse. Longitudinal, community-based studies that have examined these associations over time are consistent with this notion (for a review see White, 2016). It seems likely that CD symptoms tend to begin prior to the onset of substance use; substance use then, in turn, predicts increasing severity of CD-related behaviors, which then predict the development of substance use disorders (Brook et al., 1998; Costello, Erkanli, Federman, & Angold, 1999).

Oppositional Defiant Disorder

Possible associations between ODD and substance abuse have received much less research attention than links between CD and substance abuse. This lack of research is likely because of the clearly demonstrated developmental pathway from ODD to CD (e.g., Burke, Loeber, Lahey, & Rathouz, 2005; Rowe, Maughan, Pickles, Costello, & Angold, 2002), making links between ODD and substance abuse less proximal. However, some research demonstrates that ODD is associated with certain measures of substance use and/or use-related problems. For example, White and colleagues (2001) found that ODD was associated with the level of alcohol (but not marijuana) use; however, it was not associated with growth in the use of these substances over time. Using the National Comorbidity Survey Replication data, one study found a significant ODD–substance use disorder association (Nock, Kazdin, Hiripi, & Kessler, 2007), and there was a significant association between ODD and substance use and abuse in the Great Smoky Mountains sample as well (Costello et al., 1999).

It is unclear whether the association between ODD and substance abuse remains significant after the effect of comorbid CD is adjusted for. There was a significant association between ODD and SUDs after controlling for CD in one study (Nock et al., 2007), but, in another study, once CD was controlled for there was no significant link between ODD and substance use or abuse (Costello et al., 1999). In addition, another study using the Great Smoky Mountains community-based sample found that ODD, CD, and CD+ODD groups all had elevated rates of SUDs compared to controls (Rowe et al., 2002). There were no statistically significant differences among these three diagnostic groups in risk for SUDs, though comparisons approached significance (with odds ratios representing relative risk of over 2.0) for comparisons of ODD-only versus CD-only and ODD-only versus CD+ODD, indicating that CD may be the driving force behind these associations. Thus, research to date is mixed regarding whether or not the apparent association between ODD and substance abuse remains significant once comorbid CD is accounted for.

Possible reasons for a potential direct (i.e., not mediated by CD) link between ODD and substance abuse remain mostly unexplored. If these DBDs and substance use disorders are all part of a broader externalizing syndrome (see below), youth may simply express this liability in different ways and one of the combinations could be ODD and substance abuse, without CD. Relatedly, some youth may have subclinical levels of CD. Therefore their conduct problems would not appear in studies using categorical diagnoses, but may still mediate apparent links between ODD and substance abuse.

Newer models of ODD may shed light on this question. Specifically, ODD symptoms can be categorized into affective and behavioral dimensions (with different studies using various terminology for these categories; see Chapter 2 for a discussion of these characteristics of ODD). The behavioral symptoms (also described as defiant, oppositional, and antagonistic behavior) appear to be more closely linked with other externalizing behavior such as CD, compared to the affective symptoms (see, e.g., Burke, Hipwell, & Loeber, 2010; Leadbeater & Homel, 2015). Although we are not aware of research specifically on these subdimensions of ODD symptoms and substance abuse, it seems possible that the behavioral symptoms of

ODD are more strongly linked with substance abuse compared to the affective symptoms (e.g., irritability) owing to their closer resemblance to CD symptoms. The affective symptoms of ODD do have predictive utility to several forms of psychopathology in early adulthood (Burke, 2012); therefore, it remains possible that they could also predict future substance abuse, with this potential association perhaps being mediated by other forms of psychopathology. Future research investigating these possibilities using novel models of ODD would be useful in increasing our understanding of links between DBDs and substance abuse.

Potential Common Pathways to DBDs and Substance Use

One potential explanation for the pattern of comorbidity between DBDs and substance abuse is that many risk factors for DBDs overlap with those that predict substance use and abuse. These shared risk factors occur at the genetic, individual, family, peer, and community levels of analysis; related to this, recent research indicates that these disorders may be differing manifestations of an underlying, genetically mediated predisposition to behavioral disinhibition and a spectrum of externalizing disorders (Krueger et al., 2002; Krueger, Markon, Patrick, Benning, & Kramer, 2007). In fact, many have argued that substance use and delinquency are related because they are part of a problem behavior syndrome (Jessor & Jessor, 1977) and predicted by a similar underlying set of individual and environmental risk factors (Noyori-Corbett & Moon, 2010; White, 1997a, 1997b). Crowley and Riggs (1995) proposed that CD may also be part of this behavioral syndrome and Conner and Lochman (2010, p. 338) suggested that substance use may be "part of a pattern of antisocial and rule-breaking behavior," which is common to CD. Here we briefly review potential common risk factors at each level of analysis. Because research in this area is primarily focused on CD and delinquency, as opposed to ODD, our review focuses predominantly on these constructs.

Genetics

Twin studies indicate that approximately 35% of the phenotypic covariance between CD and drug dependence can be attributed to genetic factors (with shared environment contributing an additional 46%; Button et al., 2006). Overlap among different substance use disorders (alcohol, nicotine, and cannabis) is attributable to genetic influences that are shared with conduct disorder (Grant et al., 2015), supporting the notion that a predisposition to these disorders, as a group, is genetically influenced.

At a broader level, research on the "externalizing spectrum" supports the notion that substance dependence, antisocial behavior, and behavioral disinhibition load on a single factor (Krueger et al., 2002; Krueger et al., 2007). A general vulnerability to these externalizing disorders is highly heritable ($h^2 = .80$), though disorder-specific effects are present in some cases as well (i.e., liabilities to CD, alcohol dependence, and drug dependence were found to be related both to this general externalizing factor and to factors specific to each disorder; Hicks, Krueger, Iacono, McGue, & Patrick, 2004).

Genome-wide linkage analyses provide evidence for both general and specific effects as well. A comprehensive review of the literature indicates that two genes (GABRA2 and CHRM2) are associated with risk for a variety of externalizing disorders (Dick, 2007). Recent research indicates that these associations are likely moderated by environmental factors. For example, the association between CHRM2 and membership in higher risk externalizing trajectories was more likely among youth reporting higher levels of peer antisocial behavior (Latendresse et al., 2011). Furthermore, despite an overall association between GABRA2 and membership in a "stable high" externalizing trajectory, this association was weaker in the presence of high levels of parental monitoring (Dick et al., 2009). In addition to these associations of particular genes with disorders across the externalizing spectrum, some disorder-specific genetic effects have been found. For example, in a large sample of siblings, a linkage peak on chromosome 4q was found to be associated with alcohol dependence but not CD, providing evidence for the specificity of this gene for risk for alcohol dependence. Conversely, linkages were found for CD but not alcohol dependence in other locations, indicating that other genes appear to impact risk for CD more than risk for alcohol dependence (Kendler et al., 2006).

The mechanisms by which genes may influence both CD and SUDs are not well understood. It seems likely that genetic variation produces differences in certain neural pathways across individuals that then affect behavior (for an excellent discussion of mechanisms through which genes may affect behavior, see Hariri & Weinberger, 2003). One well-researched endophenotype underlying both DBDs and substance abuse is reduced amplitude of the P300 brain potential response. Reduced P300 amplitude has been shown to be associated with a spectrum of externalizing and substance use disorders (Patrick et al., 2006) and has been theorized to be an indicator of impairments in executive functioning that are associated with risk for both externalizing and substance use disorders (e.g., Giancola & Tarter, 1999; see below).

Individual

One common underlying factor that has been strongly linked to CD and substance use is behavioral undercontrol (for a review see Conner & Lochman, 2010). This construct encompasses several temperamental traits and personality predispositions, including impulsivity, sensation seeking, risk taking, and emotional dysregulation. For example, sensation seeking—i.e., "need for varied, novel and complex sensations and experiences and the willingness to take physical and social risks for the sake of such experience" (Zuckerman, 1979, p. 10)—is one of the best predictors of adolescent substance use (Bates, Labouvie, & White, 1986; Zuckerman, 1994) and is also linked strongly to delinquent behavior (Greene, Krcmar, Walters, Rubin, & Hale, 2000; White, Labouvie, & Bates, 1985). CD is often comorbid with hyperactivity, impulsivity, and attention problems (including ADHD; Crowley & Riggs, 1995; Gatzke-Kopp et al., 2009; Waschbuch, 2002) and impulsive behavior has been linked with CD (see Conner & Lochman, 2010; Thompson, Whitmore, Eaymond, & Crowley, 2006). Both childhood ADHD (Wilens, 1998) and impulsivity (for reviews see Thompson et al., 2006; White et al., 2011) have been strongly associated with alcohol and drug disorders, though these associations may operate via comorbidity with CD (e.g., Disney et al., 1999). Furthermore, ODD and ADHD are often comorbid in early childhood (Cunningham & Boyle, 2002) and ODD has been linked to impulse control disorders (Nock et al., 2007). In addition, Conner and Lochman (2010) highlighted the common pathways in the development of CD and SUD and suggested that early aggression in childhood may be one such pathway. Childhood aggression has also been linked to ODD (Loeber et al., 2000).

Internalizing problems, such as depression and anxiety, have been linked to CD (Loeber et al., 2000), ODD (Cunningham & Boyle, 2002; Nock et al., 2007), and substance use (Marmorstein, White, Chung, et al., 2010; Marmorstein, White, Loeber, & Stouthamer-Loeber, 2010). The temporal order between internalizing problems and CD appears to depend on the subtype of CD being examined; for example, anxiety generally precedes childhood-onset CD but adolescent-onset CD is associated with an increased risk for anxiety disorder (as reviewed in Loeber et al., 2000). Similarly, there is inconsistent evidence for the temporal association between depression and CD (see Capaldi & Kim, 2014; Loeber et al., 2000), as well as substance use disorders (SUD) and depression (e.g., Bukstein, Glancy, & Kaminer, 1992; Costello et al., 1999; Kumpulainen, 2000; Marmorstein,

Iacono, & Malone, 2010; Rao, Daley, & Hammen, 2000; Rohde, Lewinsohn, Kahler, Seeley, & Brown, 2001). Mood and anxiety disorders have also been linked to ODD (Nock et al., 2007).

School achievement problems have been associated with substance use (Fleming, Catalano, Haggerty, & Abbott, 2010; Henry, 2010) and delinquency (Maguin & Loeber, 1996). Keenan, Loeber, and Green (1999) proposed that academic failure, especially among girls, may lead to a negative response from parents and teachers, which, in turn, leads to disruptive behavior and later CD. A similar process has been identified for the relationship between academic failure and marijuana use, with deviant peers as a possible mediating mechanism (see Pardini et al., 2015).

There appear to be several common risk factors that are biologically or physiologically based. For example, neuropsychological dysfunction (e.g., deficits in executive functioning) has been linked to CD (Moffitt, 1993b), antisocial behavior (Raine et al., 2005), and substance use (Giancola, 2002). Prenatal exposure to maternal alcohol and cigarette use has also been implicated as a risk factor for CD (Freitag et al., 2012; Latimer et al., 2012) and for substance abuse (Baer, Sampson, Barr, Connor, & Streissguth, 2003).

Peer Relationships

In addition to individual-level characteristics, peer relationships are important predictors of substance use (Ennett et al., 2006; Pandina, Johnson, & White, 2009) and CD (Vitaro, Brendgen, Pagani, Tremblay, & McDuff, 1999). Several studies have found that substance-using and delinquent peers are among the strongest predictors of adolescent substance use (e.g., Dishion & Owen, 2002; Ennett & Bauman, 1996; Pandina et al., 2009; Trucco, Colder, & Wieczorek, 2011) and that delinquent peer affiliation is one of the strongest predictors of adolescent delinquency (for a review, see Gorman & White, 1995). Studies indicate, however, that youth are just as likely to choose friends whose behavior matches their own (selection) as to be socialized by their peers into both substance use and delinquent behaviors (Dishion & Owen, 2002; Gorman & White, 1995; Pandina et al., 2009).

Family Factors

Family functioning and interactions are also strongly correlated with adolescent substance use (Hemovich, Lac, & Crano, 2011; Kramer et al., 2008), CD (McCord, 1993; for a review see Conner & Lochman, 2010), and ODD (Greene et al., 2002). For example, poor parenting (e.g., low monitoring and supervision) has been related to substance use (Simons-Morton & Chen, 2005; Substance Abuse and Mental Health Services Administration, 2005), CD (Disney, Iacono, McGue, Tully, & Legrand, 2008), and ODD (Cunningham & Boyle, 2002) and parent–child conflict is associated with CD (Burt, Krueger, McGue, & Iacono, 2003) and substance use (see White, Johnson, & Buyske, 2000). Furthermore, parental substance use and substance use disorders have been shown to be significant predictors of substance use in offspring (Brook et al., 2010; Sher, 1991; White et al., 2000), as well as of CD and other conduct problems (Fuller et al., 2003; Marmorstein, Iacono, & McGue, 2009; Ritter, Stewart, Bernet, Coe, & Brown, 2002).

Community

At the larger, structural level, school and neighborhood context also influence adolescent delinquency (for a review see Sampson, Morenoff, & Gannon-Rowley, 2002) and substance use (for a review see Gardner, Barajas, & Brooks-Gunn, 2010). Neighborhood factors including residential mobility, population heterogeneity, high proportion of single-parent households, and concentrated poverty all contribute to greater opportunities for delinquency (Sampson et al., 2002) and the development of conduct problems (Schonberg & Shaw, 2007) and are often related to availability of and exposure to drugs (Ensminger, Anthony, & McCord, 1997; Freisthler, Lascala, Gruenewald, & Treno, 2005).

Potential Moderators of the Association between DBDs and Substance Use

Although DBDs and substance abuse are strongly associated, they remain separate syndromes (American Psychiatric Association, 2013). This raises questions of when, how, and for whom a DBD will lead to substance abuse (or vice-versa). In this section, we discuss several possible moderators of this association.

Gender

Given the differing rates of both CD and substance abuse among males and females, it seems possible that gender could moderate these links. Some studies do, indeed, find gender differences in particular associations; however, these are inconsistent and frequently not replicated. For example, Kandel et al. (1997) found a stronger association between illicit drug use and DBDs among females compared to males, but Whitmore et al. (1997) found that the severity of CD was associated with substance dependence in males, but not females. Overall, available research using large, community-based samples tends to indicate that CD operates similarly as a risk factor for substance use and abuse in both males and females (e.g., Disney et al., 1999), though there are exceptions (e.g., Costello et al., 1999).

Developmental Period

CD has different correlates depending on its age of onset; therefore, it seems possible that development may moderate links between CD and substance use and abuse. CD that onsets early in development may differ from that which onsets later, as posited by Moffitt's (1993a) model of adolescence-limited versus life-course-persistent antisocial behavior. Available evidence from multiple samples supports this theory's prediction that youth with early-onset antisocial behavior are at highest risk for substance abuse (e.g., Moffitt, Caspi, Harrington, & Milne, 2002; Taylor, Malone, Iacono, & McGue, 2002), though youth with antisocial behavior that begins in mid to late adolescence are also at elevated risk for substance dependence in adulthood (Marmorstein, 2006; Marmorstein & Iacono, 2005; Moffitt et al., 2002).

Substance abuse can act as a "snare," which increases antisocial behavior relative to what would have already been expected for an individual (Hussong et al., 2004). That is, substance use may entrench individuals in antisocial behavior due to the psychopharmacological properties of substances, which can increase offending (especially impulsive offending), the economic need to commit crimes to get drugs, or involvement with deviant individuals and the illegal drug markets (see White, 2016). Substance abuse may also reduce the likelihood of access to protective factors (e.g., a good marriage; Hussong et al., 2004). Alternatively, for these same reasons, substance abuse can prevent or interfere with the overall pattern of desistance from antisocial behavior that is typically seen during early adulthood (Craig, Morris, Piquero, & Farrington, 2015; Hussong, Curran, Moffitt, & Caspi, 2008; Hussong et al., 2004). The prediction from substance use to antisocial behavior may be even stronger earlier in development; for example, one study found that the effect of substance use on delinquency was limited to early (but not later) in high school (Mason & Windle, 2002).

Thus, it appears that the link between CD and substance use may vary by the developmental period of onset of symptoms of CD and onset of substance use.

Callous-Unemotional Traits

The presence or absence of callous-unemotional (CU) traits may also moderate links between CD and substance abuse. We discuss this literature only briefly; more detail can be found in another chapter in this volume, Chapter 3. Considered alone, CU traits are associated with risk for substance use (Hillege, Das, & de Ruiter, 2010), and the related construct of psychopathy is associated with a variety of negative substance use-related outcomes among adolescents (Harvey, Stokes, Lord, & Pogge, 1996; Mailloux, Forth, & Kroner, 1997; Murrie & Cornell, 2000; Roussy & Toupin, 2000). The question of whether CU traits moderate the association between DBDs and substance abuse, or whether these traits predict substance abuse over and above the effect of DBDs, is more complex and has received less research attention. Wymbs and colleagues (2012) found a pattern of complex associations such that comorbid CD symptoms accounted for many of the associations between CU traits and future substance use, but these patterns were moderated by gender and, in some cases, youth with both CD and CU traits were at risk for the most severe substance-related outcomes. A recent study of high-risk males found that CU traits interacted with conduct problems to predict the highest levels of substance use among those with both CU traits and conduct problems (Baskin-Sommers, Waller, Fish, & Hyde, 2015). Therefore, future research in this area is necessary, but evidence to date indicates that CU traits may, in fact, affect the association between CD and substance use-related outcomes, and that this moderation may differ for males and females.

Comorbid Internalizing Syndromes

The presence of comorbid internalizing syndromes may also affect associations between DBDs and substance abuse. Most research indicates that the presence of comorbid depression amplifies the risk for substance abuse that is associated with CD (Marmorstein, 2010; Marmorstein & Iacono, 2001, 2003). This intensification may be particularly true for females, compared to males (Marmorstein, 2010). However, some contradictory evidence exists. For example, Mason, Hitchings, and Spoth (2008) reported that conduct problems were most strongly associated with substance abuse among participants with low levels of depressed mood, suggesting that in some cases depressive symptoms may be protective against the development of substance abuse when conduct problems are already present.

Existing research on potential interactive effects of externalizing disorders and anxiety on risk for substance use and related problems is minimal. Pardini and colleagues (2007) failed to find evidence of an interaction between anxiety/withdrawal and CD in adolescence in predicting alcohol use disorders for men in young adulthood. In contrast, Marmorstein, White, Loeber, and Stouthamer-Loeber (2010) found that, among male adolescents, the link between social anxiety and substance use and progression to substance use-related problems was accounted for by comorbid delinquent behavior, while the link between generalized anxiety and alcohol use and progression to use-related problems was not accounted for by comorbid delinquency. In addition, research using the National Comorbidity Study data has found that adults with lifetime diagnoses of both an anxiety disorder and antisocial personality disorder (ASPD) report particularly high rates of substance use disorders, compared to those diagnosed with only one of these disorders (Goodwin & Hamilton, 2003). A similar pattern emerged in data from a representative British household sample, in which individuals with both ASPD and anxiety disorders were at particularly high risk for both alcohol and drug dependence (Coid & Ullrich, 2010). Therefore, overall, it seems likely that DBDs and anxiety combine to be associated with increased risk for substance abuse. However, there may be differences in this association by type of anxiety (e.g., social versus generalized anxiety) and/or developmental period (e.g., adolescence versus adulthood).

Conclusion and Future Directions

DBDs, in particular CD, represent strong risk factors for a range of substance use-related outcomes and problems. This association appears to be partially due to shared, genetically mediated risk for externalizing behavior, as well as other common risk factors that occur at the individual, family, peer, and community levels. CD is strongly associated with risk for a variety of substance use outcomes, ranging from early-onset use to heavy use, abuse, and dependence. Links between ODD and substance-related outcomes appear to be mostly, but not entirely, mediated by the presence or absence of CD. In addition, substance abuse can predict escalation of (or a lack of decline in) externalizing behaviors.

Evidence to date indicates that these links may be moderated by age/development, callous-unemotional traits, and comorbid internalizing syndromes. In brief, youth with early-onset CD appear to be most at risk for later substance abuse, although those with later starting CD are still at elevated risk. Although evidence is limited, those with callous-unemotional traits in addition to CD appear to be at highest risk for later substance abuse. As for internalizing syndromes, depression interacts with CD to predict particularly high levels of substance abuse; evidence regarding anxiety is mixed.

Although the basic connection between DBDs and substance abuse is well established, several aspects of this association are in particular need of research attention. First, possible interactions between anxiety and DBDs in the prediction of substance abuse are poorly understood. Currently available evidence indicates that these associations may differ by type of anxiety (e.g., social anxiety/withdrawal compared to generalized anxiety). These associations may also differ by developmental period. For example, social anxiety could be protective against substance use among adolescents with CD because it could limit their exposure to substance-using peers. But later in development, when access to alcohol is legal, this association may differ. In addition, anxiety may relate to other possible moderators of the CD–substance abuse link; for example, moderate anxiety could be an indicator of low callous-unemotional traits, which could be protective.

In addition, integration of recent research on different subtypes of ODD symptoms into the literature on ODD and substance abuse would be useful. The behavioral symptoms of ODD seem as if they would be most directly related to substance abuse, perhaps through links with CD or simply their similarity to CD symptoms. Affective symptoms of ODD could also be linked with substance abuse, though, perhaps through their comorbidity with internalizing syndromes or through individuals' attempts to self-medicate their affective instability (regardless of comorbid anxiety or depression). Additional research on this topic would increase our understanding of the nature of ODD symptom subtypes as well as their links with substance abuse.

Existing research has clearly established a strong connection between DBDs, in particular CD, and substance abuse. Research investigating potential mediators and moderators of this association is ongoing, and work that takes a developmental perspective is particularly needed. Such research will help to identify important opportunities for prevention and intervention.

Acknowledgment

The writing of this chapter was supported in part by Award Number R01 DA034608 from the National Institute on Drug Abuse (NIDA). The content is solely the responsibility of the authors and does not necessarily represent the official views of the NIDA or the National Institutes of Health.

References

American Psychiatric Association. (1994). *Diagnostic and statistical manual of mental disorders* (4th ed.). Washington, DC: Author.

American Psychiatric Association. (2013). *Diagnostic and statistical manual of mental disorders* (5th ed., text revision). Arlington, VA: Author.

Angold, A., & Costello, E. J. (2001). The epidemiology of disorders of conduct: Nosological issues and comorbidity. In J. Hill & B. Maughan (Eds.), *Conduct disorders in childhood and adolescence* (pp. 126–168). New York, NY: Cambridge University Press.

Armstrong, T. D., & Costello, E. J. (2002). Community studies on adolescent substance use, abuse, or dependence and psychiatric comorbidity. *Journal of Consulting and Clinical Psychology, 70*, 1224–1230.

Baer, J. S., Sampson, P. D., Barr, H. M., Connor, P. D., & Streissguth, A. P. (2003). A 21-year longitudinal analysis of the effects of prenatal alcohol exposure on young adult drinking. *Archives of General Psychiatry, 60*, 377–385.

Bagot, K. S., Berarducci, J. M., Franken, F. H., Frazier, M. J., Ernst, M., & Moolchan, E. T. (2007). Adolescents with conduct disorder: Early smoking and treatment requests. *The American Journal on Addictions, 16*, 62–66.

Baskin-Sommers, A. R., Waller, R., Fish, A. M., & Hyde, L. W. (2015). Callous-unemotional traits trajectories interact with earlier conduct problems and executive control to predict violence and substance use among high risk male adolescents. *Journal of Abnormal Child Psychology, 43*, 1529–1541.

Bates, M. E., Labouvie, E. W., & White, H. R. (1986). The effect of sensation seeking needs on alcohol and marijuana use in adolescence. *Society of Psychologists in Addictive Behaviors Bulletin, 5*(1), 29–36.

Boyle, M. H., & Offord, D. R. (1991). Psychiatric disorder and substance use in adolescence. *Canadian Journal of Psychiatry, 36*, 699–705.

Brinkman, W. B., Epstein, J. N., Auinger, P., Tamm, L., & Froehlich, T. E. (2015). Association of attention-deficit/hyperactivity disorder and conduct disorder with early tobacco and alcohol use. *Drug and Alcohol Dependence, 147*, 183–189.

Brook, J. S., Balka, E. B., Crossman, A. M., Dermatis, H., Galanter, M., & Brook, D. W. (2010). The relationship between parental alcohol use, early and late adolescent alcohol use, and young adult psychological symptoms: A longitudinal study. *The American Journal on Addictions, 19*, 534–542.

Brook, J. S., Cohen, P., & Brook, D. W. (1998). Longitudinal study of co-occurring psychiatric disorders and substance use. *Journal of the American Academy of Child and Adolescent Psychiatry, 25*, 666–673.

Bukstein, O. G., Glancy, L. J., & Kaminer, Y. (1992). Patterns of affective comorbidity in a clinical population of dually diagnosed adolescent substance abusers. *Journal of the American Academy of Child and Adolescent Psychiatry, 31*, 1041–1045.

Burke, J. D. (2012). An affective dimension within ODD symptoms among boys: Personality and psychopathology outcomes into early adulthood. *Journal of Child Psychology and Psychiatry, 53*, 1176–1183.

Burke, J. D., Hipwell, A., & Loeber, R. (2010). Dimensions of oppositional defiant disorder as predictors of depression and conduct disorder in preadolescent girls. *Journal of the American Academy of Child and Adolescent Psychiatry, 49*, 484–492.

Burke, J. D., Loeber, R., Lahey, B. B., & Rathouz, P. J. (2005). Developmental transitions among affective and behavioral disorders in adolescent boys. *Journal of Child Psychology and Psychiatry, 46*, 1200–1210.

Burt, S. A., Krueger, R. F., McGue, M., & Iacono, W. (2003). Parent–child conflict and the comorbidity among childhood externalizing disorders. *Archives of General Psychiatry, 60*, 505–513.

Button, T. M., Hewitt, J. K., Rhee, S. H., Young, S. E., Corley, R. P., & Stallings, M. C. (2006). Examination of the causes of covariation between conduct disorder symptoms and vulnerability to drug dependence. *Twin Research & Human Genetics: The Official Journal of the International Society for Twin Studies, 9*, 38–45.

Capaldi, D. M., & Kim, H. K. (2014). Comorbidity of depression and conduct disorder. In S. C. Richards, & M. W. O'Hara (Ed.). *The Oxford handbook of depression and comorbidity.* (pp. 186–199). New York, NY: Oxford University Press.

Chassin, L., Pitts, S. C., & Prost, J. (2002). Binge drinking trajectories from adolescence to emerging adulthood in a high-risk sample: Predictors and substance abuse outcomes. *Journal of Consulting and Clinical Psychology, 70*, 47–78.

Chassin, L., Ritter, J., Trim, R. S., & King, K. M. (2003). Adolescent substance use disorders. In E. J. Mash & R. A. Barkley (Eds.), *Child Psychopathology* (2nd ed., pp. 199–230). New York, NY: Guilford.

Coid, J., & Ullrich, S. (2010). Antisocial personality disorder and anxiety disorder: A diagnostic variant? *Journal of Anxiety Disorders, 24*, 452–460.

Conner, B. T., & Lochman, J. E. (2010). Comorbid conduct disorder and substance use disorders. *Clinical Psychology: Science and Practice, 17*(4), 337–349.

Costello, E. J., Erkanli, A., Federman, E., & Angold, A. (1999). Development of psychiatric comorbidity with substance abuse in adolescents: Effects of timing and sex. *Journal of Clinical Child Psychology, 28*, 298–311.

Craig, J. M., Morris, R. G., Piquero, A. R., & Farrington, D. P. (2015). Heavy drinking ensnares adolescents into crime in early adulthood. *Journal of Criminal Justice, 43*, 142–151.

Crowley, T. J., & Riggs, P. D. (1995). Adolescent substance use disorder with conduct disorder and comorbid conditions. *NIDA Research Monograph, 156*, 49–111.

Cunningham, C. E., & Boyle, M. H. (2002). Preschoolers at risk for attention-deficit hyperactivity disorder and oppositional defiant disorder: Family, parenting, and behavioral correlates. *Journal of Abnormal Child Psychology, 30*, 555–569.

Dick, D. M. (2007). Identification of genes influencing a spectrum of externalizing psychopathology. *Current Directions in Psychological Science, 16*, 331–335.

Dick, D. M., Latendresse, S. J., Lansford, J. E., Budde, J. P., Goate, A., Dodge, K. A., Pettit, G. S., & Bates, J. E. (2009). Role of GABRA2 in trajectories of externalizing behavior across development and evidence of moderation by parental monitoring. *Archives of General Psychiatry, 66*, 649–657.

Dishion, T. J., & Owen, L. D. (2002). A longitudinal analysis of friendships and substance use: Bidirectional influence from adolescence to adulthood. *Developmental Psychology, 38*, 480–491.

Disney, E. R., Elkins, I. J., McGue, M., Iacono, W. G. (1999). Effects of ADHD, conduct disorder, and gender on substance use and abuse in adolescence. *American Journal of Psychiatry, 156*, 1515–1521.

Disney, E. R., Iacono, W., McGue, M., Tully, E., & Legrand, L. (2008). Strengthening the case: Prenatal alcohol exposure is associated with increased risk for conduct disorder. *Pediatrics, 122*, e1225–e1230.

Elkins, I. J., McGue, M., & Iacono, W. G. (2007). Prospective effects of attention-deficit/hyperactivity disorder, conduct disorder, and sex on adolescent substance use and abuse. *Archives of General Psychiatry, 64*, 1145–1152.

Ennett, S. T., & Bauman, K. E. (1996). Adolescent social networks: Schoool, deographic and longitudinal considerations. *Journal of Adolescent Research, 11*, 194–215.

Ennett, S. T., Bauman, K. E., Hussong, A., Faris, R., Foshee, V. A., Cai, L., & DuRant, R. H. (2006). The peer context of adolescent substance use: Findings from social network analysis. *Journal of Research on Adolescence, 16*, 159–186.

Ensminger, M. E., Anthony, J. C., & McCord, J. (1997). The inner city and drug use: Initial findings from an epidemiological study. *Drug and Alcohol Dependence, 48*, 175–184.

Fleming, C., Catalano, R., Haggerty, K., & Abbott, R. (2010). Relationships between level and change in family, school, and peer factors during two periods of adolescence and problem behavior at age 19. *Journal of Youth & Adolescence, 39*, 670–682.

Freisthler, B., Lascala, E. A., Gruenewald, P. J., & Treno, A. J. (2005). An examination of drug activity: Effects of neighborhood social organization on the development of drug distribution systems. *Substance Use & Misuse, 40*, 671–686.

Freitag, C. M., Hanig, S., Schneider, A., Seitz, C., Palmason, H., Retz, W., & Meyer, J. (2012). Biological and psychosocial risk factors influence symptom severity and psychiatric comorbidity in children with ADHD. *Journal of Neural Transmission, 119*, 81–94.

Fuller, B. E., Chermack, S. T., Cruise, K. A., Kirsch, E., Fitzgerald, H. E., & Zucker, R. A. (2003). Predictors of aggression across three generations among sons of alcoholics: Relationships involving grandparental and parental alcoholism, child aggression, marital aggression and parenting practices. *Journal of Studies on Alcohol, 64*, 472–483.

Gardner, M., Barajas, R. G., & Brooks-Gunn, J. (2010). Neighborhood influences on substance use etiology: Is where you live important? In L. M. Scheier (Ed.), *Handbook of drug use etiology: Theory, methods, and empirical findings* (pp. 423–441). Washington, D.C.: American Psychological Association.

Gatzke-Kopp, L. M., Beauchaine, T. P., Shannon, K. E., Chipman, J., Fleming, A. P., Crowell, S. E., . . . & Aylward, E. (2009). Neurological correlates of reward responding in adolescents with and without externalizing behavior disorders. *Journal of Abnormal Psychology, 118*, 203–213.

Giancola, P. R. (2002). Alcohol-related aggression during the college years: Theories, risk factors, and policy implications. *Journal of Studies on Alcohol, Supplement 14*, 129–139.

Giancola, P. R., & Tarter, R. E. (1999). Executive cognitive functioning and risk for substance abuse. *Psychological Science, 10*, 203–205.

Goodwin, R. D., & Hamilton, S. P. (2003). Lifetime comorbidity of antisocial personality disorder and anxiety disorders among adults in the community. *Psychiatry Research, 117*, 159–166.

Gorman, D., & White, H. R. (1995). You can choose your friends, but do they choose your crime? Implications of differential association theories for crime prevention policy. In H. Barlow (Ed.), *Criminology and public policy: Putting theory to work* (pp. 131–155). Boulder, CO: Westview Press.

Grant, B. F., & Dawson, D. A. (1997). Age at onset of alcohol use and its association with *DSM-IV* alcohol abuse and dependence: Results from the National Longitudinal Alcohol Epidemiologic Survey. *Journal of Substance Abuse, 9*, 103–110.

Grant, B. F., Stinson, F. S., & Harford, T. C. (2001). Age at onset of alcohol use and *DSM-IV* alcohol abuse and dependence: A 12-year follow-up. *Journal of Substance Abuse, 13*, 493–504.

Grant, J. D., Lynskey, M. T., Madden, P. A. F., Nelson, E. C., Few, L. R., Bucholz, K. K., & Agrawal, A. (2015). The role of conduct disorder in the relationship between alcohol, nicotine and cannabis use disorders. *Psychological Medicine, 45*, 3505–3515.

Greene, K., Krcmar, M., Walters, L. H., Rubin, D. L., & Hale, L. (2000). Targeting adolescent risk-taking behaviors: The contributions of egocentrism and sensation-seeking. *Journal of Adolescence, 23*(4), 439–461.

Greene, R. W., Biederman, J., Zerwas, S., Monuteaux, M. C., Goring, J. C., & Faraone, S. V. (2002). Psychiatric comorbidity, family dysfunction, and social impairment in referred youth with oppositional defiant disorder. *The American Journal of Psychiatry, 159*, 1214–1224.

Hariri, A. R., & Weinberger, D. R. (2003). Functional neuroimaging of genetic variation in serotonergic neurotransmission. *Genes, Brain, and Behavior, 2*, 341–349.

Harvey, P. D., Stokes, J. L., Lord, J., & Pogge, D. L. (1996). Neurocognitive and personality assessment of adolescent substance abusers. *Assessment, 3*, 241–253.

Hemovich, V., Lac, A., & Crano, W. D. (2011) Understanding early-onset drug and alcohol outcomes among youth: The role of family structure, social factors, and interpersonal perceptions of use. *Psychology, Health & Medicine, 16*, 249–267.

Henry, K. L. (2010). Academic achievement and adolescent drug use: An examination of reciprocal effects and correlated growth trajectories. *Journal of School Health, 80*, 38–43.

Heron, J., Barker, E. D., Joinson, C., Lewis, G., Hickman, M., Munafò, M., & Macleod, J. (2013). Childhood conduct disorder trajectories, prior risk factors and cannabis use at age 16: Birth cohort study. *Addiction, 108*, 2129–2138.

Hicks, B. M., Krueger, R. F., Iacono, W. G., McGue, M., & Patrick, C. J. (2004). Family transmission and heritability of externalizing disorders: A twin-family study. *Archives of General Psychiatry, 61*, 922–928.

Hillege, S., Das, J., & de Ruiter, C. (2010). The Youth Psychopathic Traits Inventory: Psychometric properties and its relation to substance use and interpersonal style in a Dutch sample of non-referred adolescents. *Journal of Adolescence, 33,* 83–91.

Huizinga, D. H., Menard, S., & Elliott, D. S. (1989). Delinquency and drug use: Temporal and developmental patterns. *Justice Quarterly, 6,* 419–455.

Hussong, A. M., Curran, P. J., Moffitt, T. E., & Caspi, A. (2008). Testing turning points using latest growth curve models: Competing models of substance abuse and desistance in young adulthood. In Cohen, P. (Ed.), *Applied data analytic techniques for turning points research.* New York, NY: Routledge.

Hussong, A. M., Curran, P. J., Moffitt, T. E., Caspi, A., & Carrig, M. M. (2004). Substance abuse hinders desistance in young adults' antisocial behavior. *Development and Psychopathology, 16,* 1029–1046.

Jessor, R., & Jessor, S. L. (1977). *Problem behavior and psychosocial development: A longitudinal study of youth.* New York, NY: Academic Press.

Kandel, D. B., Johnson, J. G., Bird, H. R., Canino, G., Goodman, S. H., Lahey, B. B., . . . Schwab-Stone, M. (1997). Psychiatric disorders associated with substance use among children and adolescents: Findings from the Methods for the Epidemiology of Child and Adolescent Mental Disorders (MECA) study. *Journal of Abnormal Child Psychology, 25,* 121–132.

Keenan, K., Loeber, R., & Green, S. (1999). Conduct disorder in girls: A review of the literature. *Clinical Child and Family Psychology Review, 2,* 3–19.

Kendler, K. S., Kuo, P., Webb, B. T., Kalsi, G., Neale, M. C., Sullivan, P. F., . . . Prescott, C. A. (2006). A joint genomewide linkage analysis of symptoms of alcohol dependence and conduct disorder. *Alcoholism: Clinical and Experimental Research, 30,* 1972–1977.

Kramer, J. R., Chan, G., Dick, D. M., Kuperman, S., Bucholz, K. K., Edenberg, H. J., . . . Bierut, L. J. (2008). Multiple-domain predictors of problematic alcohol use in young adulthood. *Journal of Studies on Alcohol and Drugs, 69,* 649–659.

Krueger, R. F., Hicks, B. M., Patrick, C. J., Carlson, S. R., Iacono, W. G., & McGue, M. (2002). Etiologic connections among substance dependence, antisocial behavior and personality: Modeling the externalizing spectrum. *Journal of Abnormal Psychology, 111,* 411–424.

Krueger, R. F., Markon, K. E., Patrick, C. J., Benning, S. D., & Kramer, M. D. (2007). Linking antisocial behavior, substance use, and personality: An integrative quantitative model of the adult externalizing spectrum. *Journal of Abnormal Psychology, 116,* 645–666.

Kumpulainen, K. (2000). Psychiatric symptoms and deviance in early adolescence predict alcohol use 3 years later. *Addiction, 95,* 1847–1857.

Latendresse, S. J., Bates, J. E., Goodnight, J. A., Lansford, J. E., Budde, J. P., Goate, A., . . . Dick, D. M. (2011). Differential susceptibility to adolescent externalizing trajectories: Examining the interplay between CHRM2 and peer group antisocial behavior. *Child Development, 82,* 1797–1814.

Latimer, K., Wilson, P., Kemp, J., Thompson, L., Sim, F., Gillberg, C., . . . Minnis, H. (2012). Disruptive behavior disorders: A systematic review of environmental antenatal and early years risk factors. *Child: Care, Health and Development, 38,* 611–628.

Leadbeater, B. J., & Homel, J. (2015). Irritable and defiant sub-dimensions of ODD: Their stability and prediction of internalizing symptoms and conduct problems from adolescence to young adulthood. *Journal of Abnormal Child Psychology, 43,* 407–421.

Loeber, R., Burke, J. D., Lahey, B. B., Winters, A., & Zera, M. (2000). Oppositional defiant and conduct disorder: A review of the past 10 years, part I. *Journal of the American Academy of Child and Adolescent Psychiatry, 39,* 1468–1484.

Loeber, R., Stouthamer-Loeber, M., & White, H. R. (1999). Developmental aspects of delinquency and internalizing problems and their association with persistent juvenile substance use between ages 7 and 18. *Journal of Clinical Child Psychology, 28,* 322–332.

Maguin, E., & Loeber, R. (1996). Academic performance and delinquency. *Crime and Justice, 20,* 145–264.

Mailloux, D. L., Forth, A. E., & Kroner, D. G. (1997). Psychopathy and substance use in adolescent male offenders. *Psychological Reports, 81,* 529–530.

Marmorstein, N. R. (2006). Adult antisocial behavior without conduct disorder: Demographic characteristics and risk for co-occurring psychopathology. *Canadian Journal of Psychiatry, 51,* 226–233.

Marmorstein, N. R. (2010). Longitudinal associations between depressive symptoms and alcohol problems: The influence of comorbid delinquent behavior. *Addictive Behaviors, 35,* 564–571.

Marmorstein, N. R., & Iacono, W. G. (2001). An investigation of female adolescent twins with both major depression and conduct disorder. *Journal of the American Academy of Child and Adolescent Psychiatry, 40,* 299–306.

Marmorstein, N. R., & Iacono, W. G. (2003). Major depression and conduct disorder in a twin sample: Gender, functioning, and risk for future psychopathology. *Journal of the American Academy of Child and Adolescent Psychiatry, 42,* 225–233.

Marmorstein, N. R., & Iacono, W. G. (2005). Longitudinal follow-up of adolescents with late-onset antisocial behavior: A pathological yet overlooked group. *Journal of the American Academy of Child and Adolescent Psychiatry, 44,* 1284–1291.

Marmorstein, N. R., Iacono, W. G., & Malone, S. (2010). Longitudinal associations between depression and substance dependence from adolescence through early adulthood. *Drug and Alcohol Dependence, 107,* 154–160.

Marmorstein, N. R., Iacono, W. G., & McGue, M. (2009). Alcohol and illicit drug dependence among parents: Associations with offspring externalizing disorders. *Psychological Medicine, 39,* 149–155.

Marmorstein, N. R., White, H. R., Chung, T., Hipwell, A., Southamer-Loeber, M., & Loeber, R. (2010). Associations between first use of substances and change in internalizing symptoms among girls: Differences by symptom trajectory and substance use type. *Journal of Clinical Child and Adolescent Psychology, 39,* 545–558.

Marmorstein, N. R., White, H. R., Loeber, R., & Stouthamer-Loeber, M. (2010). Anxiety as a predictor of age at first use of substances and progression to substance use problems among boys. *Journal of Abnormal Child Psychology, 38,* 211–234.

Mason, W. A., Hitchings, J. E., & Spoth, R. L. (2008). The interaction of conduct problems and depressed mood in relation to adolescent substance involvement and peer substance use. *Drug and Alcohol Dependence, 96,* 233–248.

Mason, W. A., & Windle, M. (2002). Reciprocal relations between adolescent substance use and delinquency: A longitudinal latent variable analysis. *Journal of Abnormal Psychology, 111,* 63–76.

McCarty, C. A., Wymbs, B. T., Mason, W. A., King, K. M., McCauley, E., Baer, J., & Vander Stoep, A. (2013). Early adolescent growth in depression and conduct problem symptoms as predictors of later substance use impairment. *Journal of Abnormal Child Psychology, 41,* 1041–1051.

McCord, J. (1993). Conduct disorder and antisocial behavior: Some thoughts about processes. *Development and Psychopathology, 5,* 321–329.

Moffitt, T. E. (1993a). Adolescence-limited and life-course-persistent antisocial behavior: A developmental taxonomy. *Psychological Review, 100,* 674–701.

Moffitt, T. E. (1993b). The neuropsychology of conduct disorder. *Development and Psychopathology, 5,* 135–151.

Moffitt, T. E., Caspi, A., Harrington, H., & Milne, B. J. (2002). Males on the life-course-persistent and adolescence-limited antisocial pathways: Follow-up at age 26 years. *Development and Psychopathology, 14,* 179–207.

Murrie, D. C., & Cornell, D. G. (2000). The Millon adolescent clinical inventory and psychopathy. *Journal of Personality Assessment, 75,* 110–125.

Nock, M. K., Kazdin, A. E., Hiripi, E., & Kessler, R. C. (2007) Lifetime prevalence, correlates, and persistence of oppositional defiant disorder: Results from the National Comorbidity Survey Replication. *Journal of Child Psychology and Psychiatry, 48,* 703–713.

Noyori-Corbett, C., & Moon, S. (2010). Multifaceted reality of juvenile delinquency: An empirical analysis of structural theories and literature. *Child and Adolescent Social Work Journal, 27,* 245–268.

Pandina, R. J., Johnson, V. L., & White, H. R. (2009). Peer influences on substance use during adolescence and emerging adulthood. In L. M. Scheier (Ed.), *Handbook of drug use etiology* (pp. 383–401). Washington, D.C.: American Psychological Association.

Pardini, D., White, H. R., & Stouthamer-Loeber, M. (2007). Early adolescent psychopathology as a predictor of alcohol use disorders by young adulthood. *Drug and Alcohol Dependence, 88* (supp. 1), S38–S49.

Pardini, D., White, H. R., Xiong, S., Bechtold, J., Chung, T., Loeber, R., & Hipwell, A. (2015). Unfazed or dazed and confused: Does early adolescent marijuana use cause sustained impairments in attention and academic functioning? *Journal of Abnormal Child Psychology, 43,* 1203–1217.

Patrick, C. J., Bernat, E. M., Malone, S. M., Iacono, W. G., Krueger, R. F., & McGue, M. (2006). P300 amplitude as an indicator of externalizing in adolescent males. *Psychophysiology, 43*, 84–92.

Raine, A., Moffitt, T. E., Caspi, A., Loeber, R., Stouthamer-Loeber, M., & Lynam, D. (2005). Neurocognitive impairments in boys on the life-course persistent antisocial path. *Journal of Abnormal Psychology, 114*, 38–49.

Rao, U., Daley, S. E., & Hammen, C. (2000). Relationship between depression and substance use disorders in adolescent women during the transition to adulthood. *Journal of the American Academy of Child and Adolescent Psychiatry, 39*, 215–222.

Ridenour, T. A., Cottler, L. B., Robins, L. N., Campton, W. M., Spitznagel, E. L., & Cunningham-Williams, R. M. (2002). Test of the plausibility of adolescent substance use playing a causal role in developing adulthood antisocial behavior. *Journal of Abnormal Psychology, 111*, 144–155.

Ritter, J., Stewart, M., Bernet, C., Coe, M., & Brown, S. A. (2002). Effects of childhood exposure to familial alcoholism and family violence on adolescent substance use, conduct problems, and self-esteem. *Journal of Traumatic Stress, 15*, 113–122.

Rohde, P., Lewinsohn, P. M., Kahler, C. W., Seeley, J. R., & Brown, R. A. (2001). Natural course of alcohol use disorders from adolescence to young adulthood. *Journal of the American Academy of Child and Adolescent Psychiatry, 410*, 83–90.

Roussy, S., & Toupin, J. (2000). Behavioral inhibition deficits in juvenile psychopaths. *Aggressive Behavior, 26*, 413–424.

Rowe, R., Maughan, B., Pickles, A., Costello, E. J., & Angold, A. (2002). The relationship between DSM-IV oppositional defiant disorder and conduct disorder: Findings from the Great Smoky Mountains Study. *Journal of Child Psychology and Psychiatry, 43*, 365–373.

Sampson, R. J., Morenoff, J. D., & Gannon-Rowley, T. (2002). Assessing "neighborhood effects": Social processes and new directions in research. *Annual Review of Sociology, 28*, 444–478.

Schonberg, M. A., & Shaw, D. S. (2007). Do the predictors of child conduct problems vary by high- and low-levels of socioeconomic and neighborhood risk? *Clinical Child and Family Psychology Review, 10*, 101–136.

Sher, K. J. (1991). Characteristics of children of alcoholics: Putative risk factors, substance use and abuse, and psychopathology. *Journal of Abnormal Psychology, 100*, 427–448.

Simons-Morton, B., & Chen, R. (2005). Latent growth curve analyses of parent influences on drinking progression among early adolescents. *Journal of Studies on Alcohol, 66*, 5–13.

Stein, L. A. R., Hesselbrock, V., & Bukstein, O. G. (2008). Conduct disorder and oppositional defiant disorder and adolescent substance use disorders. In Y. Kaminer, & O. G. Bukstein (Eds.), *Adolescent substance abuse: Psychiatric comorbidity and high-risk behaviors* (pp. 163–194). New York, NY: Routledge.

Substance Abuse and Mental Health Services Administration. (2005). *The National Survey on Drug Use and Health report: Alcohol use and delinquent behaviors among youth*. Rockville, MD: Author.

Sung, M., Erkanli, A., & Costello, E. J. (2014). Estimating the causal effect of conduct disorder on the time from first substance use to substance use disorders using G-estimation. *Substance Abuse, 35*, 141–146.

Taylor, J., Malone, S., Iacono, W. G., & McGue, M. (2002). Development of substance dependence in two delinquency subgroups and nondelinquents from a male twin sample. *Journal of the American Academy of Child and Adolescent Psychiatry, 41*, 386–393.

Thompson, L. L., Whitmore, E. A., Raymond, K. M., & Crowley, T. J. (2006). Measuring impulsivity in adolescents with serious substance and conduct problems. *Assessment, 13*, 3–15.

Trucco, E. M., Colder, C. R., & Wieczorek, W. F. (2011). Vulnerability to peer influence: A moderated mediation study of early adolescent alcohol use initiation. *Addictive Behaviors, 36*, 729–736.

Vitaro, F., Brendgen, M., Pagani, L., Tremblay, R. E., & McDuff, P. (1999). Disruptive behaviour, peer association, and conduct disorder: Testing developmental links through early intervention. *Development and Psychopathology, 11*, 287–304.

Waschbusch, D. A. (2002). A meta-analytic examination of comorbid hyperactive–impulsive–attention problems and conduct problems. *Psychological Bulletin, 128*, 118–150.

Weinberg, N. Z., Rahdert, E., Colliver, J. D., & Myer, G. D. (1998). Adolescent substance abuse: A review of the past 10 years. *Journal of the American Academy of Child and Adolescent Psychiatry, 37*, 252–261.

White, H. R. (1997a). Alcohol, illicit drugs, and violence. In D. M. Stoff, J. Breiling, & J. D. Maser (Eds.), *Handbook of antisocial behavior* (pp. 511–523). New York, NY: John Wiley and Sons.

White, H. R. (1997b). Longitudinal perspective on alcohol use and aggression during adolescence. *Recent Developments in Alcoholism: Alcohol and Violence, 13*, 81–103.

White, H. R. (2015). Developmental approaches to understanding the substance use–crime connection. In J. Morizot & L. Kazemian (Eds.). *The development of criminal and antisocial behavior: Theory, research and practical applications* (pp. 379–397). New York, NY: Springer Press.

White, H. R. (2016). Substance use and crime. In K. J. Sher (Ed.), *The Oxford handbook of substance use and substance use disorders* (Vol. 2, pp. 347–378). Oxford, UK: Oxford University Press.

White, H. R., Johnson, V., & Buyske, S. (2000). Parental modeling and parenting behavior effects on offspring alcohol and cigarette use—A growth curve analysis. *Journal of Substance Abuse, 12*, 287–310.

White, H. R., Labouvie, E. W., & Bates, M. E. (1985). The relationship between sensation seeking and delinquency: A longitudinal analysis. *Journal of Research in Crime & Delinquency, 22*, 197–211.

White, H. R., Marmorstein, N. R., Crews, F. T., Bates, M. E., Mun, E. Y., & Loeber, R. (2011). Associations between heavy drinking and changes in impulsive behavior among adolescent males. *Alcoholism: Clinical & Experimental Research, 35*, 295–303.

White, H. R., Xie, M., Thompson, W., Loeber, R., & Stouthamer-Loeber, M. (2001). Psychopathology as a predictor of adolescent drug use trajectories. *Psychology of Addictive Behaviors, 15*, 210–218.

Whitmore, E. A., Mikulich, S. K., Thompson, L. L., Riggs, P. D., Aarons, G. A., & Crowley, T. J. (1997). Influences on adolescent substance dependence: conduct disorder, depression, attention deficit hyperactivity disorder, and gender. *Drug and Alcohol Dependence, 47*, 87–97.

Wilens, T. E. (1998). AOD use and attention deficit/hyperactivity disorder. *Alcohol Health & Research World, 22*, 127–130.

Windle, M. (1990). A longitudinal study of antisocial behaviors in early adolescence as predictors of late adolescent substance use: gender and ethnic group differences. *Journal of Abnormal Psychology, 99*, 86–91.

Wymbs, B. T., McCarty, C. A., King, K. M., McCauley, E., Vander Stoep, A., Baer, J. S., & Waschbusch, D. A. (2012). Callous-unemotional traits as unique prospective risk factors for substance use in early adolescent boys and girls. *Journal of Abnormal Child Psychology, 40*, 1099–1110.

Wymbs, B. T., McCarty, C. A., Mason, W. A., King, K. M., Baer, J. S., Stoep, A. V., & McCauley, E. (2014). Early adolescent substance use as a risk factor for developing conduct disorder and depression symptoms. *Journal of Studies on Alcohol and Drugs, 75*, 279–289.

Zuckerman, M. (1979). *Sensation seeking: Beyond the optimal level of arousal*. Hillsdale, NJ: Lawrence Erlbaum.

Zuckerman, M. (1994). *Behavioral expressions and biosocial bases of sensation seeking*. New York, NY: Cambridge University Press.

6

Intermittent Explosive Disorder and the Impulse-Control Disorders

Emil F. Coccaro and Jon E. Grant

Impulsivity has been defined as a predisposition toward rapid, unplanned reactions to either internal or external stimuli without regard for negative consequences. Given this definition of impulsivity, multiple psychiatric disorders might be characterized as exhibiting problems with impulse control. In the 5th edition of the Diagnostic and Statistical Manual of the American Psychiatric Association (DSM-5), the category of Impulse-Control Disorders Not Elsewhere Classified was dismantled and replaced with a new chapter on Disruptive, Impulse-Control, and Conduct Disorders. The classic impulse-control disorders still retained in the DSM-5 (Intermittent Explosive Disorder, Kleptomania, Pyromania) are unified by the presence of difficult, disruptive, aggressive, or antisocial behavior that is typically preceded by intense tension or arousal. Despite high prevalence rates in the general population (Kessler et al., 2005) and in psychiatric cohorts (Grant, Levine, Kim, & Potenza, 2005), Intermittent Explosive Disorder and the Impulse-Control Disorders have been relatively understudied, and the extent to which these disorders share clinical, genetic, phenomenological, and biological features is incompletely understood.

Intermittent Explosive Disorder (IED)

Human aggression consists in a behavioral act resulting in physical (or verbal) injury to self, others, or objects. It has several forms and may be defensive, premeditated (e.g., predatory), or impulsive (e.g., nonpremeditated), in nature. A converging pattern of data consistently points to critical differences between impulsive and premeditated aggression such that, while the two may appear in the same individual at different times, the underpinnings of the two are different (Barratt, Stanford, Felthous, & Kent, 1997; Raine et al., 1998). The most critical aspect of this phenomenon is that acts of impulsive aggression represent a quick—and typically angry— response, nearly always triggered by a social threat or frustration, that is out of proportion to the situation; premeditated aggressive acts, on the other hand, are thought out in advance and perpetrated for a tangible objective. Impulsive aggressive acts may include verbal attacks, temper tantrums (with or without property damage or harm to others), property assault, or assault to other living beings including animals. In fact, the severity of the aggressive outburst is less relevant than that the aggressive behavior is "explosive" in nature and that these acts cause distress to the individual or impairment in his or her psychosocial function, and are not due to another disorder (i.e., do not occur exclusively during that other disorder).

The Wiley Handbook of Disruptive and Impulse-Control Disorders, First Edition.
Edited by John E. Lochman and Walter Matthys.
© 2018 John Wiley & Sons Ltd. Published 2018 by John Wiley & Sons Ltd.

While not widely known, a disorder of impulsive aggression has been included in the Diagnostic and Statistical Manual for Psychiatric Disorders (DSM) since the outset. It was called "Passive-Aggressive Disorder—Aggressive Subtype" and "Explosive Personality" in the original DSM and in DSM-II, respectively (American Psychiaric Association, 1952, 1968). With the publication of DSM-III (American Psychiatric Association, 1980), the disorder was codified as Intermittent Explosive Disorder (IED). At the time, IED was thought to be quite rare and was conceptualized as a disorder of exclusion (e.g., if some other diagnosis better explained the aggressive behavior that was the preferred diagnosis). In fact, DSM-III criteria were limited and poorly operationalized. Most importantly, it was not clear what constituted aggressive behavior, what type of aggressive behavior defined the disorder, and how often aggressive behavior should occur and in what time frame. At the same time that DSM-III was being embraced across the nation, new research suggested that aggressive behavior was associated with reduced functioning of the central serotonin (5-HT) system. Given that 5-HT is widely distributed across the brain, that 5-HT neurons fire at a relatively constant (tonic) rate, and that enhancing 5-HT function reduces aggression in animal models, the idea that 5-HT acts as a behavioral inhibitor, or "brake," became a popular model for human aggression (Coccaro, Fanning, Phan, & Lee, 2015). Consistent with this model, empirical data supports the idea that reduced 5-HT function is associated with impulsive, but not premeditated, aggression (Linnoila et al., 1983; Virkkunen et al., 1987). In this context of new data regarding the psychobiology of impulsive aggression, researchers began to modify DSM-III criteria in order to codify a disorder of impulsive (as opposed to generalized) aggression to allow for further research to occur. This led to research criteria which focused, first, on frequent outbursts of impulsive aggressive behavior and, then, incorporated DSM-IV IED criteria to create new diagnostic criteria for DSM-5.

DSM-5 Criteria for IED

The new "A" criteria for IED in DSM-5 now clearly define the frequency and temporal nature of applicable aggressive behavior. The A_1 criteria require verbal, and/or non-assaultive and non-destructive, aggressive outbursts occurring at an average of twice weekly for at least three months while the A_2 criteria require assaultive, and/or destructive, aggressive outbursts occurring at least three times a year. About 70% of those meeting criteria for DSM-5 IED meet both the A_1 and A_2 criteria, while 20% meet the A_2 criteria only and 10% meet the A_1 only (Coccaro, 2011). Empirical studies have shown that those meeting only the A_1 criteria do not differ from those meeting only the A_2 criteria or those meeting both A_1 and A_2 (Coccaro, Lee, & McCloskey, 2014). The "B" criteria for DSM-5 do not differ from the similar criteria in DSM-IV and continue to require that the aggressive behavior be out of proportion to the situation. The remaining criteria have all been revised. The "C" criteria require that most of the aggressive outbursts be impulsive in nature so that IED may not be given to someone who predominately engages in premeditated aggressive behavior; the "D" criteria require that the aggressive outbursts cause distress and/or impairment for the individual so that the IED diagnosis is not made in the absence of clinically significant consequences; the "E" criteria require that the individual is at least six years of age before a diagnosis of IED is given so that typical aggressive behavior seen in children younger than six years of age are not considered pathological. The last criterion ("F") was revised so that the diagnosis of IED can be given as long as the aggressive outbursts do not occur only during the course of another disorder or exogenous factor known to be associated with aggression. With these changes came the immediate exclusion of individuals with selected disorders such as borderline and/or antisocial personality disorder. This was added because individuals with these disorders were frequently not particularly aggressive compared with those with only IED (Coccaro, 2012).

Epidemiology of IED

The first U.S. community survey (the National Comorbidity Study Replication: NCS-R) that included DSM-IV IED in its assessment of adult psychopathology reported a lifetime prevalence of IED at 7.3% and a past year prevalence of 3.9% by "Broad Criteria." While these prevalence rates appear high, "Broad Criteria" only require the presence of serious aggressive outbursts three times in a person's adult life, which is not very frequent and is unlikely to be associated with significant distress or impairment. The second definition used in the NCS-R study, "Narrow IED," required the presence of aggressive outbursts at least three times in a single year, and found meaningful differences between the two definitions with "Narrow IED" being far more severe than "Broad IED" (Kessler et al., 2006). The lifetime and past year prevalence of "Narrow IED" were 5.4% and 2.7% respectively. Recently, we revisited these data and have determined that lifetime and past year prevalence of DSM-5 IED are about 3.6% and 2.2%, respectively (Coccaro, Fridberg et al., 2016). The rates of IED vary across countries and range from an average of 2.9% for the broad definition and 2.1% for the narrow. Studies of adolescents estimate the lifetime and past year prevalence for the broad definition of IED at 7.8% and 6.2%, respectively; corresponding prevalence for the narrow definition of IED were 5.3% and 1.7%, respectively (McLaughlin et al., 2012)

Phenomenology

Aggressive outbursts in IED have a rapid onset and are short-lived (<30 minutes). These outbursts are frequent and of low intensity (i.e., verbal outbursts and/or non-destructive/non-assaultive outbursts occurring about twice a week for at least three months) and/or infrequent but of high intensity (i.e., physically assaultive/destructive outbursts occurring three or more times per year; Coccaro, 2011). Aggressive outbursts most commonly occur in response to a minor provocation by a close associate. Episodes are associated with substantial distress, impairment in social functioning, occupational difficulty, and legal or financial problems (Kessler et al., 2006). In a reanalysis of the National Comorbidty Study-Replication (Coccaro, Fanning, & Lee, 2016), the lifetime prevalence of DSM-5 IED was 3.6% and the past year prevalence was 2.2%. IED appears as early as childhood (e.g., prepubertal) and peaks in mid-adolescence with a mean age of onset ranging from about 13 to 18 years in adult samples (Coccaro, Posternak, & Zimmerman, 2005; Kessler et al., 2006) and lower in adolescent samples (McLaughlin et al., 2012). The average duration of symptomatic IED ranges from nearly 12 years to 20 years to nearly the whole lifetime. Clinical studies suggest that IED is more common in males than females (3:1 ratio). However, our reanalysis of the NCS-R data suggest that the lifetime prevalence rate for DSM-5 IED in males only approaches twice that in females [Odds Ratio: 1.90 (95% CI:1.50–2.38)] and that the past year prevalence rate for males is even less than that [Odds Ratio: 1.50 (95% CI: 1.14–1.98)]. IED is often comorbid with other lifetime disorders such as depressive disorder, anxiety disorder and substance use disorder (Coccaro, 2011, 2012; Coccaro, Kavoussi, Berman, & Lish, 1998; Coccaro, Posternak, & Zimmerman, 2005). However, in most cases, the age of onset of IED precedes that of these other lifetime comorbid disorders (Coccaro et al., 2005) suggesting that IED is not a consequence of these other disorders (Kessler et al., 2006).

Behavioral Genetic and Family Studies Like all personality traits, aggression has a strong genetic influence. Overall, the heritability of aggression is up to 50% (Miles & Carey, 1997). However, most studies do not distinguish between impulsive and premeditated aggression and/or did not use measures that correlate with impulsive aggression in particular. In a series of studies carried out in our group we have found significant heritability for "irritable aggressiveness" (Coccaro, Bergeman, & McCleam, 1993), for "irritability," "verbal assault," "indirect assault," and "direct assault," in twins raised apart. In the latter study we found that the degree of genetic influence increases as one goes from "verbal" to "indirect" to "direct" assault suggesting that the more severe the form of aggression, the greater the underlying degree of genetic influence. Similarly, impulsivity has substantial genetic influence. There is strong genetic correlation between impulsivity and the three different forms of aggression (Seroczynski, Bergeman, & Coccaro, 1999). More recent studies from our group support these data by showing elevated rates of IED by Research Criteria (essentially the same as DSM-5) compared with controls (Coccaro, 2010).

Comorbidity

Psychiatric Because impulsive aggressive behavior appears in patients with many diagnoses, most clinicians have been reluctant to make a diagnosis of IED in the presence of other psychiatric diagnoses. In fact, impulsive aggressive behavior is manifest in all humans, early in life, and the onset can occur prior to many other psychiatric disorders. Clinical studies suggest significant co-occurrence of IED with mood, anxiety, and substance use disorders. In most cases, the age of onset of IED is earlier than that for the co-occurring disorder suggesting the independence of IED or suggesting that IED is a risk factor for the co-occurring disorder.

Medical A relationship between impulsive aggression, or "irritability," associated with cardiovascular illness has been reported for many years. A recent analysis of a large community sample data has noted that individuals with IED have an increased risk of coronary heart disease, hypertension, stroke, diabetes, arthritis, back/neck pain, ulcer, headaches, and other chronic pain (McCloskey, Kleabir, Berman, Chen, & Coccaro, 2010). Another study reports a significant relationship between IED and diabetes (de Jonge et al., 2014). A factor tying many of these conditions together may be abnormalities of immune function (e.g., coronary heart disease, stroke, arthritis, ulcer, and others). Recently, we reported elevated plasma inflammatory markers (C-Reactive Protein: CRP and Interleukin-6: IL-6) in individuals with IED compared with psychiatric and healthy controls (Coccaro, Lee, & Coussons-Read., 2014). In addition to elevated levels of these markers, a history of aggressive behaviors and an aggressive disposition correlate directly with plasma levels of CRP and IL-6 (Coccaro, 2006; Coccaro, Lee, & Coussons-Read., 2014) and CSF levels of CRP (Coccaro, Lee, & Coussins-Read, 2015a) and of IL-1R11 protein (Coccaro, Lee, & Coussons-Read, 2015a). Recently, we reported that the presence of a latent infection with *toxoplasma gondii* was associated with an increased rate of IED compared with healthy control volunteers (Coccaro, Lee, Groer, Can, Coussons-Read, & Postolache, 2016)

Psychological Features

Not surprisingly, individuals with IED demonstrate abnormalities in a number of psychological areas. Compared with controls, individuals with IED have elevations of: (a) relational aggression aimed at damaging interpersonal relationships (Murray-Close, Ostrov, Nelson, Crick, & Coccaro, 2010); (b) hostile attribution, and negative emotional responding, to socially ambiguous stimuli (Coccaro, Fanning, & Lee, 2016; Coccaro, Noblett, & McCloskey, 2009); (c) affective lability and affective intensity (Fettich, McCloskey, Look, & Coccaro, 2015); and (d) immature defense mechanisms including acting out, dissociation, projection, and rationalization (Puhalla, McCloskey, Brickman, Fauber, & Coccaro, 2016). Most recently, individuals with IED have been reported to have reduced emotional intelligence (Coccaro,

Solis, Fanning, & Lee, 2015). All of which provide a rationale for psychological intervention, particularly those that focus on emotional and social information processing.

Biological Features

Neurotransmitters Biological studies clearly show a bio-behavioral relationship between aggression and selected brain chemicals, such as 5-HT. To date, individuals with IED are reported to have altered 5-HT function compared with Non-IED, or Healthy Control, subjects (Coccaro, Lee, & Kavoussi, 2009b, 2010; New et al., 2004). In fact, most biological studies of aggression report an association with anomalies of 5-HT including reduced levels of cerebrospinal fluid metabolites of 5-HT, reduced responsiveness of 5-HT receptors to stimulation, and reduced numbers of 5-HT transporter sites both on circulating platelets and on neurons in the brain (Duke, Bègue, Bell, & Eisenlohr-Moul, 2013). In addition, reduction of 5-HT levels, after tryptophan depletion, is associated with increased aggression on laboratory aggression tasks in "aggressive" human volunteers and is associated with greater rantings of anger in IED compared with healthy individuals (Lee, Gill, Chen, McCloskey, & Coccaro, 2012).

In addition to 5-HT, several other neurotransmitter/modulators have been found to correlate with measures of aggression. Those that correlate inversely with aggression include oxytocin (Lee, Ferris, Van de Kar, & Cocarro, 2009) and those that correlate positively with aggression include dopamine (Coccaro & Lee, 2010), vasopressin (Coccaro, Kavoussi, Hauger, Cooper, & Ferris, 1998), neuropeptide Y (Coccaro, Lee, Liu, & Mathe, 2012), substance p (Coccaro, Lee, Owens, Kinkead, & Nemeroff, 2012), glutamate (Coccaro, Lee, & Vezina, 2013), and inflammatory proteins (Coccaro, 2006; Coccaro, Fanning, Phan, & Lee, 2015; Coccaro, Lee, & Coussons-Read, 2014; Coccaro, Lee, & Coussons-Read, 2015a, 2015b; Coccaro, Lee, Fanning et al., 2016) as well as measures of oxidative stress (Coccaro, Lee, & Gozal, 2016).

Neuroimaging Structural neuroimaging studies have reported that individuals with IED have reduced grey matter volume in fronto-limbic areas including the orbital prefrontal cortex, ventromedial prefrontal cortex, anterior cingulate cortex, amygdala, insula, and uncus (Coccaro, Fitzgerald, Lee, McCloskey, & Phan, 2016). In addition, measures of aggression were found to correlate directly with grey matter volume in these areas. The shape of the amygdala is also abnormal in individuals with IED compared with healthy controls. In this morphometry study, individuals with IED have significantly more areas of inward deformation in the amygdala compared with healthy controls (Coccaro, Lee, McCloskey, Csemansky, & Wang, 2015). Diffusion tensor imaging (DTI) reveals lower fractional anisotropy in two clusters located in the superior longitudinal fasciculus when compared with psychiatric and healthy controls (Lee et al., 2016). This suggests lower white matter integrity in long-range connections between the frontal and temporo-parietal regions of the brain and likely problems with connectivity between these brain regions.

Functional magnetic resonance imaging studies report greater amygdala response to exposure to angry faces in IED compared with healthy controls. This finding is true for implicit (Coccaro, McCloskey, Fitzgerald, & Phan, 2007; McCloskey, Fitzgerald, Lee, McCloskey, & Phan, 2016) and explicit emotional processing. Life-time history of aggression correlates with amygdala response to the angry faces. Finally, acute activation of 5-HT receptors by a single dose of citalopram has been associated with an enhanced fMRI signal response to angry faces in the left temporal parietal junction (TPJ) of IED compared with healthy control individuals (Cremers, Lee, Keedy, Phan, & Coccaro, 2015). Since the TPJ is associated with social-cognitive processes, such as perspective taking and empathy, it is possible that SSRIs administration may reduce aggressive tendencies towards other people by enhancing these social-cognitive processes.

Treatments for IED in Adults

Subsequent chapters in this book (Chapters 25 through 28) address intervention programs focusing on conduct disorder and oppositional defiant disorder, and on the symptomatic behaviors associated with those disorders, including aggression. This chapter provides an overview of treatment considerations for intermittent explosive disorder, and then, in later sections, for impulse-control disorders (kleptomania; pyromania). Because of the limited literature on treatment of adolescents with these disorders, the literature on research with adults is primarily summarized, and carries implications for future research with youth.

Pharmacological While there are no medications approved by the Food and Drug Administration (FDA) for the treatment of IED, several psychopharmacologic agents appear to have effects on aggression. Double-blind, placebo-controlled, clinical trials in patients with impulsive aggression have been conducted over the past decade. The first studies reported a reduction in impulsive aggressive behavior by the serotonin-activating antidepressant, fluoxetine, in impulsive aggressive individuals with personality disorders (Coccaro, Kavoussi, & Lesser, 1992; Salzman et al., 1995) and this has been replicated in three other studies (Coccaro & Kavoussi, 1997; George et al., 2011; Silva et al., 2010) and in a study with individuals with IED (Coccaro, Lee, & Kavoussi, 2009a). Effective doses for fluoxetine are in the 20–40 mg qd range (Coccaro, Lee, & Kavoussi, 2009a).

Other classes of agents shown to have "anti-aggressive" effects in double-blind, placebo-controlled trials of individuals with "primary" aggression (i.e., not secondary to psychosis, severe mood disorder, or organic brain syndromes) include mood stabilizers (lithium: Sheard, Marini, Bridges, & Wagner, 1976) and anticonvulsants (phenytoin: Barratt et al., 1997; carbamazepine: Gardner & Cowdry, 1986; oxcarbazepine: Mattes, 2005; divalproex: Hollander et al., 2003). While NE beta-blockers (e.g., propanolol/nadolol: Mattes, 1990; Ratey et al., 1992) have also been shown to reduce aggression, these agents have exclusively been tested in patient populations with "secondary" aggression (e.g., mental retardation, organic brain syndromes, etc.). Classes of agents that may have "pro-aggressive" effects include tricyclic antidepressants (amitriptyline: Soloff, George, Nathan, Schulz, & Perel, 1986; benzodiazapines: Gardner & Cowdry, 1985), and stimulant and hallucinatory drugs of abuse (amphetamines, cocaine, phencyclidine: Fishbein & Tarter, 2009). Findings from double-blind, placebo-controlled, clinical trials suggest that anti-aggressive efficacy is specific to impulsive, rather than non-impulsive, aggression (Barratt et al., 1997).

Psychological A variety of cognitive-behavioral treatments have been found to be moderately (or more) effective in the treatment of anger and/or aggression in adults or youth. Specifically, some cognitive-behavioral techniques have demonstrated a reduction in anger or the aggressive behaviors of classroom children, juvenile delinquents, residentially placed adolescents, college students, drivers, abusive parents and spouses, and prison inmates (Beck & Fernandez, 1998; Deffenbacher, Huff, Lynch, Oetting, & Salvatore, 2000; Edmondson & Conger, 1996; Novaco, 1977). Many treatments have been found to be effective at follow-up of up to 15 months, often with additional improvement gains noted at follow-up relative to post-treatment (Deffenbacher, 1988; Deffenbacher, McNamara, Stark, & Sabadell, 1990; Deffenbacher, Oetting, Huff, Cornell, & Dallager, 1996; Deffenbacher, Oetting, Huff, & Thwaites, 1996; Deffenbacher & Stark, 1992; Hazaleus & Deffenbacher, 1986). Specific treatments have included relaxation training, social skills training, skill assembly social skills training, problem solving, negative thought reduction, self-instruction, cognitive therapy, and combined cognitive-relaxation or cognitive-behavioral treatment. Notably, however, the anger treatment literature does not discriminate between clinical anger problems without aggression and pathological aggression and so these findings may not generalize to more severely aggressive individuals with IED.

The first, and only, study of cognitive-behavioral therapy (CBT vs. wait-list control) in DSM-5 IED demonstrated that impulsive aggression, anger, and hostile thoughts are significantly reduced by a CBT package that includes relaxation training, cognitive restructuring, and coping skills training (McCloskey, Noblett, Deffenbacher, Gollan, & Coccaro, 2008). Fluoxetine and CBT demonstrated similar therapeutic responses and given that both treatments are likely working through different mechanisms, combination of the two kinds of treatments may be more effective than either alone.

Kleptomania

Epidemiology

Although the precise prevalence rates of Kleptomania remain unknown, rates in treatment-seeking samples suggest that it is fairly common. Kleptomania is also experienced by a broad range of psychiatric patient populations including 3.7% of depressed patients (n=107; Lejoyeux, Arbaretaz, McLoughlin, & Adès, 2002) and 24% of those with bulimia (Hudson, Pope, Jonas, & Yurgelun-Todd, 1983). A study of psychiatric inpatients (n=204) with a range of admitting disorders revealed that 7.8% (n=16) endorsed current kleptomania and 9.3% (n=19) met lifetime criteria (Grant et al., 2005). Approximately two-thirds of individuals with kleptomania, in clinical samples, are women (McElroy, Pope, Hudson, Keck, & White, 1991).

Phenomenology

Kleptomania is characterized by repetitive, uncontrollable stealing of items that people do not need for their personal use. Although kleptomania typically has its onset in early adulthood or late adolescence (McElroy et al., 1991), the disorder has been reported in children as young as 4 years old and in adults as old as 77 (Grant, 2006). The literature clearly suggests that the majority of patients with kleptomania are women (McElroy et al., 1991). Items stolen are typically hoarded, given away, returned to the store, or thrown away (McElroy et al., 1991). Many individuals with kleptomania (64% to 87%) have been apprehended at some time due to their stealing, and 15% to 23% report having been incarcerated (Grant, 2006). Most individuals with kleptomania try unsuccessfully to stop. The diminished ability to stop often leads to feelings of shame and guilt. Of married subjects, less than half had disclosed their behavior to their spouses due to shame and guilt (Grant, 2006). High rates of other psychiatric disorders (depression, bipolar disorder, anxiety disorders, substance use disorders, and eating disorders) are common in individuals with kleptomania (Grant, 2006; McElroy et al., 1991).

Treatments for Kleptomania

Pharmacological There have been only two placebo-controlled trials for kleptomania. One study investigated the antidepressant, escitalopram, in the treatment of kleptomania. Subjects were all given open-label escitalopram for 7 weeks and those who responded (n=15) were then randomized to either continue on the medication or be switched to placebo (Koran,

Aboujaoude, & Gamel, 2007). After randomization, 43% of those on escitalopram relapsed compared to 50% on placebo, thereby showing no drug effect in terms of response.

In an open-label study of naltrexone, 12 subjects received doses ranging 50–150 mg per day (mg/d). Naltrexone resulted in a significant decline in the intensity of urges to steal, stealing thoughts and stealing behavior (Grant & Kim, 2001). In a follow-up double-blind, placebo-controlled study of naltrexone, 25 kleptomania subjects received naltrexone or placebo for 8 weeks. The study found naltrexone significantly reduced urges to steal and stealing behavior compared to placebo (Grant, Kim, & Odlaug, 2009).

Psychological No controlled studies of psychological treatments exist for kleptomania. Case reports suggest that cognitive and behavioral therapies may be effective in treating kleptomania. Covert sensitization, where a person is instructed to imagine stealing as well as the negative consequences of stealing (e.g., being handcuffed, feeling embarrassed), has been successful in reducing kleptomania symptoms (Grant, 2006). Imaginal desensitization, where a person images the steps of stealing but also imagines her ability to resist the behavior, has also successfully reduced kleptomania behavior (Grant, Odlaug, & Donahue, 2012).

Pyromania

Epidemiology

As with Kleptomania, the precise prevalence rate of Pyromania is unknown, though studies in treatment-seeking samples suggest that pyromania is also fairly common. One study of 107 patients with depression found that 3 (2.8%) met current DSM-IV-TR criteria for pyromania (Lejoyeux et al., 2002), and a study of 204 psychiatric inpatients revealed that 3.4% (n=7) endorsed current and 5.9% (n=12) had lifetime symptoms meeting DSM-IV-TR criteria for pyromania (Grant et al., 2005). The gender ratio in pyromania is unknown.

Phenomenology

The DSM-5 describes Pyromania as a preoccupation with fire setting and characterizes the behavior with the following diagnostic criteria: (a) deliberate and purposeful fire setting on more than one occasion; (b) tension or affective arousal before the act; (c) fascination with, interest in, curiosity about, or attraction to fire and its situational contexts; and (d) pleasure, gratification, or relief when setting fires or when witnessing or participating in their aftermath.

Although long thought to be a disorder primarily affecting men, recent research suggests that the gender ratio is equal in adults and may be slightly higher among females in adolescence (Grant & Kim, 2007). Mean age of onset is generally late adolescent, and the behavior appears chronic if left untreated (Grant & Kim, 2007). Urges to set fires are common in individuals with this behavior and the fire setting is almost always pleasurable. Severe distress follows the fire setting and individuals with pyromania report significant functional impairment (Grant & Kim, 2007).

Treatment

There is no controlled pharmacological or psychological treatment data regarding pyromania. However, cognitive-behavioral treatment has been found to be useful in reducing deviant fire-related behaviors among children who had set recent fires (Kolko, 2001), suggesting such treatments could be explored and tested for these symptoms of pyromania.

Conclusions

Clinicians evaluating patients with intermittent explosive disorder and impulse-control disorders should assess the circumstances that led them to seek help. In most psychiatric disorders, patients seek treatment because they are troubled by their symptoms. Patients with impulse-control disorders, however, continue to struggle with the desire to engage in the behavior and their need to stop because of mounting social, occupational, financial, or legal problems.

In the area of intermittent explosive disorder and impulse-control disorders, the systematic study of treatment efficacy and tolerability is in its infancy. With few studies published, it is not possible to make treatment recommendations with a substantial degree of confidence. No drugs are currently approved by the FDA for the treatment of any of these disorders.

Clinicians should be aware of the limitations of our treatment knowledge. Most published studies employed relatively small sample sizes, were of limited duration, and involved possibly nonrepresentative clinical groups (e.g., those without co-occurring psychiatric disorders). Heterogeneity of treatment samples may also complicate identification of effective treatments. At present, issues such as which medication to use and for whom, or the duration of pharmacotherapy or cognitive behavior therapy cannot be sufficiently addressed with the available data.

References

American Psychiatric Association. (1952). *Diagnostic and statistical manual of mental disorders*. Washington, DC: Author.

American Psychiatric Association. (1968). *Diagnostic and statistical manual of mental disorders* (2nd ed.). Washington, DC: Author.

American Psychiatric Association. (1980). *Diagnostic and statistical manual of mental disorders* (3rd ed.). Washington, DC: Author.

Barratt, E. S., Stanford, M. S., Felthous, A. R., & Kent, T. A. (1997). The effects of phenytoin on impulsive and premeditated aggression: A controlled study. *Journal of Clinical Psychopharmacology*, 17, 341–349.

Beck, R., & Fernandez, E. (1998). Cognitive-behavioral therapy in the treatment of anger: A meta-analysis. *Cognitive Therapy and Research*, 22, 63–74.

Coccaro, E. F. (2006). Association of C-reactive protein elevation with trait aggression and hostility in personality disordered subjects: A pilot study. *Journal of Psychiatric Research*, 40, 460–465.

Coccaro, E. F. (2010). A family history study of intermittent explosive disorder. *Journal of Psychiatric Research*, 44, 1101–1105.

Coccaro, E. F. (2011). Intermittent explosive disorder: Development of integrated research criteria for *Diagnostic and Statistical Manual of Mental Disorders*, fifth edition. *Comprehensive Psychiatry*, 5, 119–125.

Coccaro, E. F. (2012). Intermittent explosive disorder as a disorder of impulsive aggression for DSM-5. *American Journal of Psychiatry*, 169, 577–588.

Coccaro, E. F., Bergeman, C. S., & McClearn, G. E. (1993). Heritability of irritable impulsiveness: A study of twins reared together and apart. *Psychiatry Research*, 48, 229–242.

Coccaro, E. F., Fanning, J. R., & Lee, R. (2016). Development of a social emotional information processing assessment for adults (SEIP-Q). *Aggressive Behavior*, 43(1), 47–59.

Coccaro, E. F., Fanning, J. R., & Lee, R. (2017). Intermittent explosive disorder and substance use disorder: Analysis of the National Comorbidity Survey Replication Sample. *Journal of Clinical Psychiatry*. E-Pub Ahead of Print. doi:10.4088/JCP.15M10306

Coccaro, E. F., Fanning, J. R., Phan, K. L., & Lee, R. (2015). Serotonin and impulsive aggression. *CNS Spectrums*, 20, 295–302.

Coccaro, E. F., Fitzgerald, D. A., Lee, R., McCloskey, M. S., & Phan, K. L. (2016). Fronto-limbic morphometric abnormalities in intermittent explosive disorder and aggression. *Biological Psychiatry: Clinical Neuroscience and Neuroimaging*, 1, 32–38.

Coccaro, E. F., Fridberg, D. J., Fanning, J. R., Grant, J. E., King, A. C., & Lee, R. (2016). Substance use disorders: Relationship with intermittent explosive disorder and with aggression, anger, and impulsivity. *Journal of Psychiatric Research, 81*, 127–132.

Coccaro, E. F., & Kavoussi, R. J. (1997). Fluoxetine and impulsive aggressive behavior in personality-disordered subjects. *Archives of General Psychiatry, 54*, 1081–1088.

Coccaro, E. F., Kavoussi, R. J., Berman, M. E., & Lish, J. D. (1998). Intermittent explosive disorder-revised: Development, reliability, and validity of research criteria. *Comprehensive Psychiatry, 39*, 368–376.

Coccaro, E. F., Kavoussi, R. J., Hauger, R. L., Cooper, T. B., & Ferris, C. F. (1998). Cerebrospinal fluid vasopressin levels: correlates with aggression and serotonin function in personality-disordered subjects. *Archives of General Psychiatry, 55*, 708–714.

Coccaro, E. F., Kavoussi, R. J., & Lesser, J. C. (1992). Self- and other-directed human aggression: The role of the central serotonergic system. *International Clinical Psychopharmacology*, Suppl. 6, 70–83.

Coccaro, E. F., & Lee, R. (2010). Cerebrospinal fluid 5-hydroxyindolacetic acid and homovanillic acid: Reciprocal relationships with impulsive aggression in human subjects. *Journal of Neural Transmission, 117*, 241–248.

Coccaro, E. F., Lee, R., & Coussons-Read, M. (2014). Elevated plasma inflammatory markers in individuals with intermittent explosive disorder and correlation with aggression in humans. *Journal of the American Medical Association: Psychiatry, 71*, 158–165.

Coccaro, E. F., Lee, R., & Coussons-Read, M. (2015a). Cerebrospinal fluid and plasma C-reactive protein and aggression in personality-disordered subjects: A pilot study. *Journal of Neural Transmission, 122*, 321–326.

Coccaro, E. F., Lee, R., Coussons-Read, M. (2015b). Cerebrospinal fluid inflammatory cytokines and aggression in personality disordered subjects. *International Journal of Neuropsychopharmacology, 18*(7). doi:10.1093/ijnp/pyv001.

Coccaro, E. F., Lee, R., Fanning, J. R., Fuchs, D., Goiny, M., Erhardt, S., . . . Coussons-Read, M. (2016). Tryptophan, kynurenine, and kynurenine metabolites: Relationship to lifetime aggression and inflammatory markers in human subjects. *Psychoneuroendocrinology, 71*, 189–196.

Coccaro, E. F., Lee, R., & Gozal, D. (2016). Elevated plasma oxidative stress markers in individuals with intermittent explosive disorder and correlation with aggression in humans. *Biological Psychiatry, 79*, 127–135.

Coccaro, E. F., Lee, R., Groer, M. W., Can, A., Coussons-Read, M., & Postolache, T. T. (2016). Toxoplasma gondii infection: relationship with aggression in psychiatric subjects. *Journal of Clinical Psychiatry, 77*, 334–341.

Coccaro, E. F., Lee, R., & Kavoussi, R. J. (2009a). A double-blind, randomized, placebo-controlled trial of fluoxetine in patients with intermittent explosive disorder. *Journal of Clinical Psychiatry, 70*, 653–662.

Coccaro, E. F., Lee, R., & Kavoussi, R. J. (2009b). Inverse relationship between numbers of 5-HT transporter binding sites and life history of aggression and intermittent explosive disorder. *Journal of Psychiatric Research, 44*, 137–142.

Coccaro, E. F., Lee, R., & Kavoussi, R. J. (2010). Aggression, suicidality, and intermittent explosive disorder: Serotonergic correlates in personality disorder and healthy control subjects. *Neuropsychopharmacology, 35*, 435–444.

Coccaro, E. F., Lee, R., Liu, T., & Mathe, A. A. (2012). CSF NPY correlates with aggression in human subjects *Biological Psychiatry, 72*, 997–1003.

Coccaro, E. F., Lee, R., & McCloskey, M. S. (2014). Validity of the new A1 and A2 criteria for DSM-5 intermittent explosive disorder. *Comprehensive Psychiatry, 55*(2), 260–267.

Coccaro, E. F., Lee, R., McCloskey, M., Csernansky, J. G., Wang, L. (2015). Morphometric analysis of amygdla and hippocampus shape in impulsively aggressive and healthy control subjects. *Journal of Psychiatric Research, 69*, 80–86.

Coccaro, E. F., Lee, R., Owens, M. J., Kinkead, B., & Nemeroff, C. B. (2012). Cerebrospinal fluid substance P-like immunoreactivity correlates with aggression in personality disordered subjects. *Biological Psychiatry, 72*, 238–243.

Coccaro, E. F., Lee, R., & Vezina, P. (2013). Cerebrospinal fluid glutamate concentration correlates with impulsive aggression in human subjects. *Journal of Psychiatric Research, 47*, 1247–1253.

Coccaro, E. F., McCloskey, M. S., Fitzgerald, D. A., & Phan, K. L. (2007). Amygdala and orbitofrontal reactivity to social threat in individuals with impulsive aggression. *Biological Psychiatry*, *62*, 168–178.

Coccaro, E. F., Noblett, K. L., & McCloskey, M. S. (2009). Attributional and emotional responses to socially ambiguous cues: Validation of a new assessment of social/emotional information processing in healthy adults and impulsive aggressive patients. *Journal of Psychiatric Research*, *43*, 915–925.

Coccaro, E. F., Posternak, M. A., & Zimmerman, M. (2005). Prevalence and features of intermittent explosive disorder in a clinical setting. *Journal of Clinical Psychiatry*, *66*, 1221–1227.

Coccaro, E. F., Solis, O., Fanning, J., & Lee, R. (2015). Emotional intelligence and impulsive aggression in intermittent explosive disorder. *Journal of Psychiatric Research*, *61*, 135–140.

Cremers, H., Lee, R., Keedy, S., Phan, K. L., & Coccaro, E. F. (2016). Effects of escitalopram administration on face processing in intermittent explosive disorder: An fMRI study. *Neuropsychopharmacology*, *41*, 590–597.

Deffenbacher, J. L. (1988). Cognitive-relaxation and social skills treatment of anger: A year later. *Journal of Counseling Psychology*, *35*, 234–236.

Deffenbacher, J. L., Huff, M. E., Lynch, R. S., Oetting, E. R., & Salvatore, N. F. (2000). Characteristics and treatment of high-anger drivers. *Journal of Counseling Psychology*, *47*, 5–17.

Deffenbacher, J. L., McNamara, K., Stark, R. S., & Sabadell, P. M. (1990). A comparison of cognitive-behavioral and process-oriented group counseling for general anger reduction. *Journal of Counseling & Development*, *69*, 167–169.

Deffenbacher, J. L., Oetting, E. R., Huff, M. E., Cornell, G. R., & Dallager, C. J. (1996). Evaluation of two cognitive-behavioral approaches to general anger reduction. *Cognitive Therapy and Research*, *20*, 551–573.

Deffenbacher, J. L., Oetting, E. R., Huff, M. E., & Thwaites, G. A. (1995). Fifteen-month follow-up of social skills and cognitive-relaxation approaches to general anger reduction. *Journal of Counseling Psychology*, *42*, 400–405.

Deffenbacher, J. L., & Stark, R. S. (1992). Relaxation and cognitive-relaxation treatments of general anger. *Journal of Counseling Psychology*, *39*, 158–167.

de Jonge, P., Alonso, J., Stein, D. J., Kiejna, A., Aguilar-Gaxiola, S., Viana, M. C., . . . Scott, K. M. (2014). Associations between DSM-IV mental disorders and diabetes mellitus: a role for impulse control disorders and depression. *Diabetologia*, *57*(4), 699–709.

Duke, A. A., Bègue, L., Bell, R., & Eisenlohr-Moul, T. (2013). Revisiting the serotonin-aggression relation in humans: A meta-analysis. *Psychological Bulletin*, *139*, 1148–1172.

Edmondson, C. B., & Conger, J. C. (1996). A review of treatment efficacy for individuals with anger problems: Conceptual, assessment, and methological issues. *Clinical Psychology Review*, *16*, 251–275.

Fettich, K. C., McCloskey, M. S., Look, A. E., & Coccaro, E. F. (2015). Emotion regulation deficits in intermittent explosive disorder. *Aggressive Behavior*, *41*, 25–33.

Fishbein, D., & Tarter, R. (2009). Infusing neuroscience into the study and prevention of drug misuse and co-occurring aggressive behavior. *Substance Use and Misuse*, *44*, 1204–1235.

Gardner, D. L., & Cowdry, R. W. (1985). Alprazolam-induced dyscontrol in borderline personality disorder. *American Journal of Psychiatry*, *142*, 98–100.

Gardner, D. L., & Cowdry, R. W. (1986). Positive effects of carbamazepine on behavioral dyscontrol in borderline personality disorder. *American Journal of Psychiatry*, *143*, 519–522.

George, D. T., Phillips, M. J., Lifshitz, M., Lionetti, T. A., Spero, D. E., Ghassemzedeh, N., . . . Rawlings, R. R. (2011). Fluoxetine treatment of alcoholic perpetrators of domestic violence: a 12-week, double-blind, randomized, placebo-controlled intervention study. *Journal of Clinical Psychiatry*, *72*, 60–65.

Grant, J. E. (2006). Understanding and treating kleptomania: new models and new treatments. *Israel Journal of Psychiatry and Related Sciences*, *43*, 81–87.

Grant, J. E., & Kim, S. W. (2001). An open-label study of naltrexone in the treatment of kleptomania. *Journal of Clinical Psychiatry*, *63*, 349–356.

Grant, J. E., & Kim, S. W. (2007). Clinical characteristics and psychiatric comorbidity of pyromania. *Journal of Clinical Psychiatry*, *68*, 1717–1722.

Grant, J. E., Kim, S. W., & Odlaug, B. L. (2009). A double-blind, placebo-controlled study of the opiate antagonist, naltrexone, in the treatment of kleptomania. *Biological Psychiatry, 65*, 600–606.

Grant, J. E., Levine, L., Kim, D., & Potenza, M. N. (2005). Impulse control disorders in adult psychiatric inpatients. *American Journal of Psychiatry, 162*, 2184–2188.

Grant, J. E., Odlaug, B. L., & Donahue, C. B. (2012). Adolescent stealing treated with motivational interviewing and imaginal desensitization. *Journal of Behavioral Addictions, 1*, 191–192.

Hazaleus, S. L., & Deffenbacher, J. L. (1986). Relaxation and cognitive treatments of anger. *Journal of Consulting and Clinical Psychology, 54*, 222–226.

Hollander, E., Tracy, K. A., Swann, A. C., Coccaro, E. F., McElroy, S. L., Wozniak, P., . . . Nemeroff, C. B. (2003). Divalproex in the treatment of impulsive aggression: Efficacy in cluster B personality disorders. *Neuropsychopharmacology, 28*, 1186–1197.

Hudson, J. I., Pope, H. G., Jr, Jonas, J. M., & Yurgelun-Todd, D. (1983). Phenomenologic relationship of eating disorders to major affective disorder. *Psychiatry Research, 9*, 345–354.

Kessler, R. C., Berglund, P., Demler, O., Jin, R., Merikangas, K. R., & Walters, E. E. (2005). Lifetime prevalence and age-of-onset distributions of DSM-IV disorders in the National Comorbidity Survey Replication. *Archives of General Psychiatry, 62*, 593–602.

Kessler, R. C., Coccaro, E. F., Fava, M., Jaeger, S., Jin, R., & Walters, E. E. (2006). The prevalence and correlates of DSM-IV intermittent explosive disorder in the National Comorbidity Survey Replication. *Archives of General Psychiatry, 63*, 669–678.

Kolko, D. J. (2001). Efficacy of cognitive-behavioral treatment and fire safety education for children who set fires: Initial and follow-up outcomes. *Journal of Child Psychology and Psychiatry, 42*, 359–369.

Koran, L. M. Aboujaoude, E. N., & Gamel, N. N. (2007). Escitalopram treatment of kleptomania: An open-label trial followed by double-blind discontinuation. *Journal of Clinical Psychiatry, 68*, 422–427.

Lee, R., Arfanakis, K., Evia, A. M., Fanning, J., Keedy, S., & Coccaro, E. F. (2016). White matter integrity reductions in intermittent explosive disorder. *Neuropsychopharmacology, 41*(11), 2697–2703.

Lee, R., Ferris, C., Van de Kar, L. D., & Cocarro, E. F.(2009). Cerebrospinal fluid oxytocin, life history of aggression, and personality disorder. *Psychoneuroendocrinology, 34*, 1567–1573.

Lee, R., Gill, A., Chen, B., McCloskey, M., & Coccaro, E. F. (2012). Modulation of central serotonin affects emotional information processing in impulsive aggressive personality disorder. *Journal of Clinical Psychopharmacology, 32*, 329–335.

Lejoyeux, M., Arbaretaz, M., McLoughlin, M., & Adès, J. (2002). Impulse-control disorders and depression. *Journal of Nervous and Mental Disease, 190*, 310–314.

Linnoila, M., Virkkunen, M., Scheinin, M., Nuutila, A., Rimon, R., & Goodwin, F. K. (1983). Low cerebrospinal fluid 5-hydroxyindoleacetic acid concentration differentiates impulsive from nonimpulsive violent behavior. *Life Science, 33*, 2609–2614.

Mattes, J. A. (1990). Comparative effectiveness of carbamazepine and propranolol for rage outbursts. *Journal of Neuropsychiatry and Clinical Neuroscience, 2*, 159–164.

Mattes, J. A. (2005). Oxcarbazepine in patients with impulsive aggression: A double-blind, placebo-controlled trial. *Journal of Clinical Psychopharmacology, 25*, 575–579.

McCloskey, M. S., Kleabir, K., Berman, M. E., Chen, E. Y., & Coccaro, E. F. (2010). Unhealthy aggression: Intermittent explosive disorder and adverse physical health outcomes. *Health Psychology, 29*, 324–332.

McCloskey, M. S., Noblett, K. L., Deffenbacher, J. L., Gollan, J. K., & Coccaro, E. F. (2008). Cognitive-behavioral therapy for intermittent explosive disorder: A pilot randomized clinical trial. *Journal of Consulting and Clinical Psychology, 76*, 876–886.

McCloskey, M. S., Phan, K. L., Angstadt, M., Fettich, K. C., Keedy, S., & Coccaro, E. F., (2016). Amygdala hyperactivation to angry faces in intermittent explosive disorder. *Journal of Psychiatric Research, 79*, 34–41.

McElroy, S. L., Pope, H. G., Jr, Hudson, J. I., Keck, P. E., Jr, & White, K. L. (1991). Kleptomania: A report of 20 cases. *American Journal of Psychiatry, 148*, 652–657.

McLaughlin, K. A., Green, J. G., Hwang, I., Sampson, N. A., Zaslavsky, A. M., & Kessler, R. C. (2012). Intermittent explosive disorder in the National Comorbidity Survey Replication Adolescent Supplement. *Archives of General Psychiatry, 69*, 1131–1139.

Miles, D. R., & Carey, G. (1997). Genetic and environmental architecture of human aggression. *Journal of Personality and Social Psychology, 72*, 207–217.

Murray-Close, D., Ostrov, J. M., Nelson, D. A., Crick, N. R., & Coccaro, E. F. (2010). Proactive, reactive, and romantic relational aggression in adulthood: Measurement, predictive validity, gender differences, and association with Intermittent Explosive Disorder. *Journal of Psychiatric Research, 44*, 393–404.

New, A., Trestman, R., Mitropoulou, V., Goodman, M., Koenigsberg, H., Silverman, J., & Siever, L. J. (2004). Low prolactin response to fenfluramine in impulsive aggression. *Journal of Psychiatric Research, 38*, 223–230.

Novaco, R. W. (1977). Stress inoculation: A cognitive therapy for anger and its application to a case of depression. *Journal of Consulting and Clinical Psychology, 45*, 600–608.

Puhalla, A. A., McCloskey, M. S., Brickman, L. J., Fauber, R., & Coccaro, E. F. (2016). Defense styles in Intermittent Explosive Disorder. *Psychiatry Research, 238*, 137–142.

Raine, A., Meloy, J. R., Bihrle, S., Stoddard, J., LaCasse, L., & Buchsbaum, M. S. (1998). Reduced prefrontal and increased subcortical brain functioning assessed using positron emission tomography in predatory and affective murderers. *Behavioral Science and the Law, 16*, 319–332.

Ratey, J. J., Sorgi, P., O'Driscoll, G. A., Sands, S., Daehler, M. L., Fletcher, J. R., . . . Lindern, K. J. (1992). Nadolol to treat aggression and psychiatric symptomatology in chronic psychiatric inpatients: A double-blind, placebo-controlled study. *Journal of Clinical Psychiatry, 53*, 41–46.

Salzman, C., Wolfson, A. N., Schatzberg, A., Looper, J., Henke, R., Albanese, M., . . . Miyawaki, E. (1995). Effect of fluoxetine on anger in symptomatic volunteers with borderline personality disorder. *Journal of Clinical Psychopharmacology, 15*, 23–29.

Seroczynski, A. D., Bergeman, C. S., & Coccaro, E. F. (1999). Etiology of the impulsivity/aggression relationship: genes or environment? *Psychiatry Research, 86*, 41–57.

Sheard, M. H., Marini, J. L., Bridges, C. I., & Wagner, E. (1976). The effect of lithium on impulsive aggressive behavior in man. *American Journal of Psychiatry, 133*, 1409–1413.

Silva, H., Iturra, P., Solari, A., Villarroel, J., Jerez, S., Jimenez, M., Bustamante, M. L. (2010). Fluoxetine response in impulsive-aggressive behavior and serotonin transporter polymorphism in personality disorder. *Psychiatric Genetics, 20*, 25–30.

Soloff, P. H., George, A., Nathan, R. S., Schulz, P. M., & Perel, J. M. (1986). Paradoxical effects of amitriptyline on borderline patients. *American Journal of Psychiatry, 143*, 1603–1605.

Virkkunen, M., Nuutila, A., Goodwin, F. K., & Linnoila, M. (1987). Cerebrospinal fluid monoamine metabolite levels in male arsonists. *Archives of General Psychiatry, 44*, 241–247.

7

Related Personality Disorders Located within an Elaborated Externalizing Psychopathology Spectrum

Martin Sellbom, Bo Bach, and Elizabeth Huxley

This chapter focuses on four adult personality disorders, which all display differential symptom manifestations that are relevant to disruptive problems affecting childhood behavior. We argue that childhood and adult behavior pathology can be framed in a broader context of externalizing psychopathology, with common mechanisms that explain symptom course from childhood to adulthood. Finally, we take the position that the formal model for personality disorders in the DSM-5 is flawed, and examining contemporary personality trait models (e.g., as presented in DSM-5 Section III) moves the field in a more productive direction for integrating child and adult behavioral pathologies.

Personality Disorders

Personality disorders (PDs) constitute a serious and widespread public health concern. Epidemiological studies have estimated that 9–15% of community adults meet diagnostic criteria for at least one disorder (see Lenzenweger, 2008, for a review); the prevalence in clinical settings is well over 50% (Mattia & Zimmerman, 2001). Furthermore, research has shown that individuals with PDs are at increased risk for inpatient hospitalization, suicidal behavior, criminal behavior, violence, and occupational and interpersonal impairment (see Hopwood & Thomas, 2012 for a review). In addition, although PDs are not impossible to treat, they frequently complicate the clinical picture and can moderate the effects of treatment of other clinical disorders (see, e.g., Cyranowski et al., 2004).

The *Diagnostic and Statistical Manual of Mental Disorders*, Fifth edition (DSM-5; American Psychiatric Association, 2013), lists the formal criteria for specific PDs in Section II (Diagnostic Criteria and Codes) of the DSM-5. There are 10 disorders that have been organized into three thematic clusters (Cluster A: paranoid, schizoid, schizotypal; Cluster B: antisocial, borderline, histrionic, narcissistic; Cluster C: avoidant, dependent, obsessive-compulsive) that have yielded marginal conceptual and empirical support (e.g., Hopwood & Thomas, 2012). The DSM-5 Section II PDs are conceptualized and operationalized as distinct diagnostic categories that have emerged through the neo-Kreaplinian descriptive nosology approach originating with the DSM-III (American Psychiatric Association, 1980). Polythetic criterion sets are used, which means that a categorical diagnosis is assigned if an individual exhibits X out of Y symptoms (e.g., 5 of 9 for borderline PD) coupled with a qualitative level of associated subjective distress or impairment.

This atheoretical descriptive approach is not without advantages, in light of the fairly straightforward mode of communication among clinicians and the possibility of clear criteria for research on epidemiology, etiology, and intervention. However, this categorical model has also engendered decades of well-founded and substantial criticism (see, e.g., Krueger, 2013 and Skodol, 2012 for reviews). These criticisms include (but are not limited to) excessive diagnostic overlap, excessive within-diagnosis heterogeneity (e.g., it is possible for individuals with antisocial PD and obsessive-compulsive PD diagnoses not to share a single symptom), inadequate coverage of personality psychopathology variance (a large proportion of patients meet criteria for PD Not Otherwise Specified), a lack of clear boundary between normal and pathological personality (owing to polythetic criterion sets), marked temporal instability, and poor convergent and discriminant validity across diagnostic categories.

As a result of these rather significant concerns, scholars have been arguing for dimensional approaches to considering personality psychopathology for decades now (e.g., Krueger, 2013; Skodol, 2012). Dimensional personality traits offer a major advantage for conceptualizing and operationalizing PDs, in that they provide a range from adaptivity to maladaptivity, are culturally universal, can be organized into meaningful hierarchies that facilitate interpretative meaning, can be reliability assessed, and are associated with a plethora of meaningful outcomes (Roberts, Kuncel, Shiner, Caspi, & Goldberg, 2007). The alternative model of PD presented in DSM-5 Section III (Emerging Models and Measures) is in part grounded in personality trait theory and provides an important blueprint for the future (and is therefore discussed in a later section of this chapter). Indeed, the personality trait portion has already amassed an impressive body of validity evidence (e.g., Krueger & Markon, 2014). However, for now, the traditional PD model printed in Section II remains the formal method for diagnosis and continues to generate important research output; as such, it will serve as the basis for this chapter.

Disruptive Behavior Disorders, Personality Disorders, and the Externalizing Spectrum

There is reason to believe that certain PDs (most notably antisocial PD/psychopathy, but see arguments for others below) are adult manifestations of symptoms and traits associated with the DSM-5 Disruptive Behavior Disorders from the perspective of an externalizing spectrum of psychopathology. Indeed, this spectrum was initially conceived in research with children and adolescents (e.g., Achenbach, 1966), and encompasses attention-deficit hyperactivity disorder (ADHD), oppositional defiant disorder, intermittent explosive disorder, and conduct disorder (see Beauchaine & McNulty, 2013 for a review). In adulthood, this spectrum is extended to include antisocial PD and alcohol and substance use disorders (SUDs) (Krueger et al., 2002; Krueger, Markon, Patrick, Benning, & Kramer, 2007), but also, to a large degree, psychopathy (Patrick & Drislane, 2015). Moreover, various studies have revealed consistent support for a higher order externalizing factor that explains a large proportion of variance in individual disorders in both children and adults (see, e.g., Krueger et al., 2002; Lahey et al., 2008; Sellbom, 2016). This latent externalizing factor is highly heritable, with over 80% of the latent externalizing variance being attributable to genetic effects in adulthood (Krueger et al., 2002). Disinhibition (or trait impulsivity) has been proposed as a temperamental liability factor shared among externalizing disorders (Beauchaine & McNulty, 2013).

Recent research has accumulated evidence for an expanded or elaborated conceptualization of the externalizing spectrum (Krueger et al., 2007; Sellbom, 2016). Hierarchical analyses of mental disorders indicate that externalizing/disinhibition and antagonism/interpersonal disturbance represent two separate but strongly related first-order domains (Kendler et al., 2011; Kotov et al., 2011) that load on the same second-order domain (Wright et al., 2012). Behavior genetics studies have revealed some separation of these domains (Kendler et al., 2011) with phenotypic support for potential unique liabilities (Krueger et al., 2007; Sellbom, 2016). The most consistent indicators on the antagonism/interpersonal disturbance domain are PDs, with narcissistic, histrionic, and paranoid loading prominently; and antisocial and borderline loading on both antagonism and externalizing/disinhibition. Conceptually, the most immediate phenotypic cognates of the antagonism domain are callous-unemotional (CU) traits (as separate from conduct disorder) in childhood (Frick, Ray, Thornton, & Kahn, 2014; see Chapter 3 in this book for an overview of CU traits) and affective-interpersonal psychopathy traits in adulthood (e.g., "meanness"; Patrick & Drislane, 2015).

There are four PDs that are broadly conceptually relevant to the externalizing spectrum and will therefore be discussed in detail in this chapter: antisocial PD/psychopathy, borderline PD, narcissistic PD, and paranoid PD. Briefly, antisocial and borderline PDs are both marked by disinhibition and, to a lesser degree, interpersonal antagonism as reflected in aggressive, deceitful, and hostile interactions with others. Psychopathy, which is often viewed as a more severe manifestation of antisocial PD, particularly in terms of the antagonism domain (Lynam & Miller, 2015), is defined by core characteristics that are labeled callous-unemotional traits in youth. Narcissistic PD is more narrowly linked to antagonistic expressions of externalizing, especially in light of excessive anger reactions in the context of ego threats (e.g., Millon, 1996) as well as an entitled and unreasonably demanding personality style (Hart & Joubert, 1996). Finally, although perhaps the most peripheral, paranoid PD is partly defined by cognitive and attributional biases that can lead to disproportional and severe anger reactions with even the slightest provocation (e.g., Bentall & Taylor, 2006; Millon, 1996) and parallel those observed in some children with conduct disorder (e.g., Dodge, 1993). In the next four sections, we discuss the phenomenology, epidemiology, and developmental course (focused primarily on childhood/adolescence) of these four PDs.

Antisocial/Psychopathic Personality Disorder

Phenomenology

Definition/Criteria Psychopathic personality disorder (henceforth, psychopathy) represents a constellation of personality traits that can be organized into at least three broad phenotypic domains of interpersonal (e.g., superficial charm, grandiose self-worth, manipulativeness/deceitfulness), affective (e.g., callousness, lack of empathy and remorse, shallow affect), and behavioral/lifestyle (e.g., impulsivity, irresponsibility, nonplanfulness, parasitic lifestyle, aggression) traits (Cooke, Michie, & Hart, 2006). Others have also written about more superficially adaptive traits, including absence of serious emotional health problems, low stress reactivity, and fearlessness (e.g., Cleckley, 1941; Patrick, Fowles, & Krueger, 2009).

The most overt expressions of psychopathy involve flagrant violations of societal rules; however, many psychopathic individuals manage to avoid incarceration, using interpersonal manipulation to exploit and otherwise cause distress in others (Hare, 2007). In the business world, psychopathic individuals can be responsible for creating hostile work environments, corruption, malfeasance, and other egregious violations of the public trust that cause financial hardship (Babiak, Neumann, & Hare, 2010). These manifestations/outcomes are very much adult parallels to children with conduct disorder and callous-unemotional traits (Frick et al., 2014).

Since DSM-III was released in 1980, psychopathy has been operationalized as antisocial PD with very little change across subsequent editions (including DSM-5). Unfortunately, it has been well documented that the diagnostic criteria for this disorder do not provide sufficient coverage of most conceptual models of psychopathy (Hare & Neumann, 2009). Indeed, these criteria emphasize the behavioral features of psychopathy (impulsivity, recklessness, irresponsibility, failure to conform to social norms), and de-emphasize the core affective (callousness, shallow affect) and interpersonal (superficial charm, grandiosity, manipulativeness) traits that many believe represent the essence of the construct (e.g., Lynam & Miller, 2015). Conduct disorder is the childhood parallel for this operationalization; indeed, for a diagnosis of antisocial PD, there must have been evidence for conduct disorder prior to age 15 (American Psychiatric Association, 2013).

Submanifestations Psychopathy is not a unitary construct. Indeed, virtually every single psychopathy instrument, whether operationalized via clinician-rating or self-report, is multifactorial (typically ranging between 2–4 factors depending on indicators and underlying theory; Boduszek & Debowska, 2016; Sellbom, Lilienfeld, Fowler, & McCrary, in press). Consequently, it is not surprising that multiple manifestations (via differing constellations of underlying traits) among those scoring high on psychopathy measures have been identified in various person-centered analyses (see, e.g., Hare, 2016). Indeed, two subtypes have generally emerged with a high degree of similarity across studies (Hicks, Markon, Patrick, Krueger, & Newman, 2004; Mokros et al., 2015). These have typically been referred to as "primary" and "secondary" psychopathy consistent with Karpman's (1941) clinical formulations—the former typically reflecting emotional stability/low anxiety and high degrees of manipulativeness, whereas high levels of impulsivity and aggression typically mark the latter. Most of these studies indicate rather clearly that the "secondary" manifestation is typically more akin to the DSM's antisocial PD operationalization, whereas the "primary" variant would be the more fearless, bold, and calculating phenotype with characteristics that go beyond the externalizing spectrum.

Gender Differences With respect to gender manifestations of psychopathy, the literature is somewhat mixed. Several studies have failed to find any observable differences in associations between psychopathy measures and external outcome measures in a range of community, forensic, and correctional samples (e.g., Marion & Sellbom, 2011; Phillips, Sellbom, Ben-Porath, & Patrick, 2014). In those studies that have revealed differences, the major distinction in the manifestation of psychopathy across men and women appears to occur in the expression of externalizing behavior. For instance, in a sample of Swedish offenders high on psychopathy, Strand and Belfrage (2005) found that male psychopaths displayed a greater level of antisocial behavior during adolescence than did their female counterparts. They also noted that women were more likely to use relational aggression, whereas men were more likely to use physical aggression. Furthermore, women high on externalizing features (i.e. mostly antisocial PD traits) of psychopathy are more psychologically maladjusted than their male counterparts, with increased risk of victimization (McClellan, Farabee, & Crouch, 1997), and more pronounced symptoms of somatization (Lilienfeld & Hess, 2001). More research, however, is definitely needed in this area.

Epidemiology

Antisocial PD in DSM-5 requires the presence of at least 3 of 7 diagnostic criteria in addition to evidence of conduct disorder before age 15. The only non-DSM (or ICD-10) method proposed to "diagnose" psychopathy is the Hare Psychopathy Checklist – Revised (PCL-R; Hare, 1991, 2003). The PCL-R is a 20-item clinician rating form based on a semi-structured interview and institutional file information; it was developed for correctional samples. Hare (1991) originally proposed a score of 30 (of 40) for a psychopathy diagnosis, which represented one standard deviation above the mean in Canadian offender samples; this cut score remained when the second edition of the manual was published (Hare, 2003).

Prevalence rates for antisocial PD tend to be higher than for PCL-estimated psychopathy, indicating that the former clearly operationalizes a broader phenotype. The DSM-5 estimates that the 12-month prevalence rate for antisocial PD is 0.2 to 3.3% (American Psychiatric Association, 2013), with lifetime prevalence estimates of DSM-IV Antisocial PD to be 1.3 to 5.5% for adult men and 0 to 1.9% for adult women (Coid, Yang, Tyrer, Roberts, & Ullrich, 2006; Grant et al., 2004; Robins, Tipp, & Przybeck, 1991; Torgersen, Kringlen, & Cramer, 2001) depending on measurement and sampling. Research with the PCL: Screening Version (PCL:SV; Hart, Cox, & Hare, 1995) instrument has indicated lower rates than for antisocial PD in the community. More specifically, studies from the US (Neumann and Hare, 2008) and UK (Coid, Yang, Ullrich, Roberts, & Hare, 2009) estimated prevalence rates of 1.0–1.3% for men and 0.0–1.2% for women for "potential" psychopathy. Unfortunately, these rates are difficult to evaluate because they both used much lower than recommended cut-off scores for a psychopathy diagnosis. Furthermore, prevalence rates in offender samples provide better comparison for PCL-R and DSM-operationalized psychopathy. Estimates for psychopathy have suggested that about 25% of correctional inmates would meet criteria for the disorder, whereas DSM-based estimates for Antisocial PD are typically between 50 and 80% (Hare, 2016). With respect to gender, Strand and Belfrage (2005) found that 16% of a female offender sample and 25% of a male offender sample met the traditionally used PCL-R cut-off for psychopathy, but, in light of smaller gender differences in the community, it may very well be dissimilarities in externalizing tendencies that drive these differences. Finally, in terms of comorbidity, epidemiological studies have shown that less than 10% of antisocial PD cases show no co-occurrence with other mental disorders (e.g., Robins et al., 1991), with substance use disorders (SUD) being far the most common (up to 80%; Kessler et al., 1996; Robins et al., 1991). Such research has also found increased risk for antisocial PD being associated with mood and anxiety disorders (approximately 25-50%; e.g., Lenzenweger, Lane, Loranger, & Kessler, 2007). No formal comorbidity studies are available for PCL-based psychopathy.

Developmental Course

According to the DSM-5, personality disorders should generally not be diagnosed prior to age 18. There is certainly evidence to indicate some stability of personality traits that give rise to PDs that can be identified in childhood (e.g., De Clerq, De Fruyt, & Widiger, 2009), but the malleability of personality at this developmental age (e.g., Roberts & DelVecchio, 2000) and the potential trajectories through which antisocial youth can progress (e.g., Moffitt, 1993) make it difficult to discuss developmental course prior to adulthood with any confidence. For antisocial PD, the DSM-5 requires some level of stability from childhood, at least with respect to antisocial/delinquent behavior, but the literature on conduct disorder indicates different trajectories into adulthood, with antisocial PD being a minority path (Quinton, Pickles, Maughan, & Rutter, 1993; Robins & Price, 1991). Indeed, a plethora of longitudinal studies have found evidence for different developmental trajectories for youth with antisocial proclivities more broadly (e.g., Moffitt, 1993). There is substantial evidence for a childhood-persistent or life-course-persistent offender pattern that entails the greatest risk of maintaining stability into adulthood and manifesting in antisocial PD/psychopathy (Lynam, 1996; Moffitt, 1993). These youth are associated with the most significant genetic, biological, and environmental risk factors (Moffitt, 1993). Furthermore, there has been some (albeit rather limited) research on the stability of psychopathic personality traits from childhood into adulthood. Although these studies have mostly focused on late adolescence (e.g., Loney, Taylor,

Butler, & Iacono, 2007), Lynam, Caspi, Moffitt, Loeber, & Stouthamer-Loeber (2007) demonstrated moderate stability ($r=.31$) from early adolescence (age 13) to adulthood (age 24) using data from the Pittsburgh Youth Study. Although this correlation might appear small, one must consider that they used vastly different measurements (with moderate concurrent associations at best) with unknown test–retest reliabilities over a very long time period.

It is potentially more useful to consider research on the externalizing spectrum of psychopathology with respect to development, which clearly indicates major genetic vulnerability towards such proclivities that can seemingly be traced to disinhibition (Beauchaine & McNulty, 2013). Beauchaine and McNulty (2013) proposed an ontological developmental model incorporating neurobiological factors that, coupled with environmental antecedents, can shape the course and manifestation of externalizing behavior over time. More specifically, they argued that dysfunction in the midbrain mesolimbic (and possibly, mesocortical by adulthood) dopaminergic system leads to hyperactive reward sensitivity, which underlies disinhibited/externalizing behavior; thus, excessive reward seeking accounts for impulsive behavior. In adulthood, there is also substantial evidence (possibly as the brain matures; see Beauchaine & McNulty, 2013) for various prefrontal cortical dysfunctions that reflect response inhibition, delayed discounting, and affective decision making (Castellanos-Ryan & Seguin, 2016), which lead to externalizing behavior. Furthermore, neurobiology interacts with a host of environmental influences to develop and maintain externalizing, including important negative childhood relationships and family and abuse histories (Beauchaine & McNulty, 2013).

Borderline Personality Disorder

Phenomenology

Definition/Criteria Borderline personality disorder (BPD) is a serious and complex mental illness characterized by a pervasive pattern of instability in affect regulation, relationships, self-image, and impulse control (Skodol, Gunderson et al., 2002). In order to meet the DSM-5 criteria for BPD one must have at least five of the following nine symptoms: affective instability, self-damaging impulsivity, lack of control of anger, recurrent suicidal threats or gestures, identity disturbance, unstable relationships, feelings of emptiness, fear of abandonment, and stress-induced paranoia or psychotic-like episodes. Like other PDs, the symptoms should emerge by early adulthood and be present in different contexts (American Psychiatric Association, 2013). A rather unique characteristic of BPD is that it comprises both internalizing features (e.g., intense bouts of depression and anxiety) and externalizing features (e.g., aggression, drug or alcohol abuse, excessive spending, and risky sex).

Gender Issues. Sansone and Sansone's (2011a) review of gender differences indicated that men with BPD were more likely to demonstrate explosive behavior and higher levels of novelty seeking than women with BPD. Moreover, men with BPD more often have substance use disorders whereas women with BPD are more likely to have eating, mood, anxiety, and posttraumatic stress disorders. Men with BPD are more likely to have a comorbid antisocial PD diagnosis than similarly affected women. Furthermore, in regard to treatment utilization, men with BPD are more likely to have treatment histories relating to substance abuse whereas women are more likely to have treatment histories characterized by medication and psychotherapy (Sansone & Sansone, 2011a). For example, Wetterborg and colleagues (2015) found that one fifth of Swedish male offenders on probation met criteria for BPD, 91% of whom also met criteria for antisocial PD. In other words, men with BPD are primarily found in prisons and addiction treatment institutions, whereas women with BPD are primarily found in psychotherapy clinics and psychiatric hospitals.

Externalizing Manifestations of BPD Impulsivity is considered a core personality component in BPD (Lieb, Zanarini, Schmahl, Linehan, & Bohus, 2004; Links, Heslegrave, & Reekum, 1999), which is how it overlaps with externalizing psychopathology more broadly. According to the DSM-5 BPD operationalization, impulsivity may manifest in a variety of life areas, including sexual behavior (e.g., promiscuity and sexual compulsion), spending behavior (e.g., compulsive shopping), eating behavior (e.g., bulimia nervosa), and substance usage (American Psychiatric Association, 2013). There seems to be a common clinical understanding of BPD-related impulsivity, which is not easy to define. Research suggests that basic mechanisms of impulse control seem not to be disturbed in BPD (Sebastian, Jacob, Lieb, & Tüscher, 2013); rather, the clinically observed impulsive behaviors may potentially be explained as a consequence of dysregulated BPD emotionality or in terms of comorbid ADHD (Sebastian et al., 2013). Thus, the specific nature of impulsivity and behavioral self-control in BPD warrants further research.

Impulsive aggression is another common feature of BPD, which can manifest in a variety of behaviors, including destruction of property, domestic violence, and assault (Perez-Rodriguez et al., 2012; Skodol, Siever, et al., 2002). In contrast to the more instrumental aggression in psychopathy, the aggression in BPD is typically of the reactive type related to emotional lability and intermittent explosive tendency (Allen & Links, 2012). Accordingly, aggression in BPD primarily emerges in close relationships and is directed against significant others or acquaintances (Mancke, Herpertz, & Bertsch, 2015).

Based on a review of findings across 11 studies, Sansone and Sansone (2011b) concluded that, in comparison to controls, those with BPD show greater sexual impulsivity as indicated by higher levels of early sexual exposure, casual sexual relationships, a greater number of different sexual partners, and homosexual experiences. These differences also involve a higher likelihood of having been coerced to have sex, experiencing date rape, being raped by a stranger, or contracting sexually transmitted diseases. Consequently, the sexual behavior in BPD is characterized by both impulsivity and victimization.

Research overall suggests that externalizing features of BPD (i.e. impulsivity and aggression) are primarily driven by interpersonally traumagenic and affective sensitive aspects (e.g., fear of abandonment, self-harm, and disordered eating behavior) whereas in ADHD, deficits in cognitive and attentional processing account for the behavior inhibition problems referred to as impulsivity (Matthies & Philipsen, 2016).

Epidemiology

BPD is estimated to occur in 0.5–4% of non-clinical populations (Lenzenweger, 2008), but is the most common PD in clinical settings, estimated to affect 10–25% of individuals in mental health care, and approximately 20% of psychiatric inpatients (Kernberg & Michels, 2009; Torgersen et al., 2001). Women have generally been considered to account for 70% of individuals with BPD in most clinical settings (Lieb et al., 2004). Yet, a more recent well-executed community-representative study found that BPD is equally prevalent among men and women (Grant, Chou et al., 2008). Moreover, BPD is particularly prevalent among individuals with drug and alcohol addiction, but it is important to determine whether the disordered behavior is accounted for by addiction alone (including intoxication or withdrawal symptoms) or actual premorbid personality dysfunction (Trull, Sher, Minks-Brown, Durbin, & Burr, 2000). Finally, a number of studies indicate a considerable overlap between ADHD and BPD symptoms (Storebo & Simonsen, 2014), which particularly applies to features of impulsivity and emotional instability (Matthies & Philipsen, 2016). It has been proposed that (a) ADHD and BPD are expressions of an underlying disorder or phenotype, (b) both disorders have common clinical features, etiology, and risk factors, (c) ADHD is an early developmental stage of BPD, or (d) that ADHD simply raises the risk of a BPD diagnosis (O'Malley, McHugh, Mac Giollabhui, & Bramham, 2016; Storebo & Simonsen, 2014). The potential role of ADHD along with ODD and CD is further discussed in the section on developmental course.

Developmental Course

Research suggests that BPD features emerge in the late latency period of childhood but that treatment is typically not sought until late adolescence (Winsper et al., 2016). Generally, longitudinal research indicates that the developmental course of BPD from childhood to adolescence is heterogeneous, pointing at various potential prodromal indicators of later BPD (e.g., Haltigan & Vaillancourt, 2016). In a recent longitudinal study, Cramer (2016) found specific childhood traits of impulsivity and aggression/nonconformity to predict BPD in adulthood.

Some studies have shown that 40–50% of adult BPD patients reported childhood ADHD when retrospectively assessed (e.g., Philipsen et al., 2008). This finding is consistent with prospective studies showing that childhood ADHD symptoms predict higher rates of BPD during young adulthood (e.g., Stepp, Burke, Hipwell, & Loeber, 2012). In addition, ODD has been found to share core features with BPD in terms of poorly controlled anger and hostility (Burke, Hipwell, & Loeber, 2010). Dysregulation in frontolimbic regions, including regions of the amygdala, is common for both BPD and ODD, suggesting a shared neurobiological pathway for emotion dysregulation (Lieb et al., 2004; Stepp et al., 2012). Consequently, it is plausible that childhood manifestations of ODD may be a precursor of BPD. Furthermore, some studies have also demonstrated associations between BPD and CD (e.g., Ceballos, Houston, Hesselbrock, & Bauer, 2006; Newhill, Vaughn, & DeLisi, 2010). Newhill et al. (2010), for example, were able to identify an antisocial subgroup of BPD individuals characterized by a history of childhood-onset CD.

Finally, a vast amount of research indicates that childhood adversities (e.g., emotional or sexual abuse) play a substantial role in the development of emotional dysregulation, which may also lead to the harmful impulsivity associated with BPD. Accordingly, a comprehensive review by Ball and Links (2009) concluded that evidence supports a causal relationship between childhood trauma and BPD, particularly if this relationship is considered as part of a multifactorial model.

Taken together, research suggests that there are at least two developmental routes to pathological impulsivity and emotional dysregulation in BPD: (a) a disinhibition route involving deficits in response inhibition functioning (including ADHD, ODD, and CD symptoms) originating in a vulnerable genotype, prenatal injury, and/or environmental factors; (b) a traumatogenic route involving childhood adversities that causes affect dysregulation, which in return may cause problems with impulse control. It seems highly plausible that those two routes interact with one another. For example, growing up with difficulties associated with ADHD may increase the risk of experiencing adversities in school and at home (i.e. parental scolding, physical abuse, peer victimization, and various defeats).

Narcissistic Personality Disorder

Phenomenology

Definition/Criteria   Narcissism can manifest in various ways, leading to a large number of definitions and conceptualizations (Cain, Pincus, & Ansell, 2008). Broadly, narcissism can be defined as a personality construct comprised of a range of interpersonal and internal processes that help individuals maintain a positive sense of self, and search for validation and self-enhancement in their environment (Pincus & Lukowitsky, 2010). Narcissistic PD occurs when high levels of narcissism impair interpersonal functioning or cause distress.

Two main subtypes of narcissism have been identified: grandiose and vulnerable. Grandiose narcissism includes behaviors and cognitions such as seeking excessive admiration and validation from others, having an inflated or grandiose sense of self, high levels of entitlement, and low empathy for others (Cain et al., 2008; Pincus & Lukowitsky, 2010). In contrast, vulnerable narcissism may include hypersensitivity to criticism, rejection and unmet needs, an unstable or fragile sense of self, and high levels of shame and negative affect (Cain et al., 2008; Pincus & Lukowitsky, 2010). Research has primarily focused on the grandiose features of narcissism, despite indications that there is significant clinical utility in considering how both vulnerable and grandiose aspects of narcissism operate within individuals (Pincus, Cain, & Wright, 2014).

Within the DSM-5, narcissistic PD is operationalized as, "a pervasive pattern of grandiosity (in fantasy and behavior), need for admiration, and lack of empathy, beginning by early adulthood and present in a variety of contexts" (American Psychiatric Association, 2013, p. 669). Narcissistic PD requires the presence of at least 5 of 9 diagnostic criteria: a grandiose sense of self, preoccupation with grandiose fantasies, regarding oneself as special and unique, requiring excessive admiration, feelings of entitlement, low empathy, exploitation of others, envying others or believing that one is envied, and arrogant behaviors and attitudes (American Psychiatric Association, 2013). Narcissistic PD is defined primarily by grandiose symptoms, and has been criticized for neglecting vulnerable manifestations of narcissism (e.g., Cain et al., 2008).

Gender Issues   Gender differences have been observed for narcissistic PD and grandiose narcissism. The DSM-5 indicates that 50–75% of those who meet diagnostic criteria are male (American Psychiatric Association, 2013). In Stinson et al.'s (2008) sample, 7.7% of men met criteria for narcissistic PD compared to 4.8% of women; however, Torgensen et al. (2001) found similar prevalence rates for men (0.9%) and women (0.8%). A recent meta-analysis (Grijalva et al. 2015) found higher levels of narcissism in males, but this effect was small. There is limited information on gender differences in adolescent samples, but a slightly higher prevalence of NPD in males has been reported (Grilo et al., 1996).

Externalizing Manifestations of NPD   Narcissism has been associated with aggression and violence in a range of populations (e.g., Bushman & Baumeister, 1998; Warren et al., 2002). The relationship between narcissism and aggression is thought to stem from protecting an overly positive or grandiose sense of self. A situation wherein an individual perceives an ego threat, such as a personal flaw that does not fit with their view of themselves, individuals higher in narcissism are thought to react with anger or aggression to protect their sense of self (e.g., Bushman & Baumeister, 1998). Shame regarding personal flaws (e.g., Krizan & Johar, 2015), and unstable or fragile self-esteem (e.g., Bushman & Baumeister, 1998) often found in highly narcissistic individuals may contribute to this aggressive response.

In adult populations, narcissism tends to be associated with anger in situations that are provocative or threatening to self-concept (Bettencourt, Talley, Benjamin, & Valentine, 2006), and this relationship is significant when controlling for self-esteem (Lambe, Hamilton-Giachritsis, Garner, & Walker, 2016). Although most research has focused on grandiose narcissism and narcissistic PD, vulnerable narcissism may also be a predictor of aggression (Krizan & Johar, 2015). The association between narcissism and aggression has also been observed in prison samples. For example, Warren et al. (2002) found that female inmates who met criteria for narcissistic PD were significantly more likely to have been convicted of a violent crime than those who did not meet such criteria.

Narcissism in children has been found to predict proactive and reactive aggression (Washburn, McMahon, King, Reinecke, & Silver, 2004), bullying in males (Reijntjes et al., 2015), and future delinquency (Barry, Frick, Adler, & Grafeman, 2007). The relationship between narcissism and conduct problems holds when controlling for callous-unemotional traits; and some facets of narcissism, such as exploitativeness, entitlement, and exhibitionism, may be more predictive of conduct issues than others (Barry, Frick, & Killian, 2003).

Narcissism has been associated with externalizing disorders in childhood and adolescence; however, this research has primarily examined narcissism as a component of psychopathy (in addition to callous-unemotional traits and impulsivity, e.g., Frick & Hare, 2001). For example, Frick, Bodin, and Barry (2000) found that narcissistic traits were positively associated with ODD, CD, and ADHD in their sample of community children. Cluster analyses revealed that high narcissism scores (and moderate scores on CU and impulsivity) were associated with higher rates of ODD and CD, with 25% of this cluster meeting criteria for either ODD or CD. Similar patterns were reported using psychiatric inpatient samples; for instance, Becker et al. (2013) found higher levels of narcissism were associated with higher levels of ODD and ADHD symptoms in a sample of child psychiatric inpatients. Although narcissism, ODD, and CD are associated with increased aggression and conduct issues, there is evidence to suggest that the link between narcissism and aggression in adolescents exists when controlling for ODD and CD. Johnson et al. (2000) found that higher levels of narcissistic PD symptoms in adolescents and young adults was a significant predictor of higher levels of violent behavior when controlling for demographic variables, and that this relationship held when controlling for CD, ODD, and other Axis I disorders. Further research is required to understand the relationship between narcissism and externalizing disorders, including whether ODD and/or CD are precursors to Narcissistic PD.

Epidemiology

The DSM-5 (American Psychiatric Association, 2013) reports that the prevalence rate for narcissistic PD is between 0 and 6.2% based on studies of community samples. Most epidemiological studies, however, report rates towards the lower end of this range (e.g., Coid et al., 2006; Lenzenweger, 2008; Torgersen et al. 2001). Higher prevalence rates of narcissistic PD (2 to 16%) appear in clinical samples with the DSM-IV-TR (American Psychiatric Association, 2000). Gender differences were described earlier. Research on narcissistic PD and its comorbidity with other disorders is limited, but available literature suggests substance use disorders, depression, bipolar I disorder, and other personality disorders, particularly other cluster B disorders and paranoid PD, are common comorbid conditions (e.g., Grant, Goldstein et al., 2008 ; Ronningstam, 1996; Stinson et al., 2008; Zimmerman, Rothschild, & Chelminski, 2005).

Developmental Course

Relatively little is known about the development of narcissism and narcissistic PD. Narcissism appears to decline with age (e.g., Stinson et al., 2008), and higher levels of narcissism during adolescence have led some to caution that narcissistic PD should be diagnosed only from early adulthood onwards (Campbell & Baumeister, 2006). However, symptoms associated with pathological narcissism and narcissistic PD are present prior to adulthood (Thomaes, Bushman, Stegge, & Olthof, 2008) and are associated with lower reports of wellbeing in adolescents (Crawford, Cohen, Johnson, Sneed, & Brook, 2004).

Both genetic vulnerability and early childhood experiences may influence the development of narcissistic PD. Heritability coefficients for narcissistic PD of .53 (Jang, Livesley, Vernon, & Jackson, 1996) in adult and .66 (Coolidge, Thede, & Jang, 2001) in child samples have been found.

Some theorists argue that parental rejection and a lack of warmth leads to the development of high narcissism to protect the sense of self (e.g., Kernberg, 1975), whereas others (e.g., Millon, 1981) argue that children who grow up in an indulgent environment see themselves as grandiose because this has been modeled for them. Research in subclinical samples has primarily used retrospective reporting and produced mixed findings: both cold and rejecting experiences (e.g., Otway & Vignoles, 2006) and parental warmth (e.g., Horton, Bleau, & Dwrecki, 2006) are associated with narcissism. Longitudinal research indicates parental overvaluation predicts increased narcissism in children (Brummelman et al., 2015) and that childhood sexual and emotional abuse and neglect have been associated with adult narcissistic PD diagnosis (Waxman, Fenton, Skodol, Grant, & Hasin, 2014), but further research is needed.

Paranoid Personality Disorder

Phenomenology

Paranoid PD symptoms can be summarized into two broad domains: cognitive and affective functioning. From a cognitive perspective, paranoid individuals exhibit extreme levels of interpersonal suspiciousness, in that they believe (usually without sufficient basis, albeit not to a delusional degree) that others are taking advantage of them, manipulating them, and otherwise harming them. They typically discern malevolence and attacks on their character where these are not obvious to other people. Moreover, they are resentful, bear grudges, and are generally unforgiving of perceived misdeeds. Such individuals also tend to externalize blame onto others for their mishaps, assuming that they are being maliciously victimized (American Psychiatric Association, 2013; Triebwasser, Chemerinski, Roussos, & Siever, 2013). From an affective perspective, and of most relevance to externalizing psychopathology, individuals with paranoid PD tend to exhibit significant levels of anger and hostility, which is typically attributed to their interpersonal suspiciousness (American Psychiatric Association, 2013). Moreover, pathological jealousy is often (albeit not in every case) attributed to paranoid PD, and can times reach a delusional degree (White & Mullen, 1989). However, it is important to disentangle paranoid PD from delusional disorders in manifestation, even though they likely appear on the same psychotic spectrum (Kendler, Myers, Torgersen, Neale, & Reichborn-Kjennerud, 2007), because the traits and features most relevant to externalizing disorders are rooted in personality rather than psychosis. Unfortunately, no research has documented gender differences in the manifestation of paranoid PD.

Paranoid PD is associated with important underlying cognitive attribution biases (Bentall, 2001) that are remarkably similar to what has been observed in children and adolescents with significant anger dysregulation (Howells, 2009), including those with behavior disruptive disorders (Dodge, 1993). Indeed, the hostile attribution bias (HAB) is the overattribution of hostile or malicious intent to others in ambiguous situations when this attribution would not be warranted from others' perspectives (Dodge, 1993). Children with this bias misinterpret benign provocations from their peers as hostile while ignoring disconfirming information or clues that point to the interaction being nonthreatening (Dodge & Newman, 1981). For instance, Dodge and Newman (1981) showed that in ambiguous situations, aggressive boys were more likely to respond quickly, pay less attention to social cues, and overattribute the hostile intent of their peers. Extensive research on children and adolescents has been conducted showing that maladaptive social processing systems and HAB often result in reactive aggression (see Dodge, 1993 for a review). Consequently, similar social information processes might, at least in part, tie paranoid PD to a developmental externalizing spectrum (see Johnson et al., 2000).

Individuals with paranoid PD are also hypervigilant to threats in their environment, sensitive to interpersonal humiliation and rejection, and socially anxious, possibly (if not likely) as a result of poorly developed social skills (e.g., Bentall & Taylor, 2006; Carroll, 2009). It is therefore not surprising that, like children with HAB, individuals with paranoid PD have a higher risk for violence and aggression (Bentall & Taylor, 2006; Carroll, 2009). Indeed, Johnson et al. (2000) reported that paranoid personality traits in adolescents were associated with future violence in early adulthood. Moreover, Berman, Fallon, & Coccaro (1998) suggested that the aggression observed in paranoid individuals might be both proactive and reactive in nature. Such individuals are indeed hypersensitive to perceived slights, infidelity, and other forms of victimization and, in addition to reactive aggression, they might also choose to engage in proactive aggression to minimize a potential threat.

Epidemiology

The prevalence rate for paranoid PD in the general community is between 0.7 and 5.0% based on national comorbidity studies (American Psychiatric Association, 2013; Lenzenweger, 2008). In clinical settings, the prevalence in general psychiatric outpatients was estimated at 4.2% overall, with 0.7% meeting criteria for paranoid PD as their only personality disorder (Zimmerman et al., 2008). Moreover, the DSM-5 states that paranoid PD "appears to be more commonly diagnosed in males" but offer no actual specifics (American Psychiatric Association, 2013, p. 651). Available community data from the US and Europe reports 1.2–3.8% (mdn. = 2.2%) for men and 0.3–5.0% (mdn. = 2.3%) for women (Coid et al., 2006; Grant et al., 2004; Torgersen et al., 2001). Furthermore, comorbidity studies with paranoid PD have been scarce, with no documented gender differences. Oldham et al. (1992) found that paranoid PD was highly comorbid with avoidant, borderline, narcissistic, and schizotypal PDs (25–40%) in a clinical sample. Behavior genetic studies (especially family studies) have indicated clear associations between paranoid PD and the schizophrenia spectrum of disorders, particularly delusional disorder, but these associations have not been as clear as for schizotypal PD (see Triebwasser et al., 2013, for a review).

Developmental Course

Very little is known about the developmental course of paranoid PD. Like other PDs, it should generally not be diagnosed prior to age 18, and the developmental precursors to trait paranoia/suspiciousness have not been clear. Negative emotionality, which is a superordinate personality domain under which suspiciousness/alienation often falls, can be traced back to childhood with good stability (Rothbart & Ahadi, 1994; Shiner, 2009). Moreover, the DSM-5 states that Paranoid PD "may be first apparent in childhood and adolescence with solitariness, poor peer relationships, social anxiety, underachievement in school, hypersensitivity, peculiar thoughts and language, and idiosyncratic fantasies" (APA, 2013, p. 651). In a review, Triebwasser et al. (2013) indicated that there has been consistent evidence for early physical and emotional childhood trauma (even more so than for other PDs) and some evidence for traumatic brain injury as risk factors for paranoid PD.

The role of childhood trauma and victimization, which is common in other PDs with paranoid elements as well (e.g., borderline PD; Zanarini, Williams, Lewis, & Reich, 1997), in underpinning a dispositional proclivity towards paranoia is not surprising. The cognitive attribution biases reviewed earlier are clearly evident in childhood and adolescence and would possibly arise from childhood victimization experiences, especially by those close to the individual (e.g., parents). Indeed, early exposure to victimization could lead to early internalized representations of others as being malevolent, feelings of rejection, and associated social anxiety, which, as a result of their interactional style, could be further confirmed and turn into a self-fulfilling prophecy (Triebwasser et al., 2013). Of course, this hypothesis is speculative at best, and research into the developmental precursors to paranoid PD is sorely needed.

Dimensional Personality Traits: A Developmentally Sounder Way Forward

We hope that, having come thus far, the reader is somewhat persuaded that at least four of the DSM-5 PDs are to various degrees related to the externalizing spectrum of psychopathology, which can be reliably identified in both children and adults. However, it has likely not gone unnoticed that our attempt to map these PDs onto this framework has (with the possible exception of antisocial PD) been awkward and not entirely conclusive. Moreover, discussion of developmental course has been difficult, as there is often no straightforward manner in which these PDs can clearly be mapped onto childhood precursors. This ambiguity might strike some readers as surprising in light of evidence suggesting that PDs are already prevalent and stable by adolescence (Shiner, 2009). We believe that some of these difficulties stem from the serious problems associated with the DSM-5 Section II PD model more generally including strong overlap among PDs and natural co-occurrence with other mental disorders. A shift towards dimensional personality traits might make for improved research on personality pathology and externalizing behavior that is better developmentally translated and can be more easily examined in longitudinal frameworks.

Personality traits are domains of individual differences that that can be identified as early as infancy (Rothbart & Ahadi, 1994) and research has already begun to show that maladaptive personality traits are relatively stable in childhood and adolescence (De Clerq et al., 2009). Moreover, many efforts have already been underway to transform our view of personality pathology from distinct and somewhat arbitrary categories to a personality style description based on a dimensional trait model (American Psychiatric Association, 2013; Skodol, 2012). The externalizing psychopathology spectrum disorders and PDs discussed here can be understood from the perspective of dimensional traits with a maladaptive range. As mentioned at the beginning of this chapter, disinhibition has been identified as a trait domain that underlies what the externalizing disorders have in common. The various PDs discussed in this chapter have various overlapping and unique trait facets (see more specifics later). These traits are transdiagnostic and could provide for better descriptions and links to both neurobiological and environmental factors that can be studied across the lifespan and provide better information about the onset, stability, and course of pathology than the arbitrary demarcations that currently exist in the DSM-5 (DeYoung, 2010). Indeed, an individual high on impulsivity, anger/hostility, grandiosity, and suspiciousness might not neatly fit into a particular PD, but has a trait profile that likely provides for a more specific and informative description of an individual than three comorbid PDs (Clark et al., 2015). Furthermore, a developmental focus on individual traits also allows for an understanding of underlying mechanisms to a much greater degree for any constellation of traits and not just those that map onto a particular disorder (De Clercq et al., 2009).

The DSM-5 Section III personality trait model appears to be a promising one within which to consider externalizing from a trait perspective. Indeed, both cross-sectional and longitudinal studies have already investigated associations between DSM-5 Section III trait dimensions and different externalizing problems. In one study, Decuyper, De Caluwé, De Clercq, & De Fruyt (2013) found that callous-unemotional features, as reported by adolescents and their mothers, were particularly associated with traits of callousness, restricted affectivity, irresponsibility, and distractibility, whereas negative associations were observed for anxiety, submissiveness, depressivity, and separation insecurity. The authors proposed that these associations are consistent with the description of psychopaths as being hostile, affectively shallow, prone to coldhearted aggression, and not able to feel or show genuine emotions. Additionally, the findings also indicated that traits of restricted affectivity, intimacy avoidance, and anhedonia might help improve the operationalization of such psychopathic features among adolescents. Moreover, Smith and Samuel (2017) have identified the trait of distractibility as a unique predictor of ADHD, which potentially makes it useful for understanding the developmental pathways of this externalizing disorder.

More broadly, the utility of DSM-5 Section III traits has also been examined in relation to various externalizing problems in adulthood including psychopathy/antisocial PD (Wygant et al., 2016), narcissistic PD (Morey, Benson, & Skodol, 2016), borderline PD (Bach, Sellbom, Bo, & Simonsen, 2016), paranoid PD (Hopwood, Thomas, Markon, Wright, & Krueger, 2012), alcohol and substance abuse (Creswell, Bachrach, Wright, Pinto, & Ansell, 2015), pathological gambling (Carlotta et al., 2015), and impulsivity problems in general (Few, Lynam, & Miller, 2015). These results have been promising not only with respect to mapping onto conceptual expectations but also in showing how traits can be useful in understanding similarities and differences across these conditions.

Table 7.1 shows a mapping of traits onto various externalizing conditions and PDs in accordance with both conceptual and empirical findings just reviewed. The various overlapping associations between DSM-5 Section III trait dimensions and externalizing problems reveal a highly transdiagnostic pattern, which can serve to illustrate what these disorders have in common (e.g., traits reflective of disinhibition) as well as how they diverge from a trait perspective. For instance, psychopathy and BPD share several disinhibition and hostility traits, but they diverge (in outright opposition) with respect to negative affectivity. This type

Table 7.1 Proposed Associations between DSM-5 Section III Traits and Externalizing Psychopathology

	APD/Psychopathy	BPD	NPD	PPD	ADHD	ODD	CD
Impulsivity	+	+			+		+
Irresponsibility	+				+		+
Distractibility					+		
Risk Taking	+	+					+
(low) Perfectionism					+		
Manipulativeness	+						+
Deceitfulness	+						+
Grandiosity			+				
Attention seeking			+				
Callousness	+		+				+***
Hostility	+	+		+		+	+
Restricted affectivity	+	−					+***
Suspiciousness			+	+			
Anxiousness	−*	+	+**				
Emotional lability	−*	+	+**			+	
Unusual beliefs/experiences				+			

Note. APD = Antisocial PD; BPD = Borderline PD; NPD = Narcissistic PD; PPD = Paranoid PD; ADHD = Attention Deficit Hyperactivity Disorder; ODD = Oppositional Defiant Disorder; CD = Conduct Disorder.
*Psychopathy should be low on anxiousness and emotional lability
**NPD in vulnerable manifestations would be high on traits reflective of negative affectivity
***When CU traits are present

of scientific inquiry should dictate the future of PD research, which will allow for a more informed developmental perspective, including better linkage with putative childhood disorders (e.g., ADHD, ODD, CD) as well as externalizing psychopathology in general. Indeed, a trait-based study throughout the lifetime would provide a unified language for understanding the development and trajectories of externalizing maladaptivity (Krueger, 2013).

Conclusion

In this chapter, we have mapped relevant symptoms of four adult PDs onto an externalizing psychopathology spectrum shared with childhood behavior disruptive disorders. The disinhibitory and emotional dysregulation processes from antisocial and borderline PDs are particularly relevant to the impulsive behavioral expressions of externalizing psychopathology, as are the cognitive mechanisms driving anger and aggression behaviors in narcissistic and paranoid PDs. However, as illustrated in Table 7.1, we contend that personality trait models serve as an improved and more scientifically useful means of linking these symptom manifestations across childhood and adulthood. We therefore encourage future research to pursue these links more systematically for a better developmental model of personality psychopathology.

References

Achenbach, T. M. (1966). The classification of children's psychiatric symptoms: A factor analytic study. *Psychological Monographs, 80*, 1–37.

Allen, A., & Links, P. S. (2012). Aggression in borderline personality disorder: Evidence for increased risk and clinical predictors. *Current Psychiatry Reports, 14*, 62–69.

American Psychiatric Association. (1952). *Diagnostic and statistical manual of mental disorders*. Washington, DC: Author.

American Psychiatric Association. (1968). *Diagnostic and statistical manual of mental disorders* (2nd ed.). Washington, DC: Author.

American Psychiatric Association. (1980). *Diagnostic and statistical manual of mental disorders* (3rd ed.). Washington, DC: Author.

American Psychiatric Association. (2013). *Diagnostic and statistical manual of mental disorders* (5th ed.). Arlington, VA: Author.

Bach, B., Sellbom, M., Bo, S., & Simonsen, E. (2016). Utility of DSM-5 Section III personality traits in differentiating borderline personality disorder from comparison groups. *European Psychiatry, 37*, 22–27.

Babiak, P., Neumann, C. S., & Hare, R. D. (2010). Corporate psychopathy: Talking the walk. *Behavioral Sciences & the Law, 28*(2), 174–193.

Ball, J. S., & Links, P. S. (2009). Borderline personality disorder and childhood trauma: Evidence for a causal relationship. *Current Psychiatry Reports, 11*(1), 63–68.

Barry, C. T., Frick, P. J., & Killian, A. L. (2003). The relation of narcissism and self-esteem to conduct problems in children: A preliminary investigation. *Journal of Clinical Child & Adolescent Psychology, 32*, 139–152.

Barry, C. T., Frick, P. J., Adler, K. K., & Grafeman, S. J. (2007). The predictive utility of narcissism among children and adolescents: Evidence for a distinction between adaptive and maladaptive narcissism. *Journal of Child and Family Studies, 16*, 508–521.

Beauchaine, T. P., & McNulty, T. (2013). Comorbidities and continuities as ontogenic processes: Toward a developmental spectrum model of externalizing psychopathology. *Development and psychopathology, 25*, 1505–1528.

Becker, S. P., Luebbe, A. M., Fite, P. J., Greening, L., & Stoppelbein, L. (2013). Oppositional defiant disorder symptoms in relation to psychopathic traits and aggression among psychiatrically hospitalized children: ADHD symptoms as a potential moderator. *Aggressive Behavior, 39*(3), 201–211.

Bentall, R. P. (2001). Social cognition and delusional beliefs. In P. W. Corrigan & D. L. Penn (Eds.), *Social cognition and schizophrenia* (pp. 123–148). Washington, DC: American Psychological Association.

Bentall, R. P., & Taylor, J. L. (2006). Psychological processes and paranoia: implications for forensic behavioural science. *Behavioral Sciences & The Law, 24*, 277–294.

Berman, M., Fallon, A. E., & Coccaro, E. F. (1998) The relationship between personality psychopathology and aggressive behavior in research volunteers. *Journal of Abnormal Psychology, 107*, 651–658.

Bettencourt, B. A., Talley, A., Benjamin, A. J., & Valentine, J. (2006). Personality and aggressive behavior under provoking and neutral conditions: A meta-analytic review. *Psychological Bulletin, 132*(5), 751–777.

Boduszek, D., & Debowska, A. (2016). Critical evaluation of psychopathy measurement (PCL-R and SRP-III/SF) and recommendations for future research. *Journal of Criminal Justice, 44*, 1–12.

Brummelman, E., Thomaes, S., Nelemans, S. A., Orobio de Castro, B., Overbeek, G., & Bushman, B. J. (2015). Origins of narcissism in children. *Proceedings of the National Academy of Sciences, 112*, 3659–3662.

Burke, J. D., Hipwell, A. E., & Loeber, R. (2010). Dimensions of oppositional defiant disorder as predictors of depression and conduct disorder in preadolescent girls. *Journal of the American Academy of Child and Adolescent Psychiatry, 49*(5), 484–92.

Bushman, B. J., & Baumeister, R. F. (1998). Threatened egotism, narcissism, self-esteem, and direct and displaced aggression: Does self-love or self-hate lead to violence? *Journal of Personality and Social Psychology, 75*, 219–229.

Cain, N. M., Pincus, A. L., & Ansell, E. B. (2008). Narcissism at the crossroads: Phenotypic description of pathological narcissism across clinical theory, social/personality psychology, and psychiatric diagnosis. *Clinical Psychology Review, 28*, 638–656.

Campbell, W. K., & Baumeister, R. F. (2006). Narcissistic personality disorder. In J. E. Fisher & W. T. O'Donohue (Eds.), *Practitioner's guide to evidence-based psychotherapy* (pp. 423–431). New York: Springer.

Carlotta, D., Krueger, R. F., Markon, K. E., Borroni, S., Frera, F., Somma, A., . . . Fossati, A. (2015). Adaptive and maladaptive personality traits in high-risk gamblers. *Journal of Personality Disorders, 29*(3), 378–392.

Carroll, A. (2009). Are you looking at me? Understanding and managing paranoid personality disorder. *Advances in Psychiatric Treatment, 15*, 40–48.

Castellanos-Ryan, N., & Seguin, J. R. (2016). Prefrontal and anterior cingulate cortex mechanisms of impulsivity. In T. P. Beauchaine & S. P. Hinshaw (Eds.), *The Oxford handbook of externalizing spectrum disorders* (pp. 201–219). New York, NY: Oxford University Press.

Ceballos, N. A., Houston, R. J., Hesselbrock, V. M., & Bauer, L. O. (2006). Brain maturation in conduct disorder versus borderline personality disorder. *Neuropsychobiology, 53*(2), 94–100.

Clark, L. A., Vanderbleek, E. N., Shapiro, J. L., Nuzum, H., Allen, X., Daly, E., . . . Ro, E. (2015). The brave new world of personality disorder-trait specified: Effects of additional definitions on coverage, prevalence, and comorbidity. *Psychopathology Review, 2*, 52–82.

Cleckley, H. (1941). *The mask of sanity*. St. Louis, MO: Mosby.

Coid, J., Yang, M., Tyrere, P., Roberts, A., & Ullrich, S. (2006). Prevalence and correlates of personality disorder in Great Britain. *The British Journal of Psychiatry, 188*, 423–431.

Coid, J., Yang, M., Ullrich, S., Roberts, A., & Hare, R. D. (2009). Prevalence and correlates of psychopathic traits in the household population of Great Britain. *International Journal of Law and Psychiatry, 32*(2), 65–73.

Cooke, D. J., Michie, C., & Hart, S. D. (2006). Facets of clinical psychopathy. In C. J. Patrick (Ed.), *Handbook of Psychopathy* (pp. 91–106). New York, NY: Guilford Press.

Coolidge, F. L., Thede, L. L., & Jang, K. L. (2001). Heritability of personality disorders in childhood: A preliminary investigation. *Journal of Personality Disorders, 15*, 33–40.

Cramer, P. (2016). Childhood precursors of adult borderline personality disorder features. *The Journal of Nervous and Mental Disease, 204*(7), 494–499.

Crawford, T. N., Cohen, P., Johnson, J. G., Sneed, J. R., & Brook, J. S. (2004). The course and psychosocial correlates of personality disorder symptoms in adolescence: Erikson's developmental theory revisited. *Journal of Youth and Adolescence, 33*, 373–387.

References

Creswell, K. G., Bachrach, R. L., Wright, A. G. C., Pinto, A., & Ansell, E. (2015). Predicting problematic alcohol use with the DSM–5 alternative model of personality pathology. *Personality Disorders: Theory, Research, and Treatment, 7*(1), 103–111.

Cyranowski, J. M., Frank, E., Winter, E., Rucci, P., Novick, D., Pilkonis, P., . . . Kupfer, D. J. (2004). Personality pathology and outcome in recurrently depressed women over 2 years of maintenance interpersonal psychotherapy. *Psychological Medicine, 34*(4), 659–669.

De Clercq, B., De Fruyt, F., & Widiger, T. A. (2009). Integrating a developmental perspective in dimensional models of personality disorders. *Clinical Psychology Review, 29*, 154–162.

Decuyper, M., De Caluwé, E., De Clercq, B., & De Fruyt, F. (2013). Callous-unemotional traits in youth from a DSM-5 trait perspective. *Journal of Personality Disorders, 28*(3), 334–357.

DeYoung, C. G. (2010). Personality neuroscience and the biology of traits. *Social and Personality Psychology Compass, 4*(12), 1165–1180.

Dodge, K. A. (1993). Social-cognitive mechanisms in the development of conduct disorder and depression. *Annual Review of Psychology, 44*(1), 559–584.

Dodge, K. A., & Newman, J. P. (1981). Biased decision-making processes in aggressive boys. *Journal of Abnormal Psychology, 90*(4), 375–379.

Few, L. R., Lynam, D. R., & Miller, J. D. (2015). Impulsivity-related traits and their relation to DSM–5 Section II and III personality disorders. *Personality Disorders: Theory, Research, and Treatment, 6*(3), 261–266.

Frick, P. J., Bodin, S. D., & Barry, C. T. (2000). Psychopathic traits and conduct problems in community and clinic-referred samples of children: Further development of the Psychopathy Screening Device. *Psychological Assessment, 12*, 382–393.

Frick, P. J., & Hare, R. D. (2001). *Antisocial process screening device*. Toronto, ON: Multi-Health Systems.

Frick, P. J., Ray, J. V., Thornton, L. C., & Kahn, R. E. (2014). Annual Research Review: A developmental psychopathology approach to understanding callous-unemotional traits in children and adolescents with serious conduct problems. *Journal of child Psychology and Psychiatry, 55*, 532–548.

Grant, B. F., Hasin, D. S., Stinson, F. S., Dawson, D. A., Chou, S. P., Ruan, W. J., & Pickering, R. P. (2004). Prevalence, correlates, and disability of personality disorders in the United States: results from the National Epidemiologic Survey on Alcohol and Related Conditions. *The Journal of Clinical Psychiatry, 65*, 948–958.

Grant, B. F., Chou, S. P., Goldstein, R. B., Huang, B., Stinson, F. S., Saha, T. D., . . . Ruan, W. J. (2008). Prevalence, correlates, disability, and comorbidity of DSM-IV borderline personality disorder: Results from the Wave 2 National Epidemiologic Survey on Alcohol and Related Conditions. *The Journal of Clinical Psychiatry, 69*(4), 533–545.

Grant, B. F., Goldstein, R. B., Chou, S. P., Huang, B., Stinson, F. S., Dawson, D. A., . . . Compton, W. M. (2008). Sociodemographic and psychopathologic predictors of first incidence of DSM-IV substance use, mood and anxiety disorders: Results from the Wave 2 National Epidemiologic Survey on Alcohol and Related Conditions. *Molecular Psychiatry, 14*, 1051–1066.

Grijalva, E., Newman, D. A., Tay, L., Donnellan, M. B., Harms, P. D., Robins, R. W., & Yan, T. (2015). Gender differences in narcissism: A meta-analytic review. *Psychological Bulletin, 141*, 261–310.

Grilo, C. M., Becker, D. F., Fehon, D. C., Walker, M. L., Edell, W. S., & McGlashan, T. H. (1996). Gender differences in personality disorders in psychiatrically hospitalized adolescents. *American Journal of Psychiatry, 153*, 1089–1091.

Hare, R. D. (1991). *Manual for the revised psychopathy checklist*. Toronto: Multi-Health Systems.

Hare, R. D. (2003). *Manual for the revised psychopathy checklist* (2nd ed.). Toronto: Multi-Health Systems.

Hare, R. D. (2007). Forty years are not enough: Recollections, random musings, and prognostications. In H. Hervé & J. Yuille (Eds.), *The psychopath: Theory, research, and practice* (pp. 3–29). Mahwah, NJ: Lawrence Erlbaum and Associates.

Hare, R. D. (2016). Psychopathy, the PCL-R, and criminal justice: Some new findings and current issues. *Canadian Psychology/Psychologie canadienne, 57*(1), 21–34.

Hare, R. D., & Neumann, C. S. (2009). Psychopathy: Assessment and forensic implications. *The Canadian Journal of Psychiatry, 54*(12), 791–802.

Hart, P. L., & Joubert, C. E. (1996). Narcissism and hostility. *Psychological Reports, 79*(1), 161–162.
Hart, S. D., Cox, D. N., & Hare, R. D. (1995). *The Hare psychopathy checklist: Screening version.* Toronto: Multi-Health Systems.
Haltigan, J. D., & Vaillancourt, T. (2016). Identifying trajectories of borderline personality features in adolescence: Antecedent and interactive risk factors. *Canadian Journal of Psychiatry, 61,* 166–175.
Hicks, B. M., Markon, K. E., Patrick, C. J., Krueger, R. F., & Newman, J. P. (2004). Identifying psychopathy subtypes on the basis of personality structure. *Psychological Assessment, 16,* 276–288.
Hopwood, C. J., & Thomas, K. M. (2012). Personality disorders. In D. Beidel & M. Hersen (Eds.), *Adult Psychopathology and Diagnosis* (6th ed., pp. 681–716). Hoboken, NJ: John Wiley & Sons.
Hopwood, C. J., Thomas, K. M., Markon, K. E., Wright, A. G. C., & Krueger, R. F. (2012). DSM-5 personality traits and DSM-IV personality disorders. *Journal of Abnormal Psychology, 121,* 424–32.
Horton, R. S., Bleau, G., & Drwecki, B. (2006). Parenting Narcissus: What are the links between parenting and narcissism? *Journal of Personality, 74,* 345–376.
Howells, K. (2009). Angry affect, aggression and personality disorder. In M. McMurran & R. Howard (Eds), *Personality, personality disorder and violence* (pp. 191–212). Chichester, UK: Wiley.
Jang, K. L., Livesley, W. J., Vernon, P. A., & Jackson, D. N. (1996). Heritability of personality disorder traits: A twin study. *Acta Psychiatrica Scandinavica, 94,* 438–444.
Johnson, J. G., Cohen, P., Smailes, E., Kasen, S., Oldham, J. M., Skodol, A. E., & Brook, J. S. (2000) Adolescent personality disorders associated with violence and criminal behavior during adolescence and early adulthood. *American Journal of Forensic Psychiatry, 157,* 1406–1412.
Karpman, B. (1941). On the need of separating psychopathy into two distinct clinical types: the symptomatic and the idiopathic. *Journal of Criminal Psychopathology, 3,* 112–137.
Kendler, K. S., Myers, J., Torgersen, S., Neale, M. C., & Reichborn-Kjennerud, T. (2007). The heritability of cluster A personality disorders assessed by both personal interview and questionnaire. *Psychological Medicine, 37,* 655–665.
Kendler, K. S., Aggen, S. H., Knudsen, G. P., Røysamb, E., Neale, M. C., & Reichborn-Kjennerud, T. (2011). The structure of genetic and environmental risk factors for syndromal and subsyndromal common DSM-IV axis I and all axis II disorders. *American Journal of Psychiatry, 168*(1), 29–39.
Kernberg, O. F. (1975). *Borderline conditions and pathological narcissism.* Northvale, NJ: Jason Aronson.
Kernberg, O. F., & Michels, R. (2009). Borderline personality disorder. *The American Journal of Psychiatry, 166*(5), 505–508.
Kessler, R. C., Nelson, C. B., McGonagle, K. A., Edlund, M. J., Frank, R. G., & Leaf, P. J. (1996). The epidemiology of co-occurring addictive and mental disorders: Implications for prevention and service utilization. *American Journal of Orthopsychiatry, 66,* 17–31.
Kotov, R., Ruggero, C. J., Krueger, R. F., Watson, D., Qilong, Y., Zimmerman, M. (2011). New dimensions in the quantitative classification of mental illness. *Archives of General Psychiatry, 68,* 1003–1011.
Krizan, Z., & Johar, O. (2015). Narcissistic rage revisited. *Journal of Personality and Social Psychology, 108,* 784–801.
Krueger, R. F. (2013). Personality disorders are the vanguard of the post-DSM-5.0 era. *Personality Disorders: Theory, Research, and Treatment, 4,* 355–362.
Krueger, R. F., & Markon, K. E. (2014). The role of the DSM-5 personality trait model in moving toward a quantitative and empirically based approach to classifying personality and psychopathology. *Annual Review of Clinical Psychology, 10,* 477–501.
Krueger, R. F., Hicks, B. M., Patrick, C. J., Carlson, S. R., Iacono, W. G., & McGue, M. (2002). Etiologic connections among substance dependence, antisocial behavior, and personality: Modeling the externalizing spectrum. *Journal of Abnormal Psychology, 111,* 411–474.
Krueger, R. F., Markon, K. E., Patrick, C. J., Benning, S. D., & Kramer, M. D. (2007). Linking antisocial behavior, substance use, and personality: An integrative quantitative model of the adult externalizing spectrum. *Journal of Abnormal Psychology, 116,* 645–666.
Lambe, S., Hamilton-Giachritsis, C., Garner, E., & Walker, J. (2016). The role of narcissism in aggression and violence: A systematic review. *Trauma, Violence, & Abuse, 17,* 1–22.
Lahey, B. B., Rathouz, P. J., Van Hulle, C., Urbano, R. C., Krueger, R. F., Applegate, B., Garriock, H. A., . . . Waldman, I. D. (2008). Testing structural models of DSM-IV symptoms of common forms of child and adolescent psychopathology. *Journal of Abnormal Child Psychopathology, 36,* 187–206.

Lenzenweger, M. F. (2008). Epidemiology of personality disorders. *Psychiatric Clinics of North America*, *31*, 395–403.

Lenzenweger, M. F., Lane, M. C., Loranger, A. W., & Kessler, R. C. (2007). DSM-IV personality disorders in the National Comorbidity Survey Replication. *Biological Psychiatry*, *62*, 553–564.

Lieb, K., Zanarini, M. C., Schmahl, C., Linehan, M. M., & Bohus, M. (2004). Borderline personality disorder. *Lancet*, *364*(9432), 453–461.

Lilienfeld, S. O., & Hess, T. H. (2001). Psychopathic personality traits and somatization: Sex differences and the mediating role of negative emotionality. *Journal of Psychopathology and Behavioral Assessment*, *23*(1), 11–24.

Links, P. S., Heslegrave, R., & van Reekum, R. (1999). Impulsivity: Core aspect of borderline personality disorder. *Journal of Personality Disorders*, *13*(1), 1–9.

Loney, B. R., Taylor, J., Butler, M. A., & Iacono, W. G. (2007). Adolescent psychopathy features: 6-year temporal stability and the prediction of externalizing symptoms during the transition to adulthood. *Aggressive Behavior*, *33*(3), 242–252.

Lynam, D. R. (1996). Early identification of chronic offenders: Who is the fledgling psychopath?. *Psychological Bulletin*, *120*, 209–234.

Lynam, D. R., & Miller, J. D. (2015). Psychopathy from a basic trait perspective: The utility of a five-factor model approach. *Journal of Personality*, *83*(6), 611–626.

Lynam, D. R., Caspi, A., Moffitt, T. E., Loeber, R., & Stouthamer-Loeber, M. (2007). Longitudinal evidence that psychopathy scores in early adolescence predict adult psychopathy. *Journal of Abnormal Psychology*, *116*, 155–165.

Mancke, F., Herpertz, S. C., & Bertsch, K. (2015). Aggression in borderline personality disorder: A multidimensional model. *Personality Disorders*, *6*(3), 278–291.

Marion, B. E., & Sellbom, M. (2011). An examination of gender-moderated test bias on the Levenson Self-Report Psychopathy Scale. *Journal of Personality Assessment*, *93*, 235–243.

Mattia, J. I., & Zimmerman, M. (2001). Epidemiology. In W. Livesley (Ed.), *Handbook of personality disorders: Theory, research, and treatment* (pp. 107–123). New York, NY: Guilford Press.

Matthies, S. D., & Philipsen, A. (2016). Comorbidity of personality disorders and adult attention deficit hyperactivity disorder (ADHD)—Review of recent findings. *Current Psychiatry Reports*, *18*, 1–7.

McClellan, D. S., Farabee, D., & Crouch, B. M. (1997). Early victimization, drug use, and criminality a comparison of male and female prisoners. *Criminal justice and behavior*, *24*, 455–476.

Millon, T. (1981). *Disorders of personality: DSM III: Axis II*. Chichester, UK: John Wiley.

Millon, T. (1996). *Disorders of personality: DSM IV and beyond* (2nd ed.). Washington, DC: American Psychological Association.

Moffitt, T. E. (1993). Adolescence-limited and life-course-persistent antisocial behavior: A developmental taxonomy. *Psychological Review*, *100*, 674–701.

Mokros, A., Hare, R. D., Neumann, C. S., Santtila, P., Habermeyer, E., & Nitschke, J. (2015). Variants of psychopathy in adult male offenders: A latent profile analysis. *Journal of Abnormal Psychology*, *124*, 372–386.

Morey, L. C., Benson, K. T., & Skodol, A. E. (2016). Relating DSM-5 section III personality traits to section II personality disorder diagnoses. *Psychological Medicine*, *46*(3), 647–655.

Neumann, C. S., & Hare, R. D. (2008). Psychopathic traits in a large community sample: links to violence, alcohol use, and intelligence. *Journal of Consulting and Clinical Psychology*, *76*(5), 893–899.

Newhill, C. E., Vaughn, M. G., & DeLisi, M. (2010). Psychopathy scores reveal heterogeneity among patients with borderline personality disorder. *Journal of Forensic Psychiatry and Psychology*, *21*(2), 202–220.

Oldham, J. M., Skodol, A. E., Kellman, D., Hyler, S. E., Rosnick, L., Davies, M. (1992). Diagnosis of DSM-III-R personality disorders by two semi-structured interviews: Patterns of comorbidity. *American Journal of Psychiatry*, *149*, 213–220.

O'Malley, G. K., McHugh, L., Mac Giollabhui, N., & Bramham, J. (2016). Characterizing adult attention-deficit/hyperactivity-disorder and comorbid borderline personality disorder: ADHD symptoms, psychopathology, cognitive functioning and psychosocial factors. *European Psychiatry*, *31*, 29–36.

Otway, L. J., & Vignoles, V. L. (2006). Narcissism and childhood recollections: A quantitative test of psychoanalytic predictions. *Personality and Social Psychology Bulletin*, *32*, 104–116.

Patrick, C. J., & Drislane, L. E. (2015). Triarchic model of psychopathy: Origins, operationalizations, and observed linkages with personality and general psychopathology. *Journal of Personality, 82*(6), 627–643.

Patrick, C. J., Fowles, D. C., & Krueger, R. F. (2009). Triarchic conceptualization of psychopathy: Developmental origins of disinhibition, boldness, and meanness. *Development and Psychopathology, 21*(03), 913–938.

Perez-Rodriguez, M. M., Hazlett, E. A., Rich, E. L., Ripoll, L. H., Weiner, D. M., Spence, N., . . . New, A. S. (2012). Striatal activity in borderline personality disorder with comorbid intermittent explosive disorder: Sex differences. *Journal of Psychiatric Research, 46*(6), 797–804.

Philipsen, A., Limberger, M. F., Lieb, K., Feige, B., Kleindienst, N., Ebner-Priemer, U., . . . Bohus, M. (2008). Attention-deficit hyperactivity disorder as a potentially aggravating factor in borderline personality disorder. *British Journal of Psychiatry, 192*(2), 118–123.

Phillips, T. R., Sellbom, M., Ben-Porath, Y. S., & Patrick, C. J. (2014). Further development and construct validation of MMPI-2-RF indices of global psychopathy, fearless-dominance, and impulsive-antisociality in a sample of incarcerated women. *Law and Human Behavior, 28*, 34–46.

Pincus, A. L., & Lukowitsky, M. R. (2010). Pathological narcissism and narcissistic personality disorder. *Annual Review of Clinical Psychology, 6*, 421–446.

Pincus, A. L., Cain, N. M., & Wright, A. G. C. (2014). Narcissistic grandiosity and narcissistic vulnerability in psychotherapy. *Personality Disorders: Theory, Research, and Treatment, 5*, 439–443.

Quinton, D., Pickles, A., Maughan, B., & Rutter, M. (1993). Partners, peers, and pathways: Assortative pairing and continuities in conduct disorder. *Development and Psychopathology, 5*, 763–783.

Reijntjes, A., Vermande, M., Thomaes, S., Goossens, F., Olthof, T., Aleva, L., & Van der Meulen, M. (2015). Narcissism, bullying, and social dominance in youth: A longitudinal analysis. *Journal of Abnormal Child Psychology, 44*, 63–74.

Roberts, B. W., & DelVecchio, W. F. (2000). The rank-order consistency of personality traits from childhood to old age: a quantitative review of longitudinal studies. *Psychological Bulletin, 126*, 3–25.

Roberts, B. W., Kuncel, N. R., Shiner, R., Caspi, A., & Goldberg, L. R. (2007). The power of personality: The comparative validity of personality traits, socioeconomic status, and cognitive ability for predicting important life outcomes. *Perspectives on Psychological Science, 2*(4), 313–345.

Robins, L. N., & Price, R. K. (1991). Adult disorders predicted by childhood conduct problems: results from the NIMH Epidemiologic Catchment Area project. *Psychiatry, 54*(2), 116–132.

Robins, L. N., Tipp, J., & Przybeck, T. (1991). Antisocial personality. In L. N. Robins & D. Regier (Eds.), *Psychiatric disorders in America* (pp. 258–290). New York, NY: The Free Press.

Ronningstam, E. (1996). Pathological narcissism and narcissistic personality disorder in Axis I disorders. *Harvard Review of Psychiatry, 3*, 326–340.

Rothbart, M. K., & Ahadi, S. A. (1994). Temperament and the development of personality. *Journal of Abnormal Psychology, 103*(1), 55–66.

Sansone, R., & Sansone, L. (2011a). Gender patterns in borderline personality disorder. *Innovations in Clinical Neuroscience, 8*(5), 16–20.

Sansone, R., & Sansone, L. (2011b). Sexual behavior in borderline personality disorder: A review. *Innovations in Clinical Neuroscience, 8*(2), 14–18.

Sebastian, A., Jacob, G., Lieb, K., & Tüscher, O. (2013). Impulsivity in borderline personality disorder: A matter of disturbed impulse control or a facet of emotional dysregulation? *Current Psychiatry Reports, 15*(2), 339. doi:10.1007/s11920-012-0339-y

Sellbom, M. (2016). Elucidating the validity of the externalizing spectrum of psychopathology in correctional, forensic, and community samples. *Journal of Abnormal Psychology, 125*(8), 1027–1038.

Sellbom, M., Lilienfeld, S. O., Fowler, K., & McCrary, K. L. (in press). Self-Report Assessment of Psychopathy: Challenges, Pitfalls, and Promises. To appear in C. J. Patrick (Ed.), *Handbook of Psychopathy* (2nd ed.). New York, NY: Guilford Press.

Shiner, R. L. (2009). The development of personality disorders: Perspectives from normal personality development in childhood and adolescence. *Development and Psychopathology, 21*, 715–734.

Skodol, A. E. (2012). Personality disorders in DSM-5. *Annual Review of Clinical Psychology, 8*, 317–344.

Skodol, A. E., Gunderson, J. G., Pfohl, B., Widiger, T. A., Livesley, W. J., & Siever, L. J. (2002). The borderline diagnosis I: Psychopathology, comorbidity, and personality structure. *Biological Psychiatry, 51*, 936–950.

Skodol, A. E., Siever, L. J., Livesley, W. J., Gunderson, J. G., Pfohl, B., & Widiger, T. A. (2002). The borderline diagnosis II: Biology, genetics, and clinical course. *Biological Psychiatry*, *51*(12), 951–963.

Smith, T. E., & Samuel, D. B. (2017). A multi-method examination of the links between ADHD and personality disorder. *Journal of Personality Disorders*, *31*(1), 36–48.

Stepp, S. D., Burke, J. D., Hipwell, A. E., & Loeber, R. (2012). Trajectories of attention deficit hyperactivity disorder and oppositional defiant disorder symptoms as precursors of borderline personality disorder symptoms in adolescent girls. *Journal of Abnormal Child Psychology*, *40*(1), 7–20.

Stinson, F. S., Dawson, D. A., Goldstein, R. B., Chou, S. P., Huang, B., Smith, S. M., . . . Grant, B. F. (2008). Prevalence, correlates, disability, and comorbidity of DSM-IV narcissistic personality disorder: Results from the Wave 2 national epidemiologic survey on alcohol and related conditions. *The Journal of Clinical Psychiatry*, *69*, 1033–1045.

Storebo, O., & Simonsen, E. (2014). Is ADHD an early stage in the development of borderline personality disorder? *Journal of Psychiatry*, *68*(5), 289–295.

Strand, S., & Belfrage, H. (2005). Gender differences in psychopathy in a Swedish offender sample. *Behavioral Sciences & the Law*, *23*(6), 837–850.

Thomaes, S., Bushman, B. J., Stegge, H., & Olthof, T. (2008). Trumping shame by blasts of noise: Narcissism, self-esteem, shame, and aggression in young adolescents. *Child Development*, *79*, 1792–1801.

Torgersen, S., Kringlen, E., & Cramer, V. (2001). The prevalence of personality disorders in a community sample. *Archives of General Psychiatry*, *58*, 590–596.

Triebwasser, J., Chemerinski, E., Roussos, P., & Siever, L. J. (2013). Paranoid personality disorder. *Journal of Personality Disorders*, *27*(6), 795–805.

Trull, T. J., Sher, K. J., Minks-Brown, C., Durbin, J., & Burr, R. (2000). Borderline personality disorder and substance use disorders: A review and integration. *Clinical Psychology Review*, *20*(2), 235–253.

Warren, J. I., Burnette, M., South, S. C., Chauhan, P., Bale, R., & Friend, R. (2002). Personality disorders and violence among female prison inmates. *Journal of the American Academy of Psychiatry and the Law Online*, *30*, 502–509.

Washburn, J. J., McMahon, S. D., King, C. A., Reinecke, M. A., & Silver, C. (2004). Narcissistic features in young adolescents: Relations to aggression and internalizing symptoms. *Journal of Youth and Adolescence*, *33*, 247–260.

Waxman, R., Fenton, M. C., Skodol, A. E., Grant, B. F., & Hasin, D. (2014). Childhood maltreatment and personality disorders in the USA: Specificity of effects and the impact of gender. *Personality and Mental Health*, *8*, 30–41.

Wetterborg, D., Långström, N., Andersson, G., & Enebrink, P. (2015). Borderline personality disorder: Prevalence and psychiatric comorbidity among male offenders on probation in Sweden. *Comprehensive Psychiatry*, *62*, 63–70.

White, G. L., & Mullen, P. E. (1989). *Jealousy: Theory, research, and clinical strategies*. New York: Guilford Press.

Winsper, C., Lereya, S. T., Marwaha, S., Thompson, A., Eyden, J., & Singh, S. P. (2016). The aetiological and psychopathological validity of borderline personality disorder in youth: A systematic review and meta-analysis. *Clinical Psychology Review*, *44*, 13–24.

Wright, A. G., Thomas, K. M., Hopwood, C. J., Markon, K. E., Pincus, A. L., & Krueger, R. F. (2012). The hierarchical structure of DSM-5 pathological personality traits. *Journal of Abnormal Psychology*, *121*(4), 951–957.

Wygant, D. B., Sellbom, M., Sleep, C. E., Wall, T. D., Applegate, K. C., Krueger, R. F., & Patrick, C. J. (2016). Examining the DSM-5 alternative personality disorder model operationalization of antisocial personality disorder and psychopathy in a male correctional sample. *Personality Disorders: Theory, Research, & Practice*, *7*(3), 229–239.

Zanarini, M. C., Williams, A. A., Lewis, R. E., & Reich, R. B. (1997). Reported pathological childhood experiences associated with the development of borderline personality disorder. *The American Journal of Psychiatry*, *154*, 1101–1106.

Zimmerman, M., Rothschild, L., & Chelminski, I. (2005). The prevalence of DSM-IV personality disorders in psychiatric outpatients. *The American Journal of Psychiatry*, *162*, 1911–1918.

Zimmerman, M., Chelminski, I., & Young, D. (2008). The frequency of personality disorders in psychiatric patients. *Psychiatric Clinics of North America*, *31*, 405–420.

Part 3
Etiological and Maintenance Factors
Child-Level Factors

8

Genetic and Gene–Environment Influences on Disruptive Behavior Disorders

Edward D. Barker, Charlotte A. M. Cecil, Esther Walton, and Alan J. Meehan

Understanding the etiology of a disorder is an important step in developing and implementing effective prevention and intervention strategies (Tremblay, 2010). Like most complex phenotypes, disruptive behavior disorders (DBDs), such as conduct disorder (CD) and oppositional defiant disorder (ODD), have been found to reflect both genetic and environmental influences. Our goal in this chapter is to provide an overview of these influences on the manifestation of DBDs in children and adolescents, with a focus on CD and ODD. We also include research that has examined related phenotypes, such as physical aggression, conduct problems, and callous-unemotional (CU) traits. We first cover twin designs, which allow an estimation of the degree to which DBDs reflect genetic and environmental components. Next we review molecular genetic approaches—including candidate gene (hypothesis-driven) and genome-wide (hypothesis-free) studies. Finally, we examine studies of gene–environment interplay. We close with a discussion on current challenges and propose three key ways to move the area forward in the future.

This chapter is not an exhaustive review of DBDs. We refer the reader to recent high-quality reviews on genetic and environmental influences underlying CD (Salvatore & Dick, 2016), externalizing psychopathology including CD, ODD and attention deficit hyperactivity disorder (Veroude et al., 2016), and aggression (Fernàndez-Castillo & Cormand, 2016).

Heritability of DBDs

The twin design uses data from siblings who differ in 'genetic relatedness' in order to disentangle and quantify the respective contributions that genes and environment make to complex disorders like DBDs. More specifically, the classical twin study compares phenotypic resemblances of monozygotic (MZ) and dizygotic (DZ) twins. MZ twins derive from a single fertilized egg (zygote) and are therefore genetically identical. In contrast, DZ twins derive from two distinct fertilized eggs, and consequently share around half of their genetic material (like non-twin siblings). If genetic influence is important for a given trait, the genetically identical MZ pairs must therefore be more similar in levels of that trait than DZ twins. The correlation between phenotypes (e.g., CD, ODD) of MZ twins encompasses additive genetic factors (a^2 or h^2; the influence on a trait stemming from one or more gene loci), common environmental factors (c^2; environmental influence that both twins experience), and the non-shared environment (e^2), which also includes measurement error. Genetic influences can also be non-additive (d^2), which can reflect epistasis variation (interaction between different loci to influence a trait in a nonadditive way). Of interest, one can also estimate the proportion of a correlation (r) between two phenotypes (e.g. ODD and CD) that is due to a^2, c^2, and e^2. Twin studies that have examined DBDs have varied widely in terms of the age range, sample characteristics, and comorbidities examined. We begin by considering studies that have focused on DBDs in early childhood and adolescence. We then cover studies that have assessed the genetic and environmental overlaps of CD and ODD. Last, we discuss the inclusion of DBDs in general factors of psychopathology, also known as syndromes.

DBDs in Childhood and Adolescence

Surprisingly, the heritability coefficient for aggression among 3-year-olds is 69% (van den Oord, Verhulst, & Boomsma, 1996) and for conduct problems among 5-year-olds is 82% (Arseneault et al., 2003). Thus, according to these studies, heritability estimates for DBDs in young children is high. The heritability of DBDs appears to stay high after childhood as well. For example, a recent study by Porsch et al. (2016) compared genetic contributions in the variation and stability of aggressive behaviors and conduct problems in two large twin cohorts from the Netherlands and the United Kingdom, between 7 and 12 years of age. In studies, the year-to-year stability of heritability was high (50–80% for the Netherlands, and ~60% UK). Another twin study examined genetic influence on the developmental course (i.e., initial levels and subsequent increases or decreases) in conduct problems in 10,038 twin pairs between ages 4 and 16 (Pingault, Rijsdijk, Zheng, Plomin, & Viding, 2015). These researchers reported strong genetic influence for baseline levels (78%) and the developmental course (73%). Lacourse et al. (2014) similarly reported that the developmental course of physical aggression in early childhood through mid childhood was strongly influenced by the genetic factors, but that the genetic factors after childhood were different from those in childhood, perhaps because new types of environmental influences emerge later on (such as peer groups).

DBDs: ODD and CD

Twin studies examining both ODD and CD suggest that, based on the relative contribution of genetic and environmental influences, the two disorders are both highly related but can also have distinct genetic and environmental influences. For example, Singh and Waldman (2010) focused on ODD and CD symptoms in 4–17-year-olds, as reported by parents. Although the additive heritability was roughly the same (~50%) for ODD and CD, non-additive factors (i.e., d^2) were found underlying CD but not ODD. Bornovalova, Hicks, Iacono, and McGue (2010) examined ODD and CD in a large sample of twins age 11. A higher heritability (0.73_{ODD} vs 0.51_{CD}) was found for ODD vs. CD, whereas the common environment was similar but significant only for CD (0.24_{CD} vs. 0.30_{ODD}). Moreover, research has been mixed with regards to sex differences; it has been suggested that both the genetic and non-shared environmental influences in CD are higher for girls than boys (Tuvblad, Zheng, Raine, & Baker, 2009), whereas Anckarsäter et al. (2011) reported that both ODD and CD are more influenced by genetic factors in boys than girls.

Considering the high rate of comorbidity between ODD and CD, it is of interest to investigate genetic and environmental influences in the association between the two disorders. Using data from 1,446 female, adolescent twin pairs, Knopik et al. (2014) reported genetic influence on both disorders, with stronger effects on ODD (60%) compared to CD (28%). Importantly, they found a genetic correlation between ODD and CD of 0.52, meaning that 27% of the genetic variance in ODD was accounted for by genetic influences on CD, and vice versa.

DBDs as Part of the Externalizing Syndrome

Given that many externalizing problems, such as ODD, CD, and attention deficit hyperactivity disorder (ADHD) often co-occur, research has tested the degree to which these problems can be classified together under the rubric of externalizing disorders. The main idea is that etiologic commonalities should be a major consideration in classifying psychopathologies (Krueger, Markon, Patrick, & Iacono, 2005). Based on 2,750 adolescent twin and sibling pairs, Cosgrove et al. (2011) reported that a single externalizing factor, encompassing ODD, CD, and ADHD, was explained mainly by common additive genetic factors (65%) followed by non-shared environmental influences (35%). Similarly, Tuvblad et al. (2009) examined 1,219 twins age 9 and 10 and also reported that ODD, CD, and ADHD could be fit to a single externalizing spectrum. These researchers, however, reported that specific genetic and environmental influences still remained after accounting for the genetic and environmental commonalities. The authors interpreted these findings as suggesting that these disorders still maintain a degree of etiological independence, which may potentially reflect the influence of distinct genes.

Genetic Studies and DBDs

Although twin studies can be used as an indication of genetic influence, specific genes are not elucidated. Candidate genes studies make up the majority of research on the molecular architecture of ODD and CD. The selection of genes has been typically based on a-priori hypotheses, informed by empirical evidence regarding their biological function. The two most commonly investigated types of genetic variability are *single-nucleotide polymorphisms* (SNPs) and *variable number tandem repeats* (VNTRs). An SNP is a variation within a single nucleotide at a specific genomic location. A VNTR is also a type of genetic variation, but it occurs within a short nucleotide *sequence* as opposed to a single base pair. VNTRs are organized as tandem repeats (the length of which can vary between individuals in a population), each representing a different allele.

Candidate Genes

MAOA   The most consistent genetic association to emerge from candidate studies on DBDs involves the monoamine oxidase-A (*MAOA*) gene (Ficks & Waldman, 2014). This gene is located on the X chromosome and encodes a major enzyme that breaks down dopamine and serotonin, as well as other monoamine neurotransmitters (e.g., norepinephrine). In humans, the promoter region of *MAOA* contains a 30-base pair VNTR sequence giving rise to a *low*-activity allele—which produces less *MAOA* enzyme—and a *high*-activity allele, which instead causes the gene to be transcribed more efficiently. Studies on *MAOA* variability have typically focused on CD and aggression. For example, longitudinal studies have found that the low-activity *MAOA* allele predicts higher CD symptoms during adolescence and antisocial behavior in adulthood, including rates of arrest, incarceration, and number of violent offences (Beaver et al., 2013; Ouellet-Morin et al., 2016). Consistent with this, a recent meta-analysis of 31 studies reported that the low-activity *MAOA* allele is modestly but significantly associated with higher aggression and antisocial behavior (Ficks & Waldman, 2014). Interestingly, associations are thought to relate more to reactive/impulsive aggression, as opposed to proactive aggression and CU traits (Beaver et al., 2013). However, it is important to note that several studies report null findings (Vassos, Collier, & Fazel, 2014). Inconsistencies may stem from a number of factors, including X-linked dosage compensation effects in females, which may explain why studies looking at females have produced particularly inconsistent findings (González-Tapia & Obsuth, 2015).

COMT Another enzyme that metabolizes dopamine and other catecholamines (e.g., epinephrine, norepinephrine) is Catechol-O-methyltransferase (*COMT*).

Associations with ODD in the context of CD and ADHD have been reported (Iofrida, Palumbo, & Pellegrini, 2014; Waltes, Chiocchetti, & Freitag, 2016). For example, the low-activity allele has been found to associate with higher levels of ODD and CD symptoms in children (Caspi et al., 2008), and aggression in adults (Singh, Volavka, Czobor, & Van Dorn, 2012). Interestingly, it has been shown that—among children with ADHD—the effect of *COMT* Val158Met polymorphism on levels of aggression is mediated by socio-emotional functioning and impaired fear-related mechanisms (van Goozen et al., 2016). As with *MAOA*, however, studies have typically focused exclusively on males, and null findings have also been reported (Iofrida et al., 2014).

Other Dopaminergic Pathway Genes

The dopamine transporter gene *SLC6A3* (also known as *DAT1*) that regulates dopamine reuptake has received considerable attention due to its observed association with impulsivity. In particular, a 9-repeat VNTR in this gene has been found to associate with a range of externalizing problems, including childhood aggression, delinquent behavior, affiliation with delinquent peers, drug use and other risky behaviors (Guo, Cai, Guo, Wang, & Harris, 2010; Young et al., 2002). We note that other studies have reported negative findings (Zai et al., 2012).

Dopamine receptor genes (*DRD1* through to *DRD5*) play an important role in dopaminergic transmission in the brain, by regulating the density of dopamine receptors on neurons as well as affecting dopamine synthesis, storage, and release into the synaptic cleft. *DRD2* has been associated with early-onset and pervasive aggression in children (Zai et al., 2012), serious and violent delinquency in males (but not females) in a large sample of youth (Guo, Roettger, & Shih, 2007), and greater physical aggression in young adults—a relationship that was mediated by higher sensation-seeking (Chester et al., 2016). With regard to *DRD4*, genetic variants that confer a low-activity enzyme have been associated with more severe ODD behavior in children with autism spectrum disorder (Gadow, Devincent, Olvet, Pisarevskaya, & Hatchwell, 2010) and higher delinquency in adolescents (Hohmann et al., 2009). When examined together, an interaction between *DRD2* and *DRD4* predicted risk for CD in a sample of children with comorbid ADHD (Mota et al., 2013).

Serotonergic Pathway Genes

Serotonergic transmission is hypothesized to relate to the affective processing and punishment sensitivity features of externalizing behaviors (Matthys, Vanderschuren, & Schutter, 2013). The majority of molecular genetic studies in this area have examined the *SLC6A4* gene (also known as *5-HTT* and *SERT*), which plays a key role in the transport and re-uptake of serotonin from the synaptic cleft to the presynaptic neuron. *5-HTTLPR* has two main variations—a short ("s"; 14-repeats) allele vs. a long ("l"; 16-repeats) allele (Iofrida et al., 2014).

At a behavioral level, the short allele has been found to associate with higher aggression in school-age children (Haberstick, Smolen, & Hewitt, 2006); extreme and persistent aggression in clinically referred children (Beitchman et al., 2006) and CD in adolescents undergoing treatment for serious substance and behavior problems (Sakai et al., 2006). However, associations between externalizing behaviors and the long allele have also been reported (e.g., Åslund et al., 2013), as well as non-replications (Vassos et al., 2014). Besides *5-HTT*, there is also some evidence for serotonin receptor genes having a role in externalizing behaviors (e.g., Hakulinen et al., 2013).

Neuroendocrine System

The neuroendocrine system, which mediates stress response through hormone production, has also been implicated in DBDs. In particular, studies have focused on vasopressin and oxytocin as they are thought to play a key role in complex social behaviors, including attachment, emotional recognition, empathy, and prosociality. Severe and persistent childhood aggression has been found to associate with genetic polymorphisms in both the vasopressin receptor genes *AVPR1A* (Malik et al., 2014) and *AVPR1B* (Luppino, Moul, Hawes, Brennan, & Dadds, 2014). Variation in the oxytocin receptor gene *OXTR* has also received considerable attention, with studies reporting associations with early-onset aggression (Malik et al., 2014), CU traits in children, and delinquency in male adolescents across two large independent samples (Hovey et al., 2016).

Genome-Wide and Polygenic Studies

Over time, it has become increasingly clear that the genetic architecture of DBDs is highly complex and likely to reflect many genetic variants with small effects, so that candidate gene studies may only provide limited insight into the pathophysiology of complex traits (Dick et al., 2015). With the decrease in genotyping cost over the past decade, it has become increasingly possible to conduct association tests across the entire genome. In these genome-wide association studies (GWASs) hundreds of thousands to millions of SNPs are genotyped and analyzed in a hypothesis-free way, allowing for the identification of previously unconsidered genetic variants.

Few published GWASs have targeted DBDs. Anney et al. (2008) examined three measures of conduct problems in 1,043,963 genetic markers. No loci met genome-wide statistical significance, although 54 markers reached a level of suggestive significance, one of which, *PAWR*, is involved in the regulation of dopamine receptor signalling. Using retrospectively reported DSM-IV CD criteria in 4,816 individuals, Dick et al. (2011) reported that four SNPs (on chromosomes 4, 11 and 13) associated with CD after genome-wide correction, two of which are located in the gene *C1QTNF7* (C1q and tumor necrosis factor-related protein 7). Tielbeek et al. (2012) used data based on 4,816 individuals from the Australian Twin Registry to examine two measures of conduct problems. No genetic variants met genome-wide significance, with the strongest association implicating the tyrosine-phosphorylation-regulated kinase 1A (*DYRK1A*) gene. The authors also checked a list of candidate genes (e.g., *DRD1, DRD4, DRD4, 5-HTTPLR, COMT, MAOA*), with none reaching nominal level of significance ($p < 0.05$). In a sample of 18,988 children from nine different cohorts that comprise the EAGLE consortium, Pappa et al. (2016) used a meta-analysis and identified "suggestive" evidence for SNP rs11126630, located near *LRRTM4* (involved in excitatory synapse development) and *SNAR-H* (implicated in transcriptional processes). Pappa et al. also examined a list of 22 candidate genes previously associated with DBDs, and indicated an association with *AVPR1A*. Finally, Viding et al. (2013) examined genetic contributions to CU traits, using behavioral and molecular genetic analyses. While they identified substantial heritability of CU traits in their twin-based analyses (>60%), no significant polymorphisms emerged from the genome-wide analysis.

To increase power to detect small genetic effects, some studies have used a "polygenic risk score," which captures the *additive* contribution of genetic variants to a phenotype of interest.

Salvatore et al. (2015) found that, while no single polymorphism reached genome-wide significance, the polygenic risk score (a sum of all nominally significant loci) accounted for 6% of the variance in externalizing disorder. In addition to exerting a significant main effect, this polygenic risk score also interacted with environmental factors, such as peer substance use, to predict CD severity. Interestingly, another study found that polygenic risk for ADHD was strongest in subjects who had co-occurring CD compared to those without, suggesting pleiotropic genetic influence (Hamshere et al., 2013).

Genome-Environment Interaction Studies

Isolating genes that have a "main effect" on DBDs has proven difficult, and these genes typically only explain a small fraction of heritability that is estimated by twin studies. Gene–environment (G×E) interactions occur when an environmental influence on a trait or phenotype is dependent on an individual's genotype, or when an individual's genetic predispositions are expressed differently under distinct environmental conditions (Caspi & Moffitt, 2006). Theoretical underpinnings of G×E have most often been articulated within the *diathesis–stress* model, whereby genetic vulnerability (or diathesis) for phenotype is activated or exacerbated in the presence of certain environmental stressors. Conversely, *differential susceptibility* theory (Belsky et al., 2009) posits that 'risk' genes confer behavioral plasticity, such that the presence of a supportive environment can also confer *greater* benefits for "risk" carriers compared to non-carriers.

G×E: MAOA With regard to ODD, one study examined the potential interaction between *MAOA* and harsh parenting for the ODD subdimension of irritable opposition. Here it was observed that, for boys, increased irritable opposition was associated with harsh parenting, but this association was not moderated by *MAOA* (Whelan, Kretschmer, & Barker, 2014). One of the first G × E findings (Caspi et al., 2002) reported that male children with a history of maltreatment and a low-activity *MAOA* genotype were more likely to develop antisocial problems, including CD, antisocial personality disorder and violent crime in adulthood, compared to maltreated high-activity genotype carriers. Subsequent studies have replicated this finding, with meta-analyses reporting a small to medium effect size (Kim-Cohen et al., 2006). However, certain studies have failed to reproduce this interaction (Young et al., 2006). Risk environments implicated in this G×E interaction for the low-activity *MAOA* genotype have subsequently been extended to include parental physical/sexual abuse (Ouellet-Morin et al., 2016) and social exclusion (Gallardo-Pujol, Andrés-Pueyo, & Maydeu-Olivares, 2013), suggesting that it involves a wider conceptualization of "adversity" compared to the original study. In contrast, however, Lee (2011) found that among carriers of the *high*-activity *MAOA* genotype, deviant peer affiliation associated with aggressive behavior more robustly. Finally, while findings have been used to suggest a *diathesis–stress* model, there is evidence that low-activity *MAOA* offers protective effects, such that it may convey *differential susceptibility* depending on the environment. For example, with regard to marital status, married male offenders were more likely to desist from crime when carrying the low-activity vs. the high-activity allele (Beaver, Wright, DeLisi, & Vaughn, 2008).

G×E: Dopamine Genes ODD features in a handful of G×E studies of the dopaminergic system, mainly through somewhat tangential findings. A secondary finding in a study of ADHD by Martel et al. (2011) also showed that homozygosity for the *DRD4* ne120-bp tandem repeat insertion allele increased vulnerability for ODD, though only in the presence of inconsistent parenting. In another ADHD study, additional analysis of ODD symptoms by

Langley et al. (2008) found interaction effects for both maternal smoking and birth weight as a function of *DRD5* genotype. Testing the interaction between *COMT* Val158Met polymorphism and socioeconomic status on ADHD/CD development from age 10–14 years, Nobile et al. (2010) included ODD as a phenotypic outcome. However, no significant interactions, or indeed direct gene associations, were observed. With regard to CD, predictive associations between parenting at 4–6 years of age and child CD symptoms 5–8 years later varied as a function of the 9r allele of the *DAT1* 3' VNTR (Lahey et al., 2011). The association between negative *and* positive parenting and later CD was stronger among children with two copies of the 9r allele compared to other genotypes. Elsewhere, *DAT1* was predictive of chronic antisocial behavior only for youth who had few delinquent peers (Vaughn, DeLisi, Beaver, & Wright, 2009). For *DRD2*, those with the A2/A2 genotype were more vulnerable to low parental support and consequently developed more delinquent behavior (Chhangur et al., 2015). Elsewhere, having a criminal father interacted with the *DRD2* A1 allele to predict greater violent delinquency among a sample of African American females (DeLisi, Beaver, Vaughn, & Wright, 2009). For *DRD4*, greater aggression has been observed in *DRD4* 7r carriers raised in disadvantaged socioeconomic circumstances (Nobile et al., 2007). Furthermore, in a preschool sample, while all children showed more aggressive behavior when peer aggression was high regardless of genotype, those carrying a long *DRD4* allele (6–8 repeats), compared to short allele carriers (2–4 repeats), were more aggressive during peer-play where peer aggression levels were low (DiLalla, Elam, & Smolen, 2009). Conversely, Kretschmer, Dijkstra, Ormel, Verhulst, and Veenstra (2013) found that adolescents *without* the 7r allele, rather than carriers, were more susceptible to the effects of both victimization and positive peer experiences on later delinquency. While the outlined *DRD4* and *DRD2* alleles have been characterized as "risk alleles," it is interesting to note that a study of adolescents with histories of criminal offences found that those carrying these polymorphisms who were exposed to low-risk family environments showed later criminal onset than non-carriers (DeLisi, Beaver, Wright, & Vaughn, 2008). In conjunction with other findings (e.g. DiLalla et al., 2009), this implies that so-called 'risk' polymorphisms may enhance environmental sensitivity, in line with *differential susceptibility* theory. Longitudinal data from a preventive intervention project supported this argument: carriers of at least one copy of the *DRD4* 7r allele who were exposed to intervention showed a decline in aggressive behaviors (Schlomer et al., 2015). *COMT* is less studied with regard to DBDs. Previously, in a high-risk clinical ADHD group, the impact of lower birth weight on risk of early-onset antisocial behavior was highest for the val/val *COMT* genotype (Thapar et al., 2005). Wagner et al. (2010) also showed that female border personality disorder (BPD) patients carrying the Val158Val genotype, who had experienced childhood physical or sexual maltreatment, manifested greater impulsive aggression than non-carriers.

GxE: Serotonin Genes In a study of GxE for a range of phenotypic outcomes using polymorphisms of *5-HTTLPR*, dopamine genes and *MAOA*, Lavigne et al. (2013) reported that the long (*l/l*) form of *5-HTTLPR*, compared to short forms (*s/s, s/l*), was associated with increased ODD symptoms in combination with family stress. At the same time, no interaction was observed with family conflict, caretaker depression, or socioeconomic status. These findings contrast with CD research, where short forms of the allele generally confer greater risk, suggesting the potential for novel and divergent results in GxE of ODD compared to other DBDs. Elsewhere, the *s*-allele of the *5-HTTLPR* genotype has been found to moderate the pathway between self-blame for parental conflict and ODD symptoms (Martel, Nikolas, Jernigan, Friderici, & Nigg, 2012). It was inferred from this that this low-functioning allele represented a biological vulnerability for psychopathology following exposure to interparental conflict via higher neuroticism, which partially accounted for this pathway.

Other studies examining 5–HTTLPR report an association between the s-allele and higher antisocial behavior as a result of exposure to adversity in childhood (Cicchetti, Rogosch, & Thibodeau, 2012). In a latent class analysis of antisocial behavior, maltreated girls homozygous for the s-allele (s/s) were twelve times more likely to belong to an "exclusive covert antisocial behavior" group compared to a non-antisocial group (Li & Lee, 2010). Sonuga-Barke et al. (2009) reported that boys who carried a short 5-HTTLPR allele (s/s or s/l) were more responsive to maternal emotion, such that maternal hostility produced elevated levels of conduct problems. However, no such association was evidenced for l/l genotypes. This effect was also strongest when the susceptibility alleles of *both* 5-HTTLPR and *DAT1* were carried.

G×E: Other Genes Significant G×E effects have emerged for further genes. Recently, a significant prospective interaction was reported whereby carriers of the G allele of the oxytocin receptor gene (*OXTR*) rs53576 polymorphism who experienced social stress exhibited higher levels of antisocial behavior compared to A allele carriers (Smearman, Winiarski, Brennan, Najman, & Johnson, 2015). Kretschmer, Vitaro, and Barker (2014) reported that the association between deviant peer affiliation in late childhood and adolescent aggressive behavior was greater in carriers of the met-met variant of the *BDNF* genotype, compared to Val/Val homozygote carriers. *BDNF* has been discussed as a moderator of the HPA axis, the pathway that regulates responses to stress.

Limitations of Approaches

Each method reviewed here for examining genetic influence has limitations that are important to bear in mind when interpreting study results. For example, while twin studies can estimate general genetic and environmental influences, and even the potential presence of G×E (Caspi et al., 2002), the exact genes and environments are not elucidated. Although results of twin studies have been fruitfully used as a basis for exploring molecular genetic influence on a trait (Kim-Cohen et al., 2006), twin analyses also have many assumptions, some of which may affect heritability estimates by enhancing the similarities of MZ vs. DZ twins. For example, the "equal environments" assumption postulates that MZ and DZ twins experience similar environments. However, some research suggests that parents, teachers, peers, and others may treat MZs more similarly than DZs—although this is an ongoing debate (Young et al., 2006). Candidate gene approaches (including G×E) have several limitations, three of which are mentioned here. First, a focus on a handful of candidate genes limits the ability to appreciate that more complex biological processes are likely to influence complex traits (Gallardo-Pujol et al., 2013). Second, there is a low replication rate among attempted direct replications of candidate gene studies. Indeed, while the majority of first studies of a candidate gene report positive findings, the proportion of positive replication attempts is much lower (McDermott, Dawes, Prom-Wormley, Eaves, & Hatemi, 2013; Ouellet-Morin et al., 2016). Weeland, Overbeek, de Castro, and Matthys (2015) stated that differences between G×E studies in terms of sample composition, conceptualizations, and power, make it difficult to determine if G×E findings are inconsistent or if the different study designs are simply incomparable. They suggested that one way to help inconsistent G×E findings is to develop a priori theory-driven research designs that could create more comparable findings. The third limitation is that, to date, few well-powered GWAS results have corroborated candidate gene findings, which are typically on smaller samples sizes. This has led to suggestion that false discovery rates in the G×E literature may be unacceptably high (Schwartz & Beaver, 2011). Conclusions drawn from GWAS designs can also have limitations. First, as with candidate genes, GWAS results are often not replicated by subsequent GWASs, pointing yet again toward the potential for false positives and the low validity of novel associations. For example, GWAS results for CD from Anney et al. (2008), Dick et al. (2011), and Pappa et al. (2016) showed low convergence, possibly due to differences in sample characteristics (e.g., sample size, age), the types of measures (e.g., psychiatric vs. non-diagnostic) and the types of analyses employed (e.g., meta-analyses vs. analysis of variance). Secondly, significant GWAS loci tend to additively explain only a small proportion of the heritability of complex traits, suggesting other genetic processes (e.g. rare loci, genetic mutations, epistatic relationships) might be overlooked. Last, a GWAS can involve testing up to millions of SNPs and the consideration of multiple comparisons is an essential part of determining statistical significance. The validity of genetic loci that do not pass the conservative GWAS correction levels is often not assessed. Of interest, Fernàndez-Castillo and Cormand (2016), using nominally significant loci from six GWAS studies examining DBDs (i.e., CD, ADHD, aggression, CU), performed a bioinformatics analysis that highlighted potential risk gene-pathways involved in neurodevelopmental processes, such as neuron projection and synaptic plasticity, not previously considered in candidate gene studies. Nominally significant GWAS loci might—under certain circumstances—be an important additional source of information for complex phenotypes.

Summary and Recommendations

This chapter highlights that different scientific methods (twin, candidate gene, genome-wide) converge on the idea that genes can influence complex traits such as DBDs. We have three suggestions that might further promote knowledge about the genetic basis of DBDs. First and foremost, we suggest that additional research on existing data resources is necessary for a better understanding of the genetic basic of ODD, which has received far less attention that CD. That is, researchers can (and should) utilize existing GWAS consortium data (e.g., EAGLE) to test hypothesis-free scans for complex traits, including ODD. More broadly, many longitudinal birth cohorts (such as the Avon Longitudinal Study of Parents and Children and Generation R) have collected extensive biological information and psychiatric phenotypes, which can be utilized by the international research community. These data resources have high potential value to early-career researchers seeking new data and career opportunities.

Second, taking into account risk environments in the context of investigating genetic influence on complex traits is necessary for an ecologically valid model. Indeed, the fact that "main effects" have not been identified in certain candidate and genome-wide approaches does not necessarily indicate that genes have no influence on the trait (Moffitt, Caspi, & Rutter, 2005). Theoretical models suggest that genes have evolved for different functions, depending on the nature of the experienced environment (Ellis & Boyce, 2008). The differential susceptibility framework states that genes do not only engender "susceptibility" or "vulnerability" to a psychiatric disease, but rather that these "vulnerable" individuals are more responsive to both positive and negative environmental conditions. Hence, genetic effects may depend on how well fit a person is to the environment in which he or she is raised. Examination of a range of social environments—especially with regard to positive or negative parenting strategies for children showing high rates of DBDs—may be of particular relevance to future genetically focused research (Belsky et al., 2009). Of note, environmental risk interactions can be incorporated into GWASs (Thomas, 2010). For example, an ADHD GWAS by Sonuga-Barke et al. (2008) assessed exploratory gene-environmental interactions with maternal warmth. One gene identified in this study (*A2BP1*) was also associated with CD in the GWAS study by Anney et al. (2008), described above.

Third, there is likely a large gap between candidate genes, or the top hits of a GWAS, and the manifestation of complex psychiatric traits (Waldman & Rhee, 2006). It is highly desirable to find a valid and meaningful intermediary construct between the genes and the complex trait. The term "endophenotype" is used to describe those intermediary constructs that are thought to underlie psychiatric disorders and to be more directly influenced by genes than the disorder itself (Gottesman & Gould, 2003). Endophenotypes are meant to be heritable, stable and observable in unaffected relatives of patients (i.e., whether or not the disorder is present). Executive functions such as attention, working memory, impulse control, organization and planning are all plausible neurodevelopmental mechanisms that could underlie childhood DBDs (Nigg, Blaskey, Huang-Pollock, & Rappley, 2002). The subdimensions of ODD (e.g., Irritability and Headstrong) may afford even more specific endophenotypes. For example, given that Irritability appears to have a genetically mediated association with depression (Stringaris, Zavos, Leibenluft, Maughan, & Eley, 2012), endophenotypes for depression may be of particular interest. In depression, brain-imaging endophenotypes encompass a broad range of neural structures (cortical and subcortical), as well as their connectivity and function (e.g., Hasler & Northoff, 2011). Future research should evaluate the relevance of these brain measures as potential endophenotypes for ODD and other DBDs.

Conclusion

In summary, existing twin research suggests that DBDs are under substantial genetic influence, but is somewhat mixed as to the degree of genetic control. While comorbid patterns between ODD and CD appear to be genetically mediated, these disorders also appear to feature distinct genetic and environmental influences. There is evidence that genes involved in neurotransmitter function may be involved in DBDs, but this research has mainly been hypothetically driven and focused around a handful of candidate genes, thus providing only limited insights into their genetic complexity. Novel genes have recently emerged through the use of GWAS studies, although the biological validity of these loci is in need of more research. Further studies should advance current findings by (a) making use of large longitudinal consortium data, (b) taking environmental factors into account, and (c) studying endophenotypes that are proximal to the underlying genetics of DBDs.

References

Anckarsäter, H., Lundström, S., Kollberg, L., Kerekes, N., Palm, C., Carlström, E., . . . Bölte, S. (2011). The child and adolescent twin study in Sweden (CATSS). *Twin Research and Human Genetics*, *14*(06), 495–508.

Anney, R. J. L., Lasky-Su, J., Ó'Dúshláine, C., Kenny, E., Neale, B. M., Mulligan, A., . . . Christiansen, H. (2008). Conduct disorder and ADHD: Evaluation of conduct problems as a categorical and quantitative trait in the international multicentre ADHD genetics study. *American Journal of Medical Genetics Part B: Neuropsychiatric Genetics*, *147*(8), 1369–1378.

Arseneault, L., Moffitt, T. E., Caspi, A., Taylor, A., Rijsdijk, F. V., Jaffee, S. R., . . . Measelle, J. R. (2003). Strong genetic effects on cross-situational antisocial behaviour among 5-year-old children according to mothers, teachers, examiner-observers, and twins' self-reports. *Journal of Child Psychology and Psychiatry*, *44*(6), 832–848.

Åslund, C., Comasco, E., Nordquist, N., Leppert, J., Oreland, L., & Nilsson, K. W. (2013). Self-reported family socioeconomic status, the 5-HTTLPR genotype, and delinquent behavior in a community-based adolescent population. *Aggressive Behavior*, *39*(1), 52–63. doi:10.1002/ab.21451

Beaver, K. M., Wright, J. P., DeLisi, M., & Vaughn, M. G. (2008). Desistance from delinquency: The marriage effect revisited and extended. *Social Science Research*, *37*(3), 736–752. doi:10.1016/j.ssresearch.2007.11.003

Beaver, K. M., Wright, J. P., Boutwell, B. B., Barnes, J. C., DeLisi, M., & Vaughn, M. G. (2013). Exploring the association between the 2-repeat allele of the MAOA gene promoter polymorphism and psychopathic personality traits, arrests, incarceration, and lifetime antisocial behavior. *Personality and Individual Differences, 54*(2), 164–168.

Beitchman, J. H., Baldassarra, L., Mik, H., De Luca, V., King, N., Bender, D., . . . Kennedy, J. L. (2006). Serotonin transporter polymorphisms and persistent, pervasive childhood aggression. *American Journal of Psychiatry, 163*(6), 1103–1105. doi:10.1176/ajp.2006.163.6.1103

Belsky, J., Jonassaint, C., Pluess, M., Stanton, M., Brummett, B., & Williams, R. (2009). Vulnerability genes or plasticity genes. *Molecular Psychiatry, 14,* 746–754.

Bornovalova, M. A., Hicks, B. M., Iacono, W. G., & McGue, M. (2010). Familial transmission and heritability of childhood disruptive disorders. *American Journal of Psychiatry, 167*(9), 1066–1074.

Caspi, A., Langley, K., Milne, B., Moffitt, T. E., O'Donovan, M., Owen, M. J., . . . Thapar, A. (2008). A replicated molecular genetic basis for subtyping antisocial behavior in children with attention-deficit/hyperactivity disorder. *Archives of General Psychiatry, 65*(2), 203–210. doi:10.1001/archgenpsychiatry.2007.24

Caspi, A., McClay, J., Moffitt, T. E., Mill, J., Martin, J., Craig, I. W., . . . Poulton, R. (2002). Role of genotype in the cycle of violence in maltreated children. *Science, 297*(5582), 851–854. doi:10.1126/science.1072290297/5582/851 [pii]

Caspi, A., & Moffitt, T. E. (2006). Gene-environment interactions in psychiatry: Joining forces with neuroscience. *Nature Reviews Neuroscience, 7*(7), 583–590. doi:10.1038/nrn1925

Chester, D. S., DeWall, C. N., Derefinko, K. J., Estus, S., Lynam, D. R., Peters, J. R., & Jiang, Y. (2016). Looking for reward in all the wrong places: Dopamine receptor gene polymorphisms indirectly affect aggression through sensation-seeking. *Social Neuroscience, 11*(5), 487–494. doi:10.1080/17470919.2015.1119191

Chhangur, R. R., Overbeek, G., Verhagen, M., Weeland, J., Matthys, W., & Engels, R. C. (2015). DRD4 and DRD2 genes, parenting, and adolescent delinquency: Longitudinal evidence for a gene by environment interaction. *Journal of Abnormal Psychology, 124*(4), 791–802. doi:10.1037/abn0000091

Cicchetti, D., Rogosch, F. A., & Thibodeau, E. L. (2012). The effects of child maltreatment on early signs of antisocial behavior: Genetic moderation by tryptophan hydroxylase, serotonin transporter, and monoamine oxidase A genes. *Development and Psychopathology, 24*(3), 907–928. doi:10.1017/s0954579412000442

Cosgrove, V. E., Rhee, S. H., Gelhorn, H. L., Boeldt, D., Corley, R. C., Ehringer, M. A., . . . Hewitt, J. K. (2011). Structure and etiology of co-occurring internalizing and externalizing disorders in adolescents. *Journal of Abnormal Child Psychology, 39*(1), 109–123.

DeLisi, M., Beaver, K. M., Vaughn, M. G., & Wright, J. P. (2009). All in the family: Gene × environment interaction between DRD2 and criminal father is associated with five antisocial phenotypes. *Criminal Justice and Behavior, 36*(11), 1187–1197. doi:10.1177/0093854809342884

DeLisi, M., Beaver, K. M., Wright, J. P., & Vaughn, M. G. (2008). The etiology of criminal onset: The enduring salience of nature and nurture. *Journal of Criminal Justice, 36*(3), 217–223. doi:10.1016/j.jcrimjus.2008.04.001

Dick, D. M., Agrawal, A., Keller, M. C., Adkins, A., Aliev, F., Monroe, S., . . . Sher, K. J. (2015). Candidate gene–environment interaction research reflections and recommendations. *Perspectives on Psychological Science, 10*(1), 37–59.

Dick, D. M., Aliev, F., Krueger, R. F., Edwards, A., Agrawal, A., Lynskey, M., . . . Nurnberger, J. (2011). Genome-wide association study of conduct disorder symptomatology. *Molecular Psychiatry, 16*(8), 800–808.

DiLalla, L. F., Elam, K. K., & Smolen, A. (2009). Genetic and gene-environment interaction effects on preschoolers' social behaviors. *Developmental Psychobiology, 51*(6), 451–464. doi:10.1002/dev.20384

Ellis, B. J., & Boyce, W. T. (2008). Biological sensitivity to context. *Current Directions in Psychological Science, 17,* 183–187. doi:10.1111/j.1467-8721.2008.00571.x

Fernàndez-Castillo, N., & Cormand, B. (2016). Aggressive behavior in humans: Genes and pathways identified through association studies. *American Journal of Medical Genetics Part B: Neuropsychiatric Genetics, 171*(5), 676–696. doi:10.1002/ajmg.b.32419

Ficks, C. A., & Waldman, I. D. (2014). Candidate genes for aggression and antisocial behavior: A meta-analysis of association studies of the 5HTTLPR and MAOA-uVNTR. *Behavior Genetics*, *44*(5), 427–444.

Gadow, K. D., Devincent, C. J., Olvet, D. M., Pisarevskaya, V., & Hatchwell, E. (2010). Association of DRD4 polymorphism with severity of oppositional defiant disorder, separation anxiety disorder and repetitive behaviors in children with autism spectrum disorder. *European Journal of Neuroscience*, *32*(6), 1058–1065. doi:10.1111/j.1460-9568.2010.07382.x

Gallardo-Pujol, D., Andrés-Pueyo, A., & Maydeu-Olivares, A. (2013). MAOA genotype, social exclusion and aggression: An experimental test of a gene-environment interaction. *Genes, Brain and Behavior*, *12*(1), 140–145. doi:10.1111/j.1601-183X.2012.00868.x

González-Tapia, M. I., & Obsuth, I. (2015). "Bad genes" and criminal responsibility. *International Journal of Law and Psychiatry*, *39*, 60–71. doi:10.1016/j.ijlp.2015.01.022

Gottesman, I. I., & Gould, T. D. (2003). The endophenotype concept in psychiatry: Etymology and strategic intentions. *American Journal of Psychiatry*, *160*(4), 636–645.

Guo, G., Cai, T., Guo, R., Wang, H., & Harris, K. M. (2010). The dopamine transporter gene, a spectrum of most common risky behaviors, and the legal status of the behaviors. *PLoS One*, *5*(2), e9352. doi:10.1371/journal.pone.0009352

Guo, G., Roettger, M. E., & Shih, J. C. (2007). Contributions of the DAT1 and DRD2 genes to serious and violent delinquency among adolescents and young adults. *Human Genetics*, *121*, 125–136.

Haberstick, B. C., Smolen, A., & Hewitt, J. K. (2006). Family-based association test of the 5HTTLPR and aggressive behavior in a general population sample of children. *Biological Psychiatry*, *59*(9), 836–843. doi:10.1016/j.biopsych.2005.10.008

Hakulinen, C., Jokela, M., Hintsanen, M., Merjonen, P., Pulkki-Raback, L., Seppala, I., . . . Keltikangas-Jarvinen, L. (2013). Serotonin receptor 1B genotype and hostility, anger and aggressive behavior through the lifespan: The Young Finns study. *Journal of Behavioral Medicine*, *36*(6), 583–590. doi:10.1007/s10865-012-9452-y

Hamshere, M. L., Langley, K., Martin, J., Agha, S. S., Stergiakouli, E., Anney, R. J., . . . Thapar, A. (2013). High loading of polygenic risk for ADHD in children with comorbid aggression. *American Journal of Psychiatry*, *170*(8), 909–916. doi:10.1176/appi.ajp.2013.12081129

Hasler, G., & Northoff, G. (2011). Discovering imaging endophenotypes for major depression. *Molecular Psychiatry*, *16*(6), 604–619.

Hohmann, S., Becker, K., Fellinger, J., Banaschewski, T., Schmidt, M. H., Esser, G., & Laucht, M. (2009). Evidence for epistasis between the 5-HTTLPR and the dopamine D4 receptor polymorphisms in externalizing behavior among 15-year-olds. *Journal of Neural Transmission*, *116*(12), 1621–1629. doi:10.1007/s00702-009-0290-1

Hovey, D., Lindstedt, M., Zettergren, A., Jonsson, L., Johansson, A., Melke, J., . . . Westberg, L. (2016). Antisocial behavior and polymorphisms in the oxytocin receptor gene: Findings in two independent samples. *Molecular Psychiatry*, *21*(7), 983–988. doi:10.1038/mp.2015.144

Iofrida, C., Palumbo, S., & Pellegrini, S. (2014). Molecular genetics and antisocial behavior: Where do we stand? *Experimental Biology and Medicine*, *239*(11), 1514–1523. doi:10.1177/1535370214529508

Kim-Cohen, J., Caspi, A., Taylor, A., Williams, B., Newcombe, R., Craig, I. W., & Moffitt, T. E. (2006). MAOA, maltreatment, and gene-environment interaction predicting children's mental health: New evidence and a meta-analysis. *Molecular Psychiatry*, *11*(10), 903–913. doi:10.1038/sj.mp.4001851

Knopik, V. S., Bidwell, L. C., Flessner, C., Nugent, N., Swenson, L., Bucholz, K. K., . . . Heath, A. C. (2014). DSM-IV defined conduct disorder and oppositional defiant disorder: An investigation of shared liability in female twins. *Psychological Medicine*, *44*(05), 1053–1064.

Kretschmer, T., Dijkstra, J. K., Ormel, J., Verhulst, F. C., & Veenstra, R. (2013). Dopamine receptor D4 gene moderates the effect of positive and negative peer experiences on later delinquency: The Tracking Adolescents' Individual Lives Survey study. *Development and Psychopathology*, *25*(4), 1107–1117. doi:10.1017/s0954579413000400

Kretschmer, T., Vitaro, F., & Barker, E. D. (2014). The association between peer and own aggression is moderated by the BDNF Val-met polymorphism. *Journal of Research on Adolescence*, *24*(1), 177–185. doi:10.1111/jora.12050

Krueger, R. F., Markon, K., Patrick, C. J., & Iacono, W. G. (2005). Externalizing psychopathology in adulthood: A dimensional-spectrum conceptualization and Its implications for DSM–V. *Journal of Abnormal Psychology*, *114*, 537–550.

Lacourse, E., Boivin, M., Brendgen, M., Petitclerc, A., Girard, A., Vitaro, F., . . . Tremblay, R. E. (2014). A longitudinal twin study of physical aggression during early childhood: Evidence for a developmentally dynamic genome. *Psychological Medicine, 44*(12), 2617–2627.

Lahey, B. B., Rathouz, P. J., Lee, S. S., Chronis-Tuscano, A., Pelham, W. E., Waldman, I. D., & Cook, E. H. (2011). Interactions between early parenting and a polymorphism of the child's dopamine transporter gene in predicting future child conduct disorder symptoms. *Journal of Abnormal Psychology, 120*(1), 33–45. doi:10.1037/a0021133

Langley, K., Turic, D., Rice, F., Holmans, P., van den Bree, M. B. M., Craddock, N., . . . Thapar, A. (2008). Testing for gene × environment interaction effects in attention deficit hyperactivity disorder and associated antisocial behavior. *American Journal of Medical Genetics Part B: Neuropsychiatric Genetics, 147*(1), 49–53. doi:10.1002/ajmg.b.30571

Lavigne, J. V., Herzing, L. B. K., Cook, E. H., Lebailly, S. A., Gouze, K. R., Hopkins, J., & Bryant, F. B. (2013). Gene × environment effects of serotonin transporter, dopamine receptor D4, and monoamine oxidase A genes with contextual and parenting risk factors on symptoms of oppositional defiant disorder, anxiety, and depression in a community sample of 4-year-old children. *Development and Psychopathology, 25*(2), 555–575. doi:10.1017/S0954579412001241

Lee, S. S. (2011). Deviant peer affiliation and antisocial behavior: Interaction with Monoamine Oxidase A (MAOA) genotype. *Journal of Abnormal Child Psychology, 39*(3), 321–332. doi:10.1007/s10802-010-9474-2

Li, J. J., & Lee, S. S. (2010). Latent class analysis of antisocial behavior: Interaction of serotonin transporter genotype and maltreatment. *Journal of Abnormal Child Psychology, 38*(6), 789–801.

Luppino, D., Moul, C., Hawes, D. J., Brennan, J., & Dadds, M. R. (2014). Association between a polymorphism of the vasopressin 1B receptor gene and aggression in children. *Psychiatric Genetics, 24*(5), 185–190.

Malik, A. I., Zai, C. C., Berall, L., Abu, Z., Din, F., Nowrouzi, B., . . . Beitchman, J. H. (2014). The role of genetic variants in genes regulating the oxytocin-vasopressin neurohumoral system in childhood-onset aggression. *Psychiatric Genetics, 24*(5), 201–210. doi:10.1097/ypg.0000000000000044

Martel, M. M., Nikolas, M., Jernigan, K., Friderici, K., & Nigg, J. T. (2012). Diversity in pathways to common childhood disruptive behavior disorders. *Journal of Abnormal Child Psychology, 40*(8), 1223–1236. doi:10.1007/s10802-012-9646-3

Martel, M. M., Nikolas, M., Jernigan, K., Friderici, K., Waldman, I., & Nigg, J. T. (2011). The dopamine receptor D4 gene (DRD4) moderates family environmental effects on ADHD. *Journal of Abnormal Child Psychology, 39*(1), 1–10. doi:10.1007/s10802-010-9439-5

Matthys, W., Vanderschuren, L. J., & Schutter, D. J. (2013). The neurobiology of oppositional defiant disorder and conduct disorder: Altered functioning in three mental domains. *Development and Psychopathology, 25*(1), 193–207. doi:10.1017/S0954579412000272

McDermott, R., Dawes, C., Prom-Wormley, E., Eaves, L., & Hatemi, P. K. (2013). MAOA and aggression: A gene-environment interaction in two populations. *Journal of Conflict Resolution, 57*(6), 1043–1064.

Moffitt, T. E., Caspi, A., & Rutter, M. (2005). Strategy for investigating interactions between measured genes and measured environments. *Archives of General Psychiatry, 62*(5), 473–481.

Mota, N. R., Bau, C. H., Banaschewski, T., Buitelaar, J. K., Ebstein, R. P., Franke, B., . . . Asherson, P. (2013). Association between DRD2/DRD4 interaction and conduct disorder: A potential developmental pathway to alcohol dependence. *American Journal of Medical Genetics Part B: Neuropsychiatric Genetics, 162*(6), 546–549. doi:10.1002/ajmg.b.32179

Nigg, J. T., Blaskey, L. G., Huang-Pollock, C. L., & Rappley, M. D. (2002). Neuropsychological executive functions and DSM-IV ADHD subtypes. *Journal of the American Academy of Child & Adolescent Psychiatry, 41*(1), 59–66.

Nobile, M., Giorda, R., Marino, C., Carlet, O., Pastore, V., Vanzin, L., . . . Battaglia, M. (2007). Socioeconomic status mediates the genetic contribution of the dopamine receptor D4 and serotonin transporter linked promoter region repeat polymorphisms to externalization in preadolescence. *Development and Psychopathology, 19*(4), 1147–1160. doi:10.1017/S0954579407000594

Nobile, M., Rusconi, M., Bellina, M., Marino, C., Giorda, R., Carlet, O., . . . Battaglia, M. (2010). COMT Val158Met polymorphism and socioeconomic status interact to predict attention deficit/hyperactivity problems in children aged 10–14. *European Child and Adolescent Psychiatry, 19*(7), 549–557. doi:10.1007/s00787-009-0080-1

Ouellet-Morin, I., Cote, S. M., Vitaro, F., Hebert, M., Carbonneau, R., Lacourse, E., . . . Tremblay, R. E. (2016). Effects of the MAOA gene and levels of exposure to violence on antisocial outcomes. *British Journal of Psychiatry, 208*(1), 42–48. doi:10.1192/bjp.bp.114.162081

Pappa, I., St Pourcain, B., Benke, K., Cavadino, A., Hakulinen, C., Nivard, M. G., . . . Tiemeier, H. (2016). A genome-wide approach to children's aggressive behavior: The EAGLE consortium. *American Journal of Medical Genetics Part B: Neuropsychiatric Genetics, 171*(5), 562–572. doi:10.1002/ajmg.b.32333

Pingault, J.-B., Rijsdijk, F., Zheng, Y., Plomin, R., & Viding, E. (2015). Developmentally dynamic genome: Evidence of genetic influences on increases and decreases in conduct problems from early childhood to adolescence. *Scientific reports, 5*. doi:10.1038/srep10053

Porsch, R. M., Middeldorp, C. M., Cherny, S. S., Krapohl, E., van Beijsterveldt, C. E. M., Loukola, A., . . . Bartels, M. (2016). Longitudinal heritability of childhood aggression. *American Journal of Medical Genetics Part B: Neuropsychiatric Genetics, 171*(5), 697–707. doi:10.1002/ajmg.b.32420

Sakai, J. T., Young, S. E., Stallings, M. C., Timberlake, D., Smolen, A., Stetler, G. L., & Crowley, T. J. (2006). Case-control and within-family tests for an association between conduct disorder and 5HTTLPR. *American Journal of Medical Genetics Part B: Neuropsychiatric Genetics, 141*(8), 825–832. doi:10.1002/ajmg.b.30278

Salvatore, J. E., Aliev, F., Bucholz, K., Agrawal, A., Hesselbrock, V., Hesselbrock, M., . . . Dick, D. M. (2015). Polygenic risk for externalizing disorders: Gene-by-development and gene-by-environment effects in adolescents and young adults. *Clinical Psychological Science, 3*(2), 189–201. doi:10.1177/2167702614534211

Salvatore, J. E., & Dick, D. M. (2016). Genetic influences on conduct disorder. *Neuroscience & Biobehavioral Reviews*. doi:10.1016/neubiorev.2016.06.034

Schlomer, G. L., Cleveland, H. H., Vandenbergh, D. J., Feinberg, M. E., Neiderhiser, J. M., Greenberg, M. T., . . . Redmond, C. (2015). Developmental differences in early adolescent aggression: A gene × environment × intervention analysis. *Journal of Youth and Adolescence, 44*(3), 581–597.

Schwartz, J. A., & Beaver, K. M. (2011). Evidence of a gene × environment interaction between perceived prejudice and MAOA genotype in the prediction of criminal arrests. *Journal of Criminal Justice, 39*(5), 378–384. doi:10.1016/j.jcrimjus.2011.05.003

Singh, A. L., & Waldman, I. D. (2010). The etiology of associations between negative emotionality and childhood externalizing disorders. *Journal of Abnormal Psychology, 119*(2), 376.

Singh, J. P., Volavka, J., Czobor, P., & Van Dorn, R. A. (2012). A meta-analysis of the Val158Met COMT polymorphism and violent behavior in schizophrenia. *PLoS One, 7*(8), e43423. doi:10.1371/journal.pone.0043423

Smearman, E. L., Winiarski, D. A., Brennan, P. A., Najman, J., & Johnson, K. C. (2015). Social stress and the oxytocin receptor gene interact to predict antisocial behavior in an at-risk cohort. *Development and Psychopathology, 27*(1), 309–318. doi:10.1017/s0954579414000649

Sonuga-Barke, E. J., Oades, R. D., Psychogiou, L., Chen, W., Franke, B., Buitelaar, J., . . . Anney, R. (2009). Dopamine and serotonin transporter genotypes moderate sensitivity to maternal expressed emotion. *Journal of Child Psychology and Psychiatry, 50*(9), 1052–1063.

Sonuga-Barke, E. J. S., Lasky-Su, J., Neale, B. M., Oades, R., Chen, W., Franke, B., . . . Faraone, S. V. (2008). Does parental expressed emotion moderate genetic effects in ADHD? An exploration using a genome wide association scan. *American Journal of Medical Genetics Part B: Neuropsychiatric Genetics, 147B*(8), 1359–1368.

Stringaris, A., Zavos, H., Leibenluft, E., Maughan, B., & Eley, T. C. (2012). Adolescent irritability: Phenotypic associations and genetic links with depressed mood. *American Journal of Psychiatry, 169*(1), 47–54.

Thapar, A., Langley, K., Fowler, T., Rice, F., Turic, D., Whittinger, N., . . . O'Donovan, M. (2005). Catechol O-Methyltransferase gene variant and birth weight predict early-onset antisocial behavior in children with attention-deficit/hyperactivity disorder. *Archives of General Psychiatry, 62*, 1275–1278. doi:10.1001/archpsyc.62.11.1275

Thomas, D. (2010). Methods for investigating gene–environment interactions in candidate pathway and genome-wide association studies. *Annual Review of Public Health, 31*, 21–36.

Tielbeek, J. J., Medland, S. E., Benyamin, B., Byrne, E. M., Heath, A. C., Madden, P. A. F., . . . Verweij, K. J. H. (2012). Unraveling the genetic etiology of adult antisocial behavior: A genome-wide association study. *PloS one, 7*(10), e45086.

Tremblay, R. E. (2010). Developmental origins of disruptive behaviour problems: The "original sin" hypothesis, epigenetics and their consequences for prevention. *Journal of Child Psychology and Psychiatry, 51*, 341–367.

Tuvblad, C., Zheng, M., Raine, A., & Baker, L. A. (2009). A common genetic factor explains the covariation among ADHD ODD and CD symptoms in 9–10 year old boys and girls. *Journal of Abnormal Child Psychology, 37*(2), 153–167.

van den Oord, E. J. C. G., Verhulst, F. C., & Boomsma, D. I. (1996). A genetic study of maternal and paternal ratings of problem behaviors in 3-year-old twins. *Journal of Abnormal Psychology, 105*(3), 349–357.

van Goozen, S. H., Langley, K., Northover, C., Hubble, K., Rubia, K., Schepman, K., . . . Thapar, A. (2016). Identifying mechanisms that underlie links between COMT genotype and aggression in male adolescents with ADHD. *Journal of Child Psychology and Psychiatry, 57*(4), 472–480. doi:10.1111/jcpp.12464

Vassos, E., Collier, D. A., & Fazel, S. (2014). Systematic meta-analyses and field synopsis of genetic association studies of violence and aggression. *Molecular Psychiatry, 19*(4), 471–477.

Vaughn, M. G., DeLisi, M., Beaver, K. M., & Wright, J. P. (2009). DAT1 and 5HTT are associated with pathological criminal behavior in a nationally representative sample of youth. *Criminal Justice and Behavior, 36*(11), 1113–1124.

Veroude, K., Zhang-James, Y., Fernàndez-Castillo, N., Bakker, M. J., Cormand, B., & Faraone, S. V. (2016). Genetics of aggressive behavior: An overview. *American Journal of Medical Genetics Part B: Neuropsychiatric Genetics, 171*(1), 3–43.

Viding, E., Price, T. S., Jaffee, S. R., Trzaskowski, M., Davis, O. S. P., Meaburn, E. L., . . . Plomin, R. (2013). Genetics of callous-unemotional behavior in children. *PloS one, 8*(7), e65789.

Wagner, S., Baskaya, O., Anicker, N. J., Dahmen, N., Lieb, K., & Tadic, A. (2010). The catechol o-methyltransferase (COMT) val(158)met polymorphism modulates the association of serious life events (SLE) and impulsive aggression in female patients with borderline personality disorder (BPD). *Acta Psychiatrica Scandinavica, 122*(2), 110–117.

Waldman, I. D., & Rhee, S. H. (2006). Genetic and environmental influences on psychopathy and antisocial behavior. In C. J. Patrick (Ed.), *Handbook of Psychopathy* (pp. 205–228). New York, NY: Guilford Press.

Waltes, R., Chiocchetti, A. G., & Freitag, C. M. (2016). The neurobiological basis of human aggression: A review on genetic and epigenetic mechanisms. *American Journal of Medical Genetics Part B: Neuropsychiatric Genetics, 171*(5), 650–675.

Weeland, J., Overbeek, G., de Castro, B. O., & Matthys, W. (2015). Underlying mechanisms of gene–environment interactions in externalizing behavior: A systematic review and search for theoretical mechanisms. *Clinical Child and Family Psychology Review, 18*(4), 413–442.

Whelan, Y. M., Kretschmer, T., & Barker, E. D. (2014). MAOA, early experiences of harsh parenting, irritable opposition, and bullying-victimization: A moderated indirect-effects analysis. *Merrill-Palmer Quarterly, 60*(2), 217–237.

Young, S. E., Smolen, A., Corley, R. P., Krauter, K. S., DeFries, J. C., Crowley, T. J., & Hewitt, J. K. (2002). Dopamine transporter polymorphism associated with externalizing behavior problems in children. *American Journal of Medical Genetics, 114*(2), 144–149.

Young, S. E., Smolen, A., Hewitt, J. K., Haberstick, B. C., Stallings, M. C., Corley, R. P., & Crowley, T. J. (2006). Interaction between MAO-A genotype and maltreatment in the risk for conduct disorder: Failure to confirm in adolescent patients. *American Journal of Psychiatry, 163*(6), 1019–1025.

Zai, C. C., Ehtesham, S., Choi, E., Nowrouzi, B., de Luca, V., Stankovich, L., . . . Beitchman, J. H. (2012). Dopaminergic system genes in childhood aggression: Possible role for DRD2. *World Journal of Biological Psychiatry, 13*(1), 65–74.

9

The Neurobiology of Oppositional Defiant Disorder and Conduct Disorder

Leah M. Efferson and Andrea L. Glenn

In recent years, researchers have focused on examining neurobiology in an effort to understand the etiology of Oppositional Defiant Disorder (ODD) and Conduct Disorder (CD). For example, brain imaging technology has allowed us to study the structure and function of the brain in relation to ODD and CD. Also, studies of the hormone and neurotransmitter systems underlying brain functioning have further contributed to our understanding of the biological abnormalities observed in these disorders. In this chapter, we will discuss how the structure and functioning of the brain has been found to differ between youth with ODD and CD and those without, and how these differences may contribute to deficits in emotion processing, problem solving, self-control, reward and punishment processing, and error monitoring in this population. We will also discuss how levels of cortisol, serotonin, and dopamine differ in youth with ODD/CD.

We will address how neurobiological studies of youth with ODD/CD have improved our understanding of several key issues. First, we will discuss the similarities and differences in the neurobiology underlying ODD/CD and Attention Deficit Hyperactivity Disorder (ADHD). Second, we will discuss neurobiological differences in youth with CD with and without callous-unemotional traits. Callous-unemotional (CU) traits involve a lack of guilt, deficits in empathy and fear, poor recognition of fear in others, thrill seeking, insensitivity to punishment, and manipulating others for personal gain (Frick & White, 2008). Children with both CD and CU traits exhibit a more severe and stable pattern of aggression and antisocial behavior throughout childhood than children without CU traits and are more likely to develop psychopathic traits in adolescence and adulthood (Forsman, Lichtenstein, Andershed, & Larsson, 2010). Finally, gender differences in brain structure and functioning in youth with CD will be discussed.

Brain Structure

A number of studies have used magnetic resonance imaging (MRI) to examine differences in the structure of the brain in youth with disruptive behavior disorders. Findings have revealed volumetric and morphological differences primarily in the frontal and temporal regions of the brain. The prefrontal cortex is involved in many functions that are often adversely affected in youth with disruptive behavior disorders including attention, inhibition, associative learning, and decision making (Kane & Engle, 2002). In the temporal lobe, the amygdala is involved in fear conditioning, in which a neutral stimulus is paired with an aversive event and eventually becomes feared (LaBar, Gatenby, Gore, LeDoux, & Phelps, 1998). A number of studies have found reduced temporal gray matter volume, including reductions in the amygdala and hippocampus, and reduced prefrontal gray matter volume in children with CD compared to controls (Kruesi, Casanova, Mannheim, & Johnson-Bilder, 2004; Huebner et al., 2008). Deficits in the hippocampus are also apparent in children with autism, schizophrenia, and bipolar disorder, and therefore may reflect an overall delay in structural development in many disorders including CD (Huebner et al., 2008).

Different symptoms of CD have been associated with different structural impairments. Sterzer, Stadler, Poutska, and Kleinschmidt (2007) found that aggression was most strongly associated with reduced gray matter in the insula, whereas attention deficits were most strongly associated with reduced volume in the left amygdala in adolescents with CD. The insula is involved in feelings of empathy, so it might be that reduced insula volume results in less empathic responses during aggressive acts. Because the amygdala is important in attending to emotional stimuli, it might be that youth who are aggressive have trouble paying attention to the emotions of others and may not associate fearful expressions in others with their aggressive behaviors. Subsequently, they may not feel aversive emotions such as guilt or remorse when they inflict pain on others. This is supported by one study that found children with higher levels of CU traits (which are associated with increased aggression) demonstrated poorer recognition of fearful facial expressions, but performed as well as children with lower levels of CU traits on a fear recognition task when specifically told to look at the eye region of the face—the region that provides the most information regarding fear (Dadds et al., 2006). It may be that deficits in the amygdala contribute to problems attending to emotionally salient information in youth with conduct disorder.

Another study (Boes, Tranel, Anderson, & Nopolous, 2008) found reduced gray matter volume in the anterior cingulate cortex (ACC) in boys who had high levels of aggressive and defiant behavior. The ACC is involved in both cognitive and affective processes, including attention, error detection, working memory, emotion regulation, and assessing the salience of emotional stimuli (Bush, Luu, & Posner, 2000). It may be, therefore, that youth who display aggressive behaviors have trouble recognizing the importance of emotional stimuli, paying attention to these stimuli, and regulating their reactions to aversive stimuli.

Dalwani et al. (2011) found reduced gray matter volume in the left dorsolateral prefrontal cortex and bilateral cerebellum in adolescents who had conduct and substance abuse problems compared to healthy adolescents, controlling for ADHD symptoms. Reduced volume in these regions may contribute to the impulsivity, disinhibition, and impaired decision making observed in these youth. Michalska, Decety, Zeffiro, and Lahey (2015) found a negative association between CD symptoms and the superior temporal sulcus (STS) while controlling for ADHD. This pattern was stronger for girls. The STS is involved in determining where emotions are being directed and where others are gazing (Engell & Haxby, 2007). This suggests that, for girls, reduced volumes in this area may contribute to CD more than for boys. Overall, these studies provide evidence that certain anatomical abnormalities are associated with antisocial behaviors and may predispose children to engage in these delinquent acts and continue on this trajectory throughout the lifespan.

However, not all studies have found reduced gray matter volumes in youth with ODD/CD. Dalwani et al. (2011) found increased volume in the right precuneus in boys with serious conduct problems and substance dependence. The precuneus is associated with self-referential thinking, and may imply that these youth spend more time thinking about themselves. Michalska, Decety et al. (2015) did not find that gray matter volume was associated with a diagnosis of ODD/CD in the amygdala, insula, and frontal cortex. Thus, inconsistencies in findings remain.

In addition to identifying brain regions that may be larger or smaller in youth with ODD/CD, structural brain imaging studies have also been useful in improving our understanding of the similarities and differences between ODD/CD and other disorders. For example, given the high rates of comorbidity between CD and ADHD, it is unclear whether the structural brain abnormalities observed in youth with CD are specific to that disorder, or whether they partly reflect deficits associated with ADHD. Noordermeer, Luman, and Oosterlaan (2016) conducted a meta-analysis of 29 studies that examined youth with ODD/CD with and without comorbid ADHD to see which brain regions contribute uniquely to ODD/CD. The meta-analysis comprised 643 youth (334 patients and 309 controls) with an age range of 6 to 21 years. For children/adolescents with ODD/CD without ADHD, one out of three studies reported a reduction in total gray matter. The specific brain regions that demonstrated reduced gray matter volume included the insula, amygdala, the cingulate cortex, the inferior frontal gyrus, and the dorsomedial prefrontal cortex. In youth with ODD/CD *and* ADHD there were smaller gray matter volumes in the temporal lobe (four out of nine studies found this) and the cerebellum (three out of nine studies found this), indicating these regions may be specific to the comorbidity of ODD/CD and ADHD. Overall, the meta-analysis concluded that the reduced gray matter in the bilateral amygdala, bilateral insula and left medial/superior frontal gyrus were specifically associated with ODD/CD but not ADHD (Noordermeer et al., 2016). The medial/superior frontal gyrus is important in response inhibition and introspection, which allows individuals to self-reflect on how their actions affect others (Passamonti et al. 2012) and inhibit an aggressive response (Goldberg, Harel, & Malach, 2006). Impairments in this region might contribute to a difficulty in inhibiting aggressive responses in youth with ODD/CD. The meta-analysis also indicated that youth with ODD/CD had smaller gray matter volumes in the right striatum and left precuneus. The right striatum might contribute to the abnormalities in reinforcement processing in youth with ODD/CD. Abnormalities in the striatum may contribute to reduced sensitivity to rewards. Youth with reduced reward sensitivity may have trouble learning how to change their inappropriate behaviors to more appropriate ones (Matthys, Vanderschuren, Schutter, & Lochman, 2012). The left precuneus is associated with self-awareness and reflection; deficits may result in difficulty understanding how one's behavior affects others. The left precuneus was also found to be larger in the Dalwani et al. (2011) study, although it was not included in the meta-analysis because youth in that sample also had substance dependence.

Another review also concluded there are distinct structural abnormalities in youth with ADHD versus CD. Rubia (2011) suggested that youth with ADHD typically have reduced gray matter in "cool" areas that involve cognitive processes such as inhibition and attention including inferior frontal, striatal, parieto-temporal, and cerebellar regions. In contrast, youth with conduct disorder are more likely to have decreased gray matter in "hot" areas that are associated with motivation and emotions, such as the lateral orbital and ventromedial prefrontal cortices, superior temporal lobes, and the amygdala. Overall, many of the symptoms observed in youth with ODD/CD might be the result of structural impairments in the areas described above. However, it should be emphasized that CD is often comorbid with ADHD symptoms, making it difficult to determine which abnormalities are specific to CD per se. Thus far, studies suggest that there are distinct structural abnormalities associated with each disorder.

One study has also examined brain structure in youth with CU traits. In it boys with CU traits and conduct problems had *increased* gray matter concentration in the medial orbitofrontal cortex (OFC), ACC, temporal lobes, and superior temporal gyrus (angular gyrus) compared to healthy controls (De Brito et al., 2009). This is different from findings in adults with psychopathic traits, which generally find reductions in these regions (Ermer, Cope, Nyalakanti, Calhoun, & Kiehl, 2012; Müller et al., 2008). The increased gray matter may reflect delayed cortical maturation in these brain regions. These youth also had reduced white matter concentrations in the superior frontal lobe, precuneus, right superior temporal gyrus, and ACC, which may also indicate that the brains of those higher in CU traits are maturing slower than those without CU traits. In contrast, the dorsolateral prefrontal cortex demonstrated increased white matter in boys with high CU traits compared to healthy controls, suggesting that this region may develop faster in these youth. The authors suggest that this more rapid development in the dorsolateral prefrontal cortex may compensate for reduced gray and white matter in other brain regions in this population. Increased dorsolateral prefrontal cortex functioning during moral decision making has been associated with psychopathic traits in adults (Glenn, Raine, Schug, Young, & Hauser, 2009), implying that this compensation may continue into adulthood.

Diffusion Tensor Imaging

Diffusion tensor imaging (DTI) is another form of structural brain imaging that allows researchers to examine the development of white matter pathways in the brain that connect brain regions. A metric that is commonly used is called fractional anisotropy (FA) which provides information about the degree of myelination and coherency of fiber tracts. A few studies have used DTI to study antisocial youth. Li, Mathews, Wang, Dunn, & Kronenberger (2005) found a 13% reduction in FA in the left arcuate fasciculus in the prefrontal cortex in adolescents with ODD/CD. The arcuate fasciculus has projections that extend from the temporal lobe to the frontal lobe; reduced FA indicates that communication between these areas is weaker in adolescents with ODD/CD, which may contribute to developmental deficits such as impairments in language and emotional processing. Conversely, Decety, Yoder, and Lahey (2015) did not find CD symptoms to be associated with the FA of white matter anywhere in the brain. FA is an indirect measure of microstructural integrity of white matter and can be measured using either radial diffusivity, which assesses myelination levels, or axial diffusivity which measures the axonal integrity of white matter tracts. This study found CD symptoms to be associated with more axial diffusivity (or less axonal integrity) in the superior longitudinal fasciculus (SLF), which connects the prefrontal and parietal regions and matures during adolescence. They also found more axial diffusivity in the tracts of the corpus callosum that connect the frontal lobes to the occipital lobes. This association was stronger for girls than boys. This may be because girls may exhibit severe CD symptoms only when they have large deficits in these white matter tracts since they tend to have more protective factors for CD than boys. Another study using DTI found that the corpus callosum and SLF increased less with age for youth with ODD/CD than with healthy controls (Hummer, Wang, Kronenberger, Dunn, & Mathews, 2015) which also points to a potential developmental delay in these areas. The integrity of the SLF is associated with performance on neuropsychological measures such as working memory (Mabbott, Noseworthy, Bouffet, Laughlin, & Rockel, 2006) and selective attention deficits in children (Klarborg et al., 2013). However, youth with ODD/CD did not perform worse on tests of working memory which indicates that the SLF is not as strongly related to working memory in this ODD/CD sample compared to controls. This suggests greater variability in brain regions that are used in working memory performance in youth with ODD/CD, which may be due to ADHD symptoms or difficulties with paying attention to the task.

Another study found that youth with CD had increased FA in the uncinate fasciculus (UF) which connects the amygdala with the OFC (Sarkar, Craig, Catani, Dell'Acqua, Fahy, Deeley, & Murphy, 2013) This increase was not found in children without CD and suggests that a lack of myelination in this tract in youth with CD may contribute to engagement in risky behaviors based off a study that reported increased FA was associated with more risky behaviors in a healthy sample (Berns, Moore, & Capra, 2009). However, Finger et al. (2012) did not find abnormalities in the UF or any white matter tracts in youth with ODD/CD and psychopathic traits. They indicate that functional connectivity measures may be more sensitive than structural connectivity measures in this population of youth.

Overall, results from structural brain imaging studies suggest that youth with ODD/CD have decreased gray matter volume primarily in frontal and temporal areas. Deficits in these areas may contribute to the difficulties in emotion processing, problem solving, self-control, introspection, and error monitoring observed in youth with ODD/CD. There are also white matter tracts that have been shown to be reduced in ODD/CD youth including the arcuate fasciculus and SLF that may contribute to deficits in emotional processing and language abilities.

Functional Brain Imaging

Although structural brain imaging can identify differences in the size of different brain regions, it does not provide information about whether these regions actually function differently. For example, it is not necessarily the case that increased brain volume in a particular region is indicative of superior functioning. Furthermore, structural imaging studies cannot provide information about the particular context in which a brain region may function differently. In order to determine whether brain regions might be dysfunctional in youth with ODD/CD symptoms, researchers have used functional magnetic resonance imaging (fMRI). This allows for the examination of brain functioning while individuals are engaged in specific tasks. A number of brain regions have shown decreased activation in particular tasks in youth with ODD/CD, which might contribute to the behaviors observed in these youth. However, youth with conduct disorder represent a heterogeneous group. There are often discrepancies in findings from brain imaging studies; this may be due to a failure to account for differences in the types of antisocial traits and behaviors present in each sample. For example, youth with conduct problems and CU traits have been found to demonstrate different patterns of brain abnormalities than youth without CU traits.

One of the regions most consistently identified in fMRI studies of youth with ODD/CD is the amygdala. The amygdala is important in the ability to learn the association between inappropriate behaviors and subsequent punishment (Phelps & LeDoux, 2005). It is also involved in emotional responding. As in structural imaging studies, several studies have found abnormalities in the amygdala in youth with CD. These studies have generally found reduced activity in the amygdala when participants are viewing different types of emotional stimuli. One study found reduced activation in the amygdala in children with CD when viewing negative emotional pictures but this was only found for those who had low anxiety levels (Sterzer, Stadler, Krebs, Kleinschmidt, & Poustka, 2005). Reduced amygdala functioning has been found to be particularly evident in youth with comorbid CU traits. Jones, Laurens, Herba, Barker, and Viding (2009) found that children with both CD and CU traits had reduced activity in the amygdala while viewing fearful faces. Similarly, Marsh et al. (2008) found that children with CU traits had less amygdala activity when viewing fearful faces but not angry or neutral faces. Responding to fearful faces may be important in understanding when one's actions are causing harm to another individual, and thus in learning to avoid such actions.

Reduced amygdala activity has been found to be more pronounced in youth in whom antisocial behavior began in childhood compared to those in whom it began in adolescence. Passamonti et al. (2010) found that a childhood- and an adolescent-onset group both demonstrated decreased amygdala activity when viewing sad facial expressions compared to controls, but reductions were more pronounced for those whose antisocial behavior started in childhood. This greater impairment in amygdala functioning in the childhood-onset group may partly explain why conduct disorder is more severe and persistent when it begins in childhood versus adolescence.

Not all studies have found reduced amygdala activity, however. Herpertz et al. (2008) found *increased* activation in the left amygdala in boys with CD while viewing negative pictures. Another study found increased activation in the amygdala and temporal pole in adolescents with CD compared to healthy adolescents when viewing people in pain (Decety, Michalska, Akitsuki, & Lahey, 2009). The authors suggest that these results may reflect increased arousal and excitement when seeing others in pain. However, another study did not find significant correlations between amygdala activity and ODD/CD symptoms when participants viewed video clips of people being harmed intentionally and by accident (Michalska, Zeffiro, & Decety, 2016). This may be because, unlike the study by Decety et al. (2009), this study did not use stimuli that depicted the fearful facial expressions of the person in pain. The amygdala may be more active when viewing fearful facial expressions (Morris et al., 1996) than when viewing body movements that depict harm.

Reduced functioning has also been consistently observed in regions of the prefrontal cortex in youth with ODD/CD, primarily in orbitofrontal/ventromedial regions. One study found that during a passive avoidance task children and adolescents with psychopathic traits and ODD/CD exhibited decreased orbitofrontal cortex (OFC) and dorsal striatum activation in response to stimulus-reinforcement exposure and rewards (Finger et al., 2011). Another study found reduced activation in the OFC in youth with CD during a rewarded continuous performance task (Rubia et al., 2009). In the study by Decety et al. (2009), adolescents with CD had reduced activity in the medial prefrontal cortex and lateral OFC while viewing scenes of people intentionally inflicting pain on each other. Another study found girls with CD demonstrated decreased medial OFC functioning while viewing facial expressions, regardless of valance (Fairchild et al., 2014). This differs from males with CD who showed less neural activity to angry expressions and increased activity when viewing neutral expressions (Passamonti et al., 2010). The medial OFC plays a role in facial expression decoding (Adolphs, 2002) and it might be that girls with CD have deficits in an overall recognition of emotions, whereas boys might have trouble specifically with recognizing angry emotions. Another study conducted by White et al., (2013) found increased activity in the dorsal striatum (caudate) during negative prediction errors or unexpected punishment. This increase was not found in healthy controls and suggests those with ODD/CD have abnormalities in brain responses when unexpected punishment occurs. The authors suggest this increased activity could be influenced by the dopamine system that is dysfunctional in youth with ODD/CD (White et al., 2013). Prediction error signaling is important in detecting whether an action will result in negative consequences and, if disrupted, might lead toward poor decision making and antisocial behaviors (White et al., 2013).

Reduced functioning of the orbitofrontal/ventromedial region of the prefrontal cortex may contribute to many of the symptoms of ODD/CD. Those who have damage to the OFC have been found to display more impulsive and aggressive behavior than those who do not (Izquierdo, Suda, & Murray, 2005) and to be less aware of the moral implications of their actions (Anderson, Bechara, Damasio, Tranel, & Damasio, 1999). Researchers have speculated that the decreased activation of the OFC could contribute to abnormalities in reward computations which can increase frustration and aggression often seen in youth with CD (Rubia et al., 2008).

There are other brain regions that have demonstrated reduced functioning during certain fMRI tasks in youth with ODD/CD. In boys with CD, reduced activity in the ACC, insula, and inferior frontal gyrus was found when viewing the infliction of pain (Lockwood et al., 2013). Other studies have found less activity in the ACC in youth with CD compared to controls when viewing negative pictures (Stadler et al., 2007; Sterzer et al., 2005). Reduced activity in the ACC may contribute to difficulties in cognitively controlling emotional responses.

Another study found that CD symptoms were associated with decreased activation in the insula when viewing clips of people being harmed vs. no harm and intentional harm vs. accidental harm. Interestingly, CU traits were associated with less activation in the insula whereas reactive aggression scores were associated with increased activation in the insula (Michalska, Zeffiro, & Decety, 2015). Children with CU traits and CD may demonstrate less empathy due to a dampening of brain activity in the insula, whereas children with CD who are more reactively aggressive may have trouble regulating their emotional responses.

Another study found that more severe conduct problems, but not CU traits, were related to performing worse on a passive avoidance task (White et al., 2016). Conduct problems were also associated with reduced representation of expected values (EVs), or the average value one expects after many rounds. This reduced EV was associated with less activation in the bilateral anterior insula, inferior frontal gyrus, and striatum when making avoidance responses. These areas have been shown to influence the decision of avoiding stimuli or actions that will result in punishment. These impairments in decision making in youth with ODD/CD may be due to difficulties in utilizing value information that is associated with activation in these brain regions. In turn, choosing to respond to stimuli that are punishing or suboptimal might increase the probability of future aggression and antisocial behaviors in youth with ODD/CD. The same meta-analysis described above also examined differences in brain function of ODD/CD youth (Noordermeer et al., 2016). In all the studies (17) there were a total of 68 brain regions that showed different activation patterns in those with ODD/CD with and without ADHD. There were five clusters that were the most reliably reported in the literature. These consisted of the right globus pallidus (part of the striatum), right and left amygdala, the left caudate (part of the striatum), and the left fusiform gyrus. When examining the "hot" executive functioning brain areas that are involved in emotional aspects of cognition, such as reinforcement learning, emotional processing and decision making, the amygdala and insula showed abnormal functioning but the left fusiform gyrus did not. These studies used different tasks that included the processing of contingencies (5 studies), passive viewing of emotional pictures (3), passive avoidance learning (2), actively viewing and rating of painful situations (1), implicit emotional processing, and interference control with emotional stimuli (1). For areas designated as the "cool" executive functioning regions involved in problem solving and self-regulation, the area most consistently reported to be abnormally functioning in ODD/CD was the precuneus.

Finally, Rubia (2011) reviewed the literature examining differences in brain functioning between youth with noncomorbid ADHD and CD on a variety of executive functioning tasks including motor response inhibition, sustained attention, cognitive switching, interference inhibition, and attentional oddball. Performance on the tasks did not differ between the two groups but, in the majority of the tasks, youth with ADHD tended to show reduced activation in the inferior frontal cortex (IFC) compared to youth with CD. The IFC is involved in many "cool" cognitive processes including motor response inhibition, inhibitory control, cognitive switching, and updating information during cognition. In contrast, youth with CD tended to show reduced activation in limbic areas such as such as the hippocampus, insula, and superior temporal lobe that are involved in "hot" processes and also the dorsal ACC which is involved in the motivation to sustain attention. Therefore, it may be that impairments in executive functioning in youth with CD may primarily result from deficits in limbic areas. Overall, the neurobiological impairments in youth with ADHD may directly influence their ability to pay attention and switch back and forth between information, whereas the impairments in youth with CD first influence their motivation to pay attention which then influences cognition.

Functional Connectivity

Researchers have also used fMRI to examine the connections between brain activity in different regions. A study by Marsh et al. (2008) found decreased connectivity between the amygdala and the vmPFC while viewing fearful facial expressions in children with more severe levels of CU traits who had either ODD or CD. Connections between the amygdala and vmPFC are important because they transfer emotional information from the amygdala, which is important in guiding behavioral selection processes and interpreting social cues (Saddoris, Gallagher, & Schoenbaum, 2005). Therefore, impairments in the vmPFC and its connection to the amygdala may contribute to hostile attribution biases and less awareness of the effects of one's actions on others, which might lead to an increased tendency to be aggressive in youth with ODD/CD. Another study found reduced functional connectivity between the amygdala and prefrontal cortex and superior temporal cortex during an instrumental learning task (Finger et al., 2012) which supports the previous study.

Neurotransmitters

Research examining the neurochemistry of ODD and CD has mainly focused on the neurotransmitter serotonin, which is often associated with aggression. Serotonin is involved in aversive processing and sensitivity to punishment. Studies have found that aversive events activate neurons that release serotonin (Takase et al., 2004) and animals with depleted serotonin levels do not respond as well to cues of punishment compared to those with more serotonin (Soubrié, 1986). Overall, research suggests a negative association between serotonin measures and aggression in youth with ODD/CD.

Children with ODD/CD have been shown to have lower plasma levels of 5-hydroxyindoleacetic acid (5-HIAA), the main metabolite of serotonin, than normal controls (Van Goozen, Matthys, Cohen-Kettenis, Westenberg, & van Engeland, 1999). Low levels of 5-HIAA in cerebrospinal fluid have also been associated with higher levels of aggression as assessed by the Child Behavior Checklist (CBCL; Kruesi et al., 1990, 1992).

Findings are less consistent when examining blood levels of serotonin. Whereas one study found a negative association between aggression and serotonin levels in aggressive children (Hanna, Yuwiler, & Coates, 1995), others have found positive associations (Hughes, Petty, Shiekha, & Kramer, 1996; Pliszka, Rogeness, Renner, Sherman, & Broussard, 1988; Unis et al., 1997), or no differences in serotonin levels in aggressive children versus normal controls (Cook, Stein, Ellison, Unis, & Leventhal, 1995; Rogeness, Hernandez, Macedo, & Mitchell, 1982). These mixed results may be because whole-blood serotonin is a peripheral measure of serotonin.

Those who have childhood-onset CD have been found to have higher blood levels of serotonin than those who have adolescent-onset CD, and more serotonin in childhood is associated with increased aggression in adolescence (Unis et al., 1997). Prolactin levels are a measure of synaptic serotonin levels; the drug fenfluramine has been shown to increase prolactin levels, thereby increasing serotonin. One study found that in a sample of boys at age 8 and later age 10, aggression was positively correlated with prolactin responses to a fenfluramine challenge (Pine et al., 1997). The administration of fenfluramine, that is to say, increased prolactin responses and was associated with increased serotonin. This increase in serotonin was associated with more aggressive behaviors. These findings are different from the adult literature which finds that aggression is negatively associated with prolactin responses and serotonin levels (Coccaro, Kavoussi, Cooper, & Hauger, 1997).

One study used a selective 5-$HT_{1B/1D}$ receptor agonist, sumatriptan, to investigate neuroendocrine responses in children with ODD/CD (Snoek et al., 2002). Animal studies have shown that the 5-$HT_{1B/1D}$ receptor plays a role in the development of reactive aggression (Saudou et al., 1994). This study found that the growth hormone response to sumatriptan, which is an indication of 5-HT receptor sensitivity, was stronger for children with ODD/CD compared to controls, suggesting children with ODD/CD may have enhanced postsynaptic sensitivity of 5-$HT_{1B/1D}$ receptors. This may be due to deficits in serotonin levels that lead to greater numbers of serotonin receptors in the brain.

Another way to measure serotonin functioning is by examining platelet membranes that reflect the pre- and postsynaptic membranes of 5-HT neurons. One study found that fewer platelet markers of 5-HT were associated with increased aggression in youth with CD and ADHD (Birmaher et al., 1990). Another study did not find differences in platelet markers of 5-HT between youth with ODD/CD and controls (Stoff et al., 1991).

Overall, there is evidence for a negative association between serotonin measures and aggression in youth with ODD and CD. This makes sense in light of the drugs risperidon and lithium, which influence 5-HT function and tend to decrease aggressive behaviors in children with ODD/CD (Findling et al., 2000; Malone, Delaney, Luebbert, Cater, & Campbell, 2000). Reduced serotonin over a long period of time may influence the aggressive behavior of youth with ODD and CD by reducing sensitivity to punishment (Spoont, 1992).

Research has also examined whether dopamine functioning is different in youth with ODD/CD. Less dopamine may contribute to less arousal to natural stimuli in the environment, which may motivate youth to engage in risky and stimulation seeking activities. It is also released in anticipation of reward (de la Fuente-Fernández et al., 2002), and is important in learning the rewarding value of stimuli (Flagel et al., 2011) and in detecting the salience of incentives (Berridge & Robinson, 1998). Dopamine is measured using homovanillic acid (HVA), which is its metabolite. Kruesi et al., (1990) did not find a relationship between HVA in cerebrospinal fluid and aggression in youth with ODD/CD and Pliszka et al. (1998) did not find lower plasma levels of dopamine in youth with CD and comorbid ADHD. However, van Goozen et al., (1999) found that children with ODD/CD had lower plasma levels of HVA compared to controls. Using indirect measures of dopamine, Rogeness, Javors, Maas, & Macedo, (1990) found lower plasma levels of dopamine in youth with CD compared to those without. Therefore, this early research is unclear as to whether or not youth with ODD/CD have decreased dopamine levels.

Studies examining the effects of psychostimulants, which enhance dopamine neurotransmission, also provide information about the relationship between dopamine and CD. Connor, Glatt, Lopez, Jackson, and Melloni (2002) conducted a meta-analysis that included studies of youth with ODD/CD who had comorbid ADHD and found that youth who were given dopamine psychostimulants demonstrated significantly lower levels of overt aggression than youth who were not (Cohen's d = .84). Because these psychostimulants are thought to increase dopamine levels, this provides indirect evidence that youth with comorbid ODD/CD and ADHD may have low levels of dopamine. However, the effect of psychostimulants was not as strong for youth who had higher levels of ODD/CD symptoms, suggesting that these treatments may be more helpful for the ADHD component of comorbid ODD/CD and ADHD. Matthys, Vanderschuren, Schutter, and Lochman (2012) suggest that psychostimulants that block the reuptake of dopamine may improve functioning of paralimbic regions that influence attention in youth with ODD/CD.

Overall, there is evidence suggesting that ODD/CD may be associated with decreased dopaminergic functioning including decreased dopamine levels and decreases in aggression after administration dopamine reuptake inhibitors.

Stress Response System

There are two primary theories regarding the stress response system that explain why children with ODD and/or CD engage in antisocial behavior. One theory postulates that these children may be less fearful (Raine, 1996) and are therefore less sensitive to the negative consequences of their actions and the punishment that results. This fearlessness would also result in problems with conditioning, in that children would not learn to associate their antisocial or aggressive behaviors with punishment, and therefore punishment would have little to no effect on changing behavior (Raine, 1996). Individuals with low levels of arousal or fear may have trouble learning the associations between their antisocial behaviors and punishments. This association is important for children to develop fear in anticipation of inappropriate behaviors they may engage in. Learning the association between a particular action and punishment can decrease the likelihood of that behavior reoccurring. This learning may be disrupted in ODD/CD children because they have a decreased sensitivity to punishment cues, so they feel less fear before they engage in antisocial behavior and less guilt after (Kochanska, 1993).

Another theory postulated by Raine (1996) states that children with ODD and/or CD have low levels of arousal, and therefore may engage in more sensation seeking. Low levels of arousal may result in discomfort, leading individuals to seek out potentially risky or dangerous, thrill-seeking behaviors (i.e., jumping off high places, stealing from a store).

The stress response system includes the hypothalamic-pituitary-adrenal (HPA) axis and the autonomic nervous system (ANS). The HPA axis releases cortisol in response to stress, which serves to mobilize the body's resources. A number of studies have examined how the HPA system may function differently in those with ODD and/or CD compared to those without. Tennes, Kreye, Avitable, & Wells, (1986) found a negative association between baseline cortisol levels and aggressive behavior in school children towards teachers and peers. Vanyukov et al., (1993) found a negative relationship between the severity of CD symptoms assessed by the Kiddie-Schedule for Affective Disorders and Schizophrenia (K-SADS-E) and baseline cortisol levels. These studies suggest that children with ODD/CD who display aggression may have lower stress levels, may be less sensitive to stress-inducing situations, and may desire stimulation to increase their levels of arousal.

Callous-unemotional traits may be especially associated with low baseline cortisol levels. In a sample of youth aged 12–18, Loney, Butler, Lima, Counts, & Eckel (2006) found that CU traits were associated with low baseline cortisol levels, and that this was independent of conduct problem severity. Similarly, Stadler et al. (2011) found that CU traits were associated with blunted cortisol reactivity to experimentally induced stress in a sample of youth with ADHD and disruptive behavior problems.

Two studies using tasks designed to produce a stress response found that children with ODD/CD had lower cortisol responses to stressors than controls (Van Goozen et al., 1998; van Goozen, Matthys, Cohen-Kettenis, Buitelaar, & van Engeland, 2000). However, they did not find differences between the two groups on baseline cortisol levels. Blunted cortisol reactivity may be the result of habituation to negative experiences, as children with ODD/CD are often exposed to stressful events over a long period of time (van Goozen & Fairchild, 2006). Particularly stressful situations such as physical or sexual abuse and neglect have been found to influence the development of the HPA axis (Bremner & Vermetten, 2001). Many children with ODD/CD have been abused or neglected early in life (Ford et al., 2000) and it is possible that these life experiences may alter the functioning of the HPA axis.

Studies have also examined whether the subjective experience of emotions in ODD/CD children is consistent with their reactivity. Interestingly, two studies found that children who do not display a large cortisol response to a computer stress task report more intense emotions toward their opponents (Snoek et al., 2004; Van Goozen et al., 2000). Therefore, the physiology of the child is not always consistent with the reported emotions of the child.

Studies have shown that cortisol influences how accurate one is in interpreting social events, including conflicts (Haller, van de Schraaf, & Kruk, 2001). That is, adequate cortisol responses are necessary to correctly interpret the social situation and without these responses it is more likely one will incorrectly evaluate a social situation. It has been shown that children with ODD/CD are more likely to evaluate ambiguous situations as hostile and threatening and they are more likely to engage in and start social conflict (Dodge, Price, Bachorowski, & Newman, 1990).

Cortisol responsiveness to a stressor has been found to predict who benefits the most from a structured intervention aimed to decrease aggressive behavior. Children with ODD/CD who had a stronger cortisol response to a psychosocial stressor had fewer behavior problems after a psychotherapeutic intervention than children with ODD/CD who had a weaker cortisol response and participated in the same treatment (Van de Wiel, van Goozen, Matthys, Snoek, & Van Engeland, 2004). Therefore, biological factors such as cortisol may be able to help predict who will benefit the most from treatment, and these treatments could then be tailored to provide the most benefits for children with specific neuroendocrine responses.

Conclusion

In sum, research on the structural and functional brain differences in youth with ODD/CD suggests there is decreased gray matter and reduced brain activity in the amygdala, prefrontal cortex (primarily orbitofrontal/ventromedial regions), insula, striatum, precuneus, and ACC. Impairments in these regions may contribute to the deficits in emotion processing, problem solving, self-control, reward and punishment processing, and error monitoring that are seen in youth with ODD/CD. Abnormalities are also present in white matter tracts such as the arcuate fasciculus, SLF, and uncinate fasciculus. These may contribute to impairments in emotional processing and language abilities. Finally, there is evidence that youth with ODD/CD demonstrate low cortisol levels and decreased serotonin and dopamine functioning that may contribute to decreased sensitivity to punishment and increased risk taking, novelty seeking, hostile attribution biases and aggression.

As highlighted by Matthys, Vanderschuren, and Schutter (2013), many neurobiological studies of ODD/CD involve youth with comorbid ODD/CD and ADHD, making it difficult to differentiate the deficits that are specific to each disorder. Although a few studies have examined neurobiology that is particular to each disorder, additional studies are needed. Furthermore, research often assumes that ODD and CD are the same disorder, but more research on the neurobiological differences between ODD and CD is needed.

References

Adolphs, R. (2002). Neural systems for recognizing emotion. *Current Opinion in Neurobiology, 12*(2), 169–177.

Anderson, S. W., Bechara, A., Damasio, H., Tranel, D., & Damasio, A. R. (1999). Impairment of social and moral behavior related to early damage in human prefrontal cortex. *Nature Neuroscience, 2*(11), 1032–1037.

Berns, G. S., Moore, S., & Capra, C. M. (2009). Adolescent engagement in dangerous behaviors is associated with increased white matter maturity of frontal cortex. *PloS one, 4*(8), e6773.

Berridge, K. C., & Robinson, T. E. (1998). What is the role of dopamine in reward: Hedonic impact, reward learning, or incentive salience? *Brain Research Reviews, 28*(3), 309–369.

Birmaher, B., Stanley, M., Greenhill, L., Twomey, J., Gavrilescu, A., & Rabinovich, H. (1990). Platelet imipramine binding in children and adolescents with impulsive behavior. *Journal of the American Academy of Child & Adolescent Psychiatry, 29,* 914–918.

Boes, A. D., Tranel, D., Anderson, S. W., & Nopoulos, P. (2008). Right anterior cingulate cortex volume is a neuroanatomical correlate of aggression and defiance in boys. *Behavioral Neuroscience, 122,* 677–684.

Bremner, J. D., & Vermetten, E. (2001). Stress and development: Behavioral and biological consequences. *Development and Psychopathology, 13,* 473–489.

Bush, G., Luu, P., & Posner, M. I. (2000). Cognitive and emotional influences in anterior cingulate cortex. *Trends in cognitive sciences, 4*(6), 215–222.

Coccaro, E. F., Kavoussi, R. J., Cooper, T. B., & Hauger, R. L. (1997). Central serotonin activity and aggression: inverse relationship with prolactin response to D-fenfluramine, but not CSF 5-HIAA concentration, in human subjects. *American Journal of Psychiatry, 154,* 1430–1435.

Connor, D. F., Glatt, S., Lopez, I., Jackson, D., & Melloni, R. (2002). Psychopharmacology and aggression. I. A meta analysis of stimulant effects on overt–covert aggression-related behaviors in ADHD. *Journal of the American Academy of Child & Adolescent Psychiatry, 41,* 253–261.

Cook, E. H., Jr., Stein, M. A., Ellison, T., Unis, A. S., Leventhal, B. L., (1995). Attention deficit hyperactivity disorder and whole-blood serotonin levels: Effects of comorbidity. *Psychiatry Research, 57,* 13–20.

Dadds, M. R., Perry, Y., Hawes, D. J., Merz, S., Riddell, A. C., Haines, D. J., . . . Abeygunawardane, A. I. (2006). Attention to the eyes and fear-recognition deficits in child psychopathy. *The British Journal of Psychiatry, 189*(3), 280–281.

Dalwani, M., Sakai, J. T., Mikulich-Gilbertson, S. K., Tanabe, J., Raymond, K., McWilliams, S. K., . . . Crowley, T. J. (2011). Reduced cortical gray matter volume in male adolescents with substance and conduct problems. *Drug and Alcohol Dependence, 118,* 295–305.

De Brito, S. A., Mechelli, A., Wilke, M., Laurens, K. R., Jones, A. P., Barker, G. J., . . . Viding, E. (2009). Size matters: Increased grey matter in boys with conduct problems and callous-unemotional traits. *Brain, 132,* 843–852.

Decety, J., Michalska, K. J., Akitsuki, Y., Lahey, B. B. (2009). Atypical empathic responses in adolescents with aggressive conduct disorder: A functional MRI investigation. *Biological Psychology, 80,* 203–11.

Decety, J., Yoder, K. J., & Lahey, B. B. (2015). Sex differences in abnormal white matter development associated with conduct disorder in children. *Psychiatry Research: Neuroimaging, 233*(2), 269–277.

de la Fuente-Fernández, R., Phillips, A. G., Zamburlini, M., Sossi, V., Calne, D. B., Ruth, T. J., & Stoessl, A. J. (2002). Dopamine release in human ventral striatum and expectation of reward. *Behavioural Brain Research, 136*(2), 359–363.

Dodge, K. A., Price, J. M., Bachorowski, J. A., & Newman, J. P. (1990). Hostile attributional biases in severely aggressive adolescents. *Journal of Abnormal Psychology, 99*(4), 385–392.

Engell, A. D., & Haxby, J. V. (2007). Facial expression and gaze-direction in human superior temporal sulcus. *Neuropsychologia, 45*(14), 3234–3241.

Ermer, E., Cope, L. M., Nyalakanti, P. K., Calhoun, V. D., & Kiehl, K. A. (2012). Aberrant paralimbic gray matter in criminal psychopathy. *Journal of Abnormal Psychology, 121*(3), 649.

Fairchild, G., Hagan, C. C., Passamonti, L., Walsh, N. D., Goodyer, I. M., & Calder, A. J. (2014). Atypical neural responses during face processing in female adolescents with conduct disorder. *Journal of the American Academy of Child & Adolescent Psychiatry, 53*(6), 677–687.

Findling, R. L., McNamara, N. K., Branicky, L. A., Schluchter, M. D., Lemon, E., & Blumer, J. (2000). A double-blind pilot study of risperi- done in the treatment of conduct disorder. *Journal of the American Academy of Child & Adolescent Psychiatry, 39,* 509–516.

Finger, E. C., Marsh, A. A., Blair, K. S., Reid, M. E., Sims, C., Ng, P., . . . Blair, J. R. (2011). Disrupted reinforcement signaling in the orbitofrontal cortex and caudate in youths with conduct disorder or oppositional defiant disorder and a high level of psychopathic traits. *American Journal of Psychiatry, 168,* 152–162.

Finger, E. C., Marsh, A., Blair, K. S., Majestic, C., Evangelou, I., Gupta, K., . . . Sinclair, S. (2012). Impaired functional but preserved structural connectivity in limbic white matter tracts in youth with conduct disorder or oppositional defiant disorder plus psychopathic traits. *Psychiatry Research: Neuroimaging, 202*(3), 239–244.

Flagel, S. B., Clark, J. J., Robinson, T. E., Mayo, L., Czuj, A., Willuhn, I., . . . Akil, H. (2011). A selective role for dopamine in stimulus-reward learning. *Nature, 469*(7328), 53–57.

Ford, J. D., Racusin, R., Ellis, C. G., Daviss, W. B., Reiser, J., Fleischer, A., & Thomas, J. (2000). Child maltreatment, other trauma exposure, and posttraumatic symptomatology among children with oppositional defiant and attention deficit hyperactivity disorders. *Child Maltreatment, 5*(3), 205–217.

Forsman, M., Lichtenstein, P., Andershed, H., & Larsson, H. (2010). A longitudinal twin study of the direction of effects between psychopathic personality and antisocial behaviour. *Journal of Child Psychology and Psychiatry, 51,* 39–47.

Frick, P. J., & White, S. F. (2008). Research review: The importance of callous-unemotional traits for developmental models of aggressive and antisocial behavior. *Journal of Child Psychology and Psychiatry, 49,* 359–375.

Glenn, A. L., Raine, A., Schug, R. A., Young, L., & Hauser, M. (2009). Increased DLPFC activity during moral decision-making in psychopathy. *Molecular Psychiatry, 14*(10), 909.

Goldberg, I. I., Harel, M., & Malach, R. (2006). When the brain loses its self: Prefrontal inactivation during sensorimotor processing. *Neuron, 50*(2), 329–339.

Haller, J., van de Schraaf, J., & Kruk, M. R., (2001). Deviant forms of aggression in glucocorticoid hyporeactive rats: A model for "pathological" aggression? *Journal of Neuroendocrinology, 13,* 102–107.

Hanna, G. L., Yuwiler, A., & Coates, J. K., (1995). Whole blood serotonin and disruptive behaviors in juvenile obsessive-compulsive disorder. *Journal of the American Academy of Child and Adolescent Psychiatry, 34,* 28–35.

Herpertz, S. C., Huebner, T., Marx, I., Vloet, T. D., Fink, G. R., Stoecker, T., . . . Herpertz-Dahlmann, B. (2008). Emotional processing in male adolescents with childhood-onset conduct disorder. *Journal of Child Psychology and Psychiatry, 49,* 781–791.

Huebner, T., Vloet, T. D., Marx, I., Konrad, K., Fink, G. R., Herpertz, S. C., & Herpertz-Dahlmann, B. (2008). Morphometric brain abnormalities in boys with conduct disorder. *Journal of the American Academy of Child and Adolescent Psychiatry, 47,* 540–547.

Hughes, C. W., Petty, F., Shiekha, S., & Kramer, G. L. (1996). Whole-blood serotonin in children and adolescents with mood and behavior disorders. *Psychiatry Research, 65,* 79–95.

Hummer, T. A., Wang, Y., Kronenberger, W. G., Dunn, D. W., & Mathews, V. P. (2015). The relationship of brain structure to age and executive functioning in adolescent disruptive behavior disorder. *Psychiatry Research: Neuroimaging, 231*(3), 210–217.

Izquierdo, A., Suda, R. K., Murray, E. A. (2005) Comparison of the effects of bilateral orbitofrontal cortex lesions and amygdala lesions on emotional responses in rhesus monkeys. *Journal of Neuroscience, 25,* 8534–8542.

Jones, A. P., Laurens, K. R., Herba, C. M., Barker, G. J., & Viding, E. (2009) Amygdala hypoactivity to fearful faces in boys with conduct problems and callous-unemotional traits. *American Journal of Psychiatry, 166,* 95–102.

Kane, M. J., & Engle, R. W. (2002). The role of prefrontal cortex in working-memory capacity, executive attention, and general fluid intelligence: An individual-differences perspective. *Psychonomic Bulletin & Review, 9*(4), 637–671.

Klarborg, B., Skak Madsen, K., Vestergaard, M., Skimminge, A., Jernigan, T. L., & Baaré, W. F. (2013). Sustained attention is associated with right superior longitudinal fasciculus and superior parietal white matter microstructure in children. *Human Brain Mapping, 34*(12), 3216–3232.

Kochanska, G. (1993). Toward a synthesis of parental socialization and child development in early development of conscience. *Child Development, 64,* 325–347.

Kruesi, M. J., Casanova, M. F., Mannheim, G., & Johnson-Bilder, A. (2004). Reduced temporal lobe volume in early onset conduct disorder. *Psychiatry Research Neuroimaging, 132,* 1–11.

Kruesi, M. J., Hibbs, E. D., Zahn, T. P., Keysor, C. S., Hamburger, S. D., Bartko, J. J., & Rapoport, J. L., (1992). A 2-year prospective follow-up study of children and adolescents with disruptive behavior disorders. Prediction by cerebrospinal fluid 5-hydroxyindole-acetic acid, homo-vanillic acid, and autonomic measures? *Archives of General Psychiatry, 49,* 429–435.

Kruesi, M. J., Rapaport, J. L., Hamburger, S., Hibbs, E., Potter, W. Z. E., Lenane, M., & Brown, G. L. (1990). Cerebrospinal fluid monoamine metabolites, aggression, and impulsivity in disruptive behavior disorders of children and adolescents. *Archives of General Psychiatry, 47,* 419–426.

LaBar, K. S., Gatenby, J. C., Gore, J. C., LeDoux, J. E., & Phelps, E. A. (1998). Human amygdala activation during conditioned fear acquisition and extinction: A mixed-trial fMRI study. *Neuron*, *20*(5), 937–945.

Li, T., Mathews, V. P., Wang, Y., Dunn, D., & Kronenberger, W. (2005). Adolescents with disruptive behavior disorder investigated using an optimized MR diffusion tensor imaging protocol. *Annals of the New York Academy of Sciences*, *1064*, 184–192.

Lockwood, P. L., Sebastian, C. L., McCrory, E. J., Hyde, Z. H., Gu, X., De Brito, S. A., & Viding, E. (2013). Association of callous traits with reduced neural response to others' pain in children with conduct problems. *Current Biology*, *23*(10), 901–905.

Loney, B. R., Butler, M. A., Lima, E. N., Counts, C. A., & Eckel, L. A. (2006). The relation between salivary cortisol, callous-unemotional traits, and conduct problems in an adolescent non-referred sample. *Journal of Child Psychology and Psychiatry*, *47*(1), 30–36.

Mabbott, D. J., Noseworthy, M., Bouffet, E., Laughlin, S., & Rockel, C. (2006). White matter growth as a mechanism of cognitive development in children. *Neuroimage*, *33*(3), 936–946.

Malone, R. P., Delaney, M. A., Luebbert, J. F., Cater, J., & Campbell, M. (2000). A double-blind placebo-controlled study of lithium in hospitalized aggressive children and adolescents with conduct disorder. *Archives of General Psychiatry*, *57*(7), 649–654.

Marsh, A. A., Finger, E. C., Mitchell, D. G. V., Reid, M. E., Sims, C., Kosson, D. S., . . . Blair, R. J. R. (2008). Reduced amygdala response to fearful expressions in children and adolescents with callous-unemotional traits and disruptive behavior disorders. *American Journal of Psychiatry*, *165*, 712–20.

Matthys, W., Vanderschuren, L. J., & Schutter, D. J. (2013). The neurobiology of oppositional defiant disorder and conduct disorder: altered functioning in three mental domains. *Development and psychopathology*, *25*(01), 193–207.

Matthys, W., Vanderschuren, L. J., Schutter, D. J., & Lochman, J. E. (2012). Impaired neurocognitive functions affect social learning processes in oppositional defiant disorder and conduct disorder: Implications for interventions. *Clinical Child and Family Psychology Review*, *15*(3), 234–246.

Michalska, K. J., Decety, J., Zeffiro, T. A., & Lahey, B. B. (2015). Association of regional gray matter volumes in the brain with disruptive behavior disorders in male and female children. *NeuroImage*, *7*, 252–257.

Michalska, K. J., Zeffiro, T. A., & Decety, J. (2015). Brain response to viewing others being harmed in children with conduct disorder symptoms. *Journal of Child Psychology and Psychiatry*, *57*(4), 510–519.

Müller, J. L., Gänßbauer, S., Sommer, M., Döhnel, K., Weber, T., Schmidt-Wilcke, T., & Hajak, G. (2008). Gray matter changes in right superior temporal gyrus in criminal psychopaths. Evidence from voxel-based morphometry. *Psychiatry Research: Neuroimaging*, *163*(3), 213–222.

Noordermeer, S. D., Luman, M., & Oosterlaan, J. (2016). A systematic review and meta-analysis of neuroimaging in oppositional defiant disorder (ODD) and conduct disorder (CD) taking attention-deficit hyperactivity disorder (ADHD) into account. *Neuropsychology Review*, *26*(1), 44–72.

Passamonti, L., Fairchild, G., Goodyer, I. M., Hurford, G., Hagan, C. C., Rowe, J. B., & Calder, A. J. (2010). Neural abnormalities in early-onset and adolescence-onset conduct disorder. *Archives of General Psychiatry*, *67*, 729–738.

Passamonti, L., Fairchild, G., Fornito, A., Goodyer, I. M., Nimmo-Smith, I., Hagan, C. C., & Calder, A. J. (2012). Abnormal anatomical connectivity between the amygdala and orbitofrontal cortex in conduct disorder. *PLoS One*, *7*(11), e48789. doi: 10.1371/journalpone.0048789

Phelps, E. A., & LeDoux, J. E. (2005). Contributions of the amygdala to emotion processing: From animal models to human behavior. *Neuron*, *48*, 175–187.

Pine, D. S., Coplan, J. D., Wasserman, G. A., Miller, L. S., Fried, J. E., Davies, M., . . . Parsons, B., (1997). Neuroendocrine response to fenfluramine challenge in boys. Associations with aggressive behavior and adverse rearing. *Archives of General Psychiatry*, *54*, 839–846.

Pliszka, S. R., Rogeness, G. A., Renner, P., Sherman, J., & Broussard, T. (1988). Plasma neurochemistry in juvenile offenders. *Journal of the American Academy of Child and Adolescent Psychiatry*, *27*, 588–594.

Raine, A., (1996). Autonomic nervous system activity and violence. In D. M. Stoff & R. B. Cairns (Eds.), Aggression and violence. Genetic, neurobiological and biological perspectives (pp. 145–168). Mahwah, NJ: Lawrence Erlbaum.

Morris, J. S., Frith, C. D., Perrett, D. I., & Rowland, D. (1996). A differential neural response in the human amygdala to fearful and happy facial expressions. *Nature, 383*(6603), 812–815.
Rogeness, G. A., Hernandez, J. M., Macedo, C. A., Mitchell, E. L., (1982). Biochemical differences in children with conduct disorder socialized and undersocialized. *American Journal of Psychiatry, 139*, 307–311.
Rogeness, G. A., Javors, M. A., Maas, J. W., & Macedo, C. A. (1990). Catecholamines and diagnoses in children. *Journal of the American Academy of Child & Adolescent Psychiatry, 29*, 234–241.
Rubia, K. (2011). "Cool" inferior frontostriatal dysfunction in attention-deficit/hyperactivity disorder versus "hot" ventromedial orbitofrontal-limbic dysfunction in conduct disorder: a review. *Biological Psychiatry, 69*(12), e69–e87.
Rubia, K., Halari, R., Smith, A. B., Mohammad, M., Scott, S., Giampietro, V., . . . Brammer, M. J. (2008). Dissociated functional brain abnormalities of inhibition in boys with pure conduct disorder and in boys with pure attention deficit hyperactivity disorder. *American Journal of Psychiatry, 165*, 889–97.
Rubia, K., Smith, A. B., Halari, R., Matsukura, F., Mohammad, M., Taylor, E., & Brammer, M. J. (2009). Disorder-specific dissociation of orbitofrontal dysfunction in boys with pure conduct disorder during reward and ventrolateral prefrontal dysfunction in boys with pure ADHD during sustained attention. *American Journal of Psychiatry, 166*, 83–94.
Saddoris, M. P., Gallagher, M., & Schoenbaum, G. (2005). Rapid associative encoding in basolateral amygdala depends on connections with orbitofrontal cortex. *Neuron, 46*(2), 321–331.
Sarkar, S., Craig, M. C., Catani, M., Dell'Acqua, F., Fahy, T., Deeley, Q., & Murphy, D. G. (2013). Frontotemporal white-matter microstructural abnormalities in adolescents with conduct disorder: A diffusion tensor imaging study. *Psychological Medicine, 43*(02), 401–411.
Saudou, F., Amara, D. A., Dierich, A., LeMeur, M., Ramboz, S., Segu, L., Buhot, M.-C.,
Hen, R., (1994). Enhanced aggressive behavior in mice lacking 5-HT1B receptor. *Science, 265*, 1875–1878.
Snoek, H., van Goozen, S. H. M., Matthys, W., Sigling, H. O., Koppeschaar, H. P. F., Westenberg, H. G. M., & van Engeland, H., (2002). Serotonergic functioning in children with oppositional defiant disorder: A sumitriptan challenge study. *Biological Psychiatry, 51*, 319–325.
Soubrie, P. (1986). Reconciling the role of central serotonin neurons in human and animal behavior. *Behavioral and Brain Sciences, 9*(02), 319–335.
Spoont, M. R., (1992). Modulatory role of serotonin in neural information processing: Implications for human psychopathology. *Psychological Bulletin, 112*, 330–350.
Stadler, C., Kroeger, A., Weyers, P., Grasmann, D., Horschinek, M., Freitag, C., & Clement, H. W. (2011). Cortisol reactivity in boys with attention-deficit/hyperactivity disorder and disruptive behavior problems: The impact of callous unemotional traits. *Psychiatry Research, 187*(1), 204–209.
Stadler, C., Sterzer, P., Schmeck, K., Krebs, A., Kleinschmidt, A., & Poustka, F. (2007). Reduced anterior cingulate activation in aggressive children and adolescents during affective stimulation: Association with temperament traits. *Journal of Psychiatric Research, 41*, 410–417.
Sterzer, P., Stadler, C., Krebs, A., Kleinschmidt, A., & Poustka, F. (2005) Abnormal neural responses to emotional visual stimuli in adolescents with conduct disorder. *Biological Psychiatry, 57*, 7–15.
Sterzer, P., Stadler, C., Poustka, F., & Kleinschmidt, A. (2007). A structural neural deficit in adolescents with conduct disorder and its association with lack of empathy. *Neuroimage, 37*, 335–342.
Stoff, D. M., Ieni, J., Friedman, E., Bridger, W. H., Pollock, L., & Vitiello, B. (1991). Platelet ³H-imipramine binding, serotonin reuptake, and plasma alpha 1 acid glycoprotein in disruptive behaviour disorders. *Biological Psychiatry, 29*, 494–498.
Takase, L. F., Nogueira, M. I., Baratta, M., Bland, S. T., Watkins, L. R., Maier, S. F., . . . Jacobs, B. L. (2004). Inescapable shock activates serotonergic neurons in all raphe nuclei of rat. *Behavioural Brain Research, 153*(1), 233–239.
Tennes, K., Kreye, M., Avitable, N., & Wells, R., (1986). Behavioral correlates of excreted catecholamines and cortisol in second-grade children. *Journal of the American Academy of Child and Adolescent Psychiatry, 25*, 764–770.
Unis, A. S., Cook, E. H., Vincent, J. G., Gjerde, D. K., Perry, B. D., Mason, C., Mitchell, J., (1997). Platelet serotonin measures in adolescents with conduct disorder. *Biological Psychiatry, 42*, 553–559.

Van de Wiel, N. M. H., Van Goozen, S. H. M., Matthys, W., Snoek, H., & Van Engeland, H. (2004). Cortisol and treatment effect in children with disruptive behavior disorders: A preliminary study. *Journal of the American Academy of Child and Adolescent Psychiatry, 43*, 1011–1018.

Van Goozen, S. H., & Fairchild, G. (2006). Neuroendocrine and neurotransmitter correlates in children with antisocial behavior. *Hormones and Behavior, 50*(4), 647–654.

Van Goozen, S. H., Matthys, W., Cohen-Kettenis, P. T., Westenberg, H., & van Engeland, H. (1999). Plasma monoamine metabolites and aggression: Twxo studies of normal and oppositional defiant disorder children. *European Neuropsychopharmacology, 9*, 141–147.

Van Goozen, S. H. M., Matthys, W., Cohen-Kettenis, P. T., Buitelaar, J. K., & Van Engeland, H. (2000). Hypothalamic–pituitary–adrenal axis and autonomic nervous system activity in disruptive children and matched controls. *Journal of the American Academy of Child and Adolescent Psychiatry, 39*, 1438–1445.

Van Goozen, S. H. M., Matthys, W., Cohen-Kettenis, P. T., Gispen-de Wied, C., Wiegant, V. M., & Van Engeland, H. (1998). Salivary cortisol and cardiovascular activity during stress in oppositional-defiant disorder boys and normal controls. *Biological Psychiatry, 43*, 531–539.

Vanyukov, M. M., Moss, H. B., Plail, J. A., Blackson, T., Mezzich, A. C., & Tarter, R. E. (1993). Antisocial symptoms in preadolescent boys and in their parents: associations with cortisol. *Psychiatry Research, 46*, 9–17.

White, S. F., Pope, K., Sinclair, S., Fowler, K. A., Brislin, S. J., Williams, W. C., . . . Blair, R. J. (2013). Disrupted expected value and prediction error signaling in youths with disruptive behavior disorders during a passive avoidance task. *American Journal of Psychiatry, 170*(3), 315–323.

White, S. F., Tyler, P. M., Erway, A. K., Botkin, M. L., Kolli, V., Meffert, H., . . . Blair, R. J. (2016). Dysfunctional representation of expected value is associated with reinforcement-based decision-making deficits in adolescents with conduct problems. *Journal of Child Psychology and Psychiatry, 57*, 938–946.

10

Cognitive Functions

Matthew A. Jarrett and Dane C. Hilton

Externalizing behavior problems have historically included a range of problematic behaviors such as hyperactivity/impulsivity, aggression, defiance, disruptive behavior, and conduct problems (Achenbach, 1991). When such problems are conceptualized in diagnostic terms, they have often been referred to as disruptive and impulse-control disorders. Recently, advances in our understanding of the neurocognitive underpinnings of these disorders have led to greater differentiation between problems such as hyperactivity/impulsivity and disruptive behaviors. For example, in the *Diagnostic and Statistical Manual of Mental Disorders*, 4th Edition (American Psychiatric Association, 2000), attention-deficit/hyperactivity disorder (ADHD) was included in the same section as other disruptive behavior disorders such as oppositional defiant disorder (ODD) and conduct disorder (CD). In the more recent DSM-5 (American Psychiatric Association, 2013), ADHD was separated from these disruptive behavior disorders and included under the neurodevelopmental disorders, thus being combined with disorders such as autism spectrum disorder, intellectual disability, and language/communication disorders. This change reflects the growing recognition of the neurodevelopmental roots of ADHD symptomatology (Nigg, 2012). At the same time, a growing body of literature has documented specific neurocognitive impairments that are unique to ODD and CD (e.g., what have been termed "hot" executive functioning deficits; see below for details), suggesting that this distinction may be somewhat premature.

Given this growing differentiation between ADHD and ODD/CD, a key focus of this chapter on the cognitive functioning of those with disruptive and impulse-control disorders will be examining intellectual, language, and executive functioning (EF) impairments that are *unique* to those with ADHD and those with ODD/CD. In addition, we explore whether impairments in those with ADHD + ODD/CD are greater than those with either disorder alone (i.e., additive) or interactive. We subdivide each of our review areas (i.e., intelligence, language, and EF) into sections on ADHD, ODD/CD, and ADHD + ODD/CD. When data are limited on these distinct diagnostic entities and/or comorbid profiles, we draw upon dimensional research examining domains relevant to these disorders (e.g., inattention, hyperactivity/impulsivity, conduct problems). When possible, we also highlight differences between ODD and CD, but given that many studies have combined ODD and CD into a single entity, such studies are often limited in the current literature.

Intellectual Functioning

ADHD

As noted by Barkley (2006), it is now clear that children and adults with ADHD exhibit lower levels of intellectual functioning relative to controls. In their meta-analysis of intellectual functioning for children and adults with ADHD, Frazier, Demaree, and Youngstrom (2004) found an average difference of 9 points (range = 7 to 15 points) on standardized intelligence tests (weighted $d = .61$) between those with ADHD and controls. In a more specific meta-analysis of adults, Hervey, Epstein, and Curry (2004) found a somewhat smaller effect size (weighted $d = .39$), corresponding to an average difference of 6 points. Such a developmental difference may partially reflect emerging evidence for ADHD as a developmental delay in cortical maturation that appears to improve during the adolescent period for at least a subset of adolescents with ADHD (Shaw et al., 2007).

While some have argued that intellectual differences between those with ADHD and controls may be due to comorbid learning disorders (Bohline, 1985), studies comparing those with ADHD to those with learning disorder (LD) have found evidence for greater impairment in those with LD relative to those with ADHD only (Barkley, DuPaul, & McMurray, 1990; Purvis & Tannock, 1997). Although there is evidence for a mild decrease in intelligence for those with ADHD, it should be noted that individuals with ADHD cover the range of intellectual functioning (e.g., some have low intelligence, others are in the gifted range). Another important issue to consider is that measures of intelligence often include aspects that intersect with EF (e.g., working memory), making it difficult to determine unique differences in overall intelligence. Further, impairments in areas such as working memory that contribute to IQ estimation may be at least partially remediated by stimulant medication. For example, Adams (2008) found evidence for increased Wechsler Intelligence Scale for Children – Fourth Edition (WISC-IV) scores in children with ADHD who were on stimulant medications compared to those not taking stimulants. Consistent with the speculation above, this effect appeared to be driven by higher scores on the Working Memory Index. In a more recent study of adults with ADHD, Biederman et al. (2012) found an average IQ score difference of 6.1 points between medicated and nonmedicated adults with ADHD, and no differences were found between verbal and performance IQ. Although there is some evidence that stimulant medication may partially normalize IQ deficits in those with ADHD, more rigorous designs are needed to infer causation (e.g., those with higher IQ and/or better EF may seek out stimulant medication treatment).

ODD/CD

While a body of research has explored intellectual deficits in those with ODD/CD (Hogan, 1999), one of the challenges in this area of research is whether intellectual deficits are *unique* to ODD/CD or explained by the common comorbidity with ADHD. Hogan (1999) noted that in a review of 27 studies examining the relationship between ODD/CD and IQ, 60% of the studies found significantly negative associations. Among those with significant associations, 80% failed to control for comorbid ADHD. When ADHD symptoms were controlled for, 73% of the studies did not find ODD/CD to be uniquely linked to lower IQ. Of the studies that did find unique relations, Lynam, Moffit, and Stouthamer-Loeber (1993) found in a sample of preadolescent boys (ages 12 and 13) that the significantly negative relationship between verbal IQ and delinquency was not attenuated by including a measure of behavioral impulsivity in the predictive model. The authors concluded that only 17–25% of the effect of verbal IQ on delinquency operated indirectly through impulsivity. Further, Frick et al. (1991) reported nonsignificant differences between those with CD ($n = 68$), ADHD ($n = 101$), and clinic controls ($n = 42$) on full scale IQ from the WISC-R.

Some additional longitudinal studies have examined how lower IQ predicts future ODD/CD. Fergusson, Horwood, and Lynskey (1993) found that lower IQ was associated with greater risk of CD, both concurrently and over time, even after controlling for the correlation between CD and ADHD. Loeber, Green, Keenan, and Lahey (1995) found that boys who eventually develop CD had lower IQs than boys who did not, and these groups did not differ on ADHD symptoms. At the same time, IQ did not uniquely predict future CD in boys when socioeconomic status (SES), parental substance abuse, and ODD were considered. Lahey and colleagues (1995) found that, when SES was controlled for, there was not a difference on IQ between boys who did and boys who did not develop CD. At the same time, they found an interaction between verbal IQ and parental psychopathology in predicting the *persistence* of CD. Overall, after controlling for demographic and family variables, lower verbal IQs were not uniquely related to CD prior to the onset or at the time of diagnosis, but lower IQs did appear to affect the persistence of CD.

Overall, the bulk of the evidence to date suggests that overall IQ deficits appear to be associated more with ADHD than ODD/CD symptomatology, but it should be noted that some studies have found no differences. At the same time, though, there does appear to be some evidence specifically for verbal IQ impairment in relation to ODD/CD, particularly in relation to the persistence of conduct problems and when in combination with other risk factors such as parental psychopathology.

ADHD + ODD/CD

Few studies have examined whether ADHD + ODD/CD is associated with greater intellectual impairment than ADHD or ODD/CD alone. Hogan (1999) reviewed the five studies that examined group comparisons. The majority of these five studies found evidence of greater impairment in groups with ADHD (either alone or with ODD/CD) relative to groups with ODD/CD alone (Anderson, Williams, McGee, & Silva, 1989; Moffitt, 1990; Taylor, Chadwick, Heptinstall, & Danckaerts, 1996). In contrast, Schachar and Tannock (1995) found no significant IQ differences among those with CD only ($n = 5$), ADHD only ($n = 22$), ADHD + CD ($n = 18$), and normal controls ($n = 16$). It should be noted, though, that this study had relatively small groups for comparison, particularly for those with CD only (n = 5). Since this review, Matthys, Cuperus, and van Engeland (1999) have compared those with ODD/CD ($n = 48$), ADHD ($n = 27$), ADHD + ODD/CD ($n = 29$), and normal controls ($n = 37$) on full scale IQ (FSIQ) and verbal IQ. All three groups had lower FSIQ scores than a normal control group, suggesting that those with ADHD + ODD/CD do not have *greater* intellectual impairments than those with ADHD or ODD/CD alone. In a study examining CD alone, Dolan and Lennox (2013) compared those with ADHD + CD ($n = 35$), CD alone ($n = 72$), and normal controls ($n = 20$). The control group was significantly higher on IQ than those with CD alone and ADHD + CD, but there were no differences between those with ADHD + CD and CD only. In perhaps the largest study to date, Jensen et al. (2001) utilized data from the Multimodal Treatment of ADHD (MTA) Study and compared those with ADHD ($n = 184$) to those with ADHD + ODD/CD ($n = 171$). These groups did not differ on either verbal or performance IQ from the Wechsler Intelligence Scale for Children, Third Edition (WISC-III). Finally, in a study of preschoolers, Skogan et al. (2014) found no differences on IQ between those with ADHD ($n = 150$), ADHD + ODD ($n = 235$), ODD ($n = 205$), and controls ($n = 455$).

Overall, studies examining those with ADHD + ODD/CD suggest that those with this comorbid profile do not appear to have *greater* deficits than those with ADHD alone. In addition, and consistent with the larger literature, many (but not all) of these studies support the contention that those with ADHD + ODD/CD appear to have greater deficits than those with ODD/CD alone.

Language

ADHD

Research to date suggests that children and adolescents with ADHD do not appear to have serious language delays (Barkley, 2006). While some studies have found evidence for delayed speech in childhood (Hartsough & Lambert, 1985; Szatmari, Offord, & Boyle, 1989), other studies have found no differences (Barkley et al., 1990), suggesting that there is not convincing evidence of language delay in those with ADHD. At the same time, studies suggest that children with ADHD are broadly more prone to exhibit difficulties with expressive language relative to controls (Barkley et al., 1990; Hartsough & Lambert, 1985; Szatmari et al., 1989). While children with ADHD are more likely to talk more during spontaneous conversations relative to controls (Barkley, Cunningham, & Karlsson, 1983), they often become less proficient and talkative when facing specific task demands, suggesting that the language difficulties of those with ADHD may partially reflect difficulties with higher order cognitive processes (e.g., organizing, self-monitoring; Barkley, 2006).

While ADHD is not broadly associated with significant language delays, there are some domains that show specificity to ADHD. In relation to verbal fluency, Frazier et al. (2004) evaluated 13 studies examining letter fluency and 9 categories of semantic fluency. Although the mean effect size for semantic fluency (.46) was not significant for those with ADHD vs. controls, letter fluency (.54) was significant, suggesting that ADHD is associated with moderate impairment in this domain. Related to fluency, children with ADHD also show some difficulty with sentence completion tasks. Clark, Prior, and Kinsella (2000) found that adolescents with ADHD perform worse than those with ODD/CD and controls, suggesting some specificity of this deficit to ADHD. Another area of research suggests that children with ADHD and/or those with elevated impulsivity often exhibit a delayed internalization of speech relative to controls (Barkley, 2006; Berk & Potts, 1991). It also appears that those with ADHD have difficulty with pragmatic aspects of speech such as conversational pragmatics (Tannock & Schachar, 1996). Finally, when compared to children with learning disorders, children with ADHD show difficulties with organizing and monitoring their verbal productions (e.g., story recall), while children with reading disorders show more deficits in receptive and expressive semantic language abilities (Purvis & Tannock, 1997).

Overall, studies to date suggest that ADHD is more likely associated with language problems that overlap with the common EF impairments associated with ADHD (e.g., story recall and working memory) as well as deficits in areas such as verbal fluency, sentence completion, and conversational pragmatics.

ODD/CD

While a body of literature has explored verbal IQ impairments in relation to ODD/CD (see the section on Intellectual Functioning above), relatively few studies have examined language impairment specifically. Early studies highlighted the links between ODD/CD and reading difficulties, but such difficulties often involve multiple causal influences beyond language impairment. At the same time, reading disorders are associated with CD, even when controlling for SES and ethnicity (Burke, Loeber, & Birmaher, 2002; Sanson, Prior, & Smart, 1996). There is also evidence for a longitudinal relationship. In boys, disruptive behavior has been found to be a risk factor for later reading problems but not vice versa (Maughan, Pickles, Hagell, Rutter, & Yule, 1996; Sanson et al., 1996). In contrast, there is some evidence that early reading problems are a risk factor for later disruptive behavior problems in girls (Maughan et al., 1996).

In relation to low verbal IQ, Pine et al. (1997) hypothesized that the link between low verbal IQ and disruptive behavior may be due to dysfunction in brain areas related to language functioning. Using a dichotic listening test, the authors found that boys with disruptive behavior disorders showed a reduced ability to perceive syllables presented to the right ear, implicating dysfunction in the left temporal cortex. It should be noted, though, that only a subset of children with language delay exhibit abnormalities on dichotic listening tests (Tallal et al., 1996). Overall, these results suggest that the linkage between language deficits and ODD/CD may be due to processes that are related to the dichotic listening task (e.g., selective attention, left hemisphere processing deficits). At the same time, though, Pine et al. (1997) noted that their study and others have shown limited evidence for specificity (i.e., is the deficit shared by ADHD as well?).

While initial studies examined low verbal IQ and reading difficulties, other studies during the same time period began to specifically focus on language impairment in relation to disruptive behavior (Beitchman et al, 1996). In a review of broad emotional/behavioral problems, Benner, Nelson, and Epstein (2002) found that 71% of children with emotional/behavioral problems experienced clinically significant language difficulties, and 57% of children with language difficulties evidenced clinically significant emotional/behavioral problems. In addition, children with language difficulties are at increased risk for disruptive behavior problems later in life (Beitchman et al., 1996). In a recent meta-analysis of controlled prospective studies, Yew and O'Kearney (2013) found that 3- to 8-year-olds with specific language impairments were twice as likely to show clinical levels of conduct problems when followed up between 2 and 12 years relative to typical language peers. At the same time, most studies have not controlled for the initial level of disruptive behavior. To address this issue, Yew and O'Kearney (2015) examined the trajectories of conduct problems over time for children with early language difficulties and those with typical language. On average, children's conduct problems showed a curvilinear decline over time, consistent with past research. In comparing those with language impairment to those without, children with language impairment showed a similar declining trajectory over time between ages 4 and 11 but showed persistently higher levels of conduct problems. In addition, boys with language difficulties exposed to harsh parenting and low SES showed even greater levels of conduct problems, while amplification was also found for girls with language impairment and low levels of prosocial responding.

Overall, the research to date implicates language processing (i.e., dichotic listening impairment), low verbal IQ, reading problems, and language impairment as etiological contributors to the development of ODD/CD, although more research is needed to determine the unique contributions. Longitudinal research suggests that these contributors are more impactful when combined with factors such as low SES, harsh parenting, and parental psychopathology.

ADHD + ODD/CD

Few studies have compared those with ADHD to those with ADHD + ODD/CD on language impairment. Children with ADHD + CD have been shown to have lower reading scores than children with CD alone (who were not different from controls; Schachar & Tannock, 1995). More recently, in the MTA Study, no differences between ADHD and ADHD + ODD/CD were found for verbal IQ, percentage of LD diagnosis, or reading on the Wechsler Individual Achievement Test (Jensen et al., 2001).

While few studies are noted in the literature, emerging conceptual models may prove helpful for understanding the language impairments of those with ADHD + ODD/CD. Carpenter and Drabick (2011) reviewed the co-occurrence of language and behavioral difficulties in early childhood. The authors highlighted three of the common hypotheses regarding the connection between language problems and behavioral difficulties: (a) language difficulties increase risk for behavior problems (e.g., difficulty communicating leads to disruptive behavior), (b) behavior problems increase the risk for language difficulties (e.g., behaviors problems interfere with the acquisition of language skills), and (c) a shared risk factor explains their co-occurrence. In relation to the third hypothesis, the authors noted that factors such as temperamental negative emotionality and working memory deficits may operate together to increase the risk of co-occurring language impairment and disruptive behavior. In the following section, we note how working memory deficits are one of the strongest EF impairments associated with ADHD (Willcutt et al., 2012), and there is a large literature to support the role of temperamental negative emotionality in relation to ODD/CD (see Chapter 11, this volume). Given this conceptual framework, it is likely that those with ADHD + ODD/CD combine these more disorder-specific deficits to compound language impairment, although future studies are needed to determine if such influences are additive or interactive.

Finally, Carpenter and Drabick (2011) highlight moderating and mediating factors such as parent–child interactional processes that might lead to unique developmental pathways. This conclusion is consistent with the research reviewed above implicating factors such as low SES, harsh parenting, and parental psychopathology in the connection between language impairment and disruptive behavior.

Executive Functioning

In this section, we review evidence for EF impairments in disruptive and impulse-control disorders. While some models of EF include aspects such as emotion regulation (Barkley, 1997), we do not cover this domain as there is a separate chapter on it in this *Handbook* (Chapter 14). In addition, EFs also contribute to social-cognitive processes in disruptive and impulse-control disorders (Matthys, Vanderschuren, Schutter, & Lochman, 2012), but again, we do not cover this area of research, given that Chapter 15 is devoted to it. Finally, some research in this area has attempted to link EFs to structural and functional brain activity, but given the scope of this chapter and the fact that brain-related differences are covered in Chapter 9 of the *Handbook*, we also chose not to cover this area of research.

ADHD

A large number of studies have implicated EFs such as inhibition and working memory as etiological factors in relation to ADHD (Barkley, 1997; Castellanos & Tannock, 2002; Pennington & Ozonoff, 1996). A meta-analysis by Willcutt and colleagues (2005) found support for EF differences between those with and without ADHD across all measured domains (i.e., inhibition, vigilance, set shifting, planning, organization, verbal and spatial WM), with the strongest and most consistent differences found for inhibition, vigilance, spatial WM, and planning. These results are consistent with a past meta-analysis implicating EF deficits in ADHD and autism but not in CD or Tourette syndrome (Pennington & Ozonoff, 1996). In a more recent meta-analysis examining DSM-IV subtypes of ADHD, more nuanced differences were found between the subtypes of ADHD and control groups on measures of EF, with ADHD Combined Type (ADHD-C) showing larger group differences than the Predominantly Hyperactive/Impulsive Type (ADHD-H) and Predominantly Inattentive Type (ADHD-I) on most measures of EF, with some minor exceptions (Willcutt et al., 2012). Such results have led to views of ADHD-C as a more severe presentation of ADHD and a decreased emphasis on the importance of ADHD subtypes/presentations (at least from an etiological standpoint). Finally, this most recent meta-analysis found the largest/consistent EF effect sizes for working memory (g = .61–.71 across subtypes), response variability or sustained attention ($g = .48-.81$), response inhibition ($g = .56-.67$), planning ($g = .12-.61$), and set-shifting ($g = -.03-.46$).

Despite evidence for significant executive impairments found in these reviews, the results were widely variable and none accounted for the majority of the variance possible. Altogether, these findings suggest that while executive dysfunction is certainly one significant aspect of ADHD, EF alone cannot explain the complexity and heterogeneity of those with the disorder (Willcutt et al., 2005), and it is unlikely that ADHD is explained by a single EF deficit. These findings have spurred additional theories that attempt account for this complexity (Castellanos & Tannock, 2002; Nigg, Willcutt, Doyle, & Sonuga-Barke, 2005; Sergeant, 2005; Sonuga-Barke, 2005). These newer theories integrate previous research from single deficit models and emphasize subcortical influences such as motivational pathways (Sonuga-Barke, 2005), endophenotypes (Castellanos & Tannock, 2002), deficits in both top-down and bottom-up processes at multiple intrapersonal levels (Sergeant, 2005), and the possibility of multiple etiological pathways (Nigg et al., 2005). Although these theories propose somewhat differing and, at times, competing models, it is clear that the field is moving away from single-deficit models and toward more scientifically precise research through the integration of genetics, neurobiology, neuroanatomy, and neuropsychological functioning (Nigg et al., 2005).

Although a review of these emerging models would be outside of the scope of the current chapter, we review the evidence to date for the individual EF deficits present in ADHD, beginning with the EFs that have shown the greatest evidence for impairment.

Working Memory A number of theories of ADHD implicate working memory (WM) deficits as a driving force behind ADHD symptomatology and impairments (Barkley, 1997; Rapport et al., 2008; Willcutt et al., 2005). WM is typically split into verbal WM (i.e., phonological) and spatial WM (i.e., visuospatial) and, from the perspective of Baddeley's model (2003), the phonological (PH) and visuospatial (VS) components of WM are coordinated and controlled further by a shared system called the central executive. This system is responsible for the general oversight of the two other subsystems, the coordination of the system in response to changing attentional demands, and is the theoretical link between the WM system and long-term memory (Baddeley, 2003).

As mentioned earlier in this section, stronger and more consistent differences between those with ADHD and controls have been found for spatial WM (Martinussen, Hayden, Hoggs-Johnson, & Tannock, 2005; Willcutt et al., 2005), with a mean effect size of $d = .63$, and 75% of the studies surveyed have found significant group differences (Willcutt et al., 2005). Consistent with results reported for other EFs, there is considerable variability across both WM domains. In one study of verbal WM, the authors found a considerably large effect size between groups ($d = 1.73$; McInnes, Humphries, Hogg-Johnson, & Tannock, 2003), though most differences fell in the medium range (Willcutt et al., 2005). As expected, given the overall findings of the meta-analysis, the results of studies utilizing spatial WM were consistently in the medium to large range (Willcutt et al., 2005), with a few studies reporting effect sizes over 1.0. Interestingly, in their meta-analysis of ADHD subtypes, Willcutt et al. (2012) found very consistent group differences between all subtypes of ADHD and control groups, which may lend some support to the idea of a common deficit in WM across ADHD presentations.

In relation to Baddeley's model specifically, examinations of the different components of WM have led to mixed results regarding the impairments found in ADHD. As mentioned in the previous paragraph, meta-analytic studies have reported larger effect size differences for the VS relative to PH subsystems (Martinussen et al., 2005; Wilcutt et al., 2005), with the central executive, along with the buffer/rehearsal facets of the other two subsystems, leading to the deficits in WM performance typically observed in children with ADHD (Martinussen et al., 2005). A study by Karatekin (2004) that addressed some methodological issues in the meta-analyses actually found no difference between PH and VS WM performance for children with ADHD. It did, however, find impairment in central executive performance relative to control children, supporting the idea that central executive impairments may be a fundamental aspect of WM deficits in children with ADHD.

In a more recent study of the different WM components, Rapport and colleagues (2008) found significant differences in all three subsystems of WM when comparing children with ADHD to control children, with statistically corrected effect size differences for the VS and PH components reflecting similar results to the previously mentioned meta-analyses ($g = .89$ and .55, respectively). In regard to the central executive specifically, the authors found very large differences between ADHD and controls ($g = 2.76$), reflecting past results and further emphasizing the importance of central executive impairments in children with ADHD (Rapport et al., 2008). Additionally, this study found the central executive to play a larger part in the VS system relative to the PH system, likewise consistent with the aforementioned meta-analyses (Martinussen, et al., 2005; Willcutt et al., 2005) and more recent literature (Alloway et al., 2006). Despite these differential relations, both VS and PH systems have been found to be impaired in children with ADHD compared to control children independent of the central executive (Rapport et al., 2008). Future studies should seek to continue to explore these distinct WM components.

Sustained Attention Another consistently demonstrated difference between ADHD and controls in the Wilcutt et al. (2005) meta-analysis was that of sustained attention. The meta-analysis found that 23 of 30 studies found significant group differences on sustained attention as measured by continuous performance test (CPT) omission errors, with effect sizes in the medium range ($d = .64$). In the more recent analysis of ADHD subtypes, the largest differences on sustained attention (as indexed by response variability) were found between ADHD-C ($g = .81$) and controls, with ADHD-I showing somewhat smaller group differences ($g = .55$) and ADHD-H showing the smallest group differences ($g = .48$; Willcutt et al., 2012).

Response Inhibition As stated earlier in this section, Willcutt and colleagues (2005) found that response inhibition was one of the most consistent deficits in children with ADHD relative to controls. A total of 27 studies examining response inhibition using a stop signal reaction time (SSRT) paradigm found significant differences in the majority of these samples with mean effect sizes in the medium range (Wilcutt et al., 2005). Group differences using CPT commission errors as a measure of response inhibition have found less consistent group differences (61% of studies) and smaller effect sizes (mean = .51) but also show a range of effects. In their meta-analysis of ADHD subtypes, Willcutt and colleagues examined response inhibition across studies that employed stop signal tasks, CPT commissions, antisaccade tasks, and others, and found comparably large mean effects as those mentioned above between ADHD-C and control groups ($g = .65$), with smaller group differences between ADHD-I ($g = .53$) and ADHD-H ($g = .36$; Willcutt et al., 2012).

Planning Planning skills are typically measured using tasks such as the Tower of Hanoi/London, Porteus Mazes, or the Rey-Osterrieth Complex Figures Test (ROCFT), though these tasks may reflect somewhat different aspects of planning (Bull, Espy, & Senn, 2004). The largest mean difference between those with and without ADHD was found using the Tower of Hanoi task ($d = .69$), which was consistent when looking at ADHD subtypes as well (Willcutt et al., 2012). The Porteus Maze and Tower of London tasks found relatively similar medium mean effects between ADHD and non-ADHD groups ($d = .58, .51$ respectively;

Willcutt et al., 2005). When examining planning across the different subtypes of ADHD, a similar pattern was found as with other EF tasks such that ADHD-C appears to have the most consistently large difference when compared to controls (Willcutt et al., 2012). The smallest mean effect size between groups was found for the ROCFT ($d = .43$) and across the nine studies analyzed, this task consistently showed effect sizes in this medium range unlike other tasks which seem to have more variability across studies (Willcutt et al., 2005).

Set Shifting Set shifting is another commonly studied EF skill in research on individuals with ADHD that reflects cognitive flexibility. Most studies have used the Wisconsin Card Sorting Task (WCST; Heaton, 1981) or Trails B to measure this skill (Willcutt et al., 2005, 2012). In their meta-analysis, Willcutt and colleagues (2005) found that roughly half of the studies examined found significant group differences on planning across both the WCST and Trails B. The authors found a slightly larger mean effect size for Trails B ($d = .55$) compared to the WCST ($d = .46$). In a more recent meta-analysis, the authors found smaller and more variable group differences when examining the subtypes of ADHD versus controls for set shifting, with a medium mean effect found for ADHD-C ($g = .46$), a somewhat smaller mean effect for ADHD-I ($g = .37$), and a nonsignificant difference between those with ADHD-H and controls (Willcutt et al., 2012).

In summary, EF models have been highly influential in the study of ADHD etiology. Although many have moved away from a single-deficit conceptualization, current theories emphasize the important role of EFs, particularly in areas such as working memory, sustained attention, inhibition, planning, and set shifting/cognitive flexibility.

ODD/CD

Historically, theories of ODD and CD have relied on environmental etiologies based in the parent–child relationship (Reid, Patterson, & Snyder, 2002) or individual factors such as those described by Lochman and Wells (2002) within the contextual social-cognitive model. These models focus heavily on social learning driven by operant conditioning as the source of problematic behavior found in ODD and CD (Kazdin, 2005). More recently, however, there has been increased interest in the potential for factors such as EF to affect learning in these populations and lead to the symptoms of ODD and CD (Matthys et al., 2012). Although ODD and CD are less extensively studied for EF correlates than ADHD, the following section will briefly review the current literature on them.

In a recent review, Matthys, Vanderschuren, and Schutter (2013) emphasized three domains relevant to ODD/CD: punishment processing, reward processing, and cognitive control. Of most interest to us here is the cognitive control domain, which could alternatively be referred to as EF, though the authors take a broader perspective in describing this domain fully (Matthys et al., 2012). One drawback of the literature to date has been the lack of control for ADHD comorbidity when examining EF impairments in ODD/CD (Matthys et al., 2012). Even when controlling for ADHD, results have been mixed, with some meta-analyses and studies finding that EF impairment in ODD/CD is explained by the presence of comorbid ADHD (Pennington & Ozonoff, 1996; Hummer et al., 2011), while other studies have found that children with ODD/CD display EF impairment without comorbid ADHD (Oosterlaan, Logan, & Sergeant, 1998; Raaijmakers et al., 1998). More recently, Schoemaker, Mulder, Dekovic, and Matthys (2013) found that preschool children with ADHD exhibit similar levels of EF impairment to children with disruptive behavior disorder symptoms. While the number of studies that separate ADHD and disruptive behavior disorders symptoms has been small, future studies should continue to examine differences in the preschool age range.

In relation to specific domains, research on inhibitory control has found that such impairments are not related to ODD (with or without CD) independent of ADHD (van Goozen et al., 2004), while other studies have not found differences between ADHD and ODD/CD, though both groups performed worse than controls on EF tasks (Oosterlaan et al., 1998; Raaijmakers et al., 1998). In studies of cognitive flexibility using the WCST, one study found impairments in children with CD after controlling for ADHD (Toupin, Dery, Pauze, Mercier, & Fortin, 2000), while others have not (e.g., Dery, Toupin, Pauze, Mercier, & Fortin, 1999). In Schoemaker et al. (2013), those with disruptive behavior disorder symptoms did not differ from those with ADHD (in terms of effect size) with respect to overall EF impairment (.19 vs. .21), working memory (.15 vs. .21), inhibition (.22 vs. .24), and cognitive flexibility (.13 vs. .14). Again, though, the number of studies in this meta-analysis was relatively small for ADHD vs. disruptive behavior disorder comparisons and the findings were specific to preschool children.

Although the research to date has been mixed, the overall findings have generally linked EF impairment more with ADHD than ODD/CD, although some findings suggest that differences are less pronounced, particularly in the preschool age range. Beyond these traditional EF comparisons, an interesting area in the EF literature relevant to ODD/CD is the distinction between "hot" and "cool" EFs. Hot EFs are typically understood as including qualities of motivation and emotion, while cool EFs are cognitive tasks that do not explicitly activate motivation or emotion (Matthys et al., 2012).

In general, there seems to be stronger evidence for hot EF deficits in ODD/CD than ADHD. In a study of children with ODD, ODD + ADHD, and normal controls, the authors found no differences between the groups on cool EF tasks with the exception of significantly worse performance on a set-shifting task for the comorbid group. However, on a task that involved motivation and reward processing (the Door Opening Task [DOT]; Daughtery & Quay, 1991), the authors found that performance on the DOT task could predict ODD vs. control status with a high degree (i.e., 77%) of accuracy (van Goozen et al., 2004). Similar results were found in another study using the DOT, with boys diagnosed with ODD showing higher perseveration during the task, despite response punishment, and lower skin conductance during punishment, suggesting low punishment sensitivity and reward dysfunction in this group (Matthys, van Goozen, Snoek, & Engeland, 2004). More recently, Hobson, Scott, and Rubia (2011) examined performance across a range of cool and hot EF tasks in those with ADHD and/or ODD/CD. Compared to controls, both those with ODD/CD alone and with ADHD (with or without ODD/CD) were impaired on cool EF (i.e., inhibition response time, intra-subject variability) and hot EF (risky decision making on the Iowa Gambling Test). In regression analyses, ODD/CD but not ADHD symptoms were independently related to hot EF deficits. In addition, ODD/CD was independently related to deficits in specific cool EF measures (i.e., inhibitory control, sustained attention), but ADHD was related to a wider range of cool EF tasks. It should be noted, though, that no differential effects for reward based on CPT performance was found, and cognitive flexibility was not related to either ADHD or ODD/CD. Although some literature links cognitive flexibility and ADHD (as reviewed above), such a linkage is often smaller in magnitude than other EF deficits and does not appear to differ from ODD/CD (Schoemaker et al., 2013). Finally, a recent study by Schoemaker et al. (2012) found that preschoolers with disruptive behavior disorders displayed deficits in inhibition, but when IQ was controlled, the deficits were most pronounced on a task that combined both EF and motivational demands (i.e., the Snack Delay task). This finding suggests that inhibition deficits in those with ODD/CD might be most pronounced when EF tasks also have motivational demands.

Overall, the current state of literature on EF in ODD/CD samples is mixed. Despite this, more recent studies have examined ADHD and ODD/CD simultaneously and have started to examine different domains of EF such as hot and cool. In general, results to date suggest that cool EF impairments tend to be more broadly associated with ADHD than ODD/CD (although some deficits such as inhibition and sustained attention may cut across both disorders), while hot EF impairments may be more strongly linked to ODD/CD, particularly in relation to risky decision making. Future experimental studies are needed that manipulate the key influences outlined by Matthys and colleagues (2012; i.e., reward sensitivity, punishment sensitivity, and cognitive control).

ADHD + ODD/CD

Given the assumption that cool EFs are more strongly associated with ADHD than ODD/CD, one may wonder whether the combination of ADHD + ODD/CD is associated with any greater cool EF impairment than ADHD alone. Among studies that have examined whether children with ADHD + ODD/CD exhibit greater EF deficits than those with ADHD only, some studies have found no differences (Barnett, Maruff, & Vance, 2009; Clark et al., 2000; Kalff et al., 2002; Newcorn et al., 2001; Nigg, Hinshaw, Carte, & Treuting, 1998; Oosterlaan et al., 1998; Qian, Shuai, Cao, Chan, & Wang, 2010; Salum et al., 2014), while others have found the comorbid group to have more severe deficits (Jennings, van der Molen, Pelham, Debski, & Hoza, 1997; Noordermeer et al., 2015; Schoemaker et al., 2012; Skogan et al., 2014; van der Meere, Marzocchi, & De Meo, 2005). In addition, some studies have found those with ADHD + ODD/CD perform better than those with ADHD only (Munkvold, Manger, & Lundervold, 2014; Oosterlaan, Scheres, & Sergeant, 2005; Shuai, Chan, & Wang, 2011). Adding to this literature with a longitudinal study, Breaux, Griffith, and Harvey (2016) examined how EF measures in preschool predict elementary school ADHD or ADHD + ODD/CD status. The authors did not find any evidence for early EF differences in the prediction of ADHD only vs. ADHD + ODD youth. Overall, the majority of the research to date suggests that the presence of ODD/CD does not add to the overall level of cool EF impairment compared to those with ADHD alone.

In relation to hot EF, relatively few studies have examined those with ADHD + ODD/CD relative to other clinical groups. Dolan and Lennox (2013) compared those with CD ($n = 62$) to those with ADHD + CD ($n = 35$) and healthy controls ($n = 20$). On EF planning tasks, the ADHD + CD group was significantly worse than controls while the CD only group was not. The two CD groups did not differ though. No group differences were found for set-shifting tasks or inhibition tasks. On hot EF tasks, no differences were found on a card-playing task emphasizing reward, but both the CD and ADHD + CD groups performed worse than controls on a punishment-based task. Additional studies are needed to determine whether those with ADHD + ODD/CD exhibit greater hot EF impairments than ADHD and ODD/CD alone.

Conclusion

As noted in the introduction to this chapter, recent advances in our understanding of the etiology of disruptive and impulse-control disorders has led to greater differentiation between disorders such as ADHD and ODD/CD. While the evidence to date finds overall intelligence impairments to be more strongly linked to ADHD than ODD/CD, there is some evidence for verbal IQ deficits being independently linked with ODD/CD and the overall IQ impairments of those with ADHD may be partially explained by impaired EF (e.g., impaired working memory). In relation to ODD/CD, the effect of low verbal IQ appears to be particularly pronounced when combined with the known psychosocial risk factors for

ODD/CD (e.g., low SES, parental psychopathology, etc.). With respect to language, both ADHD and ODD/CD appear to be linked with language difficulties, although future research is needed to determine how much of this linkage is due to factors such as EF impairment (e.g., working memory), temperament (e.g., negative affectivity), and environmental experiences (e.g., dysfunctional parent–child interactions). Finally, while EF impairments have been more frequently studied and linked to ADHD than ODD/CD, emerging research has focused on the differentiation between hot and cool EF, with hot EF being more frequently linked to ODD/CD than ADHD. While more research is needed to understand the cognitive functioning of those with disruptive and impulse-control disorders, the future appears promising. With continued progress, basic research advances should prove beneficial in developing innovative treatments that target the unique cognitive impairments of those with disruptive and impulse-control disorders.

References

Achenbach, T. M. (1991). *Manual for the Child Behavior Checklist, 4–18 and 1991 profile*. Burlington: University of Vermont.

Adams, J. (2008). *An examination of the effects of stimulant medication on the IQ test performance of children with ADHD* (Doctoral dissertation The University of North Carolina at Greensboro). Retrieved from https://libres.uncg.edu/ir/uncg/f/Adams_uncg_0154D_10016.pdf

Alloway, T. P., Gathercole, S. E., & Pickering, S. J. (2006). Verbal and visuospatial short-term and working memory in children: Are they separable? *Child Development, 77*, 1698–1716.

American Psychiatric Association. (2000). *Diagnostic and statistical manual of mental disorders* (4th ed., text rev.) Washington, DC: Author.

American Psychiatric Association. (2013). *Diagnostic and statistical manual of mental disorders* (5th ed.). Arlington, VA: Author.

Anderson, J., Williams, S., McGee, R., & Silva, P. A. (1989). Cognitive and social correlates of DSM-III disorders in preadolescent children. *Journal of the American Academy of Child and Adolescent Psychiatry, 28*, 842–846.

Baddeley, A. (2003). Working memory: Looking back and looking forward. *Nature Reviews Neuroscience, 4*, 829–839.

Barkley, R. A. (1997). Behavioral inhibition, sustained attention, and executive function: Constructing a unified theory of ADHD. *Psychological Bulletin, 121*, 65–94.

Barkley, R. A. (2006). *Attention-deficit hyperactivity disorder: A handbook for diagnosis and treatment* (3rd ed.). New York, NY: Guilford Press.

Barkley, R. A., Cunningham, C., & Karlsson, J. (1983). The speech of hyperactive children and their mothers: Comparisons with normal children and stimulant drug effects. *Journal of Learning Disabilities, 16*, 105–110.

Barkley, R. A., DuPaul, G. J., & McMurray, M. B. (1990). A comprehensive evaluation of attention deficit disorder with and without hyperactivity. *Journal of Consulting and Clinical Psychology, 58*, 775–789.

Barnett, R., Maruff, P., & Vance, A. (2009). Neurocognitive function in attention-deficit-hyperactivity disorder with and without comorbid disruptive behaviour disorders. *Australian and New Zealand Journal of Psychiatry, 43*, 722–730.

Beitchman, J. H., Wilson, B., Brownlie, E. B., Walters, H., Inglis, A., & Lancee, W. (1996). Long-term consistency in speech/language profiles, II: Behavioral, emotional, and social outcomes. *Journal of the American Academy of Child & Adolescent Psychiatry, 35*, 815–825.

Benner, G. J., Nelson, J., & Epstein, M. H. (2002). Language skills of children with EBD: A literature review. *Journal of Emotional and Behavioral Disorders, 10*, 43–59.

Berk, L. E., & Potts, M. K. (1991). Development and functional significance of private speech among attention-deficit/hyperactivity disorder and normal boys. *Journal of Abnormal Child Psychology, 19*, 357–377.

References

Biederman, J., Fried, R., Petty, C. R., Henin, A., Wozniak, J., Corkum, L., . . . Faraone, S. V. (2012). Examining the association between stimulant treatment and cognitive outcomes across the life cycle of adults with attention-deficit/hyperactivity disorder. *The Journal of Nervous and Mental Disease, 200*, 69–75.

Bohline, D. S. (1985). Intellectual and effective characteristics of attention deficit disordered children. *Journal of Learning Disabilities, 18*, 604–608.

Breaux, R. P., Griffith, S. F., & Harvey, E. A. (2016). Preschool neuropsychological measures as predictors of later attention deficit hyperactivity disorder. *Journal of Abnormal Child Psychology, 44*(8), 1455–1471.

Bull, R., Espy, K. A., & Senn, T. E. (2004). A comparison of performance on the Towers of London and Hanoi in young children. *Journal of Child Psychology and Psychiatry, 45*, 743–754.

Burke, J. D., Loeber, R., & Birmaher, B. (2002). Oppositional defiant disorder and conduct disorder: A review of the past 10 years, part II. *Journal of the American Academy of Child & Adolescent Psychiatry, 41*, 1275–1293.

Carpenter, J. L., & Drabick, D. A. G. (2011). Co-occurrence of linguistic and behavioral difficulties in early childhood: A developmental psychopathology perspective. *Early Child Development and Care, 181*, 1021–1045.

Clark, C., Prior, M., & Kinsella, G. J. (2000). Do executive function deficits differentiate between adolescents with ADHD and oppositional defiant/conduct disorder? A neuropsychological study using the six elements test and Hayling sentence completion test. *Journal of Abnormal Child Psychology, 28*, 403–414.

Castellanos, F. X., & Tannock, R. (2002). Neuroscience of attention-deficit/hyperactivity disorder: The search for endophenotypes. *Natural Review of Neuroscience, 3*, 617–628.

Daugherty, T. K., & Quay, H. C. (1991). Response perseveration and delayed responding in childhood behavior disorders. *Journal of Child Psychology and Psychiatry, 32*, 453–461.

Dery, M., Toupin, J., Pauze, R., Mercier, H., & Fortin, L. (1999). Neuropsychological characteristics of adolescents with conduct disorder: Association with attention-deficit-hyperactivity and aggression. *Journal of Abnormal Child Psychology, 27*, 225–236.

Dolan, M., & Lennox, C. (2013). Cool and hot executive function in conduct-disordered adolescents with and without co-morbid attention deficit hyperactivity disorder: Relationships with externalizing behaviours. *Psychological Medicine, 43*, 2427–2436.

Fergusson, D. M., Horwood, L. J., & Lynskey, M. T. (1993). The effects of conduct disorder and attention deficit in middle childhood on offending and scholastic ability at age 13. *Journal of Child Psychology and Psychiatry, 34*, 899–916.

Frazier, T. W., Demaree, H. A., & Youngstrom, E. A. (2004). Meta-analysis of intellectual and neuropsychological test performance in attention-deficit/hyperactivity disorder. *Neuropsychology, 18*, 543–555.

Frick, P. J., Kamphaus, R. W., Lahey, B. B., Loeber, R., Christ, M. A., Hart, E. L., & Tannenbaum, L. E. (1991). Academic underachievement and the disruptive behavior disorders. *Journal of Consulting and Clinical Psychology, 59*, 289–294.

Hartsough, C. S., & Lambert, N. M. (1985). Medical factors in hyperactive and normal children: Prenatal, developmental, and health history findings. *American Journal of Orthopsychiatry, 55*, 190–210.

Heaton, R. K. (1981): *Wisconsin Card Sorting Test manual*. Odessa, FL: Psychological Assessment Resources.

Hervey, A. S., Epstein, J. N., & Curry, J. F. (2004). Neuropsychology of adults with attention deficit/hyperactivity disorder: A meta-analytic review. *Neuropsychology, 18*, 485–503.

Hobson, C. W., Scott, S., & Rubia, K. (2011). Investigation of cool and hot executive function ion in ODD/CD independently of ADHD. *Journal of Child Psychology and Psychiatry, 52*, 1035–1043.

Hogan, A. E. (1999). Cognitive functioning in children with oppositional defiant disorder and conduct disorder. In H. C. Quay & A. E. Hogan (Eds.), *Handbook of Disruptive Behavior Disorders* (pp. 317–355). New York: Kluwer.

Hummer, T. A., Kronenberger, W. G., Wang, Y., Dunn, D. W., Mosier, K. M., Kalnin, A. J., & Mathews, V. P. (2011). Executive functioning characteristics associated with ADHD comorbidity in adolescents with disruptive behavior disorders. *Journal of Abnormal Child Psychology, 39*, 11–19.

Jennings, J. R., van der Molen, M. W., Pelham, W., Debski, K. B., & Hoza, B. (1997). Inhibition in boys with attention deficit hyperactivity disorder as indexed by heart rate change. *Developmental Psychopathology, 33,* 308–318.

Jensen, P. S., Hinshaw, S. P., Kraemer, H. C., Lenora, N., Newcorn, J. H., Abikoff, H. B., et al. (2001). ADHD comorbidity findings from the MTA Study: Comparing comorbid subgroups. *Journal of the American Academy of Child and Adolescent Psychiatry, 40,* 147–158.

Kalff, A. C., Hendriksen, J. G., Kroes, M., Vles, J. S., Steyaert, J., Feron, F. J., & Jolles, J. (2002). Neurocognitive performance of 5- and 6- year-old children who met criteria for attention deficit/hyperactivity disorder at 18 months follow-up: Results from a prospective population study. *Journal of Abnormal Child Psychology, 30,* 589–598.

Karatekin, C. (2004). A test of the integrity of the components of Baddeley's model of working memory in attention-deficit/hyperactivity disorder (ADHD). *Journal of Child Psychology & Psychiatry, 45,* 912–926.

Kazdin, A. E. (2005). *Parent management training. Treatment for oppositional, aggressive, and antisocial behaviour in children and adolescents.* New York, NY: Oxford University Press.

Lahey, B. B., Loeber, R., Hart, E. L., Frick, P. J., Applegate, B., Zhang, Q., . . . Russo, M. F. (1995). Four year longitudinal study of conduct disorder in boys: Patterns and predictors of persistence. *Journal of Abnormal Psychology, 104,* 83–93.

Lochman, J. E., & Wells, K. C. (2002). Contextual social-cognitive mediators and child outcome: A test of the theoretical model in the Coping Power Program. *Development and Psychopathology, 14,* 971–993.

Loeber, R., Green, S., Keenan, K., & Lahey, B. B. (1995). Which boys will fare worse? Early predictors of the onset of conduct disorder in a six year longitudinal study. *Journal of the American Academy of Child and Adolescent Psychiatry, 34,* 499–509.

Lynam, D., Moffitt, T., & Stouthamer-Loeber, M. (1993). Explaining the relation between IQ and delinquency: Class, race, test motivation, school failure, or self-control? *Journal of Abnormal Psychology, 102,* 187–196.

Martinussen, R., Hayden, J., Hogg-Johnson, S., & Tannock, R. (2005). A meta-analysis of working memory impairments in children with attention-deficit/hyperactivity disorder. *Journal of the American Academy of Child & Adolescent Psychiatry, 44,* 377–384.

Matthys, W., Cuperus, J. M., & van Engeland, H. (1999). Deficient social problem-solving in boys with ODD/CD, with ADHD, and with both disorders. *Journal of the American Academy of Child and Adolescent Psychiatry, 38,* 311–321. 27

Matthys, W., Vanderschuren, L. J. M. J., & Schutter, D. J. L. G. (2013). The neurobiology of oppositional defiant disorder and conduct disorder: Altered functioning in three mental domains. *Development and Psychopathology, 25,* 193–207.

Matthys, W., Vanderschuren, L. J. M. J., Schutter, D. J. L. G., & Lochman, J. E. (2012). Impaired neurocognitive functions affect social learning processes in oppositional defiant disorder and conduct disorder: Implications for interventions. *Clinical Child and Family Psychology Review, 15,* 234–246.

Matthys, W., van Goozen, S. H. M., Snoek, H., & van Engeland, H. (2004). Response perseveration and sensitivity to reward and punishment in boys with oppositional defiant disorder. *European Child and Adolescent Psychiatry, 13,* 362–364.

Maughan, B., Pickles, A., Hagell, A., Rutter, M., & Yule, W. (1996). Reading problems and antisocial behavior: Developmental trends in comorbidity. *Journal of Child Psychology & Psychiatry, 37,* 405–418.

McInnes, A., Humphries, T., Hogg-Johnson, S., Tannock, R. (2003). Listening comprehension and working memory are impaired in attention-deficit/hyperactivity disorder irrespective of language impairment. *Journal of Abnormal Child Psychology, 31,* 427–443.

Moffitt, T. E. (1990). Juvenile delinquency and attention deficit disorder: Developmental trajectories from age 3 to age 15. *Child Development, 61,* 893–910.

Munkvold, L. H., Manger, T., & Lundervold, A. J. (2014). Conners' continuous performance test (CCPT-II) in children with ADHD/ODD, or a combined ADHD/ODD diagnosis. *Child Neuropsychology, 20,* 106–126.

Newcorn, J. H., Halperin, J. M., Jensen, P. S., Abikoff, H. B., Arnold, E., Cantwell, D. P., . . . Vitiello, B. (2001). Symptom profiles in children with ADHD: Effects of comorbidity and gender. *Journal of the American Academy of Child & Adolescent Psychiatry, 40*, 137–146.

Nigg, J. T. (2012). Future directions in ADHD etiology research. *Journal of Clinical Child and Adolescent Psychology, 41*, 524–533.

Nigg, J. T., Hinshaw, S. P., Carte, E. T., & Treuting, J. J. (1998). Neuropsychological correlates of childhood attention-deficit/hyperactivity disorder: explainable by comorbid disruptive behavior or reading problems? *Journal of Abnormal Psychology, 107*, 468–480.

Nigg, J. T., Willcutt, E. G., Doyle, A. E., Sonuga-Barke, E. J. S. (2005). Causal heterogeneity in attention-deficit/hyperactivity disorder: Do we need neuropsychologically impaired subtypes. *Biological Psychiatry, 57*, 1224–1230.

Noordermeer, S. D., Luman, M., Buitelaar, J. K., Hartman, C. A., Hoekstra, P. J., Franke, B., . . . Oosterlaan, J. (2015). Neurocognitive deficits in attention-deficit/hyperactivity disorder with and without comorbid oppositional defiant disorder. *Journal of Attention Disorders.* doi:10.1177/1087054715606216

Oosterlaan, J., Logan, G. D., & Sergeant, J. A. (1998). Response inhibition in AD/HD, CD, comorbid AD/HD + CD, anxious and normal children: A meta-analysis of studies with the stop task. *Journal of Child Psychology and Psychiatry, 39*, 411–426.

Oosterlaan, J., Scheres, A., & Sergeant, J. A. (2005). Which executive functioning deficits are associated with AD/HD, ODD/CD and comorbid AD/HD + ODD/CD? *Journal of Abnormal Child Psychology, 33*, 69–85.

Pennington, B. F., & Ozonoff, S. (1996). Executive functions and developmental psychopathology. *Journal of Child Psychology and Psychiatry, 37*, 51–87.

Pine, D. S., Bruder, G. E., Wasserman, G. A., Miller, L. S., Musabegovic, A., & Waston, J. B. (1997). Verbal dichotic listening in boys at risk for behavior disorders. *Journal of the American Academy of Child & Adolescent Psychiatry, 36*, 1465–1473.

Purvis, K. L., & Tannock, R. (1997). Language abilities in children with attention deficit hyperactivity disorder, reading disabilities, and normal controls. *Journal of Abnormal Child Psychology, 25*, 133–144.

Qian, Y., Shuai, L., Cao, Q., Chan, R. C., & Wang, Y. (2010). Do executive function deficits differentiate between children with attention deficit hyperactivity disorder (ADHD) and ADHD comorbid with oppositional defiant disorder? A cross-cultural study using performance-based tests and the behavior rating inventory of executive function. *Clinical Neuropsychology, 24*, 793–810.

Raaijmakers, M. A. J., Smidts, D. P., Sergeant, J. A., Maassen, G. H., Posthumus, J. A., van Engeland, H., & Matthys, W. (2008). Executive functions in preschool children with aggressive behavior: Impairments in inhibitory control. *Journal of Abnormal Child Psychology, 36*, 1097–1107.

Rapport, M. D., Alderson, R. M., Kofler, M. J., Sarver, D. E., Bolden, J., & Sims, V. (2008). Working memory deficits in boys with attention-deficit/hyperactivity disorder (ADHD): The contribution of central executive and subsystem processes. *Journal of Abnormal Child Psychology, 36*, 825–837.

Reid, J. B., Patterson, G. R., & Snyder, J. (2002). *Antisocial behavior in children and adolescents. A developmental analysis and model of intervention.* Washington: American Psychological Association.

Salum, G. A., Sergeant, J., Sonuga-Barke, E., Vandekerckhove, J., Gadelha, A., Pan, P. M.,. . .Rohde, L. A. P. (2014). Specificity of basic information processing and inhibitory control in attention deficit hyperactivity disorder. *Psychological Medicine, 44*, 617–631.

Sanson, A., Prior, M., & Smart, D. (1996). Reading disabilities with and without behavior problems at 7–8 years: Prediction from longitudinal data from infancy to 6 years. *Journal of Child Psychology & Psychiatry, 37*, 529–541.

Schachar, R., & Tannock, R. (1995). Test of four hypotheses for the comorbidity of attention-deficit/hyperactivity disorder and conduct disorder. *Journal of the American Academy of Child & Adolescent Psychiatry, 34*, 639–648.

Schoemaker, K., Bunte, T., Wiebe, S. A., Espy, K. A., Dekovic, M., & Matthys, W. (2012). Executive function deficits in preschool children with ADHD and DBD. *Journal of Child Psychology & Psychiatry, 53*, 111–119.

Schoemaker, K., Mulder, H., Dekovic, M., & Matthys, W. (2013). Executive functions in preschool children with externalizing behavior problems: A meta-analysis. *Journal of Abnormal Child Psychology, 41*, 457–471.

Sergeant, J. A. (2005). Modeling attention-deficit/hyperactivity disorder: A critical appraisal of the cognitive energetic model. *Biological Psychiatry, 57*, 1248–1255.

Shaw, P., Eckstrand, K., Sharp, W., Blumenthal, J., Lerch, J. P., Greenstein, D., . . . Rapoport, J. L. (2007). Attention-deficit/hyperactivity disorder is characterized by a delay in cortical maturation. *Proceedings of the National Academy of Sciences, 104*, 19649–19654.

Shuai, L., Chan, R. K., & Wang, Y. (2011). Executive function profile of Chinese boys with attention-deficit hyperactivity disorder: Different subtypes and comorbidity. *Archives of Clinical Neuropsychology, 26*, 120–132.

Skogan, A. H., Zeiner, P., Egeland, J., Rohrer-Baumgartner, N., Urnes, A., Reichborn-Kjennerud, T., & Aase, H. (2014). Inhibition and working memory in young preschool children with symptoms of ADHD and/or oppositional-defiant disorder. *Child Neuropsychology, 20*, 607–624.

Sonuga-Barke, E. J. S. (2005). Causal models of attention-deficit/hyperactivity disorder: from common simple deficits to multiple developmental pathways. *Biological Psychiatry, 57*, 1231–1238.

Szatmari, P., Offord, D. R., & Boyle, M. H. (1989). Correlates, associated impairments, and patterns of service utilization of children with attention deficit disorders: Findings from the Ontario Child Health Study. *Journal of Child Psychology and Psychiatry, 30*, 205–217.

Tallal, P., Miller, S. L., Bedi, G., Byma, G., Wang, X., Srikantan, S., . . . Merzenich, M. M. (1996). Language comprehension in language-learning impaired children improved with acoustically modified speech. *Science, 271*, 81–84.

Tannock, R., & Schachar, R. (1996). Executive dysfunction as an underlying mechanism of behavior and language problems in attention deficit hyperactivity disorder. In J. H. Beitchman, N. J. Cohen, M. M. Konstantareas, & R. Tannock (Eds.), *Language learning and behavior disorders: Developmental, biological, and clinical perspective* (pp. 128–155). New York, NY: Cambridge University Press.

Taylor, E., Chadwick, O., Heptinstall, E., & Danckaerts, M. (1996). Hyperactivity and conduct problems as risk factors for adolescent development. *Journal of the American Academy of Child and Adolescent Psychiatry, 35*, 1213–1226.

Toupin, J., Dery, M., Pauze, R., Mercier, H., & Fortin, L. (2000). Cognitive and familial contributions to conduct disorder in children. *Journal of Child Psychology and Psychiatry, 41*, 333–344.

van der Meere, J., Marzocchi, G., & De Meo, T. (2005). Response inhibition and attention deficit hyperactivity disorder with and without oppositional defiant disorder screened from a community sample. *Developmental Neuropsychology, 28*, 459–472.

van Goozen, S. H. M., Cohen-Kettenis, P. T., Snoek, H., Matthys, W., Swaab-Barneveld, H., & van Engeland, H. (2004). Executive functioning in children: A comparison of hospitalized ODD and ODD/ADHD children and normal controls. *Journal of Child Psychology and Psychiatry, 45*, 284–292.

Willcutt, E. G., Doyle, A. E., Nigg, J. T., Faraone, S. V., & Pennington, B. F. (2005). Validity of the executive function theory of attention-deficit/hyperactivity disorder: A meta-analytic review. *Biological Psychiatry, 57*, 1336–1346.

Willcutt, E. G., Nigg, J. T., Pennington, B. F., Solanto, M. V., Rohde, L. A., Tannock, R., . . . Lannock, B. B.(2012). Validity of DSM–IV attention deficit/hyperactivity disorder symptom dimensions and subtypes. *Journal of Abnormal Psychology, 121*, 991–1010.

Yew, S. G., & O'Kearney, R. (2013). Emotional and behaivoral outcomes later in childhood and adolescence for children with specific language impairments: Meta-analyses of controlled prospective studies. *Journal of Child Psychology and Psychiatry, 54*, 516–524.

Yew, S. G., & O'Kearney, R. (2015). The role of early language difficulties in the trajectories of conduct problems across childhood. *Journal of Abnormal Child Psychology, 43*, 1515–1527.

11

Temperament

Jinhong Guo and Sylvie Mrug

Extensive theoretical and empirical work has highlighted the importance of temperament in developmental psychopathology. This chapter focuses on the role of temperament in the development of Oppositional Defiant Disorder (ODD) and Conduct Disorder (CD). We begin by introducing the concept of temperament and its dimensions. We follow with a review of contemporary theoretical models that link temperament with psychopathology. In the next section, we review the most relevant and recent literature on temperament and ODD and CD, including studies that document distinct temperamental profiles in children with ODD and CD; the predictive utility of temperament for ODD and CD; the joint effects of temperament and parenting; and finally the gender-specific links from temperament to ODD and CD. Finally, we discuss the limitations and implications of current research findings and provide suggestions for future research.

Definition of Temperament

Temperament refers to constitutionally based individual differences in reactivity and self-regulation, including emotionality, activity, attention, and self-regulation (Rothbart & Bates, 2006). These differences are detectable early in development (within the first year) and are influenced by genetic, biological, and environmental factors over time (Shiner et al., 2012). Temperament is believed to represent the emotional and behavioral foundations of adult personality and contributes to social and emotional development in childhood and beyond (Kiff, Lengua, & Zalewski, 2011; Rothbart & Bates, 2006; Shaffer, 2005).

Although the broad conceptualization of temperament has delineated its main characteristics, more specific dimensions have been proposed in order to better understand its genetic basis and stability over time and across situations (Sanson & Prior, 1999). The earliest model of temperament dimensions can be traced back to Thomas, Chess, and their colleagues on the New York Longitudinal Study (Thomas, Chess, Birch, Hertzig, & Korn, 1963). They identified nine characteristics that could reliably profile temperament in infants as early as two months—activity, distractibility, intensity, regularity, sensory threshold, approach/withdrawal, adaptability, persistence, and mood. Their work challenged the traditional environmentalistic view of child development, directing attention to the active role of children in their socioemotional development (Sanson, Hemphill, & Smart, 2004). The Infant Temperament Questionnaire (ITQ; Carey, 1970) was one of the first questionnaires designed to assess Thomas and Chess's nine temperament characteristics. It was subsequently revised by Carey and McDevitt (1978). Later on, Rothbart and Bates (2006) described six infant temperament dimensions—fearful distress, irritable distress, positive affect, activity level, attention span/persistence, and rhythmicity. The first five dimensions also provided a useful description of individual differences in preschoolers and older children, whereas rhythmicity was deemed less relevant beyond infancy (Rothbart & Bates, 2006).

Broader temperamental profiles have also emerged. Thomas and Chess (1977) later clustered their nine dimensions into three broader temperamental patterns—easy temperament, slow-to-warm-up temperament, and difficult temperament. This "easy–difficult" classification has gained general support among both researchers and clinicians (Sanson et al., 2004). Children with difficult temperament have been typically described as irritable, irregular in daily routines, and slow to adapt to new environments (Thomas & Chess, 1977). However, some empirical studies failed to replicate this categorization and have provided their own definitions of difficult temperament (Martin, Wisenbaker, & Huttunen, 1994; Sanson & Rothbart, 1995). For example, Guerin, Gottfried and Thomas (1997) defined difficult temperament as comprising difficultness, unsociability, unadaptability, and resistance to control, whereas Kochanska and Kim (2013) defined it as including proneness to anger, poor effort control, and negative emotionality. Caution is thus warranted when comparing research using different conceptualizations of "difficult temperament."

Another widely used system specifies three broad basic dimensions of temperament—surgency/extraversion, negative emotionality, and effortful control/self-regulation. Surgency refers to positive emotionality, activity level, and impulsivity. Negative emotionality is related to negative emotions such as fearfulness and anger. Finally, effortful control includes inhibitory control, sensitivity to perception, and attention shifting (Rothbart & Derryberry, 1981). This structure has been supported in studies using the Revised Infant Behavior Questionnaire and Children's Behavior Questionnaire (Gartstein & Rothbart, 2003; Rothbart, Ahadi, Hershey, & Fisher, 2001). Furthermore, Eisenberg and colleagues (Eisenberg et al., 1996, 2005) differentiated two types of control. The first type is "reactive control", referring to a relatively automatic modulation of emotional and behavioral responses to immediate incentives. The second, "effortful control", refers to a more deliberate modulation of emotions and behaviors. Their model also included resilience and negative emotionality. The former refers to the flexibility in modulating (reactive or effortful) control to meet context demands. The latter is defined as the tendency to experience negative emotions.

Cloninger, Svrakic, and Przybeck (1993) first developed a model reflecting heritable differences in initiating, maintaining, and inhibiting behaviors and emotions in responses to stimuli (Rettew, Copeland, Stanger, & Hudziak, 2004). This model was based on research into temperament heritability and neuropsychological findings on behavioral learning (Cloninger, 1987). The first dimension is novelty seeking, which refers to approach behaviors activated by novelty. The second is reward dependence, which is related to activation of social attachment. The third is persistence, representing maintenance of behavior in spite of frustration. Finally, harm avoidance refers to inhibitive behaviors caused by punishment or nonreward signals.

Temperament has a biological foundation (Rothbart & Bates, 2006). Behavioral genetics research indicates that most dimensions of temperament are moderately heritable throughout infancy and childhood, with heritability estimates ranging from .20 to .60 (Goldsmith, Buss, & Lemery, 1997; Saudino, 2005). Twin studies show that genetically identical twins are more similar than fraternal twins on a broad range of temperamental attributes, such as activity, irritability, sociability, and positive affect (Shaffer, 2005). One study (Scott et al., 2016) using twin-factor mixture modeling identified four temperamental profiles in school-aged twins: a "regulated, typical reactive" group, characterized by average level of reactivity, surgency, and regulation; a "well-regulated, positive reactive" group, characterized by low negative reactivity and surgency, but high positive reactivity and self-regulation; a "regulated, surgent" group, characterized by low negative reactivity, high positive reactivity and surgency, and average level of self-regulation; and, finally, a "dysregulated, negative reactive" group, characterized by high negative reactivity, average level of surgency, and low self-regulation. A moderate degree of heritability was found in all four profiles, with estimates of heritability in identical twins being twice as high as in fraternal twins.

The fact that the heritability of temperament is only moderate indicates that the environment also plays a key role in shaping children's temperament. In particular, family environment during childhood has an important effect on temperament development. Shared home environment explains similarities in siblings' positive temperamental attributes (e.g., positive affect, interest in others), whereas nonshared home environmental influences explain variability in negative temperamental characteristics (e.g., negative affect; Goldsmith et al., 1997). These differential effects may occur because parents are more likely to use similar responses to positively valenced temperamental traits, but adjust their parenting strategies in face of behavioral challenges. For example, if a mother notices that her three-year-old daughter Lily is more easily agitated than her elder sister was at that age, she may adopt a stricter parenting style to inhibit Lily's negative emotions. This may further impede Lily's development of emotion regulation abilities.

In addition, family environment may moderate the heritability of children's temperament. For example, negative affectivity is less heritable in warm, secure, and structured homes, whereas effortful control is more heritable in more chaotic and disorganized homes (Lemery-Chalfant, Kao, Swann, & Goldsmith, 2013). Temperament may also influence what type of environment the individual selects (Sanson & Prior, 1999). For example, an active and extroverted child may engage in physical sports, whereas a shy and introverted child may prefer reading at home. The extent to which heritability and environment contribute to the expression of temperament may also differ based on the specific dimension studied, analysis level (e.g., broad factors vs. narrow band factors), nature of assessment (e.g., subjective report vs. objective evaluation), and developmental stage (Scott et al., 2016).

In general, temperament is viewed as a relatively stable construct. Longitudinal studies indicate that most temperament dimensions are moderately stable across infancy and childhood, and sometimes even into early adult years, with variations depending on the dimension of temperament and developmental period (Roberts & DelVecchio, 2000; Shaffer, 2005). For example, positive and negative affectivity factors were generally stable during infancy (especially over shorter interassessment intervals) and were apparent across gender, birth order, term status, and socioeconomic status (Bornstein et al., 2015). Some researchers claim that children with extreme temperamental characteristics (e.g., highly active/inactive) are more likely to display long-term stability, whereas the temperament of children with moderate temperamental traits will fluctuate somewhat over time (Kagan, 1998; Pfeifer, Goldsmith, Davidson, & Rickman, 2002). It is also possible that temperament becomes more stable over time (Caspi et al., 2003). In summary, temperament shows some plasticity to environmental influences. Nevertheless, the general stability of temperament is responsible for its remarkable influence on later development.

Theoretical Models of Temperament and Psychopathology

Temperament and psychopathology have been viewed as related domains (Kim et al., 2010; Lavigne, Gouze, Hopkins, Bryant, & LeBailly, 2012), yet the underlying mechanisms remain inconclusive. Several theoretical models have been proposed, including the "goodness of fit" model, spectrum model, vulnerability/resilience model, and pathoplasty/exacerbation model.

The "goodness of fit" model attributes the development of psychopathology to the incompatibility between parenting and a child's temperament (Chess & Thomas, 1984). Negative temperamental attributes are more likely to lead to behavioral problems when parents respond in an unconcerned or forceful manner. On the other hand, parenting that is sensitive to the child's temperament may attenuate the risks of negative temperamental characteristics. Although the model is widely accepted, it is difficult to operationalize goodness of fit, especially when considering it from a broad multicultural perspective.

In the spectrum model (Watson, Kotov, & Gamez, 2006), the normal and abnormal processes fall at different points on the same underlying continuum, with disorders regarded as the extremes of temperamental characteristics. In other words, temperament and psychopathology share the same etiological determinants, such as genetic influences. In this case, there might be a confounding effect between extreme temperamental characteristics in young children (such as anger proneness, poor effort control, and negative emotionality) and early manifestations of behavioral disorders (such as anger and loss of temper). Such a conceptual overlap between temperament and disorder symptoms is especially problematic for cross-sectional studies. The vulnerability/resilience model argues that temperament can act as either a risk or protective factor for the initial development of psychopathology (Watson et al., 2006). For example, a child with high impulsivity may face greater risk of developing a behavioral disorder, whereas a child with high effort control may be less likely to develop one. Nevertheless, the pathoplasty/exacerbation model proposes that temperament can alter the course or symptom expression of a disorder once it occurs (Watson et al., 2006). For example, poor regulatory abilities may exacerbate the severity of behavioral disorders. Although the vulnerability/resilience and pathoplasty/exacerbation models differ in the critical periods where temperament is influential, both models hold the view that temperament exerts causal influences on psychopathology.

Research on Temperament and Disruptive Behavior Disorders

In this section, we review the most relevant and recent literature on temperament and disruptive behavior disorder. Methodologically, studies predicting ODD or CD from temperamental characteristics are either cross-sectional or longitudinal. Cross-sectional studies examine the concurrent linkages at a certain developmental period; longitudinal studies focus on the predictive effect of temperament on ODD and CD over time, delineating developmental trajectories. It should be noted, however, that direct causal linkages cannot be inferred even from longitudinal studies. Another important consideration is that temperamental characteristics can either potentiate or attenuate the development of ODD and CD. In the current literature review, we focus on the potentiating role of temperament. In addition, accumulating evidence indicates that ODD and CD are highly comorbid with a wide variety of disorders. In particular, ODD and ADHD are highly comorbid conditions, as are CD and depression. In this chapter, we try to include the latest advances in the impact of temperament on ODD and CD with and without comorbidities. Finally, temperament does not work in isolation, but is constantly interacting with parenting and other aspects of the social environment (Sanson & Prior, 1999). Therefore, we also discuss the influences of parenting and gender on the relationship between temperament and ODD and CD from a developmental perspective.

Temperamental predictors of ODD and CD

Several cross-sectional studies have documented distinct temperamental profiles in children with ODD and CD. ODD has been reported to have temperamental profiles including high negative emotionality, high novelty seeking, low persistence, and low effortful control (Hirshfeld-Becker et al., 2002; Schmeck & Poustka, 2001). Notably, a recent study found that high surgency is linked to behavioral ODD symptoms, whereas low agreeableness is linked to affective ODD symptoms in children aged 3–6 (Zastrow, Martel, & Widiger, 2016). Typically, CD demonstrates a pattern of high novelty seeking, coupled with low harm avoidance and high negative emotionality (INSERM Collective Expert Reports, 2005). It should be noted that many of the studies summarized in this section used parent reports for both temperamental characteristics and ODD/CD symptoms, and therefore caution is needed when interpreting these findings considering the issue of shared method variance.

Despite the temperamental profiles observed in ODD and CD, recent attention has been directed to investigating whether those characteristics are related specifically to ODD and CD pathology or are due to comorbidities. One cross-sectional study (Kim et al., 2010) examined the temperamental characteristics of ODD excluding the effect of comorbid ADHD in a Korean sample. After adjusting for the effect of ADHD, children and adolescents with ODD were characterized by high novelty seeking, low cooperativeness, and low self-directedness compared to the control group. In addition, participants with both ODD and ADHD showed lower levels of self-directedness and persistence compared to those with ODD alone. Similarly, Melegari et al. (2015) identified high novelty seeking as a common feature of preschool children with ODD and ADHD in a cross-sectional study. However, preschool children with ODD showed higher persistence and harm avoidance compared to those with ADHD. This study also indicated that temperamental profiles associated with ODD may emerge at a young age. Lavigne and colleagues (2012) developed a cross-sectional model of risk factors for ODD symptoms in 4-year-olds, with temperament emerging as a significant risk factor. In this model, low effortful control had the strongest predictive effect on ODD symptoms. Negative emotionality and poor sensory regulation had weak but also significant effects. Contrary to prior research (Zeman, Cassano, Perry-Parrish, & Stegall, 2006), inhibitory control was not a significant predictor. The authors noted that this may be because inhibitory control was solely related to ADHD but not ODD (Oosterlaan, Scheres, & Sergeant, 2005; Wåhlstedt, Thorell, & Bohlin, 2009).

For CD, researchers compared the temperamental profiles of four clinical groups in a cross-sectional study: CD, emotional disorder, eating disorder, and personality disorder. Children and adolescents with CD showed higher novelty seeking compared to the other three clinical groups and the normative group, and lower harm avoidance compared to the other clinical groups, but not to the normative group (Schmeck & Poustka, 2001). In summary, these findings indicate that ODD and CD are linked to specific temperamental profiles, independent of comorbidities.

Longitudinal studies have also been conducted to elucidate the possible causal relationships between temperament and ODD and CD. One study found significant associations between lack of control (negative emotionality, restlessness, and short attention span) measured at age 3 and CD measured at age 15 (Caspi, Henry, McGee, Moffitt, & Silva, 1995). The Avon Longitudinal Study (Stringaris, Maughan, & Goodman, 2010) found that two early temperament dimensions—high emotionality and activity—predicted ODD in middle childhood as well as its associations with other psychopathology. In particular, high emotionality predicted the overlap between ODD and internalizing disorders, whereas high activity was highly predictive of the co-occurrence between ODD and ADHD. These findings support the "convergence–divergence" model of oppositionality. That is, different risk factors may converge by giving rise to the phenotype of oppositionality in middle childhood, but they may also diverge by determining different comorbidities.

For CD, longitudinal studies have demonstrated the unique role of negative emotionality. For example, fearfulness and irritability showed stronger effects over positive emotionality and self-regulation in predicting conduct problems over a one year period in middle childhood (Lengua & Kovacs, 2005). These findings are consistent with prior research indicating that dysregulated temperament, especially difficulty in regulating negative emotions, may promote early disruptive problems to CD (Cole & Zahn-Waxler, 1992). Nigg (2006) proposed two temperamental pathways for CD: one route including low fear and low affiliation, and the second route involving high anger reactivity. On the one hand, children with low temperamental fear may be less sensitive to punishment cues and others' feelings; on the other, children with high temperamental anger may perceive ambiguous social cues as more threatening, which may provoke more aggressive behaviors.

However, inconsistent findings have also emerged, especially with regard to difficult temperament. For example, difficult temperament reported by parents at age 2 did not predict oppositional and conduct problems reported by teachers at age 5 (Fagot & Leve, 1998). In addition, difficult temperament measured at 18 and 24 months did not discriminate between children with ODD and those without any psychopathology at age 6 (Shaw, Owens, Giovannelli, & Winslow, 2001). Because difficult temperament combines multiple temperamental dimensions with possibly different influences, it may not be a good predictor of ODD and CD. It is also possible that other variables have more proximal influence on ODD and CD. For example, Wiesner et al. (2015) examined the relationship between temperament and ODD and CD symptoms in fifth graders. In this study, temperament dimensions did not predict ODD and CD symptoms when social skills were taken into account.

In the reviewed literature, high emotionality and low effort control are the two most salient predictors of ODD/CD. This is consistent with the contemporary theoretical view that both reactive temperamental dimensions, such as emotionality, and self-regulative dimensions, such as effort control, contribute to a person's vulnerability to psychopathology (Calkins & Fox, 2002; Frick, 2004; Muris & Ollendick, 2005). Two models have been proposed delineating the roles of reactive and self-regulative factors in the development of psychopathology (Muris & Ollendick, 2005). The first is an additive model where both emotionality and effort control have a unique impact on the etiology of child psychopathology. This model is generally supported by findings in the present literature review. Therefore, the addictive model may provide a possible explanation for the association between temperament and ODD/CD. High emotionality may have direct impact on ODD/CD by reducing the response threshold to stimuli. It may also have indirect effects through other mechanisms, such as deficits in the development of social skills. The influence of effort control may be considered as part of executive functions (Frick, 2004), but it is unclear whether low effort control is a domain-general or domain-specific deficit in executive functions.

The second model posits that emotionality and effort control work in an interacting way. For example, a stressor may arouse negative emotions in children, especially those with high emotionality. However, these negative emotions may be reduced in children with high effort control, but exaggerated in those with low effort control. Although appealing, this model lacks adequate empirical support in existing literature.

Joint Effects of Temperament and Parenting on ODD and CD

Parenting behaviors and parental mental health have demonstrated tremendous effects in moderating the relationship between children's temperament and disruptive behavior disorders. For example, 2-year-old children with high irritability who experienced harsh parenting exhibited more externalizing problems than similarly irritable children who did not receive harsh parenting (Hemphill & Sanson, 2001). Similarly, studies found that frustration reactivity was more strongly predictive of externalizing problems for children who received high maternal control or low maternal positive guiding (Calkins, 2002; Rubin, Burgess, Dwyer, & Hastings, 2003).

Another study examined the moderating effect of parental psychopathology on the relationship between temperament and ODD symptoms in preschoolers (Antúnez, de la Osa, Granero, & Ezpeleta, 2016). Negative emotionality and effortful control at age 3 predicted

ODD symptoms at age 5. The effect of low effortful control on ODD was further enhanced by higher levels of paternal depression and anxiety. However, maternal psychopathology did not moderate the effects of temperament on ODD. These findings indicate the important role of parental caregivers in modifying the effect of temperament on ODD symptoms, which has been understudied in prior research.

In addition, the "difficult" temperamental characteristics of the child also pose challenges to parenting practices (Burke, Pardini, & Loeber, 2008; Rothbart & Bates, 2006). Children who are more disobedient and aggressive tend to provoke or exacerbate rejection and negative emotions from caregivers, which have been found to predict later behavioral problems (Sanson & Prior, 1999; Scaramella & Leve, 2004). One study showed that increases in child noncompliance from age 2 to age 4 predicted increases in maternal negative control (Smith, Calkins, Keane, Anastopoulos, & Shelton, 2004). Similarly, callous-unemotional traits have been associated with changes in three domains of parenting (inconsistent discipline, punishment, and parental involvement) in a 12-month follow-up among children aged 3 to 10 years (Hawes, Dadds, Frost, & Hasking, 2011).

In summary, the reviewed literature lends support to the transactional model where the interplay between children's and parents' characteristics and behaviors contributes to children's development (Sameroff, Lewis, & Miller, 2000). On the one hand, parents provide gene-environment interactions for temperament to develop (Burnette, Oshri, Lax, Richards, & Ragbeer, 2012). On the other, children's temperament can also alter parenting behaviors (Childs, Fite, Moore, Lochman, & Pardini, 2014). Based on the "goodness of fit" model (Chess & Thomas, 1984), disruptive behavior disorders are more likely to occur when parenting is not compatible with children's temperament.

Gender-Specific Effects

Early research demonstrated gender differences in temperament. Using parental ratings and laboratory observations, female infants were less approaching to novel stimuli than male infants (Prior, Sanson, & Oberklaid, 1989). In a meta-analysis conducted by Eaton and Enns (1986), males were found to be more active than females. These gender differences in activity level were smallest in infants and increased with age through childhood. Maccoby and Jacklin (1974) found similar levels of negative emotionality in boys and girls up to 18 months, but higher negative emotional reactions in boys after 18 months. Hagekull and Bohlin (1992) found that girls showed more shyness, fearfulness, and inhibition than boys at age 5 years and older. Else-Quest, Hyde, Goldsmith, and Van Hulle (2006) examined gender differences in children from 3 months to 13 years old, finding that boys exhibited lower effortful control and higher surgency than girls. In addition, mothers and teachers reported more externalizing problems in boys than girls in toddlerhood and later (Juliano, Werner, & Cassidy, 2006; Bongers, Koot, Van der Ende, & Verhulst, 2003).

Some researchers propose that gender differences in temperament may predispose boys and girls to the development of different psychopathologies. For example, boys tend to display lower effortful control than girls (Else-Quest et al., 2006). In turn, lower effortful control has been linked to conduct problems and attention deficit hyperactivity disorder, which are more common in males (Frick & Morris, 2004; Nigg, Goldsmith, & Sachek, 2004). By contrast, girls typically are more affiliative than boys, especially during adolescence (McClure, 2000). This affiliative tendency may heighten girls' sensitivity to interpersonal stressors (Hoffmann & Su, 1998) and increase their vulnerability to internalizing disorders (Oldehinkel, Wittchen, & Schuster, 1999). Overall, this view tends to depict boys as generally having temperament characteristics that could lead to externalizing problems, and girls as having more temperament characteristics that lead to internalizing problems.

Other studies suggest that the same temperament features can differentially influence the development of psychopathology in boys and girls. For example, negative affectivity was predictive of internalizing problems in girls at age 6–7, but oppositional behaviors in boys (Rothbart, Ahadi, & Hershey, 1994). In another study, low approach contributed to externalizing problems in girls only, whereas irritability and inflexibility were associated with externalizing problems more strongly in boys than in girls at 11–12 years (Sanson, Smart, Prior, Oberklaid, & Amos, 1996). More recently, high cognitive and affective empathy were found to be associated with lower CD symptoms in adolescent girls, but not in adolescent boys (Gambin & Sharp, 2016). Finally, one study found that self-regulation at 24 and 42 months moderated the association between exuberant temperament at 20 months and externalizing behaviors at kindergarten entry for girls, but not boys (Morales, Beekman, Blandon, Stifter, & Buss, 2015).

However, gender differences in the relationship between temperament and problem behaviors are far from conclusive. For instance, one study found significant associations between difficult temperament in infants and maladjustment at 3–4 years old in girls, but not in boys (Scholom, Zucker, & Stollak, 1979), whereas another reported that the association was generally stronger for boys than for girls (Fagan, 1990). Finally, there are also studies that find no gender differences in the relationship between temperament and psychopathology (Oldehinkel, Hartman, De Winter, Veenstra, & Ormel, 2004; Ormel et al., 2005; Vitaro, Barker, Boivin, Brendgen, & Tremblay, 2006).

Despite consistent evidence of gender differences in both temperament and psychopathology, the moderating role of gender in the relationship between temperament and disruptive behavior disorders has not shown a consistent pattern of results. Several factors may contribute to those inconsistencies. For example, conduct problems may be expressed differently by boys and girls. In particular, boys tend to show direct and physical aggression, whereas girls engage more in indirect and relational aggression (Crick & Zahn-Waxler, 2003). In addition, parents and teachers may hold different role expectations for boys and girls that may differentially influence their ratings of children's behaviors.

The gender differences that are obtained may be explained by two types of process. First, gender differences may reflect biological dispositions. Males may show more externalizing problems than females because they intrinsically have higher irritability and lower effort control (Campbell, 2006; Vitaro et al., 2006). Second, gender differences may be an outcome of socialization experience. Typically, boys receive more tolerance, sometimes even reward, for exhibiting aggressive behaviors, whereas girls are socialized to be less aggressive and more affiliative (Fivush & Buckner, 2000). Thus, the association between certain temperament characteristics and conduct problems may be stronger for boys because girls are socialized more strongly to inhibit difficult temperament and antisocial behaviors.

Limitations of Current Literature

The reviewed literature has several limitations. First, some temperamental precursors of ODD and CD overlap (e.g., negative emotionality is predictive of both ODD and CD), but little research has examined if the underlying pathway differs. A better understanding of how the same temperamental precursors are linked to different behavioral outcomes would be beneficial in guiding interventions. Second, few studies have controlled for multiple comorbidities of ODD and CD (Drabick, Ollendick, & Bubier, 2010). Therefore, research that examines the concurrence of ODD/CD and ADHD should also evaluate and control the potential influences of other comorbidities, such as anxiety and mood disorders. Third, most studies have focused on dimensional measures of ODD/CD symptoms (Kim et al., 2010; Lavigne et al., 2012) rather than actual clinical diagnoses (Melegari et al., 2015), which may be differentially related to temperament. Fourth, studies of gender differences in the association between temperament and behavioral problems have not yielded consistent results. More research is needed to examine the potential causes of these inconsistencies. Fifth, some studies reviewed in this chapter relied on parent report for both temperamental characteristics and ODD/CD symptoms, which might inflate their relationships due to shared method variance. Finally, it remains unclear whether and how early temperament can be distinguished from the early demonstrations of ODD/CD behaviors. The conceptual overlap between temperament and ODD/CD is a critical issue particularly for cross-sectional studies.

Implications

Despite those limitations, findings of current literature have important theoretical and practical implications. First, a large body of literature reviewed indicates distinct temperamental profiles in children with ODD and CD, even at an early age. In addition, significant and consistent associations between temperament and disruptive behaviors were found both concurrently and longitudinally. These findings indicate that it may be possible to identify children at risk for ODD and CD at an early age by evaluating temperamental characteristics. High novelty seeking, high persistence, and low effortful control are some important predictors of ODD. Negative emotionality, especially low fear and high anger, is uniquely related to the development of CD. In addition, evaluation of those temperament characteristics may assist in implementing a patient-tailored treatment program (Kim et al., 2010). For example, intervention programs focusing on promoting emotion regulation skills may be more effective for CD children with high anger reactivity, whereas positive reinforcement may be beneficial in encouraging prosocial behaviors for CD children with low temperamental fear, as they tend to be less sensitive to punishment (Pardini & Frick, 2013). Furthermore, higher persistence in ODD children indicates that their behaviors may be highly resistant to change, and long-term intervention strategies may be needed.

Second, the literature reviewed suggests that parenting could either buffer or exacerbate the effects of temperament on ODD and CD. Antúnez and colleagues' (2016) study also indicates the important role of paternal caregivers in moderating the association between temperament and ODD, which has generally been neglected in prior research. The available findings underscore the importance of including parents, and especially fathers, in interventions for disruptive behavior disorders. Indeed, some interventions for conduct problems have focused on parenting (Eyberg, Boggs, & Algina, 1995; Webster-Stratton, Reid, & Hammond, 2004), but with only moderate effect sizes (Greene & Doyle, 1999; Lavigne et al., 2012). These interventions typically focus on improving parenting skills in a broad sense, but fail to consider the specific temperamental characteristics of each child, which is a serious limitation in current parent training research. It is possible that the effectiveness of parent training for disruptive behaviors would be enhanced by adapting the parenting skills specific to children's temperamental characteristics. For example, a child with low task persistence may improve gradually if parents can patiently and consistently assist him or her in completing a difficult task in small incremental steps. It is also possible that the interaction between parents and children's temperament may differ across development. For example, the impact of parents may be most salient during early years of life. Thus, longitudinal research is needed to examine the specific developmental timing of interactions between parenting and temperament. This information would help further guide the timing and content of parent interventions.

Finally, although the evidence of gender differences in associations between temperament and behavioral problems remains inconsistent, future studies should examine the influence of temperament on ODD/CD separately for boys and girls. Since boys and girls face different social expectations and pressures in forming gender roles (Fivush & Buckner, 2000), it is understandable that gender differences in temperament increase with age as children become exposed to more social influences. Gender differences in temperament may contribute to the way boys and girls perceive, interpret, and cope with social stressors that hold implications for their socioemotional behaviors. At the same time, it is also important to investigate if temperament is associated with different ODD/CD comorbidities for boys and girls, as well as to explore and establish possible theories to explain gender-specific effects and developmental trajectories.

Conclusion

In summary, the research reviewed in this chapter demonstrates the fundamental contributions of temperament to the development and treatment of ODD/CD symptoms. Evaluation of early temperamental characteristics may be an important first step in identifying children at risk of ODD/CD symptoms and tailoring treatment strategies to prevent the development of disruptive behavior disorders. In addition, although temperament may predispose children to develop ODD/CD, it is important to consider the joint influences of family and society. Elucidating interactions between temperament and contextual factors across childhood and adolescence would facilitate the development of individualized prevention and intervention strategies.

References

Antúnez, Z., de la Osa, N., Granero, R., & Ezpeleta, L. (2016). Parental psychopathology levels as a moderator of temperament and oppositional defiant disorder symptoms in preschoolers. *Journal of Child and Family Studies*, 25(10), 3124–3135. doi:10.1007/10826-016-1461-2

Bongers, I. L., Koot, H. M., van der Ende, J., & Verhulst, F. C. (2003). The normative development of child and adolescent problem behavior. *Journal of Abnormal Psychology*, 112(2), 179–192.

Bornstein, M. H., Putnick, D. L., Gartstein, M. A., Hahn, C. S., Auestad, N., & O'Connor, D. L. (2015). Infant temperament: Stability by age, gender, birth order, term status, and socioeconomic status. *Child Development*, 86(3), 844–863.

Burke, J. D., Pardini, D. A., & Loeber, R. (2008). Reciprocal relationships between parenting behavior and disruptive psychopathology from childhood through adolescence. *Journal of Abnormal Child Psychology*, 36(5), 679–692.

Burnette, M. L., Oshri, A., Lax, R., Richards, D., & Ragbeer, S. N. (2012). Pathways from harsh parenting to adolescent antisocial behavior: A multidomain test of gender moderation. *Development and Psychopathology*, 24(03), 857–870.

Calkins, S. D. (2002). Does aversive behavior during toddlerhood matter? The effects of difficult temperament on maternal perceptions and behavior. *Infant Mental Health Journal*, 23(4), 381–402.

Calkins, S. D., & Fox, N. A. (2002). Self-regulatory processes in early personality development: A multilevel approach to the study of childhood social withdrawal and aggression. *Development and Psychopathology*, 14(03), 477–498.

Campbell, A. (2006). Sex differences in direct aggression: What are the psychological mediators? *Aggression and Violent Behavior*, 11(3), 237–264.

Carey, W. B. (1970). A simplified method for measuring infant temperament. *The Journal of Pediatrics*, 77(2), 188–194.

Carey, W. B., & McDevitt, S. C. (1978). Revision of the infant temperament questionnaire. *Pediatrics*, 61(5), 735–739.

Caspi, A., Harrington, H., Milne, B., Amell, J. W., Theodore, R. F., & Moffitt, T. E. (2003). Children's behavioral styles at age 3 are linked to their adult personality traits at age 26. *Journal of Personality*, 71(4), 495–514.

Caspi, A., Henry, B., McGee, R. O., Moffitt, T. E., & Silva, P. A. (1995). Temperamental origins of child and adolescent behavior problems: From age three to age fifteen. *Child Development*, 66(1), 55–68.

Chess, S., & Thomas, R. (1984). *Origins and evolution of behavior disorders*. New York, NY: Brunner/Mazel.

Childs, A. W., Fite, P. J., Moore, T. M., Lochman, J. E., & Pardini, D. A. (2014). Bidirectional associations between parenting behavior and child callous-unemotional traits: Does parental depression moderate this link? *Journal of Abnormal Child Psychology*, 42(7), 1141–1151.

Cloninger, C. R. (1987). A systematic method for clinical description and classification of personality variants: A proposal. *Archives of General Psychiatry*, 44(6), 573–588.

Cloninger, C. R., Svrakic, D. M., & Przybeck, T. R. (1993). A psychobiological model of temperament and character. *Archives of General Psychiatry*, 50(12), 975–990.

Cole, P. M., & Zahn-Waxler, C. (1992). Emotional dysregulation in disruptive behavior disorders. In D. Cicchetti and S. Toth (Eds.), *Rochester symposium on developmental psychopathology: Developmental perspectives on depression* (pp. 173–209). Rochester, NY: University of Rochester Press.

Crick, N. R., & Zahn-Waxler, C. (2003). The development of psychopathology in females and males: Current progress and future challenges. *Development and Psychopathology*, 15(3), 719–742.

Drabick, D. A., Ollendick, T. H., & Bubier, J. L. (2010). Co-occurrence of ODD and anxiety: Shared risk processes and evidence for a dual-pathway model. *Clinical Psychology: Science and Practice*, 17(4), 307–318.

Eaton, W. O., & Enns, L. R. (1986). Sex differences in human motor activity level. *Psychological Bulletin*, 100(1), 19–28.

Eisenberg, N., Fabes, R. A., Guthrie, I. K., Murphy, B. C., Maszk, P., Holmgren, R., & Suh, K. (1996). The relations of regulation and emotionality to problem behavior in elementary school children. *Development and Psychopathology*, 8, 141–162.

Eisenberg, N., Sadovsky, A., Spinrad, T. L., Fabes, R. A., Losoya, S. H., Valiente, C., Reiser, M., Cumberland, A., & Shepard, S. A. (2005). The relations of problem behavior status to children's negative emotionality, effortful control, and impulsivity: Concurrent relations and prediction of change. *Developmental Psychology*, 41, 193–211.

Else-Quest, N. M., Hyde, J. S., Goldsmith, H. H., & Van Hulle, C. A. (2006). Gender differences in temperament: a meta-analysis. *Psychological Bulletin*, 132(1), 33–72.

Eyberg, S. M., Boggs, S. R., & Algina, J. (1995). Parent–child interaction therapy: A psychosocial model for the treatment of young children with conduct problem behavior and their families. *Psychopharmacology Bulletin*, 31(1), 83–91.

Fagan, J. (1990). The interaction between child sex and temperament in predicting behavior problems of preschool-age children in day care. *Early Child Development and Care*, 59(1), 1–9.

Fagot, B. I., & Leve, L. D. (1998). Teacher ratings of externalizing behavior at school entry for boys and girls: Similar early predictors and different correlates. *Journal of Child Psychology and Psychiatry*, 39(4), 555–566.

Fivush, R., & Buckner, J. P. (2000). Gender, sadness and depression: Developmental and sociocultural perspectives. In A. H. Fischer (Ed.), *Gender and emotion: Social psychological perspectives* (pp. 232–253). Cambridge, UK: Cambridge University Press.

Frick, P. J. (2004). Integrating research on temperament and childhood psychopathology: Its pitfalls and promise. *Journal of Clinical Child and Adolescent Psychology*, 33, 2–7.

Frick, P. J., & Morris, A. S. (2004). Temperament and developmental pathways to conduct problems. *Journal of Clinical Child and Adolescent Psychology*, 33(1), 54–68.

Gambin, M., & Sharp, C. (2016). The differential relations between empathy and internalizing and externalizing symptoms in inpatient adolescents. *Child Psychiatry & Human Development*, 47(6), 966–974.

Gartstein, M. A., & Rothbart, M. K. (2003). Studying infant temperament via the revised infant behavior questionnaire. *Infant Behavior and Development*, 26(1), 64–86.

Goldsmith, H. H., Buss, K. A., & Lemery, K. S. (1997). Toddler and childhood temperament: Expanded content, stronger genetic evidence, new evidence for the importance of environment. *Developmental Psychology*, 33(6), 891–905.

Greene, R. W., & Doyle, A. E. (1999). Toward a transactional conceptualization of oppositional defiant disorder: Implications for assessment and treatment. *Clinical Child and Family Psychology Review*, 2(3), 129–148.

Guerin, D. W., Gottfried, A. W., & Thomas, C. W. (1997). Difficult temperament and behaviour problems: A longitudinal study from 1.5 to 12 years. *International Journal of Behavioral Development*, *21*(1), 71–90.

Hagekull, B., & Bohlin, G. (1992). Prevalence of problematic behaviors in four-year-olds. *Scandinavian Journal of Psychology*, *33*(4), 359–369.

Hawes, D. J., Dadds, M. R., Frost, A. D., & Hasking, P. A. (2011). Do childhood callous-unemotional traits drive change in parenting practices? *Journal of Clinical Child & Adolescent Psychology*, *40*(4), 507–518.

Hemphill, S., & Sanson, A. (2001). Matching parenting to child temperament. *Family Matters*, *59*, 42–47.

Hirshfeld-Becker, D. R., Biederman, J., Faraone, S. V., Violette, H., Wrightsman, J., & Rosenbaum, J. F. (2002). Temperamental correlates of disruptive behavior disorders in young children: preliminary findings. *Biological Psychiatry*, *51*(7), 563–574.

Hoffmann, J. P., & Su, S. S. (1998). Stressful life events and adolescent substance use and depression: Conditional and gender differentiated effects. *Substance Use & Misuse*, *33*(11), 2219–2262.

INSERM Collective Expertise Centre. (2005). *Conduct: Disorder in children and adolescents*. Paris: Institut national de la santé et de la recherche médicale, Retrieved from http://www.ncbi.nlm.nih.gov/books/NBK7133/

Juliano, M., Werner, R. S., & Cassidy, K. W. (2006). Early correlates of preschool aggressive behavior according to type of aggression and measurement. *Journal of Applied Developmental Psychology*, *27*(5), 395–410.

Kagan, J. (1998). Biology and the child. In W. Damon (Series Ed.) & N. Eisenberg (Vol. Ed.), *Handbook of child psychology*, Vol. 3. *Social, emotional, and personality development* (5th ed., pp. 177–235). New York, NY: Wiley.

Kiff, C. J., Lengua, L. J., & Zalewski, M. (2011). Nature and nurturing: Parenting in the context of child temperament. *Clinical Child and Family Psychology Review*, *14*(3), 251–301.

Kim, H. W., Cho, S. C., Kim, B. N., Kim, J. W., Shin, M. S., & Yeo, J. Y. (2010). Does oppositional defiant disorder have temperament and psychopathological profiles independent of attention deficit hyperactivity disorder? *Comprehensive Psychiatry*, *51*(4), 412–418.

Kochanska, G., & Kim, S. (2013). Difficult temperament moderates links between maternal responsiveness and children's compliance and behavior problems in low-income families. *Journal of Child Psychology and Psychiatry*, *54*(3), 323–332.

Lavigne, J. V., Gouze, K. R., Hopkins, J., Bryant, F. B., & LeBailly, S. A. (2012). A multi-domain model of risk factors for ODD symptoms in a community sample of 4-year-olds. *Journal of Abnormal Child Psychology*, *40*(5), 741–757.

Lemery-Chalfant, K., Kao, K., Swann, G., & Goldsmith, H. H. (2013). Childhood temperament: Passive gene–environment correlation, gene–environment interaction, and the hidden importance of the family environment. *Development and Psychopathology*, *25*(1), 51–63.

Lengua, L. J., & Kovacs, E. A. (2005). Bidirectional associations between temperament and parenting and the prediction of adjustment problems in middle childhood. *Journal of Applied Developmental Psychology*, *26*(1), 21–38.

Maccoby, E. E., & Jacklin, C. N. (1974). *The psychology of sex differences*, Vol. 1. Stanford, CA: Stanford University Press.

Martin, R. P., Wisenbaker, J., & Huttunen, M. (1994). Review of factor analytic studies of temperament measures based on the Thomas-Chess structural model: Implications for the Big Five. In C. F. Halverson, G. A. Kohnstamm, & R. P. Martin (Eds.), *The developing structure of temperament and personality from infancy to adulthood* (pp. 157–172). Hillsdale, NJ: Erlbaum.

McClure, E. B. (2000). A meta-analytic review of sex differences in facial expression processing and their development in infants, children, and adolescents. *Psychological Bulletin*, *126*(3), 424–453.

Melegari, M. G., Nanni, V., Lucidi, F., Russo, P. M., Donfrancesco, R., & Cloninger, C. R. (2015). Temperamental and character profiles of preschool children with ODD, ADHD, and anxiety disorders. *Comprehensive Psychiatry*, *58*, 94–101.

Morales, S., Beekman, C., Blandon, A. Y., Stifter, C. A., & Buss, K. A. (2015). Longitudinal associations between temperament and socioemotional outcomes in young children: The moderating role of RSA and gender. *Developmental Psychobiology*, *57*(1), 105–119.

Muris, P., & Ollendick, T. H. (2005). The role of temperament in the etiology of child psychopathology. *Clinical Child and Family Psychology Review, 8*(4), 271–289.

Nigg, J. T. (2006). Temperament and developmental psychopathology. *Journal of Child Psychology and Psychiatry, 47*(3–4), 395–422.

Nigg, J. T., Goldsmith, H. H., & Sachek, J. (2004). Temperament and attention deficit hyperactivity disorder: The development of a multiple pathway model. *Journal of Clinical Child and Adolescent Psychology, 33*(1), 42–53.

Oldehinkel, A. J., Hartman, C. A., De Winter, A. F., Veenstra, R., & Ormel, J. (2004). Temperament profiles associated with internalizing and externalizing problems in preadolescence. *Development and Psychopathology, 16*(2), 421–440.

Oldehinkel, A. J., Wittchen, H. U., & Schuster, P. (1999). Prevalence, 20-month incidence and outcome of unipolar depressive disorders in a community sample of adolescents. *Psychological Medicine, 29*(03), 655–668.

Ormel, J., Oldehinkel, A. J., Ferdinand, R. F., Hartman, C. A., De Winter, A. F., Veenstra, R., . . . Verhulst, F. C. (2005). Internalizing and externalizing problems in adolescence: General and dimension-specific effects of familial loadings and preadolescent temperament traits. *Psychological Medicine, 35*(12), 1825–1835.

Oosterlaan, J., Scheres, A., & Sergeant, J. A. (2005). Which executive functioning deficits are associated with AD/HD, ODD/CD and comorbid AD/HD+ ODD/CD? *Journal of Abnormal Child Psychology, 33*(1), 69–85.

Pardini, D., & Frick, P. J. (2013). Multiple developmental pathways to conduct disorder: Current conceptualizations and clinical implications. *Journal of the Canadian Academy of Child & Adolescent Psychiatry, 22*(1), 20–25.

Pfeifer, M., Goldsmith, H. H., Davidson, R. J., & Rickman, M. (2002). Continuity and change in inhibited and uninhibited children. *Child Development, 73*(5), 1474–1485.

Prior, M., Sanson, A., & Oberklaid, F. (1989). The Australian Temperament Project. In G. A. Kohnstamm, J. E. Bates, & M. K. Rothbart (Eds.), *Temperament in childhood* (pp. 537–554). Chichester, UK: Wiley.

Rettew, D. C., Copeland, W., Stanger, C., & Hudziak, J. J. (2004). Associations between temperament and DSM-IV externalizing disorders in children and adolescents. *Journal of Developmental and Behavioral Pediatrics, 25*(6), 383–391.

Roberts, B. W., & DelVecchio, W. F. (2000). The rank-order consistency of personality traits from childhood to old age: A quantitative review of longitudinal studies. *Psychological Bulletin, 126*(1), 3–25.

Rothbart, M. K., Ahadi, S. A., & Hershey, K. L. (1994). Temperament and social behavior in childhood. *Merrill-Palmer Quarterly, 40*(1), 21–39.

Rothbart, M. K., Ahadi, S. A., Hershey, K. L., & Fisher, P. (2001). Investigations of temperament at three to seven years: The Children's Behavior Questionnaire. *Child Development, 72*(5), 1394–1408.

Rothbart, M. K., & Bates, J. E. (2006). Temperament. In W. Damon, R. M. Lerner, & N. Eisenberg (Eds.), *Handbook of child psychology*, Vol. 3: *Social, emotional, and personality development* (5th ed., pp. 105–176). New York, NY: Wiley.

Rothbart, M. K., & Derryberry, D. (1981). Development of individual differences in temperament. In M. Lamb & A. Brown (Eds.), *Advances in developmental psychology* (pp. 37–86). Hillsdale, NJ: Erlbaum.

Rubin, K. H., Burgess, K. B., Dwyer, K. M., & Hastings, P. D. (2003). Predicting preschoolers' externalizing behaviors from toddler temperament, conflict, and maternal negativity. *Developmental Psychology, 39*(1), 164–176.

Sameroff, A. J., Lewis, M., & Miller, S. M. (Eds.) (2000). *Handbook of developmental psychopathology*. New York, NY: Kluwer Academic/Plenum.

Sanson, A., Hemphill, S. A., & Smart, D. (2004). Connections between temperament and social development: A review. *Social Development, 13*(1), 142–170.

Sanson, A., & Prior, M. (1999). Temperament and behavioral precursors to oppositional defiant disorder and conduct disorder. In H. C. Quay & A. E. Hogan (Eds.), *Handbook of disruptive behavior disorders* (pp. 397–417). New York, NY: Springer US.

Sanson, A., & Rothbart, M. K. (1995). Child temperament and parenting. In M. Bornstein (Ed.). *Handbook of parenting* (pp. 299–321). Hillsdale, NJ: Erlbaum.

Sanson, A., Smart, D., Prior, M., Oberklaid, F., & Amos, D. (1996, October). *Temperamental precursors of externalizing and internalizing behavior problems at 11–12 years*. Paper presented at the 11th Occasional Temperament conference, Eugene, OR.

Saudino, K. J. (2005). Behavioral genetics and child temperament. *Journal of Developmental and Behavioral Pediatrics, 26*(3), 214–223.

Scaramella, L. V., & Leve, L. D. (2004). Clarifying parent–child reciprocities during early childhood: The early childhood coercion model. *Clinical Child and Family Psychology Review, 7*(2), 89–107.

Schmeck, K., & Poustka, F. (2001). Temperament and disruptive behavior disorders. *Psychopathology, 34*(3), 159–163.

Scholom. A., Zucker. R. A., & Stollak, G. E. (1979). Relating early child adjustment to infant and parent temperament. *Journal of Abnormal Child Psychology, 7*, 297–308.

Scott, B. G., Lemery-Chalfant, K., Clifford, S., Tein, J. Y., Stoll, R., & Goldsmith, H. H. (2016). A twin factor mixture modeling approach to childhood temperament: Differential heritability. *Child Development, 87*(6), 1940–1955.

Shaffer, D. R. (2005). *Social and personality development* (4th ed.). Belmont, CA: Wadsworth/Thomson Learning.

Shaw, D. S., Owens, E. B., Giovannelli, J., & Winslow, E. B. (2001). Infant and toddler pathways leading to early externalizing disorders. *Journal of the American Academy of Child & Adolescent Psychiatry, 40*(1), 36–43.

Shiner, R. L., Buss, K. A., McClowry, S. G., Putnam, S. P., Saudino, K. J., & Zentner, M. (2012). What is temperament *now*? Assessing progress in temperament research on the twenty-fifth anniversary of Goldsmith et al. *Child Development Perspectives, 6*(4), 436–444.

Smith, C. L., Calkins, S. D., Keane, S. P., Anastopoulos, A. D., & Shelton, T. L. (2004). Predicting stability and change in toddler behavior problems: Contributions of maternal behavior and child gender. *Developmental Psychology, 40*(1), 29–42.

Stringaris, A., Maughan, B., & Goodman, R. (2010). What's in a disruptive disorder? Temperamental antecedents of oppositional defiant disorder: findings from the Avon Longitudinal Study. *Journal of the American Academy of Child & Adolescent Psychiatry, 49*(5), 474–483.

Thomas, A., & Chess, S. (1977). *Temperament and development*. New York, NY: Bruner/Mazel.

Thomas, A., Chess, S., Birch, H. G., Hertzig, M. E., & Korn, S. (1963). *Behavioural individuality in early childhood*. New York, NY: New York University Press.

Vitaro, F., Barker, E. D., Boivin, M., Brendgen, M., & Tremblay, R. E. (2006). Do early difficult temperament and harsh parenting differentially predict reactive and proactive aggression? *Journal of Abnormal Child Psychology, 34*(5), 681–691.

Wåhlstedt, C., Thorell, L. B., & Bohlin, G. (2009). Heterogeneity in ADHD: Neuropsychological pathways, comorbidity and symptom domains. *Journal of Abnormal Child Psychology, 37*(4), 551–564.

Watson, D., Kotov, R., & Gamez, W. (2006). Basic dimensions of temperament in relation to personality and psychopathology. In R. F. Krueger & J. L. Tackett (Eds.), *Personality and psychopathology* (pp. 7–38). New York, NY: Guilford Press.

Webster-Stratton, C., Reid, M. J., & Hammond, M. (2004). Treating children with early-onset conduct problems: Intervention outcomes for parent, child, and teacher training. *Journal of Clinical Child and Adolescent Psychology, 33*(1), 105–124.

Wiesner, M., Elliott, M. N., McLaughlin, K. A., Banspach, S. W., Tortolero, S., & Schuster, M. A. (2015). Common versus specific correlates of fifth-grade conduct disorder and oppositional defiant disorder symptoms: Comparison of three racial/ethnic groups. *Journal of Abnormal Child Psychology, 43*(5), 985–998.

Zastrow, B. L., Martel, M. M., & Widiger, T. A. (2016). Preschool oppositional defiant disorder: A disorder of negative affect, surgency, and disagreeableness. *Journal of Clinical Child & Adolescent Psychology*. doi:10.1080/15374416.2016.1225504

Zeman, J., Cassano, M., Perry-Parrish, C., & Stegall, S. (2006). Emotion regulation in children and adolescents. *Journal of Developmental & Behavioral Pediatrics, 27*(2), 155–168.

12

Prenatal and Perinatal Risk Factors

D. Anne Winiarski, Cassandra L. Hendrix,
Erica L. Smearman, and Patricia A. Brennan

Our chapter focuses on prenatal and perinatal risk factors that can directly impact the fetus (e.g., teratogens), as well as maternal factors that can indirectly impact the child (e.g., maternal psychopathology and stress). In addition to clear links between prenatal teratogen exposure and later physical and cognitive anomalies, there is ample evidence to suggest long-term behavioral consequences. Our aim is to review literature that has shown a link between exposures during these periods of development and later aggressive, impulsive, and disruptive behaviors. We begin with a review of the literature on prenatal risk factors for disruptive and impulsive behaviors. We then discuss perinatal risk factors, and end with a brief discussion of the role of genetic variables in shaping and interacting with environmental risk factors in the prediction of behavioral problems.

Prenatal Risk Factors

Maternal Psychological Distress/Physiological Dysregulation

Pregnancy and the perinatal period are associated with significant life changes, which can oftentimes be accompanied by stress. This stress can be positive or negative for the mother depending on a variety of contextual factors (e.g., planned vs. unplanned pregnancy, financial resources, access to prenatal care, etc.). When negative stress levels are chronically high, they may manifest in depression. In addition to the characteristic cognitive and behavioral features of depression that most clinicians are familiar with, depression also has physiological correlates, one of which is dysregulated cortisol. When a mother is depressed, she typically experiences elevated levels of cortisol that can enter the fetal system through the placenta (Ponder et al., 2011). One mechanism by which this can occur is through a downregulation of a placental enzyme that typically oxidizes maternal cortisol (11 β –Hydroxysteroid dehydrogenase), which results in increased levels of maternal cortisol circulating in the uterine environment (Buss et al., 2012; Glover, O'Connor, & O'Donnell, 2010; Ponder et al., 2011). Prenatal exposure to high levels of depression has been linked to a variety of maladaptive outcomes including developmental delay at 18 months (Deave, Heron, Evans, & Emond, 2008). In addition, there is a growing body of literature that links exposure to elevated prenatal cortisol to dysregulated behaviors in late childhood, though the mechanisms by which this long-term behavioral outcome develops have not been clearly delineated.

In one longitudinal study, mothers' depressive symptomatology was assessed throughout pregnancy, immediately postpartum, and when the children were both 6 months and 5 years

---

The Wiley Handbook of Disruptive and Impulse-Control Disorders, First Edition.
Edited by John E. Lochman and Walter Matthys.
© 2018 John Wiley & Sons Ltd. Published 2018 by John Wiley & Sons Ltd.

of age. Both severity and chronicity of maternal depression were related to lower vocabulary scores and higher rates of parent-reported child behavior problems, but more recent reports of elevated depression symptomatology (as opposed to reports during pregnancy) were related to higher rates of behavior problems (Brennan et al., 2000). Similarly, researchers have found that high levels of maternal anxiety during the prenatal period predicted emotional and behavioral problems in both boys and girls, and suggested that altered fetal brain development (which could be related to increased stress hormones circulating in the uterus) was one potential mechanism by which these changes occurred (O'Connor, Heron, Golding, Beveridge, & Glover, 2002).

Of course, an important point to consider when evaluating this research is how much of the effect of maternal distress is physiological (e.g., maternal cortisol alters fetal brain development, which in turns relates to higher rates of disruptive behavior problems later in life), and how much is environmental (e.g., depressed and highly stressed mothers are less likely to interact with and model appropriate coping mechanisms for their children). A third, and more likely, option is that both of these risk factors interact to shape the development of externalizing psychopathologies across childhood. Lastly, an additional variable that comes into play is the confounding role of genetic factors—in other words, whether maternal distress can be passed on to offspring through genetic or epigenetic processes, thus increasing the risk for later externalizing psychopathology. We discuss the role of genetics at the end of this chapter.

Maternal Malnutrition

Maternal malnutrition during pregnancy is an additional perinatal risk factor for the development of externalizing problems. Research shows that low maternal folate levels during pregnancy are correlated with decreased head circumference, increased hyperactivity/inattention, and more frequent problems with peers during school age (Schlotz et al., 2011). Low iron levels have also been implicated in the development of attention problems (Monk, Georgieff, & Osterholm, 2013). Exposure to wartime famine during pregnancy is linked to elevated risk for a number of health and psychological concerns (Roseboom, Rooij, & Painter, 2006), including antisocial personality disorder (Neugebauer, Hoek, & Susser, 1999), but it is not yet clear if prenatal exposure to famine also increases risk for other externalizing behaviors.

Because individual nutrients are rarely consumed in isolation, some researchers argue that studies in this area should focus on overall maternal diet across pregnancy rather than single nutrient intake (Jacka et al., 2013; Steenweg-de Graaff et al., 2014). In fact, several studies have linked overall prenatal diet to the development of child behavior problems. One large prospective study of over 20,000 mother–child pairs suggests that the content of mothers' diet during pregnancy may be associated with child externalizing disorders in particular. Children of women who consumed a "western" diet high in processed meat products, sweet drinks, salty snacks, and refined cereals were more likely to show externalizing behaviors during preschool compared to children whose mothers consumed large amounts of vegetables, fruits, and vegetable oils. Moreover, this "western" diet was associated with a trajectory of high externalizing problems that was stable across 1.5, 3, and 5 years of age (Jacka et al., 2013). An independent research group from Denmark found strikingly similar results in a different European population a year later. This research group found that following a Mediterranean diet during pregnancy—i.e., eating a lot of fruit, vegetables, vegetable oils, and fish, as well as low amounts of processed meats—was associated with lower rates of externalizing disorders in young children. Conversely, eating large amounts of meat, potatoes, and margarine during pregnancy was associated with higher rates of externalizing, but not internalizing, problems in early childhood (Steenweg-de Graaff et al., 2014).

The mechanisms by which prenatal malnutrition may increase risk for externalizing problems are not yet established. However, several possibilities have been proposed. First, prenatal malnutrition may cause neurocognitive deficits by interfering with neurotransmitter functioning and reducing the number of neurons in the developing brain. These neurocognitive deficits may then increase risk for externalizing disorders like Oppositional Defiant Disorder/Conduct Disorder (ODD/CD) and Attention Deficit Hyperactivity Disorder (ADHD) (Liu & Raine, 2006). It is also possible that mothers who are malnourished during pregnancy continue to be malnourished after delivery, and therefore have less energy with which to model appropriate behaviors and consistently respond to their infants. These potential alterations in postnatal mother–child interactions and attachment may in turn increase child risk for externalizing disorders (Wachs, 2009).

Teratogenic Substances

Use of both prescription and illicit drugs frequently continues throughout pregnancy. Results of a 2006 study found that 5.2% of women reported methamphetamine use in pregnancy, 25% smoked tobacco, 22.8% drank alcohol, 6.0% used marijuana, and 1.3% used barbiturates (Arria et al., 2006). Results of several cross-sectional and longitudinal designs suggest poor long-term outcomes among children exposed to noxious substances *in utero*, though the exact outcomes have not been agreed on. Alcohol and cigarettes in particular continue to be the most dangerous drugs for the developing fetus.

Alcohol Maternal consumption of alcohol during pregnancy negatively impacts thedeveloping fetal brain, and heavy use can result in the diagnosis of fetal alcohol syndrome (FAS) at birth. FAS is diagnosed if there is a clearly documented exposure history, growth retardation (e.g., smaller than expected birth weight and length), facial dysmorphia (e.g., smooth, wide philtrum), and evidence of central nervous system (CNS) impairment (Coles, 1993). Though prenatal alcohol exposure has clear physical effects on the child, the "invisible" effects are even more worrisome.

Children with prenatal alcohol exposure, and especially those who meet criteria for FAS, are more likely to evidence learning difficulties, have lower average IQs relative to same-age peers, and have problems with impulsivity and inattention that are frequently diagnosed as ADHD (Coles, 1993). Behaviorally, these children are more likely to have social problems at school (e.g., frequently getting into trouble and having problems with peers), and are at greater risk of having legal problems as adolescents and adults (Streissguth et al., 2004). In a hallmark study, Cadoret, Cain and Groce (1980) found significant associations between prenatal alcohol exposure and childhood conduct problems, as well as later legal problems in adulthood. This finding remained significant even when controlling for other important sociodemographic factors (such as the adoptive family's socioeconomic status, disruptions in caregiving early in development, etc.), suggesting that alcohol has a very strong role in shaping delinquent outcomes, irrespective of later environmental factors that may come into play.

It is also important to note that mothers who abuse alcohol during pregnancy are more likely to use other substances, such as cigarettes. Nevertheless, results indicate that alcohol exposure uniquely relates to child ADHD symptoms over and above prenatal cigarette exposure (Knopik et al., 2006). Lastly, though the long-term physical, cognitive, and behavioral outcomes of prenatal alcohol exposure are unfavorable, evidence suggests that receiving an FAS diagnosis, and subsequently intervention services, earlier in life, as well as being reared in a stable and supportive home environment can be especially potent protective factors (Streissguth et al., 2004).

Cigarette Smoking When one understands both the pharmacodynamics and pharmacokinetics of nicotine, it is easy to see why prenatal exposure to cigarettes is so detrimental to a developing fetus. Nicotine has the ability to cross the placenta, thereby reducing the blood flow, nutrients, and oxygen that can reach the fetus. Follow-up studies of children exposed to cigarette smoke prenatally illustrate structural differences (i.e., decreased cortical thickness) in the frontal regions of the brain, which are necessary for behavioral inhibition (Toro et al., 2008). Many studies have found links between prenatal cigarette exposure and conduct disorder (Linnet et al., 2003; Wakschlag et al., 1997; Wakschlag & Hans, 2002). In a Finnish birth cohort, children born to mothers who reported smoking during pregnancy were twice as likely to have engaged in criminal activity in early adulthood (Rantakallio, Laara, Isohanni, & Moilanen, 1992).

The number of cigarettes smoked daily seems to be an important variable to consider in this relationship. After controlling for relevant sociodemographic variables, Brennan, Grekin, and Mednick (1999) found a dose-dependent relationship between maternal prenatal smoking and arrests for both violent and nonviolent crimes. Of note, this relationship was strongest for *persistent* criminal behavior rather than adolescent-limited delinquent behaviors, which suggests that early exposure to nicotine impacts behavioral functioning across the lifespan, and is not just limited to behavioral problems in childhood. Similarly, researchers found a greater than fourfold increase for conduct disorder among adolescent boys and a fivefold increase for drug dependence among adolescent girls only when mothers reported smoking ten or more cigarettes daily during pregnancy (Weissman, Warner, Wickramaratne, & Kandel, 1999).

Given the comorbidity between different types of externalizing behavior (e.g., ADHD and CD), it is also important to tease apart whether cigarette smoking uniquely contributes to the development of each type of externalizing behavior when controlling for these comorbid diagnoses. Previous studies have found that antisocial behaviors and ADHD among children and adolescents were each *independently* influenced by maternal cigarette smoking during pregnancy (Button, Thapar, & McGuffin, 2005). It is also important to note the contributive role of genetic effects when examining the relationship between cigarette smoking and impulsive/aggressive behaviors. Specifically, Maughan, Taylor, Caspi, and Moffitt (2004) found that cigarette smoking was a proxy measure for genetic and environmental risks for antisocial behavior. In other words, it may be inaccurate to assume that cigarette smoking directly impacts the development of aggression. Instead, mothers who smoke during pregnancy may be exposed to similar genetic and/or environmental risk factors for aggression that are passed on to the child and subsequently influence the development of child antisocial behaviors.

Illicit Drugs In addition to nicotine and alcohol, children can also be prenatally exposed to illicit drugs, which include methamphetamines, cocaine, and heroin. A thorough review of these literatures is beyond the scope of the present chapter but, overall, the results from these bodies of research suggest that the long-term behavioral outcomes of children prenatally exposed to these substances are mixed. Children who have been exposed to cocaine have been found to demonstrate altered arousal states in infancy (Eiden, Lewis, Croff, & Young, 2002; Mayes, Bornstein, Chawarska, Haynes, & Granger, 1996), and this finding persisted into school age. Specifically, children who were prenatally exposed to cocaine, together with a group of socioeconomically and behaviorally matched control children, were administered a series of stressor tasks, and their heart rate and electrodermal responses were measured. Overall, while the children with severe behavioral problems had the highest heart rate across conditions and were hyporesponsive to the stressor tasks, the cocaine-exposed children demonstrated greater skin conductance responses to the stressors (Kable, Coles, Lynch, & Platzman, 2008).

At a neural level, results of a recent functional magnetic resonance imaging (fMRI) and diffusion tensor imaging (DTI) study found that, compared to healthy controls, adolescents who were prenatally exposed to cocaine demonstrated a decreased ability to inhibit in the ventromedial prefrontal cortex and had less suppressed amygdala activation in a working memory task with emotional distractors (Li et al., 2013). Behaviorally, this might manifest as poor emotion regulation and difficulty in suppressing impulsive behaviors.

Heroin exposure *in utero* also appears to be related to the manifestation of ADHD symptoms in the long term. Ornoy, Segal, Bar-Hamburger, and Greenbaum (2001) found higher rates of ADHD in children born to mothers who abused heroin during pregnancy. However, children who continued to reside with the biological mother were twice as likely to develop ADHD as were those who were prenatally exposed but then adopted into a different family. This exposure–environment interaction is not limited to heroin exposure, as we will see in the discussion on birth complications below.

Prenatal Exposure to Psychotropic Medications

Although the focus of this section of our chapter has been on illicit drug use, tobacco, and alcohol, it is also important to comment on the emerging literature that has suggested links between prescription medication use during pregnancy and deleterious outcomes among children. The focus of our discussion will be on the use of antidepressant medication and its links to behavioral outcomes in children. Although the exact numbers are unknown, researchers report that 1–8% of pregnant women take antidepressant medications (Lupattelli et al., 2015), with some estimates as high as 13.4% (Cooper, Willy, Pont, & Ray, 2007). On account of their relative safety profile and low risk of congenital effects (Harrington, Lee, Crum, Zimmerman, & Hertz-Picciotto, 2013; Lattimore et al., 2005), selective serotonin reuptake inhibitors (SSRIs) are the most commonly prescribed antidepressant medication. Nevertheless, relatively little is known about the long-term neuropsychological profiles of children who were exposed to psychotropic medication *in utero*.

The question of whether antidepressant use impacts child cognitive, emotional, and behavioral outcomes has been studied for several years. Researchers have not been able to consistently link prenatal antidepressant exposure to one specific long-term developmental outcome. More recent studies have found links between prenatal SSRI exposure and ASD symptoms (Man et al., 2015), broader expressive language delays (Johnson, Smith, Stowe, Newport, & Brennan, 2016) as well as poor motor development (Casper et al., 2003). There is also variable evidence linking prenatal antidepressant exposure to long-term behavioral outcomes. For example, some researchers have found that exposure to tricyclic antidepressants or fluoxetine did not increase the risk of poorer cognitive, language, or behavioral outcomes among young children (Nulman et al., 1997). Similarly, Nulman and colleagues (2012) recently found that prenatal exposure to neither Venlafaxine (a serotonin-norepinephrine reuptake inhibitor) nor SSRIs resulted in behavioral differences in children, but that severity of maternal depressive symptomatology during pregnancy *did* increase the risk of externalizing behavior problems in preschoolers.

A recent study likewise found that prenatal exposure to SSRIs was not related to ADHD symptomatology at age 5, whereas bupropion use, particularly in the second trimester, was significantly related (Figueroa, 2010). It is important to recognize the impact that these conflicting reports have on mothers' decisions to pursue pharmacotherapy during pregnancy. Women oftentimes overestimate the terotogenic effects of antidepressant medication use on the developing fetus, and cite this as one reason for discontinuing treatment (Lupattelli et al., 2015). Given the lack of conclusive information about antidepressant medication use and outcomes, it is important to recognize that suddenly terminating pharmacological mental health treatment can result in a relapse of depressive or anxious symptamatology, which as we discussed above, comes with its own long-term behavioral risks for the developing fetus.

Prenatal Exposure to Environmental Toxicants

Researchers and the general public have voiced growing concern over recent years about the effects of commonly used synthetic materials on the developing fetus and child. A simultaneous increase in the prevalence of neurodevelopmental disorders such as ADHD and the use of synthetic materials has raised the question of whether these two phenomena are related. The recent Flint Water Crisis, which has led to elevated blood lead levels in children living in Flint, Michigan (Hanna-Attisha, Lachance, Sadler, & Schnepp, 2016) has also reignited interest in the well-documented association between early lead exposure and child cognitive/behavioral development. This section will discuss the potential influence of endocrine-disrupting chemicals (e.g., pesticides, phthalates) and lead on the development of disruptive behavior disorders.

One of the most commonly recognized endocrine disruptors is bisphenol A (BPA). BPA is an industrial chemical used in the production of many plastics and resins that can influence the regulation of androgens, estrogens, and thyroid hormones in the body. Some research suggests that prenatal exposure to BPA is associated with increased rule breaking, ODD traits, CD traits, and other externalizing problems in school-age boys, but not in girls (Evans et al., 2014; Polańska, Jurewicz, & Hanke, 2012; Roen et al., 2015).

Prenatal exposure to phthalates, which are used commercially in plasticizers, solvents, alcohol denaturants, and anti-foam agents, is also associated with heightened aggression, conduct problems, and attention problems in boys, but not girls. The mechanism by which phthalates may increase risk for disruptive behavior disorders is unknown, but prenatal disruption of the maternal thyroid system has been suggested as a potential mechanism (Engel et al., 2010).

Additionally, there appears to be a link between prenatal, but not postnatal, exposure to organochlorine pesticides (such as polychlorinated biphenyl) and later ADHD (Froehlich et al., 2012). Children who were prenatally exposed to polychlorinated biphenyl show more problems with concentration, higher rates of impulsivity, and poorer working memory than children not exposed (Jacobson & Jacobson, 2003). However, not all studies have supported this association (Boucher et al., 2012). Longitudinal studies have also linked prenatal exposure to organophosphate pesticides to higher incidence of attention problems and externalizing behaviors (Rauh et al., 2006), with several effects stronger for boys than girls (Froehlich et al., 2012). It is unclear why these sex-specific effects are present, but heightened prenatal exposure to testosterone (which may slow brain development and thus leave it vulnerable to teratogens for longer periods of time) has been proposed as one mechanism that increases boys' risk of externalizing problems following early exposure to endocrine-disrupting chemicals (Martel, Klump, Nigg, Breedlove, & Sisk, 2009).

Many essential aspects of brain development occur during the prenatal period, including cell proliferation, migration, differentiation, and myelination. Early exposure to endocrine disruptors may interfere with these processes, leading to lasting neural alterations that increase risk for cognitive and behavioral disorders (Winneke, 2011). However, prospective studies that examine the long-term behavioral outcomes of prenatal exposure to endocrine disruptors are still fairly new, so additional research is required to fully elucidate the effects of endocrine-disrupting chemicals.

A small body of research suggests that both prenatal and postnatal exposure to lead is associated with higher rates of antisocial and delinquent behavior in adolescence (Dietrich, Ris, Succop, Berger, & Bornschein, 2001) and adulthood (Wright et al., 2008). The majority of studies on this topic suggest that postnatal, rather than prenatal, exposure to lead is more strongly tied to the development of externalizing problems (Boucher et al., 2012; Winneke, 2011). However, prenatal lead exposure may increase risk of preterm delivery by 2.8 times for every 10-μg/dL increase in lead (National Research Council, 1993). Given associations between preterm birth and ADHD risk, it is possible that prenatal lead exposure could indirectly influence risk for attention problems by decreasing infant gestational age.

Perinatal Risk Factors

Delivery Complications and Preterm Birth

This broad category includes problems like umbilical cord prolapse, umbilical cord compression, breech delivery, forceps extraction, etc. Previous studies have directly linked perinatal complications with an increased risk of violent offending in adulthood (Kandel & Mednick, 1991). More recent research suggests that child IQ mediates the pathway from birth complications to elevated levels of externalizing behavior in middle childhood (Liu, Raine, Wuerker, Venables, & Mednick, 2009). Other studies suggest that birth complications are most deleterious when combined with poor parenting. For example, Hodgins and colleagues (2001) found that pregnancy complications alone did not predict to violent and nonviolent offending at 30 years of age. However, when combined with poor parenting, pregnancy complications predicted to criminal offending, but only slightly more than poor parenting alone. This would suggest that poor parenting is an especially strong predictor of later behavioral problems, and that pregnancy complications only contribute a small amount of predictive variance over and above parenting. Other researchers have also found that birth complications were most predictive of future violent and antisocial behavior when adverse familial factors were also taken into account (Arseneault, Tremblay, Boulerice, & Saucier, 2002; Beck & Shaw, 2005). Collectively, these results suggest that delivery complications have long-lasting outcomes when combined with poor parenting.

Preterm birth, or birth before 37 weeks gestation, has repeatedly been identified as a risk factor for ADHD (Aarnoudse-Moens, Weisglas-Kuperus, van Goudoever, & Oosterlaan, 2009; Johnson et al., 2010; Silva, Colvin, Hagemann, & Bower, 2013), over and above other risk factors such as socioeconomic status and other perinatal complications (Lindstrom, Lindblad, & Hjern, 2011). It has been estimated that prematurity is associated with a two- to fourfold increase in risk for ADHD (Johnson & Marlow, 2014), possibly due to alterations in brain development following preterm birth, such as decreases in white matter and overall brain volume (Anjari et al., 2007; Kieviet, Zoetebier, Elburg, Vermeulen, & Oosterlaan, 2012; Loe, Lee, & Feldman, 2013; Ment, Hirtz, & Hüppi, 2009; Nagy et al., 2009; Peterson et al., 2003).

Literature yields more mixed findings regarding the association between preterm birth and other externalizing disorders, such as CD and ODD. In one large prospective study of 85,535 children in the United States, preterm birth was associated with slightly to moderately increased risk for most psychological disorders, including CD/ODD. According to this study, the prevalence of CD/ODD was 4.5% in preterm children, compared to 2.95% in term children (Singh, Kenney, Ghandour, Kogan, & Lu, 2013). In other prospective birth cohorts, however, preterm birth is associated with attention, social, and thought problems, but not with delinquent or aggressive behavior. Quantitative meta-analyses have yet to support a consistent relationship between preterm birth and externalizing problems other than ADHD (Aarnoudse-Moens et al., 2009). One group of researchers has even proposed that the comorbidity that commonly occurs between ADHD and conduct problems in the general population is often absent in preterm cohorts (Johnson & Marlow, 2011), again suggesting that preterm birth may be a risk factor for ADHD, but not for delinquent behaviors.

One study that identified a significant relationship between preterm birth and conduct problems found that this relationship became nonsignificant when cognitive functioning was controlled (Samara, Marlow, & Wolke, 2008). This finding suggests that lower cognitive functioning, which has been frequently identified in children born preterm (Bhutta, Cleves, Casey, Cradock, & Anand, 2002), is what contributes to the development of conduct problems rather than preterm birth in and of itself. The development of attention problems in children born preterm may also be mediated by child cognition. For example, child working memory and general intellectual delay at 5 years of age mediate the associations between preterm birth and child inattention and hyperactivity at 7 years of age, respectively (Nadeau, Michel, Tessier, Lefebvre, & Robaey, 2001).

Some studies report that preterm birth may differentially affect boys' and girls' risk for ADHD symptoms. For example, one study found decreased caudate volume to associate with greater hyperactivity and lower social adjustment in preterm boys, but not in preterm girls (Nosarti, Allin, Frangou, Rifkin, & Murray, 2005). An epidemiological study also identified significantly higher rates of mental disorders in males born preterm (27.5%) than in females born preterm (18%; Singh et al., 2013). A separate epidemiological study conducted in Australia further found that rates of ADHD in girls born preterm were lower if oxytocin was used to augment labor, suggesting that oxytocin administration may act as a protective agent for girls, but not boys (Silva et al., 2013). However, the majority of studies have not found a sex difference in the association (or lack thereof) between preterm birth and externalizing problems (Loe, Lee, Luna, & Feldman, 2011; Scott et al., 2013).

It is difficult to determine whether preterm delivery truly causes any externalizing disorder. All of the studies discussed thus far are correlational for ethical and practical reasons. Additionally, infants who are born preterm often have more health problems (Clark, Woodward, Horwood, & Moor, 2008), lower intellectual functioning (Bhutta et al., 2002; Johnson & Marlow, 2014), and are of lower socioeconomic status than infants born at full term (Clark et al., 2008). These factors are often associated with risk for disruptive behavior disorders (Bradley & Corwyn, 2002; Loe et al., 2011), making it difficult to disentangle the effects of preterm birth from the effects of these other confounding variables.

Early parenting and environment likely ameliorate or exacerbate any association that may be present between preterm birth and externalizing problems in children. Maternal education, for instance, moderates risk of ADHD in children born preterm. Specifically, children who are born preterm are at heightened risk for ADHD if their mothers are less educated (Lindstrom et al., 2011). A preliminary randomized control trial shows that parent–child interaction training, a type of parent training program that uses in vivo coaching to increase parent responsiveness, reduces attention problems, aggressive behaviors, and other externalizing problems in children born preterm (Bagner, Sheinkopf, Vohr, & Lester, 2010). These studies suggest that preterm birth likely interacts with other factors to increase child risk for ADHD rather than acting in isolation.

Low Birth Weight

The findings linking low birth weight to later behavioral problems are mixed at best. Some studies suggest that there is a link. For example, among a sample of 136 very low birth weight children, Botting, Powls, Cooke, and Marlow (1997) found that 23% of the children met diagnostic criteria for ADHD, whereas only 6% of control children did. In another study, researchers found that low birth weight children were three times as likely to be diagnosed with ADHD than non-low birth weight children (Mick, Biederman, Prince, Fischer, & Farone, 2002). These results held even after controlling for relevant sociodemographic variables and prenatal exposure histories (e.g., cigarette smoking). The results of other studies suggest that the rater of behavioral and impulsive behavior problems matters. For example, in a study of low birth weight adolescents, only parent-report measures of ADHD and depression were significantly related to low birth weight. When teen reports of behavior were analyzed, the results were nonsignificant (Saigal, Pinelli, Hoult, Kim, & Boyle, 2003).

In another study, delivery, early life, and sociodemographic data were collected on 7–8 year-old twins to test for predictors of ODD, CD, and ADHD. Low birth weight was only associated with ADHD symptoms, and not with ODD or CD. There was also no evidence of an accumulating risk for ADHD or ODD, so that a greater number of obstetrical complications did not necessarily relate to a higher rate of diagnosis (Wagner, Schmidt, Lemery-Chalfant, Leavitt, & Goldsmith, 2009). Silva and colleagues (2013) similarly did not find support for low birth weight increasing risk for ADHD in either male or female children. Lastly, Hack and colleagues' (2004) findings suggest that very low birth weight actually makes both young adult males and females *less likely* to have a history of self-reported delinquency.

The Role of Genetics in Prenatal and Perinatal Risk

Although the focus of this chapter was largely on how environmental risk factors (e.g., social stress, exposure to toxins, etc.) may play a role in emergent behavioral problems in children, we cannot conclude our discussion without noting the interactive role that genetic factors play, as well as how the environment shapes the epigenome. For a more in-depth discussion of specific genetic and epigenetic factors, please see Chapter 8. While a number of prenatal and perinatal factors are associated with an increased risk of impulsive behaviors in children, not all children with these exposures go on to develop them. Further, it is possible that some of these findings may be more suggestive of underlying genetic factors rather than environmental exposure. Understanding factors that moderate and underlie exposure–outcome associations can give us greater insight into who is most at risk and can allow for more targeted intervention approaches and greater mechanistic understanding. There are a number of factors that are important to consider, including variation at a biological level.

For example, in the prenatal smoking literature, D'Onofrio Van Hulle, Goodnight, Rathouz, and Lahey (2012) suggest that familial or other confounding factors may account for the association between maternal prenatal smoking and adolescent antisocial behavior, rather than maternal smoking per se (see also Ellingson, Goodnight, Van Hulle, Waldman, & D'Onofrio, 2014). As mentioned above, Maughan and colleagues (2004) attribute nearly 50% of the predictive effects of cigarette smoking on antisocial behavior to correlated genetic effects. Further, a growing number of studies have reported gene by environment interactions between prenatal smoking exposure and genetic variation in the dopamine system, a brain system involved in reward or impulse control. In a number of studies, the long-repeat allele of the dopamine transporter gene (*DAT*) has been reported to interact with prenatal smoking exposure so that children with this allele are at heightened risk for impulsive, inattentive, and oppositional behaviors when exposed to prenatal maternal smoking (Becker, El-Faddagh, Schmidt, Esser, & Laucht, 2008; Kahn, Khoury, Nichols, & LanPhear, 2003; Neuman et al., 2006). The dopamine transporter gene has been of interest in these studies as it is the site of action for neurostimulants (Vandenbergh et al., 1992) and has also been associated with an increased risk for ADHD in children (Gill, Daly, Heron, Hawi, & Fitzgerald, 1997; Waldman et al., 1998). Along with the *DAT* gene, prenatal smoking and genetic interactions have also been reported for the monoamine oxidase A (*MAOA*) gene, a gene which codes for the enzyme that breaks down dopamine and other monoamine neurotransmitters. As with *DAT*, variation in the *MAOA* and *COMT* gene has been implicated in differential risk for the development of impulsive and antisocial outcomes following exposure to maternal prenatal smoking (Brennan et al., 2011; Wakschlag et al., 2010). These studies suggest that variation at a biological level, such as genetic variation in the dopamine system, may be an important factor to consider when evaluating environmental risk and outcome associations. Considering the contribution of biological variation may continue to provide a deeper understanding of how exposures influence later outcomes, and who may be most at risk.

In addition to variation in the gene sequence, a growing literature has begun to explore the role of epigenetic variation in exposure–outcome relationships. Epigenetics, translated as "on top of the genome," refers to structural modifications to DNA that do not alter the gene sequence but rather regulate and influence gene expression (Jaenisch & Bird, 2003). One of the most commonly studied epigenetic modifications is methylation, where a methyl group binds to DNA and tends to block the binding of transcription factors, reducing gene expression (Klose & Bird, 2006). While the gene sequence remains consistent over life, one of the exciting aspects of epigenetic patterns is their reported dynamic nature. Specifically, epigenetic patterns may change in response to certain environmental exposures for some genes, thus providing a mechanism by which the environment can "get under our skin" and change biology. Epigenetics may therefore be an interesting avenue to explore in early exposure and later outcome associations. Early exposures, including those that occur during the prenatal and perinatal time period, can be physiological, such as to diet or chemical exposures, or psychosocial exposures, such as to high levels of stress. For example, our diet provides the source of methyl groups, which are needed for methylation to occur. Given reported associations between prenatal nutrition and ADHD outcomes (Neugebauer et al., 1999; Vermiglio et al., 2004), exploring the epigenome as a potential mediator may be an interesting future area of research. Further, as noted above, studies have linked prenatal psychosocial stress with increased risk for child ADHD, and a number of studies have begun exploring associations between prenatal and early life stress and differential epigenetic patterns across a variety of genes (Beach et al., 2010; Essex et al., 2013; Francis, Champagne, & Meaney, 2000; Schroeder et al., 2012). Therefore, exploring the potential role of epigenetics in this and other prenatal exposure and later impulsive behavioral outcomes may also be of value (Mill & Petronis, 2008)

Conclusion

Our primary aim has been to demonstrate how a variety of prenatal and postnatal variables can influence long-term behavioral outcomes in children. While an exhaustive overview of these factors was not possible, it is our hope that we have demonstrated how biological, chemical, and social factors can both directly and indirectly place a developing fetus and newborn at risk for future complications, including ADHD, ODD, and other disruptive behavior disorders. Though there are clearly established links in the literature between certain teratogenic substances (e.g., alcohol and cigarettes) and future maladaptive behavioral outcomes, the evidence remains far less conclusive about the effects of other substances, such as SSRI medication. Moreover, as developmental psychopathology research continues to rapidly evolve into an increasingly interdisciplinary science, more work must be done to understand how genetic variables shape, interact with, and exacerbate these prenatal and perinatal risk factors. A better understanding of these complex interrelationships is crucial for interventions at both the clinical and policy levels.

References

Aarnoudse-Moens, C. S. H., Weisglas-Kuperus, N., van Goudoever, J. B., & Oosterlaan, J. (2009). Meta-Analysis of neurobehavioral outcomes in very preterm and/or very low birth weight children. *Pediatrics, 124*(2), 717–728. doi:10.1542/peds.2008-2816

Anjari, M., Srinivasan, L., Allsop, J. M., Hajnal, J. V., Rutherford, M. A., Edwards, A. D., & Counsell, S. J. (2007). Diffusion tensor imaging with tract-based spatial statistics reveals local white matter abnormalities in preterm infants. *NeuroImage*. doi:10.1016/j.neuroimage.2007.01.035

Arria, A. M., Derauf, C., Lagasse, L. L., Grant, P., Shah, R., Smith, L., Hanning, W. . . . Lester, B. (2006). Methamphetamine and other substance use during pregnancy: Preliminary estimates from the infant development, environment, and lifestyle (IDEAL) study. *Maternal and Child Health Journal*, *10*(3), 293–302. doi:10.1007/s10995-005-0052-0

Arseneault, L., Tremblay, R. E., Boulerice, B., & Saucier, J.-F. (2002). Obstetrical complications and violent delinquency: Testing two developmental pathways. *Child Development*, *73*(2), 496–508.

Bagner, D. M., Sheinkopf, S. J., Vohr, B. R., & Lester, B. M. (2010). Parenting intervention for externalizing behavior problems in children born premature: An initial examination. *Journal of Developmental and Behavioral Pediatrics*, *31*(3), 209–216. doi:10.1097/DBP.0b013e3181d5a294. Parenting

Beach, S. R. H., Brody, G. H., Gunter, T. D., Packer, H., Wernett, P., & Philibert, R. A. (2010). Child maltreatment moderates the association of MAOA with symptoms of depression and antisocial personality disorder. *Journal of Family Psychology*, *24*(1), 12–20. doi:10.1037/a0018074

Beck, J. E., & Shaw, D. S. (2005). The influence of perinatal complications and environmental adversity on boys' antisocial behavior. *Journal of Child Psychology and Psychiatry*, *46*(1), 35–46. doi:10.1111/j.1469-7610.2004.00336.x

Becker, K., El-Faddagh, M., Schmidt, M. H., Esser, G., & Laucht, M. (2008). Interaction of dopamine transporter genotype with prenatal smoke exposure on ADHD symptoms. *The Journal of Pediatrics*, *152*(2), 263–269.

Bhutta, A. T., Cleves, M. A., Casey, P. H., Cradock, M. M., & Anand, K. J. S. (2002). Cognitive and behavioral outcomes of school-aged children who were born preterm: A meta-analysis. *Journal of the American Medical Association*, *288*(6), 728–737.

Botting, N., Powls, A., Cooke, R. W. I., & Marlow, N. (1997). Attention Deficit Hyperactivity Disorder and other psychiatric outcomes in very low birthweight children at 12 years. *Journal of Child Psychology and Psychiatry*, *38*(8), 931–941.

Boucher, O., Jacobson, S. W., Plusquellec, P., Dewailly, E., Ayotte, P., Forget-Dubois, N., . . . Muckle, G. (2012). Prenatal methylmercury, postnatal lead exposure, and evidence of Attention Deficit/Hyperactivity Disorder among Inuit children in Arctic Quebec. *Environmental Health Perspectives*, *120*(10), 1456–1461.

Bradley, R. H., & Corwyn, R. F. (2002). Socioeconomic status and child development. *Annual Review of Psychology*, *53*, 371–399.

Brennan, P. A., Hammen, C., Sylvers, P., Bor, W., Najman, J., Lind, P. . . . Smith, A. K. (2011). Interactions between the COMT Val108/158Met polymorphism and maternal prenatal smoking predict aggressive behavior outcomes. *Biological Psychology*, *87*(1), 99–105. doi:10.1016/j.biopsycho.2011.02.013

Brennan, P. A., Grekin, E. R., & Mednick, S. A. (1999). Maternal smoking during pregnancy and adult male criminal outcomes. *Archives of General Psychiatry*, *56*(3), 215–219.

Brennan, P. A., Hammen, C., Andersen, M. J., Bor, W., Najman, J. M., & Williams, G. M. (2000). Chronicity, severity, and timing of maternal depressive symptoms: Relationships with child outcomes at age 5. *Developmental Psychology*, *36*(6), 759–766. doi:10.1037//0012-1649.36.6.759

Buss, C., Davis, E. P., Shahbaba, B., Pruessner, J. C., Head, K., & Sandman, C. A. (2012). Maternal cortisol over the course of pregnancy and subsequent child amygdala and hippocampus volumes and affective problems. *Proceedings of the National Academy of Sciences of the United States of America*, *109*(20), E1312–E1319. doi:10.1073/pnas.1201295109

Button, T. M. M., Thapar, A., & McGuffin, P. (2005). Relationship between antisocial behaviour, attention-deficit hyperactivity disorder and maternal prenatal smoking. *British Journal of Psychiatry*, *187*, 155–160.

Cadoret, R. J., Cain, C. A., & Grove, W. M. (1980). Development of alcoholism in adoptees raised apart from alcoholic biologic relatives. *Archives of General Psychiatry*, *37*(5), 561–563.

Casper, R. C., Fleisher, B. E., Lee-Ancajas, J. C., Gilles, A., Gaylor, E., DeBattista, A., & Hoyme, H. E. (2003). Follow-up of children of depressed mothers exposed or not exposed to antidepressant drugs during pregnancy. *The Journal of Pediatrics*, *142*, 402–408.

Clark, A. C. C., Woodward, L. J., Horwood, L. J., & Moor, S. (2008). Development of emotional and behavioral regulation in children born extremely preterm and very preterm: Biological and social influences. *Child Development, 79*(5), 1444–1462.

Coles, C. D. (1993). Impact of prenatal alcohol exposure on the newborn and the child. *Clinical Obstetrics and Gynecology, 36*(2), 255–266.

Cooper, W. O., Willy, M. E., Pont, S. J., & Ray, W. A. (2007). Increasing use of antidepressants in pregnancy. *American Journal of Obstetrics and Gynecology, 196*(6), 544–e1. doi:10.1016/ajog.2007.01.033

D'Onofrio, B. M., Van Hulle, C. A., Goodnight, J. A., Rathouz, P. J., & Lahey, B. B. (2012). Is maternal smoking during pregnancy a causal environmental risk factor for adolescent antisocial behavior? Testing etiological theories and assumptions. *Psychological Medicine, 42*(7), 1535–1545. doi:10.1017/S0033291711002443.Is

Deave, T., Heron, J., Evans, J., & Emond, A. (2008). The impact of maternal depression in pregnancy on early child development. *BJOG: An International Journal of Obstetrics and Gynaecology, 115*(8), 1043–1051.

Dietrich, K. N., Ris, M. D., Succop, P. A., Berger, O. G., & Bornschein, R. L. (2001). Early exposure to lead and juvenile delinquency. *Neurotoxicology and Teratology, 23*, 511–518.

Eiden, R. D., Lewis, A., Croff, S., & Young, E. (2002). Maternal cocaine use and infant behavior. *Infancy, 3*(1), 77–96.

Ellingson, J. M., Goodnight, J. A., Van Hulle, C. A., Waldman, I. D., & D'Onofrio, B. M. (2014). A sibling-comparison study of smoking during pregnancy and childhood psychological traits. *Behavioral Genetics, 44*(1), 25–35. doi:10.1007/s10519-013-9618-6.A

Engel, S. M., Miodovnik, A., Canfield, R. L., Zhu, C., Silva, M. J., Calafat, A. M., & Wolff, M. S. (2010). Prenatal phthalate exposure is associated with childhood behavior and executive fucntioning. *Environmental Health Perspectives, 118*(4), 565–571. doi:10.1289/ehp.0901470

Essex, M. J., Boyce, W. T., Hertzman, C., Lam, L. L., Armstrong, J. M., Neumann, S. M. A., & Kobor, M. S. (2013). Epigenetic vestiges of early developmental adversity: Childhood stress exposure and DNA methylation in adolescence. *Child Development, 84*(1), 58–75. doi:10.1111/j.1467-8624.2011.01641.x.Epigenetic

Evans, S. F., Kobrosly, R. W., Barrett, E. S., Thurston, S. W., Calafat, A. M., Weiss, B., . . . Swan, S. H. (2014). Prenatal Bisphenol A exposure and maternally reported behavior in boys and girls. *Neurotoxicology, 45*, 91–99. doi:10.1016/j.neuro.2014.10.003

Figueroa, R. (2010). Use of antidepressants during pregnancy and risk of Attention-Deficit/Hyperactivity Disorder in the offspring. *Journal of Developmental and Behavioral Pediatrics, 31*(8), 641–648.

Francis, D. D., Champagne, F. C., & Meaney, M. J. (2000). Variations in maternal behaviour are associated with differences in oxytocin receptor levels in the rat. *Journal of Neuroendocrinology, 12*, 1145–1148.

Froehlich, T. E., Anixt, J. S., Loe, I. M., Chirdkiatgumchai, V., Kuan, L., & Gilman, R. C. (2012). Update on environmental risk factors for Attention-Deficit/Hyperactivity Disorder. *Current Psychiatry Reports, 13*(5), 333–344. doi:10.1007/s11920-011-0221-3.Update

Gill, M., Daly, G., Heron, S., Hawi, Z., & Fitzgerald, M. (1997). Confirmation of association between Attention Deficit Hyperactivity Disorder and a dopamine transporter polymorphism. *Molecular Psychiatry, 2*, 311–313.

Glover, V., O'Connor, T. G., & O'Donnell, K. (2010). Prenatal stress and the programming of the HPA axis. *Neuroscience and Biobehavioral Reviews, 35*(1), 17–22. doi:10.1016/j.neubiorev.2009.11.008

Hack, M., Youngstrom, E. A., Cartar, L., Schluchter, M., Taylor, H. G., Flannery, D., . . . Borawski, E. (2004). Behavioral outcomes and evidence of psychopathology among very low birth weight infants at age 20 years. *Pediatrics, 114*, 932–940. doi:10.1542/peds.2003-1017-L

Hanna-Attisha, M., Lachance, J., Sadler, R. C., & Schnepp, A. C. (2016). Elevated blood lead levels in children associated with the Flint drinking water crisis: A spatial analysis of risk and public health response. *American Journal of Public Health Research, 106*(2), 283–290. doi:10.2105/AJPH.2015.303003

Harrington, R. A., Lee, L. C., Crum, R. M., Zimmerman, A. W., & Hertz-Picciotto, I. (2013). Serotonin hypothesis of autism: Implications for selective serotonin reuptake inhibitor use during pregnancy. *Autism Research, 6*(3), 149–168.

Hodgins, S., Kratzer, L., & McNeil, T. F. (2001). Obstetric complications, parenting, and risk of criminal behavior. *Archives of General Psychiatry*, *58*(8), 746–752.

Jacka, F. N., Ystrom, E., Brantsaeter, A. L., Karevold, E., Roth, C., Haugen, M., . . . Berk, M. (2013). Maternal and early postnatal nutrition and mental health of offspring by age 5: A prospective cohort study. *Journal of the American Academy of Child & Adolescent Psychiatry*, *52*(10), 1038–1047. doi:10.1016/j.jaac.2013.07.002

Jacobson, J. L., & Jacobson, S. W. (2003). Prenatal exposure to polychlorinated biphenyls and attention at school age. *The Journal of Pediatrics*, *143*(6), 780–788.

Jaenisch, R., & Bird, A. (2003). Epigenetic regulation of gene expression: How the genome integrates intrinsic and environmental signals. *Nature Genetics Supplement*, *33*, 245–254. doi:10.1038/ng1089

Johnson, K. C., Smith, A. K., Stowe, Z. N., Newport, D. J., & Brennan, P. A. (2016). Preschool outcomes following prenatal serotonin reuptake inhibitor exposure: differences in language and behavior, but not cognitive function. *The Journal of Clinical Psychiatry*, *77*(2), e176–82.

Johnson, S., Hollis, C., Kochhar, P., Hennessy, E., Wolke, D., & Marlow, N. (2010). Psychiatric disorders in extremely preterm children: Longitudinal finding at age 11 years in the EPICure study. *Journal of American Academic Child and Adolescent Psychiatry*, *49*(5), 453–463.e1. doi:10.1016/j.jaac.2010.02.002

Johnson, S., & Marlow, N. (2011). Preterm birth and childhood psychiatric disorders. *Pediatric Research*, *69*(5), 11R–18R.

Johnson, S., & Marlow, N. (2014). Growing up after extremely preterm birth: Lifespan mental health outcomes. *Seminars in Fetal and Neonatal Medicine*, *19*(2), 97–104. doi:10.1016/j.siny.2013.11.004

Kable, J. A., Coles, C. D., Lynch, M. E., & Platzman, K. (2008). Physiological responses to social and cognitive challenges in 8-year olds with a history of prenatal cocaine exposure. *Developmental Psychobiology*, *50*, 251–265.

Kahn, R. S., Khoury, J., Nichols, W. C., & LanPhear, B. P. (2003). Role of dopamine transporter genotype and maternal prenatal smoking in childhood hyperactive-impulsive, inattentive, and oppositional behaviors. *The Journal of Pediatrics*, *3476*, 104–110.

Kandel, E., & Mednick, S. A. (1991). Perinatal complications predict violent offending. *Criminology*, *29*(3), 519–529.

Kieviet, J. F. D. E., Zoetebier, L., Elburg, R. M. V. A. N., Vermeulen, R. J., & Oosterlaan, J. (2012). Brain development of very preterm and very low-birthweight children in childhood and adolescence: a meta-analysis. *Developmental Medicine & Child Neurology*, *54*, 313–323. doi:10.1111/j.1469-8749.2011.04216.x

Klose, R. J., & Bird, A. P. (2006). Genomic DNA methylation: The mark and its mediators. *TRENDS in Biochemical Sciences*, *31*(2), 89–97. doi:10.1016/j.tibs.2005.12.008

Knopik, V. S., Heath, A. C., Jacob, T., Slutske, W. S., Bucholz, K. K., Madden, P. A. F., Waldron, M., & Martin, N. G. (2006). Maternal alcohol use disorder and offspring ADHD: Disentangling genetic and environmental effects using a children-of-twins design. *Psychological Medicine*, *36*(10), 1461–1471.

Lattimore, K. A., Donn, S. M., Kaciroti, N., Kemper, A. R., Neal, C. R., & Vazquez, D. M. (2005). Selective serotonin reuptake inhibitor (SSRI) use during pregnancy and effects on the fetus and newborn: A Meta-Analysis. *Journal of Perinatology*, *25*(9), 595–604.

Li, Z., Santhanam, P., Coles, C. D., Lynch, M. E., Hamann, S., Peltier, S., & Hu, X. (2013). Prenatal cocaine expsoure alters functional activation in the ventral prefrontal cortex and its structural connectivity with the amygdala. *Psychiatry Research—Neuroimaging*, *213*, 47–55.

Lindstrom, K., Lindblad, F., & Hjern, A. (2011). Preterm birth and Attention-Deficit/ Hyperactivity Disorder in schoolchildren. *Pediatrics*, *127*(5), 858–865. doi:10.1542/peds.2010-1279

Linnet, K. M., Dalsgaard, S., Obel, C., Wisborg, K., Henriksen, T. B., Rodriguez, A., . . . Jarvelin, M. R. (2003). Maternal lifestyle factors in pregnancy risk of Attention Deficit Hyperactivity Disorder and associated behaviors: Review of the current evidence. *American Journal of Psychiatry*, *160*, 1028–1040.

Liu, J., & Raine, A. (2006). The effect of childhood malnutrition on externalizing behavior. *Current Opinion in Pediatrics*, *18*, 565–570. doi:10.1097/01.mop.0000245360.13949.91

Liu, J., Raine, A., Wuerker, A., Venables, P. H., & Mednick, S. (2009). The association of birth complications and externalizing behavior in early adolescents: Direct and mediating effects. *Journal of Research on Adolescence, 19*(1), 93–111. doi:10.1111/j.1532-7795.2009.00583.x.

Loe, I. M., Lee, E. S., & Feldman, H. M. (2013). Attention and internalizing behaviors in relation to white matter in children born preterm. *Journal of Developmental & Behavioral Pediatrics, 34,* 156–164.

Loe, I. M., Lee, E. S., Luna, B., & Feldman, H. M. (2011). Behavior problems of 9-16 year old preterm children: Biological, sociodemographic, and intellectual contributions. *Early Human Development, 87*(4), 247–252. doi:10.1016/j.earlhumdev.2011.01.023.Behavior

Lupattelli, A., Spigset, O., Bjornsdottir, I., Hameen-Anttila, K., Mardby, A.-C., Panchaud, A., . . . Nordeng, H. (2015). Patterns and factors associated with low adherence to psychotropic medications during pregnancy: A cross-sectional, multinational web-based study. *Depression and Anxiety, 32*(6), 1–11. doi:10.1002/da.22352

Man, K. K. C., Tong, H. H. Y., Wong, L. Y. L., Chan, E. W., Simonoff, E., & Wong, I. C. K. (2015). Exposure to selective serotonin reuptake inhibitors during pregnancy and risk of autism spectrum disorder in children: A systematic review and meta-analysis of observational studies. *Neuroscience and Biobehavioral Reviews, 49,* 82–89. doi:10.1016/j.neubiorev.2014.11.020

Martel, M. M., Klump, K., Nigg, J. T., Breedlove, S. M., & Sisk, C. L. (2009). Potential hormonal mechanisms of Attention-Deficit/Hyperactivity Disorder and Major Depressive Disorder: A new perspective. *Hormones & Behavior, 55*(4), 465–479. doi:10.1016/j.yhbeh.2009.02.004

Maughan, B., Taylor, A., Caspi, A., & Moffitt, T. E. (2004). Prenatal smoking and early childhood conduct problems: Testing genetic and environmental explanations of the association. *Archives of General Psychiatry, 61,* 836–843.

Mayes, L. C., Bornstein, M. H., Chawarska, K., Haynes, O. M., & Granger, R. H. (1996). Impaired regulation of arousal in 3-month-old infants exposed prenatally to cocaine and other drugs. *Development and Psychopathology, 8*(1), 29–42.

Ment, L. R., Hirtz, D., & Hüppi, P. S. (2009). Imaging biomarkers of outcome in the developing preterm brain. *The Lancet Neurology, 8,* 1042–1055. doi.org/10.1016/S1474-4422(09)70257-1

Mick, E., Biederman, J., Prince, J., Fischer, M. J., & Farone, S. V. (2002). Impact of low birth weight on Attention-Deficit Hyperactivity Disorder. *Developmental and Behavioral Pediatrics, 23*(1), 16–22.

Mill, J., & Petronis, A. (2008). Pre- and peri-natal environmental risks for attention-deficit hyperactivity disorder (ADHD): The potential role of epigenetic processes in mediating susceptibility. *Journal of Child Psychology and Psychiatry, 49*(10), 1020–1030. doi.org/10.1111/j.1469-7610.2008.01909.x

Monk, C., Georgieff, M. K., & Osterholm, E. A. (2013). Maternal prenatal distress and poor nutrition: mutually influencing risk factors affecting infant neurocognitive development. *Journal of Child Psychology and Psychiatry, 54*(2), 115–130. doi.org/10.1111/jcpp.12000

Nadeau, L., Michel, B., Tessier, R., Lefebvre, F., & Robaey, P. (2001). Mediators of behavioral problems in 7-year-old children born after 24 to 28 weeks of gestation. *Developmental and Behavioral Pediatrics, 22*(1), 1–10.

Nagy, Z., Ashburner, J., Andersson, J., Jbabdi, S., Draganski, B., Skare, S., . . . Lagercrantz, H. (2009). Structural correlates of preterm birth in the adolescent brain. *Pediatrics, 124*(5). doi: 10.1542/peds.2008-3801

National Research Council. (1993). *Measuring lead exposure in infants, children, and other sensitive populations.* Washington, DC: National Academies Press.

Neugebauer, R., Hoek, H. W., & Susser, E. (1999). Prenatal exposure to wartime famine and development of antisocial personality disorder in early adulthood. *Journal of the American Medical Association, 281*(5), 455–462.

Neuman, R. J., Lobos, E., Reich, W., Henderson, C. A., Sun, L., & Todd, R. D. (2006). Prenatal smoking exposure and dopaminergic genotypes interact to cause a severe ADHD subtype. *Biological Psychiatry, 61*(12), 1320–1328. doi:10.1016/j.biopsych.2006.08.049

Nosarti, C., Allin, M. P., Frangou, S., Rifkin, L., & Murray, R. M. (2005). Hyperactivity in adolescents born very preterm is associated with decreased caudate volume. *Biological Psychiatry, 57,* 661–666. doi:10.1016/j.biopsych.2004.12.003

Nulman, I., Koren, G., Rovet, J., Barrera, M., Pulver, A., Streiner, D., & Feldman, B. (2012). Neurodevelopment of children following prenatal exposure to venlafaxine, selective serotonin reuptake inhibitors, or untreated maternal depression. *The American Journal of Psychiatry, 169*(11), 1165–1174. doi:10.1176/appi.ajp.2012.11111721

Nulman, I., Rovet, J., Stewart, D. E., Wolpin, J., Gardner, H. A., Theis, J. G. W., . . . Koren, G. (1997). Neurodevelopment of children exposed in utero to antidepressant drugs. *The New England Journal of Medicine, 336*, 258–262.

O'Connor, T. G., Heron, J., Golding, J., Beveridge, M., & Glover, V. T. E. (2002). Maternal antenatal anxiety and children's behavioural/emotional problems at 4 years: Report from the Avon Longitudinal Study of Parents and Children. *British Journal of Psychiatry, 180*, 502–508.

Ornoy, A., Segal, J., Bar-Hamburger, R., & Greenbaum, C. (2001). Developmental outcome of school-age children born to mothers with heroin dependency: Importance of environmental factors. *Developmental Medicine & Child Neurology, 43*, 668–675.

Peterson, B. S., Anderson, A. W., Ehrenkranz, R., Staib, L. H., Tageldin, M., Colson, E., . . . Ment, L. R. (2003). Regional brain volumes and their later neurodevelopmental correlates in term and preterm infants. *Pediatrics, 111*(5), 939–948.

Polańska, K., Jurewicz, J., & Hanke, W. (2012). Exposure to environmental and lifestyle factors and Attention-Deficit/Hyperactivity Disorder in children—A review of epidemiological studies. *International Journal of Occupational Medicine and Environmental Health, 25*(4), 330–355. doi:10.2478/S13382-012-0048-0

Ponder, K. L., Salisbury, A., McGonnigal, B., Laliberte, A., Lester, B., & Padbury, J. F. (2011). Maternal depression and anxiety are associated with altered gene expression in the human placenta without modification by antidepressant use: Implications for fetal programming. *Developmental Psychobiology, 53*(7), 711–723.

Rantakallio, P., Laara, E. S. A., Isohanni, M., & Moilanen, I. (1992). Maternal smoking during pregnancy and delinquency of the offspring: An association without causation? *International Journal of Epidemiology, 21*(6), 1106–1113.

Rauh, V. A., Garfinkel, R., Perera, F. P., Andrews, H. F., Hoepner, L., Barr, D. B., . . . Whyatt, R. W. (2006). Impact of prenatal chlorpyrifos exposure on neurodevelopment in the first 3 years of life among inner-city children. *Pediatrics, 118*(6). doi:10.1542/peds.2006-0338

Roen, E. L., Wang, Y., Calafat, A. M., Wang, S., Margolis, A., Herbstman, J., . . . Perera, F. P. (2015). Bisphenol A exposure and behavioral problems among inner city children at 7–9 years of age. *Environmental Research, 142*, 739–745. doi:10.1016/j.envres.2015.01.014

Roseboom, T., de Rooij, S., & Painter, R. (2006). The Dutch famine and its long-term consequences for adult health. *Early Human Development, 82*, 485–491. doi:10.1016/j.earlhumdev.2006.07.001

Saigal, S., Pinelli, J., Hoult, L., Kim, M. M., & Boyle, M. (2003). Psychopathology and social competencies of adolescents who were extremely low birth weight. *Pediatrics, 111*(5), 969–976.

Samara, M., Marlow, N., & Wolke, D. (2008). Pervasive behavior problems at 6 years of age in a total-population sample of children born at <25 weeks of gestation. *Pediatrics, 122*(3), 562–573. doi:10.1542/peds.2007-3231

Schlotz, W., Jones, A., Phillips, D. I. W., Gale, C. R., Robinson, S. M., & Godfrey, K. M. (2011). Lower maternal folate status in early pregnancy is associated with childhood hyperactivity and peer problems in offspring. *Journal of Child Psychology and Psychiatry, 51*(5), 594–602. doi:10.1111/j.1469-7610.2009.02182.x.Lower

Schroeder, J. W., Smith, A. K., Brennan, P. A., Conneely, K. N., Kilaru, V., Knight, B. T., . . . Stowe, Z. N. (2012). DNA methylation in neonates born to women receiving psychiatric care. *Epigenetics, 7*(4), 409–414. doi:10.4161/epi.19551

Scott, M. N., Taylor, H. G., Fristad, M. A., Klein, N., Espy, K. A., Minich, N., & Hack, M. (2013). Behavior disorders in extremely preterm/extremely low birth weight children in kindergarten. *Journal of Developmental & Behavioral Pediatrics, 33*(3), 202–213. doi:10.1097/DBP.0b013e3182475287.Behavior

Silva, D., Colvin, L., Hagemann, E., & Bower, C. (2013). Environmental risk factors by gender associated with Attention-Deficit/Hyperactivity Disorder. *Pediatrics, 133*(1), 1–9. doi:10.1542/peds.2013-1434

Singh, G. K., Kenney, M. K., Ghandour, R. M., Kogan, M. D., & Lu, M. C. (2013). Mental health outcomes in US children and adolescents born prematurely or with low birthweight. *Depression Research and Treatment,* 7–18. doi:10.1155/2013/570743

Steenweg-de Graaff, J., Tiemeier, H., Steegers-Theunissen, R. P. M., Hofman, A., Jaddoe, V. W. V., Verhulst, F. C., & Roza, S. J. (2014). Maternal dietary patterns during pregnancy and child internalising and externalising problems. The Generation R Study. *Clinical Nutrition, 33*(1), 115–121. doi:10.1016/j.clnu.2013.03.002

Streissguth, A. P., Bookstein, F. L., Barr, H. M., Sampson, P. D., O'Malley, K., & Young, J. K. (2004). Risk factors for adverse life outcomes in Fetal Alcohol Syndrome and fetal alcohol effects. *Developmental and Behavioral Pediatrics, 25*(4), 228–238.

Toro, R., Leonard, G., Lerner, J. V., Lerner, R. M., Perron, M., & Pike, G. B. (2008). Prenatal exposure to maternal cigarette smoking and the adolescent cerebral cortex. *Neuropsychopharmacology, 33,* 1019–1027. doi:10.1038/sj.npp.1301484

Vandenbergh, D. J., Perslco, A. M., Hawkins, A. L., Griffin, C. A., Li, X., Jabs, E. W., & Uhl, G. R. (1992). Human Dopamine Transporter Gene (DAT1) maps to chromosome 5pl 5.3 and displays a VNTR. *Genomics, 7*(10), 1104–1106.

Vermiglio, F., Presti, V. P. L. O., Moleti, M., Sidoti, M., Tortorella, G., Scaffidi, G., . . . Trimarchi, F. (2004). Attention deficit and hyperactivity disorders in the offspring of mothers exposed to mild-moderate iodine deficiency: A possible novel iodine deficiency disorder in developed countries. *The Journal of Clinical Endocrinology & Metabolism, 89*(12), 6054–6060. doi:10.1210/jc.2004-0571

Wachs, T. D. (2009). Models linking nutritional deficiencies to maternal and child mental health. *American Journal of Clinical Nutrition, 89,* 935–939. doi:10.3945/ajcn.2008.26692B.1

Wagner, A. I., Schmidt, N. L., Lemery-Chalfant, K., Leavitt, L. A., & Goldsmith, H. H. (2009). The limited effects of obstetrical and neonatal complications on conduct and ADHD symptoms in middle childhood. *Journal of Developmental and Behavioral Pediatrics, 30*(3), 217–225. doi:10.1097/DBP.0b013e3181a7ee98.The

Wakschlag, L. S., & Hans, S. L. (2002). Maternal smoking during pregnancy and conduct problems in high-risk youth: A developmental framework. *Development and Psychopathology, 14*(2), 351–369.

Wakschlag, L. S., Kistner, E. O., Pine, D. S., Biesecker, G., Pickett, K. E., Skol, A. D., . . . Cook, E. H., Jr. (2010). Interaction of prenatal exposure to cigarettes and MAOA genotype in pathways to youth antisocial behavior. *Molecular Psychiatry, 15*(9), 928–937. doi:10.1038/mp.2009.22

Wakschlag, L. S., Lahey, B. B., Loeber, R., Green, S. M., Gordon, R. A., & Leventhal, B. L. (1997). Maternal smoking during pregnancy and the risk for conduct disorder in boys. *Archives of General Psychiatry, 54*(7), 670–676.

Waldman, I. D., Rowe, D. C., Abramowitz, A., Kozel, S. T., Mohr, J. H., Sherman, S. L., . . . Stever, C. (1998). Association and linkage of the dopamine transporter gene and Attention-Deficit Hyperactivity Disorder in children: Heterogeneity owing to diagnostic subtype and severity. *American Journal of Human Genetics, 63,* 1767–1776.

Weissman, M., Warner, V., Wickramaratne, P., & Kandel, D. (1999). Maternal smoking during pregnancy and psychopathology in offspring followed to adulthood. *Journal of the American Academy of Child & Adolescent Psychiatry, 38*(7), 892–899.

Winneke, G. (2011). Developmental aspects of environmental neurotoxicology: Lessons from lead and polychlorinated biphenyls. *Journal of the Neurological Sciences, 308*(1–2), 9–15. doi:10.1016/j.jns.2011.05.020

Wright, J. P., Dietrich, K. N., Ris, M. D., Hornung, R. W., Wessel, S. D., Lanphear, B. P., . . . Rae, M. N. (2008). Association of prenatal and childhood blood lead concentrations with criminal arrests in early adulthood. *PLoS Medicine, 5*(5). doi:10.1371/journal.pmed.0050101

13

Attachment and Disruptive Disorders

Marleen G. Groeneveld and Judi Mesman

In early childhood, low to moderate levels of disruptive behaviors such as aggression, temper tantrums, and defiance are quite normal, and thus seen in many children (Alink et al., 2006). In most children these disruptive behaviors decline across early childhood. However, high levels of disruptive behavior in early childhood are predictive of problematic behavior (such as disruptive and impulse-control disorders) in adolescence and adulthood (Broidy et al., 2003; NICHD, 2004). It is important to identify and understand the antecedents of these disorders, and to develop effective prevention and interventions programs.

A number of factors can play an important role in the development of disruptive behaviors and related disorders in early childhood, including child factors such as genetic, cognitive, and temperamental characteristics (see Chapters 8, 10, and 11 respectively), and family factors such as parent psychopathology and parenting practices (see Chapters 17 and 19). The early parent–child relationship is central to the development of children's personality and behaviors in many theoretical frameworks, and one particularly prominent framework in this field is attachment theory (Bowlby, 1969). In this framework, attachment refers to a child's innate tendency to seek proximity to one or more specific caregivers in times of distress or danger (Bowlby, 1969). These early experiences of parent–child interactions set the stage for later healthy development versus psychopathology. A central element of these interactions is parental sensitivity, defined as a parent's ability to notice a child's signals, interpret these signals correctly, and respond to them promptly and appropriately (Ainsworth, Bell, & Stayton, 1974). Sensitive parenting fosters a secure attachment between child and parent in which children use the parent as a secure base from which to explore, and a safe haven to return to in times of need (Ainsworth, Blehar, Waters, & Wall, 1978). Secure attachment is associated with positive child development; insecure attachment is related to negative child development, including child disruptive behavior problems (Fearon, Bakermans-Kranenburg, van IJzendoorn, Lapsley, & Roisman, 2010; Kochanska & Kim, 2013; Sroufe, Egeland, Carlson, & Collins, 2005).

In the current chapter we will first introduce the concept of attachment theory, including the role of caregiver sensitivity. Second, we will discuss the influence of the attachment relationship between children and their caregiver on child disruptive behavior problems and disruptive behavior. Third, we present a model in which we discuss several explanatory mechanisms that link early attachment and sensitivity to later disruptive behavior problems and moderators that influence this association. Finally, we will address several avenues of research that require more attention when trying to understand the role of attachment in the development of behavior problems.

The Wiley Handbook of Disruptive and Impulse-Control Disorders, First Edition.
Edited by John E. Lochman and Walter Matthys.
© 2018 John Wiley & Sons Ltd. Published 2018 by John Wiley & Sons Ltd.

Attachment

Attachment theory was developed by John Bowlby (1969), and has provided a theoretical foundation for understanding the importance of interpersonal attachments across the lifespan. According to Bowlby, all infants are predisposed to become attached to one or more primary caregivers: their attachment figure(s). He suggested that all normally developing infants show attachment behaviors like crying, smiling, reaching, and crawling. From an evolutionary perspective, these attachment behaviors are adaptive, because they ensure protection, support, and care from their primary caregiver(s), thus promoting infant survival. Based on daily interactions with their attachment figures, infants develop a mental representation of this relationship, called an internal working model (Bowlby, 1973). This model includes expectations about a caregiver's availability in times of distress, reflecting the extent to which the caregiver functions as a safe haven, and influencing the infant's behavioral decisions regarding attachment displays and exploration accordingly (Bretherton & Munholland, 2016).

This internal working model of an attachment relationship can be measured using a laboratory procedure, the Strange Situation Procedure (SSP), developed by Ainsworth et al. (1978). This procedure was designed to capture the balance between infants' attachment and exploration behaviors (12–20 months of age). The SSP consists of eight episodes: (1) caregiver and infant are introduced to the laboratory, (2) caregiver and child settle in, (3) a stranger enters the room and plays with the infant, (4) parent leaves the room, (5) parent returns, stranger leaves, (6) parent leaves again, (7) stranger returns, and (8) parent returns. This means there are two separation and reunion episodes. The status of the infant's relationship with the attachment figure is based on his or her behavior toward the caregiver during the two reunion episodes, evaluated in the context of behavior in the preceding episodes and in responses to the caregiver's current behavior. Ainsworth et al.'s system distinguishes three types of attachment: one "secure" type (B), and two insecure types, "avoidant" (A), and "resistant" or "ambivalent" (C). Subsequent research by Main and Solomon (1986; 1990) added a fourth type of attachment to these three "organized" varieties: "disorganized" or "disoriented" attachment (D).

Securely attached infants (B) are characterized by using the caregiver as a secure base for exploration. During the separation episode, they show signs of missing the parent, especially after the second separation. During reunion, they actively seek proximity to their attachment figure with simple vocalization or gesture. If they were upset by the separation, they seek contact, but are relatively quick to recover and return to the exploration of the toys and room. These infants show a *balance* between attachment and exploration. When infants with an avoidant classification (A) are introduced to the room, they explore readily and show little affect or secure-base behavior. During the separation episodes there is a minimal visible response: infants show little distress when left alone. During the reunion episodes they display avoidant behavior: they may look away from the parent or actively avoid the parent, for example when the parent picks up the child, the child may stiffen or lean away. These infants *minimize* attachment behavior. The third group of children, ambivalent or resistant attached infants (C) are visibly distressed when they are introduced to the room and often fail to engage in exploration. During the two separation episodes they are very distressed. During reunion, these infants show a mixture of proximity seeking and resistant, angry behavior toward the caregiver. Sometimes they may alternate bids for contact with signs of angry rejection and tantrums, they are difficult to soothe (or too upset to signal or make contact), and they generally fail to resume exploration. These infants *maximize* attachment behavior.

Children in all these three classifications of attachment (A, B, and C) reveal patterns of organized behavior. In the fourth group of children this is not the case; children who show disorganized or disoriented (D) attachment to their caregiver do not display a consistent strategy for dealing with the stress induced by the separation episodes. During the SSP they show a combination of avoidant and ambivalent behavior, or show disorganized behavior; they freeze for example, or show indicators of fear of the caregiver or stereotypic behavior (Solomon & George, 1999). It should be noted that the correct application of these attachment classifications requires extensive training and that relevant behaviors are not easily observed outside of standardized procedures like the SSP.

Consistent with theoretical predictions, the different types of attachment are related to caregiver behavior towards the infants. Several studies have shown that caregiver sensitivity is a key aspect. According to Mary Ainsworth, sensitivity is characterized by prompt and adequate responses to the child's emotional and behavioral signals (Ainsworth et al., 1974). A sensitive caregiver understands that children's attachment signals (for example crying after separation) should be met with soothing efforts (e.g., picking up the child, cuddling, or in many non-Western cultures breastfeeding), whereas exploration behavior only requires intervention when there is danger. A sensitive parent can thus see the world from the infant's point of view, respects the infant's autonomy when appropriate, but steps in and intervenes when the infant needs adult support. Self-reports of sensitive parenting are not feasible because an insensitive parent will inherently not recognize misinterpreting or missing their infant's signals, given that the core of insensitive parenting is a lack of awareness of infant signals. Trained observers are needed to evaluate a caregiver's behavior, ideally across different contexts. Several standardized instruments are available for this purpose (Mesman & Emmen, 2013).

Meta-analyses have shown that sensitivity is an important factor in the development of attachment security for the relationship between infants and their mothers ($r = 0.24$, $p < .001$, $k = 16$, $N = 837$; De Wolff & Van IJzendoorn, 1997) as well as the relationship between infants and their fathers ($r = 0.12$, $p < .001$, $k = 16$, $N = 1,355$; Lucassen et al., 2011). Effect sizes are small to moderate, but the attachment-based sensitivity construct also directly relates to child development in many domains (Mesman, Van IJzendoorn, & Bakermans-Kranenburg, 2012), including disruptive behavior problems (Campbell, 2002; Cassidy & Shaver, 2016; DeKlyen & Greenberg, 2016).

Attachment and Disruptive behaviors

Many empirical studies have examined the influence of the attachment relationship between children and their primary caregiver on children's disruptive behavior problems and disruptive behavior (Guttmann-Steinmetz & Crowell, 2006). One well-known longitudinal study on this topic is the Minnesota Longitudinal Study of Risk and Adaptation by Erickson, Sroufe, and Egeland, started in 1975. They recruited a sample of 267 first-time mothers in a high-risk environment, and followed the development of their children until adulthood. Poverty was the main risk factor, but often co-occurred with others such as young and single motherhood and low educational levels (Egeland, Carlson, & Sroufe, 1993). Extensive assessments were made of children's cognitive, social, and behavioral development using parent and teacher questionnaires and observations in homes, the laboratory, summer camps, and schools (Sroufe et al., 2005). The research team showed that attachment security of the children (measured at 12 months of age and 18 months of age) predicted future behavior problems: insecurely attached children scored higher than securely attached children on assessments of behavior problems at preschool age. When comparing ambivalent and avoidant children, the avoidant preschoolers showed the most behavior problems; they were less compliant, scored higher on hostility and isolation, and had more problems overall (Erickson, Sroufe, and Egeland, 1985). At six years of age there was only an association for boys, not girls: boys with an insecure attachment history at 12 months of age showed more behavior problems at age six years than boys with secure relationship history. When comparing boys in the two insecure attachment classifications, the boys with an ambivalent attachment classification scored higher on disruptive behavior problems (Lewis, Feiring, McGuffog, & Jaskir, 1984).

In a more recent study, the National Institute of Child Health and Human Development (NICHD) conducted a very large longitudinal study, measuring infant attachment in more than 1,000 infants. In this study, the disorganized (D) classification was also included. They showed that infants' Strange Situation attachment classifications predicted mothers' reports of children's social competence and teachers' reports of disruptive behavior problems from preschool age through 1st grade (NICHD, 2006). Further, in a meta-analysis focusing on adults, attachment insecurity emerged as a clear predictor of violent offending (Ogilvie, Newman, Todd, & Peck, 2014), showing that attachment relations remain salient in the prediction of disruptive behaviors into adulthood.

In addition to these two longitudinal studies, many others were published about the association between attachment and disruptive behavior problems. Study outcomes were mixed: some did find an association while others did not. To make sense of such inconsistencies, Fearon, Bakermans-Kranenburg, van IJzendoorn, Lapsley, and Roisman (2010) conducted a meta-analysis combining and analyzing the data from previous studies. They analyzed over 60 independent studies and showed that the association between attachment insecurity and disruptive behavior problems was significant ($d = 0.31$), so they concluded that attachment plays a significant role in the development of children's behavior problems. More specifically, they showed that especially disorganized children were at elevated risk ($d = 0.34$), while effects for children with avoidant attachment were smaller ($d = 0.12$), and the association for resistant attachment ($d = 0.11$) was not significant.

Fearon and colleagues (2010) only included mothers in their meta-analyses, since there was only one study that reported on outcome data for father–child attachment security and met their entry criteria (Avazier, Sagi, Resnick, & Gini, 2002). In this study, Avazier et al. looked at 66 young adolescents who were raised in infancy in Israeli kibbutzim with collective sleeping. The SSP was used to evaluate early attachment to mothers and fathers and teachers' reports evaluated school functioning and emotional maturity. Results showed that infant attachment to mother, but not to father, predicted children's scholastic skills and emotional maturity (including behavioral difficulties). This is consistent with another nonclinical study, which found that mother–child attachment was related to problem behaviors in preschoolers (and to quality of play, conflict resolution, and social perception), but that father–child attachment was not related to any of the domains. Additionally, these authors studied "double-classification": attachment classification to mother and father, and they showed that problems were best predicted by attachment to both mother and father (Suess, Grossmann, & Sroufe, 1992).

Other studies (not represented in the meta-analyses) did find an effect of the father–child attachment relationship on child behavior problems. Evidence from the Preschool Families Project, a longitudinal study of clinic-referred preschool boys at risk for conduct disorder, showed that father–child attachment classifications of boys with disruptive behavior problems differed from those of nonproblem dyads, and was related to their disruptive behavior scores. When combining attachment scores with fathers and mothers, only 25% of the clinic boys were securely attached to both parents, while 75% of the comparison boys were (DeKlyen, Speltz, & Greenberg, 1998). Recently, Kochanska and Kim (2013) have also examined the association between children's attachment security with mothers and fathers, assessed in Strange Situation with each parent at 15 months, and children's behavior problems, reported by teachers, fathers, mothers, and children themselves at age 8. These authors showed that attachment security with fathers or mothers did not predict problem behavior rated by parents, but father–child attachment (and not mother–child attachment) did predict disruptive behavior problems reported by the teacher. In addition, when analyzing the children's self reported behavior problems they found that mother–child and father–child attachment was related to behavior problems. In addition, there was an interaction effect. Children with insecure attachment classification with both fathers and mothers reported more overall problems, than those with a secure attachment with at least one parent. Security with either parent could offset such risks, while security with both parents conferred no additional benefits.

With regard to the parenting process most closely associated with the development of attachment security, many studies have shown that caregiver sensitivity is related to children's disruptive behavior (Campbell, 2002). An early meta-analysis showed that responsive parenting predicts lower levels of externalizing problems (Rothbaum & Weisz, 1994). Since then, multiple studies have confirmed this finding. Most notably, in the large longitudinal NICHD Study of Early Child Care and Youth Development, children's externalizing behavior was rated by mothers and caregivers/teachers across childhood. Several sets of analyses showed that lower levels of maternal sensitivity predicted higher levels of externalizing behavior problems at later ages (e.g., Bradley & Corwyn, 2007; Miner & Clarke-Stewart, 2008. Further, many studies have shown that sensitive parenting promotes child competencies related to lower risk for disruptive disorders, such as executive functioning (Bernier, Carlson, & Whipple, 2010), empathy (Kochanska, 2002), and general social competence (Raby, Roisman, Fraley, & Simpson, 2015; Van Berkel et al., 2015).

Explanatory Mechanisms

Figure 13.1 summarizes explanatory mechanisms that link early attachment and sensitivity to later disruptive behavior problems. These mechanisms include internal working models, emotion regulation, modeling, attention, motivational processes, behavioral contingencies, and genetics and related neuroscience.

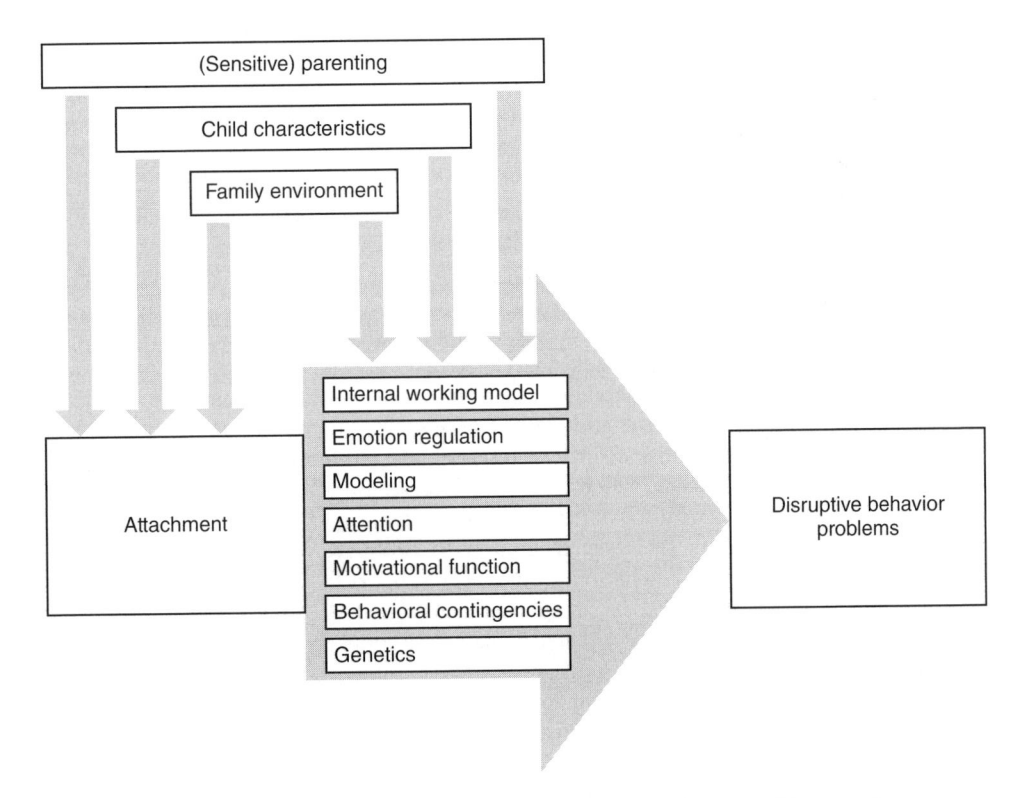

Figure 13.1 The association between attachment and disruptive behavior problems: explanatory constructs and moderators.

First, based on the interactions with their attachment figure, infants develop a mental representation of this relationship, their so-called internal working model (Bowlby, 1973). This internal working model is thought of as a set of organized cognitive-affective psychological schemata that organize thinking, feeling, and behavior about the self and others. This model influences the child's expectations regarding interactions with other persons (besides the parents) and is believed to affect perception, cognition, and motivation selectively (Bretherton, 1985; Sroufe & Fleeson, 1986).

Securely attached children hold positive models of the self and others. They approach social situations with confidence and openness, reflecting positive rather than disruptive social behaviors. Children with an avoidant attachment classification have working models of relationships that are characterized by anger and mistrust, due to insensitivity, neglect, or rejection by their caregivers (Bowlby, 1973). As a result, they are more likely to enter social interactions with heightened sensitivity to rejection (Downey, Lebolt, Rincon, & Freitas, 1998), and with attributional biases that makes them interpret the intent of other people's actions as negative or hostile (Cassidy, Kirsh, Scolton, & Parke, 1996; Suess et al., 1992). As a consequence, children with an avoidant attachment classification may show hostile, aggressive behavior towards other people, which, in turn, may also lead to peer rejection. Children with a resistant attachment classification may have internal working models that are characterized by a desire for a high level of closeness and fear of abandonment due to inconsistent caregiving (alternating sensitive and insensitive parenting). These children may show extremely high activation of emotional strategies and display frustration, overstimulation, and impulsivity (Cassidy, 1994). Finally, children with disorganized attachment classification have disorganized working models, due to a frightening, unpredictable, abusive parent. These children have been placed in a paradox: the caregiver should be a safe haven, but is also the source of fear (Main & Hesse, 1990). Children with this classification may respond to this frightening or unpredictable caregiving by developing a controlling-punitive attitude toward the parent (Main & Cassidy, 1988), they are angry and domineering, with attempts to humiliate, embarrass, or reject the parent. Such behavioral patterns toward the caregiver may then spill over to peer relations and potentially develop into disruptive disorders (Lyons-Ruth & Jacobvitz, 2016).

A second mechanism that has been suggested might explain the association between attachment security and children's disruptive behaviors is emotion regulation (Cassidy, 1994). In securely attached dyads, the caregiver is available for the child and helps him or her to calm down in stressful situations and to gain mastery over his or her emotions and the situation. If a caregiver is not available or not sensitively responsive (or inconsistent), this dyadic regulation does not take place. Research, however, shows that dyadic regulation is an important precursor of future successful self-regulation (Diamond & Aspinwall, 2003; Kochanska & Kim, 2014). As a consequence, the child is left with his or her own immature regulatory resources, unable to inhibit impulses and manage potentially difficult situations, which reflect key symptoms of several disruptive disorders. Interestingly, although it seems that avoidantly attached children are not affected when their parent leaves the room during the SSP, seemingly distracting themselves with toys, there is evidence that their heart rates do increase, just as those of securely and resistantly attached children do (Sroufe & Waters, 1977). Importantly however, the avoidantly attached children do not seek support from their parents to regulate this stress and, in the absence of experiencing dyadic regulation, do not learn to effectively self-regulate. Similarly, ambivalent or disorganized children are unlikely to count on their parents' support (because the parent is inconsistent or a source of fear and stress) and thus are at risk of failing to develop effective self-regulation and associated disruptive behaviors.

Other possible mechanisms underlying the association of attachment security and parental sensitivity with disruptive behavior are modeling, attention, motivation, and behavioral contingencies. First, when a caregiver shows sensitive and responsive care to a child, characterized by empathy and prosocial behavior, children may imitate that behavior (Guttmann-Steinmetz & Crowell, 2006) and, as a result, manifest the opposite of antisocial behavior. Second, children with sensitive parents will get attention from their parents for appropriate and positive behavior, so there is no need to show externalizing behavior to get attention. Third, children of sensitive parents may simply be more motivated to follow directions and rules (instead of engaging in oppositional defiant behavior). Based on primate studies, Mary Ainsworth, for example, hypothesized that children are inherently motivated to comply with their caregivers' directions as part of evolutionary adaptedness (i.e, making sure an infant does what is required to remain safe and healthy), and that this tendency is fostered by a secure attachment bond that helps develop mature moral behavior (Ainsworth et al., 1974). Finally, having a sensitive parent teaches children about cause and consequence (behavioral contingencies) in a positive way. The child's behavior is followed by predictable and supportive consequences, and such interaction patterns have been shown to predict the detection of contingencies in other contexts (Tarabulsy, Tessier, & Kappas, 1996). In its turn, detecting contingencies is important to adaptive functioning, as it will facilitate rule-learning and compliance, and as such limit disruptive behaviors.

Each of the mechanisms described above refers in some way to the importance of a parent's sensitive responsiveness in daily caregiving, suggesting that interventions aimed at enhancing parental sensitivity would reduce children's disruptive behaviors. Testing this notion in experimental designs (i.e., intervention studies) would provide evidence for the causal nature of the relation between parental sensitivity and child disruptive behaviors. Several randomized control trials have indeed confirmed this causality, showing that intervention-induced improvement in parental sensitivity relates to a decline in behavior problems in children (e.g., Bakermans-Kranenburg, Van IJzendoorn, Pijlman, Mesman, & Juffer, 2008; Moss et al., 2011).

A final explanatory mechanism for the relation between attachment and child disruptive behaviors lies in genetics and related neurobiology. There is some evidence that both the parental factors related to children's insecure attachment (e.g., parental psychopathology, lack of interpersonal sensitivity) and the child behaviors associated with disruptive disorders (e.g., aggression, disobedience) might be explained by genetically determined neurobiological characteristics shared by parents and their children (Moffit, 2005). In other words: the same set of genes may be responsible for both the development of insecure attachment and disruptive behaviors. This means that certain genetically vulnerable families might benefit especially from comprehensive therapeutic approaches that target the underlying social and behavioral deficiencies in all family members.

Greenberg, Speltz, and DeKlyen (1993) proposed a risk factor model that emphasizes the quality of the parent–child attachment relationship as precursor of the early onset and persistence of disruptive behavior problems. They included four general risk domains: (1) child characteristics (e.g., temperament, biological vulnerability, neurocognitive function); (2) quality of early attachment relations; (3) parenting practices (e.g., harsh and ineffective practices, lack of warmth); and (4) family ecology (e.g., family life stress and trauma, instrumental resources, social support). They state that children can experience none, one, or more risk factors, but that a single risk domain will usually not directly cause later problems, but that more risk domains will increase the probability of psychopathology during childhood.

In one of their own studies, Greenberg, Speltz, DeKlyen, and Jones (2001) used this four-factor model when they compared preschool boys with ODD and normally behaving boys. They found that all four risk domains correlated with parent and teacher ratings of conduct problems. Three out of four risk domains differed between the boys with ODD and the normally behaving boys, to the disadvantage of ODD boys: child characteristics (i.e., developmental history e.g., parental concerns and child attainments), parental management strategies (i.e., questionnaires about harshness, ineffective discipline, lack of warmth, punitive parenting, and physical abuse) and attachment security. There were no differences in family ecology (i.e., life stress, family characteristics, and family psychiatric status) between the boys with ODD and the non-ODD boys. In addition, they demonstrated that increasing the number of risk domains substantially increased the likelihood of a disorder: the ODD children were a staggering 34 times more likely than the comparison children to have risk in all four domains.

Moderators: Child, Parents, Family Environment

In addition to studies that found that attachment and parental sensitivity had the main effect on later disruptive psychopathology, many studies have shown that attachment is particularly likely to predict children's disruptive behaviors in the context of other risk factors within the child and the family ecology (Cicchetti & Rogosch, 1996; Greenberg et al., 2001). Several factors influence the association between attachment and disruptive behavior problems: parenting, child characteristics, and family environment (see Figure 13.1). In terms of child characteristics, gender is an important factor in the prevalence of disruptive behavior problems. While young boys and girls below the age of 2 years have been found equally likely to exhibit disruptive behavior problems, differences emerge at age 2–3 years (Alink et al., 2006; Lahey et al., 2000; Loeber & Hay, 1997; Mesman, Bongers, & Koot, 2001). Gender can also be a moderator in the relation between attachment and disruptive behavior problems. The meta-analysis by Fearon, Bakermans-Kranenburg, van IJzendoorn, Lapsley, & Roisman (2010) clearly showed that attachment was more strongly associated with disruptive behavior problems in samples of boys ($d = 0.35$) than in samples of girls ($d = -0.03$). However, they also included mixed samples (boys and girls) and suggest that the association between attachment and disruptive behavior problems cannot be ascribed to boys only, since these mixed samples showed equally strong effect sizes as those with only boys. The lower rates of disruptive behavior problems in girls may impose a range restriction in the studies, which may attenuate the effect size, but it is also suggested that insecurity in girls is more associated with internalizing problems than disruptive behavior problems (DeKlyen & Greenberg, 2008). A second meta-analysis undertaken by Groh, Roisman, van IJzendoorn, Bakermans-Kranenburg, and Fearon (2012), however, showed that attachment insecurity was not found to be more strongly correlated with internalizing symptoms among girls than boys.

Another relevant child characteristic is temperament. It has been shown that infant negativity, or negative mood, irritability, and high-intensity reactions like anger, is a risk factor for the development of disruptive behavior (Keller, Spieker, & Gilchrist, 2005; Sanson, Hemphill, & Smart, 2004; see also Chapter 11). On the other hand, it has also been suggested that temperament is a protective factor. For example, the Australian Temperament Project showed that boys without behavior problems at 11 to 12 years were more likely to have an inhibited temperament (at age 3–4 years) than boys with later behavior problems (Sanson, Oberklaid, Prior, Amos, & Smart, 1996). Temperament may also act a moderator in the relation between attachment and disruptive behavior problems. Burgess, Marshall, Rubin, and Fox (2003) reported that insecure attachment interacted with difficult temperament in predicting high levels of disruptive behavior problems. Temperament is often seen as a proxy for genotype, and increasingly studies examine actual genetic characteristics as potential moderators of relations between attachment and child outcomes relevant for the development of disruptive behaviors. In one study, for example, insecurely attached children who also carried a short 5-HTTLPR allele developed poor self-regulation, whereas this was not the case for those who were homozygotic for the long allele (Kochanska, Philibert, & Barry, 2009). In another study, warm-responsive parenting (which is very similar to sensitive parenting) was related to decreased externalizing problems only in children with the short polymorphism of the dopamine D4 receptor gene (Propper et al., 2007).

In the Minnesota Longitudinal Study of Risk and Adaptation (Erickson et al., 1985), main effects of attachment on disruptive behavior problems were found, but also interaction effects with parenting. Not all children with insecure attachment classification showed behavior problems. It was shown that insecurely attached children without behavior problems had mothers who were warmer, more supportive, more involved, and more appropriate in limit setting than the mothers of insecurely attached children with behavior problems. Children who have a secure attachment relationship with their mothers can also develop behavior problems, however. Comparisons between securely attached children with and without behavior problems showed that the securely attached children who showed behavior problems had mothers who scored lower on several parenting skills: they provided less support, were less involved at home, and less consistent, firm and confident in teaching tasks.

The broader family environment is the third factor that may influence disruptive behaviors, and the association between attachment and the development of disruptive behaviors. Disruptive behavior problems and disorders are more often reported in high-risk samples, including families with low socioeconomic status, low maternal education, a high incidence of stressful life events, low partner support, and who were living in neighborhoods characterized by high crime rates and social disorganization (Aguilar, Sroufe, Egeland, & Carlson, 2000; Côté, Vaillancourt, LeBlanc, Nagin, & Tremblay, 2006; Frick et al., 1993; Jouriles et al., 1991; Lahey et al., 2000). Although contextual characteristics have been found to have main effects on disruptive behavior problems, these effects seem smaller than the effects of parenting and child characteristics (Shaw, Owens, Vondra, Keenan, & Winslow, 1996).

This family environment may act as a moderator in the association of attachment and disruptive behavior problems. Keller and colleagues (2005) studied the role of child characteristics, parenting, and family environment in the development of preschoolers' disruptive behavior. They made a distinction between preschoolers with a typical trajectory of disruptive behavior (decline of problem behavior from 24 to 54 months of age) and a high problem trajectory (increase in problem behavior). They showed that children were more likely to be in the high problem trajectory when they were insecurely attached in addition to showing high levels of infant negativity. Analyses including child gender indicated that boys were particularly vulnerable to this combination. In addition, this study showed that insecurely attached children with high infant negativity were especially at risk when these two factors were also combined with high-risk parenting. As expected, they found that insecurely attached children with positive parenting were significantly less likely to develop the problematic trajectory of disruptive behavior problems and that securely attached children with positive parenting had the smallest chance of developing it. Finally, Keller and colleagues (2005) revealed that the combination of insecure attachment and family environment was a predictor of the trajectory, and that children with risks in three domains (infant negativity, parenting, and family environment) had the greatest likelihood of being on it: they showed increasing levels of disruptive behavior problems from 24 months of age.

The examination of moderators in the relation between attachment/sensitivity and disruptive behavior problems is particularly important for the understanding of resilience (Masten, 2014): the process by which some children show adaptive development—not disruptive disorders when faced with risk, attachment insecurity, and insensitive parenting. Uncovering protective characteristics and contexts that foster resilience are crucial for the development of targeted interventions that do not assume that universally problematic outcomes must follow suboptimal attachment relations, and that can target additional factors known to alleviate the potentially negative effects of attachment insecurity or insensitive parenting.

Future Directions

Although there is a substantial number of studies linking attachment security and parental sensitivity to children's disruptive behaviors, several avenues of research require more attention if we wish to try to understand the nature of such associations and their context. One factor that has received very little attention in research is cultural context. This is unfortunate, because cultural factors are relevant in understanding both attachment security (e.g., Keller, 2013; LeVine, 2004) and disruptive behaviors (e.g., Bird et al., 2001; Zwirs, Burger, Buitelaar, & Schulpen, 2006), but most research focuses only on Western samples. Several studies in the domain of harsh parenting have shown that cultural context and the related normativity of such parenting practices are salient moderators in their association with child behavioral outcomes (e.g., Deater-Deckard & Dodge, 1997; Lansford et al., 2005, 2010). Such cross-cultural work on the subject of attachment and the development of disruptive behaviors is, unfortunately, scarce (see Mesman, Van IJzendoorn, & Sagi-Schwartz, 2016 for an overview). There is, nevertheless, some evidence of insecure attachment constituting a risk for such problems in non-Western cultural contexts, such as China (Gu et al., 1997; Yue, Zhang, Chen, Liang, & Zhang, 2010) and Israel (Oppenheim, Sagi, & Lamb, 1990). Regarding sensitivity, the most recent insight is that, although its behavioral manifestations may vary across cultures, its function in promoting adaptive child development may be universal (Mesman et al., 2015, 2017). Indeed, a literature review has shown that the positive behavioral outcomes of sensitive parenting commonly found in Western ethnic majority families are also found in studies on ethnic minority families from various cultural backgrounds (Mesman et al., 2012). Nevertheless, there is a conspicuous lack of studies explicitly examining the role of culture in the relation between attachment-related constructs and children's disruptive behaviors. This line of research deserves more attention in the future to test the universality versus cultural specificity of relevant attachment processes.

It is further important to note that the direction of effects in attachment studies of behavior problems is not always straightforward. There is evidence that parenting children with social and behavior problems is challenging and may result in less adequate parenting in general (Pettit & Arsiwalla, 2008), and less sensitive parenting in particular (Newton et al., 2014), suggesting that child effects are important to consider. One symmetric longitudinal study showed that child externalizing problems at age 3 years predicted maternal distress at age 4 years, which in turn predicted lower levels of maternal sensitivity at age 5 years (Ciciolla, Gerstein, & Crnic, 2014). Importantly, such child effects are not necessarily intuitive. For example, Van der Voort et al. (2013) found that lower levels of effortful control in infants actually predicted higher levels of parental sensitivity. In their sample of highly educated adoptive families, parents may have been especially motivated and able to actively compensate for their children's lack of control by increased sensitive responsiveness, which, in turn, led to lower levels of delinquency in adolescence. Thus, the nature of bidirectional pathways may also depend on the particular context in which parent–child interactions occur. Future studies on attachment and disruptive behavior would ideally test bidirectional pathways and consider contextual variables that might explain pathway variations.

Additionally, there is still a dearth of studies that deal with the role of fathers in addition to mothers as attachment figures and sources of sensitive responsiveness in relation to children's behavioral development. Evidence is slowly emerging that it is vital to cover both parents in research of this kind (Suess et al., 1992). Similarly, the role of siblings deserves more attention. Van Berkel et al. (2015), for example, showed that father–child sensitivity predicted more compliance and more sharing in children, but only if the father treated the child's younger sibling less sensitively. Such findings may be explained by several theoretical frameworks that emphasize how dyadic parent–child relations are influenced by other parent–child dyads within the family (Boyle et al., 2004; Fearon, Bakermans-Kranenburg,

Van IJzendoorn, 2010; Feinberg, Neiderhiser, Simmens, Reiss, & Hetherington, 2000; Minuchin, 1985; Reiss et al., 1995; Volling, Kennedy, & Jackey, 2010).

Finally, it is interesting to note that the study of sensitive parenting, attachment security, and disruptive disorders rarely includes investigation of their relations with the DSM-identified attachment disorders, namely Reactive Attachment Disorder and Disinhibited Social Engagement Disorder. This is probably due to the rather controversial definitions and assumptions underlying these latter disorders (e.g., Minnis et al., 2006; Van IJzendoorn & Bakermans-Kranenburg, 2003), which have set them apart from "mainstream" studies of attachment. To foster a comprehensive understanding of the role of attachment processes in clinical disorders, it would be helpful to examine multiple diagnoses and their comorbidity as potential outcomes of suboptimal attachment and insensitive parenting.

Conclusion

As this chapter shows, the relevance of attachment theory and its constructs to the understanding of children's behavioral development in general and the emergence of disruptive behaviors and disorders in particular, has been established in many empirical studies. The literature to date shows that both attachment security and parental sensitivity predict fewer disruptive behaviors, as well as more positive functioning in several domains that relate to a lower risk for disruptive disorders, including self-regulation, empathy, contingency detection, and compliance motivation. The fact that a number of moderators have been established in the relation between attachment constructs and disruptive behaviors reveals that this is not a straightforward process, and that many other factors are important if we are to fully understand in which cases, in which contexts, and under which circumstances problems in the attachment relationship lead to disruptive behaviors and disorders. Such moderating effects are especially important for the early detection and targeted prevention of disruptive problems. The investigation of contextual variables, such as culture, socioeconomic factors, and wider social networks, represents an important avenue for future research that will help us understand the meaning of attachment processes in children's behavioral development, and prevent the field from assuming universality in processes that might very well be context-specific. Understanding the role of contextual factors may also be informative regarding the origins of potential bidirectional effects, and the complexity of multiple family relations that constitute the proximal context of parent–child dyadic interactions.

References

Aguilar, B., Sroufe, L. A., Egeland, B., & Carlson, E. (2000). Distinguishing the early-onset/persistent and adolescence-onset antisocial behaviour types: From birth to 16 years. *Development and Psychopathology, 12*, 109–132.

Ainsworth, M. D. S., Bell, S. M., & Stayton, D. J. (1974). Infant–mother attachment and social development: Socialization as a product of reciprocal responsiveness to signals. In M. P. M. Richards (Ed.), *The integration of a child into a social world* (pp. 99–135). Cambridge, UK: Cambridge University Press.

Ainsworth, M. D. S., Blehar, M. C., Waters, E., & Wall, S. (1978). *Patterns of attachment: A psychological study of the strange situation*. Hillsdale, NJ: Erlbaum.

Alink, L. R. A., Mesman, J., Van Zeijl, J., Stolk, M. N., Juffer, F., Koot, J. M., . . . van Ijzendoom, M. H. (2006). The early childhood aggression curve: Development of physical aggression in 10- to 50-month-old children. *Child Development, 77*, 954–966.

Avazier, O., Sagi, A., Resnick, G., & Gini, M. (2002). School competence in young adolescence: Links to early attachment relationships beyond concurrent self-perceived competence and representations of relationships. *International Journal of Behavioral Development, 26*, 397–409.

Bakermans-Kranenburg, M. J., Van IJzendoorn, M. H., Pijlman, F. T. A., Mesman, J., & Juffer, F. (2008). Experimental evidence for differential susceptibility: Dopamine D4 receptor polymorphism (DRD4 VNTR) moderates intervention effects on toddlers' externalizing behavior in a randomized control trial. *Developmental Psychology, 44,* 293–300.

Bernier, A., Carlson, S. M., & Whipple, N. (2010). From external regulation to self-regulation: Early parenting precursors of young children's executive functioning. *Child Development, 81,* 326–339.

Bird, H. R., Canino, G. J., Davies, M., Zhang, H., Ramirez, R., & Lahey, B. B. (2001). Prevalence and correlates of antisocial behaviors among three ethnic groups. *Journal of Abnormal Child Psychology, 29,* 465–478.

Bowlby, J. (1969). *Attachment and loss* (Vol. 1, rev. ed.). *Attachment.* Harmondsworth, UK: Penguin.

Bowlby, J. (1973). *Attachment and loss* (Vol. 2). *Separation, anxiety and anger.* New York, NY: Basic Books.

Boyle, M. H., Jenkins, J. M., Georgiades, K., Cairney, J., Duku, E., & Racine, Y. A. (2004). Differential maternal parenting behavior: Estimating within and between family effects. *Child Development, 75,* 1457–1476.

Bradley, R. H., & Corwyn, R. F. (2007). Externalizing problems in 5th grade: Relations with productive activity, maternal sensitivity, and harsh parenting from infancy through middle childhood. *Developmental Psychology, 43,* 1390–1401.

Bretherton, L. (1985). Attachment theory: Retrospect and prospect. In L. Bretherton & E. Waters (Eds.), Growing points of attachment theory and research. *Monographs of the Society for Research in Child Development, 50,* 3–35.

Bretherton, I., & Munholland, K. A. (2016). The internal working model construct in light of contemporary neuroimaging research. In J. Cassidy & P. R. Shaver (Eds.), *Handbook of attachment: Theory, research and clinical applications* (3rd ed., pp. 63–89). New York, NY: Guilford.

Broidy, L. M., Nagin, D. S., Tremblay, R. E., Bates, J. E., Brame, B., Dodge, K. A., . . . Vitaro, F. (2003). Developmental trajectories of childhood disruptive behaviors and adolescent delinquency: A six-site, cross-national study. *Developmental Psychology, 39,* 222–245.

Burgess, K. B., Marshall, P. J., Rubin, K. H., & Fox, N. A. (2003). Infant attachment and temperament as predictors of subsequent externalizing problems and cardiac physiology. *Journal of Child Psychology and Psychiatry, 44,* 819–831.

Campbell, S. B. (2002). Behavior problems in preschool children. New York, NY: Guilford Press.

Cassidy, J. (1994). Emotion regulation: Influences of attachment relationships. *Monographs of the Society for Research in Child Development, 59,* 228–249.

Cassidy, J., Kirsh, S. J., Scolton, K. L., & Parke, R. D. (1996). Attachment and representations of peer relationships. *Developmental Psychology, 32,* 892–904.

Cassidy, J., & Shaver, P. R. (2016). *Handbook of attachment: Theory, research, and clinical applications.* New York, NY: Guilford Press.

Cicchetti, D., & Rogosch, F. A. (1996). Equifinality and multifinality in developmental psychopathology. *Development and Psychopathology, 8,* 597–600.

Ciciolla, L., Gerstein, E. D., & Crnic, K. A. (2014). Reciprocity among maternal distress, child behavior, and parenting: Transactional processes and early childhood risk. *Journal of Clinical Child & Adolescent Psychology, 43,* 751–764.

Côté, S. M., Vaillancourt, T., LeBlanc, J. C., Nagin, D. S., & Tremblay, R. E. (2006). The development of physical aggression from toddlerhood to pre-adolescence: A nationwide longitudinal study of Canadian children. *Journal of Abnormal Child Psychology, 34,* 71–85.

Deater-Deckard, K., & Dodge, K. A. (1997). Externalizing behavior problems and discipline revisited: Nonlinear effects and variation by culture, context, and gender. *Psychological Inquiry, 8,* 161–175.

DeKlyen, M., & Greenberg, M. T. (2008). Attachment and psychopathology in childhood. In J. Cassidy & P. R. Shaver (Eds.), *Handbook of attachment: Theory, research and clinical applications* (2nd ed., pp. 637–663). New York, NY: Guilford.

DeKlyen, M., & Greenberg, M. T. (2016). Attachment and psychopathology in childhood. In J. Cassidy & P. R. Shaver (Eds.), *Handbook of attachment: Theory, research and clinical applications* (3rd ed., pp. 639–665). New York, NY: Guilford.

DeKlyen, M., Speltz, M. L., & Greenberg, M. T. (1998). Fathering and early onset conduct problems: Positive and negative parenting, father–son attachment, and the marital context. *Clinical Child and Family Psychology Review, 1,* 3–21.

De Wolff, M. S., & Van IJzendoorn, M. H. (1997). Sensitivity and attachment: A meta-analysis on parental antecedents of infant attachment. *Child Development, 68,* 571–591.

Diamond, L. M., & Aspinwall, L. G. (2003). Emotion regulation across the life span: An integrative perspective emphasizing self-regulation, positive affect, and dyadic processes. *Motivation and Emotion, 27,* 125–156.

Downey, G., Lebolt, A., Rincon, C., & Freitas, A. L. (1998). Rejection sensitivity and children's interpersonal difficulties. *Child Development, 69,* 1074–1091

Egeland, B., Carlson, E., & Sroufe, L. A. (1993). Resilience as a process. *Development and Psychopathology, 5,* 517–528.

Erickson, M. F., Sroufe, L. A., & Egeland, B. (1985). The relationship between quality of attachment and behavior problems in preschool in a high-risk sample. *Monographs of the Society for Research in Child Development, 50,* 147–156.

Fearon, R. M., Bakermans-Kranenburg, M. J., & Van IJzendoorn, M. H. (2010). Jealousy and attachment. The case of twins. In S. L. Hart & M. Legerstee (Eds.), *Handbook of jealousy: Theory, research, and multidisciplinary approaches* (pp. 362–386). New York, NY: Wiley.

Fearon, R. M. P., Bakermans-Kranenburg, M. J., van IJzendoorn, M. H., Lapsley, A. M., & Roisman, G. I. (2010). The significance of insecure attachment and disorganization in the development of children's externalizing behavior: A meta-analytic study. *Child Development, 81,* 435–456.

Feinberg, M. E., Neiderhiser, J. M., Simmens, S., Reiss, D., & Hetherington, E. M. (2000). Sibling comparison of differential parental treatment in adolescence: Gender, self-esteem, and emotionality as mediators of the parenting–adjustment association. *Child Development, 71,* 1611–1628.

Frick, P. J., Van Horn, Y., Lahey, B. B., Christ, M. A. G., Loeber, R., Hart, E. A., . . . Hanson, K. (1993). Oppositional defiant disorder and conduct disorder: A meta-analytic review of factor analyses and cross-validation in a clinic sample. *Clinical Psychology Review, 13,* 319–340.

Greenberg, M. T., Speltz, M. L., & DeKlyen, M. (1993). The role of attachment in the early development of disruptive behavior problems. *Development and Psychopathology, 5,* 191–213.

Greenberg, M. T., Speltz, M. L., & Deklyen, M., & Jones, K. (2001). Correlates of clinic referral for early conduct problems: Variable- and person-oriented approaches. *Development and Psychopathology, 13,* 255–276.

Groh, A. M., Roisman, G. I., van IJzendoorn, M. H., Bakermans-Kranenburg, M. J. & Fearon, R. P. (2012). The significance of insecure and disorganized attachment for children's internalizing symptoms: A meta-analytic study. *Child Development, 83,* 591–610.

Gu, H., Cen, G., Li, D., Gao, X., Li, Z., & Chen, X. (1997). Two-year-old children's social behaviour development and related family factors. *Psychological Science, 20,* 519–524.

Guttmann-Steinmetz, S., & Crowell, J. A. (2006). Attachment and externalizing disorders: A developmental psychopathology perspective. *Journal of the American Academy of Child and Adolescent Psychiatry, 45,* 440–451.

Jouriles, E. N., Murphy, C. M., Farris, A. M., Smith, D. A., Richters, J., & Waters, E. (1991). Marital adjustment, parental disagreements about child rearing, and behavior problems in boys: Increasing the specificity of the marital assessment. *Child Development, 62,* 1424–1433.

Keller, H. (2013). Attachment and culture. *Journal of Cross-Cultural Psychology, 44,* 175–194.

Keller, T. E., Spieker, S. J., & Gilchrist, L. (2005). Patterns of risk and trajectories of preschool problem behaviors: A person-oriented analysis of attachment in context. *Development and Psychopathology, 17,* 349–384.

Kochanska, G., & Kim, S. (2013). Early attachment organization with both parents and future behavior problems: From infancy to middle childhood. *Child Development, 84,* 283–296.

Kochanska, G., Philibert, R. A., & Barry, R. A. (2009). Interplay of genes and relationships in the development of self-regulation: Attachment organization moderates the effect of 5-HTTLPR status. *Journal of Child Psychology and Psychiatry, 50*(11), 1331–1338.

Kochanska, G. (2002). Mutually responsive orientation between mothers and their young children: A context for the early development of conscience. *Current Directions in Psychological Science, 11,* 191–195.

Kochanska, G., & Kim, S. (2014). Complex interplay among the parent–child relationship, effortful control, and internalized, rule-compatible conduct in young children: Evidence from two studies. *Developmental Psychology, 50,* 8–21.

Lahey B. B., Schwab-Stone, M., Goodman, S. H., Waldman, I. D., Canino, G., et al. (2000). Age and gender differences in oppositional behavior and conduct problems: a cross-sectional household study of middle childhood and adolescence. *Journal of Abnormal Psychology, 109,* 488–503.

Lansford, J. E., Chang, L., Dodge, K. A., Malone, P. S., Oburu, P., Palmerus, K., . . .Quinn, N. (2005). Physical discipline and children's adjustment: cultural normativeness as a moderator. *Child Development, 76,* 1234–1246.

Lansford, J. E., Malone, P. S., Dodge, K. A., Chang, L., Chaudhary, N., Tapanya, S., Oburu, P., & Deater-Deckard, K. (2010). Children's perceptions of maternal hostility as a mediator of the link between discipline and children's adjustment in four countries. *International Journal of Behavioral Development, 34,* 452–461.

LeVine, R. A. (2004). Challenging expert knowledge: Findings from an African study of infant care and development. In U. P. Gielen & J. Roopnarine (Eds.). *Childhood and adolescence, Cross-cultural perspectives and applications* (pp. 149–165). Westport, CT: Praeger.

Lewis, M., Feiring, C., McGuffog, C., & Jaskir, J. (1984). Predicting psychopathology in six-year-olds from early social relations. *Child Development, 55,* 123–136.

Loeber, R., & Hay, D. (1997). Key issues in the development of aggression and violence from childhood to early adulthood. *Annual Review of Psychology, 48,* 371–410.

Lucassen, N., Tharner, A., Van IJzendoorn, M. H., Bakermans-Kranenburg, M. J., Volling, B. L., Verhulst, F. C., Lambregtse-Van den Berg, M. P., & Tiemeier, H. (2011). The association between paternal sensitivity and infant–father attachment security: A meta-analysis of three decades of research. *Journal of Family Psychology, 25,* 986–992.

Lyons-Ruth, K., & Jacobvitz, D. (2016). Attachment disorganization from infancy to adulthood: Neurobiological correlated, parenting contexts, and pathways to disorder. In J. Cassidy & P. R. Shaver (Eds.), *Handbook of attachment: Theory, research and clinical applications* (3rd ed., pp. 667–695). New York: Guilford.

Main, M., & Cassidy, J. (1988). Categories of response to reunion with the parent at age 6: Predictable from infant attachment classifications and stable over a 1-month period. *Developmental Psychology, 24,* 415–426.

Main, M., & Hesse, E. (1990). Parents' unresolved traumatic experiences are related to infant disorganized attachment status: Is frightened and/or frightening parental behavior the linking mechanism? In M. Greenberg, D. Cicchetti, & E. M. Cummings (Eds.), *Attachment in the preschool years: Theory, research, and intervention* (pp. 161–182). Chicago, IL: University of Chicago Press.

Main, M., & Solomon, J. (1986). Discovery of a disorganized/disoriented attachment pattern. In T. B. Brazelton & M. W. Yogman (Eds.), *Affective development in infancy* (pp. 95– 124). Norwood, NJ: Ablex.

Main, M., & Solomon, J. (1990). Procedures for identifying infants as disorganized/disoriented during the Ainsworth Strange Situation. In M. Greenberg, D. Cicchetti, & M. Cummings (Eds.), *Attachment during the preschool years* (pp. 121–160). Chicago: University of Chicago Press.

Masten, A. S. (2014). Global perspectives on resilience in children and youth. *Child Development, 85,* 6–20.

Mesman, J., Bongers, I. L., & Koot H. M. (2001). Preschool developmental pathways to preadolescent internalizing and externalizing problems. *Journal of Child Psychology and Psychiatry, 42,* 679–689.

Mesman, J., & Emmen, R. A. G. (2013). Mary Ainsworth's legacy: A systematic review of observational instruments measuring parental sensitivity. *Attachment and Human Development, 15,* 485–506.

Mesman, J., Van IJzendoorn, M. H., & Bakermans-Kranenburg, M. J. (2012). Unequal in opportunity, equal in process: Parental sensitivity promotes positive child development in ethnic minority families. *Child Development Perspectives, 6,* 239–250.

Mesman, J., Van IJzendoorn, M. H., Behrens, K., Carbonell, O. A., Carcamo, R., Cohen-Paraira, I., . . . Zreik, G. (2015). Is the ideal mother a sensitive mother? Beliefs about early childhood parenting in mothers across the globe. *International Journal of Behavioral Development, 40,* 385–397.

Mesman, J., Van IJzendoorn, M. H., & Sagi-Schwartz, A. (2016). Cross-cultural patterns of attachment. Universal and contextual dimensions. In J. Cassidy & P. Shaver (Eds), *Handbook of attachment. Theory, research, and clinical applications* (3rd ed., pp. 852–877. New York, NY: Guilford.

Mesman, J., Minter, T., Anngned, A., Cissé, I. A. H., Salali, G. D., & Migliano, A.B. (2017). Universality without uniformity: A culturally inclusive approach to sensitive responsiveness in infant caregiving. *Child Development.* doi:10.1111/cdev.12795

Miner, J. L., & Clarke-Stewart, K. A. (2008). Trajectories of externalizing behavior from age 2 to age 9: Relations with gender, temperament, ethnicity, parenting, and rater. *Developmental Psychology, 44,* 771–786.

Minnis, H., Marwick, H., Arthur, J., & McLaughlin, A. (2006). Reactive attachment disorder: A theoretical model beyond attachment. *European Child & Adolescent Psychiatry, 15,* 336–342.

Minuchin, P. (1985). Families and individual development: Provocations from the field of family therapy. *Child Development, 56,* 289–302.

Moffit, T. E. (2005). The new look of behavioral genetics in developmental psychopathology: Gene-environment interplay in antisocial behaviors. *Psychological Bulletin, 131,* 533–554.

Moss, E., Dubois-Comtois, K., Cyr, C., Tarabulsy, G. M., St-Laurent, D., & Bernier, A. (2011). Efficacy of a home-visiting intervention aimed at improving maternal sensitivity, child attachment, and behavioral outcomes for maltreated children: a randomized control trial. *Developmental Psychopathology, 23,* 195–210.

Newton, E., Laible, D., Carlo, G., Steele, J., & McGinley, M. (2014). Do sensitive parents foster kind children, or vice versa? Bidirectional influences between children's prosocial behavior and parental sensitivity. *Developmental Psychology, 50,* 1808–1816.

NICHD Early Childcare Research Network (2004). Trajectories of physical aggression from toddlerhood to middle childhood. *Monographs of the Society for Research in Child Development, 69,* 1–128.

NICHD Early Child Care Research Network (2006). Infant–mother attachment classification: Risk and protection in relation to changing maternal caregiving quality. *Developmental Psychology, 42,* 38–58.

Ogilvie, C. A., Newman, E., Todd, L., & Peck, D. (2014). Attachment and violent offending: A meta-analysis. *Aggression and Violent Behavior, 19,* 322–339.

Oppenheim, D., Sagi, A., & Lamb, M. E. (1990). Infant–adult attachments on the kibbutz and their relation to socioemotional development four years later. In S. Chess & M. E. Hertzig (Eds.), *Annual progress in child psychiatry and child development* (pp. 92–106). New York, NY: Brunner/Mazel.

Pettit, G. S., & Arsiwalla, D. D. (2008). Commentary on special section on "bidirectional parent–child relationships": The continuing evolution of dynamic, transactional models of parenting and youth behavior problems. *Journal of Abnormal Child Psychology, 36,* 711–718.

Propper, C., Willoughby, M., Halpern, C., Carbone, M. E., & Cox, M. (2007). Parenting quality, DRD4, and the prediction of externalizing and internalizing behaviors in early childhood. *Developmental Psychobiology, 49,* 619–632.

Raby, K. L., Roisman, G. I., Fraley, R. C., & Simpson, J. A. (2014). The enduring predictive significance of early maternal sensitivity: Social and academic competence through age 32 years. *Child Development, 17,* 695–708.

Reiss, D., Hetherington, E. M., Plomin, R., Howe, G. W., Simmens, S. J., Henderson, S. H., . . . Law, T. (1995). Genetic questions for environmental studies. Differential parenting and psychopathology in adolescence. *Archives of General Psychiatry, 52,* 925–936.

Rothbaum, F., & Weisz, J. R. (1994). Parental caregiving and child externalizing behavior in nonclinical samples: A meta-analysis. *Psychological Bulletin, 116,* 55–74.

Sanson, A., Hemphill, S. A., & Smart, D. (2004). Connections between temperament and social development: A Review. *Social Development, 13,* 1–29.

Sanson, A., Oberklaid, F., Prior, M., Amos, D., & Smart, D. (1996, August). *Risk factors for 11–12 year olds' internalising and externalising behaviour problems.* Paper presented at the biennial meeting of the International Society for the Study of Behavioural Development, Quebec City, Quebec, Canada.

Shaw, D. S., Owens, E. B., Vondra, J. I., Keenan, K., & Winslow, E. B. (2009). Early risk factors and pathways in the development of early disruptive behavior problems. *Development and Psychopathology, 8,* 679–699.

Solomon, J., & George, C. (1999). The measurement of attachment security in infancy and childhood. In J. Cassidy & P. R. Shaver (Eds.). *Handbook of attachment: Theory, research, and clinical applications* (pp. 287–318). New York, NY: Guilford Press.

Sroufe, L. A., & Waters, E. (1977). Heart rate as a convergent measure in clinical and developmental research. *Merrill-Palmer Quarterly, 23,* 3–27.

Sroufe, L. A., Egeland, B., Carlson, E. A., & Collins, W. A. (2005). *The development of the person: The Minnesota study of risk and adaptation from birth to adulthood.* New York, NY: Guilford Press.

Sroufe, L. A., & Fleeson, J. (1986). Attachment and the construction of relationships. In W. Hartup and Z. Rubin (Eds.), *Relationship and development* (pp. 51–71). Hillsdale, NJ: Erlbaum.

Suess, G. J., Grossmann, K., & Sroufe, L. A. (1992). Effects of infant attachment to mother and father on quality of adaptation in preschool: From dyadic to individual organisation of self. *International Journal of Behavioral Development, 15,* 43–65.

Tarabulsy, G. M., Tessier, R., & Kappas, A. (1996). Contingency detection and the contingent organization of behavior in interactions: Implications for socioemotional development in infancy. *Psychological Bulletin, 120,* 25–41.

Van Berkel, S. R., Groeneveld, M. G., Mesman, J., Endendijk, J. J., Hallers-Haalboom, E. T., Van der Pol, L. D., & Bakermans-Kranenburg, M. J. (2014). Parental sensitivity towards toddlers and infant siblings predicting toddler sharing and compliance. *Journal of Child and Family Studies, 24,* 2270–2279.

Van der Voort, A., Linting, M., Juffer, F., Bakermans-Kranenburg, M. J., & Van IJzendoorn, M. H. (2013). Delinquent and aggressive behaviors in early-adopted adolescents: Longitudinal predictions from child temperament and maternal sensitivity. *Children and Youth Services Review, 35,* 439–446. doi:10.1016/j.childyouth.2012.12.008

Van IJzendoorn, M. H., & Bakermans-Kranenburg, M. J. (2003). Attachment disorders and disorganized attachment: Similar and different. *Attachment & Human Development, 5,* 313–320.

Volling, B. L., Kennedy, D. E., & Jackey, L. M. H. (2010). The development of sibling jealousy. In M. Legerstee & S. Hart (Eds.), *Handbook of jealousy. Theory, research, and multidisciplinary approaches* (pp. 387–417). New York, NY: Wiley.

Yue, Y., Zhang, G., Chen, H., Liang, Z., & Zhang, P. (2010). The relations between children's attachment and problem behaviour. *Psychological Science, 33,* 318–320.

Zwirs, B. W., Burger, H., Buitelaar, J. K., & Schulpen, T. W. J. (2006). Ethnic differences in parental detection of externalizing disorders. *European Child & Adolescent Psychiatry, 15,* 418–426.

14
Emotion Regulation
Megan K. Bookhout, Julie A. Hubbard, and Christina C. Moore

We begin this chapter reviewing literature characterizing emotion dysregulation as a core feature of children's and adolescents'[1] externalizing problems and disruptive behavior disorders,[2] emphasizing critical issues including involuntary reactivity versus voluntary control, the importance of anger, the role of effortful control, and biological correlates. Next, we consider the distinction between the reactive and proactive functions of aggression, the role and biological markers of emotion dysregulation in reactive aggression in particular, and the "unemotional" nature of proactive aggression. The third section of the chapter focuses on multiple pathways to disruptive behavior disorders and the importance of emotion dysregulation to each of these pathways. We conclude with a discussion of implications for prevention and intervention.

Defining Emotion Regulation

Emotion regulation encompasses the processes used to maintain or modify the valence or intensity of emotion (Cole, Martin, & Dennis, 2004; Eisenberg & Spinrad, 2004; Frick & Morris, 2004). The construct involves the modulation of internal experience and physiological states as well as overt expressive behaviors (Eisenberg & Spinrad, 2004). Furthermore, definitions emphasize adaptive responding, whether that response entails suppression, enhancement, or change in emotional experience and expression (Frick & Morris, 2004).

Another demarcation, based in the literature on temperament, distinguishes between involuntary reactivity, or initial autonomic responses to emotion-evoking events, and voluntary control of reactivity (Rothbart & Bates, 2006). These voluntary and involuntary components may interact, so that children who are both highly reactive and unskilled in control may struggle the most with emotion regulation (Derryberry & Rothbart, 1997; Eisenberg et al., 2000).

---

[1] Hereafter, references to "children" encompass both children and adolescents, unless a purely adolescent sample is being described.
[2] To narrow and focus the literature review, specific disruptive behavior disorders covered include Oppositional Defiant Disorder (ODD) and Conduct Disorder (CD) but exclude Attention Deficit Hyperactivity Disorder.

The Wiley Handbook of Disruptive and Impulse-Control Disorders, First Edition.
Edited by John E. Lochman and Walter Matthys.
© 2018 John Wiley & Sons Ltd. Published 2018 by John Wiley & Sons Ltd.

Emotion Regulation and Disruptive Behavior Disorders

Difficulties with emotion regulation have been identified as a core feature of most if not all forms of child psychopathology (Beauchaine, 2015; Cole, Michel, & Teti, 1994). Moreover, a vast literature characterizes emotion dysregulation as essential to both general externalizing psychopathology and specific disruptive behavior disorders such as ODD and CD. Within this literature, there is a focus on the challenges that externalizing children face when attempting to regulate anger, frustration, and hostility in particular (e.g., Casey & Schlosser, 1994; Eisenberg et al., 2005; Keltner, Moffitt, & Stouthamer-Loeber, 1995; Rothbart, Ahadi, & Hershey, 1994).

Much of this literature assesses emotion dysregulation as a unitary construct without regard to the distinctions between involuntary reactivity and voluntary control. It is easiest to make this distinction when studying infants, who do not yet self-regulate. From infancy, children display individual differences in their emotional responses to environmental stimuli (Cole et al., 2004), which may be considered a relatively pure index of trait-like reactivity at very young ages. Individual differences in this reactivity predict later externalizing problems, with young children who are susceptible to anger being more likely than other children to develop externalizing behaviors and disorders later in childhood (Arsenio, Cooperman, & Lover, 2000; Lengua & Kovacs, 2005; Rothbart et al., 1994).

Although involuntary reactivity develops early in life, voluntary control appears later (Derryberry & Rothbart, 1997). Thus, children's initial regulatory experiences are dyadic, and the quality of these experiences serves as a precursor to children's eventual regulatory skill (Feldman, Greenbaum, & Yirmiya, 1999; Field, 1994). Moreover, as children begin to self-regulate, the caregiver as a coregulator, model, and coach remains essential and predicts children's growing emotion regulation capability (Calkins & Johnson, 1998; Denham, 1993; Morris et al., 2011). When children do not receive strong regulatory assistance from caregivers in their earliest years, particularly around anger, their risk for externalizing problems increases (Cole, Teti, & Zahn-Waxler, 2003; Gilliom, Shaw, Beck, Schonberg, & Lukon, 2002).

Once children progress beyond the infancy period, however, observed expression of emotion becomes difficult to categorize as either involuntary reactivity or voluntary control (Beauchaine, 2015; Cole et al., 2004). Investigations have converged to suggest that children with externalizing problems display more negative emotion than controls in frustrating situations (Cole, Zahn-Waxler, & Smith, 1994; Gilliom et al., 2002; Rubin, Burgess, Dwyer, & Hastings, 2003). Whether these externalizing children are more emotionally reactive than their peers, less able to control their negative emotions, or a combination of the two is hard to determine.

An important advance in attempts to separate these components of children's emotion regulation can be seen in investigations of effortful control, which develops throughout maturation. Effortful control refers to a child's efficiency at modulating attention, inhibiting behavioral responses, and activating alternative behavioral responses, particularly in the context of emotion-evoking situations (Rothbart & Bates, 2006). Children's effortful control capabilities have been inversely linked to their externalizing behaviors across numerous studies (Duncombe, Havighurst, Holland, & Frankling, 2013; Eisenberg et al., 1996; Eisenberg et al., 2001; Gilliom et al., 2002; Rothbart et al., 1994; Valiente et al., 2003), including longitudinal prospective investigations (Eisenberg et al., 2000; Henry, Caspi, Moffitt, & Silva, 1996). This association may be particularly strong for children who exhibit high levels of negative emotionality or reactivity (Valiente et al., 2003). Moreover, separate components of effortful control, such as attentional control and inhibitory behavioral control, have demonstrated unique negative associations with externalizing behaviors (Eisenberg et al., 2001, 2005, 2009). Strong inhibitory control in particular may buffer children who tend to experience negative emotions from engaging in externalizing behaviors; in one study of preadolescent boys, a link from increased anger and decreased fearfulness to alcohol use initiation was found only for boys without strong inhibitory control (Pardini, Lochman, & Well, 2004). As a caveat, effortful control is merely one component of the broader construct of executive functioning, which also relates to conduct problems (e.g., Lynam, 1996; Nigg, 2000). Therefore, it is hard to know whether externalizing children's difficulties with effortful control are specific to the management of emotions or are a sign of broader executive functioning problems.

Another valuable development in the assessment and understanding of emotional control is our growing knowledge of the role of vagal tone, the fundamental element of the parasympathetic nervous system. The most common index of vagal tone, respiratory sinus arrhythmia (RSA), measures heart rate variability by assessing the ebb and flow of heart rate during respiration (Murray-Close, 2013). RSA has been proposed as a psychophysiological marker of emotion regulation (Beauchaine, 2001), an idea supported by a growing empirical foundation. On the one hand, higher resting levels of RSA and less RSA withdrawal in response to emotion-evoking events are associated with more adaptive functioning and emotional control capacity (El-Shiekh, Hinnant, & Erath, 2011; Gordis, Feres, Olezeski, Rabkin, & Trickett, 2010; Porges, Doussard-Roosevelt, Portales, & Greenspan, 1996) and, longitudinally, improvements in emotion regulation have been linked to improvements in RSA (Vasilev, Crowell, Beauchaine, Mead, & Gatzke-Kopp, 2009). On the other, both low resting RSA (Beauchaine, 2001; Beauchaine, Gatze-Kopp, & Mead, 2007; Beauchaine, 2015; de Wied, van Boxtel, Matthys, & Meeus, 2012; Hastings et al., 2008) and greater RSA withdrawal in anger-inducing situations (Gatzke-Kopp, Greenberg, & Bierman, 2015) have been linked to externalizing symptoms (See Chapter 9 of this book for a review of neurobiological factors related to disruptive behaviors).

The neural circuitry of both effortful control and RSA have been mapped to the prefrontal cortex (PFC), which has been associated with explicit emotion regulation processes (Etkin, Buchel, & Gross, 2015) such as reappraising and cognitively controlling emotions (Johnstone & Walter, 2014). Specifically, children's effortful control appears to operate through orbitofrontal and dorsolateral prefrontal inhibition of striatal activity and reactivity (Davidson, 2002; Heatherton, 2011), and positive correlations have been demonstrated between RSA and medial PFC activity in functional magnetic resonance imaging (fMRI) studies (Beauchaine & Thayer, 2015; Lane et al., 2009). Children with disruptive behavior disorders evidence less functional connectivity in striatal-anterior cingulate connections than comparison children (e.g., Shannon, Sauder, Beauchaine, & Gatzke-Kopp, 2009). More broadly, the typical reductions in PFC volume that begin in preadolescence as a result of gray matter pruning are not seen in children with conduct disorder (De Brito et al., 2009), and this maturational lag may well be implicated in the deficits that these children exhibit.

Hypothalamic-pituitary-adrenal (HPA) indices of emotion dysregulation in externalizing children have been uncovered as well. In particular, cortisol levels have been proposed to index emotion regulation, with both decreased baseline cortisol levels and increased cortisol reactivity to stress suggesting dysregulation (de Veld, Riksen-Walraven, & deWeerth, 2012; Zeman, Cassano, Perry-Parrish, & Stegall, 2006). In fact, reduced baseline cortisol levels have been linked to externalizing behavior including ODD and conduct problems (Alink et al., 2008; McBurnett, Lahey, Rathouz, & Loeber, 2000; Stoppelbein, Greening, Luebbe, Fite, & Becker, 2014). This relation may be mediated by behavioral control (Shoal, Giancola, & Kirillova, 2003) and moderated by testosterone, with more pronounced effects for adolescents with higher testosterone levels (Platje et al., 2015; Popma et al., 2007). Furthermore, elevated cortisol response has also been associated with externalizing behavior (McBurnett et al., 2005), and this response is moderated by emotional control (Poon, Turpyn, Hansen,

Jacangelo, & Chaplin, 2016), with stronger relations emerging for children who struggle with emotional control.

This discussion of biological markers does not imply, however, that the struggles children with disruptive behavior problems face with emotional control are trait-like or present from birth. Rather, theory suggests that, although individual differences in reactivity to emotion-eliciting stimuli may be present from infancy (Arsenio et al., 2000; Lengua & Kovacs, 2005; Rothbart et al., 1994), voluntary control of that reactivity develops later and is less heritable and largely socialized (Beauchaine, 2015). In fact, parental emotion coaching shows positive effects on youth anger regulation and externalizing problems well into adolescence (Shortt, Stoolmiller, Smith-Shine, Mark Eddy, & Sheeber, 2010). Moreover, Beauchaine argues that temperamental traits such as emotional reactivity are not sufficient to lead to disruptive behaviors disorders. Instead, he emphasizes that externalizing disorders result from the coupling of these temperamental qualities with emotional control deficits conferred through socialization processes including poor parenting and early life stressors such as poverty (Hanson, Hair, et al., 2013) and neglect (Hanson, Adluru, et al., 2013). In particular, Beauchaine (2015) argues that emotion dysregulation is learned through repetitive cycles in which aggressive children escape from negative affective exchanges with family members and peers by escalating anger and hostility until the interactions terminate, resulting in negative reinforcement of the escalating behavior (Patterson, DeBaryshe, & Ramsey, 1989; Snyder, Edwards, McGraw, Kilgore, & Holton, 1994; Snyder & Patterson, 1995; Snyder, Schrepferman, & St. Peters, 1997). Moreover, recent work suggests that externalizing children are reinforced not only by escape from others' negative emotions and behaviors, but also by escape from their own aversive physiological state (Beauchaine & Zalewski, 2016; Skowron et al., 2011).

Emotion Regulation and Reactive versus Proactive Aggression

The literature reviewed above paints a clear picture of emotion dysregulation as a core feature of externalizing problems in general and disorders such as ODD and CD in particular. However, externalizing psychopathology is comprised of a wide variety of behaviors, only some of which emerge from dysregulated emotion. As a key example, we turn now to the distinction between reactive and proactive aggression. Reactive aggression is defensive, retaliatory, and in response to real or perceived provocation. In contrast, proactive aggression is initiated to reach a goal, whether that goal involves material or territorial gain or social dominance (Hubbard, McAuliffe, Morrow, & Romano, 2010). Based on these theoretical definitions, emotion dysregulation may be an important mechanism driving the reactive aggression of externalizing children, whereas it may play little role in their proactive aggression.

Reactive Aggression In fact, a growing body of literature supports the contention that emotion dysregulation is central to children's displays of reactive aggression but unrelated to their displays of proactive aggression. Several studies have related negative emotionality and expression to reactive aggression specifically, both concurrently and prospectively (Evans et al., 2016; Shields & Cicchetti, 1998; Vitaro, Barker, Boivin, Brendgen, & Tremblay, 2006). In particular, children's reactive aggression has been linked to their experience and expression of anger (Dane & Marini, 2014; Hubbard et al., 2002; Marsee & Frick, 2007; Orobio de Castro, Merk, Koops, Veerman, & Bosch, 2005). Moreover, the link between children's anger and reactive aggression has been supported both longitudinally (Calvete & Orue, 2012) and cross-culturally (e.g., in China; Fung, Gerstein, Chan, & Engebretson, 2015).

Beyond negative emotional experience and expression, voluntary emotion regulation has been consistently linked to reactive aggression more strongly than proactive aggression, a finding supported in a meta-analysis of 11 studies (Card & Little, 2006), which further demonstrated that this relation increased with age. Some studies suggest that emotion dysregulation is related only to reactive but not proactive aggression (Nas, Orobio de Castro, & Koops, 2005; Xu & Zhang, 2008), while other studies indicate a stronger link for reactive than proactive aggression, although relations between emotion dysregulation and both subtypes of aggression are found (Fite et al., 2016; Marsee & Frick, 2007). In one important study, the relation over time between children's anger and reactive aggression was moderated by their ability to regulate emotion, such that the longitudinal association was weaker for children with stronger emotion regulation skills (Calvete & Orue, 2012). Studies examining effortful control specifically as an index of emotion regulation have also revealed unique links to reactive but not to proactive aggression in middle childhood(Rathert, Fite, Gaertner, & Vitulano, 2011) and adolescence (Dane & Marini, 2014), with the latter study suggesting that the association is specific to the overt, but not the relational, form of aggression. In addition, effortful control has been shown to moderate the relation between anger and reactive aggression (Xu, Farver, & Zhang, 2009), such that the relation is significant at low and moderate but not at high levels of effortful control.

The connection between emotion dysregulation and reactive aggression has also been evidenced in work on psychophysiology, the HPA axis, and neural circuitry. In the first study to investigate the psychophysiological correlates of reactive and proactive aggression, children's sympathetic nervous system (SNS) reactivity in response to a laboratory-based peer provocation predicted teacher-rated reactive but not proactive aggression (Hubbard et al., 2002). More recent work suggests that children with low resting heart rate variability or vagal tone are more likely to engage in reactive aggression in particular (Scarpa, Haden, & Tanaka, 2010; Xu, Raine, Yu, & Krieg, 2014), a finding implicating RSA in the regulatory deficits of this subtype of aggression. The most current work on the psychophysiology of reactive aggression examined the interaction of children's sympathetic reactivity and parasympathetic RSA in-the-moment as they were given the opportunity to engage in reactive aggression against a provocative virtual peer; RSA moderated the in-the-moment relation between SNS reactivity and reactive aggression, with children displaying both elevated SNS reactivity and blunted RSA being particularly likely to respond with reactive aggression when provoked (Moore et al., 2016).

Turning to HPA correlates, a study by Lopez-Duran, Olson, Hajal, Felt, and Vazquez (2009) suggests that a heightened cortisol response to stress is linked to reactive aggression in particular. Consistent with this finding, van Goozen, Matthys, Cohen-Kettenis, Gispen-de Wied, Wiegant, and van Engeland (1998) found that children high on both externalizing and anxious symptoms displayed an elevated cortisol response to stress, whereas children high on externalizing but low on anxious symptoms displayed a blunted response; anxiety and depression have both been linked to reactive but not proactive aggression (Dodge, Lochman, Harnish, Bates, & Pettit,1997; McAuliffe, Hubbard, Rubin, Morrow, & Dearing, 2007; Morrow, Hubbard, McAuliffe, Rubin, & Dearing, 2006; Raine et al., 2006; Vitaro et al., 2002). Thus, the link between elevated HPA axis responding may be implicated when children aggress in response to provocation but not when they aggress for instrumental or social gain.

In terms of neural circuitry, the amygdala, which may be involved in eliciting, monitoring, and stopping emotional arousal, serves both as a target of emotion regulation and as a regulatory influence (Thompson, Lewis, & Calkins, 2008; Zeman et al., 2006). The amygdala is thought to be associated with reactive aggression in particular through elevated threat responding (Crowe & Blair, 2008). In fact, Herpertz et al. (2005) demonstrated that boys with both CD and comorbid internalizing problems were most likely to display enhanced amygdala activity in response to emotional images, and this symptom pattern is most closely linked to the reactive subtype of aggression.

Before proceeding, a brief comment on hostile attributional bias seems warranted. As reviewed by Orobio de Castro and van Dijk in this volume (see Chapter 15), reactive but not proactive aggression is linked to children's tendency to attribute hostile intent to others when ambiguously provoked. While this social cognitive process can be theoretically separated from emotional reactivity, hostile attributional biases undoubtedly play an essential role in triggering reactive aggression in children by leading them to perceive situations as anger-inducing more often than their peers.

Proactive Aggression While emotion dysregulation may be an important mechanism underlying reactive aggression, the display of proactive aggression appears considerably more unemotional. In fact, proactive aggression is closely linked to the construct of callous-unemotional (CU) traits reviewed by Frick and Wall in Chapter 3 of this volume (and see also Marsee & Frick, 2007; Thornton, Frick, Crapanzano, & Terranova, 2013).

The theory that proactive aggression is unemotional in nature is borne out by psychophysiological work. The low resting heart rate that characterizes aggressive children has been linked to proactive aggression in particular (Raine, Fung, Portnoy, Choy, & Spring, 2014). Furthermore, in the first study to assess the SNS reactivity of children as they were given the opportunity to engage in unprovoked aggression for instrumental gain, Moore et al. (2016) found that children's in-the-moment skin conductance was inversely related to the level of proactive aggression they displayed toward a virtual peer. Theorists suggest that this blunted physiology may be a marker of temperamental fearlessness (Pardini, 2006) or the tendency to sensation-seek to increase arousal to normal thresholds (Beauchaine et al., 2007). Relatedly, children high in proactive aggression have been found to display elevated resting RSA, suggesting a strong capacity to regulate arousal (Scarpa et al., 2010).

In fact, in a 2006 meta-analysis, although a small positive zero-order correlation emerged between emotion dysregulation and proactive aggression, this association disappeared when reactive aggression was taken into account (Card & Little, 2006). More recent individual studies are equivocal on the relation between emotion regulation and proactive aggression taking reactive aggression into account. Two studies suggest a positive relation (Ostrov, Murray-Close, Godleski, & Hart, 2013; Rathert et al., 2011). These authors theorized that children skillful in regulating emotion may be more adept at carrying out the purposeful, goal-oriented behaviors that characterize proactive aggression. In contrast, another study revealed a modest negative relation (Calvete & Orue, 2012). However, this study differed from the majority of those reported above in that the sample was adolescent, emotion regulation was assessed via self-report responses to hypothetical vignettes, and proactive aggression was measured with a combination of self and peer report.

Of note, children who display proactive aggression or CU traits tend to be unable to identify others' sad or fearful facial expressions accurately (Blair, Colledge, Murray, & Mitchell, 2001; Blair & Coles, 2000; Dadds et al., 2006; Marsh & Blair, 2008) and to be less responsive to negative emotional images (Herpertz et al., 2005). This deficit may be critical to the characterization of proactive aggression as unemotional; it may be easier for children to remain emotionally unaroused and aggress for instrumental or social gain if they are not aware of the negative emotional reactions of their victims. In fact, when viewing videos of others being harmed, children's level of CU traits is inversely related to activity in the posterior insula, a region that plays a key role in empathy (Michalska, Zeffiro, & Decety, 2016). Furthermore, children with CD display hyporesponsiveness in the amygdala when processing fearful facial expressions (Stadler, Poustka, & Sterzer, 2010), and these authors speculate that this deficit may be linked to displays of "unemotional aggression" in particular. In support of this idea, this reduced amygdala response has been shown to be specific to externalizing children with CU traits (Hwang et al., 2016) and to mediate the relation between CU traits and proactive aggression (Lozier, Cardinale, Van Meter, & Marsh, 2014). More generally, theorists have speculated that the enhanced amygdala response associated with reactive aggression and the diminished amygdala response linked to proactive aggression may indicate differential pathways to externalizing disorders (Crowe & Blair, 2008; Frick & White, 2008).

Emotion Regulation and Pathways to Disruptive Behavior Disorders

The literature reviewed above may lead readers to conclude that two distinct groups of aggressive children exist, with one engaging in primarily reactive aggression and the other engaging in predominantly proactive aggression. In fact, researchers originally hypothesized that such well-defined groups would emerge (Dodge, 1991). However, the correlation between reactive and proactive aggression is consistently high across studies (Card & Little, 2006; Polman, Orobio de Castro, Koops, van Boxtel, & Merk, 2007), suggesting that many aggressive children engage in both subtypes of aggressive behavior. To some degree, then, the subtypes of aggression may be more accurately conceptualized as continuous measures of the extent to which children display each subtype, rather than as categories into which children are placed.

In fact, when the SNS arousal of children diagnosed with disruptive behavior disorders was assessed in both a baseline condition and a peer provocation, findings suggested that externalizing children demonstrated both lower baseline arousal and greater reactivity to the peer provocation than controls (van Goozen, Matthys, Cohen-Kettenis, Buitelaar, & van Engeland, 2000). Although these authors did not assess the reactive and proactive functions of aggression, their results suggest that aggressive children's blunted baseline SNS arousal may put them at risk of displaying proactive aggression when faced with the opportunity to aggress for instrumental gain, but that their sympathetic arousal in response to peer provocation may also increase the chance that they will display reactive aggression. In fact, if aggressive children's SNS profiles are characterized by both of these patterns, then it follows that many aggressive children may aggress for both reactive and proactive reasons, albeit in different contexts, as the consistently high correlation between the subtypes of aggression across studies suggests.

However, two recent rigorous investigations suggest that some aggressive children may display reactive aggression only, while others display both reactive and proactive aggression. In a study by Smeets et al. (2017), self-report data on reactive and proactive aggression from a large sample of adolescents were analyzed using latent class analysis; two latent classes of aggressive adolescents emerged, one that engaged primarily in reactive aggression and a second that displayed both reactive and proactive aggression. Similarly, in a recent study of adolescents in community, at-risk residential, and detained samples, cluster analyses of reactive and proactive aggression revealed three groups, with the first low on aggression overall, the second elevated on reactive aggression only, and the third elevated on both reactive and proactive aggression. With a few exceptions, these findings were replicated across the three samples, across boys and girls, and across physical and relational aggression (Marsee et al., 2014). Further analyses suggested that these three groups differed in severity, with the combined group displaying higher levels of emotion dysregulation, CU traits, and delinquency than the reactive-only group, which, in turn, exhibited higher levels of these constructs than the low-aggression group (Marsee et al., 2014). Both studies converged to suggest that few if any children display proactive aggression only.

These findings may have important implications for our understanding of multiple pathways to disruptive behavior disorders such as CD. This work suggests a first and less severe pathway characterized primarily by reactive aggression and a second and more severe one marked by both reactive and proactive aggression. It may well be that some externalizing children aggress predominantly when provoked while other disruptive children aggress both when provoked and to achieve instrumental or social gain. Importantly, both of these pathways toward disruptive behavior disorders are typified by emotion dysregulation.

Of note, a recent fMRI study supports the notion that children with and without CU traits evidence emotion dysregulation when provoked. Compared to a control sample, all adolescents with disruptive behavior disorders displayed reduced amygdala–ventromedial PFC connectivity when provoked, regardless of whether they had CU traits, and this reduction predicted both their tendency to retaliate during a laboratory task and parent ratings of reactive aggression. These results suggest that all youth with disruptive behavior disorders may be at risk for reactive aggression and propose one neural mechanism behind this risk (White et al., 2016).

This theory parallels in many ways Frick's hypothesis of two pathways toward CD, with one marked by anger dysregulation and the other by CU traits (see Frick, 2012; Frick & Morris, 2004; Frick & White, 2008; Pardini & Frick, 2013; and Chapter 3 of this volume for elegant reviews of this theory and empirical work supporting it). Notably, both of these models are supported by literature suggesting that the divergent pathways are denoted by differential familial precursors, cognitive mechanisms, and outcomes, although a review of these findings is beyond the scope of the current chapter (see Hubbard et al., 2010; Frick & White, 2008 for reviews).

However, the models diverge in that we emphasize that aggressive children with CU traits also struggle with emotion regulation, perhaps particularly when provoked, and in fact, that their regulatory deficits may be more serious than those of children who do not evidence CU traits or proactive aggression. Thus, we deviate from Frick's thinking by emphasizing that both pathways toward disruptive behavior disorders are characterized by emotion dysregulation, making this construct particularly critical to our understanding of the full continuum of externalizing problems.

Clearly, careful longitudinal work utilizing rigorous measurement approaches is needed to determine the extent to which the constructs of reactive-versus-proactive aggression and CU-traits-versus-anger dysregulation overlap, as well as the distinctness of the pathways characterized by one or more of these constructs. In our view, this effort represents a critically important direction for future research on emotion regulation and externalizing behaviors.

Implications for Prevention and Intervention

Because of the important role that emotion dysregulation plays in the development of children's disruptive behavior disorders, it is critical to target emotion regulation skills in prevention and intervention programs for externalizing disorders. Current best practice recommendations suggest that interventions for disruptive behavior are more effective when they occur earlier in childhood (Eyberg, Nelson, & Boggs, 2008). For this reason, one possible and infrequently considered target may be the quality of the parent–child relationship. In fact, an intervention program termed Attachment and Biobehavioral Catch-Up which aims to improve attachment quality has shown effects on toddlers' negative affect (Lind, Bernard, Ross, & Dozier, 2014) and cortisol regulation (Bernard, Dozier, Bick, & Gordon, 2015), although it is too soon to know whether these effects will translate into lower levels of disruptive behavior disorders. More generally, intervention programs directed at improving general parenting skills have shown effects on children's emotion dysregulation and reactive aggression (e.g., Barker et al., 2010; Scott & O'Connor, 2012). However, as emotion regulation is thought to be highly socialized (Beauchaine, 2015), it may be wise to target parental coaching of emotion regulation more directly (Gottman, Katz, & Hooven, 1996). Of note, one series of studies has demonstrated the effectiveness of the "Tuning In" program, with increases in parental emotion coaching predicting reductions in externalizing behaviors for toddlers (Lauw, Havighurst, Wilson, Harley, & Northam, 2014), children (Havighurst, Wilson, Harley, & Prior, 2009), and adolescents (Havighurst, Kehoe, & Harley, 2015). However, these studies did not directly assess emotion regulation, leaving open the question of whether emotion coaching lowered externalizing behaviors through the mechanism of increased emotion regulation.

Of course, efforts to increase children's emotion regulation skills and decrease their aggressive behaviors should also target the children themselves. In fact, when a child component was added to the Tuning In program targeting the identification and regulation of emotions, similar reductions in behavior problems resulted (Havighurst, Duncombe, et al., 2015). Interestingly, Lewis et al. (2008) combined parent management training with child cognitive-behavior therapy to reduce children's behavior problems. Their results revealed that those children who benefitted from the intervention displayed ventral prefrontal activation reduction at the peak of the N2 (an event-related potential marker of inhibitory control) that was similar to comparison children, while children whose behavior problems were not changed did not show similar reductions. These findings suggest that programs do not have to directly target emotion regulation skills to produce measurable effects on biological markers of emotion regulation. Finally, no discussion of programs aimed at teaching children emotion regulation skills in the service of decreasing externalizing behaviors would be complete without mention of the Coping Power program, reviewed thoroughly in Chapter 27 of this volume by Boxmeyer and colleagues. This program targets the emotion regulation deficits of aggressive children, along with cognitive and social-problem-solving skills, to produce reductions in externalizing behaviors at postintervention (Lochman et al., 2009), one-year follow-up (Lochman & Wells, 2003), and three-year follow-up (Lochman, Wells, Qu, & Chen, 2013).

In addition, the body of work on reactive and proactive aggression reviewed above suggests that it may be fruitful to target children's reactive and proactive aggression separately in intervention efforts. Treatment for reactive aggression could focus on anger dysregulation and hostile attributional biases, while efforts to reduce proactive aggression could emphasize reading others' distress cues, empathy-building, and balancing instrumental and social goals. Although numerous calls for separate treatment packages have been made (Dodge, 1991; Phillips & Lochman, 2003; Vitaro & Brendgen, 2005), little progress has followed, perhaps owing to concern that many children need treatment for both subtypes of aggression, given their high correlation, as well as findings suggesting that these children may display the most severe symptoms. However, research is needed to determine whether these treatments could be delivered more effectively in separate modules.

Conclusions

As we conclude, it seems appropriate to note the remarkable progress made over the past decades in our understanding of the role of emotion dysregulation in children's disruptive behavior disorders, and celebrate those researchers who have advanced our field to this point. Twenty years ago, it would have been impossible to imagine that we could know all that we do now about the nature of emotion regulation, its biological markers, and links to children's externalizing behavior in general and reactive versus proactive aggression in particular. Much work remains as we continue to move forward in our understanding of the multiple pathways toward disruptive behavior disorders and complementary treatment approaches for different subtypes of aggressive behavior. We feel certain that our field is up to the task and look forward to the exciting advances that are sure to come in the years ahead.

References

Alink, L. R. A., van Ijzendoorn, M. H., Bakermans-Kranenburg, M., Mesman, J., Juffer, F., & Koot, H. M. (2008). Cortisol and externalizing behavior in children and adolescents: Mixed meta-analytic evidence for the inverse relation of basal cortisol and cortisol reactivity with externalizing behavior. *Developmental Psychobiology, 50,* 427–450.

Arsenio, W. F., Cooperman, S., & Lover, A. (2000). Affective predictors of preschoolers' aggression and peer acceptance: Direct and indirect effects. *Developmental Psychology, 36,* 438–448.

Barker, E. D., Vitaro, F., Lacourse, E., Fontaine, N. M. G., Carbonneau, R., & Tremblay, R. E. (2010). Testing the developmental distinctiveness of male proactive and reactive aggression with a nested longitudinal experimental intervention. *Aggressive Behavior, 36,* 127–140.

Beauchaine, T. P. (2001). Vagal tone, development, and Gray's motivational theory: Toward an integrated model of autonomic nervous system functioning in psychopathology. *Development and Psychopathology, 13,* 183–214.

Beauchaine, T. P. (2015). Future directions in emotion dysregulation and youth psychopathology. *Journal of Clinical Child and Adolescent Psychology, 44,* 875–896.

Beauchaine, T. P., Gatzke-Kopp, L., & Mead, H. K. (2007). Polyvagal theory and developmental psychopathology: Emotion dysregulation and conduct problems from preschool to adolescence. *Biological Psychology, 74,* 174–184.

Beauchaine, T. P., & Thayer, J. F. (2015). Heart rate variability as a transdiagnostic biomarker of psychopathology. *International Journal of Psychophysiology, 98,* 338–350.

Beauchaine, T. P., & Zalewski, M. (2016). Physiological and developmental mechanisms of emotional lability in coercive relationships. In T. J. Dishion & J. J. Snyder (Eds.), *Oxford handbook of coercive relationship dynamics.* New York, NY: Oxford University Press.

Bernard, K., Dozier, M., Bick, J., & Gordon, M. K. (2015). Intervening to enhance cortisol regulation among children at risk for neglect: Results of a randomized clinical trial. *Development and Psychopathology, 27,* 829–841.

Blair, R. J. R., & Coles, M. (2000). Expression recognition and behavioural problems in early adolescence. *Cognitive Development, 15,* 421–434.

Blair, R. J. R., Colledge, E., Murray, L., & Mitchell, D. G. V. (2001). A selective impairment in the processing of sad and fearful expressions in children with psychopathic tendencies. *Journal of Abnormal Child Psychology, 29,* 491–498.

Calkins, S. D., & Johnson, M. C. (1998). Toddler regulation of distress to frustrating events: Temperamental and maternal correlates. *Infant Behavior & Development, 21,* 379–395.

Calvete, E., & Orue, I. (2012). The role of emotion regulation in the predictive association between social information processing and aggressive behavior in adolescents. *International Journal of Behavioral Development, 36,* 338–347.

Card, N. A., & Little, T. D. (2006). Proactive and reactive aggression in childhood and adolescence: A meta-analysis of differential relations with psychosocial adjustment. *International Journal of Behavioral Development, 30,* 466–480.

Casey, R. J., & Schlosser, S. (1994). Emotional responses to peer praise in children with and without a diagnosed externalizing disorder. *Merrill-Palmer Quarterly, 40,* 60–81.

Cole, P. M., Martin, S. E., & Dennis, T. A. (2004). Emotion regulation as a scientific construct: Methodological challenges and directions for child development research. *Child Development, 75,* 317–333.

Cole, P. M., Michel, M. K., & Teti, L. O. (1994). The development of emotion regulation and dysregulation: A clinical perspective. *Monographs of the Society for Research in Child Development, 59*(2/3), 73–100.

Cole, P. M., Teti, L. O., & Zahn-Waxler, C. (2003). Mutual emotion regulation and the stability of conduct problems between preschool and early school age. *Development and Psychopathology, 15,* 1–18.

Cole, P. M., Zahn-Waxler, C., & Smith, K. D. (1994). Expressive control during a disappointment: Variations related to preschoolers' behavior problems. *Developmental Psychology, 30,* 835–846.

Crowe, S. L., & Blair, R. J. R. (2008). The development of antisocial behavior: What can we learn from functional neuroimaging studies? *Development and Psychopathology, 20,* 1145–1159.

Dadds, M. R., Perry, Y., Hawes, D. J., Merz, S., Riddell, A. C., Haines, D. J., . . . Abeygunawardane, A. I. (2006). Attention to the eyes and fear-recognition deficits in child psychopathy. *The British Journal of Psychiatry: The Journal of Mental Science, 189*(3), 280–281.

Dane, A. V., & Marini, Z. A. (2014). Overt and relational forms of reactive aggression in adolescents: Relations with temperamental reactivity and self-regulation. *Personality and Individual Differences, 60,* 60–66.

Davidson, R. J. (2002). Anxiety and affective style: Role of prefrontal cortex and amygdala. *Biological Psychiatry, 51,* 68–80.

De Brito, S. A., Mechelli, A., Wilke, M., Laurens, K. R., Jones, A. P., Barker, G. J., . . . Viding, E. (2009). Size matters: Increased grey matter in boys with conduct problems and callous-unemotional traits. *Brain, 132,* 843–852.

Denham, S. A. (1993). Maternal emotional responsiveness and toddlers' social-emotional competence. *Child Psychology & Psychiatry & Allied Disciplines, 34,* 715–728.

Derryberry, D., & Rothbart, M. K. (1997). Reactive and effortful processes in the organization of temperament. *Development and Psychopathology, 9,* 633–652.

de Veld, D .J. M., Riksen-Walraven, J. M., & de Weerth, C. (2012). The relation between emotion regulation strategies and physiological stress responses in early childhood. *Psychoneuroendocrinology, 37,* 1309–1319.

de Wied, M., van Boxtel, A., Matthys, W., & Meeus, W. (2012). Verbal, facial and autonomic responses to empathy-eliciting film clips by disruptive male adolescents with high versus low callous-unemotional traits. *Journal of Abnormal Child Psychology, 40,* 211–223.

Dodge, K. A. (1991). The structure and function of reactive and proactive aggression. In D. J. Pepler & K. H. Rubin (Eds.), *Earlscourt symposium on childhood aggression* (pp. 201–218). Hillsdale, NJ: Lawrence Erlbaum Associates, Inc.

Dodge, K. A., Lochman, J. E., Harnish, J. D., Bates, J. E., & Pettit, G. S. (1997). Reactive and proactive aggression in school children and psychiatrically impaired chronically assaultive youth. *Journal of Abnormal Psychology, 106,* 37–51.

Duncombe, M., Havighurst, S. S., Holland, K. A., & Frankling, E. J. (2013). Relations of emotional competence and effortful control to child disruptive behavior problems. *Early Education and Development, 24,* 599–615.

Eisenberg, N., Cumberland, A., Spinrad, T. L., Fabes, R. A., Shepard, S. A., Reiser, M., . . . Guthrie, I. K. (2001). The relations of regulation and emotionality to children's externalizing and internalizing problem behavior. *Child Development, 72,* 1112–1134.

Eisenberg, N., Fabes, R. A., Guthrie, I. K., Murphy, B. C., Maszk, P., Holmgren, R., & Suh, K. (1996). The relations of regulation and emotionality to problem behavior in elementary school children. *Development and Psychopathology, 8,* 141–162.

Eisenberg, N., Guthrie, I. K., Fabes, R. A., Shepard, S., Losoya, S., Murphy, B. C., . . . Reiser, M. (2000). Prediction of elementary school children's externalizing problem behaviors from attention and behavioral regulation and negative emotionality. *Child Development, 71,* 1367–1382.

Eisenberg, N., Sadovsky, A., Spinrad, T. L., Fabes, R. A., Losoya, S. H., Valiente, C., . . . Shepard, S. A. (2005). The relations of problem behavior status to children's negative emotionality, effortful control, and impulsivity: Concurrent relations and prediction of change. *Developmental Psychology, 41,* 193–211.

Eisenberg, N., & Spinrad, T. L. (2004). Emotion-related regulation: Sharpening the definition. *Child Development, 75,* 334–339.

Eisenberg, N., Valiente, C., Spinrad, T. L., Cumberland, A., Liew, J., Reiser, M., . . . Losoya, S. H. (2009). Longitudinal relations of children's effortful control, impulsivity, and negative emotionality to their externalizing, internalizing, and co-occurring behavior problems. *Developmental Psychology, 45,* 988–1008.

El-Sheikh, M., Hinnant, J. B., & Erath, S. (2011). Developmental trajectories of delinquency symptoms in childhood: The role of marital conflict and autonomic nervous system activity. *Journal of Abnormal Psychology, 120,* 16–32.

Etkin, A., Büchel, C., & Gross, J. J. (2015). The neural bases of emotion regulation. *Nature Reviews Neuroscience, 16,* 693–700.

Evans, S. C., Blossom, J. B., Canter, K. S., Poppert-Cordts, K., Kanine, R., Garcia, A., & Roberts, M. C. (2016). Self-reported emotion reactivity among early-adolescent girls: Evidence for convergent and discriminant validity in an urban community sample. *Behavior Therapy, 47*, 299–311.

Eyberg, S. M., Nelson, M. M., & Boggs, S. R. (2008). Evidence-based psychosocial treatments for children and adolescents with disruptive behavior. *Journal of Clinical Child and Adolescent Psychology, 37*, 215–237.

Feldman, R., Greenbaum, C. W., & Yirmiya, N. (1999). Mother–infant affect synchrony as an antecedent of the emergence of self-control. *Developmental Psychology, 35*, 223–231.

Field, T. (1994). The effects of mother's physical and emotional unavailability on emotion regulation. *Monographs of the Society for Research in Child Development, 59*, 208–227, 250–283.

Fite, P. J., Poquiz, J., Cooley, J. L., Stoppelbein, L., Becker, S. P., Luebbe, A. M., & Greening, L. (2016). Risk factors associated with proactive and reactive aggression in a child psychiatric inpatient sample. *Journal of Psychopathology and Behavioral Assessment, 38*, 56–65.

Frick, P. J. (2012). Developmental pathways to conduct disorder: Implications for future directions in research, assessment, and treatment. *Journal of Clinical Child & Adolescent Psychology, 41*, 378–389.

Frick, P. J., & Morris, A. S. (2004). Temperament and developmental pathways to conduct problems. *Journal of Clinical Child and Adolescent Psychology, 33*, 54–68.

Frick, P. J., & White, S. F. (2008). Research review: The importance of callous-unemotional traits for developmental models of aggressive and antisocial behavior. *Journal of Child Psychology and Psychiatry, 49*, 359–375.

Fung, A. L. C., Gerstein, L. H., Chan, Y., & Engebretson, J. (2015). Relationship of aggression to anxiety, depression, anger, and empathy in Hong Kong. *Journal of Child and Family Studies, 24*, 821–831.

Gatzke-Kopp, L., Greenberg, M., & Bierman, K. (2015). Children's parasympathetic reactivity to specific emotions moderates response to intervention for early-onset aggression. *Journal of Clinical Child and Adolescent Psychology, 44*, 291–304.

Gilliom, M., Shaw, D. S., Beck, J. E., Schonberg, M. A., & Lukon, J. L. (2002). Anger regulation in disadvantaged preschool boys: Strategies, antecedents, and the development of self-control. *Developmental Psychology, 38*, 222–235.

Gordis, E. B., Feres, N., Olezeski, C. L., Rabkin, A. N., & Trickett, P. K. (2010). Skin conductance reactivity and respiratory sinus arrhythmia among maltreated and comparison youth: Relations with aggressive behavior. *Journal of Pediatric Psychology, 35*, 547–558.

Gottman, J. M., Katz, L. F., & Hooven, C. (1996). Parental meta-emotion philosophy and the emotional life of families: Theoretical models and preliminary data. *Journal of Family Psychology, 10*, 243–268.

Hanson, J. L., Adluru, N., Chung, M. K., Alexander, A. L., Davidson, R. J., & Pollak, S. D. (2013). Early neglect is associated with alterations in white matter integrity and cognitive functioning. *Child Development, 84*, 1566–1578.

Hanson, J. L., Hair, N., Shen, D. G., Shi, F., Gilmore, J. H., Wolfe, B. L., & Pollak, S. D. (2013). Family poverty affects the rate of human infant brain growth. *PLoS ONE, 8*, e80954. doi: 10.1371/journal.pone.0080954

Hastings, P. D., Nuselovici, J. N., Utendale, W. T., Coutya, J., McShane, K. E., & Sullivan, C. (2008). Applying the polyvagal theory to children's emotion regulation: Social context, socialization, and adjustment. *Biological Psychology, 79*, 299–306.

Havighurst, S. S., Duncombe, M., Frankling, E., Holland, K., Kehoe, C., & Stargatt, R. (2015). An emotion-focused early intervention for children with emerging conduct problems. *Journal of Abnormal Child Psychology, 43*, 749–760.

Havighurst, S. S., Kehoe, C. E., & Harley, A. E. (2015). Tuning in to teens: Improving parental responses to anger and reducing youth externalizing behavior problems. *Journal of Adolescence, 42*, 148–158.

Havighurst, S. S., Wilson, K. R., Harley, A. E., & Prior, M. R. (2009). Tuning in to kids: An emotion-focused parenting program—Initial findings from a community trial. *Journal of Community Psychology, 37*, 1008–1023.

Heatherton, T. F. (2011). Neuroscience of self and self-regulation. *Annual Review of Psychology, 62,* 363–390.

Henry, B., Caspi, A., Moffitt, T. E., & Silva, P. A. (1996). Temperamental and familial predictors of violent and non-violent criminal convictions: From age 3 to age 18. *Developmental Psychology, 32,* 614–623.

Herpertz, S .C, Mueller, B., Qunaibi, M., Lichterfeld, C, Konrad, K., & Herpertz-Dahlman, B. (2005). Response to emotional stimuli in boys with conduct disorder. *American Journal of Psychiatry, 162,* 1100–1107.

Hubbard, J. A., McAuliffe, M. D., Morrow, M. T., & Romano, L. J. (2010). Reactive and proactive aggression in childhood and adolescence: Precursors, outcomes, processes, experiences, and measurement. *Journal of Personality, 78,* 95–118.

Hubbard, J. A., Smithmyer, C. M., Ramsden, S. R., Parker, E. H., Flanagan, K. D., Dearing, K. F., . . . Simons, R. F. (2002). Observational, physiological, and self-report measures of children's anger: Relations to reactive versus proactive aggression. *Child Development, 73,* 1101–1118.

Hwang, S., Nolan, Z. T., White, S. F., Williams, W. C., Sinclair, S., & Blair, R. J. R. (2016). Dual neurocircuitry dysfunctions in disruptive behavior disorders: Emotional responding and response inhibition. *Psychological Medicine, 46,* 1485–1496.

Johnstone, T., & Walter, H. (2014). The neural basis of emotion dysregulation. In J. J. Gross (Ed.), *Handbook of emotion regulation* (pp. 58–71). New York, NY: Guilford Press.

Keltner, D., Moffitt, T. E., & Stouthamer-Loeber, M. (1995). Facial expressions of emotion and psychopathology in adolescent boys. *Journal of Abnormal Psychology, 104,* 644–652.

Lane, R., McRae, K., Reiman, E., Chen, K., Ahern, G., & Thayer, J. (2009). Neural correlates of heart rate variability during emotion. *Neuroimage, 44,* 213–222.

Lauw, M. S. M., Havighurst, S. S., Wilson, K. R., Harley, A. E., & Northam, E. A. (2014). Improving parenting of toddlers' emotions using an emotion coaching parenting program: A pilot study of tuning in to toddlers. *Journal of Community Psychology, 42,* 169–175.

Lengua, L. J., & Kovacs, E. A. (2005). Bidirectional associations between temperament and parenting and the prediction of adjustment problems in middle childhood. *Journal of Applied Developmental Psychology, 26,* 21–38.

Lewis, M. D., Granic, I., Lamm, C., Zelazo, P. D., Stieben, J., Todd, R. M., . . . Pepler, D. (2008). Changes in the neural bases of emotion regulation associated with clinical improvement in children with behavior problems. *Development and Psychopathology, 20,* 913–939.

Lind, T., Bernard, K., Ross, E., & Dozier, M. (2014). Intervention effects on negative affect of CPS-referred children: Results of a randomized clinical trial. *Child Abuse and Neglect, 38,* 1459–1467.

Lochman, J. E., Boxmeyer, C., Powell, N., Qu, L., Wells, K., & Windle, M. (2009). Dissemination of the Coping Power program: Importance of intensity of counselor training. *Journal of Consulting and Clinical Psychology, 77,* 397–409.

Lochman, J. E., & Wells, K. C. (2003). Effectiveness study of Coping Power and classroom intervention with aggressive children: Outcomes at a one-year follow-up. *Behavior Therapy, 34,* 493–515.

Lochman, J. E., Wells, K. C., Qu, L., & Chen, L. (2013). Three-year follow-up of Coping Power intervention effects: Evidence of neighborhood moderation? *Prevention Science, 14,* 364–376.

Lopez-Duran, N., Olson, S. L., Hajal, N. J., Felt, B. T., & Vazquez, D. M. (2009). Hypothalamic pituitary adrenal axis functioning in reactive and proactive aggression in children. *Journal of Abnormal Child Psychology, 37,* 169–182.

Lozier, L. M., Cardinale, E. M., Van Meter, J. W., & Marsh, A. A. (2014). Mediation of the relationship between callous-unemotional traits and proactive aggression by amygdala response to fear among children with conduct problems. *Journal of the American Medical Association Psychiatry, 71,* 627–636.

Lynam, D. R. (1996). Early identification of chronic offenders: Who is the fledgling psychopath? *Psychological Bulletin, 120,* 209–234.

Marsee, M. A., & Frick, P. J. (2007). Exploring the cognitive and emotional correlates to proactive and reactive aggression in a sample of detained girls. *Journal of Abnormal Child Psychology, 35,* 969–981.

Marsee, M. A., Frick, P. J., Barry, C. T., Kimonis, E. R., Muñoz Centifanti, L. C., & Aucoin, K. J. (2014). Profiles of the forms and functions of self-reported aggression in three adolescent samples. *Development and Psychopathology, 26,* 705–720.

Marsh, A. A., & Blair, R. J. R. (2008). Deficits in facial affect recognition among antisocial populations: A meta-analysis. *Neuroscience and Biobehavioral Reviews, 32,* 454–465.

McAuliffe, M. D., Hubbard, J. A., Rubin, R. M., Morrow, M. T., & Dearing, K. F. (2007). Reactive and proactive aggression: Stability of constructs and relations to correlates. *The Journal of Genetic Psychology: Research and Theory on Human Development, 167,* 365–382.

McBurnett, K., Lahey, B. B., Rathouz, P. J., & Loeber, R. (2000). Low salivary cortisol and persistent aggression in boys referred for disruptive behavior. *Archives of General Psychiatry, 57,* 38–43.

McBurnett, K., Raine, A., Stouthamer-Loeber, M., Loeber, R., Kumar, A. M., Kumar, M., & Lahey, B. B. (2005). Mood and hormone responses to psychological challenge in adolescent males with conduct problems. *Biological Psychiatry, 57,* 1109–1116.

Michalska, K. J., Zeffiro, T. A., & Decety, J. (2016). Brain response to viewing others being harmed in children with conduct disorder symptoms. *Journal of Child Psychology and Psychiatry, 57,* 510–519.

Moore, C. C., Hubbard, J. A., Morrow, M. T., Barhight, L. R., Lines, M. M., Rubin, R. M., . . . Hyde, C. T (2016). The interaction of sympathetic and parasympathetic psychophysiology on reactive and proactive aggression in real time. Manuscript submitted for publication.

Morris, A. S., Silk, J. S., Morris, M. D. S., Steinberg, L., Aucoin, K. J., & Keyes, A. W. (2011). The influence of mother–child emotion regulation strategies on children's expression of anger and sadness. *Developmental Psychology, 47,* 213–225.

Morrow, M. T., Hubbard, J.A., McAuliffe, M. D., Rubin, R. M., & Dearing, K. F. (2006). Childhood aggression, depressive symptoms, and peer rejection: The mediational model revisited. *International Journal of Behavioral Development, 30,* 240–248.

Murray-Close, D. (2013). Psychophysiology of adolescent peer relations I: Theory and research findings. *Journal of Research on Adolescence, 23,* 236–259.

Nas, C. N., Orobio de Castro, B., & Koops, W. (2005). Social information processing in delinquent adolescents. *Psychology, Crime & Law, 11,* 363–375.

Nigg, J. T. (2000). On inhibition/disinhibition in developmental psychopathology: Views from cognitive and personality psychology and a working inhibition taxonomy. *Psychological Bulletin, 126,* 220–246.

Orobio de Castro, B., Merk, W., Koops, W., Veerman, J. W., & Bosch, J. D. (2005). Emotions in social information processing and their relations with reactive and proactive aggression in referred aggressive boys. *Journal of Clinical Child and Adolescent Psychology, 34,* 105–116.

Ostrov, J. M., Murray-Close, D., Godleski, S. A., & Hart, E. J. (2013). Prospective associations between forms and functions of aggression and social and affective processes during early childhood. *Journal of Experimental Child Psychology, 116,* 19–36.

Pardini, D. A. (2006). The callousness pathway to severe violent delinquency. *Aggressive Behavior, 32,* 590–598.

Pardini, D., & Frick, P. J. (2013). Multiple developmental pathways to conduct disorder: Current conceptualizations and clinical implications. *Journal of the Canadian Academy of Child and Adolescent Psychiatry, 22,* 20–25.

Pardini, D., Lochman, J., & Wells, K. (2004). Negative emotions and alcohol use initiation in high-risk boys: The moderating effect of good inhibitory control. *Journal of Abnormal Child Psychology, 32,* 505–518.

Patterson, G. R., DeBaryshe, B. D., & Ramsey, E. (1989). A developmental perspective on antisocial behavior. *American Psychologist, 44,* 329–335.

Phillips, N. C., & Lochman, J. E. (2003). Experimentally manipulated change in children's proactive and reactive aggressive behavior. *Aggressive Behavior, 29,* 215–227.

Platje, E., Popma, A., Vermeiren, R. R. J. M., Doreleijers, T. A. H., Meeus, W. H. J., van Lier, P. A., . . . Jansen, L. M. C. (2015). Testosterone and cortisol in relation to aggression in a non-clinical sample of boys and girls. *Aggressive Behavior, 41,* 478–487.

Polman, H., Orobio de Castro, B., Koops, W., van Boxtel, H. W., & Merk, W. W. (2007). A meta-analysis of the distinction between reactive and proactive aggression in children and adolescents. *Journal of Abnormal Child Psychology, 35,* 522–535.

Poon, J. A., Turpyn, C. C., Hansen, A., Jacangelo, J., & Chaplin, T. M. (2016). Adolescent substance use & psychopathology: Interactive effects of cortisol reactivity and emotion regulation. *Cognitive Therapy and Research, 40,* 368–380.

Popma, A., Vermeiren, R., Geluk, C., Rinne, T., van, den Brink, W., Knol, D. L., . . . Doreleijers, T. (2007). Cortisol moderates the relationship between testosterone and aggression in delinquent male adolescents. *Biological Psychiatry, 61,* 405–411.

Porges, S. W., Doussard-Roosevelt, J. A., Portales, A. L., & Greenspan, S. I. (1996). Infant regulation of the vagal "brake" predicts child behavior problems: A psychobiological model of social behavior. *Developmental Psychobiology, 29,* 697–712.

Raine, A., Dodge, K., Loeber, R., Gatzke-Kopp, L., Lynam, D., Reynolds, C., . . . Liu, J. (2006). The reactive–proactive aggression questionnaire: Differential correlates of reactive and proactive aggression in adolescent boys. *Aggressive Behavior, 32,* 159–171.

Raine, A., Fung, A. L. C., Portnoy, J., Choy, O., & Spring, V. L. (2014). Low heart rate as a risk factor for child and adolescent proactive aggressive and impulsive psychopathic behavior. *Aggressive Behavior, 40,* 290–299.

Rathert, J., Fite, P. J., Gaertner, A. E., & Vitulano, M. (2011). Associations between effortful control, psychological control, and proactive and reactive aggression. *Child Psychiatry and Human Development, 42,* 609–621.

Rothbart, M. K., Ahadi, S. A., & Hershey, K. L. (1994). Temperament and social behavior in childhood. *Merrill-Palmer Quarterly, 40,* 21–39.

Rothbart, M. K., & Bates, J. E. (2006). Temperament. In W. Damon, R. M. Lerner, and N. Eisenberg (Eds.), *Handbook of child psychology: Social, emotional, and personality development* (pp. 99–166). New York: Wiley.

Rubin, K. H., Burgess, K. B., Dwyer, K. M., & Hastings, P. D. (2003). Predicting preschoolers' externalizing behaviors from toddler temperament, conflict, and maternal negativity. *Developmental Psychology, 39,* 164–176.

Scarpa, A., Haden, S. C., & Tanaka, A. (2010). Being hot-tempered: Autonomic, emotional, and behavioral distinctions between childhood reactive and proactive aggression. *Biological Psychology, 84,* 488–496.

Scott, S., & O'Connor, T. G. (2012). An experimental test of differential susceptibility to parenting among emotionally-dysregulated children in a randomized controlled trial for oppositional behavior. *Journal of Child Psychology and Psychiatry, 53,* 1184–1193.

Shannon, K. E., Sauder, C., Beauchaine, T. P., & Gatzke-Kopp, L. (2009). Disrupted effective connectivity between the medial frontal cortex and the caudate in adolescent boys with externalizing behavior disorders. *Criminal Justice and Behavior, 36,* 1141–1157.

Shields, A., & Cicchetti, D. (1998). Reactive aggression among maltreated children: The contributions of attention and emotion dysregulation. *Journal of Clinical Child Psychology, 27,* 381–395.

Shoal, G. D., Giancola, P. R., & Kirillova, G. P. (2003). Salivary cortisol, personality, and aggressive behavior in adolescent boys: A 5-year longitudinal study. *Journal of the American Academy of Child & Adolescent Psychiatry, 42,* 1101–1107.

Shortt, J. W., Stoolmiller, M., Smith-Shine, J., Mark Eddy, J., & Sheeber, L. (2010). Maternal emotion coaching, adolescent anger regulation, and siblings externalizing symptoms. *Journal of Child Psychology and Psychiatry, 51,* 799–808.

Skowron, E. A., Loken, E., Gatzke-Kopp, L., Cipriano-Essel, E., Woehrle, P.L., Van Epps, J. J., . . . Ammerman, R. T. (2011). Mapping cardiac physiology and parenting processes in maltreating mother–child dyads. *Journal of Family Psychology, 25,* 663–674.

Smeets, K. C., Oostermeijer, S., Lappenschaar, M., Cohn, M., Meer, J. M. J., Popma, A., . . . Buitelaar, J. K. (2017). Are proactive and reactive aggression meaningful distinctions in adolescents? A variable- and person-based approach. *Journal of Abnormal Child Psychology, 45*(1), 1–14. doi: 10.1007/s10802-016-0149-5

Snyder, J., Edwards, P., McGraw, K., Kilgore, K., & Holton, A. (1994). Escalation and reinforcement in mother–child conflict: Social processes associated with the development of physical aggression. *Development and Psychopathology, 6,* 305–321.

Snyder, J. J., & Patterson, G. R. (1995). Individual differences in social aggression: A test of a reinforcement model of socialization in the natural environment. *Behavior Therapy, 26,* 371–391.

Snyder, J., Schrepferman, L., & St. Peter, C. (1997). Origins of antisocial behavior: Negative reinforcement and affect dysregulation of behavior as socialization mechanisms in family interaction. *Behavior Modification, 21,* 187–215.

Stadler, C., Poustka, F., & Sterzer, P. (2010). The heterogeneity of disruptive behavior disorders: Implications for neurobiological research and treatment. *Frontiers in Psychiatry, 1,* 21. doi: 10.3389/fpsyt.2010.00021

Stoppelbein, L., Greening, L., Luebbe, A., Fite, P., & Becker, S. P. (2014). The role of cortisol and psychopathic traits in aggression among at-risk girls: Tests of mediating hypotheses. *Aggressive Behavior, 40*(3), 263–272.

Thompson, R. A., Lewis, M. D., & Calkins, S. D. (2008). Reassessing emotion regulation. *Child Development Perspectives, 2,* 124–131.

Thornton, L. C., Frick, P. J., Crapanzano, A. M., & Terranova, A. M. (2013). The incremental utility of callous-unemotional traits and conduct problems in predicting aggression and bullying in a community sample of boys and girls. *Psychological Assessment, 25,* 366–378.

Valiente, C., Eisenberg, N., Smith, C. L., Reiser, M., Fabes, R. A., Losoya, S., . . . Murphy, B. C. (2003). The relations of effortful control and reactive control to children's externalizing problems: A longitudinal assessment. *Journal of Personality, 71,* 1171–1196.

van Goozen, S. H. M., Matthys, W., Cohen-Kettenis, P. T., Buitelaar, J. K., & van Engeland, H. (2000). Hypothalamic-pituitary-adrenal axis and autonomic nervous system activity in disruptive children and matched controls. *Journal of the American Academy of Child and Adolescent Psychiatry, 39,* 1438–1445.

van Goozen, S. H. M., Matthys, W., Cohen-Kettenis, P. T., Gispen-de Wied, C., Wiegant, V. M., & van Engeland, H. (1998). Salivary cortisol and cardiovascular activity during stress in oppositional-defiant disorder boys and normal controls. *Biological Psychiatry, 43,* 531–539.

Vasilev, C. A., Crowell, S. E., Beauchaine, T. P., Mead, H. K., & Gatzke-Kopp, L. (2009). Correspondence between physiological and self-report measures of emotion dysregulation: A longitudinal investigation of youth with and without psychopathology. *Journal of Child Psychology and Psychiatry, 50,* 1357–1364.

Vitaro, F., Barker, E. D., Boivin, M., Brendgen, M., & Tremblay, R. E. (2006). Do early difficult temperament and harsh parenting differentially predict reactive and proactive aggression? *Journal of Abnormal Child Psychology, 34,* 685–695.

Vitaro, F., & Brendgen, M. (2005). Proactive and reactive aggression: A developmental perspective. In R. E. Tremblay, W. Hartup, & J. Archer (Eds.), *Developmental origins of aggression* (pp. 178–201). New York, NY: Guilford Press.

Vitaro, F., Brendgen, M., & Tremblay, R. E. (2002). Reactively and proactively aggressive children: Antecedent and subsequent characteristics. *Journal of Child Psychology and Psychiatry, 43,* 495–505.

White, S. F., van Tieghem, M., Brislin, S. J., Sypher, I., Sinclair, S., Pine, D. S., . . . Blair, R. J. (2016). Neural correlates of the propensity for retaliatory behavior in youths with disruptive behavior disorders. *The American Journal of Psychiatry, 173,* 282–290.

Xu, Y., Farver, J. A. M., & Zhang, Z. (2009). Temperament, harsh and indulgent parenting, and Chinese children's proactive and reactive aggression. *Child Development, 80,* 244–258.

Xu, Y., Raine, A., Yu, L., & Krieg, A. (2014). Resting heart rate, vagal tone, and reactive and proactive aggression in Chinese children. *Journal of Abnormal Child Psychology, 42,* 501–514.

Xu, Y., & Zhang, Z. (2008). Distinguishing proactive and reactive aggression in Chinese children. *Journal of Abnormal Child Psychology, 36,* 539–552.

Zeman, J., Cassano, M., Perry-Parrish, C., & Stegall, S. (2006). Emotion regulation in children and adolescents. *Journal of Developmental and Behavioral Pediatrics, 27,* 155–168.

15

"It's Gonna End Up with a Fight Anyway"

Social Cognitive Processes in Children with Disruptive Behavior Disorders

Bram Orobio de Castro and Anouk van Dijk

"What were you thinking?" may be the question children with disruptive behavior disorders (DBDs) hear most often when they have misbehaved. Unfortunately, this question is usually a rhetorical expression of incomprehension about what led the child to this disruptive behavior: Was he out of his mind? Did he fail to notice what exactly happened? Did he feel insulted? Did he feel no empathy for his victim? Did he expect to gain something by this behavior? Actually understanding the social cognitions that drive children's disruptive behavior may help to share their perspective, prevent recurrence of these behaviors, and treat disruptive behavior disorders.

The present chapter aims to provide an overview of social-cognitive processes in children with disruptive behavior problems and the development of these processes. To this end we introduce an overarching theoretical model, examine the current empirical evidence for it, and discuss its implications.

A General Model of Social Cognition in Disruptive Behavior Problems

Several theoretical models aim to explain how individual differences in the processing of social information lead to disruptive behaviors. We use an overarching model based on the Social Information Processing model (Crick & Dodge, 1994), the General Aggression model (Anderson & Bushman, 2002), and incorporating numerous additions and changes to these models that have been suggested in order, for example, to accommodate emotional processes (Lemerise & Arsenio, 2000). This model, presented in Figure 15.1, consists of an online situation-specific and an offline person-specific part. The online part describes the social-cognitive processes leading from a specific social situation to a behavioral response. The offline part describes the stable characteristics and processes that are believed to determine individual differences in online processing.

The Wiley Handbook of Disruptive and Impulse-Control Disorders, First Edition.
Edited by John E. Lochman and Walter Matthys.
© 2018 John Wiley & Sons Ltd. Published 2018 by John Wiley & Sons Ltd.

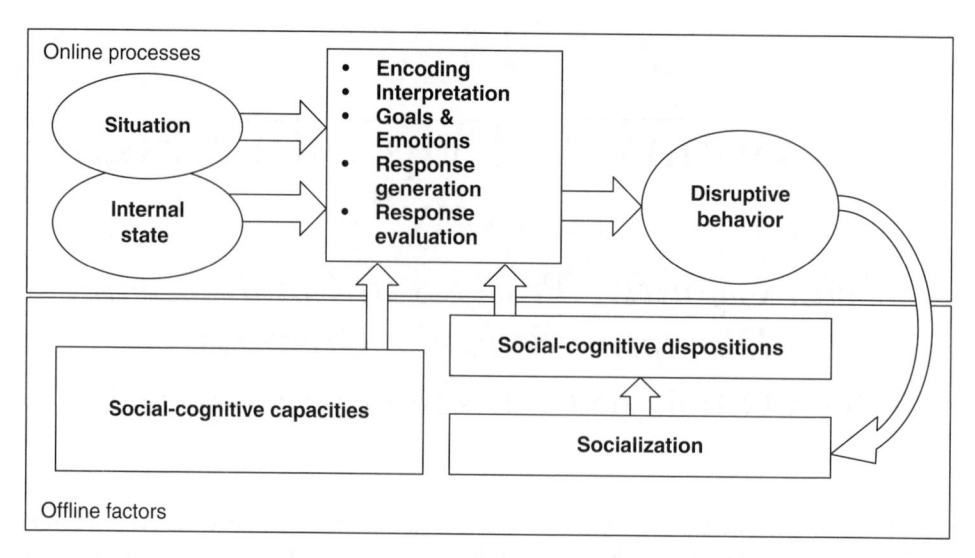

Figure 15.1 Model of social cognition in disruptive behavior disorders. Adapted from Crick and Dodge (1994), Anderson & Bushman (2002), and Frijda (1993).

Online Social-Cognitive Processing

The model assumes that social situations lead to adaptive behavioral responses when an orderly sequence of "online" processing steps is followed. Disruptive behaviors (as well as other problematic social behaviors) are thought to result from deviations in one or more of these processing steps. In any social situation, the most relevant social cues first need to be perceived and encoded as meaningful information units. The meaning of the encoded information for the child then needs to be interpreted. This interpretation clarifies which goals are at stake for the child and evokes emotions such as anger or sadness when the child's goals are threatened, or happiness when those goals are promoted. These goals and emotions activate the generation of the dominant response the child is used to giving when these goals and emotions are at stake. Often, this dominant response will be enacted. However, children may also generate multiple responses simultaneously, and then select the most appropriate for enactment through response evaluation and decision processes. To do so, they may need to inhibit their dominant response and reappraise the situation at hand more thoroughly before they respond behaviorally. Finally, the enacted response is *responded to* by the social environment, thus providing new social cues to continue this cyclic process. How information in a given situation is processed will also depend on the *internal state* of a child at the onset of the event, for instance, being frustrated, tired, or hungry.

Numerous studies have examined social cognitive processing in relation to disruptive (primarily aggressive) behavior, although only a limited number of these studies included samples of children formally diagnosed with a DBD. These studies have generally used a similar methodological approach: Standardized social situations are presented to participants in the form of hypothetical vignettes, videos, or experimental settings. These are derived from fundamental research into the specifics of situations that evoke marked individual differences between children in disruptive behavioral responses (Dodge, McClaskey, & Feldman, 1985; Matthys, Maassen, Cuperus, & Van Engeland, 2001). Most diagnostic situations are so-called "ambiguous provocations," interactions with a peer whose intentions are unclear, which involve, for instance, being hindered (e.g., a peer bumping into a child, or a ball being thrown against the child's head), entering a peer group (e.g., trying to join in on a game), and handling criticism or compliments (e.g., being told you have lost a game).

The way in which social situations are processed is examined by means of explicit open-ended and closed format questions to participants ("Why did person X in the vignette do Y?"), indirect measures of cognitive processes (eye movement, response length, speed), or behavioral responses (such as giving or refusing credit to a peer, or actual aggressive behavior). Convergent validity of these methods seems reasonable, with larger effects found when social situations are more realistic and personally involving, and when participants have more severe behavior problems (De Castro, Veerman, Koops, Bosch, & Monshouwer, 2002).

In the following sections we summarize the empirical evidence for atypical social-cognitive processing patterns by children with DBD step by step. For each step of social-cognitive processing, we focus on studies including children with DBD, but use findings from the general population and from studies of severely violent youth as additional evidence when clinical studies are scarce.

Steps in Online Social-Cognitive Processing

Encoding Encoding refers to the process of attending to relevant social cues and encoding them as accessible units for further processing. Individual differences in encoding may lead children to experience a single situation very differently. Consider the example of Pete, who wants to join a ball game. When he asks whether he can join, another kid tells him "no, wait until we finish this round," smiles apologetically, and then turns around to continue playing. Pete will experience a very different situation if he only encoded not being allowed to join the game and the kid turning his back towards him, than if he also encoded that he will get to play if he waits for his turn and noticed the friendly smile.

Two contrasting hypotheses about encoding by children with DBD have been put forward. On the one hand, children with DBD have been suggested to be hypervigilant to cues of threat or hostility, and to miss out on benign or reconciliatory cues (Crick & Dodge, 1994). On the other hand, it has been suggested that they do not miss benign or reconciliatory cues, but, in fact, initially attend to them. However, as these benign cues do not fit their expectations, they ignore this information and encode only hostile or threatening ones (Horsley, De Castro, & Van der Schoot, 2010; Lochman & Dodge, 1998).

In line with the latter hypothesis, two recent eye-tracking studies found that nonreferred children with aggressive behavior problems paid as much visual attention to relevant social cues as their peers, but then selectively remembered and recalled only the cues that fit a hostile interpretation (Horsley et al., 2010; Troop-Gordon, Gordon, Vogel-Ciernia, Ewing Lee, & Visconti, 2016). Children with DBD and severely violent behavior recall fewer cues when asked to do so (Lochman & Dodge, 1994; Matthys, Cuperus, & Van Engeland, 1999). Moreover, children with DBD prefer to use fewer cues and to selectively use cues suggesting hostility or threat in their social decision making (Dodge & Newman, 1981; Dodge, Price, Bachorowski, & Newman, 1990; Van Goozen, Cohen-Kettenis, Matthys, & Van Engeland, 2002).

Interpretation How a social situation is experienced and responded to depends critically on one's interpretation of the intentions and emotions of others in the situation. For example, Pete has a very different experience if he interprets that the kid telling him to wait for a turn at a game is pleased to see him and intends to let him join, than if he interprets the very same behavior as the kid hating his guts and looking for a way to reject him.

Children with DBD are hypothesized to overinterpret others' behaviors as hostile and others' feelings as less empathic towards them. Over 70 studies have examined the relation between such hostile intent attributions and behavior problems, including nine studies with clinical samples. A meta-analysis of these studies (De Castro et al., 2002) demonstrated a robust relation between hostile intent attribution and aggressive behavior problems, that was found to be strongest for clinical groups ($d = .47$). A recent cross-cultural comparison revealed that hostile intent attribution prospectively partly predicted changes in aggressive behavior in nine culturally diverse countries, as well as differences in the prevalence of aggression between cultural groups (Dodge et al., 2015).

Hostile intent attribution occurs primarily when children are provoked personally (so not when the provocation concerns other children; Dodge & Frame, 1982) and is stronger when participants are emotionally involved (Yaros, Lochman, Rosenbaum, & Jimenez-Camargo, 2014) or made to feel frustrated beforehand (De Castro, Slot, Bosch, Koops, & Veerman, 2003; Dodge & Somberg, 1987). Hostile intent attribution also seems to be particularly strong when it concerns provocation by specific peers, such as disliked peers (Peets, Hodges, Kikas, & Salmivalli, 2007), but is also robustly found in response to provocation by unknown others (De Castro et al., 2002, secondary analyses).

In addition to hostile intent attribution, children with DBD attribute more feelings of glee and happiness at their misfortune to others (De Castro, Merk, Koops, Veerman, & Bosch, 2005; Lochman & Dodge, 1994). In emerging conflicts they misinterpret reconciliatory emotional signals like regret or sympathy as lies, which, in turn, predicts escalation of peer conflicts (Kempes, De Castro, & Sterck, 2008). For an extensive review of emotions and emotion attributions in DBD, see Chapter 14 of this *Handbook*.

Goals and Emotions Interpretations of a social event automatically trigger goals and action tendencies that help to safeguard one's personal concerns and interests (Frijda, 1993). These goals and inclinations are reflected in physiological changes in arousal and subjective emotional experiences. In our example, if Pete interprets having to wait for a turn at a game as unfair treatment, this may activate the goal of getting back at the peer and an emotional action tendency to fight, which is reflected in arousal and experienced as anger. Conversely, if Pete interprets the same event as a benign request to wait for his turn with the ball, more prosocial goals and emotions will be activated.

Children with DBD have been found to set different goals and experience different emotional action tendencies than other children.

Children with DBD emphasize goals directed at punishing peers for alleged wrongdoing. Such goals may focus on injustice or "setting the record straight" by inflicting the same harm to peers that allegedly caused harm to the child with DBD. This may also serve an "educative" purpose when the goal is to "teach" other children to be more respectful (De Castro, Verhulp, & Runions, 2012). Moreover, children with DBD set more instrumental goals such as material gains or gains in social status. Social and cooperative goals are mentioned less often by these children than by their peers (De Castro et al., 2012). Similarly, in nonreferred samples disruptive behavior is associated with more egocentric and less prosocial goals (McDonald & Lochman, 2012; Ojanen, Gronroos, & Salmivalli, 2005).

As far as emotional action tendencies are concerned, children with DBD report feeling more angry in response to social setbacks (De Castro et al., 2005; see also, for nonreferred children, Lochman & Dodge, 1998), evidence more anger and anxiety according to parents and teachers—see Granic (2014), for an overview—and show more physiological signs of anger in response to provocation (see Chapter 14 of this book on emotional dysregulation). A subgroup of children with DBD described as callous-unemotional (see Chapter 3 of this book on conduct disorder) by definition experiences *fewer* emotional action tendencies in response to provocation, as well as less guilt or remorse when misbehaving (American Psychiatric Association, 2013).

Response generation Interaction goals and emotions trigger *response generation*, defined as the retrieval of behavioral response sequences from long-term memory. In our example, Pete's anger because he did not get a turn may lead to the dominant response to lash out aggressively and grab the ball for himself, while other children's anger may lead them to express verbally how they feel.

Children with DBD activate more aggressive and less assertive dominant responses (Matthys et al., 1999). This pattern has been noted to be more common for children with CD than for children with ODD (Dunn, Lochman, & Colder, 1997). Moreover, they generate fewer responses and their alternative responses are also more aggressive and less assertive when they are probed to generate alternative responses in addition to their first aggressive response (e.g., Matthys et al., 1999). In addition, children with DBD generate fewer responses aimed at downregulating anger, such as cognitive reappraisal or calm-down routines. In contrast, they more often opt for venting anger as an (unfortunately ineffective) way to handle such emotional tendencies (De Castro et al., 2005).

Response Evaluation and Decision When provoked, strong emotions may push children towards direct enactment of a dominant response, but—with some effort—strong anger or fear may also be interpreted as detrimental and help children to inhibit their dominant response. Children may then generate and select a response from multiple available responses. If children evaluate and decide on responses, they may consider numerous aspects of these different alternatives (for a theoretical overview, see: Fontaine, Burks, & Dodge, 2002), such as the expected outcomes for self and others, the moral acceptability of responses, and self-efficacy for responses. In our example, Pete may consider whether grabbing the ball or asking for a turn again may best further his goals of playing the game and getting along with the other kids. He may consider how likely he is to succeed in getting the ball and keeping it. He may consider whether grabbing the ball would be wrong, or would be a justified punishment for kids who do not let him join. And he may weigh these different aspects of response evaluation against each other before selecting a response. Importantly, the very length of this example suggests that such elaborate evaluations may rarely be made spontaneously by children with DBD (De Castro, 2004).

Children with DBD typically engage in more direct enactment of generated responses and consequently in less response evaluation and decision. When children with DBD do engage in response evaluation they generally expect less positive outcomes for assertive and prosocial responses than their peers, but they appear to be equally negative about the probable outcomes of aggressive responses (De Castro et al., 2012; Dodge, Lochman, Harnish, Bates, & Pettit, 1997; Matthys et al., 1999). As one participant aptly summarized "its gonna end up with a fight anyway." Thus, even though children with DBD expect little from aggressive responses, they experience no incentive to select more social responses instead. Children with DBD also are more confident than controls in their ability to enact an aggressive response (self-efficacy); and when they are given the opportunity to select a response among various responses shown, they more often select an aggressive response and less often a prosocial response (Matthys et al., 1999).

In contrast, some children seem to behave aggressively because they expect positive emotions as a consequence, for example by expecting to get enjoyment from bullying (i.e., happy victimizer emotions; Malti & Krettenauer, 2013). Perhaps not surprisingly, children with DBD consider aggressive responses more morally acceptable than their peers, specifically when they see aggression as a response to an (alleged) moral transgression by a peer

(Arsenio & Fleiss, 1996). Thus, paradoxically, children with DBD do in fact appear to have a strong moral basis for their disruptive behavior, as they aim to "punish" or "set straight" others' alleged hostile behaviors (De Castro et al., 2012).

Enactment Enactment of aggressive responses can be predicted from all of the preceding steps of social-cognitive processing. When asked to enact assertive or prosocial responses, children with DBD enact these behaviors less skillfully and with less positive outcomes (Connor, Steingard, Cunningham, Anderson, & Melloni, 2004; Kempes et al., 2008;).

Individual Differences in Online Social-Cognitive Processing

Our account of online processing by children with DBD may seem to suggest that such children follow the same sequence of processing steps as other children, but with different content. However, considerable individual differences in online processing between children with DBD have been found, suggesting that individualized profiles of specific social-cognitive processing patterns in individual clients may be more informative than a grand average of the social-cognitive processing problems of children with DBD as a group.

Reactive and Proactive Aggression Detailed hypotheses have been formulated as to which disruptive behavior patterns are related to which specific deviations in online social-cognitive processing (cf., De Castro, 2004; Dodge et al., 1997; Fontaine, 2008). Specifically, reactive aggression is hypothesized to be related to difficulties in the first steps of social-cognitive processing, so that it is characterized by difficulty in accurately *encoding* relevant social cues and in *interpreting* others' intentions, regarding them as hostile when this is not warranted, and misinterpreting others' emotions, as well as by setting more revenge *goals*, having stronger *emotions*, having less flexible *response generation* and preemptive *response evaluation and decision*, and being more affected by their *internal state*. Likewise, proactive aggression is presumed to be primarily related to later steps in social-cognitive processing, being characterized by setting more egocentric and less prosocial *interaction goals*, generating more aggressive *dominant responses*, and a series of deviations in *response evaluation and decision*, such as expecting relatively better outcomes from aggressive responses than from other responses, finding disruptive behaviors more morally acceptable, and feeling more self-efficacy in disruptive behaviors. Dysfunctional response evaluation processes have also been noted among convicted youth with higher levels of callous-unemotional traits (Pardini, Lochman, & Frick, 2003), a key component of the Low Prosocial Emotions specifier for Conduct Disorder (see Chapter 3 of this book).

Preemptive Processing It appears that children who are specifically reactively aggressive may simply skip processing steps "in the heat of the moment." Self-reported accounts of processes leading up to aggressive behaviors by children with DBD and reactive aggression describe a fast, automatic emotional response to provocation. These children report an instant flush of anger in response to being hindered or provoked, resulting in their not having the time to take a proper look at the situation before they lash out (De Castro et al., 2012). Moreover, a study with referred children found that they respond aggressively to provocation vignettes twice as often as their peers, even when they attribute benign intent afterwards, suggesting that they responded to provocation prior to any in-depth interpretation of intentions (Waldman, 1996). Similarly, in a detective game in which children had to judge whether or not a peer had acted with hostility, aggressive children were quick to judge without reviewing the available evidence (Dodge & Newman, 1981). Thus, indirect evidence suggests preemptive processing to be an important aspect of specifically reactive aggression.

Effects of Internal State The above steps of online processing appear to be influenced by a child's internal state. Children's processing may have been primed by preceding events, thus steering online processing in a specific direction. For example, if Pete was accused of being a nuisance by his mother at breakfast, he might more readily expect rejection when he tries to join the ball game at school. Similarly, it has been suggested that physiological factors such as arousal, stress, frustration, fatigue, and low blood sugar may increase the likelihood that social cues are processed as aversive.

Some children with DBD may be particularly susceptible to such effects produced by their internal state. The effect of frustration on the making of hostile intent attributions is greater for children with DBD than for their peers (De Castro, Slot et al., 2003). In nonreferred samples, online processing is likewise affected by priming with social threat (Dodge & Somberg, 1987), as well as priming with violence on TV and in video games (Kirsh & Mounts, 2007; Martins, 2013). In nonreferred adults, similar effects have been detected for low blood glucose, known as being "hangry" (Bushman, DeWall, Pond, & Hanus, 2014). A better understanding of the effects of internal states on online processing by children with DBD may potentially contribute to relatively simple strategies to improve their processing by "setting the stage" for social interactions more carefully with regard to such basic issues as TV, games, food, and structuring interactions when children are tired.

Offline Processes

We have just described the online social-cognitive processes leading from a specific social stimulus to a behavioral response. Next, we describe the offline processes or stable characteristics that are believed to determine individual differences in online processing.

Social-cognitive Dispositions

Social-cognitive dispositions are defined as stable individual differences underlying children's online social-cognitive processing. Social-cognitive dispositions are typically measured as children's general perceptions of their social worlds (e.g., "most peers are mean," "aggression is okay"), whereas social-cognitive processing is typically measured as children's perceptions of specific situations (e.g., "the peer in this story is mean," "it is okay to aggress toward this peer"). It is thought that children's social-cognitive dispositions are shaped by their social experiences, which build up to a "database" of social knowledge that, in turn, affects how they process social information in the situation at hand (Crick & Dodge, 1994). As a child's database is derived from past experience and used to guide future behavior, it is believed to contribute to stability in children's behavior over time (Dodge & Pettit, 2003). We discuss literature on three social-cognitive dispositions that may be seen as part of a child's database of social cognitive dispositions: schemas, normative beliefs, and social self-views (Crick & Dodge, 1994; Huesmann & Guerra, 1997).

Schemas Schemas are defined as memory structures that guide children's social-cognitive processing (Crick & Dodge, 1994), and have also been referred to as social knowledge structures (Dodge & Pettit, 2003), scripts (Huesmann, 1988), and working models (Bowlby, 1980). Schemas may influence children's online processing of social situations by filtering which cues are attended to and which not (Fiske & Taylor, 1984; Lochman & Dodge, 1998), by filling in children's interpretations if situational cues are unclear (Burks, Laird, Dodge, Pettit, & Bates, 1999), and by prompting children with scripts of how they can behave, which consequences are likely to follow, and how morally acceptable certain behaviors are (Huesmann, 1988). Schemas, therefore, facilitate social-cognitive processing, but may also induce errors. For instance, children may readily interpret their peers' behavior as hostilely intended, based on their schema that most peers are mean; or they may decide to respond aggressively, based on their schema that peer interactions typically end in fights. This theorized effect of schemas on social-cognitive processing has received some support from longitudinal research showing that children's hostile schemas predict biased online social-cognitive processing (Burks et al., 1999; Calvete & Orue, 2012).

Children with DBD are thought to have acquired maladaptive schemas that bias their social-cognitive processing (Dodge & Pettit, 2003; Huesmann, 1988). In line with this reasoning, studies have found that children with DBD endorsed more hostile beliefs than typically developing children (e.g., "most people are against me"; Schniering & Rapee, 2002) and that children with higher levels of disruptive symptoms more strongly expected other people to treat them badly (mistrust schema; Muris, 2006). Moreover, longitudinal research has shown that maladaptive schemas contribute to the stability of aggressive behavior across early childhood (Burks et al., 1999) and to increases in aggression in preadolescence (Troop-Gordon & Ladd, 2005). Last, there is indirect evidence suggesting that aggressive children's social-cognitive processing is more schema-driven from studies showing that these children are less affected by situational cues such as explicit "eye-witness" information about others' intentions (Dodge & Tomlin, 1987), the priming of nonhostile interpretations (Graham & Hudley, 1994), and actual behavior during peer interactions as rated by objective observers (Lochman & Dodge, 1998).

Normative Beliefs In addition to schemas (beliefs about how people are expected to behave), a child's database contains normative beliefs (beliefs about how people ought to behave). Normative beliefs refer to children's personal standards about the acceptability of a behavior, and include (but are not limited to) moral beliefs (Huesmann & Guerra, 1997). Like schemas, normative beliefs may function as stable social-cognitive dispositions affecting children's social-cognitive processing. For instance, the belief that aggression is normative may increase the likelihood that children interpret other people's behavior as aggressive, as well as the likelihood that children decide to respond aggressively themselves (Crick & Dodge, 1994; Zelli, Dodge, Lochman, Laird, & CPPRG, 1999). In line with this reasoning, longitudinal research has shown that aggression-supporting normative beliefs predict later deviant social-cognitive processing (Calvete & Orue, 2012; Zelli et al., 1999).

Children with DBD are thought to hold aggression-supporting beliefs that contribute to deviant social-cognitive processing and subsequent aggression (Huesmann & Guerra, 1997). Longitudinal research in nonclinical samples has found support for this claim (Calvete & Orue, 2012; Zelli et al., 1999), as did research comparing aggressive to nonaggressive children (Huesmann & Guerra, 1997). Clinical research with children with DBD is lacking; most clinical studies on normative beliefs have been conducted with juvenile delinquents. One study found that juvenile offenders endorsed antisocial beliefs more strongly than typically developing youth did (Butler, Parry, & Fearon, 2015). Relatedly, a meta-analysis has shown that juvenile delinquents have lower levels of moral reasoning than their typically developing peers. On average, their reasoning is closer to stage 2 (self-interest orientation) whereas their peers' reasoning is closer to stage 3 (interpersonal orientation; $d = .76$; Stams et al., 2006).

Another line of research addresses children's beliefs about their own aggressive behavior: It is thought that antisocial youth rationalize their behavior to reduce the stress resulting from committing antisocial acts (e.g., "if I don't hit first, they will think I'm an easy target"; Barriga & Gibbs, 1996). Such cognitive distortions would then lower the threshold to commit antisocial behaviors again. Cognitive distortions have been extensively researched, referred to by various paradigms as neutralization techniques (Sykes & Matza, 1957), moral disengagement (Bandura, Barbaranelli, Caprara, & Pastorelli, 1996), and secondary self-serving cognitive distortions (Barriga & Gibbs, 1996). Although cognitive distortions have not been investigated in children with DBD, there is clear evidence that cognitive distortions are related to children's antisocial behavior: two meta-analyses found a moderate effect ($d = .70$ in Helmond, Overbeek, Brugman, & Gibbs, 2015; $r = .28$ in Gini, Pozzoli, & Hymel, 2014).

Social Self-views An important determinant of social behavior is how children view themselves in social interactions: their social self-views. It is thought that children use their social interactions with peers to discover whether their own behavior leads to desirable outcomes, such as being liked (Crick & Dodge, 1994). After repeated social interactions, children are thought to build up a view of their own social competence that becomes part of their database.

Although most children with DBD have many negative social interactions, they do not generally seem to hold negative social self-views. Many children with DBD actually seem to overestimate their own social competence. This overestimation effect is a robust finding: it is replicated in both clinical samples (Renouf, Kovacs, & Mukerji, 1997; Webster-Stratton & Woolley Lindsay, 1999) and nonclinical samples (e.g., David & Kistner, 2000; Diamantopoulou, Rydell, & Henricsson, 2008). One possible explanation for this seemingly paradoxical finding is that many children with behavior problems attribute their social problems to the people they interact with rather than to themselves (Baumeister, 1997). Preliminary evidence for this view comes from studies that simultaneously investigated children's peer schemas and social self-views. These studies found that children who had positive views of themselves but negative views of their peers had the highest levels of aggressive behavior (Bradshaw & Hazan, 2006; Salmivalli, Ojanen, Haanpää, & Peets, 2005). Another possible explanation is that children's social problems cause them to inflate their self-views as a way of coping with these negative experiences ("I'm cool, screw them"; Salmivalli, 2001).

Even though children with DBD seem to hold positive social self-views, their self-views are not necessarily "healthy" (Salmivalli, 2001). The positive self-views of aggressive children are unstable (Kernis, 1993) and their high but fragile self-views (narcissism) are easily threatened by negative feedback from peers, which directly evokes aggressive responses (Thomaes, Bushman, Stegge, & Olthof, 2008). Thus, although the exact role of inflated self-views for the development of disruptive behavior is unclear, the evidence to date does falsify the commonly held assumption that aggression stems from negative self-views.

Social-Cognitive Capacities

Social situations are complex and unfold quickly. It must be cognitively demanding to accurately process all this information. Doing so requires social-cognitive capacities that may be less adequate in some children with DBD. Here, we review literature on higher-order cognitive capacities that affect social-cognitive processing as well as literature on empathy (perspective-taking abilities).

Higher Order Cognitive Capacities Children's ability to accurately process social information likely is affected by higher order cognitive capacities such as intelligence or executive functions (Huesmann, Eron, & Yarmel, 1987). Indeed, one longitudinal study showed that low intelligence put children at risk for the development of maladaptive social-cognitive processing and disruptive behavior problems (Hyde, Shaw, & Mollanen, 2010). Similarly, executive functions may impact children's social-cognitive processing. Children with low inhibition evaluate aggressive responses more positively (Van Nieuwenhuijzen et al., 2017), children with limited working memory capacities have impaired social problem solving skills (Yaghoub Zadeh,

Im-Bolter, & Cohen, 2007), and children's inhibitory control and planning abilities interact with their levels of hostile encoding and hostile attributional biases to predict their degree of reactive and proactive aggression (Ellis, Weiss, & Lochman, 2009). As researchers have only recently started to investigate the relations between higher order cognition and social cognition in children with DBD, current evidence is inconclusive with respect to which aspects of higherorder cognition affect which aspects of social-cognitive processing. Yet, for clinicians it is worthwhile to consider that children who have intellectual disabilities or impaired executive functions may be at increased risk for maladaptive social-cognitive processing.

Empathy To accurately process social information, children need to be able to understand other people's emotions (cognitive empathy) and to feel other people's emotions (affective empathy). It is often assumed that children with DBD lack empathy because empathizing with their victim would impede them from inflicting harm (e.g., Miller & Eisenberg, 1988). However, there is little evidence to support this assumption for children with DBD in general: A recent meta-analysis found that empathy explained only 1% of variance in people's aggressive behavior ($r = -.11$; Vachon, Lynam, & Johnson, 2014). Similarly, a narrative review concluded that there is no consistent evidence for an affective empathy deficit in children with DBD (Lovett & Sheffield, 2006) and studies on cognitive empathy using performance tasks (rather than parent-report) also found no deficits in children with DBD (e.g., Happé & Frith, 1996). These findings may imply that empathy is too distal a mechanism to strongly predict aggressive behavior (Vachon et al., 2014): For instance, children who lack empathy may have many reasons not to aggress (for example wanting to maintain successful relationships) and children who are very empathic may still have reasons to aggress (for example, out of a flash of anger, or to stand up for someone else). Another view is that only a subgroup of children with DBD has empathy deficits. Recently, the DSM-5 added a new specifier to the diagnosis conduct disorder: limited prosocial emotions (American Psychiatric Association, 2013). This subgroup of children with less empathy appears to differ from other children with DBD in multiple ways, as described in Chapter 3.

Socialization and the Development of Social-Cognitive Dispositions

So far, we have shown that specific social-cognitive dispositions have important roles in disruptive behavior problems. This begs the question how these dispositions emerge during children's development. According to Dodge and Pettit (2003), the differential development of social-cognitive dispositions is driven by interactions between social experiences and the development of cognitive capacities.

Children with DBD may have had adverse social experiences that shaped their deviant social-cognitive dispositions. Several longitudinal studies have shown that children who have been exposed to adverse social experiences such as peer rejection, harsh parental discipline, and community violence, later develop deviant social-cognitive dispositions such as hostile schemas or aggression-supporting beliefs, that, in turn, predict the development of disruptive behavior problems (Dodge & Pettit, 2003; Guerra, Huesmann, & Spindler, 2003; Troop-Gordon & Ladd, 2005; Weiss, Dodge, Bates, & Pettit, 1992). However, this impact of adverse social experiences on children's development is most likely not unidirectional: Children's deviant social cognitions may also evoke hostile responses from the environment that, in turn, strengthen the very social-cognitive dispositions that evoked children's aggression in the first place (a "self-fulfilling prophecy effect"). For instance, longitudinal research has shown that children's tendency to attribute hostile intent not only followed from peer rejection but also predicted future peer rejection (Lansford, Malone, Dodge, Pettit, &

Bates, 2010). Consequently, social-cognitive dispositions may maintain and reinforce the development of disruptive behavior disorders.

In addition, some children may be more sensitive to this vicious cycle than others. Limited cognitive capacities may make it harder for children to learn adaptive social-cognitive processing from their social experiences, for example, when limited working memory capacities impede children's ability to combine the multiple chunks of relevant social information needed to understand complex situations (Schuiringa, Van Nieuwenhuijzen, De Castro, & Matthys, 2016). Similarly, some children may experience stronger emotional action tendencies than other children, due to temperamental dispositions (see Chapter 11 of this book). When these children are tired or frustrated, it may be harder for them to encode, interpret, and evaluate responses adequately.

Although hostile schemas and antisocial beliefs seem deviant from a normative frame of reference, for some children with DBD such schemas and beliefs may be accurate and even adaptive, considering these children's social context (Frankenhuis & De Weerth, 2013). For instance, if children experience much hostile behavior directed toward them on a daily basis, they may infer hostile rather than benign intent in case of doubt, in line with the adage "better safe than sorry" (Frankenhuis, Panchanathan, & Nettle, 2016). Probably both perspectives are true in different contexts: Hostile schemas may be adaptive in a hostile environment, yet simultaneously limit children's possibilities to function in less hostile environments (cf. "mobility of function"; Rutter & Sroufe, 2000).

Clinical Implications

The model in Figure 15.1 draws a detailed picture of what goes on in a child's mind when he or she behaves disruptively. This picture provides many starting points for clinical assessment and intervention, the most important of which will be highlighted below (see also Chapters 23, 26, 27, and 28).

As far as assessment is concerned, children with DBD differ markedly in exactly which situations trigger problematic social cognitions, the specific nature of these cognitions, and their function in social interactions. For instance, one child may aggress because she incorrectly interprets others' intentions as hostile, whereas another child may aggress because he expects to gain dominance by doing so. It is therefore essential to conduct individual assessment of social-cognitive processing with children with DBD, using function analyses and standardized assessments. This kind of individual assessment may provide a direct route to cognitive behavioral intervention, as it highlights the exact situations, contingencies, and cognitions to be addressed in individualized treatment.

As far as intervention is concerned, experimental and intervention research have shown that changing deviant social cognitions at each online step of the model can reduce children's disruptive behavior. For instance, hostile intent and emotion attributions have been found to be malleable to some extent in aggressive children in the general population, with marked positive effects on aggressive behavior as a consequence (Hudley & Graham, 1993; Penton-Voak et al., 2013). Also, influencing response evaluation and decision processes has been shown to reduce aggressive responding in experimental studies (e.g., De Castro, Bosch, Veerman, & Koops, 2003). When multiple aspects of social-cognitive processing are targeted simultaneously, enduring effects have been obtained in both intervention and prevention studies (e.g., Kam, Greenberg, & Kusche, 2004; Lochman & Wells, 2002).

As this chapter has illustrated, children's deviant social cognitions are shaped, maintained, and reinforced by their social experiences. This implies that intervention programs for children with DBD should not ignore those children's social context. Solely targeting children's social cognitions without considering their social context is like committing the fundamental attribution error: ascribing children's disruptive behavior to dispositional rather than contextual factors (Maruna & Mann, 2006). Interventions targeting children's context are, in fact, more effective in reducing disruptive behavior. A meta-analysis has found that disruptive problems were more effectively reduced by parent training ($d = .45$) than by cognitive-behavioral therapy alone ($d = .23$; McCart, Priester, Davies, & Azen, 2006).

Research Directions

This chapter has summarized present research on social cognition in children with DBD. Although much research has been conducted to show how deviant social cognitions may explain disruptive behavior, several issues remain open to future inquiry.

First, children with DBD are often considered as a single group having similar patterns of maladaptive social cognition. However, most studies find considerable differences in social cognition among children with DBD, suggesting that their disruptive behavior problems may stem from various individual profiles of deviant social-cognitive processing. With at least eleven variables in the online processing part of the model alone, there clearly is room for considerably more individual variation than just one or two patterns associated with reactive or proactive aggression. Future research into individualized social-cognitive processing profiles may contribute to a better understanding and treatment of individual disruptive behavior problems.

Second, for many deviant social-cognitive dispositions and capacities in children with DBD, it is not known whether they are causes or mere correlates of aggression. It would be interesting to complement current observational and longitudinal studies with more small-scale experimental investigations to increase our knowledge of causal mechanisms in the development of disruptive behavior disorders. If cleverly designed, such experiments may also help us find innovative ways to change the social cognitions related to disruptive behavior. Exciting developments in this direction include, for example, implicit attentional bias retraining (Penton-Voak et al., 2013).

Third, children's social-cognitive processing is affected by situation-specific factors such as the interaction partner's relationship with the child (e.g., friend or enemy) or the nature of the interaction (e.g., competitive or provocative; Matthys et al., 1999; Peets et al., 2007). These situational effects should not be overlooked, because they may explain why some children are more aggressive in the first place (i.e., as a result of more aversive environments), and may help identify child-specific triggers for disruptive behavior. For instance, one child may quickly aggress during competition, whereas another is triggered by being laughed at (Matthys et al., 2001).

Fourth, early childhood may be an especially important age period to study social cognition, as children's social-cognitive capacities are rapidly developing and relatively large differences exist among children, which may set them on a path of deviant development. For instance, children lagging behind in the development of theory of mind skills at an early age may be at risk for negative peer interactions and consequent cascades of disruptive behavior and deviant social-cognitive processing. A better understanding of such early development may also help us interpret whether children with specific social-cognitive profiles are merely somewhat delayed in their development or are developing in truly different ways.

Fifth, we have discussed the fact that socialization experiences shape children's database of social knowledge and impact on their social-cognitive processing. However, little is known of how this shaping process occurs. What kind of experiences are likely to have a large impact on children's knowledge structures? Are there certain developmental periods when children's databases are more sensitive to socialization, such as early childhood (parents) or puberty (peers)? Is repeated exposure needed for experiences to be stored in the database or is the emotional salience of the experience more important? Do differences between children exist in the extent to which past experiences impact future processing?

Last, social-cognitive processes are only one aspect of a complex neurocognitive system. Given the emotional nature of social-cognitive processing, physiological processes must clearly play important roles in, for example, steering attention, evoking emotional action tendencies, and generating responses. Understanding the interplay between the cognitive and physiological aspects of these processes is clearly in its infancy. Intriguing findings on, for example, heart-rate variability, cortisol, and localization of activity in the brain during social-cognitive processing suggest that much is to be gained by integrating these perspectives (Crozier et al., 2008; Herpertz et al., 2008; Snoek, Van Goozen, Matthys, Buitelaar, & Van Engeland, 2004).

Conclusion

This chapter has presented a model of social cognition that describes what might go on in the minds of children with DBD. This model may help us to be more understanding of these children when they engage in conflicts and to identify promising ways in for intervention, targeting specific cognitions and situational contingencies. Ultimately, increasing the understanding of the roles of social cognition in development may even help prevent social-cognitive problems that maintain disruptive behavior problems. We hope this chapter may inspire the reader to adopt the perspective of children with disruptive behavior problems in everyday interactions, treatment, and research.

References

American Psychiatric Association. (2013). *Diagnostic and statistical manual of mental disorders* (5th ed.). Arlington, VA: Author.
Anderson, C. A., & Bushman, B. J. (2002). Human aggression. *Annual Review of Psychology, 53*, 27–51.
Arsenio, W. F., & Fleiss, K. (1996). Typical and behaviourally disruptive children's understanding of the emotional consequences of socio-moral events. *British Journal of Developmental Psychology, 14*, 173–186.
Bandura, A., Barbaranelli, C., Caprara, G. V., & Pastorelli, C. (1996). Mechanisms of moral disengagement in the exercise of moral agency. *Journal of Personality and Social Psychology, 71*, 364–374.
Barriga, A. Q., & Gibbs, J. C. (1996). Measuring cognitive distortion in antisocial youth: Development and preliminary validation of the "How I Think" questionnaire. *Aggressive Behavior, 22*, 333–343.
Baumeister, R. (1997). *Evil. Inside human cruelty and violence*. New York, NY: Freeman.
Bowlby, J. (1980). *Attachment and loss* (Vol, III). *Loss*. New York, NY: Basic Books.
Bradshaw, C. P., & Hazan, C. (2006). Examining views of self in relation to views of others: Implications for research on aggression and self-esteem. *Journal of Research in Personality, 40*, 1209–1218.
Burks, V. S., Laird, R. D., Dodge, K. A., Pettit, G. S., & Bates, J. E. (1999). Knowledge structures, social information processing, and children's aggressive behavior. *Social Development, 8*, 220–236.
Bushman, B. J., DeWall, C. N., Pond, R. S., & Hanus, M. D. (2014). Low glucose relates to greater aggression in married couples. *Proceedings of the National Academy of Sciences, 111*, 6254–6257.
Butler, S. M., Parry, R., & Fearon, R. M. P. (2015). Antisocial thinking in adolescents: Further psychometric development of the Antisocial Beliefs and Attitudes Scale (ABAS). *Psychological Assessment, 27*, 291–301.
Calvete, E., & Orue, I. (2012). Social information processing as a mediator between cognitive schemas and aggressive behavior in adolescents. *Journal of Abnormal Child Psychology, 40*, 105–117.

Connor, D. F., Steingard, R. J., Cunningham, J. A., Anderson, J. J., & Melloni, R. H. (2004). Proactive and reactive aggression in referred children and adolescents. *American Journal of Orthopsychiatry, 74*, 129–136.

Crick, N. R., & Dodge, K. A. (1994). A review and reformulation of social information-processing mechanisms in children's social adjustment. *Psychological Bulletin, 115*, 74–101.

Crozier, J. C., Dodge, K. A., Fontaine, R. G., Lansford, J. E., Bates, J. E., Pettit, G. S., & Levenson, R. W. (2008). Social information processing and cardiac predictors of adolescent antisocial behavior. *Journal of Abnormal Psychology, 117*, 253–267.

David, C. F., & Kistner, J. A. (2000). Do positive self-perceptions have a "dark side"? Examination of the link between perceptual bias and aggression. *Journal of Abnormal Child Psychology, 28*, 327–337.

De Castro, B. O. (2004). The development of social information processing and aggressive behaviour: Current issues. *European Journal of Developmental Psychology, 1*, 87–102.

De Castro, B. O., Bosch, J. D., Veerman, J. W., & Koops, W. (2003). The effects of emotion regulation, attribution, and delay prompts on aggressive boys' social problem solving. *Cognitive Therapy and Research, 27*, 153–166.

De Castro, B. O., Merk, W., Koops, W., Veerman, J. W., & Bosch, J. D. (2005). Emotions in social information processing and their relations with reactive and proactive aggression in referred aggressive boys. *Journal of Clinical Child and Adolescent Psychology, 34*, 105–116.

De Castro, B. O., Slot, N. W., Bosch, J. D., Koops, W., & Veerman, J. W. (2003). Negative feelings exacerbate hostile attributions of intent in highly aggressive boys. *Journal of Clinical Child & Adolescent Psychology, 32*, 56–65.

De Castro, B. O., Veerman, J. W., Koops, W., Bosch, J. D., & Monshouwer, H. J. (2002). Hostile attribution of intent and aggressive behavior: A meta-analysis. *Child Development, 73*, 916–934.

De Castro, B. O., Verhulp, E. E., & Runions, K. (2012). Rage and revenge: Highly aggressive boys' explanations for their responses to ambiguous provocation. *European Journal of Developmental Psychology, 9*, 331–350.

Diamantopoulou, S., Rydell, A. M., & Henricsson, L. (2008). Can both low and high self-esteem be related to aggression in children? *Social Development, 17*, 682–698.

Dodge, K.A., & Frame, C.L. (1982). Social cognitive biases and deficits in aggressive boys. *Child Development, 53*, 620–635.

Dodge, K. A., Lochman, J. E., Harnish, J. D., Bates, J. E., & Pettit, G. S. (1997). Reactive and proactive aggression in school children and psychiatrically impaired chronically assaultive youth. *Journal of Abnormal Psychology, 106*, 37–51.

Dodge, K. A., Malone, P. S., Lansford, J. E., Sorbring, E., Skinner, A. T., Tapanya, S., . . . Pastorelli, C. (2015). Hostile attributional bias and aggressive behavior in global context. *Proceedings of the National Academy of Sciences, 112*, 9310–9315.

Dodge, K. A., McClaskey, C. L., & Feldman, E. (1985). Situational approach to the assessment of social competence in children. *Journal of Consulting and Clinical Psychology, 53*, 344–353.

Dodge, K. A., & Newman, J. P. (1981). Biased decision-making processes in aggressive boys. *Journal of Abnormal Psychology, 90*, 375–379.

Dodge, K. A., & Pettit, G. S. (2003). A biopsychosocial model of the development of chronic conduct problems in adolescence. *Developmental Psychology, 39*, 349–371.

Dodge, K. A., Price, J. M., Bachorowski, J. A., & Newman, J. P. (1990). Hostile attributional biases in severely aggressive adolescents. *Journal of Abnormal Psychology, 99*, 385–392.

Dodge, K. A., & Somberg, D. R. (1987). Hostile attributional biases among aggressive boys are exacerbated under conditions of threats to the self. *Child Development, 58*, 213–224.

Dodge, K. A., & Tomlin, A. M. (1987). Utilization of self-schemas as a mechanism of interpretational bias in aggressive children. *Social Cognition, 5*, 280–300.

Dunn, S. E., Lochman, J. E., & Colder, C. (1997). Social problem-solving skills in boys with conduct and oppositional defiant disorders. *Aggressive Behavior, 23*, 457–469.

Ellis, M. L., Weiss, B., & Lochman, J. E. (2009). Executive functions in children: Associations with aggressive behavior and social appraisal processing. *Journal of Abnormal Child Psychology, 37*, 945–956.

Fiske, S. T., & Taylor, S. E. (1984). *Social cognition*. Reading, MA: Addisson-Wesley.

Fontaine, R. G. (2008). On-line social decision making and antisocial behavior: Some essential but neglected issues. *Clinical Psychology Review, 28*, 17–35.

Fontaine, R. G., Burks, V. S., & Dodge, K. A. (2002). Response decision processes and externalizing behavior problems in adolescents. *Development and Psychopathology, 14*, 107–122.

Frankenhuis, W. E., & De Weerth, C. (2013). Does early-life exposure to stress shape or impair cognition? *Current Directions in Psychological Science, 22*, 407–412.

Frankenhuis, W. E., Panchanathan, K., & Nettle, D. (2016). Cognition in harsh and unpredictable environments. *Current Opinion in Psychology, 7*, 76–80.

Frijda, N. H. (1993). The place of appraisal in emotion. *Cognition and Emotion, 7*, 357–387.

Gini, G., Pozzoli, T., & Hymel, S. (2014). Moral disengagement among children and youth: A meta-analytic review of links to aggressive behavior. *Aggressive Behavior, 40*, 56–68.

Graham, S., & Hudley, C. (1994). Attributions of aggressive and nonagressive African-American male early adolescents: A study of construct accessibility. *Developmental Psychology, 30*, 365–373.

Granic, I. (2014). The role of anxiety in the development, maintenance, and treatment of childhood aggression. *Development and Psychopathology, 26*, 1515–1530.

Guerra, N. G., Huesmann, L. R., & Spindler, A. (2003). Community violence exposure, social cognition, and aggression among urban elementary school children. *Child Development, 74*, 1561–1576.

Happé, F., & Frith, U. (1996). Theory of mind and social impairment in children with conduct disorder. *British Journal of Developmental Psychology, 14*, 385–398.

Helmond, P., Overbeek, G., Brugman, D., & Gibbs, J. C. (2015). A meta-analysis on cognitive distortions and externalizing problem behavior: Associations, moderators, and treatment effectiveness. *Criminal Justice and Behavior, 42*, 245–262.

Herpertz, S. C., Huebner, T., Marx, I., Vloet, T. D., Fink, G. R., Stoecker, T., . . . Herpertz-Dahlmann, B. (2008). Emotional processing in male adolescents with childhood-onset conduct disorder. *Journal of Child Psychology and Psychiatry, 49*, 781–791.

Horsley, T., de Castro, B., & Van der Schoot, M. (2010). In the eye of the beholder: Eye-tracking assessment of social information processing in aggressive behavior. *Journal of Abnormal Child Psychology, 38*, 587–599.

Hudley, C., & Graham, S. (1993). An attributional intervention to reduce peer-directed aggression among African-American boys. *Child Development, 64*, 124–138.

Huesmann, L. R. (1988). An information processing model for the development of aggression. *Aggressive Behavior, 14*, 13–24.

Huesmann, L. R., & Guerra, N. G. (1997). Children's normative beliefs about aggression and aggressive behavior. *Journal of Personality and Social Psychology, 72*, 408–419.

Huesmann, L. R., Eron, L. D., & Yarmel, P. W. (1987). Intellectual functioning and aggression. *Journal of Personality and Social Psychology, 52*, 232–240.

Hyde, L. W., Shaw, D. S., & Moilanen, K. L. (2010). Developmental precursors of moral disengagement and the role of moral disengagement in the development of antisocial behavior. *Journal of Abnormal Child Psychology, 38*, 197–209.

Kam, C. M., Greenberg, M. T., & Kusche, C. A. (2004). Sustained effects of the PATHS curriculum on the social and psychological adjustment of children in special education. *Journal of Emotional and Behavioral Disorders, 12*, 66–78.

Kempes, M. M., de Castro, B. O., & Sterck, E. H. M. (2008). Conflict management in 6-8-year-old aggressive Dutch boys: Do they reconcile? *Behaviour, 145*, 1701–1722.

Kernis, M. H. (2005). Measuring self-esteem in context: The importance of stability of self-esteem in psychological functioning. *Journal of Personality, 73*, 1569–1605.

Kirsh, S. J., & Mounts, J. R. W. (2007). Violent video game play impacts facial emotion recognition. *Aggressive Behavior, 33*, 353–358.

Lansford, J. E., Malone, P. S., Dodge, K. A., Pettit, G. S., & Bates, J. E. (2010). Developmental cascades of peer rejection, social information processing biases, and aggression during middle childhood. *Development and Psychopathology, 22*, 593–602.

Lemerise, E. A., & Arsenio, W. F. (2000). An integrated model of emotion processes and cognition in social information processing. *Child Development, 71*, 107–118.

Lochman, J. E., & Dodge, K. A. (1994). Social-cognitive processes of severely violent, moderately aggressive and nonaggressive boys. *Journal of Consulting and Clinical Psychology, 62,* 366–374.

Lochman, J. E., & Dodge, K. (1998). Distorted perceptions in dyadic interactions of aggressive and nonaggressive boys: Effects of prior expectations, context, and boys' age. *Development and Psychopathology, 10,* 495–512.

Lochman, J. E., & Wells, K. C. (2002). Contextual social-cognitive mediators and child outcome: A test of the theoretical model in the Coping Power program. *Development and Psychopathology, 14,* 945–967.

Lovett, B. J., & Sheffield, R. A. (2007). Affective empathy deficits in aggressive children and adolescents: A critical review. *Clinical Psychology Review, 27,* 1–13.

Malti, T., & Krettenauer, T. (2013). The relation of moral emotion attributions to prosocial and antisocial behavior: A meta-analysis. *Child Development, 84,* 397–412.

Martins, N. (2013). Televised relational and physical aggression and children's hostile intent attributions. *Journal of Experimental Child Psychology, 116,* 945–952.

Maruna, S., & Mann, R. E. (2006). A fundamental attribution error? Rethinking cognitive distortions. *Legal and Criminological Psychology, 11,* 155–177.

Matthys, W., Cuperus, J. M., & Van Engeland, H. (1999). Deficient social problem-solving in boys with ODD/CD, with ADHD, and with both disorders. *Journal of the American Academy of Child & Adolescent Psychiatry, 38,* 311–321.

Matthys, W., Maassen, G. H., Cuperus, J. M., & Van Engeland, H. (2001). The assessment of the situational specificity of children's problem behaviour in peer–peer context. *Psychiatry: Interpersonal and Biological Processes, 42,* 413–420.

McCart, M. R., Priester, P. E., Davies, W. H., & Azen, R. (2006). Differential effectiveness of behavioral parent-training and cognitive-behavioral therapy for antisocial youth: A meta-analysis. *Journal of Abnormal Child Psychology, 34,* 527–543.

McDonald, K. L., & Lochman, J. E. (2012). Predictors and outcomes associated with trajectories of revenge goals from fourth grade through seventh grade. *Journal of Abnormal Child Psychology, 40,* 225–236.

Miller, P. A, & Eisenberg, N. (1988). The relation of empathy to aggressive and externalizing/antisocial behavior. *Psychological Bulletin, 103,* 324–344.

Muris, P. (2006). Maladaptive schemas in non-clinical adolescents: Relations to perceived parental rearing behaviours, big five personality factors and psychopathological symptoms. *Clinical Psychology and Psychotherapy, 13,* 405–413.

Ojanen, T., Gronroos, M., & Salmivalli, C. (2005). An interpersonal circumplex model of children's social goals: Links with peer-reported behavior and sociometric status. *Developmental Psychology, 41,* 699–710.

Pardini, D. A., Lochman, J. E., & Frick, P. J. (2003). Callous/unemotional traits and social cognitive processes in adjudicated youth. *Journal of the American Academy of Child and Adolescent Psychiatry, 42,* 364–371.

Peets, K., Hodges, E. V. E., Kikas, E., & Salmivalli, C. (2007). Hostile attributions and behavioral strategies in children: Does relationship type matter? *Developmental Psychology, 43,* 889–900.

Penton-Voak, I. S., Thomas, J., Gage, S. H., McMurran, M., McDonald, S., & Munafò, M. R. (2013). Increasing recognition of happiness in ambiguous facial expressions reduces anger and aggressive behavior. *Psychological Science, 24,* 688–697.

Renouf, A. G., Kovacs, M., & Mukerji, P. (1997). Relationship of depressive, conduct, and comorbid disorders and social functioning in childhood. *Journal of the American Academy of Child & Adolescent Psychiatry, 36,* 998–1004.

Rutter, M., & Sroufe, L. A. (2000). Developmental psychopathology: Concepts and challenges. *Development and Psychopathology, 12,* 265-296.

Salmivalli, C. (2001). Feeling good about oneself, being bad to others? Remarks on self-esteem, hostility, and aggressive behavior. *Aggression and Violent Behavior, 6,* 375–393.

Salmivalli, C., Ojanen, T., Haanpää, J., & Peets, K. (2005). "I'm OK but you're not" and other peer-relational schemas: Explaining individual differences in children's social goals. *Developmental Psychology, 41,* 363–375.

Schniering, C. A., & Rapee, R. M. (2004). The relationship between automatic thoughts and negative emotions in children and adolescents: A test of the cognitive content-specificity hypothesis. *Journal of Abnormal Psychology, 113,* 464–70.

Schuiringa, H., Van Nieuwenhuijzen, M., De Castro, B. O., & Matthys, W. (2016). Executive functions and processing speed in children with mild to borderline intellectual disabilities and externalizing behavior problems. *Child Neuropsychology, 23*(4), 442–462. doi:0.1080/09297049.2015.1135421

Snoek, H., Van Goozen, S. H., Matthys, W., Buitelaar, J. K., & Van Engeland, H. (2004). Stress responsivity in children with externalizing behavior disorders. *Development and Psychopathology, 16,* 389–406.

Stams, G. J., Brugman, D., Deković, M., Van Rosmalen, L., Van der Laan, P., & Gibbs, J. C. (2006). The moral judgment of juvenile delinquents: A meta-analysis. *Journal of Abnormal Child Psychology, 34,* 697–713.

Sykes, G. M., & Matza, D. (1957). Techniques of neutralization: A theory of delinquency. *American Sociological Review, 22,* 664–670.

Thomaes, S., Bushman, B. J., Stegge, H., & Olthof, T. (2008). Trumping shame by blasts of noise: Narcissism, self-esteem, shame, and aggression in young adolescents. *Child Development, 79,* 1792–1801.

Troop-Gordon, W., & Ladd, G. W. (2005). Trajectories of peer victimization and perceptions of the self and schoolmates: Precursors to internalizing and externalizing problems. *Child Development, 76,* 1072–1091.

Troop-Gordon, W., Gordon, R. D., Vogel-Ciernia, L., Ewing Lee, E., & Visconti, K. J. (2016). Visual attention to dynamic scenes of ambiguous provocation and children's aggressive behavior. *Journal of Clinical Child & Adolescent Psychology.* doi:10.1080/15374416.2016.1138412

Vachon, D. D., Lynam, D. R., & Johnson, J. A. (2014). The (non)relation between empathy and aggression: Surprising results from a meta-analysis. *Psychological Bulletin, 140,* 751–773.

Van Goozen, S. H. M., Cohen-Kettenis, P. T., Matthys, W., & Van Engeland, H. (2002). Preference for aggressive and sexual stimuli in children with disruptive behavior disorder and normal controls. *Archives of Sexual Behavior, 31,* 247–253.

Van Nieuwenhuijzen, M., Van Rest, M. M., Embregts, P. J. C. M., Vriens, A., Oostermeijer, S., Van Bokhoven, I., & Matthys, W. (2017). Executive functions and social information processing in adolescents with severe behavior problems. *Child Neuropsychology, 23*(2), 228–241.

Waldman, I. D. (1996). Aggressive boys' hostile perceptual and response biases: The role of attention and impulsivity. *Child Development, 67,* 1015–1033.

Webster-Stratton, C., & Woolley Lindsay, D. (1999). Social competence and conduct problems in young children: Issues in assessment. *Journal of Clinical Child Psychology, 28,* 25–43.

Weiss, B., Dodge, K. A., Bates, J. E., & Pettit, G. S. (1992). Some consequences of early harsh discipline: Child aggression and a maladaptive social information processing style. *Child Development, 63,* 1321–1335.

Yaghoub Zadeh, Z., Im-Bolter, N., & Cohen, N. J. (2007). Social cognition and externalizing psychopathology: An investigation of the mediating role of language. *Journal of Abnormal Child Psychology, 35,* 141–152.

Yaros, A., Lochman, J. E., Rosenbaum, J., & Jimenez-Camargo, L. A. (2014). Real-time hostile attribution measurement and aggression in children. *Aggressive Behavior, 40,* 409–420.

Zelli, A., Dodge, K. A., Lochman, J. E., Laird, R. D., & Conduct Problems Prevention Research Group. (1999). The distinction between beliefs legitimizing aggression and deviant processing of social cues: Testing measurement validity and the hypothesis that biased processing mediates the effects of beliefs on aggression. *Journal of Personality and Social Psychology, 77,* 150–166.

Etiological and Maintenance Factors

Family Factors

16

Family Poverty and Structure

Barbara Maughan, Richard Rowe, and Joseph Murray

Family poverty and family structure are among the best established socio-demographic correlates of child and adolescent antisocial behavior. On average, children growing up in poverty, or who face instability in their family lives, are more likely to show disruptive behavior disorders (DBDs), to score highly on dimensional ratings of aggression and rule-breaking, and to be involved in delinquency than their peers in more stable and affluent families. The broad pattern of these associations is long established, but important research and policy questions still remain. First, investigators have recognized the need to move beyond patterns of association to test for causal influences. Many family-level risks covary with other factors—including, for example, parents' age and educational levels, but also aspects of their personality and parenting, and even of their genetic make-up—that may impact child behavior in other ways, confounding associations and leading to potentially spurious conclusions. And second, where causal influences are identified, we need to know more about the more proximal processes that contribute to these effects. Does poverty, for example, impact children's development directly, or do effects primarily run through impacts on parents, or parenting, or the wider family system? Do mediating mechanisms vary with development or between demographic subgroups? Answering these questions is also crucial if research is to provide useful guidance to policy and clinical practice.

This chapter provides an overview of recent evidence on these themes. Focusing on family poverty and family structure in turn, we begin by outlining cross-sectional findings on links with child behavior problems, and the extent to which such associations are consistent across child age and gender, and in key population subgroups. We then turn to studies that have set out to test causal hypotheses. Finally we explore the range of more proximal processes—from impacts on brain development to aspects of parenting and peer influence—that may mediate the associations observed.

While we focus on DBDs, we also draw on informative data from studies using dimensional measures of disruptive behavior problems and delinquency. Much current evidence comes from North America and, to a lesser extent, Europe. But risk factors for DBDs are a global concern. Increasingly, relevant research is also being carried out in low and middle income countries (LMICs), where the majority of the world's children live. We have capitalized on a recent systematic review of risk factors for youth conduct problems in LMICs (see Shenderovich et al., 2016) to set alongside evidence from high-income countries.

Interpreting the Evidence

We begin by considering some general issues that arise in evaluating evidence on links between DBDs and family-level variables. At base, these stem from the fact that child behavior problems are multifactorially determined: family poverty and structure are just two strands in the complex nexus of individual and "contextual" risks implicated in the etiology and maintenance of DBDs. Because risk factors often co-occur, teasing out the specific contributions of any individual risks inevitably presents challenges.

Findings from both high-income countries and LMICs have consistently confirmed strong overlaps between family poverty and aspects of family structure and stability. Two sets of recent findings, one from the US and one from the UK, illustrate these trends. In the US Fragile Families and Child Wellbeing Study just over half of single parents (53%) were living in poverty at the time of their child's birth, by contrast with 14% of married parents and 33% of unmarried cohabiting couples (Kalil & Ryan, 2010). In the UK Millennium Cohort Study, 63% of single-parent families were classified as poor at the age 7 follow-up, by contrast with 18% of married parents and 35% of those in reconstituted families (Pearce, Lewis, & Law, 2013). Despite differences in the metrics used to assess poverty, the picture painted by these two studies is clear: in both societies, children in single-parent households were markedly more likely to experience poverty than their counterparts living with married parents, while those in cohabiting or reconstituted families fell between these two extremes.

In highlighting the strong overlap between these two potential sources of risk, these findings also hint at the challenges involved in unraveling their individual effects. In practice, of course, the full picture is yet more complex. Many other risk factors for DBDs also covary with family-level indicators (Evans & Kim, 2010): parental age and education are among the most widely reported, but similar effects are found for factors as varied as exposure to maternal smoking and stress in pregnancy, parental psychopathology, family atmosphere, neighborhood disadvantage, and affiliation with deviant peers. Any or all of these may confound associations between family-level variables and child outcomes; because antisocial behavior is moderately heritable, genetic influences may also play some part.

In the past, investigators typically approached these challenges by including indicators of other known risk factors as covariates in regression models. While this goes some way to identifying the independent contribution of specific risks, it is far from a satisfactory solution. In particular, it fails to account for unmeasured confounders (including, but not limited to, genetic confounding) that may contribute to both predictors and child outcomes; it also fails to deal with possible reciprocal effects of child behavior on family-level variables. Over time, a variety of new statistical models and research designs have been developed to overcome these difficulties and strengthen causal inferences.

Jaffee, Strait, and Odgers (2012), and McLanahan, Tach, and Schneider (2013) discuss these new approaches in detail. Most depend on repeated measures of child behaviors and/or postulated risks. Where the risk factor of interest is an "event"—family breakdown, for example, or the arrival of a new parent in the family—repeated measurements make it possible to take account of the child's behavior *before* the event (lagged dependent variable models), or (with a more extended series of behavioral indicators) to use growth curves to estimate patterns of change in behavior problems. More powerful for assessing causality are *fixed-effects models*, that remove all time-constant differences among children, leaving only within-child variation on the outcomes of interest as an indicator of the effects of the selected risk. This approach can be extended to sibling fixed-effects models, where, for example, outcomes for siblings experiencing an event at different ages can be compared, with unmeasured family-level variables removed from the estimation. Finally, *propensity score matching* can be used to approximate some of the strengths of experimental designs in observational studies. Here, investigators match participants on their propensity to experience the exposure of interest, then construct "treatment" and "control" groups matched as closely as possible on this propensity, but differing in exposure to the postulated risk.

Each of these approaches moves closer to identifying causal effects of risk exposures, though each also has limitations (see Jaffee et al., 2012 and McLanahan et al., 2013 for discussions). For strong tests of causality, randomized controlled trials constitute the gold standard. In the main, these are neither ethical nor feasible in studies of family-level variables, though experimental programs have evaluated effects of income supplementation. Even in the absence of formal experiments, however, many of the advantages of experimental designs can be achieved by capitalizing on *natural experiments*. In some instances, serendipitous events (such as sudden changes in economic conditions) can provide valuable insights of this kind. In others, investigators have sought out informative contrasts (such as, for example, between father absence following divorce and following death). In yet others, they have employed genetically informative designs to take account of genetic confounding. For example, studies have compared the impact of divorce on children in adoptive families (where there is no genetic link between parents and children) and natural-parent families, and used children-of-twins designs (McAdams et al., 2014) to estimate the effects of divorce net of the effects of both genetic and other familial confounding.

As this brief overview suggests, although there are numerous challenges in interpreting evidence on the impact of family-level risks, innovative approaches are increasingly being used to strengthen causal inference. With these possibilities in mind, we next consider the evidence on links with child behavior problems, beginning with poverty.

Family Poverty

The Social Gradient in Disruptive Disorders and Antisocial Behavior

A large number of studies have examined the relationship between family economic background and antisocial behavior in offspring (Piotrowska, Stride, Croft, & Rowe, 2015). Some focus solely on income poverty, while others use related indicators of low socio-economic status (SES); we draw on findings using this broader range of indicators here. Many studies find that poverty is associated with conduct disorder (CD), oppositional defiant disorder (ODD) and antisocial behavior measured in many other ways. As has been documented with a range of health variables, social inequalities in child antisocial behavior are not confined to those in the direst economic circumstances, but are evident across the range, albeit to different degrees. For example, analysis of the large-scale British Child and Adolescent Mental Health Survey (BCAMHS) found an S-shaped relationship, as shown in Figure 16.1 (Piotrowska, Stride, Maughan et al., 2015). The gradient was steepest across the mid-income range and shallower at the higher and lower ends for both CD and ODD, with no difference in the shape of the gradient between the two disorders. The shape of the gradient remained the same after controls for a range of other factors, including number of children in the household, family composition, parental employment and parental education. In these adjusted analyses, children in the second income quintile were estimated to be 26% less likely to meet diagnostic criteria for CD/ODD than those in the lowest quintile; differences were even more marked (at 51% differences in risk) for contrasts between children in different quintiles in the middle of the income range.

Results across studies are not all consistent, however. A cohort study of children born in 1993 in Pelotas, Brazil, for example, found that low family income at birth was associated with child conduct problems at age 11 years for both boys and girls (Murray et al., 2015), but other studies in LMICs have not found a significant relationship. For example, in Puerto Rico, family welfare receipt among 5–13-year-old children did not predict delinquency over the next two years (Maldonado-Molina, Piquero, Jennings, Bird, & Canino, 2009). A recent meta-analysis of studies conducted worldwide identified 133 studies (the great majority in high-income countries) published between 1960 and 2012 that provided 139 independent

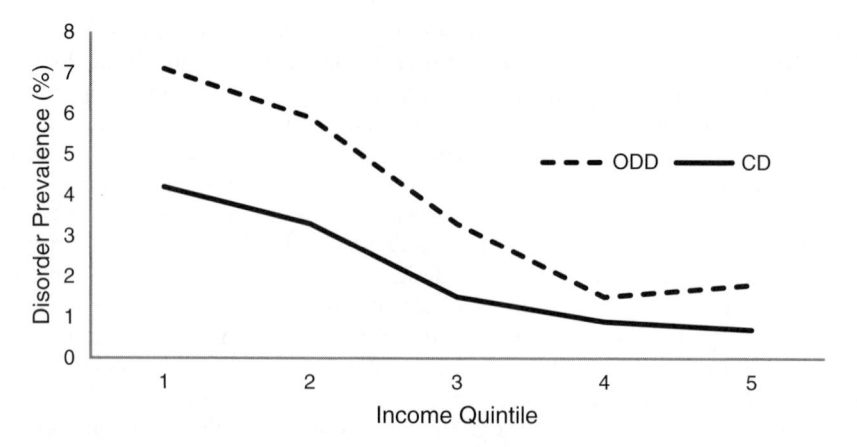

Figure 16.1 The Social Gradient in DSM-IV for CD and ODD The gradient for CD is shown by the solid line and for ODD by the broken line across 5 family income quintiles (1 = lowest income and 5 = highest) in the British Child and Adolescent Mental Health Survey, 2004 sweep, including nearly 8000 observations of children aged 5–16 years.

estimates of the relationship between SES and child antisocial outcomes, based on 339,868 individual observations (Piotrowska, Stride, Croft, & Rowe, 2015). A mean weighted effect size of –.10 (95% confidence intervals –.08 to –.12) was found.

Does Family Poverty Cause Antisocial Behavior in Offspring?

Many theories of antisocial development have assumed that poverty causes antisocial behavior. As discussed above, however, many other causal pathways could give rise to these cross-sectional associations. Family poverty may indeed lead to antisocial behavior in children, but it is also possible that antisocial children have a deleterious effect on family income, or that other correlated factors confound the association.

From a policy perspective, a key question is whether income has *any* causal effect on antisocial behavior, rather than whether this pathway explains the totality of the association. Jaffee et al. (2012, p. 285) reviewed studies using causally informative designs, and concluded that the "data from a variety of quasi-experimental designs converge in a identifying a causal role for family income in children's antisocial behavior." The evidence reviewed included the Minnesota Family Investment Partnership Study, which documented lower levels of child externalizing behaviors in families randomized to receive enhanced welfare benefit (Gennetian & Miller, 2002). Also included were findings from the Great Smoky Mountains Study, which incorporated a natural experimental reduction in poverty for a proportion of the sample. Income on an American Indian reservation was raised following the construction of a casino, with the profits distributed widely across families on the reservation. This led to long-lasting improvements in antisocial behavior (Costello, Erkanli, Copeland, & Angold, 2010). Other reviewed studies included comparisons of family members differentially exposed to poverty in the Children of the National Longitudinal Survey of Youth study. Two reports from these data concluded that differential income exposure between family members was related to the differences in their levels of conduct problems (D'Onofrio et al., 2009; Hao & Matsueda, 2006).

Since Jaffee et al.'s (2012) review, further studies have been published using variations in family financial situation across time to predict changes in child behavior. In the Pittsburgh Youth Study of boys aged 8–17 years, for example, it was found that delinquency was related to changes in family SES (Rekker et al., 2015). All the evidence considered so far has come from North American samples. While we are not aware of any causality tests in LMICs, the final two studies to be discussed come from Northern Europe, where income inequalities are less marked, and a smaller percentage of children grow up in poverty. Zachrisson and Dearing (2015) used the Norwegian Mother and Child Cohort Study (N>75000) to show that within-family variations in income-to-needs ratio were related to changes in externalizing behaviors in young children (between ages 18 and 36 months), with the effects stronger amongst lower rather than higher income families. In a Swedish total population study (N>526,000) of adolescents (15–21 years), Sariaslan, Larsson, D'Onofrio, Langstrom, and Lichtenstein (2014) reported a simple negative association between family income and violent criminality. However, once unobserved familial risk was taken into account by sibling comparison, no association with family income remained. It is unclear at this stage why this study came to a different conclusion on causality from those discussed above. The study is distinguished by a focus on a relatively rare outcome—officially recorded violent crime in adolescents and young adults—when the majority of the other studies have focused on less serious behavior problems in younger age groups. Further work will be needed to replicate this result. At this stage, however, the majority of evidence remains consistent with Jaffee et al.'s (2012) conclusion that poverty has a causal effect on antisocial behavior.

The findings summarized above highlight the possibility that the strength of the SES/antisocial behavior relationship may vary by type of antisocial outcome. This was addressed in Piotrowska, Stride, Croft, and Rowe's (2015) meta-analysis. Measures of child behavior problems were classified into those focusing on aggression, nonphysical aggression, mixed constructs, and callous-unemotional traits. The analysis found a somewhat complex pattern of results, where aggression and nonphysical aggression showed similar, small associations with SES (both rs approximately –.06) and the mixed construct showed a stronger relationship (r = –.12). Callous unemotional traits showed the strongest relationship (r = –.23), although this estimate was based on only five effect sizes, so should be treated with some caution. Grouping the measures of behavior problems used in different studies is challenging, and the authors noted marked within-category heterogeneity of effect sizes for both aggressive and nonaggressive behaviors. Interpretation was also complicated by the fact that "mixed" antisocial constructs were reported more commonly in younger samples, when, as discussed below, the meta-analysis also found stronger links between antisocial behavior and low SES at younger ages.

To examine how effects of poverty may vary across different forms of antisocial behavior, much closer control over potential confounds is offered by within-study comparisons. Piotrowska, Stride, Maughan et al. (2015) took this approach in their BCAMHS analyses. This study examined social gradients in both diagnostic and dimensional measures of antisocial behavior. Confirmatory factor analysis supported a configuration of aggressive CD symptoms, nonphysically aggressive CD symptoms, dimensions within ODD representing irritability, headstrongness, and hurtfulness and a separate factor of callous and unemotional traits. All of these traits showed an equivalent social gradient across income quintiles, with a shape similar to that shown for CD and ODD in Figure 16.1. Further studies of this sort will be required to provide a definitive evidence base on whether social gradients do indeed differ across different forms of antisocial behavior.

Factors That Moderate the SES/Antisocial Behavior Relationship

The Piotrowska, Stride, Croft, and Rowe (2015) meta-analysis also examined other potential moderators of the SES/child antisocial behavior relationship. There was no evidence that the strength of the association varied as a function of children's sex but, as noted above, there was variation by age. The relationship with child behavior problems was strongest in preschool children (r = −.13) and declined in childhood (r = −.11) and again adolescence (r = −.07). Once again, however, comparisons across studies were complicated by methodological issues. In addition to age variations in the types of antisocial behavior being assessed, age was also correlated with reporter: self-reports of antisocial outcomes were more likely in older samples. This was important because child behavior problems were more strongly linked to SES when they were rated by teachers and parents (both rs = −.14) than by self-report (r = −.05). In a meta-regression testing the effect of both of these moderators, reporter effects remained significant, but age differences did not. One potential mechanism for these effects could be that parents and teachers expect more antisocial behavior in young people they perceive to be from low SES backgrounds.

Although not currently studied with sufficient frequency to test in meta-analyses, there is growing evidence that other factors may also moderate the relationship between family SES and offspring antisocial behavior. Analyses of the UK Millennium Cohort Study found that links between low family SES and child behavior problems were weaker for children high in self-regulation (Flouri, Midouhas, & Joshi, 2014) and intelligence (Flouri, Midouhas, & Joshi, 2015). In a smaller study, the effects of low family SES on externalizing behavior at age 5 varied according to mother–child communication at age 8 months. The effects of low SES were mitigated when mothers' communications showed greater sensitivity to their babies' internal states (Meins, Centifanti, Fernyhough, & Fishburn, 2013).

Neighborhood characteristics may also moderate links between family SES and child antisocial behavior. In terms of moderation, more advantaged neighborhoods could mitigate the effects of low family SES by providing access to better quality schooling or other positive experiences. Alternatively, children from low SES families may fare less well in high SES neighborhoods because the close proximity of advantaged peers may highlight their relative disadvantage. Some evidence suggests the latter model may apply to boys but not girls; boys from low SES backgrounds have been found to be more antisocial if they live in more advantaged neighborhoods than if they live in areas where others face similar financial hardships (Kling, Ludwig, & Katz, 2005; Odgers, Donley, Caspi, Bates, & Moffitt, 2015).

How Might Family Poverty Lead to Antisocial Behavior in Children?

The evidence discussed so far indicates that family poverty is implicated in risk for antisocial behavior, albeit with an effect size that may be moderated by a number of factors. It is likely that SES is a relatively distal factor that increases antisocial behavior via intermediate variables. For example, low SES may contribute to more proximal risks such as marital discord or family break-up that, in turn, lead to antisocial behavior. As well as having theoretical importance, this issue has policy relevance. If mediating variables can be identified, then targeting these through interventions may offer a useful addition to policies that aim to reduce poverty and social inequality directly.

At an extremely proximal level, recent evidence suggests that poverty may impact brain structure and functioning. A number of studies have found associations between poverty and brain structure in children and adolescents (Johnson, Riis, & Noble, 2016). For example, Noble and colleagues (2015) reported that income was positively associated with brain surface area among 3 to 20-year-olds (N >1000). The relationship was nonlinear, such that each dollar had a greater impact on brain surface at lower levels of income than at higher levels. Brain structures of particular relevance to antisocial behavior include the amygdala (Jones, Laurens, Herba, Barker, & Viding, 2009), involved in processing emotions, and the prefrontal cortex (Raine, 2002), that has been linked to executive functioning. There is evidence that poverty is related to functional disruption in both of these structures (Johnson et al., 2016). For example, Kim and colleagues (2013) found reduced prefrontal cortex activity, and failure to regulate amygdala function during processing of negative emotions in young adults who had been exposed to poverty in childhood. While much is still to be learned about these associations, these emerging findings suggest a neural basis for the observed association between family SES and child antisocial behavior.

Effects on brain structure, and potentially on aspects of brain function, are likely to be proximal mediators in the causal chain(s) linking SES and child antisocial behavior. The identification of mechanisms whereby low SES affects brain structure and function remains a key goal. These are likely to vary across development, with some effects beginning in the prenatal period. Prenatal exposures that may be influenced by low SES and predispose to the development of antisocial behavior include maternal stress (O'Donnell, Glover, Barker, & O'Connor, 2014), poor diet (Marques, O'Connor, Roth, Susser, & Bjorke-Monsen, 2013), and smoking in pregnancy (Gaysina et al., 2013). Similar perinatal risk factors for conduct problems have been identified in developed (UK) and LMIC (Brazil) countries (Murray et al., 2015), and are related to SES in both the former (Ewart & Suchday, 2002) and the latter (Lovisi, López, Coutinho, & Patel, 2005).

During childhood, close interaction with parents makes it likely that the effects of low SES are transmitted at least in part via parental behaviors. In contrast to the limited research on the mediational role of perinatal risks, numerous studies have investigated the role of family functioning (see Shaw & Shelleby, 2014, and Chapter 19 of this book). Economic hardship is hypothesized to impact family functioning, which in turn increases risk for antisocial behavior in children, for example via reductions in parental monitoring of children's activities and lower levels of maternal warmth. A potential route via family stress has been well articulated (Conger & Donnellan, 2007; Shaw & Shelleby, 2014). It is also possible, however, that parenting is to some extent a response to the behavior of the child as well as an antecedent of it (Kerr, Stattin, & Burk, 2010). In part, then, child behavior problems may mediate the effect of poverty on parental behaviors, as well as the reverse.

Conger and Donnellan (2007) discuss a second route through which SES may influence child behavior, via family investment. This model hypothesizes that higher SES families will be better placed to provide resources ranging from food and housing to parent–child contact time and educational opportunities to support children's health and well-being. Although this path has been studied more often in terms of cognitive development (Gershoff, Aber, Raver, & Lennon, 2007), there is evidence that it may also be relevant to behavioral difficulties (Linver, Brooks-Gunn, & Kohen, 2002).

In adolescence the peer context grows in importance, and may be implicated in transmitting the effects of family SES at this stage. Peer dominance hierarchies are ubiquitous across species, with subordinates more vulnerable to a range of physical and mental challenges (Sapolsky, 2004). There is substantial evidence of human peer hierarchies, and social position may reflect perceived family SES (Goodman, Huang, Schafer-Kalkhoff, & Adler, 2007) among other factors. Social status in adolescence may be most strongly determined by popularity, academic ability and sporting prowess rather than family SES (Sweeting & Hunt, 2014). These measures better predict smoking and drinking alcohol (both correlates of antisocial behavior) than traditional SES (Sweeting & Hunt, 2015).

Finally, broader social influences may also be involved in mediating effects of family SES on child behavioral outcomes. Shaw and Shellby (2014) discuss a cultural transmission route, whereby, for example, the cultural norms of low SES families might value aggression more highly (Dodge, Pettit, & Bates, 1994). Sociocultural influences on delinquency risk may also, however, arise in high SES groups. Findings from the Dunedin Multidisciplinary Health and Development Study suggested that the effects of SES may be heterogeneous, with some aspects of high SES backgrounds working to reduce levels of antisocial behavior while others function to increase it (Wright, Caspi, Moffitt, Miech, & Silva, 1999). In particular, the authors identified a taste for risk-taking, social power, and low perceived risk of detection as mediators of the effect of higher SES on delinquency in their sample.

In practice, of course, these differing types of mediation are by no means mutually exclusive: many poor children will be exposed to multiple risk processes and to consequences of family poverty that cumulate across development. Charting these more complex risk processes constitutes a key challenge for empirical research.

Family Structure

Variations in family structure have also long been explored as correlates of, and potential risk factors for, antisocial behavior in young people. Links between "broken homes" and delinquency were noted as early as the 1920s (Wells & Rankin, 1991), and since that time numerous studies have examined the extent to which family disruption and "nontraditional" family forms[1] are associated with variations in rates of child behavior problems. These issues have become more complex—and arguably more pressing—in the wake of the major changes in patterns of family formation and stability taking place in many Western societies in recent decades (see, e.g., Furstenberg, 2014; Thomson, 2014). Families are now formed later, and are smaller, than in the past; in addition, fewer parents marry, and more separate or divorce, meaning that many children face transitions and complexity in their family lives. Parental separation is typically followed by periods in single-parent households, and then by the establishment of new families that may include half- and step-siblings as well as step-parents. And finally—though less widely represented in the research literature to date—small but increasing numbers of children are growing up in families with same-sex parents.

These changes mean that assessing the impact of "family structure" on contemporary child outcomes has become more complex. On the one hand, the range of family forms is markedly more diverse; on the other, there is growing recognition that while family instability often challenges children's development, different *types* of family transition may differ markedly in their effects. Variations between countries and racial/ethnic groups add further to the mix. As Lundberg and Pollack (2015) note, by comparison with other wealthy countries, the US is something of an outlier on many dimensions of family dynamics: the proportion of children born outside any union in the US is relatively high, patterns of cohabitation differ, and the stability of both marriages and cohabitations is relatively low. To illustrate just one of these variations, Figure 16.2 shows rates of first marriages among unmarried women in the US, Japan, England and Wales, and Sweden between 1970 and the early years of the 21st century.

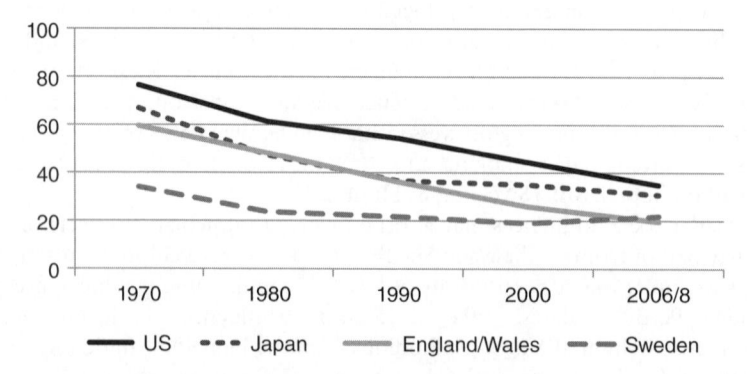

Figure 16.2 Number of marriages per 1000 unmarried women, 1970–2006/8: United States, Japan, England and Wales, and Sweden. Adapted from Lee & Payne, 2010.

---

[1] A generic term used in the literature on family structure to encompass single-parent and step-families, nonmarital cohabitation between parents, families with same-sex parents, and other family forms.

While marriage rates have converged between these countries over time, the proportion of the population that ever marries remains higher in the US than in northern Europe, while in Europe, cohabitation has progressed much further in the direction of becoming a replacement for marriage. As a result, many children in cohabiting couple families in Europe grow up with both biological parents, whereas in the US the most common pattern is still for cohabiting unions to involve one biological and one step-parent (Manning, 2015). All of these variations (along with international differences in family-related welfare provisions) need to be borne in mind in considering evidence on child outcomes.

Cross-Sectional Associations

Cross-sectional associations between variations in family structure/stability and child outcomes have been identified on many indicators of behavior problems. Beginning with diagnostic measures, epidemiologic studies in a range of Western societies provide evidence of elevated rates of CD and/or ODD among children in nontraditional family settings or who have experienced family disruption. These links are evident in preschoolers (see, e.g., Wichstrøm et al., 2012: Norway), in middle and late childhood (see, e.g., Ford, Goodman, & Meltzer, 2004: UK), and in adolescence (see, e.g., Farbstein et al., 2010: Israel). In the US National Comorbidity Survey—Adolescent Supplement, parental divorce or separation was associated with an increased risk of behavioral disorders (including CD, ODD, and ADHD) in 13–18 year-olds (Merikangas et al., 2010), and this association persisted in multivariate analyses controlled for race, urbanicity, parental education, and poverty (OR = 1.6, CI = 1.1–2.2). Evidence from non-Western countries is limited at this stage, but a recent large-scale study of 6–17-year-olds in northeast China found an elevated risk of externalizing disorders among children whose parents were single or divorced (Xiaoli et al., 2014).

The largest body of evidence on more specific aspects of family structure and stability comes from studies of parental divorce. Amato and Keith (1991) undertook the first meta-analysis of evidence in this area, bringing together findings on associations between divorce and child well-being published between the 1950s and 1980s. Divorce was associated with some decrements in children's functioning across a range of outcomes; estimated effect sizes were generally weak, however, and considerable heterogeneity was noted throughout, with more modest effects reported in methodologically stronger studies. Associations with conduct problems and delinquency showed the largest effects, with a mean effect size of –.21 in unselected samples. Amato (2001) updated this picture with studies published in the 1990s. These showed a very similar weighted effect size for overall associations with conduct problems (–.22), suggesting that links with child antisocial behavior had changed little across a period when rates of divorce rose dramatically. A yet more recent update (Amato, 2014) focused on European studies, where divorce rates are generally lower than in the US. Across child outcomes, weighted effect sizes were comparable to US estimates. Taken together, these findings point to a modest mean-level increase in risk for externalizing behavior problems among children exposed to parental divorce; multiple family transitions may carry particularly deleterious consequences (see, e.g., Fomby & Cherlin, 2007).

Children may live in single-parent families from the time of their birth or transition to this situation following parental divorce or separation. Chapple (2009) examined outcomes for children in single-parent families across the OECD. Rates of, and reasons for, sole parenthood varied markedly between countries, though almost all OECD countries saw increases in the proportion of sole-parent families between the 1980s and the early 2000s. A meta-analysis of findings from non-US OECD countries produced a mean effect size of –.29 for associations of single-parent family status with conduct problems, delinquency, and ADHD. At this stage, evidence on sole parenthood in LMICs comes largely from Brazil, and centers on mothers' marital status at birth. In the 2004 Pelotas Birth Cohort Study, having a single mother at birth was associated with child conduct problems at age four, adjusting for other sociodemographic factors, maternal psychiatric disorder, and child birth characteristics (Matijasevich et al., 2014). In the 1993 Pelotas Birth Cohort Study, having a single mother at birth was associated with child conduct problems at ages 11 (Murray et al., 2015) and 15 years (Anselmi et al., 2012). Other studies, however, failed to find links with child conduct problems (Rodriguez et al., 2011), and single motherhood at birth was unrelated to youth violence in two Pelotas studies (Caicedo, Gonçalves, González, & Victora, 2010; Murray et al., 2015).

Most single-parent families are headed by women, but a small but gradually increasing proportion are headed by men; in the US in 2013, for example, 23.7% of children lived in mother-only households, and 4.1% in father-only families (Coles, 2015). Single-father families tend to be less economically disadvantaged than single-mother households, and to have fewer children, pointing to the possibility of more positive outcomes for children. In a narrative review Coles (2015) found few differences between single-mother and single-father families on measures of children's academic attainment or internalizing problems. Against expectations, however, externalizing problems (including substance use as well as disruptive behaviors and delinquency) were consistently elevated in single-father families.

With prison populations rising in many countries, the impact of parental incarceration—which can cause temporary or permanent single parenthood for children—has become an increasing concern. In the US in 2007, 1.7 million children (2.3% of the nation's child population) had a parent in a federal or state prison (Murray, Farrington, & Sekol, 2012). In a meta-analysis Murray et al. (2012) found no evidence of associations between parental incarceration and child mental health problems, drug use or educational attainment. Levels of antisocial behaviors were elevated, however, with studies that controlled for parental criminality or children's antisocial behavior before parental incarceration giving a pooled effect size of OR = 1.4 (95% CI = 1.2, 1.6).

Three other nontraditional family forms have attracted research attention: step-families, families where parents are cohabiting but not married, and families where both parents are of the same sex.

The emerging literature suggests that children growing up with same-sex parents generally show positive behavioral adjustment, with no signs of increased rates of conduct problems or related difficulties (see Lamb, 2012; Gates, 2015). Turning to children in step-families, outcomes are less positive (Coleman, Ganong, & Fine, 2000). Both early and more recent studies report higher rates of disruptive behavior problems and delinquency among children in step-families than in intact two-parent homes. Amato and Keith (1991) noted that levels of conduct problems were higher for children in step- than in single-parent families, though these contrasts fell just short of statistical significance; similar trends have, however, been identified in some more recent research. Though often discussed separately, step-family status and parental cohabitation often overlap; recent findings from the US, for example, show that over half of children living with cohabiting parents were in step-families, while only just over 40% lived with both biological parents. This distinction appears to be an important one. Manning (2015) concluded that, for young children, parents' marital status had little if any impact on outcomes if they lived with both biological parents: children whose parents were cohabiting fared just as well as those whose parents were married. Children in cohabiting step-families, however, had much poorer outcomes. At older ages, rates of externalizing problems are also higher among youth living with one biological parent and a cohabiting step-parent, especially when the custodial parent is the biological father (see, e.g., Apel & Kaukinen, 2008).

Do Variations in Family Structure/Stability Cause Antisocial Behavior in Offspring?

These cross-sectional associations suggest that family structure and stability affect child behavior, but—as in the case of family poverty—by no means clinch the argument. Family breakdown is associated with a range of parental characteristics (including antisocial tendencies) that might impact child behavior via other routes (Jaffee et al., 2012). Some studies report that children in divorcing families showed poor adjustment *before* their parents' divorce, and reverse causation is also plausible, with problematic child behaviors putting parents' relationships under stress. Direct experimental manipulations are clearly not feasible in this area, but a variety of quasi-experimental and statistical approaches have provided more stringent tests. Reviewing this evidence, both Jaffee et al. (2012) and McLanahan et al. (2013) concluded that, though findings are not entirely consistent, on balance, results point to a likely causal impact of divorce and father absence on risk for child behavioral outcomes. We outline some key exemplars from this literature below.

Beginning with genetically sensitive designs, Burt, Barnes, McGue, and Iacono (2008) used two different approaches to assess whether common genes might underlie associations between offspring delinquency and parental divorce: an adoption design, and variations in the timing of divorce. Both pointed to environmentally mediated effects: divorce was associated with increases in offspring antisocial behavior in both adoptive and biologically related families, and effects were only seen when young people had directly experienced parental divorce, but not when parents divorced before their birth (when shared genes might still impact risk). Using a children-of-twins design, D'Onofrio et al. (2005) concluded that neither genetic nor parental family background factors confounded the association between divorce and child behavior problems. More recently, Goodnight et al. (2013), using a cousin-comparison analysis, found associations between multiple maternal relationship transitions and antisocial behavior in childhood and early adolescence could largely be explained by confounding, but that links with late adolescent delinquency were more robust. We must await further findings from similar designs to resolve these apparent inconsistencies.

Other studies have used growth curves, individual and sibling fixed-effects models, and propensity score matching in longitudinal data to assess the impact of family disruption on trajectories of child behavior over time (see McLanahan et al., 2013). Once again, results differ somewhat between studies; at this stage, however, the balance of evidence from fixed-effects analyses of child externalizing behaviors appears to favor a causal interpretation (Amato & Anthony, 2014), but with overall effect sizes estimated to be modest or small.

Factors That Moderate Associations between Family Structure/Instability and Child Behavior Problems

A number of commentators have argued that these modest effect sizes may mask heterogeneity in effects: some children may be especially vulnerable to the effects of family transitions, while others remain relatively untroubled. Although tests for moderators are still limited, there are pointers that they are likely to be important; in one recent study, for example, while almost one in five children did indeed show increased levels of conduct problems following parental divorce, a small proportion showed decreases, and the most common pattern was for no marked change (Amato & Anthony, 2014). If these findings are in any sense typical, it is clearly important to identify factors that underlie resilience.

Beginning with child characteristics, most recent findings suggest few systematic gender differences in responses to father absence (see Amato, 2010). Family transitions that occur early in childhood may have more deleterious consequences for behavior than those experienced later in development (Ryan, Claessens, & Markowitz, 2015), and a number of US studies point to racial or ethnic differences in effects, though specific findings differ somewhat across reports. In addition, there is evidence that a higher IQ and maternal sensitivity may buffer children against the adverse consequences of parental divorce (Weaver & Schofield, 2015), and that gene variants in the serotonergic and dopamine systems may contribute to individual differences in response to family transitions (Mitchell et al., 2015).

Differing types of family change, and the contexts in which change occurs, have also been examined as moderators. In general, changes involving parental "exits" show stronger associations with risk for child behavior problems than those involving the "entrance" of a new parent figure. Within the broad category of parental exits, however, other factors may also be important. A number of studies have found parental divorce to be more deleterious for child outcomes in high- than in low-income families (see, e.g., Ryan et al., 2015), while maternal education appears to buffer effects (Weaver & Schofield, 2015), and the quality of family relationships prior to breakdown is also likely to be important (Amato, 2010). Early studies suggested that, when divorce ends a high-conflict marriage, child behavior may change relatively little, or may even improve. Increases in problem behavior seem more likely following the breakdown of low-conflict marriages, or when children are separated from parent figures to whom they had strong emotional bonds. And, finally, effects may vary with parental characteristics, and in particular with parents' own antisocial tendencies. Jaffee, Moffitt, Caspi and Taylor (2003), for example, found that the less time young children lived with their fathers, the more conduct problems they had—but only when fathers were themselves low in antisocial behavior; for children with highly antisocial fathers, it was time living *with* their father that predicted child disruptiveness.

How Might Variations in Family Structure and Stability Lead to Antisocial Behavior in Children?

In an early commentary, Hetherington, Bridges, and Insabella (1998) identified several different veins of theorizing on the factors that affect the adjustment of children post-divorce. In addition to individual parental risk and vulnerability, these centered on the effects of family composition, exposure to socio-economic disadvantage and stress, parental distress, and disruptions to family processes. With the addition of a broader "instability hypothesis" put forward to account for effects of multiple parental relationship transitions (see, e.g., Fomby & Cherlin, 2007), these perspectives have continued to guide much subsequent research.

Family structure models highlight the impact of father absence on family functioning and child adjustment. Single parents lack the supports for parenting and supervision available in two-parent families, and children have diminished access to role models and parental involvement. If these were the prime drivers of the effects of single parenthood, children who lose parents from death or other causes should fare as poorly as those whose parents separate or divorce. Beginning with Amato and Keith's (1991) early meta-analysis, numerous studies have used comparisons between parental death and divorce to evaluate these arguments. Supporting the father absence hypothesis, findings indicate that children's attainments and adjustment do indeed suffer following the death of a parent; in the main, however, outcomes tend to be poorer for children whose parents divorce, suggesting that father absence alone is unlikely to account for all of the effects observed. The higher levels of difficulty found for children in step-families also argue against father absence as the sole contributor to child outcomes. Coleman et al. (2000) discuss the range of processes that may be involved in step-families, ranging from stresses associated with multiple family transitions, lower involvement and interaction with step-children than biological children or, from an evolutionary perspective, reduced investment by step-parents in nonbiologically related children. In addition, reconstituted families often involve new siblings as well as new parents. Sibling relationships have long been explored as influences on child development, though the more complex sibship patterns found in contemporary families have only recently begun to be explored. Current evidence suggests, however, that they warrant attention; Fomby, Goode and Mollborn (2016), for example, found that complex sibships were linked with risk for aggression in early childhood independent of the effects of parents' union status.

Hetherington et al.'s (1998) second model, focusing on exposure to socioeconomic disadvantage and stress, brings together the two main themes of this chapter. Family disruption is frequently followed by substantial losses of income and other resources, such as parental time; such losses contribute to rates of poverty in single-parent and reconstituted families in contemporary samples, as illustrated in our opening paragraphs. Given these consistent associations, it seems plausible that lack of economic resources is implicated in links between family structure and child outcomes, via any or all of the mechanisms discussed above. When income is treated as a covariate in multivariable analyses, a number of studies have found that links between single-parent family status and child behavior problems are reduced to nonsignificance (see, e.g., Pearce et al., 2013), though associations with step-family status persist. Where other more proximal correlates of family disruption are evaluated alongside income, their effects tend to predominate as predictors of child outcomes (see, e.g., Weaver & Schofield, 2015). And finally, comparing the effects of different risk factors on outcomes for 9-year-olds in the Fragile Families Study, Lee and McLanahan (2015) found that, while family poverty most strongly predicted internalizing problems, and maternal education most strongly predicted cognitive outcomes, family disruption proved the strongest (albeit still modest) predictor of externalizing behaviors.

Other models focus on the roles of parental distress, and disruptions to family relationships, routines, and parenting as mediators of effects of family structure. Numerous studies attest to the plausibility of these accounts. Parental discord has consistently emerged as a key mediator of the adverse consequences of divorce (Lansford, 2009); predivorce parental conflict may contribute to the elevated levels of externalizing problems seen in some children prior to divorce, and, as noted earlier, disruptive behavior problems are often reduced when children are released from high-conflict families. In addition, a cascade of other disruptions often follow when parents separate: many children face house and school moves, daily routines change, and parenting stress is often increased, with implications for parent–child relationships and styles of parenting (see, e.g., Beck, Cooper, McLanahan, & Brooks-Gunn, 2010). Weaver and Schofield (2015) explored postdivorce maternal sensitivity, maternal depression, home stimulation and support, and family income as mediators of the effects of divorce on child behavior problems. All four factors were associated with divorce, and each, considered separately, showed some mediating effects. In a joint model including all four potential mediators, however, maternal sensitivity and quality of the home environment emerged as independent mediators of teacher-rated externalizing problems, and maternal depression and home stimulation as mediators of mother-rated behavioral difficulties. In a study of mediators of the effects of parental incarceration, parenting and peer relations after parental imprisonment accounted for around half of the observed increase in youth theft (Murray, Loeber, & Pardini, 2012).

Conclusions

Family poverty and family structure were among the earliest identified family correlates of antisocial behavior in childhood. Extensive literatures have examined their links with child outcomes, and, as we have seen, new insights into the implications of these associations continue to emerge. In low- and middle-income countries, investigators are mapping basic patterns of associations between sociodemographic factors and child behavior, and testing how far models developed in high-income settings are applicable in different cultural and resource conditions. In high-income countries, the research agenda has turned to synthesizing findings from cross-sectional studies, assessing their likely causal status, and exploring the more proximal processes that function to mediate their effects.

In relation to both family poverty and family structure and stability, syntheses of evidence point to modest overall associations with child antisocial outcomes. Importantly, although different family forms vary markedly in average income levels, associations between child outcomes and family poverty and family structure seem—in statistical terms at least—somewhat distinct. In both areas, however, meta-analyses have highlighted considerable heterogeneity in effect sizes. In part, this seems likely to reflect variations in methodological issues and study quality; in part, it may also reflect variations in contextual factors and individual differences in children's response. As we have seen, evidence on moderators of effects is now beginning to emerge, with indications that factors such as maternal sensitivity, children's regulatory capacities and cognitive abilities, and aspects of their genetic make-up may all help to buffer the effects of family adversities. Much clearly still remains to be understood in this area; from a clinical perspective, however, learning more about the factors that enable some children to remain resilient in the face of family disadvantage must be a high priority for the next generation of research.

Other key areas for further study include continued research on the likely causal status of family poverty and family structure, and studies of the pathways that mediate their effects. Much current evidence points to the likelihood of causal influences, but not all findings concur. Once again, we need to know more about the reasons for such inconsistencies, and what conclusions they imply; one possibility, for example, is that it would be valuable to link causal studies more closely to work on moderators, so that tests for causality are targeted more closely on those children most likely to be at risk.

Finally, extensive efforts have gone into exploring possible mediating mechanisms. Both poverty and family structure and stability are relatively "distal" risks, whose effects are likely to be mediated via a chain of more proximal processes. As we have seen, a wide spectrum of possibilities has been examined here, from prenatal exposures to influences of neighborhoods, peers, and cultural norms. Some are specific to poverty or family structure, but many are shared; in particular, both poverty and relationship breakdowns can place stress on family relationships, parenting, and parental mental health, which have more proximal effects on children. Many of these proximal risks, and the strategies now available to remediate them, are explored in more detail in the chapters that follow.

References

Amato, P. R. (2001). Children of divorce in the 1990s: An update of the Amato and Keith (1991) meta-analysis. *Journal of Family Psychology, 15,* 355–370.

Amato, P. R. (2010). Research on divorce: Continuing trends and new developments. *Journal of Marriage and Family, 72,* 650–666.

Amato, P. R. (2014). The consequence of divorce for adults and children: An update. *Drustvena Istrazivanja, 23,* 5–24.

References

Amato, P. R., & Anthony, C. J. (2014). Estimating the effects of parental divorce and death with fixed effects models. *Journal of Marriage and Family, 76,* 370–386.

Amato, P. R., & Keith, B. (1991). Parental divorce and the well-being of children: A meta-analysis. *Psychological Bulletin, 110,* 26–46.

Anselmi, L., Menezes, A. M. B., Hallal, P. C., Wehrmeister, F., Gonçalves, H., Barros, F.C., . . . Rohde, L.A. (2012). Socioeconomic changes and adolescent psychopathology in a Brazilian Birth Cohort Study. *Journal of Adolescent Health, 51,* S5–S10.

Apel, R., & Kaukinen, C. (2008). On the relationship between family structure and antisocial behaviour: Parental cohabitation and blended households. *Criminology, 46,* 35–70.

Beck, A. N., Cooper, C. E., McLanahan, S., & Brooks-Gunn, J. (2010). Partnership transitions and maternal parenting. *Journal of Marriage and Family, 72,* 219–233.

Burt, S. A., Barnes, A. R., McGue, M., & Iacono, W. G. (2008). Parental divorce and adolescent delinquency: Ruling out the impact of common genes. *Developmental Psychology, 44,* 1668–1677.

Caicedo, B., Gonçalves, H., González, D. A., & Victora, C. G. (2010). Violent delinquency in a Brazilian birth cohort: The roles of breast feeding, early poverty and demographic factors. *Paediatric and Perinatal Epidemiology, 24,* 12–23.

Chapple, S. (2009). Child well-being and sole-parent family structure in the OECD: An analysis. *OECD Social, Employment and Migration Working Papers,* No. 82. Paris: OECD Publishing.

Coleman, M., Ganong, L., & Fine, M. (2000). Reinvestigating remarriage: Another decade of progress. *Journal of Marriage and the Family, 62,* 1288–1307.

Coles, R. L. (2015). Single father families: A review of the literature. *Journal of Family Theory and Review, 7,* 144–166.

Conger, R. D., & Donnellan, M. B. (2007). An interactionist perspective on the socioeconomic context of human development. *Annual Review of Psychology, 58,* 175–199.

Costello, E. J., Erkanli, A., Copeland, W., & Angold, A. (2010). Association of family income supplements in adolescence with development of psychiatric and substance use disorders in adulthood among an American Indian population. *Journal of the American Medical Association, 303,* 1954–1960.

Dodge, K. A., Pettit, G. S., & Bates, J. E. (1994). Socialization mediators of the relation between socio-economic status and child conduct problems. *Child Development, 65,* 649–665.

D'Onofrio, B. M., Goodnight, J. A., Van Hulle, C. A., Rodgers, J. L., Rathouz, P. J., Waldman, I. D., & Lahey, B. B. (2009). A quasi-experimental analysis of the association between family income and offspring conduct problems. *Journal of Abnormal Child Psychology, 37,* 415–429.

D'Onofrio, B. M., Turkheimer, E., Emery, R. E., Slutske, W. S., Heath, A. C., Madden, P. A., & Martin, N. G. (2005). A genetically informed study of marital instability and its association with offspring psychopathology. *Journal of Abnormal Psychology, 114,* 570–586.

Evans, G. W., & Kim, P. (2010). Multiple risk exposure as a potential explanatory mechanism for the socioeconomic status–health gradient. *Annals of the New York Academy of Sciences,1186,* 174–189.

Ewart, C. K., & Suchday, S. (2002). Discovering how urban poverty and violence affect health: Development and validation of a neighborhood stress index. *Health Psychology, 21,* 254–262.

Farbstein, I., Mansbach-Kleinfeld, I., Levinson, D., Goodman, R., Levav, I., Vograft, I., . . . Apter, A. (2010). Prevalence and correlates of mental disorders in Israeli adolescents: Results from a national mental health survey. *Journal of Child Psychology and Psychiatry, 51,* 630–639.

Flouri, E., Midouhas, E., & Joshi, H. (2014). Family poverty and trajectories of children's emotional and behavioural problems: The moderating roles of self-regulation and verbal cognitive ability. *Journal of Abnormal Child Psychology, 42,* 1043–1056.

Flouri, E., Midouhas, E., & Joshi, H. (2015). Family and neighbourhood risk and children's problem behaviour: The moderating role of intelligence. *Intelligence, 53,* 33–42.

Fomby, P., & Cherlin, A. J. (2007). Family instability and child well-being. *American Sociological Review, 72,* 181–204.

Fomby, P., Goode, J. A., & Mollborn, S. (2016). Family complexity, siblings, and children's aggressive behavior at school entry. *Demography, 53,* 1–26.

Ford, T., Goodman, R., & Meltzer, H. (2004). The relative importance of child, family, school and neighbourhood correlates of childhood psychiatric disorder. *Social Psychiatry and Psychiatric Epidemiology, 39,* 487–496.

Furstenberg F. F. (2014). Fifty years of family change: From consensus to complexity. *Annals of the American Academy of Political and Social Science, 654,* 12–30.

Gates, G. J. (2015). Marriage and family: LGBT individuals and same-sex couples. *Future of Children, 25,* 67–87.

Gaysina, D., Fergusson, D. M., Leve, L. D., Horwood, J., Reiss, D., . . . Harold, G. T. (2013). Maternal smoking during pregnancy and offspring conduct problems: Evidence from 3 independent genetically sensitive research designs. *Journal of the American Medical Association, Psychiatry, 70,* 956–963.

Gennetian, L. A., & Miller, C. (2002). Children and welfare reform: A view from an experimental welfare program in Minnesota. *Child Development, 73,* 601–620.

Gershoff, E. T., Aber, J. L., Raver, C. C., & Lennon, M. C. (2007). Income is not enough: Incorporating material hardship into models of income associations with parenting and child development. *Child Development, 78,* 70–95.

Goodman, E., Huang, B., Schafer-Kalkhoff, T., & Adler, N. E. (2007). Perceived socioeconomic status: A new type of identity that influences adolescents' self-rated health. *Journal of Adolescent Health, 41,* 479–487.

Goodnight, J. A., D'Onofrio, B. M., Cherlin, A. J., Emery, R. E., Van Hulle, C. A., & Lahey, B. B. (2013). Effects of multiple maternal relationship transitions on offspring antisocial behavior in childhood and adolescence: A cousin-comparison analysis. *Journal of Abnormal Child Psychology, 41,* 185–198.

Hao, L. X., & Matsueda, R. L. (2006). Family dynamics through childhood: A sibling model of behavior problems. *Social Science Research, 35,* 500–524.

Hetherington, E. M., Bridges, M., & Insabella, G. M. (1998). What matters? What does not? Five perspectives on the association between marital transitions and children's adjustment. *American Psychologist, 53,* 167–184.

Jaffee, S. R., Moffitt, T. E., Caspi, A., & Taylor, A. (2003). Life with (or without) father: The benefits of living with two biological parents depend on the father's antisocial behavior. *Child Development, 74,* 109–126.

Jaffee, S. R., Strait, L. B., & Odgers, C. L. (2012). From correlates to causes: Can quasi-experimental studies and statistical innovations bring us closer to identifying the causes of antisocial behavior? *Psychological Bulletin, 138,* 272–295.

Johnson, S. B., Riis, J. L., & Noble, K. G. (2016). State of the art review: Poverty and the developing brain. *Pediatrics, 137.* doi:10.1542/peds.2015–3075

Jones, A. P., Laurens, K. R., Herba, C. M., Barker, G. J., & Viding, E. (2009). Amygdala hypoactivity to fearful faces in boys with conduct problems and callous-unemotional traits. *American Journal of Psychiatry, 166,* 95–102.

Kalil, A., & Ryan, R. M. (2010). Mothers' economic conditions and sources of support in fragile families. *Future of Children, 20,* 39–61.

Kerr, M., Stattin, H., & Burk, W. J. (2010). A reinterpretation of parental monitoring in longitudinal perspective. *Journal of Research on Adolescence, 20,* 39–64.

Kim, P., Evans, G. W., Angstadt, M., Ho, S. S., Sripada, C. S., Swain, J. E., . . . Phan, K. L. (2013). Effects of childhood poverty and chronic stress on emotion regulatory brain function in adulthood. *Proceedings of the National Academy of Sciences of the United States of America, 110,* 18442–18447.

Kling, J. R., Ludwig, J., & Katz, L. F. (2005). Neighborhood effects on crime for female and male youth: Evidence from a randomized housing voucher experiment. *Quarterly Journal of Economics, 120,* 87–130.

Lamb, M. E. (2012). Mothers, fathers, families, and circumstances: Factors affecting children's adjustment. *Applied Developmental Science, 16,* 98–111.

Lansford, J. E. (2009). Parental divorce and children's adjustment. *Perspectives on Psychological Science, 4,* 140–152.

Lee, D., & McLanahan, S. (2015). Family structure transitions and child development: instability, selection, and population heterogeneity. *American Journal of Sociology, 80,* 738–763.

Lee, G. G., & Payne, K. K. (2010). Changing marriage patterns since 1970: What's going on—and why? *Journal of Comparative Family Studies, 41*(4), 537–555.

Linver, M. R., Brooks-Gunn, J., & Kohen, D. E. (2002). Family processes as pathways from income to young children's development. *Developmental Psychology, 38,* 719–734.

Lovisi, G. M., López, J. R. R. A., Coutinho, E. S. F., & Patel, V. (2005). Poverty, violence and depression during pregnancy: A survey of mothers attending a public hospital in Brazil. *Psychological Medicine, 35,* 1485–1492.

Lundberg, S., & Pollak, R. A. (2015). The evolving role of marriage: 1950–2010. *Future of Children, 25,* 29–50.

Maldonado-Molina, M. M., Piquero, A. R., Jennings, W. G., Bird, H., & Canino, G. (2009). Trajectories of delinquency among Puerto Rican children and adolescents at two sites. *Journal of Research in Crime and Delinquency, 46,* 144–181.

Manning, W. (2015). Cohabitation and child well-being. *Future of Children, 25,* 51–66.

Marques, A. H., O'Connor, T. G., Roth, C., Susser, E., & Bjorke-Monsen, A.-L. (2013). The influence of maternal prenatal and early childhood nutrition and maternal prenatal stress on offspring immune system development and neurodevelopmental disorders. *Frontiers in Neuroscience, 7.* doi:10.3389/fnins.2013.00120

Matijasevich, A., Murray, E., Stein, A., Anselmi, L., Menezes, A. M., Santos, I. S., . . . Victora, C. G. (2014). Increase in child behavior problems among urban Brazilian 4-year-olds: 1993 and 2004 Pelotas birth cohorts. *Journal of Child Psychology and Psychiatry, 55,* 1125–1134.

McAdams, T. A., Neiderhiser, J. M., Rijsdijk, F. V., Narusyte, J., Lichtenstein, P., & Eley, T. C. (2014). Accounting for genetic and environmental confounds in associations between parent and child characteristics: A systematic review of children-of-twins studies. *Psychological Bulletin, 140,* 1138–1173.

McLanahan, S., Tach, L., & Schneider, D. (2013). The causal effects of father absence. *Annual Review of Psychology, 39,* 399–427.

Meins, E., Centifanti, L. C. M., Fernyhough, C., & Fishburn, S. (2013). Maternal mind-mindedness and children's behavioral difficulties: Mitigating the impact of low socioeconomic status. *Journal of Abnormal Child Psychology, 41,* 543–553.

Merikangas, K. R., He, J., Burstein, M., Swanson, S. A., Avenevoli, S., Cui, L., . . . Swendsen, J. (2010). Lifetime prevalence of mental disorders in U.S. adolescents: Results from the National Comorbidity Survey Replication–Adolescent Supplement (NCS-A). *Journal of the American Academy of Child and Adolescent Psychiatry, 49,* 980–989.

Mitchell, C., Brooks-Gunn, J., Garfinkel, I., McLanahan, S., & Notterman, D., & Hobcraft, J. (2015). Family structure instability, genetic sensitivity, and child well-being. *American Journal of Sociology, 120,* 1195–1225.

Murray, J., Farrington, D. P., & Sekol, I. (2012). Children's antisocial behavior, mental health, drug use, and educational performance after parental incarceration: A systematic review and meta-analysis. *Psychological Bulletin, 138,* 175–210.

Murray, J., Loeber, R., & Pardini, D. (2012). Parental involvement in the criminal justice system and the development of youth theft, maijuana use, depression, and poor acdemic performance. *Criminology, 50,* 255–302.

Murray, J., Maughan, B., Menezes, A. M. B., Hickman, M., MacLeod, J., Matijasevich, A., . . . Barros, F. C. (2015). Perinatal and sociodemographic factors at birth predicting conduct problems and violence to age 18 years: Comparison of Brazilian and British birth cohorts. *Journal of Child Psychology and Psychiatry, 56,* 914–922.

Noble, K. G., Houston, S. M., Brito, N. H., Bartsch, H., Kan, E., Kuperman, J. M., . . . Sowell, E. R. (2015). Family income, parental education and brain structure in children and adolescents. *Nature Neuroscience, 18,* 773–778.

Odgers, C. L., Donley, S., Caspi, A., Bates, C. J., & Moffitt, T. E. (2015). Living alongside more affluent neighbors predicts greater involvement in antisocial behavior among low-income boys. *Journal of Child Psychology and Psychiatry, 56,* 1055–1064.

O'Donnell, K. J., Glover, V., Barker, E. D., & O'Connor, T. G. (2014). The persisting effect of maternal mood in pregnancy on childhood psychopathology. *Development and Psychopathology, 26,* 393–403.

Pearce, A., Lewis, H., & Law, C. (2013). The role of poverty in explaining health variations in 7-year-old children from different family structures: Findings from the UK Millennium Cohort Study. *Journal of Epidemiology and Community Health, 67,* 181–189.

Piotrowska, P. J., Stride, C. B., Croft, S. E., & Rowe, R. (2015). Socioeconomic status and antisocial behaviour among children and adolescents: A systematic review and meta-analysis. *Clinical Psychology Review, 35,* 47–55.

Piotrowska, P. J., Stride, C. B., Maughan, B., Goodman, R., McCaw, L., & Rowe, R.(2015). Income gradients within child and adolescent antisocial behaviours. *The British Journal of Psychiatry, 207,* 385–391.

Raine, A. (2002). Annotation: The role of prefrontal deficits, low autonomic arousal, and early health factors in the development of antisocial and aggressive behavior in children. *Journal of Child Psychology and Psychiatry, 43,* 417–434.

Rekker, R., Pardini, D., Keijsers, L., Branje, S., Loeber, R., & Meeus, W. (2015). Moving in and out of poverty: The within-individual association between socioeconomic status and juvenile delinquency. *Plos One, 10*(11). doi:10.1371/journal.pone.0136461.

Rodriguez, J. D. M., da Silva, A. A. M., Bettiol, H., Barbieri, M. A., & Rona, R. J. (2011). The impact of perinatal and socioeconomic factors on mental health problems of children from a poor Brazilian city: A longitudinal study. *Social Psychiatry and Psychiatric Epidemiology, 46,* 381–391.

Ryan, R. M., Claessens, A., & Markowitz, A. J. (2015). Associations between family structure change and child behavior problems: The moderating effects of family income. *Child Development, 86,* 112–127.

Sapolsky, R. M. (2004). Social status and health in humans and other animals. *Annual Review of Anthropology, 33,* 393–418.

Sariaslan, A., Larsson, H., D'Onofrio, B., Langstrom, N., & Lichtenstein, P. (2014). Childhood family income, adolescent violent criminality and substance misuse: quasi-experimental total population study. *British Journal of Psychiatry, 205,* 286–290.

Shaw, D. S., & Shelleby, E. C. (2014). Early-starting conduct problems: Intersection of conduct problems and poverty. *Annual Review of Clinical Psychology, 10,* 503–528.

Shenderovich, Y., Eisner, M., Mikton, C., Gardner, F., Liu, J., & Murray, J. (2016). Methods for conducting systematic reviews of risk factors in low- and middle-income countries. *BMC Medical Research Methodology, 16,* 32. doi:10.1186/s12874-016-0134-2

Sweeting, H., & Hunt, K. (2014). Adolescent socio-economic and school-based social status, health and well-being. *Social Science & Medicine, 121,* 39–47.

Sweeting, H., & Hunt, K. (2015). Adolescent socioeconomic and school-based social status, smoking, and drinking. *Journal of Adolescent Health, 57,* 37–45.

Thomson, E. (2014). Family complexity in Europe. *Annals of the American Academy of Political and Social Science, 654,* 245–258.

Weaver, J. M., & Schofield, T. J. (2015). Mediation and moderation of divorce effects on children's behavior problems. *Journal of Family Psychology, 29,* 39–48.

Wells, L. E. and Rankin, J. (1991). Families and delinquency: A meta-analysis of the impact of broken homes. *Social Problems, 38,* 71–93.

Wichstrøm, L., Berg-Nielsen, T. S., Angold, A., Egger, H. L., Solheim, E., & Sveen, T. R. (2012). Prevalence of psychiatric disorders in pre-schoolers. *Journal of Child Psychology and Psychiatry, 53,* 695–705.

Wright, B. R. E., Caspi, A., Moffitt, T. E., Miech, R. A., & Silva, P. A. (1999). Reconsidering the relationship between SES and delinquency: Causation but not correlation. *Criminology, 37,* 175–194.

Xiaoli Y., Chao J., Wen P., Wenming X., Fang L., Ning, L. . . .Guowei, P. (2014). Prevalence of psychiatric disorders among children and adolescents in northeast China. *PLoS ONE, 9*(10), e111223. doi:10.1371/journal.pone.0111223

Zachrisson, H. D., & Dearing, E. (2015). Family income dynamics, early childhood education and care, and early child behavior problems in Norway. *Child Development, 86,* 425–440.

17
Parent Psychopathology
Tammy D. Barry, Rebecca A. Lindsey, Elizabeth C. Fair, and Kristy M. DiSabatino

Parent Psychopathology

Psychopathology among parents has been established as a contributing factor to disruptive behavior problems in children and adolescents (e.g., Breaux, Harvey, & Lugo-Candelas, 2014; Harold, Elam, Lewis, Rice, & Thapar, 2012; Harvey, Stoessel, & Herbert, 2011), including the diagnoses of oppositional defiant disorder (ODD) and conduct disorder (CD; Frick et al., 1992; Marmorstein, & Iacono, 2004). There is a strong evidence base linking maternal depression specifically to the development of ODD and CD, but other internalizing and externalizing types of psychopathology among parents—including both clinically significant and subclinical levels of symptoms among mothers and fathers—are also associated with these disorders in youth (e.g., O'Connor, Heron, Golding, Beveridge, & Glover, 2002; Ohannessian et al., 2005). Furthermore, once a child or adolescent has a diagnosis of ODD or CD, parental psychopathology may be a maintenance factor for the diagnosis through a reciprocal process (Kazdin, 2005; McKee, Colletti, Rakow, Jones, & Forehand, 2008), in addition to perhaps presenting as a barrier to treatment (Kazdin & Wassell, 1999). For these reasons, parental psychopathology deserves further research so that its role in the diagnoses of ODD and CD among youth can be better understood.

To this end, this chapter examines how parental psychopathology forms an important part of the etiological background to ODD and CD, underscoring the importance of considering it as one of the contextual factors that may contribute to the development of these disruptive behavior disorders. Reflective of the literature, maternal depression is a primary focus, but the chapter also discusses the links between maternal anxiety, general stress and distress, and other forms of parental psychopathology, as well as the evidence linking paternal psychopathology to ODD and CD. The way in which parental psychopathology may serve to maintain these problem child behaviors once established (i.e., the reciprocal linkage between parent psychopathology and child disruptive behaviors) is also covered, and the various mediating processes in the association between parental psychopathology and both ODD and CD as well as moderating variables that may attenuate or exacerbate the relation are examined in the final section.

Maternal Depression

By and large, the most common aspect of parental psychopathology linked to externalizing behaviors in general and, in particular, to ODD and CD among children and adolescents is maternal depression. Perhaps this focus in the research reflects the prevalence rates for depression and the fact that it is more likely that a parent will experience depression than other forms of psychopathology. Indeed, depression is one of the most common psychological disorders with a lifetime prevalence rate of almost 20% among U.S. adults (Kessler et al., 2003; Kessler et al., 2005), with rates ranging from 17 to 24% among mothers of young children (McLennan, Kotelchuck, & Cho, 2001). Furthermore, a systematic review examining perinatal depression found that 19% of women had experienced either minor or major depression within three months of giving birth (Gavin et al., 2005). Even more mothers experience periods of heightened—albeit subclinical—depression at some point in their child's development (Campbell, Morgan-Lopez, Cox, & McLoyd, 2009). In light of these prevalence rates, understanding the role of maternal depression in the development of youth ODD and CD is crucial.

There is substantial evidence connecting maternal depression with child externalizing behaviors (e.g., Malik et al., 2007; Singh et al., 2011; Slatcher & Trentacosta, 2011; van der Molen, Hipwell, Vermeiren, & Loeber, 2011), including indications that severer and more chronic depression is related to severer behavior problems in children (e.g., Brennan et al., 2000; van der Waerden et al., 2015). These associations are not limited to mothers diagnosed with major depressive disorder. Mothers with subclinical levels of depression have children who exhibit higher rates of externalizing behaviors compared to mothers with no symptoms of depression (Conners-Burrow, Swindle, McKelvey, & Bokony, 2015). Furthermore, maternal depression has been found to predict both concurrent and future general externalizing behaviors in children (Blatt-Eisengart, Drabick, Monahan, & Steinberg, 2009). Specifically, maternal depression was shown to have an effect on externalizing behaviors for both boys (especially younger boys) and girls (especially older girls).

In addition to studies linking maternal depression to externalizing and disruptive behaviors among youth, a large literature supports maternal depression as a risk factor for the clinical diagnoses of both ODD and CD in children and adolescents (e.g., Hirshfeld-Becker et al., 2008; Kopp & Beauchaine, 2007; Marmorstein, & Iacono, 2004; Ohannessian et al., 2005; Singh et al., 2011; Wickramaratne & Weissman, 1998). For example, when compared to non-depressed mothers, mothers with high depressive symptoms during their child's preschool period have children with higher levels of conduct problems prospectively at age 5 years (van der Waerden et al., 2015). Indeed, a diagnosis of parental major depressive disorder (not necessarily specific only to mothers) is associated with a fivefold increase in CD (Wickramaratne & Weissman, 1998). That said, understanding the role of depression among mothers specifically may be of particular interest, given that maternal depression has been shown to independently predict a diagnosis of a disruptive behavior disorder, even when accounting for paternal antisocial behavior (Kopp & Beauchaine, 2007).

Temporal studies indicate that maternal depression may be a causal agent in the development of ODD and CD. For example, a link between maternal depression and the externalizing behaviors associated with ODD and CD among very young children has been established (Breaux et al., 2014; Conners-Burrow et al., 2015; Harvey et al., 2011). Likewise, maternal depression appears to relate to preschooler aggression, both directly and indirectly (Malik et al., 2007). Even among infants, maternal depression is related to a difficult temperament, and a large-scale cohort study indicated that this relation is most likely accounted for by significant parent-to-child rather than child-to-parent effects (Hanington, Ramchandani, & Stein, 2010). This association between maternal depression and temperament is particular noteworthy given that a difficult child temperament can be a precursor to an ODD or CD diagnosis (Antúnez, de la Osa, Granero, & Ezpeleta, 2016).

In addition to the studies linking maternal depression to externalizing behaviors among young children, prospective, longitudinal studies support maternal depression as an etiological factor in diagnoses of ODD and CD in youth (e.g., Antúnez et al., 2016; van der Waerden et al., 2015). Finally, higher levels of maternal depression predict poorer treatment outcomes among children with a disruptive behavior disorder treated with a multi-component program targeting both child and parental processes (Muratori et al., 2015). Thus, maternal depression may not only increase the likelihood of disruptive behaviors, such as those found with ODD and CD, but may also complicate intervention efforts.

Maternal Anxiety

There is significantly less research on the link between maternal anxiety and child externalizing behaviors than on maternal depression. This difference is surprising as anxiety disorders are some of those most commonly diagnosed, are most common in women (Michael, Zetsche, & Margraf, 2007), and may at times co-occur with depression.

Although the preponderance of research on maternal anxiety within this context has connected higher levels of anxiety with short- and long-term negative outcomes for children, overall research into the effects of maternal anxiety on child externalizing symptoms, such as those associated with ODD and CD, appears to be more mixed. Like maternal depression, maternal anxiety has been connected to symptoms associated with ODD and CD among children (see, e.g., O'Connor, Heron, Glover, & Alspac Study Team, 2002) as well as the disorders themselves (Latimer et al., 2012). Furthermore, maternal anxiety has been shown to relate to child behavioral problems independent of maternal depression, suggesting that anxiety could be a unique risk factor for child behavior problems (O'Connor, Heron, Glover et al., 2002). Another study found that both antenatal and postnatal maternal anxiety was significantly related to the symptoms associated with ODD and CD for boys and girls at age 4 years (O'Connor, Heron, Golding et al., 2002). However, it is important to note that some other studies have found no relation between maternal anxiety and child externalizing disorders (Burstein, Ginsburg, & Tein, 2010), and others still have indicated that maternal anxiety is actually related to lower levels of externalizing behaviors (Manassis, Bradley, Goldberg, & Hood, 1995). As the literature remains divided, more research is needed to understand the unique contribution a parent's anxiety may have on a child's risk for developing a disruptive behavior disorder.

General Stress and Distress among Mothers

Interestingly, a mother's internalizing psychopathology does not have to be clinically significant to increase the likelihood that her child will exhibit symptoms of ODD or CD. Subclinical levels of general stress and distress have been associated with aggression (Malik et al., 2007), externalizing behaviors (Baker et al., 2003; Calzada, Eyberg, Rich, & Querido, 2004; Eyberg, Boggs, & Rodriguez, 1993; Morgan, Robinson, & Aldridge, 2002), and diagnoses of ODD (Ross, Blanc, McNeil, Eyberg, & Hembree-Kigin, 1998) and CD (Sayed, Hussein, El-Batrawy, Zaki, & El Gaafary, 2006). One study indicated that parenting stress among mothers predicted unique variance in boys' disruptive behavior problems above and beyond demographic factors and that maternal distress (continuous measure of depression, anxiety, and somatization which was subclinical for the majority of the sample) accounted for additional unique variance (Barry, Dunlap, Cotten, Lochman, & Wells, 2005).

A study examining risk factors for ODD symptoms in children found that, although parental stress did not directly affect ODD symptoms in children, there was a statistically significant indirect effect (Lavigne, Gouze, Hopkins, Bryant, & LeBailly, 2012). Specifically, maternal stress was related to parental depression which, in turn, was related to ODD symptoms. The mechanism for the influence of parental depression was also examined, and greater parental depression was associated with greater negative affect in children, and greater negative affect was related to more ODD symptoms. Furthermore, elevated scores on the Parenting Stress Index (PSI) have been found among mothers of children with CD relative to a control group or normative scores (Sayed et al., 2006).

Stress, distress, and psychopathology among parents have also been linked to other externalizing disorders, such as attention-deficit/hyperactivity disorder (ADHD; Deault, 2010). However, Deault (2010) suggests that this association with ADHD may be due to comorbid ODD and CD. For example, Chronis et al. (2003) examined children aged 3 to 7 years with ADHD only, and with ADHD and ODD or CD, comparing them with non-ADHD control children and found that it may be the disruptive behaviors (i.e., ODD or CD symptoms), which are often comorbid in children with ADHD, that are more strongly linked with parental distress and psychopathology than the ADHD symptoms themselves. Overall, studies have demonstrated that parental distress, even when subclinical, still contributes to disruptive behaviors in children.

Internalizing Psychopathology among Fathers

Currently, there is less research on the effect of paternal depression on child psychopathology and behavior problems in general than on depression among mothers (Brennan, Hammen, Katz, & Le Brocque, 2002). Furthermore, studies investigating paternal depression and child externalizing behaviors have found conflicting results. One study, for instance, found that maternal depression significantly increased the risk of both adopted and non-adopted adolescents developing ODD and CD, whereas paternal depression did not increase the risk of either disorder (Tully, Iacono, & McGue, 2008). However, other studies have demonstrated that both maternal and paternal depression are predictors of child CD (e.g., Ohannessian et al., 2005). Maternal depression and paternal depression have also been shown to have an additive effect on youth externalizing disorders such that children were most at risk if depression was present among both parents (Brennan et al., 2002).

In a large-scale, large-sample, longitudinal study, Ramchandani and colleagues (2008) investigated the influence of paternal depression during the postnatal period by following a population-based cohort of 10,975 fathers and their children for seven years. Results demonstrated that postnatal paternal depression was related to an increased risk of child ODD and CD, even after accounting for maternal depression. In fact, ODD and CD were the most common childhood psychiatric disorders associated with postnatal paternal depression (Ramchandani et al., 2008). Similarly, Mezulis, Hyde, and Clark (2004) found that maternal depression when a child was an infant predicted externalizing behaviors at age 5 years, and this relation was exacerbated by paternal depression, particularly when it affected those fathers who spent more time caring for the infants. These compelling findings underscore the importance of considering psychopathology, specifically depression, among fathers.

Other Forms of Parental Psychopathology

Although the focus on this chapter thus far has been on parental internalizing symptoms and youth ODD and CD, a large-scale meta-analysis of maternal depression, specifically, and childhood psychopathology indicated that the relation between maternal depression and child externalizing behaviors is significant but small (Goodman et al., 2011). Thus, other factors explain the variance found in externalizing behaviors among youth, including those with ODD and CD. Although some of these additional factors are external to the parents or even the home environment, it is nonetheless the case that other forms of parental psychopathology are also implicated in these disorders.

Disruptive Behavior Disorders Parents with a childhood history of disruptive behavior disorders are more likely to have children who are similarly affected (Hirshfeld-Becker et al., 2008). It is more interesting, however, to consider the influence of disruptive behavior disorders in parents above and beyond the influence of parental depression, particularly given the fact that depression and disruptive behavior disorders are highly comorbid (Vander Stoep et al., 2012). Hirshfeld-Becker and colleagues found that parents with major depressive disorder, as well as a childhood history of a disruptive behavior disorder, were more likely to have a child with a disruptive behavior disorder in general. Furthermore, the presence of depression and a childhood history of a disruptive behavior disorder among the parents each conferred independent risk for (i.e., accounted for unique variance in) the child's disruptive behavior disorder. When considering youth ODD and CD separately, only parental major depressive disorder conferred independent risk for ODD, and only a history of parental disruptive behavior disorder conferred independent risk for CD (Hirshfeld-Becker et al., 2011). Thus, the increase in risk for ODD or CD associated with parental depression may not only be due to shared variance based on the parent's own history of disruptive behaviors; these two types of parent psychopathology, in fact, appear to be unique predictors of youth ODD and CD.

The association between parent and youth disruptive behaviors may not be limited to a history of ODD and CD symptoms among parents. ADHD is often a comorbid diagnosis of ODD and CD among youth (Chronis et al., 2003). Thus, it is not surprising that the presence of current ADHD among parents increases the risk of externalizing behaviors among children (Humphreys, Mehta, & Lee, 2012).

Substance Abuse Externalizing behaviors among children also have been linked to parental substance use disorder (Bornovalova, Hicks, Iacono, & McGue, 2010; Bountress & Chassin, 2015). Clinical diagnoses of ODD and CD are also specifically associated with substance abuse (Ohannessian et al., 2005), albeit this relation does not appear to be as robust as that found for other parental psychiatric diagnoses, such as depression. For example, Ohannessian and colleagues (2005) found that parental alcohol dependence related to adolescent conduct disorder but did not predict unique variance when accounting for parental depression.

Nevertheless, the relation between parental substance abuse and youth disruptive behaviors deserves consideration. Bountress and Chassin (2015) found that parental substance use disorder predicts externalizing behaviors in children, both when parents currently meet criteria for a substance use disorder and when they have recovered (i.e., compared to parents who were never diagnosed). This latter finding is especially compelling evidence for the link between parental substance abuse and child externalizing behaviors, particularly given that having a parent in recovery did not relate to internalizing symptoms in children (Bountress & Chassin, 2015). Although both a current and a recovered substance use disorder status among parents predicted child externalizing behaviors, the mechanisms mediating that relation may differ. For parents with a current diagnosis, the impact on children may be through a disrupted home environment, whereas for recovered parents, the pathway may be a shared genetic risk (Bountress & Chassin, 2015).

Personality disorders Several personality disorders among parents have been linked to ODD and CD among youth. Most evidence is found for the link between parental antisocial personality disorder (APD; Bornovalova et al., 2010; Bornovalova et al., 2014)—which is more typical of fathers than mothers—and youth ODD and CD. This association is expected, given that fathers with APD may have developed the disorder along a trajectory of childhood ODD and CD (Diamantopoulou, Verhulst, & van der Ende, 2010).

Bornovalova and colleagues (2010) examined the prediction of specific disruptive behavior disorders in preadolescent twins by a combined parental externalizing construct (i.e., antisocial behavior and substance use disorder). They concluded that parents pass on a "general liability to externalizing psychopathology that is then manifested in their offspring" (p. 1071). When teasing apart the genetic versus shared environment effect, however, they found some disorder-specific differences. For both ODD and CD, there was a significant genetic contribution (i.e., externalizing problems in parents were highly heritable), but a significant influence based on shared environment was found only for CD (Bornovalova et al., 2010).

Likewise, paternal APD has been linked to comorbid CD among children with ADHD, albeit there was no support for an increased risk of comorbid ODD associated with paternal APD, thus the connection may exist only for the more extreme symptoms (Pfiffner, McBurnett, Rathouz, & Judice, 2005). Antisocial behavior among fathers also appears to predict a disruptive behavior diagnosis among children, independently of maternal depression, while paternal antisocial behavior exacerbates the likelihood that maternal depression will lead to child conduct problem diagnoses (Kopp & Beauchaine, 2007).

In addition to APD, borderline personality disorder (BPD) among parents, especially mothers, has been linked to disruptive behaviors in youth (Barnow, Spitzer, Grabe, Kessler, & Freyberger, 2006). Although maternal BPD and its link to the symptoms of ODD and CD have garnered less research attention than the link to maternal depression, children of mothers with BPD actually have been shown to have more externalizing problems than children of mothers with depressive disorders (Barnow et al., 2006).

Consideration of the Complexities of the Relation between Parental Psychopathology and Child Disruptive Behaviors

Parent Psychopathology as a Maintenance Factor and the Reciprocal Process Whereas there are many nuanced questions remaining, the literature clearly supports parental psychopathology as an etiological factor in the development of ODD and CD. However, does it maintain the behaviors associated with these disorders once they are established? The answer appears to be yes. Indeed, many of the hypotheses put forward in the literature on parental psychopathology and ODD and CD, as previously reviewed, assume that parental psychopathology plays a causal role in the development of the disorders. Considerably less research considers the possibility that ODD and CD among children and adolescents may be an etiological or maintenance factor of parental psychopathology, particularly maternal depression. Yet, child behavior problems and parental psychopathology often have a bidirectional relation, with higher levels of distress being linked to more behavior problems, and more frequent problematic behaviors being associated with increased parental distress over time (e.g., Blacher, Neece, & Paczkowski, 2005; Neece, Green, & Baker, 2012). As there is sufficient evidence that maternal psychopathology is related to child externalizing behaviors (e.g., Connell & Goodman, 2002), it is imperative to consider this bidirectional relation given that it may account for the maintenance of ODD and CD symptoms in children once such symptoms exist. Again, much of the research in this area focuses on maternal depression, which, when present, has been found to increase the odds that youth's ODD and CD are maintained relative to youth in a home with a non-depressed mother.

Several mechanisms, both direct and indirect, have been suggested to contribute to the bidirectional relation between parental psychopathology and child externalizing behaviors. For example, parental psychopathology has been associated with inconsistent and harsh parenting (e.g., Lovejoy, Graczyk, O'Hare, & Neuman, 2000), and negative parenting behaviors have been linked with increased child behavior problems (e.g., August, Realmuto,

Joyce, & Hektner, 1999; Johnston & Mash, 2001; Rothbaum & Weisz, 1994; Stormshak, Bierman, McMahon, Lengua, & Conduct Problems Prevention Research Group, 2000). However, some studies examining parenting behavior as a mediator between parental psychopathology and child behavior have failed to find support for such a model (e.g., Crnic, Gaze, & Hoffman, 2005), suggesting that further research is needed to better understand these variables. Furthermore, mothers with depression may interact with their children in an insensitive (Embry & Dawson, 2002) or hostile manner (Downey & Coyne, 1990; Sellers et al., 2014), which has been associated with strained parent–child relationships (e.g., Lyons-Ruth, 1996; Miller-Slough, Dunsmore, Ollendick, & Greene, 2016). Having a strained parent–child relationship and a resultant insecure attachment style—particularly a coercive pattern—have been linked to more severe behavioral problems in children (DeVito & Hopkins, 2001). A similar pattern has been found for mothers with ADHD, with these mothers being more likely to discipline their children inconsistently compared to mothers without ADHD, which was related to significantly more ODD and CD symptoms in children (Murray & Johnston, 2006).

It is also important to recognize that maternal psychopathology exists within other contextual circumstances, and there are several familial and societal constructs that contribute to both maternal psychopathology and child externalizing behaviors including lower socioeconomic status (e.g., Lovejoy et al., 2000), intimate partner violence (Holmes, 2013), and lower levels of social support (e.g., Duchovic, Gerkensmeyer, & Wu, 2009), among others (see Chapters 16 and 18 for a full discussion of the role of poverty and of intimate partner violence). One study found that intimate partner violence indirectly influenced children's aggressive behaviors through self-reported maternal mental health concerns (depression and substance use; Holmes, 2013). Certainly the broader context in which both parent psychopathology and child behavioral outcomes, including ODD and CD symptoms, occurs should be considered. Such a consideration is consistent with current research that emphasizes the importance of integrating multiple risk factors when evaluating the etiology of child behavior problems (Cummings, Davies, & Campbell, 2000).

Mediators in the Relation between Parent Psychopathology and ODD and CD To gain a more nuanced understanding of parental psychopathology as an etiological factor, it is important not only to examine its direct effect on youth ODD and CD but also how it relates to youth ODD and CD indirectly through mediating mechanisms. Indeed, ultimately understanding the mechanisms by which this relation occurs will better inform interventions.

As discussed above regarding the reciprocal process between parent psychopathology and youth disruptive behaviors, one well-established mediator in that relation is parenting practices. Depressed parents tend to display higher levels of negative and lower levels of positive parenting behaviors compared to non-depressed parents (e.g., Lovejoy et al., 2000), both of which may contribute to increased externalizing behaviors in children over time and across age ranges (e.g., Eisenberg et al., 2005; Pugh & Farrell, 2011)—including diagnoses of ODD and CD (Falk & Lee, 2012; Miller-Slough et al., 2016). Depressed mothers implement disciplinary strategies more inconsistently and report lower levels of confidence related to parenting (e.g., Muratori et al., 2015). Additionally, mothers with more depressive symptoms (i.e., who are more distressed) respond more arbitrarily than mothers without high levels of depression or distress, which has been shown to predict to more child behavior problems and noncompliance (Dumas, Gibson, & Albin, 1989).

Depressed mothers may implement harsh or coercive disciplinary techniques when children misbehave, resulting in children developing more severe conduct problems (e.g., Downey & Coyne, 1990). For example, a survey of 3,412 mothers found that mothers who reported higher levels of depression were more likely to report implementing harsh disciplinary acts such as slapping their child or spanking their child using an object (McLearn, Minkovitz, Strobino, Marks, & Hou, 2006).

Furthermore, children of depressed mothers may undergo disrupted parent–child bonding (e.g., Moehler, Brunner, Wiebel, Reck, & Resch, 2006) due to parental disengagement (Lovejoy et al., 2000). These children may develop an insecure attachment (Manassis et al., 1995) and experience strained parent–child interactions (e.g., Murray, Sinclair, Cooper, Ducournau, & Turner, 1999), all of which could initiate a trajectory of behavior problems that develop into ODD or CD. The risk for such disruptive behavior disorder symptoms in depressed mothers also may be due to increased parent–child conflict (Marmorstein, & Iacono, 2004). Finally, parental psychopathology also may relate to youth ODD and CD indirectly through marital/interparental conflict (Fisher, Brock, O'Hara, Kopelman, & Stuart, 2015), diminished marital quality or partnership satisfaction (Herwig, Wirtz, & Bengel, & 2004), and other stressful contexts in the children and adolescent's lives (Goodman & Gotlib, 1999).

Importantly, despite the aforementioned environmental and familial contextual factors, the potential contribution of a genetic risk to the development of disruptive behavior disorder symptoms, specifically in relation to internalizing symptomatology among parents, cannot be dismissed. For example, in a large-scale twin study, Singh and colleagues (2011) found that parental depression related to child conduct disorder via genetic factors, whereas parental depression's link to child depression was due to environmental causes. Thus, despite the internalizing-externalizing distinction, genetics clearly plays a role in the intergenerational association between parental depression and child externalizing behaviors.

Parent Psychopathology as a Moderator Finally, parent psychopathology and other known etiologies of ODD and CD may interact to further increase the likelihood of these disruptive behavior disorders in children relative to the presence of either risk factor alone. For example, difficult child temperament is more likely to develop into ODD or CD in the presence of parental psychopathology (Antúnez et al., 2016) (see Chapter 11 in this *Handbook* for more research on child temperament). A study examining a large sample of preschoolers and their parents found, both cross-sectionally and longitudinally across three time points, that children with more difficult temperaments (e.g., higher negative affect, poorer effortful control) had higher levels of ODD symptoms when parental depression and anxiety were also higher (Antúnez et al., 2016). Similarly, children with early emotional and behavioral dysregulation who live in a home with parents with psychopathology are more likely to develop externalizing behaviors consistent with a diagnosis of ODD or CD (Han & Shaffer, 2013). Furthermore, an interaction between social-cognitive deficits (i.e., those associated with the development of externalizing behaviors) among children and parent psychopathology increases the risk for child psychopathology (e.g., Goodman & Gotlib, 1999). Although peer relationships become increasingly important as children age, the established influence of delinquent peers on the development of disruptive behavior disorders like ODD or CD may be exacerbated by parental psychopathology (Burke, Loeber, & Birmaher, 2002).

Thus, parental psychopathology functions not only as a predictor but also as a risk factor, interacting with other known predictors of ODD and CD to increase the risk of developing these disruptive behavior disorders. Indeed, the psychopathology of one parent may also exacerbate the relation between the psychopathology of another parent and their child's risk for ODD and CD. As discussed earlier, maternal depression and paternal depression have an additive effect on youth externalizing disorders (Brennan et al., 2002) and interact in predicting disruptive behavior symptoms (Mezulis et al., 2004).

Conclusions, Clinical Implications, and Future Directions

Parent psychopathology is a definitive etiological factor to be considered in the development of ODD and CD in children and adolescents. Furthermore, an understanding of parent psychopathology is imperative when considering the context in which ODD and CD in youth occur. A wide range of parental psychopathology, among both mothers and fathers, has been associated with these disruptive behavior disorders among youth. However, the preponderance of evidence links maternal depression to child ODD and CD. The literature reviewed suggests that parental psychopathology likely exhibits both a direct and indirect effect on youth ODD and CD. Furthermore, the relation between these pathologies appears to be reciprocal. Finally, parental psychopathology not only predicts the development of youth ODD and CD but also exacerbates risk and symptomatology when it co-occurs with other known predictors.

Clearly, given these findings, parental psychopathology should be considered in the diagnosis and treatment of youth ODD and CD. A comprehensive psychological assessment should assess the child or adolescent's symptoms within the familial context, including parents' own psychopathology (see Chapter 23 for a full discussion of the assessment process). The parental contextual factors should be considered in an integrative case conceptualization, with the presence of parental psychopathology being considered a risk factor and the lack of any parental psychopathology being considered a protective factor.

Treatment planning should also take into consideration that parental psychopathology, if present, can be a treatment barrier—perhaps by directly minimizing therapeutic change to the child or adolescent (Kazdin & Wassell, 1999) or by impeding improvement in factors known to relate to better child outcomes (e.g., parenting behaviors; Reyno & McGrath, 2006). For example, one study found that depressed mothers reacted differently to their child's compliant or noncompliant behaviors when compared to mothers whose depression was in remission or mothers who were never depressed (Thomas, O'Brien, Clarke, Liu, & Chronis-Tuscano, 2015). Specifically, the depressed mothers were not only more likely to respond coercively when their child was noncompliant but also were less likely to reinforce their child when compliant.

If parent psychopathology is severe enough, it may warrant referral of the parent to their own treatment, which would have the added benefit of reducing risk for the child or adolescent (Gunlicks & Weissman, 2008). Research supports the argument that treating psychopathology among parents (including maternal depression) may reduce symptomatology in their children, even when children do not receive direct treatment (Kim, Szigethy, Meltzer-Brody, Pilowsky, & Verhulst, 2013). Even if the parent does not seek their own treatment or displays only subclinical symptoms themselves, therapy with the child or adolescent with ODD or CD may need to take into account the parent's functioning. Parent-focused aspects of treatment may require modifications to remain feasible for a parent struggling to function with his or her own psychopathology. Certain aspects of treatment, such as improving parent–child interactions (Kazdin, 2005), may require more focus than would be typical, due to their potential direct link to the child's problems in the context of parental psychopathology. Clinicians may have to process children's reactions to their parent's psychopathology and help them to develop adaptive skills—rather than disruptive behavior and acting out—to cope with it.

It will be important for future outcome studies to use the literature on parental psychopathology to modify, improve, and support evidenced-based assessment and interventions with ODD and CD. In addition, research should continue to build knowledge on the association between parental psychopathology and early signs of externalizing behaviors among preschool children—and even infants via their temperament—to better understand the complexity of parental psychopathology and the eventual development of ODD and CD among youth. Such research will be important in informing both prevention and early intervention efforts.

Although research has been growing in recent years, there remains relatively less of it that specifically focuses on father's psychopathology as it relates to child externalizing outcomes, including ODD and CD (i.e., in comparison to the research on mothers). Some of the research considering fathers does so by examining their presence or absence in the home but more work is needed in considering the co-psychopathology of parents (Goodman et al., 2011). With the continued reduction of traditional marital roles and fathers having ever-increasing involvement in their children's direct care (Puhlman & Pasley, 2016), they must earn equal billing in future research efforts. In addition, in considering the gender of youth with ODD and CD, more research is needed to understand the relation between parental psychopathology and the development of ODD and CD symptoms specifically in females. Likewise, how the relation between parental psychopathology and ODD and CD could be attenuated by other factors, including demographic and cultural ones, requires further study. Finally, although this chapter considered mediators of the relation between parental psychopathology and symptoms of ODD and CD, it is also essential that research consider parental psychopathology itself as a mediator that may explain an indirect influence of some other factors (e.g., low socioeconomic status; Barry et al., 2005) known to predict ODD or CD in youth. Such studies will contribute to a more complete understanding of the contextual factors in which ODD and CD in youth develop.

References

Antúnez, Z., de la Osa, N., Granero, R., & Ezpeleta, L. (2016). Parental psychopathology levels as a moderator of temperament and oppositional defiant disorder symptoms in preschoolers. *Journal of Child and Family Studies, 25,* 3124–3135.

August, G. J., Realmuto, G. M., Joyce, T., & Hektner, J. M. (1999). Persistence and desistance of oppositional defiant disorder in a community sample of children with ADHD. *Journal of the American Academy of Child & Adolescent Psychiatry, 38,* 1262–1270.

Baker, B. L., McIntyre, L. L., Blacher, J., Crnic, K., Edelbrock, C., & Low, C. (2003). Pre-school children with and without developmental delay: Behaviour problems and parenting stress over time. *Journal of Intellectual Disability Research, 47,* 217–230.

Barnow, S., Spitzer, C., Grabe, H. J., Kessler, C., & Freyberger, H. J. (2006). Individual characteristics, familial experience, and psychopathology in children of mothers with borderline personality disorder. *Journal of the American Academy of Child & Adolescent Psychiatry, 45,* 965–972.

Barry, T. D., Dunlap, S. T., Cotten, S. J., Lochman, J. E., & Wells, K. C. (2005). The influence of maternal stress and distress on disruptive behavior problems in boys. *Journal of the American Academy of Child & Adolescent Psychiatry, 44,* 265–273.

Blacher, J., Neece, C. L., & Paczkowski, E. (2005). Families and intellectual disability. *Current Opinion in Psychiatry, 18,* 507–513.

Blatt-Eisengart, I., Drabick, D. A., Monahan, K. C., & Steinberg, L. (2009). Sex differences in the longitudinal relations among family risk factors and childhood externalizing symptoms. *Developmental Psychology, 45,* 491–502.

Bornovalova, M. A., Cummings, J. R., Hunt, E., Blazei, R., Malone, S., & Iacono, W. G. (2014). Understanding the relative contributions of direct environmental effects and passive genotype–environment correlations in the association between familial risk factors and child disruptive behavior disorders. *Psychological Medicine, 44,* 831–844

Bornovalova, M. A., Hicks, B. M., Iacono, W. G., & McGue, M. (2010). Familial transmission and heritability of childhood disruptive disorders. *The American Journal of Psychiatry, 167,* 1066–1074.

Bountress, K., & Chassin, L. (2015). Risk for behavior problems in children of parents with substance use disorders. *American Journal of Orthopsychiatry, 85*, 275–286.

Breaux, R. P., Harvey, E. A., & Lugo-Candelas, C. (2014). The role of parent psychopathology in the development of preschool children with behavior problems. *Journal of Clinical Child and Adolescent Psychology, 43*, 777–790.

Brennan, P. A., Hammen, C., Andersen, M. J., Bor, W., Najman, J. M., & Williams, G. M. (2000). Chronicity, severity, and timing of maternal depressive symptoms: Relationships with child outcomes at age 5. *Developmental Psychology, 36*, 759–766.

Brennan, P. A., Hammen, C., Katz, A. R., & Le Brocque, R. M. (2002). Maternal depression, paternal psychopathology, and adolescent diagnostic outcomes. *Journal of Consulting and Clinical Psychology, 70*, 1075–1085.

Burke, J. D., Loeber, R., & Birmaher, B. (2002). Oppositional defiant disorder and conduct disorder: A review of the past 10 years, part II. *Journal of the American Academy of Child & Adolescent Psychiatry, 41*, 1275–1293.

Burstein, M., Ginsburg, G. S., & Tein, J. Y. (2010). Parental anxiety and child symptomatology: An examination of additive and interactive effects of parent psychopathology. *Journal of Abnormal Child Psychology, 38*, 897–909.

Calzada, E. J., Eyberg, S. M., Rich, B., & Querido, J. G. (2004). Parenting disruptive preschoolers: Experiences of mothers and fathers. *Journal of Abnormal Child Psychology, 32*, 203–213.

Campbell, S. B., Morgan-Lopez, A. A., Cox, M. J., & McLoyd, V. C. (2009). A latent class analysis of maternal depressive symptoms over 12 years and offspring adjustment in adolescence. *Journal of Abnormal Psychology, 118*, 479–493

Chronis, A. M., Lahey, B. B., Pelham, W. E., Kipp, H. L., Baumann, B. L., & Lee, S. S. (2003). Psychopathology and substance abuse in parents of young children with attention-deficit/hyperactivity disorder. *Journal of the American Academy of Child and Adolescent Psychiatry, 42*, 1424–1432.

Connell, A. M., & Goodman, S. H. (2002). The association between psychopathology in fathers versus mothers and children's internalizing and externalizing behavior problems: A meta-analysis. *Psychological Bulletin, 128*, 746.

Conners-Burrow, N. A., Swindle, T., McKelvey, L., & Bokony, P. (2015). A little bit of the blues: Low-level symptoms of maternal depression and classroom behavior problems in preschool children. *Early Education and Development, 26*, 230–244.

Crnic, K. A., Gaze, C., & Hoffman, C. (2005). Cumulative parenting stress across the preschool period: Relations to maternal parenting and child behaviour at age 5. *Infant and Child Development, 14*, 117–132.

Cummings, E. M., Davies, P. T., & Campbell, S. B. (2000). *Developmental psychopathology and family process: Theory, research, and clinical implications.* New York, NY: Guilford.

Deault, L. C. (2010). A systematic review of parenting in relation to the development of comorbidities and functional impairments in children with attention-deficit/hyperactivity disorder (ADHD). *Child Psychiatry and Human Development, 41*, 168–192.

DeVito, C., & Hopkins, J. (2001). Attachment, parenting, and marital dissatisfaction as predictors of disruptive behavior in preschoolers. *Development and Psychopathology, 13*, 215–231.

Diamantopoulou, S., Verhulst, F. C., & van der Ende, J. (2010). Testing developmental pathways to antisocial personality problems. *Journal of Abnormal Child Psychology, 38*, 91–103.

Downey, G., & Coyne, J. C. (1990). Children of depressed parents: An integrative review. *Psychological Bulletin, 108*, 50–76.

Duchovic, C. A., Gerkensmeyer, J. E., & Wu, J. (2009). Factors associated with parental distress. *Journal of Child and Adolescent Psychiatric Nursing, 22*, 40–48.

Dumas, J. E., Gibson, J. A., & Albin, J. B. (1989). Behavioral correlates of maternal depressive symptomatology in conduct-disorder children. *Journal of Consulting and Clinical Psychology, 57*, 516–521.

Eisenberg, N., Zhou, Q., Spinrad, T. L., Valiente, C., Fabes, R. A., & Liew, J. (2005). Relations among positive parenting, children's effortful control, and externalizing problems: A three-wave longitudinal study. *Child Development, 76*, 1055–1071.

Embry, L., & Dawson, G. (2002). Disruptions in parenting behavior related to maternal depression: Influences on children's behavioral and psychobiological development. In J. G. Borkowski & S. L. Ramey (Eds.), *Parenting and the child's world: Influences on academic, intellectual, and social-emotional development* (pp. 203–212). Mahwah, NJ: Lawrence Erlbaum Associates, Inc.

Eyberg, S. M., Boggs, S. R., & Rodriguez, C. M. (1993). Relationships between maternal parenting stress and child disruptive behavior. *Child & Family Behavior Therapy, 14*, 1–9.

Falk, A. E., & Lee, S. S. (2012). Parenting behavior and conduct problems in children with and without attention-deficit/hyperactivity disorder (ADHD): Moderation by callous-unemotional traits. *Journal of Psychopathology and Behavioral Assessment, 34*, 172–181.

Fisher, S. D., Brock, R. L., O'Hara, M. W., Kopelman, R., & Stuart, S. (2015). Longitudinal contribution of maternal and paternal depression to toddler behaviors: Interparental conflict and later depression as mediators. *Couple and Family Psychology: Research and Practice, 4*, 61–73.

Frick, P. J., Lahey, B. B., Loeber, R., Stouthamer-Loeber, M., Christ, M. G., & Hanson, K. (1992). Familial risk factors to oppositional defiant disorder and conduct disorder: Parental psychopathology and maternal parenting. *Journal of Consulting and Clinical Psychology, 60*, 49–55.

Gavin, N. I., Gaynes, B. N., Lohr, K. N., Meltzer-Brody, S., Gartlehner, G., & Swinson, T. (2005). Perinatal depression: A systematic review of prevalence and incidence. *Obstetrics & Gynecology, 106*, 1071–1083.

Goodman, S. H., & Gotlib, I. H. (1999). Risk for psychopathology in the children of depressed mothers: A developmental model for understanding mechanisms of transmission. *Psychological Review, 106*, 458.

Goodman, S. H., Rouse, M. H., Connell, A. M., Broth, M. R., Hall, C. M., & Heyward, D. (2011). Maternal depression and child psychopathology: A meta-analytic review. *Clinical Child and Family Psychology Review, 14*, 1–27.

Gunlicks, M. L., & Weissman, M. M. (2008). Change in child psychopathology with improvement in parental depression: A systematic review. *Journal of the American Academy of Child & Adolescent Psychiatry, 47*, 379–389.

Han, Z. R., & Shaffer, A. (2013). The relation of parental emotion dysregulation to children's psychopathology symptoms: The moderating role of child emotion dysregulation. *Child Psychiatry and Human Development, 44*, 591–601.

Hanington, L., Ramchandani, P., & Stein, A. (2010). Parental depression and child temperament: Assessing child to parent effects in a longitudinal population study. *Infant Behavior & Development, 33*, 88–95

Harold, G. T., Elam, K. K., Lewis, G., Rice, F., & Thapar, A. (2012). Interparental conflict, parent psychopathology, hostile parenting, and child antisocial behavior: Examining the role of maternal versus paternal influences using a novel genetically sensitive research design. *Development and Psychopathology, 24*, 1283–1295.

Harvey, E., Stoessel, B., & Herbert, S. (2011). Psychopathology and parenting practices of parents of preschool children with behavior problems. *Parenting: Science and Practice, 11*, 239–263.

Herwig, J. E., Wirtz, M., & Bengel, J. (2004). Depression, partnership, social support, and parenting: Interaction of maternal factors with behavioral problems of the child. *Journal of Affective Disorders, 80*, 199–208.

Hirshfeld-Becker, D. R., Petty, C., Micco, J. A., Henin, A., Park, J., Beilin, A., . . . Biederman, J. (2008). Disruptive behavior disorders in offspring of parents with major depression: Associations with parental behavior disorders. *Journal of Affective Disorders, 111*, 176–184.

Holmes, M. R. (2013). Aggressive behavior of children exposed to intimate partner violence: An examination of maternal mental health, maternal warmth and child maltreatment. *Child Abuse & Neglect, 37*, 520–530.

Humphreys, K. L., Mehta, N., & Lee, S. S. (2012). Association of parental ADHD and depression with externalizing and internalizing dimensions of child psychopathology. *Journal of Attention Disorders, 16*, 267–275.

Johnston, C., & Mash, E. J. (2001). Families of children with attention-deficit/hyperactivity disorder: Review and recommendations for future research. *Clinical Child and Family Psychology Review, 4*, 183–207.

Kazdin, A. E. (2005). *Parent management training: Treatment for oppositional, aggressive, and antisocial behavior in children and adolescents.* New York, NY: Oxford University Press.

Kazdin, A. E., & Wassell, G. (2000). Therapeutic changes in children, parents, and families resulting from treatment of children with conduct problems. *Journal of the American Academy of Child & Adolescent Psychiatry, 39,* 414–420.

Kessler, R. C., Berglund, P., Demler, O., Jin, R., Koretz, D., Merikangas, K. R., . . . Wang, P. S. (2003). The epidemiology of major depressive disorder: Results from the National Comorbidity Survey Replication (NCS-R). *Journal of the American Medical Association, 289,* 3095–3105.

Kessler, R. C., Berglund, P., Demler, O., Jin, R., Merikangas, K. R., & Walters, E. E. (2005). Lifetime prevalence and age-of-onset distributions of DSM-IV disorders in the National Comorbidity Survey Replication. *Archives of General Psychology, 62,* 593–602.

Kim, S. R., Szigethy, E., Meltzer-Brody, S., Pilowsky, D. J., & Verhulst, F. (2013). Supporting the mental health of children by treating mental illness in parents. *Psychiatric Annals, 43,* 534–537.

Kopp, L. M., & Beauchaine, T. P. (2007). Patterns of psychopathology in the families of children with conduct problems, depression, and both psychiatric conditions. *Journal of Abnormal Child Psychology, 35,* 301–312.

Latimer, K., Wilson, P., Kemp, J., Thompson, L., Sim, F., Gillberg, C., . . . Minnis, H. (2012). Disruptive behaviour disorders: A systematic review of environmental antenatal and early years risk factors. *Child: Care, Health and Development, 38,* 611–628.

Lavigne, J. V., Gouze, K. R., Hopkins, J., Bryant, F. B., & LeBailly, S. A. (2012). A multi-domain model of risk factors for ODD symptoms in a community sample of 4-year-olds. *Journal of Abnormal Child Psychology, 40,* 741–757.

Lovejoy, M. C., Graczyk, P. A., O'Hare, E., & Neuman, G. (2000). Maternal depression and parenting behavior: A meta-analytic review. *Clinical Psychology Review, 20,* 561–592.

Lyons-Ruth, K. (1996). Attachment relationships among children with aggressive behavior problems: The role of disorganized early attachment patterns. *Journal of Consulting and Clinical Psychology, 64,* 64–73.

Malik, N. M., Boris, N. W., Heller, S. S., Harden, B. J., Squires, J., Chazan-Cohen, R., . . . Kaczynski, K. J. (2007). Risk for maternal depression and child aggression in Early Head Start families: A test of ecological models. *Infant Mental Health Journal, 28,* 171–191.

Manassis, K., Bradley, S., Goldberg, S., & Hood, J. (1995). Behavioural inhibition, attachment and anxiety in children of mothers with anxiety disorders. *The Canadian Journal of Psychiatry, 40,* 87–92.

Marmorstein, N. R., & Iacono, W. G. (2004). Major depression and conduct disorder in youth: associations with parental psychopathology and parent–child conflict. *Journal of Child Psychology and Psychiatry, 45,* 377–386.

McKee, L., Colletti, C., Rakow, A., Jones, D. J., & Forehand, R. (2008). Parenting and child externalizing behaviors: Are the associations specific or diffuse? *Aggression and Violent Behavior, 13,* 201–215.

McLearn, K. T., Minkovitz, C. S., Strobino, D. M., Marks, E., & Hou, W. (2006). The timing of maternal depressive symptoms and mothers' parenting practices with young children: Implications for pediatric practice. *Pediatrics, 118,* e174–e182.

McLennan, J. D., Kotelchuck, M., & Cho, H. (2001). Prevalence, persistence, and correlates of depressive symptoms in a national sample of mothers of toddlers. *Journal of the American Academy of Child & Adolescent Psychiatry, 40,* 1316–1323.

Mezulis, A. H., Hyde, J. S., & Clark, R. (2004). Father involvement moderates the effect of maternal depression during a child's infancy on child behavior problems in kindergarten. *Journal of Family Psychology, 18,* 575–588.

Michael, T., Zetsche, U., & Margraf, J. (2007). Epidemiology of anxiety disorders. *Psychiatry, 6,* 136–142.

Miller-Slough, R. L., Dunsmore, J. C., Ollendick, T. H., & Greene, R. W. (2016). Parent–child synchrony in children with oppositional defiant disorder: Associations with treatment outcomes. *Journal of Child and Family Studies, 25,* 1880–1888.

Moehler, E., Brunner, R., Wiebel, A., Reck, C., & Resch, F. (2006). Maternal depressive symptoms in the postnatal period are associated with long-term impairment of mother–child bonding. *Archives of Women's Mental Health, 9,* 273–278.

Morgan, J., Robinson, D., & Aldridge, J. (2002). Parenting stress and externalizing child behaviour. *Child & Family Social Work, 7,* 219–225.

Muratori, P., Milone, A., Nocentini, A., Manfredi, A., Polidori, L., Ruglioni, L., . . . Lochman, J. E. (2015). Maternal depression and parenting practices predict treatment outcome in Italian children with disruptive behavior disorder. *Journal of Child and Family Studies, 24,* 2805–2816.

Murray, C., & Johnston, C. (2006). Parenting in mothers with and without attention-deficit/hyperactivity disorder. *Journal of Abnormal Psychology, 115,* 52–61.

Murray, L., Sinclair, D., Cooper, P., Ducournau, P., Turner, P., & Stein, A. (1999). The socioemotional development of 5-year-old children of postnatally depressed mothers. *Journal of Child Psychology and Psychiatry, 40,* 1259–1271.

Neece, C. L., Green, S. A., & Baker, B. L. (2012). Parenting stress and child behavior problems: A transactional relationship across time. *American Journal on Intellectual and Developmental Disabilities, 117,* 48–66.

O'Connor, T. G., Heron, J., Glover, V., & Alspac Study Team. (2002). Antenatal anxiety predicts child behavioral/emotional problems independently of postnatal depression. *Journal of the American Academy of Child & Adolescent Psychiatry, 41,* 1470–1477.

O'Connor, T. G., Heron, J., Golding, J., Beveridge, M., & Glover, V. (2002). Maternal antenatal anxiety and children's behavioural/emotional problems at 4 years. *The British Journal of Psychiatry, 180,* 502–508.

Ohannessian, C. M., Hesselbrock, V. M., Kramer, J., Kuperman, S., Bucholz, K. K., Schuckit, M. A., & Nurnberger, J. I. (2005). The relationship between parental psychopathology and adolescent psychopathology: An examination of gender patterns. *Journal of Emotional and Behavioral Disorders, 13,* 67–76.

Pfiffner, L. J., McBurnett, K., Rathouz, P. J., & Judice, S. (2005). Family correlates of oppositional and conduct disorders in children with attention deficit/hyperactivity disorder. *Journal of Abnormal Child Psychology, 33,* 551–563.

Pugh, K. L., & Farrell, A. D. (2011). The impact of maternal depressive symptoms on adolescents' aggression: Role of parenting and family mediators. *Journal of Child and Family Studies, 21,* 589–602.

Puhlman, D. J., & Pasley, K. (2016). Father role, History of. In C. L. Shehan (Ed.), *The Wiley Blackwell Encyclopedia of Family Studies*. 1–5. Chichester, UK: John Wiley & Sons, Inc.

Ramchandani, P. G., Stein, A., O'Connor, T. G., Heron, J. O. N., Murray, L., & Evans, J. (2008). Depression in men in the postnatal period and later child psychopathology: A population cohort study. *Journal of the American Academy of Child & Adolescent Psychiatry, 47,* 390–398.

Reyno, S. M., & McGrath, P. J. (2006). Predictors of parent training efficacy for child externalizing behavior problems–a meta-analytic review. *Journal of Child Psychology and Psychiatry, 47,* 99–111.

Ross, C. N., Blanc, H. M., McNeil, C. B., Eyberg, S. M., & Hembree-Kigin, T. L. (1998). Parenting stress in mothers of young children with oppositional defiant disorder and other severe behavior problems. *Child Study Journal, 28,* 93–111.

Rothbaum, F., & Weisz, J. R. (1994). Parental caregiving and child externalizing behavior in nonclinical samples: a meta-analysis. *Psychological Bulletin, 116,* 55.

Sayed, M., Hussein, H., El-Batrawy, A., Zaki, N., & El Gaafary, M. (2006). Parenting stress index among mothers of conduct disorder children. *Current Psychiatry, 13,* 255–270.

Sellers, R., Harold, G. T., Elam, K., Rhoades, K. A., Potter, R., Mars, B., . . . Collishaw, S. (2014). Maternal depression and co-occurring antisocial behaviour: Testing maternal hostility and warmth as mediators of risk for offspring psychopathology. *Journal of Child Psychology and Psychiatry, 55,* 112–120.

Singh, A. L., D'Onofrio, B. M., Slutske, W. S., Turkheimer, E., Emery, R. E., Harden, K. P., . . . Martin, N. G. (2011). Parental depression and offspring psychopathology: A Children of Twins study. *Psychological Medicine, 41,* 1385–1395.

Slatcher, R. B., & Trentacosta, C. J. (2011). A naturalistic observation study of the links between parental depressive symptoms and preschoolers' behaviors in everyday life. *Journal of Family Psychology, 25,* 444–448.

Stormshak, E. A., Bierman, K. L., McMahon, R. J., Lengua, L. J., and the Conduct Problems Prevention Research Group (2000). Parenting practices and child disruptive behavior problems in early elementary school. *Journal of Clinical Child Psychology, 29,* 17–29.

Thomas, S. R., O'Brien, K. A., Clarke, T. L., Liu, Y., & Chronis-Tuscano, A. (2015). Maternal depression history moderates parenting responses to compliant and noncompliant behaviors of children with ADHD. *Journal of Abnormal Child Psychology, 43,* 1257–1269.

Tully, E. C., Iacono, W. G., & McGue, M. (2008). An adoption study of parental depression as an environmental liability for adolescent depression and childhood disruptive disorders. *American Journal of Psychiatry, 165,* 1148–1154.

van der Molen, E., Hipwell, A. E., Vermeiren, R., & Loeber, R. (2011). Maternal characteristics predicting young girls' disruptive behavior. *Journal of Clinical Child & Adolescent Psychology, 40,* 179–190.

van der Waerden, J., Galéra, C., Larroque, B., Saurel-Cubizolles, M. J., Sutter-Dallay, A. L., Melchior, M., & EDEN Mother–Child Cohort Study Group. (2015). Maternal depression trajectories and children's behavior at age 5 Years. *The Journal of Pediatrics, 166,* 1440–1448.

Vander Stoep, A., Adrian, M. C., Rhew, I. C., McCauley, E., Herting, J. R., & Kraemer, H. C. (2012). Identifying comorbid depression and disruptive behavior disorders: Comparison of two approaches used in adolescent studies. *Journal of Psychiatric Research, 46,* 873–881.

Wickramaratne, P. J., & Weissman, M. M. (1998). Onset of psychopathology in offspring by developmental phase and parental depression. *Journal of the American Academy of Child & Adolescent Psychiatry, 37,* 933–942.

18

Relationship Discord, Intimate Partner Physical Aggression, and Externalizing Problems of Children

K. Daniel O'Leary and Ingrid Solano

This chapter will, first, address the prevalence of relationship discord. Second, data will be presented on the prevalence of intimate partner aggression (IPA). Third, the associations of these two problems will be addressed. Fourth, the prevalence of oppositional defiant disorder (ODD) and conduct disorder (CD) will be very briefly reviewed. Fifth, the association between relationship discord and externalizing problems of children will be examined. Sixth, meta- analyses on the associations of marital discord with ODD and CD will be summarized and suggestions for future directions made. Seventh, the association of IPA and externalizing problems of children will be investigated. Eighth, a summary of meta-analyses on the associations of IPA and externalizing problems will be followed by suggestions for future directions. The meta-analyses will be presented after some examples of the research areas in order to document the overall effects of marital discord, marital conflict, and IPA on externalizing behaviors of children.

Relationship Discord

Numerous articles describe the positive effects of being in a satisfying intimate relationship, and the effects are salutary for both men and women (Foran, Whisman, & Beach, 2015). Alternatively viewed, being in a discordant relationship is associated with more depression, anxiety, and substance abuse (Whisman, 1999) and more inadequate immune function (Glaser & Kiecolt-Glaser, 2014). And, relationship discord is not simply a correlate of depressive symptomatology. In longitudinal research, relationship discord is predictive of later depressive symptomatology as well as clinical diagnoses of depression (Beach, 2014). And individuals who divorce are likely to die earlier than those who remain married (Waite, 1995).

When one looks at the prevalence of discord at any specific time, it is very clear from numerous studies that only a small minority of individuals report themselves to be quite unhappy in their relationships. One way to document this point about unhappiness in relationships is to look at studies in which individuals report their unhappiness in a relationship ranging from 1–5 or 1–7 on a Likert scale. In a 2003–2004 survey of the National Fatherhood Initiative, over 1500 individuals in the US were surveyed. The 890 married individuals surveyed produced the following relationship results: "not at all satisfied,"

1.0%; "not very satisfied," 1.9%; "somewhat satisfied," 9.0%; "very satisfied," 38.4%; and "completely satisfied," 49.7%.

In research with a randomly recruited NY sample, only a small percentage of the respondents reported being quite unhappy in their relationship (O'Leary, Acevedo, Aron, Huddy, & Mashek, 2011). More specifically, less than 5% of women and 3% of men reported being a little unhappy, fairly unhappy, or extremely unhappy in their relationship with their partner. By contrast, 5.9% of females said they were "perfectly happy" in their relationship with their partner," 12.7% said that they were "extremely happy," 19.8% said they were "very happy," and 7.8% said they were "happy." For men, we have the following: 13.6% "perfectly happy," 7.9% "extremely happy," 9.3% "very happy," and 6.2% "happy." The main point here is that only a very small percentage of men and women at any single point in time report being unhappy in their relationship.

If the majority of men and women report being very happy in a relationship, then one may ask why the divorce rate has approximated 50% (Kennedy & Ruggles, 2014). Further, given the small percentages of individuals who report being discordant at any point, a natural question that comes to mind is what factors lead to divorce and how could individuals who report being quite satisfied in their relationship move on to the divorce court. A 2003–2004 national survey of over 1500 adults, sponsored by the National Fatherhood Initiative (2005) and referred to above, found that the most common reason for divorce given by the 170 subjects who had ever divorced was "lack of commitment" (73%). Other significant reasons included too much arguing (56%), infidelity (55%), marrying too young (46%), unrealistic expectations (45%), lack of equality in the relationship (44%), lack of preparation for marriage (41%), and abuse (29%).

In addition to the reasons for divorce cited above, it has been shown that there is a group of 10–15% of individuals who show a honeymoon effect followed by a rapid decrease in marital satisfaction in the first few years of marriage. This rapid decrease in satisfaction was reportedly associated with intimate partner violence, depression, and partner's relationship satisfaction (Lorber, Erlanger, Heyman, & O'Leary, 2014). Thus, while the vast majority of individuals report being quite satisfied at any specific point, approximately 50% of individuals in the United States are divorcing (Kennedy & Ruggles, 2004), and satisfaction can turn sour very quickly for some.

Intimate Partner Aggression

Intimate partner aggression (IPA) comprises psychological, physical, and sexual aggression. Psychological aggression is clearly the most common form in relationships, with physical aggression being second in terms of frequency, and sexual aggression being least common (Monson, Langhinrichsen-Rohling, & Taft, 2009; O'Leary & Woodin, 2009). In fact, because psychological aggression is so common, and because, several decades ago, it seemed difficult to measure, psychological aggression had less research attention than physical or sexual aggression. Further, the effects of sexual aggression against a partner and on children are much less studied than physical aggression. This chapter, therefore, will focus only on physical aggression against a partner. Physical aggression in the form of acts such as pushing, slapping, shoving, kicking, hitting with a fist, threatening with a knife or gun seemed easier to measure as hundreds of studies have been published on its prevalence, impact, and correlates.

Based on several nationally representative studies, the percentage of men and women who perpetrate IPA is roughly 10% of the population, and the percentage of *young* men and women who perpetrate IPA is roughly 35–45% (Jose & O'Leary, 2009). To the surprise and dismay of many, the prevalence of self-reported physical aggression among women was almost the same as that of men (Archer, 2000). Data like this sparked great controversy, and the similarity of prevalence rates of physical aggression by men and women in representative studies led to various articles on gender symmetry or asymmetry in IPA (Johnson, 2006). The debates still occur but they are less vociferous and more nuanced. Importantly, the differential impact of physical aggression by men and women is clear, with greater injury being inflicted on women in population (Coker et al., 2002) and marital clinic samples (Cascardi, Langhinrichsen, & Vivian, 1992). Physically victimized women reported more fear of their partners than physically victimized men and nonvictimized women (Kar & O'Leary, 2010). Finally, at the extreme end of the continuum, murder of women by their intimate male partners is approximately three times that of murder of men by their female partners (1,247 vs. 400 in 2000; Rennison, 2003).

The field of intimate partner aggression has sometimes been characterized by research that relied on representative samples versus research that relied on clinical samples, such as those of battered women and batterers. In fact, as in almost any field, if one uses a representative sample from which to draw conclusions, the conclusions will likely be quite different from the conclusions one would draw from a clinical sample. Of course, there are individuals in representative samples who have characteristics that are similar to those of subjects in clinical samples such as men and women who seek marital therapy. Between 40 and 60% of couples seeking marital therapy report intimate partner aggression (Jose & O'Leary, 2009). In this chapter, we will characterize the types of samples from which we draw conclusions.

The Association of Relationship Discord and Intimate Partner Violence

If one frequently engages in aggression against an intimate partner, the relationship is likely to be poor or will soon become discordant. The data do indeed support this assumption. There is evidence that the extent of IPA is correlated with the extent of relationship discord. However, research on engaged and newly married individuals has shown that many individuals who describe their relationship as quite positive sometimes engage in physical aggression (Lawrence & Bradbury, 2001).

Even individuals who report being intensely in love are sometimes in relationships characterized by IPA. In a sample of over 2000 couples from the Madrid area, Grana, Montesino, Rediondo, and O'Leary (2016), found that a small but significant percentage of men and women, namely, about 15%, who said they were intensely in love reported that they had been the objects of physical aggression by their partner in the past year. Multi-level models confirmed that individuals who were less intensely in love reported a higher level of psychological aggression. And even though some individuals in aggressive relationships reported being intensely in love, men who reported they were less intensely in love reported a higher level of physical aggression by their partners.

On the other hand, across the years of a relationship, discord can ensue for many reasons as discussed earlier in this chapter. Arguing, being critical, and yelling, which are forms of psychological aggression, can lead to IPA. Psychological and physical aggression are generally quite highly correlated across many studies and there is longitudinal evidence that, when psychological aggression becomes quite intense, IPA will occur even in couples who have never previously engaged in it (Murphy & O'Leary, 1989). In short, across many studies there is evidence that relationship discord and IPA are significantly correlated, and a meta-analysis by Stith et al. (2000) has shown that the effect size of marital/relationship discord and perpetration of IPA by men was .30 and by women .25. In samples of men mandated to a batterer program, the relationship between the mandated man and his partner or previous partner is often hard to measure accurately because the couple may have split voluntarily or the husband may be unable to have any contact with the partner as a result of a "refrain from" or "stay away" order from a judge. Nonetheless, on the basis of many clinical assessments of men in batterer programs by colleagues who have conducted groups for batterers, there is little question that many if not the majority of men mandated to batterer treatments have been in highly discordant relationships.

Prevalence of ODD/CD

The lifetime prevalence of ODD is estimated to be 10.2% (males = 11.2%; females = 9.2%) and ODD is associated with risk factors such as temperament, parenting issues, and family problems (Nock, Kazdin, Hiripi, & Kessler, 2007; see Chapters 2 and 3 of this book for a full discussion of the definition and characteristics of conduct disorder and oppositional defiant disorder). Prior to puberty, ODD is more common in boys (1.4:1), while prevalence rates after puberty are equal across genders (APA, 2015). ODD symptoms are quite stable across time in males and females (Diamantopoulou, Verhulst, & van der Ende, 2011). The estimated lifetime prevalence of CD is 9.5% (males = 12%, females = 7.1%) and is associated with low education, marital disruption, and urban residence (Nock et al., 2006). ODD usually appears by age 8, while the median age-of-onset for CD is 11.6 years old. CD is divided into childhood-onset which manifests as one or more symptoms before the age of 10, and adolescent-onset. Conduct disorder co-occurs at greater than chance levels with ODD, attention deficit hyperactivity disorder (ADHD), anxiety disorders, and depressive disorders in both clinical and population-based samples (Lahey, Loeber, Burke, Rathouz, & McBurnett, 2002).

In general, conduct concerns fall along a continuous spectrum of externalizing problems with CD accounting for the more extreme symptomology later in childhood (Nock et al., 2007). In a 2002 study, Lahey and colleagues found that only ODD predicted later CD diagnoses. Yet, diagnoses of both ODD and CD predict future psychopathology and impaired life functioning, with CD being the more detrimental (Burke, Waldman, & Lahey, 2010).

Due to the high degree of overlap between symptoms, there is some concern as to whether ODD is a separate disorder from CD (Waldman & Lahey, 2013). Since ODD symptoms emerge first, it may be a precursor of CD. Notably, CD is often conceptualized as the longitudinal progression of ODD in adolescence. Approximately 30% of children who were diagnosed with ODD will go on to develop CD. Among children with ODD, 50% maintain their ODD diagnosis without progressing to CD, and 25% cease to display conduct problems entirely (Burke et al., 2010). However, nearly half of all children with CD have no prior ODD diagnosis (Rowe, Costello, Angold, Copeland, & Maughan, 2010), and most children who display ODD do not progress to CD, making the argument for separate diagnoses more cogent. Though the progression is not simple, there do seem to be temporal and symptom-severity vectors of externalizing behavior that may be more informative than individual diagnoses. For example, the risk of developing CD is three times greater for children who were initially diagnosed with ODD in preschool (Connor, 2002), but not for those diagnosed later on. Considering ODD and CD as externalizing problems that arise at different time points and with differential severity is relevant for this chapter, as ODD and CD have been found to share marital discord as a common environmental risk factor.

Family-related difficulties are among the strongest and most consistent correlates of conduct problems (Dishion & Patterson, 2006). Understandably, the systemic maintenance and exacerbation of externalizing problems includes marital conflict. Exposure to conflict between parents increases verbal and physical aggression in children of ages 2 to 18 (Davis, Hops,

Alpert, & Sheeber, 1998). Children predominantly have aggressive responses to destructive conflict tactics between parents (96%) rather than constructive responses (4%) (Cummings & Davies, 2010; Cummings, Davies, & Campbell, 2000). It would seem logical to theorize that the later onset and increased severity of symptoms in CD possibly stem from longer exposure to such destructive conflicts.

Association of Marital Discord/Conflict and ODD/CD

Conflict is a regular occurrence in marriage and intimate relationships. When handled well and resolved constructively, exposure to conflict may have little to no effect, in fact may even have a positive effect (Grych & Fincham, 1990). However, poorly managed conflict increases risk for child emotional and behavioral problems (Braithwaite, Steele, Spjut, Dowdle, & Harper, 2015; Emery, 1982; Kitzmann, 2000). Most research regarding risk factors for conduct problems explores the relationship between the family environment and antisocial behavior. Marital/parental-related risk factors include family discord and disruption, child abuse and neglect, coercive/hostile styles of parenting, lack of parental monitoring and supervision, and marriage maladaptation (Farrington, 1995; Loeber & Stouthamer-Loeber, 1986; Meyer et al., 2000; Patterson, 1996; Patterson & Yoerger, 1997). Indeed, having more than one of the aforementioned factors increases risk, and, taken in isolation, no one environmental risk factor has a major effect (Coln, Jordan, & Mercer, 2013).

The association between parental factors and child behavioral adjustment is a robust one. Recent research has focused on exploring mediation and causal relationships between parental problems and child maladjustment (Coln, Jordan, & Mercer, 2013; Cui & Conger, 2008; Kaczynski, Lindhal, Malik, & Laurenceau, 2006). This large body of work has found that specific aspects of parenting (e.g. harshness, poor parental behavioral control, inconsistent discipline, lax parental supervision, psychological intrusiveness, low acceptance and support, rejection, coercion, and inconsistency) as well as paternal stress (Camisasca, Miragoli, & Di Blasio, 2016) mediate the associations between marital conflict and the externalizing behaviors of children. Both high levels of interparental conflict and low levels of marital satisfaction have been consistently associated with behavior problems (Cummings & Davies, 1994, 2002; Rhoades et al., 2011) with few exceptions (Burt, Wildey, & Klump, 2015).

There has also been a more recent focus on interactional and genetically informed studies that indicate a child-driven effect (Harden et al., 2007). Children's maladaptive emotion regulation has been found to mediate the association between negative parental conflict resolution styles and children's externalizing problems (Siffert & Schwarz, 2011). Further, there is emerging literature that temperament and parenting styles interact to influence externalizing behavior (Bradley & Corwyn, 2007; Lengua & Kovacs, 2005; Stright, Gallagher, & Kelley, 2008). Ultimately, adolescent externalizing problems have been found to exacerbate parental conflicts over child rearing (Cui, Donnellan, & Conger, 2007). These dynamic links between marital conflict and child outcomes provides a more nuanced understanding of these complex associations.

The most prominent theoretical approaches for explaining these mechanisms involve children's cognitive appraisals (Grych & Fincham, 1990) and their emotional security (Davies & Cummings, 1994). Though a large amount of research has focused on child perceptions of conflict, there is some evidence that parent-reported connectedness (with the child) may mediate the relationship between marital conflict and externalizing behavior (Braithwaite et al., 2015). Nevertheless, the most widely discussed mechanism for the relationship between marital conflict and externalizing behavior in children is "spill-over." Emotions aroused in family conflict can "spill over" into other areas (Margolin, Christensen, & John, 1996).

This spill-over can transfer mood, affect, or behaviors to other individuals in the family (Cox, Paley, & Harter, 2001; Erel & Burman, 1995). Of concern in this context, parental/marital realm risk factors can transfer to the parent–child relationship. This mechanism, consequently, can account for diminished parent–child relationships and increased negative parenting practices (Camisasca et al., 2015).

Meta Analyses of the Association of Marital Discord/Conflict and Externalizing Behavior

Reid and Crisafulli (1990) conducted a meta-analysis that assessed marital dissatisfaction/conflict and child conduct problems. They examined 33 published articles spanning from 1957 to 1988. They found the overall effect size of marital dissatisfaction and childhood behavior problems to be .16 for boys compared to .05 for girls. Only 5% of effect sizes from all papers were significant for girls as compared to 25% for boys. Additionally, there appeared to be a significant increase in effect size when studies obtained behavioral information from parents rather than relying on self-report data. Buehler and colleagues (1997) argue that Reid and Crisafulli's use of both marital dissatisfaction and marital conflict may have contributed to a lower effect size than might be expected, and, in fact, Buehler et al. (1997) did find larger effect sizes though they examined interparental conflict rather than marital discord.

Buehler and colleagues (1997) conducted a meta-analysis of interparental conflict and childhood problems in youth aged 5 to 18. They examined 68 studies and found an average effect size of .32. The effect size for externalizing problems was .39 and for internalizing problems, .31. Buehler et al. noted that the effect size for the association of interparental conflict and childhood problems was twice as large as the effect size for marital conflict in the Reid and Crisafulli analysis. Such results are in accord with the view that overt marital conflict would have a greater impact on children then general marital discord (Cummings & Davies, 1994; Emery & O'Leary, 1982). In contrast to the gender difference found by Reid and Crisafulli (1990), no gender difference was found in this meta-analysis, and there was no effect of age. Of special interest to the authors of this chapter was the finding that the association between parental conflict and childhood problems was stronger for recently separated families than families in which the separation or divorce was more distant. They also found that the overall effect size varied with educational level across samples. In samples in which most subjects had not completed high school, the effect size was .60; in those in which most subjects had completed high school, the effect size was .03; and in those in which most subjects had completed some college, the effect size was .30. Given these large differences, the effects are certainly worthy of replication. Finally, when they analyzed the types of conflict to which children were exposed, overt conflicts were more strongly associated with childhood problems than were covert conflicts.

Rhoades (2008) continued to explore the link between marital conflict and children's behavioral and emotional dysfunction with a meta-analysis that focused on the child's own responses to parental conflict. The direct focus on parental conflict occurred in part because the children's own responses to conflict would seem most proximal to their own psychosocial and physical adjustment. Rhoades identified 71 studies that explored these relationships in children of 5–19 years of age, and age was found to significantly moderate the majority of effect sizes with older children showing stronger associations. Notably, effect sizes were generally larger for internalizing than for externalizing behavior problems. The meta-analysis found no significant differences between aggregate effect sizes for girls or boys. Negative responses to marital conflict may be more likely, over repeated experiences, to become characteristic response patterns to a variety of life events, thus resulting in generalized externalizing and internalizing problems. There is some evidence that children under 10 years of age may lack the cognitive sophistication necessary for generating as well as processing maladaptive cognitions about marital conflict. It may be the case that younger children generate maladaptive cognitions during, but not after, conflict and thus avoid additional processing. Additionally, Rhoades noted that the age difference may be influenced by the fact that younger children have had less opportunity to witness marital conflict than older children.

In summary, based on the two meta-analyses on marital problems and childhood problems discussed above, the following conclusions can be made:

- There is a significant albeit small association, <.20, between marital discord and childhood problems, with a larger effect for boys than girls. Age was not a significant moderator. Exposure to overt parental conflicts has a stronger association with externalizing problems, >.30, than being in a home in which the parents have a discordant marriage but may not display their problems in front of the children.
- When one examines the direct association of marital conflict and children's reactions to the conflict, the results suggest that older children are more affected than younger children. Internalizing problems were more strongly associated with marital conflict than externalizing problems.

Future Directions

As stated earlier, it will be useful to explore conduct issues in children in a temporal and externalizing symptom framework. More specifically, the extent of marital conflict and the length of exposure to it would help elucidate the etiology of the ODD and CD diagnoses. With nearly identical risk factors, it may be more informative to explore associations, correlates, and risk factors based on these dimensional approaches rather than individual diagnoses. In fact, transdiagnostic research suggests that internalizing and externalizing factors may be more predictive of all diagnoses except those characterized by thought disorder (Krueger & Eaton, 2015).

A major limitation of all included meta-analyses is the dearth of experimental design and thus the inability to ascertain the directionality of the findings. Some research indicates that children with externalizing behavior may adversely affect their parents and peers. For example, longitudinal research using survival analyses, showed that children with ADHD are more likely to be in families in which parents divorce than families without ADHD, and symptoms of ODD and CD were predictors of divorce (Wymbs et al., 2008). Aggressive children have also been found to make more hostile attributions to peers than nonaggressive children (Dodge & Somberg, 1987) and thus may be differentially affected by a heightened perception of a hostile environment.

The Relationship between IPA and Externalizing Problems of Children

The research on IPA and its effects on children has not been broken down into the impact of IPA on ODD and/or CD. Instead, this area of research has paid more attention to the broad-ranging impact of IPA on various behavior problems of children. Consequently, the focus in this section of the chapter will be on the different effects of IPA on children, with an emphasis on their externalizing problems, and, where possible, effects on CD and ODD will be noted.

The most studied impact of IPA on offspring is whether children who observe violence between their parents learn to act in similar ways. That is, if a child sees his or her parents engaging in IPA, will that child be more likely to engage in acts of physical aggression against a dating partner or even a marriage partner later? This issue has long been described as the intergenerational transmission of violence, and meta-analyses have shown that this it has an effect size of .21 for men and .11 for women (Stith et al., 2000). Thus, while the data across many studies support the concept of the intergenerational transmission of violence, the actual effects are small. Stated positively, the majority of individuals who observe violence do not go on to engage in such behavior.

Engaging in acts of physical aggression against dating partners or spouses can be characterized as one form of externalizing behavior that is actually associated with a number of other externalizing behaviors, but a key issue in this chapter is whether IPA is associated with CD and ODD in children. This specific issue has been addressed in the context of women in shelters for IPA and the kinds of problem that the children of the abused women have. Literature reviews show that approximately 35–65% of fathers whose wives or partners are in shelters physically abuse their children (e.g., Jouriles, Spiller, Stephens, McDonald, & Swank, 2000) But even if a child is in a shelter and has experienced some physical abuse by the father, not all such children have ODD or CD.

The types of problem that children of abused women experience were evaluated by Grych, Jouriles, Swank, McDonald, and Norwood (2000) in a sample of 228 children aged 8–14 years residing in a battered women's shelter. Using cluster analyses, five behavior patterns were found: multi-problem externalizing, multi-problem internalizing, externalizing, mild distress, and no problems reported. In a neat methodological manner, the results were cross-validated in independent halves of the sample, and the effects were similar for boys and girls. It is very important to note that the children in the largest group (31%) had no patterns of maladjustment. The second largest group (21%) had externalizing problems, and the third group (19%) had both internalizing and externalizing problems. The fourth group (18%) had mild distress with only slightly elevated means for internalizing and very low levels of externalizing problems. The fifth group (11%) was labeled multi-problem because of high scores on depressive symptoms and somewhat elevated externalizing scores.

In examining the role of partner violence on the childhood problem types, the investigators found that the children's reports of IPA by fathers was different across the groups with multi-problem externalizing and multi-problem internalizing having the highest levels of father aggression toward the mother; the other three groups were indistinguishable. In addition, child appraisal of parent conflict was examined as a possible differentiator across the childhood problem types: no problems and externalizing problem groups reported the lowest level of parental conflict. The multi-problem externalizing, multi-problem internalizing, and mild distress groups did not differ among themselves. Overall, Grych et al. (2000) interpreted the data to support a dose-effect model in which IPA on the part of fathers and appraisal of conflict are associated with level of child maladjustment. Finally, this research points to the need to study and capitalize on the resiliency of a significant percentage of children, namely the 31%, who had no level of clinical problems. While it is true that they experienced less IPA and may have been subjected to less risk than others, they may also have had better coping skills and their mothers may have been better able to provide support for them during the time they resided in a shelter.

Evidence (Jouriles, Murphy, & O'Leary, 1989) shows that IPA contributes to conduct disorders in boys even after marital discord, child's age, child's sex, and marital discord by child's sex interaction was controlled for. The participants (n = 87 couples) in the research sought marital therapy and their children were between 5 and 12 years of age. Although IPA clearly had a uniquely negative effect on children's behavior, it was also interesting to note that, when the data were analyzed for the clinical level of the childhood problems, approximately 50% of the children from maritally aggressive homes were not evidencing problems at a clinical level. The childhood problems assessed were conduct problems, personality problems, and inadequacy-immaturity, and all three problems were predicted by marital aggression, with CD and personality problems being predicted for boys and inadequacy-immaturity for girls. Viewed differently, the likelihood of having a clinical-level childhood problem in the non-aggressive families was 15%, whereas 50% of the children in maritally aggressive families had clinical levels of childhood problems. Thus, as the above analyses of problem types show, while marital aggression does correlate with CD, it is not uniquely associated with it. It has wide-ranging negative effects. And, as we shall now see from a 20-year longitudinal study, CD is a predictor of later partner violence.

In a longitudinal study that followed over 500 children across 20 years, Ehrensaft et al. (2003) tested the effects of exposure to domestic violence between parents, adolescent disruptive behavior disorders, and emerging substance abuse on later partner violence. Conduct disorder was the strongest risk for perpetrating partner violence for both sexes, followed by exposure to domestic violence between parents, and power-assertive punishment. This research extended the findings of Magdol, Moffitt, Caspi, and Silva (1998) showing that childhood behavior problems are among the most robust predictors of later interpartner violence. In short, while partner aggression is associated with CD and is often seen as an important etiological risk for CD, CD in children is also a risk for later IPA in these individuals when they became parents.

Meta Analyses of the Association of IPA with Externalizing Problems

Wolfe, Crooks, Lee, McIntyre-Smith and Jaffee (2003) identified 41 studies that were deemed worthy of inclusion in a meta-analysis regarding the effects of exposure of children to domestic violence. Forty such studies showed that exposure was related to emotional and behavioral problems with a small overall effect. While there were only four studies that allowed for a parsing of exposure to IPA and the effects of child abuse directly, as might be expected, co-occurrence of child abuse increased the extent of emotional and behavioral problems over and above the effects of exposure alone.

Based on a number of literature reviews there is a general consensus that exposure to IPA has significant negative effects on children compared to children who grow up in families without IPA. The negative effects are wide-ranging and include emotional and behavioral functioning, as well as social and achievement problems. The literature also supports a position that the effects of IPA go beyond other co-existing factors like marital discord, which we have discussed earlier. However, Wolfe and colleagues noted that conclusions about the effects of exposure to IPA need to be examined with some caution for a number of reasons. First, much of the research comes from children whose mothers were in shelters for battered women. Second, there were no nationally representative samples in the meta-analytic review. Third, the community samples were often small; of the 13 community samples, seven had surveyed less than 100 subjects. While age and gender were able to be evaluated as moderators of outcome, other moderators were not examined. Gender was not found to be a significant moderator when the studies that included only boys were removed. The aggregate weighted mean correlation for boys was .11 and for girls .09. Of special relevance to this chapter on the effects of IPA on ODD and CD, the effect size for internalizing and externalizing was examined and not found to be different—with an aggregate mean correlation for internalizing of .19 and an effect size for externalizing of .21.

In 2003 another meta-analysis was published on the effects of exposure to IPA by Kitzmann, Gaylord, Holt, and Kenny who reported that d was .50 for internalizing symptoms and was .43 for externalizing symptoms. Further, in 2008, Evans, Davies, and DiLillo found similar but larger effect sizes in a meta-analysis with a larger data base with weighted effect sizes of

.48 and .47 for childhood internalizing and externalizing symptoms, respectively, indicating moderate effects. A larger mean weighted effect size d value of 1.54 was obtained for the relationship between exposure to domestic violence and childhood trauma symptoms, though this figure was based on only six studies.

The results across three meta-analytic studies are quite consistent with regard to the effects of witnessing domestic violence on children's externalizing behavior, as Evans et al. (2008) concluded. They noted that Wolfe et al. (2003) weighted mean correlations of .19 for internalizing problems and .21 for externalizing problems corresponds to effect sizes of .38 and .42, respectively, not very different from the other two meta-analytic studies. Moderator analyses for gender by Evans et al. (2008) showed that the relationship between exposure to domestic violence and externalizing symptoms was significantly stronger for boys than for girls, but they urged caution in interpreting the gender differences, which may have been due to methodological differences. Evans et al. (2008) concluded that the effects found in community samples were not different from those from samples of battered women. While such results may have been found, it seems premature to conceptualize that the effects of a child seeing frequent physical aggression against a mother that leads to fear and injury would be the same as the effects of a child seeing an occasional push or shove by the father or mother. As will be discussed later, there is a clear need to examine the level of exposure a child has to intimate partner physical aggression.

Conclusions and Future Research Directions

One way to interpret data presented in this chapter is that many children fortunately escape any adverse effects of exposure to IPA. As illustrated by Murphy et al. (1989), 50% of the children exposed to IPA whose parents sought treatment at a marital clinic did not experience behavior or emotional problems. And when a sample of children whose mothers were in a shelter was examined, the percentage of children without significant problems was 31%. In fact, the group without significant behavioral or emotional problems was the largest group found in the cluster analyses of Grych et al. (2000). The data on the groups of children without significant clinical problems may point, in part, to the resilience of many children.

The issue of resilience was addressed by Alaggia, Scott, Donahue, and Niepage (2016) who analyzed 18 studies on exposure to IPA. A thematic analysis examined definitions of resilience and protective factors. Their search terms included resilience, emotional adjustment, and protective factors. They used a social ecological lens to interpret their data, and their main finding were as follows: there were incongruencies regarding definitions of resilience; intra and interpersonal factors dominate the literature with little emphasis on contextual and environmental factors; and poly-victimization should be expected and explored. Since the literature on exposure to IPA is sparse regarding resilience factors, some are listed here:

1. Intrapersonal Factors: easy temperament, agreeable; socially competent; academically successful; accurately assigns abuse responsibility
2. Interpersonal Factors: access to one safe adult, protective mother; one secure attachment; peer and social support
3. Contextual and Cultural Factors: Safe haven; community resources; educated mother with stable employment; connection to spirituality and faith.

Given that a significant percentage of children exposed to IPA do not evidence clinical levels of childhood symptomatology, it would seem worthwhile in future research to examine whether protective and resilience factors like those just discussed are predictive of children not having problems despite some exposure to IPA. The field seems ripe for such work with the emergence of a new journal, *Journal of Adversity and Resilience*, edited by Sherry Hamby, and the publication of the *Resilience Portfolio Model* (Grych, Hamby, & Banyard, 2015). In that model, resilience requires measurement of three components: adversity; a positive (or at least not a negative outcome; and one protective factor that can be related to a positive outcome.

In addition, it would seem worthwhile for future research to contain a much greater delineation of the level of exposure to IPA as reported by both parents and children, since exposure can vary dramatically. For example, one could imagine at least the following different levels of exposure from a child or teenager's perspective:

1. Heard fighting of some kind and no injury (Most likely exposure in randomly selected community samples)
2. Heard but did not see IPA (Heard parents fighting but did not see it; knew mother was injured since child saw that she was)
3. Did not hear or see IPA (Was not at home but saw injury on mother and believed that father caused injury)
4. Saw physical fighting between parents but there was no injury to mother
5. Saw physical fighting between parents and there was injury observable to the children or teens.

In accordance with the need to examine levels of exposure to IPA, it would seem valuable to ascertain the extent of intervention by the child or teen attempting to stop verbal and physical fighting between the parents. Further, it would be useful to examine the perceptions of the child or teen about the extent to which the physical aggression between the parents was mutual or unilateral. The data from nationally representative samples indicates that in approximately 50% of the cases where any physical aggression occurs, the aggression is engaged in by both partners (Straus & Gelles, 1990), yet the exposure-to-IPA literature is basically silent on this matter.

Finally, an area that has not been evaluated is the relative negative effects on children of psychological aggression compared to physical aggression. Research in the partner abuse area has shown that the effects of psychological aggression are often more deleterious to women than the effects of physical aggression, and it seems likely that exposure to intense arguing on a weekly or more frequent basis could have more deleterious effects on children than exposure to acts of physical aggression a few times a year (a common pattern in community samples). For example, in a sample of 68 women residing in a shelter for battered women, the frequency and severity of physical abuse was not a significant predictor of posttraumatic stress disorder symptoms nor of the women's intentions to terminate their abusive relationships (Arias & Pape, 1989). However, psychological abuse was a significant predictor of both PTSD symptoms and intentions to permanently leave abusive partners even after controlling for the effects of physical abuse.

References

Alaggia, R., Scott, K., Donahue, M., & Niepage, M. (2016, July). *Take these broken wings and learn to fly: A review on resilience and child exposure to IPA through a social ecological lens. Poster presented at International Family Violence Research*, Portsmouth, NH.

Arias, I., & Pape, K. T. (1999). Psychological abuse: Implications for adjustment and commitment to leave violent partners. *Violence and Victims, 14*(1), 55–67.

Archer, J. (2000). Sex differences in aggression between heterosexual partners: A meta-analytic review. *Psychological Bulletin, 126,* 651–680.

Beach, S. R. H. (2014). The couple and family discord model of depression: Updates and future directions. In C. R. Agnew and S. C. South (Eds.), *Interpersonal relationships and health: Social and clinical psychological mechanisms* (pp 133–155). Oxford, UK: Oxford University Press.

Bradley, R. H., & Corwyn, R. F. (2007). Infant temperament, parenting, and externalizing behavior in first grade: A test of the differential susceptibility hypothesis. *Journal of Child Psychology and Psychiatry, 49,* 124–131.

Braithewaite, S. R., Steele, E., Spjut, K., Dowdle, K. K., & Harper, J. (2015). Parent–child connectedness mediates the association between marital conflict and children's internalizing/externalizing outcomes. *Journal of Family Studies, 24,* 3690–3699.

Buehler, C., Anthony, C., Krishnakumar, A., Stone, G., Gerard, J., & Pemberton, S. (1997). Interparental conflict and youth problem behaviors: A meta-analysis. *Journal of Child and Family Studies, 6*(2), 233–247.

Burke, J. D., Waldman, I., & Lahey, B. B. (2010). Predictive validity of childhood oppositional defiant disorder and conduct disorder: Implications for the DSM-V. *Journal of Abnormal Psychology, 119*(4), 739–751.

Burt, S. A., Wildey, M. N., & Klump, K. L. (2015). The quality of the interparental relationship does not moderate the etiology of child conduct problems. *Psychological Medicine, 45,* 319–332.

Camisasca, E., Miragoli, S., & Di Blasio, P. (2016). Families with distinct levels of marital conflict and child adjustment: Which role for maternal and paternal stress? *Journal of Child and Family Studies, 25,* 733–745.

Cascardi, M., Langhinrichsen, J., & Vivian, D. (1992). Marital aggression: Impact, injury, and health correlates for husbands and wives. *Archives of Internal Medicine, 152,* 1178–1184.

Coker, A. L., Davis, K. E., Arias, I., Desai, S., Sanderson, M., Brandt, H. M, & Smith, P. H. (2002). Physical and mental health effects of intimate partner violence for men and women. *American Journal of Preventive Medicine, 23,* 260–268.

Coln, K. L., Jordan, S. S., & Mercer, S. H. (2013). A unified model exploring parenting practices as mediators of marital conflict and children's adjustment. *Child Psychiatry and Human Development, 44,* 419–429.

Connor, D. F. (2002). *Aggression and antisocial behavior in children and adolescents: Research and treatment.* New York, NY: The Guilford Press.

Cox, M. J., Paley, B., & Harter, K. (2001). Interparental conflict and parent–child relationships. In J. H. Grych & F. D. Fincham (Eds.), *Interparental conflict and child development: Theory, research, and application.* New York, NY: Cambridge University Press.

Crockenberg, S., & Langrock, A. (2001). The role of specific emotions in children's responses to interparental conflict: A test of the model. *Journal of Family Psychology, 15,* 163–182.

Cui, M., & Conger, R. D. (2008). Parenting behavior as mediator and moderator of the association between marital problems and adolescent maladjustment. *Journal of Research on Adolescence, 18*(2), 261–284.

Cui, M., Donnellan, M. B., & Conger, R. D. (2007). Reciprocal influences between parents' marital problems and adolescent internalizing and externalizing behavior. *Developmental Psychology, 43*(6), 1544–1552.

Cummings, E. M., & Davies, P. (1994). *Children and marital conflict: The impact of family dispute and resolution.* New York, NY: The Guilford Press.

Cummings, E. M., Davies, P. T. (2002). Effects of marital conflict on children: Recent advances and emerging themes in process-oriented research. *Journal of Child Psychology and Psychiatry, 43,* 31–63.

Cummings, E. M., & Davies, P. T. (2010). *Marital conflict and children: An emotional security perspective.* New York, NY: Guilford Press.

Cummings, E. M., Davies, P. T., & Campbell, S. B. (2000). *Developmental psychopathology and family process: Theory, research, and clinical applications.* New York, NY: Guilford Press.

Davies, P. T., & Cummings, E. M. (1994). Marital conflict and child adjustment: An emotional security hypothesis. *Psychological Bulletin, 116,* 387–411.

Davis, B. T., Hops, H., Alpert, A., & Sheeber, L. (1998). Child responses to parental conflict and their effect on adjustment: A study of triadic relations. *Journal of Family Psychology, 12,* 163–177.

Diamantopoulou, S., Verhulst, F. C., & van der Ende, J. (2011). The parallel development of ODD and CD symptoms from early childhood to adolescence. *European Child & Adolescent Psychiatry, 20,* 301–309.

Dishion, T. J., & Patterson, G. R. (2006). The development and ecology of antisocial behavior. In D. Cicchetti & D. J. Cohen (Eds.), *Developmental psychopathology* (Vol. 3). *Risk, disorder, and adaptation.* New York, NY: Wiley.

Dodge, K. A., & Somberg, D. R. (1987). Hostile attribution biases among aggressive boys are exacerbated under conditions of threat to self. *Child Development, 58,* 213–224.

Ehrensaft, M., K., Cohen, P., Brown, J., Smailes, E., Chen, H., & Johnson, J. G. (2003). Intergenerational transmission of partner violence: A 20-year prospective study. *Journal of Consulting and Clinical Psychology, 71,* 741–753.

Emery, R. E. (1982). Interparental conflict and the children of discord and divorce. *Psychological Bulletin, 92,* 310–330.

Emery, R. E., & O'Leary, K. D. (1982). Children's perceptions of marital discord and behavior problems of boys and girls. *Journal of Abnormal Child Psychology, 10,* 11–24.

Erel, O., & Burman, B. (1995). Interrelatedness of marital relations and parent–child relations: A meta-analytic review. *Psychological Bulletin, 118,* 108–132.

Evans, S. E., Davies, C., & DiLillo, D. (2008). Exposure to domestic violence: A meta-analysis of child and adolescent outcomes. *Aggression and Violent Behavior, 13,* 131–140.

Farrington, D. P. (1995). The development of offending and antisocial behavior from childhood: Key findings from the Cambridge study in delinquent development. *Journal of Child Psychology, 36,* 929–964.

Foran, H. M., Whisman, M. A., & Beach, S. R. H. (2015). Intimate partner relationship distress in the DSM-V. *Family Process, 54*(1), 48–63.

Glaser, R., & Kiecolt-Glaser, J. (2014). *Handbook of human stress and immunity.* New York, NY: Academic Press.

Grana, J. L., Montesino, M. L. C., Redondo, N., & O'Leary, K. D. (2016). Can you be hit by your partner and be intensely in love? *Journal of Interpersonal Violence, 31*(12), 2156–2174.

Grych, J. H., & Fincham, F. D. (1990). Marital conflict and children's adjustment: A cognitive-contextual framework. *Psychological Bulletin, 108,* 267–290.

Grych, J. H., Hamby, S., & Banyard, V. (2015). The resilience portfolio model: Understanding healthy adaptation in victims of violence. *Psychology of Violence, 5*(4), 343–354.

Grych, J. H., Jouriles, E. N., Swank, P. R. McDonald, R., & Norwood, W. D. (2000). Patterns of adjustment among children of battered women. *Journal of Consulting and Clinical Psychology, 68*(1), 84–94.

Harden, K. P., Lynch, S. K., Turkheimer, E., Emery, R. E., Slutske, W. S., Waldron, M. D., . . . Martin, N. G. (2007). A behavior genetic investigation of adolescent motherhood and offspring mental health problems. *Journal of Abnormal Psychology, 116,* 667–683.

Johnson, M. P. (2006). Conflict and control: Gender symmetry and asymmetry in domestic violence. *Violence against Women, 12*(1), 1003–1018.

Jouriles, E. N., Murphy, C. M., & O'Leary, K. D. (1989). Interspousal aggression, marital discord, and childhood problems. *Journal of Consulting and Clinical Psychology, 57*(3), 453–455.

Jouriles, E. N., Spiller, L. C., Stephens, N., McDonald, R., & Swank, P. (2000). Variability in adjustment of children of battered women: The role of child appraisals of interparent conflict. *Cognitive Therapy and Research, 24,* 233–249.

Jose, A., & O'Leary, K. D. (2009). Prevalence of partner aggression in representative and clinic samples. In K. D. O'Leary & E. M. Woodin (Eds.). *Psychological and physical aggression in couples: Causes and interventions.* Washington, DC, American Psychological Association.

Kaczynski, K. J., Lindahl, K. M., Malik, N. M., & Laurenceau, J. P. (2006). Marital conflict, maternal and paternal parenting, and child adjustment: a test of mediation and moderation. *Journal of Family Psychology, 20,* 199–208.

Kar, H. L., & O'Leary, K. D. (2010). Gender symmetry or asymmetry in intimate partner victimization? Not an either/or answer. *Partner Abuse, 1*(2), 152–168.

Kennedy, S., & Ruggles, S. (2014). Breaking up is hard to count: The rise of divorce in the United States, 1980–2010. *Demography, 51,* 587–598.

Kitzmann, K. M. (2000). Effects of marital conflict on subsequent triadic family interactions and parenting. *Developmental Psychology, 36,* 3–13.

Kitzman, K. M., Gaylord, N. K., Holt, A. R., & Kenny, D. R. (2003). Child witness to domestic violence. A meta-analytic review. *Journal of Consulting and Clinical Psychology, 71,* 339–352.

Krueger, R. F., & Eaton, N. R., (2015). Transdiagnostic factors of mental disorders. *World Psychiatry, 14*(1), 27–29.

Lahey, B. B., Loeber, R., Burke, J., Rathouz, P. J., & McBurnett, K. (2002). Waxing and waning in concert: dynamic comorbidity of conduct disorder with other disruptive and emotional problems over 7 years among clinic-referred boys. *Journal of Abnormal Psychology, 111*(4), 556–567.

Lawrence, E., & Bradbury, T. N. (2001). Physical aggression and marital dysfunction: A longitudinal analysis. *Journal of Family Psychology, 15,* 135–154.

Lengua, L. J., & Kovacs, E. A. (2005). Bidirectional associations between temperament and parenting and the prediction of adjustment problems in middle childhood. *Journal of Applied Developmental Psychology, 26,* 21–38.

Loeber, R., & Stouthamer-Loeber, M. (1986). Family factors as correlates and predictors of juvenile conduct problems and delinquency. In M. H. Tonry & N. Morris (Eds.), *Crime and justice: An annual review of research* (Vol. 7). Chicago, IL: University of Chicago Press.

Lorber, M. F., Erlanger, A. C. E., Heyman, R. E., & O'Leary, K. D. (2015). The honeymoon effect: does it exist and can it be predicted? *Prevention Science, 16*(4), 550–559.

Magdol, L., Moffit, T. E., Caspi, A., & Silva, P. (1999). Developmental antecedents of partner abuse: A prospective longitudinal study: *Journal of Abnormal Psychology, 107,* 375–389.

Margolin, G., Christensen, A., & John, R. S. (1996). The continuance and spillover of everyday tensions in distressed and non-distressed families. *Journal of Family Psychology, 10,* 304–321.

Meyer, J. M., Rutter, M., Silberg, J. L., Maes, H. H., Simonoff, E., Shillady, L. L., . . . Eaves, L. J. (2000). Familial aggregation for conduct disorder symptomatology: The role of genes, marital discord and family adaptability. *Psychological Medicine, 30,* 759–774.

Monson, C. M., Langhinrichsen-Rohling, J. L., & Taft, C. T. (2009). Sexual aggression in intimate relationships. In K. D. O'Leary & E. M. Woodin (Eds.), *Psychological and physical aggression in couples* (pp. 37–57). Washington, DC: American Psychological Association.

Murphy, C. M., & O'Leary, K. D. (1989). Psychological aggression predicts physical aggression in early marriage. *Journal of Consulting and Clinical Psychology, 5,* 579–582.

National Fatherhood Initiative. *With this ring . . . A national survey on marriage in America.* (2005). Gaithersburg, MD: Author.

Nock, M. K., Kazdin, A. E., Hiripi, E., & Kessler, R. C. (2007). Lifetime prevalence, correlates, and persistence of oppositional defiant disorder: Results from the National Comorbidity Survey Replication. *Journal of Child Psychology and Psychiatry, 48*(7), 703–713.

O'Leary, K. D., Acevedo, B., Aron, A., Huddy. L., & Mashek, D. (2012). Is long term love more than just a rare phenomenon? *Social Psychological and Personality Science, 3*(2), 241–249.

O'Leary, K. D., & Woodin, E. M. (2009). *Psychological and physical aggression in couples: Causes and interventions.* Washington, DC: American Psychological Association.

Patterson, G. R. (1996) Some characteristics of a developmental theory for early onset delinquency. In M. F. Lenzenweger & J. J. Haugaard (Eds.), *Frontiers of developmental psychopathology* (pp. 81–124). New York, NY: Oxford University Press.

Patterson, G. R., & Yoerger, K. A. (1997). Developmental model for late-onset delinquency. *Nebraska Symposium on Motivation, 44,* 119–177.

Reid, W. J., & Crisafulli, A. (1990). Marital discord and child behavior problems: A meta-analysis. *Journal of Abnormal Child Psychology, 18*(1), 105–117.

Rennison, C. M. (2003, February). *Intimate partner violence, 1993–2001.* Bureau of Justice Statistics. Retrieved from https://www.bjs.gov/content/pub/pdf/ipv01.pdf

Rhoades, K. A. (2008). Children's responses to interparental conflict: A meta-analysis of their associations with child adjustment. *Child Development, 79*(6), 1942–1956.

Rhoades, K. A., Leve, L. D., Harold, G. T., Neiderhiser, J. M., Shaw, D. S., & Reiss, D. (2011). Longitudinal pathways from marital hostility to child anger during toddlerhood: Genetic susceptibility and indirect effects via harsh parenting. *Journal of Family Psychology, 25*, 282–291.

Rowe, R., Costello, E. J., Angold, A., Copeland, W. E., & Maughan, B. (2010). Developmental pathways in oppositional defiant disorder and conduct disorder. *Journal of Abnormal Psychology, 119*, 726–738.

Siffert, A., & Schwarz, B. (2011). Parental conflict resolution styles and children's adjustment: Children's appraisals and emotion regulation as mediators. *The Journal of Genetic Psychology, 172*(1), 21–39.

Stith, S. M., Rosen, K. H., Middleton, K. A., Busch, A. L., Lundeberg, K., & Carlton, R. P. (2000). The intergenerational transmission of spouse abuse: A meta-analysis. *Journal of Marriage and the Family, 62*, 640–654.

Straus, M. A., & Gelles, R. J. (1990). How violent are American families? Estimates from the National Family Violence Resurvey and other studies. In M. A. Straus & R. J. Gelles (Eds.), *Physical violence in American families: Risk factors and adaptations to violence in 8,145 families* (pp. 95–112). New Brunswick, NJ: Transaction.

Stright, A. D., Gallagher, K. C., & Kelley, K. (2008). Infant temperament moderates relations between maternal parenting in early childhood and children's adjustment in first grade. *Child Development, 79*, 186–200.

Waite, L. J. (1995). Does marriage matter? *Demography, 32*, 483–507.

Waldman, I., & Lahey, B. (2013). Oppositional defiant disorder, conduct disorder, and juvenile delinquency. In T. P. Beauchaine & S. P. Hinshaw (Eds.), *Child and adolescent psychopathology* (2nd ed.). Hoboken, NJ: Wiley.

Whisman, M. (1999). Marital dissatisfaction and psychiatric disorders: Results from the national comorbidity survey. *Journal of Abnormal Psychology, 108*(4), 701–706.

Wolfe, D. A., Crooks, C. V., Lee, V., McIntyre-Smith, A., & Jaffee, P. G. (2003). The effects of children's exposure to domestic violence: A meta-analysis and critique. *Clinical Child and Family Psychology Review, 6*(3), 171–187.

Wymbs, B. T., Pelham, W. E., Molina, B., Gnagy, E. M., Wilson, T. K., & Greenhouse, J. B. (2008). Rate and predictors of divorce among parents of youths with ADHD. *Journal of Consulting and Clinical Psychology, 7*, 735–744.

19

Parenting Practices and the Development of Problem Behavior across the Lifespan

Elizabeth A. Stormshak, Elisa DeVargas, and Lucía E. Cárdenas

Being a parent: It's one of the most important jobs people have in their lives, yet one of the most challenging, for which many are unprepared. Integrally connected to culture, values, family, and community, parenting skills emerge from the relationships between all these developmental contexts. The "science" of parenting has come a long way during the past 30 years, and we now understand many of the parenting skills and strategies that lead to healthy child development and the skill deficits that lead to problem behavior among children. Yet, despite a robust literature on the topic of parenting, there is much left to learn. In this chapter we discuss effective parenting strategies used throughout a child's lifespan that predict reductions in child externalizing behavior, cultural variations in parenting skills, and effective approaches to parent training with various ages and groups of people.

History of Parenting Literature

The concept of "parenting" as a topic of research can be traced to the beginnings of the field of psychology and has strong roots in the foundations of psychology as a science. Asking the question, "Why do people act a certain way?" naturally leads to curiosity about the influence of family and parents on human behavior. Although much of the literature on parenting skills has been written from a behavioral perspective, one might argue that even the early writings of Freud focused on parenting, family relationships, and the effects of these relationships on a person's development over time.

During the late 1960s and early 1970s there was a renewed focus on parenting skills, rather than on parenting relationships, and the impact that parenting skills have on human behavior. This literature led to a proliferation of research and publications about effective parenting. Several key researchers during this era influenced and shaped the way we think about parenting today. One prominent researcher was Diana Baumrind, who categorized parenting styles in three groups: permissive, authoritarian, and authoritative. She hypothesized that authoritative parenting, which is associated with calm, controlled parenting skills that are reasonable, encourage verbal communication, exert control without coercion or abuse, and support healthy child autonomy, is the most effective for reducing child behavior problems and supporting healthy child development (Baumrind 1966; 1967). Before Baumrind's pioneering work, research had emphasized the important role of parents but had failed to identify actual skills or strategies associated with effective parenting. Her work on parenting styles was arguably one of the most influential areas of research in child development, and it continues to be well referenced today in the literature linking parenting styles with child problem behavior.

Another preeminent researcher, Gerald Patterson, was simultaneously working on understanding environmental factors that lead to conduct problems in young boys. Among Patterson's novel methods was the use of videotaped family observations to understand parenting skills that predict problem behavior. Guided by a social learning framework, he developed coercion theory, a behavioral escape conditioning theory that links parent and child behavioral escalation to the entrainment of problem behavior over time (Patterson, 1976, 1982). Rather than see children as "blank slates" in their environment, or recipients of environmental shaping, Patterson articulated the dynamic influence of parenting on children, and children on parents. He was one of the first to describe the dyadic interaction between parent and child during which each is training the other in coercive behavior that escalates over time. He applied his theories to interventions for delinquency and conduct problems and hypothesized that changing the environment and caretaker behavior would reduce antisocial behavior over time (Patterson, 1974). His model formed the foundation for most of the evidence-based parent training programs used today to treat problem behavior, and he is certainly one of the most well-known and published scientists in the area of parenting, child development, and conduct problems.

Many others contributed to this literature in earlier years, but these two pioneers set the stage for the next 40 years of research about parenting skills and problem behavior. In this chapter we discuss the work that extended these early models and continues to influence the way we conceptualize parenting in models that predict externalizing behavior.

Parenting across the Lifespan

Parenting is a job that lasts a lifetime. From their child's infancy to the adult years, parents are expected to adapt their skills and expectations to the developmental needs of their offspring. Parenting that begins in infancy with warm, nurturing behaviors forms the foundation for a baby's healthy attachment, security, and satisfaction of basic needs. It then progresses through childhood and adolescence to the adult years, during which time parenting involves communication, listening skills, and autonomy-promoting behaviors. Figure 19.1. illustrates the unique parenting skills associated with each developmental period and summarizes research that links specific parenting skills to healthy child development and reduction in problem behavior. The lifespan parenting model recognizes that parenting does not end when children reach age 18, and for most families continues with direct guidance and support well

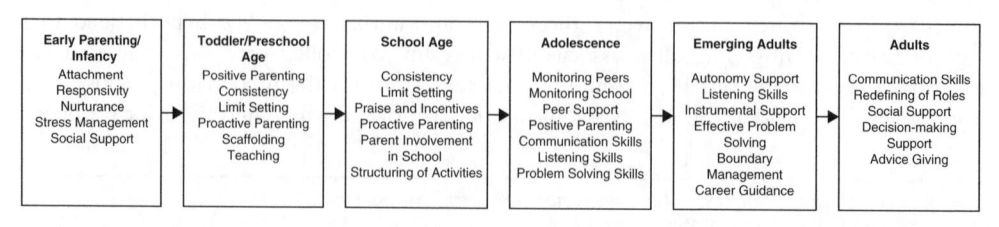

Early Parenting/ Infancy	Toddler/Preschool Age	School Age	Adolescence	Emerging Adults	Adults
Attachment Responsivity Nurturance Stress Management Social Support	Positive Parenting Consistency Limit Setting Proactive Parenting Scaffolding Teaching	Consistency Limit Setting Praise and Incentives Proactive Parenting Parent Involvement in School Structuring of Activities	Monitoring Peers Monitoring School Peer Support Positive Parenting Communication Skills Listening Skills Problem Solving Skills	Autonomy Support Listening Skills Instrumental Support Effective Problem Solving Boundary Management Career Guidance	Communication Skills Redefining of Roles Social Support Decision-making Support Advice Giving

Figure 19.1 Parenting through the lifespan: a developmental perspective.

into emerging adulthood. Parenting continues as long as there is no major disruption in the relationship during the course of the lifespan, and it changes with each major developmental transition and new set of tasks.

Parenting Skills as a Target of Interventions

It is increasingly clear that parenting practices can enhance the risk of problem behavior from early childhood to late adolescence; consequently, parenting skills are one of the best targets for intervention and prevention (Dishion & Stormshak, 2007). In fact, much of what we have learned about parenting skills and child development has been derived from intervention research. Figure 19.2. depicts a theoretical model that forms the foundation for many skills-based parenting training programs. Parenting skills, or deficits, emerge from predictable risk environments in the family that include multiple risk factors such as poverty, family stress, substance use, and parent mental health problems. Contextual stress and early child risk factors directly limit parents' ability to use effective parenting strategies at home and lead to poor self-regulation and behavioral control in children. Some of these risk factors are nearly impossible for educational and mental health systems to address (e.g., poverty), but ample research has shown that enhancing parenting skills can have a positive impact on later child behavior problems despite these early challenges. Developmental research suggests that this model, and variations of this model, are relatively robust and significant across various ages and cultural groups (Ackerman, Brown, & Izard, 2004; Raver, Gershoff, & Aber, 2007). Even in the face of poverty and high levels of neighborhood risk, warm and supportive parenting mediates the link between socioeconomic status (SES) and later antisocial behavior from early development to adolescence (Odgers et al., 2012). The implication of the model is that motivation and support to improve parenting skills can reduce the negative impact of sociocultural stress and early risk on children by enhancing self-regulation skills and behavioral competence indicators, thereby decreasing the risks of developing externalizing behavior problems over the lifespan.

In this model, child self-regulation is the *mechanism* of change, but parenting skills are the target of the intervention. Self-regulation lies at the core of health, positive development, and behavioral health problems (Blair, 2002). Individual differences in self-regulation and temperament are central features of several early childhood externalizing behavior problems, including attention deficit hyperactivity disorder (ADHD), conduct disorder, oppositional defiant disorder, and social skill deficits (Barkley, 1997). Effective parenting in early childhood and the quality of the parent–child relationship form the foundation for the development

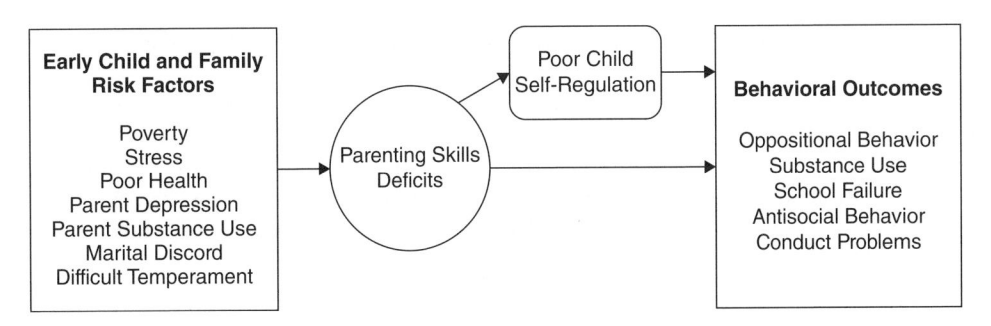

Figure 19.2 Theoretical model of parenting as a key intervention target.

of self-regulation throughout the lifespan (Eisenberg et al., 2003; Eisenberg et al., 2005). Parents contribute to the development of self-regulation in multiple ways. First, parents socialize children through the structure, shaping of behavior, and support for emotional development that occurs in the home and provides skill-based learning to support school adjustment (Morris, Silk, Steinberg, Myers, & Robinson, 2007). Second, effective parents establish behavioral routines by creating and monitoring environments that include consistent limits and support for productive behaviors (e.g., homework routines). Parents also provide positive support for children engaging and persisting in activities that result in skill development and adaptation (Zeman, Cassano, & Adrian, 2013). Third, parents can work in partnership with schools to establish predictable cross-setting routines that encourage appropriate behavior and home-to-school planning. These parenting strategies support children's attention and effortful control while promoting the development of self-regulation skills from childhood through adolescence (Spear, 2010). This, in turn, improves school achievement and adolescent adaptation. Parent interventions have shown direct effects on self-regulation constructs in early childhood, including negative emotionality and behavioral control (Blair, 2002; Chang, Shaw, Dishion, Gardner, & Wilson, 2014). Support for this model has been growing in recent years, with multiple studies suggesting strong links from parenting skills to self-regulation, and subsequent reductions in regulatory problems and externalizing behavior as a result of parent skills training (Fosco, Frank, Stormshak, & Dishion, 2013; Sulik, Blair, Mills-Koonce, Berry, & Greenberg, 2015).

From infancy to adolescence, randomized trials that follow children and families longitudinally, implement parenting skills interventions, and measure changes in behavior and parenting skills have expanded our understanding of the skill deficits that lead to externalizing behavior. This body of research provides one of the strongest arguments for the important role that parenting skills play in the development and maintenance of problem behavior. In early childhood, parenting interventions that improve positive parenting, such as warmth and praise, have been shown to change patterns of externalizing behavior over time for children as they enter school and as parents learn to identify and support positive behavior in their children, thereby reducing aggression and oppositional behavior (Dishion et al., 2008; Kazdin, 2005). Parenting interventions that reduce commands and harsh discipline predict fewer conduct problems at school entry (Webster-Stratton, 1998). In adolescence, interventions that increase parental monitoring predict improvements in antisocial behavior over time (Dishion, Nelson, & Kavanagh, 2003; Fosco, Stormshak, Dishion, & Winter, 2012). In each of these examples, comparison to a control group provides insight into the typical course of development of children, the potential preventative impact of parenting interventions on behavior, and the role that effective parenting can play in reducing the risk of externalizing behavior and later antisocial behavior in children and adolescents.

Parenting Skills That Affect the Development of Problem Behavior

The robust literature about parenting skills is too expansive to review in one chapter; however, several critical skills emerge from the literature as significant predictors of externalizing behavior problems across the lifespan. They can be summarized into the following categories: positive parenting, limit setting and consistency, and monitoring and supervision. These three skills, and variations in them, have formed the foundation of curricula for most evidence-based parent training programs.

Positive Parenting   Positive parenting includes behaviors such as rewards, incentives, praise, and positive relationships with children that support healthy development. A wealth of literature shows that negative parenting behaviors, such as punitive parenting (McKee et al., 2007) and inconsistent discipline (Stormshak, Bierman, McMahon, & Lengua, 2000), along with an insecure parent–child relationship (Zisser & Eyberg, 2010), are significant risk factors for the development of externalizing or oppositional behaviors in children (Granic & Patterson, 2006), However, it is critical to acknowledge not only the role of negative parenting practices in the emergence of externalizing behaviors in children, but also that of positive parenting practices (Boeldt et al., 2012) that influence the development of a healthy child (Castro-Schilo et al., 2013; Jones et al., 2008 ; Skinner, Johnson, & Snyder, 2005). In a 2008 meta-analysis that reviewed 77 parent-training programs, Kaminski, Valle, Filene, and Boyle (2008) found that parent–child positivity was the most effective aspect of parenting programs for child well-being and the parent–child relationship.

Positive parenting is a general term that encompasses parenting behaviors, such as parental warmth and affection (McKee et al., 2007); parent involvement (Yong, Fleming, McCarty, & Catalano, 2013); positive reinforcement, which involves reacting in a positive way when a child uses a new skill or demonstrates a new behavior (Chamberlain et al., 2010; Dishion & Stormshak, 2007); proactive structuring, or the management of a child's environment to mitigate behavior problems (Dishion & Stormshak, 2007); and acceptance (Morrill, Hawrilenko, & Córdova, 2015). Positive parenting behaviors are associated with the development of prosocial skills, such as self-esteem and emotion regulation, that are necessary for success in academic and social settings (Morrill et al., 2015).

In the literature, consistent findings demonstrate how positive parenting practices are associated with reduced externalizing problems in children. In a study conducted by Chronis et al. (2007) with a sample of children with ADHD, children of mothers who demonstrated the highest levels of positive parenting exhibited less externalizing and conduct behaviors in later years. Extant studies have identified relationships between high levels of parental warmth and lower levels of child externalizing behaviors and between low levels of parental warmth and higher levels of child externalizing behaviors (Caspi et al., 2004; McKee et al., 2007). A risk factor for the development of externalizing behaviors is a high level of coercion in the parent–child relationship, which is marked by parental withdrawal or failure to follow through with a request when a child is noncompliant (Granic & Patterson, 2006). Research suggests that parents who are warm and who engage in positive reinforcement are less likely to engage in a coercive cycle with their children (Patterson, 1982). Parental warmth, affection, and involvement are facets of the parent–child relationship that help parents establish effective discipline and limit setting (Dishion & Stormshak, 2007; Zisser & Eyberg, 2010). McNeil and Hembree-Kigin (2010) found that parents are more likely to use effective discipline strategies when the parent–child relationship is positive.

Limit Setting and Consistency *Limit setting* is defined as a set of skills used by parents to establish boundaries on children's behavior that involves saying "no," establishing and reinforcing clear expectations for child behavior, requesting behavior change, using contingencies for child compliance/noncompliance, and maintaining consistency in strategies used to enforce rules (Bolsoni-Silva & Marturano, 2010; Denham et al., 2000; Harris-McKoy & Cui, 2013). Evidence shows that this parenting strategy prevents and reduces problem behaviors (e.g., Janssen, Dekovic, & Bruinsma, 2014). Structuring children's environments so behaviors can be tracked through monitoring and supervision enables parents to adequately enforce rules and attend to misbehaviors. The ways in which parents address child behavior vary depending on child age and can be achieved by modifying the environment for young children and by verbal mediators, such as rules, for older children (Dishion & McMahon, 1998). Proactive parenting, marked by provision of a structured environment and a de-emphasis on harsh, reactive methods of child rearing, predicts decreases in children's antisocial behavior problems over time, even among children who present with greater levels of problem behavior (Denham et al., 2000).

Conversely, a lack of rules set forth by parents, in addition to negative parenting practices, is a key contributing factor to child externalizing behaviors (Bor, Sanders, & Markie-Dadds, 2002). Permissive disciplinary practices and inconsistency in setting limits places children at increased risk of engaging in antisocial behaviors and is linked with anger reactivity among youths (Houltberg, Morris, Cui, Henry, & Criss, 2014; Tilton-Weaver, Burk, Kerr, & Stattin, 2013; Walton & Flouri, 2010). Similarly, adolescents who spend more time in settings with high rates of crime are significantly more likely to have parents who provide fewer rules and fewer consequences for misbehavior (Janssen et al., 2014). Researchers posit that children whose behavior problems appear early in development may experience greater levels of adverse effects as a result of negative parenting (Denham et al., 2000). Specifically, a lack of limit setting along with punitive strategies for discipline, such as spanking, may exacerbate children's externalizing behaviors over time (Gershoff, Lansford, Sexton, Davis-Kean, & Sameroff, 2012).

Monitoring and Supervision   Parental monitoring is a strategy by which parents stay informed of their child's behavior, friendships, and activities by tracking the child's whereabouts and attending to the child's conduct (Dishion & McMahon, 1998). For younger children, monitoring skills involve supervision of activities in the home and at school. Strategies for monitoring children vary, based on the type of knowledge parents are seeking (Bourdeau, Miller, Duke, & Ames, 2011), and the structure of monitoring changes as children transition into adolescence and gain more independence. During childhood, parental monitoring primarily takes place in home and school settings, whereas in adolescence, parents must adapt monitoring strategies to include tracking activities with peers and unsupervised activities in the community (Racz & McMahon, 2011). Solicitation and control are the most commonly used strategies (Stattin & Kerr, 2000). *Solicitation* refers to active efforts by parents to gather information from their children, and *control* refers to parent-initiated structure of children's daily activities that facilitates the ease with which parents stay abreast of children's behavior (Stattin & Kerr, 2000).

Debate continues in the literature about what parental monitoring represents and how the construct should be measured. Some studies have evaluated parental monitoring by assessing parent knowledge of child activities (Abar, Jackson, Colby, & Barnett, 2014), and others have measured it as specific monitoring efforts, such as time spent together as a family (e.g., family dinner frequency), solicitation, and control (Hair, Moore, Garrett, Ling, & Cleveland, 2008; Kerr, Stattin, & Burk, 2010). Child and youth self-disclosure of activities is a construct that most relates to the amount of knowledge parents have about their children (Stattin & Kerr, 2000); therefore, researchers have proposed that parent knowledge should be conceptualized separately from monitoring because knowledge is primarily imparted by children and teens themselves rather than by parents' efforts (Kerr et al., 2010).

Despite debates about how to conceptualize knowledge and monitoring, both constructs have been found to be important in shaping child and adolescent behavior. Research has demonstrated links between parental monitoring and child safety, antisocial behavior, and substance use (Dishion & McMahon, 1998). Some theories suggest that being informed of children's activities, in turn, enables parents to appropriately address misbehavior and ensure safety (e.g., Fosco et al, 2012). Conversely, parents who are not well informed of their children's whereabouts, day-to-day activities, and friendships are more likely to have children who engage in delinquency and other problem behaviors (Crouter, Bumpus, Davis, & McHale, 2005). Parental monitoring positively associates with greater youth connectedness to parents and negatively relates to youth antisocial behavior and deviant peer relationships (e.g., Fosco et al., 2012; Tharp & Noonan, 2012). Youths who perceive greater parental solicitation are significantly less likely to engage in antisocial behavior over time, particularly among adolescents who report having significant amounts of unsupervised time (Laird, Marrero, & Sentse, 2010). In a study that investigated differences in parenting skills between mothers and fathers, researchers found that monitoring strategies of opposite-gender parents were indirectly related to child behavioral control variables, such as impulsiveness and alcohol consumption (Patock-Peckham, King, Morgan-Lopez, Ulloa, & Filson Moses, 2011). Specifically, Patock-Peckham and colleagues (2011) found that monitoring by their mother indirectly related to impulsiveness and drinking control of sons while monitoring by their father indirectly related to impulsiveness and drinking control of daughters.

Parental monitoring and knowledge of children's day-to-day activities, whereabouts, and friendships are aspects of parenting that are reliably related to behavioral outcomes. Parents who engage in more surveillance through solicitation of information and control of child and youth activities are better able to address misbehavior and prevent future conduct problems. Knowledge of behavior predicts decreases in externalizing behavior, especially for boys (Lansford, Laird, Pettit, Bates, & Dodge, 2014). Furthermore, parents' behavioral control predicts reductions in the growth of externalizing behavior, even when children are already showing initial levels of behavior problems that are significant (Galambos, Barker, & Almeida, 2003). The amount of child self-disclosure also affects how well informed parents are about their children and often mediates the relationship between child delinquency and parent knowledge (Kerr et al. 2010). The interaction between parenting efforts to stay abreast of child behaviors and child and youth openness to sharing information about the activities they are engaging in is a salient factor to consider when working with children who have conduct problems, in that both are potential areas for intervention work (Kerr et al., 2010; Pearl et al., 2014).

Parenting during the Transition to Adulthood and Interventions to Reduce Risk

Although many studies have documented parental influence on *adolescent* problem behavior, far fewer studies have examined these connections after youths leave high school. Developmental tasks associated with this period, such as self-sufficiency and identity development, necessitate a realignment of the parent–child relationship, yet these relationships remain important for promoting a successful transition to adulthood (Bartle-Haring, Brucker, & Hock, 2002; O'Connor, Allen, Bell, & Hauser, 1996). Substantial research shows that parents continue to play a significant role in the lives of their children after they leave high school, with many providing housing, material assistance, time, and emotional support. In 2010, the U.S. Census Bureau found that 57% of men and 49% of women between ages 18 and 24 were living with their parents, and parents were offering an average of 367 hours of help per year to emerging adult children living away from home (Schoeni & Ross, 2004).

In addition to various kinds of instrumental support, parents also continue to provide emotional support (Levitt, Silver, & Santos, 2007; Wintre & Yaffe, 2000) and health information (Lefkowitz & Espinosa-Hernandez, 2007), and set expectations for maturity, educational attainment, and dating behavior (Agliata & Renk, 2008). Research suggests that family relationships influence emerging adults' psychosocial development, including psychological well-being and adjustment to new roles, health behavior, capacity for intimacy, and commitment to career development (Caruthers, Van Ryzin, & Dishion, 2014; Hargrove, Creagh, & Burgess, 2002; Larose & Boivin, 1998; Pascarella & Terenzini, 1991; Scharf, Mayseless, & Kivenson-Baron, 2004; Strage & Brandt, 1999; Wintre & Yaffe, 2000). Thus, one cannot discount parents' influence during this lengthy period of transition to independent living.

Problem behaviors during the emerging adulthood years tend to cluster around the use of alcohol and illicit substances. Research suggests that many of the same family processes and parenting practices that contribute to substance use during adolescence also contribute to early-adult substance use and risk behavior. Parents influence alcohol-related beliefs (Turrisi, Wiersma, & Hughes, 2000), and parental permissiveness about drinking has been linked to increased levels of heavy drinking, greater binge drinking, and greater alcohol-related consequences over time (Turrisi, Jaccard, Taki, Dunnam, & Grimes, 2001; Walls, Fairlie, & Wood, 2009). Parent–child conflict and poor relationships with parents have both been associated with heavier drinking and negative behavioral consequences (Fischer, Forthun, Pidcock, & Dowd, 2007; Turner, Larimer, & Sarason, 2000), and a permissive parenting style—one in which children are allowed to regulate their own activities with few parental demands, rules, or consequences—has been found to influence college student drinking and students' self-regulation (Patock-Peckham, Cheong, Balhorn, & Nagoshi, 2001; Patock-Peckham & Morgan-Lopez, 2006). In contrast, parental disapproval of drinking has been negatively associated with college student alcohol use and the consequences of use (Boyle & Boekeloo, 2006; Jessor, Costa, Krueger, & Turbin, 2006; Wood et al., 2009), and parental monitoring or knowledge has been related to lower levels of alcohol use and binge drinking, fewer alcohol-related problems, and reduced drug use (Sessa, 2005; White et al., 2006; Wood et al., 2009; Wood, Read, Mitchell, & Brand, 2004).

Even though it has been established that parents continue to influence their children's behavior during emerging adulthood, researchers and practitioners alike appear to underappreciate the potential role of parents in preventing growth in conduct problems and substance use during this period. Few studies have applied a family-centered approach to the prevention of problem behavior during the young adult years (Brody, Chen, Kogan, Smith, & Brown, 2010). In fact, colleges and universities tend to engage parents only after substance-use–related problems have occurred. Future research is needed to develop family-centered approaches to reducing substance use and problem behavior during the emerging adult years.

Culture and Parenting

To successfully implement interventions that target parenting behaviors and child behavior problems in diverse populations, it is imperative for researchers to consider the various cultural factors that may affect implementation, such as language or cultural beliefs about disciplinary practices (Zisser & Eyberg, 2010). An overrepresentation of White, middle-class samples in developmental research has led to assumptions about the relationship between various forms of discipline and negative outcomes for youths that might not be true. Research suggests that the association between harsh parenting and externalizing behavior outcomes may not be the case for all children and that spanking will have less negative effects on child outcomes in cultural contexts in which harsh parenting behaviors are culturally standardized (Deater-Deckard & Dodge, 1997; Lansford, Deater-Deckard, Dodge, Bates, & Pettit, 2004). Other studies have demonstrated an association between negative externalizing behaviors and harsh parenting across White, African American, and Hispanic children (Grogan-Kaylor, 2005). These contradictory findings indicate the need for more research to examine other variables that may be moderating the effects of harsh parenting on externalizing behaviors, aside from ethnicity. For instance, although harsh parenting is associated with negative behavioral outcomes in Latino families, in the context of a relationship with high maternal warmth there is no link between harsh discipline and externalizing behaviors for Mexican American adolescents (Germán, Gonzales, McClain, Dumka, & Millsap, 2013; McLoyd & Smith, 2002). Similarly, maternal warmth has been shown to be a moderator of the effects of harsh parenting on externalizing behaviors in African American families (Deater-Deckard, Ivy, & Petrill, 2006; McLoyd & Smith, 2002).

Consideration of the social and cultural contexts of family processes helps us understand how family interactions may have an impact on child development (Bronfenbrenner, 1979). For instance, *familismo* in Mexican-origin families comprises family closeness and ultimately fosters family well-being (Cauce & Domenech-Rodriguez, 2002; Sabogal, Marín, Otero-Sabogal, Marín, & Perez-Stable, 1987). This family-based form of decision making cultivates a more collectivistic, as opposed to individualistic, social context (Smith-Morris, Morales-Campos, Alvarez, & Turner, 2012). Evidence also suggests that *familismo* contributes to positive family dynamics, effective parenting, and positive associations with a child's attachment to school (Santisteban, Mena, & Abalo, 2012; Taylor, Larsen-Rife, Conger, & Widaman, 2012).

A study that examined the cultural values of 48 Dominican and Mexican mothers of preschoolers found that the value of *respeto* was salient in regard to parenting socialization messages and parenting practices (Calzada, Fernandez, & Cortes, 2010). *Respeto* highlights obedience and emphasizes that children should not argue with or interrupt adults (Delgado-Gaitan, 1994). It dictates the types of child behavior that are appropriate in formalized situations and in public settings (Calzada et al., 2010). According to Marin and Marin (1991), *respeto* serves to preserve harmony and minimize conflict in the family and influences how parents may socialize their child (i.e., to prioritize obedience and deference, as opposed to negotiation and assertiveness), ultimately shaping the nature of their parenting practices. For instance, parents who encourage their child to demonstrate deference to adults and authoritative figures may be less likely to invite a child's opinion. In a study that examined parenting and culture in relation to child's externalizing problems among Latino, specifically Mexican American and Dominican American, mothers of preschoolers, researchers found a negative association between authoritarian parenting practices and externalizing behaviors (Calzada, Huang, Anicama, Fernandez, & Brotman, 2012). These results were surprising in that past studies have found no association, or even positive associations, between authoritarian practices and child externalizing behaviors in Latino children (Calzada et al., 2012).

With a more holistic understanding of cultural values and how they inform parenting, researchers and clinicians can incorporate these values into parent training programs and make appropriate modifications to the programs to optimize child outcomes (Calzada et al., 2010). Although it is rare for evidence-based parenting training programs to have undergone rigorous cultural adaptation processes (Baumann et al., 2015), it is also the case that few evidence-based treatments find that race moderates outcomes, and the majority appear to be equally effective with families for a variety of cultural groups (Huey & Polo, 2008; Smith, Knoble, Zerr, Dishion, & Stormshak, 2014). This is likely because universal parenting skills impact child development in similar ways regardless of culture.

Conclusion

Parenting skills, parent–child relationships, and development that occurs in the context of the family are some of the strongest predictors of outcomes throughout the life span. This connection has been established through rigorous longitudinal, developmental research that has followed children through multiple years and helped parents improve their skills and thus change the trajectory of their children's lives, reducing the risks associated with problem behavior well into the adult years. Conduct problems and related behaviors are detrimental to both the individual child and family and to society and include later adult outcomes such as antisocial behavior, substance abuse, incarceration, and chronic poor health. Although SES plays a key role in later health, parenting skills appear to have independent effects on health outcomes, including reduced cardiovascular risk (Doom, Gunnar, & Clark, 2016).

Clearly, the positive benefits of effective parenting last a lifetime and are associated with a wide range of healthy outcomes for children, adolescents, and young adults.

Although much of the current literature points to parenting practices as predictors of child behavior, it is also clear that bidirectionality is part of the developmental course of problem behavior and parenting skills. For example, parental monitoring is a key parenting skill linked to problem behavior in adolescence, yet children who engage in less antisocial behavior are more likely to communicate with parents and be open about their activities, thus parental monitoring is increased (Crouter et al., 2005; Kerr et al., 2010). Delinquency predicts decreases in parental knowledge, and parental knowledge predicts decreases in delinquency (Kerr et al., 2010). These findings support a developmental model in which parenting skills and child externalizing behaviors are shaped through a series of complex and dynamic interactions.

Given the clear relationship between parenting skills and later externalizing behavior, implementation and dissemination are of utmost importance. Parenting interventions are effective at every stage of life and are cost-effective because they reduce outcomes that are costly to society. Future research will likely focus on how to implement these interventions widely in community settings, schools, pediatric offices, and early-childhood centers to increase the reach of this content to the general population while increasing the benefits to society over time.

Acknowledgment

The authors gratefully acknowledge research funding from the National Institute of Child Health and Human Development, grant HD075150 to the first author.

References

Abar, C. C, Jackson, K. M., Colby, S. M., & Barnett, N. P. (2014). Parent–child discrepancies in reports of parental monitoring and their relationship to adolescent alcohol-related behaviors. *Journal of Youth and Adolescence, 44*(9), 1688–1701. doi: 10.1007/s10964-014-0143-6.

Ackerman, B. P., Brown, E. D., & Izard, C. E. (2004). The relations between contextual risk, earned income, and the school adjustment of children from economically disadvantaged families. *Developmental Psychology, 40*(2), 204–216. doi: 10.1037/0012-1649.40.2.204

Agliata, A. K., & Renk, K. (2008). College students' adjustment: The role of parent–college student expectation discrepancies and communication reciprocity. *Journal of Youth and Adolescence, 37*(8), 967–982. doi: 10.1007/s10964-007-9200-8

Barkley, R. A. (1997). Behavioral inhibition, sustained attention, and executive functions: Constructing a unifying theory of ADHD. *Psychological Bulletin, 121*(1), 65–94. doi: 10.1037/0033-2909.121.1.65

Bartle-Haring, S., Brucker, P., & Hock, E. (2002). The impact of parental separation anxiety on identity development in late adolescence and early adulthood. *Journal of Adolescent Research, 17*(5), 439–450. doi: 10.1177/0743558402175001

Baumann, A. A., Powell, B. J., Kohl, P. L., Tabak, R. G., Penalba, V., Proctor, E. K., . . . Cabassa, L. J. (2015). Cultural adaptation and implementation of evidence-based parent-training: A systematic review of guiding evidence. *Children and Youth Services Review, 53,* 113–120. doi: https://dx.doi.org/10.1016/j.childyouth.2015.03.025

Baumrind, D. (1966). Effects of authoritative parental control on child behavior. *Child Development, 37*(4), 887–907. doi: 10.2307/1126611

Baumrind, D. (1967). Child care practices anteceding three patterns of preschool behavior. *Genetic Psychology Monographs, 75*(1), 43–88.

Blair, C. (2002). School readiness: Integrating cognition and emotion in a neurobiological conceptualization of children's functioning at school entry. *American Psychologist, 57*(2), 111–127. doi: 10.1037/0003-066X.57.2.111

Boeldt, D. L., Rhee, S. H., DiLalla, L. F., Mullineaux, P. Y., Schulz-Heik, R. J., Corley, R. P., . . . Hewitt, J. K. (2012). The association between positive parenting and externalizing behaviour. *Infant and Child Development, 21*(1), 85–106. doi: 10.1002/icd.764

Bolsoni-Silva, S. T. & Marturano, E. M. (2010). Evaluation of group intervention for mothers/caretakers of kindergarten children with externalizing behavioral problems. *Interamerican Journal of Psychology, 44*(3), 411–417.

Bor, W., Sanders, M. R., & Markie-Dadds, C. (2002). The effects of the Triple P-Positive Parenting Program on preschool children with co-occurring disruptive behavior and attentional/hyperactive difficulties. *Journal of Abnormal Child Psychology, 30*(6), 571–587. doi: https://dx.doi.org/10.1023/A:1020807613155

Bourdeau, B., Miller, B. A., Duke, M. R., & Ames, G. M. (2011). Parental strategies for knowledge of adolescent's friends: Distinct from monitoring? *Journal of Child and Family Studies, 20*, 814–821. doi: 10.1007/s10826-011-9449-0.

Boyle, J. R., & Boekeloo, B. O. (2006). Perceived parental approval of drinking and its impact on problem drinking behaviors among first-year college students. *Journal of American College Health, 54*(4), 238–244. doi: 10.3200/JACH.54.4.238-244

Brody, G. H., Chen, Y.-F., Kogan, S. M., Smith, K., & Brown, A. C. (2010). Buffering effects of a family-based intervention for African American emerging adults. *Journal of Marriage and Family, 72*, 1426–1435. doi: 10.1111/j.1741-3737.2010.00774.x

Bronfenbrenner, U. (1979). *The ecology of human development: Experiments by nature and design.* Cambridge, MA: Harvard University Press.

Calzada, E. J., Fernandez, Y., & Cortes, D. E. (2010). Incorporating the cultural value of respeto into a framework of Latino parenting. *Cultural Diversity and Ethnic Minority Psychology, 16*(1), 77–86. doi: 10.1037/a0016071

Calzada, E. J., Huang, K. Y., Anicama, C., Fernandez, Y., & Brotman, L. M. (2012). Test of a cultural framework of parenting with Latino families of young children. *Cultural Diversity and Ethnic Minority Psychology, 18*(3), 285–296. doi: 10.1037/a0028694

Caruthers, A. S., Van Ryzin, M. J., & Dishion, T. J. (2014). Preventing high-risk sexual behavior in early adulthood with family interventions in adolescence: Outcomes and developmental processes. *Prevention Science, 15*, 59–69. doi: https://dx.doi.org/10.1007/s11121-013-0383-9

Caspi, A., Moffitt, T. E., Morgan, J., Rutter, M., Taylor, A., Arseneault, L., . . . Polo-Tomas, M. (2004). Maternal expressed emotion predicts children's antisocial behavior problems: Using monozygotic-twin differences to identify environmental effects on behavioral development. *Developmental Psychology, 40*, 149–161. doi: https://dx.doi.org/10.1037/0012-1649.40.2.149

Castro-Schilo, L., Taylor, Z. E., Ferrer, E., Robins, R. W., Conger, R. D., & Widaman, K. F. (2013). Parents' optimism, positive parenting, and child peer competence in Mexican-origin families. *Parenting, 13*(2), 95–112. doi: 10.1080/15295192.2012 .709151

Cauce, A. M., & Domenech-Rodriguez, M. (2002). Latino families: Myths and realities. In J. M. Contreras, K. A. Kerns, & A. M. Neal-Barnett (Eds.), *Latino children and families in the United States: Current research and future directions* (pp. 3–25). Westport, CT: Praeger.

Chamberlain, P., Snowden, L. R., Padgett, C., Saldana, L., Roles, J., Holmes, L., . . . Landsverk, J. (2010). A strategy for assessing the costs of implementing new practices in the child welfare system: Adapting the English Cost Calculator in the United States. *Administration and Policy in Mental Health and Mental Health Services Review, 38*, 24–31. doi: 10.1007/s10488-010-0318-8

Chang, H., Shaw, D. S., Dishion, T. J., Gardner, F., & Wilson, M. N. (2014). Direct and indirect effects of the Family Check-Up on self-regulation from toddlerhood to early school-age. *Journal of Abnormal Child Psychology, 42*, 1117–1128. doi: https://dx.doi.org/10.1007/s10802-014-9859-8

Chronis, A. M., Lahey, B. B., Pelham, W. E., Jr., Williams, S. H., Baumann, B. L., Kipp, H., . . . Rathouz, P. J. (2007). Maternal depression and early positive parenting predict future conduct problems in young children with attention-deficit/hyperactivity disorder. *Developmental Psychology, 43*(1), 70–82. doi: 10.1037/0012-1649.43.1.70

Crouter, A. C., Bumpus, M. F., Davis, K. D., & McHale, S. M. (2005). How do parents learn about adolescent's experiences? Implications of parental knowledge and adolescent risky behavior. *Child Development, 76*(4), 869–882. doi: https://dx.doi.org/10.1111/j.1467-8624.2005.00883.x

Deater-Deckard, K., & Dodge, K. A. (1997). Externalizing behavior problems and discipline revisited: Nonlinear effects and variation by culture, context, and gender. *Psychological Inquiry, 8,* 161–175. doi: 10.1207/s15327965pli0803_1

Deater-Deckard, K., Ivy, L., & Petrill, S. A. (2006). Maternal warmth moderates the link between physical punishment and child externalizing problems: A parent–offspring behavior genetic analysis. *Parenting: Science and Practice, 6*(1), 59–78. doi:10.1111/j.1469-7610.2006.01668.x

Delgado-Gaitan, C. (1994). Socializing young children in Mexican-American families: An intergenerational perspective. In P. Greenfield & R. Cocking (Eds.), *Cross-cultural roots of minority child development* (pp. 55–86). Hillside, NJ: Erlbaum.

Denham, S. A., Workman, E., Cole, P. M., Weissbrod, C., Kendziora, K. T., & Zahn-Waxler, C. (2000). Prediction of externalizing behavior problems from early to middle childhood: The role of parental socialization and emotion expression. *Development and Psychopathology, 12,* 23–45. doi: 10.1017/S0954579400001024

Dishion, T. J. & McMahon, R. J. (1998). Parental monitoring and the prevention of child and adolescent problem behavior: A conceptual and empirical formulation. *Clinical Child and Family Psychology Review, 1*(1), 61–75. doi: 10.1023/A:1021800432380.

Dishion, T. J., Nelson, S. E., & Kavanagh, K. (2003). The Family Check-Up with high-risk young adolescents: Preventing early-onset substance use by parent monitoring. *Behavior Therapy, 34,* 553–571. doi: https://dx.doi.org/10.1016/S0005-7894(03)80035-7

Dishion, T. J., Shaw, D., Connell, A., Gardner, F., Weaver, C., & Wilson, M. (2008). The Family Check-Up with high-risk indigent families: Preventing problem behavior by increasing parents' positive behavior support in early childhood. *Child Development, 79*(5), 1395–1414. doi: 10.1111/j.1467-8624.2008.01195.x

Dishion, T. J., & Stormshak, E. A. (2007). *Intervening in children's lives: An ecological, family-centered approach to mental health care.* Washington, DC: American Psychological Association.

Doom, J. R., Gunnar, M. R., & Clark, C. J. (2016). Maternal relationship during adolescence predicts cardiovascular disease risk in adulthood. *Health Psychology, 35*(4), 376–386. doi: 10.1037/hea0000285

Eisenberg, N., Valiente, C., Morris, A. S., Fabes, R. A., Cumberland, A., Reiser, M., . . . Losoya, S. (2003). Longitudinal relations among parental emotional expressivity, children's regulation, and quality of social emotional functioning. *Developmental Psychology, 39,* 3–19. doi: https://dx.doi.org/10.1037/0012-1649.39.1.3

Eisenberg, N., Zhou, Q., Spinrad, T. L., Valiente, C., Fabes, R. A., & Liew, J. (2005). Relations among positive parenting, children's effortful control, and externalizing problems: A three-wave longitudinal study. *Child Development, 76*(5), 1055–1071. doi: 10.1111/j.1467-8624.2005.00897.x

Fischer, J. L., Forthun, L. F., Pidcock, B. W., & Dowd, D. A. (2007). Parent relationships, emotion regulation, psychosocial maturity and college student alcohol use problems. *Journal of Youth and Adolescence, 36*(7), 912–926. doi: 10.1007/s10964-006-9126-6

Fosco, G. M., Frank, J. L., Stormshak, E. A., & Dishion, T. J. (2013). Opening the "black box": Family Check-Up intervention effects on self-regulation that prevents growth in problem behavior and substance use. *Journal of School Psychology, 51*(4), 455–468. doi: https://dx.doi.org/10.1016/j.jsp.2013.02.001

Fosco, G. M., Stormshak, E. A., Dishion, T. J., & Winter, C. E. (2012). Family relationships and parental monitoring during middle school as predictors of early adolescent problem behavior. *Journal of Child Clinical and Adolescent Psychology, 42*(1), 202–212. doi: 10.1080/15374416.2012.651989.

Galambos, N. L., Barker, E. T., & Almeida, D. M. (2003). Parents do matter: Trajectories of change in externalizing and internalizing problems in early adolescence. *Child Development, 74*(2), 578–594. doi: 10.1111/1467-8624.7402017

Germán, M., Gonzales, N. A., Bonds McClain, D., Dumka, L., & Millsap, R. (2013). Maternal warmth moderates the link between harsh discipline and later externalizing behaviors for Mexican American adolescents. *Parenting, 13*(3), 169–177. doi: 10.1080/15295192.2013.756353

Gershoff, E. T., Lansford, J. E., Sexton, H. R., Davis-Kean, P., & Sameroff, A. J. (2012). Longitudinal links between spanking and children's externalizing behaviors in a national sample of White, Black, Hispanic, and Asian American families. *Child Development, 83*(3), 838–843. doi: 10.1111/j.1467-8624.2011.01732.x.

Granic, I., & Patterson, G. R. (2006). Toward a comprehensive model of antisocial development: A dynamic systems approach. *Psychological Review, 113*(1), 101–131. doi: 10.1037/0033-295X.113.1.101

Grogan-Kaylor, A. (2005). Corporal punishment and the growth trajectory of children's antisocial behavior. *Child Maltreatment, 10*(3), 283–292. doi: https://dx.doi.org/10.1177/1077559505277803

Hair, E. C., Moore, K. A., Garrett, S. B., Ling, T., & Cleveland, K. (2008). The continued importance of quality parent–adolescent relationships during late adolescence. *Journal of Research on Adolescence, 18*(1), 187–200. doi: 10.1111/j.1532-7795.2008.00556.x.

Hargrove, B. K., Creagh, M. G., & Burgess, B. L. (2002). Family interaction patterns as predictors of vocational identity and career decision-making self-efficacy. *Journal of Vocational Behavior, 61*(2), 185–201. doi: 10.1006/jvbe.2001.1848

Harris-McKoy, D., & Cui, M. (2013). Parental control, adolescent delinquency, and young adult criminal behavior. *Journal of Child and Family Studies, 22*(6), 836–843. doi: 10.1007/s10826-012-9641-x

Houltberg, B. J., Morris, A. S., Cui, L., Henry, C. S., & Criss, M. M. (2014). The role of youth anger in explaining links between parenting and early adolescent prosocial and antisocial behavior. *Journal of Early Adolescence*, 1–22. doi: 10.1177/0272431614562834.

Huey S. J., Jr., & Polo, A. J. (2008). Evidence-based psychosocial treatments for ethnic minority youth. *Journal of Clinical Child & Adolescent Psychology, 37*(1), 262–301. doi: 10.1080/15374410701820174

Janssen, H. J., Dekovic, M., & Bruinsma, G. J. (2014). Parenting and time adolescents spend in criminogenic settings: A between and within person analysis. *British Journal of Criminology, 54*, 551–567. doi: 10.1093/bjc/azu032.

Jessor, R., Costa, F. M., Krueger, P. M., & Turbin, M. S. (2006). A developmental study of heavy episodic drinking among college students: The role of psychosocial and behavioral protective and risk factors. *Journal of Studies on Alcohol, 67*(1), 86–94. doi: 10.15288/jsa.2006.67.86

Jones, D. J., Forehand, R., Rakow, A., Colletti, C. J. M., McKee, L., & Zalot, A. (2008). The specificity of maternal parenting behavior and child adjustment difficulties: A study of inner-city African American families. *Journal of Family Psychology, 22*, 181–192. doi:10.1037/0893-3200.22.2.181

Kaminski, J. W., Valle, L. A., Filene, J. H., & Boyle, C. L. (2008). A meta-analytic review of components associated with parent training program effectiveness. *Journal of Abnormal Child Psychology, 36*(4), 567–589. doi: 10.1007/s10802-007-9201-9

Kazdin, A. E. (2005). *Parent management training: Treatment for oppositional, aggressive, and antisocial behavior in children and adolescents.* New York, NY: Oxford University Press.

Kerr, M., Stattin, H., & Burk, W. J. (2010). A reinterpretation of parental monitoring in longitudinal perspective. *Journal of Research on Adolescence, 20*(1), 39–64. doi: 10.1111/j.1532-7795.2009.00623.x.

Laird, R. D., Marrero, M. D., & Sentse, M. (2010). Revisiting parental monitoring: Evidence that parental solicitation can be effective when needed most. *Journal of Youth and Adolescence, 39*, 1431–1441. doi: 10.1007/s10964-009-9453-5.

Lansford, J. E., Deater-Deckard, K., Dodge, K. A., Bates, J. E., & Pettit, G. S. (2004). Ethnic differences in the link between physical discipline and later adolescent externalizing behaviors. *Journal of Child Psychology and Psychiatry, 45*(4), 801–812. doi: 10.1111/j.1469-7610.2004.00273.x

Lansford, J. E., Laird, R. D., Pettit, G. S., Bates, J. E., & Dodge, K. A. (2014). Mothers' and fathers' autonomy-relevant parenting: Longitudinal links with adolescents' externalizing and internalizing behavior. *Journal of Youth and Adolescence, 43*(11), 1877–1889. doi: https://dx.doi.org/10.1007/s10964-013-0079-2

Larose, S., & Boivin, M. (1998). Attachment to parents, social support expectations, and socioemotional adjustment during the high school–college transition. *Journal of Research on Adolescence, 8*(1), 1–27. doi: 10.1207/s15327795jra0801_1

Lefkowitz, E. S., & Espinosa-Hernandez, G. (2007). Sex-related communication with mothers and close friends during the transition to university. *Journal of Sex Research, 44*(1), 17–27. doi: https://dx.doi.org/10.1207/s15598519jsr4401_3

Levitt, M. J., Silver, M. E., & Santos, J. D. (2007). Adolescents in transition to adulthood: Parental support, relationship satisfaction, and post-transition adjustment. *Journal of Adult Development, 14*(1–2), 53–63. doi: 10.1007/s10804-007-9032-5

Marin, G., & Marin, B. (1991). *Research with Hispanic populations.* Newbury Park, CA: Sage.

McKee, L., Roland, E., Coffelt, N., Olson, A. L., Forehand, R., Massari, C., . . . Zens, M. S. (2007). Harsh discipline and child problem behaviors: The roles of positive parenting and gender. *Journal of Family Violence, 22*(4), 187–196. doi:10.1007/s10896-007-9070-6

McLoyd, V. C., & Smith, J. (2002). Physical discipline and behavior problems in African American, European American, and Hispanic children: Emotional support as a moderator. *Journal of Marriage and Family, 64*(1), 40–53. doi: 10.1111/j.1741-3737.2002.00040.x

McNeil, C. B., & Hembree-Kigin, T. L. (2010). *Parent–child interaction therapy.* New York, NY: Springer. doi: 10.1007/978-0-387-88639-8

Morrill, M. I., Hawrilenko, M., & Córdova, J. V. (2015). A longitudinal examination of positive parenting following an acceptance-based couple intervention. *Journal of Family Psychology, 30*(1), 104–113. doi: 10.1037/fam0000162.supp

Morris, A. S., Silk, J. S., Steinberg, L., Myers, S. S., & Robinson, L. R. (2007). The role of the family context in the development of emotion regulation. *Social Development, 16*(2), 361–388. doi: 10.1111/j.1467-9507.2007.00389.x

O'Connor, T. G., Allen, J. P., Bell, K. L., & Hauser, S. T. (1996). Adolescent–parent relationships and leaving home in young adulthood. *New Directions for Child and Adolescent Development, 71,* 39–52.

Odgers, C. L., Caspi, A., Russell, M. A., Sampson, R. J., Arseneault, L., & Moffit, T. E. (2012). Supportive parenting mediates neighborhood socioeconomic disparities in children's antisocial behavior from ages 5–12. *Development and Psychopathology, 24*(3), 705–721. doi: https://dx.doi.org/10.1017/S0954579412000326

Pascarella, E. T., & Terenzini, P. T. (1991). *How college affects students: Findings and insights from twenty years of research.* San Francisco, CA: Jossey-Bass.

Patock-Peckham, J. A., Cheong, J., Balhorn, M. E., & Nagoshi, C. T. (2001). A social learning perspective: A model of parenting styles, self-regulation, perceived drinking control, and alcohol use and problems. *Alcoholism: Clinical and Experimental Research, 25*(9), 1284–1292. doi: 10.1111/j.1530-0277.2001.tb02349.x

Patock-Peckham, J. A., King, K. M., Morgan-Lopez, A. A., Ulloa, E. O., & Filson Moses, J. M. (2011). Gender-specific mediational links between parenting styles, parental monitoring, impulsiveness, drinking control, and alcohol-related problems. *Journal of Studies on Alcohol and Drugs, 72*(2), 247–258. doi: https://dx.doi.org/10.15288/jsad.2011.72.247.

Patock-Peckham, J. A., & Morgan-Lopez, A. A. (2006). College drinking behaviors: Mediational links between parenting styles, impulse control, and alcohol-related outcomes. *Psychology of Addictive Behaviors, 20*(2), 117–125. doi: 10.1037/0893-164X.20.2.117

Patterson, G. R. (1974). Interventions for boys with conduct problems: Multiple settings, treatments, and criteria. *Journal of Consulting and Clinical Psychology, 42,* 471–481. doi: 10.1037/h0036731

Patterson, G. R. (1976). The aggressive child: Victim and architect of a coercive system. *Behavior Modification and Families, 1,* 267–316.

Patterson, G. R. (1982). *Coercive family processes.* Eugene, OR: Castalia Publishing Co.

Pearl, A. M., French, B. F., Dumas, J. E., Moreland, A. D., & Prinz, R. (2014). Bidirectional effects of parenting quality and child externalizing behavior in predominantly single parent, under-resourced African American families. *Journal of Child and Family Studies, 23,* 177–188. doi: 10.1007/s10826-012-9692-z.

Racz, S. J. & McMahon, R. J. (2011). The relationship between parental knowledge and monitoring and child and adolescent conduct problems: A 10-year update. *Clinical Child and Family Psychology Review, 14,* 377–398. doi: 10.1007/s10567-011-0099-y

Raver, C. C., Gershoff, E. T., & Aber, J. L. (2007). Testing equivalence of mediating models of income, parenting, and school readiness for White, Black, and Hispanic children in a national sample. *Child Development, 78*(1), 96–115. doi: 10.1111/j.1467-8624.2007.00987.x

Sabogal, F., Marín, G., Otero-Sabogal, R., Marín, B. V., & Perez-Stable, E. J. (1987). Hispanic familism and acculturation: What changes and what doesn't? *Hispanic Journal of Behavioral Sciences, 9,* 397–412. doi: 10.1177/07399863870094003

Santisteban, D. A., Mena, M. P., & Abalo, C. (2012). Bridging diversity and family systems: Culturally informed and flexible family based treatment for Hispanic adolescents. *Couple & Family Psychology, 2*(4), 246–263. Doi: http://doi.org/10.1037/cfp0000013

Scharf, M., Mayseless, O., & Kivenson-Baron, I. (2004). Adolescents' attachment representations and developmental tasks in emerging adulthood. *Developmental Psychology, 40*(3), 430–444. doi: 10.1037/0012-1649.40.3.430

Schoeni, R., & Ross, K. (2004). Family support during the transition to adulthood. *Network on Transitions to Adulthood Policy Brief,* (12). Retrieved from http://www.npc.umich.edu/publications/policy_briefs/brief3/brief3.pdf

Sessa, F. M. (2005). The influence of perceived parenting on substance use during the transition to college: A comparison of male residential and commuter students. *Journal of College Student Development, 46,* 62–74. doi: https://dx.doi.org/10.1353/csd.2005.0010

Skinner, E., Johnson, S., & Snyder, T. (2005). Six dimensions of parenting: A motivational model. *Parenting: Science and Practice, 5*(2), 175–235. doi: 10.1207/s15327922par0502_3

Smith, J. D., Knoble, N. B., Zerr, A. A., Dishion, T. J., & Stormshak, E. A. (2014). Family Check-Up effects across diverse ethnic groups: Reducing early-adolescence antisocial behavior by reducing family conflict. *Journal of Clinical Child and Adolescent Psychology, 43*(3), 400–414. doi: https://dx.doi.org/10.1080/15374416.2014.888670

Smith-Morris, C., Morales-Campos, D., Alvarez, E. A. C., & Turner, M. (2012). An anthropology of familismo: On narratives and description of Mexican/immigrants. *Hispanic Journal of Behavioral Sciences, 35,* 35–60. doi: 10.1177/0739986312459508

Spear, L. (2010). *The behavioral neuroscience of adolescence.* New York, NY: WW Norton.

Stattin, H., & Kerr, M. (2000). Parental monitoring: A reinterpretation. *Child Development, 71*(4), 1072–1085. dou: 10.1111/1467-8624.00210.

Stormshak, E. A., Bierman, K. L., McMahon, R. J., & Lengua, L. J. (2000). Parenting practices and child disruptive behavior problems in early elementary school. *Journal of Clinical Child Psychology, 29*(1), 17–29. doi: 10.1207/S15374424jccp2901_3

Strage, A., & Brandt, T. S. (1999). Authoritative parenting and college students' academic adjustment and success. *Journal of Educational Psychology, 91*(1), 146–156. doi: 10.1037/0022-0663.91.1.146

Sulik, M. J., Blair, C., Mills-Koonce, R., Berry, D., & Greenberg, M. (2015). Early parenting and the development of externalizing behavior problems: Longitudinal mediation through children's executive function. *Child Development, 86*(5), 1588–1603. doi: 10.1111/cdev.12386

Taylor, Z. E., Larsen-Rife, D., Conger, R. D., & Widaman, K. F. (2012). Familism, interparental conflict, and parenting in Mexican-origin families: A cultural–contextual framework. *Journal of Marriage and Family, 74*(2), 312–327. doi: 10.1111/j.1741-3737.2012.00958.x

Tharp, A. T., & Noonan, R. K. (2012). Associations between three characteristics of parent–youth relationships, youth substance use, and dating attitudes. *Health Promotion Practice, 13,* 515–523. doi: 10.1177/1524839910386220.

Tilton-Weaver, L. C., Burk, W. J., Kerr, M., Stattin, H. (2013). Can parental monitoring and peer management reduce the selection or influence of delinquent peers? Testing the question using a dynamic social network approach. *Developmental Psychology, 49*(11), 2057–5070. doi: 10.1037/a0031854.

Turner, A. P., Larimer, M. E., & Sarason, I. G. (2000). Family risk factors for alcohol-related consequences and poor adjustment in fraternity and sorority members: Exploring the role of parent–child conflict. *Journal of Studies on Alcohol, 61*(6), 818–826. doi: 10.15288/jsa.2000.61.818

Turrisi, R., Jaccard, J., Taki, R., Dunnam, H., & Grimes, J. (2001). Examination of the short-term efficacy of a parent intervention to reduce college student drinking tendencies. *Psychology of Addictive Behaviors, 15*(4), 366–372. https://dx.doi.org/10.1037/0893-164X.15.4.366

Turrisi, R., Wiersma, K. A., & Hughes, K. K. (2000). Binge-drinking-related consequences in college students: Role of drinking beliefs and mother–teen communications. *Psychology of Addictive Behaviors, 14*(4), 342–355. doi: 10.1037/0893-164X.14.4.342

Walls, T. A., Fairlie, A. M., & Wood, M. D., (2009). Parents do matter: A longitudinal two-part mixed model of early college alcohol participation and intensity. *Journal of Studies on Alcohol and Drugs, 70,* 908–919. doi: 10.15288/jsad.2009.70.908

Walton, A. & Flouri, E. (2010). Contextual risk, maternal parenting and adolescent externalizing behavior problems: The role of emotion regulation. *Child: Care, Health and Development, 36*(2), 275–284. doi:10.1111/j.1365-2214.2009.01065.x.

Webster-Stratton, C. (1998). Preventing conduct problems in Head Start children: Strengthening parenting competencies. *Journal of Consulting and Clinical Psychology, 66*(5), 715–730. doi: 10.1037/0022-006X.66.5.715

White, H. R., McMorris, B. J., Catalano, R. F., Fleming, C. B., Haggerty, K. P., & Abbott, R. D. (2006). Increases in alcohol and marijuana use during the transition out of high school into emerging adulthood: The effects of leaving home, going to college, and high school protective factors. *Journal of Studies on Alcohol, 67,* 810–822. doi: https://dx.doi.org/10.15288/jsa.2006.67.810

Wintre, M. G., & Yaffe, M. (2000). First-year students' adjustment to university life as a function of relationships with parents. *Journal of Adolescent Research, 15*(1), 9–37. doi: https://dx.doi.org/10.1177/0743558400151002

Wood, M. D., DeJong, W., Fairlie, A. M., Lawson, D., Lavigne, A. M., Cohen, F. (2009). Common Ground: An investigation of environmental management alcohol prevention initiatives in a college community. *Journal of Studies on Alcohol and Drugs, S16,* 96–105.

Wood, M. D., Read, J. P., Mitchell, R. E., & Brand, N. H. (2004). Do parents still matter? Parent and peer influences on alcohol involvement among recent high school graduates. *Psychology of Addictive Behaviors, 18*(1), 19–30. doi: 10.1037/0893-164X.18.1.19

Yong, M., Fleming, C. B., McCarty, C. A., & Catalano, R. F. (2013). Mediators of the associations between externalizing behaviors and internalizing symptoms in late childhood and early adolescence. *The Journal of Early Adolescence, 34,* 967–1000. doi: 10.1177/0272431613516827

Zeman, J., Cassano, M., & Adrian, M. C. (2013). Socialization influences on children's and adolescents' emotional self-regulation processes. In K. C. Barrett, N. A. Fox, G. A. Morgan, D. J. Fidler, & L. A. Daunhauer, *Handbook of self-regulatory processes in development: New directions and international perspectives* (pp. 70–106). New York, NY: Psychology Press.

Zisser, A., & Eyberg, S. M. (2010). Parent–child interaction therapy and the treatment of disruptive behavior disorders. In A. E. Kazdin & J. R. Weisz (Eds.), *Evidence-based psychotherapies for children and adolescents* (pp. 179–193). New York, NY: Guilford.

Etiological and Maintenance Factors
Peer Factors

20

Peer Rejection and Disruptive Behavioral Disorders

Kristina L. McDonald and Carolyn E. Gibson

Within the field of peer relationships, a great deal of research attention has been given to understanding why some children are well liked by their peers whereas others are rejected. Generally, this line of work has found that children who are kind, trustworthy, and cooperative are liked more by peers than children who do not behave prosocially. Children who are interpersonally aggressive, disruptive, annoying, and oppositional with teachers are often disliked by their classmates in childhood (see Asher & McDonald, 2009 for a review). A more complicated and interesting question arises about how troubled peer relationships, marked by peer dislike, may contribute to the growth of aversive and troubled behavior patterns over time.

This chapter will address this question, reviewing research that has examined how peer relationships are both affected by, and influence, behavior disorders like Conduct Disorder (CD) and Oppositional Defiant Disorder (ODD) (see Chapters 2 and 3 for a description of these disorders). This chapter will outline several models that explain the relationship between peer rejection and CD/ODD symptoms and review the empirical evidence supporting these models. To accomplish this task, we draw on literature that has examined peer rejection and broadband externalizing behaviors, including aggression, delinquency, and rule-breaking behaviors. As only a small sample of studies have used clinical diagnoses of CD or ODD, this additional literature may facilitate a better understanding of the larger phenomenon.

A second issue that we address in this chapter is that CD and ODD are often comorbid with attention deficit hyperactivity disorder (ADHD). For instance, 50% of children and adolescents with CD/ODD also have ADHD. Similarly, 50% of children diagnosed with ADHD also have either CD or ODD (Angold, Costello, & Erkanli, 1999; Kutcher et al., 2004). As both CD/ODD and ADHD are associated with peer rejection, it is important to disentangle the unique effects that these problems have in relation to it.

Finally, there are several promising lines of research that may speak to the more micro-level processes that explain how peer group experiences foster aggressive, delinquent, and oppositional behavior in childhood and adolescence. We conclude the chapter with ideas about the underlying processes by which peer rejection may contribute to the development of CD/ODD over time. Before addressing these topics however, we start with a brief review of how peer acceptance and rejection are operationalized and measured within the peer group.

The Wiley Handbook of Disruptive and Impulse-Control Disorders, First Edition.
Edited by John E. Lochman and Walter Matthys.
© 2018 John Wiley & Sons Ltd. Published 2018 by John Wiley & Sons Ltd.

Operationalization of Peer Acceptance and Rejection

Peer acceptance is the degree to which a child is liked versus disliked by his or her peers. When a child is disliked by many peers and liked by few, this state is referred to as peer rejection. Peer acceptance and rejection are typically measured via one of two ways. In the sociometric nomination method, researchers ask children in a peer group, often within a class or a school grade, to nominate peers that they "like the most" and peers that they "like the least." Nominations are counted and proportions are calculated to control for group size. Proportions may also be standardized within nominating groups as another means to control for systematic differences between the nominating groups.

The number of nominations that children can give for each question varies by study. Some ask children to limit their nominations to three peers per question whereas others allow children to give an unlimited number of names for each item. There is growing consensus in the field that allowing children to use unlimited nominations has measurement advantages. Sociometric scores that use unlimited nominations are more stable over multiple years and are more highly correlated to measures of social behavior than are scores derived from limited nominations (see Cillessen, 2009, for a review).

Coie, Dodge, and Coppotelli (1982) and Newcomb and Bukowski (1983) outlined procedures that are commonly used to group children into sociometric categories based on extreme sociometric scores for "liked most" and "liked least." Generally, sociometrically popular kids are those who are liked by many and disliked by few, rejected children are those who are disliked by many and only liked by a few, and controversial youth are those who are nominated often as both being liked and disliked. Neglected children are those who are nominated infrequently in both categories, and finally, average children are youth who are near the mean for both types of nominations or do not fall into any of the other categories. In addition to categorizing children, these nominations can be used to compute continuous scores for social preference and social impact. Social preference is calculated by subtracting the standardized "liked least" nominations from the standardized "liked most" nominations, and again standardizing the result within the nominating group. Social impact is calculated by adding the standardized scores for "liked most" and "liked least" and standardizing again within the nominating group.

A second way to assess peer acceptance is through a rating-scale assessment. With this method, children are given a list of peers' names (typically, their whole class or a randomly generated list of grademates) and asked to rate how much they like each peer on a Likert scale. The ratings that children receive are averaged and standardized within their nominating group (Oden & Asher, 1977). Researchers treat this score as a continuous measure of peer acceptance or group children into extreme groups based on their received ratings. Scores and classifications generated from rating-scale measures seem to be more stable over time than those generated from nominations alone (Maassens, van Boxtel, & Goossens, 2005).

There are other ways that have been used to assess child social acceptance and competence, namely teacher-, peer-, or self-reports. However, teachers and parents may not be privy to a large portion of peer interactions and may be unlikely to witness covertly aggressive behaviors. Furthermore, self-reports, especially those of aggressive youth, may be biased or inaccurate (e.g., Bagwell, Molina, Pelham, & Hoza, 2001; Murray-Close et al., 2010). Thus, sociometric methods are considered the gold standard for assessing the peer group's attitude toward a child. In this chapter, we focus attention on research that has used sociometric nominations or the rating-scale assessment to measure peer acceptance or rejection.

The Complex Relationship of Peer Rejection with Externalizing Problems

There is a long history of research that has tied peer rejection to later psychopathology, particularly juvenile delinquency, crime, and externalizing problems like ODD and CD (see Parker & Asher, 1987 for a review of early research on this topic). To make sense of how and why peer rejection is associated with later adjustment issues, several models have been proposed. First, the incidental model suggests that behavior and underlying psychopathology are present early and are the root of later adjustment difficulties. According to the incidental model, peer rejection is just a by-product of the underlying behavioral and adjustment problems that are evident in children early on. There is some support for the incidental model. Kupersmidt and Coie (1990) followed children from fifth grade through late adolescence. They found that peer rejection in fifth grade was related to police contact and externalizing behaviors in late adolescence. However, when initial level of aggression or disruptive behavior was controlled, fifth-grade peer rejection did not uniquely predict either externalizing problems or police contact, suggesting that being rejected by peers did not contribute to these later adjustment problems. Others have also found support for an incidental model predicting to early adolescent delinquency; peer rejection in elementary school did not predict to delinquency early in adolescence beyond the effects of early disruptive behavior (Pederson, Vitaro, Barker, & Borge, 2007).

In contrast, the causal model outlined by Parker and Asher (1987) posits that behavioral tendencies early in childhood may cause peers to dislike a child. In turn, peer rejection, which often includes, or co-occurs with, being excluded by peers, negative peer treatment, and missing out on other important peer socialization opportunities, causes youth to develop psychopathology and behavioral problems over time. In this way, rejection may mediate, or explain, the association between early behavior and later externalizing problems. For instance, Ettekal and Ladd (2015) found the number of years a child was rejected in elementary school explained how aggression and disruptiveness in kindergarten was related to later rule-breaking behavior in early adolescence.

Researchers have also suggested that rejection contributes to maladjustment above and beyond initial behavioral or dispositional tendencies. Ladd and Burgess (2001) called this the additive model. Contrary to the causal model, in which the link between early behavior and later externalizing problems is explained by rejection, in the additive model early behavior and peer rejection both uniquely predict later outcomes. Within the additive model, there may be some overlapping influence; more specifically, investigations of the causal model that do not find that rejection completely mediates how early behavior predicts later behavior, would support an additive model.

Although there is some support for causal or incidental models, most empirical evidence has supported the additive model, finding that both initial behavioral tendencies and peer rejection predict increases in behavior problems over time. The additive effect of peer rejection can be seen in both short-term and long-term longitudinal studies. Initial behavior problems and peer rejection in early elementary school both predict increases in externalizing problems later in childhood (Bierman & Wargo, 1995; Powers, Bierman, and the Conduct Problems Prevention Research Group, 2013; Sturaro, van Lier, Cuikpers, & Koot; 2011). There is also some evidence that both early childhood aggressive behavior and peer rejection may directly predict later delinquent behaviors in early adolescence (Bierman, Kalvin, & Heinrichs, 2015).

However, there is evidence that rejection seems to increase externalizing problems comparatively more in early childhood than it does in adolescence. Laird, Jordan, Dodge, Pettit, and Bates (2001) followed a sample from kindergarten through early adolescence. They found that kindergarten externalizing problems were predictive of peer rejection in elementary school. Peer rejection made a unique contribution above early externalizing problems to broadband externalizing behaviors at age 14. They also found that rejection was a stronger predictor of aggression in the early school years than in early adolescence (Laird et al., 2001).

Similarly, Ladd (2006) examined how withdrawal, aggression, peer rejection, internalizing problems, and externalizing problems were interrelated longitudinally. Measuring each of the central variables once a year for seven years, from kindergarten through sixth grade, he found that rejection and aggression made unique predictions to externalizing problems and but that rejection was a stronger predictor of aggression in the early school years than it was in early adolescence.

It may therefore be that rejection increases aggressive or externalizing tendencies earlier in childhood, but by adolescence the effect of peer group rejection is weaker. Sullivan (1953) suggested that middle childhood is characterized by the need for acceptance, which can be fulfilled by participation in peer groups. He also suggested that, during the transition to the preadolescent period, the need for acceptance moves more toward a need for interpersonal intimacy. At this developmental period, friendships may be more important for adjustment. If Sullivan was correct, this may explain why the additive effect of rejection on later externalizing behaviors seems to be stronger in childhood than in adolescence.

The final model is the moderated risk-adjustment model and it suggests that peer rejection exacerbates the risks associated with early behavioral issues (Ladd & Burgess, 2001). More specifically, this model states that certain children, those that are most aggressive for instance, will be more negatively affected by rejection than other children. There is growing support for this model, as evidence is building that peer rejection may magnify how early behavior problems are associated with later externalizing problems. Miller-Johnson, Coie, Maumary-Gremaud, Lochman, and Terry (1999) found that rejection exacerbated how early aggressive behavior predicted adolescent delinquent behavior. In a sample of urban, African American youth, childhood aggression was a significant predictor of both serious and the non-serious delinquency offenses in early adolescence. However this effect was exacerbated by peer rejection for boys. Rates were higher for boys who were also rejected by peers (45%) compared to boys who were highly aggressive but not rejected (41 %) or were rejected but not aggressive (34%). Similarly, rates for serious offenses were highest for rejected-aggressive boys (41%), whereas probabilities for other boys were lower (rejected-nonaggressive, 30%; nonrejected-aggressive, 33%). In contrast for girls, only aggression was predictive of later serious offenses.

Evidence also suggests that it is important to consider how chronically, or for how long, a child has been highly disliked by peers. In support of a moderated-risk adjustment model, the chronicity of rejection seems to exacerbate how early behavioral problems are associated with later dysfunction. For instance, DeRosier, Kupersmidt, and Patterson (1994) found that aggression and disruptive behaviors in elementary school were predictive of later aggressive and disruptive behaviors, but the association was strengthened the more years a child had been rejected by peers. Dodge et al. (2003) also found that, for children who were below the median on aggression in kindergarten, social rejection did not predict increases in aggressive behavior in third grade. However for children high on aggression at school entry, the chronicity of peer rejection exacerbated these aggressive tendencies, increasing their aggression over time.

Gender Differences in the Effects of Rejection on Externalizing Problems

Miller-Johnson et al. (1999) were not the first to find that peer rejection may differentially affect externalizing problems for boys and girls. For example, following an African American sample from childhood to adolescence, Coie, Lochman, Terry, and Hyman (1992) and Coie, Terry, Lenox, Lochman, and Hyman (1995) found that both childhood aggression and peer rejection in third grade predicted externalizing problems in sixth grade. Later in adolescence, the combination of peer rejection and aggression predicted greater externalizing behaviors among 10th-grade boys than did aggression or rejection alone. For girls, however, the additive effects of behavior and rejection were absent. More specifically, peer rejection led to higher parent ratings of externalizing problems, whereas initial aggression led to greater self-reports of externalizing problems.

Miller-Johnson et al. (1999) suggested that peer rejection may be different experiences for boys and girls. For boys, peer rejection may be more likely to lead to associations with deviant peers, whereas for girls rejection may be more socially isolating and, thus, may increase internalizing problems as well as externalizing problems. We suggest that girls may partake in other types of risk-behaviors when they show signs of early aggression and are also rejected by peers. For example, girls' childhood aggression predicted later externalizing behaviors and substance use when girls were highly disliked by peers, but this effect was not found for girls who were highly liked by peers in early adolescence (Prinstein & LaGreca, 2004).

According to Moffitt and Caspi (2001) girls are more likely to partake in adolescent-limited delinquency than in life-course-persistent forms. Childhood peer rejection is a risk factor associated with life-course-persistent delinquency whereas deviant peer influences are the primary contributor to adolescent-limited delinquency (see Chapter 21 for full discussion of deviant peer effects). Although research seems to suggest that deviant peer affiliations are equally influential for boys and girls (Ettekal & Ladd, 2015; Laird et al., 2001; Vitaro, Pedersen, & Brendgen, 2007), it may be that deviant friends may be more likely to influence growth in externalizing behaviors for girls compared to the effect of peer rejection.

Popularity and Aggression

Finally, we note that, although aggressive behavior is negatively correlated with peer acceptance, not all aggressive children are low in social status. There are subtypes of aggressive youth who are not actively disliked by peers and some may even be considered "popular" or "cool" by their peers (e.g., Bierman, Smoot, & Aumiller, 1993; Rodkin, Farmer, Pearl, & Van Acker, 2000). First, aggressive children who are rejected tend to be more dysregulated than aggressive youth who are not rejected by peers. For instance, Bierman et al. (1993) found that rejected aggressive boys were more physically aggressive, argumentative, inattentive, disruptive and less prosocial compared to their non-rejected aggressive counterparts. In contrast, non-rejected aggressive youth tended to be more proactively or instrumentally aggressive than their rejected counterparts.

Second, Rodkin and colleagues (2000) identified a subgroup of teacher-identified "popular" boys that were aggressive. These "tough" boys were considered "cool" and were socially central in their peer groups. Additionally, relational aggression may be positively associated with perceived popularity in adolescence, even though it remains associated with peer dislike (e.g., Cillessen & Mayeux, 2004). Thus, interpersonally aggressive behavior may actually be reinforced through peers' perceptions of popularity and enhanced social dominance over time (Cillessen & Mayeux, 2004).

Although research into the long-term effects of perceived popularity is new, there is evidence that popularity, like peer rejection, may also add to or exacerbate initial aggressive tendencies. Popularity predicts increases in relational aggression over time (e.g., Cillessen & Mayeux, 2004; Troop-Gordon & Ranney, 2014), perhaps because popular youth are reinforced in their relational aggression through continued dominance in the peer group. Research also has found that perceived popularity in high school predicts increased risk-taking behaviors late in high school and after high school, even when controlling for prior levels of risk taking (Mayeux, Sandstrom, & Cillessen, 2008; Sandstrom & Cillessen, 2010). It may be that adolescents perceived as popular socialize with others who partake in risky behaviors and these socialization experiences continue to affect them into adulthood.

Comorbidity with ADHD

One difficulty in understanding how peer rejection is related to CD and ODD is that a significant portion of children with these disorders are also diagnosed with ADHD (Hoza et al. 2005; Milich & Landau, 1982) (see Chapter 4 for more information on ADHD comorbidity with disruptive behavior disorders). Research comparing children with and without ADHD has found that ADHD children are liked less by peers (Grygiel, Humenny, Rebisz, Bajcar, & Switaj, 2014; Hoza, 2007; Hoza et al., 2005) and their rejection may manifest quite quickly in group settings. For instance, summer camp studies have found that ADHD boys are highly disliked by peers within the first day of interaction (Hinshaw, 1994; Hinshaw & Melnick, 1995) and this is even more pronounced when ADHD boys are also high in aggression (Erhardt & Hinshaw, 1994).

High rates of rejection amongst ADHD youth are likely because ADHD children are more disruptive in class (Abikoff et al., 2002; Whalen, Henker, Collins, McAuliffe, & Vaux, 1979), are less socially skilled than non-ADHD peers (DuPaul, McGoey, Eckert, & VanBrakle, 2001; Murray-Close et al., 2010) and demonstrate impaired social problem solving (Matthys, Cuperus, & van Engeland, 1999) and social decision making (Humphreys, Galán, Tottenham, & Lee, 2015; Sibley, Evans, & Serpell, 2010). Furthermore, youth with ADHD may not be attentive to social feedback and may not recognize that peers dislike them. For instance, parents, peers, and teachers rate ADHD adolescents as being more rejected than non-ADHD youth, yet a majority of ADHD youth do not self-report being more disliked by peers (e.g., Bagwell et al., 2001; Murray-Close et al., 2010).

It is worthwhile to note that children with subtypes of ADHD may have different social impairments that may affect their peer relationships in different ways. For instance, children with the inattentive type of ADHD may have more difficulty attending to and actively participating in social interaction, whereas those with the combined type have more difficulty regulating emotions and inhibiting aggressive and disruptive behavior (Hodgens, Cole, & Boldizar, 2000; McQuade & Hoza, 2008). These differences may be reflected in peers' attitudes towards them. While ADHD youth are more rejected than their peers without ADHD, children with the combined type of ADHD may be even more at risk for rejection than children with the inattentive type (Gaub & Carlson, 1997; Hinshaw, 2002).

Are ADHD youth who are aggressive or have CD/ODD more likely to be disliked than ADHD children who are not? Results seem inconclusive (see Becker, Luebbe, & Langberg, 2012 for a review). There is evidence that hyperactive symptoms are uniquely associated with rejection, even when aggression or CD/ODD is controlled (Pope, Bierman, & Mumma, 1989; Stormshak & Bierman, 1998). However, ADHD children who are aggressive or have CD/ODD are more likely to be rejected or be low in peer acceptance than those with ADHD alone (Hinshaw & Melnick, 1995; Hoza et al., 2005; McArdle, O'Brien,

Macmillan, & Kolvin, 2000; Mrug et al., 2009), and this effect may be stronger for girls (Mikami & Lorenzi, 2011). Similarly, other researchers find that aggression (or low levels of prosocial behavior) predicts peer acceptance more than ADHD symptoms. For instance, when Diamantopoulou, Henricsson, and Rydell (2005) controlled for aggression, internalizing symptoms, and prosocial behavior, peer liking scores did not vary as a function of ADHD symptoms for girls. For boys, when aggression, internalizing symptoms, and prosocial behavior were controlled, ADHD symptoms actually predicted higher peer liking. The authors suggest that boys with ADHD are also high in initiative, which has been associated with high peer acceptance. Thus there is some evidence that other comorbidities may explain why ADHD is typically associated with peer rejection.

We suggest that discrepancies in findings may be due to methodology. For instance, using Fast Track data Stormshak, Bierman, and the Conduct Problems Prevention Research Group (1998) found that hyperactivity uniquely predicted social preference, but aggression did not. However, when children were put into extreme groups, those who were high on both hyperactive and aggressive behaviors we more likely to be rejected by peers than those who were only high on aggression or only high on hyperactivity. Thus, studies that use extreme groups may find that aggressive ADHD children are more disliked than non-aggressive ADHD children, but when these constructs are measured continuously these independent effects may be lost because of the high correlations amongst constructs. It is likely that the aggressive and oppositional behavior that is associated with ADHD adds to the peer problems of these youth.

In light of the comorbidity of ADHD, CD/ODD, and rejection, one may ask whether peer rejection uniquely contributes to the development of CD/ODD beyond the effects of ADHD. There is some evidence to suggest that inattention and hyperactivity are stronger predictors of later conduct problems than rejection for girls. Lee and Hinshaw (2006) followed a sample of ADHD and comparison girls for five years after they had participated in a summer camp. Although peer preference at summer camp was negatively correlated with conduct problems four to five years later, it had no effect when initial levels of inattention/hyperactivity and noncompliance were controlled. Thus, it may be that rejection does not contribute to the development of conduct problems above the effects of ADHD and initial rule-breaking behaviors, at least for girls.

Mikami and Hinshaw (2006) also examined how childhood peer rejection (as assessed at a summer camp) and ADHD predicted internalizing and externalizing problems in adolescence for girls. They found that both childhood peer rejection and ADHD were related to externalizing problems in adolescence. However, when childhood externalizing behaviors were controlled, neither rejection nor ADHD remained significant predictors. As there was quite a bit of variability in the ages of girls at baseline (6–12 years old), it may be that externalizing problems are already established by middle childhood and are stable through early adolescence. Conversely, peer rejection as assessed at a summer camp may not be indicative of the overall peer experiences of these youth. Longer-term peer experiences, such as those encountered every day at school, may have more effects on the development of behavioral problems.

When peer relations are assessed in school contexts, it seems that peer rejection makes unique and direct contributions, beyond the effects of ADHD, to the development of CD/ODD. Miller-Johnson, Coie, Maumary-Gremaud, Bierman and the Conduct Problems Prevention Research Group (2002) found that ADHD diagnoses in first grade predicted conduct problems in fourth grade, and this effect was partially explained by social preference. Thus, it may be that early ADHD symptoms negatively impact peer relationships, and these negative social experiences give rise to later conduct problems over time. Similarly, Mrug et al. (2012) examined how peer rejection and friendships predicted functioning in a sample of ADHD children followed over eight years. They found that peer rejection predicted delinquent behaviors in middle adolescence, above and beyond childhood levels of ADHD, ODD, and CD. However, the effect of peer rejection on late adolescent delinquency was not significant. Perhaps childhood peer rejection increases delinquency beyond the influence of ADHD symptoms, but this effect is stronger earlier in development.

Finally, as has been found with CD/ODD, there is also evidence of a bidirectional relationship of peer rejection and ADHD symptoms. Tseng, Kawabata, Fen, and Crick (2014) followed youth over 18 months. They found that ADHD symptoms predicted increases in peer rejection over time. They also found peer rejection predicted increases in inattention and hyperactivity/impulsivity symptoms over time. The authors suggest that children who are inattentive and hyperactive are liked less by peers, and because of this they miss out on socialization opportunities to learn behavioral control. This opportunity loss may contribute to worsening symptoms over time. Alternatively, it may be that peer rejection for ADHD youth leads them to feel uncomfortable and anxious at school. Negative affect can make it even more difficult for them to concentrate and attend to what is happening around them (Jarrett, Wolff, Davis, Cowart, & Ollendick, 2016). However, although cross-sectional analyses find that anxiety is related to ADHD symptoms, findings about the longitudinal relationships between anxiety and ADHD are inconsistent (e.g., Baldwin & Dadds, 2008; Wichstrom, Belsky, & Berg-Nielsen, 2013). Thus, future research should continue to explore how ADHD, peer problems, and anxiety are interrelated over time.

Thus, enough evidence has accumulated to demonstrate that peer rejection has negative effects on behavioral adjustment over time, contributing to the development of CD/ODD, and possibly worsening ADHD symptoms. Rejection also seems to negatively impact CD/ODD even when early ADHD symptoms are accounted for.

To conclude, we briefly address a few underlying mechanisms that explain why and how rejection may contribute to these behavioral adjustment problems.

The Mechanisms for Peer Rejection's Effect on CD/ODD

The most commonly discussed means by which rejection may contribute to CD/ODD is through deviant peer associations (Dodge & Petitt, 2003; Patterson, DeBaryshe, & Ramsey, 1989). Rejection by peers may lead children to affiliate with other peers who have been rejected. If these peers are also prone to behavioral problems, their friends or social groups may further socialize conduct problems over time. In support of this model, Ettekal and Ladd (2015) found that moderate peer rejection in grade school predicted more deviant friend groups in early adolescence, which, in turn, predicted more rule-breaking behavior later in adolescence. Chapter 21 in this book, speaks more to the process by which deviant peers may influence the development of CD/ODD over time.

Another means by which peer rejection may increase CD/ODD is through the lost opportunities for youth to interact in positive ways with peers. Through interactions with peers, children improve their perspective-taking abilities and learn how to resolve conflict (Rubin, Bukowski, & Parker, 1998). If rejection decreases these opportunities, it may negatively affect their social competence, compounding the challenges they face in social life.

Furthermore, and as alluded to in the section on ADHD, the experience of active rejection is, in itself, stressful for children. Low peer acceptance increases the risk of internalizing disorders and loneliness (e.g., Fontaine et al., 2009), and this may be explained in part through increasing conduct problems (Gooren, Lier, van Stegge, Meerum Terwogt, & Koot, 2011). This stress may be further exacerbated by the fact that rejected and friendless children lack support from a strong social network (Bukowski, Newcomb, and Hartup, 1996; Coie, 1990). Thus, the stress that accompanies peer rejection, as well as the low support network, may explain why youth who are actively disliked by peers increase in behavioral problems as time goes on. More research should study these issues over time in attempt to better understand the mechanisms of influence.

There are also social-cognitive biases characteristic of aggressive rejected children that may further the development of behavioral problems over time. For example, aggressive children tend to overestimate their social acceptance relative to how peers perceive them (David & Kistner, 2000), and this is especially so for aggressive-rejected youth (e.g., Orobio de Castro, Brendgen, Van Boxtel, Vitaro, & Schaepers, 2007). As children with ADHD also evidence these positive self-biases (Owens, Goldfine, Evangelista, Howa, & Kaiser, 2007), some have suggested that their inaccuracy may be due to problems attending to social feedback. However, others have suggested that positively biased self-perceptions may be self-protective (see Zakriski & Coie, 1996). Overly positive, inaccurate self-views are likely fragile and thus these biases may contribute to aggression because aggression is a means to defend the ego (Baumeister, Smart, & Boden, 1996).

Peer rejection also affects how children think about their social worlds. Being rejected and mistreated by peers can lead youth to develop negative and hostile social schemas that support the use of aggression as a coping mechanism. Aggressive children, in particular, are more likely than their peers to attribute hostile intent in situations which they have suffered ambiguous harm by a peer (e.g., for a review see Orobio de Castro, Veerman, Koops, Bosch, & Monshouwer, 2002) and these attributional processes exacerbate conduct problems over time (Dodge & Pettit, 2003). For instance, peer rejection predicts changes in how competently children encode social information, make attributions about others' behavior, and generate strategies to peer conflict over time (Dodge et al., 2003; Lansford, Malone, Dodge, Pettit, & Bates, 2010). Thus, peer rejection may negatively affect these social information processing patterns, leading to more aggressive or oppositional behavior across development.

Finally, we suggest that part of the process by which strained peer relationships might affect later behavior may be reflected in the teacher-child relationships of these youth. Teachers, as directors of the classroom setting, influence peer relationships (Farmer, Lines, & Hamm, 2011). Children with behavioral problems typically receive considerable negative attention from teachers (Flicek & Landau, 1985). Peers may pick up on teachers' reactions, biasing their perceptions of their classmates. In this way teachers may act as social referents for children, influencing their affective reactions to peers (Hughes, Cavell, & Willson, 2001). Negative attention from teachers may influence peer relationships and ultimately contribute to increasing behavioral issues over time.

There is evidence of the interplay between peer relationships and student-teacher relationships in elementary school. Social preference contributes to better student-teacher relationships over time, and student-teacher relationships also predict increases in peer acceptance from year to year (De Laet et al., 2014; Hughes & Chen, 2011; Kiuru et al., 2015; Mercer & DeRosier, 2008). Teacher-student relationships may also affect the development of externalizing problems over time, either buffering children through close relationships or exacerbating the problems (Silver, Measelle, Armstrong, & Essex, 2005). However, studies that consider peer relations, teacher support, and externalizing problems over time are rare and results about how teacher-student relationships may affect externalizing behavior are inconsistent (Mercer & DeRosier, 2008; Leflot et al., 2011). Thus, it is still unclear how peer relationships and teacher-student relationships uniquely and together impact the development of CD/ODD over time.

Conclusion

In conclusion, the peer acceptance of youth is both influenced by, and contributes to, their social behaviors. Youth prone to aggressive or oppositional behaviors are more likely to be rejected by peers in school; these negative social experiences add to or exacerbate these tendencies over time. ADHD youth are also often rejected by their peers, however rejection seems to contribute to behavioral problems, even when co-morbidity with ADHD is accounted for. There are many mechanisms that may explain the bidirectional relationship between peer experiences and behavior problems, including deviant peers, lost opportunities for positive peer interactions, stress, social-cognitive mediators, and poor relationships with teachers. In general, continued research will be critical to a better understanding of these processes and the ability to intervene to improve the social and behavioral functioning of CD/ODD youth.

References

Abikoff, H. B., Jensen, P. S., Arnold, E. L. L., et al. (2002). Observed classroom behavior of children with ADHD: Relationship to gender and comorbidity. *Journal of Abnormal Child Psychology, 30,* 349–359.

Angold, A., Costello, E. J., & Erkanli, A. (1999). Comorbidity. *Journal of Child Psychology and Psychiatry, 40*(1), 57–87.

Asher, S. R., & McDonald, K. L. (2009). The behavioral basis of acceptance, rejection, and perceived popularity. In K. H. Rubin, W. Bukowski, & B. Laursen (Eds.), *The handbook of peer interactions, relationships, and groups* (pp. 232–248). New York, NY: Guilford.

Bagwell, C. L., Molina, B. S. G., Pelham, W. E., Jr., & Hoza, B. (2001). Attention-deficit hyperactivity disorder and problems in peer relations: Predictions from childhood to adolescence. *Journal of the American Academy of Child and Adolescent Psychiatry, 40*(11), 1285–1292.

Baldwin, J. S., & Dadds, M. R. (2008). Examining alternative explanations of the covariation of ADHD and anxiety symptoms in children: A community study. *Journal of Abnormal Child Psychology, 36,* 67–79.

Baumeister, R. F., Smart, L., & Boden, J. M. (1996). Relation of threatened egotism to violence and aggression: The dark side of high self-esteem. *Psychological Review, 103,* 5–33.

Becker, S. P., Luebbe, A., & Langberg, J. M. (2012). Co-occurring mental health problems and peer functioning among youth with attention-deficit/hyperactivity disorder: A review and recommendations for future research. *Clinical Child and Family Psychological Review, 15,* 279–302.

Bierman, K. L., Kalvin, C. B., & Heinrichs, B. S. (2015). Early childhood precursors and adolescents sequelae of gradeschool peer rejection and victimization. *Journal of Clinical Child and Adolescent Psychology, 44*(3), 367–379.

Bierman, K. L., Smoot, D. L., & Aumiller, K. (1993). Characteristics of aggressive-rejected, aggressive (nonrejected), and rejected (nonaggressive) boys. *Child Development, 64*(1), 139–151.

Bierman, K. L., & Wargo, J. B. (1995). Predicting the longitudinal course associated with aggressive-rejected, aggressive (nonrejected), and rejected (nonaggressive) status. *Development and Psychopathology, 7,* 669–682.

Bukowski, W. M., Newcomb, A. F., & Hartup, W. W. (1996). Friendship and its significance in childhood and adolescence: Introduction and comment. In W. M. Bukowski, A. F. Newcomb, & K. Aumiller (Eds.), *The company they keep: Friendship in childhood and adolescence* (pp. 1–15). New York, NY: Cambridge University Press.

Cillessen, A. H. N. (2009). Sociometric methods. In K. H. Rubin, W. M. Bukowski, & B. Laursen (Eds.), *Handbook of peer interactions, relationships, and groups* (pp. 82–99). New York, NY: The Guilford Press.

Cillessen, A. H., & Mayeux, L. (2004). From censure to reinforcement: Developmental changes in the association between aggression and social status. *Child Development, 75*(1), 147–163.

Coie, J. D. (1990). Toward a theory of peer rejection. In S. R. Asher, & J. D. Coie (Eds.), *Peer Rejection in Childhood* (pp. 365–401). New York, NY: Cambridge University Press.

Coie, J. D., Dodge, K. A., & Coppotelli, H. (1982). Dimensions and types of social status: A cross-age perspective. *Developmental Psychology, 18,* 557–570.

Coie, J. D., Lochman, J. E., Terry, R., & Hyman, C. (1992). Predicting early adolescent disorder from childhood aggression and peer rejection. *Journal of Consulting and Clinical Psychology, 60,* 783–792.

Coie, J. D., Terry, R., Lenox, K., Lochman, J., & Hyman, C. (1995). Childhood peer rejection and aggression as predictors of stable patterns of adolescent disorder. *Development and Psychopathology, 7,* 697–713.

David, C. F., & Kistner, J. A. (2000). Do positive self-perceptions have a "dark side"? Examination of the link between perceptual bias and aggression. *Journal of Abnormal Child Psychology, 28,* 327–337.

De Laet, S., Doumen, S., Vervoort, E., Colpin, H., Van Leeuwen, K., Goossens, L., & Verschueren, K. (2014). Transactional links between teacher–child relationship quality and perceived versus sociometric popularity: A three-wave longitudinal study. *Child Development, 85*(4), 1647–1662.

DeRosier, M., Kupersmidt, J. B., & Patterson, C. J. (1994). Children's academic and behavioral adjustment as a function of the chronicity and proximity of peer rejection. *Child Development, 65*(6), 1799–1813.

Diamantopoulou, S., Henricsson, L., & Rydell, A. M. (2005). ADHD symptoms and peer relations of children in a community sample: Examining associated problems, self-perceptions, and gender differences. *International Journal of Behavioral Development, 29*(5), 388–398.

Dodge, K. A., Lansford, J. E., Burks, V. S., Bates, J. E., Pettit, G. S., Fontaine, R., & Price, G. M. (2003). Peer rejection and social information-processing factors in the development of aggressive behavior problems in children. *Child Development, 74*(2), 374–393.

Dodge, K. A., & Pettit, G. S. (2003). A biopsychosocial model of the development of chronic conduct problems in adolescence. *Developmental Psychology, 39*(2), 349–371.

DuPaul, G. J., McGoey, K. E., Eckert, T. L., & VanBrakle, J. (2001). Preschool children with Attention-Deficit/Hyperactivity Disorder: Impairments in behavioral, social, and school functioning. *Journal of the American Academy of Child and Adolescent Psychiatry, 40*(5), 508–515.

Erhardt, D., & Hinshaw, S. P. (1994). Initial sociometric impressions of attention-deficit hyperactivity disorder and comparison boys: Predictions from social behaviors and from nonbehavioral variables. *Journal of Consulting Clinical Psychology, 62*(4), 833–842.

Ettekal, I., & Ladd, G. W. (2015). Developmental pathways from childhood aggression-disruptiveness, chronic peer rejection, and deviant friendships to early-adolescent rule breaking. *Child Development, 86*(2), 614–631.

Farmer, T. W., Lines, M. M., & Hamm, J. V. (2011). Revealing the invisible hand: The role of teachers in children's peer experiences. *Journal of Applied Developmental Psychology, 32*(5), 247–256.

Flicek, M., & Landau, S. (1985). Social status problems of learning disabled children and adolescents: A review. *Learning Disability Quarterly, 8,* 189–204.

Fontaine, R. G., Yang, C., Burks, V. S., Dodge, K. A., Price, J. M., Pettit, G. S., & Bates, J. E. (2009). Loneliness as a partial mediator of the relation between low social preference in childhood and anxious/depressed symptoms in adolescence. *Development and Psychopathology, 21,* 479–491.

Gaub, M., & Carlson, C. L. (1997). Behavioral characteristics of DSM-IV ADHD subtypes in a school-based population. *Journal of Abnormal Child Psychology, 25,* 103–111.

Gooren, E. M. J. C., Lier, P. A. C., van Stegge, G. T. M., Meerum Terwogt, M., & Koot, H. M. (2011). The development of conduct problems and depressive symptoms in early elementary school children: The role of peer rejection. *Journal of Clinical Child and Adolescent Psychology, 40,* 245–253.

Grygiel, P., Humenny, G., Rebisz, S., Bajcar, E., & Switaj, P. (2014). Peer rejection and perceived quality of relations with schoolmates among children with ADHD. *Journal of Attention Disorders.* doi:10.1177/1087054714563791

Hinshaw, S. P. (1994). Conduct disorder in childhood: Conceptualization, diagnosis, comorbidity, and risk status for antisocial functioning in adulthood. In D. C. Fowles, P. Sutker, & S. H. Goodman (Eds.), *Progress in experimental personality and psychopathology research* (Vol. 17, pp. 3–44). New York, NY: Springer.

Hinshaw, S. P. (2002). Preadolescent girls with attention-deficit/hyperactivity disorder: I. Background characteristics, comorbidity, cognitive and social functioning, and parenting practices. *Journal of Consultant and Clinical Psychology, 70*(5), 1086–1098.

Hinshaw, S. P., & Melnick, S. M. (1995). Peer relationships in boys with attention-deficit hyperactivity disorder with and without comorbid aggression. *Development and Psychopathology, 7*(4), 627–647.

Hodgens, J. B., Cole, J., & Boldizar, J. (2000). Peer-based differences among boys with ADHD. *Journal of Clinical Child Psychology, 29*(3), 443–452.

Hoza, B. (2007). Peer functioning in children with ADHD. *Journal of Pediatric Psychology, 32*(6), 655–663.

Hoza, B., Mrug, S., Gerdes, A. C., Hinshaw, S. P., Bukowski, W. M., Gold, J. A., . . . Arnold, L.E. (2005). What aspects of peer relationships are impaired in children with Attention-Deficit/Hyperactivity Disorder? *Journal of Consulting and Clinical Psychology, 73*(3), 411–423.

Hughes, J. N., Cavell, T. A., & Willson, V. (2001). Further support for the developmental significance of the quality of the teacher-student relationship. *Journal of School Psychology, 39*(4), 289–301.

Hughes, J. N., & Chen, Q. (2011). Reciprocal effects of student-teacher and student-peer relatedness: Effects on academic self-efficacy. *Journal of Applied Developmental Psychology, 32*(5), 278–287.

Humphreys, K. L., Galán, C. A., Tottenham, N., & Lee, S. S. (2015). Impaired social decision-making mediates the association between ADHD and social problems. *Journal of Abnormal Child Psychology, 44*(5), 1023–1032.

Jarrett, M. A., Wolff, J. C., Davis, T. E., Cowart, M. J., & Ollendick, T. H. (2016). Characteristics of children with ADHD and comorbid anxiety. *Journal of Attention Disorders, 20,* 636–644.

Kiuru, N., Aunola, K., Lerkkanen, M.-K., Pakarinen, E., Poskiparta, E., Ahonen, T., Poikkeus, A.-M., & Nurmi, J.-E. (2015). Positive teacher and peer relations combine to predict primary school students' academic skill development. *Developmental Psychology, 51*(4), 434–446.

Kupersmidt, J., & Coie, J. D. (1990). Preadolescent peer status, aggression, and school adjustment as predictors of externalizing problems in adolescence. *Child Development, 61,* 1350–1362.

Kutcher, S., Aman, M., Brooks, S. J., Buitelaar, J., van Daalen, E., Fegert, J., . . . Tyrano, S. (2004). International consensus statement on attention-deficit/hyperactivity disorder (ADHD) and disruptive behavior disorders (DBDs): Clinical implications and treatment practice suggestions. *European Neuropsychopharmacology, 14*(1), 11–28.

Ladd, G. W. (2006). Peer rejection, aggressive or withdrawn behavior, and psychological maladjustment from ages 5 to 12: An examination of four predictive models. *Child Development, 77*(4), 822–846.

Ladd, G. W., & Burgess, K. B. (2001). Do relational risks and protective factors moderate the linkages between childhood aggression and early psychological and school adjustment? *Child Development, 72*(5), 1579–1601.

Ladd, G. W., & Troop-Gordon, W. (2003). The role of chronic peer difficulties in the development of children's psychological adjustment problems. *Child Development, 74,* 1344–1367.

Laird, R. D., Jordan, K. Y., Dodge, K. A., Pettit, G. S., & Bates, J. E. (2001). Peer rejection in childhood, involvement with antisocial peers in early adolescence, and the development of externalizing behavior problems. *Development and Psychopathology, 13,* 337–354.

Lansford, J. E., Malone, P. S., Dodge, K. A., Pettit, G. S., & Bates, J. E. (2010). Developmental cascades of peer rejection, social information processing biases, and aggression during middle childhood. *Developmental Psychopathology, 22*(3), 593–602.

Lee, S. S., & Hinshaw, S. P. (2006). Predictors of adolescent functioning in girls with attention deficit hyperactivity disorder (ADHD): The role of childhood ADHD, conduct problems, and peer status. *Journal of Clinical Child and Adolescent Psychology, 35*(3), 356–368.

Leflot, G., van Lier, P. A. C., Verschueren, K., Onghena, P., & Colpin, H. (2011). Transactional associations among teacher support, peer social preference, and child externalizing behavior: A four-wave longitudinal study. *Journal of Clinical Child and Adolescent Psychology, 40,* 87–99.

Maassen, G. H., van Boxtel, H. W., & Goossens, F. A. (2005). Reliability of nominations and two-dimensional rating scale methods for sociometric status determination. *Journal of Applied Developmental Psychology, 26*(1), 51–68.

Matthys, W., Cuperus, J., & van Engeland, H. (1999). Deficient social problem-solving in boys with ODD/CD, with ADHD, and with both disorders. *Journal of the American Academy of Child and Adolescent Psychiatry, 38,* 311–321.

Mayeux, L., Sandstrom, M. J., & Cillessen, A. H. N. (2008). Is being popular a risky proposition? *Journal of Research on Adolescence, 18*(1), 49–74.

McArdle, P., O'Brien, G., Macmillan, A., & Kolvin, I. (2000). The peer relations of disruptive children with reference to hyperactivity and conduct disorder. *European Child and Adolescent Psychiatry, 9,* 91–99.

McQuade, J. D., & Hoza, B. (2008). Peer problems in attention deficit hyperactivity disorder: Current status and future directions. *Developmental Disabilities Research Reviews, 14,* 320–324.

Mercer, S. H., & DeRosier, M. E. (2008). Teacher preference, peer rejection, and student aggression: A prospective study of transactional influence and independent contributions to emotional adjustment and grades. *Journal of School Psychology, 46*(06), 661–685.

Mikami, A. Y., & Lorenzi, J. (2011). Gender and conduct problems predict peer functioning among children with attention-deficit/hyperactivity disorder. *Journal of Clinical Child and Adolescent Psychology, 40*(5), 777–786.

Mikami, A. Y., & Hinshaw, S. P. (2006). Resilient adolescent adjustment among girls: Buffers of childhood peer rejection and attention-deficit/hyperactivity disorder. *Journal of Abnormal Child Psychology, 34*(6), 825–839.

Milich, R., & Landau, S. (1982). Socialization and peer relations in hyperactive children. In K. D. Gadow & I. Bialer (Eds.), *Advances in learning and behavior disabilities* (Vol. 1, pp. 283–339). Greenwich, CT: JAI Press.

Miller-Johnson, S., Coie, J. D., Maumary-Gremaud, A., Bierman, K., & Conduct Problems Prevention Research Group. (2002). Peer rejection and aggression and early starter models of conduct disorder. *Journal of Abnormal Child Psychology, 30*(3), 217–230.

Miller-Johnson, S., Coie, J. D., Maumary-Gremaud, A., Lochman, J., & Terry, R. (1999). Relationship between childhood peer rejection and aggression and adolescent delinquency severity and type among African American youth. *Journal of Emotional and Behavioral Disorders, 7*(3), 137–146.

Moffitt, T. E., & Caspi, A. (2001). Childhood predictors differentiate life-course persistent and adolescence-limited antisocial pathways among males and females. *Development and psychopathology, 13*(2), 355–375.

Mrug, S., Hoza, B., Gerdes, A. C., Hinshaw, S., Arnold, L. E., Hechtman, L., & Pelham, W. E. (2009). Discriminating between children with ADHD and classmates using peer variables. *Journal of Attention Disorders, 12*(4), 372–380.

Mrug, S., Molina, B. S. G., Hoza, B., Gerdes, A. C., Hinshaw, S. P., Hechtman, L., & Arnold, L. E. (2012). Peer rejection and friendships in children with attention-deficit/hyperactivity disorder: Contributions to long-term outcomes. *Journal of Abnormal Child Psychology, 40*(6), 1013–1026.

Murray-Close, D., Hoza, B., Hinshaw, S. P., Arnold, L. E., Jensen, P. S., Hechtman, L., & Wells, K. (2010). Developmental processes in peer problems of children with ADHD in the MTA study: Developmental cascades and vicious cycles. *Developmental Psychopathology, 22*(4), 785–802.

Newcomb, A. F., & Bukowski, W. M. (1983). Social impact and social preference as determinants of children's peer group status. *Developmental Psychology, 19,* 856–867.

Oden, S., & Asher, S. R. (1977). Coaching children in social skills in friendship making. *Child Development, 48*(2), 495–506.

Orobio de Castro, B., Brendgen, M., Van Boxtel, H., Vitaro, F., & Schaepers, L. (2007, April). "Accept me, or else": Disputed overestimation of social competence predicts increases in proactive aggression. *Journal of Abnormal Child Psychology, 35*(2), 165–178.

Orobio de Castro, B., Veerman, J. W., Koops, W., Bosch, J. D., & Monshouwer, H. J. (2002). Hostile attribution of intent and aggressive behavior: A meta-analysis. *Child Development, 73,* 916–934. doi:10.1111/1467-8624.00447

Owens, J. S., Goldfine. M. E., Evangelista, N. M., Hoza B., & Kaiser, N. M. (2007). A critical review of self-perceptions and the positive illusory bias in children with ADHD. *Clinical Child and Family Psychology Review, 10,* 335–51.

Parker, J. G., & Asher, S. R. (1987). Peer relations and later personal adjustment: Are low accepted children at risk? *Psychological Bulletin, 102,* 357–389.

Patterson, G. R., DeBaryshe, B. D., & Ramsey, E. (1989). A developmental perspective on antisocial behavior. *American Psychologist, 44,* 329–335.

Pederson, S., Vitaro, F., Barker, E. D., & Borge, A. I. (2007). The timing of middle-childhood peer rejection and friendship: Linking early behavior to early-adolescent adjustment. *Child Development, 78*(4), 1037–1051.

Pope, A. W., Bierman, K. L., & Mumma, G. H. (1989). Relations between hyperactive and aggressive behavior and peer relations at three elementary grade levels. *Journal of Abnormal Child Psychology, 17*(3), 253–267.

Powers, C. J., Bierman, K. L., & the Conduct Problems Prevention Research Group. (2013). The multifaceted impact of peer relations on aggressive-disruptive behavior in early elementary school. *Developmental Psychology, 49,* 1174–1186.

Prinstein, M. J., & La Greca, A. M. (2004). Childhood rejection, aggression, and depression as predictors of adolescent girls' externalizing and health risk behaviors: A six-year longitudinal study. *Journal of Consulting and Clinical Psychology, 72,* 103–112.

Rodkin, P. C., Farmer, T. W., Pearl, R., & Van Acker, R. (2000). Heterogeneity of popular boys: Antisocial and prosocial configurations. *Developmental Psychology, 36,* 14–24.

Rubin, K. H., Bukowski, W., & Parker, J. G. (1998). Peer interactions, relationships, and groups. In W. Damon & N. Eisenberg (Eds.), *Handbook of child psychology: Social, emotional, and personality development* (5th ed., pp. 619–700). New York, NY: Wiley.

Sandstrom, M. J., & Cillessen, A. H. (2010). Life after high school: Adjustment of popular teens in emerging adulthood. *Merrill-Palmer Quarterly, 56*(4), 474–499.

Sibley, M. H., Evans, S. W., & Serpell, Z. N. (2010). Social cognition and interpersonal impairment in young adolescents with ADHD. *Journal of Psychopathological Behavioral Assessment, 32,* 193–202.

Silver, R. B., Measelle, J. R., Armstrong, J. M., & Essex, M. J. (2005). Trajectories of classroom externalizing behavior: Contributions of child characteristics, family characteristics, and the teacher-child relationship during the school transition. *Journal of School Psychology, 43,* 39–60.

Stormshak, E. A., Bierman, K. L., and the Conduct Problems Prevention Research Group (1998). The implications of different developmental patterns of disruptive behavior problems for adjustment. *Development and Psychopathology, 10,* 451–467.

Sturaro, C., van Lier, P. A., Cuijpers, P., & Koot, H. M. (2011). The role of peer relationships in the development of early school-age externalizing problems. *Child Development, 82*(3), 758–765.

Sullivan, H. S. (1953). *The interpersonal theory of psychiatry.* New York, NY: Norton.

Troop-Gordon, W., & Ranney, J. D. (2014). Popularity among same-sex and cross-sex peers: A process-oriented examination of links to aggressive behaviors and depressive affect. *Developmental Psychology, 50*(6), 1721–1733.

Tseng, W. L., Kawabata, Y., Fen, S. S., & Crick, N. R. (2014). Symptoms of attention-deficit/hyperactivity disorder and peer functioning: A transactional model of development. *Journal of Abnormal Child Psychology, 42*(8), 1353–1365.

Vitaro, F., Pedersen, S., & Brendgen, M. (2007). Children's disruptiveness, peer rejection, friends' deviancy, and delinquent behaviors: A process-oriented approach. *Development and Psychopathology, 19*(02), 433–453.

Whalen, C. K., Henker, B., Collins, B. E., McAuliffe, S., & Vaux, A. (1979). Peer interactions in structured communication tasks: Comparisons of normal and hyperactive boys and of methylphenidate (Ritalin) and placebo effects. *Child Development, 50,* 388–401.

Wichstrom, L., Belsky, J., & Berg-Nielsen, T. S. (2013). Preschool predictors of childhood anxiety disorders: A prospective community study. *The Journal of Child Psychology and Psychiatry, 54,* 1327–1336.

Zakriski, A. L., & Coie, J. D. (1996). A comparison of aggressive-rejected and nonaggressive-rejected children's interpretations of self-directed and other-directed rejection. *Child Development, 67,* 1048–1070.

21

The Role of Deviant Peers in Oppositional Defiant Disorder and Conduct Disorder

Damir S. Utržan, Timothy F. Piehler, and Thomas. J. Dishion

Conduct problems associated with Oppositional Defiant Disorder (ODD) and Conduct Disorder (CD) are a serious public health concern in the United States. In youth, they are associated with crime, substance use, socio-emotional impairment, and academic underachievement. Although critical to the successful transition from childhood and adolescence to adulthood, peer relationships are also a powerful socializing agent in the development of conduct problems. This chapter provides an introduction to the role of deviant peers in the development of conduct problems associated with ODD and CD. We briefly outline the developmental and ecological context for understanding peer influence processes in adolescence as well as risk factors for deviant peer association. We also introduce the mechanisms of deviancy training and coercion, along with the social augmentation hypothesis. We review research identifying several types of moderators of peer influence. Finally, we suggest several future research directions.

Conduct Disorder, Oppositional Defiant Disorder, and Deviant Peers

Oppositional Defiant Disorder (ODD) and Conduct Disorder (CD), defined in more detail elsewhere in this volume (see Chapters 2 and 3), reflect patterns of behavioral problems that result in functional impairment in multiple settings (American Psychiatric Association [APA], 2013). Common behaviors associated with ODD are defiance, spitefulness, negativity, and hostility or verbal aggression (APA, 2013). When untreated, ODD can progress to CD, a more severe pattern of behavioral problems that include persistent violations of others' basic rights and social expectations such as physical aggression, theft, vandalism, and other rule violations (APA, 2013; Rogge, 2015). The lifetime prevalence of ODD and CD is approximately 10% in the general population (Nock, Kazdin, Hiripi, & Kessler, 2007). These diagnoses reflect a spectrum of serious behavior problems that we refer to broadly as conduct problems for the purposes of this chapter. Conduct problems in children and adolescents are a major public health concern because they disrupt multiple domains of positive adjustment during development (Dishion & Patterson, 2016). These behaviors are associated with academic underachievement (Masten et al., 2005), socioemotional impairment (Dodge &

The Wiley Handbook of Disruptive and Impulse-Control Disorders, First Edition.
Edited by John E. Lochman and Walter Matthys.
© 2018 John Wiley & Sons Ltd. Published 2018 by John Wiley & Sons Ltd.

Pettit, 2003), crime (Murray, Irving, Farrington, Colman, & Bloxsom, 2010), substance use (Hawkins, Catalano, & Miller, 1992), and negative relationship and occupational outcomes in adulthood (Fergusson, John Horwood, & Ridder, 2005).

Deviant peer affiliations are among the most reliable risk factors in the development of conduct problems (Dishion & Patterson, 2016; Haynie & Osgood, 2005). Association with peers who engage in problematic conduct serves to introduce, escalate, and maintain problem behaviors. When compared to other risk factors, deviant peer affiliations are often the most robust predictor of conduct problems in youth (Aseltine, 1995; Deković, 1999). This chapter outlines the complex nature of the relationship between deviant peer associations and the development and maintenance of conduct problems. We review risk factors for associations with deviant peers, specific mechanisms of deviant peer influence, as well as several types of moderators of influence effects.

A Developmental-Ecological Perspective

While peer risk factors have been identified as particularly salient in the development of conduct problems, peer risk most often occurs within a complex constellation of neurobiological, familial, and other contextual risk factors (Loeber, Burke, Lahey, Winters, & Zera, 2000; Loeber, Burke, & Pardini, 2009). Low sensitivity to punishment and reward, increased sensation seeking, and executive functioning deficits (e.g., impulsivity, impaired cognitive control over emotions) have been identified as neurobiological contributors to the development of conduct problems (Matthys, Vanderschuren, & Schutter, 2013). Familial risk includes inadequate parental supervision and maladaptive discipline strategies (Smith & Stern, 1997). Intra-individual and family factors not only contribute independently to the development of conduct problems, but may also heighten the impact of deviant peer affiliations. Youth with neurobiological risk factors may be the most susceptible to peer influence processes (Piehler, Véronneau, & Dishion, 2012). Parent disengagement from monitoring youth in early adolescence may also accelerate the peer socialization processes (Dishion, Nelson, & Bullock, 2004). For many youth, these risk factors co-occur, with peers playing a central component in the ecology of risk that contributes to the development of conduct problems (Aseltine, 1995).

Developmental considerations are also critical in understanding peer influences on conduct problems. As children enter adolescence, familial relationships tend to become less influential, while peers become the predominant socializing agents (Deković, Janssens, & Van As, 2003; Fosco, Stormshak, Dishion, & Winter, 2012). This transition requires parents to modify aspects of their parenting approach. Where monitoring their child's behavior may have previously occurred primarily within the family home, activities with peer groups increasingly occur in settings outside of the home during adolescence. Youth with antisocial behavior may actively avoid parent oversight of their activities and whereabouts (Stoolmiller, 1994). Parents who do not adjust their monitoring structure while decreasing their involvement place their children at greater risk for exposure to and corresponding influence from deviant peers. Indeed, decreases in family management practices associated with monitoring in early- to mid-adolescence (i.e., 15–16 years of age) were associated with deviant peer association two years later (Dishion et al., 2004). The combination of decreased monitoring and deviant peer associations predicted growth in substance use and antisocial behavior at 18 years of age. Thus, parental disengagement appears to facilitate youth access to deviant friendships during early adolescence, which contributes to the development of conduct problems.

Risk Factors for Deviant Peer Involvement

From an ecological perspective, it is important to consider the broader context that may lead youth to socialize with deviant peers. Figure 21.1 outlines a conceptual model of both risk factors for deviant peer affiliations and moderators of the relationship between deviant peers and conduct problems which are detailed in later in the chapter. Three primary categories of risk factors for deviant peer involvement have been identified in previous research, including individual, family-based, and broader contextual risk factors.

Individual Risk Factors

Early peer rejection has been consistently identified as a risk factor for deviant peer involvement (Dishion, Patterson, Stoolmiller, & Skinner, 1991). Youth often begin a trajectory toward rejection from mainstream peers due to poor social skills and aggressive behavior (Bierman, 2004). Early academic failure also reliably predicts subsequent deviant peer involvement (Dishion et al., 1991). Hill, Howell, Hawkins, and Battin-Pearson (1999) identified several individual risk factors for gang membership, an especially pernicious form of deviant peer affiliation. They found that early development of problem behaviors, such as aggression and marijuana use, were associated with gang involvement later in adolescence. Early antisocial beliefs (e.g., positive beliefs about rule breaking) and poor peer refusal skills were also associated with later gang involvement.

Family Risk Factors

Ineffective parenting practices have been identified as significant risk factors for deviant peer involvement (Brown & Bakken, 2011; Dishion et al., 2004). Parental monitoring, defined as a broad set of behaviors that include maintenance of structure across different contexts (e.g., home, school, community) and tracking behaviors in those contexts, is the parenting practice

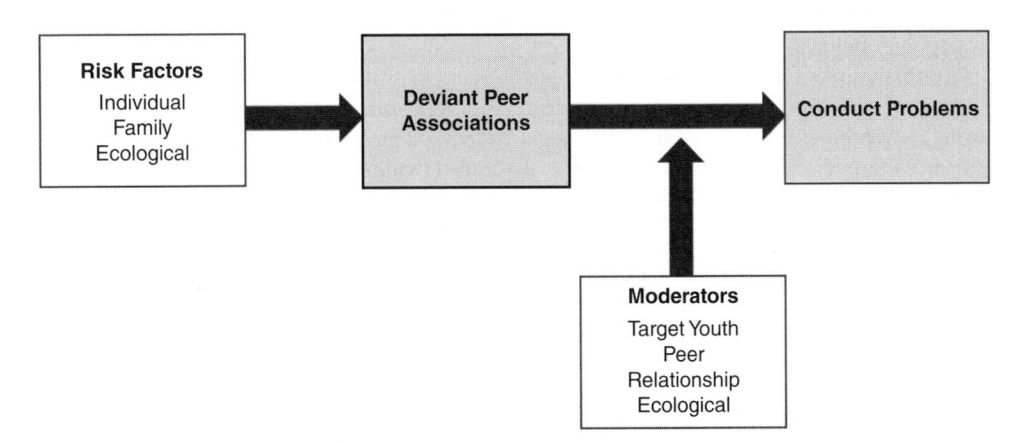

Figure 21.1 Conceptual model detailing risk factors for deviant peer association and moderators of the relationship between deviant peer association and conduct problems.

most closely linked to deviant peer involvement (Dishion & McMahon, 1998). With limited awareness of their children's activities and associates, parents are less effective in discouraging activities with deviant peers. Stattin and Kerr (2000) offer a reinterpretation of findings involving monitoring. They note that effective monitoring largely depends upon a child's disclosure of his or her activities to a parent. They also suggest that effective monitoring does not simply reflect parental behavior but a dynamic embedded within the parent–child relationship. Supporting this view, Dishion et al. (2004) highlighted the reciprocal nature of family management practices, including parental monitoring, and youth involvement with deviant peers. In this study, poor family management practices were associated with growth in deviant peer involvement. In turn, high levels of deviant peer involvement lead to a degradation of family management practices.

Other aspects of family functioning and the parent–child relationship have also been identified as predictors of deviant peer involvement. Cashwell and Vacc (1996) found a relationship between family cohesion and adolescent delinquency that was mediated by deviant peer involvement. They suggest that poor family cohesion influences peer group selection through adolescents' limited development of the requisite interpersonal skills necessary for acceptance by prosocial peers. Similarly, longitudinal work has revealed that youth perceptions of parental warmth are associated with subsequent deviant peer involvement, which, in turn, predicts problem behaviors later in adolescence (Goldstein, Davis-Kean, & Eccles, 2005). Youth who perceived their parents as demonstrating more warmth and caring in their relationship were less likely to subsequently affiliate with deviant peers.

Ecological Risk Factors

Family risk factors tend not to occur in isolation but in combination with other broader ecological factors that also increase the likelihood of deviant peer association. Structural characteristics of family contexts, including low socioeconomic status, poor housing quality, and limited availability of resources, increase the likelihood of youth becoming involved with deviant peers (Sampson, 1993). Ge, Brody, Conger, Simons, and Murry (2002) similarly reported that disadvantaged neighborhood conditions (e.g., low income, high unemployment, etc.) are significantly associated with deviant peer affiliation among African-American youth. In these high-risk communities, the available peer groups may be more likely to be characterized by problem behaviors.

Contextual risk for involvement with deviant peers may also occur in settings designed to support at-risk youth. When lacking structure and appropriate adult supervision and monitoring, environments that aggregate at-risk youth may lead to formation of deviant friendships and provide peer reinforcement of antisocial values (Dodge, Dishion, & Lansford, 2006). Often referred to as peer contagion (see Dishion & Tipsord, 2011), these dynamics may reduce the effectiveness of group-based intervention programming and potentially even result in iatrogenic effects (Dishion, McCord, & Poulin, 1999). It is important to note that many well-executed group-based programs for youth with conduct problems demonstrate positive effects (e.g., Lochman & Wells, 2004). However, the evidence suggests that even well-run, evidence-based interventions show a diminished effect size in a group format when compared to individual formats in the context of a randomized trial (Lochman et al., 2015). A review of group-based programs targeting adolescent delinquency found that those programs that demonstrated the strongest outcomes took steps to limit unstructured peer interactions (Lipsey & Wilson, 1998).

Mechanisms of Peer Influence

Selection versus Influence Effects

Research into peer social networks has consistently identified significant homophily (i.e., similarities) between youth. Homophily develops through either peer selection or peer influence, both of which operate within a mutually recursive relationship (Brechwald & Prinstein, 2011; De Klepper, Sleebos, van de Bunt, & Agneessens, 2009). Youth are similar because they seek out peers who are similar (i.e., through selection). But they also become similar to peers through their associations (i.e., through influence). While the relationship between association with deviant peers and conduct problems is generally interpreted as evidence of peer influence, this neglects the possibility that youth choose friends who are similar to themselves.

Both of these processes have been found to contribute to the onset or maintenance of conduct problems in youth. Studies that employ longitudinal social network analyses may allow researchers to most effectively isolate the relative contributions of selection and influence effects. When examined in these models, both processes have been clearly identified as contributors to homophily (Dijkstra et al., 2010; Sijtsema et al., 2010). When looking at several different types of aggressive behaviors, influence tended to show a greater impact when compared to selection for most types of aggression (Sijtsema et al., 2010).

Monahan, Steinberg, and Cauffman (2009) used longitudinal data to examine the relative contributions of selection and influence effects on antisocial behavior during different developmental periods from adolescence to adulthood. While both selection and influence effects were present in mid-adolescence (i.e., at 14–15 years of age), only influence effects were noted in late adolescence (i.e., at 16–20 years of age). Neither influence nor selection effects were reliably found in early adulthood (i.e., at 20–22 years of age). These findings highlight that peer networks may be in formation earlier in adolescence as youth seek out like-minded friends who are also highly influential. Friendship networks solidify by late adolescence, though these friendships continue to be influential in shaping behavior. Other findings support youth's unique susceptibility to peer influence during adolescence in addition to the waning of that influence during early adulthood (Steinberg & Monahan, 2007).

Peer Deviancy Training

Specific mechanisms of peer influence have been identified through observational research. In deviancy training, peers shape and encourage deviant behavior through positive reinforcement (Dishion et al., 1996). This type of interaction occurs when youth discuss deviant topics or display behaviors that violate social norms and receive a positive response from a peer (e.g., laughter). Deviancy training has been observed in peer interactions from early childhood through adolescence (Dishion, Spracklen, Andrews, & Patterson, 1996; Piehler & Dishion, 2007; Snyder et al., 2005).

Systematic research in a public school setting revealed that deviancy training can occur as early as kindergarten and influences the emergence of conduct problems in the ensuing years (Snyder et al., 2005). When observed in kindergarteners, deviant talk (e.g., discussion of deviant behaviors) evoked a positive response from peers nearly 40% of the time across all youth. Furthermore, peer reinforcement of deviant talk during kindergarten increased school-based conduct problems, such as aggression, swearing, and stealing, in the first two years of elementary school. During adolescence, deviant peers were also more likely to reject prosocial discussions while simultaneously reinforcing deviant talk (Dishion et al., 1996). Deviancy training during adolescence has been associated with growth in antisocial behavior, violence, and substance use (Dishion, Eddy, Haas, Li, & Spracklen, 1997; Granic & Dishion, 2003).

Coercion

Coercion represents another mechanism of peer influence that relies upon escape conditioning rather than positive reinforcement. Coercive interactions occur when aversive behaviors are used to control another person's behavior (Patterson, 1982; Patterson, Reid, & Dishion, 1992). This type of exchange has been classically studied in parent–child interaction. In this context, a parent's request is met with noncompliance from the child. This elicits anger from the parent, increases defiance from the child, and leads to a mutually reinforcing pattern of interaction in an attempt to gain control over the situation (Patterson, 1982). Such negative interactions model and reinforce the child's defiance and subsequently conduct problems (Webster-Stratton, Reid, & Hammond, 2004).

Children subsequently learn to apply these patterns of interaction to other social relationships. Coercion is a powerful method in altering the behavior of other people and shaping conduct problems, particularly covert behaviors such as lying and stealing (Patterson, 2016). When measured in early childhood, observed coercive behaviors included negative interpersonal behaviors such as teasing, threats, name calling, and physical aggression (Snyder et al., 2008). Children who experienced coercive behaviors from their peers in kindergarten demonstrated higher levels of conduct problems by third and fourth grade, even when controlling for initial levels of conduct problems in kindergarten (Snyder et al., 2008).

Van Ryzin and Dishion (2013) examined the cascading effects of coercion in family and peer relationships in adolescence. During this developmental period, coercion was observed through a process they labeled *coercive joining*. Coercive joining is an interpersonal process that involves youth using an aggressive interaction style in attempts to gain dominance over one another. The researchers theorized that this process serves to connect youth through shared enjoyment in treating others negatively. Van Ryzin and Dishion (2013) found that coercive peer interactions in middle adolescence mediated the relationship between coercive family interactions in early adolescence and violent behavior in young adulthood. Coercive family interactions were associated with the development of coercive peer interactions, which, in turn, predicted the development of violent behavior (e.g., committing acts of violence, arrests, use of weapons) by young adulthood.

Social Augmentation Hypothesis

Friendships characterized by deviancy training or coercion would seem to be undesirable for youth. But this raises the question of why youth would choose to engage in friendships that promote antisocial values or that are characterized by aversive interactions. The social augmentation hypothesis suggests that youth enter into deviant friendships because they are in some sense functionally adaptive within their immediate environment (Dishion, Piehler, & Myers, 2008). Youth with poor social skills or aggressive behaviors with others are likely to be marginalized or rejected by their peers. These youth experience few positive social interactions and engage in a process of "niche finding" in an effort to find a peer group.

Youth also often seek out others they perceive to be similar to themselves. They try to find peers who will be at least superficially accepting and provide a reinforcing environment. This process, often referred to as the confluence model, leads to formation of deviant peer groups

(Dishion, Patterson, & Griesler, 1994). Youth in these groups find that antisocial values are positively reinforced, and aversive social interactions, rather than leading to rejection, serve instead as tools used to gain power and control over others. Furthermore, joining a peer group, even an antisocial one, typically carries with it at least some level of status within a social network. Thus, when viewed from this broader perspective, these maladaptive friendships serve an adaptive purpose within a marginalizing social network.

Recent longitudinal analyses of a multiethnic community sample systematically linked middle school marginalization with early adolescent gang involvement (Dishion, Ha, & Véronneau, 2012). In this study, peer nominations of rejection, teacher ratings of low acceptance, and academic failure formed a construct describing school marginalization during grades six, seven, and eight. Second, family attenuation was measured by the youth report of low parent monitoring, poor relationships with parents, and low rates of positive behavior support at the same age. Controlling for family socioeconomic status, it was found that both school marginalization and family attenuation predicted a multi-agent and -method measure of gang involvement. Interestingly, gang involvement at age 14 was by far the strongest predictor of sexual activity at age 16 to 17, which in turn was highly predictive of having children in late adolescence (Dishion, 2012). Thus, for marginalized youth, organization into deviant peer groups may lead to increased access to sexual partners, an adaptive short-term outcome with a high potential cost in early parenthood. These analyses suggest that sexual partners may play an important role in the social augmentation model as sexual interest promotes self-organization into deviant peer groups that amplify problem behavior in adolescence.

Moderators of Deviant Peer Influence

A number of factors have been identified that may either increase or decrease the relative impact of deviant peer affiliations on the development of conduct problems (see Figure 21.1). These moderators may be particularly important not only for gaining a deeper understanding of peer influence processes but also in targeting prevention efforts. Four primary categories of moderators of deviant peer effects have been identified in previous research: target, peer, relationship, and contextual (Brechwald & Prinstein, 2011; Heilbron & Prinstein, 2008).

Target and Peer Moderators

A variety of psychological characteristics of the influenced (i.e., target) youth may moderate the impact of exposure to deviant peers. Aspects of self-regulatory ability and executive functioning generally serve as protective factors for youth. Gardner, Dishion, and Connell, (2008) found that a multi-informant measure of self-regulation (focused on inhibition, activation control, and attention) was associated with a reduced impact of deviant peer associations on conduct problems across a large community sample of youth. These skills may allow youth to resist the short-term gains of yielding to peer expectations in favor of behavior that may be less immediately reinforcing but more promotive of long-term success. Other psychological indices such as social anxiety, depression, and poor self-esteem have also been linked to increased susceptibility to peer influence (Cohen & Prinstein, 2006; Prinstein, 2007; Prinstein, Boergers, & Spirito, 2001). Youth with more limited confidence in themselves and their identity may be more susceptible to pressure from peers and the immediate positive feedback provided by conforming to peer demands (Heilbron & Prinstein, 2008).

The severity of existing conduct problems may also have a bearing on individual susceptibility to influence from deviant peers. Youth with moderate levels of conduct problems tend to be more vulnerable to associations with deviant peers when compared to youth with high levels of conduct problems (Vitaro, Tremblay, Kerr, Pagani, & Bukowski, 1997). This finding may be particularly important when considering the composition of intervention groups for at-risk youth. Indeed, when comparing outcomes between youth involved in intervention groups uniformly composed of youth with high levels of conduct problems and those involving a mix of youth with moderate to high levels, the mixed groups demonstrated notably poorer outcomes (Mager, Milich, Harris, & Howard, 2005).

While less studied than target moderators, characteristics of the influencing peer have also been identified as moderators of influence. Peer moderators have generally reflected social status. Cohen and Prinstein (2006) found that influence toward aggression and other health-risking behaviors was more likely to occur when peers' likability and reputation-based popularity were high. It is not surprising that high-status peers are more likely to be influential within their social networks.

Relationship Moderators

The characteristics of the relationship between the target youth and influencing peer are a third type of moderator. Research in this area has generally supported the idea that closer, higher quality friendships support higher levels of influence among peers. In one observational study of adolescent friendship interactions, dyadic mutuality (i.e., the extent to which peer interactions were reciprocal, responsive, and mutually engaging) and deviant discussion topics were coded (Piehler & Dishion, 2007). For those friendships with low levels of deviant discussion, dyadic mutuality was a protective factor and was associated with lower levels of conduct problems. However, for those friends who spoke extensively about deviant topics (e.g., rule breaking, aggression towards others, substance use, etc.), dyadic mutuality was associated with greater engagement in problem behaviors. Responsive and engaging interactions seemed to be associated with heightened influence surrounding friendship norms.

Ecological Moderators

Ecological features, such as the family and broader peer group environment, may also moderate the impact of deviant peer affiliations. Within the family context, parental monitoring not only reduces the risk for deviant peer affiliation (see above), it may also lessen the impact of existing affiliations with deviant peers. Laird, Criss, Pettit, Dodge, and Bates (2008) reported that parents who increased their monitoring over the course of their children's adolescence tended to disrupt deviant influence processes that occurred between their child and the peer group.

Increasing monitoring also tended to disrupt the formation of new friendships between their children and deviant peers. These results support previous findings that parents' ability to maintain or increase their level of monitoring during adolescence is a critical factor in disrupting risk from deviant peers (Dishion et al., 2004).

Features of the broader peer group may also impact the extent of influence that occurs within it. Using social network analysis, Ellis and Zarbatany (2007) evaluated characteristics of early adolescent peer groups and their association with the extent of influence of different behaviors within the groups. They found that high-status peer groups characterized by greater centrality within the larger social network were associated with greater socialization effects (i.e., influence) for both prosocial and deviant behaviors. These highly visible peer groups seemed to have greater influence on individual behaviors within the group that helped maintain the group's elevated social status. Interestingly, youth who were a part of poorly accepted (i.e., marginalized) peer groups demonstrated enhanced influence of deviant behaviors only, not prosocial ones. When peer groups are largely rejected by other peers, group norms surrounding deviant behaviors seem to prevail and result in greater socialization of those behaviors.

Conclusion and Future Directions

This chapter described the role of deviant peers in the development of conduct problems. While there is a broad body of literature supporting this area, there are also several important directions of future research that will benefit from additional focus. First, research in this area has largely concentrated on understanding deviant peer associations. We know much less about the development of prosocial peer groups and the mechanisms of prosocial peer socialization. It is clear that positive peer influence does not simply reflect a lack of deviant peer processes. Mechanisms such as deviancy training do not seem to apply in the same fashion to prosocial socialization (Piehler & Dishion, 2007). A better understanding of prosocial peer processes is an important first step in developing strategies to support prosocial peer influence.

A second related future direction has to do with effectively intervening deviant peer processes. While there are clear indications of parenting behaviors that combat deviant peer influence, intervention work has been notably less effective when trying to address these peer processes more directly. Efforts outside of the family, such as utilizing peer group leaders and altering group norms in addressing conduct problems, have tended to be less successful and occasionally even result in harm for some high-risk youth (e.g., Valente et al., 2007).

Future intervention work in this area may benefit from several strategies. First, it will be important to address risks for peer contagion more effectively within interventions that aggregate at-risk youth. While a variety of strategies have been identified to reduce risk in these contexts, they have received little empirical evaluation. Second, as noted above, a better understanding of prosocial peer processes may allow for youth-focused interventions to specifically target these dynamics. School-based intervention efforts in particular may benefit from moving beyond more general social skill building to targeting specifically identified interpersonal dynamics. Finally, a broader focus on contextual factors, such as characteristics of the social network, family functioning, and school and neighborhood environments would allow programming to capitalize most effectively on existing strengths and target areas of risk supporting deviant peer processes. These types of advance may hold considerable promise for improving our intervention efforts and maximizing positive outcomes for youth.

References

American Psychiatric Association. (2013). *Diagnostic and statistical manual of mental Disorders* (5th ed.). Arlington, VA: Author.

Aseltine, R. H. (1995). A reconsideration of parental and peer influences of adolescent deviance. *Journal of Health and Social Behavior, 36*(2), 103–121.

Bierman, K. L. (2004). *Peer rejection: Developmental processes and intervention strategies.* New York, NY: Guilford Press.

Brechwald, W. A., & Prinstein, M. J. (2011). Beyond homophily: A decade of advances in understanding peer influence processes. *Journal of Research on Adolescence, 21*(1), 166–179.

Brown, B. B., & Bakken, J. P. (2011). Parenting and peer relationships: Reinvigorating research on family-peer linkages in adolescence. *Journal of Research on Adolescence, 21*(1), 153–165. doi:10.111/j.1532-7795.2010.00720.

Cashwell, C. S., & Vacc, N. A. (1996). Family influences on adolescent delinquent behavior. *The Family Journal: Counseling and Therapy for Couples and Families, 4*(3), 217–225. doi:10.1177/1066480796043005

Cohen, G. L., & Prinstein, M. J. (2006). Peer contagion of aggression and health risk behavior among adolescent males: An experimental investigation of effects on public conduct and private attitudes. *Child Development, 77*(4), 967–983. doi:10.1111/j.1467-8624.2006.00913.x

De Klepper, M., Sleebos, E., van de Bunt, G., & Agneessens, F. (2010). Similarity in friendship networks: Selection or influence? The effect of constraining contexts and non-visible individual attributes. *Social Networks, 31*(1), 82–90. doi:10.1016/j.socnet.2009.06.003

Deković, M. (1999). Risk and protective factors in the development of problem behavior during adolescence. *Journal of Youth and Adolescence, 28*(6), 667–685. doi:10.1023/a:1021635516758

Deković, M., Janssens, J. M. A. M., & Van As, N. M. C. (2003). Family predictors of antisocial behaviors in adolescence. *Family Process, 42*(2), 223–235. doi:10.1111/j.1545-5300.2003.42203.x

Dijkstra, J. K., Lindenberg, S., Veenstra, R., Steglich, C., Isaacs, J., Card, N. A., & Hodges, E. V. E. (2010). Influence and selection processes in weapon carrying during adolescence: The roles of status, aggression, and vulnerability. *Criminology, 48*(1), 187–220. doi:10.1111/j.1745-9125.2010.00183.x

Dishion, T. J., Eddy, J. M., Haas, E., Li, F., & Spracklen, K. (1997). Friendships and violent behavior during adolescence. *Social Development, 6*(2), 207–223. doi:10.1111/j.1467-9507.1997.tb00102.x

Dishion, T. J., Ha, T., & Véronneau, M.H. (2012). An ecological analysis of the effects of deviant peer clustering on sexual promiscuity, problem behavior, and childbearing from early adolescence to adulthood: An enhancement of the life history framework. *Developmental Psychology, 48*(3), 703–717. doi:10.1037/a0027304

Dishion, T. J., McCord, J., & Poulin, F. (1999). When interventions harm: Peer groups and problem behavior. *American Psychologist, 54*(9), 755–764.

Dishion, T. J., & McMahon, R. J. (1998). Parental monitoring and the prevention of child and adolescent problem behavior: A conceptual and empirical formulation. *Clinical Child and Family Psychology Review, 1*(1), 61–75. doi:10.1023/A:1021800432380

Dishion, T. J., Nelson, S. E., & Bullock, B. M. (2004). Premature adolescent autonomy: Parent disengagement and deviant peer process in the amplification of problem behaviour. *Journal of Adolescence, 27*(5), 515–530. doi:10.1016/j.adolescence.2004.06.005

Dishion, T. J., & Patterson, G. R. (2016). The development and ecology of problem behavior: Linking etiology, prevention, and treatment. In D. Cicchetti (Ed.), *Development psychopathology, risk, resilience, and intervention* (Vol. 3, pp. 647–678). Hoboken, NJ: John Wiley & Sons.

Dishion, T. J., Patterson, G. R., & Griesler, P. C. (1994). Peer adaptations in the development of antisocial behavior. In L. R. Huesmann (Ed.), *Aggressive behavior: Current perspectives* (pp. 61–95). Boston, MA: Springer US.

Dishion, T. J., Patterson, G. R., Stoolmiller, M., & Skinner, M. L. (1991). Family, school, and behavioral antecedents to early adolescent involvement with antisocial peers. *Developmental Psychology, 27*(1), 172–180. doi:10.1037/0012-1649.27.1.172

Dishion, T. J., Piehler, T. F., & Myers, M. W. (2008). Dynamics and ecology of adolescent peer influence. In M. J. Prinstein & K. A. Dodge (Eds.), *Understanding peer influence in children and adolescents* (pp. 72–93). New York, NY: Guilford Press.

Dishion, T. J., Spracklen, K. M., Andrews, D. W., & Patterson, G. R. (1996). Deviancy training in male adolescent friendships. *Behavior Therapy, 27*(3), 373–390. doi:10.1016/S0005-7894(96)80023-2

Dishion, T. J., & Tipsord, J. M. (2011). Peer contagion in child and adolescent social and emotional development. *Annual Review of Psychology, 62*, 189–214. doi:10.1146/annurev.psych.093008.100412

Dodge, K. A., Dishion, T. J., & Lansford, J. E. (2006). *Deviant peer influences in programs for youth: Problems and solutions.* New York, NY: Guilford Press.

Dodge, K. A., & Pettit, G. S. (2003). A biopsychosocial model of the development of chronic conduct problems in adolescence. *Developmental Psychology, 39*(2), 349–371. doi:10.1037/0012-1649.39.2.349

Ellis, W. E., & Zarbatany, L. (2007). Peer group status as a moderator of group influence on children's deviant, aggressive, and prosocial behavior. *Child Development, 78*(4), 1240–1254. doi:10.1111/j.1467-8624.2007.01063.x

Fergusson, D. M., Horwood, L. J., & Ridder, E. M. (2005). Show me the child at seven: The consequences of conduct problems in childhood for psychosocial functioning in adulthood. *Journal of Child Psychology and Psychiatry, 46*(8), 837–849. doi:10.1111/j.1469-7610.2004.00387.x

Fosco, G. M., Stormshak, E. A., Dishion, T. J., & Winter, C. E. (2012). Family relationships and parental monitoring during middle school as predictors of early adolescent problem behavior. *Journal of Clinical Child & Adolescent Psychology, 41*(2), 202–213. doi:10.1080/15374416.2012.651989

Gardner, T. W., Dishion, T. J., & Connell, A. M. (2008). Adolescent self-regulation as resilience: Resistance to antisocial behavior within the deviant peer context. *Journal of Abnormal Child Psychology, 36*(2), 273–284. doi:10.1007/s10802-007-9176-6

Ge, X., Brody, G. H., Conger, R. D., Simons, R. L., & Murry, V. M. (2002). Contextual amplification of pubertal transition effects on deviant peer affiliation and externalizing behavior among African-American children. *Developmental Psychology, 38*(1), 42–54. doi:10.1037/0012-1649.38.1.42

Goldstein, S. E., Davis-Kean, P. E., & Eccles, J. S. (2005). Parents, peers, and problem behavior: A longitudinal investigation of the impact of relationship perceptions and characteristics on the development of adolescent problem behavior. *Developmental Psychology, 41*(2), 401–413. doi:10.1037/0012-1649.41.2.401

Granic, I., & Dishion, T. J. (2003). Deviant talk in adolescent friendships: A step toward measuring a pathogenic attractor process. *Social Development, 12*(3), 314–334. doi:10.1111/1467-9507.00236

Haynie, D. L., & Osgood, D. W. (2005). Reconsidering peers and delinquency: How do peers matter? *Social Forces, 84*(2), 1109–1130. doi:10.1353/sof.2006.0018

Hawkins, J. D., Catalano, R. F., & Miller, J. Y. (1992). Risk and protective factors for alcohol and other drug problems in adolescence and early adulthood: Implications for substance abuse prevention. *Psychological Bulletin, 112*(1), 64–105. doi:10.1037/0033-2909.112.1.64

Heilbron, N., & Prinstein, M. J. (2008). Peer influence and adolescent nonsuicidal self-injury: A theoretical review of mechanisms and moderators. *Applied and Preventive Psychology, 12*(4), 169–177. doi:10.1016/j.appsy.2008.05.004

Hill, K. G., Howell, J. C., Hawkins, J. D., & Battin-Pearson, S. R. (1999). Childhood risk factors for adolescent gang membership: Results from the Seattle Social Development Project. *Journal of Research in Crime and Delinquency, 36*(3), 300–322. doi:10.1177/0022427899036003003

Laird, R. D., Criss, M. M., Pettit, G. S., Dodge, K. A., & Bates, J. E. (2008). Parents' monitoring knowledge attenuates the link between antisocial friends and adolescent delinquent behavior. *Journal of Abnormal Child Psychology, 36*(3), 299–310. doi:10.1007/s10802-007-9178-4

Lipsey, M. W., & Wilson, D. B. (1998). Effective intervention for serious juvenile offenders: A synthesis of research. In R. Loeber & D. P. Farrington (Eds.), *Serious & violent juvenile offenders: Risk factors and successful interventions* (pp. 313–345). Thousand Oaks, CA: Sage.

Lochman, J. E., Dishion, T. J., Powell, N. P., Boxmeyer, C. L., Qu, L., & Sallee, M. (2015). Evidence-based preventive intervention for preadolescent aggressive children: One-year outcomes following randomization to group versus individual delivery. *Journal of Consulting and Clinical Psychology, 83*(4), 728–735. doi:10.1037/ccp0000030

Lochman, J. E., & Wells, K. C. (2004). The coping power program for preadolescent aggressive boys and their parents: outcome effects at the 1-year follow-up. *Journal of Consulting and Clinical Psychology, 72*(4), 571.

Loeber, R., Burke, J. D., Lahey, B. B., Winters, A., & Zera, M. (2000). Oppositional defiant and conduct disorder: A review of the past 10 years, Part I. *Journal of the American Academy of Child and Adolescent Psychiatry, 39*(12), 1468–1484. doi:10.1097/00004583-200012000-00007

Loeber, R., Burke, J. D., & Pardini, D. A. (2009). Development and etiology of disruptive and delinquent behavior. *Annual Review of Clinical Psychology, 5*(1), 291–310. doi:10.1146/annurev.clinpsy.032408.153631

Mager, W., Milich, R., Harris, M. J., & Howard, A. (2005). Intervention groups for adolescents with conduct problems: Is aggregation harmful or helpful? *Journal of Abnormal Child Psychology, 33*(3), 349–362. doi:10.1007/s10802-005-3572-6

Masten, A. S., Roisman, G. I., Long, J. D., Burt, K. B., Obradović, J., Riley, J. R., . . . Tellegen, A. (2005). Developmental cascades: Linking academic achievement and externalizing and internalizing symptoms over 20 years. *Developmental Psychology, 41*(5), 733–746. doi:10.1037/0012-1649.41.5.733

Matthys, W., Vanderschuren, L. J. M. J., & Schutter, D. J. L. G. (2013). The neurobiology of oppositional defiant disorder and conduct disorder: Altered functioning in three mental domains. *Development and Psychopathology, 25*(1), 193–207. doi:10.1017/S0954579412000272

Monahan, K. C., Steinberg, L., & Cauffman, E. (2009). Affiliation with antisocial peers, susceptibility to peer influence, and antisocial behavior during the transition to adulthood. *Developmental Psychology, 45*(6), 1520–1530. doi:10.1037/a0017417

Murray, J., Irving, B., Farrington, D. P., Colman, I., & Bloxsom, C. A. J. (2010). Very early predictors of conduct problems and crime: Results from a national cohort study. *Journal of Child Psychology and Psychiatry, 51*(11), 1198–1207. doi:10.1111/j.1469-7610.2010.02287.x

Nock, M. K., Kazdin, A. E., Hiripi, E., & Kessler, R. C. (2007). Lifetime prevalence correlates, and persistence of oppositional defiant disorder: Results from the National Comorbidity Survey Replication. *Journal of Child Psychology and Psychiatry, 48*(7), 703–713. doi:10.1111/j.1469-7610.2007.01733.x

Patterson, G. R. (1982). *Coercive family process.* Eugene, OR: Castalia Publishing Company.

Patterson, G. R. (2016). Coercion theory: The study of change. In T. J. Dishion & J. J. Snyder (Eds.), *Oxford handbook of coercive relationship dynamics* (pp. 7–22). New York, NY: Oxford University Press.

Patterson, G. R., Reid, J. B., & Dishion, T. J. (1992). *Antisocial boys: A social interaction approach.* Eugene, OR: Castalia Publishing Company.

Piehler, T. F., & Dishion, T. J. (2007). Interpersonal dynamics within adolescent friendships: Dyadic mutuality, deviant talk, and patterns of antisocial behavior. *Child Development, 78*(5), 1611–1624.

Piehler, T. F., Véronneau, M. H., & Dishion, T. J. (2012). Substance use progression from adolescence to early adulthood: Effortful control in the context of friendship influence and early-onset use. *Journal of Abnormal Child Psychology, 40*(7), 1045–1058. doi:10.1007/s10802-012-9626-7

Prinstein, M. J. (2007). Moderators of peer contagion: A longitudinal examination of depression socialization between adolescents and their best friends. *Journal of Clinical Child & Adolescent Psychology, 36*(2), 159–170. doi:10.1080/15374410701274934

Prinstein, M. J., Boergers, J., & Spirito, A. (2001). Adolescents' and their friends' health-risk behavior: Factors that alter or add to peer influence. *Journal of Pediatric Psychology, 26*(5), 287–298. doi:10.1093/jpepsy/26.5.287

Rogge, T. (2015). *Conduct disorder.* United States National Library of Medicine. Retrieved from www.nlm.nih.gov/medlineplus/ency/article/000919.htm.

Sampson, R. J. (1993). The community context of violent crime. In W. J. Wilson (Ed.), *Sociology and the public agenda* (pp. 259–286). Newbury Park, CA: Sage.

Sijtsema, J. J., Ojanen, T., Veenstra, R., Lindenberg, S., Hawley, P. H., & Little, T. D. (2010). Forms and functions of aggression in adolescent friendship selection and influence: A longitudinal social network analysis. *Social Development, 19*(3), 515–534. doi:10.1111/j.1467-9507.2009.00566.x

Smith, C. A., & Stern, S. B. (1997). Delinquency and antisocial behavior: A review of family processes and intervention research. *Social Sciences Review, 71*(3), 382–420. doi:10.1086/604263

Snyder, J., Schrepferman, L., McEachern, A., Barner, S., Johnson, K., & Provines, J. (2008). Peer deviancy training and peer coercion: Dual processes associated with early-onset conduct problems. *Child Development, 79*(2), 252–268. doi:10.1111/j.1467-8624.2007.01124.x

Snyder, J., Schrepferman, L., Oeser, J., Patterson, G., Stoolmiller, M., Johnson, K., & Snyder, A. (2005). Deviancy training and association with deviant peers in young children: Occurrence and contribution to early-onset conduct problems. *Development and Psychopathology, 17*(02), 397–413. doi:10.1017/S0954579405050194

Stattin, H., & Kerr, M. (2000). Parental monitoring: A reinterpretation. *Child Development, 71*(4), 1072–1085.

Steinberg, L., & Monahan, K. C. (2007). Age differences in resistance to peer influence. *Developmental Psychology, 43*(6), 1531–1543. doi:10.1037/0012-1649.43.6.1531

Stoolmiller, M. (1994). Antisocial behavior, delinquent peer association, and unsupervised wandering for boys: Growth and change from childhood to early adolescence. *Multivariate Behavioral Research, 29*(3), 263–288. doi:10.1207/ s15327906mbr2903_4

Valente, T. W., Ritt-Olson, A., Stacy, A., Unger, J. B., Okamoto, J., & Sussman, S. (2007). Peer acceleration: Effects of a social network tailored substance abuse prevention program among high-risk adolescents. *Addiction, 102*(11), 1804–1815. doi:10.1111/j.1360-0443.2007.01992.x

Van Ryzin, M. J., & Dishion, T. J. (2013). From antisocial behavior to violence: A model for the amplifying role of coercive joining in adolescent friendships. *Journal of Child Psychology and Psychiatry, 54*(6), 661–669. doi:10.1111/jcpp.12017

Vitaro, F., Tremblay, R. E., Kerr, M., Pagani, L., & Bukowski, W. M. (1997). Disruptiveness, friends' characteristics, and delinquency in early adolescence: A test of two competing models of development. *Child Development, 68*(4), 676–689. doi:10.1111/j.1467-8624.1997.tb04229.x

Webster-Stratton, C., Reid, M. J., & Hammond, M. (2004). Treating children with early-onset conduct problems: Intervention outcomes for parent, child, and teacher training. *Journal of Clinical Child & Adolescent Psychology, 33*(1), 105–124. doi:10.1207/S15374424JCCP3301_11

Etiological and Maintenance Factors

Broader Social Context

22

The Broader Context
School and Neighborhood Factors Contributing to ODD and CD Symptomatology

Paula J. Fite, Sonia L. Rubens, Spencer C. Evans, and Jonathan Poquiz

There is ample research indicating contextual contributions to the development of child and adolescent problem behavior. In fact, larger contextual factors, such as school and neighborhood, have been found to be related to problem behavior above and beyond individual characteristics, family, and peers (e.g., Kupersmidt, Griesler, DeRosier, Patterson, & Davis, 1995; Maughan, 2004). Developmental ecological models provide an overarching framework for understanding the influence of larger contextual factors, in addition to individual and familial ones, on child problem behavior (Henry, Gorman-Smith, Schoeny, & Tolan, 2014). An extension of social ecological models, which posit that layers of social settings interact with one another (and also directly and indirectly affect one another) to shape and formulate a child's behavior (Bronfenbrenner & Morris, 1998), developmental ecological models emphasize the developmental timing of effects (Bronfenbrenner, 1995). Consistent with this framework, the present chapter provides an overview of extant literature supporting the influence (direct, indirect, and interactive effects) of school and neighborhood factors on Oppositional Defiant Disorder (ODD) and Conduct Disorder (CD) symptomatology. However, given the limited research focusing specifically on contextual risk factors of ODD and CD symptom clusters, we review the larger literature examining associations between school and neighborhood factors and aggression, delinquency, and other antisocial behavior. Research specific to the diagnostic categories and symptom clusters are highlighted when available.

Additionally, researchers have put forth a variety of taxonomies that have been useful for our understanding of the development, phenomenology, and course of youth antisocial behavior (Frick & Ellis, 1999; Hyde et al., 2015). Theories regarding developmental trajectories, pathways, subtypes, and dimensions of antisocial behavior were instrumental in formulating the basic conceptualization of ODD and CD, which has been in place for over two decades (Loeber, Lahey, & Thomas, 1991). There is some, albeit very limited, research regarding contextual associations with two of these taxonomies: (a) callous-unemotional (CU) traits, a characteristic pattern of deficits in empathy, emotional expressiveness, and concern which has formed the basis of the "limited prosocial emotions" subtype in DSM-5 conduct disorder (see Frick, Ray, Thornton, & Kahn, 2014 for a comprehensive review as

---

The Wiley Handbook of Disruptive and Impulse-Control Disorders, First Edition.
Edited by John E. Lochman and Walter Matthys.
© 2018 John Wiley & Sons Ltd. Published 2018 by John Wiley & Sons Ltd.

well as Chapter 3 of this book); and (b) age-of-onset as a marker for different subtypes and trajectories of conduct disorder (Moffit, 1993, 2007). Accordingly, we include the research regarding these taxonomies when available.

School Factors

School Factors and Problem Behavior

Simply by virtue of the sheer amount of time youth spend at school, the school context will have direct influences on child/adolescent behavior. Moreover, the school context provides opportunities for social interaction outside of one's family, which can be positive and/or negative in nature. Indeed, in addition to the strong intellectual and cognitive ability factors as well as peer influences discussed in Chapters 20 and 21, a multitude of factors at the school-wide, classroom, and individual level have been linked to child problem behaviors (Barth, Dunlap, Dane, Lochman, & Wells, 2004; Maughan, 2004; Payne & Welch, 2015).

From a school-wide perspective, poorly resourced schools (i.e., with low economic support and greater student to teacher ratios) that serve high numbers of at-risk youth (including economically disadvantaged and aggressive students) are associated with increased risk for poorer overall student outcomes, including aggression (Colder, Lengua, Fite, Mott, & Bush, 2000; Gottfredson & Gottfredson, 1985; Rutter, 1983). These effects may be attributed to the link between exposure to violence and peer support for, and reinforcement of, aggression and other disruptive behaviors. That is, youth who attend poorly resourced schools tend to reside in disadvantaged neighborhoods that model violence, which becomes the social norm and a culture that provides reinforcement for such behavior within the school setting (Barth et al., 2004; Kellam, Ling, Merisca, Brown, & Ialongo, 1998; Snyder, 2002).

Alternatively, creating an overall environment at school in which youth feel safe, supported, and respected should create a culture that has more positive attitudes about school and less tolerance for aggression and other problem behavior (Meehan, Hughes, & Cavell, 2003; Reinke & Herman, 2002; Vassallo, Smart, & Sanson, 2002). However, findings appear to be somewhat mixed with regard to the magnitude of these effects, and there may be differences across informants. For example, school commitment to bullying prevention was associated with lower levels of teacher-reported bullying and fighting among middle-school-age youth, and these effects were stronger than teacher perceptions of positive student–teacher relationships (Espelage, Polanin, & Low, 2014). However, when examining youth reports of behavior, demographic characteristics accounted for 50% of the variance (with females and Black students reporting less fighting than males and students of other racial/ethnic backgrounds), leaving little unique influence of school commitment to bullying prevention and positive student–teacher relationships.

Further still, research among 4th and 5th grade students indicates that classroom norms of behavior (i.e., acceptance of aggressive behavior) is more influential on problem behavior than other aspects of the overall school environment (i.e., including school-wide rates of free/reduced lunch and a school's average achievement test scores; Barth et al., 2004). Additional research shows that high levels of aggressive behavior within the classroom are associated with increases in individual levels of aggression (e.g., Kellam et al., 1998; Werthamer-Larsson, Kellam, & Wheeler, 1991). Barth and colleagues (2004) suggest that the overall school environment may be playing a secondary role to the immediate classroom environment in contributing to problem behavior.

Although the classroom environment has been conceptualized in a multitude of different ways, there is ample evidence supporting the importance of classroom-level influences (e.g., Barth et al., 2004). In a study of Spanish adolescents, a positive classroom environment (as defined by student involvement, student affiliation, and teacher support) was negatively associated with aggression for boys (Lopez, Perez, Ochoa, & Ruiz, 2008). For girls, however, a positive family environment appeared to be more strongly linked to lower levels of aggression. Classroom quality (defined by observations of overcontrol, positive emotional climate, classroom management, literacy instruction, evaluative feedback, instructional quality, and child responsibility) in kindergarten classrooms has also been found to influence child behavior, with higher quality classrooms resulting in fewer child problem behaviors, such as noncompliance (Rimm-Kaufman, La Paro, Downer, & Pianta, 2005).

Within the classroom environment, teachers are the authority figures that provide the structure for the classroom climate and help establish acceptable norms of behavior. Further, teachers are the personnel in the school with whom the students will have the most direct contact. Accordingly, it is reasonable to assume that specific teaching styles and teacher relationships with the students will impact child behavior. Indeed, teachers' behavior management styles are important, with constructive and consistent, but not overly severe, styles associated with positive outcomes (Jack et al., 1996; Mortimore, 1998). Overly harsh discipline by teachers in response to misbehavior has been found to increase levels of student delinquency, while effectively establishing, communicating, and enforcing rules and rewarding appropriate behavior is associated with lower levels of problem behavior (Gottfredson, Gottfredson, Payne, & Gottfredson, 2005; Payne & Welch, 2015; Skiba & Knesting, 2001).

Teacher–child relationships also appear to be important for the prevention of problem behavior, with students exhibiting behavior problems reporting less positive attitudes about teachers as well as about the school in general (Jack et al., 1996; Samdal, 1998). In fact, teacher–child relationships appear to be bidirectionally related, such that child problem behaviors negatively impact the teacher–child relationship (Henricsson & Rydell, 2004). In turn, teacher rejection and conflictual teacher–child interactions are associated with child problem behaviors (Henricsson & Rydell, 2004; Pace, Mullines, Beesley, Hill, & Carson, 1999). On the other hand, there is evidence that a positive teacher–child relationship can help to improve problem behavior (Baker, 2006).

It is important to note that these larger school and classroom contexts also influence how strongly individuals bond and connect with the school, with poor school bonding repeatedly found to be associated with problem behavior, such as delinquency and criminality (Ayers et al, 1999; Chung, Hills, Hawkins, Gilchrist, & Nagin, 2002; Hawkins et al., 1998; Loeber & Farrington, 2001; Payne & Welch, 2015).

Finally, school mobility (or changing the schools that the child attends) is associated with increased risk for a variety of adjustment difficulties (e.g., Gruman, Harachi, Abbott, Catalano, & Fleming, 2008; South, Haynie, & Bose, 2007), including problem behavior (Herbers, Reynolds, & Chen, 2013; Leonard & Elias, 1993; Wood, Halfron, Scarlata, Newacheck, & Nessim, 1993). For example, the more school changes an individual experiences between kindergarten and 12th grade, the more likely he or she is to be arrested as an adult (Herbers et al., 2013). The disruption in the learning experiences and social relationships likely affects students adjustment and well-being (Herbers, et al., 2013). Further, residential instability and economic disadvantage, which are also likely to contribute to school mobility, are risk factors for problem behavior; however, school mobility has been found to be associated with maladaptive outcomes above and beyond the effects of economic difficulties (Alexander, Entwisle, & Dauber, 1996; Mehana & Reynolds, 2004; Rumberger & Larson, 1998).

School Context and ODD/CD

Although we are not aware of any studies looking specifically at the link between school factors and ODD and CD symptomatology, there is some research examining taxonomical distinctions. With regard to the age of onset diagnostic taxonomy, one multilevel meta-analysis of 55 studies (Assink et al., 2015) identified 14 domains of risk as predictors of life-course-persistent conduct problems compared to the adolescent-limited course. Notably, criminal history, aggression, and substance use were among the strongest and most robust predictors of persistent conduct problems, whereas school variables (e.g., academic achievement, attitude/interest/motivation toward school) were weak predictors.

School Context and CU Traits

There is also evidence to suggest that children with CU traits have lower quality relationships with their teachers, and worse performance on standardized math and reading exams, even after controlling for conduct problems (Horan, Brown, Jones, & Aber, 2016). Longitudinally, a persistent pattern of CU traits over time predicts lower levels of school connectedness, as well as poorer outcomes on various social, academic, and cognitive variables (Fanti, Colins, Andershed, & Sikki, 2017); however, the converse longitudinal question of whether school connectedness predicts CU traits has not been examined.

Thus, there is clear evidence of the school context influencing various problem behaviors. However, it is not clear which factors are most impactful, under what conditions, and for whom. Further, studies examining how these school factors are related specifically to ODD and CD diagnoses are virtually nonexistent, and it would be beneficial to further evaluate how these factors are related to the various taxonomies of these diagnostic groups.

Neighborhood Factors

Neighborhood Context and Problem Behaviors

The neighborhoods in which youth reside can also have a significant influence on behavior and psychological adjustment (e.g., Aneshensel & Sucoff, 1996). Extant literature supports the effect of neighborhood characteristics on various psychological outcomes, including internalizing and externalizing symptomology (e.g., Fowler, Tompsett, Braciszewski, Jacques-Tiura, & Baltes, 2009; Wilson & Rosenthal, 2003).

To understand the relations between neighborhood factors and externalizing problems, it is important to take into account the way in which neighborhood is conceptualized. According to Aneshensel and Sucoff (1996), the neighborhood consists of two components: structure and subjective experience. Structural characteristics include stratification or segregation of neighborhoods by socioeconomic status or racial/ethnic identities, while subjective experiences consist in the presence of threatening conditions (e.g., gang activity, violent crime, drug dealing). The conceptualization of neighborhood will also influence the way it is measured. Measurement of the neighborhood context can be based on subjective reports and/or objective measures (e.g., census data; Leventhal & Brooks-Gunn, 2000). This variability in measurement may make it difficult to compare findings across studies (e.g., Ingoldsby & Shaw, 2002). Thus, it is important to consider the methods of measuring neighborhood context to understand its effects on problem behavior.

Massey and Denton (1993) emphasize the components of structural characteristics and cultural makeup of neighborhoods and how these factors may create a deleterious environment of beliefs and behaviors. They argue that segregation within neighborhoods (e.g., by socioeconomic class, racial/ethnic identity) may limit access to resources and lead to exposure to problematic behaviors, which, in turn, may impact psychological adjustment. More specifically, segregation may lead to concentrated poverty, which can contribute to social disorder in the neighborhood (e.g., high crime rates, graffiti). This pattern of constraints in the neighborhood can also be understood within the neighborhood disorder model (Wandersman & Nation, 1998), which posits that aspects of disadvantage encountered in the neighborhood (e.g., robberies, vandalism, gang activity) can negatively influence feelings of safety, which, likewise, is associated with externalizing problems in youth. Indeed, residing in neighborhoods with high levels of disadvantage and violence and low community support has been shown to be associated with a host of problem behaviors, including delinquency, aggression, and other antisocial conduct, through both cross-sectional and longitudinal studies (Attar, Guerra, & Tolan, 1994; Barry, Lochman, Fite, Wells, & Colder, 2012; Colder et al., 2006; Elliot et al., 1996; Farrell & Bruce, 1997; Fowler et al., 2009; Goodnight et al., 2012; Kilpatrick et al., 2000; Rubens, Fite, Cooley, & Canter, 2014; Singer, Anglin, Song, & Lunghofer, 1995). These associations are evident even when accounting for prior levels of problem behaviors (Gorman-Smith & Tolan, 1998; Miller, Wasserman, Neugebauer, Gorman-Smith, & Kamboukos, 1999) and when controlling for other factors such as family context (e.g., income, education, race, ethnicity; Leventhal & Brooks-Gunn, 2000), and even genetics (Goodnight et al., 2012).

Notably, the neighborhood context may have differential effects on subtypes of aggressive behavior. In particular, research has found that exposure to disadvantaged and unsafe neighborhoods is associated with proactive (goal-oriented, calculated), but not reactive (in response to perceived threat), aggression in youth (Fite et al., 2010; Fite, Wynn, Lochman, & Wells, 2009). This may be due to differences in the development of these aggressive behaviors. Proactive aggression may be best explained by social learning theory, which suggests that individuals learn, through modeling, that aggression can help them achieve their goals and objectives (Bandura, 1973; Card & Little, 2007; Fite et al., 2012). Based on this theory, neighborhoods that are characterized as having high levels of violence or crime may provide a model of aggressive behaviors. For instance, youth may learn to engage in aggressive behaviors after being exposed to them through witnessing gang activity or theft in their neighborhoods. In contrast, reactively aggressive behavior is supported by the frustration-aggression hypothesis, which suggests that aggression occurs in response to anger and frustration (Berkowitz, 1978; Card & Little, 2007; Vitaro & Brendgen, 2011). Overall, youth residing in more disadvantaged neighborhoods may be exposed to more violence and aggression there, which provides a model for engaging in proactively aggressive behavior (Matthys & Lochman, 2010).

Moderating and Indirect Effects

In addition to the direct effects of the neighborhood context on problem behaviors, researchers in the last two decades have responded to the call for an increase in research examining factors that moderate and/or mediate these associations (Leventhal & Brooks-Gunn, 2000). Individual factors, such as gender, age, and temperament, can influence the effect of the neighborhood context on problem behaviors. The association between the neighborhood context and problem behavior may differ by gender (Kroneman, Hipwell, Loeber, Koot, & Pardini, 2004), with some research showing this relation to be stronger for boys compared to girls (Beyers, Bates, Pettit, & Dodge, 2003). This may be related to the larger amount of unsupervised time boys spend in their neighborhoods compared to girls (Beyers et al., 2003), the earlier onset and more persistent pathways of antisocial behavior among boys compared to girls (Moffitt & Caspi, 2001), and peer relations (e.g., boys' have higher involvement in gangs than girls; Esbensen, Deschenes, & Winfree, 1999; Kroneman et al., 2004). With regard to age differences, adolescents may be more susceptible to engaging in problem behavior in the context of neighborhood disadvantage than younger children (Fowler et al., 2009), perhaps due to their spending more time outside the home as their desire for autonomy increases (Leventhal, Dupéré, & Brooks-Gunn, 2009) and the general rise in problem behaviors found in adolescence (Moffitt & Caspi, 2001).

Aspects related to culture, race, and ethnicity may also influence outcomes associated with the neighborhood context. Discrimination within one's neighborhood can influence problem behavior among adolescents (Riina, Martin, Gardner, & Brooks-Gunn, 2013). In a study of African American adolescents enrolled in the Project on Human Development in Chicago Neighborhoods, participants who experienced racial discrimination within their neighborhood had higher externalizing problems compared to those who did not. This association was moderated by neighborhood cohesion, such that the link between discrimination within one's neighborhood and externalizing problems was significant at low, but not high, levels of neighborhood cohesion. Further, differences in cultural background, values, beliefs, and lifestyles may play a moderating role in the relation between neighborhood disadvantage and childhood outcomes (Roosa et al., 2005). For example, among Mexican American families in the United States, the significant amount of perceived support from extended family members (known as familism) that is common in traditional Mexican society may help to buffer the risks of neighborhood effects on youth outcomes (Sabogal, Marín, Otero-Sabogal, Marín, & Perez-Sable, 1987; Roosa et al., 2005). Because the disproportionately high rate of poverty among racial and ethnic minority youth (US Census Bureau, 2011) serves to increase their risk of residing in disadvantaged neighborhoods, research is needed to further understand the role of culture, race, and ethnicity in the link between neighborhood disadvantage and problem behaviors.

Other individual factors, such as internal processes, can also play a role in this relation. Colder et al. (2006) found that the relation between neighborhood disadvantage and antisocial behavior appears to be most evident in children who demonstrate infant temperaments characterized by either (a) high fear and low positive affect or (b) low fear and high positive affect. Social cognition may also help explain the link between exposure to violence and aggressive behavior in youth, with exposure to violence being associated with the belief that aggression is an acceptable behavior, which in turn is associated with aggression (Guerra, Rowell Huesmann, & Spindler, 2003).

Outside of the individual context, parenting practices, such as parental monitoring, positive parenting, and harsh parenting, can also play a role in the relation between the neighborhood context and problem behaviors (Barry et al., 2012, Beyers et al., 2003; Gayles, Coatsworth, Pantin, & Szapocznik, 2009; Lee et al., 2014; Mrug & Windle, 2009; Plybon & Kliewer, 2001). Among a sample of moderately to highly aggressive youth, for instance, high levels of neighborhood problems were associated with high levels of aggression among youth exposed to harsh parenting (Barry et al., 2012). On the other hand, using census-tract data, Plybon and Kliewer. (2001) found that family cohesion acted as a protective factor in the relation between neighborhood disadvantage and problem behavior. Consistent with the developmental ecological framework, it is important to consider the parenting context in understanding risk and protective factors in the link between the neighborhood context and problem behavior.

Studies have also found peer relationships, particularly relationships with deviant peers, to play a role in the relation between neighborhood disadvantage and problem behaviors. This is likely due to the increasing importance of peers as children get older, as well as findings that problem behaviors tend to occur in the company of peers (Moffit, 1993). A number of studies have examined the mediating role of peers in this relation (e.g., Ingoldsby et al., 2006;

Mrug & Windle, 2009; Roosa et al., 2005). When using a stress process model, for example, Roosa and colleagues (2005) found that associating with delinquent peers mediated the relation between neighborhood risk and problem behavior. Several studies too have examined the moderating role of deviant peers within the neighborhood context. For instance, residing in disadvantaged and unsafe neighborhoods has been shown to interact with peer delinquency in predicting engagement in delinquency (Fite et al., 2012) and proactive, but not reactive, aggression (Fite et al., 2010). It appears that residing in disadvantaged neighborhoods can increase the risk of associating with deviant peers who may influence a child's engagement in problem behavior, and the risk of engaging in problem behaviors is highest through an interaction between neighborhood disadvantage and peer deviance.

Exposure to personal stressors is also an important aspect to consider. Children living in highly disadvantaged neighborhoods are at increased risk of exposure to a variety of stressors (King & Ogle, 2014), which, in turn, can exacerbate problem behavior (Attar et al., 1994). Indeed, several studies have found that exposure to stressful life events mediates the link between neighborhood risk and problem behavior (Katz, Esparza, Carter, Grant, & Meyerson, 2012; Roosa et al., 2005). Further, exposure to child maltreatment was found to moderate the relation between neighborhood disadvantage and marijuana use in a sample of adolescents, such that the positive association between neighborhood disadvantage and marijuana-dependence symptoms was only evident among adolescents with a maltreatment history (Handley, Rogosch, Guild, & Cicchetti, 2015). Consideration of exposure to stressors and trauma both within and above and beyond the neighborhood context is essential for identifying youth at risk for problem behaviors.

Health behaviors may also affect the relation between the neighborhood context and problem behaviors. In a sample of low-income, Latino adolescents, community violence exposure was associated with sleep problems, which, in turn, was associated with engagement in delinquency (Rubens et al., 2014). This may be related to the increased levels of impulsivity, emotional lability, and impaired decision making associated with poor sleep (Gruber, Cassoff, Frenette, Wiebe, & Carrier, 2012; Venkatraman, Chuah, Huettel, & Chee, 2007). Continuing to examine health behaviors in this relation may provide insight into other mechanisms for intervention for problem behavior.

Neighborhood Context and ODD/CD

Although there have been several studies assessing neighborhood characteristics and their impact on problem behavior, the current literature examining how neighborhood characteristics relate specifically to ODD and CD diagnoses is limited. In a nationally representative sample of adolescents, Russell and colleagues (2015) sought to fill this gap in the literature by examining neighborhood correlates (e.g., neighborhood safety, neighborhood cohesion and camaraderie, prevalence of crime, prenatal drug exposure) that could impact the onset of ODD. The researchers found that parents' report of the sale and use of drugs within the neighborhood predicted a diagnosis of ODD in their adolescents. Defying authority is a core symptom of ODD, and one can argue that criminal activity like the sale and use of drugs creates an environment in which defiance of authority (e.g., parents, teachers, police), becomes commonplace. This emphasizes the process of social learning in which the modeling of defiant behaviors can influence the development of symptoms of ODD.

Pajer and colleagues (2008) examined the relation between the neighborhood context and CD diagnosis. When examining neighborhood disadvantage among a sample of Caucasian and African American female adolescents, findings suggested that CD was not associated with neighborhood disadvantage. Nonetheless, Pajer et al. (2008) suggest that future research continue to examine problem behaviors related to CD, such as aggression and delinquency, in addition to determining whether these behaviors meet diagnostic criteria for CD, in order to elucidate whether neighborhood disadvantage is related to particular symptoms of CD or to a CD diagnosis. Another study that examined the relation between the neighborhood context, measured as household income, and ODD and CD symptoms found that household income was a specific correlate of CD symptoms, but not ODD symptoms (Wiesner et al., 2015). Further research is needed to examine these relationships to gain a better understanding of whether neighborhood factors relate to single behaviors and symptoms of ODD and CD or clusters of them, with and without meeting diagnostic criteria.

Neighborhood Context and Callous/Unemotional Traits

Lastly, a small body of evidence has explored the connection between neighborhood factors and CU or psychopathic traits. Research shows that CU traits are associated with higher levels of community violence exposure (Davis, Ammons, Dahl, & Kliewer, 2015; Kimonis, Frick, Munoz, & Aucoin, 2008), stressful negative life events (Frick & Dantagnan, 2005; Kimonis, Centifanti, Allen, & Frick, 2014), and composite measures of neighborhood risk (Kroneman et al., 2011). Notably, among youth with CU traits, stability in conduct problems was predicted by higher rates of stressful life events, whereas among youth without CU traits, impulsivity and socioeconomic status were the strongest predictors (Frick & Dantagnan, 2005).

Ray, Thornton, Frick, Steinberg, & Cauffman (2016) applied latent class analysis to a large sample of justice-involved adolescents and found that CU traits and neighborhood disorder both contributed independently, with no interactions, to predicting more severe profiles of delinquency. In a study of girls, CU traits predicted trajectories of ODD/CD behaviors over time, but neighborhood risk did not moderate the association, nor was it a significant unique predictor (Kroneman et al., 2011). However, other studies have found evidence in support of neighborhood-moderation hypotheses. In large samples, CU traits were associated with more violent forms of delinquent behavior in low-income neighborhoods only (Markowitz, Ryan, & Marsh, 2015), and the association between callousness and delinquent behavior was strongest among boys who lived in neighborhoods with low levels of social control and social cohesion (Meier, Slutske, Arndt, & Cadoret, 2008). Similarly, exposure to community violence appears to be associated with emotional processing deficits at high, but not low, levels of CU traits (Kimonis et al., 2008). In sum, limited and mixed evidence supports direct and moderating roles of neighborhood risk factors in relation to CU traits and antisocial behavior.

Conclusion

To summarize, there is clear evidence indicating the importance of both school and neighborhood context on the development of oppositional, aggressive, disruptive, and other problem behaviors. School-wide (low economic support, greater student to teacher ratios, and high levels of aggressive students), classroom (acceptance of aggressive behavior, teacher support, student involvement, teacher behavior management style, instructional quality, student teacher relationships), and individual-level (school bonding/connectedness, school mobility) factors all contribute to the development of problem behavior to some extent. Further, both the structure (socioeconomic status and racial/ethnic identities) and subjective experiences (safety, rates of crime/violence, resources available, cohesion, and levels of support) of the neighborhood context play a role in child and adolescent problem behavior.

However, the literature does not provide a clear picture of what factors are most relevant, particularly when one is also considering individual and family factors. More comprehensive studies are needed that include a multitude of risk factors across domains and are assessed by multiple informants and methods with a large sample size. This research would aid in developing more effectively targeted prevention and intervention strategies. For instance, Lochman, Wells, Qu, & Chen (2013) examined the moderating role of neighborhood disadvantage in outcomes associated with participation in the Coping Power intervention program. Findings suggested that families living in less disadvantaged neighborhoods showed improved family support over time compared with families living in more disadvantaged neighborhoods. Additionally, potential moderators and mediators of these associations, including individual characteristics (e.g., age, genetic predisposition, gender, racial/ethnic background) and social influences (i.e., parents, peers), is in need of much greater investigation. Brady, Gorman-Smith, Henry, and Tolan (2008), for example, found that coping moderated the link between community violence exposure and violent behavior in a sample of urban African American and Latino adolescent males. Although there is a growing body of literature examining the moderating effects of individual factors, parents, and peers in the link between neighborhood factors and problem behavior, research examining factors that impact the links between school factors and problem behavior is extremely limited. It would be helpful to know the mechanisms involved in these associations and if there are factors that make individuals more or less vulnerable to these influences from a prevention/intervention standpoint. Furthermore, research identifying resiliency factors that can buffer the negative impact of both school and neighborhood risk factors on problem behavior is lacking.

In order to truly advance the understanding of contextual influences from an ecological perspective (in which elements in multiple overlapping systems may influence youth behavior in different ways over time), researchers may need to employ more sophisticated, creative, and rigorous study designs and analytic methods. Although the present chapter has separately summarized the literatures on school and neighborhood influences, the reality is that these contexts overlap and interact with one another, as well as with other variables at different levels of emphasis. For example, multi-level modeling is needed to evaluate the impact of neighborhood risk, school, and classroom variables, as well as the effects of youth being nested within particular neighborhoods, schools, and classrooms (e.g., Maughan, 2004). In addition, while there are some longitudinal studies examining these associations (e.g., Attar et al., 1994; Barry et al., 2012; Barth et al., 2004; Colder et al., 2006; Farrell & Bruce, 1997), the vast majority of research is cross-sectional in design. Additional longitudinal studies are needed to further understand the impact of these school and neighborhood characteristics on the development and maintenance of these behavioral difficulties as individuals age.

Finally, from a diagnostic perspective, more research focusing specifically on contextual risk factors and differential associations with ODD versus CD symptom clusters, as well as their taxonomies, would be useful to understand the unique etiologies of these disorders. There are a handful of studies examining neighborhood risk factors that may be differentially associated with these diagnostic groups, while the literature pertaining to school factors has generally focused primarily on specific behaviors rather than diagnostic categories. Therefore, studies are greatly needed to help understand the link between school and neighborhood context and ODD/CD diagnoses. One exciting current direction of the taxonomy research is the identification of the irritable and headstrong dimensions of symptoms of Oppositional Defiant Disorder (see Chapter 2; Burke et al., 2014; Evans, Pederson, Fite, Blossom, & Cooley, 2016; Leadbeater & Hommel, 2014; Stringaris & Goodman, 2009), which may help account for the inconsistent links between ODD symptomatology and symptoms of anxiety and depression (Burke & Loeber, 2010; Fraire & Ollendick, 2013). To our knowledge, however, no studies have directly examined school or neighborhood influences on the development of irritable or headstrong dimensions of oppositional defiant behavior. Evidence is particularly limited with regard to neighborhood influences on ODD symptom dimensions; however, it is notable that ODD dimensions appear to convey unique risk for subsequent antisocial behavior, independent of socioeconomic factors (Burke, Hipwell, & Loeber, 2010). Further evaluation of the contextual influences of these symptom clusters and their taxonomies will be an important direction for future research.

Overall, the literature demonstrates support for the link between the larger contextual factors of school and neighborhood in predicting problem behavior in youth. Future research should continue to examine factors contributing to these associations and seek ways to intervene at the contextual level in order to prevent and/or reduce problem behavior in youth.

References

Alexander, K. L., Entwisle, D. R., & Dauber, S. L. (1996). Children in motion: School transfers and elementary school performance. *Journal of Educational Research, 90,* 3–12.

Aneshensel, C. S., & Succoff, C. A. (1996). The neighborhood context of adolescent mental health. *Journal of Health and Social Behavior, 27,* 293–310.

Assink, M., van, der Put, C. E., Hoeve, M., de Vries, S. L., Stams, G. J. J. M., & Oort, F. J. (2015). Risk factors for persistent delinquent behavior among juveniles: A meta-analytic review. *Clinical Psychology Review, 42,* 47–61.

Attar, B. K., Guerra, N. G., & Tolan, P. H. (1994). Neighborhood disadvantage, stressful life events, and adjustment in urban elementary-school children. *Journal of Clinical Child Psychology, 23,* 391–400.

Ayers, C. D., Williams, J. H., Hawkins, J. D., Peterson, P. L., Catalano, R. F., & Abbott, R. D. (1999). Assessing correlates of onset, escalation, de-escalation, and desistance of delinquency behavior. *Journal of Quantitative Criminology, 15,* 277–306.

Baker, J. A. (2006). Contributions of teacher-child relationships to positive school adjustment during elementary school. *Journal of School Psychology, 44,* 211–229.

Bandura, A. (1973). *Aggression: A social learning analysis.* Prentice-Hall.

Barry, T. D., Lochman, J. E., Fite, P. J., Wells, K. C., & Colder, C. R. (2012). The influence of neighborhood characteristics and parenting practices on academic problems and aggression outcomes among moderately to highly aggressive children. *Journal of Community Psychology, 40,* 372–379.

Barth, J., Dunlap, S. T., Dane, H., Lochman, J. E., & Wells, K. C. (2004). Classroom environment influences on aggression, peer relations, and academic focus. *Journal of School Psychology, 42,* 115–133.

Berkowitz, L. (1978). Whatever happened to the frustration–aggression hypothesis? *American Behavioral Scientist, 32,* 691–708.

Beyers, J. M., Bates, J. E., Pettit, G. S., & Dodge, K. A. (2003). Neighborhood structure, parenting processes, and the development of youths' externalizing behaviors: A multilevel analysis. *American Journal of Community Psychology, 31,* 35–53.

Brady, S. S., Gorman-Smith, D., Henry, D. B., & Tolan, P. H. (2008). Adaptive coping reduces the impact of community violence exposure on violent behavior among African American and Latino male adolescents. *Journal of Abnormal Child Psychology, 36,* 105–115.

Bronfenbrenner, U. (1995). Developmental ecology through space and time: A future perspective. In P. Moen, G. H., Elder, Jr., & K. Luscher (Eds.), *Examining lives in context: Perspectives on the ecology of human development* (pp. 619–647). Washington, DC: American Psychological Association.

Bronfenbrenner, U., & Morris, P. (1998). Ecological processes of development. In W. Damon, (Ed.), *Handbook of child psychology: Theoretical issues* (Vol. 1, pp. 993–1028). New York, NY: Wiley.

Burke, J. D., Boylan, K., Rowe, R., Duku, E., Stepp, S. D., Hipwell, A. E., & Waldman, I. D. (2014). Identifying the irritability dimension of ODD: Application of a modified bifactor model across five large community samples of children. *Journal of Abnormal Psychology, 123,* 841–851.

Burke, J. D., Hipwell, A. E., & Loeber, R. (2010). Dimensions of oppositional defiant disorder as predictors of depression and conduct disorder in preadolescent girls. *Journal of the American Academy of Child & Adolescent Psychiatry, 49,* 484–492.

Burke, J., & Loeber, R. (2010). Oppositional defiant disorder and the explanation of the comorbidity between behavioral disorders and depression. *Clinical Psychology: Science and Practice, 17,* 319–326.

Card, N. A., & Little, T. D. (2007). Differential relations of instrumental and reactive aggression with maladjustment: Does adaptivity depend on function? In P. H. Hawley, T. D. Little, & P. C. Rodkin (Eds.), *Aggression and adaptation: The bright side to bad behavior* (pp. 107–134). Mahwah, NJ: Lawrence Erlbaum.

Chung, I. J., Hills, K. G., Hawkins, J. D., Gilchrist, L. S., & Nagin, D. (2002). Childhood predictors of offensive trajectories. *Journal of Research in Crime and Delinquency, 39,* 60–90.

Colder, C. R., Lengua, L. J., Fite, P. J., Mott, J. A., & Bush, N. R. (2006). Temperament in context: Infant temperament moderates the relationship between perceived neighborhood quality and behavior problems. *Journal of Applied Developmental Psychology, 27,* 456–467.

Colder, C. R., Mott, J., Levy, S., & Flay, B. (2000). The relation of perceived neighborhood danger to childhood aggression: A test of mediating mechanisms. *American Journal of Community Psychology, 28,* 83–104.

Davis, T., Ammons, C., Dahl, A., & Kliewer, W. (2015). Community violence exposure and callous-unemotional traits in adolescents: Testing parental support as a promotive versus protective factor. *Personality and Individual Differences, 77,* 7–12.

Elliott, D. S., Wilson, W. J., Huizinga, D., Sampson, R. J., Elliott, A., & Rankin, B. (1996). The effects of neighborhood disadvantage on adolescent development. *Journal of Research in Crime and Delinquency, 33,* 389–426.

Esbensen, F. A., Deschenes, E. P., & Winfree, L. T. (1999). Differences between gang girls and gang boys: Results from a multisite survey. *Youth & Society, 31*(1), 27–53.

Espelage, D. L., Polanin, J. R., & Low, S. K. (2014). Teacher and staff perceptions of school environment as predictors of student aggression, victimization, and willingness to intervene in bullying situations. *School Psychology Quarterly, 29,* 287–305.

Evans, S. C., Pederson, C. A., Fite, P. J., Blossom, J. B., & Cooley, J. L. (2016). Teacher-reported irritable and defiant dimensions of oppositional defiant disorder: Social, behavioral, and academic correlates. *School Mental Health, 8*(2), 292–304.

Fanti, K. A., Colins, O. F., Andershed, H., & Sikki, M. (2017). Stability and change in callous-unemotional traits: Longitudinal associations with potential individual and contextual risk and protective factors. *American Journal of Orthopsychiatry, 87*(1), 62–75.

Farrell, A. D., & Bruce, S. E. (1997). Impact of exposure to community violence on violent behavior and emotional distress among urban adolescents. *Journal of Clinical Child Psychology, 26*(1), 2–14.

Fite, P. J., Wynn, P., Lochman, J. E., & Wells, K. C. (2009). The effect of neighborhood disadvantage on proactive and reactive aggression. *Journal of Community Psychology, 37*(4), 542–546.

Fite, P. J., Vitulano, M., Wynn, P., Wimsatt, A., Gaertner, A., & Rathert, J. (2010). Influence of perceived neighborhood safety on proactive and reactive aggression. *Journal of Community Psychology, 38*(6), 757–768.

Fite, P. J., Preddy, T., Vitulano, M., Elkins, S., Grassetti, S., & Wimsatt, A. (2012). Perceived best friend delinquency moderates the link between contextual risk factors and juvenile delinquency. *Journal of Community Psychology, 40*(6), 747–761.

Fowler, P. J., Tompsett, C. J., Braciszewski, J. M., Jacques-Tiura, A. J., & Baltes, B. B. (2009). Community violence: A meta-analysis on the effect of exposure and mental health outcomes of children and adolescents. *Development and Psychopathology, 21,* 227–259.

Fraire, M. G., & Ollendick, T. (2012). Anxiety and oppositional defiant disorder: A transdiagnostic conceptualization. *Clinical Psychology Review, 33,* 229–240.

Frick, P. J., & Dantagnan, A. L. (2005). Predicting the stability of conduct problems in children with and without callous-unemotional traits. *Journal of Child and Family Studies, 14,* 469–485.

Frick, P. J., & Ellis, M. (1999). Callous-unemotional traits and subtypes of conduct disorder. *Clinical Child and Family Psychology Review, 2,* 149–168.

Frick, P. J., Ray, J. V., Thornton, L. C., & Kahn, R. E. (2014). Can callous-unemotional traits enhance the understanding, diagnosis, and treatment of serious conduct problems in children and adolescents? A comprehensive review. *Psychological Bulletin, 140,* 1–57.

Gayles, J. G., Coatsworth, J. D., Pantin, H. M., & Szapocznik, J. (2009). Parenting and neighborhood predictors of youth problem behaviors within Hispanic families. *Hispanic Journal of Behavioral Sciences, 31*(3), 277–296.

Goodnight, J. A., Lahey, B. B., Van Hulle, C. A., Rodgers, J. L., Rathouz, P. J., Waldman, I. D., & D'Onofrio, B. M. (2012). A quasi-experimental analysis of the influence of neighborhood disadvantage on child and adolescent conduct problems. *Journal of Abnormal Psychology, 121*(1), 95–108. doi: 10.1037/a0025078

Gorman-Smith, D., & Tolan, P. (1998). The role of exposure to community violence and developmental problems among inner-city youth. *Development and Psychopathology, 10,* 101–116.

Gottfredson, G. D., & Gottfredson, D. C. (1985). *Victimization in Schools.* New York, NY: Plenum.

Gottfredson, G. D., Gottfredson, D. C., Payne, A. A., & Gottfredson, N. C. (2005). School climate predictors of school disorder: Results from the national student of delinquent prevention in schools. *Journal of Research in Crime and Delinquency, 42,* 412–444.

Gruber, R., Cassoff, J., Frenette, S., Wiebe, S., & Carrier, J. (2012). Impact of sleep extension and restriction on children's emotional lability and impulsivity. *Pediatrics, 130*(5), e1155–e1161.

Gruman, D. H., Harachi, T. W., Abbott, R. D., Catalano, R. F., & Fleming, C. B. (2008). Longitudinal effects of student mobility on three dimensions of elementary school engagement. *Child Development, 79,* 1833–1852.

Guerra, N. G., Rowell Huesmann, L., & Spindler, A. (2003). Community violence exposure, social cognition, and aggression among urban elementary school children. *Child development, 74,* 1561–1576.

Handley, E. D., Rogosch, F. A., Guild, D. J., & Cicchetti, D. (2015). Neighborhood disadvantage and adolescent substance use disorder: The moderating role of maltreatment. *Child Maltreatment, 20*(3), 193–202.

Hawkins, J. D., Herrenkohl, T. I., Farrington, D. P., Brewer, D., Catalano, R. F., & Harachi, T. W. (1998). A review of predictors of youth violence. In R. Loeber & D. Farrington (Eds.), *Serious and Violent Juvenile Offenders: Risk Factors and Successful Interventions* (pp. 106–146). Thousand Oaks, CA: Sage.

Henry, D., Gorman-Smith, D., Schoeny, M., & Tolan, P. (2014). "Neighborhood matters": Assessment of neighborhood social processes. *American Journal of Community Psychology, 54,* 187–204.

Henricsson, L., & Rydell, A. M. (2004). Elementary school children with behavior problems: Teacher–child relations and self-perception. A prospective study. *Merrill-Palmer Quarterly, 50,* 111–138.

Herbers, J. E., Reynolds, A. J., & Chen, C. (2013). School mobility and developmental outcomes in young adulthood. *Developmental Psychopathology, 25,* 501–515.

Horan, J. M., Brown, J. L., Jones, S. M., & Aber, J. L. (2016). The influence of conduct problems and callous-unemotional traits on academic development among youth. *Journal of Youth and Adolescence, 45*(6), 1245–1260.

Hyde, L. W., Burt, S. A., Shaw, D. S., Donnellan, M. B., & Forbes, E. E. (2015). Early starting, aggressive, and/or callous–unemotional? Examining the overlap and predictive utility of antisocial behavior subtypes. *Journal of Abnormal Psychology, 124,* 329–342.

Ingoldsby, E. M., Shaw, D. S., Winslow, E., Schonberg, M., Gilliom, M., & Criss, M. M. (2006). Neighborhood disadvantage, parent–child conflict, neighborhood peer relationships, and early antisocial behavior problem trajectories. *Journal of Abnormal Child Psychology, 34*(3), 303–319.

Jack, S. L., Shores, R. E., Denny, R. K., Gunter, P. L., DeBriere, T., & DePaepe, P. (1996). An analysis of the relationships of teachers' reported use of classroom management strategies on types of classroom interactions. *Journal of Behavioral Education, 6,* 67–87.

Katz, B. N., Esparza, P., Carter, J. S., Grant, K. E., & Meyerson, D. A. (2012). Intervening processes in the relationship between neighborhood characteristics and psychological symptoms in urban youth. *Journal of Early Adolescence, 32*(5), 650–680.

Kellam, S. G., Ling, X., Merisca, R., Brown, C. H., & Ialongo, N. (1998). The effect of level of aggression in the first grade classroom on the course and malleability of aggressive behavior into middle school. *Development and Psychopathology, 10,* 164–186.

Kilpatrick, D. G., Acierno, R., Saunders, B., Resnick, H. S., Best, C. L., & Schnurr, P. P. (2000). Risk factors for adolescent substance abuse and dependence: Data from a national sample. *Journal of Consulting and Clinical Psychology, 68,* 19–30.

Kimonis, E. R., Centifanti, L. C., Allen, J. L., & Frick, P. J. (2014). Reciprocal influences between negative life events and callous-unemotional traits. *Journal of Abnormal Child Psychology, 42,* 1287–1298.

Kimonis, E. R., Frick, P. J., Munoz, L. C., & Aucoin, K. J. (2008). Callous-unemotional traits and the emotional processing of distress cues in detained boys: Testing the moderating role of aggression, exposure to community violence, and histories of abuse. *Development and Psychopathology, 20,* 569–589.

King, K., & Ogle, C. (2014). Negative life events vary by neighborhood and mediate the relation between neighborhood context and psychological well-being. *PLoS ONE, 9,* e93539. doi:10.1371/journal.pone.0093539

Kroneman, L. M., Hipwell, A. E., Loeber, R., Koot, H. M., & Pardini, D. A. (2011). Contextual risk factors as predictors of disruptive behavior disorder trajectories in girls: The moderating effect of callous-unemotional features. *Journal of Child Psychology and Psychiatry, 52,* 167–175.

Kroneman, L., Loeber, R., & Hipwell, A. E. (2004). Is neighborhood context differently related to externalizing problems and delinquency for girls compared with boys? *Clinical Child and Family Psychology Review, 7*(2), 109–122.

Kupersmidt, J. B., Griesler, P. C., DeRosier, M. E., Patterson, C. J., & Davis, P. W. (1995). Childhood aggression and peer relations in the context of family and neighborhood factors. *Child Development, 66,* 360–375.

Leadbeater, B. J., & Homel, J. (2015). Irritable and defiant sub-dimensions of ODD: Their stability and prediction of internalizing symptoms and conduct problems from adolescence to young adulthood. *Journal of Abnormal Child Psychology, 43,* 407–421.

Lee, E. H., Zhou, Q., Ly, J., Main, A., Tao, A., & Chen, S. H. (2013). Neighborhood characteristics, parenting styles, and children's behavioral problems in Chinese American immigrant families. *Cultural Diversity and Ethnic Minority Psychology, 20*(2), 202–212.

Leonard, C. P., & Elias, M. J. (1993). Entry into middle school: Student factors predicting adaptation to an ecological transition. In L. A. Jason, K. E. Danner, & K. S. Kurasaki, (Eds.), *Prevention in Human Services Series: Prevention and School Transitions* (pp. 39–57). New York, NY: Haworth Press.

Leventhal, T., & Brooks-Gunn, J. (2000). The neighborhoods they live in: the effects of neighborhood residence on child and adolescent outcomes. *Psychological Bulletin, 126*(2), 309–337.

Leventhal, T., Dupéré, V., & Brooks-Gunn, J. (2009). Neighborhood influences on adolescent development. *Handbook of Adolescent Psychology, 2,* 411–443.

Lochman, J. E., Wells, K. C., Qu, L., & Chen, L. (2013). Three year follow-up of coping power intervention effects: evidence of neighborhood moderation? *Prevention Science, 14,* 364–376.

Loeber, R., & Farrington, D. P. (2001). *Child delinquents: Development, intervention, and service needs.* Thousand Oaks, CA: Sage.

Loeber, R., Lahey, B. B., & Thomas, C. (1991). Diagnostic conundrum of oppositional defiant disorder and conduct disorder. *Journal of Abnormal Psychology, 100,* 379–390.

Lopez, E. E., Perez, S. M., Ochoa, G. M., & Ruiz, D. M. (2008). Adolescent aggression: Effects of gender and family and school environments. *Journal of Adolescence, 31,* 433–450.

Macartney, S. E. (2011). *Child poverty in the United States 2009 and 2010: Selected race groups and Hispanic origin.* Washington, DC: US Department of Commerce, Economics and Statistics Administration, US Census Bureau.

Markowitz, A. J., Ryan, R. M., & Marsh, A. A. (2015). Neighborhood income and the expression of callous–unemotional traits. *European Child & Adolescent Psychiatry, 24,* 1103–1118.

Massey, D. S., & Denton, N. A. (1993). *American apartheid: Segregation and the making of the underclass.* Cambridge, MA: Harvard University Press.

Matthys, W., & Lochman, J. E. (2010). *Oppositional defiant disorder and conduct disorder in childhood.* Oxford, UK: Wiley-Blackwell.

Maughan, B. (2004). Conduct disorder in context. In J. Hill & B. Maughan (Eds.), *Conduct disorders in childhood and adolescence* (pp.169–201). Cambridge, UK: Cambridge University Press.

Meehan, B. T., Hughes, J. N., & Cavell, T. A. (2003). Teacher-student relationships as compensatory resources for aggressive children. *Child Development, 74,* 1145–1157.

Mehana, M., & Reynolds, A. J. (2004). School mobility and achievement: A meta-analysis. *Children and Youth Services Review, 26,* 93–119.

Meier, M. H., Slutske, W. S., Arndt, S., & Cadoret, R. J. (2008). Impulsive and callous traits are more strongly associated with delinquent behavior in higher risk neighborhoods among boys and girls. *Journal of Abnormal Psychology, 117,* 377–385.

Miller, L. S., Wasserman, G. A., Neugebauer, R., Gorman-Smith, D., & Kamboukos, D. (1999). Witnessed community violence and antisocial behavior in high-risk, urban boys. *Journal of Clinical Child Psychology, 28*, 2–11.

Moffitt, T. E. (1993). Adolescence-limited and life-course-persistent antisocial behavior: A developmental taxonomy. *Psychological Review, 100*, 674–701.

Moffitt, T. E. (2007). A review of research on the taxonomy of life-course persistent versus adolescent limited antisocial behavior. In D. J. Flannery, A. T. Vazsonyi, and I. D. Waldman (Eds.), *The Cambridge handbook of violent behavior and aggression* (pp. 49–74). New York, NY: Cambridge University Press.

Moffitt, T. E., & Caspi, A. (2001). Childhood predictors differentiate life-course persistent and adolescence-limited antisocial pathways among males and females. *Developmental Psychopathology, 13*, 355–375.

Mortimore, P. (1998). *The road to school improvement: Reflections on school effectiveness.* Lisse: Swets & Zeitlinger.

Mrug, S., & Windle, M. (2009). Mediators of neighborhood influences on externalizing behavior in preadolescent children. *Journal of Abnormal Child Psychology, 37*, 265–280.

Pace, T. M., Mullines, L. L., Beesley, D., Hill, J. S., & Carson, K. (1999). The relationship between children's emotional and behavioral problems and the social responses of elementary school teachers. *Contemporary Educational Psychology, 24*, 140–155.

Pajer, K., Stein, S., Tritt, K., Chang, C., Wang, W., & Gardner, W. (2008). Conduct disorder in girls: Neighborhoods, family characteristics, and parenting behaviors. *Child and Adolescent Psychiatry and Mental Health, 2*. doi:10.1186/1753-2000-2-28

Payne, A. A., & Welch, K. (2015). How school and education impact the development of criminal and antisocial behavior. In J. Morizot & L. Kazemian (Eds.), *The development of criminal and antisocial behavior* (pp. 237–251). Cham, Switzerland: Springer International Publishing.

Plybon, L. E., & Kliewer, W. (2001). Neighborhood types and externalizing behavior in urban school-age children: Tests of direct, mediated, and moderated effects. *Journal of Child and Family Studies, 10*(4), 419–437.

Ray, J. V., Thornton, L. C., Frick, P. J., Steinberg, L., & Cauffman, E. (2016). Impulse control and callous-unemotional traits distinguish patterns of delinquency and substance use in justice involved adolescents: Examining the moderating role of neighborhood context. *Journal of Abnormal Child Psychology, 44*, 599–611.

Reinke, W. M., & Herman, K. C. (2002). Creating school environment that deter antisocial behaviors in youth. *Psychology in the Schools, 39*, 549–559.

Riina, E. M., Martin, A., Gardner, M., & Brooks-Gunn, J. (2013). Context matters: Links between neighborhood discrimination, neighborhood cohesion and African American adolescents' adjustment. *Journal of Youth and Adolescence, 42*, 136–146.

Rimm-Kaufman, S. E., La Paro, K. M., Downer, J. T., & Pianta, R. C. (2005). The contribution of classroom setting and quality of instruction to children's behavior in kindergarten classrooms. *The Elementary School Journal, 105*, 377–394.

Roosa, M. W., Deng, S., Ryu, E., Burrell, G. L., Tein, J., Jones, S., Lopez, V., & Crowder, S. (2005). Family and child characteristics linking neighborhood context and child externalizing behavior. *Journal of Marriage and Family, 67*, 515–529.

Rubens, S. L., Fite, P. J., Cooley, J. L., & Canter, K. S. (2014). The role of sleep in the relation between community violence exposure and delinquency among Latino adolescents. *Journal of Community Psychology, 42*, 723–734.

Rumberger, R. W., & Lawson, K. A. (1998). Student mobility and the increased risk of high school dropout. *American Journal of Education, 107*, 1–35.

Russell, A. A., Johnson, C. L., Hammad, A., Ristau, K. I., Zawadzki, S., Del, A. V., & Coker, K. L. (2015). Prenatal and neighborhood correlates of oppositional defiant disorder (ODD). *Child & Adolescent Social Work Journal, 32*(4), 375–381.

Rutter, M. (1983). School effects on pupil progress: Research findings and policy implications. *Child Development, 54*, 1–29.

Sabogal, F., Marín, G., Otero-Sabogal, R., Marín, B. V., & Perez-Stable, E. J. (1987). Hispanic familism and acculturation: What changes and what doesn't? *Hispanic Journal of Behavioral Sciences, 9*(4), 397–412.

Samdal, O. (1998). *The school environment as a risk or resource for students' health-related behaviors and subjective well-being.* Bergen, Norway: University of Bergen.

Singer, M. I., Anglin, T. M., Song, L. Y., & Lunghofer, L. (1995). Adolescents' exposure to violence and associated symptoms of psychological trauma. *Journal of the American Medical Association, 273,* 477–482.

Skiba, R. J., & Knesting, K. (2001). Zero tolerance, zero evidence: An analysis of school discipline practice. *New Directions for Mental Health Services, 92,* 17–43.

Snyder, J. (2002). Reinforcement and coercion mechanisms in the development of antisocial behavior: Peer relationships. In J. B. Reid, G. R., Patterson, & J. Snyder (Eds.), *Antisocial Behavior in Children and Adolescents* (pp.101–122). Washington, DC: American Psychological Association.

South, S. J., Haynie, D. L., & Bose, S. (2007). Student mobility and school dropout. *Social Science Research, 36,* 68–94.

Stringaris, A., & Goodman, R. (2009). Three dimensions of oppositionality in youth. *Journal of Child Psychology and Psychiatry, 50,* 216–223.

U.S. Census Bureau (2011). *United States Census 2010.* Retrieved from https://www.census.gov/2010census/.

Vassallo, S., Smart, D., & Sanson, A. (2002). *Patterns and precursors of adolescent antisocial behavior.* Melbourne, Australia: Australian Institute of Family Studies.

Venkatraman, V., Chuah, Y. M. L., Huettel, S. A., & Chee, M. W. L. (2007). Sleep deprivation elevates expectation of gains and attenuates response to losses following risky decisions. *Sleep, 50,* 603–609.

Vitaro, F., & Brendgen, M. (2011). Subtypes of aggressive behaviors: Etiologies, development and consequences. In T. Bliesnder, A. Beelman, & M. Stemmler (Eds.), *Antisocial behavior and crime: Contributions of theory and evaluation research to prevention and intervention* (pp. 17–38). Goettingen, Germany: Hogrefe.

Wandersman, A., & Nation, M. (1998). Urban neighborhoods and mental health. *American Psychologist, 53,* 647–656.

Werthamer-Larsson, L., Kellam, S. G., & Wheeler, L. (1991). Effect of classroom environment on shy behavior, aggressive behavior and concentration problems. *American Journal of Community Psychology, 19,* 585–602.

Wiesner, M., Elliott, M. N., McLaughlin, K. A., Banspach, S. W., Tortolero, S., & Schuster, M. A. (2015). Common versus specific correlates of fifth-grade conduct disorder and oppositional defiant disorder symptoms: Comparison of three racial/ethnic groups. *Journal of Abnormal Child Psychology, 43*(5), 985–998.

Wilson, W. C., & Rosenthal, B. S. (2003). The relationship between exposure to community violence and psychological distress among adolescents: A meta-analysis. *Violence and Victims, 18*(3), 335–352.

Wood, D., Halfron, N., Scarlata, D., Newacheck, P., & Nessim, S. (1993). Impact of family relocation on children's growth, development, school function, and behavior. *Journal of the American Medical Association, 270,* 1334–1340.

Part 4
Assessment Processes

23

Problem-Solving Structure of Assessment

Walter Matthys and Nicole P. Powell

The clinical assessment of a child or adolescent can be considered to be a decision-making process in which the clinician assesses for the presence (or not) of one or more psychiatric disorders, considers the underlying etiology, and plans treatment. We describe this decision process in eight steps:

1. the collection of written information from the parents;
2. the initial interview with the parents and the child;
3. the formulation of a hypothesis on possible diagnoses and comorbidities;
4. the clinical interview and observation of the child;
5. the completion of additional assessments, if necessary;
6. a DSM-5 or ICD-11 orientated interview with the parents (and the older child or adolescent separately);
7. the integration of all available information with a view to a categorical (DSM-5 or ICD-11) diagnosis and a diagnostic formulation including considerations regarding etiology, together with the decision on a treatment plan;
8. the discussion of the diagnosis and treatment plan with the parents, and the provision of psychoeducation in order to facilitate engagement with the treatment.

First, however, we discuss some general issues.

General Issues

The clinical assessment of a child or adolescent results in three decisions. First, the clinician decides whether the behavioral problems of the child are severe enough to qualify as oppositional defiant disorder (ODD) or conduct disorder (CD) and whether one or more comorbid disorders may be diagnosed. Second, the clinician tries to understand the factors involved in the development of the disorder and makes a diagnostic formulation. Third, the clinician proposes a treatment plan to the parents resulting from the diagnosis and the considerations about etiology.

Although most psychopathological phenomena in youth can best be regarded as quantitative variations, many clinical decisions have to be categorical. Deciding on whether a child or adolescent has ODD, CD, and/or one or more comorbid disorders is based on whether his or her symptoms meet the criteria for a given diagnosis. Thus, the disorder is either present or it is not. This decision is needed for practical purposes: whether treatment or special education is indicated and whether resources for these and other purposes (e.g., social services) should be made available.

Although the distinction between normative and clinically significant misbehavior is crucial in all evaluations, specific attention to this issue is required in preschool children. Noncompliance, temper loss, and physical aggression commonly occur in this group and may be considered normative misbehaviors unless they surpass a threshold of typical severity and frequency (Wakschlag et al., 2007). Clinicians, therefore, must have a comprehensive understanding of normative presentations of these behaviors in preschoolers in terms of frequency, duration, and response to intervention, in order to discern whether a clinical problem is present.

In line with these considerations regarding the distinction between normative misbehavior and behavior that is symptomatic, DSM-5 (American Psychiatric Association, 2013) provides guidance on a minimal level of frequency to define symptoms of ODD. For children younger than 5 years, a given symptom should occur on most days for at least 6 months, while for children 5 years and older, a given symptom should occur once a week or more for at least 6 months. An exception is the vindictiveness symptom; this must have shown itself at least twice in the past 6 months. In addition, it is specified that the intensity of the behaviors should be outside the normative range for the child's developmental level, gender, and culture. It should be noted that DSM-5 does not specify that symptoms of CD should be defined by frequency criteria.

The dichotomy between normality and pathology that characterizes classification systems does not, however, preclude a dimensional approach. It is important to assess the severity of the disorder with a view to making decisions about the urgency, type, and intensity of treatment. DSM-5 specifies ODD as mild, moderate, or severe in terms of occurrence of symptoms in one, two, or three or more settings (e.g., at home, at school, with peers), respectively. Severity for CD is specified from mild to severe based on (a) the number of conduct problems in excess of those required to make the diagnosis and (b) the harm caused by the conduct problems.

Related to severity is the issue of impairment. In all DSM-5 disorders, a generic diagnostic criterion requiring distress or impairment is used to establish disorder thresholds. It is insufficient for the clinician to check whether a child or adolescent fulfils four criteria of ODD or three criteria of CD in order to make a diagnosis. For a diagnosis of CD, the disturbance must cause clinically significant impairment in social, academic, or occupational functioning, while for ODD, distress in the child, or others in his or her family or peer group, must additionally be present.

But a diagnostic classification is not enough to draw conclusions about the treatment needed for a particular child or adolescent. A diagnostic formulation, by contrast, also includes hypotheses about causal processes and therapeutic interventions (Rutter & Taylor, 2008). With respect to causal processes, a distinction needs to be made between the factors involved in the initiation of the disorder and those involved in its maintenance. To make hypotheses that can assist with planning therapeutic interventions, we need also to distinguish proximal factors (i.e., factors that are proximal to the child's problem behavior such as inconsistent discipline) from distal risk factors (i.e., contextual factors such as maternal depression, marital disharmony, and low socioeconomic status), as well as modifiable from stable factors. Thus, when planning treatment we should focus on the factors that play a role in the maintenance of the disorder and are modifiable and proximal.

Our present knowledge does not allow us to clearly identify the specific causal processes underlying the disorder in each child or adolescent. The issue for the clinician is how extensive the assessment needs to be be to generate a hypothesis on the etiology in the child that is good enough to form the basis of a rational treatment plan. In this context, however, we need to bear in mind the large number of young people who are referred for assessment and treatment of ODD or CD and ADHD and try to avoid the long waiting lists caused by unnecessarily lengthy assessments. We therefore advocate an assessment which, on the one hand, is good enough for a satisfactory understanding of etiological factors involved in the development of the disorder in this particular individual but, on the other, is not unnecessarily detailed. The identification of factors that are associated with the maintenance of the disorders (e.g., the child's borderline intellectual functioning; insufficient parental skills) and have consequences for the treatment and education of the child or adolescent is essential.

An Overview of the Assessment Procedure

Below we describe eight decision-making steps that may be followed.

1. Parents are asked to give *written information* (questionnaire, comprehensive standardized rating scale) on the youth and his or her family prior to the first visit to the clinic.
2. The assessment starts with an *initial interview with the parents and the child or adolescent*.
3. Based on this information and scores on one of the comprehensive standardized rating scales, the clinician generates a differential diagnosis, i.e., *a hypothesis on possible diagnoses and comorbidities*.
4. This hypothesis helps the clinician to decide which issues he or she needs to focus on in the *clinical interview and observation of the child or adolescent*.
5. An evaluation is made of whether *additional assessments* are needed.
6. With a view to a categorical diagnosis, the clinician administers a *DSM-5 orientated interview with the parents (and with the older child or adolescent separately)*.
7. The clinician integrates all the information available with respect to a *DSM-5 or ICD-11 categorical diagnosis and diagnostic formulation, including etiological considerations, and generates a treatment plan*.
8. The clinician *discusses the diagnosis and treatment plan with the parents*, and provides *psychoeducation in order to facilitate treatment engagement*.

The identification of these various steps in the decision-making process does not mean that we are in favor of an assessment procedure that takes many weeks to conduct. As already stated, we are in favor of a succinct assessment procedure. Thus, steps 2 to 6 can even be undertaken in a single day, together with some additional assessments (e.g., cognitive and neuropsychological assessments). More time, however, would be needed to collect other additional information, for instance, from observation at school.

Written Information

To save time and actively involve the parents in the assessment procedure, it is appropriate to send both a questionnaire and a comprehensive standardized rating scale to be completed by the parents and the youth's teacher or, in case of young children, their professional daycare-giver. Relevant reports from previous medical assessments, the school, and previous psychological and educational evaluations may also be sent either by the parents or the referring agent. This information is used in the initial interview with the parents and child or adolescent, or prior to the DSM-5 orientated interview with the parents.

Questionnaire

The questionnaire will ideally request information on both the child or adolescent and his or her family. A comprehensive questionnaire will cover the youth's prenatal and perinatal period, early development, medical, school, and psychosocial (e.g., foster care, parental divorce) history, as well as the presenting behavioral problems (e.g., age of onset, previous treatments, response to the treatment). Important family information will include family composition, medical history, and psychiatric history.

Comprehensive Rating Scales

It is often appropriate to use a comprehensive standardized rating scale (Verhulst & Van der Ende, 2008). Widely used, well-validated examples include the Achenbach System of Empirically Based Assessment (ASEBA; Achenbach & Rescorla, 2000, 2001), the Behavior Assessment System for Children (BASC-2; Reynolds & Kamphaus, 2004), the Strengths and Difficulties Questionnaire (SDQ; Goodman, 1997), and the Conners' Rating Scales–Revised (CRS-R; Conners, 1997). Such rating scales assess a number of areas of adjustment rather than a single domain of behavior. Moreover, because they have been standardized using large normative samples, the referred child's ratings on a given scale can be compared with those of typically developing children and adolescents. Thus, scores give a quick view on whether the youth functions within the clinical or normal range of various domains.

Parents and teachers are useful as informants, and adolescents generally have the cognitive capacity to report on their own behavior, though they may be motivated to underreport conduct problems or to respond in a socially desirable manner (Collett, Ohan, & Myers, 2003). When information is collected in a developmentally appropriate manner, children as young as 5 years of age can provide valid information on their own conduct problems (Arseneault, Kim-Cohen, Taylor, Caspi, & Moffitt, 2005). Low levels of agreement amongst different informants do not invalidate the reports of any of them (Verhulst & Van der Ende, 2008). The different views of parents and teachers on the youth's problems are the result not only of different standards and different levels of professionalism, but also of the fact that children and adolescents behave differently at home and at school. Further, youths' self-reports may differ from those of adults on behaviors that parents and teachers may not have the opportunity to observe (e.g., stealing, fire-setting, aggression between peers; Collett et al., 2003).

Initial Interview with the Parents and the Child or Adolescent

The initial clinical interview is important not only for gathering information, but also for building rapport and empathizing with the family. The clinician may start by asking the parents to share their thoughts and concerns about their child's behavior and factors that may have contributed to the child's behavioral problems, as well as their opinions about possible diagnoses and treatment options. Parents are typically worried and want to express their concerns about the future of their child. Some parents have strong negative feelings about their child, while others feel the need to also stress their child's positive characteristics. The clinician's attitude towards the child's misbehavior is neutral and nonjudgmental; the clinician also empathizes with the child's feelings of helplessness in regard to anger and frustration.

The clinician needs to be sensitive to possible biases on the part of the parents from the outset. Various biases with respect to psychiatric disorders, specifically ODD and CD, can exist. For example, ODD and CD often are thought to be the result of bad parenting and to inevitably result in criminality or drug abuse. It is important to clarify that, in clinical psychology and psychiatry and medicine in general, causation is most often considered in a probabilistic rather than deterministic way. If we do diagnose a disorder in the child or adolescent we will try to identify factors that have increased his or her risk of developing the disorder, but will not be able to find the one single factor that caused it. Moreover, we will also pay attention to the strengths of the child and the family. In other words, we will also assess the protective and promotive factors in the child and his or her environment, such as well-developed motor skills or sense of humor or the parents' mutual support in parenting. Parents of young children in particular feel the need to stress the strengths of their child, such as his or her cheerfulness or enthusiasm.

Using the written information the parents have sent to the clinic, the clinician will next focus on clarification about who initiated the referral, the reasons for referral, and why the referral was made at this particular time. Additional information is obtained on pregnancy, birth, medical history, and developmental milestones, when needed.

In-depth information is obtained on the onset and development of behavior problems over time. Specifically, the clinician asks at what age the various problems first occurred, in which settings, and with whom (parents, other adults in the family, other adults outside the family, teachers, siblings, peers). The course of each behavior over the years is discussed and whether the problem persists in terms of frequency, interactions with particular individuals, and consequences for overall functioning (e.g., peer relations, academic achievement). In this context, it is also important to gather information on the youth's current social and communication skills (e.g., as regards entering a group of peers who are already playing together, asking to play with a peer, competing with peers) and social-problem-solving skills (appropriately interpreting social situations, adequately taking the perspective of the other person and inferring his or her thoughts and feelings, feeling with the other person). Likewise, the child's characteristic responses to a parent's management of his or her misbehavior is asked for, that is, the child's sensitivity to punishment cues, as well as the child's responses to the parents' praise or reward of appropriate behaviors, for there is evidence that ODD and CD are characterized by decreased sensitivity to punishment and reward. In line with the discussion of the reasons for referral and the current problems, information on prior care and contacts with health, mental health, and educational professionals is gathered.

Information on the parents and the wider family, based on sensitive information (e.g., family psychiatric history) can be gathered at the DSM-5 interview with the parents, when the child or adolescent is not present. Spontaneous information given by the parents assists in evaluating the parental relationship, the social support they receive, and their parenting skills (consistency, amount of praise, punishing techniques, supervision). To assess parental style, one may ask parents to describe situations that resulted in the child being disciplined, including how the parents handled the situation, how the child reacted, and how the situation was resolved. In this initial interview the clinician may also observe how the parents support each other.

During this initial meeting it is also appropriate to involve the child or adolescent, allowing the clinician to observe how the parents present their reasons for referral and their concerns in the child's presence, how the child responds to this, whether the parents encourage the child to express his or her views, whether they spontaneously mention the child's strengths, and how they manage any behavior problems the child manifests. Likewise, the clinician has the opportunity to observe the child. In general in child psychiatry and clinical psychology there are many symptoms that cannot be observed during the assessment, but this applies especially to children with ODD or CD. Indeed, one seldom observes actual physical aggression, though milder symptoms such as deliberately annoying the parents while they are talking with the clinician or blaming others for the misbehavior that is being discussed may occur during the initial interview.

At the end of the initial interview it is important to give parents the opportunity to provide additional information, as they may feel that important issues have been overlooked. Some parents feel embarrassed that attention has been focused onesidedly on their child's problems, and may appreciate the opportunity to report on their child's positive qualities and strengths. Encouraging parental input can have the added benefit of helping parents to engage in the evaluation process. Sharing observations of parents' strengths can also help to facilitate connection during the assessment (see Chapter 24 for a full discussion of parental engagement in therapy).

Hypotheses regarding Possible Diagnoses and Comorbidities

Based on the information gathered, the clinician generates a differential diagnosis. The issue not only is which possible psychiatric diagnoses should be taken into consideration, but also which disorders may co-occur. The differential diagnosis is to be considered as a clinical hypothesis that needs further testing during the next steps of the assessment.

Besides ODD and CD, the following diagnostic categories should be considered as possible first diagnoses when a child or adolescent presents with symptoms of disruptive behavior, hyperactivity, impulsivity, and attention problems:

- ADHD: mild forms of oppositional and aggressive behaviors frequently occur as associated features;
- Autism spectrum disorder: disruptive behaviors such as aggression may frequently occur as associated features;
- Bipolar disorder, major depressive disorder, and persistent depressive disorder (dysthymia): in children depressed mood may manifest as irritability and related disruptive behavior;
- Intermittent explosive disorder: high rates of anger and serious aggression toward others are characteristics of this disorder;
- Substance-related disorder: intoxication or withdrawal from substances may result in aggression, anger, irritability, restlessness, impulsivity, and impairments in attention;
- Eating disorder: irritability may occur as an associated feature; oppositional and argumentative behaviors may be displayed around eating and meals;
- Social anxiety disorder and separation anxiety disorder: anxiety may be expressed by disruptive behaviors;
- Language disorder: failure to follow directions is the result of impaired language comprehension;
- Intellectual disability: disruptive behavior is the result of difficulties with social judgment and communication;
- Adjustment disorder with disturbance of conduct or with mixed disturbance of emotions and conduct: behavioral symptoms develop in response to an identifiable stressor;
- Parent–child relational problem: although not a psychiatric disorder this category is used when the main focus of clinical attention is on addressing the quality of the parent–child relationship (e.g., parental overprotection and disruptive behavior in the child) or when the quality of the parent–child relationship is affecting the course, prognosis, or treatment of a disorder.

Of note, if symptoms of ODD occur exclusively during the course of a mood disorder such as persistent depressive disorder (dysthymia), a diagnosis of ODD should not be made. Further, disruptive mood dysregulation disorder has been added in DSM-5. This disorder is defined by severe temper outbursts and persistent irritability. The developers of DSM-5 elected to address concerns about increasing rates of diagnosis of childhood bipolar disorder and the related overmedication of children by adding this new category of disorder. It, however, is based on limited research and a task group has recommended that the WHO should not accept it as a diagnostic category in ICD-11 (Lochman et al., 2015). Instead, the group has proposed that ICD-11 include a specifier to indicate whether or not the presentation of ODD includes chronic irritability and anger (see Chapter 2 of this book for an overview of this important diagnostic issue).

Other disorders that co-occur with ODD and CD should also be considered. Special attention should be given to Specific Learning Disorder (with impairment in reading, written expression, or mathematics). Since there is much evidence that the co-occurrence of specific learning disorder with ODD or CD is largely attributable to the presence of comorbid ADHD (for a review of studies see Hinshaw, 1992), the clinician should be specifically attentive to Learning Disorders in children with ODD or CD comorbid with ADHD. With respect to specific learning disorder, it should be noted that developmental delays in, say, reading might not be severe enough to be diagnosed as a clear disorder but nevertheless are important to acknowledge and to include in the clinician's understanding of the child's dysfunctioning. Reading problems may lead to disruptive behavior as a result of frustration and marginalization engendered by school failure. Likewise, language problems specifically in preschool children may lead to disruptive behavior as a result of difficulties in understanding the rules and requests made by adults, in understanding complex social interactions with peers, and in communicating the child's needs. Finally, individuals with mild to borderline intellectual disabilities (IQ score 55–85) are at increased risk for aggressive and antisocial behaviors. Below we give the list of comorbid disorders to be considered. It should be noted that DSM-5 allows the co-occurrence of ODD and CD.

- ADHD;
- Bipolar disorder, major depressive disorder and persistent depressive disorder (dysthymia);
- Anxiety disorders;
- Specific learning disorder (with impairment of reading, written language, or mathematics);
- Language disorder;
- Intellectual disability;
- Substance-related disorders.

Interview and Observation of the Child or Adolescent

The clinical interview and observation of the child or adolescent is needed for several purposes: for the exclusion of other disorders such as an autism spectrum disorder, for the identification of comorbid disorders such as ADHD, and for the observation of symptoms and other features that are characteristic of ODD and CD. Even though clinicians do not expect to observe the symptoms of ODD or CD that have been reported by the parents, they may want to see at least "the tip of the iceberg." Thus, although the presumption of the presence of ODD or CD may be generated on the basis of information from parents and teachers, the clinical interview may be used to support this presumption or not. Importantly, the child or adolescent is also given the opportunity to express his or her view on (and concerns about) family members.

Preschool Children

In general, observational methods are appropriate for the assessment of preschool children whereas a mixture of observation and interview is appropriate for children over 6 and for adolescents. A structured observation assessment has been developed for the clinical assessment of preschool children (the disruptive behavior diagnostic observation schedule [DB-DOS]; Wakschlag, Briggs-Gowan, et al., 2008; Wakschlag, Hill, et al., 2008). The DB-DOS allows the child's behavior (e.g., compliance, frustration, social interaction, and internalization of rules) to unfold during a variety of challenging and pleasurable tasks that take place between the child and parent, and between the child and the examiner. In the first examiner module, the examiner is normally responsive to child behavior. This is the examiner active support module. Then, in a context of minimal support, the child is observed while working independently, the examiner being busy doing his or her own work. The DB-DOS has been developed for research purposes and is difficult to use in clinical settings since specialized training and ongoing monitoring of administration are needed. However, familiarity with this method can help clinicians set up an observation of a preschool child (Matthys, Bunte, & Schoemaker, 2016).

Children over 6 Years Old

With children over six one can chat without playing, but observation of the child while playing may provide additional information. In general, open questions are preferred to closed questions as they offer the chance to give a wide range of answers (Angold, 2002). It is important not to rush into difficult topics (such as the reason for referral) but instead to focus initially on neutral or pleasant topics in order to engage the child (Goodman & Scott, 2004). Thus, one may start with questions about the name of the child's school, which grade the child is in, and what he or she likes doing at school. One may then go on to the more difficult questions such as how he or she gets along with the teacher and whether he or she has friends in class. In this way issues known to be problematic for the child come to be explored. The topics to be discussed are: the school; friends; hobbies, activities, and clubs; relations with parents, siblings, and other family members; anxieties and worries; self-esteem; mood; defiant behavior; aggression; antisocial behavior.

Adolescents

The majority of adolescents can participate in a discussion-based interview; however, engaging in a board game, card game, or art activity can help to "break the ice" for adolescents who are anxious or guarded. In many cases, adolescents may be unhappy about participating in an evaluation. Clinicians can validate these feelings by acknowledging them and providing empathy. Adolescents often have concerns about how the information they provide will be used, and clinicians should be prepared to discuss the general plan for the evaluation (e.g., obtaining information about the adolescent and his or her family; developing a treatment plan). The clinician should also talk with the adolescent about whether information from the interview will be shared with the adolescent's parents or school, and should ensure that the adolescent understands the limits of confidentiality. As in interviews with younger children, it is important to establish a rapport. Questions about friends, music, favorite sports teams, and the like can help the adolescent to feel comfortable while also providing information about his or her psychosocial functioning to the clinician. The adolescent can be asked for his or her thoughts about the reason for the evaluation, factors contributing to the problems, and what he or she thinks might help the situation to improve. If the adolescent has previously participated in treatment, it can be enlightening to ask for his or her impressions of the intervention and what he or she previously found helpful or challenging. In addition to the topics to be discussed with children listed above, the adolescent interview should explore substance use; delinquency, truancy, and gang involvement; sexual activity; risk-taking behaviors; self-harm (e.g., "cutting"); and suicidal and/or homicidal ideation or intent.

Behavioral Observation during Interviews with Children and Adolescents

When observing and clinically interviewing the child or adolescent, the clinician can attend to the features of other disorders than ODD, CD, and ADHD. The following are features characteristic of ODD, CD, and ADHD:

- hyperactivity: fidgets, is restless, leaves seat, runs about, talks excessively;
- impulsivity: blurts out answers before question has been completed, has difficulty waiting his or her turn during a competitive game, interrupts the clinician;
- attention: easily distracted by noises outside the room, has difficulty sustaining attention during play activity or while talking;
- oppositional behaviors: refuses to comply with parent's or clinician's requests and persists in this behavior;
- hostile behaviors: blames others for his or her mistakes when these are discussed; deliberately annoys parents when asked to wait;
- emotional dysregulation: is touchy or loses temper while performing a task that is frustrating;
- negative mood: is annoyed, miserable, surly;
- threatening attitude: verbal aggression with threat to harm;
- physical aggression towards objects: rough handling of toys, slapping, banging;
- rule breaking: touching prohibited objects;
- lack of problem awareness and distress: does not acknowledge behavioral problems or minimizes their severity and negative consequences (e.g. peer rejection), and his or her responsibility for them;
- low sensitivity to negative cues: is not sensitive to negative feedback or threats of punishment, careless about mistakes, lack of fear in situations that normally elicit fear, high pain threshold (does not cry when hurt);
- low sensitivity to praise: is unresponsive when praised;
- callous-unemotional traits: lacks empathy (does not feel concern for family members when ill or did hurt), lacks remorse or guilt, is unconcerned about (poor) performance at school, demonstrates shallow or deficient affect (does not express feelings or show emotions);
- less display of negative emotions: shows little disappointment and sadness;
- narcissistic traits: arrogant, requires excessive admiration, expects automatic compliance with his or her expectations (entitlement);
- deficient social information processing: attributes hostile intent to others, shows impaired perspective-taking, generates aggressive responses to social problems, thinks about aggressive solutions (finds them acceptable, feels confident in his or her ability to enact them);
- deficient conscience: standards and norms are in line with those generally accepted in society but these are not adequately internalized, i.e., child needs adult's prompts; these standards and norms are not used because of impulsivity in responding; standards and norms are deviant from those generally accepted in society.

Physical examination and additional investigations vary largely from patient to patient and depend on whether medical information (from a pediatrician, physiotherapist, speech therapist, and/or paediatric neurologist) is already available at referral. Most children and adolescents referred for psychiatric or clinical psychological assessment have already been physically examined. In all patients attention should be paid to signs of neglect or abuse, to minimal physical anomalies or dysmorphic features, and to motor behavior (gait disturbance, clumsiness) suggestive of a developmental coordination disorder (Baird & Gringras, 2008). It is advisable always to measure the youth's height, weight, and head circumference. A basic neurological examination is indicated in children and adolescents with a history of seizures, developmental delay, abnormal gait, difficulty in using both hands well, dysmorphic features, and skin signs of a neurocutaneous disorder (Bailey, 2002; Goodman & Scott, 2005). If an abnormality is found, the youth should be referred to a pediatrician or a pediatric neurologist. Likewise, if visual or hearing problems are suspected, the child or adolescent should be referred to an appropriate clinic.

Additional Assessments

A number of additional assessments and rating scales may be used. Some of these assessment procedures, such as cognitive assessment, are standardized but others have been developed for research purposes and do not have clinical cut-off points.

Doubts about overall cognitive developmental level and language development may arise during the assessment process, possibly on the basis of teacher reports or low scores on standardized testing of academic achievement. Psychological testing using standardized assessment of intellectual ability (IQ) is then indicated. Results of a test of intelligence or the need to get more insight into possible deficits in executive functioning may lead to additional neuropsychological testing (attention, visuo-spatial skills, inhibition, working memory, cognitive flexibility) and speech–language assessment (Charman, Hood, & Howlin, 2008).

In addition, the clinician may feel the need to have a more differentiated insight into the variety of the disruptive symptoms. For the assessment of callous-unemotional traits various rating scales have been developed for children and adolescents either as subscales from broader measures of psychopathy such as the antisocial process screening device (APSD; Frick & Hare, 2001) and the child psychopathy scale (CPS; Lynam, 1997) or as a separate scale, i.e., the inventory of callous-unemotional traits (ICU; Kimonis et al., 2008). For preschool children, the low concern for others dimension of the Multidimensional Assessment Profile of Disruptive Behavior (MAP-DB; Wakschlag et al., 2014) has been developed as well as a preschool version of the ICU (Ezpeleta, de la Osa, Granero, Penelo, & Domenech, 2013). For the distinction between proactive and reactive aggression, Dodge and Coie (1987) developed a teacher-rating scale. Other rating scales are the parent-rating scale of reactive and proactive aggression (PRPA; Kempes, Matthys, Maassen, van Goozen, & van Engeland, 2006) and the teacher-report instrument for reactive and proactive aggression (IRPA; Polman, Orobio de Castro, Thomaes, & Van Aken, 2009). To assess social skills, the clinician may use the social skills rating scale (SSRS; Gresham & Elliot, 1990). To identify the specific social situations that are problematic (e.g., peer group entry, response to peer provocations), the taxonomy of problem situations (TOPS) (Dodge, McClasky, & Feldman, 1985) or the TOPS short form (Matthys, Maassen, Cuperus, & van Engeland, 2001) may be used.

The clinician may want to have a more specific insight into parents' parenting skills. Various instruments are available to assess them: the Alabama parenting questionnaire (APQ; Frick, 1991) and the parenting practices interview (PPI; Webster-Stratton, Reid, & Hammond, 2001; www.incredibleyears.com). To measure caregiver stress, the parenting stress index (Abidin, 1990) may be used.

If there is a discrepancy between scores on rating scales completed by teachers and parents' reports of the child's or adolescent's problem behavior at school, then contact with school is useful and observation at school may be needed. Nock and Kurtz (2005) have developed clinical procedures including not only behavioral observation but also description of the school and classroom context and collaboration with teachers and school psychologists.

To determine whether the symptoms result in impairment, overall functioning may be assessed using the children's global assessment scale (C-GAS; Shaffer et al., 1983). Likewise, the impact on the family scale (IFS; Sheeber & Johnson, 1992) is available to assess the impact of the behavior problems on the functioning of the family.

DSM-5 Orientated Interview

To confirm a DSM-5 diagnosis, the criteria of various disorders need to be checked. Information from parents is crucial as the criteria of DSM-5 are described in terms of behaviors that occur in everyday life. Before the criteria for psychiatric disorders are checked, it is important that parents should be given the opportunity to provide additional information on relevant issues not discussed at the initial interview, such as any problems of their own. In general, adolescents and children from the age of 9 can accurately report on their emotional and behavioral problems, although the test–retest reliability of psychiatric disorders (including ODD) is somewhat lower when highly structured interviews are administered to children rather than to parents (Jensen et al., 1995).

Two types of structured diagnostic method, respondent-based and interviewer-based, have been developed for use in research contexts. Respondent-based interviews such as the diagnostic schedule for children (DISC; Shaffer, Fisher, Lucas, Dulcan, & Schwab-Stone, 2000) and the diagnostic interview schedule for children and adolescents (DICA; Reich, 2000) do not allow any interpretation of the parent's or child's response. The wording of questions is predetermined, and the range of responses is limited. These highly structured interviews are also called lay interviews as no in-depth knowledge of psychopathology is needed for their administration.

By contrast, interviewer-based interviews such as the Kiddie-Schedule for Affective Disorders and Schizophrenia (K-SADS; Ambrosini, 2000) and the child and adolescent psychiatric assessment (CAPA; Angold & Costello, 2000) leave the interviewer free to ask any questions needed to decide whether or not a particular criterion is present. Therefore, only experienced clinicians can administer these types of interview. The disruptive behavior module of the K-SADS has been adapted for assessment of disruptive behaviors in preschool children (Kiddie Disruptive Behavior Disorders Schedule; Keenan et al., 2007); clinical usefulness has been demonstrated by studying validity on an individual level (Bunte, Schoemaker, Hessen, van der Heijden, & Matthys, 2013). The CAPA has also been revised for the assessment of most disorders in preschoolers (preschool age psychiatric assessment; Egger et al., 2006). Importantly, none of these interviews cover the autism spectrum disorders, which may be assessed with the autism diagnostic interview-revised (ADI-R; Lord, Rutter, & LeCouteur, 1994).

Child and adolescent versions of the structured interviews described above are available for use with youth over age 9. These structured interviews are DSM-oriented and generate a DSM diagnosis for the disruptive behavior disorders. It should be noted that none of the structured parent- or child- /adolescent-report interviews have been revised for consistency with DSM-5 criteria.

Most institutions do not have the resources for the training and ongoing monitoring of the administration of these structured diagnostic methods. Therefore, in everyday clinical practice clinicians use nonstructured, open interviews. To ensure diagnostic accuracy, it is extremely important for clinicians to carefully check each criterion separately with the parents by asking for specific examples and by probing for the frequency of behaviors.

Categorical Diagnosis, Diagnostic Formulation, and the Treatment Plan

Categorical Diagnosis

How should clinicians proceed in obtaining a final DSM-5 or ICD-11 categorical diagnosis? Based on the information available, the clinician needs to decide whether or not the referred youth qualifies for a diagnosis. It is necessary to integrate the information from different sources (standardized questionnaires, interview and observation of the child or adolescent, the DSM-orientated interview with the parents or the youth) at the level of each criterion or symptom and to decide whether the criterion is met. In this respect it should be noted that while considering standardized questionnaires one should not only look at whether the scores from the scales (e.g., the broadband or narrowband scales of the ASEBA) fall within the clinical domain, but check, at the level of items, whether behaviors (or symptoms, criteria) are scored as clearly present or not.

One issue is what to do with disagreement among informants. According to Angold (2002), a symptom can be considered present if reported by any informant—thus the source can be "ignored" and all positive symptoms from any source can simply be added up. Although this rule seems attractive because of its simplicity, bias in reporting symptoms may occur—by teachers because of school characteristics and by parents because of personality characteristics, psychiatric disorders, or personal interests may occur. In the event of disagreement among informants, we suggest that the clinician interpret this discrepancy and make a decision whether or not the specific symptom should be considered present.

With respect to disagreement among informants, we should like to point out that, first, to diagnose ODD the symptoms need not be present in two settings. According to the DSM-5, symptoms may be confined to only one setting; in that case, symptom severity is specified as mild. Second, with respect to ADHD, according to the DSM-5 several inattentive or hyperactive-impulsive symptoms need to be present in two or more settings.

In cases where the child or adolescent has a number of clinical meaningful characteristics of ODD or CD that cause clinically significant distress or impairment but still do not fulfill DSM-5 criteria for either diagnosis, the "other specified disruptive, impulse-control, and conduct disorder" category is used. The clinician should communicate the specific reason why the youth does not meet the criteria for either of these disorders. If the clinician decides not to specify the reason that the criteria are not met, for example, in an emergency room setting, then the category "unspecified disruptive, impulse-control, and conduct disorder" should be used.

According to the DSM-5, if more than one diagnosis is present, the clinician should indicate the principal diagnosis by listing it first. In an inpatient setting, the principal diagnosis is the condition responsible for the admission of the child or adolescent. In an outpatient setting, the principal diagnosis is the condition responsible for the visit.

Diagnostic Formulation

Besides a categorical DSM-5 or ICD-11 diagnosis, a diagnostic or case formulation is needed that includes a hypothesis regarding the risk and protective factors that play a role in the development of the disorders. Although our understanding of the etiology of ODD and CD is increasing, the application of this knowledge at the level of the individual and his or her family is limited. Some risk factors can be identified during the assessment (e.g., language delay, parental disharmony), but even then it may remain unclear to what extent these factors have played a role in causing the disorder(s) in this particular case. Therefore, clinicians should be extremely cautious in explaining to parents why the disorder(s) developed in their child. Instead, a more general framework about etiology may be presented in which a distinction is made between factors that may have played a role in the initiation of the disorder(s) and factors that probably play a role in its/their maintenance. The factors that play a role in the maintenance of the disorder(s) will be the targets of interventions; the factors that played a role in initiating it or them many years ago will not. Thus, in the case formulation, the assessment report, and in the discussion of the assessment with the parents, priority will be given to the factors that maintain the disorder(s) above those that may have played an initiating role, as the former will determine the intervention(s) proposed to the parents and the child or adolescent. A distinction should also be made between proximal factors, such as inconsistent discipline, and distal risk factors, such as marital disharmony, and between modifiable and stable factors. Finally, strengths in the youth (e.g., acknowledgment of misbehavior), in the parents (e.g., agreement about managing their child's misbehavior) and in the school (e.g., good cooperation with the parents) should be acknowledged for they are important for treatment as well.

Treatment Plan

Four evidence-based intervention methods, and their combination, are discussed: behavioral parent training, cognitive behavioral therapy, multisystem intervention, and pharmacotherapy (see Chapters 25 to 28 for a full overview of the individual treatment programs for the disruptive behavior disorders). Here we give an outline of the decision the clinician needs to make with respect to the selection of interventions, depending on the age of the child (preschool age or school-age children and adolescents), the presence of ADHD, and the severity of the symptoms.

In preschool children with ODD or CD without ADHD comorbidity the treatment consists of behavioral parent training. In preschool children with ODD or CD with ADHD comorbidity behavioral parent training is proposed as a first step. Starting a trial with psychostimulants is indicated in severe forms of ODD or CD comorbid with ADHD that do not respond to behavioral parent training.

In school-aged children with ODD or CD without ADHD comorbidity one may start with behavioral parent training and add cognitive behavior therapy when symptoms and impairment are severe or when the effect of behavioral parent training is insufficient. When youth do not respond to these methods and still manifest severe physical aggression, pharmacotherapy is indicated, either with psychostimulants (or atomoxetine) or, for a limited time, one of the antipsychotic medications.

In adolescents with ODD or CD without ADHD comorbidity one may start with a multisystem intervention. When youth do not respond to these methods and still manifest severe physical aggression, pharmacotherapy is indicated, either with psychostimulants (or atomoxetine) or, for a limited time, one of the antipsychotic medications.

In school-age children and adolescents with ODD or CD and ADHD comorbidity behavioral parent training or a multisystem intervention is indicated and psychostimulants or atomoxetine are added when the impairment associated with ADHD is severe. Cognitive behavior therapy may be added for children either when symptoms and impairment associated with ODD or CD are severe or when the effect of behavioral parent training is insufficient. When youth do not respond to these methods and still manifest severe physical aggression, pharmacotherapy is indicated with one of the antipsychotic medications, for a limited time.

School interventions are often are needed for children of all ages with a view to managing disruptive behavior and improving underachievement. Most children and adolescents may be treated in outpatient settings or by school-based mental health clinicians. However, when the combination of the above-mentioned methods is not effective because of the severity of the disorder(s) or when there are severe barriers to outpatient treatment attendance and adherence, then day treatment or inpatient/residential treatment is indicated. These settings, when compared with the outpatient setting, offer more opportunities to integrate the various interventions discussed above.

Discussion of Diagnosis and Treatment Plan with the Parents, and Use of Psychoeducation in Order to Improve Treatment Engagement

The diagnosis and the proposed treatment plan are discussed with the parents and the youth. Information parents may have gathered from the media, especially from the Internet, may become part of this discussion. This information sometimes engenders extremely negative biases about ODD and CD. Parents, for example, may assume that negative outcomes such as delinquency and substance use disorders are an inescapable future for their child. In addition, ODD and CD are still thought of as the result of bad parenting only while the active role played by the child or adolescent in the onset of ODD and CD is often ignored. Thus, it is necessary to give accurate general information as regards our present knowledge of the etiology and outcome of ODD and CD; this is called psychoeducation.

Use of psychoeducation helps to address barriers to treatment engagement. It is more important to focus on the youth, family, and other environmental factors that probably play a role in the *maintenance* of the disorder(s), rather than factors likely involved in the *development* of the disorder(s), because the maintaining factors will be the targets of intervention. Thus, it should be made clear that an indication of behavioral parent training does not imply that inappropriate parenting actually caused the onset of ODD and CD; instead discussion should focus on how improving the parents' skills will change the behavior of their child while inappropriate parenting would be likely to maintain the child's misbehavior. Similarly, deviant social cognitions probably did not cause the youth's disorders(s) but have developed over the years and thus have come to play a role in the maintenance of the disorder(s). Cognitive behavior therapy targets these deviant social cognitions and improving these skills will likely result in behavioral change.

When discussing specific treatment methods with parents and youth, clinicians should be prepared to encounter barriers. Some parents of children diagnosed with ODD or CD may not accept that they themselves should invest in treatment (behavioral parent training) while the child or adolescent is left out of it. To motivate parents, the distinction may be made between ordinary parenting that is good enough for "typical" youth and the additional parenting qualities (e.g., praising the "positive opposites" of inappropriate behaviors, using mild punishment procedures for inappropriate behaviors, stress-management in the parents) needed for youth with ODD or CD. Participating in behavioral parent training for parents is easier to accept when the youth is also involved in treatment (cognitive behavior therapy). Thus, the parents' and the youth's engagement in treatment, and their motivation to attend and adhere to treatment, are important issues to assess when the proposed treatment plan is discussed (see Chapter 24 for more discussion of treatment engagement).

Finally, when discussing with the parents the possible outcome of the disorder(s) in their child, clinicians should be reluctant to give a prognosis as so many factors are involved in the outcome. Instead, the various factors involved in the outcome may be discussed as well as the need to target these factors (e.g., supervision, appropriate education).

Conclusion

In this chapter, we have presented important considerations in the clinical assessment of children and adolescents. The assessment process involves a series of steps in which clinicians gather information from multiple informants (e.g., parents, the child/adolescent, teachers) through multiple methods (e.g., questionnaires, standardized measures, interviews, observations) to formulate diagnoses, etiological impressions, and treatment recommendations. It is important for clinicians to conduct the evaluation process thoroughly yet efficiently, so that an adequate understanding of contributing factors (particularly those that are modifiable and proximal) is reached in a timely manner. Clinicians need to give consideration to differential and comorbid diagnoses, and to confirm diagnostic impressions by careful validation of diagnostic criteria. Informants may give conflicting information about the presence of a given symptom, requiring the clinician's clinical judgment to determine whether the criterion has been met. The evaluation process also includes development of a case formulation outlining risk and protective factors involved in the development and maintenance of the disorder(s). Maintaining factors are often natural targets for intervention, as in the case of behavioral parent training. Other treatments for ODD and CD include cognitive behavioral therapy, multisystem intervention and, when comorbidity with ADHD is present or when there are problems with severe aggression, medication trials.

References

Abidin, R. R. (1990). *Parenting stress index: Manual* (3rd ed.). Charlottesville, VA: Pediatric Psychology Press.

Achenbach, T. M., & Rescorla, L. A. (2000). *Manual for the ASEBA preschool forms and profiles*. Burlington, VT: ASEBA.

Achenbach, T. M., & Rescorla, L. A. (2001). *Manual for the ASEBA school age forms and profiles*. Burlington, VT: ASEBA.

Ambrosini, P. J. (2000). Historical development and present status of the schedule for affective disorders and schizophrenia for school-age children (K-SADS). *Journal of the American Academy of Child and Adolescent Psychiatry, 39,* 49–58.

American Psychiatric Association (2013). *Diagnostic and statistical manual of mental disorders* (5th ed., DSM-5). Washington, DC: Author.

Angold, A. (2002). Diagnostic interviews with parents and children. In M. Rutter and E. Taylor (Eds.), *Child and adolescent psychiatry* (pp. 32–51). Oxford: Blackwell.

Angold, A., & Costello, E. J. (2000). The child and adolescent psychiatric assessment (CAPA). *Journal of the American Academy of Child and Adolescent Psychiatry, 39,* 39–48.

Arseneault, L., Kim-Cohen, J., Taylor, A., Caspi, A., & Moffitt, T. E. (2005). Psychometric evaluation of 5- and 7-year-old children's self-reports of conduct problems. *Journal of Abnormal Child Psychology, 33,* 537–550.

Bailey, A. (2002). Physical examination and medical investigations. In M. J. Rutter, D. Bishop, D. Pine, S. Scott, J. S. Stevenson, E. A. Taylor, & A. Thapar (Eds.), *Rutter's child and adolescent psychiatry* (5th ed., pp. 141–160). Malden, MA: Blackwell.

Baird, G., & Gringras, P. (2008). Physical examination and medical investigation. In M. J. Rutter, D. Bishop, D. Pine, S. Scott, J. S. Stevenson, E. A. Taylor, & A. Thapar (Eds.) *Rutter's child and adolescent psychiatry* (5th ed., pp. 317–335). Malden, MA: Blackwell.

Bunte, T. L., Schoemaker, K., Hessen, D. J., van der Heijden, P. G. M., & Matthys, W. (2013). Clinical usefulness of the Kiddie-Disruptive Behavior Disorder Schedule in the diagnosis of DBD and ADHD in preschool children. *Journal of Abnormal Child Psychology, 41,* 681–690.

Charman, T., Hood, J., & Howlin, P. (2008). Psychological assessment in a clinical context. In M. J. Rutter, D. Bishop, D. Pine, S. Scott, J. S. Stevenson, E. A. Taylor, & A. Thapar, (Eds.) *Rutter's child and adolescent psychiatry* (5th ed., pp. 299–316). Malden, MA: Blackwell.

Collett, B. R., Ohan, J. L., & Myers, K. M. (2003). Ten-year review of rating scales. VI: Scales assessing externalizing behaviors. *Journal of the American Academy of Child & Adolescent Psychiatry, 42,* 1143–1170.

Conners, C. K. (1997). *Conners' rating scales-revised: Technical manual.* North Tonawanda, NY: Multi-Health Systems.

Dodge, K. A., & Coie, J. D. (1987). Social-information-processing factors in reactive and proactive aggression in children's peer groups. *Journal of Personality and Social Psychology, 53*(6), 1146–1158.

Dodge, K. A., McClasky, C. L., & Feldman, E. (1985). Situational approach to the assessment of social competence in children. *Journal of Consulting and Clinical Psychology, 53,* 344–353.

Egger, H. L., Erkanli, A., Keeler, G., Potts, E., Walter, B. K., & Angold, A. (2006). Test-retest reliability of the preschool age psychiatric assessment (PAPA). *Journal of the American Academy of Child and Adolescent Psychiatry, 45,* 538–549.

Ezpeleta, L., de la Osa, N., Granero, R., Penelo, E., & Domenech, J. M. (2013). Inventory of callous-unemotional traits in a community sample of preschoolers. *Journal of Clinical Child & Adolescent Psychology, 42,* 91–105.

Frick, P. J. (1991). *The Alabama parenting questionnaire.* University of Alabama, Author. Retrieved from https://cyfar.org/sites/default/files/PsychometricsFiles/Parenting%20Questionnaire-Alabama%20(parents%20of%20children%206-18)_0.pdf

Frick, P. J., & Hare, R. D. (2001). *The antisocial process screening device.* Toronto: Multi-Health Systems.

Goodman, R. (1997). The strengths and difficulties questionnaire: A research note. *Journal of Child Psychology and Psychiatry, 38*(5), 581–586.

Goodman, R., & Scott, S. (2005). *Child psychiatry.* Oxford: Blackwell.

Gresham, F. M., & Elliott, S. N. (1990). *The social skills rating system.* Circle Pines, MN: American Guidance Service.

Hinshaw, S. P. (1992). Externalizing behavior problems and academic underachievement in children and adolescents: Causal relationships and underlying mechanisms. *Psychological Bulletin, 111,* 127–155.

Jensen, P., Roper, M., Fisher, P., Piacentini, J., Canino, G., Richters, J., . . . Rae, D. (1995). Test-retest reliability of the diagnostic interview schedule for children (DISC 2.1): Parent, child, and combined algorithms. *Archives of General Psychiatry, 52*(1), 61–71.

Keenan, K., Wakschlag, L. S., Danis, B., Hill, C., Humphries, M., Duax, J., & Donald, R. (2007). Further evidence of the reliability and validity of DSM-IV ODD and CD in preschool children. *Journal of the American Academy of Child and Adolescent Psychiatry, 46,* 457–468.

Kempes, M., Matthys, W., Maassen, G., van Goozen, S. H. M., & van Engeland, H. (2006). A parent questionnaire for distinguishing between reactive and proactive aggression in children. *European Child and Adolescent Psychiatry, 13,* 38–45.

Kimonis, E. R., Frick, P. J., Skeem, J., Marsee, M. A., Cruise, K., Muñoz, L. C., . . . Morris, A. S. (2008). Assessing callous-unemotional traits in adolescent offenders: Validation of the inventory of callous-unemotional traits. *Journal of the International Association of Psychiatry and Law, 31,* 241–252.

Lochman, J. E., Evans, S. C., Burke, J. D., Roberts, M. C., Fite, P. J., Reed, G. M., . . . Garralda, E. M. (2015). An empirically based alternative to DSM-5's disruptive mood dysregulation disorder for ICD-11. *World Psychiatry, 14,* 30–33.

Lord, C., Rutter, M., & LeCouteur, A. (1994). Autism diagnostic interview-revised: A revised version of a diagnostic interview for caregivers of individuals with possible pervasive developmental disorders. *Journal of Autism and Developmental Disorders, 24,* 659–685.

Lynam, D. R. (1997). Pursuing the psychopath: Capturing the fledging psychopath in a nomological net. *Journal of Abnormal Psychology, 116,* 155–165.

Matthys, W., Bunte, T., & Schoemaker, K. (2016). Oppositional defiant disorder and conduct disorder. In J. L. Luby (Ed.). *Handbook of preschool mental health: Development, disorders and treatment* (2nd ed.). New York, NY: Guilford Press.

Matthys, W., Maassen, G. H., Cuperus, J. M., & van Engeland, H. (2001). The assessment of the situational specificity of children's problem behaviour in peer-peer context. *Journal of Child Psychology and Psychiatry, 42,* 413–420.

Nock, M., & Kurtz, S. M. S. (2005). Direct observation in school settings: Bringing science to practice. *Cognitive and Behavioral Practice, 12,* 359–370.

Polman, H., Orobio de Castro, B., Thomaes, S. E., & Van Aken, M. A. G. (2009). New directions in measuring reactive and proactive aggression: Validation of a teacher questionnaire. *Journal of Abnormal Child Psychology, 37*(2), 183–193.

Reich, W. (2000). Diagnostic interview for children and adolescents (DICA). *Journal of the American Academy of Child and Adolescent Psychiatry, 39,* 59–66.

Reynolds, C. R., & Kamphaus, R. W. (2004). *Behavior assessment system for children–2.* Bloomington, MN: Pearson Assessments.

Rutter, M., & Taylor, E. (2008). Clinical assessment and diagnostic formulation. In M. J. Rutter, D. Bishop, D. Pine, S. Scott, J. S. Stevenson, E. A. Taylor, & A. Thapar, (Eds.) *Rutter's child and adolescent psychiatry* (5th ed., pp. 42–57). Malden, MA: Blackwell.

Shaffer, D., Fisher, P., Lucas, C. P., Dulcan, M. K., & Schwab-Stone, M. E. (2000). NIMH diagnostic interview schedule for children version IV (NIMH DISC-IV): Description, differences from previous versions and reliability of some common diagnoses. *Journal of the American Academy of Child and Adolescent Psychiatry, 39,* 28–38.

Shaffer, D., Gould, M. S., Brasic, J., Ambrosini, P., Fisher, P., Bird, H., & Aluwahlia, S. (1983). A children's global assessment scale (CGAS). *Archives of General Psychiatry, 40,* 1228–1231.

Sheeber, L., & Johnson, J. (1992). Applicability of the impact on family scale for assessing families with behaviorally difficult children. *Psychological Reports, 71,* 155–159.

Verhulst, F. C., & Van der Ende, J. (2008). Using rating scales in a clinical context. In M. J. Rutter, D. Bishop, D. Pine, S. Scott, J. S. Stevenson, E. A. Taylor, & A. Thapar, (Eds.) *Rutter's child and adolescent psychiatry* (5th ed., pp. 289–298). Malden, MA: Blackwell.

Wakschlag, L. S., Briggs-Gowan, M. J., Carter, A. S., Hill, C., Danis, B., Keenan, K., . . . Leventhal, B. L. (2007). A developmental framework for distinguishing disruptive behavior from normative misbehavior in preschool children. *Journal of Child Psychology and Psychiatry, 48,* 976–987.

Wakschlag, L. S., Briggs-Gowan, M. J., Choi, S. W., Nichols, S. R., Kestler, J., Burns, J. L., . . . Henry, D. (2014). Advancing a multidimensional, developmental spectrum approach to preschool disruptive behavior. *Journal of the American Academy of Child and Adolescent Psychiatry, 53,* 82–96.

Wakschlag, L. S., Briggs-Gowan, M. J., Hill, C., Danis, B., Leventhal, B. L., Keenan, K., . . . Carter, A. S. (2008). Observational assessment of preschool disruptive behavior, Part II: Validity of the disruptive behavior diagnostic schedule (DB-DOS). *Journal of the American Academy of Child and Adolescent Psychiatry, 47,* 632–641.

Wakschlag, L. S., Hill, C., Carter, A. S., Danis, B., Egger, H. L., Keenan, . . . Briggs-Gowan, M. J. (2008). Observational assessment of preschool disruptive behavior, Part I: Reliability of the disruptive behavior diagnostic observation schedule (DB-DOS). *Journal of the American Academy of Child and Adolescent Psychiatry, 47,* 622–631.

Webster-Stratton, C., Reid, M. J., & Hammond, M. (2001). Preventing conduct problems, promoting social competence: A parent and teacher training partnership in Head Start. *Journal of Clinical Child Psychology, 30,* 283–302.

Part 5
Treatment and Prevention

24

Engaging Families in Treatment for Child Behavior Disorders

A Synthesis of the Literature

Mary Acri, Anil Chacko, Geetha Gopalan, and Mary McKay

Oppositional Defiant Disorder (ODD) and Conduct Disorder (CD), which are part of the Disruptive Behavior Disorders (DBDs) diagnostic category, are chronic and impairing conditions associated with significant burden to children, their families, and society. Children living in poverty face up to four times the risk of the onset of a DBD compared to children of higher socioeconomic status (SES), mainly due to stressors associated with living in communities with scarce resources, violence, and crime. Efficacious treatments do exist, and many require the active collaboration of service providers with parents and adult caregivers in order to address serious child behavioral challenges. Unfortunately, there are many obstacles to the full engagement of parents and family members with participation in treatment, and families in poverty frequently experience multiple barriers. In this chapter, we synthesize the literature pertaining both to parental engagement in treatments for child DBDs, and to the importance of parental engagement for child treatment outcomes. In addition, we present a set of promising efforts to enhance engagement, particularly for those families who struggle with the challenges associated with poverty and chronic stress and who are least likely to utilize the current child mental health service system. We conclude with a review of future directions for practice.

Prevalence of Disruptive Behavior Disorders and Families at Risk

As described in Chapters 2 and 3 in this book, disruptive behavior disorders are among the most common of child mental health challenges; there is wide variation regarding their prevalence, with studies offering population figures ranging between 1% and 21% depending on geographic characteristics, child age, gender, and diagnostic tool. According to the DSM-5 (American Psychiatric Association [APA], 2013), males are more likely than females to present with ODD prior to adolescence, at a ratio of 1.4:1, and for CD, 1-year prevalence rates range from 2–20%, with higher prevalence rates reported for males. These gender differences increase in adulthood. Based on the National Comorbidity Survey Replication (Nock, Kazdin, Hiripi, & Kessler, 2006), for example, lifetime prevalence rates for CD among English-speaking adults in the US aged 18–44 were estimated at 9.5% (males, 12%; females, 7.1%), with a median age of onset at 11.6 years.

Family poverty is among the greatest risk factors for childhood externalizing behavior problems (Linver, Brooks-Gunn, & Kohen, 2002; Mistry, Vandewater, Huston, & McLoyd, 2002; National Institute of Child Health and Human Development Early Child Care Research Network, 2005; see also Chapter 16 in this book), at rates up to four times higher than among children of higher socioeconomic status (Ghandour, Kogan, Blumberg, Jones, & Perrin, 2012). Rates of disruptive, aggressive, and delinquent behavior have been found to be as high as 40% among economically disadvantaged populations (Bannon & McKay, 2007; Tolan & Henry, 2000).

The Relationship between Poverty and Child Disruptive Behavior Disorders

The development and maintenance of child behavioral difficulties have been associated with parenting challenges, including struggles to develop child management skills and disciplinary practices, difficulties related to family communication, child supervision and monitoring, and reduced positive parental involvement and warmth (Frick & Muñoz, 2006). Poverty is often linked to child behavioral difficulties because of its impact on caregivers, where chronic exposure to the adverse events and stressors that burden parents (e.g., economic stress, community violence, unemployment, inadequate housing, and/or limited health and mental health resources) increases the perception of stress and the reporting of depressive symptoms (Conger et al., 2002; Siefert, Finlayson, Williams, Delva, & Ismail, 2007). More specifically, parental depression has been associated with emotional preoccupation and reduced positive expression, increased use of coercive parenting and overreliance on physical discipline practices (Chronis, Chacko, Fabiano, Wymbs, & Pelham, 2004; Cummings & Davies, 1994; Feng, Shaw, Skuban, & Lane, 2007; Lovejoy, Graczyk, O'Hare, & Neuman, 2000). Heightened maternal stress and diminished social networks can interfere with the ability of caregivers to be comfortable, spontaneous, nurturing or responsive to their children (Evans, Boxhill, & Pinkava, 2008). This increases the caregiver's susceptibility to irritability and leads to the intensification of emotionally charged parent–child interactions (Kazdin & Whitley, 2003). As a result, low-income communities and their inherent stressors undermine parenting and the parent/child relationship, putting children at serious risk for externalizing behavior problems.

While parenting has a clear impact on child behavioral difficulties, poverty also exerts its influence through the multiple other hardships associated with impoverished or violence-impacted communities. These hardships include social isolation, lack of social support, housing and economic instability, elevated rates of community violence, and limited youth-centered support resources and mental health treatment options (Bell & Jenkins, 1993; Black & Krishnakumar, 1998; Evans, 2004; Gorman-Smith, Tolan, & Henry, 1999; Yoshikawa, Aber, & Beardslee, 2012). Consequently, it is not surprising that the impact of family risk factors is particularly magnified in poverty-impacted contexts (Beyers, Loeber, Wikstrom, & Stouthamer-Loeber, 2001; Burke, Loeber, & Birmaher, 2002; Grant et al., 2005). This underscores the urgency and importance of treating child behavioral difficulties by addressing family risk factors in low-income, resource-poor communities.

Treatments for DBDs and Parent Engagement

Parent training programs, which are also referred to as parent management training or Behavior Parent Training (BPT), are among the best studied and most efficacious treatments for DBDs (Brestan & Eyberg, 1998; see Chapters 26, 27, and 28 in this book for further explorations of evidence-based psychosocial intervention practices for DBDs from early childhood through adolescence). Developed in the 1960s, BPT draws on the theory, amply supported by research noted above, that parenting practices influence and can modify child behavior (Chacko et al., 2015; Jones et al., 2013). Within anywhere from 6 to 14 weekly sessions, depending on the program (clinical samples include cases involving up to 25 sessions), clinical staff model and teach parenting strategies for caregivers to implement, with the aim of decreasing their child's externalizing behavior problems and enhancing positive, prosocial behaviors (Chacko et al., 2015; Jones et al., 2013).

Parental engagement is considered essential to BPT treatments, either with or without the child present during sessions, depending on the program (Danko, Brown, Van Schoick, & Budd, 2016; Staudt, 2007). Engagement, also referred to as participation, involvement, and, if lacking, resistance, is categorized within the BPT literature as physical engagement, meaning initial and ongoing attendance at sessions, and behavioral and cognitive engagement in treatment.

Several studies of parental attendance at sessions and related therapeutic outcomes suggest that BPT is not as effective for families who drop out of treatment prematurely, compared to families who complete the course (Assenany & McIntosh, 2002; Prinz & Miller, 1994). However, the general consensus on session attendance is that, while it is a necessary prerequisite, it is not sufficient for therapeutic change (Haine-Schlagel & Walsh, 2015). Consequently, a growing area of inquiry covers the relationship between participation in the therapeutic process and child outcomes, with participation encompassing cognitive indicators of engagement (e.g., motivation to attend and to participate fully), and behavioral indicators, such as practicing and role-playing in session, and the completion of homework.

Some studies have examined these types of engagement separately, but behavioral and cognitive indicators of engagement are generally assumed to be related, and usually examined together. Haine-Schlagel and Walsh (2015) theorize that, along with seeking treatment, what they refer to as attitudinal engagement (e.g., motivation, perception of treatment as helpful) influences attendance and behavioral engagement. This theory has been supported, as attendance and participation in the therapeutic process have been shown to be interrelated. Prinz and Miller (1994), for example, found that families who dropped out of treatment prematurely were more dissatisfied with the therapeutic approach than those who completed it, while Danko et al. (2016) found that the relationship between treatment completion and behavioral indicators of participation, namely homework completion, approached significance, in that families who completed treatment were also more likely to have completed homework between sessions. Moreover, Chacko, Feirsen, Rajwan, Wymbs and Wymbs (2017), found that parents who dropped out of treatment were more likely to perceive the treatment as less helpful than those who completed it. In addition, He, Gewirtz, Lee, Morrell, and August (2016) found that families who were given a choice as to whether to receive parent training or the usual services, and where to receive the intervention (e.g., in the home vs. the clinic), were more likely to be retained in treatment, suggesting that parents' preference may influence attendance, retention, and completion.

Treatment Engagement Difficulties for Poverty-Affected Families

Despite the elevated levels of need and the risk of child behavioral difficulties in families residing in poverty-affected communities, data indicate that these families are particularly unlikely to attend child mental health services. No-show rates for initial intake appointments in urban, low-income communities range from 48% to 62% (McKay & Bannon, 2004), and most families only remain in treatment, on average, for three to four sessions, with up to

60% of families nationwide reported to have terminated treatment prematurely (Gopalan et al., 2010). By the end of a 12-week course of treatment, less than one-tenth of families who initiate services in urban, low-income settings remain (McKay, Lynn, & Bannon, 2005).

There are a number of reasons why families living in poverty-impacted communities have substantial difficulties in engaging with and participating throughout the treatment process. As indicated earlier, families struggle to manage numerous, often concurrent stressors. This chronic strain becomes debilitating, limiting the resources and motivation needed to seek and maintain treatment or to follow through with treatment instructions (Harrison, McKay, & Bannon, 2004; Leslie, Aarons, Haine, & Hough, 2007; Thompson et al., 2007). Logistical barriers include insufficient time, lack of transportation and child care, conflicting commitments, community violence, and extensive agency waiting lists (McKay & Bannon, 2004). However, research also demonstrates that parental perceptions of treatment are far more formidable barriers to service utilization than logistical factors (Kazdin, Holland, & Crowley, 1997). For example, weak therapeutic alliance, little perceived need for treatment, and negative expectations of therapy and the therapeutic process all impact on engagement (Chacko et al., 2017; Kazdin et al., 1997; Kerkorian, McKay, & Bannon, 2006; MacNaughton & Rodrigue, 2001; Nock & Kazdin, 2001). Often, ethnocultural beliefs, such as how mental health disorders are caused, for example, or the conviction that parents should overcome difficulties on their own rather than seeking outside help, can pose further barriers to seeking help and maintaining treatment (McCabe, 2002; Snowden, 2001; Yeh et al., 2005). For adolescents, barriers to seeking and maintaining mental health treatment include anticipating stigma from others and fears of being labeled (Boldero & Fallon, 1995; Yeh, McCabe, Hough, Dupuis, & Hazen, 2003), as well as insufficient knowledge about the need for treatment, how services can be beneficial, and how the treatment process actually works (Goldstein, Olfson, Martens, & Wolk, 2006).

The Need to Engage with Support Services

There has been a significant history of efforts to identify strategies to improve engagement with interventions and to study them empirically. In this section we focus on methods to improve engagement in both prevention and treatment, and studies that have attempted to improve engagement by families at high risk. It is important to note that engagement is a continuous process with key phases (pretreatment; ongoing treatment) and key outcomes (attendance, adherence). We review the literature on these areas below.

Preparing parents for treatment is essential; approximately 25% of parents who are eligible for BPT never enroll, and, of those who initially attend, almost half drop out after the first session (Chacko et al., 2016). Low rates of parent attendance also constitute a challenge for research into intervention with these children, often leading to creative efforts to address dosage in outcome analyses (Lochman, Boxmeyer, Powell, Roth, & Windle, 2006). As suggested in recent practice-based reviews of this literature (e.g., Axford, Lehtonen, Kaoukji, Tobin, & Berry, 2012), efforts to improve initial enrollment in prevention-focused BPT should include collaboration and the development of relationships between BPT providers and key stakeholders who interface with the target population, such as educators and community-leaders. In particular, BPT must be fully integrated into routine service settings. This will require clear recruitment efforts and multiple opportunities for families to enroll in BPT; it will need to include recruiters with the training and interpersonal skills to identify barriers to family involvement, who can frame BPT in language that resonates with the needs of parents. Flexible scheduling of BPT is required to increase accessibility. "Accessibility promotion" (Becker et al., 2015; Lindsey et al., 2014), that is, strategies to make services convenient and accessible (e.g., weekend sessions, child care, financial support for transportation), must be carefully considered. To disseminate BPT on a broader scale in order to meet its intended goals, initial enrollment must be more carefully promoted, documented, and systematically evaluated.

There have been several efforts to increase initial engagement, primarily in prevention studies, through methods such as monetary incentives programs (Heinrichs, 2006). However, these methods have had limited impact on parents' ongoing engagement. Some data also suggests that the format of treatment (e.g., group vs. individual) has no effect on enrollment, although other studies suggest that group-based formats implemented in the community enroll more of the families who are traditionally at higher risk for poor engagement (Cunningham et al., 2000). Families from ethnic-minority, lower SES backgrounds may perceive groups as less stigmatizing and allowing more social support from peers. These perceptions may influence preference for group-based formats, particularly in community-based settings.

There has been a growing emphasis on understanding the role of more malleable factors related to engagement in treatment. Two important factors related to poor engagement, namely practical/perceived barriers to treatment and parental cognitions (attribution for their child's behavior; perceived parenting competency; expectations for treatment) have begun to receive particular attention in the literature (Chacko et al., 2017; Chronis et al., 2004; Ingoldsby, 2010; Morrissey-Kane & Prinz, 1999; Nock & Ferriter, 2005). Based on the seminal work of Kazdin and colleagues (e.g., Kazdin, Holland, & Crowley, 1997; Kazdin, Holland, Crowley, & Brenton, 1997), practical and perceived barriers to treatment have been found to be predictive of engagement in BPT and to contribute to dropout rates even after other familial, parental, and child variables have been controlled for (e.g., single-parent status, SES). According to the barriers to treatment model, perceived parental barriers fall into four domains: (1) experience of stressors and obstacles (e.g., conflict with significant others), (2) relationship with the clinician (including perceived lack of support from, and disclosure to, the therapist), (3) treatment relevance, and (4) treatment demands. Perceived relevance of treatment was found to be the best factor discriminating between treatment dropouts and treatment completers, suggesting that parental perception are an important target prior to initiating BPT.

Parental attributions have also been shown to be related to engagement in BPT (Morrissey-Kane & Prinz, 1999). Research has shown that some parents of children with ADHD are more likely to attribute the causes of their child's behavior to enduring symptoms of the disorder and therefore to factors beyond the child's control (Johnston & Freeman, 1997). These parents manifest a lower level of acceptance of interventions such as BPT that emphasize improving child behavior through altering contingencies in the environment (Johnston, Mah, & Regambal, 2010). Parents who assume more responsibility for their child's behavior are more likely to engage with and complete BPT (Chacko et al., 2017; Peters, Calam, & Harrington, 2005). It also appears that, in order to find interventions focused on parenting behaviors acceptable, parents must feel some competence in their own parenting efficacy: both Chacko et al., (2017) and Johnston, Mah, and Regambal (2010) have demonstrated that mothers' parenting efficacy is significantly and positively correlated with engagement and/or the acceptability of BPT. Finally, parental expectations also play a key role in a parent's willingness to participate in treatment. Studies have found that parent's inaccurate expectations regarding the content, format, and process of treatment, as well as of the potency, rate, and expected course of therapeutic benefit/change, are all related to premature termination from BPT (Morissey-Kane, & Prinz, 1999; Nock & Kazdin, 2001).

There have been notable efforts to prepare parents for treatment by addressing these attributions. In particular, the effective assessment of the strengths, needs, and goals of both children and parents appears to improve initial enrollment and attendance as well as ongoing engagement (Becker et al., 2015 Chacko et al., 2009; Chacko, Wymbs, Chimiklis, Wymbs, &

Pelham, 2012; Lindsey et al., 2014; McKay, McCadam, & Gonzales, 1996; McKay, Nudelman, McCadam, & Gonzales, 1996). Psychoeducation—that is, informing parents about the content, process, roles of participants and expectations of treatment—also appears to improve initial engagement. Services should, therefore, adopt these relatively low-cost and minimally intensive (in terms of time and effort) methods to prepare parents for BPT; written or audio-visual materials that describe the content and process of BPT as well as how parents are involved during the training, can be developed and offered. However, a one-time discussion of these issues is likely to be insufficient (Chacko et al., 2009); these themes typically need to be revisited throughout therapy.

Addressing practical barriers to engagement at the time of intake is effective in improving initial engagement (Chacko et al., 2009; McKay et al., 1996a, 1996b). In addition, asking parents open-ended questions about their expectations concerning their involvement in treatment (e.g., What role do you think you will have in treatment?), their expectations for the rate and potency of treatment-related improvements for their child (e.g., How fast do you expect to observe improvements in your child's behavior? How much of an improvement do you expect you and your child to make during the course of treatment?), and about their attributions regarding the locus of control of their child's behavior and the effect of their parenting (e.g., What do you think causes your child to misbehave? Do you believe your parenting can make a difference in the way your child behaves?) can enhance parental engagement. These questions are intended to open a dialogue between the therapist and parent(s) that attempts to clarify the reasons for seeking treatment, and allows parents to appreciate the rationale, the course, and expected outcomes of treatment. This in turns helps to develop parental motivation, to anticipate the common challenges experienced by parents, to develop and implement a plan to address common barriers, and to begin the process of building a therapeutic alliance. It is likely that assessment, psychoeducation, and addressing barriers increases engagement by improving family–therapist allegiance (although, to our knowledge, this has not been empirically evaluated) and by preparing families for the process of treatment.

Several initiatives have been successful in reducing both initial and ongoing BPT attrition rates. As with studies reporting low levels of recruitment attrition, the vast majority of studies reporting significantly attenuated initial and ongoing BPT dropout do not provide explicit information about the methods utilized to achieve this improvement. A small number of studies do, however, offer some important insights. For example, Chacko et al. (2009) used various methods to engage parents actively in understanding how BPT matched their current needs, to clarify their expectations regarding the content, process and expected benefits from BPT, and to find solutions to practical obstacles to attendance (e.g., child care, transportation). In a randomized controlled trial, they found that these additional approaches led to a significant improvement in attrition prior to the start of BPT (2%) compared to families who did not receive these additional approaches (30%). In another study, Martinez, Lau, Chorpita, and Weisz (2015) reported that psychoeducation in early phases of treatment (i.e., discussing causes of problems and describing the rationale for treatment) in addition to other engagement strategies (e.g., collaborative goal-setting, managing expectations) predicted parent engagement in treatment.

A further set of studies suggest that ongoing attendance can be improved by utilizing multiple methods to address barriers to participation, to ensure readiness to participate in treatment, and to provide parents with skills in problem solving and coping (Chacko et al., 2009; 2012; Cunningham, Bremner, & Secord, 1998; Kazdin & Whitley, 2003; Nock & Kazdin, 2005; Prinz & Miller, 1994). For example, the Family Check-Up intervention (FCU; Sitnick et al., 2014) starts with a comprehensive ecological inquiry into, and assessment of, parental concerns, followed by feedback sessions utilizing motivational interviewing techniques to enhance parents' readiness to change. If parents are interested in follow-up treatment, clinicians provide instruction in family management skills (see Chapter 19 for further information on how the FCU can be integrated into typical treatment). Nock and Kazdin (2005) implemented enhancements to address practical barriers to treatment, maladaptive cognitions, and motivation for treatment during the course of individually administered BPT. Their study reports how the enhancement intervention was implemented in three individual sessions, interspersed throughout BPT. The enhancement sessions consisted of the therapist eliciting self-motivational statements to improve attributions in parents (e.g., "What steps can you take to help change your child's behavior?"). Therapists also inquired about practical barriers to participation and assisted parents in removing them. Results showed that, compared to the basic BPT group, families in the enhanced BPT group attended treatment more reliably. All in all, it appears that approaches that focus on preparing parents for BPT, addressing practical barriers to engagement, assisting in aligning parent's involvement with their own goals for treatment, and providing parents with skills to manage their own problems/stressors can significantly affect initial and ongoing BPT attendance.

Initiatives have also attempted to improve outcomes (including engagement) by utilizing adjunctive treatments to address other areas of parental functioning, including targeting parental depression (Chronis-Tuscano et al., 2013; Sanders & McFarland, 2001), parental isolation (Dadds & McHugh, 1992), or multiple factors such as skills relating to communication and self-control (Sanders, Markie-Dadds, Tully, & Bor, 2000; Webster-Stratton, 1994). In general, these studies do not show incremental benefits for engagement, but it is important to note that engagement outcomes were not uniformly assessed in these studies; it is possible that utilizing these adjunctive treatments may have resulted in improvements in engagement.

There are very few studies that report between- and within-session engagement; of those, even fewer discuss methods designed explicitly to improve this aspect of engagement (Chacko et al., 2016). Interestingly, studies that report higher levels of between- and within-session engagement suggest that addressing practical barriers to between-session engagement (e.g., homework completion) and explicitly discussing the purpose and goals of homework can improve attendance (Chacko et al., 2009; Nock & Kazdin, 2005).

Future Directions

We conclude this chapter by presenting a set of promising initiatives with the potential to enhance engagement, particularly for families who are at highest risk for DBDs, yet are the least likely to access mental health services.

Consumer-Driven Approaches

One method that may prove beneficial is the application of consumer-driven methods for ascertaining preferences in terms of the parameters and goals of BPT. This field often uses small focus groups, whose members are considered "exemplars," and whose input is used to develop interventions. The approach offers significant advantages, but the assumption is that these individuals' opinions represent the larger population and that, often enough, only one type of intervention needs to be developed. This may not be the case. By analogy, in product development, there are often different types of a particular product that represent the preferences of segments of the population (e.g., there are approximately 40 different pasta sauces made by Prego© that vary based on price, flavor, etc.). As with most products, different consumers prefer different sauces. In order to identify the preferences for different segments of a population, systematic input from various potential consumers will be needed. Reliance on focus groups may miss the preferences of key segments of a population.

Nonetheless, the emergent use of consumer research methods for the development of children's mental health services and interventions may have particular relevance for understanding engagement. Wymbs et al. (2015), for example, utilized a consumer preference method (in this case, discrete-choice experiments) to examine how parental preferences a format of treatment (group vs. individual) influenced participation in BPT. Data suggested that parents preferred individual (58.7%) to group-based (19.4%) BPT, with further data suggesting that parents also have different preferences as regards the goals of BPT (e.g., acquisition of information and understanding vs. active skill development and problem solving). This study highlights the potential of utilizing parent preference in the development and implementation of BPT as a function of population and setting. Future studies using consumer preference methods to explore choice on the basis of key factors (e.g., family/child demographics, presenting problem, setting of intervention) may allow for a more systematic evaluation of these factors and their relationship with engagement. This line of inquiry may ultimately prove useful in tailoring/matching BPT more closely to the needs of different families and children.

Mobile Health Strategies

Smartphone technology has facilitated recent advances in mobile health ("mHealth") strategy; soon there may be opportunities to capture real-time, ongoing data, on a large scale, to understand, and ultimately to support, better engagement in BPT (Chacko, Isham, Cleek, & McKay, 2016; Mohr, Burns, Schueller, Clarke, & Klinkman, 2013). Mobile phones offer increasingly novel methods of interfacing with treatment recipients, through features available on smartphones such as camera/video/voice recording, Internet access, global positioning, and bio-sensing technology. Specifically, mHealth applications can be used to facilitate the systematic, periodic assessment of factors (i.e., the ongoing perceived and practical barriers) that often impede engagement with BPT (Kazdin & Wassell, 2000); to offer initial opportunities to educate parents about BPT (e.g., to provide psychoeducation through written/audio/visual materials, which can be accessed on demand based on parents' schedules); and to provide reminders about sessions and homework implementation. These methods may be particularly helpful during the early stages of the engagement process, allowing families an opportunity to understand the content, process and the potential benefits of BPT more clearly, as well as allowing BPT developers and therapists a better understanding of which families might benefit from BPT but are at higher risk of not enrolling. As in other areas, such as substance use (see Gustafson et al., 2011), mHealth applications may provide a unique opportunity to capture ongoing information which can be used to develop predictive models and thereby permit clinicians to intervene immediately throughout the BPT process, to improve engagement.

Peer Support

Increasingly present within the child mental health service system are a new cadre of professionals who possess the shared/lived experience of being consumers of the child mental health system. Parent peer support partners (PPSPs) are caregivers who have had personal experience of caring for a child with a mental health difficulty (Hoagwood et al., 2009; Obrochta et al., 2011; Olin et al., 2014). Programs utilizing PPSPs are proliferating across the US, helping other families to navigate the mental health service system, linking them to other support systems, coordinating care, and ensuring substantial family involvement in treatment (Hoagwood et al., 2009; Jensen & Hoagwood, 2008; Obrochta et al., 2011; Olin et al., 2014). Because of their unique personal experience, PPSPs often engender greater credibility and trust among caregivers than traditional professionals and, as a result, they are seen as an important resource to help families become more actively engaged in the treatment process (Gopalan, Acri, Lalayants, Hooley, & Einbinder, 2014; Hoagwood et al., 2008; Koroloff, Elliott, Koren, & Friesen, 1994; Robbins et al., 2008). There is also evidence that the use of PPSP support increases the likelihood that caregivers will seek mental health services for their children (Koroloff, Elliott, Koren, & Friesen, 1996; Kutash, Duchnowski, Green, & Ferron, 2011; Kutash et al., 2013).

Likewise, youth peers may be young adults who have had prior mental health challenges and service experiences and can provide support, education, advocacy, and guidance to youth who are currently struggling with mental health difficulties (Roussos, Berger, & Harrison, 2008). Programs utilizing youth peers have reported high program satisfaction levels (Klodnick et al., 2015; Radigan, Wang, Chen, & Xiang, 2014), and increased engagement in program activities (Geenen et al., 2013; Philips, Oca, Geenan, & Powers, 2013; Powers et al., 2001; Powers et al., 2012).

The 4Rs and 2Ss Program for Strengthening Families

The 4Rs and 2Ss program for strengthening families (4R2S) is an evidence-based, manualized, family-based treatment targeting children aged 7–11 with disruptive behaviors (Chacko et al., 2015; Franco, Dean-Assael, & McKay, 2008; Gopalan et al., 2015; McKay, Gonzales, Quintana, Kim, & Abdul-Adil, 1999; McKay, Harrison, Gonzales, Kim, & Quintana, 2002; McKay et al., 2011). Recently listed in the Substance Abuse and Mental Health Services Administration (SAMHSA) National Registry of Evidence-based Programs and Practices (see http://nrepp.samhsa.gov/ProgramProfile.aspx?id=41), the 4R2S intervention aims to improve engagement outcomes among low-income, predominantly minority families with children manifesting ODD and CD.

In this model, 6–8 families meet in a series of 16 weekly group sessions focused on addressing key family and parenting factors linked to the development and persistence of behavioral difficulties (e.g., inconsistent discipline, strained parent-child relationships, family disorganization, and dysfunctional family communication; Lanza, Rhoades, Nix, Greenberg, & Conduct Problems Prevention Research Group, 2010; Montague, Cavendish, Enders, & Dietz, 2010; Patterson, Reid, & Dishion, 1992; Patterson, Crosby, & Vuchinich, 1992). At the same time, session content addresses important factors known to hinder engagement and retention in treatment among vulnerable families (e.g., lack of social support, high stress levels; Kazdin & Whitley, 2003; Wahler & Dumas, 1989). At each session, families are provided with a meal, free childcare, and transportation expenses, in order to obviate some of the most common logistical barriers to utilizing child mental health services (McKay & Bannon, 2004). Moreover, common perceptual barriers, such as stigma and the fear of being blamed for children's difficulties, are targeted through group processes which normalize family difficulties, validate families' existing expertise in solving problems, and promote mutual aid among families in order to maximize change (Gopalan & Franco, 2009). Finally, the 4R2S model also encourages the use of parent peer support partners as co-facilitators, taking advantage of the unique peer ability to build relationships with other parents (Frame, Conley, & Berrick, 2006).

Evaluations of the 4R2S model indicate its superior ability to engage low-income, minority families in child mental health services compared to traditional engagement styles. In one study of 138 children with behavioral difficulties and their families, families receiving the 4R2S intervention attended an average of 7 sessions, compared to an average of 3–4 sessions for treatment as usual during the 16-week intervention period (McKay et al., 2002). A larger-scale effectiveness study (n = 320) demonstrated that families receiving 4R2S intervention attended 59% of sessions on average, compared to "typical" families who dropped out after 25% of sessions with interventions of the same length. Such findings underscore the ability of 4R2S to elicit relatively high rates of attendance (Chacko et al., 2015).

The 4R2S model has also been shown to be particularly good at engaging high-risk families, such as those involved in the child welfare system, who are often significantly harder to engage than families without child welfare involvement (Lau & Weisz, 2003). In addition to the typical logistical and perceptual barriers that hinder engagement with child mental health treatment for low-income families, families involved in child welfare services also struggle with additional multiple, concurrent stressors (e.g., poverty, housing instability, parental mental illness and/or substance abuse, domestic violence; Kemp, Marcenko, Hoagwood, & Vesneski, 2009). These families are often mandated to services that they may not identify themselves as requiring (Dawson & Berry, 2002; Rooney, 2009); they may have had prior negative experiences with formal service providers that inhibit future help-seeking (Kemp et al., 2009; Kerkorian et al., 2006; Palmer, Maiter, & Manji, 2006). However, in spite of the fact that families involved in child welfare services report a greater number of barriers to accessing child mental health services than those families not involved in child welfare services, Gopalan et al. (2011) found no differences in rates of attendance between the two groups when both received the 4R2S intervention. Child welfare-involved caregivers receiving the 4R2S intervention indicated that their experiences within the group promoted their retention within the program; these experiences included the opportunity to receive much-needed information, a reduction in isolation, shame, and stigma, participation in a fun and interactive atmosphere, as well as encouragement from their children to attend sessions (Gopalan, Fuss, & Wisdom, 2015).

Training Intervention for the Engagement of Families

The last model examined here, the Training Intervention for the Engagement of Families (TIES), involves educating mental health professionals in regard to the common barriers faced by families. Providers are further trained in specific skills for overcoming barriers at two different stages of accessing child mental health services. The first intervention focuses on engaging families who have made initial phone contact to set up an intake appointment (McKay, McCadam, & Gonzales, 1996a). At this initial phone contact, providers focus on four goals: (1) clarifying the caregiver's concern about the child's mental health need (e.g., Why are you here? Why now? What does your family need); (2) enhancing the caregiver's sense of investment and self-efficacy (e.g., reinforcing what they have done well); (3) identifying attitudes relating to previous service experiences (e.g., previous attempts to seek treatment; expectations, concerns, hopes); and (4) working with caregivers to resolve existing barriers to accessing treatment services (e.g., lack of transportation, conflicts with other time commitments, child care problems). Compared to families randomly assigned to receive the usual telephone intake procedure (45%), a significantly higher percentage (73%) of families receiving the new telephone engagement strategy attended the first appointment or called to reschedule (McKay et al., 1996a).

The second stage of accessing child mental health services focuses on the face-to-face intake session (McKay, Nudelman, McCadam, & Gonzales, 1996b). At this point in the process, providers are trained in a second engagement strategy aimed at increasing overall treatment retention by addressing expectations of treatment and engaging family members to help in the process. The goals of the second intervention involve: (1) providing a breakdown of the intake process, the service options, and the specific roles of providers and agency staff; (2) establishing a relationship in which providers and family members work together to achieve goals; (3) ascertaining which tangible and practical family needs can be met right away; and (4) collaborating with family members on strategies to resolve any impediments to continued involvement in treatment. In a randomized controlled study, significantly more families who received the first intake TIES engagement returned for the next appointment and attended more treatment sessions overall, compared to families receiving the clinical comparison condition (McKay et al., 1996b).

Conclusion

In summary, collaboration and full participation on the part of parents and adult caregivers appear to be key to addressing the serious behavioral health concerns of children. However, the successful engagement of parents with evidence-based approaches such as BPT has often proven challenging. There is a robust literature exploring many of the factors that influence initial and ongoing engagement, as well as the completion of treatment. These factors are now being actively addressed in a number of ways. Emerging evidence suggests that interventions that directly address barriers or that assist the parent to develop their own strategies for managing obstacles can be successful. Furthermore, the incorporation of peer support and/or group-based models also appears to help increase the likelihood that families will engage with and more fully participate in their child's treatment.

A challenge remains in this area of inquiry. There is considerable evidence that poverty and its associated stressors and burdens undermine parenting and, ultimately, child behavioral success. There are emerging efforts, particularly in the global child mental health field, to integrate parent- and family-strengthening interventions and poverty-reducing measures in order to enhance outcomes for the child (Ssewamala et al., 2016); this may be an important line of inquiry to pursue in the US.

References

American Psychiatric Association. (2013). *Diagnostic and statistical manual of mental disorders* (DSM-5). Washington, DC: Author.

Assenany, A. E., & McIntosh, D. E. (2002). Negative treatment outcomes of behavioral parent training programs. *Psychology in the Schools, 39*(2), 209–219.

Axford, N., Lehtonen, M., Kaoukji, D., Tobin, K., & Berry, V. (2012). Engaging parents in parenting programs: Lessons from research and practice. *Children and Youth Services Review, 34*(10), 2061–2071.

Bannon, W. M. J., & McKay, M. M. (2007). Addressing urban African American youth externalizing and social problem behavioral difficulties in a family-oriented prevention project. *Social Work in Mental Health, 5*(1–2), 221–240.

Becker, K. D., Lee, B. R., Daleiden, E. L., Lindsey, M., Brandt, N. E., & Chorpita, B. F. (2015). The common elements of engagement in children's mental health services: Which elements for which outcomes? *Journal of Clinical Child and Adolescent Psychology, 44*(1), 30–43.

Bell, C. C., & Jenkins, E. J. (1993). Community violence and children on Chicago's Southside. *Psychiatry: Interpersonal and Biological Processes, 56*(1), 46–54.

Beyers, J. M., Loeber, R., Wikstrom, P., & Stouthamer-Loeber, M. (2001). What predicts adolescent violence in better-off neighborhoods? *Journal of Abnormal Child Psychology, 29*(5), 369–381.

Black, M. M., & Krishnakumar, A. (1998). Children in low-income, urban settings. Interventions to promote mental health and well-being. *American Psychologist, 53*(6), 635–646.

Boldero, J., & Fallon, B. (1995). Adolescent help-seeking: What do they get help for and from whom? *Journal of Adolescence, 18*(2), 193–209.

Brestan, E. V., & Eyberg, S. M. (1998). Effective psychosocial treatments of conduct-disordered children and adolescents: 29 years, 82 studies, and 5,272 kids. *Journal of Clinical Child Psychology, 27*(2), 180–189.

Burke, J. D., Loeber, R., & Birmaher, B. (2002). Research review update: Oppositional defiant disorder and conduct disorder: A review of the past 10 years, part II. *Journal of the American Academy of Child & Adolescent Psychiatry, 41*, 1275–1293.

Chacko, A., Alan, C., Uderman, J., Cornwell, M., Anderson, L., & Chimiklis, A. (2015). Training parents of children with ADHD. In R. Barkley (Ed.), *Attention deficit hyperactivity disorder: A handbook for diagnosis and treatment* (4th ed., pp. 513–536). New York, NY: Guilford Press.

Chacko, A., Feirsen, N., Rajwan, E., Wymbs, B.T, & Wymbs, F.A. (2017). Distinguishing never-attenders, dropouts, and completers to behavioral parent training: The importance of parental cognitions. *Journal of Child and Family Studies, 26*(3), 950–960.

Chacko, A., Isham, A., Cleek, A., & Mckay, M. (2016). Using mobile health technology to improve homework implementation in evidence-based parenting intervention for disruptive behavior disorders in youth. *Pilot and Feasibility Studies, 2*, 1–11.

Chacko, A., Jensen, S., Lowry, L.S., Cornwell, M., Chimiklis, A., Chan, E., Lee, D., . . . Pulgarin, B. (2016). Engagement in Behavioral Parent Training: Review of the literature and implications for practice. *Clinical Child and Family Psychology Review, 19*, 204–2015.

Chacko, A., Gopalan, G., Franco, L. M., Dean-Assael, K. M., Jackson, J. M., Marcus, S., . . . McKay, M. M. (2015). Multiple family group service model for children with disruptive behavior disorders: Child outcomes at post-treatment. *Journal of Emotional and Behavioral Disorders, 23*(2), 67–77.

Chacko, A., Wymbs, B. T., Wymbs, F. A., Pelham, W. E., Swanger-Gagne, M. S., Girio, E., . . . O'Connor, B. (2009). Enhancing traditional behavioral parent training for single mothers of children with ADHD. *Journal of Clinical Child & Adolescent Psychology, 38*(2), 206–218.

Chacko, A., Wymbs, B. T., Chimiklis, A., Wymbs, F. A., & Pelham, W. E. (2012). Evaluating a comprehensive strategy to improve engagement to group-based behavioral parent training for high-risk families of children with ADHD. *Journal of Abnormal Child Psychology, 40*, 1351–1362.

Chronis-Tuscano, A., Clarke, T. L., O'Brien, K. A., Raggi, V. L., Diaz, Y., Mintz, A. D., . . . Seeley, J. (2013). Development and preliminary evaluation of an integrated treatment targeting parenting and depressive symptoms in mothers of children with attention-deficit/hyperactivity disorder. *Journal of Consulting and Clinical Psychology, 81*(5), 918–925.

Chronis, A. M., Chacko, A., Fabiano, G. A., Wymbs, B. T., & Pelham, W. E. J. (2004). Enhancements to the behavioral parent training paradigm for families of children with ADHD: Review and future directions. *Clinical Child and Family Psychology Review, 7*(1), 1–27.

Conger, R. D., Wallace, L. E., Sun, Y., Simons, R. L., McLoyd, V. C., & Brody, G. H. (2002). Economic pressure in African American families: A replication and extension of the family stress model. *Developmental Psychology, 38*(2), 179–193.

Cummings, E. M., & Davies, P. T. (1994). Maternal depression and child development. *Journal of Child Psychology and Psychiatry, 35*(1), 73–112.

Cunningham, C. E., Bremner, R., & Secord, M. (1998). *COPE: The Community Parent Education Program: A school-based family systems oriented workshop for parents of children with disruptive behavior disorders.* Hamilton, Ontario: COPE Works.

Cunningham, C. E., Boyle, M., Offord, D., Racine, Y, Hundert, J., Secord, M., & McDonald, J. (2000). Tri-ministry Study: Correlates of school-based parent course utilization. *Journal of Consulting and Clinical Psychology, 68*, 928–933.

Dadds, M. R., & McHugh, T. A. (1992). Social support and treatment outcome in behavioral family therapy for child conduct problems. *Journal of Consulting and Clinical Psychology, 60*(2), 252.

Danko, C. M., Brown, T., Van Schoick, L., & Budd, K. S. (2016). Predictors and correlates of homework completion and treatment outcomes in parent–child interaction therapy. *Child Youth Care Forum, 45*(3), 467–485.

Dawson, K., & Berry, M. (2002). Engaging families in child welfare services: An evidence-based approach to best practice. *Child Welfare, 81*(2), 293.

Evans, G. W. (2004). The environment of childhood poverty. *American Psychologist, 59*(2), 77–92.

Evans, G. W., Boxhill, L., & Pinkava, M. (2008). Poverty and maternal responsiveness: The role of maternal stress and social resources. *International Journal of Behavioral Development, 32*(3), 232–237.

Feng, X., Shaw, D. S., Skuban, E. M., & Lane, T. (2007). Emotional exchange in mother–child dyads: Stability, mutual influence, and associations with maternal depression and child problem behavior. *Journal of Family Psychology, 21*(4), 714–725.

Frame, L., Conley, A., & Berrick, J. D. (2006). "The real work is what they do together": Peer support and birth parent change. *Families in Society: The Journal of Contemporary Social Services, 87*(4), 509–520.

Franco, L. M., Dean-Assael, K. M., & McKay, M. (2008). Multiple family groups to reduce youth disruptive difficulties. In C. W. LeCroy (Ed.), *Handbook of evidence-based treatment manuals for children and adolescents* (pp. 546–590). New York, NY: Oxford University Press.

Frick, P. J., & Muñoz, L. (2006). Oppositional defiant disorder and conduct disorder. In C. A. Essau (Ed.), *Child and Adolescent Psychopathology: Theoretical and Clinical Implications* (pp. 26–51). New York, NY: Routledge/Taylor & Francis Group.

Geenen, S., Powers, L. E., Powers, J., Cunningham, M., McMahon, L., Nelson, M., . . . Fullerton, A. (2013). Experimental study of a self-determination intervention for youth in foster care. *Career Development and Transition for Exceptional Individuals, 36*(2), 84–95.

Ghandour, R. M., Kogan, M. D., Blumberg, S. J., Jones, J. R., & Perrin, J. M. (2012). Mental health conditions among school-aged children: Geographic and sociodemographic patterns in prevalence and treatment. *Journal of Developmental and Behavioral Pediatrics, 33*(1), 42–54.

Goldstein, R. B., Olfson, M., Martens, E. G., & Wolk, S. I. (2006). Subjective unmet need for mental health services in depressed children grown up. *Administration and Policy in Mental Health and Mental Health Services Research, 33*(6), 666–673.

Gopalan, G., Acri, M., Lalayants, M., Hooley, C., & Einbinder, E. (2014). Child welfare involved caregiver perceptions of family support in child mental health treatment. *Journal of Family Strengths, 14*(1), 1–25.

Gopalan, G., Bannon, W. M., Dean-Assael, K., Fuss, A., Gardner, L., LaBarbera, B., & McKay, M. M. (2011). Multiple family groups: An engaging mental health intervention for child welfare involved families. *Child Welfare, 90*(4), 135–156.

Gopalan, G., Chacko, A., Franco, L. M., Rotko, L., Marcus, S., & McKay, M. M. (2015). Multiple family groups service delivery model to reduce childhood disruptive behavioral disorders: Outcomes at 6-months follow-up. *Journal of Child and Family Studies, 24*(9), 2721–2733.

Gopalan, G., & Franco, L. (2009). Multiple family groups to reduce disruptive behaviors. In A. Gitterman, & R. Salmon (Eds.), *Encyclopedia of social work with groups* (pp. 86–89). New York: Routledge.

Gopalan, G., Fuss, A., & Wisdom, J. P. (2015). Multiple family groups to reduce child behavior difficulties: Influences on retention for child welfare-involved caregivers. *Research on Social Work Practice, 25*(5), 564–577.

Gopalan, G., Goldstein, L., Klingenstein, K., Sicher, C., Blake, C., & McKay, M. M. (2010). Engaging families into child mental health treatment: Updates and special considerations. *Journal of the Canadian Academy of Child and Adolescent Psychiatry /Journal de l'academie canadienne de psychiatrie de l'enfant et de l'adolescent, 19*(3), 182–196.

Gorman-Smith, D., Tolan, P. H., & Henry, D. (1999). The relation of community and family to risk among urban-poor adolescents. In P. Cohen, C. Slomkowski, & L. N. Robins (Eds.), *Historical and geographical influences on psychopathology* (pp. 349–367). Mahwah, NJ: Lawrence Erlbaum Associates Publishers.

Grant, K. E., McCormick, A., Poindexter, L., Simpkins, T., Janda, C. M., Thomas, K. J., . . . Taylor, J. (2005). Exposure to violence and parenting as mediators between poverty and psychological symptoms in urban African American adolescents. *Journal of Adolescence, 28*, 507–521.

Gustafson, D. H., Boyle M. G., Shaw B. R., Isham, A., McTavish, F., Richards, S., . . . Johnson, K. (2011). An e-Health solution for people with alcohol problems. *Alcohol Research and Health, 33*, 327–337.

Haine-Schlagel, R., & Walsh, N. E. (2015). A review of parent participation engagement in child and family mental health treatment. *Clinical Child and Family Psychology Review, 18*(2), 133–150.

Harrison, M. E., McKay, M. M., & Bannon, W. M., Jr. (2004). Inner-city child mental health service use: The real question is why youth and families do not use services. *Community Mental Health Journal, 40*(2), 119–131.

He, Y., Gewirtz, A., Lee, S., Morrell, N., & August, G. (2016). A randomized preference trial to inform personalization of a parent training program implemented in community mental health clinics. *Translational Behavioral Medicine, 6*, 1–8.

Heinrichs, N. (2006). The effects of two different incentives on recruitment rates of families into a prevention program. *Journal of Primary Prevention, 27*(4), 345–365.

Hoagwood, K. E., Cavaleri, M. A., Olin, S. S., Burns, B. J., Slaton, E., Gruttadaro, D., & Hughes, R. (2009). Family support in children's mental health: A review and synthesis. *Clinical Child and Family Psychology Review, 13*(1), 1–45.

Hoagwood, K. E., Green, E., Kelleher, K., Schoenwald, S., RollsReutz, J., Landsverk, J., ... Research Network on Youth Mental Health, Chicago. (2008). Family advocacy, support and education in children's mental health: Results of a national survey. *Administration and Policy in Mental Health and Mental Health Services Research, 35*(1–2), 73–83.

Ingoldsby, K. M. (2010). Review of interventions to improve family engagement and retention in parent and child mental health programs. *Journal of Child and Family Studies, 19,* 629–645.

Jensen, P. S., & Hoagwood, K. E. (2008). *Improving children's mental health through parent empowerment: Trainer's guide.* Unpublished manuscript.

Johnston, C., & Freeman, W. (1997). Attributions for child behavior in parents of children without behavior disorders and children with attention deficit-hyperactivity disorder. *Journal of Consulting and Clinical Psychology, 65*(4), 636–645.

Johnston, C., Mah, J. W., & Regambal, M. (2010). Parenting cognitions and treatment beliefs as predictors of experience using behavioral parenting strategies in families of children with attention-deficit/hyperactivity disorder. *Behavior Therapy, 41*(4), 491–504.

Jones, D. J., Forehand, R., Guellar, J., Kincaid, C., Parent, J., Fenton, N., & Goodrum, N (2013). Harnessing innovative technologies to advance children's mental health: Behavioral parent training as an example. *Clinical Psychology Review, 33,* 241–252.

Kazdin, A. E., Holland, L., & Crowley, M. (1997). Family experience of barriers to treatment and premature termination from child therapy. *Journal of Consulting and Clinical Psychology, 65*(3), 453–463.

Kazdin, A. E., Holland, L., Crowley, M., & Breton, S. (1997). Barriers to treatment participation scale: Evaluation and validation in the context of child outpatient treatment. *Journal of Child Psychology and Psychiatry, 38*(8), 1051–1062.

Kazdin, A. E., & Whitley, M. K. (2003). Treatment of parental stress to enhance therapeutic change among children referred for aggressive and antisocial behavior. *Journal of Consulting and Clinical Psychology, 71*(3), 504–15.

Kemp, S. P., Marcenko, M. O., Hoagwood, K., & Vesneski, W. (2009). Engaging parents in child welfare services: Bridging family needs and child welfare mandates. *Child Welfare, 88*(1), 101–126.

Kerkorian, D., McKay, M., & Bannon, W. M., Jr. (2006). Seeking help a second time: Parents'/caregivers' characterizations of previous experiences with mental health services for their children and perceptions of barriers to future use. *American Journal of Orthopsychiatry, 76*(2), 161–166.

Klodnick, V. V., Sabella, K., Brenner, C. J., Krzos, I. M., Ellison, M. L., Kaiser, S. M., ... Fagan, M. A. (2015). Perspectives of young emerging adults with serious mental health conditions on vocational peer mentors. *Journal of Emotional and Behavioral Disorders, 23*(4), 226–237.

Koroloff, N. M., Elliott, D. J., Koren, P. E., & Friesen, B. J. (1994). Connecting low-income families to mental health services: The role of the family associate. *Journal of Emotional and Behavioral Disorders, 2*(4), 240–246.

Koroloff, N. M., Elliott, D. J., Koren, P. E., & Friesen, B. J. (1996). Linking low-income families to children's mental health services: An outcome study. *Journal of Emotional and Behavioral Disorders, 4*(1), 2–11.

Kutash, K., Duchnowski, A. J., Green, A. L., & Ferron, J. M. (2011). Supporting parents who have youth with emotional disturbances through a parent-to-parent support program: A proof of concept study using random assignment. *Administration and Policy in Mental Health and Mental Health Services Research, 38*(5), 412–427.

Kutash, K., Garraza, L. G., Ferron, J. M., Duchnowski, A. J., Walrath, C., & Green, A. L. (2013). The relationship between family education and support services and parent and child outcomes over time. *Journal of Emotional & Behavioral Disorders, 21*(4), 264–276.

Lanza, S. T., Rhoades, B. L., Nix, R. L., Greenberg, M. T., & Conduct Problems Prevention Research Group (2010). Modeling the interplay of multilevel risk factors for future academic and behavior problems: A person-centered approach. *Development and Psychopathology, 22,* 313–335.

Lau, A. S., & Weisz, J. R. (2003). Reported maltreatment among clinic-referred children: Implications for presenting problems, treatment attrition, and long-term outcomes. *Journal of the American Academy of Child & Adolescent Psychiatry, 42*(11), 1327–1334.

Leslie, L. K., Aarons, G. A., Haine, R. A., & Hough, R. L. (2007). Caregiver depression and medication use by youths with ADHD who receive services in the public sector. *Psychiatric Services, 58*(1), 131–134.

Lindsey, M. A., Brandt, N. E., Becker, K. D., Lee, B. R., Barth, R. P., Daleiden, E. L., & Chorpita, B. F. (2014). Identifying the common elements of treatment engagement interventions in children's mental health services. *Clinical Child and Family Psychology Review, 17,* 283–298.

Linver, M. R., Brooks-Gunn, J., & Kohen, D. E. (2002). Family processes as pathways from income to young children's development. *Developmental Psychology, 38*(5), 719–734.

Lochman, J. E., Boxmeyer, C., Powell, N., Roth, D. L., & Windle, M. (2006). Masked intervention effects: Analytic methods addressing low dosage of intervention. *New Directions for Evaluation, 110,* 19–32.

Lovejoy, M. C., Graczyk, P. A., O'Hare, E., & Neuman, G. (2000). Maternal depression and parenting behavior. A meta-analytic review. *Clinical Psychology Review, 20,* 561–592.

Luthar, S. S. (1999). *Poverty and children's adjustment.* Thousand Oaks, CA: Sage.

MacNaughton, K. L., & Rodrigue, J. R. (2001). Predicting adherence to recommendations by parents of clinic-referred children. *Journal of Consulting and Clinical Psychology, 69,* 262–270.

Martinez, J. I., Lau, A. S., Chorpita, B. F., & Weisz, J. R. (2015). Psychoeducation as a mediator of treatment approach on parent engagement in child psychotherapy for disruptive behavior. *Journal of Clinical Child & Adolescent Psychology,* 1–15. doi: 10.1080/15374416.2015. 10388826

McCabe, K. M. (2002). Factors that predict premature termination among Mexican-American children in outpatient psychotherapy. *Journal of Child and Family Studies, 11,* 347–359.

McKay, M. M., & Bannon, W. M. J. (2004). Engaging families in child mental health services. *Child and Adolescent Psychiatric Clinics of North America, 13*(4), 905–921.

McKay, M. M., Gonzales, J., Quintana, E., Kim, L., & Abdul-Adil, J. (1999). Multiple family groups: An alternative for reducing disruptive behavioral difficulties of urban children. *Research on Social Work Practice, 9*(5), 593–607.

McKay, M. M., Gopalan, G., Franco, L., Dean-Assael, K., Chacko, A., Jackson, J. M., & Fuss, A. (2011). A collaboratively designed child mental health service model: Multiple family groups for urban children with conduct difficulties. *Research on Social Work Practice, 21*(6), 664–674.

McKay, M. M., Harrison, M. E., Gonzales, J., Kim, L., & Quintana, E. (2002). Multiple-family groups for urban children with conduct difficulties and their families. *Psychiatric Services, 53*(11), 1467–1468.

McKay, M. M., Lynn, C. J., & Bannon, W. M. (2005). Understanding inner city child mental health need and trauma exposure: Implications for preparing urban service providers. *American Journal of Orthopsychiatry, 75*(2), 201–210.

McKay, M. M., McCadam, I., & Gonzales, J. (1996a). Addressing the barriers to mental health services for inner-city children and their caretakers. *Community Mental Health Journal, 32,* 353–361.

McKay, M. M., Nudelman, R., McCadam, K., & Gonzales, J. (1996b). Evaluating a social work engagement approach to involving inner-city children and their families in mental health care. *Research on Social Work Practice, 6*(4), 462–472.

Mistry, R. S., Vandewater, E. A., Huston, A. C., & McLoyd, V. C. (2002). Economic well-being and children's social adjustment: The role of family process in an ethnically diverse low-income sample. *Child Development,* (3), 935.

Mohr, D. C. Burns, M. N., Schueller, S. M., Clarke G., & Klinkman, M. (2013). Behavioral intervention technologies: Evidence review and recommendations for future research in mental health. *General Hospital Psychiatry, 35,* 332–338.

Montague, M., Cavendish, W., Enders, C., & Dietz, S. (2010). Interpersonal relationships and the development of behavior problems in adolescents in urban schools: A longitudinal study. *Journal of Youth and Adolescence, 39*(6), 646–657.

Morrissey-Kane, E., & Prinz, R. J. (1999). Engagement in child and adolescent treatment: The role of parental cognitions and attributions. *Clinical Child and Family Psychology Review, 2,* 183–198.

National Institute of Child Health and Human Development Early Child Care Research Network. (2005). Duration and developmental timing of poverty and children's cognitive and social development from birth through third grade. *Child Development, 76*(4), 795–810.

Nock, M. K., & Ferriter, C. (2005). Parent management of attendance and adherence in child and adolescent therapy: A conceptual and empirical review. *Clinical Child and Family Psychology Review, 8*(2), 149–166.

Nock, M. K., & Kazdin, A. E. (2001). Parent expectancies for child therapy: Assessment and relation to participation in treatment. *Journal of Child and Family Studies, 10,* 155–180.

Nock, M. K., & Kazdin, A. E. (2005). Randomized controlled trial of a brief intervention for increasing participation in parent management training. *Journal of Consulting and Clinical Psychology, 73*(5), 872–879.

Nock, M. K., Kazdin, A. E., Hiripi, E., & Kessler, R. C. (2006). Prevalence, subtypes, and correlates of DSM-IV conduct disorder in the national comorbidity survey replication. *Psychological Medicine, 36*(5), 699–710.

Obrochta, C., Anthony, B., Armstrong, M., Kalil, J., Hust, J., & Kernan, J. (2011, October). *Issue brief: Family-to-family peer support: Models and evaluation.* Atlanta, GA: ICF Macro, Outcomes Roundtable for Children and Families.

Olin, S. S., Kutash, K., Pollock, M., Burns, B. J., Kuppinger, A., Craig, N., . . . Hoagwood, K. E. (2014). Developing quality indicators for family support services in community team-based mental health care. *Administration and Policy in Mental Health and Mental Health Services Research, 41*(1), 7–20.

Palmer, S., Maiter, S., & Manji, S. (2006). Effective intervention in child protective services: Learning from parents. *Children and Youth Services Review, 28*(7), 812–824.

Patterson, G. R., Crosby, L., & Vuchinich, S. (1992). Predicting risk for early police arrest. *Journal of Quantitative Criminology, 8*(4), 335–355.

Patterson, G. R., Reid, J. B., & Dishion, T. J. (1992). *A social learning approach: IV. Antisocial boys.* Eugene, OR: Castalia.

Peters, S., Calam, R., & Harrington, R. (2005). Maternal attributions and expressed emotion as predictors of attendance at parent management training. *Journal of Child Psychology and Psychiatry, 46*(4), 436–448.

Philips, L. A., Oca, S., Geenan, S., & Powers, L. (2013). Better futures: Helping young people in foster care with mental health challenges prepare for and participate in higher education. *Focal Point: Youth, Young Adults, & Mental Health, Education, and Employment, 27*(1), 5–8.

Powers, L. E., Geenen, S., Powers, J., Pommier-Satya, S., Turner, A., Dalton, L. D., . . . Swank, P. (2012). My life: Effects of a longitudinal, randomized study of self-determination enhancement on the transition outcomes of youth in foster care and special education. *Children and Youth Services Review, 34,* 2179–2187.

Powers, L. E., Turner, A., Westwood, D., Matuszewski, J., Wilson, R., & Phillips, A. (2001). Take charge for the future: A controlled fieldtest of a model to promote student involvement in transition planning. *Career Development for Exceptional Individuals, 24*(1), 89–104.

Prinz, R. J., & Miller, G. E. (1994). Family-based treatment for childhood antisocial behavior: Experimental influences on dropout and engagement. *Journal of Consulting and Clinical Psychology, 62*(3), 645.

Radigan, M., Wang, R., Chen, Y., & Xiang, J. N. (2014). Youth and caregiver access to peer advocates and satisfaction with mental health services. *Community Mental Health Journal, 50*(8), 915–921.

Robbins, V., Johnston, J., Barnett, H., Hobstetter, W., Kutash, K., Duchnowski, A. J., . . . Annis, S. (2008). *Parent to parent: A synthesis of the emerging literature.* Tampa, FL: University of South Florida, The Louis de la Parte Florida Mental Health Institute Department of Child & Family Studies.

Rooney, R. H. (Ed.). (2009). *Strategic work with involuntary clients* (2nd ed.). New York, NY: Columbia University Press.

Roussos, A., Berger, S., & Harrison, M. (2008). *Family support report: A call to action.* New York, NY: New York City Department of Health and Mental Hygiene, Division of Mental Hygiene, Bureau of Child and Adolescent Services.

Sanders, M. R., Markie-Dadds, C., Tully, L. A., & Bor, W. (2000). The triple P-positive parenting program: A comparison of enhanced, standard, and self-directed behavioral family intervention for parents of children with early onset conduct problems. *Journal of Consulting and Clinical Psychology, 68*(4), 624.

Sanders, M. R., & McFarland, M. (2001). Treatment of depressed mothers with disruptive children: A controlled evaluation of cognitive behavioral family intervention. *Behavior Therapy, 31,* 89–112.

Siefert, K., Finlayson, T. L., Williams, D. R., Delva, J., & Ismail, A. I. (2007). Modifiable risk and protective factors for depressive symptoms in low-income African American mothers. *American Journal of Orthopsychiatry, 77*(1), 113–123.

Sitnick, S. L., Shaw, D. S., Gill, A., Dishion, T., Winter, C., Waller, R., . . . Wilson, M. (2014). Parenting and the Family Check-Up: Changes in observed parent-child interaction following early childhood intervention. *Journal of Clinical Child & Adolescent Psychology, 44*(6), 970–984.

Snowden, L. R. (2001). Barriers to effective mental health services for African Americans. *Mental Health Services Research, 3*(4), 181–187.

Ssewamala, F. M., Karimli, L., Neilands, T.B., Wang, J. S-H., Han, C-K., Ilic, V., & Nabunya, P. (2016). Applying a family-level economic strengthening intervention to improve education and health-related outcomes of orphaned children: Lessons from a randomized experiment in southern Uganda. *Prevention Science, 17,* 134–143.

Staudt, M. (2007). Treatment engagement with caregivers of at-risk children: Gaps in research and conceptualization. *Journal of Child and Family Studies, 16*(2), 183–196.

Thompson, R., Lindsey, M. A., English, D. J., Hawley, K. M., Lambert, S., & Browne, D. C. (2007). The influence of family environment on mental health need and service use among vulnerable children. *Child Welfare, 86*(5), 57–74.

Tolan, P., & Henry, D. (2000). *Patterns of psychopathology among urban poor children: Community, age, ethnicity and gender effects.* Unpublished manuscript.

Wahler, R. G., & Dumas, J. E. (1989). Attentional problems in dysfunctional mother–child interactions: An interbehavioral model. *Psychological Bulletin, 105*(1), 116–130.

Webster-Stratton, C. (1994). Advancing videotape parent training: A comparison study. *Journal of consulting and clinical psychology, 62*(3), 583–593.

Wymbs, F. A., Cunningham, C. E., Chen, Y., Rimas, H. M., Deal, K., Waschbusch, D. A., & Pelham, W. E., Jr. (2015). Examining parents' preferences for group and individual parent training for children with ADHD symptoms. *Journal of Clinical Child & Adolescent Psychology, 45*(5), 614–631.

Yeh, M., McCabe, K., Hough, R. L., Dupuis, D., & Hazen, A. (2003). Racial/ethnic differences in parental endorsement of barriers to mental health services for youth. *Mental Health Services Research, 5*(2), 65–77.

Yeh, M., McCabe, K., Hough, R. L., Lau, A., Fakhry, F., & Garland, A. (2005). Why bother with beliefs? Examining relationships between race/ethnicity, parental beliefs about causes of child problems, and mental health service use. *Journal of Consulting and Clinical Psychology, 73*(5), 800–807.

Yoshikawa, H., Aber, J. L., & Beardslee, W. R. (2012). The effects of poverty on the mental, emotional, and behavioral health of children and youth implications for prevention. *American Psychologist, 67*(4), 272–284.

25

Pharmacotherapy of Disruptive and Impulse Control Disorders

Gloria M. Reeves, Heidi J. Wehring, and Mark A. Riddle

Pharmacologic treatment of Oppositional Defiant Disorder (ODD) and Conduct Disorder (CD) is challenging for several reasons. First, the evidence base to guide medication treatment is limited compared to that of other pediatric mental health disorders. There are no medications approved by the Food and Drug Administration (FDA) for ODD/CD treatment, so prescribers must rely on emerging research data, expert consensus guidelines, and personal clinical experience to guide patient care. In addition, clinical pharmacologic studies to date have generally been short-term, acute treatment trials, so there is also limited information on long-term tolerability and safety issues. Additionally, youth with ODD/CD have high rates of psychiatric comorbidity. Prescribers must monitor for symptom changes across multiple disorders and domains (e.g., mood, anxiety, impulsivity), potential drug interactions with polypharmacy treatment (e.g., a drug interfering with the metabolism of a coprescribed agent), and additional side effects (e.g., sedation).

Despite these challenges, pharmacologic treatments remain an important option for the management of ODD/CD behaviors that impair functioning in multiple settings (home, school, community) and that fail to respond to first-line treatments (e.g., behavioral services; treatment with medication of co-occurring attention deficit hyperactivity disorder [ADHD]). Judicious treatment with appropriate dosing, monitoring, and duration can be used to target behaviors that cause significant impairment in child/family functioning and are associated with the frequent use of crisis services (e.g., emergency room visits, hospitalizations). Pharmacologic intervention may also help stabilize high-risk behaviors (e.g., impulsive aggression leading to injury) while behavioral strategies are being adjusted and optimized.

This chapter reviews the evidence base for pharmacologic treatment of ODD/CD. Clinical trial data and recently published expert opinion/practice guidelines are discussed, with attention to specific patient subgroups (e.g., youth with ODD/CD and co-occurring ADHD or intellectual disability) and different medication classes studied. Related information is presented on the treatment of maladaptive aggression and irritability, cardinal symptoms of CD and ODD respectively. General principles and strategies to support safe and effective pharmacologic treatment are reviewed, as are future directions of ODD/CD treatment.

Pharmacologic Treatment of ODD/CD

Clinical Trial Data

The Agency for Healthcare Research and Quality of the U.S. Department of Health and Human Services funded a 2015 review by Epstein et al. of pharmacologic and psychosocial interventions for disruptive behavior disorders, including ODD and CD. Studies of youth with ADHD were only included if the child had co-occurring ODD or CD (Epstein et al., 2015). They excluded studies of youth with disruptive behavior secondary to another condition (e.g., autism, intellectual disability, substance abuse), studies of youth residing in an institutional setting (e.g., inpatient or residential treatment facility), and any pharmacologic studies published prior to 1994. They only reviewed studies that included a treatment comparison group (placebo or head-to-head comparison). The authors identified 13 pharmacologic studies. Pharmacologic studies were generally short-term (4–10 weeks; there was one study with 6-month maintenance treatment), industry-sponsored (one trial was exclusively funded by the federal government), and enrolled mainly male participants. Medications studied came from a wide array of classes (antipsychotic medications, mood stabilizers, stimulants, and non-stimulant ADHD medications), but the only medications studied in more than one controlled trial were risperidone, atomoxetine, and divalproex. Most studies of youth with ODD/CD had co-occurring diagnosis of ADHD, and two studies investigated pharmacologic augmentation of stimulant treatment. The authors concluded that there are "very few studies supporting effectiveness of pharmacologic interventions, but small studies of antipsychotics and stimulants reported positive effect in short term" (Epstein et al., p. 176). Of note, this review did not include randomized controlled trials (RCTs) of lithium or first-generation antipsychotic medication. Four lithium trials were not included because three took place in an inpatient setting and one study was published prior to 1994. In these studies, lithium was superior to placebo in reducing CD symptoms, but treatment studies were of very brief duration (2–6 weeks). One study included a head-to-head comparison with haloperidol, which was also superior to placebo in decreasing CD symptoms. Thioridazine and molindone have also been studied in controlled trials for ODD/CD, but molindone was discontinued by the manufacturer for non-safety reasons and thioridazine is generally avoided in pediatric patients because of cardiovascular side effect risk, namely, risk of prolonged QTc interval.

A 2016 review of pharmacotherapy specifically for treatment of CD identified 12 RCTs with sample sizes ranging from 12–180 participants and study durations ranging from 4 to 19 weeks (Hambly, Khan, McDermott, Bor, & Haywood, 2016). Psychiatric comorbidity with ADHD, ODD, Post Traumatic Stress Disorder (PTSD), and Disruptive Behavior Disorder Not Otherwise Specified (NOS) were included, and one study included youth with "sub-average" intelligence. Study medications included atomoxetine, divalproex, lithium, methylphenidate plus clonidine, methylphenidate, molindone, quetiapine, and risperidone. The authors concluded that antipsychotic medications demonstrated efficacy in short-term studies, but cautioned about the potential for significant side effects. Studies on other medications were inconclusive.

Table 25.1 provides a review of clinical trial design (participant age, study design, outcomes measured) and results for selected controlled trials of mood stabilizers and antipsychotic medications studied for primary treatment of ODD/CD or maladaptive aggression. These two medication classes are highlighted because they have been the most widely studied for this indication.

ADHD medication trials generally do not require all participants to have co-occurring ODD/CD, but psychiatric comorbidity is high, so ODD/CD symptom outcomes are often

Table 25.1 Selected Clinical Trials: Antipsychotics and Mood Stabilizing Medications in CD/ODD

Author	Diagnosis	Study design	N	Age	Dose	Assessments	Outcome
Mood Stabilizers: Lithium							
Campbell et al., 1984	CD	2 wks PLB, 4 wks DBL-BL lithium/haloperidol/PLB	61	5–12	Lithium: 500–2,000 mg/day; mean 1,166 (serum 0.32–1.51 mEq/L, mean 0.99) Haloperidol: optimal dose 1–6 mg/day (mean 2.95) (0.04–0.21 mg/kg/d, mean 0.096)	Timed Objective Rating Scale for Aggression; CPRS clusters; CGI-S; CGI-I; CGI-Efficacy index; GCJS; CTQ, CPTQ	Lithium and haloperidol superior vs PLB for hyperactivity, aggression, hostility, unresponsive clusters from CPRS; CGI-severity, improvement, efficacy index significant for drug vs PLB; haloperidol group greater side effects GCJ highly significant for medication vs PLB
Campbell et al., 1995	CD, hospitalized aggressive children	2 wks PLB, 6 wks DBL-BL lithium vs PLB, 2 wks post-treatment PLB	50	5–12	Lithium mean 1,248 mg/day; mean serum level 1.12 mEq/L	CCJS; CPRS; CGI CTQ; CPTQ; POMS	Lithium was superior to placebo for global clinical judgments, CGI-Global Improvement; and Aggression factor from CPRS items
Rifkin et al., 1997	CD, hospitalized	1 wk PLB, 2 wks R-DBL-BL lithium or PLB	33	12–17	Lithium mean level 0.79 mEq/L (range 0.6–1.25)	OAS, BRS, CTRS, ADD/H Adolescent Self-Report Scale	No significant effects for OAS, BRS, CTRS

(Continued)

Table 25.1 Continued

Author	Diagnosis	Study design	N	Age	Dose	Assessments	Outcome
Malone, Delaney, Luebbert, Cater, & Campbell, 2000	CD, admitted to hospital	2 wks PLB, 4 wks R-DBL-BL lithium or PLB	40	10–17	Lithium dose 900–2100 mg/d; mean 1425 (321) mg/day; serum levels 0.78–1.55 mEq/L; mean 1.07 (0.19)	CGI GCJS OAS	Lithium significant in reducing aggression; OAS, GCJCS, CGI-I

Mood Stabilizers: Divalproex

Author	Diagnosis	Study design	N	Age	Dose	Assessments	Outcome
Donovan et al., 2000	ODD, CD explosive temper/mood lability	DBL-BL crossover of divalproex 6 wks and {;B 6 wks	20	10–18	Divalproex 750–1500 mg/day; 82.2 mcg/ml	M-OAS; SCL-90 (6 items from anger-hostility subscale)	12/15 completers had superior response during divalproex treatment
Steiner, Petersen, Saxena, Ford, & Matthews, 2003	CD	Randomized open clinical management of high- or low-dose divalproex for 7 wks; participants and raters were blinded	61	14–18	Divalproex high dose (500–1500 mg/day, or levels 50–120 mcg/ml) or low-dose (up to 250 mg/day); mean drug level was 71.2 (22.8) in high dose and 13.8 (5.12) in low-dose condition	CGI-S; CGI-I, WAI	Significant improvements on impulse control (high-dose group), significant associations between assignment to high-dose condition and CGI-S and CGI-I
Khanzode, Saxena, Kraemer, Chang, & Steiner, 2006	CD (analysis of sample from Steiner et al., 2003)	(see Steiner et al., 2003)	58	14–18	(see Steiner et al., 2003)	(see Steiner et al., 2003)	No significant improvements in anxiety, anger, happiness, consideration for others states; high dose group showed larger improvement in self-reported depression and impulse control

Blader, Schooler, Jensen, Pliszka, & Kafantaris, 2009	ADHD and ODD/CD aggression refractory to stimulant	R-DBL-BL-PLB-CTL, flexible dose divalproex adjunct to stimulant for 8 wks + family therapy	27	6–13	Mean divalproex daily dose 567 mg (291); 68.11 mg/l (21.26)	R-M-OAS	Significantly higher proportion divalproex met remission criteria compared to placebo
Saxena et al., 2010	ODD or CD	12 wks open divalproex vs comparison control group	40			(CGI-S) and CGI-C (Change) scales;	Improvement in divalproex group per CGI-S and CGI-C

Mood Stabilizers: Carbamazepine

Cueva et al., 1996	CD	6 wks DBL-BL, PLB-CTL CBZ vs PLB	22	5–12	Carbamazepine 400–800 mg/day; mean dose 683 mg; serum levels 4.98 to 9.1 mcg/ml	OAS, GCJC, CPRS	CBZ was not superior to placebo

Antipsychotics: Risperidone

Findling et al., 2000	CD	10 wks DB-BL, PLB-CTL risperidone vs placebo	20	5–15	Risperidone 0.75–1.5 mg/day	RAAPPS	Risperidone group significantly less aggressive over last 4 wks; greater reductions in symptoms from baseline
Buitelaar, Van der Gaag, & Melman, 2001	Hospitalized adolescents with CD, ODD, ADHD, IQ 60-90 with severe persistent aggression	Six wks R-DBL-BL, PLB-CTL trial of risperidone	38	12–18	Risperidone mean dose 29 mg/day (range 1.5–4)	CGI; ABC; MOAS	Risperidone associated with improvement on CGI-S and at school ABC overall and hyperactivity scales

(Continued)

Table 25.1 Continued

Author	Diagnosis	Study design	N	Age	Dose	Assessments	Outcome
Van Bellinghen and De Troch, 2001	Behavioral disturbances in children with borderline intellectual functioning	R-DBL-BL, PLB-CTL 4 wks risperidone or PLB	6–14	13	Risperidone 0.05 mg/kg or 1.2 mg/ay	ABC symptom cluster for irritation and hyperactivity; CGI, VAS score for individual target symptoms, PAC	Improvement in risperidone for ABC symptom cluster scores for irritation and hyperactivity, CGI, VAS for individual target symptoms, PAC
Snyder et al., 2002	Conduct and disruptive behavior disorders and subaverage IQ (80% comorbid ADHD)	1 wk PLB then 6 wks DBL-BL, PLB-CTL risperidone	5–12	110	Risperidone mean dose was 0.98 mg/day (0.06), or 0.033 mg/kg/day (0.001); dose range 0.4 to 4.8 mg/day	NCBRF, ABC, Behavior Problems Inventory, CGI, CPT	Risperidone showed significant reduction on Conduct Problem subscale of NCBRF; CGI improvement was significant
Aman & Gharabawi, 2004	Combined results from Snyer et al., 2002 and Buitelaar et al., 2001)	Combined results of above studies to examine risperidone effects in presence/absence of stimulants in ADHD and other disorder;		155 of the original 208	Risperidone as above		Patients treated with risperidone had significant reductions in disruptive and hyperactive subscale scores regardless of stimulant use; addition of risperidone resulted in better control of hyperactivity than stimulant alone

Reyes, Buitelaar, Toren, Augustyns, & Eerdeken, 2006	Disruptive behavior disorder	5–17	Random assignment to 6 months of DBL-BL risperidone or PLB in patients who had responded to 12 wks of risperidone treatment previously	335 pts randomized		Time to recurrence of symptoms as measured by CGI-S or conduct problem subscale of NCBRF	Time to symptom recurrence was significantly longer in patients who took risperidone
Armentero, Lewis, & Davalos, 2007	ADHD and significant aggressive behaviors	7–12	4 wks R-DBL-BL, PLB-CTL risperidone or PLB	25	Risperidone mean dose 1.08 mg/day	CAS-P and CAS-T scores	CAS-P improved; 100% of RIS improved by >30% vs 77% of PLB; no differences on CAS-T
Aman et al., 2014	ADHD and ODD or CD, aggression	6–12	9-wk trial of parent training, stimulant and PLB or risperidone; first 3 wks stimulant and parent training, if still symptomatic either PLB or risperidone added (TOSCA study)	168 (n=124 comorbid OD, n=44 with comorbid CD)	Risperidone 1.65 (0.75) mg/day	Parent ratings-NCBRF; Disruptive-total subscale; ABS; CGI	Risperidone showed significant improvement on the NCBRF-Disruptive-total subscale and social competence subscale, and reactive aggression.

Antipsychotics: First-Generation Antipsychotics (see lithium section for haloperidol results)

| Greenhill, Solomon, Pleak, & Ambrosini, 1985 | Hospitalized Conduct Disorder | 6–11 | 8 wks DBL-BL molindone vs thioridazine | 31 | Molindone 27 mg; Thioridazine 170 mg | Behavioral and treatment emergent symptoms | Molindone and thioridazine were equally effective |

(Continued)

Table 25.1 Continued

Author	Diagnosis	Study design	N	Age	Dose	Assessments	Outcome
Stocks, Taneja, Baroldi, & Findling, 2012	ADHD and persistent serious conduct problems	9-12 wks of molindone, open label, parallel group, randomized, 4 different dose groups	78 randomized (55 completers)	6-12	Molindone at 4 different doses; at end point, molindone 5-20 mg/day (<30 kg) and 20-40 mg/day (at least 30 kg) well tolerated	Primary outcomes safety and tolerability; secondary efficacy endpoints	Molindone was well tolerated, preliminary efficacy results suggest dose-related improvements; CGI-S and SNAP-IV scores improved in all treatment groups, CGI-I scores improved to greatest extent in highest dose group; NCBRF-TQ Conduct Problem subscale scores improved in all groups.

Antipsychotics: Quetiapine

Author	Diagnosis	Study design	N	Age	Dose	Assessments	Outcome
Connor, McLaughlin, & Jeffers-Terry, 2008	CD with moderate to severe aggressive behavior	7 wks DBL-BL, PLB-CTL 7-wk study of quetiapine vs PLB	19	12-17	Quetiapine 200-600 mg/d; mean dose 294 (78) mg/d	CGI-Severity CGI-Improvement	Quetiapine was superior to placebo

ABC = Aberrant Behavior Checklist; ABS = Antisocial Behavior Scale ; CGA-S =Children's Global Assessment-Severity; CPRS = Child Psychiatric Rating Scale; CAS-P = Children's Aggression Scale-Parent; CAS-T= Children's Aggression Scale-Teacher; CBCL= Child Behavior Checklist; CGI-C = Clinical Global Impression-Change; CGI-I Clinical Global Impressions-Improvement; CGI-S Clinical Global Impressions-Severity; CRS = Conners Rating Scale; CPTQ = Conners Parent Teachers Questionnaire; CTQ = Conners Teachers Questionnaire; GCJs = Global Clinical Judgments; M-OAS = Modified Overt Aggression Scale; NCBRF = Nisonger Child Behavior Rating Form; OAS = Overt Aggression Scale; PAC = Personal Assessment Checklist; POMS = Profile of Mood States; RAAPPS = Rating of Aggression against People and/or Property Scale; R-MOAS = Retrospective-Modified Overt Aggression Scale; SCL90 = Symptoms Checklist 90; TRF = Teacher's Report Form; Turgay DSM-IV = Turgay DSM-IV-Based Child and Adolescent Behavior Disorders Screening and Rating Scale; VAS = Visual Analogue Scale; WAI = Weinberger Adjustment Inventory Ratings; YMRS = Young Mania Rating Scale reported as secondary outcomes in ADHD trials. The multimodal treatment of ADHD (MTA) study was one of the largest ADHD medication trials conducted to date (Group, 1999; MTA, 1999). Youth aged 7–9.9 years old were randomized to one of four active treatment options, with three evidence-based, systematically delivered ADHD treatment modalities (behavioral-only, medication-only, and combined behavior and medication treatment), and a community care referral comparison group. The behavioral and medication interventions were developed to provide optimal care in a highly rigorous and systematic fashion (e.g., the medication protocol included a double-blinded, placebo-controlled medication titration protocol with randomized dose order, and the behavioral protocol included individual, group, family, and school-based interventions); the community referral option allowed parents to select their preferred treatment for their child. Most medication-treated youth received methylphenidate, although protocols allowed alternative ADHD medications for non-responders (there were no restrictions on medication options for the community referral comparison group). The primary ADHD outcome was measured by reporting from both parent and teacher; an ODD subscale and other functional measures were included. ADHD symptoms improved in all four intervention groups, but parent/teacher report of ADHD symptoms showed greatest improvement in the two interventions that involved systematic pharmacologic treatment (medication-only and combined treatment).

Subgroup analysis (Jensen et al., 2001) indicated that youth with ADHD only or with ADHD plus ODD/CD responded best to medication treatment (with or without behavioral treatment), but youth with complex ADHD plus ODD/CD and anxiety disorder responded optimally to combined treatment. In contrast, youth with ADHD plus anxiety disorders (and no ODD/CD) responded equally well to medication and behavioral treatments. A caveat to these findings is that the behavioral interventions were not developed specifically for any ADHD subgroup, so it is unclear if a behavioral treatment designed for youth ADHD plus ODD/CD might have had a greater impact on symptoms.

The Treatment of Severe Child Aggression (TOSCA) study (Aman et al., 2014; Gadow et al., 2014) investigated multimodal treatment designed specifically for youth with ADHD plus co-occurring ODD/CD and significant aggressive behavior. All youth received parent training and stimulant treatment. Youth were randomized to stimulant medication plus risperidone or placebo after 3 weeks if symptoms persisted. The study enrolled 169 youths aged 6–12 with ADHD (124 had comorbid ODD, and 44 had comorbid CD). Over the 6 weeks of treatment, risperidone was found to be superior to placebo in the improvement of reactive aggression and as measured on social competence subscales (Aman et al., 2014). Outcomes differed between parent and teacher report. Parents reported superior improvement of ODD severity and peer aggression, compared to placebo, but no significant difference in ADHD or CD symptoms. Teachers reported significant improvement of ADHD symptoms only, compared to placebo, with no significant improvement on ODD, CD, or aggression scales (Gadow et al., 2014). At 12-month naturalistic follow-up, both treatment groups demonstrated significant improvement compared to baseline, but differences between the primary behavioral outcomes did not persist (Gadow et al., 2016).

Practice Parameters

The American Academy of Child and Adolescent Psychiatry (AACAP) published practice parameters for Conduct Disorder in 1997 and for Oppositional Defiant Disorder in 2007. Both parameters emphasized that pharmacologic interventions should be reserved for "adjunctive treatment" to comprehensive psychosocial treatments (e.g., family engagement, psychoeducation, behavior management) and that the greatest evidence to support pharmacologic intervention is for stimulant treatment of youth with co-occurring ADHD. To date, these historical parameters have not been updated.

In England, the National Institute for Health and Care Excellence (NICE) provides quality standards and guidance to the National Health Service on health topics where there is significant variation in care. The NICE and Social Care Institute for Excellence (NICE-SCIE) guidelines for the management of ODD/CD were published in 2013 (NICE-SCIE, 2013). These guidelines also emphasize the importance of psychosocial interventions as both first-line treatment and an essential component of any multimodal treatment for these conditions. Quality standards for psychosocial treatments emphasize the importance of a strong family/developmental approach to care, adequate frequency of therapy appointments, and an appropriately trained provider workforce. . For youth who fail to respond to psychosocial and evidence-based treatment of co-occurring conditions, the guidelines recommend risperidone for short-term pharmacologic management of youth with conduct disorder who have "explosive anger and severe emotional dysregulation." The authors strongly recommend monitoring medication adherence and side effects (including metabolic, cardiovascular, hormonal, and extrapyramidal). They advise that efficacy should be monitored every 3–4 weeks and medication discontinued if no significant improvement is observed by 6 weeks.

Summary Points

- Pharmacologic studies are largely comprised of short-term studies; there are, therefore, very limited data on maintenance treatment.
- "Off-label" pharmacologic treatment of ODD/CD should only be considered after first-line, approved pharmacologic treatments have been attempted for co-occurring disorders, including ADHD.
- Pharmacologic treatment of ODD/CD should only occur as part of multimodal treatment alongside evidence-based child/family psychosocial interventions.
- Risperidone is the most widely studied non-ADHD pharmacologic intervention for youth with ODD/CD treated in an outpatient setting. However, comprehensive and especially metabolic side effect monitoring, including blood work (as described in the medication monitoring section of this chapter) is required.

Pharmacologic Treatment of Maladaptive Aggression and Irritability

Clinical Trial Data

Research into the pharmacologic treatment of the target symptoms of maladaptive aggression and irritability have primarily focused on (a) youth with intellectual disability and/or developmental delay, and (b) youth with ADHD.

Fung et al. (2016) completed a systematic review and meta-analysis of pharmacologic interventions for severe irritability and problem behaviors in youth with autism. This review has been used to support the development of primary care practice guidelines (discussed below). Compared to the research on the pharmacologic treatment of ODD/CD in youth without developmental disabilities, there is a more extensive evidence base to guide the treatment of irritability/aggression symptoms among youth with autism. The authors identified 46 RCTs, using 11 in the meta-analysis. The best evidence of effectiveness was for aripiprazole and risperidone, the two medications that currently have an FDA-approved indication for the treatment of irritability and aggression due to autism (see Table 25.2 for FDA-approved

Table 25.2 Off-Label Pharmacologic Treatment of ODD/CD

	Pediatric Approved Atypical Antipsychotics		
Antipsychotic	*Irritability due to autism (ages approved)*	*Bipolar I (ages approved)*	*Schizophrenia (ages approved)*
Aripiprazole (Abilify)	6–17	10–17	13–17
Risperidone (Risperdal)	5–17	10–17	13–17
Olanzapine (Zyprexa)		13–17	13–17
Quetiapine (Seroquel)		13–17	13–17
Asenapine (Saphris)		10–17	
Paliperidone (Invega)			12–17
Lurasidone (Latuda)			13–17

indications for pediatric antipsychotic treatment). The primary outcome applied in most studies was change as measured on the Aberrant Behavioral Checklist Irritability (ABC-I) sub-scale. The ABC was developed specifically to measure pharmacologic and other treatment effects in studies of youth with severe intellectual disability. The irritability subscale covers a broad range of symptoms, including mood lability, self-harm, impulsivity, and aggression.

Research has also been carried out into the pharmacologic treatment of youth with co-occurring ADHD and irritability/aggression. Forty RCTs have studied the effects of stimulants on symptoms such as aggression, oppositional behavior, and conduct in children and adolescents with ADHD with or without ODD and CD. A meta-analysis of studies between 1970 and 2001 included 28 RCTs examining effect size for stimulants in treating aggression (overt/covert) in children with ADHD, using agents such as methylphenidate (21 studies), amphetamine (5 studies), and pemoline (2 studies); 75% of the 683 participants had comorbid ODD or CD (Connor, Glatt, Lopez, Jackson, & Melloni, 2002). Overt aggression improved with stimulants vs. placebo, based on the ratings of clinicians (18 studies), parents (13 studies) and teachers (16 studies); comorbidity with ODD or CD correlated negatively with effect size. The seven studies reporting on covert aggression all found positive effects for stimulants compared to placebo (Connor et al., 2002). In their guidelines for assessment and treatment of ODD and CD in the Netherlands, Matthys and van de Glind (2013) recommend stimulants as the medication of first choice in children who have ODD or CD with comorbid ADHD symptoms but who are not formally diagnosable with ADHD, owing to the evidence for the effects of stimulants on aggression, independent of their effects on ADHD symptoms, in children and adolescents with CD (Klein et al., 1997). Matthys and van de Glind (2013) recommend a trial of risperidone if methylphenidate is ineffective in these situations.

Practice Guidelines

Treatment of Maladaptive Aggression in Youth The Treatment of Maladaptive Aggression in Youth (T-MAY) project (Rosato, Correll, & Group, 2012) provides guidance on treatment of impulsive/reactive aggression among youths aged 6–18 who are receiving services in an outpatient setting. Recommendations were based on a systematic review of the published literature, a survey of experts recommended practices, a consensus stakeholder conference, and review by the steering committee. The T-MAY guidelines include 18 recommendations. The first 11 recommendations focus on family engagement, evaluation/monitoring of aggressive symptoms, referral strategies for acute aggressive behavior (e.g., ER visit), identification of community supports for the family, and implementation of child and parenting skills training.

Further, the T-MAY guidelines recommend evidence-based pharmacologic and psychosocial treatment for underlying psychiatric disorders (e.g., ADHD and depression) as the initial intervention. For youth with symptoms of severe aggression that fail to respond to psychosocial treatment and first-line medication, the guidelines recommend considering a trial of antipsychotic medication. For youth who fail to respond to an adequate dose/duration of antipsychotic treatment, they recommend switching to another antipsychotic medication. For youth with a partial response to antipsychotic medication, the addition of a mood stabilizer can be considered. The guidelines specifically mention lithium as an option either to augment an antipsychotic or as monotherapy if the child is unable to tolerate antipsychotic treatment. The T-MAY strongly advises against the use of more than two medications to target severe aggression. Comprehensive side-effect monitoring is strongly advised, and families should be given "accessible" information on how to identify and monitor side effects. The T-MAY toolkit (http://www.thereachinstitute.org/images/pdfs/T-MAY-final.pdf) provides guidelines on dosing strategy, a recommended aggression outcome scale, and algorithms to manage aggression for youth with co-occurring ADHD or mood/anxiety disorders.

Special Populations Psychosocial and pharmacologic clinical approaches to managing challenging behaviors may need to be modified or adjusted to take into consideration the special needs of specific patient populations. For example, youth with developmental delay may need specialized educational services and therapy approaches appropriate for the child's cognition level and communication ability. The Autism Intervention Research Network on Physical Health and the Autism Speaks Autism Treatment Network convened a work group to develop a practice pathway for primary care providers to manage irritability and "problem behavior" in youth with autism (McGuire et al., 2016). The guidelines recommend an initial evaluation of safety concerns, monitoring changes in level of functioning, the identification of specific behaviors requiring intervention, and careful assessment of the etiology of and potential stressors related to behavior problems (i.e., medical symptoms, communication difficulties, psychosocial stressors, maladaptive reinforcement patterns, and/or co-occurring psychiatric disorder). Psychosocial, educational, and pharmacologic interventions are included in the guidelines.

Very young children with disruptive behavior constitute another patient population that may require more specialized services. Expertise in normal development is critical in order to distinguish pathologic from typically developmental behaviors (e.g., aggressive behaviors are more common among toddlers/preschool youth than older children), to identify communication difficulties or other developmental delays that may be fueling concerning behavioral patterns, and to provide appropriate parenting guidance. There is a stark contrast between the paucity of safety and efficacy data for pharmacologic treatments for disruptive behaviors in very young children, and the robust evidence base supporting psychosocial interventions for this population (Comer, Chow, Chan, Cooper-Vince, & Wilson, 2013); much greater caution is warranted, therefore, in exposing these children to pharmacologic treatments.

The Preschool ADHD Treatment Study (PATS) (Greenhill et al., 2006) provides promising data on the benefits of methylphenidate for improving core ADHD symptoms, as well as secondary aggression symptoms, among preschool age youth with moderate to severe ADHD who manifest inadequate response to parental training interventions. However, tolerance levels for this medication were lower than those reported in studies of older children; and the benefits of this medication for CD symptoms is not known, as the percentage of comorbid CD cases was very low in this study.

Summary Points

- Youth with maladaptive aggression/irritability who are sub-threshold for ODD/CD should be screened carefully for other psychiatric disorders.
- "Off-label" pharmacologic treatment of aggression/irritability in youth with developmental disability also requires careful screening for underlying medical, communication, and environmental triggers of behavior that may be more appropriately treated with educational and psychosocial intervention.
- Youth with co-occurring ADHD may experience improvement in other disruptive behavior symptoms (e.g., overt aggression) as a result of first-line ADHD treatment.
- It is important to confirm that an adequate trial (i.e., appropriate dose and duration) of medication has taken place before designating a child as "treatment refractory" and switching agents.

Strategies for Treatment

This section of the chapter offers general strategies to support the safe and effective care for youth with ODD/CD, with an emphasis on family engagement and ongoing monitoring of the risk-to-benefit treatment ratio.

Family Engagement

Family engagement may be the most important clinical intervention to obtain long-term improvement in aggressive/disruptive behaviors. Patient engagement may be difficult because of the nature of ODD/CD symptoms. Youth with ODD display a pattern of argumentative and oppositional behaviors, and youth with CD have problems with deceitful, aggressive, and rule-violating behaviors. Youth may be uncooperative and have difficulties in participating in a lengthy evaluation. In some cases, mental health referrals are mandated by an outside agency (e.g., Department of Juvenile Justice); patients and parents may have concerns, therefore, about confidentiality and about the potentially negative consequences of disclosing information. These challenges can be significant barriers to family engagement.

Strategy 1: Support Family Engagement through Collaborative and Transparent Communication It is important to seek feedback from the youth and parent about their aims in seeking help from professional services, and to be attentive to any concerns, expressed either verbally or through non-verbal cues, that may make a youth or parent uncomfortable about participating in the evaluation. A discussion of the evaluation process, including information on the boundaries of confidentiality, may be helpful in alleviating anxiety by letting the child and family know what to expect. Family engagement can also be supported by focusing on patient and family strengths, asking, for example, "What are some activities you are especially good at? What are things you enjoy doing together as a family?" It is important to acknowledge the seriousness and potential consequences of maladaptive behaviors, but it is equally important to project a balanced view of the youth and the family that highlights its strengths and instills hope for positive change.

Providers have an excellent opportunity for positive reinforcement of appropriate communication and behavior as they observe the child, for example, "It's really helpful that you could describe so many details about the incident at school. This information will be useful for us to come up with an effective plan;" or, "I noticed that you were being very respectful and didn't interrupt your mother while she was sharing her point of view. I will be interested to hear your perspective also."

Diagnostic Evaluation

The American Academy of Child and Adolescent Psychiatry practice parameters are a helpful resource to guide clinicians through screening/evaluation for different child psychiatric disorders (http://www.aacap.org/aacap/resources_for_primary_care/practice_parameters_and_resource_centers/practice_parameters.aspx; see also Chapter 23).

Strategy 2: The Diagnostic Evaluation Should Determine Whether or Not Behaviors Occur in More Than One Setting and also Whether or Not They Cause Functional Impairment Clinical evaluation using symptom rating scales can be very helpful in screening for ODD/CD. However, clinical diagnosis is also based on whether or not the child has symptoms that occur in multiple settings and whether there is a clear pattern of functional impairment. Problem behaviors that occur in only one setting should prompt exploration of possible environmental triggers for the behaviors. When aggression and irritability are isolated to the school setting, common underlying issues may include peer conflict, undiagnosed learning or speech/language disorders, or conflict with a specific teacher or authority figure. Behavior concerns that only emerge at home may be related to inconsistent parenting or sibling conflict. Behaviors that occur in one setting only generally do not require pharmacotherapy. Identification of environmental triggers for maladaptive behavior at home or school can help guide the selection of appropriate psychosocial interventions.

In some cases, a child may be sub-threshold for a diagnosis of ODD/CD because they do not meet the given criteria for a number or a duration of symptoms, and yet still experience significant functional impairment. For example, a child may have new-onset aggression that results in suspension from school and delinquent behavior in the community. ODD/CD psychosocial prevention strategies may be indicated as high-priority within the treatment plan if the emerging behaviors cause safety concerns (e.g., harm toward peers).

Strategy 3: A Comprehensive Diagnostic Evaluation Should Include Screening for Violence Exposure, Especially for Youth with Aggressive Behavior Exposure to violence can occur at school (e.g., bullying), at home (e.g., domestic violence), or in the community (e.g., exposure to criminal activity). Unfortunately, violence toward youth is not uncommon. The National Survey of Children's Exposure to Violence (Finkelhor, Turner, Shattuck, & Hamby, 2015) reported that 37.3% of youth experienced physical assault and 15.2% experienced maltreatment during the one-year study period. Approximately one in ten youth surveyed reported an assault-related injury, and one in twenty females aged 14–17 experienced sexual assault or abuse during that year. It may be difficult to identify a child's exposure to violence or victimization during initial evaluation because the child involved or their family may feel uncomfortable about disclosing this information. Follow-up screening for exposure to violence can be helpful in cases where a child has poor response to initial treatment (e.g., worsening aggression). Providers can utilize information disclosed during ongoing screening to guide safety planning and the choice of psychosocial interventions (e.g., trauma-informed therapy), saying, for instance, "I understand it was difficult for you to talk about what happened, but now that I understand the situation better I can help you with your goal of keeping your family safe."

Strategy 4: The Diagnostic Evaluation Should Systematically Screen for Co-Occurring Psychiatric Disorders This information will help determine first-line psychosocial and medication interventions. As noted above, practice guidelines recommend that youth with co-occurring ADHD, anxiety, or mood disorders should receive evidence-based, approved pharmacologic interventions, in addition to first-line psychosocial treatment, before being treated for ODD/CD with "off-label" medication. Youth who have co-occurring substance use or trauma-related disorders may also require additional medical screening and referral (e.g., in the case of an adolescent who reports a history of sexual assault, or of blackouts when intoxicated).

Informed Consent

The informed consent process reviews the diagnosis and indication for treatment and the risks and benefits of treatment options for the particular child. Prescribers act as a "consultant" to the parent or guardian by providing expert information about different treatment options so that they can make an informed decision about what is best for their child. A parallel "informed assent" process is completed with the youth in order to educate her/him about treatment options and provide an opportunity to ask questions or give feedback.

Strategy 5: Informed Consent Should Be an Ongoing Process over the Course of Treatment Because all pharmacologic treatment options for ODD/CD are "off-label," it is especially important to develop a plan to monitor responses to treatment and to limit maintenance treatment to those pharmacologic agents that have clear benefits. Recording ongoing data on symptom improvement (benefit) and side effects (risk) can be helpful to support reassessment of the treatment plan. Youth participation is also critical during these discussions for early identification of side effects and to assess changes in overall functioning.

Pharmacologic Dosing and Polypharmacy Issues

Polypharmacy, that is, concurrent treatment with multiple agents, is not uncommon within community care for youth with serious and complex mental illness. For example, in a large retrospective observational study of over 30,000 youth with autism spectrum disorder, 35% of cases had prescriptions for two or more psychotropic medications and 15% for three or more classes of medication (Spencer et al., 2013). Polypharmacy treatment is challenging because of adherence issues (multiple dosing) and potential drug interactions. A careful review of medication schedules and the use of organizational tools (e.g., pill boxes) may help families to administer medication consistently. Online drug interaction checking programs can be very helpful in keeping providers up to date on newly discovered safety or drug interaction issues.

Antipsychotic polypharmacy, that is, treatment with multiple antipsychotic medications, has not been well studied in youth (except for acute cross-over titration). The American Academy of Child and Adolescent Psychiatry (2011, p. 12) practice parameter on pediatric atypical antipsychotic treatment includes the recommendation that, "The simultaneous use of multiple AAAs [atypical antipsychotic agents] has not been rigorously studied and should generally be avoided."

Strategy 6: Off-Label Pharmacologic Treatment of ODD/CD Should Generally Be Confined to Medications with FDA-Approved Pediatric Indications (see Table 25.2) and Dosing Should Not Exceed Package Insert Guidelines Prescribers may have concerns about using conservative dosing strategies for youth with severe behavior problems (e.g., recent assault of a family member). However, rapid or high dosing is likely to cause problems with medication tolerability, and the youth or parents may then be unwilling to continue treatment. In addition, the safety of high-dose treatment (above package-insert guidelines) is not known. To address acute safety concerns prescribers may alternatively utilize more intensive treatment settings (e.g., partial or full hospitalization) or increase the frequency of follow-up. Conservative, stepwise dosing will also provide clearer data on whether or not the treatment is beneficial.

Medication Monitoring

Strategy 7: Medication Adherence Should Be Assessed at Each Follow-Up Appointment Adherence simply refers to whether or not a medication is being taken at the prescribed dose and frequency. Nonadherence to medication treatment is relatively common. In the MTA Study, stimulant adherence for youth with ADHD was monitored four times within 14 months using an objective measure (saliva assay). Approximately 25% of participants who were randomized to stimulant medication treatment were deemed "nonadherent" on at least half of repeated saliva assays, and only around half (53%) of youth were deemed "adherent" on all assays (Pappadopulos et al., 2009). There was also a significant correlation between adherence and treatment response.

Nonadherence may be due to several factors, including side effects, inconvenient medication scheduling, stigma about medication treatment, and family stress. Adherence may be more problematic for youth who manifest behavior problems and are in conflict with parents/authority figures.

Youth engagement via the medication assent process can be used to identify any concerns the child has about taking the medication and to encourage them to give feedback if new concerns develop. A non-judgmental approach with an emphasis on accurate reporting, rather than a focus on "compliance," is important. The prescriber should convey the message that accurate adherence data will help to ensure that the most appropriate medication and the lowest effective dose is used.

Strategy 8: Safety Monitoring Should Assess for Visible and "Silent" Side Effects Many side effects can be difficult for a child or parent to detect. For example, second-generation antipsychotic medications may cause increases in blood sugar or lipids, such as cholesterol, which are asymptomatic. Blood work is needed for early detection of these types of side effects. Recommendations for monitoring side effects of the most commonly prescribed medication classes (stimulants, alpha agonists, and second-generation antipsychotic medications) are provided in Table 25.3. These recommendations offer guidance on side-effect monitoring through clinical history taking, laboratory data records, and physical assessment (e.g., vital signs, weight, height). Practitioners are referred to the medication's package insert for comprehensive information on specific safety issues and potential drug interactions.

Of note, antipsychotic medications and mood stabilizers require periodic blood work for safety monitoring. Lithium and divalproex also require blood tests to monitor drug levels. Second-generation antipsychotic medications, one of the most extensively studied classes of medication for "off-label" treatment of ODD/CD, have a propensity to cause significant metabolic side effects. Adverse effects include weight gain, increased blood sugar/cholesterol, and even, though rarely, new-onset diabetes, all with long-lasting impacts on future physical health. Monitoring should follow recommended guidelines for the early detection of metabolic side effects since these adverse events often occur early (in the first 3–6 months of treatment).

Treatment Outcomes

Prescribers should assess the frequency and severity of ODD/CD symptoms at baseline and during acute treatment. Rating scales should be appropriate for the age, cognitive/communication status, and developmental ability of the youth. A review of ratings scales for assessment of aggression is provided by Gurnani, Ivanov, and Newcorn (2016).

Strategy 9: Prescribers Can Utilize Outcomes-Based Assessments to Insure That Only Efficacious "Off-Label" Treatments Are Utilized for Maintenance Treatment Most practice guidelines for treatment of youth with ODD/CD recommend the assessment of treatment outcome

Table 25.3 Safety Monitoring

MEDICATION CLASS	SIDE EFFECTS	BASELINE ASSESSMENT	FOLLOW-UP MONITORING	COMMENTS
Stimulants	• Decreased appetite • Decreased sleep • Increased pulse/blood pressure • Worsening of tics or compulsive behaviors (e.g. skin picking) • Irritability	<u>Measurements</u>: weight, height, blood pressure, pulse <u>Observation</u>: involuntary movements <u>Clinical</u>: Assess sleep, appetite, and mood; Screen for risk factors to vulnerability for cardiovascular effects of medication (e.g., history of heart murmur, syncope, family history of premature heart disease); and assess family history of tic disorders	• Repeat baseline measurements at therapeutic dose • Measure weight at each visit and height quarterly	Pediatric consultation: Refer <u>prior to</u> starting medication if child is underweight (BMI% <5%), hypertensive, or if a cardiovascular disease risk factor is identified that has not been evaluated (e.g., history of syncopal episodes) Refer during maintenance treatment if child develops cardiovascular abnormalities (e.g., hypertension). Refer as clinically indicated for decrease in BMI% (e.g., child becomes underweight or child fails to gain weight as expected)
Alpha agonists	• Decreased blood pressure and/or pulse • Sedation	<u>Measurements</u>: blood pressure and pulse <u>Clinical</u>: Assess for daytime sedation and baseline sleep	• Repeat blood pressure and pulse at therapeutic dose (re-assess as clinically indicated) • Assess for sleep and daytime sedation (e.g. impact on school performance)	Pediatrics consultation as clinically indicated for hypotension/bradycardia Medication should be tapered and not stopped abruptly to avoid rebound hypertension

(*Continued*)

Table 25.3 Continued

MEDICATION CLASS	SIDE EFFECTS	BASELINE ASSESSMENT	FOLLOW-UP MONITORING	COMMENTS
Second-generation antipsychotic medications	• Metabolic • Cardiovascular • Endocrine (prolactin) • Involuntary movements • Cognitive	<u>Measurements</u>: Weight, height <u>Labs</u>: Fasting glucose, LDL/HDL cholesterol, triglycerides, liver function tests <u>Observation</u>: Assess for involuntary movements (e.g. AIMS scale) and screen for restlessness (akathisia) <u>Clinical</u>: Assess for sleep, appetite, daytime sedation, gynecomastia	• Repeat baseline labs at 3 months and then every 6 months • Measure weight at each visit and height at least quarterly • Obtain AIMS scale at 3 months and then every 6 months • Repeat clinical assessments and screen for akathisia (e.g., Smith-Barnes akathisia scale) at follow-up medication appointments	Pediatrics consultation for confirmed abnormal lab results and obesity Obtain ECG at baseline and therapeutic dose for ziprasidone Clozapine is <u>not</u> recommended as an option for pharmacologic treatment of ODD/CD

every three months, and the discontinuation of ineffective treatment(s). Given the risk of side effects, especially in antipsychotic treatment, it is important to taper off treatment that has a poor risk-to-benefit ratio rather than to continue the youth's exposure to ineffective medication. In maintenance treatment, quarterly assessments of efficacy can provide feedback to parents within the ongoing informed consent process.

Conclusions and Future Directions

Although multiple medication options for the treatment of ODD/CD have been explored in research studies and in community care, data are still limited. Efficacy data is strongest for stimulants and select antipsychotic medication, followed by alpha agonists and mood stabilizers. Promising pharmacologic agents, including n-acetylcysteine, should be retested in future studies. Practitioners should take into consideration the risk-to-benefit ratio of any treatment, and discuss with patients/families any potential short-term (e.g., weight gain) and/or future (e.g., increased risk of diabetes) health risks associated with it. The high prevalence of ODD/CD and high levels of service utilization by youth with these conditions underscores the public health requirement for evidence-based treatments.

Further research into pharmacologic interventions for ODD/CD is also needed in order to replicate studies using larger sample sizes and monitoring longer periods of treatment. There are limited data available on predictors of treatment response. Since youth with ODD/CD are a very heterogeneous population, research focused on specific subgroups (e.g., ODD/CD with co-occurring mood disorder) would be very beneficial to guide clinical care. Within CD, different sub-types have been proposed, based on the presence of callous-unemotional traits, ADHD comorbidity, aggressive and nonaggressive antisocial behavior, etiologic factors, and age of onset (Hambly et al., 2016). In addition, especially in young children, ODD has been characterized as having two dimensions: one affective, one behavioral (Lavigne, Bryant, Hopkins, & Gouze, 2015). The current DSM-5 diagnostic criteria for ODD/CD also describe a very heterogenous population. For example, youth with ODD may display symptoms from either two or all three categories of symptom (mood, argumentativeness/defiance, and vindictiveness). Based on symptom heterogeneity, some experts have suggested that ODD should be considered a mixed (i.e., emotional and behavioral) disorder (Matthys, Vanderschuren, Schutter, & Lochman, 2012; Matthys, Vanderschuren, & Schutter, 2013). Research into more specific patient subgroups, defined, for example, by ODD/CD criteria and/or by the presence of psychiatric comorbidity, could help practitioners to identify which pharmacologic strategies might be effective for their particular patient.

Research into maintenance treatment strategies and further studies to compare different combinations of multimodal treatments (e.g., stimulant plus parenting skills training vs. stimulant plus school-based behavioral therapy) are also needed to guide treatment of youth with chronic and more severe illness (e.g., young people attracting repeated attention from the juvenile justice system). Longitudinal outcomes studies offering data on long-term tolerance/safety issues would also inform pharmacologic options. Furthermore, a comparison of strategies focusing on how best to sequence multimodal treatments would help tackle common challenges to clinical decision making.

The current evidence base for pharmacologic treatments of ODD/CD and maladaptive aggression/irritability is strongest with respect to the use of stimulants and select antipsychotic medications. Replication studies are needed further explore the efficacy of alpha agonists, mood stabilizers, N-acetylcysteine, and other agents.

New biological therapies may include "cognitive training" through the use of exogenous agents (e.g., procognitive drugs, dietary supplements) to target mental health disorders associated with impairment in cognitive control and socio-affective processing (Keshavan, Vinogradov, Rumsey, Sherrill, & Wagner, 2014). Dietary supplements may be an attractive option for pediatric populations, but more research is clearly needed.

Finally, little is known about the effectiveness of first-line pharmacologic treatments for the *prevention* of ODD/CD. Research into "critical windows" for the treatment of early-onset conditions (e.g., ADHD, autism, separation anxiety, etc.), and into longitudinal ODD/CD symptom outcomes, is required in order to improve strategies for the treatment of young children.

References

Aman, M. G., Bukstein, O. G., Gadow, K. D., Arnold, L. E., Molina, B. S., McNamara, N. K., . . . Findling, R. L. (2014). What does risperidone add to parent training and stimulant for severe aggression in child attention-deficit/hyperactivity disorder? *Journal of the American Academy of Child & Adolescent Psychiatry, 53*(1), 47–60.e1. doi:10.1016/j.jaac.2013.09.022

Aman, M. G., De Smedt, G., Derivan, A., Lyons, B., & Findling, R. L. (2002). Double-blind, placebo-controlled study of risperidone for the treatment of disruptive behaviors in children with subaverage intelligence. *American Journal of Psychiatry, 159*(8), 1337–1346.

Aman, M. G., & Gharabawi, G. M. (2004). Treatment of behavior disorders in mental retardation: Report on transitioning to atypical antipsychotics, with an emphasis on risperidone. *Journal of Clinical Psychiatry, 65*(9), 1197–1210.

American Academy of Child and Adolescent Psychiatry. (2011). Practice parameter for the use of atypical antipsychotic medications in children and adolescents. Retrieved from http://www.aacap.org/App_Themes/AACAP/docs/practice_parameters/Atypical_Antipsychotic_Medications_Web.pdf

Armenteros, J. L., Lewis, J. E., & Davalos, M. (2007). Risperidone augmentation for treatment-resistant aggression in attention-deficit/hyperactivity disorder: A placebo-controlled pilot study. *Journal of the American Academy of Child & Adolescent Psychiatry, 46*(5), 558–565.

Blader, J. C., Schooler, N. R., Jensen, P. S., Pliszka, S. R., & Kafantaris, V. (2009). Adjunctive divalproex versus placebo for children with ADHD and aggression refractory to stimulant monotherapy. *American Journal of Psychiatry,166*(12), 1392–1401.

Buitelaar, J. K., Van der Gaag, R. J., & Melman, C. T. (2001). A randomized controlled trial of risperidone in the treatment of aggression in hospitalized adolescents with subaverage cognitive abilities. *The Journal of Clinical Psychiatry, 62*(4), 239–248.

Campbell, M., Adams, P. B., Small, A. M., Kafantaris, V., Silva, R. R., Shell, J., . . . Overall, J. E. (1995). Lithium in hospitalized aggressive children with conduct disorder: a double-blind and placebo-controlled study. *Journal of the American Academy of Child & Adolescent Psychiatry, 34*(4), 445–453.

Campbell, M., Small, A. M., Green, W. H., Jennings, S. J., Perry, R., Bennett, W. G., & Anderson, L. (1984). Behavioral efficacy of haloperidol and lithium carbonate: A comparison in hospitalized aggressive children with conduct disorder. *Archives of General Psychiatry, 41*(7), 650–656.

Comer, J. S., Chow, C., Chan, P. T., Cooper-Vince, C., & Wilson, L. A. (2013). Psychosocial treatment efficacy for disruptive behavior problems in very young children: A meta-analytic examination. *Journal of the American Academy of Child & Adolescent Psychiatry, 52*(1), 26–36.

Connor, D. F., Glatt, S. J., Lopez, I. D., Jackson, D., & Melloni, R. H. (2002). Psychopharmacology and aggression. I: A meta-analysis of stimulant effects on overt/covert aggression–related behaviors in ADHD. *Journal of the American Academy of Child & Adolescent Psychiatry, 41*(3), 253–261.

Connor, D. F., McLaughlin, T. J., & Jeffers-Terry, M. (2008). Randomized controlled pilot study of quetiapine in the treatment of adolescent conduct disorder. *Journal of Child and Adolescent Psychopharmacology, 18*(2), 140–156.

Cueva, J. E., Overall, J. E., Small, A. M., Armenteros, J. L., Perry, R., & Campbell, M. (1996). Carbamazepine in aggressive children with conduct disorder: A double-blind and placebo-controlled study. *Journal of the American Academy of Child & Adolescent Psychiatry, 35*(4), 480–490.

Donovan, S. J., Stewart, J. W., Nunes, E. V., Quitkin, F. M., Parides, M., Daniel, W., . . . Klein, D. F. (2000). Divalproex treatment for youth with explosive temper and mood lability: A double-blind, placebo-controlled crossover design. *American Journal of Psychiatry,157*(5), 818–820.

Epstein, R., Fonnesbeck, C., Williamson, E., Kuhn, T., Lindegren, M. L., Rizzone, K., . . . Ness, G. L. (2015). *Psychosocial and Pharmacologic Interventions for Disruptive Behavior in Children and Adolescents.* Rockville, MD: Agency for Healthcare Research and Quality (US).

Findling, R. L., McNamara, N. K., Branicky, L. A., Schluchter, M. D., Lemon, E., & Blumer, J. L. (2000). A double-blind pilot study of risperidone in the treatment of conduct disorder. *Journal of the American Academy of Child & Adolescent Psychiatry, 39*(4), 509–516.

Finkelhor, D., Turner, H. A., Shattuck, A., & Hamby, S. L. (2015). Prevalence of childhood exposure to violence, crime, and abuse: Results from the National Survey of Children's Exposure to Violence. *Journal of the American Medical Association Pediatrics, 169*(8), 746–754.

Fung, L. K., Mahajan, R., Nozzolillo, A., Bernal, P., Krasner, A., Jo, B., . . . Hardan, A. Y. (2016). Pharmacologic treatment of severe irritability and problem behaviors in autism: A systematic review and meta-analysis. *Pediatrics, 137* (Supplement 2), S124–S135.

Gadow, K. D., Arnold, L. E., Molina, B. S., Findling, R. L., Bukstein, O. G., Brown, N. V., . . . Kipp, H. L. (2014). Risperidone added to parent training and stimulant medication: Effects on attention-deficit/hyperactivity disorder, oppositional defiant disorder, conduct disorder, and peer aggression. *Journal of the American Academy of Child & Adolescent Psychiatry, 53*(9), 948–959.

Gadow, K. D., Brown, N. V., Arnold, L. E., Buchan-Page, K. A., Bukstein, O. G., Butter, E., . . . Molina, B. S. (2016). Severely aggressive children receiving stimulant medication versus stimulant and risperidone: 12-month follow-up of the TOSCA trial. *Journal of the American Academy of Child & Adolescent Psychiatry, 55*(6), 469–478.

Greenhill, L., Kollins, S., Abikoff, H., McCracken, J., Riddle, M., Swanson, J., . . . Cooper, T. (2006). Efficacy and safety of immediate-release Methylphenidate treatment for preschoolers with ADHD. *Journal of the American Academy of Child and Adolescent Psychiatry, 45*(11), 1284–1293.

Greenhill, L. L., Solomon, M., Pleak, R., & Ambrosini, P. (1985). Molindone hydrochloride treatment of hospitalized children with conduct disorder. *Journal of Clinical Psychiatry, 46*(8), 20–25.

Group, M. C. (1999). A 14-month randomized clinical trial of treatment strategies for attention-deficit/hyperactivity disorder. *Archives of General Psychiatry, 56*(12), 1073–1086.

Gurnani, T., Ivanov, I., & Newcorn, J. H. (2016). Pharmacotherapy of aggression in child and adolescent psychiatric disorders. *Journal of Child and Adolescent Psychopharmacology, 26*(1), 65–73.

Hambly, J. L., Khan, S., McDermott, B., Bor, W., & Haywood, A. (2016). Pharmacotherapy of conduct disorder: Challenges, options and future directions. *Journal of Psychopharmacology, 30*(10). doi:10.1177/0269881116658985.

Jensen, P. S., Hinshaw, S. P., Kraemer, H. C., Lenora, N., Newcorn, J. H., Abikoff, H. B., . . . Conners, C. K. (2001). ADHD comorbidity findings from the MTA study: Comparing comorbid subgroups. *Journal of the American Academy of Child & Adolescent Psychiatry, 40*(2), 147–158.

Keshavan, M. S., Vinogradov, S., Rumsey, J., Sherrill, J., & Wagner, A. (2014). Cognitive training in mental disorders: Update and future directions. *American Journal of Psychiatry, 171*(5), 510–522.

Khanzode, L. A., Saxena, K., Kraemer, H., Chang, K., & Steiner, H. (2006). Efficacy profiles of psychopharmacology: Divalproex sodium in conduct disorder. *Child Psychiatry and Human Development, 37*(1), 55–64.

Klein, R. G., Abikoff, H., Klass, E., Ganeles, D., Seese, L. M., & Pollack, S. (1997). Clinical efficacy of methylphenidate in conduct disorder with and without attention deficit hyperactivity disorder. *Archives of General Psychiatry, 54*(12), 1073–1080.

Lavigne, J. V., Bryant, F. B., Hopkins, J., & Gouze, K. R. (2015). Dimensions of oppositional defiant disorder in young children: Model comparisons, gender and longitudinal invariance. *Journal of Abnormal Child Psychology, 43*(3), 423–439.

Malone, R. P., Delaney, M. A., Luebbert, J. F., Cater, J., Campbell, M. (2000). A double-blind placebo-controlled study of lithium in hospitalized aggressive children and adolescents with conduct disorder. *Archives of General Psychiatry, 57*(7), 649–654.

Matthys, W., Vanderschuren, L. J., & Schutter, D. J. (2013). The neurobiology of oppositional defiant disorder and conduct disorder: Altered functioning in three mental domains. *Development and Psychopathology, 25*(1), 193–207.

Matthys, W., Vanderschuren, L. J., Schutter, D. J., & Lochman, J. E. (2012). Impaired neurocognitive functions affect social learning processes in oppositional defiant disorder and conduct disorder: Implications for interventions. *Clinical child and family psychology review, 15*(3), 234–246.

Matthys, W., & van de Glind, G. (2013). *Richtlijn oppositioneel-opstandige stoornis (ODD) en gedragsstoornis (CD) bij kinderen en jongeren.* Utrecht, Netherlands: Nederlandse Vereniging voor Psychiatrie/De Tijdstroom.

McGuire, K., Fung, L. K., Hagopian, L., Vasa, R. A., Mahajan, R., Bernal, P., . . . Hardan, A. Y. (2016). Irritability and problem behavior in autism spectrum disorder: A practice pathway for pediatric primary care. *Pediatrics, 137* (Supplement 2), S136–S148.

MTA (the MTA Cooperative Group). (1999). A 14-month randomized clinical trial of treatment strategies for attention-deficit/hyperactivity disorder. *Archives of General Psychiatry, 56*(12), 1073–1086.

NICE-SCIE (2013). Antisocial behaviour and conduct disorders in children and young people: Recognition, intervention and management. *NICE Clinical Guideline 158.* NICE: London.

Pappadopulos, E., Jensen, P. S., Chait, A. R., Arnold, L. E., Swanson, J. M., Greenhill, L. L., . . . Pelham, W. (2009). Medication adherence in the MTA: Saliva methylphenidate samples versus parent report and mediating effect of concomitant behavioral treatment. *Journal of the American Academy of Child & Adolescent Psychiatry, 48*(5), 501–510.

Reyes, M., Buitelaar, J., Toren, P., Augustyns, I., & Eerdekens, M. (2006) A randomized, double-blind, placebo-controlled study of risperidone maintenance treatment in children and adolescents with disruptive behavior disorders. *American Journal of Psychiatry, 163*(3), 402–410.

Rifkin, A., Karajgi, B., Dicker, R., Perl, E., Boppana, V., Hasan, N., & Pollack S. (1997). Lithium treatment of conduct disorders in adolescents. *American Journal of Psychiatry,154*(4), 554–555.

Rosato, N. S., Correll, C., & Group, T. M. S. (2012). Treatment of Maladaptive Aggression in Youth (T-MAY). CERT guidelines II. Psychosocial interventions, medication treatments, and side effects management. *Pediatrics, 129*, e1577–e1586.

Safavi, P., Hasanpour-Dehkordi, A., & AmirAhmadi, M. (2016). Comparison of risperidone and aripiprazole in the treatment of preschool children with disruptive behavior disorder and attention deficit-hyperactivity disorder: A randomized clinical trial. *Journal of Advanced Pharmaceutical Technology & Research, 7*(2), 43–47.

Saxena, K., Mora, L., Torres, E., Hall, R., Delizonna, L., Torres, A., & Steiner H. (2010). Divalproex sodium-ER in outpatients with disruptive behavior disorders: A three month open label study. *Child Psychiatry & Human Development, 41*(3), 274–284.

Snyder, R., Turgay, A., Aman, M., Binder, C., Fisman, S., & Carroll, A. (2002). Effects of risperidone on conduct and disruptive behavior disorders in children with subaverage IQs. *Journal of the American Academy of Child & Adolescent Psychiatry, 41*(9), 1026–1036.

Spencer, D., Marshall, J., Post, B., Kulakodlu, M., Newschaffer, C., Dennen, T., . . . Jain, A. (2013). Psychotropic medication use and polypharmacy in children with autism spectrum disorders. *Pediatrics, 132*(5), 833–840.

Steiner, H., Petersen, M., Saxena, K., Ford, S., & Matthews, Z. (2003). A randomized clinical trial of divalproex sodium in conduct disorders. *Journal of Clinical Psychiatry, 64,* 1183–1191.

Stocks J. D., Taneja, B. K., Baroldi, P., Findling, R. L. (2012). A phase 2a randomized, parallel group, dose-ranging study of molindone in children with attention-deficit/hyperactivity disorder and persistent, serious conduct problems. *Journal of Child and Adolescent Psychopharmacology, 22*(2), 102–111.

Van Bellinghen, M., & De Troch, C. (2001). Risperidone in the treatment of behavioral disturbances in children and adolescents with borderline intellectual functioning: A double-blind, placebo-controlled pilot trial. *Journal of Child and Adolescent Psychopharmacology, 11*(1), 5–13.

West, A. E., Weinstein, S. M., Celio, C. I., Henry, D., & Pavuluri, M. N. (2011). Co-morbid disruptive behavior disorder and aggression predict functional outcomes and differential response to risperidone versus divalproex in pharmacotherapy for pediatric bipolar disorder. *Journal of Child and Adolescent Psychopharmacology, 21*(6), 545–553.

26

Psychosocial Treatment and Prevention of Conduct Problems in Early Childhood

Danielle Cornacchio, Laura J. Bry, Amanda L. Sanchez, Bridget Poznanski, and Jonathan S. Comer

Conduct problems (CPs) and disruptive behavior disorders—characterized by problems of aggression, oppositionality, noncompliance, and/or serious rule-breaking behavior—collectively constitute one of the most prevalent classes of problems affecting very young children (Egger & Angold, 2006; see Chapters 2 and 3 of this *Handbook* for extended descriptions of Conduct Disorder and Oppositional Defiant Disorder). Conduct problems can be reliably assessed as early as infancy (Bagner, Rodríguez, Blake, Linares, & Carter, 2012) and formal disruptive behavior disorders can be reliably diagnosed as early as age 2 (Egger et al., 2006). Estimates suggest that roughly 1 in 11 preschoolers meets the formal diagnostic criteria for a disruptive behavior disorder, with 1 in 14 meeting the criteria for Oppositional Defiant Disorder and 1 in 30 meeting those for Conduct Disorder (Egger & Angold, 2006).

When left untreated, early-onset CPs (i.e., those presenting prior to age 7) tend to persist. Stability estimates suggest that roughly 50–60% of toddlers with disruptive behavior disorders continue to meet the criteria for their diagnoses at two-year follow-up (e.g., Bunte, Schoemaker, Hessen, Van Der Heijden, & Matthys, 2014), and CPs observed in early childhood show substantial concordance with CPs subsequently observed in middle childhood and adolescence (e.g., Lavigne et al., 2001). Moreover, early-onset CPs are associated with considerable impairment and increased service utilization into middle childhood (Essex et al., 2009), and, in later life, are associated with increased psychopathology (e.g., Hofstra, van der Ende, & Verhulst, 2002), delinquency and criminality (e.g., Copeland, Miller-Johnson, Keeler, Angold, & Costello, 2007), substance misuse (Fergusson, Horwood, & Riddler, 2007), unemployment (Kokko & Pulkkinen, 2000), and family dysfunction (Kim-Cohen, Moffitt, Taylor, Pawlby, & Caspi, 2005).

Given the early onset and pernicious course of CPs across the lifespan, effective early intervention is critical. Despite daunting statistics relating to the prevalence, scope, and impact of early-onset CPs, the past few decades, fortunately, have seen tremendous advances in the development and evaluation of evidence-based psychosocial procedures, with demonstrable success in treating aggression, oppositionality, noncompliance, and rule-breaking behaviors in very young children (Comer, Chow, Chan, Cooper-Vince, & Wilson, 2013). These procedures have drawn largely upon developmentally informed behavioral models for intervention, often

---

The Wiley Handbook of Disruptive and Impulse-Control Disorders, First Edition.
Edited by John E. Lochman and Walter Matthys.
© 2018 John Wiley & Sons Ltd. Published 2018 by John Wiley & Sons Ltd.

evidencing the negative and/or coercive parenting practices associated with the maintenance of CPs prove to be malleable when targeted early (Reid, Webster-Stratton, & Baydar, 2004).

In this chapter we offer a review of the behavioral model of psychosocial treatment for early-onset CPs. We then turn our attention to three common formats of psychosocial treatment for them: individual family-based treatment, group-based treatment, and school-based treatment. This is followed by an overview of some of the leading evidence-based psychosocial intervention protocols for early-onset CPs. We then highlight a number of promising trends in, and future directions for, the psychosocial treatment of early childhood CPs, including technology-based treatments to expand the scope and reach of care and intensive treatment formats. We conclude by discussing areas in need of further empirical attention in order to optimize psychosocial procedures for redressing CPs that present in early childhood.

The Behavioral Model of Psychosocial Treatment for Early-Onset CPs

The intervention programs for young children with CPs best supported by the outcomes of clinical trials are behavioral in nature (Comer et al., 2013), and incorporate social learning theory (Bandura, 1977) and coercion theory (Patterson, 1982). These programs specifically focus on rewarding positive child behaviors, ignoring relatively minor child misbehaviors, and implementing consistent consequences for more serious misbehaviors. Most supported programs for early child CPs focus specifically on the family context, incorporating attachment theory and scientific findings regarding effective parenting styles (e.g., Baumrind, 1978; see also Chapter 19 of this book). The cognitive limitations of preschool-aged children make it difficult to engage them directly in cognitively mediated self-control strategies, self-statements, perspective-taking, and coping skills, as one might if treating an older child or adolescent with conduct problems (e.g., Lochman, Wells, & Lenhart, 2008; although by the early elementary school period, there are developmentally sensitive programs that show success with issues of emotion management and problem solving). Simple "downward" extensions of treatments designed for older individuals are therefore inappropriate (see Cornacchio, Sanchez, Chou, & Comer, 2017). Instead, evidence-based behavioral treatments for early child CPs will typically target child behavior indirectly, by reshaping parenting practices and patterns that may serve to promote or maintain the problems. These programs work to disrupt negative and coercive family dynamics that inadvertently reinforce and perpetuate negative child behaviors.

Evidence-based psychosocial programs for early child CPs work to improve structure, consistency, predictability, and follow-through in children's lives, and these programs share several key components typical of behaviorist principles and social learning theory. Supported programs emphasize *positive reinforcement* as a primary mechanism of change, in which the adults in children's lives are taught to attend to and reward desired child behaviors (e.g., sharing, using kind words, using gentle hands). Rewards can be either social (e.g., praise, attention, special time with parents) or tangible (e.g., toys) but, for younger children, social reinforcements tend to be more salient and effective than tangible rewards. Positive reinforcement—even if for very brief instances of positive behavior—is particularly important for young children with CPs, because these children generally receive excessive negative attention in their environments (e.g., yelling, tense parent–child and teacher–child relationships, isolation from peers). This can serve to maintain and exacerbate negative child behaviors and to foster low self-efficacy and low self-esteem. Parents are taught to focus on the *positive opposites* of negative child behavior (e.g., praising a typically aggressive child for using gentle hands;

Kazdin, 2005). Supported psychosocial programs also emphasize *differential attention*, in which the adults in children's lives are taught not only to give positive attention to desired child behaviors, but also to deliberately ignore instances of minor misbehavior (e.g., removing attention from a child who is whining or raising its voice). Increased attention, whether negative (e.g., yelling, spanking) or positive (e.g., praise, affection), can maintain child behavior problems. The swift removal of active attention from negative child behaviors, on the other hand, promotes learning, by offering an important sharp contrast to the positive attention afforded to desired child behaviors.

Supported behavioral programs for early child CPs also emphasize consistency within and across child settings in order to optimize the predictability of expectations and consequences. Adults learn to set limits and use clear commands to direct children's behavior and implement effective, structured, and predictable discipline strategies for child misconduct. Research suggests that "time-out" procedures are the best supported discipline strategies for misconduct in early childhood (Quetsch, Wallace, Herschell, & McNeil, 2016). Arthur Staats (1971) originally coined the term "time-out," an abbreviation of what behavior analysts describe as "time-out from positive reinforcement" (Kazdin, 2001, p. 210). It refers to the removal of a positive reinforcer for a brief and specific period of time. In supported psychosocial treatment for early child CPs, adults are taught to remove children from positively reinforcing environments immediately following their misconduct or noncompliance, for a structured period of 1–7 minutes. Importantly, time-out as specified in supported behavioral interventions does not involve the active introduction of a negative environment, but, rather, the removal of the child from a positively reinforcing environment in a calm and controlled manner. Given the restricted attention spans characteristic of early childhood, immediate removal from a positive environment is typically more effective than the withdrawal of privileges or the application of consequences that unfold across longer periods of time.

Treatment Formats for the Psychosocial Treatment of Early-Onset CPs

Although the common behavioral principles and strategies of positive attention, differential attention, and time-out underlie many of the supported psychosocial treatments for early child CPs, these principles and strategies can be implemented via a number of varied treatment formats, including individual family-based formats, group-based formats, and school-based formats. We now consider each of these treatment formats in turn for the psychosocial treatment of early child CPs.

Individual Family-Based Formats

Many of the best supported psychosocial interventions for early child CPs utilize the individual family-based format, in which the therapist works directly with a single family, and focuses on parents as the primary agents of change. Therapy is designed to reshape parenting practices and household patterns that can trigger or maintain child behavior problems.

A family-based approach is useful for many reasons. First, young children with CPs are often referred by their parents for treatment of problems that they do not agree that they have, and consequently they often show little motivation to engage directly in treatment or to collaborate with a therapist. Second, as noted above, young children with CPs typically lack the cognitive sophistication to engage directly in child-focused psychosocial intervention. Third, successful treatment of child CPs requires extensive practice and work outside of treatment sessions, and younger children lack the executive functioning and organizational skills to complete treatment homework tasks independently (Cornacchio et al., 2017). Fourth, any gains made in treatment sessions without parents present often dissipate quickly if the child returns to an unchanged, dysfunctional family environment.

Behavioral family-based interventions are typically structured around the Hanf two-stage model of parental intervention (Hanf, 1969; Reitman & McMahon, 2013). Stage I focuses on differential reinforcement, positive attending, improving parental responsiveness, and on building a pattern of warm parent–child interactions. Parents are taught specifically to describe and praise their child's appropriate behaviors, to reflect their child's appropriate language, and to actively ignore unwanted behaviors. Building on the newly improved foundations of positive parent–child interaction generated by Stage I, Stage II then focuses on giving parents the skills to guide children's behavior, to promote compliance, and to develop effective time-out contingency plans for incidences of noncompliance and misbehavior. Parents are specifically taught how to give effective commands (e.g., clear, direct, and developmentally compatible "do" commands), how to be consistent in giving their child the opportunity to comply, and how either to praise compliance or follow through with a consistent time-out procedure if necessary (Reitman & McMahon, 2013).

In the two-stage Hanf sequence, therapists also systematically conduct structured observations of parent and child behaviors to inform the course and nature of subsequent treatment sessions and identify areas in need of focused clinical attention. This empirical approach also guides clinical decisions about when to move from Stage I to Stage II, and when to consider treatment complete. Out-of-session practice of skills learned in treatment is considered an essential ingredient of treatment.

Individual family-based formats for treatment for early child CPs are generally clinic-based, and take place as scheduled outpatient appointments within a community-, hospital-, or university-based treatment setting (e.g., Eyberg & Funderburk, 2011; McMahon & Forehand, 2005). Clinic-based intervention allows treatment to take place in a controlled environment that optimizes children's chances for a successful outcome. For example, many clinic-based interventions allow for the teaching and practicing of skills in rooms specifically designed for the treatment of young children with CPs (e.g., rooms with few distractions and only the necessary treatment materials; nothing breakable, such as windows or computers, no objects that could result in serious injury or destruction of property if thrown by the child). Further, clinic-based intervention can involve discreet *in vivo* coaching of parents, via a "bug-in-the-ear" while therapists observe parent–child interactions from behind a one-way mirror.

Some individual family-based formats of treatment for early child CPs are delivered directly in families' homes (Bagner, Rodríguez, Blake, & Rosa-Olivares, 2013). Home-based delivery of intervention expands the reach of supported care for affected families by overcoming many typical barriers that undermine the accessibility of clinic-based treatment (e.g., transportation, geographical obstacles, cost). Home-based intervention is particularly useful strategy when targeting at-risk families who may not self-identify as needing treatment, may not present at clinical settings for services, and/or may have concerns about the stigma related to attending a mental health clinic. Importantly, home-based intervention can also improve the ecological validity of treatment by providing services to families directly in the home where many early child CPs naturally occur. Some individual family-based treatments were designed from the outset for home-based delivery (e.g., Dishion & Kavanagh, 2003), whereas other home-based interventions have been adapted from clinic-based treatment protocols (Bagner et al., 2013).

Group-Based Formats

In addition to treatments that focus on one family at a time, group-based formats simultaneously treating multiple families have also proved to be an efficient and effective strategy for delivering psychosocial treatment for early child CPs. Group formats improve the cost effectiveness of care and therapist efficiency, reduce waitlists more quickly than individual family treatment models, and optimize therapist time (Dretzke et al, 2009). Multi-family group formats also offer opportunities for social support, modeling, and group practice of skills, which are not available in individual family formats (Dretzke et al., 2009; Niec, Hemme, Yopp, & Brestan, 2005). There is evidence that minority families find group treatment formats more acceptable than individual family services (Cunningham, Bremner, & Boyle, 1995), and some research suggests that group-based formats yield lower rates of attrition (Niec et al., 2005). Most importantly, group formats do not appear to dilute the efficacy of care. Meta-analytic work reveals limited or no differences between group and individual treatment format outcomes (Comer et al., 2013; Shechtman & Ben-David, 1999; Weisz, Han, Granger, & Morton, 1995). Many group parenting interventions for early CPs are extensions or adaptations of individual family-based formats, but with the active components and their delivery (e.g., psychoeducation, skills, coaching) modified for a parent group format. There are also several group models in which children are the recipients of direct intervention, although most of these child groups are run alongside a parallel parent group (e.g., Webster-Stratton & Reid, 2003).

School-Based Formats

Despite advances in family- and group-based treatment formats for early child CPs, the overwhelming majority of young children in need do not receive services (Kataoka, Zhang, & Wells, 2002). For young children who have already started school or who are in day care for large parts of the day, delivering treatment in the school setting offers an ecologically valid treatment option that can reach more children in need and reduce traditional barriers to care, such as cost, time, and transportation. School-based options can also be useful when parents do not recognize that their child's behavior is problematic or when, for various reasons, parents are unable to participate in treatment. Indeed, families perceive school-based treatments to be very acceptable, as is evidenced by the higher rate at which they seek services for their children in the school context, compared to medical and mental health settings (Burns et al., 1995).

Effective school-based programs for early CPs utilize the same behavioral principles as family-based and group-based programs, including positive reinforcement, contingency management, differential attention, and setting-consistent consequences. Many school-based interventions for early child CPs focus on training teachers in behavior management skills in order to improve individual child behavior problems as well as to facilitate the overall learning environment of the classroom.

For young children with CPs who have already started school, daily report cards (DRCs) are a supported strategy commonly employed in the classroom. DRCs track specific behaviors throughout every school day. They also promote teacher–parent communication and school–home consistency, and inform structured reinforcement for appropriate child behavior (Cornacchio et al., 2017). It is typically recommended that one or two specific positive behaviors be tracked (e.g., keeping hands to self, using nice words) during specific time periods throughout the day. For example, for a preschool child, the day might be broken into 4–6 time periods (e.g., morning play time, circle time, lunch time, recess, story time, dismissal). For each time period the child can earn a happy (or sad) face on the record card for keeping his or her hands to him or herself (or not doing so). The number of happy faces the child earns is tracked daily, and children receive rewards at home (or at school, if parents cannot participate) for earning a specified number of happy faces (i.e., meeting specific target goals) in school. Targeted behaviors become more difficult and/or the number of points/happy faces required to earn rewards increases as the child makes behavioral gains.

Leading Psychosocial Intervention Protocols for the Treatment of Early-Onset CPs

A number of specific treatment and prevention protocols (incorporating the behavioral psychosocial strategies and the family-, group-, and school-based formats discussed above) have gained increasing empirical support and popularity in the past few decades (see Eyberg, Nelson, & Boggs, 2008). These largely overlapping and neighboring protocols share most underlying principles, but differ in some key ways. We now review some of the most widely researched and utilized protocols for the treatment of early child CPs.

Parent-Child Interaction Therapy (PCIT)

PCIT is an individual family treatment for early CPs (Eyberg & Funderburk, 2011), and one of the best supported behavioral parenting interventions for early CPs based on the Hanf two-stage model. The first stage of PCIT is referred to as Child Directed Interaction (CDI). In the CDI stage, parents are taught specific skills for giving positive attention to appropriate behaviors and for actively ignoring negative behaviors. The second stage of PCIT is referred to as Parent Directed Interaction (PDI). In this stage, parents learn specific disciplinary strategies, such as how to give effective commands and how to follow through using a consistent time-out sequence. Both CDI and PDI stages begin with a parents-only "teach" session in which parents are taught the specific skills that will be practiced and mastered during that phase of treatment. Teach sessions are followed by a series of coaching sessions, in which therapists coach parents on the use of the newly learned skills during parent–child interactions. A distinguishing feature of PCIT is the regular use of live coaching of individual parents via a bug-in-the-ear receiver by a therapist who discreetly monitors family interactions from an observation room. The bug-in-the-ear format for delivering coaching from behind a one-way mirror allows the therapist to provide direction to parents without the child hearing. The focus of each parent-coaching session is directly informed by weekly coding by the therapist of parent skills and by recording child symptoms using the Eyberg Child Behavior Inventory (ECBI). Progression through (and eventual graduation from) treatment is determined by parental mastery of CDI and PDI skills and by adequate reductions in child symptoms.

Meta-analysis has demonstrated PCIT to be a highly efficacious and effective protocol with very strong potential for dissemination (Cooley, Veldorale-Griffin, Petren, & Mullis, 2014). PCIT has also proved to be highly robust and versatile and has been adapted to meet the clinical needs of a range of different populations and problems (e.g., children with developmental delay, children born prematurely, children with early internalizing problems, and maltreating families; Bagner et al., 2016; Bagner & Eyberg, 2007; Carpenter, Puliafico, Kurtz, Pincus, & Comer, 2014; Comer et al., 2012; Thomas & Zimmer-Gembeck, 2012). For example, Bagner and colleagues (2013) adapted the CDI phase of PCIT for delivery as a brief intervention for infants exhibiting externalizing problems in the home setting. Comer and colleagues (2012) modified PCIT to incorporate live exposure tasks for treating early child anxiety problems. Some investigators have even trialed a group-based version of the PCIT format, in which 3–7 families meet simultaneously with a therapist for weekly sessions (e.g., Niec et al., 2005, 2016). Abbreviated group PCIT formats have also been tested in primary care settings (Berkovits, O'Brien, Carter, & Eyberg, 2010).

A school-based adaptation of PCIT, referred to as Teacher–Child Interaction Training (TCIT; Budd, Barbacz, & Carter, 2015), works to improve teacher–child interactions and to equip teachers with skills for managing difficult child behaviors in the classroom. In a Teacher-Directed Interaction (TDI) phase of training, teachers are given CDI skills as well as effective discipline skills. Although the specific structure of TCIT has varied across protocols, all TCIT protocols have included didactic teach sessions (usually in a group format) and live coaching at both CDI and TDI stages. TCIT has been rolled out as a universal prevention program in regular classrooms, as well as implemented as a targeted treatment.

Helping the Noncompliant Child (HNC)

HNC is another well-supported intervention for early childhood CPs that follows the Hanf two-stage model (McMahon & Forehand, 2005). HNC is an individual family-based treatment, and is similar in structure and delivery to traditional PCIT, with regular weekly sessions focused on coaching parents towards mastery of specific parenting skills. Five specific skills (attending, rewarding, ignoring, clear instructions, and time-out) are taught to parents across two phases (the differential attention phase, and the compliance training phase). Parents learn to set appropriate limits and respond with appropriate consequences to child compliance and noncompliance. They are also taught skills via role-plays and direct *in vivo* practice with their child. As in PCIT, parents must demonstrate proficiency in all of the aforementioned skills in order to progress through treatment.

The Incredible Years (IY)

The Incredible Years (Webster-Stratton & Reid, 2003) is another well-supported intervention for early childhood CPs; it incorporates multiple treatment components, including both individual and group formats across various settings. IY is a three-part treatment for children with disruptive behavior problems. There are group parent (IY-PT), group child (IY-CT), and group teacher (IY-TT) training components. Both IY-PT and IY-CT have been posited as "probably efficacious" interventions (Eyberg et al., 2008).

IY-PT consists of 18–20 two-hour sessions with 8–12 parents per group. With the assistance of video vignettes, IY-PT groups teach positive parent–child interactions and effective disciplinary strategies (Webster-Stratton & Reid, 2003). A meta-analysis of studies examining IY-PT revealed an overall large effect on reducing problematic child behavior and increasing prosocial behavior, with larger effects for children with greater severity of problem behaviors prior to treatment (Menting, Orobio de Castro, & Matthys, 2013). IY appears to be comparable across families of varying socioeconomic backgrounds and ethnicities (Leijten, Raaijmakers, Orobio de Castro, van den Ban, & Matthys, 2017).

IY-CT (also referred to as "Dinosaur School") is a 22-week program for 3–8 year olds in which six children and one therapist meet for two hours each week. IY-CT is delivered using a series of video vignettes, after which the children engage in discussion about feelings, problem solving, and role-plays. IY-CT is often delivered in conjunction with IY-PT or IY-TT, although studies have revealed benefits when IY-CT is delivered alone (Webster-Stratton, Reid, & Hammond, 2004). Gains tend to be even stronger, however, when IY-CT is delivered in parallel with an IY-PT or IY-TT group.

IY-TT (Webster-Stratton, Reid, & Hammond, 2004) is made up of a 6-day training program (offered over the course of several months by IY-certified trainers) for teachers and other school personnel (e.g., school counselors) that focuses on effective classroom management, promoting positive relationships between teachers and children with behavior problems, and promoting positive communication with parents. IY-TT has been used as a part of a series of treatments for children with behavior problems and as a prevention program among children most at risk for behavior problems (i.e., high poverty); it has demonstrated encouraging outcomes in clinical evaluations (Webster-Stratton, Reid, & Stoolmiller, 2008).

The Positive Parenting Program (Triple P)

Triple P (Sanders, Turner, & Markie-Dadds, 2002) is another popular and well-supported intervention for child CPs that focuses on positive parenting and behavior management. Triple P is unique in having been designed to be delivered in a number of different ways and for children at various levels of risk (e.g., in preventative or high-risk contexts). Triple P offers families support in various information formats (e.g., self-directed learning modules, phone consultation) and encourages parents to use positive reinforcement and effective communication, and to apply structured and consistent consequences for misbehavior. Triple P interventions are organized by levels of intensity. Level 1 is "Universal Triple P" and is *not* a targeted intervention, but rather a way of accessing a large parenting population, offering universal materials to encourage positive parenting skills, improve parenting confidence, and reduce stigma around parental help seeking. Level 2 is for parents who have mild concerns about their child's behavior; parents can attend seminars or have a brief consultation with a primary care provider. Level 3 targets parents of children with mild to moderate behavior problems, and entails multiple consultations or face-to-face intervention sessions. Level 4 care is for parents of children with severe behavior problems who need more consistent or intensive intervention. Level 5 care is for families with severe problems or dysfunction, including more serious child psychopathology, high partner conflict, and/or child maltreatment. There are various formats for intervention delivery at each level. Parents can participate in treatment in a group, online, or in a self-directed format using a workbook.

Meta-analyses indicate that Triple P programs are associated with significant improvements in child behavior, parental well-being, and parenting skills, and that these gains are maintained across over time (Sanders, Kirby, Tellegen, & Day, 2014). More pronounced improvements have been associated with a higher level of intensity in Triple P intervention (Nowak & Heinrichs, 2008).

Family Check-Up (FCU)

The early childhood version of the Family Check-Up (Dishion & Kavanagh, 2003) is a brief home-based intervention targeting child behavior problems and family engagement. Parents are interviewed in their home and goals are identified for their child and family. Feedback is subsequently provided to parents with an emphasis on motivational interviewing and engaging families in the intervention process. Follow-up intervention is then recommended based on the family's needs (e.g., services to address parental psychopathology, collaboration between parents and school). The FCU model is a family-centered approach (i.e., compared to other behavioral parent management programs such as PCIT or HNC, FCU advice is more individualized and based on each family's specific needs), and its relatively brief and home-based format—along with its focus on enhancing parental motivation and engagement—lends itself well to the goals of population-wide implementation and universal prevention. The FCU is commonly delivered by paraprofessionals or non-mental health professionals, and has shown great success in preventing and reducing behavior problems in early childhood, and improving school readiness (Lunkenheimer et al., 2008). Randomized trials have also shown that the FCU can help to prevent neglect and improve positive parent–child engagement (e.g., Dishion et al., 2015), and promote increased service utilization across time (Leijten et al., 2015).

Nurse Family Partnership (NFP)

The NFP (Olds, 2006) is another example of a home-based intervention that uses the mental health workforce to supply prevention and intervention services to a large population. The NFP utilizes registered nurses who regularly visit the families of low-income first-time mothers from pregnancy until the child turns two. Nurses provide health and prenatal care as well as parenting strategies. While the NFP does not directly target child behavior problems (i.e., instead it focuses on parent–child health and appropriate parenting), it has shown success in preventing later conduct problems (e.g., Olds et al., 1998).

Summer Treatment Program for Pre-Kindergarteners (STP-PreK)

Intensive group intervention models have also been employed to combat problem behaviors in young children, and to prevent the development of these behaviors following school entry. One example is the STP-PreK (Graziano, Slavec, Hart, Garcia, & Pelham, 2014), an intensive, full-day, 8-week, group-based intervention for children with behavior problems who are transitioning into kindergarten. The STP-PreK is a downward extension of the successful Summer Treatment Program (STP) for ADHD in elementary and middle school children (Pelham & Fabiano, 2008), and uses a behavior modification system to target problem behaviors while incorporating a school-readiness and social-emotional curriculum. The intervention is delivered to children in groups of approximately 15 with a 1:3 staff to student ratio. A *contingency management* system is used, in which children earn points for appropriate behaviors, and lose points for inappropriate behaviors. These points result in specific rewards throughout the day and the duration of the program. There is also a weekly group parent training component that focuses on improving the caregiver–child relationship and on increasing the parental use of effective behavior management skills. Preliminary studies have demonstrated improvement across domains including children's academic, social-emotional, and behavioral functioning, as well as self-regulation (Graziano, Slavec, Hart, Garcia, & Pelham, 2014). Although promising, STP-PreK is one of the newer formats and approaches for treating early child CPs; further studies are needed to examine the maintenance of treatment gains across time, and to explicate the elements of active intervention.

A variety of other supported school-based programs exist for the early elementary school years, such as the School-Wide Positive Behavioral Interventions and Supports program (SWPBIS; Sugai, Horner, & Gresham, 2002), a behavioral system comprised of primary and secondary prevention and targeted efforts at intervention, and the Good Behavior Game (GBG; Barrish, Saunders, & Wolff, 1969), a classroom-level behavior management program (see Chapter 27 for more information on these and related programs).

Promising Trends and Innovations in the Psychosocial Treatment of Early-Onset CPs

Despite tremendous progress in the development and evaluation of well-supported psychosocial options for preventing and treating CPs in young children, a gap persists between treatments in research settings and services generally available to the majority of youth in need. There are systematic barriers to evidence-based practices being widely accessible, and the majority of young children with CPs do not receive quality care (Comer & Barlow, 2014).

In fact, a recent meta-analysis examining psychosocial interventions for early disruptive behavior problems found the largest treatment effects when comparing supported psychosocial interventions with treatment-as-usual control groups, relative to experimental comparisons with inactive control groups (Comer et al., 2013). Put another way, both no-treatment control groups and supportive control groups are currently yielding stronger outcomes than "usual-care" options for young children with CPs.

A number of barriers currently limit access to quality care. First, there is a shortage of trained mental health professionals, resulting in a significant gap in the workforce relative to the extent of mental health need among families in the general population (Kazdin & Blasé, 2011). Second, the majority of trained professionals practice in urban or suburban areas, or areas centralized around academic hubs (Thomas & Holzer, 2006), leaving large numbers of youth in rural and/or other remote areas underserved. Further, given personpower workforce disparities and limited reimbursement for mental health care, frontline mental health providers are commonly overburdened; this, combined with the proliferation of overlapping psychosocial interventions, prevents providers from pursuing adequate training in and mastery of many supported interventions.

Moreover, research examining the efficacy of psychosocial interventions for early child CPs has been criticized for failing to use samples that more readily generalize to the broader populations of youth in need of services. For example, youth in real-time care settings tend to present with more complex needs and higher problem rates than youth evaluated in clinical trials (Baker-Ericzén, Hurlburt, Brookman-Frazee, Jenkins, & Hough, 2010). Research trials often exclude participants with more complex presentations (i.e., the methodology includes rule-outs at given thresholds of symptom severity or comorbidity). As a consequence, some community practitioners treating complex cases may, regrettably, disregard research-evaluated treatments (Addis & Krasnow, 2000).

Yet despite these barriers to care and limits to the dissemination of evidence-based treatments for early child CPs, the past decade has witnessed an exciting surge in innovative efforts aimed at overcoming these challenges (see also Chapter 29). We now briefly consider two of the most promising trends toward expanding the accessibility and acceptability of evidence-based practices for early child CPs: (1) the use of technology to expand the scope and reach of supported care; and (2) intensive treatment formats.

Using Technology to Expand The Scope and Reach of Supported Care

The communications revolution has brought opportunities to advance our science and to incorporate novel technological elements into existing evidence-based interventions. Technology-based or -enhanced treatments often aim to circumvent traditional barriers to care and thereby to increase access to supported interventions (Comer, 2015; Comer, Elkins, Chan, & Jones, 2014; Crum & Comer, 2016).

Internet-based or -assisted parent management training programs have shown initial efficacy, feasibility, and acceptability among participants. For example, a self-administered online adaptation of the Triple P Positive Parenting Program found positive outcomes on measures of disruptive behavior and dysfunctional parenting styles at post-treatment and 6-month follow-up, relative to a control group (Sanders, Baker, & Turner, 2012). Similarly, a self-administered Internet-based adaptation of a Swedish parent management training program, called Comet, yielded significant reductions in disruptive child behaviors and increases in positive parenting (Enebrink, Högström, Forster, & Ghaderi, 2012). A recent study points to the broader effectiveness of an Internet- and telephone-based program for 4-year-olds screened from a large primary healthcare clinic. Relative to an educational control group, intervention participants saw significant improvements on a range of behavioral and parenting outcomes at post-treatment and follow-up (Sourander et al., 2016).

Smartphone-based and related mobile phone initiatives also show great promise in terms of improving the accessibility of evidence-based care and increasing the engagement of families in parent management training (Jones et al., 2015). For example, in an innovative technology-enhanced version of HNC, Jones et al. (2014) added smartphone-based skills videos, daily surveys, text messages, video recording of practice at home and mid-week calls to promote engagement between sessions. Data from an initial study showed that, compared to the standard HNC group, participants in the technology-enhanced HNC group had higher levels of engagement on all measures and required fewer sessions to complete the program.

Videoconferencing formats offer an opportunity to extend the reach of the highest quality care options, without increasing the demand on therapist time and attention (Crum & Comer, 2016). Given that supported behavioral parent management programs rely primarily on therapist observation and verbal communication with parents, videoconferencing formats are beginning to show success in bypassing geographic barriers to care and delivering real-time treatment to families in need, regardless of their physical proximity to supported care for early child CPs (Comer et al., 2014). For example, Comer and colleagues (2015) are currently evaluating the efficacy, feasibility, and acceptability of leveraging videoconferencing technology to deliver PCIT remotely, in real time, to families in their homes. Using webcams, families broadcast their home-based parent–child interactions to therapists during weekly sessions, and therapists provide live coaching to parents via a Bluetooth earpiece worn by the parent (see also Elkins & Comer, 2014). It is anticipated that, in addition to improving the accessibility of PCIT, Internet-delivered PCIT may improve the ecological validity of care by treating families in their natural settings (i.e., in their homes, where many early CPs and dysfunctional parent–child interactions occur). A randomized trial comparing Internet-delivered PCIT (I-PCIT) with standard clinic-based PCIT recently completed, with preliminary outcomes showing support for the feasibility and positive outcomes associated with videoconferencing-based PCIT. In fact, the rate of "excellent responders" was significantly higher among children treated with I-PCIT relative to clinic-based PCIT, and parents of children treated with I-PCIT reported significantly fewer barriers to treatment participation than parents of children treated with clinic-based PCIT (Comer et al., under reviewunder review). A larger randomized trial is also currently underway, to evaluate the effectiveness of real-time videoconferencing-based PCIT for treating CPs in young children with developmental delay.

Intensive Treatment Formats

In addition to technology-assisted treatment models, intensive treatment formats—in which patients travel to attend a brief series of all-day sessions of focused treatment not offered in their local community—can also address geographic disparities in the availability of evidence-based care (Comer et al., 2014). Intensive treatment can also overcome problems of engagement in regions where quality services are available. For example, families with limited time and/or resources may not be able to commit to regular attendance and compliance with homework requirements over an extended course of weekly treatments, but may be able to engage fully when the entire course is condensed into a relatively short (e.g., one- week) period of all-day sessions.

Recent pilot work supports the preliminary feasibility of engaging families in extended parent management sessions on a daily basis for a two-week period (Graziano et al., 2015). Results so far have shown high treatment completion and satisfaction rates, positive changes in parenting, and improvements in young children's CPs at post-treatment and at 4-month follow-up. Future research, utilizing controlled designs and incorporating comparisons with traditional weekly formats is now needed, in order to examine the full potential of intensive treatment formats for early CPs as vehicles for overcoming traditional barriers to quality care and family engagement.

Conclusions

Serious conduct problems declare themselves in early childhood, are highly persistent, worsen over time, and, when left untreated, are associated with considerable costs to the individual, family, and society at large. Fortunately, the past several decades have witnessed the development and evaluation of evidence-based assessment, prevention, and treatment practices that are effective in identifying youth with early CPs and can significantly reduce aggression, oppositionality, noncompliance, and serious rule-breaking behavior in early childhood (Comer et al., 2013). More recent research incorporating long-term follow-up evaluations suggests that early psychosocial intervention for child CPs can even reduce rates of adult psychopathology, substance use, and criminality (Dodge et al., 2015). The best supported psychosocial protocols for early child CPs are behavioral (Comer et al., 2013), incorporate social learning theory (Bandura, 1977), and focus on rewarding positive child behaviors, ignoring relatively minor child misbehaviors, and implementing consistent consequences for more serious child misbehaviors. Promoting structure, predictability, and follow-through in children's environments is key. Research has demonstrated that positive outcomes are associated with a variety of treatment formats, including individual family-based formats, group-based formats, and—for young children who have started school or spend much of their time in day care—school-based treatment formats. In this chapter, we reviewed a number of the leading evidence-based prevention and treatment protocols for early child CPs that have been supported in clinical trials.

However, despite these promising developments, recent trends in service use call for a renewed sense of urgency in the development of innovative methods to improve the availability of supported psychosocial practices. Systematic barriers—including geographic disparities in quality care, and difficulties in disseminating so many very similar protocols for early child CPs—interfere with the broad availability of supported services for a considerable proportion of families in need. Limitations in the resources needed to deliver evidence-based psychosocial treatment options place a heavy clinical demand on the pharmacologic dimensions of mental health care (Comer & Barlow, 2014). For young children, pediatricians typically fill the geographic workforce gaps in mental health care, but tend to lack the time and training to adequately address the needs of young children with CPs. Indeed, in recent years we have seen a progressive expansion in the use of off-label psychotropic medications, many with unfavorable side effects, to treat early child mental health problems (Comer, Olfson, & Mojtabai, 2010; Olfson, Crystal, Huang, & Gerhard, 2010). For example, there has been a two- to fivefold increase in antipsychotic prescriptions for very young children with CPs (Olfson, Crystal, Huang, & Gerhard, 2010; Zito et al., 2007), despite the absence of controlled trials evaluating the safety and efficacy of many off-label psychotropics for very young children.

Recent years have seen the development of several promising trends addressing traditional barriers to quality psychosocial care, including the increased use of technology to extend the reach of care and the development of intensive treatment formats and facilities for families lacking local quality services. With continued empirical support and innovation, these exciting new methods and modes of service delivery hold great promise for advancing and transforming the broad relevance and public health significance of evidence-based psychosocial treatments for early child CPs.

References

Addis, M. E., & Krasnow, A. D. (2000). A national survey of practicing psychologists' attitudes toward psychotherapy treatment manuals. *Journal of Consulting and Clinical Psychology, 68,* 331–339.

Bagner, D. M., Coxe, S., Hungerford, G. M., Garcia, D., Barroso, N. E., Hernandez, J., & Rosa-Olivares, J. (2016). Behavioral parent training in infancy: A window of opportunity for high-risk families. *Journal of Abnormal Child Psychology, 44,* 901–912.

Bagner, D. M., & Eyberg, S. M. (2007). Parent–child interaction therapy for disruptive behavior in children with mental retardation: A randomized controlled trial. *Journal of Clinical Child and Adolescent Psychology, 36,* 418–429.

Bagner, D. M., Rodríguez, G. M., Blake, C. A., Linares, D., & Carter, A. S. (2012). Assessment of behavioral and emotional problems in infancy: A systematic review. *Clinical Child and Family Psychology Review, 15,* 113–128.

Bagner, D. M., Rodríguez, G. M., Blake, C. A., Rosa-Olivares, J. (2013). Home-based preventive parenting intervention for at-risk infants and their families: An open trial. *Cognitive and Behavioral Practice, 20,* 334–348.

Baker-Ericzén, M. J., Hurlburt, M. S., Brookman-Frazee, L., Jenkins, M. M., & Hough, R. L. (2010). Comparing child, parent, and family characteristics in usual care and empirically supported treatment research samples for children with disruptive behavior disorders. *Journal of Emotional and Behavioral Disorders, 18,* 82–99.

Bandura, A. (1977). *Social learning theory.* Englewood Cliffs, NJ: Prentice-Hall.

Barrish, H. H., Saunders, M., & Wolf, M. M. (1969). Good behavior game: Effects of individual contingencies for group consequences on disruptive behavior in a classroom. *Journal of applied behavior analysis, 2*(2), 119–124.

Baumrind, D. (1978). Parental disciplinary patterns and social competence in children. *Youth and Society, 9,* 238–276.

Berkovits, M. D., O'Brien, K. ., Carter, C. G., & Eyberg, S. M. (2010). Early identification and intervention for behavior problems in primary care: A comparison of two abbreviated versions of parent–child interaction therapy. *Behavior Therapy, 41,* 375–387.

Budd, K. S., Barbacz, L. L., & Carter, J. S. (2015). Collaborating with public school partners to implement Teacher–Child Interaction Training (TCIT) as universal prevention. *School Mental Health, 8,* 207–221.

Bunte, T. L., Schoemaker, K., Hessen, D. J., Van Der Heijden, P. G., & Matthys, W. (2014). Stability and change of ODD, CD, and ADHD diagnosis in referred preschool children. *Journal of Abnormal Child Psychology, 42,* 1213–1224.

Burns, B. J., Costello, E. J., Angold, A., Tweed, D., Stangl, D., Farmer, E., & Erkanli, A. (1995). Children's mental health service use across service sectors. *Health Affairs, 14,* 147–159.

Carpenter, A. L., Puliafico, A. C., Kurtz, S. M. S., Pincus, D. B., & Comer, J. S. (2014). Extending Parent–Child Interaction Therapy for early childhood internalizing problems: New advances for an overlooked population. *Clinical Child and Family Psychology Review, 17,* 340–356.

Comer, J. S. (2015). Introduction to the special section: Applying new technologies to extend the scope and accessibility of mental health care. *Cognitive and Behavioral Practice, 22,* 253–257.

Comer, J. S., & Barlow, D. H., (2014). The occasional case against broad dissemination and implementation: Retaining a role for specialty care in the delivery of psychological treatments. *American Psychologist, 69,* 1–18.

Comer, J. S., Chow, C., Chan, P. T., Cooper-Vince, C., & Wilson, L. A. (2013). Psychosocial treatment efficacy for disruptive behavior problems in very young children: A meta-analytic examination. *Journal of the American Academy of Child and Adolescent Psychiatry, 52,* 26–36.

Comer, J. S., Elkins, R. M., Chan, P. T., & Jones, D. J. (2014). New methods of service delivery for children's mental health care. In C. A. Alfano & D. Beidel (Eds.), *Comprehensive evidence-based interventions for school-aged children and adolescents.* New York, NY: Wiley.

Comer, J. S., Furr, J. M., Cooper-Vince, C., Madigan, R. J., Chow, C., Chan, P. T., . . . Eyberg, S. M. (2015). Rationale and considerations for the Internet-based delivery of Parent–Child Interaction Therapy. *Cognitive Behavioral Practice, 22,* 302–316.

Comer, J. S., Furr, J. M., Miguel, E., Cooper-Vince, C. E., Carpenter, A. L., Elkins, R. M., . . . Chase, R. (under review). Remotely delivering real-time parent training to the home: An initial randomized trial of Internet-delivered Parent-Child Interaction Therapy (I-PCIT). *Journal of Consulting and Clinical Psychology.*

Comer, J. S., Olfson, M., & Mojtabai, R. (2010). National trends in child and adolescent psychotropic polypharmacy in office-based practice, 1996–2007. *Journal of the American Academy of Child and Adolescent Psychiatry, 49,* 1001–1010.

Comer, J. S., Puliafico, A. C., Aschenbrand, S. G, McKnight, K., Robin, J. A., Goldfine, M., & Albano, A. M. (2012). A pilot feasibility evaluation of the CALM Program for anxiety disorders in early childhood. *Journal of Anxiety Disorders, 26,* 40–49.

Cooley, M. E., Veldorale-Griffin, A., Petren, R. E., & Mullis, A. K. (2014). Parent–Child Interaction Therapy: A meta-analysis of child behavior outcomes and parent stress. *Journal of Family Social Work, 17,* 191–208.

Copeland, W. E., Miller-Johnson, S., Keeler, G., Angold, A., & Costello, E. J. (2007). Childhood psychiatric disorders and young adult crime: A prospective, population-based study. *American Journal of Psychiatry, 164,* 1668–1675.

Cornacchio, D., Sanchez, A. L., Chou, T., & Comer, J. S. (2017). Cognitive-behavioral therapy for children and adolescents. In S. G. Hofmann & G. Asmundson (Eds.), *The science of cognitive behavioral therapy: From theory to therapy.* New York, NY: Elsevier.

Crum, K. I., & Comer, J. S. (2016). Using synchronous videoconferencing to deliver family-based mental health care. *Journal of Child and Adolescent Psychopharmacology, 26,* 229–234.

Cunningham, C. E., Bremner, R., & Boyle, M. (1995). Large group community-based parenting programs for families of preschoolers at risk for disruptive behaviour disorders: Utilization, cost effectiveness, and outcome. *Journal of Child Psychology and Psychiatry, 36,* 1141–1159.

Dishion, T. J., & Kavanagh, K. (2003). *Intervening in adolescent problem behavior: A family-centered approach.* New York, NY: Guilford Press.

Dishion, T. J., Mun, C. J., Drake, E. C., Tein, J. Y., Shaw, D. S., & Wilson, M. (2015). A transactional approach to preventing early childhood neglect: The Family Check-Up as a public health strategy. *Development and Psychopathology, 27,* 1647–1660.

Dodge, K. A., Bierman, K. L., Coie, J. D., Greenberg, M. T., Lochman, J. E., McMahon, R. J., . . . Conduct Problems Prevention Research Group (2015). Impact of early intervention on psychopathology, crime, and well-being at age 25. *American Journal of Psychiatry, 172,* 59–70.

Dretzke, J., Davenport, C., Frew, E., Barlow, J., Stewart-Brown, S., Bayliss, S., . . . Hyde, C. (2009). The clinical effectiveness of different parenting programmes for children with conduct problems: A systematic review of randomized control trials. *Child and Adolescent Psychiatry and Mental Health, 3,* 1–10.

Egger, H. L., & Angold, A. (2006). Common emotional and behavioral disorders in preschool children: Presentation, nosology, and epidemiology. *Journal of Child Psychology and Psychiatry, 47,* 313–337.

Egger, H. L., Erkanli, A., Keeler, G., Potts, E., Walter, B. K., & Angold, A. (2006). Test–retest reliability of the preschool age psychiatric assessment (PAPA). *Journal of the American Academy of Child and Adolescent Psychiatry, 45,* 538–549.

Elkins, R. M, & Comer, J. S. (2014). Internet-based implementation: Broadening the reach of Parent–Child Interaction Therapy for early child behavior problems. In R. S. Beidas & P. C. Kendall (Eds.), *Child and adolescent therapy: Dissemination and implementation of empirically supported treatments.* New York, NY: Oxford.

Enebrink, P., Högström, J., Forster, M., & Ghaderi, A. (2012). Internet-based parent management training: A randomized controlled study. *Behaviour Research and Therapy, 50,* 240–249.

Essex, M. J., Kraemer, H. C., Slattery, M. J., Burk, L. R., Thomas Boyce, W., Woodward, H. R., & Kupfer, D. J. (2009). Screening for childhood mental health problems: Outcomes and early identification. *Journal of Child Psychology and Psychiatry, 50,* 562–570.

Eyberg, S. M., & Funderburk, B. W. (2011). *Parent–Child Interaction Therapy Protocol.* Gainesville, FL: PCIT International.

Eyberg, S. M., Nelson, M. M., & Boggs, S. R. (2008). Evidence-based psychosocial treatments for children and adolescents with disruptive behavior. *Journal of Clinical Child and Adolescent Psychology, 37,* 215–237.

Farmer, E., Burns, B., Phillips, S., Angold, A., & Costello, E. (2003). Pathways into and through mental health services for children and adolescents. *Psychiatric Services, 54,* 60–66.

Fergusson, D. M., Horwood, L. J., & Riddler, E. M. (2007). Conduct and attentional problems in childhood and adolescence and later substance use, abuse, and dependence: Results of a 25-year longitudinal study. *Drug and Alcohol Dependence, 88,* S14–S26.

Graziano, P. A., Bagner, D. M., Slavec, J., Hungerford, G., Kent, K., Babinski, D., . . . Pasalich, D. (2015). Feasibility of intensive parent–child interaction therapy (I-PCIT): results from an open trial. *Journal of Psychopathology and Behavioral Assessment, 37,* 38–49.

Graziano, P. A., Slavec, J., Hart, K., Garcia, A., & Pelham, W. E. (2014). Improving school readiness in preschoolers with behavior problems: Results from a summer treatment program. *Journal of Psychopathological Behavioral Assessment, 36,* 555–569.

Hanf, C. A. (1969). *A two-stage program for modifying maternal controlling during mother–child (M–C) interaction*. Paper presented at the meeting of the Western Psychological Association, Vancouver.

Hofstra, M. B., van der Ende, J., & Verhulst, F. C. (2002). Child and adolescent problems predict DSM-IV disorders in adulthood: A 14-year follow-up of a Dutch epidemiological sample. *Journal of the American Academy of Child and Adolescent Psychiatry, 41*, 182–189.

Jones, D. J., Anton, M., Gonzalez, M., Honeycutt, A., Khavjou, O., Forehand, R., & Parent, J. (2015). Incorporating mobile phone technologies to expand evidence-based care. *Cognitive and Behavioral Practice, 22*, 281–290.

Jones, D. J., Forehand, R., Cuellar, J., Parent, J., Honeycutt, A., Khavjou, O., . . . Newey, G. A. (2014). Technology-enhanced program for child disruptive behavior disorders: Development and pilot randomized control trial. *Journal of Clinical Child and Adolescent Psychology, 43*, 88–101.

Kataoka, S., Zhang, L., & Wells, K. (2002). Unmet need for mental health care among U.S. children: Variation by ethnicity and insurance status. *American Journal of Psychiatry, 159*, 1548–1555.

Kazdin, A. E. (2001). *Behavior modification in applied settings* (6th ed.). Long Grove, IL: Waveland Press Inc.

Kazdin, A. E. (2005). *Parent management training. Treatment for oppositional, aggressive, and antisocial behavior in children and adolescents*. New York, NY: Oxford University Press.

Kazdin, A. E., & Blasé, S. L. (2011). Rebooting psychotherapy research and practice to reduce the burden of mental illness. *Perspectives on Psychological Science, 6*, 21–37.

Kim-Cohen, J., Moffitt, T. E., Taylor, A., Pawlby, S. J., & Caspi, A. (2005). Maternal depression and children's antisocial behavior: Nature and nurture effects. *Archives of General Psychiatry, 62*, 173–181.

Kokko, K., & Pulkkinen, L. (2000). Aggression in childhood and long-term unemployment in adulthood: A cycle of maladaptation and some protective factors. *Developmental Psychology, 36*, 463–472.

Lavigne, J. V., Cicchetti, C., Gibbons, R. D., Binns, H. J., Larsen, L., & DeVito, C. (2001). Oppositional defiant disorder with onset in preschool years: Longitudinal stability and pathways to other disorders. *Journal of the American Academy of Child and Adolescent Psychiatry, 40*, 1393–1400.

Leijten, P., Raaijmakers, M. A., Orobio de Castro, B., van den Ban, E., & Matthys, W. (2017). Effectiveness of the Incredible Years Parenting Program for families with socioeconomically disadvantaged and ethnic minority backgrounds. *Journal of Clinical Child and Adolescent Psychology, 46*(1), 59–73.

Leijten, P., Shaw, D. S., Gardner, F., Wilson, M. N., Matthys, W., & Dishion, T. J. (2015). The family check-up and service use in high-risk families of young children: A prevention strategy with a bridge to community-based treatment. *Prevention Science, 16*, 397–406.

van Lier, P. A. C., Muthén, B. O., van der Sar, R. M., & Crijnen, A. A. (2004). Preventing disruptive behavior in elementary schoolchildren: Impact of a universal classroom-based intervention. *Journal of Consulting and Clinical Psychology, 72*, 467–478.

Lochman, J. E., & Conduct Problems Prevention Research Group (1995). Screening of child behavior problems for prevention programs at school entry. The Conduct Problems Prevention Research Group. *Journal of Consulting and Clinical Psychology, 63*, 549–559.

Lochman, J. E., Wells, K., & Lenhart, L. A. (2008). *Coping Power: Child group facilitator's guide*. New York, NY: Oxford University Press.

Lunkenheimer, E. S., Dishion, T. J., Shaw, D. S., Connell, A. M., Gardner, F., Wilson, M. N., & Skuban, E. M. (2008). Collateral benefits of the family check-up on early childhood school readiness: Indirect effects of parents' positive behavior support. *Developmental Psychology, 44*, 1737–1752.

McMahon, R. J., & Forehand, R. L. (2005). *Helping the noncompliant child: Family-based treatment for oppositional behavior*. New York, NY: Guilford Press.

Menting, A. T. A., Orobio de Castro, B., & Matthys, W. (2013). Effectiveness of the Incredible Years parent training to modify disruptive and prosocial child behavior: A meta-analytic review. *Clinical Psychology Review, 33*, 901–913.

Niec, L. N., Hemme, J. M., Yopp, J. M., & Brestan, E. V. (2005). Parent–child interaction therapy: The rewards and challenges of a group format. *Cognitive and Behavioral Practice, 12*, 113–125.

Niec, L. N., Barnett, M. L., Prewett, M. S., & Shanley, C. J. (2016). Group Parent–Child Interaction Therapy: A randomized control trial for the treatment of conduct problems in young children. *Journal of Consulting and Clinical Psychology, 84*(8), 682–698.

Nowak, C., & Heinrichs, N. (2008). A comprehensive meta-analysis of Triple P-Positive Parenting Program using hierarchical linear modeling: Effectiveness and moderating variables. *Clinical Child and Family Psychology Review, 11,* 114–144.

Olds, D. L. (2006). The nurse–family partnership: An evidence-based preventive intervention. *Infant Mental Health Journal, 27,* 5–25.

Olds, D., Henderson, C. R., Jr., Cole, R., Eckenrode, J., Kitzman, H., Luckey, D., . . . Powers, J. (1998). Long-term effects of nurse home visitation on children's criminal and antisocial behavior: 15-year follow-up of a randomized controlled trial. *Journal of the American Medical Association, 280,* 1238–1244.

Olfson, M., Crystal, S., Huang, C., & Gerhard, T. (2010). Trends in antipsychotic drug use by very young, privately insured children. *Journal of the American Academy of Child and Adolescent Psychiatry, 49,* 13–23.

Patterson, G. R. (1982). *Coercive family process* (Vol. 3). Eugene, OR: Castalia Publishing Company.

Pelham, W. E., & Fabiano, G. A. (2008). Evidence-based psychosocial treatments for attention-deficit/hyperactivity disorder. *Journal of Clinical Child and Adolescent Psychology, 37,* 184–218.

Quetsch, L. B., Wallace, N. M., Herschell, A. D., & McNeil, C. B. (2016). Weighing in on the time-out controversy: An empirical perspective. *The Clinical Psychologist, 68*(2), 4–19.

Reid, J. B., Eddy, J. M., Fetrow, R. A., Stoolmiller M., (1999). Description and immediate impacts of a preventive intervention for conduct problems. *American Journal of Community Psychology, 27,* 483–517.

Reid, M. J., Webster-Stratton, C., & Baydar, N. (2004). Halting the development of conduct problems in Head Start children: The effects of parent training. *Journal of Clinical Child and Adolescent Psychology, 33,* 279–291.

Reitman, D., & McMahon, R. J. (2013). Constance "Connie" Hanf (1917–2002): The mentor and the model. *Cognitive and Behavioral Practice, 20,* 106–116.

Sanders, M. R., Baker, S., & Turner, K. M. (2012). A randomized controlled trial evaluating the efficacy of Triple P Online with parents of children with early-onset conduct problems. *Behaviour Research and Therapy, 50,* 675–684.

Sanders, M. R., Kirby, J. N., Tellegen, C. L., & Day, J. J. (2014). The Triple P-Positive Parenting Program: A systematic review and meta-analysis of a multi-level system of parenting support. *Clinical Psychology Review, 34*(4), 337–357.

Sanders, M. R., Turner, K. M., & Markie-Dadds, C. (2002). The development and dissemination of the Triple P–Positive Parenting Program: A multilevel, evidence-based system of parenting and family support. *Prevention Science, 3,* 173–189.

Shechtman, Z., & Ben-David, M. (1999). Individual and group psychotherapy of childhood aggression: A comparison of outcomes and processes. *Group Dynamics: Theory, Research, and Practice, 3,* 263–274.

Sourander, A., McGrath, P. J., Ristkari, T., Cunningham, C., Huttunen, J., Lingley-Pottie, P., . . . Fossum, S. (2016). Internet-assisted parent training intervention for disruptive behavior in 4 year old children: A randomized clinical trial. *JAMA Psychiatry, 73,* 378–387.

Staats, A. W. (1971). *Child learning, intelligence, and personality: Principles of a behavioral interaction approach.* New York, NY: Harper & Row.

Sugai, G., Horner, R., & Gresham, F. (2002). Behaviorally effective school environments. In M. Shinn, H. Walker, & G. Stoner (Eds.), *Interventions for academic and behavior problems II: Prevention and remedial approaches* (pp. 315–350). Bethesda, MD: National Association of School Psychologists.

Thomas, C. R., & Holzer, C. E. (2006). The continuing shortage of child and adolescent psychiatrists. *Journal of the American Academy of Child and Adolescent Psychiatry, 45,* 1023–1031.

Thomas, R., & Zimmer-Gembeck, M. J. (2012). Parent–child interaction therapy: An evidence-based treatment for child maltreatment. *Child Maltreatment, 17,* 253–266.

Webster-Stratton, C., & Reid, M. (2003). The Incredible Years: Parents, teachers, and children training series: A multifaceted treatment approach for young children with conduct problems. In A. E. Kazdin & J. R. Weisz (Eds.), *Evidenced-based psychotherapies for children and adolescents* (pp. 224–240). New York, NY: Guilford.

Webster-Stratton, C., Reid, M. J., & Hammond, M. (2001). Preventing conduct problems, promoting social competence: A parent and teacher training partnership in Head Start. *Journal of Clinical Child Psychology, 30,* 283–302.

Webster-Stratton, C., Reid, M. J., & Hammond, M. (2004). Treating children with early-onset conduct problems: Intervention outcomes for parent, child, and teacher training. *Journal of Clinical Child and Adolescent Psychology, 33,* 105–124.

Webster-Stratton, C., Reid, M. J., & Stoolmiller, M. (2008). Preventing conduct problems and improving school readiness: Evaluation of the Incredible Years teacher and child training programs in high-risk schools. *Journal of Child Psychology and Psychiatry, 49,* 471–488.

Weisz, J. R., Weiss, B., Han, S. S., Granger, D. A., & Morton, T. (1995). Effects of psychotherapy with children and adolescents revisited: A meta-analysis of treatment outcome studies. *Psychological Bulletin, 117,* 450–468.

Zito, J. M., Safer, D. J., Valluri, S., Gardner, J. F., Korelitz, J. J., & Mattison, D. R. (2007). Psychotherapeutic medication prevalence in Medicaid-insured preschoolers. *Journal of Child and Adolescent Psychopharmacology, 17,* 195–204.

27

Psychosocial Treatment and Prevention in Middle Childhood and Early Adolescence

Caroline L. Boxmeyer, Nicole P. Powell, Qshequilla Mitchell, Devon Romero, Cameron E. Powe, and Casey Dillon

This chapter provides an overview of the evidence-based psychosocial treatment and prevention programs for children with, or at risk for, oppositional defiant disorder (ODD) and conduct disorder (CD). The focus of this chapter is on treatment and prevention strategies for children in middle childhood and early adolescence, spanning approximately ages 9–13. There is an array of programs available that seek to address disruptive and impulse-control disorders in this age group, or their underlying mechanisms. Programs with substantial research support are highlighted here, as well as the common strategies utilized across research-supported programs. Specific cautions that have been raised for intervening with this population are also noted. The treatment and prevention programs described in this chapter include programs that are child-, parent- or family-directed, as well as programs that intervene at multiple levels. Universal prevention programs are described first, followed by indicated prevention and treatment programs for youth with identified disruptive behavior and impulse-control problems.

Many of the evidence-based psychosocial treatment and prevention programs for ODD and CD share similar theoretical underpinnings. The programs with parent-training components are often rooted in Gerald Patterson's coercion theory, which hypothesizes that aggressive behavior develops in families when parents use coercion as the primary mode for controlling their children (Patterson, 1982). Thus, most behavioral parent-training programs seek to teach parents a wider range of strategies for providing consistent, effective caregiving. Lochman and Wells' (2002) contextual social-cognitive model extends into other domains, summarizing characteristics of children's family, school, and classroom/community contexts, as well as individual child social-cognitive factors that can contribute risk for a child developing ODD and CD. Examples of family-level risk factors include family income, parental psychopathology, and effective/responsive parenting. Examples of school and community risk factors include lack of a caring, responsive classroom environment, exposure to deviant peers and neighborhood violence. Examples of individual child-level risk factors include heightened anger arousal and social information processing deficits. Most of the evidence-based

---

The Wiley Handbook of Disruptive and Impulse-Control Disorders, First Edition.
Edited by John E. Lochman and Walter Matthys.
© 2018 John Wiley & Sons Ltd. Published 2018 by John Wiley & Sons Ltd.

programs described below attempt to reduce children's risk for developing ODD and CD by addressing as many of these domains as possible, in particular those that are malleable and can be addressed with psychosocial treatment.

Universal Prevention Programs

As described in earlier chapters, there are a number of well-established risk factors for disruptive and impulse-control problems that present in early and middle childhood, including child and parent/family factors. One approach for preventing or reducing problems of this kind is to provide universal prevention programming to broad groups, regardless of their risk status. This approach has the benefit of teaching all participating children valuable social and emotional skills and/or teaching all parents effective parenting skills, while in many cases yielding the most robust effects on the children and families at highest risk. In this section, a number of universal prevention programs for preadolescent and early adolescent children are described, which have been shown to decrease the development of conduct problems in at-risk youth.

Promoting Alternate THinking Strategies (PATHS)

Promoting Alternate THinking Strategies (PATHS) is a universal prevention program that provides developmentally appropriate social and emotional skills training for preschool and elementary students (Kusché & Greenberg, 1994). PATHS is based on the affective-behavioral-cognitive-dynamic model of development (Greenberg & Kusché, 1993), which posits that children develop social and emotional competencies as they are increasingly able to integrate affect, behavior, and cognitive understanding. The PATHS program also emphasizes the role of the environmental context in addition to children's own skill development.

Separate grade-level volumes of the PATHS curriculum are available for preschool through fifth grade, each targeting five domains: emotional awareness and understanding, self-control, interpersonal problem-solving skills, positive self-esteem, and positive peer relationships. Classroom teachers lead PATHS lessons 1–2 times per week and utilize supplementary activities and parent materials to promote skill generalization. PATHS recognizes that children who demonstrate behavior problems also tend to have social-emotional skill deficits, and seeks to improve children's functioning and decrease their risk status by teaching core social and emotional competencies.

Although a number of rigorous research studies have evaluated PATHS and demonstrated its positive impact and preventive effects on conduct problems, the majority of these studies have included students younger than the focus of this chapter (i.e., preschool through third grade; e.g., Conduct Problems Prevention Research Group (CPPRG), 1999a, 2010; Domitrovich, Cortes, & Greenberg, 2007; Greenberg, Kusché, Cook, & Quamma, 1995; Kam, Greenberg, & Kusché, 2004). A recent independent evaluation by Crean and Johnson (2013) examined the effects of PATHS in third through fifth grade students, using a cluster-randomized design in 14 elementary schools. Longitudinal analyses favored PATHS relative to the control condition on a range of social information processing, aggression, and conduct problems outcomes. Another recent independent, large-scale randomized controlled trial of PATHS in third through sixth grade students yielded positive intervention effects on a number of academic outcomes (Schonfeld et al., 2014).

LifeSkills Training (LST)

The Botvin LifeSkills Training program is a prevention program designed to prevent substance abuse in early-adolescent and adolescent children. LST was primarily developed for use with middle school students, and it is typically implemented across 15 class periods during children's 6th grade year. Supplemental booster sessions are then administered over the children's 7th and 8th grade years, with 10 in their 7th and 5 in their 8th. Cognitive-behavioral techniques are the core components of this program, which aims to teach students about personal self-management, social skills, and drug resistance (Botvin, Griffin, & Nichols, 2006).

LST has been evaluated in a series of randomized controlled efficacy trials and two effectiveness studies have demonstrated its effectiveness in reducing alcohol consumption, tobacco use, marijuana use, and poly-drug use. LST's long-term effectiveness and its generalizability to diverse racial/ethnic, socioeconomic, and geographic groups has also been supported by evaluation studies (Botvin et al., 2006; Mackillop, Ryabchenko, & Lisman, 2006). Conduct problems and substance use tend to co-occur and share a similar etiology. Thus, Botvin et al. (2006) examined the effects of LST with program content specifically related to substance use and violence, such as anger management, interpersonal assertiveness, and conflict resolution skills. Significant reductions in violence and delinquency were found for intervention participants relative to controls. Stronger prevention effects were found for students who received at least half of the preventive intervention, including on verbal and physical aggression, fighting, and delinquency.

Second Step

The Second Step program is a universal prevention and intervention program for children ages 4 to 14. It is a classroom-based program designed to reduce impulsive and aggressive behavior. The program focuses on building children's skills in the following areas: empathy, impulse control, problem solving, and anger management. Sequential lessons are delivered by classroom teachers or counselors using curriculum kits, with separate kits available for elementary and middle school. Numerous research studies have examined the effects of the Second Step program, including several that included preadolescent and early adolescent students (e.g., Edwards, Hunt, Meyers, Grogg, & Jarrett, 2005; Frey, Nolen, Van Schoiack-Edstrom, & Hirschstein, 2005; McMahon & Washburn, 2003). Second Step has been found to lead to increases in prosocial behavior and social reasoning, improvement in self-regulation of emotions, decreased verbal and physical aggression, and decreased behavioral problems and is in wide-scale use in school districts across the United States. A limitation of the research evidence for Second Step is that effects on teacher-reported outcomes have not been consistent, or have not been measured.

Seattle Social Development Project (SSDP)

The Seattle Social Development Project is a universal prevention program designed to reduce aggression by creating a positive school environment. This prevention program has been predominantly used for public elementary schools serving high-crime areas of Seattle, Washington. The SSDP includes training for teachers to increase the use of non-punitive classroom behavioral management such as positive reinforcement. More recent versions of the intervention have also included parent training and problem-solving and social skills training for children (Hawkins, Catalano, Kosterman, Abbott, & Hill, 1999).

Longitudinal efficacy evaluation studies have found significant prevention effects in treated versus control children with corresponding reductions in alcohol use (Hawkins et al., 1999) and delinquency, lower frequency of sexual intercourse and number of sexual partners, and decreased reports of pregnancy for females and of males fathering children (Hawkins et al., 1999). In addition, students receiving the prevention reported more positive feelings and commitment to school compared to control groups, improved academic achievement, and less student-reported school misbehavior (Hawkins et al., 1999). A long-term follow-up study found that participants in SSDP were functioning better in a variety of life domains at age 21, including better emotional regulation, better employment outcomes, and lower rates of criminal involvement (Hawkins, Kosterman, Catalano, Hill, & Abbott, 2005).

Positive Action (PA)

Positive Action is a school-based prevention program designed to address a variety of issues in both elementary and middle school students. PA typically occurs in 15–20-minute lessons, 2–4 times per week. There are approximately 140 lessons in Kindergarten through 6th grade, and 82 lessons in 7th and 8th grade. The lessons focus on six core units: the Positive Action Philosophy and the Thoughts-Actions-Feelings about Self Circle; Positive Actions for Body and Mind; Social/Emotional Positive Actions for Managing Yourself Responsibly; Social/Emotional Positive Actions for Getting Along with Others; Social/Emotional Positive Actions for Being Honest with Yourself and Others; and Social/Emotional Positive Actions for Improving Yourself Continuously.

PA has been evaluated in two randomized controlled trials, and studies have demonstrated its effectiveness through reductions in grade retention, suspensions, and absenteeism, lower self-reported substance use and violent behavior, and improvements in self-esteem and feelings of school supportiveness. PA's long-term effectiveness and its generalizability to diverse racial/ethnic, socioeconomic, and geographic groups have also been supported by evaluation studies (Snyder, Vuchinich, Acock, Washburn, & Flay, 2012; Lewis et al., 2013).

PAX Good Behavior Game

The PAX Good Behavior Game (GBG) is a classroom-based behavior management strategy that elementary school teachers can use along with a school's standard instructional curricula (Dolan, Turkkan, Wethamer-Larsson, & Kellam, 1989; Kellam et al., 2011). GBG uses a classroom-wide game format with teams and rewards to socialize children to the role of student and to reduce aggressive, disruptive classroom behavior. The first published study examined the use of GBG in a 4th grade classroom with several students who had significant behavioral problems (Barrish, Saunders, & Wolf, 1969). GBG has since been utilized across many classroom settings, with numerous age groups, and with differing student strengths and needs (Kellam et al., 2011). Although programs for early childhood are outside the scope of this chapter, it is worth noting that students who participated in GBG in first grade in a large-scale study were found to have reduced conduct problems and need for mental health services at age 12 (Ialongo, Poduska, Werthamer, & Kellam, 2001) and improved academic outcomes at age 19 (Bradshaw, Zmuda, Kellam, & Ialongo, 2009), compared to children who participated in a family–school partnership intervention. Several studies have examined the effects of GBG for upper elementary students, finding that it had positive effects on student behavior (Barrish et al., 1969; Johnson, Turner, & Konarski, 1978; Warner, Miller, & Cohen, 1977). In some cases, however, the behavioral effects of GBG were not well sustained at follow-up (see, e.g., Johnson et al., 1978), leading to recent efforts to implement GBG in combination with social-emotional learning programs, such as PATHS.

Other Promising Approaches

Olweus Bullying Prevention Program The Olweus Bullying Prevention Program is a multilevel, multicomponent program designed to reduce and prevent school bullying in elementary and middle schools (Olweus, 1993). It was initially implemented as a nationwide universal preventive intervention in Norway. The program's objectives include reducing the acceptance of bullying among children and school staff and improving school supervision and deterrence of bullying through instilling awareness with instructional booklets, providing suggestions for preventing bullying, initiating classroom meetings, and using videos. Results from a clinical trial involving 42 elementary and middle schools in Norway showed at least a 50% decrease in bullying and decreased reports of delinquency including vandalism, fighting, intoxication, theft, and truancy. Greater positive effects were found at a 2-year compared to a 1-year follow-up (Olweus, 1993). Although a number of replication studies have been conducted, including several in the United States, they have all used quasi-experimental designs, without random assignment to treatment and comparison groups. In a non-randomized, controlled study of the program in 10 public middle schools, Bauer, Lozano, and Rivara (2007) found no overall program effects and mixed positive effects varying by gender, race/ethnicity, and grade level.

Schoolwide Positive Behavior Support (SWPBS) Also known as Positive Behavioral Interventions and Supports (PBIS or PBS), SWPBS is a rapidly growing approach to universal promotion of students' positive social and academic functioning (Sugai & Horner, 2002). It has an established record of reducing challenging behaviors in children with developmental and intellectual disabilities, and research is beginning to emerge supporting its effectiveness as a school-wide preventive intervention to reduce the incidence of problem behaviors and increase student learning. An example of a school-wide or universal application of PBS is the "teaching recess," promoting workshops for the entire school, including staff and students, outlining positive behavioral expectations for recess. Following such an intervention, recess-related office referrals were found to decrease by 80% (Todd, Haugen, Anderson, & Spriggs, 2002). A recent meta-analysis of 20 single-case studies found that SWPBS reduced misbehavior and improved school culture among elementary and middle schools, particularly in urban settings; however, teacher buy-in and implementation quality substantially affect outcomes (Solomon, Klein, Hintze, Cressey, & Peller, 2012).

Indicated Prevention and Treatment Programs

For preadolescents and early adolescents who have identifiable risk factors for disruptive and impulse-control disorders, or who already have a diagnosis, there are a number of indicated prevention and treatment programs available that have substantial research support. Many of the programs described below have been implemented for both indicated prevention and treatment purposes and are thus described together here. Like the universal prevention programs described above, these indicated prevention and treatment programs often seek to facilitate change at both the youth and the parent/family contextual levels and to provide skills training to address malleable risk factors for disruptive and impulse-control disorders in middle childhood.

A meta-analysis conducted by McCart, Priester, Davies, and Azen (2006) found that behavioral parent training has stronger effects than youth-focused cognitive behavioral therapy for preschool and school-age children with antisocial behavior. However, studies that have directly compared multimodal treatment approaches with singular treatment approaches have consistently demonstrated the benefits of combined parent and youth interventions for children with antisocial behavior (e.g., Kazdin, Siegel, & Bass, 1992; Lochman & Wells, 2004).

Fast Track

Fast Track is the most intensive multimodal preventive intervention tested with youth at high risk for conduct problems (CPPRG, 1992). In a large-scale trial conducted in four different sites across the United States, 891 kindergarteners identified as high risk for conduct problems were enrolled in the study and randomly assigned to intervention or control. Children in the intervention condition (and their families) received comprehensive multimodal programming during first through fifth grade, including the classroom PATHS social emotional curriculum, behavioral parent training, home visiting, child social skills training groups, child tutoring in reading, and child friendship enhancement in the classroom. In middle and high school, participating youth and families also received a combination of standard and individualized intervention, designed to support children's transition to middle school and to strengthen protective factors and reduce risk factors in areas of particular need for each youth (including home visiting, family problem solving and liaisons with school and community agencies).

Initial impact studies after first grade found moderate positive effects on children's social, emotional, behavioral and academic functioning, parents' parenting skills and satisfaction with parenting, and the classroom environment (CPPRG, 1999a, 1999b). Significant reductions in child aggressive and disruptive behavior were reported by both teachers and parents by the end of third grade and fewer children in the intervention condition met criteria for a clinical diagnosis such as ODD or CD (CPPRG, 2002). Long-term studies that followed the children through 12th grade found that the Fast Track program prevented externalizing psychiatric disorders, but only among the highest risk group (CPPRG, 2011). Cost-effectiveness studies show that, although comprehensive longitudinal preventive interventions such as Fast Track are expensive to implement, the cost per participant falls far below the cost of a single life of crime (Foster et al., 2006).

Coping Power

Coping Power is a multi-component intervention for preadolescent children with disruptive behavior problems and their parents. Coping Power is based on a contextual social-cognitive model, which identifies key risk factors for the development and maintenance of childhood aggression. The Coping Power child component (Lochman, Wells, & Lenhart, 2008) targets children's social-cognitive processing, problem-solving skills, emotional regulation abilities, and social skills with peers, while also including awareness-raising activities addressing peer influence and neighborhood factors. The Coping Power parent component (Wells, Lochman, & Lenhart, 2008) targets family factors and parenting skills associated with children's behavioral problems, as well as parents' emotional well-being.

Coping Power has been evaluated as a school-based indicated preventive intervention for youth with aggressive behavior problems and as a clinic-based treatment for children with ODD and CD. In a number of randomized trials conducted by the program developer and independent researchers, Coping Power has been found to have beneficial effects on children's disruptive and aggressive behavior, academic functioning, and parent/family functioning, and many of these effects are sustained well beyond treatment (for a recent review, see Powell, Lochman, Boxmeyer, Barry, & Pardini, in press).

The full Coping Power program includes 34 child group sessions and 16 parent group sessions. The child and parent components are implemented separately but concurrently, typically lasting 16 to 18 months. An abbreviated version of Coping Power with 24 child and 10 parent sessions can be delivered in a single school year with beneficial results (Lochman et al., 2014). Coping Power has been shown to be an effective intervention for children diagnosed with ODD or CD receiving clinic-based treatment (van de Wiel, Matthys, Cohen-Kettenis, Maassen et al., 2007; van de Wiel, Matthys, Cohen-Kettenis, & van Engeland, 2003) and to have preventive effects on substance use 4 years posttreatment (Zonnevylle-Bender, Matthys, van de Wiel, & Lochman, 2007).

Other versions of Coping Power have been developed for individual administration (Lochman, et al., 2015), for hybrid Internet and in-person implementation (Lochman, Boxmeyer et al., in press), for modular administration implemented in combination with the Family Check-Up (Herman et al., 2012), and with added mindfulness and yoga components (Boxmeyer et al., 2016). Coping Power has also been adapted for use with a variety of populations, including aggressive deaf children (Lochman et al., 2001), children in international settings (e.g., Italy, the Netherlands, Pakistan; for review see Powell, Lochman, Boxmeyer, Barry, & Pardini, in press), and children who are younger (Boxmeyer et al., 2015) and older (Lochman, Powell, Boxmeyer, Kelly, & Dillon, 2013) than the initial target age group for Coping Power (preadolescents).

The Coping Power-Early Adolescent (CP-EA) program is a recent developmental adaptation of Coping Power for early adolescents (middle school students, approximately ages 11–13). The CP-EA Youth Component addresses the same topics as standard Coping Power (i.e., goal setting, organizational and study skills, emotion identification, anger management, perspective-taking, social problem-solving, and resisting peer pressure) in a manner adapted for adolescents (e.g., greater use of journaling activities, media, role-plays, peer leadership opportunities and an adapted incentive system). CP-EA also includes new topics developmentally relevant to adolescents, such as social media use, cyber bullying, sexting, apologizing, active listening, assertive communication, and romantic relationships.

The CP-EA Parent Component is an adapted version of Coping Power for parents of early adolescents. The adaptations made to develop the CP-EA Parent Component center on relevant differences between academic preparation for middle school versus high school, as well as developmentally appropriate methods for behavior management (e.g., reward systems, discipline, independence/privileges) (Lochman et al., 2012).

A large-scale randomized controlled trial of CP-EA is currently underway with 720 participating families from 40 middle schools in Maryland and Alabama. Preliminary results from the first intervention cohort reveal a significant reduction in hyperactivity, aggression, and conduct problems from pre to post-intervention. Improvements in adaptability and leadership skills were also observed in CP-EA participants, as well as improvements in impulse control, emotional regulation, and social adjustment (Lochman et al., 2016). These results should be interpreted with caution, as they only include a third of the intended overall sample, however, they indicate CP-EA's potential to join a collection of research-supported programs for early adolescents with disruptive and impulse-control problems.

Incredible Years (IY) - Parent Training

The Incredible Years® (IY) Training Series is a set of interlocking and comprehensive training programs for parents, teachers, and children (Webster-Stratton, 2011). The program can be used for universal or indicated prevention, or as a treatment program for youth with conduct problems. While IY has been shown to have positive effects on child disruptive behavior in numerous research studies (see Menting, Orobio de Castro, & Matthys, 2013 for a recent meta-analysis), most samples have included children younger than the focus of this chapter (ages 3–8) (see Chapter 26). The IY program that is appropriate for preadolescent children (ages 9–12) is the school age parent-training program, thus this program is described below. IY has also been used as an indicated prevention program for children with formerly incarcerated mothers, given the increased risk for disruptive behavior problems and later delinquency among children with incarcerated parents (Menting, Orobio de Castro, Wijngaards-de Maij, & Matthys, 2014).

The IY parent-training program from Webster-Stratton's (2011) Incredible Years training series is grounded in cognitive social learning theory. The IY parent-training series is a necessary component of the Incredible Years training series consisting of group-based programs designed to strengthen parent competencies, parent–child interactions, children's independence, empathy awareness, and motivation for academic learning. Each program incorporates age-appropriate parenting skills to promote social competence, emotional regulation, and academic skills in order to prevent, reduce, and treat behavior and emotion problems in children. The parenting programs consist of group-led discussions on a series of age-appropriate video vignettes depicting parent interactions with their children in various situations. During these group sessions, training takes place through video modeling, experiential learning, rehearsal and practice, homework assignments, self-reflection and group discussion, and self-monitoring (Webster-Stratton, 2011).

The IY BASIC parent-training series includes an age-appropriate curriculum for parents of school age children (6–12 years). In the BASIC parent-training program, communication, praise, and rewards, limit setting, handling misbehavior, and logical and natural consequences are of primary focus. The school age parent program lasts on average between 12 and 16 sessions, and up to 24 sessions if the population is high-risk (Webster-Stratton, 2011). Weekly sessions are 2 to 2.5 hours in length and involve 2 group leaders and 10–14 participants. For families with unique circumstances (e.g., parental depression, marital conflict, negative life stressors, and socioeconomic status) a supplemental advanced version (ADVANCE) of the parent program is available. The IY ADVANCE program is offered after the completion of the BASIC school age program as an additional 8–12 sessions. In the IY ADVANCE parenting program, interpersonal issues such as communication, anger management, coping skills, and problem solving are emphasized (Webster-Stratton, 2011).

Parent Management Training—Oregon Model

Parent Management Training (Oregon Model; PMTO) is a manualized program based on the social interaction learning model. In PMTO, parents are the primary agents of change for their children. The program focuses on enhancing positive parenting in order to diminish coercive practices (e.g., negative reciprocity, escalation, negative reinforcement) and reduce antisocial and problematic behavior in children aged 3–16 years (Forgatch, Patterson, & DeGarmo, 2005). PMTO promotes five positive parenting practices: (1) skill encouragement; (2) discipline and setting limits; (3) monitoring; (4) problem solving; and (5) positive involvement (Forgatch & Martinez, 1999; Forgatch et al., 2005). In addition to the core components, more recent iterations of PMTO incorporate recognizing and regulating emotions, mindfulness practice, enhancing communication, giving clear directions, promoting school success, and tracking behavior as supporting skills (Forgatch & Rodriguez, 2015). The benefits of PMTO for youth with, or at risk for, conduct problems have been established in a number of randomized controlled trials, including independent evaluations, long-term follow-up studies and cultural adaptation studies (Forehand, Lafko, Parent, & Burt, 2014; Forgatch & Patterson, 2010).

PMTO can be delivered in group and individual family formats in a variety of settings (e.g., clinics, homes, schools, community centers, homeless shelters), and can be adapted to the families' needs (e.g., family context, length of treatment). Traditionally, group sessions are 1.5 to 2 hours a week with the number of sessions ranging from 6 to 14. Individual and family sessions are generally 60 minutes long, and 10 to 25 sessions are recommended. The recommended size for group sessions is 12–15 participants. The parent-training process takes place through instruction, videotaped demonstration, role-play exercises, and home-practice assignments. A typical PMTO session consists of (a) opening greetings; (b) a review of the previous session's material and home practice assignment(s); (c) introduction of new skills; (d) role plays and exercises to practice new skills; (e) addressing individual family needs; (f) assigning new home practice assignment(s) (Fossum, Kjobbli, Drugli, Handegard, Morch, & Ogden, 2014).

Problem-Solving Skills Training (PSST) plus Parent Management Training (PMT)

This approach to treating children with diagnoses of ODD and CD includes a child component offering prosocial problem-solving skills training (PSST), a parent component offering parent management training (PMT), or a combination of both (Kazdin, 2010). The program targets school-age children with antisocial behavior between aged 7–13. Children attend 25 weekly sessions lasting approximately 50 minutes each (Kazdin et al., 1992). PSST emphasizes the daily interpersonal situations that children face, and specifically focuses on individual interpersonal deficits. Techniques such as role-playing, reinforcement, modeling, and feedback are all utilized to teach and reward effective problem-solving skills. Children are also given tasks called super-solvers, which allow them to practice techniques from the sessions with other people outside the group. Parent participation is a large component of the training, and parents attend their own training and also view the child sessions, serve as co-leaders and supervise the child's use of the new skills at home (Kazdin et al., 1992).

Outcome studies suggest that PSST significantly reduces antisocial behavior during one-year follow-up periods. Although PSST has been found to do better than PMT at increasing children's social competence at school and reducing self-reports of aggression and delinquency, a combination of both treatments is optimal for most outcomes (Kazdin, Siegel, & Bass, 1992). The combination of PSST with an increased parent-focused intervention was found to produce stronger outcome effects (in terms of both statistical and clinical significance) than PSST or parent-focused interventions alone (Kazdin et al., 1992). The accumulation of evidence suggests that PSST + PMT is an effective and long-lasting treatment for antisocial behavior in children (Kazdin, 2010).

Treatment Foster Care Oregon (TFCO)

Treatment Foster Care Oregon, formerly Multidimensional Treatment Foster Care, is a community-based program developed as an alternative to group or residential treatment, incarceration, and/or hospitalization for adolescents who struggle with disruptive and criminal behavior (Chamberlain, 1990). Community families are recruited and trained to provide a structured, though relatively unrestricted, environment, in which adolescents have the opportunity to build positive relationships with adult mentors and gain separation from delinquent peers. Rigorous outcome research has yielded a range of positive results, with decreased self-reports of delinquency and criminal referrals (Chamberlain, Leve, & DeGarmo, 2007; Chamberlain & Reid, 1998), less involvement in drug use for boys (Smith, Chamberlain, & Eddy, 2010), and lower rates of teen pregnancy in girls (Kerr, Leve, & Chamberlain, 2009).

TFCO is rooted in a daily reward system that offers praise and awards points for positive behavior, while matter-of-factly deducting points for rule violations. School attendance/behavior and homework completion are incorporated into the point system via daily teacher ratings. Adolescents have the opportunity to rise through three point levels over the course of treatment, each offering more privileges (e.g., home visits, unsupervised community activities) than the last. To facilitate this upward movement through the program, TFCO parents and therapists communicate daily, which allows them to provide teens with consistent, specific feedback. Weekly individual therapy, aimed at behavioral, emotional, and relational skill building, offers further structure and support (Chamberlain, 1990).

Throughout the treatment program, therapy sessions are held with the biological family in order to prepare them for their teen's return home. Such skills as positive parenting, effective supervision, and consistency in reward and punishment are covered. Parents are encouraged to practice these techniques during home visits, which TFCO permits once adolescents reach levels two and three of the program's point system. Following completion of the program, (typically after six to nine months), families receive continued services as requested, generally lasting for approximately one year. These services encompass on-call case managers, as well as the opportunity to participate in group parent meetings that offer additional skill development, feedback, and support (Chamberlain, 1990).

Achievement Mentoring

Achievement Mentoring is a treatment program designed to address problem school behavior (i.e., disciplinary actions, attendance, tardiness, etc.) in a middle school population. It has also been implemented as a universal prevention program. Students typically meet in small groups and begin to work on changing their problem school behavior through four components. The first involves the collection of information on the school-related behavior of each student. This information is obtained from teachers, attendance records, and disciplinary action records, and is typically updated regularly. The second gives students, and their parents, feedback about their (the students') behavior and outlines behaviors the student should be performing. The third then attaches a value to the behaviors the student should be performing, and establishes an incentive should the student obtain enough points. The final component involves problem solving with the student in an effort to help him or her earn more points.

Two randomized controlled trials have demonstrated the effectiveness of Achievement Mentoring in increasing attendance rates and grades, and reducing criminal involvement and illegal drug use at follow-up (Bry, 1982; Bry & George, 1980).

Multisystemic Therapy and Functional Family Therapy

Multisystemic Therapy (MST) and Functional Family Therapy (FFT) are also effective treatment programs for youth with disruptive behavior disorders. Since these treatment programs have been primarily tested with adolescents, a comprehensive description of each program is included in Chapter 28.

Briefly, MST is an intensive, family- and community-based treatment designed to address youth antisocial behavior comprehensively by targeting the interaction between youth and their existing environmental systems (Henggeler, Melton, & Smith, 1992; Henggeler, Schoenwald, Borduin, Rowland, & Cunningham, 2009). FFT is a short-term treatment program designed for families of youth with externalizing behavior problems at risk for institutionalization (Alexander & Parsons, 1973). FFT is based on core theoretical principles from family systems theory and cognitive behavioral therapy and has produced significant positive change processes for aggressive youth (Pardini, 2016).

Conclusions and Future Directions

This chapter has reviewed evidence-based psychosocial prevention and treatment programs for disruptive and impulse-control disorders in middle childhood and early adolescence. Many of these programs target similar child, family and school/contextual risk factors and share common intervention elements, such as behavioral parent training, children's social-emotional and problem-solving skills training, and interventions at the family and school level. It is important to identify these common program elements (Chorpita, Daleiden, & Wiesz, 2005), in particular the "active ingredients" that mediate program effects, both within and across evidence-based programs. Recent work has begun to examine this, for example, Forehand and colleagues' (2014) study examining whether parenting is the mediator of change across studies of behavioral parent training for children with disruptive behavior problems. In a somewhat different vein, Sukhodolsky and colleagues (2016) have advocated the use of transdiagnostic approaches to treating anger, irritability, and aggression in children with internalizing as well as externalizing problems, such as by utilizing common elements of many of the behavioral interventions reviewed here.

Other recent studies have examined important research questions, such as what are the characteristics of the child and family participants, the providers, the provider training, and the program implementation that affect program outcomes (e.g., Leijten, Raaijmakers, de Castro, & Matthys, 2013; Lochman, Boxmeyer, Powell, Qu, Wells, & Windle, 2009; Lochman, Dishion, Boxmeyer, Powell, & Qu, 2017). There is concern that aggregating youth with disruptive behavior problems can have iatrogenic effects, by creating opportunities for peer reinforcement of deviant behavior (e.g., Dishion, Poulin, & Burraston, 2001). Although effective group leadership and the use of manualized interventions targeting key social-cognitive and contextual risk factors appear to limit deviant peer effects (Lochman et al., 2015), these circumstances are not reflective of usual care treatment for children with disruptive behavior problems (e.g., Garland et al., 2010) or common professional development practices (offering opportunities for intensive training in evidence-based practice with performance feedback during initial implementation, rather than brief initial workshop training, which is the more common practice). Thus, it will be important for future studies to identify the conditions under which children in the community who have, or are at risk for, disruptive and impulse-control disorders can receive effective psychosocial prevention and treatment services, as well as the conditions under which usual care providers can be trained to implement effective services.

Acknowledgment

The preparation of this chapter has been supported by grants from the National Institute on Drug Abuse (R34 DA035946; R34 DA045295), National Institute of Child Health and Human Development (R01 HD 079273), Institute for Education Sciences (R305A140070), and Administration for Children and Families (90YR0075).

References

Alexander, J. F., & Parsons, B. V. (1973). Short-term behavioral intervention with delinquent families: Impact on family process and recidivism. *Journal of Abnormal Psychology, 81,* 219–225.

Barrish, H. H., Saunders, M., & Wolf, M. M. (1969). Good Behavior Game: Effects of individual contingencies for group consequences on disruptive behaviors in a classroom. *Journal of Applied Behavior Analysis, 2,* 119–124.

Bauer, N. S., Lozano, P., & Rivara, F. P. (2007). The effectiveness of the Olweus Bullying Prevention Program in public middle schools: A controlled trial. *Journal of Adolescent Health, 40,* 266–274.

Botvin, G. J., Griffin, K. W., and Nichols, T. R. (2006). Preventing youth violence and delinquency through a universal school-based prevention approach. *Prevention Science, 7,* 403–408.

Boxmeyer, C., Gilpin, A., DeCaro, J., Lochman, J., Qu, L., Mitchell, Q., & Snead, S. (2015). Power PATH: Integrated two-generation social emotional intervention for Head Start preschoolers and their parents. Online paper collection of the *Association for Public Policy Analysis and Management's 37th Annual Fall Research Conference: The Golden Age of Evidence-Based Policy.* Retrieved from https://appam.confex.com/appam/2015/webprogram/Paper12784.html

Boxmeyer, C., Miller, S., Lochman, J., Powell, N., Romero, D., Jones, S., & Rowe, J. (April, 2016). *Mindful Coping Power: An integrated mindfulness, yoga, and cognitive-behavioral preventive intervention for at-risk aggressive children and their parents.* Poster presentation at the 17th Annual Rural Health Conference, Complementary and Integrative Medicine: A Whole Person Approach to Healthcare. Tuscaloosa, Alabama.

Bradshaw, C. P., Zmuda, J. H., Kellam, S. G., & Ialongo, N. S. (2009). Longitudinal impact of two universal preventive interventions in first grade on educational outcomes in high school. *Journal of Educational Psychology, 101*(4), 926–937.

Bry, B. H. (1982). Reducing the incidence of adolescent problems through preventive intervention: One- and five-year follow-up. *American Journal of Community Psychology, 10,* 265–276.

Bry, B. H., & George, F. E. (1980). The preventive effects of early intervention on the attendance and grades of urban adolescents. *Professional Psychology, 11,* 252–260.

Chamberlain, P. (1990). Comparative evaluation of specialized foster care for seriously delinquent youths: a first step. *Community Alternatives: International Journal of Family Care, 2,* 21–36.

Chamberlain, P., Leve, L. D., & DeGarmo, D. S. (2007). Multidimensional Treatment Foster Care for girls in the juvenile justice system: 2-year follow-up of a randomized clinical trial. *Journal of Consulting and Clinical Psychology, 75*(1), 187–193.

Chamberlain, P., & Reid, J. (1998). Comparison of two community alternatives to incarceration for chronic juvenile offenders. *Journal of Consulting and Clinical Psychology, 5,* 857–863.

Chorpita, B. F., Daleiden, E. L., & Weisz, J. R. (2005). Identifying and selecting the common elements of evidence based interventions: A distillation and matching model. *Mental Health Services Research, 7,* 5–20. doi:10.1007/s11020-005-1962-6

Conduct Problems Prevention Research Group (CPRG). (1992). A developmental and clinical model for the prevention of conduct disorders; The FAST Track Program. *Development and Psychopathology, 4,* 505–527.

Conduct Problems Prevention Research Group. (1999a). Initial impact of the Fast Track prevention trial for conduct problems: I. The high-risk sample. *Journal of Consulting and Clinical Psychology, 67,* 631–647.

Conduct Problems Prevention Research Group (1999b). Initial impact of the Fast Track prevention trial for conduct problems: II. Classroom effects. *Journal of Consulting and Clinical Psychology, 67,* 648–657.

Conduct Problems Prevention Research Group (2002). Evaluation of the first 3 years of the Fast Track prevention trial with children at high risk for adolescent conduct problems. *Journal of Abnormal Child Psychology, 30,* 19–35.

Conduct Problems Prevention Research Group. (2010). The effects of a multiyear universal social-emotional learning program: The role of student and school characteristics. *Journal of Consulting and Continuing Psychology, 78*(2), 156–168.

Conduct Problems Prevention Research Group. (2011). The effects of the Fast Track preventive intervention on the development of conduct disorder across childhood. *Child Development, 82,* 331–345.

Crean, H. F., & Johnson, D. B. (2013). Promoting Alternative THinking Strategies (PATHS) and elementary school aged children's aggression: Results from a cluster randomized trial. *American Journal of Community Psychology, 52,* 56–72.

Dishion, T. J., Poulin, F., & Burraston, B. (2001). Peer group dynamics associated with iatrogenic effect in group interventions with high-risk young adolescents. *New Directions for Child and Adolescent Development, 91,* 79–92.

Dolan, L., Turkkan, J., Wethamer-Larsson, L., & Kellam, S. (1989). *The good behavior game manual.* Baltimore, MD: The Johns Hopkins Prevention Research Center.

Domitrovich, C. E., Cortes, R. C., & Greenberg, M. T. (2007). Improving young children's social and emotional competence: A randomized trial of the preschool "PATHS" curriculum. *The Journal of Primary Prevention, 28,* 67–91.

Edwards, D., Hunt, M. H., Meyers, J., Grogg, K. R., & Jarrett, O. (2005). Acceptability and student outcomes of a violence prevention curriculum. *Journal of Primary Prevention, 26,* 401–418.

Forehand, R., Lafko, N., Parent, J., & Burt, K. B. (2014). Is parenting the mediator of change in behavioral parent training for externalizing problems of youth? *Clinical Psychology Review, 34*(8), 608–619. doi:10.1016/j.cpr.2014.10.001

Forgatch, M. S., & Martinez, C. R. (1999). Parent management training: A program linking basic research and practical application. *Tidsskrift for Norsk Psykologforening, 36,* 923–937.

Forgatch, M. S., & Patterson, G. R. (2010). The Oregon Model of Parent Management Training (PMTO): An intervention for antisocial behavior in children and adolescents. In J. R. Weisz & A. E. Kazdin (Eds.), *Evidence based psychotherapies for children and adolescents* (2nd. ed., pp. 159–178). New York, NY: Guilford.

Forgatch, M. S., Patterson, G. R., DeGarmo, D. S. (2005). Evaluating fidelity: Predictive validity for a measure of competent adherence to the Oregon model of parent management training. *Behavior Therapy, 36,* 3–13.

Forgatch, M. S., & Rodriguez, M. M. D. (2015). Interrupting coercion: The iterative loops among theory, science, and practice. *The Oxford handbook of coercive relationship dynamics* (pp. 194–214). doi:10.1093/oxfordhb/9780199324552.013.17

Fossum, S., Kjobbli, J., Drugli, M. B., Handegard, B. H., Morch, W. T., & Ogden, T. (2014). Comparing two evidence-based parent-training interventions for aggressive children. *Journal of Children's Services, 9,* 319–329. doi:10.1108/JCS-04-2014-0021

Foster, E. M., Jones, D. E., & the Conduct Problems Prevention Research Group. (2006). Can a costly intervention be cost-effective? An analysis of violence prevention. *Archives of General Psychiatry, 63,* 1284–1291.

Frey, K. S., Nolen, S. B., Van Schoiack-Edstrom, L., & Hirschstein, M. K. (2005). Effects of a school-based social-emotional competence program: Linking children's goals, attributions, and behavior. *Journal of Applied Developmental Psychology, 26,* 171–200.

Garland, A. F., Brookman-Frazee, L., Hurlburt, M. S., Accurso, E. C., Zoffness, R. J., Hanie-Schlagel, R., Ganger, W. (2010). Mental health care for children with disruptive behavior problems: A view inside therapists' offices. *Psychiatric Services, 8,* 788–795. doi:10.1176/appi.ps.61.8.788.

Greenberg, M. T., & Kusché, C. A. (1993). *Promoting social and emotional development in deaf children: The PATHS Project.* Seattle, WA: University of Washington Press.

Greenberg, M. T., Kusché, C. A., Cook, E. T., & Quamma, J. P. (1995). Promoting emotional competence in school-aged children: The effects of the PATHS curriculum. *Development and Psychopathology, 7,* 117–136.

Hawkins, J. D., Catalano, R. F., Kosterman, R., Abbott, R. D., & Hill, K. G. (1999). Preventing adolescent health-risk behaviors by strengthening protection during childhood. *Archives of Pediatrics and Adolescent Medicine, 153,* 226–234.

Hawkins, J. D., Kosterman, R., Catalano, R. F., Hill, K. G., & Abbott, R. D. (2005). Promoting positive adult functioning through social development intervention in childhood: Long-term effects from the Seattle Social Development Project. *Archives of Pediatrics and Adolescent Medicine, 159,* 25–31.

Henggeler, S. W., Melton, G. B., & Smith, L. A. (1992). Family preservation using multisystemic therapy: An effective alternative to incarcerating serious juvenile offenders. *Journal of Consulting and Clinical Psychology, 6,* 953–961.

Henggeler, S. W., Schoenwald, S .K., Borduin, C. M., Rowland, M. D., & Cunningham, P. B. (2009). *Multisystemic therapy for antisocial behavior in children and adolescents* (2nd ed.). New York, NY: Guilford Press.

Herman, K. C., Reinke, W. M., Bradshaw, C. P., Lochman, J. E., Boxmeyer, C. L., Powell, N. P., . . . Ialongo, N. (2012). Integrating the Family Check-Up and the Parent Coping Power program. *Advances in School Mental Health Promotion, 5,* 208–219.

Ialongo, N., Poduska, J., Werthamer, L., & Kellam, S. (2001). The distal impact of two first-grade preventive interventions on conduct problems and disorder in early adolescence. *Journal of Emotional and Behavioral Disorders, 9,* 146–160.

Johnson, M. R., Turner, P. F., & Konarski, E. A. (1978). The "good behavior game": A systematic replication in two unruly transitional classrooms. *Education and Treatment of Children, 1,* 25–33.

Kam, C., Greenberg, M. T., & Kusché, C. A. (2004). Sustained effects of the PATHS® Curriculum on the social and psychological adjustment of children in special education. *Journal of Emotional and Behavioral Disorders, 12,* 66–78.

Kazdin, A. E. (2010). Problem-solving skills training and parent management training for oppositional defiant disorder and conduct disorder. In J. R. Weisz & A. E. Kazdin (Eds.), *Evidence based psychotherapies for children and adolescents* (2nd. ed., pp. 159–178). New York, NY: Guilford.

Kazdin, A. E., Siegel, T. C., & Bass, D. (1992). Cognitive problem-solving skills training and parent management training in the treatment of antisocial behavior in children. *Journal of Consulting and Clinical Psychology, 60*(5), 733–747.

Kellam, S. G., Mackenzie, A. C. L., Brown, C. H., Poduska, J. M., Wang, W., Petras, H., & Wilcox, H. C. (2011). The Good Behavior Game and the future of prevention and treatment. *Addiction Science & Clinical Practice, 6*(1), 73–84.

Kerr, D. C. R., Leve, L. D., & Chamberlain, P. (2009). Pregnancy rates among juvenile justice girls in two randomized controlled trials of Multidimensional Treatment Foster Care. *Journal of Counseling and Clinical Psychology, 77*(3), 588–593.

Kusché, C. A., & Greenberg, M. T. (1994). *The PATHS curriculum.* South Deerfield, MA: Channing-Bete Co.

Leijten, P., Raaijmakers, M. A., de Castro, B. O., & Matthys, W. (2013). Does socioeconomic status matter? A meta-analysis on parent training effectiveness for disruptive child behavior. *Journal of Clinical Child and Adolescent Psychology, 42,* 384–392. doi:10.1080/15374416.2013.769169

Lewis, K. M., Schure, M. B., Bavarian, N., DuBois, D. L., Day, J., Ji, P., . . . Flay, B. R. (2013). Problem behavior and urban, low-income youth: A randomized controlled trial of Positive Action in Chicago. *American Journal of Preventive Medicine, 44*(6), 622–630.

Lochman, J. E., Baden, R. E., Boxmeyer, C. L., Powell, N. P., Qu. L., Salekin, K. L., & Windle, M. (2014). Does a booster intervention augment the preventive effects of an abbreviated version of the Coping Power Program for aggressive children? *Journal of Abnormal Child Psychology, 42,* 367–381.

Lochman, J. E., Boxmeyer, C. L., Jones, S., Qu, L., Ewoldsen, D., & Nelson, W. M. (in press). Promoting parent and child engagement in school-based preventive intervention with aggressive children: A hybrid intervention with face-to-face and Internet components. *Journal of School Psychology.* doi:10.1016/j.jsp.2017.03.010

Lochman, J. E., Boxmeyer, C. L., Powell, N., Qu, L., Wells, K., & Windle, M. (2009). Dissemination of the Coping Power program: Importance of intensity of counselor training. *Journal of Consulting and Clinical Psychology, 77*(3), 397–409.

Lochman, J. E., Bradshaw, C. P., Powell, N., Debnam, K., Pas, E., & Ialongo, N. (June, 2016). Can indicated prevention work for conduct problem middle school adolescents? Preliminary findings for the Early Adolescent Coping Power Program (CP-EA). Oral presentation at the *Society for Prevention Research 24th Annual Meeting: Using Prevention Science to Promote Health Equity and Improve Well-being.* San Francisco, California.

Lochman, J. E., Dishion, T. J., Boxmeyer, C. L., Powell, N. P., & Qu, L. (2017). Variation in response to evidence-based group preventive intervention for disruptive behavior problems: A view from 938 Coping Power sessions. *Journal of Abnormal Child Psychology*. doi:10.1007/s10802-016-0252-7

Lochman, J. E., Dishion, T. J., Powell, N. P., Boxmeyer, C. L., Qu, L., & Sallee, M. (2015). Evidence-based preventive intervention for preadolescent aggressive children: One-year outcomes following randomization to group versus individual delivery. *Journal of Consulting and Clinical Psychology, 83*, 728–735.

Lochman, J. E., FitzGerald, D. P., Gage, S. M., Kannaly, M. K., Whidby, J. M., Barry, T. D., ... McElroy, H. (2001). Effects of social-cognitive intervention for aggressive deaf children: The Coping Power Program. *Journal of the American Deafness and Rehabilitation Association, 35*, 39–61.

Lochman, J. E., Powell, N., Boxmeyer, C., Andrade, B., Stromeyer, S. L., & Jimenez-Camargo, L. A. (2012). Adaptations to the coping power program's structure, delivery settings, and clinician training. *Psychotherapy, 49*(2), 135–142.

Lochman, J. E., Powell, N. P., Boxmeyer, C. L., Kelly, M., & Dillon, C. (2013). Anger management in schools: The Coping Power program for children and early adolescents. In E. Fernandez (Ed.), *Treatments for anger in specific populations: Theory, application, and outcome* (pp. 176–196). New York, NY: Oxford University Press.

Lochman, J. E., & Wells, K. C. (2002). Contextual social-cognitive mediators and child outcome: A test of the theoretical model in the Coping Power Program. *Development and Psychopathology, 14*(4), 945–967.

Lochman, J. E., & Wells, K. C. (2004). The Coping Power Program for preadolescent boys and their parents: Outcome effects at the 1-year follow-up. *Journal of Consulting and Clinical Psychology, 72*(4), 571–578.

Lochman, J. E., Wells, K. C., & Lenhart, L.A. (2008). *Coping Power child group program facilitator guide*. New York, NY: Oxford University Press.

MacKillop, J., Ryabchenko, K. A., and Lisman, S. A. (2006). Life Skills Training outcomes and potential mechanisms in a community implementation: A preliminary investigation. *Substance Use and Misuse, 41*, 1921–1935.

McCart, M. R., Priester, P. E., Davies, W. H., & Azen, R. (2006). Differential effectiveness of behavioral parent-training and cognitive-behavioral therapy for antisocial youth: A meta-analysis. *Journal of Abnormal Child Psychology, 34*, 525–541.

McMahon, S. D., & Washburn, J. J. (2003). Violence prevention: An evaluation of program effects with urban African American students. *Journal of Primary Prevention, 24*, 43–62.

Menting, A. T. A., Orobio de Castro, B., & Matthys, W. (2013). Effectiveness of the Incredible Years parent training to modify disruptive and prosocial child behavior: A meta-analytic review. *Clinical Psychology Review, 33*, 901–913.

Menting, A. T. A., Orobio de Castro, B., Wijngaards-de Meij, L. D. N. V., & Matthys, W. (2014). A trial of parent training for mothers being released from incarceration and their children. *Journal of Clinical Child and Adolescent Psychology, 43*, 381–396.

Olweus, D. (1993). *Bullying at school: What we know and what we can do*. Oxford: Blackwell.

Pardini, D. (2016). Empirically based strategies for preventing juvenile delinquency. *Child and Adolescent Psychiatric Clinics of North America, 25*(2), 257–268.

Patterson, G. R. (1982). *Coercive family processes*. Eugene, OR: Castalia.

Powell, N. P., Lochman, J. E., Boxmeyer, C. L., Barry, T. D., & Pardini, D. A. (in press). The Coping Power program for aggressive behavior in children. In J. R. Weisz & A. Kazdin (Eds.) *Evidence-based psychotherapies for children and adolescents* (3rd ed.).

Schonfeld, D. J., Adams, R. E., Fredstrom, B. K., Weissberg, R. P., Gilman, R., Voyce, C., . . . Speese-Linehan, D. (2014). Cluster-randomized trial demonstrating impact on academic achievement of elementary social-emotional learning. *School Psychology Quarterly, 30*(3), 406–420.

Smith, D. K., Chamberlain, P., & Eddy, J. M. (2010). Preliminary support for Multidimensional Treatment Foster Care in reducing substance use in delinquent boys. *Journal of Child & Adolescent Substance Abuse, 19*(4), 343–358.

Snyder, F. J., Vuchinich, S., Acock, A., Washburn, I. J., & Flay, B. R. (2012). Improving elementary school quality through the use of a social-emotional and character development program: A matched-pair, cluster-randomized control trial in Hawai'i. *Journal of School Health, 82,* 11–20.

Solomon, B. G., Klein, S. A., Hintze, J. M., Cressey, J. M., & Peller, S. L. (2012). A meta-analysis of school-wide positive behavior support: An exploratory study using single-case synthesis. *Psychology in the Schools, 49*(2), 105–121.

Sugai, G., & Horner, R. H. (2002). Introduction to the special series on positive behavior support in schools. *Journal of Emotional and Behavioral Disorders, 10,* 130–135.

Sukhodolsky, D. G., Smith, S. D., McCauley, S. A., Ibrahim, K., & Piasecka, J. B. (2016). Behavioral interventions for anger, irritability, and aggression in children and adolescents. *Journal of Child and Adolescent Psychopharmacology, 26*(1), 58–64.

Todd, A., Haugen, L., Anderson, K., & Spriggs, M. (2002). Teaching recess: Low-cost efforts producing effective results. *Journal of Positive Behavioral Interventions, 4,* 46–52.

van de Wiel, N. M. H., Matthys, W., Cohen-Kettenis, P. T., Maassen, G. H., Lochman, J. E., & van Engeland, H. (2007). The effectiveness of an experimental treatment when compared with care as usual depends on the type of care as usual. *Behavior Modification, 31,* 298–312.

van de Wiel, N. M. H., Matthys, W., Cohen-Kettenis, P. T., & van Engeland, H. (2003). Application of the Utrecht Coping Power Program and care as usual to children with disruptive behavior disorders: A comparative study of cost and course of treatment. *Behavior Therapy, 34,* 421–436.

Warner, S. P., Miller, F. D., & Cohen, M. W. (1977). Relative effectiveness of teacher attention and the "good behavior game" in modifying disruptive classroom behavior. *Journal of Applied Behavior Analysis, 10,* 737.

Webster-Stratton, C. (2011). *The Incredible Years: Parents, teachers, and children's training series.* Seattle, WA: The Incredible Years.

Wells, K. C., Lochman, J. E., & Lenhart, L. (2008). *Coping Power: Parent group facilitators' guide.* New York, NY: Oxford University Press.

Zonnevylle-Bender, M. J. S., Matthys, W., van de Wiel, N. M. H., & Lochman, J. E. (2007). Preventive effects of treatment of DBD in middle childhood on substance use and delinquent behavior. *Journal of the American Academy of Child and Adolescent Psychiatry, 46,* 33–39.

28

Psychosocial Treatment and Prevention in the Adolescent Years for ODD and CD

Brian P. Daly, David DeMatteo, Aimee Hildenbrand, Courtney N. Baker, and Jacqueline H. Fisher

This chapter provides a qualitative description and review of the research evidence for psychosocial treatment and prevention programs targeted at middle to late adolescents (ages 13–21 years) diagnosed with Oppositional Defiant Disorder (ODD) or Conduct Disorder (CD). We classified programs and interventions into those that are child-focused, those that are parent-focused, and those that are delivered in combination. Modalities included in this review are individual interventions, parent training, family interventions, group interventions, and multi-component interventions. Where applicable, we note the implementation of the reviewed programs in homes, schools, and various community settings. The different modalities of treatments and programs are organized as follows: (a) interventions with at least some evidence; and, (b) interventions without any research evidence or those that are iatrogenic. Qualifiers for interventions with at least some evidence include studies that utilized a treatment comparison group or waiting list control group. It is worth noting that, even for programs categorized as having some evidence, the level of empirical support is often mixed.

While the interventions described in this chapter certainly do not represent an exhaustive list of all evidence-based prevention and treatment programs, the reader is nonetheless provided with a succinct overview of programs that are frequently employed with adolescents diagnosed with ODD or CD. For more extensive and rigorous reviews of the programs described in this chapter, the interested reader is referred to the following websites: (a) The Substance Abuse and Mental Health Services Administration's (SAMHSA) National Registry of Evidence-Based Programs and Policies (NREPP; http://www.nrepp.samhsa.gov); (b) The Blueprints for Violence Prevention Program at The Center for the Study and Prevention of Violence, Institute of Behavioral Science, University of Colorado at Buffalo (http://www.colorado.edu/cspv/blueprints); (c) What Works Clearinghouse (http://ics.ed.gov/ncee/wwc/); (d) Child Link/TRENDS (http://www.childtrends.org/); (e) National Institute of Justice (http://www.crimesolutions.gov); or, (6) the Office of Juvenile Justice and Delinquency Prevention (http://www.ojjdp.gov/mpg).

The Wiley Handbook of Disruptive and Impulse-Control Disorders, First Edition.
Edited by John E. Lochman and Walter Matthys.
© 2018 John Wiley & Sons Ltd. Published 2018 by John Wiley & Sons Ltd.

Interventions That Are Child-Focused

Interventions with At Least Some Evidence

Cognitive Behavior Therapy Strategies Cognitive therapy, behavioral therapy, and combination cognitive-behavioral therapy (CBT) are frequently utilized in the treatment of youth with disruptive behavior problems. When employed in individual interventions, the effective core elements of these approaches often focus on improving an adolescent's social skills, anger management skills, problem-solving skills, self-control skills, and providing affect education (Garland, Hawley, Brookman-Frazee, & Huburt, 2008). Systematic reviews and meta-analyses of CBT strategies that combined social learning and skills-building employed with older adolescents have found significant reductions in antisocial behaviors (McCart, Priester, Davies, & Azen, 2006), and recidivism (Armelius & Andreassen, 2007).

Social Skills and Problem-Solving Training Social skills training is commonly employed for adolescents with conduct problems because of research demonstrating that individuals who lack social skills are at increased risk for aggression, peer rejection, and contact with the legal system (Maag, 2006). This training is frequently combined with problem-solving skills training because adolescents who engage in oppositional or conduct problem behaviors also may demonstrate distortions and deficiencies in their cognitive thought processes, including in interpersonal situations (Kazdin, 1997). Instruction in these skills-training programs can be delivered as a stand-alone intervention or as a component of a group of interventions for youth with conduct problems. Intervention strategies used in these skills training include modeling, coaching, eliminating competing behaviors, and enhancing prosocial behaviors.

Problem-solving skills training (PSST; Kazdin, 2001) utilizes a cognitive-behavioral approach for youth aged 7–14 years and focuses on identifying and adjusting dysfunctional thoughts related to how adolescents perceive, code, and experience their world. PSST aims to help youth to engage in more appropriate and prosocial interactions with others. Five problem-solving steps are key to the PSST approach and are used to help the adolescent identify thoughts, feelings, and behaviors in problem social situations. These steps focus on helping him or her think differently about the situation, identify and change self-statements and reactions, alter attributions about others' motivations, learn how to be more sensitive to the feelings of others, and ultimately generate alternative and positive solutions that avoid physical aggression and conflict. Techniques used in PSST include modeling, role-playing, positive reinforcement of appropriate behavior, and teaching alternative behaviors.

PSST is supported by an extensive body of empirical research that dates back 30 years. Outcome studies have been conducted with racially diverse adolescents from both inpatient and outpatient settings. Overall, findings indicate that youth who receive PSST demonstrate significant decreases in aggression at home and school, reduced deviant behaviors, and increases in prosocial behaviors relative to control groups (Kazdin, Sigel, & Bass, 1992; Kazdin, Bass, Siegal, & Thomas, 1989).

Mentoring The goal of mentoring programs is to expose youth to, and affiliate them with, positive role models (usually adults) from outside their immediate families. These trained mentors are encouraged to develop caring and supportive relationships with their mentees. The rationale behind mentoring programs is the belief that prosocial and available individuals can help change the negative trajectories of youth with conduct problems by fostering resiliency. There are many mentoring programs and each varies in structure, points of emphasis, length of services, and delivery or programming. Mentoring organizations are located across a range of settings including schools, community agencies, faith-based organizations, and juvenile corrections facilities (Substance Abuse and Mental Health Services Administration, 2011).

Two prominent organizations that focus on connecting youth with adult mentors are Big Brothers Big Sisters of America (BBBSA) and MENTOR/The National Mentoring Partnership. Findings from an 18-month study of adolescents (n = 959, 10–16 years) from eight BBBSA agencies, randomly assigned to a mentor or waitlist control group, revealed that mentored youth were less likely to engage in physical aggression toward another person (Tierney, Grossman, & Resch, 1995). Caution is warranted, however, as the effect sizes in this study were relatively small (average standardized mean difference effect size of .06, Herrera, Grossman, Kauh, Feldman, & McMaken, 2007). Results from a meta-analysis that included 73 independent evaluations of mentoring programs indicated improvements across behavioral, social, and emotional, and academic domains of youth development (DuBois, Portillo, Rhodes, Silverthorn, & Valentine, 2011). Program impacts were noted to be stronger when the mentees had preexisting problem behaviors or were exposed to significant levels of environmental risk. It is worth highlighting that few studies of mentoring programs assessed juvenile offending as an outcome (DuBois et al., 2011).

Interventions without Research Evidence or Iatrogenic

Mindfulness-based Approaches (e.g., Dialectical Behavior Therapy; (DBT) Mindfulness has been described as the complete, nonjudgmental awareness of what is happening in the moment (Perry-Parrish, Copeland-Linder, Webb, & Sibinga, 2016). The goal of mindfulness-based approaches for youth with conduct problems is to strengthen their coping response to stress while also improving their ability to self-regulate behavior and emotions (Perry-Parrish & Sibinga, 2014). Although the application of mindfulness-based approaches to youth with disruptive behavior problems has increased in recent years (Burke, 2010), the research evidence for these approaches is limited. Much of the emerging research evaluating mindfulness-based programs for adolescents has targeted internalizing outcomes such as depression or anxiety (Biegel, Brown, Shapiro, & Schubert, 2009) or health benefits such as lower blood pressure (Barnes, Treiber, & Johnson, 2004). In one of the few studies that included adolescents with a disruptive behavior disorder, 16 weeks of an adapted version of DBT resulted in parent and self-reported reductions in externalizing symptoms (Nelson-Gray et al., 2006). Although findings from this pilot study are promising, the study design was limited by lack of a treatment comparison group or waiting list control group studies.

Moral Reasoning Interventions that provide training in moral reasoning for adolescents with significant behavior problems focus on enhancing the youth's sense of fairness and justice relative to other people's needs. The majority of studies on moral reasoning have been conducted with preadolescent children. Findings from studies that included adolescents consistently demonstrate that moral reasoning is related to their antisocial behavior (Stams et al., 2006). For example, conduct-disordered youth perform worse on tasks of moral reasoning and moral judgment relative to their non-conduct-disordered peers (Jolliffe & Farrington, 2004; Stams et al., 2006). Although results from these studies revealed that training in moral reasoning was successful in enhancing the use of more mature moral reasoning, these improvements did not always produce reductions in conduct problem behaviors for delinquent adolescents (Fonagy et al., 2015).

Interventions That Are Parent-Focused

Parent Management Training

Interventions that employ parent management training provide instruction to parents on how they can utilize contingency management techniques in the home setting to change their adolescent's behavior. Goals of this intervention include improving parent–adolescent interactions and enhancing other important parenting skills such as communication, monitoring, and supervision. The evidence base for parenting management training programs is primarily derived from studies conducted with parents of preadolescent children. However, some recent studies have examined the impact of these programs with parents of middle and older adolescents.

Parent Management Training Interventions with At Least Some Evidence

Positive Parenting Program (Triple P) Triple P (Sanders, 1999) is a multilevel system of parenting intervention, with five levels of intensity designed to match child and family needs based on problem severity. The five levels are as follows:]BL[

- Level 1: Parenting information;
- Level 2: One- to two-session intervention for mild behavior problems;
- Level 3: Four sessions for moderate behavior problems;
- Level 4: Parent training program;
- Level 5: Behavioral family intervention.

Core components of the program include guided participation, behavioral rehearsal, and self-regulation of parenting skills (Kaslow, Broth, Smith, & Collins, 2012). The research base for Triple P is extensive but the overwhelming majority of studies have focused on children. There have been several recent studies of Group Teen Triple P (GTTP; Ralph & Sanders, 2003), a broad-based parenting intervention delivered over 8 weeks for parents of teenagers up to age 16.

In a preliminary evaluation of GTTP with parents of teenagers transitioning to high school, Ralph and Sanders (2003) found parent-reported reductions in conflicts with their teenager. Findings from a randomized controlled trial (RCT) of self-administered GTTP with parents of early adolescents (ages 12–14 years) revealed that parents participating in the enhanced condition (self-directed plus brief therapist telephone consultations) reported significantly fewer adolescent behavior problems compared to parents in either the standard (self-directed alone) or waitlist condition (Stallman & Ralph, 2007). In a more recent study, Chu, Bullen, Farruggia, Dittman, and Sanders (2015) enrolled adolescents between 12 and 15 years of age with behavior problems and randomly assigned them to either GTTP (n = 35) or a treatment-as-usual control condition (n = 37). According to parent report, those who received GTTP indicated significant improvements in parenting practices, parenting confidence, the quality of family relationships, and fewer adolescent problem behaviors at postintervention relative to those in the treatment-as-usual group. In a similar set of results, adolescents whose parents received the intervention also reported significantly fewer behavioral problems than adolescents in the control condition. Reductions in behavior problems were maintained at 6-month follow up.

Parent Management Training—Oregon Model (PMTO™) There is compelling evidence to support the effectiveness of this intervention with younger children. However, as with Triple P, fewer studies have been conducted with older adolescents. The original Oregon

Parent Management Training model was modified to address the more significant conduct problems displayed by adolescents relative to younger children. This parent training intervention can be used with adolescents up to 16 years of age. New elements to this model include an increased focus on risk behaviors, higher levels of parental monitoring, and the use of more age-appropriate punishments (e.g., restriction of free time vs. time-out). The number of sessions provided in parent groups ranges from 6 to 14. A key component of this model is encouraging parents to report their adolescent's offending behaviors to the authorities and then advocate for them in court.

Bank, Marlowe, Reid, Patterson, and Weinrott (1991) compared this model to treatment as usual in a sample of 55 adolescent boys (M age = 14.0) who averaged eight previous offenses. Short-term results were encouraging with the intervention group demonstrating reductions in criminal offenses during the course of treatment. However, at the 1-year and 3-year follow-ups, rates of offending were equivalent across groups. Dishion and Andrews (1995) used this model with adolescents' aged 11–14 years with participants randomly assigned to 1 of 5 groups: (1) parent training following the Oregon model; (2) an adolescent group intervention for self-regulation enhancement; (3) combined parent and adolescent treatment; (4) a self-directed change control group; and, (5) a quasi-experimental placebo control with no intervention. Adolescents that received parent training following the Oregon model demonstrated short-term positive effects (e.g., reductions in negative family interactions).

Group Interventions

Though parents and caregivers are one of the primary sources of influence on children's behavior, this influence wanes over the course of development as the impact of peers becomes more important during adolescence. Because peers can influence teens' attitudes and behaviors (Gardner & Steinberg, 2005), leveraging peer influence through group treatment can be an efficient and effective way to address teens' behavioral health needs. Unfortunately, using group treatment for disruptive behavior problems has proven problematic due to the risk of negative peer influences, resulting in iatrogenic effects. Specifically, group therapy in which youth are surrounded by other peers with similar or more severe disruptive behavior problems can potentially worsen the symptom profiles of participating teens (Dishion & Kavanagh, 2003). Given that one of the primary treatment goals for ODD/CD is to promote contacts with prosocial peers and limit contacts with antisocial peers, the modality of group treatment does not have a strong evidence base for middle to late adolescents with these diagnoses. Below, we briefly review several group-based treatment programs that are considered promising, that is, that have shown moderate to strong evidence of their effectiveness with early adolescents but have yet to demonstrate effectiveness with older adolescents. These programs are included in the chapter because they have curriculums that are marketed for middle school students and youth up to 14 years of age.

Group Interventions with At Least Some Evidence

Second Step Second Step is a classroom-based, universal prevention and intervention program designed to reduce impulsive and aggressive behavior. The program focuses on skill building in the areas of empathy, impulse control, problem solving, and anger management. The group component of Second Step is a class-wide curriculum that is delivered sequentially by the teacher or the school mental health provider. The curriculum features lessons, videos, prompt cards, teacher-led discussion, role plays, reproducible activity sheets, and homework.

In a number of large-scale evaluations, Second Step has been associated with increased prosocial behavior, better self-regulation and social-emotional competence, decreased aggression, and fewer behavioral problems (Espelage, Polanin, & Rose, 2015; Low, Cook, Smolkowski, & Buntain-Ricklefs, 2015). Though the Second Step literature spans the early learning, elementary, and middle school curricula, there is a relatively strong representation of youth in middle school up to eighth grade in these analyses. Outcomes of these studies have included those relevant to children with ODD/CD, including decreased aggression, antisocial behavior, and bullying, and increased prosocial behavior. Shortcomings of this research for understanding Second Step's potential impact on adolescents with ODD/CD include its focus only on children up to eighth grade. In addition, the literature base does not indicate whether children with ODD/CD diagnoses, or those at risk for these diagnoses, responded in the same way as the general youth population targeted in the studies.

Coping Power Coping Power is an intervention program that has been evaluated with children ages 8 to 14 years who screen in for disruptive and aggressive behavior. The program is based on social-cognitive principles with a focus on helping children understand and address their deficits in social information processing and improve their problem-solving abilities. The program, when delivered in school settings, is intended to span up to 2 years. Four to six children are assigned to a group, which is led by a master's-level clinician. Activities in the small groups focus on goal setting, emotion vocabulary building and awareness, emotion regulation, perspective taking and social-cognitive skill building, social skills development, and problem solving. There is a complementary parent component that is delivered to the caregivers of children in the groups.

Coping Power has a strong empirical base in a diverse population of children and youth (Lochman, Boxmeyer, Powell, Roth, & Windle, 2006; Lochman & Wells, 2004). Outcomes associated with the program include improved social skills, decreases in social-cognitive problems associated with aggression, and reduced externalizing problem behaviors. Additional findings from long-term follow-up studies (three to four years postintervention) reveal reductions in children's aggressive behavior and academic behavior problems (Lochman, Wells, Qu, & Chen, 2013) as well as in children's proactive and reactive aggression, impulsivity traits and callous-unemotional traits (Lochman et al., 2014). A strength of the Coping Power literature base is that it focuses exclusively on those children who screen in due to aggressive and disruptive behavior. Therefore, it is probable that many of the children who have been helped by Coping Power were diagnosed as ODD/CD or at risk for ODD/CD. Notably, some preliminary data support the feasibility and efficacy of adapting the program for use with seventh grade students (Lochman et al., 2016).

Project ACHIEVE Project ACHIEVE is a universal, school-based intervention focused on improving academic achievement and engagement, facilitating positive behavioral supports in schools, decreasing discipline problems, increasing school safety, and improving parent and community involvement with school. The group component of Project ACHIEVE is only one in a multicomponent intervention, and it is based on the Stop & Think Social Skills Program. Project ACHIEVE is implemented by school leaders and teachers over 3 years through a series of supports provided by the Project ACHIEVE team.

One quasi-experimental study (Knoff & Batsche, 1995) and one pre–post study with a comparison group (Killian, Fish, & Maniago, 2006) demonstrated school-level outcomes directly relevant to disruptive behavior disorders, including decreases in disciplinary referrals, out-of-school suspension, undesirable behaviors, and serious offenses. However, research has been uncontrolled, samples have been relatively small, and the study population has been limited to students in elementary school grades up to sixth grade. Thus, although the program is marketed for middle schools serving children up to age 14 years, the research evidence does not currently include this population. Another limitation of this universal intervention is the lack of data specific to children diagnosed with, or at risk for, ODD/CD, to ensure that treatment effects are also present for this subpopulation.

Group Interventions without Research Evidence or Iatrogenic

Though some of the individual interventions covered in this chapter, including cognitive-behavioral therapy, social skills, and problem-solving training, can be delivered in group format, we recommend caution with group approaches, especially in treatment settings, owing to the potential risk of iatrogenic effects (Dodge, Dishion, & Lansford, 2006). When groups are used, single-gender groups are recommended (National Mental Health Association, 2004). A second consideration is that adolescents with ODD/CD may need additional treatment approaches that address their individual needs, including their verbal ability, executive functioning, emotional style, and motivation (Frick, Ray, Thornton, & Kahn, 2014).

Interventions Delivered to Youth and their Parents

Family Interventions

Given that family factors play a central role in the etiology of conduct problems among youth (Pardini, Waller, & Hawes, 2015), it is not surprising that a majority of effective interventions for this population are family-based (Henggeler, 2015). Specifically, research suggests that malleable variables including parental monitoring, supervision and involvement, discipline strategies, emotional warmth, parental conflict, and family cohesion are critical in the development and maintenance of serious behavior problems in children and adolescents (Pardini et al., 2015). Indeed, empirical evidence indicates that improvements in family functioning mediate decreases in antisocial behavior and substance use (Henggeler, 2015). The interventions described below represent the most efficacious or promising family-based treatments for addressing ODD and CD among adolescents. These programs are comparable in that they are based on well-elaborated conceptual frameworks, explicitly target specific individual, family, and broader social/environmental risk and protective factors, are multimodal in nature, can be delivered in multiple settings, and require considerable treatment fidelity to yield favorable outcomes (Henggeler, 2015).

Family Interventions with At Least Some Evidence

Functional Family Therapy Among the most extensively investigated family-based therapeutic interventions for adolescent behavior problems is Functional Family Therapy (FFT; Alexander, Waldron, Robbins, & Neeb, 2013). FFT focuses on changing maladaptive family interactions and improving family relationships, which are conceptualized as the primary mechanisms by which to reduce conduct problems in youth. A short-term (12–14 sessions, on average), structured intervention for youth aged 11–18 years, FFT is delivered by trained mental health clinicians in homes, clinics, schools, and child welfare and juvenile justice facilities. The intervention is comprised of five primary components: (1) engagement in change; (2) motivation to change; (3) relational/ interpersonal assessment and change planning; (4) behavior change; and (5) generalization across domains and systems. The engagement phase aims to facilitate positive perceptions of the program and enhance families' willingness to attend sessions (e.g., addressing barriers such as transportation, reluctance, confusion) in order to prevent early program drop-out, while the motivation phase seeks to increase therapeutic alliance and hope for lasting change. Importantly, FFT clinicians steer families away from negative and blaming discussions of adolescent behavior problems, instead refocusing treatment on building more positive relationships. The relational assessment phase of FFT helps identify individual, family system, and larger systems relational processes thought to maintain presenting problems. These relational functions and needs are then targeted during the behavior change phase through a variety of specific behavioral and cognitive-behavioral techniques (e.g., family communication, conflict resolution, and problem-solving skills training, parenting skills, behavioral contracting, response-cost and contingency management). In the final phase, clinicians focus on sustaining and generalizing positive behavior changes, increasing family resources and supports, and preventing relapse.

FFT is supported by a large body of empirical research conducted over the past four decades. To date, more than two dozen outcome studies have been conducted with adolescents with a range of problem behaviors, from status offenders to youth with more serious antisocial behavior and criminal offenses (Alexander et al., 2013). Overall, findings indicate that adolescents who receive FFT demonstrate significantly reduced recidivism rates and subsequent sibling court involvement when compared to those who receive alternative or no treatment, particularly when FFT is delivered competently and with high fidelity to the treatment model (Hansson, Cederblad, & Hook, 2000; Sexton & Turner, 2010). Of note, the efficacy of FFT is supported across diverse sites and treatment settings, clients, and service providers (Alexander et al., 2013).

Multidimensional Family Therapy Developed by Howard Liddle (see Liddle, 1992), Multidimensional Family Therapy (MDFT) is a comprehensive, family-centered, and developmentally oriented treatment for adolescent substance abuse and delinquency. MDFT is informed by multiple theoretical frameworks, including self-efficacy and family systems theory, developmental psychopathology, transactional and contextual theories, and the risk and protective model of adolescent substance abuse and related problems. A manualized treatment, MDFT is delivered 1–3 times per week over the course of 3–6 months in a wide range of treatment contexts, including drug abuse and mental health settings (e.g., outpatient clinics, in-home, day treatment, residential programs), within the juvenile justice system (e.g., detention centers, drug court), and child welfare settings (Liddle, 2016). MDFT emphasizes four interdependent treatment domains: (1) adolescent, (2) parent, (3) family, and (4) extra-familial. Individual work with adolescents involves establishing a therapeutic alliance, defining meaningful therapeutic goals for youth, generating hope, improving problem-solving and social competence skills, and preparing teens to discuss important issues with their parents. Interventions with parents aim to enhance emotional connection to teens and improve parenting skills (e.g., limit setting and monitoring). Following in the tradition of structural family therapy, joint parent–adolescent sessions focus on increasing positive and constructive family interactions through enactments. Finally, extra-familial interventions aim to establish more collaborative relationships between families and other social systems in which teens participate (e.g., school, peer, legal, employment, health). For instance, MDFT therapists help families navigate complex systems in order to obtain adjunctive services, satisfy any legal requirements, secure school or job placements, and/or address medical, immigration, or financial problems.

A strong body of empirical research indicates that MDFT is an effective treatment for adolescent substance use, with mounting evidence for related problem behaviors including antisocial, delinquent, and externalizing behaviors (Dakof et al., 2015; Liddle, Dakof, Henderson, & Rowe, 2011). In a recent RCT, adolescent group therapy and MDFT yielded comparable reductions in delinquency, rearrests, externalizing symptoms, and drug use for youth enrolled in juvenile drug court, yet the MDFT group exhibited fewer externalizing symptoms, serious crimes, and felony arrests at a 2-year follow-up (Dakof et al., 2015). While individual CBT and MDFT yield comparable reductions in substance use and delinquency, MDFT demonstrates greater reductions in functional impairment, higher treatment retention rates, and improved efficacy with youth with more severe psychiatric problem behaviors (Hendriks, van der Schee, & Blanken, 2011, 2012). Similarly, in an RCT involving youth from five western European countries, MDFT outperformed individual psychotherapy with regards to treatment retention as well as reductions in cannabis dependence and externalizing symptoms, particularly with youth with more severe drug use (Schaub et al., 2014).

Adolescent Transitions Program The Adolescent Transitions Program (ATP; Dishion, Andrews, Kavanagh, & Soberman, 1996) was designed for, and evaluated with, middle school students. ATP is a multitiered intervention that can be tailored to family needs and the severity of presenting problems (Connell, Dishion, Yasui, & Kavanagh, 2007). The program includes universal, selected, and indicated family interventions, which can be combined into a flexible menu of services after an initial assessment of strengths and needs. The universal component includes the development of a *Family Resource Center* in schools, which is staffed by parent consultants who support parents' involvement, supervision, and management of their children (Connell et al., 2007). The selected component of ATP is referred to as the *Family Check-Up* (FCU; Dishion et al., 2008), a brief intervention comprised of an initial parent interview to assess behavioral concerns, an extensive home visit to evaluate parent–child interactions (via videotaping and coding), and a structured feedback session focusing on positive parenting practices and areas for improvement in parent–child interactions. For youth with diagnosed behavior problems or high levels of family dysfunction, ATP provides a menu of family-centered services; this intervention facilitates families' self-selection into the most appropriate intervention services based on assessment of needs, resources available, and the motivation and skills of parents (Connell et al., 2007).

Several randomized trials suggest that ATP holds promise for preventing or reducing youth antisocial behavior, and other conduct problems. At-risk middle school students whose families received FCU exhibited significantly lower rates of antisocial behavior when they reached high school (9th–11th grades) compared to matched controls (Connell et al., 2007). Additionally, middle schoolers whose families participated in an indicated ATP component demonstrated reduced symptoms of conduct disorder, lower risk of drug use initiation, and reductions in depressive symptoms in ninth grade, when compared to control students (Connell & Dishion, 2008). In particular, families with high levels of engagement in ATP intervention services demonstrated substantially better youth substance abuse and behavioral outcomes, with medium to large effect sizes (Stormshak et al., 2011). For instance, high-risk sixth graders whose families were not offered FCU were six times more likely to be arrested within the next five years and used marijuana five times more frequently. These findings indicate that the selected and indicated components of ATP, when delivered to at-risk middle schoolers, can help decrease the likelihood of more significant substance use and behavior problems during middle and late adolescence. This research also highlights the utility of schools as an entry point to intervention services for at-risk youth.

Familias Unidas Familias Unidas is a family-based preventive intervention that aims to reduce risk for adverse health behaviors (i.e., substance use and unsafe sexual behaviors) in Hispanic adolescents (Pantin et al., 2003). Based in ecodevelopmental theory and specific models developed for Hispanic populations in the United States, Familias Unidas utilizes both multiparent groups and family visits to promote positive parenting, family support for youth, parental involvement, and adaptive parent–adolescent communication around health behaviors (Pantin et al., 2007). The intervention also targets cultural risk and protective processes highlighted through community-based participatory research (e.g., acculturation issues; Prado & Pantin, 2011). Parent groups emphasize participatory learning (i.e., learning through dialogue and role plays), while family visits provide opportunities for facilitators to restructure family, peer, and school risk processes and for parents to practice and implement skills learned in group sessions, thereby facilitating more nurturing and supportive family relationships (Prado & Pantin, 2011).

A growing body of research suggests that Familias Unidas effectively prevents or reduces substance use, behavior problems, and risky sexual practices in Hispanic youth when compared to treatment-as-usual control conditions. Findings from three efficacy trials indicate that Familias Unidas increases family functioning and reduces adolescent behavior problems (i.e., substance use, externalizing symptoms, and unsafe sexual behavior) for both at-risk teens and those with clinical behavior problems at baseline, relative to prevention as usual (Pantin et al., 2003; Pantin et al., 2009).

Family Behavior Therapy and Contingency Management Family behavior therapy (FBT) and family-based contingency management (CM) are related outpatient treatments founded upon cognitive behavioral and behavioral models of youth substance use. FBT (Donohue & Azrin, 2012) involves behavioral contracts, self-management training (e.g., identifying and addressing triggers for substance use), and family communication training. Family-based CM (Henggeler, Cunningham, Rowland, & Schoenwald, 2012) was developed based on the Community Reinforcement Approach, an effective intervention for adult substance abuse (Budney & Higgins, 1998). Although very similar to FBT, CM is unique in that it involves monitoring youth drug use through frequent drug testing, which directs the implementation of contingencies specified in the behavioral contract. Additionally, parents are involved with every aspect of treatment, including adolescent self-management training (Henggeler, 2015).

In a small RCT, FBT demonstrated promise in reducing drug and alcohol use and depression and improving school attendance and family relationships (Azrin, Donohue, Besalel, Kogan, & Acierno, 1994). However, these outcomes were not replicated in a larger RCT with youth diagnosed with conduct disorder and substance dependence (Azrin et al., 2001). With regard to CM, findings from a randomized trial suggested that this intervention reduces delinquent behavior in adolescents (Stanger, Budney, Kamon, & Thostensen, 2009), though whether these gains are maintained over longer periods of time is unclear. Overall, while findings are promising, additional research is needed to better understand whether FBT and CM have lasting effects on adolescent behavior problems.

Brief Strategic Family Therapy A promising intervention for addressing antisocial behavior in adolescents, Brief Strategic Family Therapy (BSFT) involves weekly clinic or in-home sessions delivered across an average of four months (Szapocznik, Hervis, & Schwartz, 2003). BSFT uses structural, strategic, and problem-focused strategies to address patterns of family interactions thought to maintain youth behavior problems. During sessions, BSFT therapists attempt to elicit and restructure typical family interactions through traditional family therapy techniques such as joining, reframing, and modifying family boundaries and alliances through enactments. BSFT also incorporates practical strategies such as helping parents set household rules (e.g., curfew).

The efficacy and effectiveness of BSFT for youth antisocial behavior has been examined through several randomized trials. For Hispanic adolescents with behavior and substance use problems, BSFT was superior to group therapy for reducing conduct problems, association with antisocial peers, and marijuana use at post-treatment as well as improving observer-rated family functioning (Santisteban et al., 2003). Valdez, Cepeda, Parrish, Horowitz, and Kaplan (2013) implemented an adapted version of BSFT with gang-affiliated Mexican American adolescents and found lower parent-reported conduct problems 6 months posttreatment. In a small RCT, BSFT reduced bullying behaviors, substance use, risky sexual behaviors, and interpersonal problems among adolescent girls at posttreatment when compared to a placebo intervention, though differences in bullying were no longer significant one year later (Nickel et al., 2006). In a community-based effectiveness trial, BSFT did not improve behavior problems for a sample of young adolescents (Coatsworth, Santisteban, McBride, & Szapocznik, 2001). Conversely, in a subsequent independent multisite effectiveness study, families who received BSFT demonstrated reduced adolescent-reported drug use and improved parent-reported family functioning one year after recruitment, relative to those who participated in community services (Robbins et al., 2011). Overall, findings are mixed, yet suggest that BSFT may be a promising approach for adolescent conduct problems warranting additional investigation.

Multicomponent Interventions

Multi-component interventions target the adolescent, their parent(s), and the wider social environment.

Multicomponent Interventions with At Least Some Evidence

Fast Track Project The Fast Track Project is a large-scale, multiyear, multimodal program combining intensive universal and targeted interventions, delivered in home and school-based settings, and originally targeted at young children at high risk for early-onset conduct problems (Conduct Problems Prevention Research Group [CPPRG], 1992). The adolescent phase of the program (grades 6–10) primarily focuses on tailoring the intervention to the needs of individual youth using criterion-based assessment, but also includes a few manual-based sessions. Findings reveal that intervention effects were mixed and sometimes null for antisocial behavior during the middle school years (CPPRG, 2010b). Prevention impacts for the Fast Track intervention among adolescent through young adulthood participants (ages 12–20) revealed reduced delinquency and number of arrests (CPPRG, 2007, 2010a) and significant reductions in antisocial behavior in Grade 9 relative to the control group (Dodge, Goodwin, CPPRG, 2013). However, further analyses found that the later program effects were primarily due to changes in targeted child, peer and parent mechanisms during the elementary school years (Sorensen, Dodge, CPPRG, 2015). Therefore, caution is warranted when interpreting findings of the adolescent phase of the Fast Track program.

Multisystemic Therapy (MST) MST is a multimodel intervention that targets youth with conduct problems who are at risk for out-of-home placements and their families (Henggeler, Melton, & Smith, 1992). It conceptualizes youth behavior as resulting from the relationship between the individual and several interrelated systems, including family, peers, school, and community. MST therapists carry a small caseload and are available to the youth and family 24 hours per day. Over a period of several months, MST therapists work to restructure the youth's environment across several levels—family (e.g., teaching parenting skills, addressing parental mental health and substance use problems), peer (e.g., distancing the youth from negative peers), and school (e.g., promoting education and/or job skills)—to reduce antisocial behavior (Henggeler, 1997).

Results from an RCT with non-court-referred adolescents (ages 11–18) found significant reductions in parent and self-report ratings of externalizing behavior problems for those in the MST group as compared to treatment as usual (Weiss et al., 2013). Sawyer and Borduin (2011) examined the long-term effects of MST for serious and violent juvenile offenders after 20 years of intervention as compared to individual therapy. Findings revealed lower recidivism rates (38.4% vs. 54.8%), and reduced frequency of misdemeanor offending for those who received MST relative to those who received individual counseling.

Multidimensional Treatment Foster Care (MTFC) MTFC is often used an alternative to residential, secure-care, or hospitalization treatment for youth with chronic and severe behavior disorders (Elliott, 1998). MTFC involves placing youth with trained and supervised families for 6 to 9 months in an effort to reduce antisocial behavior, increase prosocial engagement, and eventually return the youth to his or her family. The intervention involves individualized behavioral management programs, close supervision of activities, individual and family therapy, and rewards and punishments for youth behavior. The MTFC parents make regular reports to case managers regarding the youth's progress, and they maintain contact with a range of professionals, including behavioral-support specialists, physicians, teachers, probation officers, and work supervisors (Fisher & Chamberlain, 2000).

Rhoades, Chamberlain, Roberts, and Leve (2013) found significantly reduced offending, violence, risky sexual behavior, and self-harm among female youth enrolled in MTFC programs in both England and the United States. The National Mental Health Association (2004) reported that youth who received MTFC spent 60% fewer days incarcerated and had significantly fewer arrests than youth who did not receive services. Leve, Chamberlain, and Reid (2005) found that female youth assigned to MTFC had significantly fewer days spent in locked settings and 42% fewer criminal referrals than the control group at a 12-month follow-up.

Conclusion

Over the past two decades there has been a significant increase in the development, implementation, evaluation, and replication of psychosocial treatment and prevention programs for children and adolescents displaying disruptive, impulsive, and conduct-disordered behavior problems. Although the majority of these programs have been applied with preadolescents, there has been a recent surge in intervention strategies targeted at middle to late adolescents. An important next direction for research is to conduct long-term follow-up studies of adolescents who received treatment to determine if any gains are maintained into adulthood. Given the importance of high levels of treatment fidelity to successful intervention outcomes, more research should focus on effective dissemination strategies, including best-practice for training and supervision of practitioners. Because there are now well-established and efficacious treatments for ODD and CD, future research studies should focus on identifying which treatment best matches the needs and risk profile of the adolescent and how we can best implement the selected treatment program to produce the most favorable outcomes.

References

Alexander, J. F., Waldron, H. B., Robbins, M. S., & Neeb, A. A. (2013). *Functional family therapy for adolescent behavior problems.* Washington, D.C.: American Psychological Association.

Armelius, B. Å., & Andreassen, T. H. (2007). *Cognitive-behavioural treatment for antisocial behaviour in youth in residential care.* Chichester: The Cochrane Collaboration, John Wiley & Sons, Ltd.

Azrin, N. H., Donohue, B., Besalel, V. A., Kogan, E. S., & Acierno, R. (1994). Youth drug abuse treatment: A controlled outcome study. *Journal of Child and Adolescent Substance Abuse, 3*(3), 1–16.

Azrin, N. H., Donohue, B., Teichner, G. A., Crum, T., Howell, J., & DeCato, L. A. (2001). A controlled evaluation and description of individual-cognitive problem solving and family-behavior therapies in dually diagnosed conduct-disordered and substance-dependent youth. *Journal of Child & Adolescent Substance Abuse, 11,* 1–43.

Bank, L., Marlowe, J. H., Reid, J. B., Patterson, G. R., & Weinrott, M. R. (1991). A comparative evaluation of parent-training interventions for families of chronic delinquents. *Journal of Abnormal Child Psychology, 19,* 15–33.

Barnes, V. A., Treiber, F. A., & Johnson, M. H. (2004). Impact of transcendental meditation on ambulatory blood pressure in African-American adolescents. *American Journal of Hypertension, 17,* 366–369.

Biegel, G. M., Brown, K. W., Shapiro, S. L., & Schubert, C. M. (2009). Mindfulness-based stress reduction for the treatment of adolescent psychiatric outpatients: A randomized clinical trial. *Journal of Consulting and Clinical Psychology, 77,* 855–866.

Budney, A. J., & Higgins, S. T. (1998). *A community reinforcement plus vouchers approach: Treating cocaine addiction.* Rockville, MD: US Department of Health and Human Services, National Institutes of Health, National Institute on Drug Abuse.

Burke, C. A. (2010). Mindfulness-based approaches with children and adolescents: A preliminary review of current research in an emergent field. *Journal of Child and Family Studies, 19,* 133–144.

Chu, J. T., Bullen, P., Farruggia, S. P., Dittman, C. K., & Sanders, M. R. (2015). Parent and adolescent effects of a universal group program for the parenting of adolescents. *Prevention Science, 16,* 609–620.

Coatsworth, J. D., Santisteban, D. A., McBride, C. K., & Szapocznik, J. (2001). Brief Strategic Family Therapy versus community control: Engagement, retention, and an exploration of the moderating role of adolescent symptom severity. *Family Process, 40,* 313–332.

Conduct Problems Prevention Research Group. (1992). A developmental and clinical model for the prevention of conduct disorders: The FAST Track Program. *Development and Psychopathology, 4,* 509–527.

Conduct Problems Prevention Research Group. (2007). The Fast Track randomized controlled trial to prevent externalizing psychiatric disorders. *Journal of the American Academy of Child and Adolescent Psychiatry, 46,* 319–333.

Conduct Problems Prevention Research Group. (2010a). Fast Track intervention effects on youth arrests and delinquency. *Journal of Experimental Criminology, 6,* 131–157.

Conduct Problems Prevention Research Group. (2010b). The difficulty of maintaining positive intervention effects: A look at disruptive behavior, deviant peer relations, and social skills during the middle school years. *Journal of Early Adolescence, 30,* 593–624.

Connell, A. M., & Dishion, T. J. (2008). Reducing depression among at-risk early adolescents: Three-year effects of a family-centered intervention embedded within schools. *Journal of Family Psychology, 22,* 574–585.

Connell, A. M., Dishion, T. J., Yasui, M., & Kavanagh, K. (2007). An adaptive approach to family intervention: linking engagement in family-centered intervention to reductions in adolescent problem behavior. *Journal of Consulting and Clinical Psychology, 75,* 568–579.

Dakof, G. A., Henderson, C. E., Rowe, C. L., Boustani, M., Greenbaum, P. E., Wang, W., . . . Liddle, H. A. (2015). A randomized clinical trial of family therapy in juvenile drug court. *Journal of Family Psychology, 29,* 232–241.

Dishion, T. J., & Andrews, D. W. (1995). Preventing escalation in problem behaviors with high-risk adolescents: Immediate and 1-year outcomes. *Journal of Consulting and Clinical Psychology, 63,* 538–548.

Dishion, T. J., Andrews, D. W., Kavanagh, K., & Soberman, L. H. (1996). Preventive interventions for high-risk youth: The Adolescent Transitions Program. In R. D. Peters & R. J. McMahon (Eds.), *Preventing childhood disorders, substance abuse, and delinquency* (pp. 184–214). Thousand Oaks, CA: Sage.

Dishion, T. J., & Kavanagh, K. (2003). *Intervening in adolescent problem behavior: A family-centered approach.* New York, NY: The Guilford Press.

Dishion, T. J., Shaw, D., Connell, A., Gardner, F., Weaver, C., & Wilson, M. (2008). The family check-up with high-risk indigent families: Preventing problem behavior by increasing parents' positive behavior support in early childhood. *Child Development, 79,* 1395–1414.

Dodge, K. A., Dishion, T. J., & Lansford, J. E. (2006). *Deviant peer influences in programs for youth: Problems and solutions.* New York, NY: Guilford Press.

Dodge, K. A., & Godwin, J., & Conduct Problems Prevention Research Group. (2013). Social-information-processing patterns mediate the impact of preventive intervention on adolescent antisocial behavior. *Psychological Science, 24,* 456–465.

Donohue, B., & Azrin, N. H. (2012). *Treating adolescent substance abuse using family behavior therapy: A step-by-step approach.* Hoboken, NJ: Wiley.

DuBois, D. L., Portillo, N., Rhodes, J. E., Silverthorn, N., & Valentine, J. C. (2011). How effective are mentoring programs for youth? A systematic assessment of the evidence. *Psychological Science in the Public Interest, 12,* 57–91.

Elliott, D. S. (Ed.) (1998). *Blueprints for violence prevention: Multidimensional treatment foster care.* Denver, CO: C & M Press.

Espelage, D. L., Polanin, J. R., & Rose, C. A. (2015). Social-emotional learning program to reduce bullying, fighting, and victimization among middle school students with disabilities. *Remedial and Special Education, 36,* 1–13.

Fisher, P. A., & Chamberlain, P. (2000). Multidimensional treatment foster care: A program for intensive parenting, family support, and skill building. *Journal of Emotional and Behavioral Disorders, 8,* 155–164.

Fonagy, P., Cottrell, D., Phillips, J., Bevington, D., Glaser, D., & Allison, E. (2015). *What works for whom? A critical review of treatments for children and adolescents* (2nd ed.). New York, NY: Guilford Press.

Frick, P. J., Ray, J. V., Thornton, L. C., & Kahn, R. E. (2014). Can callous-unemotional traits enhance the understanding, diagnosis, and treatment of serious conduct problems in children and adolescents? A comprehensive review. *Psychological Bulletin, 140,* 1–57.

Gardner, M., & Steinberg, L. (2005). Peer influence on risk taking, risk preference, and risky decision making in adolescence and adulthood: An experimental study. *Developmental Psychology, 41,* 625–635.

Garland, A. F., Hawley, K. M., Brookman-Frazee, L., & Hurlbut, M. S. (2008). Identifying common elements of evidence-based psychosocial treatments for children's disruptive behavior problems. *Journal of the American Academy of Child and Adolescent Psychiatry, 47,* 505–514.

Hansson, K., Cederblad, M., & Hook, B. (2000). Functional family therapy: A method for treating juvenile delinquents. *Socialvetenskaplig Tidskrift, 3,* 231–243.

Hendriks, V., van der Schee, E., & Blanken, P. (2011). Treatment of adolescents with a cannabis use disorder: Main findings of a randomized controlled trial comparing multidimensional family therapy and cognitive behavioral therapy in the Netherlands. *Drug and Alcohol Dependence, 119,* 64–71.

Hendriks, V., van der Schee, E., & Blanken, P. (2012). Matching adolescents with a cannabis use disorder to multidimensional family therapy or cognitive behavioral therapy: treatment effect moderators in a randomized controlled trial. *Drug and Alcohol Dependence, 125,* 119–126.

Henggeler, S. W. (1997). *Treating serious antisocial behavior in youth: The MST approach.* Washington, DC: U.S. Department of Justice.

Henggeler, S. W. (2015). Effective family-based treatments for adolescents with serious antisocial behavior. In J. Morizot & L. Kazemian (Eds.), *The development of criminal and antisocial behavior* (pp. 461–475). Cham, Switzerland: Springer International Publishing.

Henggeler, S. W., Cunningham, P. B., Rowland, M. D., & Schoenwald, S. K. (2012). *Contingency management for adolescent substance abuse: A practitioner's guide.* New York, NY: Guilford.

Henggeler, S. W., Melton, G. B., & Smith, L. A. (1992). Family preservation using multisystemic therapy: An effective alternative to incarcerating serious juvenile offenders. *Journal of Consulting and Clinical Psychology, 60,* 953–961.

Herrera, C., Grossman, J. B., Kauh, T. J., Feldman, A. F., & McMaken, J. (2007). *Making a difference in schools: The Big Brothers Big Sisters school-based mentoring impact study.* Philadelphia, PA: Public/Private Ventures.

Jolliffe, D., & Farrington, D. (2004). Empathy and offending: A systematic review and meta-analysis. *Aggression and Violent Behavior, 9,* 441–476.

Kaslow, N. J., Broth, M. R., Smith, C. O., & Collins, M. H. (2012). Family-based interventions for child and adolescent disorders. *Journal of Marital and Family Therapy, 38,* 82–100.

Kazdin, A. E. (1997). Parent management training: Evidence, outcomes, and issues. *Journal of the American Academy of Child and Adolescent Psychiatry, 36,* 1349–1356.

Kazdin, A. E. (2001). *Behavior modification in applied settings* (6th ed.). Belmont, CA: Wadsworth.

Kazdin, A. E., Bass, D., Siegal, T., & Thomas, C. (1989). Cognitive-behavioral therapy and relationship therapy in the treatment of children referred for antisocial behavior. *Journal of Consulting and Clinical Psychology, 57,* 522–535.

Kazdin, A. E., Sigel, T. C., & Bass, D. (1992). Cognitive problem-solving skills training and parent management training in the treatment of antisocial behavior in children. *Journal of Consulting and Clinical Psychology, 60,* 737–747.

Killian, J. M., Fish, M. C., & Maniago, E. B. (2006). Making schools safe: A system-wide school intervention to increase student prosocial behaviors and enhance school climate. *Journal of Applied School Psychology, 23,* 1–30.

Knoff, H. M., & Batsche, G. M. (1995). Project ACHIEVE: Analyzing a school reform process for at-risk and underachieving students. *School Psychology Review, 24,* 579–603.

Leve, L. D., Chamberlain, P., & Reid, J. B. (2005). Intervention outcomes for girls referred from juvenile justice: Effects on delinquency. *Journal of Consulting and Clinical Psychology, 73,* 1181–1185.

Liddle, H. A. (1992). A multidimensional model for treating the adolescent who is abusing alcohol and other drugs. In W. Snyder & T. Ooms (Eds.), *Empowering families, helping adolescents: Family-centered treatment of adolescents with alcohol, drug abuse, and mental health problems* (pp. 91–100). Rockville, MD: U.S. Government Printing Office.

Liddle, H. A. (2016). Multidimensional family therapy. In T. Sexton & J. Lebow (Eds.), *Handbook of family therapy* (pp. 231–249). New York, NY: Routledge.

Liddle, H. A., Dakof, G. A., Henderson, C., & Rowe, C. (2011). Implementation outcomes of Multidimensional Family Therapy-Detention to Community: A reintegration program for drug-using juvenile detainees. *International Journal of Offender Therapy and Comparative Criminology, 55,* 587–604.

Lochman, J. E., Baden, R. E., Boxmeyer, C. L., Powell, N. P., Qu ,L., Salekin, K. L., &Windle, M. (2014). Does a booster intervention augment the preventive effects of an abbreviated version of the Coping Power program for aggressive children? *Journal of Abnormal Child Psychology, 42,* 367–381.

Lochman, J. E., Boxmeyer, C., Powell, N., Roth, D. L., & Windle, M. (2006). Masked intervention effects: Analytic methods for addressing low dosage of intervention. *New Directions for Evaluation, 110,* 19–32.

Lochman, J. E., Bradshaw, C. P., Powell, N., Debnam, K., Pas, E., & Ialongo, N. (2016, June). *Preventing conduct problems in middle schoolers: Preliminary effects of the Early Adolescent Coping Power Program.* Paper presented in a symposium (C. Bradshaw, chair) at the 24th Annual Meeting of the Society for Prevention Research, San Francisco, CA.

Lochman, J. E., & Wells, K. C. (2004). The coping power program for preadolescent aggressive boys and their parents: outcome effects at the 1-year follow-up. *Journal of Consulting and Clinical Psychology, 72,* 571–578.

Lochman, J. E., Wells, K. C., Qu, L., & Chen, L. (2013). Three year follow-up of Coping Power intervention effects: Evidence of neighborhood moderation? *Prevention Science, 14,* 364–376.

Low, S., Cook, C. R., Smolkowski, K., & Buntain-Ricklefs, J. (2015). Promoting social–emotional competence: An evaluation of the elementary version of Second Step®. *Journal of School Psychology, 53,* 463–477.

Maag, J. W. (2006). Social skills training for students with emotional and behavioral disorders: A review of reviews. *Behavioral Disorders, 32,* 5–17.

McCart, M. R., Priester, P. E., Davies, W. H., & Azen, R. (2006). Differential effectiveness of behavioral parent-training and cognitive-behavioral therapy for antisocial youth: A meta-analysis. *Journal of Abnormal Child Psychology, 34,* 527–543.

National Mental Health Association. (2004). *Mental health treatment for youth in the juvenile justice system: A compendium of promising practices.* Chicago, IL: Author.

Nelson-Gray, R. O., Keane, S. P., Hurst, R. M., Mitchell, J. T., Warburton, J. B., Chok, J. T., . . . Cobb, A. R. (2006). A modified DBT skills training program for oppositional defiant adolescents: Promising preliminary findings. *Behavior Research and Therapy, 44,* 1811–1820.

Nickel, M., Luley, J., Krawczyk, J., Nickel, C., Widermann, C., Lahmann, C., . . . Loew, T. (2006). Bullying girls—Changes after brief strategic family therapy: A randomized, prospective, controlled trial with one-year follow-up. *Psychotherapy & Psychosomatics, 75,* 47–55.

Pantin, H., Coatsworth, J. D., Feaster, D. J., Newman, F. L., Briones, E., Prado, G., . . . Szapocznik, J. (2003). Familias Unidas: The efficacy of an intervention to promote parental investment in hispanic immigrant families. *Prevention Science, 4,* 189–201.

Pantin, H., Prado, G., Lopez, B., Huang, S., Tapia, M. I., Schwartz, S. J., . . . Branchini, J. (2009). A randomized controlled trial of Familias Unidas for Hispanic adolescents with behavior problems. *Psychosomatic Medicine, 71,* 987–995.

Pantin, H., Schwartz, S. J., Coatsworth, J. D., Sullivan, S., Briones, E., & Szapocznik, J. (2007). Familias Unidas: A systemic, parent-centered approach to preventing problem behavior in hispanic adolescents. In P. Tolan, J. Szapocznik & S. Sambran (Eds.), *Preventing youth substance abuse: Science-based programs for children and adolescents* (pp. 211–238). Washington, DC: American Psychological Association.

Pardini, D. A., Waller, R., & Hawes, S. W. (2015). Familial influences on the development of serious conduct problems and delinquency. In J. Morizot & L. Kazemian (Eds.), *The development of criminal and antisocial behavior* (pp. 201–220). Cham, Switzerland: Springer International Publishing.

Perry-Parrish, C., Copeland-Linder, N., Webb, L., & Sibinga, E. M. S. (2016). Mindfulness-based approaches for children and youth. *Current problems in pediatric and adolescent health care, 15,* S1538–5442.

Perry-Parrish, C. K., & Sibinga, E. M. S. (2014). Mindfulness meditation for children. In R.D. Anbar (Ed.), *Functional symptoms in pediatric disease: A clinical guide* (pp. 343–352). New York, NY: Springer.

Prado, G., & Pantin, H. (2011). Reducing substance use and HIV health disparities among Hispanic youth in the USA.: The Familias Unidas program of research. *Psychosocial Intervention, 20,* 63–73.

Ralph, A., & Sanders, M. R. (2003). Preliminary evaluation of the Group Teen Triple P program for parents of teenagers making the transition to high school. *Australian e-Journal for the Advancement of Mental Health, 2,* 169–178.

Rhoades, K. A., Chamberlain, P., Roberts, R., & Leve, L. D. (2013). MTFC for high-risk adolescent girls: A comparison of outcomes in England and the United States. *Journal of Child and Adolescent Substance Abuse, 22,* 439–449.

Robbins, M. S., Feaster, D. J., Horigian, V. E., Rohrbaugh, M., Shoham, V., Bachrach, K., . . . Szapocznik, J. (2011). Brief strategic family therapy versus treatment as usual: Results of a multisite randomized trial for substance using adolescents. *Journal of Consulting and Clinical Psychology, 79,* 713–727.

Sanders, M. R. (1999). Triple P-Positive Parenting Program: Towards an empirically validated multi-level parenting and family support strategy for the prevention of behavior and emotional problems in children. *Clinical Child and Family Psychology Review, 2,* 71–90.

Santisteban, D. A., Coatsworth, J. D., Perez-Vidal, A., Kurtines, W. M., Schwartz, S. J., LaPerriere, A., & Szapocznik, J. (2003). Efficacy of brief strategic family therapy in modifying Hispanic adolescent behavior problems and substance use. *Journal of Family Psychology, 17,* 121–133.

Sawyer, A. M., & Borduin, C. M. (2011). Effects of multisystemic therapy through midlife: A 21.9 year follow-up to a randomized clinical trial with serious and violent juvenile offenders. *Journal of Consulting and Clinical Psychology, 79,* 643–652.

Schaub, M. P., Henderson, C. E., Pelc, I., Tossmann, P., Phan, O., Hendriks, V., . . . Rigter, H. (2014). Multidimensional family therapy decreases the rate of externalising behavioural disorder symptoms in cannabis abusing adolescents: outcomes of the INCANT trial. *BMC Psychiatry, 14,* 26.

Sexton, T., & Turner, C. W. (2010). The effectiveness of functional family therapy for youth with behavioral problems in a community practice setting. *Journal of Family Psychology, 24,* 339–348.

Sorensen, L. C., Dodge, K. A., & Conduct Problems Prevention Research Group (2015). How does the Fast Track intervention prevent adverse outcomes in young adulthood? *Child Development, 87,* 429–445.

Stallman, H. M., & Ralph, A. (2007). Reducing risk factors for adolescent behavioural and emotional problems: A pilot randomised controlled trial of a self-administered parenting intervention. *Australian e-Journal for the Advancement of Mental Health, 6,* 1–13.

Stams, G. J., Brugman, D., Dekovic, M., van Rosmalen, L., van der Laan, P., & Gibbs., J. C. (2006). The moral judgment of juvenile delinquents: A meta-analysis. *Journal of Abnormal Child Psychology, 34,* 697–713.

Stanger, C., Budney, A. J., Kamon, J. L., & Thostensen, J. (2009). A randomized trial of contingency management for adolescent marijuana abuse and dependence. *Drug and Alcohol Dependence, 105,* 240–247.

Stormshak, E. A., Connell, A. M., Veronneau, M. H., Myers, M. W., Dishion, T. J., Kavanagh, K., & Caruthers, A. S. (2011). An ecological approach to promoting early adolescent mental health and social adaptation: Family-centered intervention in public middle schools. *Child Development, 82,* 209–225.

Substance Abuse and Mental Health Services Administration (2011). *Interventions for disruptive behavior disorders: Evidence-based and promising practices.* HHS Pub. No. SMA-11-4634, Rockville, MD: Center for Mental Health Services, U.S. Department of Health and Human Services.

Szapocznik, J., Hervis, O., & Schwartz, S. J. (2003). *Brief Strategic Family Therapy for adolescent drug abuse.* Bethesda, MD: National Institute on Drug Abuse.

Tierney, J. P., Grossman, J., & Resch, N. (1995). *Making a difference: An impact study of Big Brothers Big Sisters.* Philadelphia, PA: Public/Private Ventures.

Valdez, A., Cepeda, A., Parrish, D., Horowitz, R., & Kaplan, C. (2013). An adapted Brief Strategic Family Therapy for gang-affiliated Mexican American adolescents. *Research on Social Work Practice, 23,* 383–396.

Weiss, B., Han, S., Harris, V., Catron, T., Ngo, V. K., Caron, A. . . . Guth, C. (2013). An independent randomized clincial trial of multisyetmic therapy with non-court referred adolescents with serious conduct problems. *Journal of Consulting and Clinical Psychology, 81,* 1027–1039.

29

Factors Influencing Intervention Delivery and Outcomes

John E. Lochman, Francesca Kassing, Meghann Sallee, and Sara L. Stromeyer

This chapter will overview key factors that influence how evidence-based interventions for children with disruptive behavior disorders (DBDs) are disseminated into real-world settings. Dissemination factors that influence outcomes include (a) those at program level that address cultural context and children's developmental processes (including delivering interventions to different types of clients and settings than those originally targeted in the efficacy research), or involve changes to the program's content or structure in order to optimize outcomes (adding booster sessions, creating abbreviated versions of a program, using different formats to deliver the program, including Internet components, applying the program to settings other than those planned); (b) those at client level (parental engagement, comorbidity, community context), and (c) those at the level of clinicians and their practice settings (clinician personality, organizational characteristics, intensity of training). These issues will be addressed in part by drawing on our experience in researching dissemination and adaptation issues with the Coping Power program. The chapter concludes with a consideration of the cost-effectiveness of interventions and their adaptations.

Dissemination to Real-World Settings

In this book, we have examined how a relatively broad set of risk factors are related to children's aggressive and disruptive behaviors and how a menu of evidence-based intervention strategies and programs has been developed to work with these children and their parents. In this chapter, we wish to address the basic question of whether this can make a difference to real-world clinical and preventive care of these children. After the efficacy and effectiveness of an intervention have been established, an important next step is the dissemination of the program for "real-world" implementation to reflect the fact that an intervention that is evidence-based can also be transportable (La Greca, Silverman, & Lochman, 2009; Lochman, Powell, Boxmeyer, Baden, 2010).

Psychotherapy with children and adolescents has traditionally been a field in which typical community-based care had consistently poor outcomes (Bickman, 2003), and use of evidence-based programs (EBPs) has remained infrequent in treatment settings (Henderson, MacKay, & Peterson-Badali, 2006). Support for their implementation has increased through the recommendations and mandates of funders, national associations, and national and state-level legislation (Bickman, 2003; Glisson & Schoenwald, 2005), but EBPs have still been found to have low rates of use in the routine clinical care of youth (Ng & Weisz, 2016; Weisz et al., 2012). As EBPs move from carefully controlled research studies to clinical practice, there is a need to identify the factors that might promote or interfere with their successful dissemination, and a growing body of research has examined this topic.

Attention has been shifting from highly controlled efficacy and effectiveness trials to an interest in understanding the effects of disseminating evidenced-based practices within "real world" settings (Moore, Bumbarger, & Cooper, 2013). Outcomes for evidence-based interventions may not be as strong when the interventions are disseminated to real-world settings (schools, clinics, community agencies). Variation in implementation effects across sites can be more important than average effect sizes across sites, and can lead to greater understanding of factors that can moderate intervention effects in the real world (Raudenbush & Willms, 1991). Thus, the challenges that exist in disseminating evidence-based interventions can shape and sharpen our understanding of the dissemination process, and of the interventions being disseminated and their developmental models.

Factors at the Intervention Program Level

How Much Adaptation Is Alright?

Manuals developed for intervention studies during efficacy and effectiveness trials have the benefit of supporting intervention integrity and promoting the transportability of the program as its broader dissemination begins. By specifically setting out the program's key features, manuals increase the likelihood that future replications of the program will yield effects similar to those realized in intervention trials (Kendall & Chu, 2000). These benefits notwithstanding, practicing clinicians have raised concerns about the use of manualized treatments in "real-world" clinical work (Addis, Wade, & Hatgis, 1999). Criticism is fueled by beliefs that manuals have a limited focus and a single therapeutic perspective, and that they de-emphasize common factors such as positive engagement and the therapeutic alliance, do not pay attention to client-specific characteristics (including comorbidity), may prolong treatment as a result of their required adherence to a linear, invariant protocol, and may limit therapists' ability to use their clinical judgment during treatment sessions (Kendall & Beidas, 2007).

Although intervention developers often insist on complete adherence to protocols, innovations inevitably emerge (Berwick, 2003), including adjustments to program materials to address participants' educational-developmental and motivational levels (Lochman & Pardini, 2008). Innovative interventions often need to be adapted to the realities of intervening with children in applied settings (Stirman, Crits-Christoph, & DeRubeis, 2004). When exporting interventions from research labs to clinical practice settings, refinements should be made to fit clinic conditions (Weisz, Donenberg, Han, & Kauneckis, 1995), and strategies should be made appropriate for the target audiences. The creative, flexible use of manuals can permit individualization of the intervention, increase its likely transportability to new settings, and reduce clinicians' resistance to new programs (Kendall, Chu, Gifford, Hayes, & Nauta, 1998). As long as rigid adherence to manuals is avoided, then clinicians may not regard a manual as a "required cookie cutter approach" (Kendall, 2002, p. 215). In other words, a manual derived from intervention research need not be regarded as something to be followed word for word in applied practice, but could instead provide a *guide* to the core skills and concepts to be covered. As Kendall and Beidas (2007) have proposed, evidence-based, manualized treatments can be designed to promote "flexibility within fidelity," allowing practitioners to use their clinical judgment to individualize an EBP for a given client, while retaining the critical features of the program.

Beyond the "garden variety" adaptations of a manualized program that clinicians make when they see different clients in clinical practice, there are times when deeper adaptations may need to be made to a program because it is going to be used in a different culture, with a clearly different clientele (e.g., in an older developmental period), or in a quite different clinical or practice setting (e.g. in a daily after-school or inpatient setting, instead of in an outpatient clinic or weekly school group). For example, one randomized control trial assessed the use and dissemination of the Coping Power program in a sample of 49 deaf children screened for high levels of aggressive behavior living in a residential school (Lochman et al., 2001). The child component of the program was adapted to meet the needs of deaf children and the parent component, although not used in the study, helped with informed training of teachers and residential staff. Based on teacher ratings, children receiving the Coping Power program demonstrated significant improvements in behavior, social-problem-solving skills, and communication skills compared to children in the control condition (Lochman et al., 2001).

In these cases, a systematic approach to adaptation is needed so that core features of the program are retained. Goldstein, Kemp, Leff, and Lochman (2013) outline a step-wise approach to adapting manualized interventions for new target populations. The nine steps include conducting a focus group with the new population to get feedback about the content and structure of the program, making initial revisions to the manual, piloting these and getting experts and staff to review a revised manual, before conducting a pilot trial and then a full randomized control trial of the adapted program.

Despite the likelihood of programs being adapted over time, and the possibility that rigid, inflexible use of manuals may lead to less effective outcomes when interventions are disseminated to applied settings, little research has examined the effects of program adaptations. Two studies, both addressing internalizing conditions, have directly addressed this issue with child interventions. Harnett and Dadds (2004) found facilitators' degree of deviation from session activities was not found to be significantly associated with program outcomes, in either a positive or negative direction. Kendall and Chu (2000) asked therapists who had used a structured evidence-based cognitive-behavioral intervention manual with 148 children (aged 9–13) who had primary anxiety disorders what kinds of adaptations they had made to their interventions. The study found that the therapists' ratings of flexible adaptation of intervention activities were not related to intervention outcome. It appeared that the combination of requiring strict adherence to session goals while permitting careful flexibility in adapting the specific activities meant to achieve those session goals could lead to successful implementation of programs in "real-world" settings.

Our own dissemination efforts with the Coping Power program have indicated that clinicians appreciate the opportunity to adapt the program content to suit case-specific needs (Boxmeyer, Lochman, Powell, Windle, & Wells, 2008; Lochman, Powell, Boxmeyer, & Baden, 2010). For example, clinicians might supplement session content with favorite activities from their clinical repertoire (e.g., adding a "feelings bingo" game to the component on emotional awareness), or adapt activities to better match client characteristics (e.g., conducting role-plays rather than discussions with children demonstrating ADHD symptoms). To make Coping Power relevant for younger or developmentally delayed children, activities may have to be more concrete, highly engaging, briefly presented, and make frequent use of stimulating books, puppets, and arts-and-crafts activities. It is important to note that flexible adaptations such as these do not extend to omissions of program content or radical departures from the protocol, which would be considered a lack of adherence and be expected to detract from the effectiveness of an EBP.

Adaptations to Address Cultural Context and Developmental Differences

Cultural Adaptations It is also important for interventions to be able to handle children from diverse ethnic, cultural, and community backgrounds. Children's cultural environment and experiences often help shape their ethnic identity, ethnically related religiosity, and social schema (Holmes & Lochman, 2012), which may directly influence their aggressive behavior. Cognitive-behavioral interventions may be limited by cultural constraints and thus need to address this issue carefully.

An international dissemination study examined the use of the Coping Power program among Dutch children with disruptive behavior disorders. Dr. Walter Matthys and his colleagues developed a Dutch version of the program and assessed its effects in a study of 77 children in a child psychiatric outpatient unit (Van De Wiel et al., 2007). Children were randomly assigned to receive the Coping Power program or case-as-usual. Children in both conditions demonstrated significant improvements in disruptiveness post-treatment; however, children who received the Coping Power program displayed greater reductions in overt aggression. This version of the program was also found to be highly cost-effective (van de Wiel, Matthys, Cohen-Kettenis, & van Engeland, 2003). After four years, a study on this sample found that children who received the Coping Power program displayed significantly lower marijuana and tobacco use compared to children in the control condition, demonstrating the preventative and long-lasting effects of the intervention (Zonnevylle-Bender, Matthys, van de Wiel, & Lochman, 2007). This Dutch adaptation of Coping Power has been further adapted for use with children with lower levels of cognitive abilities (Schuiringa, van Nieuwenhuijzen, Orobio de Castro, Lochman, & Matthys, 2017).

Coping Power has been adapted for use in other countries and territories as well. In addition to the clinic sample in the Netherlands described above, variants of Coping Power have been tested in Canada (Andrade, Browne, & Naber, 2015), Italy (Muratori, Milone, Manfredi et al., 2015; Muratori, Milone, Nocentini et al., 2015), Pakistan (Mushtaq, Lochman, Tariq, & Sabih, 2016) and Puerto Rico (Cabiya et al., 2008), with significant reductions in aggression and conduct problems for children in the intervention condition relative to those in the control conditions. These adaptations have ranged from straightforward translations of the program into a new language, to deeper level adaptations that have required changes to how material is presented. For example, in the adaptation of the program for use in Pakistan, the manual was translated into the relevant language (Urdu), and the cognitive and emotional skills were presented within the context of Islamic stories and practices (Mushtaq et al., 2016).

Developmental Adaptations Programs are typically developed and tested with children in specific age ranges, and questions often arise about whether the program can be used effectively by children who are younger or older than the original samples. Like other adaptations, these developmental adjustments should be rigorously evaluated. For example, while Coping Power has primarily been utilized with preadolescents (children aged approximately 8–12), it has recently been adapted for use with both younger and older populations. From a preventional standpoint, teaching children social and emotional skills as early as possible is important. Thus, one study is testing an integrated classroom and family intervention with preschoolers, in which the Coping Power parent program provides the basis for the parent/family intervention (Boxmeyer et al., 2015). In this study, Head Start teachers are being trained to implement the Preschool PATHS social emotional curriculum in the classroom, while students' parents are invited to take part in a corollary parent program, which integrates content from both the Coping Power parent program and the preschool PATHS curriculum. Preliminary data from the first cohort (n=219) indicate that this combined program has benefits for child executive function and classroom behavior, as well as parent and family functioning (Boxmeyer et al., 2015).

There has been a relative lack of prevention programs targeting the early- to mid-adolescence period, especially programs that include both youth and parent components. As a result, we developed and piloted a version of Coping Power with colleagues in Baltimore that extends the program through the middle school years (Coping Power–Early Adolescent version, CP-EA). This version includes increased focus on adolescent issues such as assertive communication, cyber bullying and social media use, and how to repair damaged relationships. It also uses delivery methods more appropriate for adolescents, such as journaling and greater use of video and media content. With funding from the Institute of Education Sciences, CP-EA is currently being tested in an efficacy study in 40 middle schools in Alabama and Maryland; preliminary analyses for the Alabama subsample for the first of three cohorts has indicated that CP-EA can produce reductions in children's teacher-rated aggression and conduct problems by a follow-up one year after the program ended, in comparison to the control condition (Lochman, Bradshaw, Powell, Debnam, Pas, & Ialongo, 2016). Additional grant funding will also support the development and testing of a high school version of Coping Power in Baltimore.

Adaptations to Address Program Structure to Optimize Effects

There are obstacles that complicate the expansive dissemination of evidence-based programs, and which have led to the adaptation of program content and structure in order to optimize intervention effects.

Adaptations: Booster Sessions One such adaptation is the inclusion of booster sessions. An interest in booster sessions is not surprising given that research has shown the positive treatment effects for children with disruptive behavior problems tend to weaken over time (McMahon & Wells, 1998). These sessions may serve to reinforce behavioral gains, as this may not occur naturally within the peer, family, and/or neighborhood context that potentially contributed to or maintained the child's presenting problems. Booster sessions are typically held after the formal intervention is over as a refresher of the main program content, and are provided at varying intervals, often several weeks or months apart. Theoretically, they are meant to enhance retention and memory of intervention concepts and positive reinforce newly developed skills (Lochman et al., 2014). Indeed, there is evidence to suggest that the use of booster sessions promotes the maintenance of intervention effects. For example, Lochman (1992) found that earlier intervention-produced reductions in children's disruptive off-task behavior in school settings was maintained at a 3-year follow-up only for aggressive children who had received a booster intervention.

Despite encouraging findings for the usefulness of booster sessions, research is limited and findings are mixed with regards to clinical utility. Tolan, Gorman-Smith, Henry, and Schoeny (2009) found that a lengthy family-oriented booster of over 20 sessions following a family-based preventative intervention produced further effects on some behavioral outcomes for high-risk children, although not on their aggressive behavior. Additionally, no further treatment effects were observed following a six-session booster to a classroom social problem solving program designed to reduce aggression (Daunic, Smith, Brank, & Penfield, 2009). Similarly, a recent study of a long-term 3-year follow-up of an abbreviated 24-session version of Coping Power did not find a booster intervention to be useful, as it did not augment intervention effects (Lochman et al., 2014). The absence of bolstering effects may have been due to a lack of need for a booster following a lengthy intervention, to the brief and unscripted nature of booster sessions, or possibly to the exclusion of a booster intervention for parents.

Interestingly, there is evidence to suggest that booster interventions aimed at decreasing aggressive behavior in children may be more effective if the booster includes contact with the parents (Lochman, 1992; Tolan et al., 2009). Notably, while it logically follows that booster sessions would assist in enhancing and maintaining intervention effects, further research is needed to determine effective use of booster sessions within clinical practice.

Adaptations: Technology and Internet Use A growing trend in adaptations to evidence-based programs is the integration of technology to increase child and parent engagement (e.g., Lochman, Boxmeyer et al., 2017; Jones et al., 2014). The inclusion of multimodal methods of delivering session content (i.e., verbally presented, use of media) can enhance motivation for learning and lead to improved recall along with a deeper conceptual understanding of the material. Furthermore, and importantly for developmental considerations, children and adolescents report that their preferred method of learning involves interactive multimedia (Lieberman, 2001). In addition to the enhanced learning benefits of, and young people's preference for, multimedia delivery of intervention content, technological advancements can also serve to cost-effectively facilitate greater connection of evidence-based services to low-income families within "real-world" settings (Aguilera & Muench, 2012).

Over the past decade, there has been significant progress in computer technology that lends itself to the advancement of prevention interventions. One technology-based program developed to prevent youth violence, SMART talk (Students Managing Anger and Resolution Together) aims to teach middle school students anger management and conflict resolution skills through computer-based activities. While no significant differences emerged on the frequency of aggressive behavior in a randomized controlled study of SMART talk, there were significant differences observed on mediating factors associated with violence. Specifically, students in the intervention condition were less likely to value violence as a solution to conflict, more likely to report intentions to use nonviolent strategies, and reported more self-awareness about their response to anger in conflict situations than students in the control group (Bosworth et al., 2000).

Along with the development of innovative technologically based interventions, researchers have worked to include technological features in existing evidence-based programs. Lochman and colleagues developed a hybrid version of Coping Power that included a much briefer version of the program carefully integrated with Internet-based website activities for children and parents to learn many of the program's concepts (Lochman, Boxmeyer et al., 2017). The children's website included a brief, animated, and humorous cartoon series, The Adventures of Captain Judgment, which had been developed specifically to illustrate Coping Power concepts and skills. The Coping Power-Internet Enhanced (CP-IE) program introduced a set of cognitive-behavioral skills in 12 small group sessions for children delivered within the school setting and seven group sessions for parents. An outcome study suggests that control children had significantly greater increases in conduct problem behaviors across the fifth-grade year than did CP-IE children. Of particular note, the website materials appeared to successfully engage children, and parents' use of the website predicted 'changes in children's conduct problems across the year. Use of technology can also enhance the cost-effectiveness of interventions. Use of the hybrid version of Coping Power, which included an Internet component, and the resultant 60% reduction in the frequency of face-to-face meetings between the counselor and child reduced the cost of intervention per child from $974 to $432 (a cost saving of 44%) while still producing significant intervention effects on the child's conduct problems (Lochman, Boxmeyer et al., 2017).

Further evidence of engaging parents and caregivers through technological advances is Jones and colleagues' development of a technology-enhanced version of an evidence-based behavioral parent training program, Helping the Noncompliant Child (HNC). In a pilot study, low-income families of 3- to 8-year-old children with clinically significant disruptive behaviors were randomized to, and completed, standard HNC or Technology-Enhanced HNC (TE-HNC). The TE-HNC included smartphone enhancements such as skills video series, brief daily surveys, text message reminders, video recording home practice, and midweek video calls. The TE-HNC yielded larger effect sizes than HNC for all engagement outcomes. Clinically significant improvements in disruptive behavior emerged for both groups. However, findings suggest that the greater program engagement associated with TE-HNC boosted child treatment outcome. An interesting effect associated with the smartphone enhancements was the possibility of increasing co-parent practice of the skills by providing caregivers with a mechanism (e.g., skills videos) and support (e.g., text reminders) enabling the co-parent, who might not be able to attend traditional in-office sessions, to become involved (Jones et al., 2014). It is worth noting that previous research has indicated that consistency in skill utilization between caregivers leads to greater improvements in child behavior (McMahon & Forehand, 2003).

Adaptations: Treatment Length and Delivery Format Interventions often need to be modified to meet the realities of treating children and families in applied settings (Stirman et al., 2004). One area of difficulty may be delivering lengthy evidence-based programs efficiently yet effectively. Two randomized controlled trials have examined outcomes of an abbreviated version of the Coping Power program that can be implemented in one school year (24 child sessions and 10 parent sessions). The abbreviated version has been shown to produce significant reductions in teacher-rated externalizing behavior for children who had a caregiver attend at least one parent session in comparison to children in the control condition (Lochman, Boxmeyer, Powell, Roth, & Windle, 2006). Moreover, 3 years after the end of intervention, Coping Power, in comparison to the control condition, had more generalized long-term effects on reducing children's externalizing behavior problems regardless of degree of parental attendance and also showed reductions in impulsivity and callous-unemotional traits (Lochman et al., 2014). An independent investigative team found that the 24-session Coping Power child component alone produced significant teacher-rated behavioral improvements in learning, study skills, and school problems, as well as in behavioral symptoms and social withdrawal when compared to the control condition (Peterson, Hamilton, & Russell, 2009).

Another area that may pose a challenge is the delivery format. There is often concern about iatrogenic effects when adapting an intervention that targets disruptive behavior for a group delivery format. Weiss et al. (2005), based on up-to-date treatment meta-analysis datasets, found that there was no overall difference in effect size for group versus individual treatment. However, groups tended to have worse effects as children approached adolescence, consistent with previously documented concerns. As a result of Coping Power typically being delivered in small groups, a large-scale study was conducted to investigate how children fared if they received Coping Power in a group versus individual format (Lochman, Dishion et al., 2015). Results indicated both intervention delivery methods led to similar significant reductions in parent-rated externalizing problems through a 1-year follow-up period. However, although teacher-rated externalizing problems also declined significantly for both intervention conditions, the reductions were significantly greater for children receiving Coping Power in an individual format. The main effect was moderated by children's baseline levels of inhibitory control. Children with fewer problems with inhibitory control responded in similarly positive ways to either the group or individual format. These results are encouraging in terms of effectively adapting an EBP to the specific needs of an applied setting, whether that involves working with children individually or in small groups.

Factors at the Client Level

In addition to factors at the intervention level, there are many factors at the individual level, related to the child, parent, family, or environment, that may contribute significantly to the successful delivery and implementation of evidence-based interventions.

Parent Characteristics

Many evidence-based practices for children with disruptive behavior disorders, including the Coping Power program, have a substantial focus on parental involvement. Unfortunately, research has shown that many parents will not participate in interventions, despite efforts to increase attendance (see Chapter 24 of this book). Recent research has used person-oriented analyses to examine issues related to intervention processes and how child and parent factors influence outcomes from the Coping Power program. For example, parents with lower levels of social support and who experience more stressful events show lower attendance and engagement in the Coping Power parent component (Minney, Lochman, & Guadagno, 2015). On the other hand, parents who exercise more positive parenting and less inconsistent discipline also exhibit lower attendance and engagement in the Coping Power parent component (Andradeet al., 2015). While some parents may have chaotic and stressful lives that prohibit them from having the time or resources to engage in the intervention, other parents may feel that they would benefit little from the intervention and therefore choose not to attend. In both situations, issues of parental attendance and engagement may significantly impact outcomes from the Coping Power program as a whole.

Research has shown that children's engagement in their own component of the intervention may predict parental engagement (Ellis, Lindsey, Barker, Boxmeyer, & Lochman, 2013). Cross-lag analyses have demonstrated that children who engage more in the child component during the earlier sessions have parents whose attendance significantly increases during the middle sessions. Adaptations of interventions may take this into account when implementing strategies to improve parent attendance and engagement.

Several adaptations have been made to the delivery of the Coping Power program that specifically focus on increasing parent attendance. A pilot effort in Baltimore City, for example, modified the program and incorporated it in the Family Check-Up, an approach to encourage parental involvement through motivational interviewing principles (Herman et al., 2012). Changes were made to allow parents to choose relevant components to work on (rather than complete all 16 sessions) and to revise the content to be delivered in an individual, rather than group, format. On the basis of a developed procedure manual (Herman & Reinke, 2011), the clinician works with the family after the second session to develop a plan, identify applicable components to be covered, and establish parental commitment to the chosen plan. Preliminary findings from this study suggest that the integrated Family Check-Up–Coping Power model was acceptable and feasible for urban families of children with disruptive behavior disorders (Herman et al., 2012). In addition to the level of parent engagement and attendance, other parental characteristics have also been shown to affect intervention outcomes for children involved in the program. More specifically, parents with lower baseline levels of depression and who improved in the consistency of their discipline throughout the intervention had children with greater reductions in aggressive behavior (Muratori, Milone, Nocentini et al., 2015).

Child Characteristics

In addition to parental factors that influence treatment outcomes, there are also several child-specific characteristics and factors that may affect a child's experience, engagement, and progress within the intervention. For example, children with higher levels of baseline depression have been found to have greater reductions in parent- and teacher-reported externalizing behaviors at post-intervention assessment (Jarrett, Siddiqui, Lochman, & Qu, 2014).

Another child-specific characteristic that may affect intervention outcomes is comorbid diagnoses. In some cases, manualized CBT treatments may ignore the complexities and distinguishing characteristics of individual clients (Herschell, McNeil, & McNeil, 2004). In these cases, the manual may neglect to appropriately address cases where comorbid disorders are present or cases where the targeted disorder is particularly severe (Weisz et al., 1995). In order to successfully treat a wide range of children diagnosed with disorders such as ODD and CD, future interventions should work to focus on integrating and combining treatments for youth with comorbid diagnoses and symptoms.

Transdiagnostic interventions, for example, work to address multiple disorders through the use of the same underlying treatment principles. While the Coping Power program may be considered a disorder-specific intervention given its focus on children with aggressive behavior issues, it may contain certain transdiagnostic elements that impact other presenting symptoms along with externalizing behaviors. In fact, research has shown that the program produces reductions in both externalizing *and* internalizing behaviors (Lochman, Dishion et al., 2015). There are several key reasons why it may produce these effects: (a) some other outcomes follow the development of aggressive behaviors and therefore changes in aggression may influence them, (b) there are some common active mechanisms within the program (e.g. social problem solving) that may affect multiple areas, and (c) aggressive children often have comorbid issues that may be addressed through adaptation of the program.

Community Characteristics

The child's community context (dangerous, threatening neighborhoods) may limit an intervention's ability to produce effective outcomes. However, despite higher concentrations of poverty and deviant peer groups, research has shown that children from disadvantaged neighborhoods can actually show the greatest reductions in aggression (Lochman, Wells, Qu, & Chen, 2013). Therefore, it is important to examine whether neighborhood factors (e.g. crime and poverty), moderate children's responses to intervention, as these factors may facilitate or hinder the improvement of children's behavior.

Factors at the Level of the Clinician and the Practice Setting

Finally, in addition to intervention- and client-level factors, effective dissemination of a program can be influenced by characteristics of the clinician and practice setting. Key factors relating to the clinicians include 'their perceived barriers to implementation, levels of confidence, self-efficacy, prior experience, and familiarity with the intervention and its theoretical model (Turner & Sanders, 2006).

The practitioner's attitude toward the program itself is a major factor, particularly if the program is new to him or her. Clinicians who are concerned about the appropriateness or flexibility of a new program or cynical about organizational change may be more resistant to a particular intervention. Consequently, identifying the benefits of program adoption and helping clinicians to develop favorable attitudes toward the intervention are key in effective dissemination (Stirman et al., 2004). Fortunately, research has demonstrated the substantial positive influence of "change agents," who are able to address therapist concerns early in training and provide education regarding the effectiveness of the particular intervention. This leads to altered attitudes and beliefs as far as the program is concerned, which, in turn, increase openness to adoption and implementation (Stirman et al., 2004).

Furthermore, level of intensity and type of training can impact effective implementation of a program, and therefore clinical outcomes, leading to reduced effect sizes in program evaluations. For example, one study found that workshops were not sufficient as a sole training mechanism to develop clinician competency (Sholomskas et al., 2005). However, improvements in competency and intervention adherence were noted when workshops were combined with other supports including ongoing supervision, expert consultation, and the provision of feedback on cases (e.g., Stirman et al., 2004). Certain interventions may require higher levels of training in order to establish fidelity. For example, Henggeler, Melton, Brondino, Scherer, and Hanley (1997) investigated the impact of training on the dissemination of Multisystemic Therapy (MST). The authors argued that MST training should be intense (5-day initial training), ongoing (weekly supervision by MST trained supervisors), and carefully specified. These requirements generated high levels of adherence and intervention integrity to MST.

Following training and adoption of a program, clinicians must demonstrate familiarity with the intervention and its theoretical model and have sufficient levels of confidence, self-efficacy, and prior experience to implement it effectively. A combination of these skills assists the clinician in remaining adherent to the intervention, while allowing for flexibility in treatment delivery to the identified individual or group. Another important skill concerns the practitioner's ability to identify unique social problems or negative group process issues. Clinicians who are able to do so can apply the overall objectives of the program flexibly to the individual situation, potentially using modeling or practice to demonstrate intervention goals. Aggressive children seen by clinicians who displayed higher levels of clinical skills (notably more warmth and less anger and irritability) in 936 group intervention sessions had progressively greater reductions in conduct problems through a one-year follow-up than did children seen by clinicians with less evident clinical skills (Lochman, Dishion, Boxmeyer, Powell, & Qu, 2017). These results indicate the need and importance of intensive training on the intervention process for therapists who work with aggressive children, especially in group therapy. These clinical skills, and the clinicians' close attention and constructive response to children's in-session negative behaviors, can enhance children's therapeutic relationship with the clinician. The therapeutic alliance has historically been heralded as a necessary condition for progress in therapy. In terms of treatment outcomes, a meta-analysis (Shirk, Karver, & Brown, 2011) indicated that the therapeutic alliance had small but significant effects on externalizing and internalizing problems, particularly when assessed toward the end of treatment. In sum, clinician-level factors play a role in effective dissemination of a program, which also has an impact on clinical outcomes.

In addition to clinician characteristics, aspects of the practice setting can strongly influence treatment dissemination. Once effectiveness has been established in one setting, it is relevant to consider alternative practice settings for intervention implementation. For example, the Anger Coping program and Coping Power were originally developed for school-based implementation, which has a number of advantages specific to the school setting, including context-specific intervention, opportunities for teacher and school staff collaboration, and high attendance rates. Subsequent research identified that these interventions were transportable to the outpatient setting (van de Wiel et al., 2003), which offers other benefits including the inclusion of parents, extension of session length, and incorporation of the intervention into a more comprehensive treatment plan (e.g., medication, other psychosocial treatments). Similarly, Coping Power has been successfully disseminated to after-school programs, juvenile correctional settings for girls (Goldstein, Kemp, Leff, & Lochman, 2013), and residential settings. Treatment adaptations, training and supervision issues, treatment fidelity, and implementation barriers often needed to be addressed to maximize portability to residential settings (James, Alemi, & Zepeda, 2013).

Regardless of the type of practice setting, certain organizational characteristics can influence effective dissemination of an intervention. Of course, new programs require organizational support to be adequately implemented. One study of the dissemination of a multi-site school-based intervention found that successful sites had a greater organizational structure for delivering school services, a social network of clinicians delivering the same intervention, and administrative support (Langley, Nadeem, Kataoka, Stein, & Jaycox, 2010). Although interventions are disseminated *faster* when the decision is made hierarchically (i.e., administrators exclusively decide and inform clinicians), they are less likely to be sustained than where there is a more collaborative process between administrators and clinicians (Henggeler, Lee, & Burns, 2002). High turnover of clinician and administrators in the practice setting also influences ongoing sustainability of a program.

With regard to school settings, several specific factors have been found to affect dissemination, including school size, the ethnic composition of schools, the socioeconomic level of the student body, and school-wide aggression levels among students (Barth, Dunlap, Dane, Lochman, & Wells, 2004). While these factors are not likely to be ameliorated through intervention, awareness of their relevance may assist in planning implementation efforts and clinician support. Overall, aspects of the practice setting are important to consider when disseminating a program to the "real world."

Example of Training, Clinician, and Organizational Characteristics in Dissemination A field trial study funded by the National Institute on Drug Abuse (NIDA) was conducted to examine whether Coping Power could be effectively disseminated to school systems and implemented by school staff (Lochman, Powell, et al., 2009). The program was implemented with 531 students in 57 schools within five school districts in Tuscaloosa, AL and Birmingham, AL by in-house school counselors in the fourth and fifth grade years. School counselors were randomly assigned to one of three conditions: Coping Power – Intensive Training for Counselors (CP-IT), Coping Power – Basic Training for Counselors (CP-BT), or Care-as-Usual Comparison. Counselors in the CP-IT and CP-BT conditions attended a three-day initial workshop and participated in monthly ongoing training sessions. Additionally, in the CP-IT condition only, research staff provided feedback to counselors about the quality of implementation and completion of session objectives to counselors through coding of session audiotapes.

The level of intensity of training had a large impact on dissemination outcomes. Students who received the intervention from CP-IT counselors had significantly lower levels of externalizing behavior compared to control students and to children receiving intervention from basic-trained counselors, as measured by parent, teacher, and student ratings (Lochman, Boxmeyer et al., 2009). Furthermore, these children also had better-rated social and academic skills at school, improved social cognitive abilities, and more stable grades over time (Lochman et al., 2012).

Counselor's personality characteristics influenced program implementation as well. Counselors who were conscientious and agreeable demonstrated the highest quality program implementation as indicated by number of sessions scheduled and quality of engagement with children and parents (Lochman, Powell, et al., 2009). However, counselors who were cynical about organizational change and who were in schools that had rigid managerial control and offered little autonomy to school professional staff were less likely to implement the program with high quality. In the two years following the field study, the researchers collected information about sustained use of Coping Power (Lochman et al., 2015). The likelihood of ongoing use of the program was predicted by several factors, including perceptions of program effectiveness, actual client behavior change at the end of the program, expectations about future use, perceptions of interpersonal support from teachers, and clinician conscientiousness. Therefore, both clinician-level and school climate factors played a role in the sustained implementation of Coping Power. Taken together, this example demonstrates the importance of multiple influences on effective dissemination, including clinician characteristics, intensity of training, organizational support, and characteristics of the specific practice setting.

Conclusions and Cost-effectiveness of Programs and Their Adaptations

It is apparent that careful attention to the implementation and dissemination of evidence-based interventions for children with disruptive behavior disorders in real-world settings is critically important. Implementation research needs to explore in detail how intensity of training and characteristics of clinicians and work settings can affect the quality of implementation, quality of outcomes, and degree of dissemination in community mental health settings. Even under optimal conditions, most of our evidence-based interventions do not provide strong results for all children. Thus, we need to approach potential adaptations to a program in a thoughtful, planned way, with a focus on empirical investigation of these adaptations. It is useful to approach intervention refinement in the same way that an engineer would in an effort to optimize and strengthen outcomes. Effective interventions in 10–20 years' time should not take exactly the same form that they do now, but should show evidence of rigorous evolution. And our focus ought necessarily to fall increasingly on the cost-effectiveness of interventions, especially with the children and adolescents who have the most severe disruptive behaviors.

There is a relatively small group of children who do not age out of their serious antisocial and criminal behavior, but continue their involvement in serious and persistent antisocial behavior well beyond adolescence. These youth create an enormous cost to society because of their chronic antisocial behavior and its consequences. Cohen (2005) has estimated the life-course cost of each career criminal to be over two million dollars. Thus, these especially problematic young children are those ultimately most likely to cause the great harm to and create the largest costs for society (Sherman, 2007).

The intransigence of this behavioral pattern, when left untreated, underscores the clear importance of creating increasingly effective interventions with these children and their families. And we have seen in this book, there are interventions that have been demonstrated to have significant effects on the behaviors of some of these children post-treatment and at longer term follow-up assessments. Research can explore the cost-effectiveness of these interventions and of optimized versions of the programs.

Are the amounts of funds required for the type of intensive, comprehensive, and multicomponent interventions needed to have an effect on early-onset behavioral problems really worth it? Research needs to be conducted with the variety of interventions described in the prior chapters, but initial results are encouraging. Even expensive interventions may be cost-effective, but the intervention must target a population that is particularly costly to society when left untreated, such as children with early-starting conduct disorder. For example, analyses of the costs of the multi-year Fast Track intervention and its effects on conduct disorder diagnoses indicate that the intervention is cost-effective for the highest risk children (Foster, Jones, & Conduct Problems Prevention Research Group, 2006). Experimentally investigated adaptations of interventions, using technology to optimize outcomes, may produce even more cost-effective outcomes for a range of evidence-based programs. A condition such as CD (and the subsequent violent behavior that often results from it) creates enormous public costs, and can be a cost-effective focus for these evidence-based interventions and their adaptations.

References

Addis, M. E., Wade, W. A., & Hatgis, C. (1999). Barriers to dissemination of evidence-based practices: Addressing practitioners' concerns about manual-based psychotherapies. *Clinical Psychology: Science and Practice, 6,* 430–441.

Andrade, B. F., Browne, D. T., & Naber, A. R. (2015). Parenting skills and parent readiness for treatment are associated with child disruptive behavior and parent participation in treatment. *Behavior Therapy, 46*(3), 365–378. doi.org/10.1016/j.beth.2015.01.004

Aguilera, A., & Muench, F. (2012). There's an app for that: Information technology applications for cognitive behavioral practitioners. *The Behavior therapist/AABT, 35*(4), 65–73.

Barth, J. M., Dunlap, S. T., Dane, H., Lochman, J. E., & Wells, K. C. (2004). Classroom environment influences on aggression, peer relations, and academic focus. *Journal of School Psychology, 42*(2), 115–133.

Berwick, D. M. (2003). Disseminating innovations in health care. *Journal of the American Medical Association, 289,* 1969–1975.

Bickman, L. (2003). The death of treatment as usual: An excellent first step on a long road. *Clinical Psychology: Science and Practice, 9,* 195–199.

Bosworth, K., Espelage, D., DuBay, T., Daytner, G., & Karageorge, K. (2000). Preliminary evaluation of a multimedia violence prevention program for adolescents. *American Journal of Health Behavior, 24*(4), 268–280.

Boxmeyer, C. L., Lochman, J. E., Powell, N. R., Windle, M., & Wells, K. (2008). School counselors' implementation of Coping Power in a dissemination field trial: Delineating the range of flexibility within fidelity. *Report on Emotional and Behavioral Disorders in Youth, 8,* 79–95.

Boxmeyer, C., Gilpin, A., DeCaro, J., Lochman, J., Qu, L., Mitchell, Q., & Snead, S. (2015). Power PATH: Integrated two-generation social emotional intervention for Head Start preschoolers and their parents. Online paper collection of the *Association for Public Policy Analysis and Management's 37th Annual Fall Research Conference: The Golden Age of Evidence-Based Policy.* Retrieved from https://appam.confex.com/appam/2015/webprogram/Paper12784.html

Cabiya, J. J., Padilla-Cotto, L., González, K., Sanchez-Cestero, J., Martínez-Taboas, A., & Sayers, S. (2008). Effectiveness of a cognitive-behavioral intervention for Puerto Rican children. *Revista Interamericana de Psicología, 42*(2), 195–202.

Cohen, M.A. (2005). *The costs of crime and justice.* New York, NY: Routledge.

Daunic, A. P., Smith, S. W., Brank, E. M., & Penfield, R. D. (2009). Classroom-based cognitive-behavioral intervention to prevent aggression: Efficacy and social validity. *Journal of School Psychology, 44,* 123–139.

Ellis, M. L., Lindsey, M. A., Barker, E. D., Boxmeyer, C. L., & Lochman, J. E. (2013). Predictors of engagement in a school-based family preventive intervention for youth experiencing behavioral difficulties. *Prevention Science, 14*(5), 457–467. doi:10.1007/s11121-012-0319-9

Foster, E. M., Jones, D., & Conduct Problems Prevention Research Group (2006). Can a costly intervention be cost-effective? An analysis of violence prevention. *Archives of General Psychiatry, 63,* 1284–1291.

Glisson, C., & Schoenwald, S. K. (2005). The ARC organizational and community intervention strategy for implementing evidence-based children's mental health treatments. *Mental Health Services Research, 7*(4), 243–259. doi:10.1007/s11020-005-7456-1.

Goldstein, N. E. S., Kemp, K. A., Leff, S. S., & Lochman, J. E. (2012). Guidelines for adapting manualized treatments for new target populations: A step-wise approach using anger management as a model. *Clinical Psychology: Science and Practice, 19,* 385–401.

Harnett, P. H., & Dadds, M. R. (2004). Training school personnel to implement a universal school-based prevention of depression program under real-world conditions. *Journal of School Psychology, 42,* 343–357.

Henderson, J. L., MacKay, S., & Peterson-Badali, M. (2006). Closing the research–practice gap: Factors affecting adoption and implementation of a children's mental health program. *Journal of Clinical Child and Adolescent Psychology, 35,* 2–12.

Henggeler, S. W., Lee, T., & Burns, J. A. (2002). What happens after the innovation is identified?. *Clinical Psychology: Science and Practice, 9*(2), 191–194.

Henggeler, S. W., Melton, G. B., Brondino, M. J., Scherer, D. G., & Hanley, J. H. (1997). Multisystemic therapy with violent and chronic juvenile offenders and their families: The role of treatment fidelity in successful dissemination. *Journal of Consulting and Clinical Psychology, 65*(5), 821–833.

Herman, K. C., & Reinke, W. M. (2011). *School enhanced-FCU for Coping Power manual*. Baltimore, MD: Center for Prevention and Early Intervention.

Herman, K. C., Reinke, W. M., Bradshaw, C. P., Lochman, J. E., Boxmeyer, C. L., Powell, N. P., . . . Ialongo, N. S. (2012). Integrating the Family Check-up and the parent Coping Power program. *Advances in School Mental Health Promotion, 5*(3), 208–219. doi:10.1080/1754730X.2012.707437

Herschell, A. D., McNeil, C. B., & McNeil, D. W. (2004). Clinical child psychology's progress in disseminating empirically supported treatment. *Clinical Psychology: Science & Practice, 11*(3), 267–288.

Holmes, K. J., & Lochman, J. E. (2012). The role of religiosity in African American preadolescent aggression. *Journal of Black Psychology, 38*(4). doi: 10.1177/0095798412443161

James, S., Alemi, Q., & Zepeda, V. (2013). Effectiveness and implementation of evidence-based practices in residential care settings. *Children and Youth Services Review, 35*(4), 642–656.

Jarrett, M., Siddiqui, S., Lochman, J., & Qu, L. (2014). Internalizing problems as a predictor of change in externalizing problems in at-risk youth. *Journal of Clinical Child and Adolescent Psychology, 43*(1), 27–35. doi:10.1080/15374416.2013.764823

Jones, D. J., Forehand, R., Cuellar, J., Parent, J., Honeycutt, A., Khavjou, O., . . . Newey, G. A. (2014). Technology-enhanced program for child disruptive behavior disorders: Development and pilot randomized control trial. *Journal of Clinical Child and Adolescent Psychology, 43*(1), 88–101. doi:10.1080/15374416.2013.822308.

Kendall, P. (2002). Toward a research-practice-community partnership: Goin' fishing and showing slides. *Clinical Psychology: Science and Practice, 9*, 214–216.

Kendall, P. C., & Beidas, R. S. (2007). Smoothing the trail for dissemination of evidence-based practices for youth: Flexibility within fidelity. *Professional Psychology: Research and Practice, 38*, 13–20.

Kendall, P. C., & Chu, B. C. (2000). Retrospective self-reports of therapist flexibility in a manual-based treatment for youths with anxiety disorders. *Journal of Clinical Child Psychology, 29*, 209–220.

Kendall, P. C., Chu, B., Gifford, A., Hayes, C., & Nauta, M. (1998). Breathing life into a manual: Flexibility and creativity with manual-based treatments. *Cognitive and Behavioral Practice, 5*, 177–198.

La Greca, A. M., Silverman, W. K., & Lochman, J. E. (2009). Moving beyond efficacy and effectiveness: Factors influencing the outcome of evidence-based psychological interventions with children and adolescents. *Journal of Consulting and Clinical Psychology, 77*, 373–382.

Langley, A. K., Nadeem, E., Kataoka, S. H., Stein, B. D., & Jaycox, L. H. (2010). Evidence-based mental health programs in schools: Barriers and facilitators of successful implementation. *School Mental Health, 2*(3), 105–113.

Lieberman, D.A. (2001). Management of chronic pediatric diseases with interactive health games: Theory and research findings. *Journal of Ambulatory Care Management, 24*, 26–38.

Lochman, J. E. (1992). Cognitive-behavioral intervention with aggressive boys: Three-year follow-up and preventive effects. *Journal of Consulting and Clinical Psychology, 60*(3), 426–432. doi:10.1037/0022-006X.60.3.426.

Lochman, J. E., Baden, R. E., Boxmeyer, C. L., Powell, N. P., Qu, L., Salekin, K. L., & Windle, M. (2014). Does a booster intervention augment the preventive effects of an abbreviated version of the Coping Power program for aggressive children? *Journal of Abnormal Child Psychology, 42*(3), 367–381. doi:10.1007/s10802-013-9727-y

Lochman, J. E., Boxmeyer, C. L., Jones, S., Qu, L., Ewoldsen, D., & Nelson, W. M., III (2017). Testing the feasibility of a briefer school-based preventive intervention with aggressive children: A hybrid intervention with face-to-face and Internet components. *Journal of School Psychology.* doi:10.1016/j.jsp.2017.03.010

Lochman, J. E., Boxmeyer, C. L., Powell, N. P., Qu, L., Wells, K., & Windle, M. (2009). Dissemination of the Coping Power program: Importance of intensity of counselor training. *Journal of Consulting And Clinical Psychology, 77*(3), 397–409.

Lochman, J. E., Boxmeyer, C. L., Powell, N. P., Qu, L., Wells, K., & Windle, M. (2012). Coping Power dissemination study: Intervention and special education effects on academic outcomes. *Behavioral Disorders, 37*(3), 192–205.

Lochman, J. E., Boxmeyer, C. L., Powell, N. P., Roth, D., & Windle, M. (2006). Masked intervention effects: Analytic methods for addressing low dosage of intervention. *New Directions for Evaluation, 110,* 19–32.

Lochman, J. E., Bradshaw, C. P., Powell, N., Debnam, K., Pas, E., & Ialongo, N. (2016, June). Preventing conduct problems in middle schoolers: Preliminary effects of the Early Adolescent Coping Power program. Paper presented in a symposium (C. Bradshaw, chair) at the *24th Annual Meeting of the Society for Prevention Research*, San Francisco.

Lochman, J. E., Dishion, T. J., Boxmeyer, C. L., Powell, N. P., & Qu, L. (2017). Variations in response to evidence-based group preventive intervention for disruptive behavior problems: A view from 938 Coping Power sessions. *Journal of Abnormal Child Psychology.* doi:10.1007/s10802-016-0252-7

Lochman, J. E., Dishion, T. J., Powell, N. P., Boxmeyer, C. L., Qu, L., & Sallee, M. (2015). Evidence-based preventive intervention for preadolescent aggressive children: One-year outcomes following randomization to group versus individual delivery. *Journal of Consulting and Clinical Psychology, 83*(4), 728–735. doi:10.1037/ccp0000030

Lochman, J. E., FitzGerald, D. P., Gage, S. M., Kannaly, M. K., Whidby, J. M., Barry, T. D., . . . McElroy, H. (2001). Effects of social-cognitive intervention for aggressive deaf children: The Coping Power program. *Journal of the American Deafness and Rehabilitation Association, 35,* 39–61.

Lochman, J. E., & Pardini, D. A. (2008). Cognitive behavioral therapies. In M. Rutter, D. Bishop, D. Pine, S. Scott, J. Stevenson, E. Taylor, & A. Thapar (Eds.), *Rutter's child and adolescent psychiatry* (5th ed., pp. 1026–1045). London: Blackwell.

Lochman, J. E., Powell, N. R., Boxmeyer, C.L., & Baden, R. (2010). Dissemination of evidence-based programs in the schools: The Coping Power program. In B. Doll, W. Pfohl, & J. Yoon (Eds.), *Handbook of youth prevention science* (pp. 393–412). New York, NY: Routledge.

Lochman, J. E., Powell, N. P., Boxmeyer, C. L., Qu, L., Sallee, M., Wells, K. C., & Windle, M. (2015). Counselor-level predictors of sustained use of an indicated preventive intervention for aggressive children. *Prevention Science, 16,* 1075–1085.

Lochman, J. E., Powell, N. P., Boxmeyer, C. L., Qu, L., Wells, K. C., & Windle, M. (2009). Implementation of a school-based prevention program: Effects of counselor and school characteristics. *Professional Psychology: Research and Practice, 40*(5), 476–482.

Lochman, J., Wells, K., Qu, L., & Chen, L. (2013). Three year follow-up of Coping Power intervention effects: Evidence of neighborhood moderation? *Prevention Science, 14*(4), 364–376. doi:10.1007/s11121-012-0295-0

McMahon, R. J., & Forehand, R. L. (2003). *Helping the noncompliant child.* New York, NY: Guilford.

McMahon, R. J., & Wells, K. C. (1998). Conduct problems. In E. J. Mash, R. A. Barkley, E. J. Mash, R. A. Barkley (Eds.), *Treatment of childhood disorders* (2nd ed., pp. 111–207). New York, NY: Guilford.

Minney, J. A., Lochman, J. E., & Guadagno, R. E. (2015). SEARCHing for solutions: Applying a novel person-centered analysis to the problem of dropping out of preventive parent education. *Prevention Science,* (4), 621–632. doi:10.1007/s11121-014-0526-7

Moore, J. E., Bumbarger, B. K., & Cooper, B. R. (2013). Examining adaptations of evidence-based programs in natural contexts. *The Journal of Primary Prevention, 34*(3), 147–161. doi:10.1007/s10935-013-0303-6.

Muratori, P., Milone, A., Manfredi, A., Polidori, L., Ruglioni, L., Lambruschi, F., . . . Lochman, J. E. (in press). Evaluation of improvement in externalizing behaviors and callous-unemotional traits in children with disruptive behavior disorder: A 1-year follow up clinic-based study. *Administration and Policy in Mental Health and Mental Health Services.*

Muratori, P., Milone, A., Nocentini, A., Manfredi, A., Polidori, L., Ruglioni, L., . . . Lochman, J. (2015). Maternal depression and parenting practices predict treatment outcome in Italian children with disruptive behavior disorder. *Journal of Child & Family Studies, 24*(9), 2805–2816. http://doi.org/10.1007/s10826-014-0085-3

Mushtaq, A., Lochman, J. E., Tariq, P. N., & Sabih, F. (2016). Preliminary effectiveness study of Coping Power program for aggressive children in Pakistan. *Prevention Science.* doi:10.1007/s11121-016-0721-9

Ng, M. Y., & Weisz, J. R. (2016). Annual research review: Building a science of personalized intervention for youth mental health. *Journal of Child Psychology and Psychiatry, 57*, 216–236.

Peterson, M. A., Hamilton, E. B., & Russell, A. D. (2009). Starting well: Evidenced-based treatment facilitates the middle school transition. *Journal of Applied School Psychology, 25*, 183–196.

Raudenbush, S. W., & Willms, J. D. (1991). The organization of schooling and its methodological implications. In S. W. Raudenbush & J. D. Willms (Eds.), *Schools, classrooms, and pupils: International studies of schooling from a multilevel perspective* (pp. 1–12). San Diego, CA: Academic Press.

Schuiringa, H., van Nieuwenhuijzen, M., Orobio de Castro, B., Lochman, J. E., & Matthys, W. (2017). Effectiveness of an intervention for children with externalizing behavior and mild to borderline intellectual disabilities: A randomized trial. *Cognitive Therapy and Research, 41*(2), 237–251. doi:10.1007/s10608-016-9815-8

Shirk, S. R., Karver, M. S., & Brown, R. (2011). The alliance in child and adolescent psychotherapy. *Psychotherapy, 48*(1), 17–24.

Sherman, L.W. (2007). The power few: Experimental criminology and the reduction of harm: The 2006 Joan McCord Prize Lecture. *Journal of Experimental Criminology, 3*, 299–321.

Sholomskas, D. E., Syracuse-Siewert, G., Rounsaville, B. J., Ball, S. A., Nuro, K. F., & Carroll, K. M. (2005). We don't train in vain: A dissemination trial of three strategies of training clinicians in cognitive-behavioral therapy. *Journal of Consulting and Clinical Psychology, 73*(1), 106–115.

Stirman, S. W., Crits-Christoph, P., & DeRubeis, R. J. (2004). Achieving successful dissemination of empirically supported psychotherapies: A synthesis of dissemination theory. *Clinical Psychology: Science and Practice, 11*(4), 343–359.

Tolan, P. H., Gorman-Smith, D., Henry, D., & Schoeny, M. (2009). The benefits of booster interventions: Evidence from a family-focused prevention program. *Prevention Science, 10*, 287–297.

Turner, K. T., & Sanders, M. R. (2006). Dissemination of evidence-based parenting and family support strategies: Learning from the Triple P Positive Parenting Program system approach. *Aggression and Violent Behavior, 11*(2), 176–193.

van de Wiel, N. M. H., Matthys, W., Cohen-Kettenis, P. T., Maassen, G. H., Lochman, J. E., & van Engeland, H. (2007). The effectiveness of an experimental treatment when compared with care as usual depends on the type of care as usual. *Behavior Modification, 31*, 298–312.

van de Wiel, N. M. H., Matthys, W., Cohen-Kettenis, P., & van Engeland, H. (2003). Application of the Utrecht Coping Power program and care as usual to children with disruptive behavior disorders in outpatient clinics: A comparative study of cost and course of treatment. *Behavior Therapy, 34*(4), 421–436.

Weiss, B., Caron, A., Ball, S., Tapp, J., Johnson, M., & Weisz, J. R. (2005). Iatrogenic effects of group treatment for antisocial youths. *Journal of Consulting and Clinical Psychology, 73*(6), 1036–1044.

Weisz, J. R., Chorpita, B. F., Palinkas, L. A., Schoenwald, S. K., Miranda, J., Bearman, S. K., . . . The Research Network on Youth Mental Health. (2012). Testing standard and modular designs for psychotherapy treating depression, anxiety, and conduct problems in youth: A randomized effectiveness trial. *Archives of General Psychiatry, 69*, 274–282.

Weisz, J. R., Donenberg, G. R., Han, S. S., & Kauneckis, D. (1995). Child and adolescent psychotherapy outcomes in experiments versus clinics: Why the disparity? *Journal of Abnormal Child Psychology, 23*(1), 83–106.

Zonnevylle-Bender, M. J. S., Matthys, W., van de Wiel, N. M. H., & Lochman, J. (2007). Preventive effects of treatment of DBD in middle childhood on substance use and delinquent behavior. *Journal of the American Academy of Child and Adolescent Psychiatry, 46*, 33–39.

Part 6
Concluding Comments

30

Future Directions

Walter Matthys and John E. Lochman

This chapter will address a set of conclusions and implications arising from the themes and literature cited in the chapters of this Handbook. The commentary will address whether to consider conceptualizing oppositional defiant disorder and conduct disorder as neurodevelopmental disorders, the role of assessment in diagnostic and treatment-planning processes, and a set of issues related to psychological intervention, including psychoeducation as intervention, the interpretation of effect sizes in intervention research, the emerging importance of personalizing interventions, the place of psychobiological functions as active mechanisms that can be the target of intervention, and how to broaden the scope of implementing and disseminating evidence-based interventions outside of clinic settings.

The Nature of Oppositional Defiant Disorder and Conduct Disorder

Oppositional Defiant Disorder (ODD) and Conduct Disorder (CD) may be conceptualized from two perspectives. In terms of their behavioral manifestations, these disorders are primarily characterized by behaviors that violate the rights of others and/or bring the individual into conflict with societal norms or authoritative figures (American Psychological Association [APA], 2013). On the other hand, in terms of prominent underlying factors, the expression of these disorders is very much bound up with emotional and behavioral regulation (APA, 2013). The chapters in this Handbook have richly illustrated the broad range of risk factors and potential mechanisms at both social and child level that contribute to the disruptive behavior disorders (DBDs). They suggest that there is no single underlying cause for all the DBDs that affect children. Children diagnosed with these disorders are likely, in fact, to be rather heterogeneous in their behavioral symptoms and in the risk factors they have experienced. The disordered behavior of some children seen clinically will likely have been influenced in important ways by social and environmental factors (ranging from family and peer influences to community-level effects), while the behavior of others will have been affected almost exclusively by child-level factors, and that of many more by the interaction of child and environmental factors. Extreme environmental disasters, for instance, can affect children's behaviors by interacting with child-level factors. Stressors related to a severe tornado have been found to have greater effects on aggressive children's subsequent externalizing behavior problems if those children had particularly low levels of anxiety and fear prior to the event and they were highly exposed to it (Lochman, Vernberg et al., 2017). Given the central problems with behavioral and emotional control displayed by children with DBD, and since attention deficit hyperactivity disorder (ADHD), another disorder which involves problems in behavioral control, has been conceptualized as a neurodevelopmental disorder in DSM-5 (APA, 2013), one may question why ODD and CD are not considered to be neurodevelopmental disorders as well.

Neurodevelopmental disorders typically develop before the child enters grade school, frequently co-occur and are characterized by developmental deficits (APA, 2013). This is also the case with ODD and CD. These disorders can be reliably diagnosed in preschool children and are often comorbid with ADHD (Matthys, Bunte, & Schoemaker, 2017). There is also convincing evidence for the occurrence of neurocognitive deficits in young children with ODD or CD and related conduct problems. More specifically, impairments in executive functions such as inhibitory control have been shown in these children (Schoemaker et al., 2012; Schoemaker, Mulder, Deković, & Matthys, 2013). Impaired inhibitory control has also been shown in preschool children with ADHD and in preschool children with both ADHD and ODD or CD (Schoemaker et al., 2012). In both young and older children "hot" executive functions seem to be more frequently linked to ODD/CD than ADHD (Chapter 10, this book; Schoemaker et al., 2012). According to a systematic review and meta-analysis of neuroimaging of ODD and CD taking into account ADHD, impairments of structure and function are present in most of the hypothesized hot executive-function-related structures, and to a lesser extent in cool executive-related structures (Noordermeer, Luman, & Oosterlaan, 2016). Importantly, these authors add that the reported hot executive-function brain areas are also involved in cool executive functions, and conclude that an integrated model of abnormalities in both hot and cool executive functions is more appropriate than a strict separation between these two.

Thus, careful consideration should be given to including ODD and CD alongside other neurodevelopmental disorders in future updates of the DSM and ICD diagnostic classifications. This recommendation is based on accumulating research that indicates that DBDs often co-occur with ADHD, and are characterized by developmental deficits, for instance, in inhibitory control, that produce impairments of social functioning.

One may wonder if this is really such an important point. We think it is. There is a tendency among clinicians to isolate conduct problems and the related disorders ODD and CD from other mental health problems and psychiatric/psychological conditions, and consider them as risks only for criminality or antisocial personality disorder. However, longitudinal studies have shown that adult disorders are often preceded by ODD and CD. For example, in the Dunedin study it was shown that ODD and CD were the only child disorders that precede *all* adult disorders, including depression and anxiety disorders (Kim-Cohen et al., 2003). Based on these results, Kim-Cohen and colleagues (2003, p. 715) stated that "Adult psychiatry has tended to ignore conduct disorder, assuming it leads only to adult antisocial personality disorder, a relatively rare disorder that is difficult to treat."

If ODD and CD precede all adult disorders they must be heterogeneous in nature. Over the years the heterogeneous nature of CD has been acknowledged in the various versions of the DSM by distinguishing subtypes, based on whether the children were "socialized" into antisocial behavior by others, on the age of onset, or on the presence of callous-unemotional traits (or lack of prosocial emotions). But, as noted by Lahey (2014), after all these years of research it is still not clear that subtyping CD on the basis of age of onset is valid and useful since, with the exception of one study, the subtyping has not been examined using prospective data. Likewise, according to Lahey (2014), the evidence on the validity of subtyping based on callous-unemotional traits is thin. In particular, more studies are needed to determine whether callous-unemotional traits are related to external criteria variables over and above measures of the severity of CD.

Further research on the heterogeneity of ODD is needed as well. It has become clear that the dimensions of irritability and oppositional behavior explain important differences in risk for internalizing versus externalizing disorders (see Chapter 2 of this book). But additional research can examine the relation between irritability (i.e., the so-called mood component of ODD) and later depression, and could further differentiate the mood component into dejection and low spirits on one hand and gruffness, surliness, and grumpiness on the other. In other words, attention could focus on *the quality of deviant mood itself* rather than only on its *behavioral expression* in the form of irritability and loss of temper. Gruffness, surliness, and grumpiness could be key characteristics of the deviant mood in ODD. The ongoing frustrating social experiences of children with ODD may result in an increase in their gruffness, surliness, and grumpiness and, in a subgroup, ultimately in the occurrence of dejection and low spirits. Further research on the quality of deviant mood itself (i.e., gruffness, surliness, and grumpiness) may clarify whether interventions should expand their focus on the mood component of ODD.

On the other hand, children with high levels of severe irritability and temper outbursts have been treated by medications appropriate for bipolar disorder. But these medications are probably not appropriate for these children. The developers of DSM-5 elected to address these concerns by creating a separate disorder for children with severe disruptive mood problems: disruptive mood dysregulation disorder. However, there is high overlap between this new diagnosis and other disorders (Copeland, Angold, Costello, & Egger, 2013). Therefore, an ICD-11 task group proposed to include a specifier indicating whether or not the presentation of ODD includes chronic irritability and anger (Evans et al., 2017; Lochman et al., 2015; Chapter 2, this book). Again, more research is needed into the associated or underlying quality of deviant mood typical for ODD.

The Need for Careful and In-Depth Assessment and Reassessment

In this context, continuing education is needed for clinicians in order to ensure that they do not isolate conduct problems and related disorders from the whole range of mental health problems, and thus stigmatize ODD and CD as "bad" behavior that must be morally condemned and for which there is no place in mental health care. This is crucial because the engagement of parents in treatment, for example in behavioral parent training, depends on how clinicians assess children, how clinicians discuss diagnoses with the parents, and how clinicians provide psychoeducation. Engaging families in behavioral parent training is a challenge, as many families identified as appropriate for behavioral parent training either do not start treatment or drop out before completing it (Chacko et al., 2016). But engaging parents in interventions does not start when parents have their first meeting with the psychotherapist after the clinical evaluation of their child, but must start in the course of the clinical evaluation (see next section).

In the training and ongoing education of psychiatrists and clinical psychologists attention should be paid to the clinical skills needed for the assessment of ODD and CD. These disorders are part of the whole range of mental health problems. Rather than using quick-and-dirty diagnostic practices, careful assessment is needed for children and adolescents referred because of conduct problems. Attention should be paid not only to both disruptive disorders and comorbidity, but to etiology as well.

To ensure categorical diagnostic accuracy in ODD, CD, and comorbid disorders, clinicians must carefully check each criterion separately with the parents by asking for specific examples and by probing for the frequency of behaviors (Chapter 23, this book). But parent reports may be biased due to a number of factors, such as depression (Collishaw, Goodman, Ford, Rabe-Hesketh, & Pickels, 2009). Therefore, direct observation that is not filtered through the perceptions of the parent may provide a different window on the child's functioning (Le Couteur & Gardner, 2008). In addition, clinical experience suggests that many parents desire the clinician to observe the child in order to arrive at a diagnosis, because parents who consult a clinician have difficulty accepting that the decision about the presence or absence of a disorder should be based only on parent and teacher reports; parents want clinicians themselves to "look at their child" (Bunte et al., 2013). Thus, careful assessment must include multiple reporters (parents, teacher, child/adolescent) and multiple methods (rating scales, clinical interview and observation of the child/adolescent, DSM/ICD-orientated interview).

With regard to etiology, in addition to a categorical diagnosis a diagnostic formulation or case formulation is needed that includes a hypothesis regarding the risk and protective factors that play a role in the development of the disorder (Chapter 23, this book). Particular attention should be paid to the factors that play a role in the maintenance of the disorder(s) for these will be the targets of interventions. While discussing potential risk factors with the parents, including the role of inadequate parenting behaviors, clinicians should be aware of parents' possible biases and misperceptions and correct these by giving appropriate information. For example, conduct problems and related disruptive disorders are still commonly thought by some people to be the result only of bad parenting. The active role of the child in the onset of ODD and CD is often ignored. Providing appropriate information on the disorders (i.e., psychoeducation, see next section) may already start during the clinical assessment and is part of building a working relationship between the clinician (and the clinical team) and the parents and child or adolescent.

One neglected topic is the need for clinical reassessment. ODD and CD are valid disorders that can be reliably diagnosed in preschool and elementary school children. But in the literature more attention has been given to stability of diagnosis than to change. However, the symptoms for these disorders do change over time, despite showing stability in preschool and elementary school children (Bunte, Schoemaker, Hessen, van der Heijden, & Matthys, 2014; Keenan et al., 2011; Rowe, Maughan, Costello, & Angold, 2005). Thus, children under treatment should be reassessed after an intervention has been given to determine whether there has been a remission in the symptoms and whether a diagnosis of ODD or CD is still warranted. Reassessment may also result in the identification of a comorbid disorder (e.g., ADHD), particularly among children who do not respond to a specific intervention. Instability of diagnosis may also be due to changing environmental conditions. For example, a preschool child referred for conduct problems who is not diagnosed with a disorder at the initial assessment may show an increase in symptoms and be diagnosed later on, possibly as a result of increasing environmental expectations over the preschool period (Bunte et al., 2014; Matthys et al., 2017). Finally, reassessments are not only needed for children under care in mental health centers, but also for children involved in indicated prevention programs, for example, in the school context.

Psychological Interventions

Psychoeducation

On the one hand, interventions that have been shown to be effective in randomized control trials are available. On the other hand, engaging families in interventions targeting conduct problems is a challenge. The flowcharts of randomized clinical trials show that a high proportion of families requiring intervention do not, in the end, start on one (Scott, 2016). Based on data from 262 studies, Chacko and colleagues (2016) showed that at least 25% of the parents identified as appropriate for behavioral parent training do not start treatment, and an additional 26 % begin, but drop out before completing the treatment. The participation rate of poverty-impacted families is much lower (Chapter 24, this book).

For many years, much attention has been paid to practical barriers to intervention. However, lack of mental health literacy—that is, accurate knowledge and beliefs about the nature of mental health problems and effective interventions—is also considered an important barrier to intervention (Martinez, Lau, Chorpita, Weisz, & Research Network on Youth Mental Health, 2015). Presenting factual information to parents about their child's mental health problems and effective treatments is commonly referred to as psychoeducation. Psychoeducation is increasingly considered an important tool to prepare parents for treatment.

For example, it is important for parents to understand that behavioral parent training is not being advised for them because they did a bad job as parents. Parents must be informed about the interplay between early child vulnerabilities and nonoptimal parenting characteristics. More specifically, children's temperamental characteristics may elicit negative parenting behaviors that result in conduct problems and related disorders. Parents must understand that behavioral parent training is advised for them because this intervention will equip them with skills that will enable them to decrease their child's conduct problems and increase his or her socially appropriate behavior. Importantly, parents need to understand how behavioral parent training works.

As already noted, engaging parents in interventions does not start when parents have their first meeting with the psychotherapist after the clinical evaluation of their child, but must start in the course of the clinical evaluation itself. In our view, clinicians who have built a working relationship with the parents and the child or adolescent in the course of the assessment are best suited to take the first steps in providing psychoeducation. They must have interpersonal skills, which serve as the basis for strong therapeutic alliances, and have training in identifying barriers to family involvement and in aligning parents' involvement with their own goals for treatment (Chacko et al., 2016). But, as noted in Chapter 24 of this book, a one-time discussion of relevant topics is unlikely to be sufficient; a number of topics need to be readdressed throughout the therapy by the therapist. Psychoeducation strategies employed by therapists early on have been shown to uniquely predict subsequent parent involvement in treatment (Martinez et al., 2015).

Effect Sizes of Psychological Interventions

In a meta-analysis of behavioral parent training and cognitive behavioral therapy (CBT) for children and adolescents with antisocial behavior, the mean effect size of behavioral parent training was 0.47 and of CBT 0.35 (McCart, Priester, Davies, & Azen, 2006), with older youth receiving greater effects from CBT than young children. However, these effect sizes are based on clinical trials conducted in highly controlled research settings. Therefore, it remains unclear whether the effect sizes obtained in everyday clinical practice would be as large. In clinical trials therapy sessions are thoroughly prepared and subsequently discussed, and treatment fidelity is checked. One may question whether all this is as carefully done amidst the hustle and bustle of everyday clinical practice. Importantly, it has been shown that reduced fidelity of implementation leads to smaller effect sizes (Weisz, Donenberg, Han, & Wess, 1995). So it may be that the effect sizes of these psychological interventions in everyday clinical practice are smaller.

Also, in most randomized control trials the experimental condition is compared to no treatment. However, when the control condition is usual care, effect sizes are small to medium (Weisz, Jensen-Doss, & Hawley, 2006; Weisz et al., 2013). In addition, many effect studies of psychological interventions do not include blinded measurement (for example, behavioral observation, or teacher or peer ratings conducted at longer term follow-up assessments when the teachers and peers are unaware of children's prior assignment-to-condition), although it has been shown that blinded measurement is an important factor. In a meta-analysis of psychological interventions for ADHD there was a moderate, statistically significant, positive effect on ADHD core symptoms for assessments made by the individuals most proximal to the therapeutic setting, often provided by parents who were not blinded to treatment allocation. However, these effects were not corroborated when analyses were restricted to trials with measurements made by observers or raters unaware of treatment allocation (Sonuga-Barke et al., 2013). Effect sizes of psychological interventions for conduct problems in children and adolescents may, therefore, be smaller than those found by McCart et al. (2006). There is also evidence that effect sizes are smaller in indicated prevention than in treatment settings; for example, in a meta-analysis of Incredible Years the effect size was 0.20 for indicated prevention while it was 0.50 for treatment (Menting, Orobio de Castro, & Matthys, 2013).

Personalizing Interventions

Should we be satisfied with such effect sizes? To put the above-cited effect sizes into context, let us have a look at the efficacy of psychiatric medication and somatic medication. In a systematic review the mean effect size of psychiatric medication was 0.49 and of general medicine medication 0.45 (Leucht et al., 2012). Thus, when compared to medication with general medicine the mean effect size for behavior parent training is reasonable. Although the mean effect size of cognitive behavior therapy is somewhat lower for young children, in treatment settings cognitive behavior therapy is typically combined with behavior parent training.

In medicine, the transition is being made from evidence-based medicine to personalized medicine. For example, treatments for cancers are personalized according to biological characteristics such as genotypes. In line with this, Ng and Weisz (2016) suggest personalized psychological interventions could boost the effectiveness and clinical utility of empirically supported therapies. If children do not respond to first-line evidence-based treatments, then treatments could be systematically adjusted for the poor responders, using adaptive treatment strategies, as in the case of adolescent depression (Gunlicks-Stoessel, Mufson, Westervelt, Almirall, & Murphy, 2016). But how should decisions be made about how to personalize or adapt interventions for disruptive behavior disorders?

One approach may be to use the results from research on moderators of intervention outcomes to provide information on how to tailor and adapt interventions and thus move toward personalized mental health care (e.g., La Greca, Silverman, & Lochman, 2009). Indeed, it may be that the benefits of standard evidence-based interventions are received only by subsets of children with conduct problems. A number of intervention studies have examined moderators of intervention outcomes, to explore "what works with whom." Unfortunately, very few moderators of intervention responses have been identified consistently in meta-analyses, although research on specific intervention programs have identified particular moderators for specific intervention approaches. One moderator that has emerged in meta-analyses is severity of conduct problems. Initial severity of symptoms was the strongest predictor of Incredible Years interventions effects with young children, with larger effects for studies including more severe cases (Menting et al., 2013). Disadvantaged family socioeconomic status has also been assumed to diminish the effectiveness of behavioral parent training. In a meta-analysis, parent training was equally effective for disadvantaged and nondisadvantaged families immediately post-treatment, when initial problems were severe. However, disadvantaged samples benefited less if they had low levels of initial problem severity. It may be that families' readiness to change is lower in disadvantaged families with mild child behavior problems than in nondisadvantaged families with the same problems. At follow-up, disadvantaged samples benefited less from behavioral parent training regardless of initial problem severity. Maintenance of treatment seems harder for disadvantaged families, suggesting that more sustained family support may be needed (Leijten, Raaijmakers, Orobio de Castro, & Matthys, 2013).

Research on moderators may also be useful in identifying which components of multicomponent interventions are useful (especially in studies with sequential multiple assessment randomized treatment designs), and which specific intervention delivery formats may be most useful for different children. For example, Glenn, Lochman, Dishion, Powell, Boxmeyer and Qu (2017) used a genomic approach and have found that the oxytocin receptor gene, which has been associated with many aspects of social behavior, predicted whether children would have greater reductions in teacher-rated externalizing behavior through follow-up assessment depending on whether they received the intervention in individual sessions or in small group sessions. Children with the A/A genotype responded better to group intervention (and in similar ways to their response to individual intervention) than did children with the G allele. It appears that children who are less socially bonded, and thus less prone to deviant peer effects, may be particularly good candidates for group intervention to produce the strongest effects on this particular outcome. Studies of moderators of specific interventions will be fruitful in identifying foci for future research, and ultimately assist with the personalization of interventions for children with conduct problem symptoms.

Psycho(bio)logical Functions as Mechanisms

With regard to child and adolescent factors, we need to better understand the mechanisms underlying the development and maintenance of conduct problems if we are to personalize interventions. Among these mechanisms the psychobiological functions associated with the learning of (in)appropriate behaviors are particularly relevant, such as the altered processing of punishment and reward cues and impaired executive functions that have been shown in children and adolescents with ODD and CD (Matthys, Vanderschuren, & Schutter, 2013). While actually changing altered processing of punishment and reward cues would not be a target for intervention, taking into account impaired functioning in these areas during interventions is an option. For example, with regard to punishment processing, in work with parents and teachers relatively greater emphasis can be placed on clarifying antecedent control and monitoring of children and the use of more consistent and less harsh discipline methods (e.g., withdrawal of privileges, work chores, and time-out). Likewise, with regard to reward processing, more attention than usual can be given to parent–child special time and the use of praise and point systems with rewards (Matthys, Vanderschuren, Schutter, & Lochman, 2012)

With regard to executive functions, despite the publication of many studies on executive functions in ODD and CD and, even more, in ADHD (see Chapter 10, this book), their causal role in the occurrence of symptoms has been questioned. Based on a systematic review of neurocognitive functions, Van Lieshout, Luman, Buitelaar, Rommelse and Oosterlaan (2013) concluded that executive functions, including inhibitory control, are unrelated to the developmental course of ADHD in children and adolescents. These authors therefore qualify executive functions as epiphenomena, factors that play no causal role in the developmental course of the disorder. However, two recent longitudinal studies have shown that executive functions are a mechanism linking mother–child interactions to preschoolers' externalizing behavior. Based on coded parent–child observations, executive functioning tasks, and questionnaires Sulik et al. (2015) reported that preschoolers' executive functioning mediates the relation between early parenting and conduct problems in a large community sample. Likewise, based on parent–child observations, inhibitory control tasks, and teacher questionnaires, Van Dijk et al. (2017) showed that preschoolers' inhibitory control operates as a mechanism underlying the association between mother–child interactions and hyperactive/impulsive behavior, but that there was no association between mother–child interactions and aggressive behavior over time in a sample of predominantly clinically referred preschoolers.

These studies support the relevance of early parent training programs to affect conduct problems and hyperactive/impulsive behavior (ODD, CD, and ADHD symptoms) in young children. Although it has been shown that inhibitory control improves over time, and in preschool children with ODD/CD and ADHD even more than in typically developing children (Schoemaker, Bunte, Espy, Dekovic, & Matthys, 2014), it is still unclear whether interventions targeting parents or children can actually improve executive functions such as inhibitory control (Diamond & Ling, 2016). Further research in this area is badly needed as executive functions such as inhibitory control are higher order cognitive abilities that affect other cognitive processes (Miyake & Friedman, 2012) such as those involved in social problem solving (Van Nieuwenhuijzen et al., 2017). Thus, improving inhibitory control may increase the effect of cognitive behavioral therapy in which social information processing skills are targeted that have been shown to mediate prevention intervention outcomes: interpretation of other people's intentions, generation of possible behavioral responses, and evaluation of the likely positive and negative consequences of the potential responses (Dodge, Godwin, and The Conduct Problems Prevention Research Group, 2013). Intervention-produced changes in children's attributions of hostile intent and in their outcome expectations for aggressive behaviors have been found to mediate the effects of multicomponent cognitive behavioral therapy on the behavior problems, delinquency, and substance use of aggressive children through follow-up periods (Lochman & Wells, 2002).

Opportunities for Delivering Effective Interventions

While we expect that personalizing interventions has the potential to increase effectiveness, presently it is urgent to improve other key aspects of the delivery and dissemination of evidence-based interventions, as noted in Chapter 29 of this book. To improve the reach and quality of the delivery of effective interventions, two key issues are where the services are provided and how advances in technology can aid in providing Internet delivery of interventions.

Beyond the Clinic Although the bulk of traditional mental health services are still delivered in clinic settings, there are ongoing, and in fact increasing, efforts to promote provision of psychological interventions to behavior problem children in other health and community settings, especially schools. The desire to provide community-based services has been largely driven by the recognition that only 20% of children with diagnosable mental health disorders have received appropriate mental health services (Hoagwood & Johnson, 2003). Thus, providing care in community settings can be expected to increase children's and families' access to services that can be at least as effective as those provided in clinics. It has been found that providing evidence-based services (cognitive behavioral therapy; parent behavioral management training) to children with early-onset ODD or CD within the community ecology (schools, the home, community settings) was as effective in reducing their behavioral and emotional problems, psychopathic features, and diagnostic status, as providing the same types of service to similar children who had been randomly assigned to receive them in clinic settings (Kolko et al., 2009). Home-based therapy has been a notable feature of certain evidence-based interventions for many decades (see, e.g., Henggeler, 2015), as has the role of psychological intervention in the schools.

The schools have been an important focus for prevention programs for children with behavior problems since the early years of the community psychology movement (e.g., Allen,

Chinsky, Larcen, Lochman, & Selinger, 1976). Working with children in schools, for prevention or treatment purposes, has several advantages. Schools are one of the few primary socializing systems which involve most children; hence, service provision in schools promotes the possibility of access to services by students (and their parents) and of screening children to discover those at risk. Because children are in schools for large amounts of time during the year, clinicians providing services in the schools also have an unusually rich opportunity to interact with the other students and teachers whom the target children spend much of their around. Thus, their understanding of the nature of the target children's behavioral problems is deepened and they are given notable opportunities to influence the social environment around them through teacher consultation and training and intervention with the peer group. In addition, because schools are typically closer to children's homes than outpatient clinics are, it can be easier to engage parents in services (Van Acker & Mayer, 2009).

As described in Chapter 1, prevention programs, including those deployed within schools, can be conceptualized as being at one of three levels (Allen et al., 1976; Conduct Problems Prevention Research Group, 1992). Universal prevention programs (sometimes described as primary prevention) are often delivered at the classroom level to all of the children in a classroom and are designed to stimulate improved behavioral control in children and to encourage the development of social-emotional skills that promote positive youth development. Targeted prevention programs (at the selected or indicated levels of prevention—these are similar to what is also known as secondary or tertiary prevention) are delivered in schools by identifying and intervening with at-risk children. Indicated prevention, which assists children who are already displaying subclinical characteristics of the disorder to be prevented (e.g., conduct disorder), typically requires the use of a population-wide screen across all students, often involving teacher ratings of the problem behaviors of all children, and then establishing a cut-off for receipt of prevention services. Teacher ratings, sometimes augmented by parent ratings, have been found to serve as valid and effective screens for later adolescent problem behaviors (Hill, Lochman, Coie, Greenberg, & Conduct Problems Prevention Research Group, 2004) and adult criminal behavior (Kassing, Godwin, Lochman, Coie, & Conduct Problems Prevention Research Group, under review), although the base rates of the outcome affect the accuracy of prediction. Chapters 26, 27, and 28 of this book have described some of the prominent prevention programs that have established a research base for use in schools.

Schools, in the United States, are mandated to provide programming for children with behavioral and emotional problems, if those problems impair children's academic functioning. Similar to the conceptualization of mental health practitioners who implement prevention programs in the schools, school personnel (special education teachers, school psychologists, etc) use frameworks such as Response to Intervention (RTI) for academic outcomes and Positive Behavior Supports (PBSs) for behavioral outcomes to design behavioral plans for students (Larson & Lochman, 2011). These programs are commonly based on a three-tier model. If children do not respond to the first-tier interventions addressing all children in the classroom (similar to universal prevention), then Tier 2 and, if necessary, Tier 3 interventions provide progressively greater intensity of contact and structure to subsets of at-risk children and, if necessary, their parents (similar to selected and indicated prevention programs). Tier 3 interventions can, in some cases, involve clinical treatment services (Larson & Lochman, 2011), and the use of mental health treatment services in schools (as opposed to prevention) has increased in recent decades.

It became increasingly apparent in the 1980s and 1990s that, although children's serious behavioral problems were often first identified in the school setting, schools were ill-equipped to respond effectively to the intense treatment needs presented by the children with the most severe problems (Weist et al., 2014). This recognition led to expanded school mental health approaches which integrated schools' efforts with those local community mental health centers (CMHCs; Weist et al., 2014). In these approaches, CMHC staff augment the work of school-employed staff and can provide intensive evidence-based treatment services for children's behavioral problems in the school setting itself. Mental health clinicians working in schools include those operating in areas typically related to education, including school counseling, clinical and counseling psychology, clinical social work, and child and adolescent psychiatry (Weist et al., 2009). To work effectively as a mental health clinicians within the school setting, clinicians need specialized training in how to develop and maintain relationships with school administrators, teachers, and health staff, besides having to gain insight into relevant educational regulations and understand how to integrate mental health interventions with children's busy school days and academic demands. Sometimes, however, school mental health programs are imperfectly implemented with poor-quality outcomes in the schools. Some of the deficiencies that lead to poorer outcomes are ineffective administrative and financial collaboration between the CMHC and the schools, a lack of adequate infrastructure and funding to support this model of intervention, and inadequate training for the mental health clinicians in how to work within the school environment (George, Taylor, Schmidt, & Weist, 2013; Reinke, Herman, & Ialongo, 2012). Further research is needed to examine the effectiveness of placing community-funded mental health clinicians in school settings (Weist et al., 2014).

Advocates have suggested other settings and models for community-based mental health services besides schools, and one of the areas of particular interest has been the embedding of mental health clinicians into primary medical care clinics (Asarnow et al., 2015; Kolko & Perrin, 2014). Primary care settings, such as pediatric and family medicine practices, can play a role in addressing the mental health needs of children and adolescents, especially since some of the more common behavioral problems seen in primary care include oppositional and aggressive behaviors from child patients (Kelleher & Stevens, 2009; Kolko & Perrin, 2014). It has been anticipated that providing evidence-based mental care within primary care settings might increase access to, and the acceptability of, services by reducing the long waiting times for them, the stigma attached to seeking care, and high drop-out rates, while at the same time enhancing communication between mental and physical health providers. Mental health clinicians can provide on-site intervention for DBD children, potentially on immediate referral from primary care staff during children's regular and acute medical visits, and can consult and collaborate with the primary medical care staff in real time about the cases. Research has demonstrated that behavioral health care can be provided effectively and cost-effectively within primary care clinics (Asarnow et al., 2015).

Technology-Based Intervention As described in Chapters 26 and 29 of this Handbook, technology-based interventions designed to assist children with disruptive behavior disorders have shown innovative and exciting possibilities for increasing access to services, addressing common barriers that interfere with parents and children receiving care, involving parental co-partners more easily, increasing child and parent engagement in intervention, and for reducing costs. Technology-based interventions represent an evolving set of technologies. An intervention requiring direct therapist–parent interaction, like Parent–Child Interaction Therapy, has used a video-conferencing format, while other forms of parent education and child intervention have been delivered with Internet and smart-phone platforms which can include specialized cartoons and interactive games and activities. Given the flexible nature of their delivery, Internet-based interventions have been tested in some of the community settings noted in the prior section, including in schools (Lochman, Boxmeyer et al., 2017) and in child health clinics (Sourander et al., 2016).

Research on these technology-based interventions is still in its early stages and is likely to feature prominently in the decade ahead. There have been positive findings for specific programs, as noted in Chapters 26 and 29, but, because there are relatively few studies, larger scale review papers report promising but mixed results. There have been few studies particularly devoted to disruptive behavior disorders, although more have been conducted with adults and with other forms of child psychopathology.

In a meta-analysis of intervention research on the overall effects of mobile technology, Lindheim, Bennett, Rosen, and Silk (2015) found that interventions using mobile technologies in randomized control studies had significant effects, with an overall effect size of .34. But only a minority of the reviewed studies were with children and adolescents, and only one was with children who had DBDs. These were encouraging results, though, indicating the potential value of this approach. The analysis did find that interventions that included mobile applications in addition to traditional treatment had significantly better outcomes than the traditional treatments alone, although early findings with samples of young children have been more equivocal about whether there were additive effects to traditional parent training from the technology-assisted aspect of the intervention (Hall & Bierman, 2015).

In Hollis et al.'s (2016) meta-analysis of digital health interventions with children, it was notable that again there were no studies of children with DBDs, and that the most common form of childhood psychopathology covered was childhood anxiety and depression. As another recent meta-analysis (MacDonnell & Prinz, 2016) revealed, significant effects emerged for technology-based interventions targeted at children with internalizing disorders, using both interventions that addressed parents and the family and interventions that were solely child-focused. This latter meta-analysis did include several studies focusing on parent and family interventions with children with behavior problems, and these interventions did produce encouraging behavioral improvements. The conclusions were consistent with the overall findings for technology-based interventions, and suggest that continued technology-based research on children with conduct problems is in order.

In planning for the next wave of studies on technology-based interventions, the recent reviews and meta-analyses have noted some common advantages and challenges for this form of intervention delivery. Advantages noted have been that technology-based interventions can assist with clinical staff shortages and permit self-pacing and flexible scheduling in intervention delivery (MacDonnell & Prinz, 2016). Challenges have included the "digital divide" (Hall & Bierman, 2015) that excludes families and children with limited financial resources who may not have the technological equipment and services required for the intervention. Other challenges include the limited wireless connection in some areas and the general absence of human contact, which may lead to diminishing engagement across time (MacDonnell & Prinz, 2016).

Among unknown areas and suggestions for future research are issues such as how technology can assist teachers and mental health professionals, whether these interventions are in fact cost-effective as they were anticipated to be, and what should be the optimal role of human support (Hall & Bierman, 2015; Hollis et al., 2016). It has been proposed that hybrid interventions, which include a reduced amount of clinician contact (in comparison to traditional face-to-face treatment) in addition to the technology-based intervention, may be especially important in altering the stable patterns of problem behavior associated with children's early-onset conduct problems, and such hybrid interventions have indeed produced significant behavioral improvements (Lochman, Boxmeyer et al., 2017; Taylor et al. 2008), Notably, these results have been produced with a 44% reduction in costs (Lochman, Boxmeyer et al., 2017), suggesting that further exploration of hybrid interventions and of the cost-effectiveness of technology-based interventions is clearly warranted.

References

Allen, G. J., Chinsky, J. M., Larcen, S. W., Lochman, J. E., & Selinger, H. V. (1976). *Community psychology in the schools: A behaviorally oriented multilevel preventive approach.* Hillsdale, NJ: Erlbaum.

American Psychiatric Association (2013). *Diagnostic and statistical manual of mental disorders* (5th ed.). Arlington, VA: Author.

Asarnow, J. R., Hoagwood, K. E., Stancin, T., Lochman, J. E., Hughes, J. L., Miranda, J. M., . . . Kazak, A.E. (2015). Psychological science and innovative strategies for informing health care redesign: A policy brief. *Journal of Clinical Child and Adolescent Psychology, 44,* 923–932.

Bunte, T. L., Laschen, S., Schoemaker, K., Hessen, D. J., van der Heijden, P. G. M., & Matthys, W. (2013). Clinical usefulness of observational assessment in the diagnosis of DBD and ADHD in preschoolers. *Journal of Clinical Child and Adolescent Psychology, 42,* 749–761.

Bunte, T., Schoemaker, K., Hessen, D. J., van der Heijden, P. G., & Matthys W. (2014). Stability and change of ODD, CD and ADHD diagnosis in referred preschool children. *Journal of Abnormal Child Psychology, 42,* 1213–1224.

Chacko, A., Jensen, S. A., Lowry, L. S., Cornwell, M., Chimklis, A., Chan, E., . . . Pulgarin, B. (2016). Engagement in behavioral parent training: Review of the literature and implications for practice. *Clinincal Child and Family Psychology Review, 19,* 204–15.

Collishaw, S., Goodman, R., Ford, T., Rabe-Hesketh, S., & Pickels, A. (2009). How far are associations between child, family and community factors and child psychopathology informant-specific and informant-general? *Journal of Child Psychology and Psychiatry, 50,* 571–580.

Conduct Problems Prevention Research Group (1992). A developmental and clinical model for the prevention of conduct disorders: The FAST Track Program. *Development and Psychopathology, 4,* 509–527.

Copeland, W. E., Angold, A., Costello, E. J., & Egger, H. (2013). Prevalence, comorbidity, and correlates of DSM-5 proposed disruptive mood dysregulation disorder. *American Journal of Psychiatry, 170,* 173–179.

Diamond, A., & Ling, D. S. (2016). Conclusions about interventions, programs, and approaches for improving executive functions that appear justified and those that, despite much hype, do not. *Developmental Cognitive Neuroscience, 18,* 34–48.

Dodge, K. E., Godwin, J., and The Conduct Problems Prevention Research Group (2013). Social-information-processing patterns mediate the impact of preventive intervention on adolescent antisocial behavior. *Psychological Science, 24,* 456–465.

Evans, S. C., Burke, J. D., Roberts, M. C., Fite, P. J., Lochman, J. E., de la Pena, F. R., & Reed, G. M. (2017). Irritability in child and adolescent psychopathology: An integrative review for ICD-11. *Clinical Psychology Review, 53,* 29–45.

George, M., Taylor, L., Schmidt, S. C., & Weist, M. D. (2013). A review of school mental health programs in SAMHSA's National Registry of Evidence-Based Programs and Practices. *Psychiatric Services, 64,* 483–486.

Glenn, A. L., Lochman, J. E., Dishion, T., Powell, N. P., Boxmeyer, C., & Qu, L. (2017). Oxytocin receptor gene variant interacts with intervention delivery format in predicting intervention outcomes for youth with conduct problems. *Prevention Science.* doi:10.1007/s11121-017-0777-1

Gunlicks-Stoessel, M., Mufson, L., Westervelt, A., Almirall, D., & Murphy, S. (2016). A pilot SMART for developing an Adaptive Treatment Strategy for adolescent depression. *Journal of Clinical Child and Adolescent Psychology, 45,* 480–494.

Hall, C. M., & Bierman, K. L. (2015). Technology-assisted interventions for parents of young children: Emerging practices, current research, and future directions. *Early Childhood Research Quarterly, 33,* 21–32.

Henggeler, S. W. (2015). Effective family-based treatments for adolescents with serious antisocial behavior. In J. Morizot & L. Kazemian (Eds.), *The development of criminal and antisocial behavior* (pp. 461–475). Cham, Switzerland: Springer International Publishing.

Hill, L. G., Lochman, J. E., Coie, J. D., Greenberg, M. T., & Conduct Problems Prevention Research Group (2004). Effectiveness of early screening for externalizing problems: Issues of screening accuracy and utility. *Journal of Consulting and Clinical Psychology, 72,* 809–820.

Hoagwood, K., & Johnson, J. (2003). School psychology: A public health framework: From evidence-based practices to evidence-based policies. *Journal of School Psychology, 41*, 3–21.

Hollis, C., Falconer, C. J., Martin, J. L., Whittington, C., Stockton, S., Glazebrook, C., & Davies, E. B. (2016). Annual research review: Digital health interventions for children and young people with mental health problems: A systematic and meta-review. *Journal of Child Psychology and Psychiatry*. doi:10.1111/jcpp.12663

Kassing, F., Godwin, J., Lochman, J. E., Coie, J. D., & Conduct Problems Prevention Research Group (under review). How base rates influence the accuracy of early childhood screens by predicting convictions at age 25. *Journal of Consulting and Clinical Psychology*.

Keenan, K., Boeldt, D., Chen, D., Coyne, C., Donald, R., Duax, J., . . . Humphries, M. (2011). Predictive validity of DSM-IV oppositional defiant and conduct disorders in clinically referred preschoolers. *Journal of Child Psychology and Psychiatry, 52*, 47–55.

Kelleher, K. J., & Stevens, J. (2009). Evolution of child mental health services in primary care. *Academic Pediatrics, 9*, 7–14.

Kim-Cohen, J., Caspi, A., Moffitt, T. E., Harrington, H., Milne, B. J., & Poulton, R. (2003). Prior juvenile diagnoses in adults with mental disorder: Developmental follow-back of a prospective-longitudinal cohort. *Archives of General Psychiatry, 60*, 709–717.

Kolko, D. J., Bukstein, O. G., Pardini, D., Holden, E. A., Hart, J., & Dorn, L. D. (2009). Community vs. clinic-based modular treatment of children with early-onset ODD or CD: A clinical trial with 3-year follow-up. *Journal of Abnormal Child Psychology, 37*, 591–609.

Kolko, D. J., & Perrin, E. C. (2014). The integration of behavioral health interventions in children's health care: Services, science, and suggestions. *Journal of Clinical Child and Adolescent Psychology, 43*, 216–228.

La Greca, A. M., Silverman, W. K., & Lochman, J. E. (2009). Moving beyond efficacy and effectiveness: Factors influencing the outcome of evidence-based psychological interventions with children and adolescents. *Journal of Consulting and Clinical Psychology, 77*, 373–382.

Lahey, B. B. (2014). What we need to know about callous-unemotional traits: Comment on Frick, Ray, Thornton, and Kahn (2014). *Psychological Bulletin, 140*, 58–63.

Larson, J., & Lochman, J. E. (2011). *Helping school children cope with anger: A cognitive-behavioral intervention* (2nd ed.). New York, NY: Guilford.

Le Couteur, A., & Gardner, F. (2008). Use of structured interviews and observational methods in clinical settings. In M. Rutter, D. Bishop, D. Pine, S. Scott, J. Stevenson, E. Taylor, & A. Thapar (Eds.), *Rutter's child and adolescent psychiatry* (5th ed., pp. 271–288). Oxford, UK: Blackwell.

Leijten, P., Raaijmakers, M. A., de Castro, B. O., & Matthys, W. (2013). Does economic status matter? A meta-analysis on parent training effectiveness for disruptive child behavior. *Journal of Clinical Child and Adolescent Psychology, 42*, 384–392.

Leucht, S., Hierl, S., Kissling, W., Dold, M., & Davis, J. M. (2012). Putting the efficacy of psychiatric and general medicine medication into perspective: Review of meta-analyses. *British Journal of Psychiatry, 200*, 97–106.

Lindheim, O., Bennett, C. B., Rosen, D., & Silk, J. (2015). Mobile technology boosts the effectiveness of psychotherapy and behavioral interventions: A meta-analysis. *Behavior Modification, 39*, 785–804.

Lochman, J. E., Boxmeyer, C. L., Jones, S., Qu, L., Ewoldsen, D., & Nelson, W. M., III (2017). Testing the feasibility of a briefer school-based preventive intervention with aggressive children: A hybrid intervention with face-to-face and Internet components. *Journal of School Psychology*. doi:10.1016/j.jsp.2017.03.010

Lochman, J. E., Evans, S. C., Burke, J. D., Roberts, M. C., Fite, P. J., Reed, G. M., . . . Garralda, E. M. (2015). An empirically based alternative to DSM-5's disruptive mood dysregulation disorder for ICD-11. *World Psychiatry, 14*, 30–33.

Lochman, J. E., Vernberg, E., Powell, N. P., Boxmeyer, C. L., Jarrett, M., McDonald, K., . . . Kassing, F. (2017). Pre-post tornado effects on aggressive children's psychological and behavioral adjustment through one-year postdisaster. *Journal of Clinical Child and Adolescent Psychology, 46*(1), 136–149. doi:10.1080/15374416.2016.1228460

Lochman, J. E., & Wells, K. C. (2002). Contextual social-cognitive mediators and child outcome: A test of the theoretical model in the Coping Power program. *Development and Psychopathology, 14*, 971–993.

MacDonnell, K. W., & Prinz, R. J. (2016). A review of technology-based youth and family-focused interventions. *Clinical Child and Family Psychology Review*. doi:10.1007/s10567-016-0218-x

Martinez, J. I., Lay, A. S., Chorpita, B. F., Weisz, J. R., & Research Network on Youth Mental Health (2015). Psychoeducation as a mediator of treatment approach on parent engagement in child psychotherapy for disruptive behavior. *Journal of Clinical Child and Adolescent Psychology*. doi:10.1080/15374416.2015.1038826.

Matthys, W., Bunte, T., & Schoemaker, K. (2017). Oppositional defiant disorder and conduct disorder. In J.L. Luby (Ed.), *Handbook of preschool mental health: Development, disorders, and treatment* (2nd ed., pp. 101–125). New York, NY: Guilford.

Matthys, W., Vanderschuren, L. J. M. J., & Schutter, D. J. L. G. (2013). The neurobiology of oppositional defiant disorder and conduct disorder: Altered functioning in three mental domains. *Development and Psychopathology, 25*, 193–207.

Matthys, W., Vanderschuren, L. J. M. J., Schutter, D. J. L. G., & Lochman, J. E. (2012). Impaired neurocognitive functions affect social learning processes in oppositional defiant disorder and conduct disorder: Implications for interventions. *Clinical Child and Family Psychology Review, 15*, 234–246.

McCart, M. R., Priester, P. E., Davies, W. H., & Azen, R. (2006). Differential effectiveness of behavioral parent-training and cognitive-behavioral therapy for antisocial youth: A meta-analysis. *Journal of Abnormal Child Psychology, 34*, 527–543.

Menting, A. T., Orobio de Castro, B., & Matthys, W. (2013). Effectiveness of the Incredible Years parent training to modify disruptive and prosocial child behavior: A meta-analytic review. *Clinical Psychology Review, 33*, 901–913.

Miyake, A., & Friedman, N. P. (2012). The nature and organization of individual differences in executive functions: Four general conclusions. *Current Directions in Psychological Science, 21*, 8–14.

Ng, M. Y., & Weisz, J. R. (2016). Building a science of personalized intervention for youth mental health. *Journal of Child Psychology and Psychiatry, 57*, 216–236.

Noordermeer, S. D., Luman, M., & Oosterlaan, J. (2016). A systematic review and meta-analysis of neuroimaging in Oppositonal Defiant Disorder (ODD) and Conduct Disorder (CD) taking Attention-Deficit Hyperactivity Disorder (ADHD) into account. *Neuropsychology Review, 26*, 44–72.

Reinke, W. M., Herman, K. C., & Ialongo, N. S. (2012). Developing and implementing integrated school-based mental health interventions. *Advances in School Mental Health Promotion, 5*, 158–160.

Rowe, R., Maughan, B., Costello, E. J., & Angold, A. (2005). Defining oppositional defiant disorders. *Journal of Child Psychology and Psychiatry, 46*, 1309–1316.

Scott, S. (2016). Finding out the best way to tailor psychological interventions for children and families—A commentary on Ng and Weisz (2016). *Journal of Child Psychology and Psychiatry, 57*, 237–240.

Schoemaker, K., Bunte, T., Espy, K. A., Deković, M., & Matthys W. (2014). Executive functions in preschool children with ADHD and DBD: An 18-month longitudinal study. *Developmental Neuropsychology, 39*, 302–15.

Schoemaker, K., Bunte, T., Wiebe, S. A., Espy, K. A., Deković, M., & Matthys, W. (2012). Executive function deficits in preschool children with ADHD and DBD. *Journal of Child Psychology and Psychiatry, 53*, 111–119.

Schoemaker, K., Mulder, H., Deković, M., & Matthys, W. (2013). Executive functions in preschool children with externalizing behavior problems: A meta-analysis. *Journal of Abnormal Child Psychology, 41*, 457–471.

Sonuga-Barke, E., Brandeis, D., Cortese, S., Daley, D., Ferrin, M., Holtmann, M., . . . European ADHD Guidelines Group. (2013). Nonpharmacological interventions for attention-deficit/hyperactivity disorder: Systematic review and meta-analyses of randomized controlled trials of dietary and psychological treatments. *American Journal of Psychiatry, 170*, 275–289.

Sourander, A., McGrath, P. J., Ristkari, T., Cunningham, C., Huttunen, J., Lingley-Pottie, P., . . . Unruh, A. (2016). Internet-assisted parent training intervention for disruptive behavior in 4-year-old children: A randomized clinical trial. *Journal of the American Medical Association Psychiatry, 73,* 378–387.

Sulik, M. J., Blair, C., Mills-Koonce, R., Berry, D., Greenberg, M., & the Family Life Project Investigators (2015). Early parenting and the development of externalizing behavior problems: Longitudinal mediation through children's executive function. *Child Development, 86,* 1588–1603.

Taylor, T. K., Webster-Stratton, C., Feil, E. G., Broadbent, B., Widdop, C. S., & Severson, H. H. (2008). Computer-based intervention with coaching: An example using the Incredible Years Program. *Cognitive Behavior Therapy, 37,* 233–246.

Van Acker, R., & Mayer, M. J. (2009). Cognitive-behavioral interventions and the social context of the school: A stranger in a strange land. In Mayer, M. J., Van Acker, R., Lochman, J. E., & Gresham, F. M. (2009). *Cognitive behavioral interventions for emotional and behavioral disorders: School-based practice* (pp. 82–108). New York, NY: Guilford.

Van Dijk, R., Dekovic, M., Bunte, T. L., Schoemaker, K., Zondervan-Zwijnenburg, M., Espy, K. A, & Matthys, W. (2017). Mother–child interactions and externalizing behavior problems in preschoolers over time: Inhibitory control as a mediator. *Journal of Abnormal Child Psychology.* doi:10.1007/s10802-016-0258-1

Van Lieshout, M., Luman, M., Buitelaar, J., Rommelse, N. N. J., & Oosterlaan, J. (2013). Does neurocognitive functioning predict future or persistence of ADHD? A systematic review. *Clinical Psychology Review, 33,* 539–560.

Van Nieuwenhuijzen, M., van Rest, M. M., Embregts, P. J. C. M., Vriens, A., Oostermeijer, S., van Bokhoven, I., & Matthys, W. (2015). Executive functions and social information processing in adolescents with severe behavior problems. *Child Neuropsychology, 23*(2), 228–241. doi:10.1080/09297049.2015.1135421

Weist, M., Lever, N., Stephan, S., Youngstrom, E., Moore, E., Harrison, B., . . . Stiegler, K. (2009). Formative evaluation of a framework for high quality, evidence-based services in school mental health. *School Mental Health, 1*(4), 196–211. doi:10.1007/s12310-009-9018-5

Weist, M. D., Youngstrom, E. A., Stephan, S., Lever, N., Fowler, J., Taylor, L., . . . Hoagwood, K. (2014). Challenges and ideas from a research program on high-quality, evidence-based practice in school mental health. *Journal of Clinical Child and Adolescent Psychology, 43,* 244–255.

Weisz, J. R., Donenberg, G. R., Han, S. S., & Weiss, B. (1995). Bridging the gap between laboratory and clinic in child and adolescent psychotherapy. *Journal of Consulting and Clinical Psychology, 63,* 688–701.

Weisz, J. R., Jensen-Doss, A., & Hawley, K. M. (2006). Evidence-based youth psychotherapies versus usual clinical care: A meta-analysis of direct comparisons. *Psychologist, 61,* 671–689.

Weisz, J. R., Kuppens, S., Eckshtain, D., Ugueto, A. M., Halwey, K. M., & Jensen-Doss, A. (2013). Performance of evidence-based youth psychotherapies compared with usual care: A multilevel meta-analysis. *Journal of the American Medical Association Psychiatry, 70,* 750–761.

Index

Page numbers in **bold** refer to Tables; page numbers in *italics* refer to Figures

abuse 56, 110, 113, 132, 152, 424
academic achievement 339, 345, 374,
　　454, 472–473
　　callous-unemotional traits 358
　　deviant peers 341
　　ODD/CD with ADHD comorbidity
　　　58–60
　　paranoid personality disorder 114
　　substance abuse 78
Achievement Mentoring 460
activity 175, 176, 177, 179, 181
adaptation of treatment 486–491, 492,
　　494, 508
adjustment disorder 378
adolescence
　　ADHD 160, 162
　　aggression 224, 227
　　antisocial behavior 147–148, 262
　　assessment 380
　　barriers to treatment 396
　　callous-unemotional traits 46
　　CD 38, 39
　　neighborhood context 360
　　ODD 26, 27, 28
　　ODD/CD with ADHD comorbidity
　　　58, 59–60, 66
　　parenting 308, 310, 312–314, 316
　　peers 263, 327–328, 330, 332, 340,
　　　343–344, 346
　　personality disorders 115

　　psychopathy 107–108
　　psychosocial treatment 457, 459–461,
　　　467–483, 489
　　Pyromania 96
　　serotonin levels 150
　　substance abuse 79
　　treatment plans 385
Adolescent Transitions Program (ATP) 475
adults
　　attachment insecurity 208
　　IED 94–95
　　ODD 28
　　ODD/CD with ADHD comorbidity
　　　60–61, 66
　　parenting 308, 313–314
　　serotonin levels 150
affect, shallow 39, 59, 105, 106, 116, 381
African-Americans 12, 314, 342, 360,
　　361, 363
aggression 4, 12, 381, 494
　　avoidant attachment 210
　　BPD 108, 109, 110
　　callous-unemotional traits 29, 40–43, 47,
　　　49, 59, 65, 143
　　CD 37, 38, 339, 358
　　Coping Power 456–457, 472, 488,
　　　489, 493
　　deviant peers 341, 343, 346
　　emotion regulation 224–229
　　gender differences 26, 182

The Wiley Handbook of Disruptive and Impulse-Control Disorders, First Edition.
Edited by John E. Lochman and Walter Matthys.
© 2018 John Wiley & Sons Ltd. Published 2018 by John Wiley & Sons Ltd.

aggression (*Continued*)
  genetics 128–131, 133–135
  IED 89, 91–92, 94, 95
  intimate partner 292–294, 297–301
  marital conflict 294–295
  narcissistic personality disorder 111–112, 117
  neighborhood context 359, 360, 361
  neurobiology 144, 148, 149, 153
  neurotransmitters 93
  normal behavior 205, 374
  ODD 28, 77, 339
  ODD/CD with ADHD comorbidity 58, 60
  paranoid personality disorder 113, 114
  parent psychopathology 276
  peer rejection 327–328, 329–331, 333
  pharmacotherapy 411, 419, 420–423, 429
  prenatal phthalates exposure 194
  proactive/reactive 224–229, 242, 246, 359, 361, 382
  psychopathy 105, 106, 116
  psychosocial treatment 433, 453, 461, 471–472
  schools 356–357, 424
  serotonin 150–151
  SES relationship 261, 394
  SMART talk 490
  social cognition 241–242, 244, 245, 247, 248
  stress response system 152
  substance abuse 77
Agreeableness 44, 178–179
Ainsworth, Mary 206, 207, 211
alcohol use 73–75, 116, 263, 313–314
  anxiety comorbidity 80–81
  BPD 108, 109
  externalizing spectrum 76, 77, 104
  inhibitory control 223
  parental 279
  prenatal exposure 78, 191
  psychosocial treatment 453, 454, 476
alpha agonists 426, **427**, 429
ambiguous provocations 238–239
ambivalent attachment 206, 207–208
American Academy of Child and Adolescent Psychiatry (AACAP) 419–420, 424, 425
American Psychiatric Association (APA) 6–7
amygdala 144–150, 153, 193, 225–228, 262–263

anger
  CD 4
  emotion regulation 222, 224
  IED 95
  ODD 21, 22, 23, 24
  ODD/CD with ADHD comorbidity 30, 65
  personality disorders 105, 108, 111, 113, 115, 117
  psychosocial treatment 461
  reactive aggression 224–225
  social cognition 240, 241
  temperament 176, 178, 180, 183
antagonistic behavior 75, 105
anterior cingulate cortex (ACC) 144, 145–146, 148–149, 153
anticonvulsants 94
antidepressants 94, 95, 193–4
antipsychotic medication 412, **415–418**, **421**–422, 425–426, 428, 429, 444
antisocial behavior 355, 382, 496
  callous-unemotional traits 40–41, 43, 49, 143
  CD 38, 39–40
  cognitive distortions 244–245
  deviant peers 340, 341, 343, 344–345
  family structure 265, 267–268, 270
  genetics 129, 132–134, 258
  multimodal treatment 455–456
  neighborhood context 359, 360
  neurobiology 144, 146, 147–148, 149
  ODD 363–364
  ODD/CD with ADHD comorbidity 58, 60
  parenting 308–310, 312–313, 316
  perinatal risk factors 195
  poverty 259, 260–263, 270
  prenatal risk factors 192, 197
  psychosocial treatment 459–460, 468, 473, 474, 477
  stress response system 152
  substance abuse 74, 76, 78, 79
antisocial personality disorder (APD) 25, 90, 105–108, **116**, 117, 504
  externalizing spectrum 104
  gene-environment interactions 132
  ODD/CD with ADHD comorbidity 60
  parental 279–280
  prenatal risk factors 190
  substance abuse 74, 80–81

anxiety 5, 115–116, 379, 504
    BPD 108
    callous-unemotional traits 43
    CD 39, 77
    digital interventions 513
    gender differences 27
    IED comorbidity 91, 92
    maternal 190, 277
    mindfulness 469
    ODD 22–23, 25, 78
    paternal 181
    pharmacotherapy 411, 424–425
    psychopathy 106, 107
    reactive aggression 225
    separation 65, 430
    substance abuse 80–81
argumentativeness 21, 22, 26, 58, 65
arousal 152, 226, 227, 240, 451
assessment 373–389, 505–506
    callous-unemotional traits 44–46
    ODD/CD with ADHD comorbidity 61, 67
    parent psychopathology 283
    pharmacotherapy 426–429
    social cognition 247
    see also diagnosis
Association for Psychological Science 10–11
atomoxetine 412
attachment 10, 191, 205–220, 228, 281, 282, 434
attention 175, 222, 381
    attachment *209*, 210–211
    endophenotypes 136
    neurobiology 144, 149
    prenatal risk factors 190, 194
    preterm birth 196
    selective deficits 146
    sustained 164–165, 166, 169
Attention Deficit Hyperactivity Disorder (ADHD) 14, 23, 28, 311, 503–504
    ASD comorbidity 31
    assessment 375, 379, 381
    BPD comorbidity 109–110
    callous-unemotional traits 43
    diagnosis 61–63, 159, 378, 384
    DMDD comorbidity 23–24
    executive functioning 164–169, 170, 509–510
    externalizing spectrum 104, 129
    family engagement 397

family structure 265
gender differences 26–27, 181
genetics 130, 132, 133, 135
impulsivity 109
intellectual functioning 159–160, 161, 169
language impairments 162, 163–164, 170
learning disorders 379
low birth weight 196–197
marital conflict 297
narcissism 112
neurobiology 144–146, 149, 151, 153
ODD/CD comorbidity 29–31, 55–71, 145, 151, 161, 163–164, 167–169, 179, 278, 330–332, 379, 385, 387, 412–**421**
parent psychopathology 278, 279, 281
peer rejection 330–332, 334
personality traits 116
pharmacotherapy 411, 412–420, 421, 422–423, 424–425, 426, 430
prenatal risk factors 191–195, 197–198
preterm birth 195–196
self-biases 333
self-regulation 309
substance abuse 77
subtypes/presentations 55, 57, 164, 166, 167, 330
treatment 385, 507–508
attention seeking **116**
authority figures 28, 63
autism/autism spectrum disorder (ASD) 48, 144, 159, 430
    assessment 378, 383
    executive functioning 164
    genetics 130
    ODD comorbidity 30–31
    pharmacotherapy 420–421, 422, 425
    prenatal SSRI exposure 193
avoidant attachment 206, 207–208, 210

Baumrind, Diane 307–308
Behavior Parent Training (BPT) 394–395, 396–399, 400, 403, 505, 507
    see also parent training
behavioral contingencies *209*, 210–211
behavioral disorder (BD) 178
beliefs 244–245, 246, 247, 396
beta-blockers 94
biases 62, 67, 113, 376, 384, 506
Big Brothers Big Sisters of America (BBBSA) 469

binge drinking 74
bipolar disorder 23, 112, 144, 378–379, 505
bisphenol A (BPA) 194
blaming others 26, 42, 64
booster sessions 453, 489–490
borderline personality disorder (BPD) 23, 90, 108–110, 114, **116**, 117
   externalizing spectrum 105
   genetics 133
   hyperactivity/impulsivity 66
   parental 280
boundaries 311–312
Bowlby, John 206
brain 10, 143–158, 262–263
   emotion regulation 110, 223
   endophenotypes 136
   externalizing behavior 108
   fetal development 190, 194
   IED 93–94
   language impairments 163
   social cognition 249
Brief Strategic Family Therapy (BSFT) 476–477
British Child and Adolescent Mental Health Survey (BCAMHS) 259, *260*, 261
bulimia 95
bullying 30, 112, 241, 356, 455, 477

callous-unemotional (CU) traits 29, 105, 181, 355–356, 381
   assessment 382
   CD 39–49, 504
   Coping Power 491
   genetics 131, 135
   narcissistic personality disorder 112
   neighborhood context 362
   neurobiology 143, 144, 145–147, 149–150, 152
   ODD/CD with ADHD comorbidity 59, 65, 66
   personality traits 115–116
   proactive aggression 226–227, 228
   school context 358
   SES relationship 261
   social cognition 240–241, 242
   substance abuse 80, 81
candidate gene studies 127, 129–130, 134, 135, 136
carbamazepine 94, **415**
case formulation 7, 384–385, 387, 506

Catechol-O-methyltransferase (COMT) 130, 197
categorical approaches 9–10, 384
central executive 165–166
child and adolescent psychiatric assessment (CAPA) 383
child effects on parents 214
clinical interviews 61–65, 67, 373, 375, 376–383, 506
clinical utility 8–9
clinicians 9, 384–385, 493–494, 495–496, 505–506, 507, 512, 513
clonidine 412
cocaine 192–193
coercion 344, 394, 434, 451
cognitive assessment 382
cognitive behavioral therapy (CBT) 385, 386, 468, 510
   adaptation of 487
   comorbidity 493
   effect sizes 507, 508
   emotion regulation 229
   group 473
   IED 94–95
   Impulse-Control Disorders 96, 97
   LifeSkills Training 453
   ODD/CD with ADHD comorbidity 66, 387
cognitive biases 62, 67, 113, 114
cognitive capacities 245–246
cognitive control 167, 169
cognitive distortions 244–245
cognitive flexibility 168
cognitive functioning 10, 11, 159–174, 196
cognitive training 429–430
cohabitation 264–265, 266
community 78–79, 246, 394, 451, 493
   see also neighborhood context
community-based services 510, 512
comorbidity 4, 493
   assessment 379, 387, 506
   BPD 108, 109–110
   DMDD 23–24
   genetics 128–129, 136
   IED 91, 92
   Kleptomania 95
   narcissistic personality disorder 112
   neurobiology 153
   ODD 29–31

ODD/CD with ADHD 29–30, 55–71, 145, 151, 161, 163–164, 167–169, 179, 278, 330–332, 379, 385, 387, 412–421
    paranoid personality disorder 114
    pharmacotherapy 411, 412–420, 421, 424–425, 429
    psychopathy 107
    psychostimulants 151
    substance abuse 73–88
    temperament 178, 179, 182, 184
compliance 215, 436
concentration 55, 65, 194, 332
Conduct Disorder (CD) 3, 4, 23, 37–54, 339, 503–505
    ADHD comorbidity 55–71, 145, 151, 161, 163–164, 167–169, 179, 278, 330–332, 379, 385, 387, 412–421
    age-of-onset 356
    assessment 44–46, 373–375, 376–377, 379, 381, 505–506
    callous-unemotional traits 39–49, 355
    cognitive functioning 159
    comorbidities 493
    cost-effectiveness of interventions 496
    definition of 37–38
    deviant peers 332
    diagnosis 37–39, 61–63, 384, 424
    executive functioning 167–169, 170, 509–510
    externalizing spectrum 104, 129
    family structure 265
    genetics 127–132, 133, 135, 136
    intellectual functioning 160–161, 169–70
    intimate partner aggression 297–299
    language impairments 162–164, 170
    low birth weight 197
    marital conflict 295–297
    narcissism 112
    neighborhood context 355, 361–362, 363
    neurobiology of 143–158
    ODD overlap 24–25, 29
    parent psychopathology 275–284
    pathways to 228
    peer rejection 325, 327, 332–334
    personality traits 43–44, 116
    pharmacotherapy 411–432
    poverty 259–260
    prenatal risk factors 191, 192, 194

preterm birth 195
    prevalence 37, 294, 393, 433
    proactive aggression 226
    psychoeducation 386
    psychopathy 106
    psychosocial treatment 451–452, 456, 459, 467, 471–473
    school context 355, 358, 363
    self-regulation 309
    social cognition 241
    substance abuse 73, 74–75, 76–81
    temperament 178–83
    treatment 385, 387, 393, 401, 510
Conduct Problems Prevention Research Group (CPPRG) 456, 477
conscience 39, 40, 43, 381
consistency 12, 435, 436
consumer-driven approaches 399–400
contingency management (CM) 441, 476
contingency processing 43, 215
"convergence-divergence" model of oppositionality 179
Coping Power 229, 363, 456–457, 472, 495
    adaptations 487, 488–489, 491, 494
    Internet-Enhanced 490
    parental engagement 492
    transdiagnostic elements 493
cortisol 12, 152–153, 189, 190, 223, 225, 249
cost-effectiveness 496, 512, 513
criminal behavior 37, 339–340, 358, 433, 496
    family poverty 261
    gene-environment interactions 132, 133
    neighborhood context 361
    ODD/CD with ADHD comorbidity 59, 60–61
    peer rejection 327
    perinatal risk factors 195
    personality disorders 103
    prenatal maternal smoking 192
    psychosocial treatment 444, 454, 471, 474–475, 477–478
    school context 357
    see also offenders
cultural issues 57, 263, 485
    attachment 214, 215
    neighborhood context 360

cultural issues (*Continued*)
  parenting 314–315
  reporter expectations 62
  treatment adaptations 488

daily report cards (DRCs) 437–438
deceitfulness 37, 60, **116**
decision making 149, 169
defense mechanisms 92
defiance 4, 21, 26, 58, 75, 205, 339, 344
delinquency 23, 227, 433
  assessment 380
  deviant peers 78, 342, 361
  family structure 264, 266, 267
  genetics 130, 131, 133
  LifeSkills Training 453
  low birth weight 197
  moral reasoning 244
  multicomponent CBT 510
  narcissistic personality disorder 112
  neighborhood context 359, 361, 362
  neurobiology 144
  ODD/CD with ADHD comorbidity 56, 66
  parenting 312, 313, 316
  peer rejection 327, 329, 332
  poverty 260–261, 394
  prenatal alcohol exposure 191
  psychosocial treatment 454, 459, 474–475, 476
  school context 357
  substance abuse 74, 76, 78–79, 80
delivery formats 491
delusional disorders 113, 114
depression 5, 378, 492–493, 504
  adaptive treatment 508
  assessment 505
  BPD 108
  CD 29, 39, 77
  digital interventions 513
  endophenotypes 136
  gender differences 27
  IED comorbidity 91
  Kleptomania 95
  maternal 12, 189–190, 193–194, 269, 275–278, 280, 281–282, 283
  narcissistic personality disorder 112
  ODD 22–23, 25, 29, 504–545
  parental 11, 277–278, 279, 282, 394, 399, 492
  paternal 181, 278, 282

peer influence 345
personality traits 115–116
psychosocial treatment 469, 476
Pyromania 96
reactive aggression 225
relationship discord 291, 292
severe mood dysregulation 23
substance abuse 77, 80, 81
developmental adaptations 488–489
developmental delay 160, 422
developmental ecological models 355, 360
developmental immaturity 64
developmental onset
  antisocial behavior 147–148
  assessment 377
  BPD 110
  CD 294, 356
  Kleptomania 95
  narcissistic personality disorder 112–113
  ODD 294
  ODD/CD with ADHD comorbidity 58–61
  paranoid personality disorder 114–115
  psychopathy 107–108
  Pyromania 96
  substance abuse 79–80, 81
developmental psychopathology 11, 12, 14, 198
deviant peers 258, 329, 332, 334, 339–351, 360–361, 461, 471
diagnosis 4–10, 373–375, 378–379, 383–387, 505–506
  ADHD 61–63
  BPD 108
  CD 37–39, 40, 41, 48–49, 61–63, 294
  definition of 7
  IED 90
  ODD 21–36, 61–63, 294
  ODD/CD with ADHD comorbidity 57, 63–66, 67
  personality disorders 103–104
  pharmacotherapy 424–425
  psychopathy 105–106
  substance use disorder 73
  see also assessment
Diagnostic and Statistical Manual of Mental Disorders (DSM) 6–7, 26, 27, 90, 215, 504
Diagnostic and Statistical Manual of Mental Disorders (DSM-II) 37–38, 90

Diagnostic and Statistical Manual of Mental Disorders (DSM-III) 7, 21, 22, 28, 38, 39, 90, 103–104, 105
Diagnostic and Statistical Manual of Mental Disorders (DSM-IV) 7, 73, 90, 91, 96, 159
Diagnostic and Statistical Manual of Mental Disorders (DSM-5) 3, 7, 9, 378–379
  ADHD 159, 503–504
  assessment 373, 375, 383, 384
  categorical diagnosis 384
  CD 37, 39–40, 47, 48–49, 374, 429
  DMDD 23, 24, 505
  IED 90, 91, 95
  Impulse-Control Disorders 89
  impulsivity 109
  limited prosocial emotions 29, 39–40, 41, 45, 48, 59, 246
  ODD 21–22, 24–25, 28, 62, 374, 393, 429
  personality disorders 103–104, 106–107, 108, 111, 112, 114, 115–116
  substance abuse 73
Dialectical Behavior Therapy (DBT) 469
diathesis-stress model 132
differential attention 435, 437
differential susceptibility 132, 133, 135
diffusion tensor imaging (DTI) 146–147, 193
dimensional approaches 9–10, 104, 115–117, 182–183, 297
discipline 310–311, 340, 394, 473, 509
  callous-unemotional traits 42, 181
  consistency 12, 435
  parent psychopathology 281–282
  PMTO 458
  social cognition 246
  teachers 357
discrimination 360
Disinhibited Social Engagement Disorder 215
disinhibition 104–105, 108, 110, 115, 116, 117, 144
  see also impulsivity
disorder, definition of 7
disorganized attachment 206–207, 208, 210
dispositions 243–245, 246–247
disruptive behavior
  attachment 207–215
  emotion regulation 223–224

  executive functioning 167–168
  language impairments 162–163, 164
  normal 205
  prenatal risk factors 190
  preterm birth 196
  temperament 181, 183
disruptive behavior diagnostic observation schedule (DB-DOS) 380
Disruptive Behavior Disorders (DBDs) 3–4, 6, 503
  emotion regulation 222–224, 227–229
  family context 257, 258
  genetics 127–141
  parent psychopathology 279, 280, 282
  parent training 394–395
  poverty 394
  prevalence 393
  social cognition 237–253
  substance abuse comorbidity 73–88
  temperament 178–183
  see also Attention Deficit Hyperactivity Disorder; Conduct Disorder; Oppositional Defiant Disorder
Disruptive Mood Dysregulation Disorder (DMDD) 22, 23–24, 25, 505
distractibility 64, 115, **116**
divalproex 94, 412, **414–415**, 426
divorce 259, 264–265, 267–269, 292, 296–297
dominance 12, 42
dopamine 108, 130, 132–133, 148, 151, 153, 197–198, 212–213, 268
dorsolateral prefrontal cortex 144, 146
dosing 425

early childhood
  aggression 128
  assessment 374, 379–380, 382
  attachment 207, 213
  callous-unemotional traits 47
  deviant peers 343–344
  emotion regulation 222
  executive functioning 167, 509–510
  ODD 27–28
  ODD/CD with ADHD comorbidity 58–59
  parent psychopathology 276, 283–284
  parenting 308
  peer rejection 327–328
  pharmacotherapy 422

early childhood (*Continued*)
  psychosocial treatment 433–449
  SES and antisocial behavior 261–262
  social cognition 248
  temperament 177, 179, 180
early intervention 48, 66
eating disorders 108, 378
ecological risk factors 342
education 37, 196, 213, 258, 268, 269, 296
effect sizes 507–508
effortful control 176–179, 180–181, 182, 183, 214, 222
emotion regulation 4, 10, 11, 183, 221–236, 503
  attachment *209*, 210
  callous-unemotional traits 43
  marital conflict 295
  ODD/CD with ADHD comorbidity 65
  positive parenting 311
  psychosocial treatment 454, 456, 458, 469
  temperament 177
  see also self-regulation
emotional dysregulation 222, 381
  aggression 224–225, 226, 227–228
  BPD 110, 117
  ODD/CD with ADHD comorbidity 30, 58
  parent psychopathology 282
  substance abuse 77
emotional intelligence 92–93
emotionality 175, 179, 180
  see also negative emotionality
emotions
  executive functioning 168
  neurobiology 145, 147, 152–153, 262
  social cognition *238*, 240–241, 242
empathy 209, 210–211, 215, 246
  gender differences 182
  lack of 39, 45, 59, 65, 105, 111, 143, 149, 381
  neurobiology 131, 144
  psychosocial treatment 453, 458, 471–472
  see also theory of mind
enactment 242
encoding *238*, 239, 242, 246, 333
endocrine disrupters 194
endophenotypes 136, 165

environmental factors 127–128, 129, 136, 503
  gene-environment interactions 132–134, 135, 181
  ODD/CD with ADHD comorbidity 56
  parent psychopathology 280, 282
  prenatal risk factors 192
  temperament 177
environmental toxicants 194–195
epigenetics 198
escitalopram 95–96
ethnicity 12, 360
etiology 5–6, 8, 386
  ADHD 165, 167
  assessment 373, 375, 385, 505–506
  callous-unemotional traits 41–43
evidence-based interventions 13, 14, 496, 510, 512
  adaptations 486–491
  adolescence 467–478
  early childhood 438–441, 444
  family engagement 401–402, 403
  middle childhood 452–461
  parental involvement 492
  personalization 508
  real-world settings 485–486
excitement 64–5
executive functioning (EF) 136, 159, 164–169, 170, 223, 262, 504, 509–510
  brain areas 149
  deficits 340
  effortful control 180
  intelligence 160
  sensitive parenting *209*
  social cognition 245–246
expectations 61–62, 65, 262, 397, 398, 506
  gender role 182, 184
  internal working models 206, 210
expected values (EVs) 149
externalizing behaviors 12, 14, 159, 503
  BPD 108, 109
  Coping Power 229, 491, 493, 495
  emotion regulation 222–223, 224, 227–229
  externalizing spectrum 4, 76–77, 104–105, 108, 113, 115, 129, 294
  family structure 265, 266, 267, 269
  frustration reactivity 180
  gender differences 26, 27, 181–182

genetics 129, 130–131, 132, 509
intimate partner aggression 298–300
marital conflict 295, 296–297
narcissistic personality disorder 105, 111–112
neighborhood context 358
ODD 30, 31
parent psychopathology 276–277, 278, 279, 280–281, 282, 283–284
parenting 209, 212–213, 214, 310–314, 316
peer rejection 327–330, 331
perinatal risk factors 196
personality traits 115–117
prenatal risk factors 190–191, 192, 194–195
psychopathy 106
psychosocial treatment 456, 460–461, 472, 474–475
reactive aggression 225
SES relationship 262, 394
spouses 63
substance abuse 75, 76, 80, 81
teacher-student relationships 333
extraversion 176, 177

facial expressions 147–148, 150, 226
Familias Unidas 475–476
familismo 315
family 211–212, 213, 257–274
　assessment 377
　coercion 344
　deviant peers 340, 341–342, 346
　engagement in treatment 393–409, 423–424, 492
　marital conflict 268, 269, 282, 291–297
　ODD/CD with ADHD comorbidity 56, 66
　poverty 257–258, 259–264, 269, 270
　psychosocial treatment 435–436, 437, 440–441, 443, 451, 473–478
　structure 257–258, 264–269, 270
　substance abuse 78
　temperament 177, 184
　see also parenting; parents
Family Behavior Therapy (FBT) 476
Family Check-Up (FCU) 398–399, 440–441, 475, 492
Fast Track 456, 477, 496

fathers 63, 183, 266, 268–269, 313
　attachment 208–209, 214
　intimate partner aggression 298, 300
　psychopathology 278, 280, 282, 284
　see also parents
fear 210, 226, 360
　callous-unemotional traits 42, 143, 144
　gender differences 181
　stress response system 152
　temperament 179–180, 183
Feighner criteria 7
fetal alcohol syndrome (FAS) 191
fidgetiness 65
Five Factor Model (FFM) 44
5-HT system 90, 93, 130–131, 133–134, 150–151, 212
fluoxetine 94, 95, 193
foster care 459–460, 478
4R2S model 401–402
frustration 65, 148, 176, 180, 210, 222, 243, 359
functional brain imaging 147–149, 193, 223
functional connectivity 150
Functional Family Therapy (FFT) 46, 460–461, 473–474
functional impairment 27, 28, 56, 59, 383, 424

gambling 116
gangs 341, 345, 359–360, 380
gender differences
　attachment 212, 213
　BPD 108–109
　CD 146, 393
　genetic and environmental factors 128
　IED 91
　intimate partner aggression 292–293, 299, 300
　language impairments 162
　marital conflict 296, 297
　narcissistic personality disorder 111
　neighborhood context 359–360
　neurobiology 148
　ODD 25–27, 31, 393
　ODD/CD with ADHD comorbidity 30, 57–58, 62
　ODD with depression comorbidity 29
　paranoid personality disorder 114
　peer rejection 328, 329, 331

gender differences (*Continued*)
   prenatal risk factors 194
   preterm birth 196
   psychopathy 106, 107
   Pyromania 96
   school context 357
   SES and antisocial behavior 262
   substance abuse 79
   temperament 181–182, 183–184
gene-environment interactions 132–134, 135, 181
generalized anxiety disorder 27, 80
genetics 10, 11, 127–141, 258, 509
   attachment 209, 211, 212–213
   callous-unemotional traits 41
   divorce 267
   executive functioning 165
   externalizing spectrum 104, 105
   heritability of DBDs 127–129
   IED 91–92
   irritability and depression 29
   narcissistic personality disorder 112
   ODD/CD with ADHD comorbidity 56–57
   parent psychopathology 280, 282
   prenatal and perinatal risk factors 190, 192, 197–198
   substance abuse 76–77, 81
   temperament 176–177
genome-wide association studies (GWAS) 127, 131–132, 134–135, 136
geographical factors 57
goals *238*, 240, 242
Good Behavior Game (GBG) 454
"goodness of fit" model 177–178, 181
grandiosity 111, 113, 115, **116**
group-based treatment 397, 399, 403
   deviant peers 342, 346
   psychosocial 437, 439, 441, 458, 459, 471–473
Group Teen Triple P (GTTP) 470
guilt
   Kleptomania 95
   lack of 39, 59, 65, 143, 144, 152, 240–241, 381

halo effects 64, 65
haloperidol 412, **413**
Hanf two-stage model 436, 439
Hare Psychopathy Checklist - Revised (PCL-R) 106–107

harm avoidance 176, 179
health issues 37, 92, 196, 315–316, 361
Helping the Noncompliant Child (HNC) 439, 443, 490–491
heritability 127–129, 132, 135, 258
   aggression 91–92
   endophenotypes 136
   externalizing spectrum 104
   narcissistic personality disorder 112
   temperament 176–177
   see also genetics
heroin 193
hippocampus 144, 149
Hippocrates 5
histrionic personality disorder (HPD) 105
home-based interventions 436, 510
homelessness 38–39
homophily 343
hormones 143
hostile attribution bias (HAB) 150, 153, 210, 243, 381, 510
   paranoid personality disorder 113, 114
   peer rejection 333
   reactive aggression 226, 229
   social cognition 239–240, 246
hostility 92, 153, 210, 339, 381
   emotion regulation 222, 224
   personality disorders 113, 115, **116**
   social cognition 239–240, 244, 246–247
hybrid interventions 513
hyperactivity 55, 66, 381, 457, 509–510
   adulthood 60
   gender differences 26–27
   ODD/CD with ADHD comorbidity 58, 62
   peer rejection 330, 331, 332
   prenatal risk factors 190
   preterm birth 196
   see also Attention Deficit Hyperactivity Disorder
hypothalamic-pituitary-adrenal (HPA) axis 152, 223, 225

immaturity 64
implementation science 13–14, 496
impulse control 59, 136
Impulse-Control Disorders 3, 4, 14, 89–101
impulsivity 55, 89, 362, 381, 509–510
   adulthood 60
   BPD 66, 108, 109, 110

callous-unemotional traits 43, 44
Coping Power 491
genetics 92, 197
neurobiology 144, 148
ODD/CD with ADHD comorbidity 30, 58, 62, 65
parenting 313
peer rejection 332
personality disorders 115, 116
pharmacotherapy 411
prenatal risk factors 191, 194
psychopathy 105, 106
resistant attachment 210
reward seeking 108
sleep problems 361
substance abuse 77
surgency 176
inattention 55, 190, 191, 196, 197, 331, 332
Incredible Years (IY) 439–440, 457–458, 508
indicated prevention 455–461, 508, 511
Infant Temperament Questionnaire (ITQ) 175
inferior frontal cortex (IFC) 149
informed consent 425
inhibition 164–165, 166, 168, 169, 181
inhibitory control 179, 222–223, 246, 491, 504, 509–510
insecure attachment 205, 206–209, 211, 212–214, 281, 282
Institute of Medicine (IOM) 13
insula 144, 145, 148–149, 153, 226
integrative science 10–11
intellectual disability 159, 378, 379
intellectual functioning 159–161, 169–170, 196, 245, 382
intensive treatment 443, 444
intentionality 64–65
Intermittent Explosive Disorder (IED) 3, 4, 89–95, 97, 104, 378
internal states 242, 243
internal working models 206, *209*, 210
internalizing behaviors
  BPD 108
  CD 77
  Coping Power 493
  emotionality 179
  family poverty 269
  gender differences 27, 181–182, 212
  intimate partner aggression 298, 299–300
  marital conflict 296–297

neighborhood context 358
ODD 29, 30, 31
ODD/CD with ADHD comorbidity 60
parent psychopathology 278, 282
peer rejection 331, 332
psychosocial treatment 461, 469
substance abuse 80–81
technology-based interventions 513
International Classification of Diseases (ICD) 6, 9, 29, 373, 379, 504
  assessment 375, 384
  callous-unemotional traits 48
  ODD 24, 505
internet 442, 443, 457, 490, 512
interpretation *238*, 239–240, 242
interventions 12–14, 374, 385–386, 506–513
  callous-unemotional traits 40–41, 46–47
  cortisol responsiveness 153
  cost-effectiveness 496
  deviant peers 342, 346, 347
  dissemination of 485–500, 510–513
  emotion regulation 228–229
  ODD/CD with ADHD comorbidity 66
  parenting 309–310, 316
  social cognition 247–248
  temperament 183, 184
  see also psychosocial treatment; treatment
intimate partner aggression (IPA) 281, 291, 292–294, 297–301
introversion 177
Inventory of Callous-Unemotional Traits (ICU) 45–46, 48
IQ 160–161, 162–163, 169–170, 191, 195, 268, 379, 382
irresponsibility 43, 105, 106, 115, **116**
irritability 91–92, 424, 461
  endophenotypes 136
  gender differences 182
  gene-environment interactions 132
  ODD 21–24, 28–29, 31, 363, 504–505
  ODD/CD with ADHD comorbidity 30, 65
  parenting 180, 394
  pharmacotherapy 420–423, 429
  temperament 176, 179

Kiddie-Schedule for Affective Disorders and Schizophrenia (K-SADS) 383
Kleptomania 3, 4, 14, 95–96
Kraepelin, Emil 5–6

language/communication disorders 159
language impairments 159, 162–164, 170, 193, 378, 379
Latinos 314, 315, 360, 361, 363, 475–476
lead exposure 194–195
learning disorder (LD) 160, 162, 379
LifeSkills Training (LST) 453
limit setting 311–312
limited prosocial emotions (LPE) 29, 39–41, 45, 48, 59, 246, 355
lithium 94, 151, 412, **413–414**, 422, 426
low and middle income countries (LMICs) 257–259, 261, 263, 265–266, 270
low birth weight 196–197

maintenance 13, 280–281, 375, 385, 386, 387, 429
major depressive disorder (MDD) 29, 378, 379
malnutrition 190–191
manipulativeness 43, 105, 106, **116**, 143
manualized treatment 461, 474, 486–487, 493
marijuana 78, 191, 341, 361, 453, 475, 476, 488
marital conflict 268, 269, 282, 291–297, 309
marriage rates 264–265
maturity 208
medial/superior frontal gyrus 145
mediation 12
medication 97, 385, 411–432, 444, 505, 508
  ADHD 30, 160
  adherence 426
  IED 94, 95
  Kleptomania 95–96
  ODD/CD with ADHD comorbidity 66, 385, 387
  prenatal exposure 193–194, 198
memory 136, 146, 160
  endophenotypes 136
  executive functioning 164, 165–166, 168
  language impairments 162, 164, 170
  prenatal risk factors 193, 194
  preterm birth 196
  schemas 243–244
  social cognition 245, 247
mental illness, classification of 5
mentoring 460, 468–469
methylation 198

methylphenidate 412, 419, 421
Mexican Americans 315, 360, 476–477
middle childhood 308, 433
  aggression 128, 225
  assessment 380
  ODD 27
  ODD/CD with ADHD comorbidity 59
  peer rejection 328
  psychosocial treatment 451–466
  SES and antisocial behavior 262
  temperament 179
mindfulness 457, 469
Minnesota Longitudinal Study of Risk and Adaptation 207, 213
mobile technology 400, 443, 491, 512–513
modeling *209*, 210–211, 359
molecular genetics 127, 134
molindone 412, **417–418**
monitoring 311, 312–313, 316, 340, 341–342, 346, 394, 458, 473
monoamine oxidase-A (MAOA) 129–130, 132, 133, 197–198
mood 22, 23–24, 27, 58, 381, 411, 505
mood disorders 78, 92, 107, 378, 424–425
mood stabilizers 94, 412, **413–415**, 422, 426, 429
moral reasoning 241–242, 244, 469
mothers 262, 313
  attachment 208–209, 213
  depression 12, 189–190, 193–194, 269, 275–278, 280, 281–282, 283
  education level 196, 213
  intimate partner aggression 298, 300
  malnutrition 190–191
  single 265–266
  smoking 56, 191, 192, 197, 258, 263
  stress and distress 189–190, 277–278
  see also parents
motivation 165, 168, *209*, 210–211
multicomponent interventions 277, 477–478, 509, 510
Multidimensional Family Therapy (MDFT) 474–475
Multidimensional Treatment Foster Care (MTFC) 478
multimodal treatment 66, 419, 429, 455–456, 477–478, 490, 509
Multisystemic Therapy (MST) 460–461, 477–478, 494

naltrexone 96
narcissism 43, 110–113, 245, 381
narcissistic personality disorder (NPD) 105, 110–113, 114, **116**, 117
National Institute for Health and Care Excellence (NICE) 420
National Institute of Child Health and Human Development (NICHD) 208, 209
National Institute on Drug Abuse (NIDA) 495
National Mentoring Partnership 469
negative cues 381
negative emotionality 4, 114, 116, 310, 381
  effortful control 222
  gender differences 181, 182
  language impairments 164, 170
  reactive aggression 224
  temperament 176, 177–180, 181, 183
neighborhood context 11, 213, 262, 355, 358–363
  deviant peers 342, 347
  intervention outcomes 493
  substance abuse 78–79
neurobiology 10, 11, 38, 93–94, 108, 143–158, 223, 262–263, 340
see also brain
neurodevelopmental disorders 159, 194, 503–504
neuroendocrine system 131
neuroimaging 93–94, 143, 145, 146–149, 193, 223, 504
neuropsychological dysfunction 78
neurotransmitters 93, 136, 143, 150–151, 191
New York Longitudinal Study 175
normative beliefs 244–245
norms 4, 37, 57, 106, 263, 343, 347, 356–357, 381
novelty seeking 153, 176, 178–179, 183
Nurse Family Partnership (NFP) 441

observations 61–65, 67, 373, 375, 377, 380–382, 436, 505–506
occupational problems 37, 91, 103, 374
offenders 46, 107, 108–109, 208, 477–478
see also criminal behavior
Olweus Bullying Prevention Program 455
online social-cognitive processing 238–243, 248

Openness 44
oppositional behavior 75, 197, 381, 504
Oppositional Defiant Disorder (ODD) 3, 4, 339, 503–505
  ADHD comorbidity 29–30, 55–71, 145, 151, 161, 163–164, 167–169, 179, 278, 330–332, 379, 385, 387, 412–**421**
  assessment 373–375, 376–377, 379, 381, 505–506
  cognitive functioning 159
  comorbidities 23–24, 29–31, 493
  deviant peers 332
  diagnosis 21–36, 61–63, 378–379, 384, 424
  emotional dysregulation 110
  endophenotypes 136
  executive functioning 167–169, 170, 509–510
  externalizing spectrum 104, 129
  family structure 265
  general risk domains 211–212
  genetics 127–130, 135, 136
  intellectual functioning 160–161, 169–170
  intimate partner aggression 297–299
  language impairments 162–164, 170
  low birth weight 197
  marital conflict 295–297
  narcissism 112
  neighborhood context 355, 361–362, 363–364
  neurobiology of 143–158
  parent psychopathology 275–284
  parenting 78
  peer rejection 325, 327, 332–334
  personality traits 116
  pharmacotherapy 411–432
  poverty 259–260
  prenatal risk factors 191, 194
  preterm birth 195
  prevalence 25–27, 31, 294, 393, 433
  psychoeducation 386
  psychosocial treatment 451–452, 456, 459, 467, 471–473
  school context 355, 358, 363
  self-regulation 309
  social cognition 241
  substance abuse 73, 75–76, 77, 81
  temperament 178–183
  treatment 385, 387, 393, 401, 510

orbitofrontal cortex (OFC) 148
organizational support 494–495, 496
oxytocin 131, 134, 196, 509

pain 148
paranoia 5, 108
paranoid personality disorder (PPD) 105, 113–115, **116**, 117
parent-child interaction therapy (PCIT) 196, 438–439, 443, 512
Parent Management Training—Oregon Model (PMTO) 458–459, 470–471
parent peer support partners (PPSPs) 400–401
parent training 183, 196, 248, 308, 387, 421, 510
  consumer preferences 400
  cultural issues 315
  engagement 394–395, 396–399, 403, 505
  mobile health strategies 400
  positive parenting 310–311
  psychoeducation 507
  psychosocial treatment 439–440, 451, 455–456, 457–459, 461, 470–473
  socioeconomic status 508
  technology 442–443, 490–491
  treatment plans 385, 386
parental warmth 42, 48, 113, 212–213, 311, 314, 342, 394, 473
parenting 11, 12, 269, 270, 307–322
  assessment 382, 506
  attachment 205–215
  callous-unemotional traits 42, 43, 48
  CD 44
  criminal behavior 195
  deviant peers 340, 341–342, 347
  emotion coaching 224, 228–229
  gene-environment interactions 132, 133
  language impairments 163, 164, 170
  narcissistic personality disorder 113
  neighborhood context 360
  ODD/CD with ADHD comorbidity 56, 66
  parent psychopathology 280–282
  poverty 263, 394
  risk factors 211–212
  sensitivity 205
  social cognition 246
  styles 307–308, 377, 434

substance abuse 78, 161
temperament 177–178, 180–181, 183
see also family; parent training
parents
  assessment 373, 375, 376–378, 383, 384, 505–506
  engagement in treatment 492, 505
  expectations 182, 262, 397, 398
  interparental conflict 133
  ODD/CD with ADHD comorbidity 62–63
  parent-child relational problems 378
  psychoeducation 386, 507
  psychopathology 161, 164, 180–181, 211, 258, 275–289
  psychosocial treatment 434–437, 438–441, 452, 456–460, 470–478
  temperament 177
  see also family; fathers; mothers
passive aggressive personality disorder (PAPD) 28, 90
pathoplasty/exacerbation model 178
Patterson, Gerald 308
PAX Good Behavior Game (GBG) 454
peer acceptance 326, 328, 330–331, 334, 342
peer contagion 342, 347
peer rejection 58, 59, 210, 246, 325–338, 341
peer relationships 11, 263, 452
  deviant peers 258, 329, 332, 334, 360–361, 461, 471
  neighborhood context 360–361
  paranoid personality disorder 114
  parent psychopathology 282
  prenatal risk factors 190, 191
  social cognition 245, 248
  substance abuse 78
peer support 400–401, 403
perfectionism 116
perinatal risk factors 10, 195–197, 263
persistence 176, 178, 179, 183
personality 43–44, 77, 104, 115–117
personality disorders (PDs) 4, 63, 103–123, 279–280
personalization 508–509
pesticides 194
pharmacotherapy 66, 94, 95–96, 97, 385, 411–432
  see also medication

phthalates 194
physical examination 381–382
physiology 226, 249
planning 136, 164–165, 166–167, 246
policy 14, 262
polygenic studies 131–132
polypharmacy 425
popularity 326, 329–330
Porteus Maze task 166–167
Positive Action (PA) 454
Positive Behavior Supports (PBSs) 511
positive parenting 310–311
Positive Parenting Program (Triple P) 440, 442, 470
positive reinforcement 48, 311, 343, 434–435, 437, 440, 453, 468
post-traumatic stress disorder (PTSD) 301, 412
poverty 11, 78–79, 207, 309, 393
  emotion regulation 224
  family 257–258, 259–264, 269, 270, 394
  neighborhood 359, 360
  treatment engagement 395–396, 402, 403
  see also socioeconomic status
preemptive processing 242
prefrontal cortex (PFC) 143–144, 146, 148, 150, 153, 193, 223, 228, 262–263
pregnancy 56, 189–195
prenatal risk factors 10, 78, 189–195, 197–198, 263
Preschool ADHD Treatment Study (PATS) 422
Preschool Families Project 208
preterm birth 195–196
prevention 10, 12, 13, 452–455, 489, 511
  effect sizes 508
  emotion regulation 228–229
  family engagement 396–397
  pharmacotherapy 430
  temperament 184
primary care settings 512
prison 111, 266, 269
proactive aggression 226–227, 228–229, 242, 246, 359, 361, 382
Problem-Solving Skills Training (PSST) 459, 468, 473
Project ACHIEVE 472–473
Promoting Alternate THinking Strategies (PATHS) 452, 454, 456, 488–489

property destruction 4, 37, 89–90, 109
prosocial behavior 210–211
psychobiological functions 509–510
psychoeducation 386, 398, 505, 506–507
psychological aggression 292, 301
psychopathology 47, 205, 433, 444
  developmental 11, 12, 14, 198
  externalizing spectrum 108, 115–117
  gender differences 181–182
  parental 161, 164, 180–181, 211, 258, 275–289
  peer rejection 327
  reporters 62–63
  substance abuse 74, 76
  temperament 177–178, 180
psychopathy 38, 40, 104, 105–108, 116
  assessment 44–45, 382
  callous-unemotional traits 39, 43–44, 143
  narcissism 112
  neurobiology 145
  substance abuse 80
psychosocial treatment 419–420, 422, 424–425
  adolescence 467–483
  early childhood 433–449
  middle childhood 451–466
  see also interventions; treatment
psychostimulants 151, 385
  see also stimulants
punishment 340, 377, 509
  callous-unemotional traits 41–42, 143, 181
  executive functioning 167, 168, 169
  neurobiology 147–149, 150–151, 152, 153
Pyromania 3, 4, 14, 96

questionnaires 375, 376, 384
quetiapine 412, **418**, **421**

racial discrimination 360
rating scales 61–65, 67, 326, 376, 506
reactive aggression 224–226, 227–229, 242, 246, 359, 361, 382
Reactive Attachment Disorder 215
reactivity 175, 176–177, 221, 222, 224
reading problems 379
reassessment 506
relationship discord 268, 269, 282, 291–297, 309

relationships 38, 92, 108, 114, 346, 474
  see also peer relationships
remorse 39, 45, 59, 60, 105, 144, 240–241, 381
resilience 178, 213, 267, 300–301, 363
resistant attachment 206, 208, 210
respeto 315
respiratory sinus arrhythmia (RSA) 223, 225, 226
response evaluation *238*, 241–242
response generation *238*, 241, 242
response inhibition 164–165, 166
Response to Intervention (RTI) 511
response variability 164–165
restricted affectivity 115, **116**
revenge 12, 42
rewards 340, 377, 509
  callous-unemotional traits 42
  executive functioning 167, 169
  neurobiology 145, 148, 151, 153
  psychosocial treatment 434, 444, 460
  reward dependence 176
risk factors 8, 10, 11–12
  assessment 384–385, 387, 506
  contextual 355, 362–364, 451, 461
  deviant peers 340, 341–342
  family 257–259, 270, 295, 309, 340, 341–342, 394, 451, 461
  general risk domains 211–212
  language impairments 164
  marital conflict 296, 297
  neighborhood 358–362, 363
  ODD/CD with ADHD comorbidity 56, 58
  paranoid personality disorder 114
  parent psychopathology 283
  perinatal 195–197, 198, 263
  prenatal 10, 78, 189–195, 197–198, 263
  proximal and distal 270, 374, 385
  psychopathy 107
  substance abuse 76, 78, 81
risk taking 77, **116**, 263, 380
  neurobiology 146–147, 152, 153
  peer rejection 329, 330
risperidone 151, 412, 415–417, 419, 420, **421**
routines 310
rule-breaking behavior 4, 327, 341, 381, 433
  CD 37, 339
  ODD/CD with ADHD comorbidity 60, 63

peer rejection 332
prenatal BPA exposure 194
psychopathy 105
substance abuse 76

same-sex parents 264, 266
schemas 243–244, 246, 247, 333
schizophrenia 114, 144, 383
schools 310, 355–358, 363, 382, 385–386, 424, 451
  intervention dissemination 494–495, 510–512
  peer influence 345, 347
  psychosocial treatment 437–438, 439, 441, 444, 453–455, 472–473
  see also teachers
Schoolwide Positive Behavior Support (SWPBS) 455
Seattle Social Development Project (SSDP) 453–454
Second Step 453, 471–472
secure attachment 205, 206–209, 210–211, 213
segregation 358–359
selective serotonin reuptake inhibitors (SSRIs) 193, 198
self-directedness 179
self-esteem 111, 311, 345, 434, 452, 454
self-harm 27, 380, 478
self-perception/self-view 245, 333
self-regulation 222, 309–310
  attachment 212, 215
  callous-unemotional traits 47
  deviant peers 345
  gender differences 182
  neurobiology 149
  psychosocial treatment 441, 453, 469, 471
  SES relationship 262
  temperament 175, 176–177, 179, 180
  see also emotion regulation
self-reports 63, 326, 376
sensation seeking 77, 130, 152, 226, 340
sensitive parenting 205, 207, *209*, 210–211, 212–213, 214, 269
separation anxiety 65, 430
serotonin 90, 94, 130–131, 133–134, 150–151, 153, 268
set-shifting 164–165, 167
severe mood dysregulation (SMD) 23

sexual activity 345, 380, 454, 476, 477, 478
sexual assault 424
sexual impulsivity 109
shame 111
siblings 214, 269
side effects 422, 426, **427–428**, 444
single-nucleotide polymorphisms (SNPs) 129
single parents 258, 264, 265–266, 268
sleep problems 23, 361
SMART talk 490
smartphones 399, 443, 491, 512
smoking 74, 263, 488
   ODD/CD with ADHD comorbidity 56
   prenatal exposure 56, 78, 191, 192, 197, 258, 263
"snares" 60, 74, 79
social anxiety 80, 81, 114–115, 345, 378
social augmentation hypothesis 344–345
social-cognitive processing 10, 11, 93–94, 237–253, 386
   executive functioning 164
   neighborhood context 360
   parent psychopathology 282
   peer rejection 333, 334
   psychosocial treatment 451, 456, 472
social competence 209, 245, 332, 419, 452, 458–459, 471, 474
social impairment 37, 56, 59, 91, 339–340, 374
social learning 167, 308, 359, 361, 434, 444, 458, 468
social marginalization 60
social networks 343, 345, 346, 347, 394
social self-views 245
social skills 180, 309, 330, 495
   assessment 377, 382
   deviant peers 344, 347
   psychosocial treatment 452–453, 456, 468, 472, 473
socialization *238*, 246–247, 248–249, 310, 315, 330, 340, 346–347, 511
socioeconomic status (SES) 161, 213, 281, 362, 393
   deviant peers 342
   family engagement 397
   family poverty 259–263, 269, 394
   language impairments 163, 164

parent training 508
parenting 309, 315
preterm birth 196
see also poverty
sociometric scoring 326
solicitation 312–313
spanking 56, 281–282, 312, 314
see also discipline
specific learning disorder 379
spectrum model 178
spill-over 295–296
spitefulness 22, 23, 339
startle reflex 42
step-families 264, 266, 268–269
stigma 40, 65, 396, 401, 402, 436, 512
stimulants 94, 160, 412, 419, 426, **427**, 429
Strange Situation Procedure (SSP) 206–207, 208, 210
strengths 377, 378, 385, 397, 423
stress 11, 211, 361, 394
   gene-environment interactions 134
   maternal 189–190, 263, 277–278, 394
   parenting 269, 309
   peer rejection 332–333, 334
   prenatal 198
   stress response system 152–153
substance abuse 23, 73–88, 339–340, 433
   assessment 380
   BPD 108, 109
   CD 25, 37, 39, 358
   deviant peers 340, 341, 344
   gender differences 79
   genetics 76–77, 130
   impulsivity 109
   LifeSkills Training 453
   mobile health strategies 400
   multicomponent CBT 510
   neighborhood context 361
   neurobiology 144, 145
   ODD/CD with ADHD comorbidity 66
   parental 161, 279, 309, 402
   parenting 313–314
   peer rejection 329
   personality traits 116
   pharmacotherapy 425
   prenatal exposure 191, 192–193
   psychosocial treatment 444, 457, 459, 473, 474–475, 476–477
"snares" 60

Substance Abuse and Mental Health Services Administration (SAMHSA) 401, 467
substance use disorders (SUDs) 14, 73–75, 77, 104, 379
  diagnosis 378
  IED comorbidity 91, 92
  narcissistic personality disorder 112
  psychopathy 107
suicide 38–39, 103, 108, 380
Summer Treatment Program for Pre-Kindergarteners (STP-PreK) 441
superior temporal sulcus (STS) 144
supervision 311, 312–313, 340, 394, 473
surgency 176–177, 178, 181
suspiciousness 113, 114, 115, **116**
sustained attention 164–165, 166, 169
Sydenham, Thomas 5
sympathetic nervous system (SNS) 225, 226, 227

targeted prevention 10, 13, 511
teachers 62, 357, 358, 376, 511
  assessment 382, 384
  expectations 182, 262
  psychosocial treatment 437, 439, 440
  relationships with 333, 334, 356
  see also schools
technology 400, 442–443, 444, 490–491, 512–513
temper 26, 30, 374, 505
temper tantrums 22, 23, 89, 205
temperament 175–188, 211, 212–213, 309
  callous-unemotional traits 43
  emotion regulation 224
  language impairments 170
  neighborhood context 360
  parent psychopathology 276, 282
  substance abuse 77
teratogen exposure 189, 191–193, 198
testosterone 223
theft 37, 339
theory of mind 65, 248
  see also empathy
therapeutic alliance 396, 398, 473–474, 486, 494, 507
therapy 94–95, 96, 438–439, 443, 460–461, 473–478, 485
  see also cognitive behavioral therapy
thioridazine 412, **417**
thrill seeking 143, 152

"time-outs" 435, 436
Tower of London task 166–167
toxicants 194–195
Trails B 167
training 493–494, 495, 496, 505
Training Intervention for the Engagement of Families (TIES) 402–403
transdiagnostic interventions 461, 493
trauma 110, 114, 211, 425
treatment 8–9, 13, 387, 506–513
  barriers to 396, 397, 399, 402, 442, 444, 507
  callous-unemotional traits 40–41, 46–47
  CD 46–47, 48, 49
  cortisol responsiveness 153
  dissemination of 485–500, 510–513
  emotion regulation 228–229
  family engagement 393–409, 423–424, 492, 505
  IED 94–95
  Impulse-Control Disorders 95–96, 97
  ODD/CD with ADHD comorbidity 66, 67
  parent psychopathology 277, 283
  personality disorders 103
  plans 373, 375, 385–386
  temperament 183
  see also interventions; medication; psychosocial treatment; therapy
Treatment Foster Care Oregon (TFCO) 459–460
Treatment of Maladaptive Aggression in Youth (T-MAY) 421–422
Treatment of Severe Child Aggression (TOSCA) study 419
triggers 248
"Tuning In" program 228–229
twin studies 127–129, 131–132, 134, 136
  divorce 267
  low birth weight 197
  parent psychopathology 280
  substance abuse 76
  temperament 176–177

unemployment 30, 56, 342, 433
universal prevention 452–455, 511

variable number tandem repeats (VNTRs) 129, 130
vasopressin 131

videoconferencing 443, 512
vindictiveness 21, 22, 374
violence 4, 195, 208, 424
  BPD 109
  CD 37, 38
  deviant peers 344
  intimate partner 281, 291, 292–294, 297–301
  LifeSkills Training 453
  neighborhood 359–362, 363, 394
  personality disorders 103, 111, 114
  school context 356
  social cognition 246
  see also aggression

vulnerability/resilience model 178
vulnerable narcissism 111

Wechsler Intelligence Scale for Children - Fourth Edition (WISC-IV) 160, 161
Wisconsin Card Sorting Task (WCST) 167, 168
working memory *see* memory
World Health Organization (WHO) 6, 7, 24, 379
written information 373, 375–376